HISTORY OF MANKIND

CULTURAL AND SCIENTIFIC DEVELOPMENT

VOLUME II

THE ANCIENT WORLD

1200 BC TO AD 500

PUBLISHED FOR THE

INTERNATIONAL COMMISSION FOR A HISTORY OF THE
SCIENTIFIC AND CULTURAL DEVELOPMENT
OF MANKIND

BY

HARPER & ROW, PUBLISHERS

NEW YORK

HISTORY OF MANKIND

VOLUME II

By LUIGI PARETI

Assisted By

PAOLO BREZZI and LUCIANO PETECH

THE ANCIENT WORLD

1200 BC to AD 500

Translated from the Italian
By Guy E. F. Chilver and Sylvia Chilver

HARPER & ROW, PUBLISHERS

NEW YORK

*Prepared under the auspices and
with financial assistance of the
United Nations Educational, Scientific and
Cultural Organization*

Consultants for Volume II

Dr. Guy E. F. Chilver
(Queen's College, Oxford)

Professor J. Filliozat
(College de France)

LIBRARY OF CONGRESS CATALOG CARD NUMBER: 64-12677

INTERNATIONAL COMMISSION
FOR A HISTORY OF THE SCIENTIFIC AND
CULTURAL DEVELOPMENT OF MANKIND

CORRESPONDING MEMBERS

Argentina
Dr R. Frondizi

Australia
Professor R. M. Crawford

Austria
Dr Karl Jettmar

Belgium
Professor Marcel Florkin
Professor Charles Manneback

Brazil
Professor Fernando de Azevedo
Professor Gilberto Freyre
Professor Sergio Buarque de Hollanda
Dr José Honorio Rodrigues

Burma
Dr Htin Aung

Canada
Professor Wilfrid Cantwell Smith

Chile
Dr Ricardo Donoso

China
Professor Tso-ping Tung
H.E. M. Chang Chi-yun

Colombia
Professor German Arciniegas
Professor Luis Martinez Delgado

Cuba
H.E. Dr J. Remos y Rubio

Denmark
Dr Kaj Birket-Smith

Egypt
Professor Aziz S. Atiya

France
Monseigneur Blanchet
Professor Julien Cain
Professor J. B. Duroselle
Professor C. Lévi-Strauss

Federal Republic of Germany
Dr Georg Eckert
Dr Hermann Heimpel
Dr Ludwig Dehio

Honduras
H.E. Prof. Rafael Heliodoro Valle

India
Professor J. N. Banerjea
Dr Humayun Kabir
H.E. Sir Sarvepalli Radhakrishnan
Professor K. A. Nilakanta Sastri

Indonesia
Dr S. T. Alisjahbana
Professor M. Sardjito

Iran
Professor Ali-Asghar Hekmat

Iraq
Dr Abdul Aziz al-Duri

Israel
Professor B. Mazar

Italy
Professor Domenico Demarco
Professor Giacomo Devoto
R. P. Antonio Messineo

Japan
Professor Shigeki Kaizuka
Professor Suketoshi Yajima
Dr Seeichi Iwao
Professor Daisetso Suzuki

Lebanon
Emir Maurice Chehab
H.E. Dr Charles Malik

Mexico
Dr Alfonso Caso
Professor Samuel Ramos
Professor Manuel Sandoval Vallarta
Professor Daniel Cosio Villegas

Nepal
Professor Gókal Chand

Netherlands
Professor Dr R. Hooykaas
Dr Maria Rooseboom

New Zealand
Dr J. C. Beaglehole

Norway
Professor Alf Sommerfelt

Pakistan
Dr A. Halim
Dr I. H. Qureshi
Dr S. Suhrawardy

Philippines
Professor Gabriel Bernardo

Senegal
H.E. M. L. S. Senghor

Spain
Professor Claudio Sanchez Albornoz
Professor Antonio Garcia Bellido
M. Ciriaco Pérez Bustamante
M. F. Cantera
Professor Emilio Garcia Gomez
Duke of Maura
Professor R. Menendez Pidal
Professor José Pijoan

Sweden
Professor Axel Boëthius

Switzerland
Dr Werner Kaegi
Professor Jean Piaget

Syria
H.E. Khalil Mardam Bey

Thailand
Prince Dhani Nivat

Turkey
H.E. Mehmed Fouad Köprülü

Union of South Africa
Professor A. N. Pelzer

Union of Soviet Socialist Republics
Professor A. V. Artsikhovski
Professor N. A. Figourovsky
Professor Guber
Professor B. Kedrov
Professor D. V. Sarabianov
Professor N. A. Sidorova
Professor Vinogradov
Professor V. P. Zoubov

United Kingdom
Sir Ernest Barker
Dr Joseph Needham
Bertrand Russell

United States of America
Professor Eugene Anderson
Professor Salo W. Baron
Professor Norman Brown
Professor J. K. Fairbank
Professor Harold Fisher
Professor G. Stanton Ford
Professor R. H. Gabriel
Professor Oscar Halecki
Dr C. W. de Kiewiet
Professor A. L. Kroeber
Professor Martin R. P. McGuire
Professor H. W. Schneider
Professor Richard Shryock
Professor John A. Wilson

Uruguay
Professor Carlos M. Rama

Venezuela
H.E. C. Parra-Perez
Professor Mariano Picon Salas

HISTORY OF MANKIND
CULTURAL AND SCIENTIFIC DEVELOPMENT

* Tentative title.

FOREWORD

by the

Director-General of UNESCO

At a time when man is preparing to launch out from this planet into space, it is well that History should hold him in contemplation of his trajectory through the ages.

Never before, indeed, has he shown so searching a curiosity about his past or such jealous care to preserve its vestiges. It is as though in some mysterious way a balance were now maintained in his thought between the exploration of space and that of time, the extroversion of the one being offset by the inwardness of the other.

Be that as it may, never more than now, when man finds himself hurtling at vertiginous speed towards a wondrous future, has there been a great need for the function of memory to ensure for mankind the appropriation of its creative actuality. If consciousness were not thus rooted in such reflection on its own process of becoming, many of the inventions we hail as conquests and advances would be no more than the uncontrollable workings of an alienated destiny.

To evoke this retrospective awareness is the first thing that this work which we now have the honour of introducing to the public sets out to do; it is an attempt to sum up the heritage of civilization to which we owe our present élan.

The ambition to write a universal history is a very old one indeed. Many have tried their hand at it before, particularly in the classical epochs—not without merit, nor without success. The present work belongs to that noble line of great syntheses which seek to present to man the sum total of his memories as a coherent whole.

It has the same twofold ambition, to embrace the past in its entirety and to sum up all that we know about the past. And it adopts the same intellectual approach—that of the interpretative as opposed to the descriptive historian—reducing events to their significance in a universal frame of reference, explicit or implicit.

However, this *History of Mankind* parts company with its predecessors on several essential points. In the first place, it deliberately confines itself to shedding light on one of mankind's many aspects, its *cultural and scientific development*.

In so doing it departs from the traditional approaches to the study of history, which, as we know, attach decisive importance to political, economic and even military factors. It offers itself as a corrective to the ordinary view of man's past. And those who initiated the enterprise may well have thought at first that this was, in itself, sufficiently useful and original for them to dispense with any further aim.

Admittedly, it rests with the science of history to decide objectively, *a posteriori* and according to the case, on the relative importance of the different elements and factors in particular situations. To that extent the approach deliberately adopted in this history may well be said to be an *a priori* postulate. This is the very postulate on which UNESCO itself is based, namely, the conviction that international relations, in their ultimate reality, are determined not merely by political and economic factors and considerations but spring as well, and perhaps even more surely, from the capabilities and demands of the mind.

Nevertheless, even from the strictly scientific point of view, this History, deliberately partial though it be, may well claim that, in restoring to the achievements of culture and science their full reality and significance, it has made an essential contribution to that sum of factual knowledge and right understanding which a complete history aspires to offer.

But the originality of the enterprise does not stop there. In point of fact, that is where it begins. For the facts of which this History treats are no ordinary ones. To put them back in their proper place is not merely to fill a long-standing gap and thus complete the sum, restoring its balance to the whole. It is to discover a new dimension of the historical object, perceptible only when approached from a particular intellectual angle.

Cultural or scientific facts, whatever their subject-matter, means, cause, pretext or circumstances, are essentially thoughts of man about man.

This is obvious in the cultural sphere, every value being a human ideal. But it is no less true of science; for apart from the fact that truth, too, is a value, the essence of science is not knowledge, but the method by which knowledge is gained, the rule the mind prescribes itself in order to attain it; and every rule is a form of reflection and self-discipline; that is, doubled consciousness.

Thus, the history of what has no doubt been too simply described here as 'the cultural and scientific development of mankind' is, strictly speaking, the story of how, through the ages, men—individually and collectively—have conceived of humanity. Or, to be more correct, have conceived of *their* humanity, that is, the universal aspect of their experience. In short, the subject of this work is the gradual development, in its most expressive manifestations, of the consciousness of the universal in man.

As will be seen, great care is taken to describe the exchanges and influences which link the different foci of civilization across space or time. We are shown how this web of reciprocal influences is becoming more closely woven as spatial communications grow more numerous and rapid and relations in time more intensive.* Indeed by no means the least interesting

---

* Even in time, relations are reversible—not, of course, through any real causation, but owing to the perpetual reappraisal of the significance of events that takes place in the course of man's constantly renewed, and renewing, retrospection.

feature of this work is the stress it lays upon this still too little known aspect of historical reality in which the 'intellectual and moral solidarity of mankind' referred to in the Preamble to UNESCO's Constitution can really be seen at work.

Yet even this is not the decisive discovery. That lies not so much in the evidence of interrelation between the many and varied civilizations as in the fact, manifest in all forms of culture and science, that every civilization implies, produces or invokes an image of man in terms of the universal.

This immanence of the universal in every cultural and scientific experience is what gives its essential character to the spiritual solidarity of mankind. And it is in this form that the solidarity can serve as the foundation for the true peace described in UNESCO's Constitution, whereas the effect of intercultural relations upon the interplay of the forces conducive, in a given situation, to peace is, as well we know, extremely complex and indirect, and therefore contingent. In fact it is because the object of this History, as already pointed out, is the development of the consciousness of this solidarity that UNESCO regards such an undertaking as both vital and necessary.

But straightway we are faced with another fact, no less rich in implications. In the actual experience of science and culture, sense and style, which constitute the universal element, remain indissolubly bound up with the singular act of invention or creation from which they derive. It may truly be said both of science and of culture, regarded as experiences, that 'the more one concentrates on the particular, the more universal one becomes'. And it is only by repeating the various operations of the act of creation, reduced to their objective characteristics—which make up what we call method—or by subjective communion with the mental atmosphere of that act—which is what we call intuition—that another person can understand and assimilate this sense and style.

It follows that for a history which aims to keep in constant touch with experience and restore it in its contingent truth, scientific and cultural facts have significance only for certain individuals, namely those who are capable of applying these methods and of exercising this intuition which give access to the secrets of creativeness in its unique aspects. However, to possess this ability, there is no doubt that one must belong to the particular context of civilization in which such unique phenomena occur. Accordingly a concrete history of science and culture can only be written from a plurality of viewpoints corresponding to the variety of civilizations.

To acknowledge the fact that there is more than one civilization is not to deny in any way the continuity or solidarity of human development. On the contrary, the study of the interrelations, across time and space, of ideas, values and techniques restores this sense of continuity and solidarity, which have never before been so definitely and convincingly established as in this History. Similarly, to be aware of the originality of the works and symbols which make up each civilization is not to gainsay the universality of the human mind. As we have seen, true universality is no more than a dimension of this consciousness of a sense or style, which opens out to the potential totality of mankind only by rooting itself in the particularity of its initial emergence.

The classical rationalism of the West conceived the history of the human mind as a process of development in which all scientific and cultural facts are arranged in order with reference to a single, constant subject that is universal by nature. There is no need to plunge into a philosophical discussion on ontological humanism in order to expose this myth. It would be only too easy, now of all times, to show how into this allegedly universal subject has been projected, out of pride or sheer naïveté, the subjectivity, in more or less sublimated form, of certain personalities eminently representative of their epoch, civilization or race.

The work you are about to read represents the first attempt to compose a universal history of the human mind from the varying standpoints of memory and thought that characterize the different contemporary cultures.

But in doing so, its main purpose was not to banish all subjectivity of interpretation. Indeed, such a pretension could not be entertained in a history which seeks to assess the significance of events and which takes as its starting points the positions adopted by the various cultures. For there is a kind of subjectivity, co-substantial, as it were, with culture, which causes the perspective opened by each culture on the universal in man to be a projection of that culture's humanity in its own particular circumstances. The originality of this attempt at a universal history lies in its having taken for its frame of reference the multiplicity of contemporary cultural perspectives and projections. For the first time an attempt has been made to present, with respect to the history of consciousness, the sum total of the knowledge which the various contemporary societies and cultures possess and a synthesis of the conceptions which they entertain. For the first time an attempt has been made to offer a history of human thought which is the product of the thought of mankind in every aspect of its present complexion. A universal history indeed, and doubly so—in both its object and its subject.

This aspiration, which is the essence of the whole undertaking, has determined the choice of method.

The History is the work, not of a team with a homogeneous cultural background, but of an International Commission which, by its very composition and even more by the spirit pervading it, embraces all the varied cultural traditions and modern ideologies which form the spiritual framework of our present-day world. What is more, the International Commission made it a rule that the contributions of the many scholars whose services it enlisted be submitted to the scrutiny of the National Commissions which, in the Member States of UNESCO, group together persons particularly qualified to represent the fields of education, science and culture. Subject always to the overriding considerations of scientific truth, the observations received in the course of these extensive consultations were scrupulously taken into account in drawing up the final text. Never before has what I may call the decentralization of viewpoints and interpretations been carried so far in the science of history.

Accordingly the work is also an act; for this historical study is itself a cultural achievement calculated to influence, by its spirit and its methods, the present trend of culture. And that, no doubt, is its ultimate end. For just as the awareness of mankind's intellectual and moral solidarity to which it leads stems less from the discovery of the interrelations of the past than from the effort of synthesis by which mankind seeks to apprehend the whole compass of its scientific and cultural heritage, so the essential feature of this effort is not so much the complete restitution of the object which it is designed to achieve as the fact that the whole of the subject as it exists today is taking part in it and thus affirms its own unity in the process of achieving it.

In this humanism, whose universality springs not from a unique abstract nature but is being gradually evolved, on the basis of a freely acknowledged diversity, through actual contact and a continuous effort at understanding and co-operation, UNESCO recognizes both its own *raison d'être* and its guiding principle. The unity of mankind, we believe, has to be patiently built up, through mutual respect for the cultures which diversify it without dividing it, and by the establishment of more and more centres of science which spread man's technological power throughout the world, fostering equality of opportunity for progress and for the genuine preservation of his dignity.

Such, then, are the principal ideas and essential features of this work; they are, at the same time, the very reasons which led UNESCO, as the educational, scientific and cultural organization of the United Nations, to conceive the project and assist in its execution.

The author of this History is not UNESCO; it is the International Commission which, since 1950, has directed this venture in complete intellectual independence. It is to the Commission, therefore, and to it alone, that the full credit for this work is due. And at the same time—allow me to state—it also bears the sole responsibility for its scientific worth.

UNESCO is, however, proud to have organized this work and to have made possible its accomplishment by providing the necessary funds, administrative machinery and international background. In that sense this great venture, without precedent in many respects, is also in some measure its work, too.

It is, therefore, my pleasant duty to express the Organization's gratitude to all those who have, to whatever degree, participated in this undertaking and contributed to its success. Above all its thanks are due to the distinguished members of the International Commission and to its eminent Chairman, Professor Paulo E. de Berrêdo Carneiro, who for thirteen years have given

unsparingly of the wealth of their knowledge and talents, with a devotion and
selflessness equalled only by the nobility of their thought. In this concept of
scientific and cultural development in which consciousness is an act and all
reflection a creation, it may be said without fear of exaggeration that, in
presenting this vast panorama of the past history of the human mind, such
as never was before, they have made a powerful contribution towards the
advent of a consciousness of civilization on a scale encompassing the whole
of mankind. With all my admiration, I wish to express to them UNESCO's
gratitude.

RENÉ MAHEU

Paris, 1962.

PREFACE

by the

*President of the International Commission
for a History of the Scientific and Cultural Development
of Mankind*

Among the great tasks assigned to UNESCO by its Constitution is the duty
to promote and encourage mutual knowledge and understanding throughout
the world. While many of the divergences which divide people date from
a distant past, an analysis of their historical antecedents discloses links which
draw them nearer to one another, brings to light their contributions to a
common patrimony of humanity, reveals the ebb and flow of cultural
exchanges and emphasizes their increasing tendency to become integrated
into an international community.

Beyond differences of race, climate, economic structure and systems of
ideas, history shows the fundamental identity of the various human groups,
making it possible to discern, in many cases, profound analogies among the
transformations they have undergone from the Palaeolithic era down to the
present time. If we consider the human species as a whole, we perceive that
the course of its evolution has been accomplished from one region and one
people to another by way of a series of oscillations, greater or lesser in extent,
longer or shorter in duration. The different civilizations which have arisen
in the course of the ages correspond to distinct phases and patterns of this
general movement. Almost every one of them is to be found somewhere in
the world of today. Contemporary society appears as a mosaic in which the
most widely-differing cultures adjoin and confront each other.

It was, I think, in order to know them better and to strengthen their
solidarity that UNESCO took the initiative of entrusting to historians, men
of science and of letters, recruited from all parts of the world, the task of
preparing and of publishing this work. This, at least, is how I have understood the mandate of the International Commission over which I have the
honour to preside. Our task was not to draw up a philosophy of history in
the light of the economic, intellectual and moral laws which may govern
social development, but to describe, from a universal standpoint, the contribution of each age, each region, each people to the scientific and cultural
ascent of humanity.

In the official reports which I have presented since 1951 to the General
Conference of UNESCO will be found a detailed account of the steps taken
in implementing this project which originated in a resolution submitted to
the second session of the General Conference held in Mexico City in 1947.
The idea had been put forward in 1946 by Dr Julian Huxley, then Executive
Secretary of the Preparatory Commission for UNESCO:

'The chief task before the Humanities today would seem to be to help in constructing a history of the development of the human mind, notably in its highest cultural achievements. For this task, the help of art critics and artists will be needed as well as of art historians; of anthropologists and students of comparative religion as well as of divines and theologians; of archaeologists as well as of classical scholars; of poets and creative men of letters as well as of professors of literature; as well as the whole-hearted support of the historians. Throughout, of course, the development of culture in the various regions of the Orient must receive equal attention to that paid to its Western growth. Once more, UNESCO can help by being true to its many-sidedness, and by bringing men together from all these various fields to help in one or other facet of this huge work.' (UNESCO: *Its Purpose and Its Philosophy* [London, 1946].)

Several preparatory meetings were held and preliminary studies made in 1947 and 1948 with the participation of Professors Carl J. Burckhardt, Lucien Febvre, Joseph Needham, Georges Salles, Taha Hussein, and UNESCO officials, among whom were Dr Julian Huxley, then Director-General, Mr Jean Thomas and Professor Pierre Auger. In 1949, Professors Lucien Febvre and Miguel Ozorio de Almeida were asked to prepare general reports on the basis of which the General Conference, at its fourth session, recommended that the work should proceed immediately.

In the same year a committee of experts was called to draft the plan to be submitted to the General Conference for the elaboration of a scientific and cultural history of mankind. It included the following scholars: R. Ciasca, L. Febvre, M. Florkin, J. Needham, J. Piaget, P. Rivet and R. Shryock. In opening the proceedings, Dr Jaime Torres-Bodet, at that time Director-General, evoked the spirit in which he considered the work should be accomplished:

'Through UNESCO, humanity must come to realize its common past and understand the significance of the sum total of endeavour, invention and enlightenment which have gone to make up the heritage we seek to serve today. If we can regard this moment in the world's history as UNESCO's hour, it is thanks to the slow and often unnoticed growth of an outlook shared by all men, which is now beginning to take shape as the outlook of Mankind. . . .'

'We seek only to draw up the table of the major cultural events which have shaped Man's existence and slowly brought civilization into being. . . .'

'The important thing is to embark on it with the will to succeed and in a spirit of serene and dispassionate objectivity. . . .'

'Nevertheless, by publishing today a synthesis of our present knowledge of *humanity's scientific and cultural history*, UNESCO, far from lulling the critical spirit to sleep, will spur it to new and eager research. It is my profound conviction that there is nothing in the nature or the present state of historical science precluding the making of such a synthesis; indeed all circumstances invite us to it.'

In accordance with a resolution of the General Conference of 1950, consultations were held with the International Council of Scientific Unions (ICSU) and the International Council for Philosophy and Humanistic Studies (CIPSH) as to the appointment of an international commission to undertake, on behalf of UNESCO, full responsibility for the preparation and execution of the work. The following experts nominated by these two councils were invited by the Director-General to become active members of the Commission: Professors Homi Bhabha (University of Bombay), Carl J. Burckhardt (Switzerland), Paulo E. de Berrêdo Carneiro (University of Brazil), Julian Huxley, FRS (United Kingdom), Charles Morazé (University of Paris), Mario Praz (University of Rome), Ralph E. Turner (Yale University), Silvio Zavala (University of Mexico) and Constantine K. Zurayk (University of Damascus).

The International Commission met for the first time in December 1950 and again in March 1951 in Paris. It decided during these two meetings to invite a number of distinguished persons to become Corresponding Members, and to set up an Editorial Committee, under the chairmanship of Professor Ralph E. Turner, with Professors Constantine K. Zurayk and Charles Morazé as members. The Commission did me the honour of electing me as its President, with Dr Julian Huxley and Professor Carl J. Burckhardt as Vice-Presidents. A Bureau was created comprising the President, the Vice-Presidents and the Chairman of the Editorial Committee. Dr Armando Cortesao, a member of the Department of Cultural Activities of UNESCO, initially responsible for the secretariat of the Commission, was unanimously elected Secretary-General. In 1952 he was succeeded by Dr Guy S. Métraux.

Between 1952 and 1954 new members were added to the International Commission to enlarge its geographical, cultural and philosophical representation. The following scholars were appointed in agreement with the Director-General of UNESCO: Professors E. J. Dijksterhuis (Netherlands), Jacques Freymond (Switzerland), Mahmud Husain (Pakistan), Hu-Shih (China), Erik Lönnroth (Sweden), R. C. Majumdar (India), Percy E. Schramm (Federal Republic of Germany), Ali A. Siassi (Iran), and J. Pérez Villanueva (Spain).

As early as 1952 the International Commission approached scholars of countries which, at the time, were not members of UNESCO but which represented important cultural areas. Invitations were sent to national academies of sciences and arts, but met with no response. It was only in 1955 that the International Commission was able to welcome as new members historians and scientists from the Union of Soviet Socialist Republics and the People's Republics of Czechoslovakia, Hungary and Poland.

Since 1954 the Bureau, acting as delegate of the International Commission with additional responsibilities placed on it by the General Assembly, has been enlarged to comprise the President and six Vice-Presidents as follows: Sir Julian Huxley (United Kingdom), Professor R. C. Majumdar (India),

Professor Ralph E. Turner (United States of America), Professor Gaston Wiet (France), Professor Silvio Zavala (Mexico), and Professor A. A. Zvorikine (Union of Soviet Socialist Republics). Professor Louis Gottschalk (United States of America) was unanimously elected as a further Vice-President in 1961.

The first publication which the International Commission initiated, on the proposal of Professor Charles Morazé, was a quarterly review, the *Journal of World History*. Professor Lucien Febvre was the Editor until his death in 1956, when it came under the supervision of the Bureau, with Dr François Crouzet and Dr Guy S. Métraux as its editorial staff.

The main function of the *Journal of World History* has been to provide the International Commission with material for the final compilation of the History—documentary or bibliographical details about problems which have so far remained obscure; translations of documents which may have appeared desirable; contributions to the History itself. This review has also enabled scholars in all countries to take part in an exchange of views on questions of interpretation and the actual presentation of the History.

The *Journal of World History* represents a considerable contribution on the part of the International Commission to historical knowledge and towards a better understanding of historical processes. Comprising articles of the highest scientific quality which bear the signature of scholars from every country and which express the most diverse ideological trends, it foreshadows to some extent the great work for which it has furnished basic materials.

The preparation of the History was examined in detail during the first and second meetings of the International Commission. Several courses of action presented themselves: the Commission could draft the final text, or it could be entrusted to a single editor, or to independent authors. It was decided that, while the Commission would retain the full authority conferred upon it by the General Conference of UNESCO, the wisest course would be to select individual author-editors for each of the six volumes. The author-editors would be fully responsible for the text, but they would work under the supervision of, and in collaboration with, the Editorial Committee and the Commission; they would benefit by the assistance of scholars, designated by them, to deal with certain chapters; and, if necessary, sections could be referred to specialists.

On the recommendation of the Editorial Committee, author-editors for five of the six volumes were at this time appointed. For Volume I, Jacquetta Hawkes and Henri Frankfort, both of the United Kingdom. On the death of Professor Frankfort in 1954, the late Sir Leonard Woolley (United Kingdom) was appointed to write the second part of this volume. For Volume III, René Grousset (France), with two co-authors, Vadime Elisséeff and Philippe Wolff (France). Professor Gaston Wiet (France) took over the

author-editorship of this third volume in 1953 on the death of Professor
Grousset. For Volume IV, Louis Gottschalk (United States of America);
for Volume V, Jorge Basadre (Peru), who afterwards resigned and was
replaced later by Professor Charles Morazé (France); and for Volume VI,
K. Zachariah (India), who was succeeded in 1956 by Dr Caroline F. Ware
(United States of America), H.E. Dr K. M. Panikkar (India), and the late
Dr J. M. Romein (Netherlands).

In 1953 the late Professor Luigi Pareti (Italy) was appointed author-editor
of Volume II, with Professors Paolo Brezzi and Luciano Petech of Italy as
assistants.

By the spring of 1952 a first draft plan of the History was in circulation.
Through the active interest of the author-editors, the members of the
International Commission, and scholars consulted throughout the world
on the initiative of the International Commission, this plan was slowly
revised to constitute a general guide for the elaboration of the six volumes.

At a meeting of the International Commission in February 1954 it was
decided, on my proposal, to include in its membership the author-editors
of the six volumes and the editor of the *Journal of World History*. This
measure was designed to enable those primarily responsible for the text of
the volumes to take part in discussions and so to make a more effective
contribution to the direction of the activities of the International Commission. In addition it was decided that one single body—the Bureau of the
Commission—should be made entirely responsible for the co-ordination of
the Commission's work. To ensure the unity of style and presentation
essential to a work of such high intellectual standing and covering so wide a
field, Professor Ralph E. Turner was entrusted with the task of editing the
English texts.

In the course of the execution of its programme the International Commission benefited by the co-operation of UNESCO and of the General Conference which, at several of its sessions, had the opportunity to examine the
work plans prepared for the History, and on two occasions took decisions
which markedly influenced our work. The Ninth General Conference held
in New Delhi in 1956 recommended that the texts of all volumes be submitted to the National Commissions set up in the Member States. The
objective was to assist the International Commission in obtaining for each
volume additional critical materials to enable the author-editors to revise
and to perfect their texts. While not all National Commissions responded,
the comments which were received proved most useful. All the author-
editors have conscientiously noted the criticisms received and have taken
them into account, wherever possible, when revising their texts. Furthermore, the International Commission has sought the advice of experts on
several points.

Again at the invitation of the General Conference, following its tenth
meeting held in Paris in 1958, the International Commission decided to

appoint a number of historians to advise the Bureau and the author-editors
on possible modifications of the text of each volume of the History, in the
light of comments and criticisms received, and to suggest editorial notes on
controversial issues. This step had become necessary as Professor Turner's
illness had prevented him from accomplishing the editorial work. In pur-
suance of this policy, and in agreement with the members of the Bureau and
with the author-editors, I selected a number of eminent historians, of
different nationalities, particularly qualified to act as special consultants.
Thus, at the end of each chapter of all volumes the reader will find grouped
together editorial notes and bibliographical references that will provide him
with summaries of historical opinions on those questions which can be
variously interpreted.

The International Commission plans to issue a supplement to Volume VI,
The Twentieth Century. While the first part treats of the history of our age
in the same way as the history of previous periods was considered in all the
volumes, this second tome will be devoted to an open debate on the main
trends in scientific and cultural development at mid-century.

The six volumes include line drawings prepared by Mrs Stella Robinson
at the request of the author-editors, photographic plates assembled by the
Secretariat of the International Commission in co-operation with the author-
editors and their assistants, and maps drawn specially by the Swiss firm,
Hallwag, A.G.

At the time of publication I must recall with gratitude and regret the memory
of those scholars whom the International Commission had the misfortune
to lose in the course of its work and who contributed so much to the achievement of its task: Professors René Grousset, Henri Frankfort and K.
Zachariah, Sir Leonard Woolley, Professors Luigi Pareti, Lucien Febvre,
J. M. Romein, and H.E. Dr K. M. Panikkar.

I must hereby express, on behalf of the International Commission,
my gratitude to the General Conference of UNESCO which made this
project possible, to the Directors-General, Messrs Julian Huxley, Jaime
Torres-Bodet, Luther Evans, Vittorino Veronese and René Maheu, and to
the Secretariat of UNESCO which, through ten years, has extended assistance
and guidance on every possible occasion.

The International Commission is greatly indebted to the author-editors
who, often under difficult circumstances, fulfilled their task with the highest
competence and devotion; to its Vice-Presidents, who constitute the Bureau,
for assuming with me full responsibility for every phase of the execution of
this project; and in particular to Professor Ralph E. Turner, Chairman of
the Editorial Committee, for the elaboration of the general plan of the
History and for his whole-hearted dedication to the success of the work to
which he brought his own personal outlook of an integrated world history.
I am particularly happy to acknowledge herewith the co-operation of the

Corresponding Members, the consultants and the translators, whose work proved invaluable for the completion of this project.

The International Commission benefited throughout its work by the advice of the official Observers of the International Council of Scientific Unions, Professor R. J. Forbes; of the International Council for Philosophy and Humanistic Studies, Sir Ronald Syme; and of the International Social Science Council, Professor F. H. Lawson.

Lastly, I would like on behalf of the International Commission to thank the Secretary-General, Dr Guy S. Métraux, and his staff for their active and faithful collaboration which has contributed so much to the success of this scientific and cultural history of mankind.

PAULO E. DE BERRÊDO CARNEIRO

NOTE ON THE EDITORIAL TREATMENT
PREPARATION AND EDITING

The preparation of Volume II of the *History of Mankind: Cultural and Scientific Development* was entrusted by the International Commission to Professor Luigi Pareti of the University of Naples. At his request, two associate authors were appointed: Professor Paolo Brezzi (University of Naples), to be responsible for the sections pertaining to the origins of Christianity, and Professor Luciano Petech (University of Rome), for the sections dealing with the civilizations of India, the Far East, and Central Asia.

In 1960–61 the manuscript was sent to the National Commissions in all Member States of UNESCO and to specialists nominated by members of the International Commission. The numerous comments and suggestions which were received were submitted to the author-editor and to his associates who undertook a careful revision of the text in the light of this valuable material.

Soon after completing this work, Professor Pareti died in Rome at the age of seventy-seven. Accordingly, at the request of the President of the International Commission, the final editorial work was carried out under the general responsibility of his associates, who sought the co-operation of the Secretary-General of the International Commission.

Two consultants, Dr Guy E. F. Chilver (Queen's College, Oxford[1]; translator of the volume) and Professor Jean Filliozat (Collège de France, Paris) were requested to study the revised manuscript. On the basis of available comments they prepared editorial notes which reflect some of the differences of opinion apparent in the understanding and interpretation of the scientific and cultural development of mankind. In addition, the consultants were asked to submit to the International Commission a brief report on the volume as a whole for the guidance of the authors.

With the approval of Professors Brezzi and Petech, and with the full support of the International Commission, Dr Chilver suggested additional material for the volume, and on his recommendation the following scholars were appointed:

Professor Pedro Bosch-Gimpera (University of Mexico and the National School of Anthropology of Mexico), on the art of the Tartesso-Iberian. See Chapter XII.

Dr A. G. Drachmann (sometime on the staff of the University Library, Copenhagen), on 'Mechanics in Antiquity'. See Chapter XV.

Professor Robert Etienne (University of Bordeaux) who wrote a series of comments on specific aspects of Roman religion in Chapter XVII.

Mr M. W. Frederiksen (Worcester College, Oxford) prepared the Appendix to Chapter I on the Etruscans; the section on Roman Town Planning and Housing (Chapter XV); the note on the role of freedmen in the cities of the Early Empire, and the section on population statistics (Chapter XVI).

Professor Pierre Grimal (University of Paris) wrote important sections on literature. See Chapters XII and XVIII.

Mr Alan Watson (Oriel College, Oxford) analysed Roman jurisprudence in Chapter XVI.

In addition, Dr Barbara Levick (St Hilda's College, Oxford) compiled a bibliography on the basis of preliminary notes made by Professor Pareti.

Wherever possible, all supplementary material has been integrated into the text. In each case, however, the authorship is clearly indicated by a footnote on the page itself. In order to preserve the continuity, especially in Chapters XII and XVIII, material not written by Professor Pareti or his colleagues appears between brackets *within* the original text.

[1] Dr Chilver is now Professor at the University of Kent at Canterbury.

Editorial Notes

These can be divided into two principal categories as follows:

(1) Editorial notes prepared by the consultants, Dr Guy E. F. Chilver and Professor Jean Filliozat. In most instances, the author of the original comment upon which a note is based is named.
(2) Notes that are the sole responsibility of the scholars who prepared them, and whose names appear between parentheses at the end of the notes.

In revising the text, the author and his associates benefited from the critiques of many scholars whose comments were also used in the preparation of the editorial notes:

Dr Pedro Bosch-Gimpera, University of Mexico.
Professor Christo Danov, University of Sofia, on behalf of the Academy of Sciences of Bulgaria for the Bulgarian National Commission for UNESCO.
Dr A. G. Drachmann of Copenhagen.
Professor B. A. van Groningen, University of Leiden, the Netherlands.
Professor U. N. Ghoshal, University of Calcutta.
Professor F. M. Heichelheim, University of Toronto.
Professor Björn Hougen and Mr Aslak Liestöl, both of the Museum of National Antiquities of the University of Oslo, on behalf of the Norwegian National Commission for UNESCO.
Professor F. W. König and Professor Albin Lesky, both of the University of Vienna, on behalf of the Austrian Commission for UNESCO.
Professor H. Michell, Lennoxville, Quebec.
Dr Pavel Oliva on behalf of the Czechoslovak Commission for Co-operation with UNESCO.
Professor Ch. Th. Saricakis, University of Athens, on behalf of the Hellenic National Commission for UNESCO.
Professor Antonio L. Tovar, University of Salamanca.
The Rev. Martin R. P. McGuire, University of Washington, Washington, D.C., on behalf of the United States National Commission for UNESCO.
Professor J. Vogt, University of Tübingen, on behalf of the UNESCO Commission of the Federal Republic of Germany.

On behalf of the Commission of the USSR for UNESCO the following scholars prepared editorial notes which are printed at the request of Professor A. A. Zvorikine, Vice-President of the International Commission:

I. N. J. Golubtsova, Candidate of Historical Sciences, Academy of Sciences of the USSR.
Dr K. M. Kolobova, Professor at the University of Leningrad.
Dr E. M. Shtaerman, Institute of History, Academy of Sciences of the USSR.
L. S. Vasilyev, Candidate of Historical Sciences, Institute of Asian Peoples, Academy of Sciences of the USSR.

Finally, the authors and the consultants utilized critical material supplied by Professor Herbert Hunger, University of Vienna, on behalf of the Austrian Commission for UNESCO; by Professors Minoru Hara and Shirô Hattori, University of Tokyo, and Professor Suketoshi Yajima, Tokyo College of Science and Corresponding Member of the International Commission, on behalf of the Japanese National Commission for UNESCO.

GUY S. MÉTRAUX,
Secretary-General.

Paris, September, 1963.

ACKNOWLEDGEMENTS

UNESCO, the International Commission, the authors and the publishers wish to thank all those who have kindly given permission for the reproduction of the plates in this book. Acknowledgements are made under each illustration and abbreviated as follows:

Archaeological Museum, Madrid AM

Archaeological Survey of India, New Delhi ASI

Archives Photographiques, Paris APP

Bibliothèque Nationale, Paris BNP

Bildarchiv Foto, Marburg BFM

British Information Services and the Central Office of Information BI

British Museum BM

Commissione Pontificia di Archeologia Sacra, Rome AS

Department of Archaeology, Government of India DAI

Fratelli Alinari, Florence ALINARI

Gabinetto Fotografico Nazionale, Rome GFN

Hellenic National Commission for Unesco HELLENIC

Mr Saburō Hosaka, Japan HOSAKA

India Office IO

Institute of Archaeology, Academy of Sciences, The Rumanian People's Republic IAR

John Rylands Library, Manchester JOHN RYLANDS

Lahore Museum LM

Mathura Museum, India MMI

Léonard von Matt, Switzerland VON MATT

Musée Guimet, Paris MG

Musée du Louvre, Paris LOUVRE

Musée National du Bardo MNB

Musée Saint Rémi, Reims REIMS

Musei Comunali, Rome MC

Museum für Ostasiatische Kunst, Cologne MOK

National Museum of India, New Delhi NMI

National Museum, Seoul NMS

National Museum, Tokyo NMT

Östasiatiska Museet, Stockholm OM

Prado Museum, Madrid PMM

Science Museum, London SML

Soprintendenza alle Antichità dell'Etruria Meridionale, Rome
SAEM

Soprintendenza alle Antichità della Puglia e del Materano, Taranto
SAPM

Staatliche Kunstsammlungen, Dresden DM

Staatliche Museen, Berlin BSM

Staatliche Museeum (Antikenabteilung), Berlin BSMA

Stadtbibliothek, Trier ST

Stato Maggiore Aeronautica Militare, Italy AERONAUTICA

Professor J. B. Ward Perkins, The British School at Rome
WARD PERKINS

CONTENTS

PART ONE: FROM ABOUT 1200 BC TO ABOUT 500 BC

PART TWO: FROM 500 BC TO THE CHRISTIAN ERA

PART THREE: FROM THE BEGINNING OF THE CHRISTIAN ERA TO *c*. AD 500

ILLUSTRATIONS

These illustrations follow page 146

FIGURES

All line drawings were executed especially for this work by Stella Robinson in collaboration with R. G. Hadlow.

MAPS

The maps of Volume II were prepared by Hallwag, A.G., Berne, on the basis of original material supplied by Professor Luigi Pareti and his associates.

PART ONE

MANKIND FROM ABOUT 1200 BC TO ABOUT 500 BC

AUTHORS' PREFACE

WE ask our readers to bear in mind certain facts, neglect of which would make it impossible to use our book profitably or to understand it precisely. This is a work which has been planned by persons other than those who are carrying out the actual task; and the authors have therefore found themselves, as so often happens with works of this kind, tied to a pre-ordained scheme of presentation, which is not the one they themselves would have chosen to adopt. This scheme requires a systematic exposition of the history of mankind, divided into sections each of which covers a single type of human activity; and it has the advantage of making it easier to trace the broad lines along which particular human activities evolved, both in time and in space. The disadvantage is that the interdependence of these various activities is thereby rendered less clear. Nevertheless, this defect can be remedied if the reader is patient and alert enough to compare one chapter with another, and to make proper use of the table of contents, the indexes, and the cross-references.

If on the other hand we had felt bound, in dealing with each topic, to set out the whole chain of causes and effects at large, we should have produced a work of analysis and not of synthesis. It would have been disconnected, and full of repetition.

Without doubt there are scholars who tend to place importance upon only one way of looking at history, for example those who emphasize only the social and economic factors. But though they would have preferred the book to be written according to their principles, we are sure they will recognize that they could hardly expect this from authors like ourselves, who believe these principles to be one-sided and consequently not genuinely historical.

The fair-minded reader will also, we hope, understand the position of scholars who have to deal, in a work of synthesis, with a number of historical problems which they have already attempted to solve, with minute attention, in sufficiently well-known published works. They are bound, in the work of synthesis, to give prominence to the answers they believe, all things considered, to be the nearest to the truth, though they will also mention any other views which appear to be reputable.

Lastly, we beg specialist scholars to remember that this book is indeed one of synthesis and general information. It cannot go deeply into every topic and set out all the details the specialist wants, without prejudicing the balance both of the work as a whole and of its separate parts.

LUIGI PARETI
PAOLO BREZZI
LUCIANO PETECH

CHAPTER I

THE CHIEF HISTORICAL EVENTS
1200 BC—500 BC[1]

MANY features of history can influence developments in thought, science, and culture, not only among individual peoples but over wide sections of humanity, sometimes even over the whole world. One group of people may be enabled to become leaders of progress; another may find its activities smothered or extinguished, and be obliged to yield its place to other groups. These processes often enlarge, restrict, or drastically modify the zones from which culture radiates and the exchanges between these zones; here a leap forward and there a leap back; or sometimes a people is driven by events into a dormant state which may be mortal but which could also be invigorating.[2]

It is enough to recall among such decisive events: wars with their outcomes; long fruitful times of peace; revolutions and their innovating force; migrations with the ethnic mixtures they bring; colonial undertakings; conquests by imperialist nations; the breakdown of powers once dominant; changes in homes or climates or natural environment, and thence altered conditions of production and economy; vicissitudes in state and society; the diffusion of new religious and moral concepts; and finally the spread of plagues and of the other agents by which populations are destroyed.

These considerations affect the plan of our work, which is divided into three parts, covering three successive periods. Each must be preceded by a broad survey of the main events which bear on the cultural and scientific development of the leading peoples, and of the others who came to some extent under their influence. In the subsequent chapters of each part, which are devoted to the separate aspects of human activity, attention will be paid to the connection between each aspect and the events previously surveyed. We shall of course expand our field of vision at the beginning and at the end. We shall recall some of the things said in Volume I about the events of earlier times; and when dealing with events at the end of our period we shall take account of some of the effects felt in the period of Volume III (see *History of Mankind: Cultural and Scientific Development*, London and New York, 1963, 6 volumes).

I. THE MEDITERRANEAN, THE AEGEAN AND THE NEAR EAST

a. *The Decline of Empires in the Eastern Mediterranean.*
Migrations, the Foundation of New States

The Hatti, after their victory over the state of Mitanni[3] in 1365, substituted their own colonies for those settled by the Hurri in Syria and in northern Palestine: this brought them into contact with the Egyptian possessions in southern Palestine. It also encouraged the Assyrians to free themselves from vassalage to Mitanni and to resume their expansionist tendencies. As a result the three major states, Hattic, Assyrian, and Egyptian, whose possessions now bordered on one another, had by the middle of the fourteenth century achieved a balance of power. They still often came to blows, but were normally able to carry on extensive exchange of ideas and commodities under peaceful conditions.

They constituted the three most active areas for the diffusion of ideas and commodities among their smaller neighbours. Chief among these were the Kassites (who had assimilated the composite civilization of Babylonia where they were still dominant), the small 'Minoan' states of Crete, and the 'Cycladic' communities in the Aegean islands. But the triad of dominant powers was gravely menaced. Threats gathered around them, and the most effective of these came from the hordes of new migrants who poured into their lands.

The warrior tribes, nomad and semi-nomad, scattered through the immense steppes of middle Eurasia, were perennially on the move. Their aims were various. They sought new pastures and new lands for temporary cultivation in a favourable climate; they wanted plunder; or they were escaping the attacks of hordes, more barbarous and more powerful, which pressed on their backs. In this way they had entered for some time on one of their most restless and dynamic phases. The groups who were already settled were pushed farther south or confined to narrow territories, or amalgamated with the migratory tribes. These migrations provoked a general confusion of peoples and there were further displacements for a long time to come.

Many of these migratory waves affected the so-called Indo-European peoples who, whatever their original racial elements, had lived for a considerable time in adjacent areas. They had adopted similar languages and allied civilizations.

The migrations of the Indo-Europeans who pressed into Italy and the westernmost areas of Europe, and of the group which took the eastern route as far as India, will be treated in their proper context. Let us here consider the complex middle migratory layer formed by the people of Greek, Macedonian, Thraco-Phrygian, and Illyrian dialects who drove in successive moves into the Balkans, Anatolia, and beyond.

This movement had begun in an epoch substantially farther back in time —probably already in the Copper Age or in the earliest Bronze Age—when the advance guards of the 'Hellenic' people had penetrated into the Greek peninsula. In historical times these were the Ionic-speaking inhabitants of Attica and Euboea, those behind them in Thessaly and Boeotia who used northern Aeolic dialects, and those Peloponnesians who expressed themselves in southern Aeolic or Arcadian.

These first groups of Greeks had now for a long time been fused with their indigenous predecessors, who probably belonged to the same Asian stock from which the contemporary inhabitants of the Aegean islands derived. These natives had continued to develop (partly through their own talents, and partly by direct or indirect contact with the people of Anatolia, Syria, and Egypt) those typical Bronze Age civilizations which, from their regional stamp, we call 'Minoan' when it is found in Crete, and 'Cycladic' in the island zones.

These civilizations were evolved in areas of the Hellenic peninsula nearest to the Aegean, or in those with most frequent contact with the Minoan and Cycladic lands. As a reflex from them, the Greeks had developed a civilization of their own which we normally call Mycenaean. It was above all an 'Aulic' (Palace) civilization, which expressed itself in the palaces and tombs of sovereigns from the sixteenth century onward. From several angles it fulfilled needs, tastes, and inspirations all its own, although in other respects it reflected pre-existing local usages.

But these two parallel and related cultural developments, Minoan and Greek (partly spontaneous and partly reflected), were complicated by the arrival of new waves of Greek stock who spoke Achaeo-Doric dialects and had different customs. These had up till then remained farther back along the migration route. Their slow displacement can be dated as beginning at the latest from the sixteenth century, and was roughly contemporary with the settlement of the Macedonians in the sites they possessed in historical times, and with the establishment of the Thracians farther to the east and north-east. The latter were in their turn pushed by the Illyrians, part of whom were advancing towards the south-west.

From a push of this kind a section of the Thracians crossed the Hellespont and the Bosphorus, and occupied vast tracts of western and central Anatolia. They merged with the natives of other races and bred new hybrid peoples of mixed language. The results were the Phrygians, Mysians, Bithynians, Cappadocians, Paphlagonians, and Cilicians, whose names do not appear in Hittite texts of earlier centuries.[4]

Ancient learned tradition distinguished the Achaeans from the Dorians, making the former the pre-Dorian inhabitants of the Peloponnese. But there is decisive evidence to the contrary.[5,5a] All the people who, in fully historical times, were still known as Achaeans spoke Doric dialects, and not pre-Doric or Arcadian; moreover the name of 'Dorians'—used first by the colonists of Asia Minor—was gradually adopted in Crete, the Peloponnese, and north-eastern Greece, by those who earlier were called Achaeans, while the remainder, continuing to use Doric dialects, preserved the old name of Achaeans. The fact is that the name 'Achaeans' originally meant all Greeks irrespective of their dialect, and therefore irrespectively of the invading movement to which they belonged: the names 'Ionian', 'Aeolian', and 'Dorian' grew up later, and each of these bore a definite relation to the dialect in question. If we use the terms 'Achaeo-Ionians', 'Achaeo-Aeolians', and 'Achaeo-Dorians' when speaking of these peoples' migrations, we are doing so for the sake of clarity, and with deliberate anticipation of later times.

Moving then from north-western Greece the Achaeo-Dorians followed two directions. One moved to the east until they eventually came out at the Malian Gulf, occupying Achaean Phthiotis and the district subsequently known as Doris. They split the originally compact northern Aeolic unit into two segments—Thessalians and Boeotians—and shut the Ionians into the confines of Attica. The other part went towards the south-east, penetrated by the isthmus into the Peloponnese, and there spread out, in a horse-shoe movement, to the south towards Argolis and Laconia (where they called themselves Dorians), and to the west towards Achaea and Elis. Later on, in the seventh century, they contained and limited the southern Aeolians to Arcadia alone.

The two successive penetrations began, it appears, in the fifteenth century, as is shown by adequately clear archaeological evidence. They developed by stages in the centuries which followed. Naturally these Achaeo-Dorians amalgamated more or less completely with the other Greek people of Aeolic dialect whom they found in the new territories. They even absorbed and diffused the Mycenaean civilization which for almost two centuries had been flourishing there, especially in the east.

But the two Achaeo-Dorian occupations provoked in their turn other displacements. One part of the northern Aeolians (who had once lived between Thessaly and Boeotia) moved to Lesbos and the coast of the Troad, creating the so-called Aeolian colonies for which the earliest evidence derives from the destruction of 'Stratum VIIA' of the Ilium excavations.[6] Parts of the Ionians went towards the Cyclades and the coasts of Asiatic Ionia, a fact which explains the evidence from the excavations of Mycenaean Miletus. Some of the Arcadians moved to Crete and the southern coasts of Asia Minor, as far as Pamphylia and Cyprus.

These displacements, in their early days, were marked by new constructional and artistic systems of a Graeco-Mycenaean type which replaced those of Minoan, Cycladic, Trojan and Anatolian origin in Crete, Melos, Troy, Miletus, and even on the Syrian shores at Ugarit and Alalak-Al Mina. They seem also to have provoked the exodus of a part of the pre-Greek population of Crete, who went to settle in southern Syria and so created the Philistines —who gave the country its name of Palestine.

But the Achaeo-Dorian migration was not yet exhausted. After having filled Argolis and Laconia to overflowing some invaders took to the sea towards the islands and coasts of Asia, especially the regions already occupied by the emigrants from Arcadia. This Achaeo-Dorian element was not numerous enough to modify the kinds of Greek civilization which were already dominant in Aeolis and Ionia, but in more southerly areas it gained supremacy. As a result the Arcadian colonists succeeded in preserving their identity through their dialect only in the more distant lands of Pamphylia and Cyprus. The Achaeo-Dorians, who planted themselves in Crete, Rhodes, Caria, and Lycia, became, as we shall show, one of the most dynamic and active races in the eastern Mediterranean zone in the thirteenth and twelfth centuries BC.

Meanwhile, during the thirteenth century, these migrations of new peoples, Thracian and Hellenic, into Anatolia, were a decisive factor in accelerating the decline in Hattic power. It was already undermined by rebellious subjects aiming at independence and by continuous struggles with the Kaskeans on the southern coasts of the Black Sea. But what really proved ruinous was the barrier formed towards the Aegean by the Phrygians and other kindred peoples, who came from the Balkans and took part about 1250 in the anti-Hittite coalition of Assuwa (the Dardani, Mysi, and Lyki are explicitly mentioned in this connection). Greek peoples therefore were planted in increasing masses on the Anatolian coasts and the neighbouring islands; a Graeco-Phrygian-Microasiatic belt, with a new common cultural orientation, isolated the western Hittite dominions and the Mesopotamian hinterland from the Aegean. To the south, from 1350 to 1225, the power of the Achaean Greeks (the Ahhiyava of Hittite documents), short-lived though it was, seized the coast from Caria to Cilicia and interrupted Hittite communications with Cyprus. In northern Syria the situation was aggravated by Graeco-Mycenaean outposts, like that at Ugarit (Ras Shamrah), and by the settlement of Greek people like the Danaoi. Ugarit can be shown from excavations to have existed in the fourteenth and thirteenth centuries, but to have been destroyed shortly afterwards. Danuna appear in fourteenth-century texts of Amarna, and Din'n (or Denyen) among the raiders repelled from Egypt about 1200. It is tempting to identify both these with the Danaoi, and to seek confirmation from the name 'Dananim' found on an eighth-century inscription from Karatepe in Cilicia, where traces of the wanderers of the earlier period are not surprising.[7]

The Hittite empire was soon to be catastrophically and utterly dismembered. The only survivors for any length of time were some of the so-called neo-Hittite settlements (which had ousted those of the Mitanni in northern Syria). There arose from this a completely new order, and perhaps also cultural barbarization, through the collapse of the old areas of diffusion and the rise of new ones. These events are known too superficially, but they perhaps explain not a few of the early exchanges of ideas and concepts between the Greek and Anatolian peoples, and the indirect cultural borrowings by Hellas from the Orient.

The Hittite catastrophe and the Phrygian-Greek immigrations then provoked a state of social and political chaos: a favourable background for a complex series of daring exploits and temporary coalitions, consisting of armed bands, pirates, and sometimes a mass of immigrants (with waggons,

women, and children), who swarmed over the Middle East. Of the two surviving great powers, Egypt was placed in a state of emergency, and Assyria
had its western possessions reduced.

Moreover with the dismemberment of the Hittite empire, Anatolia
proper remained divided into many small states. Of these not a few had
already been part of the Hittite dominions or had lived in its shadow; others
were of new creation, formed by the new Phrygian-speaking migrants, who
became more or less closely linked with the old population.

One of the most important states was the Phrygian, which derived, as
far as one can tell, from the fusion of the Ascani, a pre-Indo-European
people, with the new Indo-European arrivals (the Brygians). Its political
centre was first at Gordium in the Sangarios valley, and then at Nakolea;
and the state extended gradually as far as the Halys on the east and the
Aegean on the west. Greek tradition speaks of their maritime supremacy
(thalassocracy) in the ninth century. In all probability the Troad also lived
for some time in the orbit of the Phrygian state. After the fall of Hittite
rule and before the Graeco-Aeolian colonization, certain small independent
states existed there; among them were Troy and the Dardanians—recorded
in the *Iliad* but before that in the Egyptian documents of Ramses II, who
defeated 'the Peoples of the Sea', the invaders of Egypt. Their name, identical
with that of the Dardani of Thrace, suggests a fusion of pre-Indo-European
and Indo-European peoples.

Greek colonization, and the reaction of the natives to it, tended now[8]
to reduce the area of the Phrygian kingdom, especially in the west. It finally
collapsed, however, through invasions at the hands of the Cimmerians,
which began soon after 700 and resulted in the partial occupation of the
country throughout that century. This tribe came from present-day south
Russia (compare the name of the Crimean peninsula); they were probably
Indo-European nomads of an Indo-Iranian type.[9]

A second state of remarkable importance in post-Hittite western Anatolia
was that of Lydia, which had Sardis as its capital. They too, to judge from
their language, appear to derive from a fusion between indigenous Asiatic
peoples (the Maeones of Homer) and Indo-European migrants. Herodotus
speaks of an earlier dynasty of theirs, the Heracleidai, lasting five centuries;
followed by a new dynasty of Mermnadai, starting with Gyges about 685.
In these centuries, in all probability, Lydia lived in the orbit of the Phrygian
empire.

During the reign of Gyges, the Cimmerians attacked Lydia too, and to
resist them Gyges allied himself with the Assyrians, and submitted to their
hegemony. On the other hand he had already begun to extend his own power
over the Greek colonies of the Asiatic coasts of the Aegean, though at the
same time he encouraged Hellenic culture in his own land. The same policy,
struggle against the Cimmerians, expansion to the detriment of the Greek
colonies (who, however, drew great economic advantages from the extension

of their trade in Anatolia), and assimilation of Greek civilization, was followed by Gyges' successors: among them Ardys took Priene; Alyattes occupied Clazomenai and Smyrna, though he failed to occupy Miletus. Alyattes fought also against the Median king Cyaxares, and extended his power in Anatolia: in 585 he successfully fixed the limit of his influence at the river Halys; and about 590 he had decisively driven out the Cimmerians, and occupied the central zone of Phrygia. His successor Croesus inherited an empire which included all Asia Minor west of the Halys, except Lycia, Caria, Cilicia, and the Greek city of Miletus. He succeeded also in taking and depopulating Ephesus; but he then clashed with the Persian king Cyrus who besieged him at Sardis and took him prisoner, and from then on Lydia became a Persian possession (546).

Egypt. We said above that the fall of the Hittite empire encouraged a series of expeditions by armed bands in search of booty and conquest. Egypt had been fiercely attacked by such bands in the reign of the Pharaohs Merneptah (about 1234–1220) and Ramses III (c.1195–1165). On the first occasion[10] the main attack was led from the north-west by the Libyan Tehenu, prompted by an expansionist movement which was exciting the Hamitic tribes of the semi-desert region of Cyrenaica. The second invasion came from the north-east, from southern Syria. Among the aggressors at the time of Merneptah we notice the Agaiwasha, that is to say the Achaeans; the Lukku or Lycians; the Tursha, the Sherdana, and the Shekelesha, who can perhaps be connected with the inhabitants of the region Tyrrha (or Tarsos or Tarnisa) in Lydia, and with those of Sardis and Sagalassus respectively. Among the aggressors of Ramses III we find the Danuna (Danaoi), the Peleset (Philistines), the Thekel (from Syrian Dor according to Wen Amon's report), the Washasha, and again the Shekelesha. Ramses III succeeded in halting the immigration and preventing these foreigners from settling in Egypt in mass, but he could not hold back the Libyan hordes. In the course of time all the Syrian dominions of the Nile kingdom were lost, and were settled by the new Semitic invasions (see pp. 19 ff.). They erected a barrier against cultural exchanges between Egypt, Mesopotamia, and Anatolia, which lasted for more than two centuries. At the same time the established relations between Egypt and the Aegean world were coming to an end.

Here it is worth glancing at such developments in Egypt, down to the sixth century BC, as are relevant to our survey. Under the last Ramsids of the Twentieth Dynasty (1165–1085) life in Egypt degenerated; and trouble was also caused by continual disturbances of public order, by the feudal claims made by the Libyan governors of the 'nomes', and by political encroachment from the priestly colleges. With the Twenty-first Dynasty Egypt split into two states; one with a usurping Pharaoh at Tanis, the other with the priests of Ammon at Thebes. Then, in the course of the Twenty-second Dynasty (about 935 onwards), complete dynastic power passed to a

Libyan chief, Sheshonk (935–918), who placed the capital at Bubastis, and succeeded for a time in reuniting the country. This king profited from the quarrels between the kingdoms of Judah and Israel, and managed to set foot once more in Palestine, where after taking Ugarit and Byblos he sacked Jerusalem. But his policy of expansion was soon abandoned by later Libyan dynasts of the Twenty-second and Twenty-fourth Dynasties, because of dissension with the clergy, and rivalry from the indigenous Twenty-third Dynasty, which established itself at Tanis about 800. Tefnakht, a sovereign of the Twenty-fourth Dynasty, succeeded in seizing power (720 BC), but he found himself faced by a rival dynasty, the Libyo-Ethiopian Twenty-fifth. The latter, first installed at Napata, occupied Ethiopia, and then by various operations in Lower Egypt ended by reuniting the whole country (about 715), with signal effect on its cultural character. Soon afterwards these Ethiopian Pharaohs were tempted to check the Assyrian advance in Syria; but instead the Assyrian kings penetrated into Egypt; Esarhaddon took Memphis in 670, and Ashur-banipal in 667 and 663 pushed as far as Thebes, and forced the Ethiopian Pharaohs back to Nubia. Egypt then became an Assyrian province, and this encouraged direct cultural relations between the two countries. Meanwhile the decline of pharaonic power permitted grave social upheavals.

Not long afterwards the Assyrian troops, who were needed in the fight against Babylonia, were withdrawn, and thus Psamtik I (663–609), who governed Egypt on behalf of Ashur-banipal, was able to declare his independence and to found the Saite dynasty (the Twenty-sixth, 663–525). The dynasty created a strong fleet and developed a policy of expansion, not only towards Nubia, but also in Syria, and brought on the Saites frequent counterattacks from Babylonia. To meet them they made use of mercenaries, particularly Greeks; the Greeks were also allowed to open up iron mines and to station trading posts in Egypt.[11] This was of fundamental importance in bringing about the resumption of direct cultural exchanges between Egyptians and the Greeks in the seventh and sixth centuries.

In the reign of the Pharaoh Amasis in 567 the Saite dynasts suffered their last severe rebuff from the Babylonian Nebuchadnezzar. Yet they then decided to support these same Babylonians against the conquering Persians. But they, like their allies, were overthrown by Cambyses in 525. Egypt then became, for about two centuries, a satrapy of the Persian kings, and this marked a decisive turning point in the development of cultural relations between the countries of the Middle East.

The Assyrian Empire. While Egypt gradually lost its power and then also its liberty, the Assyrian empire continued to pass through alternating periods of growth and stagnation. In an early period, lasting a century and a half (1365–1207), it had profited successfully from the fall of Mitanni and the progressive decline of the Hittites. Next, with sweeping expansionist vigour the Assyrians first occupied northern Mesopotamia, which had once belonged to Mitanni; and then, under Tukulti Nimurta I (1234–1207), confronted the Hittites at Carchemish, the Nairi near Lake Van, and beyond them the Guti. In the south they defeated the Babylonian Kassites and occupied their territory.

For the cultural growth of the East, the result, particularly of the last conquests, was remarkable. Although in many important fields the new rulers[12] let themselves be absorbed by the earlier Babylonian civilization (diplomatic language, literary works, religious ideas, etc.), all the same they, too, left a clear imprint. They spread certain national cults, together with new legal, artistic, and military ideas; and they introduced a unique political organization with a feudal basis.

But towards the end of the thirteenth century, after the violent death of Tukulti Nimurta (1207), Assyrian power contracted on itself over nearly a hundred years. It lost its Syrian dominions; and large parts of the East were occupied by the Elamites, who had come down from their crags in the Iranian mountains and at one time, in 1171, took Babylonia from the Kassites.

Elamite rule was brief and was brought to an end by a simultaneous counter-attack from Babylonian elements (under the Isin dynasty, whose most famous king was Nebuchadnezzar I), and from the Assyrians under a new leader, Tiglath-Pileser I (1112–1074).[13] The latter also defeated the Nairi and the Muska, established his rule over the peoples of Anatolia and Syria as far as the Mediterranean, and several times defeated the Babylonians. After him there followed a second period of stagnation in Assyria, lasting from 1074–909, which was mostly caused by new Semitic movements, especially those of the Arameans. Once again the Assyrians lost all the conquests they had made, and found themselves in possession only of their original lands. Next came a new revival with Adad Nirari II (909–889), Ashur-nasirpal II (883–859), and Shalmaneser III (859–824). These kings offered opposition to Urartu in the north, recovered the dominions in Syria, and defeated the Arameans of Damascus and the Hebrews in Israel. They made Tyre and Sidon subject, and also occupied Babylonia down to the Persian Gulf.

There followed a new, though broken, period of decadence (824–809: 782–745). This was due to regional separatism, to struggles with Urartu and the Medes, who were now living in the mountains to the east of Mesopotamia, and to the political and cultural ascendancy of Babylonia. But there now took place the last revival of Assyrian imperialism (745–630 or 612), begun by the victories of Tiglath-Pileser III (745–727) over the Amorites, Elamites, Urartu, and Babylonians. His work was continued by Shalmaneser V and by Sargon II (721–705), who began the struggle with the Pharaohs of Lower Egypt for the possession of the Syrian zone. In two battles (722–711) they overcame the hostile coalition and transplanted the conquered people to Assyria. At the same time they withstood the Chaldeans of Babylonia and

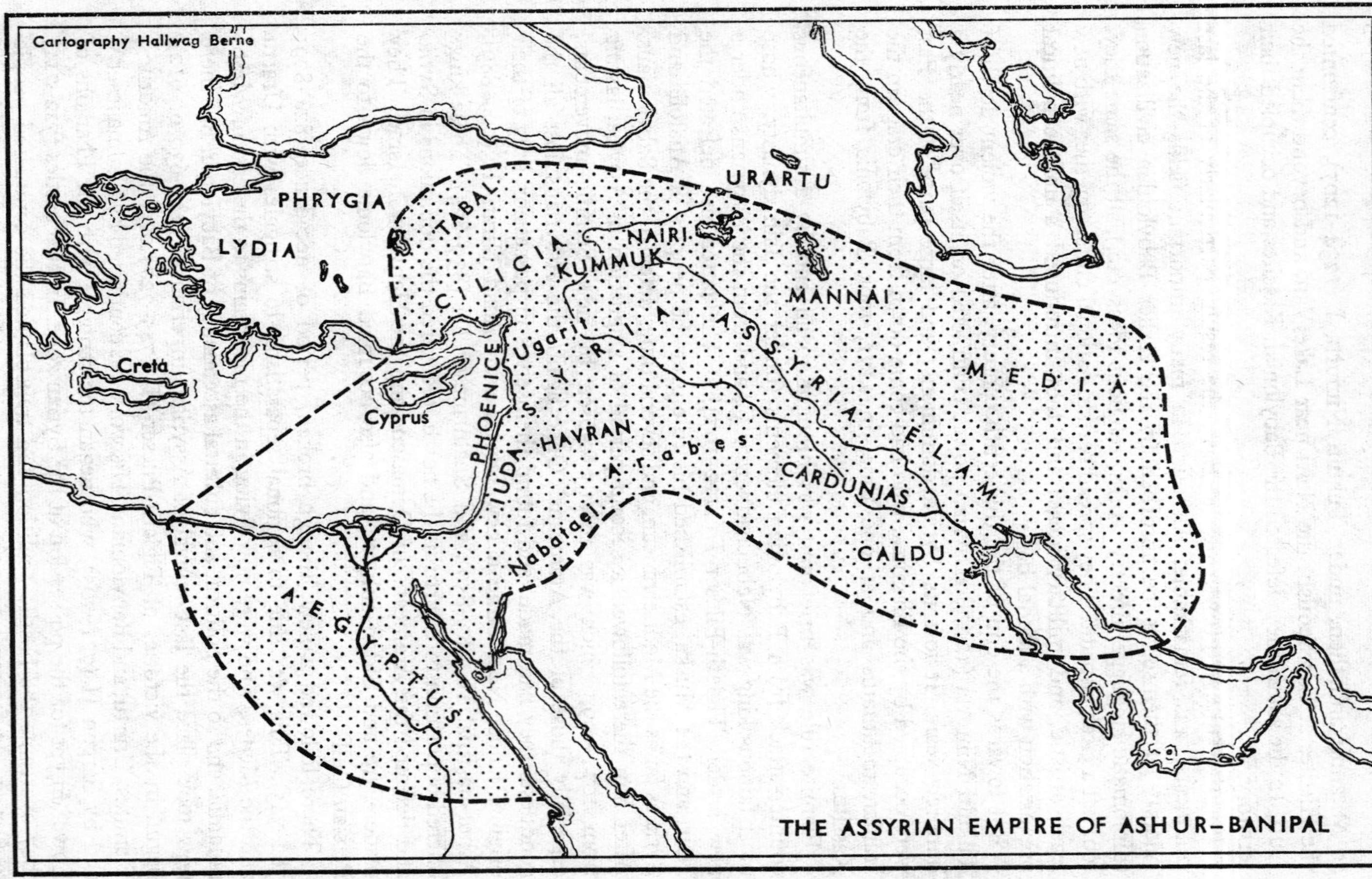

URARTU

MEDIA

MANNAI

NAIRI

KUMMUK

ASSYRIA

ELAM

CARDUNIAS

CALDU

TABAL

CILICIA

PHRYGIA

LYDIA

UGARIT

PHOENICE

JUDA

HAVRAN

Arabes

Nabataei

AEGYPTUS

Cyprus

Creta

THE ASSYRIAN EMPIRE OF ASHUR—BANIPAL

MAP I

the Elamites. Sargon's successor, Sennacherib (705–681), in his turn defeated a coalition of Chaldeans, Elamites, Sidonians, and Egyptians, destroyed Babylon, and deported 200,000 Hebrews. The struggle was continued by Esarhaddon and by Ashur-banipal (669–630), this last being the king who conquered the Egyptians in 667 and 663. (Map I.)

But at this point the Assyrians, though they allied themselves with the Pharaoh Psamtik I, were not able to withstand the Chaldeans, who were supported by the Medes and used the Cimmerian hordes and wandering Scyths as auxiliary forces. In 612 Nineveh fell, and in 603 Assyrian resistance to the Babylonians came to an end. They were worn out by their wars, and their numbers were too small and insignificant in comparison with the subject and displaced peoples living in their homelands; their forces were scattered too thinly to defend their vast possessions and by this time had become mere raiding hordes; and their decline also owed something to the incompetence of their last kings. Nevertheless, for cultural history, the importance of the Assyrian empire, even in its last phase, is confirmed by its monuments, and by the 22,000 tablets from Ashur-banipal's library, which contain writings on history, astrology, astronomy, and mathematics, as well as texts of an administrative nature.

Phoenician Colonization. Historical events and cultural development in the areas of Syria and Palestine were determined largely by the geographical position of the country, lying at the crossing of the commercial highways which allowed communication between the powers of the East and at the point at which these highways gave access to the sea. Another factor was the characteristic bent of the Semitic and pre-Semitic mind. Yet a third arose from the fluctuations in the degree of freedom these lands and peoples could enjoy during the many turns of fortune which affected the imperial powers around them. The conflicts of the great powers before the beginning of our period were often fought out in just those areas where their cultural influences overlapped and their spheres of political action met. In these periods the tiny countries and city-states in the Canaanite-Phoenician district (Acco, Tyre, Sidon, Berytus, Byblos, Ugarit, and so on), and also in the Amorite district farther inland (Aleppo, Qatna), had to get on as best they might by manœuvring between the more powerful contestants or by putting themselves at the service of one of them. In this way they came profoundly under the influence both of Mesopotamian and of Anatolian and Egyptian civilization, all of them uniting with the indigenous elements to form in these areas a cultural mixture which was markedly complex. But already in the fourteenth century, as can be seen from the Tell el Amarna records, they had to take advantage of the first symptoms of Egyptian inactivity to assume importance in their own right. Then followed the upheavals caused by the migrations of the 'Peoples of the Sea' and the renewal of more direct contacts with the Mycenaeans, who made settlements as far

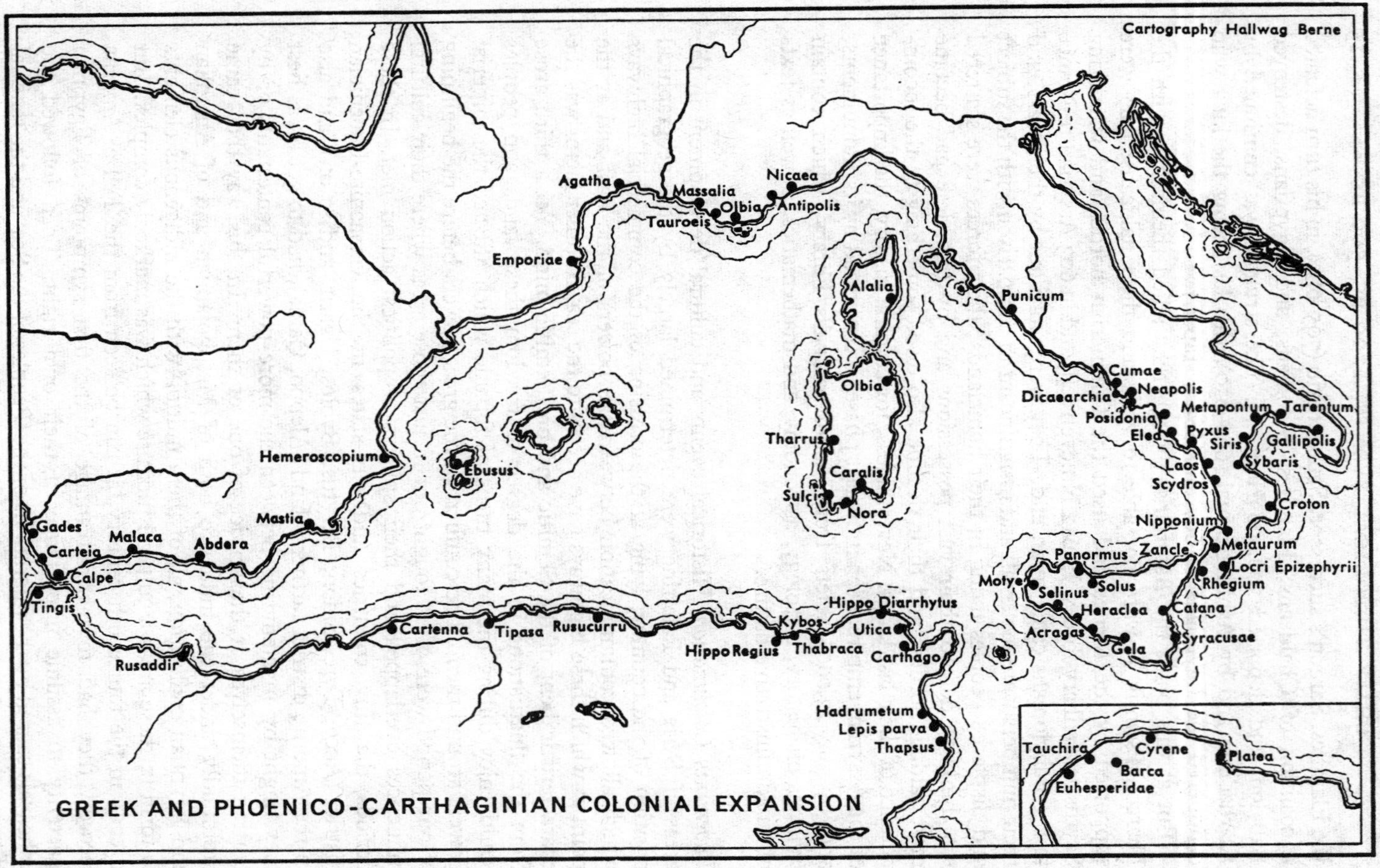

GREEK AND PHOENICO-CARTHAGINIAN COLONIAL EXPANSION

MAP II *a*

Cartography Hallwag Berne

Tarentum
Gallipolis
Siris
Sybaris
Croton
Metapontum
Pyrus
Locri Epizephyrii
Laos
Scydros
Caiaga
Neapolis
Elea
Rhegium
Cumae
Posidonia
Nipponium
Metaurum
Zancle
Syracusae
Dicaearchia
Panormus
Solus
Heraclea
Motye
Selinus
Gela
Acragas

Punicum

Alalia

Olbia

Tharrus

Caralis
Sulcis
Nora

Hippo Diarrhytus
Utica
Kybos
Thabraca
Carthago
Hadrumetum
Lepis parva
Thapsus

Hippo Regius
Cartenna
Rusucurru
Tipasa

Nicaea
Antipolis
Massalia
Olbia
Taurois
Agatha

Emporiae

Ebusus

Hemeroscopium
Mastia
Malaca
Abdera
Carteia
Calpe
Tingis
Gades
Rusaddir

Tauchira
Cyrene
Platea
Barca
Euhesperidae

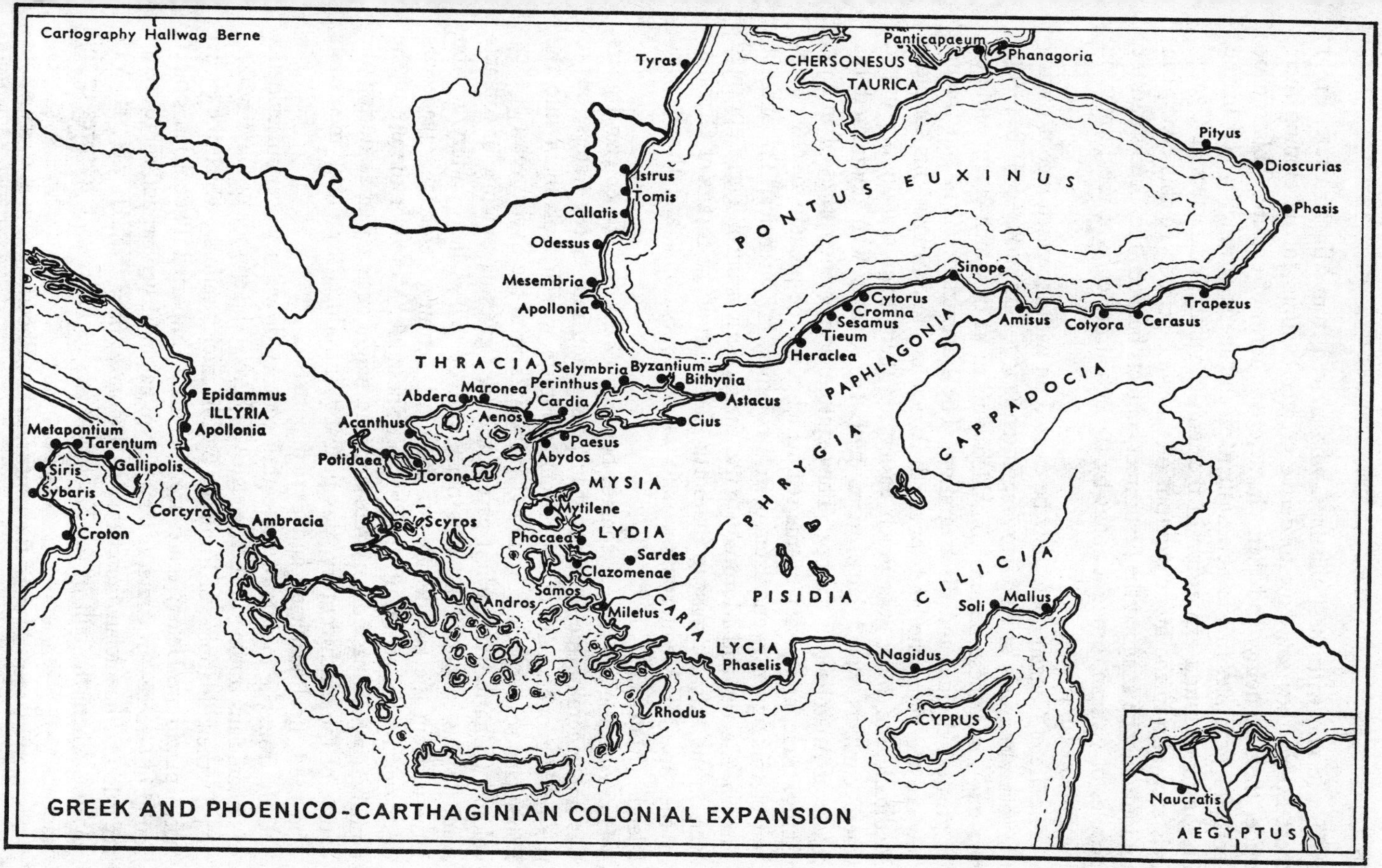

Cartography Hallwag Berne

GREEK AND PHOENICO-CARTHAGINIAN COLONIAL EXPANSION

MAP II b

as Ugarit, and with the Philistines, who arrived from Minoan Crete. From these events they saw how to derive greater facilities for developing their trade, their economy, and their characteristic form of culture. This can be seen, for example, in the new system of alphabetic writing, which in the first instance found expression in the semi-cuneiform characters at Ugarit; it is seen also in the literary output of the same period. To this epoch can undoubtedly be assigned the first direct contacts between the Greeks and the peoples of Canaan, brought about by the actual presence of the former on the Phoenician coasts.

The life of Canaan could now be carried on with increased vigour during the several periods of Assyrian stagnation (1207–1112; 1074–909; 824–809; 782–745): and these periods coincided with those in which Egypt suffered its greatest decline and disintegration. The Phoenician sailors and traders now coasted along the lands of north Africa and to Sardinia: this southern Mediterranean route was much easier for them than that in the north, where conflicts would have arisen with the Greeks who dominated the coasts of Anatolia and Europe. They started daring enterprises of mining, fishing, trade, and piracy on the sea, which were the prelude to settlements, first of trading posts and later of real colonies, in Cyrenaica, Tripolitania, Tunisia, Algeria, and Morocco (to use the modern names). These appeared even on the Atlantic coast to the north and south of the Straits of Gibraltar in the Spanish Mediterranean, and as far as Sardinia and the Balearic Islands. (Map IIa.)

However, the first direct contact between Greek and Phoenician traders was not generally due to Phoenician penetration into Greek waters, but to the trading operations of the Greek colonists, which took them into the Phoenician sea, especially round Cyprus, and on to the Syrian coast at their colony of Ugarit. The earliest part of the *Iliad* gives us a picture of contacts made in this manner: and it is borne out by 'Thessalian' pottery at Abu Howan, from the last decades of the ninth century, before this place was destroyed by the action of the Pharaoh Sheshonk. Moreover the use of the alphabet, which passed to Crete and the neighbouring islands during the course of the ninth century, was probably introduced by Greek merchants who used the Phoenician and Syrian ports.

Only from the middle of the eighth century do we have certain evidence of Phoenicians trading in the Aegean.[14] There is the episode of *Odyssey*, XV, 403 ff. (the kidnapping of Eumaeus by Phoenician sailors), which the earlier poets placed in Delos; there are the many imported Phoenician objects found in Greece—in Crete, Athens, Olympia, and Rheneia; and there are the records of Phoenician merchants in Lemnos (*Iliad*, XXIII, 744; cf. VII, 467 ff.), where the cult of the Kabeiroi owes its Phoenician features to this trade.

So, step by step through the centuries, the Phoenicians took every opportunity to develop trade and also colonization in the southern and extreme western Mediterranean. This process was of the greatest importance on account of the imports—foodstuffs and above all metals—brought from the West to the East, against the export of manufactured goods which the Phoenicians had invented or copied. Equally significant was the penetration of ideas and techniques of Middle Eastern origin into a part of the West.

This flow of trade between the Phoenician mother country and its colonies could not yet proceed without disturbance, especially in the periods in which the mother country came under the dominion of one of the great neighbouring powers and lost the unfettered control of its ports and of its ships. Even at those periods, however, commercial activity must often have been maintained, in order to satisfy the interests and needs of the overlords. That explains the continuous prosperity of the Phoenician cities, which is attested by archaeology and by tradition, especially from the twelfth to the eighth centuries; this particularly affected Sidon, and later Tyre. The periods of Assyrian expansionism, therefore, brought difficulties, but not insuperable ones, for Phoenicia's trade and its relations with its colonies. But a much graver catastrophe fell on these people when the Chaldean empire, having beaten the Assyrians, wanted to punish the allies who had assisted them: Egyptians, Syrians, and Palestinians. Tyre was then subjected by Nebuchadnezzar II in 571. The loss of sovereignty of this large metropolis, to which all the colonies had been linked, severed the relations, the mutual assistance, and the economic understanding between the colonies and the Phoenician cities. These relations had, however, already become difficult in recent years; for from the seventh century onwards the Greek colonies established in Cyrenaica formed a barrier along their lines of communication. Now however the Phoenician system, menaced previously by the Greek colonial world, fell into a state of complete collapse and dissolution. We shall explain later how one of their colonies, Carthage, which had already made itself leader and metropolis of its sister cities, succeeded in imposing a limit upon Greek growth. (Map IIb.)

Aramean Migrations. Reasons similar to those affecting the Phoenicians explain the alternations in fortune of the Aramean and Hebrew elements in Syria. The determining factor was the degree of pressure brought to bear on them by neighbouring powers.

The Arameans were semi-nomadic raiders, who had already for centuries been careering round northern Syria and in upper Mesopotamia. They appear first as participants in the actions of an alliance called Akhlâmu, directed against the Assyrians at the end of the twelfth century. Next they are found as prime movers in similar activity during the second Assyrian 'stagnation' (1074-909), for which indeed they had initially been responsible when they created a number of small new states. Some of these, with capitals at Til Barsip, at Guzana (Tell Halaf), etc., emerged in the middle basin of the Euphrates; others on the lower Tigris as far as Babylonia, where for a time (c.1083) the throne was occupied by an Aramean prince named Adadapal-iddiu; a third group is found on the Persian Gulf, where the tribe of the Kaldu (Chaldeans) appears; and lastly a whole series of such people arrived in northern Syria, behind the Phoenician country from the slopes of the Taurus to the boundaries of the Hebrews (Zincirli, Arpad, Aleppo, Hamath, Soba, and Damascus).

The recovery of Assyrian power (909–858) was naturally marked by a progressive weakening of these Aramean states, and one by one they were brought into subjection: those in the Mesopotamian zone in the first half of the twelfth century, and towards the middle of the century those of Syria. Reviving for a while during the new period of Assyrian stagnation (824–809), the western Aramean states, especially those in the Damascus zone, were again broken shortly afterwards, when Damascus submitted to Adad Nirari III (809–782). They re-emerged during the other brief period of stagnation (782–745), but again they were gradually subdued—Arpad (743), Sam'al (735), Damascus (732), and Hamath—so that all northern Syria, including the neo-Hittite survival at Carchemish, became an Assyrian possession (719). The importance of these Arameans for the cultural evolution of the Middle East was very marked, both for what they drew and for what they gave. In fact, the extension of the Aramean states from Syria to the Persian Gulf, and their repeated conquests by the Assyrians, were the fundamental reason why in all fields of culture (religion, art, science, etc.) they absorbed existing ingredients—Canaanite, Egyptian, Mitannic, Hittite, Assyrian, Accadian, Mesopotamian. On the other hand, by their ubiquity, and by the importance assumed by their Chaldean sub-group, they succeeded in introducing in all the lands of the Middle East new elements of uniformity, of which the most important was the use of Aramaic as the diplomatic and literary language. After they had adopted the Phoenician alphabet, this language became easier to write and was, therefore, more generally used.

The Hebraic States. According to biblical tradition, the Hebrew people, before their final settlement in Palestine, travelled from one home to another. From the land of Ur they made their way to that of Cheran or Harran: their route must have lain between Babylonia and Syria. Next they arrived in Canaan (hence the affinity between the Hebrew and Phoenician languages), and they then moved into the valley of the Nile (where they perhaps took part in the Hyksos invasions). In the end, led by Moses and later by Joshua, they settled once for all in the Jordan valley, the 'Promised Land' given by their own God to his 'chosen people'. The *terminus post quem* of this return emerges on the one hand from the Tell el Amarna texts of 1380–1350 BC which relate attacks by Khabiru nomads on Jerusalem, then still an Egyptian possession;[15] and on the other hand from the same texts of *c.* 1230, recording victories of Pharaoh Merneptah over Canaan, Ascalon, Gezer, and Yanuam, and also over Israel. By the later date, then, the final settlement of the Israelites had probably taken place.

All this history explains why Hebrew civilization presents a composite characteristic from the earliest times. That is the impression given, for example, if Sumerian, Accadian, and Hittite stories are compared with those told in Genesis: it is the impression derived from legal concepts, from the contrast between the characteristic Hebrew monotheism and the continuous infiltrations of polytheism, and from the designs found in Hebrew architecture, carving, and so on. To overcome their foreign enemies, the Hebrews passed through a phase of priestly government on a federal basis, and achieved union under a monarchy, which took pains to develop the country's industry, trade, and agriculture. The later schism between the two kingdoms of Israel and Judah was aggravated by the struggle between monotheism, upheld by the priests and Prophets, and the syncretism favoured by some of the rulers; a further factor was the decline of the ruling houses. Meanwhile the rivalry between the two states, which were often at war with each other, weakened both; it also forced them into alliances which were unstable and burdensome.

The kingdom of Israel had a turbulent history. It was divided into two rival sections, one pro-Aramaic which favoured Damascus, the other pro-Assyrian, until in 732 Tiglath-Pileser III reduced the kingdom to the territory of Samaria alone, and in 722 it was finally vanquished by Sargon II. He transplanted the propertied classes to Mesopotamia and settled the country with Arabian and Babylonian peoples (the 'Samaritans'): these modified the racial, cultural, and religious structure which the region had acquired.

More compact than Israel, the kingdom of Judah survived it for a century and a half, but became a sort of cushion between the empire of Egypt and that of the Assyrians and their successors the Chaldeans. A first deportation of Hebrews was carried out on the orders of Sennacherib about 700, and in 586 came the larger deportations ordained by Nebuchadnezzar.

The exile of the Hebrews in Babylonia for about half a century (586–538) was of decisive importance in shaping that people. It polarized them in the indomitable will to rise again, and in their absolute certainty that divine intervention had reserved for them a glorious future. It evoked in them the sublime conception of the indestructible link of nationality, which bound them together even when their country was lost to them. Finally it placed them in daily contact with the peoples of Mesopotamia, with obvious effects upon their output of literature and art, and upon their legal, social, and other ideas.

Mesopotamia. We have already referred several times to Babylonia. But we have still to outline the principal events from the fall of the Kassites in the mid-twelfth century, when the indigenous element reasserted itself under the Second Dynasty of Isin: this was followed by four other dynasties, lasting into the tenth century. The country was conquered by the Assyrian

Shalmaneser III (859–824), while for some time the Aramaic nomads called Kaldu (Chaldaei) were continuously invading in increasing numbers. For the next two centuries, ending in 626, it was sometimes directly subject to the neighbouring Assyrian empire (whether that empire was united or split in two); at other times it was under Assyrian influence. But meanwhile the Chaldeans sought a way of obtaining dominion over their country and turning the Assyrians out. The latter reacted by deporting Babylonians, but in vain; in the end the Chaldeans, aided by the Medes, and under the leadership of King Nabopolassar (625–605), the founder of an Aramaic dynasty, succeeded in taking Nineveh. So they brought about the fall of the Assyrian empire and occupied its territory. They then began action against Egypt, whose forces were defeated at Carchemish (605); they also imposed their dominion on Syria and Palestine, consolidating it with the victories of Nebuchadnezzar in 597 and 588–586, and with the subjection of Tyre in 573.

Yet the power of the Chaldeans was short-lived. One may explain this either by the political incapacity of Nebuchadnezzar's successors and the misfortunes caused by internal risings and the interference of the priests, or by the events which were beginning to unfold in the East, with the victory of the Persians over the Chaldeans' friends the Medes. These events were not assessed at their proper importance by King Nabunidus, who was fully absorbed in an attempt at religious revival and in the construction of temples; but the outcome was the Persian war in which the last Chaldean king was overcome and Babylon was taken (539).

But even though the Chaldean dominion lasted only three-quarters of a century, it was marked by a ferment of human existence; by religion with tendencies towards pantheism; by remarkable scientific discoveries and formulations, especially in astronomy, astrology, and mathematics; and by massive architectural constructions, such as city defences, fortresses, royal palaces, and temples.

b. *Greek Colonizations and the Recognition of Unity*

The principal events in the Middle East between *c.* 1200 and the middle of the sixth century BC have now been recorded. While they were going on, the whole Aegean Sea was the centre of important historical movements, which, spreading in almost every direction, were of concern to many peoples, and altered the peoples' development. The first plantations of Hellenic peoples on the Aegean islands, and on the eastern and southern coasts of Anatolia as far as Cyprus and beyond, had been turbulent and to some extent forced upon the emigrants. But these movements were migrations in the fullest sense, and are only loosely described as 'colonization'. In them, as we have already noted, the settlers mixed with the original inhabitants, though these were of different race. Moreover at the outset they preserved their own monarchical government and civilization of Mycenaean origin, which was typical of their courts. Meanwhile the warlike deeds and the pomp of these prince-adventurers were made glorious in the epics of the bards and became the model for men to picture the life of the gods, their enterprises and their genealogies, all anthropomorphically conceived.

But at this point nearly all the Greek world, both inside and outside Hellas, was almost completely transformed. The kings fell, being supplanted in many of their functions by magistrates who, largely through the initiative taken by the kings' subjects, arose to organize the protection of individuals, in peace and in war; moreover the dynasties themselves could not hold out in face of challenge from the nobles, who were equally laden with honours and riches. From that time on many states, instead of making a royal palace their centre, established a common citadel. This was a refuge in time of war, and the centre of their political life,—of their assemblies, markets, and magistrates, of their artisans and industry, of their cults and of their law courts. In this way arose the 'polis'.

This political and social phenomenon, the passage from kingdom to republic, was accompanied and followed by other consequences of great importance in every field. It was now that Mycenaean art gradually decayed and gave place to new artistic conceptions. It had flowered mainly as a 'palace' product; but commercial relations with the East had ceased for a time, and the courts were disappearing, together with the concentration of wealth in the hands of the kings. It was now too that the new metal iron, which revolutionized metal working, was adopted far and wide. At the same time the spread of alphabetic writing made it easier to transmit to others first epics, then other forms of literary output. Finally, it was now that the area of colonization assumed enormous dimensions. Up to the time of which we are speaking, it was simply the earliest zones of occupation, in the Aegean islands and on the Anatolian coasts, which had continued, almost to overflowing, to receive Greek peoples: they were large territories, and new settlement could make it possible to assert Greek race and culture against the threat of being swamped by foreign elements among the indigenous peoples. The result was that, united in leagues with religious backgrounds, the Greek settlements not only succeeded, generally speaking, in preserving their freedom, but also joined with the indigenous peoples to form mixed cultures, the so-called *koinai* of Greek Asia Minor. The best-known *koiné* (apart from that of Cyprus) is the Ionian, especially in the Graeco-Lydian period, when the Lydian tendency to welcome Ionian civilization was so clearly shown.[16]

For centuries the Greeks had poured in this way into the earliest colonial lands, but now new areas were needed to cope with the overpopulation which affected not a few districts in Greece.[17] They increasingly needed to find foodstuffs to exchange against manufactured goods, and new cultivable lands for the disinherited and for political malcontents, who wanted to emigrate.

A further cause was their love of expeditions which were risky, but could bring great profits. A second wave of expansion, over a wider field, now began. First came commercial ventures of piratical type which explored the way; they were followed by one lot of emigrants after another, the movement growing in intensity over three centuries, from c. 800 to 500 BC. The result was the creation of trading-stations and colonies on many islands and shores; in the western Balkans, in Sicily and south Italy from the Gulf of Taranto to Cumae, in the Adriatic and on the Ligurian, Celtic, and Iberian coasts of the Mediterranean, in Cyrenaica and even in a piece of Egypt and at Al Mina in north Syria. These were paralleled by the rise of other settlements on the northern coast of the Aegean, and in the Propontis, Pontus, and Crimea. (Map IIa and b.)

These commercial and colonial enterprises, which in their early days provided the background for the poetry of romance and adventure—a vast corpus from which we possess the *Odyssey*—had decisive importance in spreading Greek ideas, both original and at second hand, over all the Mediterranean, especially the northern coasts; and into Greece there poured produce, merchandise, ideas, and stories from all that world outside. The different sections of the new colonial Greece each encountered an environment that was peculiar. Detached from their mother countries, they had contact with indigenous peoples of every possible way of life; their new lands were not always comparable with their own in climate, and possessed quite different resources in agriculture, pasture, mining, and trade. Although, therefore, each section according to its bent and powers contributed to the general civilizing process, each developed a civilization which was in some measure its own. The result is that many specific Graeco-native cultures can be distinguished: in Magna Graecia, Sicily, the country round Marseilles, the Propontis, the Ukraine, the Crimea, Cyrenaica, and so on. In Egypt at the outset the Hellenic traders only succeeded in establishing trading-posts like those at Naucratis in the sixth century: it was later, when the country fell into anarchy and decay, that the Greeks were taken on as mercenaries and intermarried with the natives; but they could not appreciably modify a civilization which had thousands of years behind it, and consequently from the beginning they took more from it than they gave. In Cyrenaica on the other hand they co-operated with the Libyans in intercepting trade along the caravan routes. In Sicily the cultural union with the natives was close and productive, especially in the days before discord began and before competition from the Carthaginian colonists made itself felt in the north-west part of the island. In south Italy the colonies had admittedly to meet competition from the Etruscans, who had conquered down to the Gulf of Salerno (but note that the Etruscans themselves were already markedly Hellenized); yet until the Sabellians expanded in the fifth century, Graeco-Italian culture achieved a magnificent degree of prosperity. Lastly, there were the Phocaean traders, who, in their descents on the Adriatic coasts and the central Tyrrhenian

MAP III

PHRYGIA

PHRYGIA MINOR
(AD HELLESPONTUM)

MYSIA MINOR

MYSIA MAIOR

TROAS

LYDIA

CARIA

Cartography Hallwag Berne

Caunos

Rhodus

Smyrna

Ephesus

Halicarnassus

Cos sonesus

Cnidos

Lesbos

Mytilene

Phocaea

Samos

Chios

Mare N Icarium

Icaros

Tragia

Miletus

Lerus

Calymna

Cos

R O D

Syrnos

Carpathos

Thasos

Imbros

Samothrace

Lemnos

Mare A E G A E U M

Andros

Tenos

Myconos

Ceos

Syros

C Y C L A D E S

Paros

Naxos

Amorgos

Astypalaea

Anaphe

S P O R A D E S

Thera

Melos

PAEONIA

PARORBELIA

PHYLLIS

BISALTIA

CRESTONIA

MYGDONIA

D O N I A

CHALCIDICE

PALLENE

SITHONIA

ACTE

ATE

ICUS

PELAGONIA

LYNCESTIS

ORESTIS

EMATHIA

ELIMEA

M A C E D

Mare Thracicum

Scyros

Icus

Peparethus

EUBOEA

ILLYRIA

Apollonia

PARAUAEI

ATINTANIA

TYMPHAEA

PERRHAEBIA

Larissa

THESSALIA

THESSALIOTIS

MAGNESIA

ACHAIA

Thebae

BOEOTIA

Delphi

PHOCIS

LOCRIS

ATTICA

Athenae

Aegina

Megaris

CORINTHIA

ARGOLIS

Hydrea

Seriphos

Cythnos

Mare Myrtoum

EPIRUS

ATHAMANIA

MOLOSSIS

Dodona

THESPROTIA

CHAONIA

LATOA

ETHOTIA

DOLOPIA PHTHIOTIS

APERANTIA

GRAEAI

AENIS MALIS

OETAEA

AETOLIA

ACARNANIA

ACHAIA

ELIS

TRIPHYLIA

ARCADIA

PELOPONNESUS

Messene

MESSENIA

Sparta

LACONIA

Cythera

Corcyra

Leucas

Ithaca

Zacynthus

Cephallenia

M A R E I O N I U M

CRETA

GREECE

coasts of Italy, brought imports from eastern lands and provided the impetus for the orientalizing periods in local art. Moreover, by planting themselves in Corsica, on the Gulfs of Genoa and Lions, and on the coast to the north of the Ebro, they were the determining force in promoting cultural progress among the Ligurians, Celts, and Iberians, until about the middle of the sixth century they came into conflict with the Etruscans and Carthaginians in Corsica, and with the Carthaginians in Spain. No less important was the influence of the Greek colonists on the Black Sea coasts, especially in the modern Ukraine.

At the same time constitutional units on a larger scale were gradually forming in Greece. In some places these took the form of voluntary federations, religious and political; in others an imperial power expanded and imposed its rule directly on the neighbouring peoples, who were reduced to subjection or treated as members of a league directed by the dominant city; in other cases again the means were the synoecism of several small independent states, who were absorbed into a single *polis*. (Map III.)

The best-known and most typical case of the unification of a whole region by constitutional development occurred in Attica, where all the centres which once were independent were gradually 'synoecized' into a single city-state, named Athens;[18] and kingship gave place to oligarchic rule, and then to democracy.[19] The latter process occurred through the legislative work of two 'nomothetai', Draco and Solon, through the pro-democratic behaviour of the Peisistratid tyrants, and through the reforms of Cleisthenes. The work of Cleisthenes brought to an end many decades of similar upheavals.[20] It ended the domination of the Eupatridae, and was decisive in giving Athens the military, social, economic, and moral power, which in the years which followed enabled it to work towards the preservation of Greece from Persian domination.

But Athenian synoecism was only one of the many political associations, which like all manifestations of the Greek genius admitted marked variations within the type. The divergence was very largely caused, of course, by the actual conditions of environment and by the economies of the different peoples, which were in some places based mainly on commerce and abundance of movable wealth, in others on agriculture and grazing, that is to say chiefly on landed property. Thus in the neighbourhood of the isthmus various commercial and industrial cities competed for hegemony. In Corinth the ruling house of the Bacchiads and after them the Cypselid tyrants developed shipping and mercantile activities; the many colonies they sent out were kept, so far as possible, in subject status until they asserted their independence at the time of the fall of the Cypselids. Megara, which was also ruled first by its aristocrats and then by tyrants, took an active and warlike part in colonization, and was later engaged in a long struggle with Athens for the possession of Salamis and Nisaea. Sicyon, the determined enemy of Argos, was similarly dominated by aristocratic families, and was then ruled for a century by the Orthagorid tyrants, who may have survived until 520.[21] Lastly Argos, with the Temenid house at its head, in the middle of the seventh century found in Pheidon the man to secure its temporary supremacy over the Argolid, Achaea and part of Arcadia: he too was a great promoter of commercial expansion, and he introduced coinage into Greece.[22]

The great opponent of Argos was the political organization which had started its history farther to the south, around Sparta. While in other states the rise of the aristocrats had generally led to the fall of the kingly power, in Sparta two reigning families had taken their place side by side, each controlling the other, and both being controlled by the board of magistrates called the ephors. Other characteristic features of the constitution, which was attributed to Lycurgus,[23] were the strictly agricultural basis of Spartan life, and the militarist organization of the governing class, the 'Homoioi': they alone enjoyed full political rights and alone had ownership of the lots into which the greater part of the land was divided. These lots were cultivated by the 'Helots', descendants of the inhabitants who of old had been conquered and reduced to serfdom: the remaining land was held by the Perioeci, people who were free but had no political rights, though they were not forbidden to engage in trade. But with the passage of time both these methods of dealing with the conquered peoples led to a dangerous lack of numerical balance between the governors and the governed; and in the lands farther from the centre the Spartans adopted instead a system of alliances, making possible the creation of the 'Peloponnesian League'. By the end of the sixth century this had become the largest political association in Greece. Into it were gradually drawn almost all the Peloponnesian states, whether they liked it or not; the chief cause being their perpetual feuds and their wars with Argos.

The phenomenon of tyranny flourished also in the islands of the Aegean and in the Asiatic Greek cities, where the tyrants both took part in the struggle between nobles and demos and also acted as arbiters: for example at Chalcis, Lesbos, Ephesus (which was linked by close commercial ties with Lydia), Erythrae, Miletus, Samos. In Samos, Polycrates about 540 created a small maritime empire: he was the friend first of Egypt, then of Persia, and engaged in war at various times with the leading Greek powers of Sparta, Corinth, Lesbos, and Miletus. Nor were the colonies of Magna Graecia free from these struggles for power or from the class struggles which called for intervention by the law-givers and later by the tyrants. As an example may be mentioned the wars between Croton and Locri in the first half of the sixth century. A little later came the coalitions formed against Siris and against Croton (which had come into the hands of the aristocratic Pythagoreans). Finally Croton was victorious, with the destruction of Sybaris in 510.

About 500, then, the three cities in the Ionian Sea which maintained their power were Tarentum, Croton, and Locri; on the Tyrrhenian side the prominent city was Cumae, which had lately defeated the Etruscans. In Sicily, too, there were struggles for power, class wars, law-givers, and tyrants: the most notable examples of the last are found before the end of the seventh century at Leontini, followed by Phalaris at Acragas who acceded in 570.

Yet however much the Greeks, in the peninsula and in their colonies, were divided into many states which had different constitutions and were often at war with one another, they still had a deep sense of their racial unity, across a hundred modes of dialect, custom, and cult.[24] What mattered most was that all recognized a group of major Panhellenic deities, of whom the great poets sang. They had their great temples to which men flocked from every side to hear the oracles. And they had their games—great meeting-places, in which they got to know one another, where they exchanged ideas, and where artistic production and imitation were fostered.

c. *Pre-Roman Italy*

Between about 1200 and 1100 BC Italy, in broad terms, was inhabited as follows. From the Tusco-Emilian Apennines, and from the Ciminian hills on the Tyrrhenian side, as far as Sicily there were Indo-European peoples, the first wave of Italian invaders: these spoke dialects akin to Latin (Latini, Hernici, Ausones, Opici, Itali, Siculi and Sicani) and had probably already arrived in the Chalcolithic Age. To the north of the Arno, and throughout Liguria, Piedmont, and western Emilia, the Ligurians had been living at least from Neolithic times; they were the remains of a pre-Aryan race who had originally been spread over a much wider area. Around Verona were the Euganei, in Picenum the Asyli, in western Sicily the Elymians; these too were probably of Liguroid stock, the survivors of Neolithic populations, as were at least a part of the Corsicans and Sardinians. Lastly, along the routes of the central Alpine passes and in the lake districts of the Transpadana there were the *palafitticoli*; and farther to the south astride the Po their offshoot the *terramaricoli*, who constructed pile-dwellings on terra firma. These the present writer maintains were of Etruscan stock; that is, they were ancestors of the Etruscans of historical times, who believed themselves to be autochthonous inhabitants of the peninsula from remote antiquity. The Etruscans therefore rejected the pseudo-learned theory of the Greek logo-graphers, who used futile arguments, with variants which destroyed con-sistency, to support the view that at a more or less recent date the Etruscans had come from the East. Many modern scholars still believe in these Eastern origins, though they cannot agree on the chronology of the migration, which they place variously at dates ranging from 1200 to 650 BC.[25]

But about 1000 great changes and racial movements affected this distri-bution. New waves of Indo-European peoples arrived in the Balkans and in the upper Danube valley, from which a section crossed into Italy by the eastern Alpine passes. These included first the people we shall call the

'Second Italici' (Oscans followed by Umbrians), secondly the Illyrians, and thirdly the Celts. The last-named remained for the moment in the rear-guard, in the Transalpine country. But their movements, by the pressure they set up, must none the less have helped to generate the three advances into the Po valley: by the Osco-Umbrians, by the Veneti (an Illyrian race), and by a large section of those North Etruscans who till now had stayed north of the Alps or in the Alpine valleys.

The adjacent portions of these three peoples, racially distinct, had now come to live next door to one another in an area which was not particularly large. This led to the creation of an almost homogeneous regional culture, whose distinguishing features include artistic decoration of Balkan provenance, cremation of their dead, and the abundant use of iron. It is possible, however, to discern three distinct variations: the Atestine culture of the Veneti, the 'Villanovan' of the Etruscans, and the 'Pianellian' of the Oscans.

Later, while the Veneti gradually penetrated into their home of historical times, the Osco-Umbrians were pressed towards the Apennines of Umbro-Romagna. They therefore crossed the mountains and descended into Umbria, the Sabine and Marsic countries, and beyond—even sending out some offshoots to settle among the Latins.

At the same time[26] part of the Etruscans crossed the Tusco-Emilian Apennines and entered Tuscany. There they found themselves in quite new surroundings. The contours of Tuscany and its climate, and the wealth of its mines on the mainland and the island of Elba, made it a more promising country than that which they had left: so, too, did the outlets to the sea, which allowed them to start a navy and establish trade with the Mediterranean peoples.

By about 700 the first Greek colonists had begun to arrive on the Ionian coasts of Italy:[27] the Laconians at Tarentum, followed soon by the Achaeans (to use the archaic term, but really Dorians) at Metapontum, Sybaris, Croton, and other places; and the Locrians of Epizephyrian Locris. Soon afterwards the Chalcidians of Euboea settled at Rhegium and Cumae on the Tyrrhenian coast, and also in Sicily at Naxos, Catana, Leontini, Himera, and other places. They were followed in that island by the Megarians at Megara Hyblaea and later at Selinus; by the Corinthians at Syracuse and its daughter-colonies; and a little while later, about 680, by the Cretans and Rhodians at Gela (who in 580 sent an offshoot to Acragas).

Meanwhile, about 630, another stream of trader-colonists from Ionia, who started from Phocaea on the Asiatic coast, had begun to found outposts on the coasts of the Adriatic, and also on the Tyrrhenian coast to the north of Cumae at the mouth of the Tiber, on the Etruscan and Ligurian coasts, and farther to the west.

The economic relations between Etruscans and Greeks, first the Cumaeans and later the Phocaeans, were of enormous importance in the progress of Etruscan civilization. For instance they took from the Cumaeans the alphabet, together with many concepts in the field of religion, art, and literature: from the Phocaeans they derived all the features of the orientalizing period of their art. Their culture reached such heights of maturity in their new surroundings and with their new contacts that, despite political disunity, they were fired by the desire to expand. So it was that in the seventh and sixth centuries one group of armed bands subdued the principal towns on the routes between Etruria and Campania (overrunning early regal Rome in the first period of its hegemony over the Latins), and pushed down to the Gulf of Salerno: other bands pressed into western Umbria and south-eastern Liguria, and even poured into part of the Po valley to become overlords of their cousins the North Etruscans.

But after a long period of Graeco-Etruscan friendship the harmony was broken by the exploits of the Phocaeans in the northern Tyrrhenian Sea, where they were based on Alalia in Corsica and seen to be coveting the iron of Elba. Some Etruscans then allied themselves with the Carthaginians, the third sea-power of the western Mediterranean, who had for some time been fighting the Phocaeans on the coasts of Africa and Spain. The result, about 540, was the battle of Alalia, which compelled the Phocaeans to relinquish Corsica and give up commercial competition south of the Arno mouth. To this period of Etrusco-Carthaginian co-operation probably belongs the so-called Treaty of 509 between Rome and Carthage, whose terms certainly imply Etruscan domination of Rome.

Meanwhile the conflict between Etruscans and Greeks developed on the mainland. In c. 524 Aristodemus, tyrant of Cumae, repelled the Etruscans and weakened their hold on Campania. Then the Latins won a victory over them at Aricia, and the Romans expelled the Tarquins.[28] So the Campanian possessions were cut off by land from Etruria and could not be maintained for more than about thirty years (see Part II). The enmity between Greeks and Etruscans naturally diminished the borrowings between one culture and the other; and the result was that even in the coastal districts the Tyrrhenians produced work which reflected more accurately their own tastes and talents, like the earlier work produced in the more inland cities which had less contact with the Greeks.

In the eighth and seventh centuries, therefore, all the more civilized peoples of Italy looked to the Greek world as their leader. This was true directly in Magna Graecia and in Sicily on account of the strong and numerous Hellenic colonies. It was also true, though less directly, in the Latian district, in the Veneto, in Apulia, and in Picenum (where about 1000 BC other Illyrian peoples had settled), since the Etruscans and the other inhabitants of these territories had frequent commercial contacts with the Greeks.

At the end of the seventh century and more particularly in the course of the sixth, as we have already shown, the Etruscans acquired both political and cultural supremacy in the central Cispadana and in the Tyrrhenian countries down to the Gulf of Salerno; and by this time they had been indoctrinated with Greek culture. Their conquests included Latium, which is shown by its use of the alphabet and by other evidence to have been in contact with Cumae; they also conquered Rome, then engaged in establishing its first narrow hegemony in Latium, which area was extended by the Etruscans to take in Terracina. After the fall of the Tarquins this Etruscan empire broke down; but their supremacy had been long-lived enough to introduce a number of new ideas and techniques, some purely Etruscan, others Greek which the Etruscans had taken over. At the same time the Carthaginians, a new power, were making themselves felt for the first time in western Sicily, and were reinforcing the influence which their Phoenician cousins had already established in Sardinia. Finally, in all the countries which came less fully under Greek or Etruscan influence, it was largely an archaic, 'tribal', conception of living which went on: the peoples were engaged mainly in pasturage and agriculture, and were therefore scattered over the countryside, or living in villages. The villages which were sited at strong points served as refuges in case of danger, and this fact often allowed them to assert their supremacy over their neighbours, as happened with the 'Palatine city' in the early regal period of Rome.

d. *Phoenicians and Carthaginians, Phocaeans and Massiliotes in the Mediterranean*

We have already related the decay and disintegration of the Phoenician colonies resulting from the difficulties of communication with the mother country in south Syria when it came under Assyrian domination. This led, it was explained, to the establishment in the second half of the seventh century[29] of Phocaean colonies in the old zone of Phoenician activity on the west coast of Spain (which Herodotus says Colaeus of Samos found deserted about 630), and even on the shore of Tunisia, at Kybos, Hippo Diarrhytus, and other places. This explains the contemporary passage of Genesis, assigning to the Iavan (Ionians) the possession of both Elisha (Tunisia) and Tarshish (Tartessus in Spain).[30]

But at this point Carthage asserted its influence: it became the new metropolis in place of Tyre, and set about the organization of its daughter-cities around it. The establishment of its new empire was comparatively rapid. Already at the end of the seventh century, or the beginning of the sixth, Carthage in its turn had sent colonies to Pantelleria, to Motya, Panormus, and Solus in Sicily, and to Ebusus in the Balearics. It had reinforced the Phoenician settlements on the eastern coast of Sardinia, looking towards the iron island of Elba; placed an outpost at Punicum to the north of Caere, to lay hands on the Tolfa mines; and soon made an alliance with the Etruscans, checking, at the battle of Alalia, the progress of the Phocaeans in the northern Tyrrhenian Sea and in Corsica (c. 540). Finally (for this our authority is Aristotle) it concluded a series of maritime treaties with the

Etruscan cities, among which we have knowledge of the one with Rome.
Moreover in the sixth century the Carthaginians prevented any establishment
of Greek colonies in western Sicily, where they were enlarging their own
dominion.

The relationship of Carthage to the Phoenician colonies was paralleled by
that of Massilia to the Greek colonies of Phocaea. After 540 they were cut off
from normal contact with the mother country and from any easy possibility
of obtaining their customary supplies of oriental merchandise. Left therefore
to fend for themselves, and subjected to the hostile attacks of the Carthaginians and Etruscans, they united under the leadership and protection of
Massilia.

Once bases in the East were lost, the cultural significance of the new
empires, of both Carthage and Massilia, naturally began to be very different
from that of the old colonies of Tyre and Phocaea. Indeed the two powers,
the one Semitic and the other Greek, grew continually more remote from,
and independent of, their mother countries, and developed a western
outlook. This process owed something to the effect they had on one another:
it also reflected the tastes and talents and potentialities of the peoples with
whom they most often came into contact, namely those of north-west Africa,
Spain, Gaul, and the Ligurian lands.

In fact Massilia and the other Phocaean settlements, together with some
infiltration from the Etruscans, were the main forces responsible for the
civilizing movement among the Ligurian and Celtic tribes, in direct proportion to the distance of these tribes from the Greeks.

We have seen that about 1000 the Celts were concentrated north of the
Alps, in two groups with North Etruscan peoples lying between them. The
eastern group for some time maintained contact with the Osco-Umbrians
and adopted certain common forms of speech: the other group, farther to
the west, had preserved their original tongue, which bears comparison with
Latin forms. It seems that the Celts of this second group, the westerners,
were the first to penetrate into eastern France.[31] They took with them
culture of the first Hallstatt[32] period, which gives us a date about 800 or
slightly later, and pushed up through Franche Comté, Burgundy, Champagne,
and Lorraine into modern Belgium,[33] finally pressing along the coast into
Armorica. It was only later that the eastern group, following along behind
the others, entered the part of Gaul which had not yet been occupied,
though in some districts they superimposed themselves on the earlier
arrivals.

e. The Celts

The Celts naturally found it easy to conquer these large territories with
their superior military organization, which included cavalry,[34] chariots of
war, entrenched camps and so on; and their iron sabres struck fear in com-

parison with the primitive equipment of the Ligurian peoples. At this point, in the second half of the seventh century, the Phocaean merchants began to arrive and place their outposts on the Mediterranean coast, from the Gulf of Genoa to the Pyrenees; and the Celts as well as the surviving Ligurian peoples started to draw their cultural borrowings from the newcomers. In this way, by a process which began in the period 600–550 and extended gradually from the Mediterranean to the interior, the civilization of Hallstatt was gradually transformed into that of La Tène: the latter originated in the cultural 'koiné' of Celts and Phocaeans, and in the more precise combination of Celts and Massiliotes which soon followed after the Massiliote empire had been formed. But the Celtic peoples who lived relatively far from Massilia, those in Belgica and the Rhineland for example, were not appreciably affected by this influence, and were even carried back to more primitive conditions of civilization by their admixture with the Germanic peoples who were beginning at this time to cross the Rhine.

Meanwhile the population was rapidly growing, with results made more noticeable by the Germanic invasions. Partly for this reason, and partly because they still retained their semi-nomadic ways and spirit of adventure, a part of the Celts returned from Gaul to their earlier homes on the northern side of the Alps, and from there pressed into the Balkans and beyond (see Part II). At the same time other parties separated from this main body, crossed both the western and the northern Alpine passes, and began to pour into the Po valley. There in successive invasions they took possession of large tracts of country. This was not, as the Roman annalists claimed, an operation accomplished in a very short space of time just before the siege of Rome in 386. The true story is given by several independent traditions, including one also reported by Livy. They started in the first half of the sixth century, and gradually, though with difficulty, overcame the Ligurians of central and northern Piedmont, together with the North Etruscans and the Etruscans of Lombardy and Emilia, until they finally penetrated into northern Picenum. The slow progress of the advance is confirmed by archaeological evidence, which ascribes greater antiquity to the earliest Celtic remains in Piedmont and Lombardy in comparison with those in Emilia and Picenum. In any event these Celts can be shown by the hybrid character of the surviving texts to have become mixed with the earlier inhabitants, and in the cultural field they were influenced by the Etruscans and Veneti.

We now pass to Spain, where the history of culture must take account of the following events and movement of peoples. The Iberians, a Hamitic race of north African origin, were superimposed on the country's earlier inhabitants; and the result was the civilization which in the Bronze Age we call 'Almerian', from El Argar in Almeria, and in the Iron Age Tartessian; this civilization was spread over a wide area. But in the first half of the first millennium two land invasions took place. In the first, about 1000, a people penetrated into Catalonia carrying the so-called 'Urn civilization',35 which resembled that of the *terramaricoli* and the Villanovan culture of the Po valley, and also the civilization of Switzerland, south Germany, and eastern France: all these areas were the home of 'lake-dwellers' (*palafitticoli*), which in the author's view implies that the inhabitants were of Etruscan origin. The second invasion occurred about 600 at the hands of emigrants arriving from Gaul.[36] They brought the Hallstatt civilization into Catalonia, the central plateau, Portugal, and Galicia; and there over three centuries they developed Hallstatt culture with few innovations derived from La Tène. This second wave of immigrants, who are certainly to be identified with the Celts, fused with the Iberians and are the ancestors of the later Celtiberians. They were prevented by Iberian resistance from penetrating into southern Spain. ·

Meanwhile, however, there arrived by sea two sets of foreign settlers, to whom we have already alluded. The Phoenicians are said by some sources on Cadiz to have arrived about 1100, but even if this is false the date was little more than a hundred years later. The second invasion, by the Phocaeans, founded Hemeroscopeion and Mainake about 600 and Emporion about 550.[37] Relations between Phoenicians and Iberians were by no means steady. In periods where the Phoenicians were conscious of the support of Tyre, they were not content with acquiring the minerals (gold, silver, copper, tin, and lead), which were the objectives of their trade. They attempted political domination of the Iberians; and the people of Tartessus hit back at them, especially in periods when Tyre was suffering disasters. When, later on, Carthage had taken over the direction of Phoenician policy in the West, and had reinforced the trading-stations in Spain, relations with the natives became more stable, and in general more peaceful: they opened the way to important exchanges of products and ideas. But for this very reason the more southerly colonies of Phocaea, which had acquired consequence in the period of Phoenician decline, had to face the effects of the new state of affairs and the expansionist policy of their rivals. Mainake was destroyed, and though the northern colonies survived, they passed through a troubled time. To sum up, one may say broadly that the influence of the Phoenico-Carthaginians was more strongly felt in south-east Spain, and that of the Phocaeans and Massiliotes in the north-east.

Caesar distinguishes only two racial groups in Britain, one native group which claimed to be autochthonous and one Celtic group which he claims, on the strength of similarity in place-names, to come from Belgica (to which one might add Armorica). The linguistic evidence shows that Britain was invaded both by 'Goidelic' Celts, who belong to the first movement and would thus in our view have come from Belgica, and also by 'Cymric' Celts, who belong to the second movement and presumably came from Brittany or Armorica. But there is no archaeological confirmation of these crossings until the first period of La Tène. So, although many scholars disagree, our view must be that before c.500 the inhabitants of the British Isles were pre-Celtic, and pre-Aryan. They certainly belonged to several racial strata which overlay one another, and at least in the southern districts they had attained a certain level of civilization through their early trading relations with the Mediterranean people, who came to Britain from Spain and from farther afield in search of Cornish tin and Irish gold. The greater part of this trade was ultimately monopolized by the Phoenician colonies and later by those of Carthage.

This cultural history explains, among other things, how the Celts who crossed to Britain transmitted to their ancestors east of the Channel not only merchandise but religious and political ideas, for instance Druidism.

f. Northern Europe

About the remainder of Europe, central, north and east, there are no specific references in our authorities which can help to explain the progress of civilization in the period with which we are concerned. We must, therefore, try to infer the main lines of intertribal relationships from archaeological finds and their distribution, bearing in mind the natural routes along which trade could develop, and also the districts where the merchandise wanted by the civilized countries came to be discovered or produced. This kind of investigation needs great caution. There is the initial difficulty of establishing relative chronologies for the various levels of backward civilization attained by countries which are still to be accounted 'barbarian', the backwardness increasing roughly in proportion to their distance from the Mediterranean lands. Moreover, the goods exchanged are only very partially preserved. With crude and manufactured metals (for which we also know the mining and manufacturing areas), or with pottery, or with precious materials like coral, amber, and ivory (unless they have perished for some such reason as being used in cremation), we can argue from something concrete. But for many other articles of trade, like cereals, domestic animals, smoked fish, salt, slaves, textiles, or wine and oil, we have no solid data. In our period, however, transport went so far as possible by the easiest means, that is to say by water, on rivers or on the sea. If, therefore, we bear in mind archaeological finds which illustrate this commerce, and the production areas of crude metal, amber, and rock-salt, we can reconstruct (as follows) a certain number of trade-routes, and so get some idea, on very schematic lines, of the way civilization moved up from the south:

(1) The sea-route from the Mediterranean, by the Pillars of Hercules and the Atlantic coast-line, to Britain. This route was already followed in the Bronze Age to obtain Cornish tin and also Irish gold, and was later dominated by the Phoenicians and Carthaginians, who started from Spain or Africa;

(2) the sea-route from Britain to Belgica, which from that point divided in three directions: by the rivers of northern Gaul and the Rhône towards the Gulf of Lions; by the Scheldt and the Rhine towards Germany; and by the North Sea and the Baltic to Scandinavia;

(3) the routes leading from the central Po valley (the North Etruscan region) and the head of the Adriatic (where the Veneti lived) by the Danube and the Rhine towards the North Sea, or by the Danube and the Vistula to the Baltic and beyond;

(4) the routes from the Po valley by the Julian Alps and the Danube to the Black Sea—or by the Balkans to the Aegean and Anatolia;

(5) the waterway from the Adriatic up the Po and the tributaries on its left bank, leading to the country of the Alpine and North Etruscan tribes, and then across the passes to the Rhône valley;

(6) the route from the Greek colonies of Odessus, Istria, Tyras, etc., by the Dniester and the Vistula to the Baltic and Scandinavia;

(7) the routes from the Greek town of Olbia via the Dnieper, and from the Crimean colonies via the Don, to central Russia and beyond;

(8) from the Greek colonies of Colchis via the Caucasian region towards the countries beyond the Caspian;

(9) from the Middle East via the Caspian coasts and the Volga, to the country lying beyond.

But naturally the use made of these routes altered from time to time, among other things when new exportable surpluses were discovered in the barbarian countries.

2. THE BEGINNINGS OF MEDIA AND PERSIA

We have now given a broad outline of historical events in the Middle East and the West. It remains to consider the Asiatic countries lying farther east, beginning with the Medo-Persian area which served as a bridge.

We have already had occasion, in speaking of the Mitanni and Kassites, to mention the eastward movement of an eastern Indo-European group of peoples, the 'Aryans', who must be assumed to have come from the Russian steppes along the coasts of the Caspian. To this group belonged, first the Scythians and Cimmerians, who remained as nomads along the route they had travelled, secondly the Iranic people, the subject of this section, and thirdly the Indians, of whom we shall speak in a moment. The Iranic races had their rise when they migrated in various sections on to the Iranian plateau south of the Caucasus. The Medes moved into the country north-east of the Elamites; and the Persians, who first were semi-nomadic wanderers in league with the Cimmerians and Scyths to the north-west of the Medes near Lake Van, later settled down south of Media in territory which extended to the eastern shore of the Persian Gulf.[38] The identification of the Medes with the Mannei mentioned in second-millennium documents may be doubted.[39] But an inscription of the Assyrian king Shalmaneser II speaks of his victory over them, followed by the deportation of 50,000 people, in 837; Tiglath-Pileser III made them tributary, and at least for a time occupied the territory of the Parsua; and in 715 Sargon II carried off the Median king Dayakku. Vassalage to the Assyrians led the Medes to take over some parts of Assyrian culture; but they must also have possessed a considerable culture of their own to account for the lofty ideas in religion and ethics which bear the general title of Zoroastrianism. On the date of Zoroaster (Zarathustra) there was already wide disagreement in antiquity, but he cannot be put later than 1000 if we are to explain the archaic language of the 'Gathā' which are attributed to him.[40]

It then seems that Dayakku (the Deioces of Herodotus) recovered his freedom, and in the years beginning in 708 unified the Medes around Ecbatana as their capital, although they still paid tribute to Assyria. One of his successors, Phraortes (Khshathrita), advanced farther, by subduing a part of the Persians (though in the country of Anzan an independent Persian dynasty still maintained itself);[41] he also tried, without success, to throw off the Assyrian yoke. His work was carried to its conclusion by Cyaxares (653–585). This king recovered the throne he had lost to Scythian invaders, raised an excellent army, and made an alliance with the Chaldean Nabopalassar. He then defeated Assyria and in 612 destroyed Nineveh. After this he occupied Armenia, Cappadocia, and the eastern part of the domains of Alyattes, king of Lydia, as far as the Halys. He thus merged the cultures of Media, Mesopotamia, and Anatolia into a single union over a wider area than hitherto.

But his successor Astyages (585–550) could not hold his own against the action of the Persian king Cyrus II (558–529), a member of the Achaemenid family who until then had been princes of Anzan. Cyrus first achieved the unification of Persia; he then subdued Media, capturing Ecbatana in 550 or so, and took possession of the whole Median empire.

From 547 BC Cyrus continued his conquests. He started with two victories over the Lydian king Croesus, who in resisting him had relied on a coalition with the Chaldeans and Egyptians: Croesus' whole kingdom was occupied, including the Greek cities of the Asiatic coast which formed part of it. Next Cyrus pressed forward to the Caspian and almost to the Aral Sea in the north; and in the east he reached the right bank of the Indus and the left bank of the Jaxartes as far as the foothills of the Himalayas. Finally, he began to revenge himself upon Croesus' allies. He took Babylon by storm (c. 539), occupied its territories, and caused himself to be recognized as their legitimate sovereign—for he had clearly been favoured by the local gods.

After his death the vengeance was completed by Cambyses (529–521). With the help of Arabian allies he concentrated his forces at Gaza and defeated the Egyptian king Psamtik III at Pelusium. After the fall of Memphis, Psamtik was made prisoner, and the Persian secured recognition as a legitimate Pharaoh, acceptable to the gods of the country. But Cambyses could make no headway against Ethiopia in the south or Carthage in the west, beyond Nubia and Cyrenaica respectively. At his death there were difficulties over the succession, complicated by separatist attempts of Persia, Susiana,

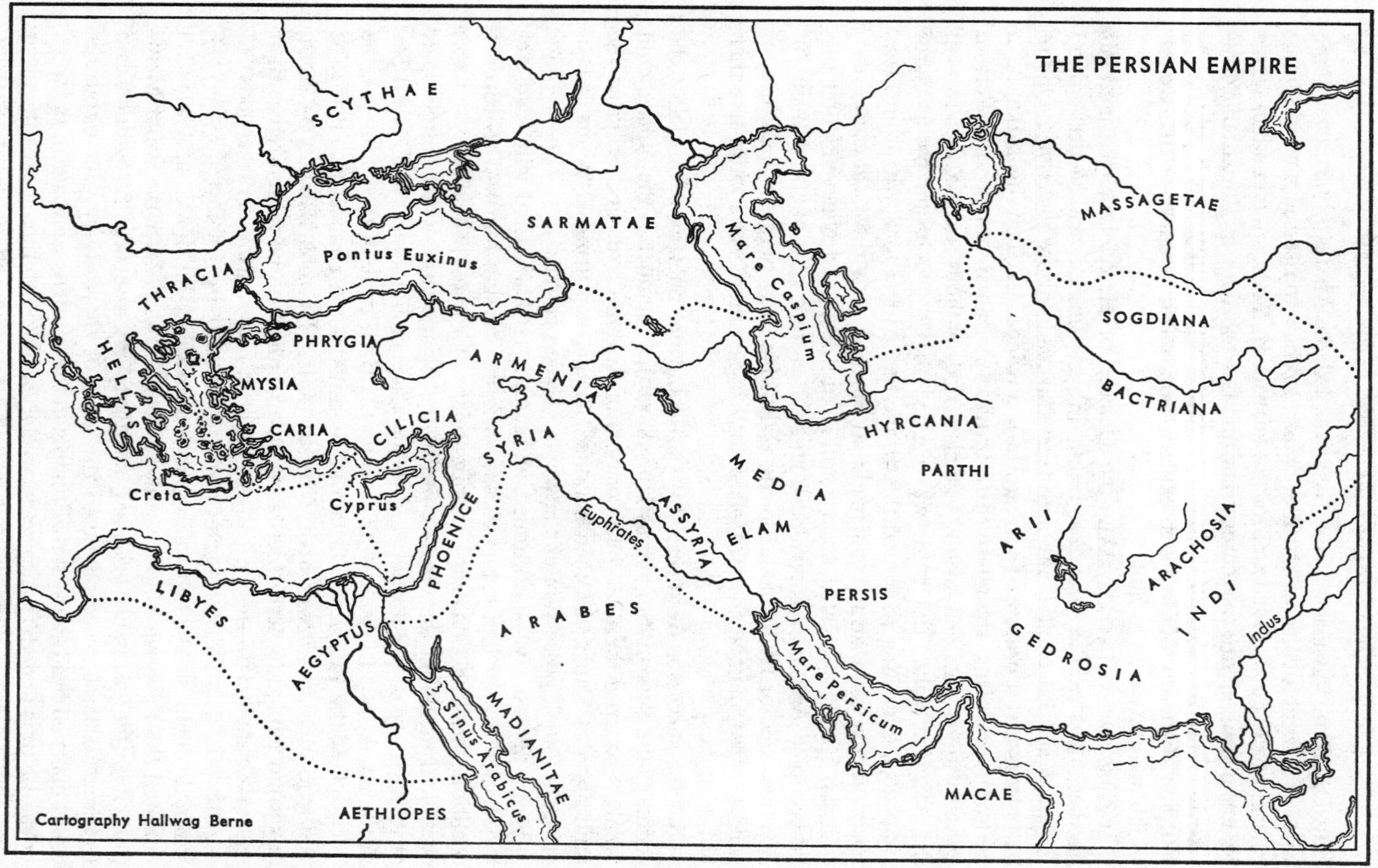

THE PERSIAN EMPIRE

MASSAGETAE
SOGDIANA
BACTRIANA
ARII
ARACHOSIA
INDI
Indus
GEDROSIA
MACAE
HYRCANIA
PARTHI
SARMATAE
Mare Caspium
MEDIA
ELAM
PERSIS
ASSYRIA
Mare Persicum
ARMENIA
Euphrates
ARABES
SCYTHAE
Pontus Euxinus
PHRYGIA
SYRIA
PHOENICE
MADIANITAE
Sinus Arabicus
THRACIA
MYSIA
CILICIA
CARIA
Cyprus
AEGYPTUS
AETHIOPES
HELLAS
Crete
LIBYES

Cartography Hallwag Berne

MAP IV

Babylonia, Hyrcania, Lydia, and Egypt.[42] Eventually the throne was won by Darius (521–486), a member of the cadet branch of the Achaemenid house and a devoted adherent to Zoroastrianism.[43] In the early part of his reign he expanded his possessions near the Indus, and also tried to put an end to the Scythian and Cimmerian raids by making an expedition across the Bosphorus and Thrace to the Danube. Then before resuming his expansionist policy abroad he sought to provide a stable organization for his empire, which by now comprised a vast area—from Egypt and the Aegean Sea to the banks of the Indus and Jaxartes, and from the Persian Gulf to the Black Sea and the Caspian. (Map IV.) It was an empire which clearly aimed at including the whole civilized world in a single political organism.

The organization had been already in large part prepared, and actually put into effect, by Cyrus II and Cambyses, not only through their conquests, but also by the use of new policies. In religion they practised toleration—the permission granted to the Hebrews to return to their country may be remembered—and they also favoured syncretism, which was made easier by the universality inherent in the Zoroastrian religion, with its monotheistic and ethical outlook. Moreover, in strong contrast to the arrogance of the Assyrians, they displayed humanity towards the conquered peoples and understanding of their customs; they employed local rulers as governors of the satrapies; and they tried to issue reasonable laws and provide justice and prosperity in all the countries they controlled. This was of great consequence in achieving an assimilation of cultures which was spontaneous and not forced, and in raising the level of civilization of their subjects, and of the neighbouring peoples too. Darius in his turn brought all this process to perfection by organizing the twenty divisions of the empire, the 'satrapies', from the various standpoints of administration, justice, defence, and finance. He paid attention to communications, and built permanent roads, with posting stations and forts: these were of immense importance for trade, which was fostered also by the adoption from Lydia of a gold coin of fixed weight, acceptable in all the provinces and called the 'daric', a name derived from the Accadian word for gold. The roads also provided for the defence of the empire, which was entrusted to a large standing army. From the military angle the army sometimes proved too loose an instrument: it was made uneven by the great differences in race, aptitude, speech, and equipment among the regional troops who composed it. But it was of the first importance in putting the people of distant countries into direct contact with one another and in bringing them together into a uniform way of life. Moreover the kings, to build their palaces and royal tombs, made use of craftsmen and materials from the most widely separated areas; and this brought about an intricate fusion of artistic ideas, and vastly increased the cultural borrowings and exchanges between all districts of the empire.[44]

3. PRE-BUDDHIST INDIA

After 1500 BC the static agricultural and urban culture of the Indus, which had long been ossified and deprived of any real possibility of growth, decayed and finally disappeared. According to some scholars the final blow was inflicted by an invader from the north-west. These were the Aryans, a group of tribes that came perhaps from the Caspian zone and whose language still formed part of the single Indo-Iranic group. Penetrating into the Punjab from across the Afghan frontier passes, it was probably they who destroyed the strongholds (*pur*) of the Indus civilization.

The Aryans were the bearers of a civilization completely different from that of the Indus. Still semi-nomads when they entered India, they were chiefly engaged, apart from war, in cattle-raising, and only secondarily in agriculture. Gradually they imposed their language and their religion on the earlier Dravidic and Munda populations of north India (the Dasyu or Dāsa).[45] For fuller statements of the linguistic and religious history see below, pp. 60 ff., pp. 226 ff. Inevitably exposed to the penetrating influence of their surroundings, they, or rather their aristocracy, reacted instinctively by constructing a rigidly compartmentalized social system. This, at a later stage, crystallized into the theory of the four castes: priests (*Brāhmaṇa*), warriors (*Kṣattriya*), merchants and farmers (*Vaiśya*), and servants (*Śūdra*): only the three first castes enjoyed full social and religious rights. This was an unconscious attempt by one race to defend itself against the others. By its nature it involved the recognition of alien elements and an attempt to control them. But despite it the Vedic culture, originally foreign to Indian soil, ended by being deeply influenced by its environment; above all, it changed its own spirit and its own religious, ethical, and economic content, although it kept up the mythology, the ritual, and the social structure on which it had been founded. The story of the Aryan society is one of gradual adaptation to environment and of deep penetration into the psychology and way of life of their Dravidian and Munda substrata.

But before that happened, in a period contemporary with the migration into the Punjab, this rude society of Aryan shepherds and soldiers conceived a series of sacred lays; and at the end of the second millennium BC these were gathered into the four great collections of the *Veda*. They were very soon accepted as revealed truth, and remained always (at least in theory) the fundamental basis of Indian religion.

Once they were fixed in their definite form by the ancient compilers, their preservation was assured. For they were handed down from generation to generation, with scrupulous care for the sound and form of the sacred text, in schools, better described as societies for oral transmission: the text was then written down several centuries after our era. Indeed, after pictographic script had vanished from the Indus, it is remarkable that writing—and therefore written sources—appear in India much later, as is indeed the case with all Indo-European languages, than in the other great cultural areas of Asia.

India, with rare exceptions, has not developed a written history.[46] Yet we can reconstruct an outline of Aryan tribal history from the Vedic hymns, from the great epics of *Mahābhārata* and the *Rāmāyaṇa*, from later works (the *Purāṇas*) of mythical, sociological and semi-historical content, and from Buddhist and Jain texts. Much of the history, however, is disconnected, uncertain and unsupported by archaeology: it is therefore largely hypothetical.

At the beginning Aryan power was limited to the Punjab; the focus of the Rigvedic culture lay on the banks of the now extinct river Sarasvatī (the Sarsuti, which today is lost in the sands of Bikaner). From this small central nucleus Aryan rule spread slowly eastward as far as Bengal and southward as far as the Vindhya Mountains, where it seems to have suffered a check. The duration of this is uncertain, but of all the history of the Deccan and of India to the middle of the third century BC we really know nothing precise other than what derives from the scanty data of prehistoric archaeology.

Aryan society was divided into little states of monarchic and aristocratic character engaged in perpetual struggles against one another. Few figures of historical import emerge from the shadows of myth. There were, for example, King Sudās of early Vedic times, and the confederacies of the Kuru and the Pancāla in the later Vedic period. We can identify the outline of a major conflict which involved almost all the Aryan tribes, the leaders of the two opposite camps being respectively the Kaurava and the Pāṇḍava (perhaps tenth century BC). This conflict is the semi-historic core round which was then constructed the vast poem of the *Mahābhārata*. Later a great dynasty descended from King Parikṣit appeared in the western part of present-day Uttar Pradesh, a dynasty adorned by the great King Janamejaya (ninth century BC). Later still we meet the figures of the wise philosopher-king Janaka (seventh century BC?) in Videha (eastern Uttar Pradesh and western Bihar). These rather uncertain data point to a progressive displacement eastward of the political centre of gravity of Aryan India. The Punjab was abandoned to obscure tribes of the Aryan rearguard and the great kingdoms were formed more and more to the east. Finally a limit was reached and a point of equilibrium found in central Bihar, which for about a thousand years from *c.* 500 BC became the imperial centre of Aryan India. Furthermore in the sixth century we can discern in outline how a balance of power took shape among the larger territorial formations (the sixteen Mahājanapada). Besides these there existed various states governed by assemblies of noblemen, sometimes but not always headed by a president with the royal title; true and real aristocratic republics of a type which did not survive for long. At the end of the period with which we have been dealing, about 500 BC, the kingdom of Magadha in central Bihar is prominent among these various states. At the same time Cyrus II and Darius I conquered the Punjab and part of Sind and annexed them to Persia as the satrapies of Gandhāra and

India. They thus started that political and cultural contact between India and Iran, often broken but always revived, which characterizes the history of the region destined in the twentieth century to become Pakistan.

In the meantime the spiritual life of the ancient Aryans had been modified by the penetration of Dravidian or at least un-Aryan ideas (metempsychosis, theory of *Karma*, sanctity of the cow, etc.), which gradually altered religious values.[47] New deities made their appearance; and Vedic religion was insensibly transformed into Brahmanism. Later, outside Brahmanic priestly circles though in close connection with them, there arose the bold monist speculations of the *Upaniṣad*. On the other hand, as an attempt to step beyond the system of caste, there emerged, about 500, the two great movements of religious reform, Jainism and Buddhism. Of these the second was destined during the following period to spread widely, within and outside the confines of India.

4. THE FAR EAST AND ASIA

a. *Pre-Confucian China*

Although China, because of its relatively isolated geographical position, had been able to develop an autonomous culture, it remained at the beginning of this period in fairly close cultural contact with the large area of steppe culture from the Ukraine to Manchuria. The Neolithic culture of Lung-Shan was followed about 1600 by a brilliant Bronze Age civilization, which is known to Chinese historical tradition by the name of Shang, and later as Yin (*c.* 1600–1027 BC). It is known to us above all by the excavations of its last capital, Anyang in Honan, as well as of minor towns in the same area. Its social organization presents strong matriarchal elements and the prevailing character of its religion was agricultural (with field and fertility divinities).

Towards the end of the Shang-Yin period the horse and the war chariot were introduced, perhaps from central Asia. This contributed to the formation of a governing class of warriors fighting from chariots and to the slow rise of a primitive form of feudalism.[48] We find pictographic writing already in full development in the Shang state, with features essentially identical with those obtaining at the present day.

The Shang-Yin state, which comprised a relatively small area in the lower valley of the Huang-ho, fell a victim in the second half of the eleventh century BC to the conquering armies of an ethnic group which was possibly related though less civilized: this was the Chou people, who lived in the valley of the Wei and on the bend of the Huang-ho. Their original culture was characterized by certain features somewhat different from the Shang: they were unfamiliar with bronze, had no system of writing, and their religion put less emphasis on the cult of the earth, and had a strong patriarchal stamp. It quickly assimilated the main features of Shang-Yin culture. Of course, the fusion of the two people encountered great difficulties and needed a considerable time. But once it was achieved, the result was the Chinese civilization of the classical period.

The Chou state, founded by King Wu, was moulded at its beginning by a great statesman, the Duke of Chou, regent and later minister of the second King Wen. To Wu and to the Duke of Chou the Chou state owes its peculiar structure. It received a typically feudal organization: its territories were governed by a large number of feudal princes, enjoying full power over their own fiefs, but under the ultimate suzerainty of the king (*Wang*). The central authority derived its revenues and its military force from contributions made by its vassals. The system functioned well in the first centuries, but then decayed; it received its death blow from a barbarian invasion in 771, which compelled the dynasty to shift its residence from the lower valley of the Wei to modern Lo-yang or Honan.

The Chou dynasty was now hemmed in by powerful vassals on every side. It lost all power of developing the small territory it directly governed and was reduced to a nonentity by the great feudal leaders. It therefore quickly lost all political importance while among the fiefs a slow process of simplification and concentration of power evolved. The Chou kingdom turned into a feudal confederation under the purely religious suzerainty of the king who was left as guardian of the state cult.

Both before and after 771 the political system of the Chou, fluid and unstable though it was, spread gradually like a spot of oil over the Huang-ho and Yangtze plains, and also over part of the coastal zone. Four different processes played their part. First, foreign territories were conquered and annexed by the feudal states on the frontiers. Secondly, the expanding populations of these countries began to emigrate, sometimes in substantial numbers, and their new settlements were placed under the protection of the nearest feudal state. Thirdly, peoples and state formations, which were independent but closely connected with Chinese civilization, would accept this civilization wholesale and obtain admittance to the system of feudal states. Lastly, states with civilizations of their own would approach China, accept its fundamental premises in politics and religion, and come in as part of the feudal confederation, although they continued for centuries to preserve their own civilizations. They were influenced by Chinese culture, but from time to time contributed new features to it. Typical of this category is the state of Ch'u on the middle Yangtze, of proto-Thai race, which was added to the confederation 'in the ninth century. It introduced a rich civilization of its own, some remains of which have been excavated near Ch'ang-sha. It is significant that from the end of the eighth century the Ch'u kings bore the royal title of *Wang*, which was also borne by the fainéant Chou kings.

Since almost the beginning, a process developed by which the smaller states tended to be conquered and annexed by the larger ones, leading thus to a simplification of the political structure of China, to a sharpening of the conflicts and to an increase of the war potentials involved in the struggle.

By the eighth century the number of feudal states had been reduced to about 200, and the recurring struggles between them made any permanent solution impossible. To cope with the absence of a central authority, an attempt was made to introduce a stable element with the election of a hegemon or prince-president (*pa*) who would act as head of a general alliance of the feudal chiefs. This is the period (722–481) called Ch'un-ch'iu (spring and autumn), from the name of an ancient chronicle. At the beginning of the seventh century BC the strongest state was that of Ch'i in modern Shan-tung, in the centre of salt production and of trade in bronze and later in iron. Through the work of the great minister Kuan-chung, Duke Huan of Ch'i became in 678 the first *pa* of the Chinese feudal confederations; but the grand alliance of which he was head did not survive his death in 643. After a brief predominance by Ch'u, the presidency passed in 635 to Duke Wen of Chin (in Shansi); the position of hegemon was inherited by his successors but became ever more nominal when the power of that state declined. Meanwhile the power of the young state of Ch'in was slowly rising: originally a small fief in the upper valley of the Wei, this had received from the Chou, when they retreated to Lo-yang in 771, the mission of reconquering from the barbarians the ancient home of the royal dynasty. Their task was accomplished after many years of hard struggle, and by now the dukes of Ch'in dominated a solid frontier march, enclosed in the natural fortress of the Wei valley. They were hemmed in on three sides by barbarians, but, for that very reason, were accustomed to warfare and possessed a good army. Chin, Ch'in, and Ch'u remained for a long time the dominant states in the kaleidoscopic movements of the Chinese political scene. King Chuang of Ch'u (613–591) obtained the supremacy and exercised hegemony, although without a formal investiture. After his death the formal hegemony of Chin revived in practice too, especially with Duke Ching (d. 581). Then Chin became a victim of internal struggles among its noble families; the dynasty lost all its authority and in the following period the state broke up into three smaller ones. This was a tendency which can be observed also in other feudal principalities. Already in the late sixth century Chin gave way gradually in face of its more solid rivals, although its formal presidency lasted until the beginning of the fifth century BC. Peace treaties and pacts of alliances against the renewal of war followed each other at brief intervals, without succeeding in giving peace to the convulsed political world of China. In the second half of the sixth century Chin moved towards dissolution, while Ch'u was temporarily enfeebled by serious internal squabbles in which a dynastic quarrel on the surface cloaked the real but obscure ethnic tensions below. Even the growth of Ch'in seemed to slow down considerably.

The end of the period saw a great ferment of ideas in philosophy and political thought: the first schools were formed, and there appear the first wandering philosopher-counsellors who offered their advice and services to any feudal princes willing to employ them. Confucius (Kung-tsu, 551–479), was one of these philosophers, and his school later became dominant in China, and formed and moulded its habits of thought and political theory down to the beginning of the twentieth century.

b. *Japanese Origins*

Japanese legend, codified in the *Kojiki* and in the *Nihongi*, fixes at about 660 BC the foundation of the Japanese empire at the hands of Jimmu Tennō. In actual fact Jimmu lived, it appears, a millennium later; and of Japanese history from 1200 to 500 BC we know absolutely nothing. Archaeology can only tell us that there was no Palaeolithic culture in Japan. In the Mesolithic period stone and pottery ware of very high artistic quality begins to appear in many parts of the country. This culture is normally given the name of Jōmon, from the cord-shaped decoration (*jōmon*) on the pottery. The greater part of the Jōmon industry belongs to the Neolithic period, and can be dated to the second and first millennia BC. This culture came to an end during the last centuries BC.

The inhabitants of Japan were originally a race whose modern descendants are the Ainu, of whom there are about 20,000 survivors on the island of Hokkaido. But in the first centuries of the last millennium BC came a series of migrations from the Chinese and Korean coasts and across the bridge of islands which join Japan with Melanesia and Indonesia. They led to the retreat of the Ainu towards the north, and to the formation of a mixed population whose original differences became substantially merged in the common characteristics produced by their isolated life in an island world: so was born the Japanese people. The question whether the Jōmon industry belongs to the ancestors of the modern Japanese or to the Ainu is still discussed; it seems that both people shared in it, but the former had the prevailing part.

c. *The Steppe Civilizations of Eurasia*

Conditions in central and northern Eurasia, within the scope of the present volume, are known directly only through archaeological discoveries which are nowhere near full enough to enable us to draw confident and detailed conclusions from them; nor have they yet been, as a rule, studied systematically.

In early times, it is true, the various methods of existence predominated in turn in this waste country: hunting and grazing on the one hand, which require relatively wide movements from place to place, and primitive agriculture on the other, keeping the tribes to settled homes. Yet it is certain that by the end of the second millennium BC they were nomad horsemen breeding cattle. This way of life first reached eastern Europe, then northeastern Asia, but soon was found on the steppes of central Asia and finally in the region of Lake Baikal. Many of the people thus acquired increased mobility in their migrations, which were also affected by the progressive growth of semi-desert areas due to desiccation.

At the present day many races and languages are intermingled in this vast area—Indo-European, Uralian, Turco-Mongolian-Tungus, Caucasian, and Tibetan—and all can be identified among the nomads who attacked China in the fourth and fifth centuries A D. They may all also have played a part, no longer definable, in cultural development and ethnic relations in the preceding centuries, and in the formation of a more or less ephemeral political whole. To attribute a precise function in time and space to each of these groups is not yet possible with any certainty, though archaeological discoveries are continually increasing. The continuous wanderings of these nomads, the repeated fusions of races and superimposition of one on the other, and the rapid evolution and mutations of speech all add to the uncertainty.

This immense area of unstable people in unsettled homes must one way or another have become the launching ground of many migrations, the impetus from each one of which was able to provoke others. In these nebulous movements lies the explanation of many reverberations which, in the course of centuries, were felt even by the people with higher civilizations in the East and in the Mediterranean world. Teggart has studied these repercussions in the period from 58 BC to AD 107; but it is to be hoped that the study will be extended to earlier and later periods, and that pertinent Soviet research will be utilized. In studies of this kind we can now go beyond archaeological evidence and the sequences provided by stratifications, and beyond the history of language; for absolute chronology is ascertainable by new scientific methods. These will permit us to identify and date the periods of climatic change, the development of communications by land and by water, and the diffusion of discoveries and of new methods for the expansion of resources, such as the exploitation of metals.

For the present we can say that the band of steppes, which stretches through northern Eurasia from the Ukraine (or even the Hungarian plain) almost to the Japanese Sea, has seen in the course of history a succession of political and cultural formations, which from about the beginning of the first millennium BC were based on nomad economy. The various states which followed each other in the steppe, although they were created by different peoples and were therefore built on various races and languages, all possessed certain characteristics which were fundamental. Their economy was pastoral; the structure of society was aristocratic; there were no cities nor urban civilizations (except for the large oases on the southern rim of this band); little or no value was attached to the possession of land itself; and bitter struggles went on with the large sedentary civilizations which adjoined them. But these factors, though perennial, cannot be directly ascertained until a later date.

For us central and northern Asia remain for the whole of this period in the sphere of prehistory. There is as yet no ray of light from outside, from the texts and documents of the great bordering civilizations. All that archaeology can tell us is almost limited to the territories which today form part of the Soviet Union, where excavations using modern scientific methods have taken place in recent times. These excavations show the importance of the metallurgical centre at Minusinsk on the upper Yenisei both in respect of its high yield and its influence on other areas.

At the beginning of the period with which we are dealing the dominant culture in Siberia was that of Karasuk (about the twelfth-seventh centuries BC), whose members were anthropologically Sinoid. Cattle-breeding began to take precedence, and later became characteristic of the whole steppe economy. Metals were already known. The Karasuk culture predominated chiefly in Transbaikalia and in northern Mongolia, and shows undoubted contacts with the Chinese Shang civilization at least in the artistic field. From about 1000, it extended also towards the west taking the place of the Andronovo culture which had survived there until then. This is the period of great cultural unity on the steppes from Pannonia to China. In this period a great military innovation began to take shape; we can detect the outlines of the man who remained dominant until the seventeenth century AD—the warrior on horseback. The western part of this area was occupied by the Scythians who were based on the steppes of south Russia. The excavations of Bernshtam in the T'ien-Shan and the Pamir have revealed the prevalence in that region since the eighth century of people who can be identified with the Sacae of western sources. In Minusinsk also there was a sudden change, with the penetration of Europoid elements, who created the Tagar I culture (about the seventh–fifth centuries), a pure Bronze Age civilization in which the horse, and the way of life that is founded on it, already played an important part. Contemporary with Tagar, there developed in the valleys of the Altai a parallel and kindred culture, that of Maiemir.

5. THE PACIFIC ISLANDS, AMERICA, AND AFRICA

Much the same confusion of peoples which we have seen brought about over many centuries by the nomads of the steppes in central and northern Eurasia must also have occurred in the vast area of the Pacific islands. Some of these were great, others small, some formed part of an archipelago, others not; and through them the sea peoples moved from one home to another using the most primitive equipment. The extent of the immigrations, the admixtures they caused, and the way one people succeeded another, are sufficiently proved by the sandwiching of languages at the present day, which shows kindred groups like the Indonesian and Polynesian separated by others of widely different speech, like that of Papua. There is also an enormous variety of dialects and anthropological formations within each group, for the migrations increased the linguistic diversity which the establishment of each language in a separate island had already caused.

For the history of America* we can now supplement the older methods of relative chronology, based on excavation and the inspection of trees, by the more exact results obtainable from work with 'Carbon 14'. In this way without having to rely on the very inadequate oral traditions, we can distinguish various civilizations with reasonable confidence in the millennium before the discovery by Columbus.

Geography, anthropology and language make it likely that the first settlers in this vast territory arrived across the Behring Straits from north-eastern Asia, and perhaps, as some scholars maintain, by 'island-hopping' from south-east Asia, Australia, and Tasmania across the south Pacific. They scattered over huge regions, which provided every kind of climate and resources; and for thousands of years lived in various primitive societies, hunting, fishing, and gathering natural fruits. What is certain is that the so-called hoe-culture was introduced or discovered not later than the middle of the third millennium, especially in Mexico, Guatemala, and Nicaragua in the northern hemisphere, and in Peru and Bolivia in the southern: this led to sedentary ways of life and a rapid development of wealth and culture. Whether the discovery was made in one of the two hemispheres and passed on to the other, or was an autonomous act in each, is a problem to be decided when we have better knowledge of the way civilization progressed in the central American corridor, which linked the two zones.

The management of agriculture, the construction of terraces and irrigation works, or the production of edible and medicinal roots—and its improvement by the use of fertilizers—undoubtedly led in time to the formation of aristocratic classes; and to them, from c. 1000 BC, was due the origin of urban life, with rapid and revolutionary development in architecture, artistic techniques, social organization, and religious ideas. Moreover about 500 Mexico began to make use of carved hieroglyphs, though these pictograms have not yet been deciphered. Our knowledge of these centres of a relatively advanced civilization, which was gradually conducted into the other regions, is now sufficiently detailed to allow a reasonable degree of precision in, for example, the classification of artistic periods.

In Africa there was a marked difference between the history of the two zones, normally called 'white' and 'black'. But though this division is more or less adequate, the frontier between the zones in the course of centuries was relatively ill-defined. In an early period the Negro or Negroid peoples may have reached the Mediterranean coast, at least at certain points: then they retreated before invaders, until they reached the present southern

* The rise and diffusion of civilization in North and South America in Pre-Columbian times will be described in Volume III of the *History of Mankind: Cultural and Scientific Development* (London and New York, 1963–,), 6 vols.

boundary of the tribes of Berber-Hamitic and Cushite speech, with the river Senegal on the west and the Juba on the east. Finally, not later than the fourth century BC, Negroes are found again north of that line, either as slaves or as descendants of earlier races: thus the Moorish tribes and the Tuareg seem to be half-caste peoples from this mixture of white and black.

In white Africa, of which we have been speaking, the most ancient civilized people were the Egyptians, with the Libyans possessing a similar culture at their side. In the Mediterranean coastal districts the Hamitic races were joined by others: to the west the Phoenicians, whose colonies came later under the direction of Carthage, to the east the Greek colonists of Cyrenaica, but not before the seventh century BC.

But as time went on some cultural importance was acquired in that part of Africa by the people of Cushite language, who inhabited the land south of Egypt down to the border of modern Somaliland. In that district, which had been for long under Egyptian influence, a powerful dynastic state with its centre at Napata was built about 730 BC; and its king Piankhi conquered Egypt, expelled the reigning Libyan house, and founded the twenty-fifth dynasty. The kingdom of Napata survived in later times, although its capital was moved to Meröe, farther south.

In 'black' Africa on the other hand we can discern even in antiquity a number of movements by peoples who had for long been separated from one another and had consequently very different ways of life. The evidence of anthropology, culture, and language makes it certain that several tribes, who in our period lived, often in a state of vassalage, in small pockets of territory, like the Pygmy hunters or the Khoisan shepherds (Boshiman and Hottentots), must in earlier times have inhabited very large areas. The Bantus and kindred tribes, after they had learned the elements of agricultural technique, had expanded into their lands.

APPENDIX

A NOTE ON THE ORIGINS OF THE ETRUSCANS

by M. W. FREDERIKSEN

The view adopted here by Professor Pareti, who identified the ancestors of the Etruscans with the *terramara* or pile-dwellers of the Po valley, was based upon supposed resemblances of culture and has been radically criticized, especially by G. Säflund, *Le Terramare* (Uppsala, 1939), and the same applies to the views of earlier scholars for whom the *Terramara* people were the original Romans. It would now be generally agreed that the *Terramaricoli*, after invading the Po valley in about 1600 BC, attained only a local importance, being finally absorbed or dispersed after 1100 BC in the obscure period of transition from the Bronze Age to the Iron

Age. On the other hand, it is now clearer that the earliest Etruscan centres were those that developed in the south such as Caere, Tarquinii, or Veii; and that the signs of Etruscan occupation north of the Apennines were the result of a later expansion towards the Alps during the sixth century BC (see also pp. 72 ff.).

The archaeological culture of the Bronze Age came to an end about 1000 BC, and most scholars would agree that this was brought about by a series of invasions by peoples who cremated their dead. After an obscure period of some two centuries, there developed in central Italy a distinctive Iron Age or Villanovan culture, and it is from this that the Etruscan civilization began to emerge in the eighth century BC. At this time are found the first recognizably Etruscan remains, of pottery and bronzes, and after a short time the earliest inscribed objects. Although it is clear that trade began early and Greek vases appear in some quantity, there is no archaeological trace of an invasion or immigration at that date. Instead there is an unbroken continuity in pottery styles and funerary rites from the Villanovan to the Etruscan periods; and in certain sites, such as Tarquinii and Veii, recent studies suggest that the early defensive system and the civic topography, and therefore the rudiments of a city organization, originated also in the Villanovan period.

There is still little agreement about the origin of the Etruscan people; the most recent views have been collected by M. Pallottino in *Studi Etruschi* (1961), p. 3 ff. To some writers the language, which is clearly unrelated to the Italic languages in the rest of Italy, shows that the Etruscans were an indigenous race like the Ligurians; but the complete change in archaeological habits and the break in occupation after the Bronze Age make this improbable. Other scholars maintain that they were a northern invasion, pointing to the great affinities between early Villanovan objects and others found in central Europe and the Danube valley; but this can only concern their remote origins and tells us little. The view of Herodotus, who says that the Etruscans migrated from Lydia at a date about 1200 BC according to his reckoning, finds many supporters. The strongest arguments for an eastern origin are non-archaeological; first, an inscription from the Greek island of Lemnos contains a language which shows close external resemblances to Etruscan; second, that Etruscan religion is very similar in certain points to the astrology and divination practised in Babylonia. But the linguistic evidence is at least ambiguous; and unfortunately their religion is only known in its later phases and could be a feature introduced in Hellenistic times. Herodotus' account, therefore, can only be defended by supposing an invasion in a remote period, some five hundred years before the Etruscans as we know them appear; or else, at a later date, by assuming a peaceful diffusion or occupation by a ruling class such as to leave no trace in the archaeological remains. Either view seems possible, but neither really saves the credit of Herodotus, whose information about prehistoric migrations was at best vague.

Attempts to recover the racial composition of the Etruscans are likewise very uncertain. Ancient writers, indeed, suggest that throughout the Italian peninsula there was a considerable mixture of peoples and ethnic groups; this is confirmed by the variety of burial rites in several places, and in the remoter areas of the peninsula, such as the central Apennines and the foothills of the Alps, earlier habits lasted for some centuries after they were abandoned elsewhere. It may, therefore, be wasted labour to seek the racial derivations of the Etruscans or other Italic peoples. The latter, it is agreed, may be identified with the groups of invaders of about 1000 BC who spread through Italy introducing the practice of cremation; but it is not yet possible to identify among them those who became the distinct peoples known to Greek and Roman writers of a later time.

The long debate about Etruscan origins, it may be said, is unlikely to be answered by a new discovery and is mainly concerned with the interpretation of already-known facts. Recent research, however, has shown that some older conceptions must be abandoned; the main development of this people certainly took place in Etruria itself, and the only problem is about their very remote origins, which is in comparison unimportant. Like the other Italic peoples, the Etruscans acquired their distinctive character comparatively recently, in the seventh and sixth centuries BC. Their civilization, as it was known to ancient writers, seemed a strange one; but it was based economically upon the wealth in agriculture and bronze of Etruria; it had taken over much from the Villanovan culture that had preceded it; they absorbed much of artistic value from their early contacts with the Greeks; the growth of the great city-states of Etruria and their organization into a league with a religious centre near Volsinii is very like the history of the Greek states in the same period, and was influenced by the same political and cultural needs. The language will offer no certain answer until it is translated; it is not yet known whether it was spoken by a small ruling class who imposed it upon a subject population, just as Latin was spread by the Romans in Spain and Gaul, or whether it was an indigenous language which was then taken over by some foreign invaders, as occurred when the Normans conquered Sicily. Mommsen said that the origin of the Etruscans 'could not be known, and was not worth knowing'; since his day further research has reduced the number of possibilities but the question is still unanswered. It is therefore more important to realize how much they owed to their experiences in Italy and to the stimulus supplied by their relations with the Greeks, which were, on any view, the determining factors in the formation of the Etruscan people.

NOTES TO CHAPTER I

1. The short historical introductions, which come at the beginning of the work's three sections, make no pretence at providing, in a few pages, a complete conspectus of world history from the twelfth century BC to the fourth century AD. Their object is the more modest, yet indispensable, one of reminding the 'ordinary reader' of the main events which form the setting for the material in the succeeding chapters, these latter chapters being the real content of the book.

2. A shortcoming of this work is that social, political, and cultural phenomena are treated in isolation from one another. In a number of cases this leads to a complete failure to formulate, even in the form of hypotheses, the causes giving rise to particular phenomena, to the changes that took place in the social and political structure of various states, or to changes in the ideology of the inhabitants of these states. Thus, for example, in the 'Historical Introduction' to Part I the author unwarrantedly divorces political from social and economic history. The history of Greece after the Persian Wars is reduced to a chronicle of successive wars, and the internal conflict between advocates of oligarchy and advocates of democracy is attributed solely to differences over foreign policy.

Instead of an account of the complex history of Hellenism we are given a history of wars. But it is precisely in Greek history that we find the clearest evidence of the proposition that, as a rule, foreign policy is merely the product of the internal relations between different social classes and groups. It is quite arbitrary to separate these two aspects. (K. M. Kolobova and E. M. Shtaerman.)

3. On Mitanni, the state established in northern Syria by the Hurri, see Sir Leonard Woolley, *History of Mankind: Cultural and Scientific Development*, Volume I, Part 2, *The Beginnings of Civilization*, pp. 370, 383, 387–9 (hereinafter cited as *History of Mankind*, I–2).

4. To Homer, however, they are neighbours of the Trojans (see *Iliad*, III. 184 ff.); and if this reflects genuine folk-memory, the Phrygian settlement in Asia Minor should be dated to the thirteenth century BC at the latest. See Seton Lloyd, *Early Anatolia* (London, 1956), pp. 71 ff.

5. Professor Pareti here follows up a line of argument first brilliantly suggested by K. J. Beloch, *Griechische Geschichte* (ed. 2, Strasbourg, 1912), i.2.76 ff. Yet the Greek tradition of a 'Dorian invasion' (and of pre-Dorian Achaeans) is surprisingly unanimous, even as to dates—about two generations after the Trojan War, i.e. about 1100 BC, see N. Hammond, *A History of Greece* (Oxford, 1959), p. 653. The strength of the linguistic case against his own view was not fully known to Professor Pareti when he wrote: see note 15 to p. 68, below. But many scholars have also seen confirmation of the Greek tradition in the archaeological evidence for widespread destruction and disorder in post-Mycenaean Greece. See A. W. Gomme, *A Historical Commentary on Thucydides*, I (Oxford, 1945), p. 118.

5a. The process of linguistic development is never rectilinear. The author states the problem too categorically. It can be solved only by taking into consideration the data obtained through decipherment of the 'Linear B' script. M. Ventris and J. Chadwick understood by 'Achaean dialect' Arcadian and Cyprian, Pamphylian and Aeolic dialects, E. Risch (*Die Gliederung der griechischen Dialekte im neueren Sicht*, 1955), who took those findings into account, drew a contrast between the Arcadian and Cyprian and the Ionian dialects—the 'southern group'—on the one hand, and Aeolic, western Greek, and Doric —the 'northern group'—on the other. S. Ya. Lurye (*Yazyk i kultura mikenskoy Gretsii* [*Language and Culture in Mycenaean Greece*], Moscow-Leningrad, USSR Academy of Sciences, 1957), follows Chadwick, with some variations and modifications in the attribution of the dialects, but considers that the difference in the dialects (between Achaean and the others) was much greater in the fourteenth–thirteenth centuries than it was in the sixth–fifth centuries BC. In any case, although a number of questions are still debatable, the Doric dialect cannot be identified with Achaean, but on the contrary stands in contrast to it.

Besides this, the 'decisive arguments' on which Professor Pareti relies do not appear conclusive to Soviet scholars. In the areas of Achaean culture that were subjected to conquest by the Dorians the language must have become Doricized. The fact that Homer mentioned 'Dorians' on Crete can be plausibly explained by the Dorian invasion of Crete, which is confirmed by early archaeological evidence. In Homer's time these were matters of long ago. Homer's Crete cannot serve as a projection of the Minoan and Mycenaean periods. (K. M. Kolobova.)

6. Troy VII A (or Homer's Troy) is the late Bronze Age city which was destroyed by fire at the end of the period known as Late Mycenaean III B, i.e. in the late thirteenth century BC. It should be noted that Professor Pareti's chronology for the Aeolian and other trans-Aegean migrations places them a century or more before that accepted by many other scholars.

7. Note also in eighth-century texts the 'Iwn and Iamani (who may be the Ionians), and the 'qws (possibly once more the Akaiwasha or Achaeans).

8. Or perhaps, as Professor F. M. Heichelheim suggests, rather later than the events so far described.

9. On the Cimmerians, see further below, p. 63. Professor P. Bosch-Gimpera questions whether they were nomads when they were ejected from south Russia.

10. Professor F. W. König would place the Libyan (Tehenu) invasion later than that of the sea raiders.

11. The first mercenaries, Ionians and Carians, arrived in the reign of Psammetichus I (663–609), and 'camps' were established at Daphnae in the eastern Delta and at Naucratis on a western arm of the Nile. Amasis (c. 569–526) concentrated all Greeks at Naucratis, which became an extremely flourishing centre of trade in this period and possessed several Greek temples.

12. I.e. the Assyrians. Professor F. W. König emphasizes the sharp difference between them and the Kassites: the latter had fully absorbed Babylonian culture. See below, p. 59.

13. As Professor F. W. König points out, however, there is no evidence of concerted action between these two kings.

14. Professor P. Bosch-Gimpera points out that there are several other mentions of Phoenicians in Homer, and that (despite the arguments below, pp. 268 ff.) it is difficult to refer all of them to memories from Mycenaean times. Greek genealogies, too, surely reflect Phoenician contacts with the Greek homelands.

15. On the Khabiru or Habiru, whom many scholars identify with the Hebrews, but who (Professor König suggests) were not necessarily nomads, see *History of Mankind*, I–2, p. 393.

16. It is not of course implied that this Graeco-Lydian *Koiné* was the result of colonization.

17. Professor K. M. Kolobova warns us against accepting any Malthusian theory of absolute overpopulation in Greece. Certainly the growth of Greek manufactures must not be overlooked in tracing the causes of Greek colonization, and there must also have been important political causes affecting many colonizing cities. But Professor Pareti undoubtedly meant to emphasize that the causes were very various.

18. Greek writers ascribed this 'synoecism' to Theseus, i.e. to one generation before the Trojan War. See C. Hignett, *History of the Athenian Constitution* (Oxford, 1952), pp. 34 ff.

19. The final fall of the kingship probably belongs to the eighth century. See Hignett, *op. cit.*, pp. 34 ff.

20. For a fuller analysis of the causes of Greek tyranny, see pp. 165 ff.

21. Although tyranny at Sicyon outlasted that in most Greek cities, many modern writers would place its fall, which was probably brought about by Sparta, about 550 rather than 520: see N. Hammond, *Classical Quarterly*, N.S. VI (1956), p. 45. Professor Pareti's view is partly based on Beloch's chronology for seventh- and sixth-century Greece (see p. 277, n. 9): but there are other considerations in its favour: see F. Schachermeyr, *Realencyclopaedie*, s.v. 'Orthagoriden' (1942), col. 1430.

22. The view that Pheidon introduced coinage goes back to the historian Ephorus and has had strong supporters in modern times: see still N. Hammond, *A History of Greece* (Oxford, 1959), p. 132. But an important article by E. S. G. Robinson, *Journal of Hellenic Studies* (1951), pp. 156 ff. (cf. *Numismatic Chronicle*, 1956, pp. 1 ff.) puts the first coinage of Asiatic Greece as late as c. 620; and since it is generally agreed that Greek coinage began in Ionia, it cannot (if Robinson is right) have reached the Peloponnese in Pheidon's time. For Pheidon's date (floruit c. 670), see A. Andrewes, *The Greek Tyrants* (London, 1956), pp. 31 ff., and for further discussion of coinage see notes to p. 138 below.

23. The origins and development of the Spartan constitution, and with it of the Spartan social system, are highly controversial questions. See bibliography in G. L. Huxley, *Early Sparta* (London, 1962).

24. Professor Ch. Th. Saricakis considers that Professor Pareti underestimates the bonds which united the Greek world by about 500 BC. A classic text is Herodotus, VIII, 144, where the Athenians speak of the ties of blood, language, religion, and customs, inescapably binding them to the other Greeks.

25. Professor Pareti has written two detailed works in refutation of these theories. See Appendix, Chapter I, pp. 49 ff.

26. Professor Pareti is here speaking of a period in the ninth century BC.

27. As Professor Ch. Th. Saricakis points out, the earliest Greek colony in the West was not on the Ionian Sea but at Cumae, just north of the Bay of Naples. See the geographer Strabo, V., p. 243.

28. The traditional date for the expulsion of the Tarquins is 510 BC.

29. Professor P. Bosch-Gimpera would date the foundation of Phocaea's Spanish colonies somewhat later, in the early sixth century, i.e. after its foundation of Massilia which is traditionally dated 600 BC. See his article in *Nouvelle Clio* (1951), pp. 260–96.

30. Professor H. Michell questions the identification of Tartessus (at the mouth of the Baetis = Guadalquivir) with the biblical Tarshish, citing his note in *The Economics of Ancient Greece* (Cambridge, 1940), p. 300. Yet Tyre's connections with Tartessus are attested also by an ancient source (Diodorus, V, 35): on the whole history of the site see A. Schulten, *Realencyclopaedie*, s.v. 'Tartessus', col. 2446.

31. The questions connected with Celtic and German migrations are discussed more fully in Chapter II, pp. 76 ff.

32. A village in Upper Austria where the earliest phase of Celtic culture was first identified by archaeologists. La Tène, which gave its name to the phases from c. 500 BC onwards, is in western Switzerland.

33. The modern view that the Belgae arrived at a later date is in conflict with the sources and cannot be accepted.

34. Professor F. M. Heichelheim emphasizes that from early La Tène days the mounts were horse-shoed.

35. Professor P. Bosch-Gimpera considers that these people were Celts, and that such Etruscan features as can be seen in Catalonia could easily have derived from trade and other contacts. But he differs from Professor Pareti about the origins of the Etruscans— see Appendix.

36. Professor P. Bosch-Gimpera believes that the only invasions of this period came over the western passes of the Pyrenees, though Catalonia naturally also had contacts with the Hallstatt civilization of southern France.

37. Professor P. Bosch-Gimpera would place the foundation of the old city of Emporion c. 570–560, but the new city (with other settlements in north-east Spain) after the battle of Alalia (535), when refugees fled to Massilia and neighbouring parts. He thinks the extent of the Greek decline in the late sixth century has been exaggerated, and that Mainake (Malaga) was Greek until the fourth century.

38. A more usual view, as Professor F. W. König points out, is that the Persians entered a century and a half earlier than the Scyths and the Cimmerians. They gave their name to Barshua on Lake Urmia, but then pushed southward and settled on the north-eastern shores of the Persian Gulf. Cyrus the Great was the fourth of his house to be king of Anshan (or Anzan), the southern part of Elam east of Babylon and around the eventual Achaemenid capital Susa; for the way in which his house progressed to power over the whole Persian homeland, see *Cambridge Ancient History*, IV (1926), pp. 2 ff.

39. Indeed it was the Persians, rather than the Medes, who first settled in the country of the Mannei south of Lake Urmia. The Medes are derived from, or related to, the Manda south of the Caspian Sea, and Astyages, father-in-law of Cyrus, is called the ruler of Umman-Manda.

40. Both the Median origin and the date of Zoroaster are much disputed. In fuller discussion below (p. 229) Professor Pareti leans more towards a seventh-century date. The contrary view, which identifies Vishtaspa, Zoroaster's royal patron, with Hystaspes, father of Darius I (acceded 522 BC) is supported by E. Herzfield, *Zoroaster and his World* (Princeton, 1947). The identification is strongly contested by A. R. Burn, *Persia and the West* (London, 1962), p. 70; but closely following R. C. Zaehner, *Zoroastrianism* (London, 1961), Mr Burn upholds the view that it was in the period of Cyrus' conquests (i.e. in the sixth century) that the religion first made itself felt.

41. Professor F. W. König questions the evidence for this statement.

42. These risings were extremely widespread, and included the Medes, Sacae, and Arachosii.

43. This view has been and continues to be strongly disputed. Despite some similarity of ideas and practices Zoroastrianism does not seem to have belonged to the Achaemenid world. The language (dialect is used in the Gātha, the work of Zoroaster) is different from ancient Achaemenid Persian. The funerary ritual of the Achaemenids which included burial in tombs was disapproved of in Zoroastrianism where the rule was to abandon the dead to birds of prey. Cf. J. Duchesne-Guillemin, *Ormazd et Ahriman* (Paris, 1953), pp. 22 ff.

44. One must none the less remember the unrest which prevailed in many parts of the Persian empire, not least among its Greek cities; moreover, whether for economic, cultural, or political reasons, many mainland Greeks, led by the Spartans, reacted very early against the danger of incorporation into that empire.

45. These are linguistic terms, and not either ethnic or social. Many writers think that the Aryans did not force a complete language and religion on the 'Dravidians' and 'Munda', and furthermore that their own religion was influenced by the peoples settled before them; indeed this is indicated later on.
    The theory that the Aryans, exposed to the influence of these peoples, reacted by constructing a rigidly compartmentalized social system, is controversial.
    The division of mankind into four functional classes which is attested for the first time in the late *Rigveda* (X, 90, see Chapter IV, p. 352) applied not to local society but to all humanity, and the *śūdra*, who formed the humblest class, were drawn from the body of cosmic man on the same principle as the other classes although playing a less noble role. They are not regarded as a different race (see J. Filliozat, 'Les classes sociales de l'Inde', in G. Olivier, *Anthropologie des Tamouls de l'Inde du Sud*, Paris 1961, pp. vi ff.).
    It is only in the classical *Dharmaśāstra*, and not in the pre-Buddhist period, that the division becomes rigid and is in theory based on birth. Birth in one class or another here still depends on acts committed in previous lives, and is not the result of racial origin.

46. However it should not be forgotten that the echoes of dynastic data which are preserved in the *Purāṇas* have already been attested by Megasthenes (end of the fourth century BC) as covering very many generations (Arrian, *Indica*, IX, 19).

47. The Dravidian, or at least non-Aryan, character of ideas such as metempsychosis, the theory of *Karma*, or the sanctity of the cow, has not been established. Their appearance in an India partially Aryanized by language and by respect for the *Veda* could as well have been due to the birth of new ideas as to an inheritance from the non-Aryan elements of whose primitive ideas we possess no information, and to whom we cannot automatically attribute all the ideas which do not appear common to the Indo-Europeans.

48. Although it is not yet clear to scholars how, when, and from where ancient China obtained horse-drawn chariots, technically well adapted for warfare, there is no reason to suppose that their appearance was the prime cause of the formation of a governing class of warriors and the origin of a feudal state. This process was much more complex. (K. M. Kolobova and L. S. Vasilyev.)

CHAPTER II

THE EVOLUTION OF LANGUAGES AND WRITING SYSTEMS TO 500 BC

THE fortunes of individual languages have depended upon the march of historical events, especially those which have altered the physical contacts between different peoples. Sometimes a people whose language is homogeneous has continuously occupied the same area over a long period, without receiving immigrants and with few outside contacts. In this case two things can happen. Either some sections in the course of time evolve dialects which are different from those of their neighbours: this happens particularly when trade between the different sections is impeded by mountain or water barriers. Or alternatively regional differences get obliterated because the dialect of one section asserts its mastery over others, for instance when it develops a literature which commands imitation and acts as a unifying and stabilizing force.[1]

On the other hand the area occupied by a people of more or less homogeneous speech is sometimes pervaded by one or more races, whose language may be either allied or utterly different. A number of possible consequences can follow. If the newcomers destroy the majority of their predecessors or reduce the survivors to slavery (the women may of course be forced into marriage with their masters), then the language of the original inhabitants will tend to disappear, though the language of the new population will still feel some effects from it. If, however, the bulk of the primitive population is allowed to survive, then the outcome will depend on the relative numbers of the various races, on the political and cultural worth of each, and on their disposition to amalgamate with others or to keep themselves distinct. The language of the original inhabitants will either give way gradually to that of the newcomers, or combine with it, or possibly obtain the mastery; or again it may become simply the language of racial and linguistic 'pockets', for example in mountainous or outlying zones used as a refuge by the indigenous people against the invaders; or, as a final possibility, it may attain equality, and then the country, at least at certain social levels, becomes genuinely bilingual.

But changes in language, and hybrid formations, and the complete or partial adoption of bilingual habits, do not arise only in the straightforward cases when a people settles, as the result of migrations, in territory already occupied by a people of different race. When a people falls under the political domination of another, or is outnumbered by its neighbours, it may be compelled, up to a point at least, to adopt the other's language in its official acts; and it thus, at least to some extent, becomes bilingual.[2] Or again, it may of its own accord, to further trade relations, adopt in part the language of another people which enjoys a favoured or monopoly position against it in commercial matters. A final instance arises when a people is starting a literature of its own and takes the existing output of another people as its model. The accompanying effects in the linguistic field will be obvious, varying from a simple amalgamation between the languages of the copiers and the copied, to the complete adoption by the former of the literary language of the latter, in which case the former's language sinks to the status of a dialect.

I. THE FORMATION OF THE PRINCIPAL LANGUAGES

a. *The Indo-European Languages*

Comparative philology has clearly shown three things: (1) the so-called Indo-European languages were once, in their earliest forms, dialects, differentiated one from another; they were spoken by peoples who, to whatever racial group they belonged from the anthropological standpoint, lived next door to one another over a territory which, though vast, was none the less limited; (2) the peoples in question had almost all reached the same levels of civilization; and (3) when numerous successive migrations led the Indo-European peoples to split up, their speech tended to grow gradually more diverse, partly through their own action and partly because of contacts with other forms of speech.

Similarities of vocabulary and pronunciation can be detected between the Indo-European and the Semitic, Hamitic, and Ugro-Finnish languages; and the Indo-Europeans have certain less important points in common with languages of different types, such as Sumerian, Altaic, Georgian and so on. Scholars have therefore believed that they can reconstruct earlier stages, each more ancient than the last, and each followed by the separation of a creative racial group, which then differentiated itself from the main body. But it seems more likely that most of the similarities in question go back to less ancient times and are the result of influences brought to bear on individual Indo-European languages, in the course of their history, by races of different speech: sometimes Indo-European elements have passed into foreign tongues, sometimes the reverse process has occurred.

The primitive homes of the Indo-Europeans, before their dispersal, are not easy to identify. They were still semi-nomadic, and must therefore have moved around; moreover, since individual groups branched off at varying dates, we must suppose that some maintained a common home after others had left. Probably therefore there was a succession of movements, starting in central Asia, to the zone north of the Black Sea and the Caucasus;[3] here the Persians put their Ajryana Vaejo, 'the home of the Aryans' (by which they meant the people we call Indo-Iranians).[4]

Linguistic features and relationships show how the Indo-European nucleus was first split into two main sections, with perhaps others of less importance lying between. At any rate in the earliest period, most peoples of the first section tended to move west and south-west, those of the second east and south-east. These two groups used once to be called the *centum* and the *satem* groups, from the different ways they spoke the word for 'hundred'. But when the two sections spread out fanwise there must have been overlapping in some districts. This can be proved by the presence of some western-group languages in the East, such as the languages called Kuchean and Agnean in central Asia, or neo-Hittite (and later Galatian) in Anatolia. The fact is that the long-drawn-out Indo-European migrations, which lasted from the beginning of metals to the Late Middle Ages, were a series of separate waves and pushes, one people following another into a district or taking up where its ancestors had left off; and their routes were complex, as can be seen, for example, in the Cimbric and Teuton wanderings at the end of the second century BC.

The eastern or 'Aryan' group may be taken to comprise the peoples who spoke Iranic dialects (Old Iranic, Median, Scythian, and Middle Iranic), with all the sub-species which will be mentioned in Parts II and III and the dialects of India. The western group on the other hand included the dialects of neo-Hittite, Phrygian, Greek, Illyrian, Italic, Celtic, Germanic and others.[5]

When the two Indo-European groups separated, they must already have known some kinds of metal, for their languages use kindred terms for what is sometimes copper, sometimes bronze, and sometimes iron (*Old Ind.* ayas; *Avest.* ayo; *Lat.* aes; *Goth.* aiz; *O.E.* ar; *O.H.G.* er). This shows that their earliest migrations cannot have preceded the Copper or Chalcolithic Age.

The evidence which has come down to us for the first periods of individual Indo-European dialects is relatively late: only for neo-Hittite and Graeco-Mycenaean can we go back to the middle of the second millennium. The first Indo-Iranic, Italic, and Old Phrygian texts belong to the first millennium BC. For all other dialects our earliest texts come from the periods of Christian and Buddhist propaganda: for Albanian this means the fifteenth, for Lettish and Lithuanian the sixteenth centuries AD.

Diffusion into Anatolia, Persia, and India. The first contacts between the Indo-Europeans and the peoples of Anatolia go back to at least the beginning of the second millennium, the time when the new conquerors became masters of the 'Hattic' country and its capital Hattusas (Boğazköy). By generous introduction of Indo-European elements they transformed the country's language from palaeo-Hittite, a pre-Indo-European tongue, to neo-Hittite, which is similar to Indo-European languages in the western group. The same migratory movement must have been responsible for the 'mixed' features in other languages. In Anatolia, for example, we have clear evidence of pre-Indo-European background and of the additions made from Indo-European sources. In particular there are the Luvian texts from the nearer parts of southern Asia Minor, and the so-called Hittite hieroglyphs of Cilicia and northern Syria, datable to the period between the fourteenth and eighth centuries BC: these last were deciphered by means of the bilingual inscription, in Hittite hieroglyphs and Phoenician letters, which was recently discovered at Karatepe.

Where, however, Semitic peoples had not succeeded in taking permanent possession in Anatolia and Mesopotamia, and before the entry there of small warrior groups of eastern type, there still flourished in most districts a set of people to whom we shall give the name 'Asianic': their language was related to proto-Hittite. This is hypothesis rather than confident assertion, for our knowledge of these people is scanty: for some of them, admittedly, we have only nomenclature (Paphlagonian, Lycaonian, Cilician, etc.), and others have writings that are not easily decipherable: only for a few do we possess texts in cuneiform or alphabetic scripts.

The following Asianic peoples deserve special mention:

(a) The *Chalds* were a pre-Indo-European people of Armenia, the Urartu of Assyrian sources: some modern writers call them Alarodians, following Herodotus (VII, 79), or Vannic because they lived near Lake Van. They have left about 200 inscriptions in cuneiform script, datable between the ninth century and the year 640 BC when they were made subject to the Assyrians. Bilingual texts in Chaldic and Assyrian made it possible to decipher their language,[6] which seems to have been akin to that of the next people.

(b) The *Hurrians*, who were called Subartu or Mitanni by the Assyrians, and lived between Syria, Mesopotamia, and the region of Kirkuk. They were earlier dominated by overlords of Indo-European race (see below) but later fell at the hands of the Assyrians.

Farther east are found:

(c) The *Elamites*, who lived in present-day Zagros, Luristan and Kuzistan, around their capital Susa, which gave them the name of Susiani. Their documents range from the third millennium to the fourth century BC, the very numerous tablets found at Persepolis being of the Achaemenid period.

(d) The *Kassites* or Koššaei, who lived in Zagros and have left texts of the period between the sixteenth and tenth centuries. Of them we have spoken in our historical introduction: at one time they were apparently ruled by Indo-European princes.[7]

The texts written by these eastern Asianic peoples may well reflect the first south-eastward penetration by the Indo-Europeans of the Indo-Iranic (or Aryan) group. For especially in Hurrian and Kassite documents[8] of the fifteenth century BC we meet names of kings and gods with a clearly Indo-Iranic or Indian ring. This seems to show that during the Indo-Iranic trek towards the homes they occupied in historical times some of their armed parties succeeded in conquering the Asianic peoples and remaining as their rulers.

The region from which these 'Aryans' came before their movement south-eastward seems to be indicated by the presence of other peoples of the same Indo-Iranic type farther north, living in the Dnieper basin and on the steppes north of the Caucasus. These are the Scyths or Sarmatians—the Śaka of the ancient Persians. They are divided by Herodotus (IV, 18–19) into Cultivators and Nomads.

The Iranic tribes must have moved in many waves, one after another: at any rate they were divided into groups with different dialects even before they appeared on the high ground east of Mesopotamia. All we know of the Median language comprises a few glosses and proper names, handed down by the Persians and the Greeks. In Old Persian, however, we have a substantial number of texts, since it became the official language of the Achaemenid kings. This was the dialect of Persia, which corresponds to the south-western portion of Iran; and it also preserved some influences of more northerly dialects. We possess also some trilingual texts, in Persian, Elamite, and Babylonian. Nevertheless Persian found difficulty in getting established as the official language of the Middle East; and in the long run the Achaemenids had to have recourse to Aramaic for this purpose (see pp. 89, 195).

By the side of imperial Persian is found another form of literary Iranic, which apparently originated not in Media but in eastern districts, and which was used for religious writings. These were eventually in the Sassanid period collected in the *Avesta*, but were considerably contaminated in the copying: the fragments which preserve a more ancient language, going back to the tenth century BC, are the verses (*Gātha*) believed to represent the preaching of Zarathustra. The hymns (*yaśt*) and moral precepts (*vidēvdad*) which compose the *Avesta* proper are of more recent date.

Languages in India. In India today there are three main families of language, which are, in their order of importance, Indo-European, Dravidian, and Munda. Behind the present picture, however, lies a dynamic period of most intense linguistic exchange, not yet entirely over. The existence of Aryan languages certainly results from an immigration at the dawn of history.[9] On the other hand it is uncertain which of the other two families arrived first: couched in these terms the question is insoluble. Indeed nothing precise can be said about the relative position of the two non-Aryan families in this early period, since ancient sources are completely lacking. The first Tamil texts do not go back beyond the beginning of our era, while the Munda languages have never been literary and 'oral' texts were first collected in the last century. Place-names in the Sanskrit texts provide useful material, but are not adequate for the generalizations which have been made. One cannot emphasize too strongly how insecurely founded these generalizations are.

The Munda family, probably but not certainly related to the Mon-Khmer group, originally occupied a very wide territory, but today it is in full decline. It is confined to linguistic pockets isolated and surrounded by Indo-European and Dravidian tongues. The largest nucleus is composed of the Khuwari languages (Santali, Mundari, and Ho) between Orissa, Bihar, and Bengal. The Munda dialects have become the language of backward peoples, outside the main lines of communication, and have never, in historical times, formed a means of civilization. Even their influence on Sanskrit vocabulary and on place-names, which Przyluski and Lévi believed was very significant, is now usually stated in more modest terms.

The Dravidian languages even today remain completely isolated, and attempts to link them with other families have been fruitless. They too in antiquity occupied a much larger area than they do now: at the beginning of history and in historical times they were pushed farther and farther southward by the Indo-Aryan group, until the present linguistic picture took shape. Today the Dravidian languages form a compact mass covering the extreme south of India and the greater part of the Deccan. Various linguistic pockets are scattered here and there, almost up to the banks of the Ganges; and a substantial isolated nucleus is formed by the Brahui dialect, though this is somewhat diverging and is markedly influenced in its vocabulary by the Iranic languages. Brahui is spoken by about 200,000 persons in Baluchistan; and it is hard to say whether it represents a survival, on the periphery, of a very large Dravidian area, or results from a late migration in an opposite direction. At any rate there is no anthropological affinity between the Brahui, whose somatic type is Iranic, and the Dravidas of south India. The theory of P. Heras, which made the carriers of the Indus culture speak a 'proto-Dravidian' language, has not yet received confirmatory evidence and has never been accepted outside India. The various Dravidian languages, literary and other, will be dealt with in Part III.

About the middle of the second millennium BC there descended into India across the passes of the Afghan frontier certain tribes who spoke an Indo-European language of the Indo-Iranic group, which we call Indian. This language and its derivatives gradually gained a foothold, by conquest or by diffusion, in the basin of the Indus—and also in that of the Ganges, although for a long time Bengal was regarded as a frontier zone whose Aryanism was doubtful. At the end of this period the Aryan languages seem to have extended south of the Vindhya mountains and begun their penetration into the Deccan. The first hymns of the *Rigveda*, the final collection of which seems to go back to the beginning of the first millennium, show us a language (Vedic Sanskrit) which is still closely related to Old Iranic: the relationship often amounts almost to identity. It is a language of the 'analytical' type, very richly inflected; but it is already a mixed language, being based on a north-western dialect with marked borrowings from dialects of regions farther east. Vedic Sanskrit was a priestly language, with its form fixed immutably in the sacred *Vedas*; yet it was able to evolve to some extent in minor religious writings, and the stage it had reached at the end of this period was rather more advanced.

The result was Classical Sanskrit, which at the outset was a language exclusively for the priests, but later had secular usages. It was in part an artificial language, spoken by particular social classes rather than by particular regions; and it was very soon codified and fixed for eternity by the Indian grammarians. By the side of Sanskrit, which was employed in the whole domain of the Aryans, there developed early the various regional languages, the Prakrits. They are derived not from Sanskrit, but from a proto-Vedic, or even pre-Vedic stage. They were spoken by the vast majority of the Aryan population, and were used earlier than Sanskrit for secular literature. But Prakrit writing proper is attested only in the ensuing period.

This is not the place to speak of the very numerous fragments of minor languages which are scattered here and there, especially on the slopes of the Himalaya and in Assam: the latter region is a real museum of languages. Mention must however be made of the Tibeto-Burman family, which is now confined to the Himalayan valleys but was once widespread. The influence of the Tibeto-Burman substratum is felt still today in place-names and even in certain linguistic peculiarities of Bengal.

b. *The Role of the Thraco-Phrygians*

While the peoples of central and eastern Anatolia were undergoing the effects of two earlier general movements of migration, the one belonging to the western section, the other Aryan, two later and less general penetrations were proceeding, side by side, in western Anatolia, which faces towards the Aegean Sea. Both were Indo-European, the Phrygians and the Greeks, as will be seen below.

The Thracians spoke an Indo-European language, perhaps one belonging to the eastern group; but apart from a short inscription of the fifth century BC, from Ezerovo in Bulgaria, we know nothing of it save glosses and proper names. According to Herodotus (V, 3) they were the most numerous people on earth after the Indians. Their penetration into the Balkans was probably responsible for the final southward movements of the Greeks, but they in their turn were pressed from behind by the Illyrians. So after gathering in mass in the districts adjoining the Black Sea, including that to the north of the Danube where their kinsmen the Getae (called Dacians by the Romans) were settled, a part crossed the Hellespont under the name of Brygians. They came in waves over more than one period, the last coinciding with the Cimmerian invasions (Strabo, XII, p. 586); and when they had found a home in Anatolia in the country which once belonged to the Asianic Ascani, they gave rise to the people called Phrygian. Of them we possess two series of inscriptions, although only the older, called Palaeo-Phrygian and belonging to the seventh and sixth centuries BC, is of concern to this first section of our history (the neo-Phrygian series is of the third and fourth centuries AD). In some Palaeo-Phrygian epigraphy the influence of Greek is evident, deriving from contact with the Hellenic colonists (see Chapter I).

Not a few of the Asianic peoples in this western Anatolian country were subjected to new racial admixtures; and they felt the effects of the Indo-European languages spoken by their Phrygian and Greek neighbours and by other less determinate Indo-European groups. Yet they preserved the original Anatolian basis of their speech, which seems to have been in part connected with the language of the pre-Hittites and kindred peoples, in part with that of the Minoans of the Aegean islands. The following such people are known: (a) the Maeones of Homer, who in classical times are called Lydians. We know about fifty inscriptions of this people, belonging to the fourth century BC, which have been partially deciphered with the aid of a bilingual text in Lydian and Aramaic; (b) the Mysians farther north. They spoke a hybrid tongue, which made the ancients wonder whether to associate them with the Phrygians or the Lydians (Xanthus in Strabo, XII, p. 572). This hybrid character appears also on the inscription found at Uyujik; (c) the Carians to the south, Homer's 'barbarophonoi'. From them have come down some inscriptions and graffiti of mercenaries who served in Egypt in the seventh and sixth centuries, and also some later texts of the fourth century BC. Some of these are bilingual, in Carian and Greek, but have not yet been completely deciphered; (d) the Termiloi or Milyai, also called Lycians (a name already attested in the form Lukki by the Tell el Amarna documents of the fourteenth century), for whom Herodotus (I, 173) suggested a racial link with the ancient Cretans. From them we possess about 180 inscriptions of the fifth to fourth centuries BC, some of them lengthy and one a bilingual text in Lydian and Greek, and also legends on coins. Two phases of their language can be detected, of which the earlier phase is attested by a famous stele of Xanthus; (e) the Pisidians, to whom should probably be attributed a collection of short and late inscriptions of imperial times, found at Sofular; these mainly consist only of proper names, but there are evident Phrygian features.

Even after the entry of the Phrygians and Greeks western Anatolia was the objective of other attempted migrations. They covered the whole area, but fell particularly on the west, under the Cimmerians, and on the east under the Armenians.

The Cimmerians (called Gimirrai by the Assyrians and Gomer in the Bible), together with the Tauri were probably Indo-Europeans of Aryan type. Their home, already mentioned in *Odyssey*, XI, 14 ff., was in south Russia, where the name Cimmerian Bosphorus (Herodotus, IV, 11) is still recalled in the modern Crimea. But with their linguistic cousins the Scythians at their backs—this explains why the Sacae of the Persians came to be called Gimirri[10]—they precipitated themselves upon Asia Minor and plundered it repeatedly in the eighth–seventh centuries BC.

These Cimmerian invasions, together with the ruin of the Chalds of the Lake Van area under the blows delivered by the Assyrians (640 BC), were very probably the factors which made possible another migration by Indo-Europeans of the Aryan group, the Armenians (Arminiya in Darius' Persian inscriptions). A tradition recorded by Herodotus connects this people with the Thracians, and makes them colonists of the Phrygians. Already at the end of the seventh century they must have occupied the country of the Chalds, which was subsequently called Armenia; but they did not destroy the indigenous population, whom they governed from the position of a ruling class. This state of affairs can be seen in a reasonable number of Armenian texts which have come down to us. They are too late (ninth century AD) to allow a detailed study of the primitive condition of the language. But they do show the dominant influence of two other forms of speech: the pre-Aryan language of the Chalds,[11] and the Iranic language spoken by the Persians and later by the Parthians, in whose sphere the Armenians were to live for centuries to come.

c. Illyrian Peoples and Dialects

The Illyrians, an Indo-European people—though whether of eastern, western, or intermediary type is not clear—must have begun their penetration of the north-western Balkans at latest in the fourteenth century BC. They pushed the Thracians southward and eastward, and this blow reverberated on the Greeks, who were driven in the same directions. Direct evidence of their language is very scanty, being confined to an extremely brief inscription from Scutari in Albania and to proper names. But for a long time it was believed that the vocabulary and pronunciation of modern Albanian (whose earliest written documents go back to the fifteenth century AD) could, when stripped of all modern borrowings from Greek, Latin, Venetian, Turkish, Slav and so on, reveal to us a purely Illyrian core. Not a few modern writers, however, think that Albanian in isolation cannot help us finally in the reconstruction of ancient Illyrian; for Albanian itself is derived from a mixture of Illyrian and Thracian. This may possibly account for the difference between the so-called ancient colonies of the Illyrians in Italy:[12] the Venetic colonies would give us the true northern Illyrian language, and those of Apulia and Messapia the hybrid southern dialect, which was a mixture between Thracian and Illyrian.

Of the dialect of the ancient Veneti we possess, apart from proper names, about 200 brief inscriptions written in the North Etruscan alphabet of the fourth to first centuries BC. But occupation of the Venetian district of Italy goes back at latest to the beginning of the Iron Age, when the characteristic 'Atestine' civilization had its rise. That the Veneti were Illyrian is stated explicitly by Herodotus (I, 196) and Polybius (II, 17), the latter of whom says their speech was different from that of the Celts though their civilization was similar. It may therefore well be that, like the Liburni near the Aternus in Picenum (who bring to mind the Liburnians in Illyricum; Pliny, *N.H.*, III, 110, 112), the Veneti were also of Illyrian origin but in Italy had mixed with the indigenous pre-Indo-European people of the two regions they inhabited; the latter were the Euganei and North Etruscans (later joined by the Celts) in the Veneto, and the Asyli in Picenum. It is not clear whether the Liburni and the survivors from among their predecessors the Asyli, were responsible for the so-called 'pre-Sabellian' inscriptions of the Adriatic coast.

A number of other peoples whose Illyrian origin is attested also came from the Balkans, but arrived by sea before the Greek colonization of Tarentum. Their names were Daunians (cf. Festus, *Epit.* 69 M), Peucetians (Pliny, III, 102), Salentini (Probus on Virgil, *Ecl.* VI, 31; Festus, 329) and Messapii (Nicander in *Antonius Liberalis*, 31). Together they are called Iapyges, a name already associated by Hecataeus with that of the Iapodes across the Adriatic. Their proper names and the 200 surviving inscriptions have allowed a convincing set of comparisons between them and the early nucleus of peoples in Albania. They probably came from the southern part of Illyricum, where admixture with Thracian races was more noticeable.

d. *Greek Peoples and Dialects: the Literary Language*

Since, as we said earlier, the Indo-Europeans before they separated already possessed some knowledge of metal, the oldest periods of Stone Age civilization attested in Hellas must beyond doubt be the work not of the Greeks, but of indigenous people who preceded them. Classical writers, mainly on the strength of wild deductions from place-names, used to give accounts of the ancient races they assumed to have inhabited the Greek peninsula, such as the Pelasgians, the Leleges, the Carians and so on. These accounts have very little value; but to prove the existence of pre-Greeks there is, in addition to inferences based on archaeology, certain evidence worth recording. In fully classical times groups of non-Greeks were still living, and speaking non-Hellenic languages, in parts of the islands of Crete, Carpathos, and Cyprus; and in the Greek vocabulary are found many names of gods, animals, and vegetables which are characteristic of the country but of obvious non-Greek etymology. Moreover a large number of people and places in Greece of historical times have names which do not admit of Greek etymologies, their roots and terminations being apparently similar to Asianic names.

We possess important literary records of the pre-Greek inhabitants of Crete (the Eteo-Cretans). There are, for example, numerous tablets and seals—as well as an inscribed discus—found mainly at Knossos and Mallia, and incised either with special hieroglyphic characters or with a linear script; there is an Egyptian medical papyrus of about 1500 BC, which records the formula of an oath taken by the Keftiu, i.e. the Cretans; and there are several inscriptions of the sixth century BC, found at Praisos, on which the alphabet is Greek but the language not.

From the pre-Greek inhabitants of Cyprus we possess eight brief inscriptions, probably of the fourth century BC, which are written in syllabic script (see also below, p. 91) and in a language which is commonly called 'Cypro-Mycenaean'. They have not yet been deciphered, although one is a bilingual with a Greek text beside the other language.

The Greeks conquered these pre-Greek populations, but did not destroy them completely. We can only partially determine how far they influenced the physical, moral, and intellectual qualities of the Greek peoples, in the peninsula or in the colonial world; but such evidence as we have suggests that the effect upon their usages and customs, including their language and religion, was significant. The Greeks, like others, arrived in many waves, and did not subject all these peoples together in a brief period of time: the peninsula had been occupied by the invaders for centuries at a time when the indigenous peoples were free inhabitants of the Aegean islands and of the Asiatic coasts. It was only in the fifteenth to fourteenth centuries that the 'Minoan' kingdoms of Crete went down and new Graeco-Mycenaean states were constructed in their place, while the first Greek cities on the Asiatic coasts were being founded. It was not until c. 1000 BC that Greek colonists arrived to settle in Cyprus;[13] and the Hellenic colonizing movement had still to establish itself in the following centuries in all the directions it took, on the shores of the Hellespont, the Euxine, Ionia, the Tyrrhenian Sea and so on.

When this Greek colonization took place, the various parties of colonists took with them dialects which were already very different from one another. For the varieties which existed of old, at the time when the many waves of Greeks had entered the Hellenic peninsula, had continually grown more diverse owing to the contours of the country, divided as it was into so many almost isolated portions.

These more ancient and basic differences allow the classification of Greek dialects under three heads, each one of which has two subdivisions: Ionic, including Attic and Ionic proper; Aeolic, of which the northern subdivision comprises Thessalian and Boeotian, and the southern is typified by Arcadian; and Doric, as spoken by north-west Greece and by the outlying districts of the Peloponnese.

Attic was spoken in Attica; the Ionic dialects in the island of Euboea, in the northern Cyclades, in the colonies of Ionia and Chalcidice, in several Euxine colonies, and in the colonies sent by Phocaea and Chalcis to the West. Attic differs from Ionic in using $\tau\tau$ for $\sigma\sigma$, forming the genitive in -ου instead of –εω, writing ὤν for ἐών and ξύν for σύν and retaining the aspirate.

The northern Aeolic dialects were spoken in Thessaly and Boeotia, and also in the colonial areas of Lesbos and of Aeolis in Asia, where initially the speech must have been intermediate between Thessalian and Boeotian. There are characteristic analogies between them and the southern Aeolic (Arcadian, and its Cypriot and Pamphylian derivatives), but characteristic differences too. In addition each of the two Aeolic groups has features, but different features, in common with Attic.

The north-western Doric dialects belonged to Epirus, Locris, Phthiotis, Aetolia, and Acarnania, to which Achaea and Elis were added in classical times: southern Doric was spoken in the Argolid, Laconia, and classical Messenia, in Crete, Melos, Thera, and Cyrene, in Rhodes and the colonies of Asiatic Doris, and in the Dorian colonies of the West (founded by Achaea, Corinth, Megara, Rhodes, Crete, etc.). The two kinds of Doric have features in common, but both also have features in common with the Aeolic dialects.

Both the geographical distribution of the Greek dialects, and the influence one group had on another, were undoubtedly affected by the form taken by the migrations and by the history of the relations between the groups. It seems certain that the first to enter Greece were the peoples of Ionic and Attic speech, who subsequently kept possession of Attica and Euboea. They were followed by the Aeolians, whose northern and southern sub-divisions adjoined one another for a short time in early days. The greater antiquity of these two migrations conforms well with the claim of both the Attic and the Arcadian people to be autochthonous; and the fact that the Cypriot and Pamphylian colonies were Arcadian seems to show that at one time the Arcadians had an outlet to the Aegean, which would mean that the whole Peloponnese was occupied by southern Aeolians.

The third and comparatively late migration, by the Doric-speaking Greeks, came therefore in several stages. From north-western Greece they infiltrated eastward, broke the link between Thessalians and Boeotians, and shut the Ionians into Attica, reducing their area to that district alone. They thus prompted the emigration of the Aeolians who occupied Lesbos and whose speech is precisely intermediate between Thessalian and Boeotian; and the remnant of the Ionians went to colonize the Cyclades and the central coast of western Anatolia. Their second stage carried the Dorians into the Peloponnese, where very gradually they wrested from the southern Aeolians all the coastal districts. This led to a colonizing movement by the Arcadians, but only their farthest foundations, those in Pamphylia and Cyprus, were able to survive. The zones between, namely the lower Aegean and the south-western coast of Asia Minor, were recolonized by the Dorians, in the third stage of their migrations.

The date of the Dorian migration still continues to be disputed among modern scholars.[14] Some accept the statements in ancient writers according to which it was 'after the Trojan Wars' that the Dorians entered Greece and conquered the Achaeans; they consequently put this migration after *c.* 1200 BC. Others, including the present writer, maintain that the name Achaeans was originally the ethnic name of the peoples who spoke Doric, and that they then in part discarded it for the new name of Dorians. For all the 'Achaeans' of classical times spoke Doric dialects; and the name Dorians, which started in Asia Minor, gradually spread from there to Crete and the Peloponnese. This school therefore dates the Dorian migration some centuries before 1200 BC. We shall be able to choose between the two views with greater confidence when full use has been made of the recent discovery that certain fourteenth-century texts from Crete, Mycenae, Asine, and Pylos, in the 'Minoan Linear B' script, are in Greek. Only if it be shown that every one of these is in Aeolic could we still believe that the Dorian migration took place only after the fourteenth century; if part turns out to be Aeolic and part Doric, the opposite view is proved.[15]

The Greek dialects, already diversified in the peninsula, naturally became still more diverse in the colonies. Every colony was of mixed population through having been a refuge for emigrants from various parts; and all had their contacts with the natives. As an example of the latter process we can see from the fragments of Epicharmus, and from other evidence, that a number of native Sicilians found their way into Syracusan territory. As regards the mixing of Greek races we must remember that when a Greek colony was called Corinthian (for example), this simply meant that the Corinthian element had gained the upper hand there. This state of affairs was not necessarily permanent, for in some Chalcidian (i.e. Ionian) colonies the Dorian element predominated later: Himera is a case in point. The same happened in Asia Minor, at Smyrna and Phocaea, the Ionian character of which is of relatively late date.

Almost all these Greek dialects were not only spoken, but were written in literary texts and on inscriptions. Indeed in the early days of Greek literature every writer made use of his own dialect, though he might ennoble its forms and borrow features from other dialects. Thus we can still catch a glimpse of an early Epic in Aeolic dialect; on its model the Homeric Epic was later developed in Ionia, and presents us with Ionic contaminated with many forms copied from Aeolic. In a later period the language of the Elegiac poets (Callinus, Mimnermus and Phocylides) was founded on Ionic, as was that of the Iambic writers (Archilochus, Semonides, Hipponax), of the lyric poet Anacreon, of the first didactic writers and philosophers, and of the first historians and geographers. A language based on Aeolic was used by the Lesbian poets Alcaeus and Sappho; the language of Alcman, Tyrtaeus, and Philoxenus of Cythera had a Laconian base,[16] that of Corinna a Boeotian, that of Telesilla an Argolic, and that of Epicharmus a Syracusan. As for the Attic dialect, it served the needs of the Athenian writers, their tragedians, comedians, orators, and historians.

Later, however, a particular district in which some form of literature had been born might attain great cultural prestige, or the dialect of an important area might spread outside its original boundaries. When that happened, writers would use, in some or all of their works, not their own dialect but a distorted and contaminated form of another one, just because that other had been elevated to be a language of literature. In this way the bards of Ionia, in imitating those who wrote in Aeolic, had created a language which was a cross between Aeolic and Ionic, the language of Homer, and this was later used not only for Epic, but for Elegy and Epigram; indeed it had its influence on the language of almost every literary genre. Similarly the Doric language of the ancient choral songs was taken up again for the choruses of Tragedy, even by non-Doric writers. In the course of the seventh and sixth centuries three literary languages were formed in the three areas of Greece which had the greatest cultural and political development, those of Ionia, the Peloponnesian League, and the West; and all three languages were disseminated at the same time. (Map V.) The first was based on Ionic, and was used by Herodotus and the first prose writers; the other two were more or less Doric, one employed in Greece proper (cf. Pindar and Bacchylides), the other in the West (cf. the two poets called Stesichorus, and later Epicharmus and Archimedes).

Only after the age of Pericles, which we shall treat in Part II, did Attic gain its supremacy, with a *koiné* which was used in almost every part of Greece.

e. *The Two Groups of 'Italic' Dialects*

Just as we can distinguish chronologically and linguistically a series of several migrations of Greeks into Hellas, so too there were separate invasions of Italic type Indo-Europeans into the peninsula of Italy. The first wave of migrants, whom we call the 'First Italici', had a language between Latin and Siculan, and practised inhumation exclusively. They must have spread over a very wide area, but they later lost a large part of it when new peoples arrived. At a period earlier than the sixth to fifth centuries, before the last phases of the migration of the 'Second Italici', various groups of First Italici could be clearly identified in the district extending from Latium north of the Tiber down to central Sicily.

In Latium and adjacent districts we still possess written testimony for these people from an archaic period. For the Falisci there are numerous epigraphic texts, markedly affected by Etruscan influence, as far back as the fourth century. For the Latins the famous inscription on a *fibula* takes us back to the seventh century at Praeneste; and at Rome we reach at least the sixth with the well-known '*cippus* of the Forum',[17] found under the Lapis Niger, and the inscribed vase discovered under the Quirinal which goes by by name of Duenos.

For their kinsmen, however, the Hernici of the Trerus valley, there are no records. Farther south, in the lower reaches of the Liris in the district

Cartography Hallwag Berne

ILLYRIA

Apollonia

PELAGONIA

LYNCESTIS

MACEDONIA

AXIUS

THRACIA

ORESTIS

Methone

BISALTAE

CRESTONIA

EDONES

PIERES

MYGDONIA

BOTTICE

Thasos

PARAUEA

ATINTANIA

CHAONIA

TYMPHAEA

ELIMEA

PERRHAEBIA

EPIRUS

Corcyra

THESPROTIA

THESSALIA

MAGNESIA

Scyros

ATHAMANIA

DOLOPIA

ACHAEA

AENIANES

Leucas

AGRAEI

APERANTIA

EUBOEA

ACARNANIA

MALIS

AETOLIA

PHOCIS

LOCRIS

LOCRIS

LOCRIS

BOEOTIA

Thebae

ATTICA

Cephallenia

ACHAEA

Athenae

Zacynthos

ELIS

ARCADIA

Argos

TRIPHYLIA

MESSENIA

Sparta

Melos

LACONIA

Doric

North Doric

Ionic

North and South Aeolic

GREEK DIALECTS C. 600 B.C.

Cythera

MAP V

of Terracina, the Ausones and Aurunci belonged to the First Italici; beyond them, in what was later Campania and part of Lucania, lived the Opici; and at the foot of the peninsula were the Itali (or Oenotrii) and other groups called Morgeti, Choni and so on. But for none of these, it seems, do we possess written texts. Beyond the straits the Siculans and Sicans belonged to this group, the former in the eastern part of Sicily, the latter in the centre and west. From them survive many glosses, and some words which passed into the speech of Epicharmus; and they have left inscriptions at Adrano, Sciri, Comiso and other places, of which the longest is on a vase at Centuripa. It seems clear that Siculan was the purer language, but that Sican showed more marked borrowings from the language of the indigenous pre-Indo-European people. But more direct evidence of that earlier language can be seen in the speech of the Elymians in western Sicily (see p. 76).

The First Italici, then, must have settled in Italy in fairly ancient times, not before the discovery and use of metals, but probably during the actual Chalcolithic Age. Their only subdivision which produced literature worthy of note was the Latin people; but that literature was formidable, and its cause was the political success and imperial expansion of Rome. It began without doubt in the period of the Kings, with popular Epic, religious hymns, and the writing of laws. But its greatest early works came later, in the fifth century, when the pontiffs edited the first part of the 'Annales Maximi' and the 'Laws of the Twelve Tables' were published. The succession of Roman conquests, however, had an inverse effect on the development of the Latin language, which gradually became infected by foreign influences, both in its vocabulary and in its grammar. Indeed this infection had set in early, as the result of the seventh- and sixth-century Etruscan domination of Rome, which lasted for more than a hundred years. All these phenomena have been closely examined by philologists.

The Second Italici must have started their migration very much later than their predecessors. There is a marked difference between the speech of the Latins and Siculans and that of the Oscans and Umbrians, who compose the second group; and a further linguistic argument can be found in the features which the latter languages, especially Umbrian, have in common with Celtic, features which are absent from the dialects of the First Italici. They are probably due to the fact that for some time the Second Italici and Celts inhabited adjoining districts, most likely in the upper valley of the Danube. The vanguard of the Oscans must have come down south of the Apennines at the time when the so-called 'Pianello civilization' appeared in these parts. This was a civilization of the First Iron Age, which cremated its dead and was related to, though distinct from, the Villanovan (or Proto-Etruscan) and First Atestine (or Proto-Venetic) civilizations. All these three developed for some time in close contact with one another, but on different lines, in the eastern part of the plain of the Po.

The Oscans, followed by the Umbrians, then penetrated farther south, and began to fuse with the native inhumators, now partly composed of First Italici. In this way they acquired the mixture of rites, inhumation and cremation together, which characterized Oscan culture in the district of central Italy that from now on remained in their hands. The process also had its effect on the culture of Latium, where the newcomers sent some offshoots. It accounts for the Oscan features in the language of Rome (Mamercus, Mamertinus, Ciprius, etc.) and in that of Praeneste (*vhevaked*); it also explains the tradition of Sabine invasions of Latium, including Rome.

Of the two groups of Second Italici the Umbrians in the rear by their southward advance accelerated the southward movement of the Oscans in the van. Herodotus (IV, 49) reflects a tradition which still places the Umbrians in the eastern Alpine country;[18] but in the first half of the fourth century our authorities treat them as occupying, with their last outposts, the district south of Spina, including Butrium, Ravenna, and Ariminum. The fact was that the majority of their tribes had been pushed southward by the settlers in the Po valley, the Etruscans and later the Celts. They had therefore crossed the Apennines and occupied Umbria, later pouring down into other districts previously occupied by the Oscans, such as the Sabine country. The movement spread to one section of the Oscans themselves, who started the 'Sabellic migration' into southern Italy. The racial affinity between the Oscans and Umbrians is attested by a number of features common to their languages, by similarity between their proper names, and by the fact that the two races had to some extent an identical Pantheon and identical religious customs. But the two groups are fairly clearly distinct, as is shown by the greater tendency to innovation in the Umbrian language. Umbrian elements joining Oscan seem to have produced the hybrid group whose character is shown by an inscription of Velitrae, and which took the name of Volscian: at the end of the sixth century this became established as a barrier in lower Latium, between the remnants of the First Italici, the Latins, and the Ausones. The 'Sabellic' migrations, which were the last stage in the wanderings of the Second Italici, will be dealt with in Part II. But already in the period before 500 BC some tribes, the Picentes, Praetuttians, Marrucini, Marsi, and Frentani must have pushed east and south and south-east: the Samnites, too, had begun to invade the country which became their home in classical times.

For the Umbrian language the famous seven 'Tables of Iguvium', which go back to the years between 200 and 70 BC, are the most notable texts: for that of the Oscan tribes which remained north of Campania and Samnium written texts are comparatively short and few (for the more southerly Oscans see Part II).

f. *The 'Prae-Italic' Languages: the Etruscans*

We maintained earlier that the Etruscans came from across the Alps to north Italy at a very early period, still in the Neolithic Age, and that at the dawn of the Iron Age, in the first stage of the Villanovan civilization, they passed on to Tuscany. If this hypothesis is right,[19] they will have been in the Po valley before the First Italici arrived there, and will have descended south of the Apennines about the same time as the Second Italici.

Every attempt so far made to decipher Etruscan by identifying it with some known language, whether Indo-European, Semitic, Hamitic, Ugro-Finnish, or Anatolian, may be taken to have failed. The extremely slender similarities on which each attempt was based are, at the most, evidence for very early contacts and meetings between the Etruscans and peoples of foreign speech. So in early times Dionysius of Halicarnassus seems to have been largely right in believing Etruscan to be a peculiar language on its own. The only parallels which are at all clear are with languages of the northern Caucasus on the one hand and with Basque on the other.

'Etruscoid' texts are found in the Transpadana and the Alpine country (from the North Etruscans), in Tuscany (from the Etruscans proper), and on the island of Lemnos.[20] The distribution suggests that one party of peoples belonging to this linguistic group came from Danubian Europe into the Balkans, where they were practically overwhelmed and cut off by the Indo-European immigrants, Greeks, Thracians, and Illyrians; but that larger bodies invaded the Po valley, from which at the dawn of the Iron Age they pushed on into Tuscany. The long period of separation between the North Etruscans, who stayed in the Po valley, and the Etruscans, who crossed the Apennines down into Tuscany, explains the strong difference between the two groups. There are, it is true, some limited but quite marked resemblances between Etruscoid and Indo-European languages not only in vocabulary but in grammatical forms. But these can quite easily be explained on our hypothesis, which puts the Etruscans in contact with Indo-Europeans, especially Italici, over long periods in many places, in the Danube and Po valleys, and in central Italy.

For the North Etruscan languages, which must have been split into dialects, we have a number of texts; but they are unfortunately late ones, in which the language has been infected by the speech of adjacent peoples, Ligurians, Celts, and Illyrians. These texts have been found in various regions of the Transpadana and the Alps, where Etruscan settlement is evident, and each region has given a name (Lepontian, Lugano, Sondrio, Bolzano) to a particular type of North Etruscan dialects.[21] It is most improbable that these texts are evidence of a late and debased phase in the Etruscan culture of Tuscany, although this culture is normally believed on the strength of a passage in Livy (V, 32), to have extended into the Po valley. Admittedly texts in all respects similar to the Etruscan documents of Tuscany have been found in the Po valley, but they go back to the period, starting in the sixth century BC, when the cities of northern Etruria were extending their hegemony on the southern side of the Po; they have nothing to do with North Etruscan texts found in quite different districts, outside those in which the Tuscan hegemony was exercised. The North Etruscan inscriptions are much more likely to represent a late phase in the language which the Etruscoids of the Transpadana and the Alpine districts spoke from the outset.

We have already suggested identifying the first North Etruscans with the inhabitants of the pile-dwellings (*palafitte*), who lived in the settlements formed on the sub-Alpine and Alpine lakes. It follows from our view that an Etruscan origin must be assigned also to the *palafitticoli* on the other side of the Alps, in Switzerland, south Germany, Austria, Croatia, eastern France, and Belgium. This hypothesis seems to be confirmed by evidence from language. In those regions one may notice the persistence of typically Etruscan place-names, such as those ending in *-enna* (Arduenna, Cevenna, Vienna, Taruenna, etc.); and in the same Alpine and Transalpine regions, in three groups (the Grisons, Tyrol, and Friuli) are found the 'Ladin' or Rhaeto-Romance dialects, which must ultimately have been founded on a compound of North Etruscan and Latin.

The Etruscans proper have left us about 10,000 texts, mostly inscriptions, dating from the seventh century BC onwards. The longest is on the covering of a mummy, now in the museum at Zagreb; and others worthy of mention include a fifth-century Capuan inscription and one on a *cippus* at Perugia. Bilingual texts are few and brief; for example an inscription of Pesaro in Etruscan and Latin contains only three words. We also possess a fair number of Etruscan glosses, with their meanings explained in classical authors.

Distinguished study has been given to possible survivals of Etruscan speech in present-day Tuscan dialects. Another source of evidence is provided by Etruscan and hybrid texts from the regions where the Etruscans ruled, such as Capua and other parts of Campania.

Other Prae-Italic Dialects. The Etruscans and Etruscoids of classical times probably represented the races and languages surviving from a large stock, which in the course of the Neolithic Age had occupied the whole of a vast arc, from the Caucasus to the Iberian peninsula (see Chapter I). Similarly in fully classical periods in Italy and adjacent areas there existed survivors of an even older period, the Palaeolithic Age, who had been in fairly unbroken possession of south-west Europe. These were the Ligurian and Liguroid peoples.

Hesiod (in Strabo, VII, p. 660), writing about 600 BC[22] spoke of the Ligurians as a people living at what, from the Greek standpoint, was the edge of the world, like the Ethiopians and Scyths. It appears from Hecataeus and from Himilco, in Avienus (*Ora Maritima*, 130 ff.), who are later supported by Lucan (I, 443-4), that all Gaul, including Belgium, was once occupied by the Ligurians, and that after the Celtic invasion they remained in certain districts and mixed with the Celts. The same is true of the Po valley, where in fully classical times they still occupied present-day Liguria as far as Pisa and the arc of the western Apennines, including the Casentino.

There is a set of place-names in *-asc*, *-osc*, *-isc* and *-usc*, which can be shown to be typically Ligurian and which allow us to envisage a still larger Liguria of early times. They are found not only in modern Liguria, but in Piedmont, Lombardy, Emilia, the Apuan region, Corsica, Switzerland, upper Bavaria, the Tyrol, the Rhône departments of France, northern Spain, and Portugal. To illustrate the Ligurian language we have a few inscriptions on menhir statues of the Luna district, a number of citations in classical texts, the evidence of place-names, and some pre-Latin features in the vocabulary of modern Ligurian dialects. The so-called Lepontian (or Lugano) inscriptions, considered by some to be Ligurian, are so only in part: they are in a mixed dialect, with obvious Celtic and Etruscoid features. The Ligurians can be shown to have been one of the oldest peoples of western Europe. We can trace the way they retired to the mountains on all sides in face of the new invaders, Etruscans, Italici, Celts, and Germans. Moreover in those districts where they held out until the Roman conquest in the last centuries BC their cultural history continues from the Palaeolithic Age without a break.

The theory that the Ligurians were Indo-Europeans[23] is repugnant to everything so far said. It attaches too much importance to Indo-European features which entered Ligurian speech; these were simply the result of long contiguity between the two races, which lived together in the same area and formed hybrid dialects.

On the other hand, scholars might find it worth while to re-examine the possibility that the Liguroid languages, spoken all the way from Italy into Spain, were closely linked with the Hamitic and Berber dialects of North Africa.

Other Prae-Italic peoples still survived in historical times from the primitive populations of the peninsula and the neighbouring islands. They can be recognized in some parts of the Veneto and the Picene coastal area, and in western Sicily, Pantelleria, Sardinia, and Corsica. It may be that most of them derive from a submerged people of ancient Ligurian origin, who had spread fairly regularly in all directions; but it may be also that, as in Spain, they were joined by a layer of immigrating Hamitic peoples. Their scanty writings show, as was *a priori* likely, that their native speech was affected by the languages of the more civilized peoples with whom they had relations.

The name 'Euganei' is Greek, but the Greeks had here distorted a native name just as they called the Ligurian 'Ingauni' by the name 'Eubioi' (as a fragment of Theopompus tells us). The Euganei were clearly Ligurian, as is shown by similarities in their material remains and by the fact that one of their tribes, the Stoeni, is called 'Ligure' in the *Fasti Triumphales*. But they bordered on the North Etruscan Rhaeti and mingled with them, with the result that their language became infected with Etruscoid elements.

Of the indigenous Asyli in Picenum, the northern section lived near modern Novilara and Pesaro, the southern near Belmonte Piceno, Fermo, and Cupra Maritima. Their Iron Age culture derived from the Neolithic culture of the district, but gradually assimilated alien features from the North Etruscans, from the Illyrian Liburnians who settled between their two sections, and from the Italic Umbrians and Picenes invading from the West; later they were influenced by the Tarentines and Phocaeans as well. The language underlying the two sets of inscriptions they have left is of a purely Indo-European type, though in the north it was affected by the Illyrians and North Etruscans, in the south by the Umbrians and Oscans. It would seem logical to connect these Asyli with the Liguroid stratum in the population, but in the last resort we know too little about them to justify such a conclusion without further evidence.

Another probable pre-Indo-European language is that of the Elymians, who were indigenous in western Sicily and must have formed pockets where their speech was used in pure or hybrid form, extending into the territory of the Italic Sicans in the centre of the island. Coins at Eryx and Segesta carry legends in a language which is not Greek and which suggests a connection with the Iberian and Iberio-Ligurian worlds: this may have been dimly in Thucydides' mind (VI. 2) when he makes the Sicans come from the Iberian peninsula, though he should have said 'pre-Sicans'. Such Elymian place-names as are known have other echoes in the Ligurian world, this time on the east coast of the Gulf of Genoa. Moreover, like the Ligurians, the Elymians are shown by archaeology to have had a continuous cultural history starting in Neolithic times or perhaps even earlier.

Corsica, as the Spaniard Seneca attests, must have been inhabited by a miscellany of peoples, Iberian and Ligurian, with a civilization which took root in the Neolithic Age and with customs similar to those of the Berbers and Iberians. As to Sardinia, ancient writers speak explicitly both of an Etruscan connection which it had in common with Corsica and also of particular immigrants, from Iberia (including the Balearics) and Libya. Direct evidence about the Sardinian language is practically confined to a couple of glosses and to place-names: the latter show signs of Iberian origin, for instance the name *Balari*, which in Corsican, we are told, meant 'fugitive' (Pausanias, X. 17. 9).

g. *The Celts and the Iberians*

Celtic languages have features in common with those both of the First and of the Second Italici, and have had strong influence on the dialects of the Germans. This shows that these four Indo-European groups[24] were in contact with one another before the Celts moved to the country called Gaul; and in all probability these contacts were established in the region north of the Alps, in the Bronze or Early Iron Age. It is clear, however, that at the moment of their passage into Gaul the Celts were in process of developing their particular form of Iron Age culture which we call Western Hallstatt (in two periods: 800–650, 650–550 BC): this was shot through with features borrowed from the Greeks, Italici, Illyrians, and Etruscans, whose culture reached them along the Adriatic and the Alpine passes. To be precise, Hallstatt appears first in the regions north of the Alps, in Bohemia, Silesia, Austria, the eastern Alps, and south Germany (including Württemberg and Baden). Soon afterwards it is found in Switzerland, and it then spreads in two directions; (a) Franche Comté, Burgundy, Champagne, the Palatinate, Lorraine, and Belgium; (b) Savoy, Dauphiné, the Auvergne. These must have been the lines along which the Celts penetrated into Gaul. Once there, they came under the influence of Massiliote culture, which spread through the country and was responsible for transforming Hallstatt into the civilization we call La Tène (first phase 550–500).[25]

From the study of Celtic dialects still surviving in Great Britain, Ireland, and in Britanny we can distinguish two groups, one represented by the Goidelic and Gaelic dialects, which at several points are in line with Latin, the other by the Breton or Cymric dialects, aligned more with Osco-Umbrian.[26] Moreover, these differences probably go back to the time of the migrations from the Danube regions, since survivals in later speech show that at an early period a Goidelic dialect was spoken in Gaul as well: compare the month named 'equus', the river Sequana, the tribe of the Sequani, the city Argentorate, and other Goidelic forms. So the earliest Celtic migrants, who brought Hallstatt culture with them, belonged to the first linguistic group, but their successors to the second.

The first wave of migrants started, as Tacitus says (*Germ.*, 18), from the region between the Hercynian forest, the Rhine, and the Main, and probably gave rise to the Helvetii, Sequani, Lingones, Leuci, Mediomatrici, and also to the Belgae: the view of some moderns that the Belgae came down from the north in the third century is based on a misunderstanding of certain passages in ancient writers (Caesar, *de Bello Gallico*, II, 4, 1; Avienus, *Ora Maritima*, 139–45; Mela, III, 6, 57, cf. 5, 36).[27] From the Belgae later were derived the people of Armorica, who also received immigrants from the second migration: they then, accompanied by some of the Belgae, crossed over to occupy southern Britain, at a time when La Tène culture was already widespread. Caesar, who was the first to call attention to the correspondence between the Celtic place-names of Britain and Belgica (*de Bello Gallico*, V, 12, 2), distinguishes only two races in southern Britain, one indigenous, the other Belgic. He did not therefore believe in an early migration by 'proto-Celts', which is supported by certain modern writers.[28]

The most compelling reason for the Celtic movement towards Gaul was undoubtedly the pressure exercised on them by the Germans. But the pressure was not thereby halted: Germans now repeatedly crossed the Rhine and settled on its left bank. These invasions, with the consequent increase in population, brought about two further migrations by some sections of the Celts: one back towards the Danube and into the Po valley, the other across the Pyrenees into Spain.

The return of part of the Celts into the Danube region, and their simultaneous descent into the Po valley, did not begin, as the Roman annalists claimed, at the beginning of the fourth century, but undoubtedly started a couple of centuries earlier (cf. Livy, V, 33–5; Justin, XX, 5, 7–9; Polybius, II, 17; Appian, Celt., 2).[29] The establishment in the Po valley took a considerable time, for the inhabitants, especially the Etruscans and Umbrians, put up a tenacious resistance. This view is confirmed by archaeological finds relating to the Celts in this region, which are noticeably earlier in the northwest, and later in the south-east.

The reconquest of the Danubian region was already known to Hecataeus slightly after 500, before its mention by Herodotus (II, 33; IV, 49). Herodotus also knows of the other movement of the Celts which took them into Spain and of which we shall speak in a moment.

Evidence about the Celtic language in classical times is not plentiful. There are names of persons, divinities, and places, about a hundred brief inscriptions and graffiti (starting in the third century BC), and some coin legends. But detailed knowledge of Celtic is given us later by the dialects which survive in Ireland, Wales, Cornwall, and Brittany: there are also Irish texts from the fifth century AD.

It was earlier than Herodotus' day, in other words about 450 BC at latest,[30] that the Celts pushed into the Iberian peninsula and settled in the valleys of the Anas (Guadiana), Tagus, and Ebro, where they joined with the indigenous races to form a group of mixed language, the Celtiberians. Apart from historical tradition, these are known to us from brief inscriptions, mainly on coins, and from a quantity of place-names of Celtic type, for instance those ending in '-briga'. In the Iberian peninsula they must have found at least two languages spoken: in some districts these were sharply distinguished, in others they had been fused. The first was the forebear of the modern 'euskara', the language of the Vascones, a tribe from which the Pyrenean races, the Basques in Spain and the Gascons in France, are descended: it was the language of a people which had taken to the hills in face of invasions from south and north, and was probably spoken in Spain from the end of the Neolithic Age. It can be regarded as the remnant of a great racial and linguistic unity which stretched in a wide arc from the Iberian peninsula to the Caucasus but from which there survived only the 'linguistic pockets', the places where Basque, Etruscoid, and Caucasian languages were spoken. We have seen, incidentally, that penetration by Etruscan peoples into Spain is not to be ruled out.

In contrast, the second kind of language found in Spain, which we shall call Iberian and which in the majority of the peninsula had blended with the language just described, seems to be comparable chiefly with languages in the Hamitic world of North Africa: in the European world it has affinities with the ancient speech of the Balearics, western Sicily, Sardinia, and Corsica.

h. *First Evidence for the Germans*

Our first records of the Germans are late, not earlier than the fourth century BC, when Pytheas of Massilia reported that in his travels he had reached the lands of the Teutones. One century later, bands of German 'gaesati' aided the Gallic expeditions against Rome; and the *Fasti Triumphales* report a victory over them in 222. Their first migrations recorded by classical sources are those by the Bastarnae about 200, and those by the Cimbri and Teutones at the end of the second century BC. In this period covered by this chapter they had not yet settled in the more southerly regions in which they are found soon afterwards; the whole district north of the Alps (south Germany, Switzerland, Austria and so on) was occupied partly by North Etruscans and partly by Celts. But Germanic contacts with those people can be proved. The burning of their dead was a custom probably learnt from the North Etruscans (and the Germans still preserved it in Tacitus' time—*Germ.*, 27); and numerous Celticisms entered German nomenclature and their language generally. Undoubtedly too ideas and goods reached the Germans from Mediterranean lands by way of the North Etruscans and Celts: but this happened on a small scale, since all Nordic civilization, though homogeneous, was apparently late in developing.

It is clear that the home of the German tribes, who believed themselves to be autochthonous, still lay in northern Germany and a part of Scandinavia. But they were already showing a tendency to fan out southwards; and in so doing they acted as a lever which started the Celtic migrations and shut the North Etruscan tribes within narrower areas than before.

The present writer believes that some Germans had crossed the Rhine before the Celts occupied the parts of Gaul on the left bank. A long strip of German, or mixed Germano-Celtic, tribes is well known in the time of Caesar, who considered all the more northerly and easterly tribes of Belgica to be Germanized; and it would follow from our view that these tribes made their first appearance quite far back in time. Two arguments confirm this theory. First, cremation was exclusively practised in Belgica from the Bronze Age onwards, while in the remainder of Gaul the Celts used both rites indiscriminately, having borrowed inhumation from the Ligurians. Secondly, in the district of which we are speaking there are many fortified posts and abandoned treasures, proof of a continual state of warfare.

The first epigraphic documents of the Germans, in the Runic alphabet which originated probably with the North Etruscans, go back only to the third century AD, so does the Gothic translation of the Bible by Wulfila. For ancient times, therefore, we have only names of persons, divinities, and places, in Greek and Latin authors, as evidence for the German language.

i. *The Semitic Languages*

In the period 1200–500 BC the languages used by the Semitic peoples, in the eastern section of the Middle Eastern lands into which they were expanded, were still those they had used in earlier times, namely Accadian and Assyrian, though Aramaic was beginning to creep in.

Accadian about 1400 had become the diplomatic language of the whole vast region from Mesopotamia to Egypt, precisely because it was employed by people whose natural speech was foreign (the Hittites, Hurrians and so on). We consequently find Accadian with local characteristics, as at Nuan south of Nineveh, at Alalakh, and at Mari on the Euphrates. It continued to be used for imperial documents even when the Assyrians were ruling in Babylonia; and it was then imposed as an official language in the neo-Babylonian or Chaldean empire, from 626 to 532, after which, under the Persian dominion, it became the learned language of the priests. Meanwhile the language of the Assyrians continued to develop side by side with Accadian,[31] to which it was fairly similar, apart from its sibilants and the general tendency to archaism shown in the 'Cappadocian tablets' of the eighteenth century found at Kultepe. But it was gradually altered in its later history, when the area of its employment depended on the changing fortunes of the Assyrian empire.

But in later times the introduction of Aramaic personages into the neo-Babylonian and Persian worlds as imperial functionaries, and the success with which their language was spreading, brought about the adoption of Aramaic as the main Achaemenid administrative language. It was employed by the Persians in the countries they had taken from the Assyrians and Chaldeans, and gradually took the place of the earlier languages in Mesopotamia and Syria.

Aramaic, Hebrew, and Phoenician. The main classification of the western Semitic languages is into two groups, northern and southern (or Arabian).

Within the northern group, in the Canaan region, we can distinguish the following tongues:

(*a*) Old Sinaitic, known from about twenty inscriptions written in an archaic semi-alphabetic script (see below, p. 92), which is hard to interpret. This was probably employed at the time of the Hyksos invasions of Egypt, but its dating is disputed (between the nineteenth and fifteenth centuries BC).

(*b*) The language of Ugarit (Ras Shamrah). Besides the Accadian and Asianic texts discovered at this site, which faces Cyprus, some others have been found of fourteenth-century date. These are in a language akin to Phoenician, but with a high degree of archaizing.

(*c*) Phoenician. Of this the earliest surviving texts were found at Byblos (about ten fragments in pseudo-hieroglyphic script, including the epitaph of King Akhiram, whose date is put at various points between the thirteenth and tenth centuries BC), at Cyprus (a ninth-century alphabetical votive inscription of Arvab), and at Karatepe (an eighth-century bilingual text). The majority of texts in this language, some of which are Punic (from Carthage and its empire), are of much later date.

(d) The languages of Moab, Ammon, and Edom. The first is known from the ninth-century *stele* of King Mesha, the second from some incised seals, and the last from a short inscription of the eighth or seventh century and from seventh-century stamps on jars.

(e) Ancient or Biblical Hebrew, from the period before the Babylonian Captivity. In this the principal inscriptions are the so-called Calendar of Gezer, dated between the eleventh and ninth centuries; fragments of ninth-century *ostraka* from Samaria; the inscription on the aqueduct of Siloam in Judaea (c. 700); a leather fragment from Marabbaat (seventh century), and the letters on *ostraka* found at Lachish in southern Palestine, some of which can be dated around 587. It is in these centuries that the greater part of the Bible was edited, the oldest sections, such as the *Song of Deborah*, possibly going back to about 1000 BC,[32] and others being as late as the seventh century. After the return of the Hebrews from captivity in 538 Ancient Hebrew was used as prayer language and to draw up the sacred texts, while in the country Aramaic began to be spoken widely.

(f) Aramaic. Accadian texts of the fourteenth century BC speak of Arameans, nomads of northern Arabia; and these people took part in invasions of Egypt in the thirteenth and twelfth centuries. They surged northwards, into the Transjordanian part of Palestine, and created in turn the small states of Petra, Palmyra, and Edessa.

In Persian times, as we have stated above, Aramaic became the official administrative language in the Assyrian and Babylonian zones; but it also gained supremacy in every Syrian country. The earliest Aramaic texts are the following: a brief inscription of Gozan (Tell Halaf), which may be tenth-century; an inscribed table of ivory belonging to King Hazael in the ninth; an inscription of Ben Hadad, king of Damascus, of about 850; the *stele* discovered near Aleppo, relating to Zakir, king of Hamath and Lu'ash, dated about 775; the sixth-century *stele* of Nerab; and the Aramaic papyri of an earlier date (c. 815) found together with Aramaic *ostraka* in Egypt.

The southern Semitic group consisted mainly of the Arabian peoples. The northern section of these, which can be subdivided further, are mentioned in ninth-century Accadian texts, and have left only inscribed seals and cylinders, which perhaps belong to the previous century. The southern Arabs included the Minaeo-Sabaitic state, which was probably not created until the sixth century BC.

j. *Caucasian Languages*

We are ignorant of the precise linguistic conditions in the Caucasian region, not only during the period 1200–500 BC, but throughout antiquity. If we are forced to conjecture, the most probable answer is that at that time Caucasian languages were not so fully diversified as they were soon to become. They were nearer to their primitive state, and furthermore had not yet been greatly affected, in the southern part of the region, by the speech of peoples of different culture with whom they were in contact over so many centuries. Moreover the northern districts cannot yet have been invaded by the Indo-European foreigners (Iranic Ossetians and Russian Slavs) and by the Turco-Tartars, who live there today.

It is also likely that at least in the early centuries of our period the surviving portions of the great linguistic arc of southern Europe covered a much wider area and yet bordered on one another. This is the arc from which, besides the Caucasians, there still survived the Etruscoids and the Basques.

k. *Chinese and Sino-Tibetan Languages*

The Chinese are probably autochthonous: every theory of a migrant origin has collapsed in face of complete absence of confirmatory evidence. At the outset the dialect, or group of dialects, on which the present literary language is founded, was spoken only in a very narrow area on the western side of the great alluvial plain of the Huang-ho. The remainder of China was covered by kindred dialects, of which we know little or nothing; and especially to the south of the Yangtze-kiang there were languages of other families, such as Tibeto-Burman, T'ai, and perhaps also Malayo-Polynesian. Chinese as the language of administration and culture spread with the same rhythm as the Chou state; and by the second century BC it had therefore become the official language of all present-day China. But as a language of the lower classes its progress was very much slower. In the north 'barbarian' (i.e. non-Chinese) groups still inhabited the mountain country a few centuries before our era; but their languages quickly died out. South China, on the other hand, for a long time remained a country whose language was not Chinese. Later on the various local forms of speech were overcome: they retired to the less accessible regions of the interior, where in more or less compact linguistic 'pockets' they even today put up a resistance to the progress of Sinization. On the other side, the Chinese *koiné* was subdivided in its turn into a number of early dialects.

The first appearance of the Chinese language is on bronzes and tortoise-shell of the Shang period: classical literature begins in the first quarter of the first millennium, at first in an oral form, being recorded in writing much later. The very nature of its ideographic script conceals the linguistic content. The ideograms are read in modern pronunciation, which means in the dialect of the readers: the script gives us only indirect evidence about the ancient pronunciation. The attempt to construct a history of the Chinese language has been going on for less than a generation; the process is laborious and the results are not always certain.

In this field the work of B. Karlgren is fundamental. From a reasonably sure reconstruction of the pronunciation current in the sixth and seventh centuries AD he argues back to the archaic pronunciation of the Chou period, making particular use of the rhymes of the *Shih-ching* and other ancient texts. The Chinese language in the Chou period had a phonetic structure much richer and more complex than it has now—with final consonants and sets of initial consonants, whereas modern Pekin Chinese allows only a single consonant at the beginning of a word, and a single vowel or diphthong or a single nasal at the end. To this generous use of consonants must be added the three or (as Chinese grammarians maintain) four tones, divided into two series, high and low. Karlgren's reconstruction met with powerful objections, particularly from Chinese scholars, and although it is a very probable one it cannot yet be regarded as definitive. It should be made clear that his theory relates to the language used by court circles in the two Chou capitals. Once again difficulties connected with the script make it difficult to grasp the dialect variations, though we get information about them from later sources.

Archaic Chinese had two methods of derivation: one through the alternation of voiced and unvoiced initials, with the addition of prefixes; the other by the alternation of vowels and by changes in the final sounds. The first method was used to form pairs of transitive and intransitive verbs, or of verbs and verbal nouns: for instance *duan* = to be cut, *tuan* = to cut; and *lön* = ice, *plön* = to freeze. The second method served for the grammatical cases of pronouns and for sundry other forms of variation. For instance *no* = I (the nominative), *na* = me (the accusative). In its syntax the literary language began to take shape in the Chou period, and was to be finally fixed in the period which followed (see Part II).

The majority of the languages spoken in south-east Asia, in south-west China, and on the Tibetan plateau can be grouped with Chinese in the large Sino-Tibetan family. This can be classified into six divisions: Sinic, T'ai, Tibetan, Burman, Bari, and Karenni (according to the scheme formulated by R. Shafer). Very little can be said about their distribution in primitive times: we only know that in the historical period the areas in which the languages were used both contracted and expanded, and also shifted. For example there were certainly no Burmese in Burma nor T'ai in Siam before our era; and there may not even have been Tibetans in central Tibet. It would seem that the primitive home of these languages, the centre from which they radiated, should be sought in the west and south-west of China. None of them has left written records earlier than the seventh century AD.

At an undefined period of the first millennium BC a small T'ai aristocracy imposed its rule and its own language on the Mon-Khmer population of the Tonking delta. This basically T'ai language, however, was heavily contaminated by the underlying Khmer layer, and eventually gave rise to the Annamite speech, though the precise position of the latter is still in dispute.

Most of the southern region where Sino-Tibetan languages are found today, that is to say the various coastal plains of south-east Asia, was originally occupied by languages of the Mon-Khmer family. These were later overwhelmed and reduced to a few remnants, of which the most noticeable today are the Khmer (or Cambogian) and the Mon (or Talaing) in lower Burma. But the first records of these two languages do not go back beyond the eighth century AD.

1. *Languages in Central and North Eurasia*

No account can possibly be given of the races and languages in the immense regions of central and northern Eurasia. Archaeological finds tell us something about the progress of civilization and the centres for its diffusion; but they provide no indications of any value about the problem of language, which is before us now. We must also remember that any hypothesis which attempts to get help from the circumstances of centuries nearer our own must inevitably be unreliable. No concrete evidence exists for the period with which we are concerned; and these nomadic and semi-nomadic tribes are so mobile that they may have shifted their homes out of recognition. In addition, the spontaneous growth of dialects not tied down by literary usage has brought about far-reaching alterations in languages; and over wide areas the influence of more civilized peoples may have had a similar effect.

If we limit ourselves to quite elementary conclusions, we might say that approximately the same races and languages as are found there today must have moved around this vast region, some chiefly in the west, others in the east. They had not yet, however, become an important factor in the districts most familiar to states of more advanced culture.

The presumption would then be that the western districts were inhabited by those Indo-European races who had not yet been in the lands of higher civilization. Besides the Germans, this means the Baltic Slavs and the Tokharic peoples (for whom the earliest written evidence, from Turkestan, is not earlier than the seventh century AD). In addition, these districts would have contained the ancestors of the present speakers of Uralic languages: the Finnish group (Lapps, Finns—already known to Tacitus, *Germ.*, 48— Mordvinians, Permians, Ostiaks and so on); the Magyar group; and the Samoyedes, who are now spread from Norway to the Yenisei basin, i.e. to longitude 90° east. Farther to the south and south-east lay probably the ancient home of the Turkish peoples, now scattered between Anatolia and longitude 100°.

On the other hand the primitive home of the Mongols (now living between longitudes 80° and 125°) should probably be pictured as lying in the eastern zone; and also that of the Tunguses (now between 85° and 165°), the Palaeo-Siberians (who apart from the Ket group on the Yenisei are between 145° and 170°), the Koreans, and the Ainu. Finally some influence would have been exerted by the Tibetans from the south. But all this is wildly hypothetical and elastic. One needs only to remember that modern scholars cannot agree whether the Huns (Hsiung-nu), the enemies of China, belonged to the Turkish or Mongolian or Tungus group (see pp. 45 ff.).

m. *Polynesia*

It is even more difficult to guess at the broad lines on which races and languages were distributed in the Polynesian and Australasian worlds in the period 1200 BC to AD 400. Although the island nature of these regions helps us in that various peoples have persisted in the same place without changing their homes, none the less some considerable migrations are attested. The natives, true-born sailors, found it easy, even with their primitive equipment, to undertake the most daring expeditions from island to island; and we also get evidence from the disordered way in which the languages of the region can be seen distributed at the present day. Not only do they show heavily marked differences between each group, caused by the independent development of speech not used in literature; but there are similarities between groups which today do not adjoin one another, their separation being clearly due to the fact that other groups have come in between them. For example the Papuans, the Melanesians, and the Australian aborigines have inserted themselves between the Malay Indonesians and the Melanesians; and there are strong resemblances between the Malay Indonesians and the far-distant inhabitants of Madagascar, and between the Papuans of New Guinea and the inhabitants of the Andaman Islands in the Indian Ocean. All this leads one to believe that many movements have occurred since antiquity, though their nature cannot be precisely determined.

One would like, then, to think it probable that the forebears of the races and languages found there today (i.e. the Malay Indonesians, Papuans, Melanesians, Australian and Tasmanian aborigines, and Polynesians) inhabited this vast region of Oceania from very early times. But we are entirely ignorant as to where each one was located at each particular period of the past. We can be more confident in assuming certain migratory movements, for example by Malay Indonesians going west to Madagascar and east to Polynesia; and certain direct contacts, in antiquity, by peoples now far apart, like the Papuans and the inhabitants of the Andamans.

n. *America before Columbus*

It would be even more hazardous to try deducing anything about linguistic conditions on the American continent in the period 1200 BC to AD 400 by using the distribution of languages there in modern times. They have been very numerous—on one calculation there were about 900 at the beginning of the sixteenth century—but knowledge of their distribution is useful only for topographical and other incidental inquiries. Nowadays one can speak of six large families of ancient languages in North America, with an enormous number of sub-species; of thirteen large families with a similar proportion of sub-species in Mexico and Central America; and of at least 108 languages in South America and the Antilles. Even if, despite all the variations brought about by people detaching themselves geographically from their main body, and despite the rapid transformations affecting languages which are only spoken (and not written), we could succeed in reducing this linguistic picture to a much more simple scheme, we should still not know how to place the various languages securely either in time or in space.

There are points to notice about the much-discussed relations between these languages and the world outside America. In North America there are the similarities noted by Sauvageot between the speech of the Aleutian Eskimos and that of the Ural peoples. There are Rivet's comparisons between Hoka-siu and Malay Polynesian speech, and Sapir's between Na-deve speech and that of the Sino-Tibetans. Moreover in South America interesting analogies have been drawn between Patagonian and Fuegian on the one hand and Australian on the other.

But it is another thing to say in what period these possible migrations to the new continent took place.

o. *Africa*

As regards the African continent, the first thing to remember is that in Egypt, besides the continued use by the scribes of the traditional literary language, there was an increasing tendency to set down familiar texts in a vernacular. This was a very different language, which must have been that of the district round Thebes; it is usually called neo-Egyptian. Later, from the time of the Saite Psamtiks of the seventh century, although the traditional language used for inscriptions was still showing a deliberate effort at purism, the vernacular was assuming marked regional features.

Some have believed that the Hamitic and Semitic languages formed a single group, within which the Semitic were more conservative. There is no adequate proof of this.[33] The older theory seems more likely, namely that the Egyptian language is a hybrid, its base being provided by the indigenous Hamitic people, its superstructure by early Semitic invaders. Other examples of Semitic immigration into Egypt are not lacking, like the one in the Hyksos period and later those by the 'Peoples of the Sea'. Semitic migrations also occurred farther south, in east Africa, such as that which started from southern Arabia and founded the languages of Ethiopia: this certainly took place several centuries before our era, though the languages are not attested until the third or fourth century AD.

We now come to North Africa, by which is meant the area from the borders of Egypt on the north-east as far as Morocco and the Canaries, and in the south from the mouth of the Senegal to Assuan on the Nile—exception being made for a part of Cyrenaica, where Greek colonies were settled, and for a part of the southern Mediterranean coast between Tunisia and Morocco, where there were Phoenico-Punic colonies and Numidians. With these exceptions Hamitic dialects, of the kind normally called Libyo-Berber, were spoken in all the area, just as they are spoken still where they have not been overwhelmed by Arabic. These are dialects akin to those which penetrated in an archaic period into part of Spain and part of Sicily. They are attested by names of places and persons, and also by brief inscriptions and graffiti, though these seem to be not earlier than the second century AD.

A group of kindred dialects, called Cushite, are spoken today east of the Nile valley along the coast of the Red Sea and Indian Ocean, as far as latitude 4° south, though they are interspersed with Semitic forms of speech. The only one of these dialects whose archaic phase is known to us is that from Meroë, in upper Nubia and the Egyptian Sudan. In the period 750 BC–AD 350 this was the home of a more or less autonomous state from which Egyptian hieroglyphic inscriptions have come down to us with examples of ancient Cushite.

Of the ancient conditions of language in 'Black Africa', on the other hand, we know practically nothing. At the present day the languages spoken in the Sudan and Guinea are divisible into sixteen groups, and each of these can again be divided into a number of dialects. The earliest evidence of what they were like is provided by the explorer Hanno, in his note on the word 'gorilla'; and there are religious writings in the Nubian language from the fourth century AD onward. South of them, on the Atlantic coast as far as Angola and on the other side down to the eastern coast of the Republic of South Africa, are about 150 species of the Bantu language; and farther south again there are the Koin languages of the Bushmen and Hottentots. The area occupied by the Bantu must have seen many changes of races and languages: the Pygmies of the tropical forests must once have spread widely over it, and these have been linked by some scholars with the Koin group. But it is not impossible that the Bantu peoples emigrated to these areas comparatively late, though this view must not be supported by the confusing comparisons which have been established between their dialects and those of other peoples of whom the Dravidians are the chief.

2. THE EVOLUTION OF WRITING SYSTEMS

a. *Persistence of Tradition*

The first thing to remember about methods of writing in the period 1200–500 BC is the extent to which the methods current in the preceding centuries persisted.

Thus the two scripts of Egypt were for half a millennium the only ones which had spread through the Nile valley. They were the hieroglyphic, which was employed for monumental records, and the hieratic, a cursive increasingly less equipped with pictorial features, which was used for both ecclesiastical and secular writings on papyrus. Neither, however, gained as such any ground outside the Nile valley, although other peoples drew inspiration from them in composing their own scripts, and the Phoenicians sometimes used hieroglyphic characters simply as ornamental and pictorial motifs.

In the course of the seventh century BC the hieratic script gave rise to a second type of cursive, which Herodotus called 'Demotic'. This was used particularly for secular purposes, and was dominant down to the fifth century AD: it had signs for words, sounds, and cases, with no apparent traces of pictorial writing, and was set down from right to left with ligatures linking the signs. No one of the three Egyptian types of script ever assumed alphabetic features.

Cuneiform. The Sumerian script, called cuneiform, had been gradually adopted by a number of peoples. They included the Semitic (Accadian and Babylonian) invaders of Mesopotamia, the Assyrians to their north, who had gradually become Semitic in culture, and the Kassites, who dominated Mesopotamia until their defeat by the Elamites in 1171. The Elamites had previously used a linear geometric script of their own, called Palaeo-Elamite, which may be derived from pictographic symbols;[34] but when from 1171 to 640 they became lords of Babylonia they too adopted the cuneiform system (neo-Elamite), though they simplified it and used only about 113 characters,[35] of which more than 80 were syllabic in nature. This they then left as a legacy to the Arameo-Chaldeans, who supplanted them as rulers of that country down to 539, the year in which Babylon was conquered by the Persians.

But the cuneiform script was not confined to the areas of Babylonia and Assyria. In early days it was disseminated as an international language of diplomacy by the various peoples who had their headquarters in those areas. In this way it was used by the Hittites, Mitanni and Hurrians, Chalds, Urartu, and Canaanites; and finally sometimes by the Egyptians, as can be seen particularly in records from the Tell el Amarna archives. Later, as we shall see, it inspired the so-called Old Persian script of the Achaemenids, which was half cuneiform and half alphabetic.

Hittite Hieroglyphic. The problems of the early methods of Hittite cuneiform are outside our field, but some mention must be made of the so-called 'Hittite hieroglyphic'. This must have been in use during the second half of the second millennium: extant records of it belong to the period between the thirteenth and seventh centuries. But as an artificial method of writing the Hittite empire was already using, especially on bilingual inscriptions, the script of the Syrian regions where vassal states of the Hittites had been created (Carchemish, Hamath, Aleppo, etc.) though the languages spoken were not those of the Hittites of Boğazköy.

Hittite hieroglyphic had 220 signs, some of them ideograms, others phonetic, and a number being syllabic. They were cut from right to left, or alternatively *boustrophedon*. The script does not seem to have been derived either from Egyptian hieroglyphs or from Minoan pictograms: at the most it may have been devised as an imperial script along Egyptian lines. As we said above, the eighth-century bilingual inscription from Karatepe, set up by a king of the Danauna, has made it possible to establish our knowledge of these Hittite hieroglyphs with full certainty.

Early Indian writing. After the middle of the second millennium BC the Indus culture, and with it its pictographic writing, became a thing of the past. The Aryan invaders, who succeeded it immediately or after a lapse of time, were in all probability without a script; and a gap of about one thousand years separates the pictograms of Harappā and Mohenjo-daro from the first Brahmī inscriptions.[36]

The origin of the Brahmī alphabet, from which all the modern Indian scripts derive, is obscure. It had been maintained once that it derived from some form of Semitic alphabet; but the resemblances are too vague. Now the recent discoveries at Lothal in Gujarat seem to provide the missing link in the history of Indian writing. They show a late simplified form of the Indus script, in which the pictographic element has nearly completely disappeared. From this simpler script the Brahmī alphabet may be descended. Of course, final proof of this derivation is still lacking.

However, since the first epigraphic occurrence of Brahmī is not earlier than the end of the fourth century, it can be more suitably dealt with in the section which follows.

The Chinese Ideogram. The first examples of writing in China are found on bones and tortoise-shells excavated at Anyang, which were used under the Shang dynasty for purposes of divination. The earliest go back to the fourteenth century BC. Even at that time the general principles behind the ideograms were already the same as those which inspire modern Chinese writing: the modern characters are in the direct line of descent from those of the Shang period and have undergone no fundamental modifications. We know of about 2,500 Shang pictograms; and all have already a style and simplicity which imply that a considerable period of development lay behind them, though of such a period no traces have yet been discovered. The Chou conquest about 1050 brought no changes of any consequence; the Chou spoke the same language as the Shang, or at any rate one which was closely akin, so no change was made necessary. From the first Chou period (c. 1050–771) there survive numerous and sometimes comparatively lengthy inscriptions on bronze vases; and to these one may add sporadic inscriptions on pottery and jade. In the later Chou period (c. 771–250) these inscriptions become shorter and less common.

The Chinese characters are the perfect response to the nature of the language, in which every word is complete by itself and is not altered by its syntactical use: the same monosyllable can serve as substantive, verb, adjective, etc., according to its position in the phrase. Moreover the existence of a large number of homophones (which are admittedly much more numerous now than they were in the archaic language) is another reason why ideo-graphic script is the method best adapted to Chinese speech.

Its origin, as far as we can see today, was entirely autochthonous. Neither its principle nor its forms seem to owe anything to inspiration from outside Shang China, that is to say from outside the lower basin of the Huang-ho. The greatest possible freedom and variety were allowed in the primitive stage of the script. The scribes all follow the same tradition and the same kind of convention, but within it they are free to modify and vary the forms as much as they please. The more the characters increased in number, the more they became conventional and lost all resemblance to the naturalistic representations of primitive times; but different kinds of 'ductus' begin to develop. The ancient script (*Ku-wen*) used under the Shang in this way gave rise to an angular 'Great Seal script' (*ta-chuan*) and a 'Small Seal script' (*hsiao-chuan*), which are attributed by later tradition to the ninth and third centuries BC respectively, but whose first origins must, it seems, be put at the end of the Shang period.

Chinese philologists traditionally divide the characters into six classes: (1) *hsiang-hsing* (resemblance of form), which are genuine pictograms in the full sense of the word and embrace the earliest characters; (2) *chih-shih* (indicative symbols), in which abstract ideas are represented either by human gestures which indicate them or by means of signs borrowed from words of analogous meaning (e.g. the signs for numerals, parts of the day, etc.); (3) *hui-i* (associative compounds), which are based on the association of ideas resulting from the sum of their component parts (e.g. two 'woman' characters with the meaning 'to quarrel'; 'sun' behind 'tree' with the meaning 'east'); (4) *chuan-chu* (mutually interpretative symbols), when a word is indicated by using the character for another word of analogous meaning, or by turning other characters upside-down or reversing them; (5) *chia-chieh* ('to seek help'), the deliberate or accidental interchange of characters which represent homophones, or even some kind of straightforward borrowing of characters which resemble the word required; (6) *hsing-sheng* (harmon-ized sounds), which are phonetic compounds, written with one element which indicates the word's pronunciation, and another which indicates the group or class to which its meaning belongs; for instance the character *fang*, = 'square', when used as a phonetic and placed next to the 'earth' character (which when it stands alone is pronounced *t'u*, but which here is used only to indicate the group of meanings), produces *fang* = place.

The vast majority of Shang period characters belong to class 1, with a small number in classes 2 to 5. Class 6 grew up almost entirely in the Chou period (there are, however, some doubts about this),[37] and has been the most fertile of all in producing later developments; today it comprises, according to Creel, about half the characters normally used in classical texts, and it may even comprise nine-tenths of all existing characters (Karlgren's figure). At the end of the Chou period Chinese had in essence become, to use Needham's words, 'a phonetic script employing some 1,000 signs rendering the sounds of all the different syllable-words, and ready to combine with determinatives which would indicate the meaning'.

'Hexagrams' have a place apart. They are composed of six parallel horizontal lines, which are each either continuous or divided, thus giving the possibility of sixty-four different combinations. They are found only in the *I-ching* or book of changes, a manual on divination which is attributed to the father of the first Chou king, but which must in fact be somewhat later. The hexagrams indicate certain basic ideas and were meant entirely for purposes of divination; they thus fall outside the field of writing, especially as they had no possibilities of further development.

The Syllabic Scripts of Mycenae and Cyprus. We have no reason to concern ourselves in this chapter with the two earliest Minoan scripts which grew up during the Early and Middle Minoan periods. But we cannot avoid mention of the two linear scripts. The first of these, called Linear A and datable to the sixteenth and succeeding centuries, was used by the pre-Greek population of Crete; it was also adopted by the Hellenes of the Greek peninsula, where it appears for example at Orchomenus. It possesses about 90 symbols, of which not a few are clearly derived from pictograms. The second script, called Linear B, has 64 signs; and of these 48 can be connected with the signs of Linear A, from which they are probably derived. This script is attested from the fourteenth century onwards by about a thousand tablets found at Knossos and by others discovered on the Greek mainland, at Mycenae, Asine, and Pylos.

Recent researches by able scholars (see pp. 68 f.) have led to the recognition that the Linear B texts are written in Greek, and that the script is a syllabic one which precedes the introduction of the alphabet: it was invented by a pre-Greek people and later taken over by the Greeks. It was therefore a method of writing already possessed by the Greeks when they began to occupy the Aegean islands and the coasts of Asia Minor.

Moreover the Greeks must still have been using some kind of syllabic method, and have been ignorant of the alphabetic one, when they settled in distant Cyprus. Cypro-Minoan and Cypro-Mycenaean inscriptions have been found there which seem to mark the intermediate stage between the Cretan Linear script and the later syllabic one—this last being a script with fifty-six signs, attested by a fair number of Greek and non-Greek inscriptions from the seventh to the third centuries. Pre-alphabetic writings are undoubtedly mentioned in a passage of the *Iliad* (VI, 166 ff.), where they are considered by the poet's time to be incomprehensible.

To very much the same period, *c.* 1350 onwards, belong the texts found at Byblos, which were once called pseudo-hieroglyphic. As Dhorme has shown, they prove that a syllabic script, with 114 signs, was used for the Phoenician language. In the second half of the second millennium, therefore, various methods of syllabic writing were independently devised to make writing more expeditious and to reduce the number of symbols it had to use.

b. *First Attempts at an Alphabet*

Older theories of the origin of the alphabet derived it from some other form of writing, Egyptian or cuneiform or Cypriot syllabic, or from Cretan syllabic transported to Palestine by the Phoenicians. Archaeology has disposed of all these theories, since recent finds show that before the definitive invention of a Semitic proto-alphabet various attempts were being made to reduce to a minimum the signs used in writing; and that these attempts were independent of one another, and spread over the whole area from the frontiers of Egypt to that of north Syria.

It is enough to mention here:

(*a*) The Sinaitic inscriptions of the nineteenth to fifteenth centuries BC, written in a Semitic language with a semi-alphabetic system which recalls Egyptian characters on the one hand and north Semitic on the other;

(*b*) The fifteenth- to thirteenth-century inscriptions of Ugarit, in a script which is a cross between alphabetic and cuneiform; its thirty-two signs are cut by persons familiar with cuneiform but are comparable with north Semitic characters; and such inscriptions are fairly widely spread, since we also find examples in Galilee;

(*c*) The Byblos inscriptions recorded above;

(*d*) Some still earlier inscriptions of Canaan, eleven in number so far, which come from Gezer, Beth-Shemesh, and Lachish, and are datable between the sixteenth and thirteenth centuries.

Contemporary with these scattered attempts came another, which had much greater success than all others like it. It appeared in some district or other belonging to the northern Semitic peoples of Syria or Palestine, and may belong to the period of the Hyksos invasions of Egypt. This system we propose to call Northern Proto-Semitic. The earliest documents in it which have come down to us belong to a slightly later date: they include the epitaph of King Akhiram (variously dated between the thirteenth and tenth centuries), the Calendar of Gezer (eleventh to ninth centuries), the ninth-century Moabite *stele* of Mesha, a ninth-century *stele* from Cyprus, and some Aramaic inscriptions from Zincirli (ninth to eighth centuries). This alphabet reduced the number of signs to twenty-two, all consonants and no vowels, a feature explained by the nature of the Semitic language. Its inventor very probably had in his mind not only one or other of the more or less contemporaneous attempts to construct an alphabet, but above all the traditional systems of writing in use by the peoples who created civilization. The Egyptians, with their acrophonic method, had essentially been the first to give the lead in simplifying writing; some Minoan forms too had been used by our inventor as his model; and from the Assyro-Babylonians were preserved the names for certain signs.

The descendant of this Northern Proto-Semitic alphabet among the north Semitic peoples themselves were the Phoenician alphabet of historical times, with its derivatives, together with the Old Hebrew and Aramaic alphabets. But in addition it gave rise to the south Semitic (or Arabian) alphabet and to the first Greek alphabets with all the consequences that followed from them.

There is no doubt that the invention of the alphabet, which made writing so much easier and quicker and so much more understandable, was of fundamental importance in the history of civilization. The new method was no longer the preserve of the priestly class, or the means by which governments conducted their propaganda. It spread abroad among the merchants composing their notes and bills, among the workmen as a means of setting down and handing on their technical processes, among the bards making known their songs, and among the middlemen and clerical classes who wanted to publish their rules, laws and customs, and the records of their work. It was thus an instrument which all the time became more widely known, and was a means of first importance in bringing distant peoples nearer to one another, in removing the differences between their levels of culture and in increasing the rate of their progress.

The Phoenician Alphabet and its Derivatives. We have already recorded the earliest documents in the historical Phoenician alphabet which appear in epigraphy. The Phoenician alphabets of the colonies provide a number of sub-species, as follows:

(1) the Cypro-Phoenician, in which we have documents from the tenth to second centuries BC;

(2) the Sardo-Phoenician, in which the earliest document can be dated probably to the ninth century;

(3) the Carthaginian or Punic, with its later form the neo-Punic;

(4) the Libyan (which shows more primitive remainders) and partly the Iberian.

The last two deserve a special note. The Libyan alphabet has been used in the cutting of about 500 inscriptions in Hamitic dialects from North Africa, all of the Roman period; but it undoubtedly goes back to a period much older than the documents which have survived. The inscriptions include some bilinguals, on which the other language is Punic, Neo-Punic, or

Latin; and in the Libyan versions only the consonants are written, with
special signs to represent certain groups of consonants. We may ignore the
theories which derive this script from Egyptian hieroglyphic, from pre-alphabetic scripts of the Aegean, or from Arabian alphabets. It is beyond doubt that
it had its origin in the alphabet used by the Phoenician colonies of the African
coast: a few special signs, however, were added, and there were changes in
the way certain letters were used; moreover some letters were affected by the
alphabet of the old Phocaean colonies on the African coast, such as Kybos.

The alphabets used by the Iberians may be divided into two types; the
southern (Turdetanian or Tartessian) which records consonants only, and
appears to be a variant of the Libyan; and the Iberian alphabet of Nearer
Spain. From the latter we have about 150 short inscriptions, some of which
are coin legends from the fourth century down to imperial times; on them
are found 30 signs (25 consonants and 5 vowels), with no f or h or v, but with
special signs for double v or double n, and for b, p, z, k, d, and t when followed
by the different vowels. In the south-western corner of the Iberian peninsula
the script of a dozen Algarve *stelae* seems to be alphabetic. On some coins
of the Cadiz region letters have been considered to be a variant of the Libyan
letters, but perhaps only their outlines are similar.

Evans thought this alphabet too came from Crete: Wilke and Cejador y
Franca believed it was connected with ancient signs of geometric pattern
and was conceived locally. It is much more likely that it had a twofold origin,
and came partly from the Semitic (Punic) population, and partly from the
Phocaean or Massiliote Greeks. From the latter both the earlier 'Red'
script and the later 'Blue' script (see below) will have made their contributions.

Old Hebrew and Aramaic Alphabets. Persian Cuneiform. We now come to the
Old Hebrew and Aramaic alphabets, about which it is enough to say this.
The former was in use up to the time of the Babylonian captivity but has left
few texts.[38] The oldest is the so-called 'Alphabet of Gezer'; and we may add
the earliest documents from Moab, Ammon, and Edom.

We have already recorded the earliest documents in the Aramaic alphabet.
According to Albright it was in use from the tenth century onwards. It was
widely used; and its greatest importance lies in the fact that it provided a
pattern for the growth of the type of script used for official purposes in the
Achaemenid empire, normally known as Old Persian Cuneiform. It is
uncertain whether the latter dates from the days of Darius I, or before him
to Cyrus the Great, or even a few decades earlier still. It is an artificial
creation, not the result of natural growth, and combines the old cuneiform
outlines with a number of alphabetic signs drawn from the Aramaic alphabet,
though the latter was simultaneously being used for writings on papyrus
and parchment. There are in fact about forty signs, of which only four
(those for dj and w) are genuine ideograms, three are signs for vowels (a, i, u),
and the rest are pure consonants or syllables formed by consonants and vowels.

Greek Alphabets. Even in ancient times tradition derived the Greek alphabet
from the Phoenician, and there is nothing to commend the view that it came
to the Greeks through the intermediary of alphabets of Asia Minor. Kirchhoff
distinguished three types of Greek alphabet, and we propose to label them
according to the colours in the chart accompanying his work: the Green
comes from the islands of the southern Aegean, the Red from the west, and
the Blue from the east. It is probable that Green, which includes the inscriptions from Thera, Crete, and Melos, is oldest, and comes next to the Phoenician original. It has only 22 letters in the Thera texts: in the Cretan a digamma
is added to make 23. It seems clear that in the original 22-letter form certain
Phoenician signs not needed in Greek had been used to represent the vowels
(aleph for a, he for e, jod for i, vav for u, and ain for o); when the Cretans
added the digamma, they were creating a variant of vav. Furthermore, het
was used for the aspirate, and tet for th. The Green alphabet has no special
signs for the compound sounds th, kh, ps (or qs), and ks, which were consequently produced by using two ordinary signs together.

This alphabet was simpler than all the others, and kept more closely to
its model: it must have been the result of direct trading relations between
the islands in question and the coasts of Syria, where the Phoenician alphabet
had been adopted. The reason for these was not any frequent voyages by the
Phoenicians in the Aegean during the tenth or ninth centuries.[39] On the
contrary, it was that the Greeks made Crete and the neighbouring islands
their base for commercial operations on the Syrian coast (see Chapter I).
Mycenaean finds at Ugarit and Al Mina are evidence for operations of this
kind, as are the Phoenician wares transported home by the Greeks.

The two other types of Greek alphabet were derived from this first type;
and it would seem that the western type, or Red, is earlier than the eastern
Blue. In actual fact, however, if certain observations made about Phocaea
and the Aeolian colonies can be our guide, these terms 'eastern' and 'western'
are irrelevant by quite early times. The colonies from Phocaea northwards
must, at any rate at the outset, have used a Red alphabet, but the general
spread of Ionian influences on the edge of this area must later have led them
to change to Blue.

We come now to the areas covered by the two types of alphabet, and to
the features of each, as Kirchhoff describes them:

(*a*) The Red or western type was used in Euboea, in the whole of the
Greek peninsula except Attica, Megara, Corinth, and Argos, and in the non-
Ionian colonies of the West. It added the three new signs φ, χ (or +), and
Ψ (or ⋁) to express ph, kh, and ps; but it kept the Green alphabet's doubling
of letters for ps (or φs), except that in Arcadia and Locris the symbol ✳
appears for this sound.

(*b*) The Blue or eastern type covered Attica (together with Salamis and
Aegina), the Peloponnesian districts excepted above, the Cyclades, the Asia

Minor coasts, and the Ionic colonies in the West. It had the four new signs
Φ, X, Ψ, Ξ for ph, kh, ps, and ks; and it added two more, for the long ē
and long ō.

The Blue type, being more highly developed and diversified, seems
clearly the later of the two. But, as we said above, one area of Asia Minor,
where in classical times texts are written in the Blue alphabet, must initially
have used a Red one because the Phocaeans came from Phocis. Later, when
the Phocaeans became Ionicized, they changed their system, but the original
arrangement had its results in the appearance of the Red alphabet in districts
with which Phocaea had relations. These included Lemnos and Phrygia,
and the stations along their western voyages—namely Elea, Neapolis, Corsica,
Tartessus in Spain, and the neighbourhood of their colony Kybos in Numidia.
The influence of the North Etruscan alphabet is discussed below.

Naturally within each one of these types of alphabet there developed local
variants. Some of these were autonomous growths, but one must also
remember that certain colonies, like Naucratis, were formed by traders
from many parts of the Greek world, and that several others must have
opened their gates to settlers from various cities, especially in early days.
Tradition on this point is confirmed by the heterogeneous elements to be
found in local cults and language, and in the usages and customs of individual
cities. These customs necessarily included their alphabets: yet this historical
truth is often forgotten by scholars who investigate the origin of alphabets
in the western Mediterranean. That a colony was called Chalcidian, for
example, or Corinthian, means only that the people who founded it or who
gained the upper hand there were Chalcidian or Corinthian; and, as we
can see at Smyrna and Phocaea, and at Himera and Zancle-Messene, this
state of affairs was not always constant.

Alphabets for non-Greeks in Asia. Examination of the evidence so far known
about the alphabets used in Asia Minor or western Anatolia leads to the
simple conclusion that they were derived from the Greek alphabets. They
were influenced from other quarters, too, but they were not the intermediate
stage between Phoenician and Greek.

In Phrygia, for example, inscriptions in Hittite hieroglyphic are found at
least as late as the ninth century. This fact is enough to show that the
Phrygian alphabet was not the source of the Greek; on the contrary, it
derived from an already existing Red-type alphabet.

The Lydian alphabet, with twenty-six letters, derives in part from a Greek
alphabet. It used 8 for f; and for this and other reasons the alphabet is
probably the Phocaean or another from the 'proto-Red' district of Asia
Minor.

The Carian alphabet included, besides the ordinary Greek letters, certain
signs of syllabic type which are survivals from an earlier method of writing.

It appears to have affinities with the Green alphabet and is likely therefore to have been influenced from the Cretan area.

The Lycian alphabet likewise shows the combined influence of Greek alphabetic forms and earlier syllabic signs. Moreover its use of E (he), instead of I (jod), to denote the i sound is clear evidence of further departure from the norm.

Alphabets Derived from the Greek in Italy—Etruscan, Oscan, and Umbrian. This is not the right place in which to reopen the old problem of the origin of the Etruscan alphabet. Etruscan inscriptions show that four basic letters from the Greek alphabet, o, g, b, and d, were not used, since they had no sounds to correspond with them. Some alphabet lists (one at Ruselle, four at Chiusi, one at Bomarzo, three at Nola, and one at Orbetello) comprise the letters used in Etruscan inscriptions but leave out the four we have mentioned. This shows that the alphabet lists found in Tuscany which do include these letters are not Etruscan but Greek: they start with the list incised on an eighth- or seventh-century ivory tablet found in the Marsigliana, and there are parallels at Viterbo, Caere, Fornello near Veii (two documents), Colle Val d'Elsa, Narce, and Leprignano.

The question is what Greek alphabet is represented by these Greek 'exemplars' found in Etruria. Kirchhoff[40] perceived—and we still maintain he was right—that they are lists originally prepared at Cumae, and that consequently the Etruscan alphabet was derived from the Cumaean. The alphabet lists, it is true, represent a more archaic phase than any for which we have evidence from Cumaean inscriptions known to us. This may be called the 'Euboean' phase, though it is impossible to verify such a view of it because the earliest Euboean inscriptions are not older than the sixth century.

Grenier believed that the alphabet of the Marsigliana list was different from the Cumaean and was a Greek 'proto-alphabet' based on forms earlier than the time when the Red alphabet diverged from the Blue. The objections made by the present writer to this theory seem to be decisive. It would be much simpler to believe, if any special explanation of the curious alphabet is needed, that Cumae, like other colonies, had a mixed population, with Euboean and non-Euboean elements in the same city.

Already nine or ten thousand Etruscan inscriptions are known. The majority were found in Tuscany, with a certain number from other regions, such as the Po valley, Latium, and Campania, into which the Etruscans extended their hegemony in the sixth and fifth centuries; but there are also some from places outside that area, as far afield as Piedmont, Sicily, Sardinia, Egypt, and Carthage. The longest text is that on the covering of a mummy, now in the museum at Zagreb; and texts of substantial size include a fifth-century tile from S. Maria at Capua, a *cippus* of Perugia, the sixth-century 'lead sheet of Magliano', a tablet from Volterra, and the so-called 'liver of

Piacenza'. The writing is sometimes *boustrophedon*, but normally from right to left. The earliest texts may go back to the seventh or eighth centuries.

The Etruscan alphabet was certainly responsible for both the Oscan and the Umbrian. In Oscan writing we have a couple of hundred inscriptions, three quarters of them from Campania, datable between the fifth century BC and the Christian era; and coin legends in this alphabet are found from the fifth to first centuries BC. The inscriptions are undoubtedly modelled on the alphabet the Etruscans were using in Campania during their hegemony there in the sixth and fifth centuries. They read from right to left. There is no d; there is a special sign for modifying the γ; and a dot over V̇ is used to indicate o which is missing in the Etruscan alphabet. However, g and b, which the Etruscans did not use either, are drawn as such from the Greek alphabets.

The most important Umbrian texts are the *Tabulae Iguvinae*. Most of these are in a fourth-century Umbrian alphabet, with the remainder in the Latin alphabet of the first century BC. Here too the debt to the classical Etruscan alphabet is obvious: there is no o, g, or d, and an Etruscan 8 is used for f.

Other Derivations from the Greeks. Herodotus (I, 163) states that Phocaean trade in the Adriatic discovered that sea for the Greeks, and undoubtedly Phocaeans were voyaging there at least half a century before they entered the Tyrrhenian Sea, which was farther from their mother city. Their activity in the Adriatic started therefore in the eighth century.

The present writer thinks that these Phocaeans were responsible for the beginnings of the Messapian and Picene alphabets, and of a North Etruscan prototype which had many descendants.

The Messapian alphabet is undoubtedly modelled on a Red Greek alphabet, but just as the Etruscans did not take over the Greek o so the Messapians did not take this alphabet's u, perhaps because o in Messapian speech had a closed sound not easily distinguishable from u and so could use one sign for two sounds. There are about 200 inscriptions in this alphabet, divisible into two groups, the southern from the district of Taranto, Brindisi, and Lecce, the northern from the neighbourhood of Lucera. Although the majority are third or fourth century BC, some appear to be much earlier, perhaps even from the period around 700. The Tarentine alphabet may have exercised some influence, for instance in shaping the Messapian lambda; but the view of Whatmough[41] that the Tarentine is actually the source of the Messapian seems impossible.

An archaic Greek alphabet of Red type was also directly copied for the inscriptions of both northern and southern Picenum, some of which have very ancient forms and 'ductus' and quite certainly go back to the seventh century. They have all the internal consonants and the Greek o, many parallel forms for the remaining vowels, and a variant of the symbol V (like that used in Umbrian); there are no special signs for ph, ps, and kh. It seems certain that the Picene alphabet was derived from the actual Greek model which with certain modifications served as a basis for the Atestine script and for writing in North Etruscan dialects.

Yet although the Atestine and Venetic inscriptions, and also those from the various North Etruscan regions, are derived from the same Greek model as the Picene texts, they cannot have been copied from it directly, but only through the medium of an alphabet constructed to meet the requirements of the Etruscan language. This intermediate language is not, however, to be confused with the one adopted in Etruria proper. It seems to have been employed before the Etruscans of Tuscany exercised their hegemony in the Po valley. For this view there is evidence in the letters incised on the bronzes discovered in the 'foundry of San Francesco' near Bologna, which go back to the seventh century: some internal consonants are missing, the alphabet has an o sign as well as a u, and it does not employ the Etruscan signs ⊞ and 8 . It is consequently Etruscoid, but markedly different from the Etruscan alphabet properly so called. The Atestine alphabet lists are of Etruscoid origin, for they do not possess all the letters needed for satisfactory recording of the Venetic language; and the model used for the North Etruscan inscriptions in the Bolzano, Magré, Sondrio, and Lugano dialects, where these letters are also missing, seems to have been Etruscoid too. Yet the markedly hybrid character of these texts, which contain partly Etruscan words, but partly also Ligurian or Celtic or Illyrian, would have made the use of internal consonants desirable; and in fact these letters are found in the latest Sondrio-type texts, which have been influenced by Latin. The original model, however, was ancient: this is proved not only by the signs on the 'foundry' inscriptions, but from the *boustrophedon* writing and other features.

Most scholars now seem to be agreed that the North Etruscan alphabets were models, in their turn, for the earliest writing of the Germanic peoples of northern Europe, with its 'runic' characters. Of these the earliest surviving examples, the inscriptions on the Negau helmet and (if it is genuine) the pen from Saalerberg in Carinthia, seem to be second century BC; but the writing is *boustrophedon* or alternatively from right to left, and such archaic features make it likely that the characters were employed from the sixth century at latest. No other explanation of the origin of runic writing carries conviction.

Latium and Latin Alphabets. The Greek alphabet was the parent of others of comparatively minor significance, like those of the Siculi, Sicani, and Elymians in Sicily. But the derivation of the Latin alphabet from the Cumaean was more important than any other process, for it spread over a vast area and allowed methods of writing to develop all over the world.

The oldest documents in Latin alphabets are the well-known inscribed *fibula* of the seventh century from Praeneste, and two fifth-century texts from Rome, the *boustrophedon cippus* of the Forum, and the inscription on the 'Duenos' vase.

The presence of signs for internal d and for o is enough to show that the Latin alphabet derived directly from a Greek original and not through the medium of Etruscan. The parallels adduced to prove dependence on Etruscan are for the most part misconceived, in the present author's opinion, since the alphabets assumed to have been the model were not Etruscan but Greek, like that of the Marsigliana. Moreover it is plain that in the period before the Etruscan domination of Latium, which belongs to the late seventh and the whole of the sixth centuries, the Latin peoples took their alphabet from the Greeks of Campania, with whom they were in direct contact.

All the same it may be that the subsequent Etruscan domination in Latium affected the development of the Latin alphabet in some of its details, for instance in its use of c for k and g and in its names for the letters. One characteristic in the texts which have come down to us is that three signs from the Greek model are not used, namely Θ, ϕ, ψ, though they are preserved as arithmetical signs with the values of 100, 1000, and 50.

The Faliscan dialect, from Falerii, where the earliest document seems to go back to the sixth century, has a status of its own. It shows differences from the Latin alphabet in its signs for f, z, h, r, and t; and like some other Italian alphabets it preserves the archaic system of writing from right to left. It disappears with the Roman conquest in 241 BC.

c. *Ancient Writing in America*

A brief note must be made about the earliest methods of writing in the American continents. Their chronology cannot be precisely determined, and we shall therefore not return to the subject in Parts II and III.

Above all we must mention certain mnemonic devices, like the notching of sticks. There were the *quipus* or *kipus*, found especially in Peru and Bolivia, which consist of a collection of strings of different colours, with various types of knot either single or in groups: these were genuine *aides-mémoire* for arithmetical data, for calculating the days or for matters of statistical importance. There were the *wampum* of the Iroquois in North America which consist of figured and striped embroidery. In North America too there were pictorial ideograms, carved mainly on rocks, which were used to illustrate story-telling and to keep records of arithmetical data: these often contain representational figures with syllabic equivalents and look like actual word-puzzles. Finally there are the illustrated books of Panama, Colombia, etc., which helped in the recitation of magical and religious texts.

But the Mayas and Aztecs of Mexico in early days possessed real books made of folded bark: these were covered with pictograms for ritual purposes, with calendars for divination, with tribute registers and with annalistic records. They also had *stelae* inscribed in bas-relief, on which pictographic and syllabic elements are found side by side.

But in all this the only objects likely to belong to late antiquity are a bas-relief on a *stele* at Vera Cruz and an inscribed plaque now at Leyda. These are assigned by some scholars to the period around AD 320.

d. *Writing Materials*

No ancient Chinese manuscript has been preserved. Bones and tortoise-shells were inscribed for purposes connected with divination, and bronze vases mainly for religious usages. But the normal writing materials were tablets of wood and bamboo; these had made their appearance under the Shang dynasty, as can be seen from a pictogram of Anyang showing a bundle of tablets held together by strings and representing 'book' or 'writing'. The damp climate of northern China has prevented any of these tablets from being preserved.

Originally the Chinese wrote with a bamboo reed sharpened and cut like a pen: the matter written with this had to be of uniform thickness. On the bones employed in divination characters were incised with a metal point. But the writing-brush, although its invention is traditionally ascribed to Meng-T'ien under the Ch'in dynasty (third century BC), already existed in the twelfth century. It is not only represented on a pictogram of Anyang, but at least three bones and a potsherd carry characters traced with a brush. So Meng-T'ien did no more than perfect the shape and composition of an instrument which was already in being.

Writing materials in the Middle Eastern and classical worlds were very varied. One reason was that after the invention and spread of alphabetic methods the use of writing proportionately increased, and consequently also demanded lower-priced material even if it was more perishable. Naturally the increase in written documents and the lower price of writing material went hand-in-hand with the increase in the number of readers.

We start, then, with writings carved with chisels or similar instruments on rocks or plates or stone and marble *stelae*. They might also be cut on the fronts of buildings, or on tablets of bronze, copper, lead, or precious metal, and later on coins and weights; or again they could be scratched or tooled on tablets and seals of unbaked clay or terracotta. To these were now added other writings achieved in diverse ways.

Some were traced with the *stilus* on smooth wooden tablets, or on tablets smeared with white paint (*tabulae dealbatae*) or coloured. Others were written with the small reed called a 'calamus', and with ink (*atramentum*), on light and plastic material. Leaves of papyrus pulp, or some similar substance, are an example (cf. the *Charta Fanniana* mentioned by Pliny, *N.H.*, XIII, 11, 21); and there was writing on olive leaves (the petalism at Syracuse for instance), on linen bandages (especially those used as coverings for

mummified corpses in Egypt), on earthenware sherds (*ostraka*) and so on.
Later on Phoenician influence was particularly responsible for the use of
calf-skin for expensive documents; and sheepskin (*Pergamena*) came in from
Pergamum in Asia Minor. Skins were used for inscribing the ancient treaty
between Rome and Gabii and also for a cypher employed at Sparta:[42] for the
latter strips of skin were wrapped in a spiral on to a cylinder of given size
and then inscribed, in such way that they could only be read if they were
wrapped once more round an identical cylinder (*scutalē*).

In ancient Egypt it was already the custom, when one wanted to write a
complete document or a definitive part of a work, to paste one pressed
papyrus leaf (*byblos*) on to another and so to construct long strips; these
were wrapped together into a roll (*volumen*) and kept in a store (*thēcē*).
Herodotus (II, 92) speaks of this device, though he does not tell us when
Greece acquired it: probably it penetrated to Ionia in the days of Polycrates
of Samos in the sixth century, and to the rest of Greece about 500. Where
tablets or smoothed skins were used, they were joined together into *codices*;
and these, on account of their high price, were often used more than once,
the first set of writings being cancelled and a further set being written over
them (*palimpsest*).

For the material used in ancient American writings see p. 100.

e. *Archives and Libraries*

As written documents, both public and private, became more common,
and as literary output increased, it was necessary to consider better ways of
preserving and consulting writings, by bringing them together in suitable
places. The classes of documents in question were varied and important.
The earliest which it was essential to construct and preserve were state
treaties, laws and decrees, administrative acts, records of foreign relations,
chronicles both lay and sacerdotal, the acts of kings, and the lists of priests
and magistrates. All these were written on relatively durable material, and
were collected in royal palaces, or in temple precincts and sacristies, or in
the seats of magistrates and of public assemblies.

Collections of official documents of these kinds are known from finds.
In Egypt the so-called Tell el Amarna archives (fourteenth century) contained
the correspondence with subject regions and neighbouring powers from the
time of Amenhotep III. In Crete we have the archives of the Minoan
palaces, and in the Hittite empire the archives of the kings and leading cities.

In the ensuing period proper libraries came into being, or at any rate
departments for the preservation of literature which adjoined the archives.
One of the most characteristic libraries known to us is that of Ashur-banipal
(668–630), who put on to its contents his stamp of ownership, his 'ex libris'.
Among these are 30,000 tablets of documents contained in chests arranged
on shelves. These include receipts, levy lists, and his official and private

correspondence. But in addition there are pieces of epic and mythological poems; of liturgies and prayers; of magical writings, psalms, oaths, and auguries; of annals, chronicles, and lists of dates; of works on grammar and dictionaries; and of astronomical calculations, tables of weights, and other arithmetical writings. The king had sent scribes to many places to copy ancient tablets. Another noteworthy library is that of Nippur; and there were others owned by private persons and by temples.

These Assyrian archives and libraries probably had their precursors at Babylon and Boğazköy. They were followed by similar institutions in the Persian capitals, among which we know best the one instituted at Persepolis in the days of Darius I.

The first collections of literature, and therefore the first libraries, in the Greek world must have been made in the time of the sixth-century tyrants, Polycrates of Samos and the Peisistratids of Athens. Later on we are told of libraries belonging to individual literary men, of whom the first is Euripides.

At the same time archives to preserve copies of important private documents were on the increase. Examples of such documents are conveyances, boundary plans, manumissions, adoptions, and wills.

f. *Writing and Schooling*

Education and the system of schools were also feeling the effect of writing, and of written documents and work.

In early days the traditional ideas about religion and techniques were learned in the family, or in priestly colleges, or in unions of artisans, by means of mnemonic methods. The teaching was oral, and the pupils committed to memory what they learned. In our period this was still the stage reached in education in India. The Indian system of education was developing along clearly defined lines. Writing was not used for religious purposes, and oral tradition was therefore completely supreme: yet instruction was confined to sacred matters. The study of the *Veda* was given only to the first three castes, the *Śūdra* being excluded. From the beginning we see the sacred texts being taught by a master and repeated by the pupils in chorus 'like the croaking of frogs' (Ṛigveda, VII, 103). In Vedic times the religious students (*Brāhmacārin*) were the educated class of India.

Their duties were to study the *Veda*, to serve their Brahmin masters (*guru*), and to maintain chastity. In very early times the acceptance of a student into a school was conditioned by a complicated initiation ceremony, the *upanayana*, through which the pupil received his second (spiritual) birth and was therefore twice-born (*dvija*). In the Late Vedic period supplementary subjects, such as mathematics, grammar, and prosody, were added to the curriculum. Education was originally confined to the Brahmans, but was widened as time went on to include the *Kṣattriya* and *Vaiśya* too: towards the end of our period a genuine intellectual aristocracy came into being, with the *Kṣattriya* occupying a position at least equal to that of the Brahmans. These are the circles in which Upanisadic thought took shape. The *sūtra* of Late Vedic times prescribe a detailed curriculum, which already embraced all traditional Indian knowledge, that is to say the six *Vedāṅga* (phonetics, ritual, grammar, etymology, prosody, astronomy), together with other ancillary sciences.

With other peoples, however, the use of writing became an aid to education at an earlier stage. With some the basis of education remained theocratic, for instance in Egypt or among the Hebrews—especially after the Captivity, when it was carried on in synagogues. On the other hand in the Graeco-Roman world lay education predominated; it was sometimes private and sometimes public, the many forms it assumed being dictated by the varying bents and environments of the different peoples.

Within the precocious culture of the Ionian Greeks we find a form apparently already known in the Homeric poems, which was intermediate between instruction at home and instruction at school, and which was provided by a 'pedagogue' privately employed. Side by side with this there existed the genuine school, where physical education (the *palestra*) was originally the main feature but gradually tended to get separated from instruction in music and grammar. A law of Charondas mentioned by Diodorus (XII, 12–13) is often cited as evidence that masters were paid by the state and experiments in compulsory education were already known in the seventh century; but in all probability this is not the original law made at Catana, but a revision of it made in the middle of the fifth century at Thurii. Doubt has also been cast on the passage of Aeschines purporting to describe Solonian legislation on education. The first certain case of a state school, recorded by Plutarch, relates to Troezen in 480. Meanwhile particular importance was assumed by the schools of a domestic, or professional, nature which were gradually created to preserve and advance the writings of various groups—the Epic poets (Homeridai), the doctors (in the Asclepieia), the philosophers, and the mathematicians (cf. the Pythagoreans).

The Dorian world, Sparta or Crete for example, presents a contrast. There, at any rate from the ninth or seventh century onwards, the paramount feature was a militarist education provided by the state; and letters were sacrificed in favour of physical and athletic instruction.

A characteristic instance of individual arrangements is provided by archaic Rome. After the end of the domination exercised in the sixth century by the more civilized Etruscans, the well-to-do families preserved the custom of sending their sons to get instruction at Caere.

NOTES TO CHAPTER II

1. The processes of ethnogenesis cannot be reduced exclusively to linguistic processes, although a common language is, of course, an important feature of any ethnic group. Ethnogenesis is primarily a social process, involving the formation of nationalities out of individual tribes and tribal federations. For this reason problems of ethnogenesis and glottogony are directly linked with the problems involved in the formation of a class society and also, in many cases, with conquest and linguistic assimilation.

   The concept of the racial group (i.e. the anthropological characteristics of the ethnos) is confused here—and throughout the chapter—with the concept of the linguistic family (i.e. the linguistic characteristics of the ethnos). But the linguistic characteristics of a particular ethnic group need not correspond with the supposed anthropological characteristics: neither of them are static or incapable of further development and modification. (K. M. Kolobova.)

2. Professor K. M. Kolobova makes the important point that in many cases only the upper section of a conquered people will become bilingual as a result of the adoption of their conqueror's language for official acts. This may well be the case with Late Minoan Crete, with Syria and Anatolia in Achaemenid times, or perhaps with various parts of Italy down to the first century B C. It seems valid for Egypt at almost all periods, and perhaps also for certain provinces of the Roman empire.

3. So, too, Sir Leonard Woolley, *History of Mankind*, vol. I, part 2, p. 387. Another possibility is the European region lying roughly between Thuringia and Kiev. See also P. Bosch-Gimpera, *El problema indoeuropeo* (Mexico, 1960, also in French translation), where the author argues against a single area of origin but favours districts of central and eastern Europe.

4. It is not certain that the term embraces the people whom comparative philology has regarded as the common ancestors of Indians and Iranians; the classification of countries given in the *Avesta* (*Vidēvdad* I) is not necessarily a genuine memory of an 'Indo-Iranian' past, given the late character of the written text (see below).

5. This classification could be disputed. Some scholars would include Thracian, Phrygian, and perhaps Illyrian in the eastern group, and Tokharic has strong claim to be considered western. On Phrygian see again p. 62.

6. These bilingual texts are very short, but they seem to confirm an interpretation of the language which had earlier been made on the strength of its similarity to Hurrian.

7. This is the view of many earlier scholars (cf. *Cambridge Ancient History*, III (1929), p. 187), but is, in Professor F. W. König's view, very doubtful.

8. The texts in question are concerned almost solely with proper names.

9. Some Indian scholars have tried to prove an Indian origin for the Indo-European languages and the people who carried them abroad: see the summary of their arguments by Srikanth Sastri in R. C. Majumdar and A. C. Pusalker, *History and Culture of the Indian People*, I, *The Vedic Languages* (London, 1951), pp. 215–17. But they have received little support in India and none in other countries.

10. The word 'Gimirri' appears in the Babylonian translation of the Achaemenid inscriptions, but (as Professor F. W. König points out) it is doubtful whether this really proves a relationship, particularly a linguistic relationship, between the Scyths and the Cimmerians.

11. Professor F. W. König is sceptical about the traces of this language in 'Armenian texts', i.e. in such writers as Moses of Chosroene.

12. The view that Venetia was colonized from Illyria was supported by J. Whatmough, *The Prae-Italic Dialects* (London, 1933), pp. 1–201, but is strongly contested by M. Beeler, *The Venetic Language* (Berkeley, 1949), and by H. Krahe, *Sitzungsberichte Heidelberg* (1950), p. 3.

13. Professor Pareti is here probably thinking of Iron Age Greek settlement in Cyprus, though his date 1000 B C seems unduly late for activity which must have formed part

of the great 'Achaean' migrations. There is also, as Professor Ch. Th. Saricakis emphasizes, evidence of much earlier contact between Cyprus and people commonly thought to be Greek: a Minoan script has been found at Enkomi, cf. N. Hammond, *A History of Greece* (Oxford, 1959), p. 32.

14. See above, p. 52, note 5.

15. Unfortunately it is now fairly clear that the issue posed by Professor Pareti has now been resolved, and in a manner adverse to his thesis. There are still some scholars who recognize Ionic elements in the Linear B language, but none who makes any claim for Doric: a usual view is that the language is 'Arcado-Cyprian'. See, for example, M. Ventris and J. Chadwick, *Documents in Mycenaean Greek* (London, 1956), pp. 67 ff.; E. Risch, 'Frühgeschichte der griechischen Sprache' in *Museum Helveticum* (1959), pp. 215 ff.; L. R. Palmer, *Mycenaeans and Minoans* (London, 1961), pp. 143 ff.

16. It would be difficult, however, to connect the writings of these authors with spoken Laconian.

17. This inscription is undoubtedly early, but may belong to the early fifth century rather than to the sixth.

18. Herodotus is here claiming that certain rivers flow from the Umbrian country into the Danube. It must be regarded as dubious whether his confused geography reflects an earlier settlement of the Umbrians in the Alpine region, especially as another passage (I, 94) makes the Etruscans arrive by sea in the Umbrian territory and therefore (on any view) surely shows awareness of the Umbrian settlement in central Italy.

19. The theory that the Etruscans migrated from the north is not generally accepted, and the question of their origin remains for the present a debatable one. But see Appendix to Chapter I (M. W. Frederiksen.)

20. See M. Pallottino, *Etruscologia* (Milan, 1955), with bibliography.

21. For detail, see J. Whatmough, *The Foundations of Roman Italy* (London, 1937), pp. 132 ff.

22. This date will be discussed in the chapter on literature; VI, pp. 273 ff.

23. See Whatmough, *op. cit.*, pp. 129 ff.

24. For this form of classification, see H. Krahe, *Indo-Germanische Sprachwissenschaft* (Berlin, 1958), I, pp. 26 ff.

25. For Hallstatt and La Tène, see p. 54, note 32.

26. For a different analysis of Celtic dialects, see R. G. Collingwood, *Oxford History of England*, I (1936), pp. 18 ff.

27. What Caesar says he was told is that *plerosque Belgas esse ortos ab Germanis, Rhenumque antiquitus traductos propter loci fertilitatem ibi consedisse, Gallosque qui ea loca incolerent expulisse.* This has commonly been taken to mean that the Belgae came across the Rhine, from the north, and expelled the existing Celtic settlers. Professor Pareti argues that Caesar does not bring the Belgae, as such, from the north: he means rather that the original Belgic invaders (who were Celts arriving from the south-east as part of a substantial Gallic invasion datable to *c.* 500 BC) later suffered an admixture from Germans who came across the Rhine from the north. The full argument is given in his articel in *Atti della reale Accademia d'Italia* (1943), pp. 203 ff.

28. Professor P. Bosch-Gimpera insists that Hallstatt remains, in Great Britain and probably in Ireland too, are only to be explained by a Celtic invasion well before 500 BC. See also R. G. Collingwood, *op. cit.*, p. 21.

29. On the many controversial questions surrounding Celtic migrations, see P. Bosch-Gimpera in *Études Celtiques* (Paris, 1950–55). The account given by Livy, who dated the beginning of the invasion of Italy to the early sixth century, is described by J. de Navarro (*Cambridge Ancient History*, VII (1930), pp. 41ff.) as 'a tissue of inaccuracies'. But Professor Pareti's view that the first crossings of the Alps must have occurred long before 400 BC has surely much to commend it, although there are reasons (elaborated by Navarro) for thinking that the passes used were in the Brenner group rather than in the west.

30. In Professor P. Bosch-Gimpera's view the main Celtic immigration into Spain, which doubtless came in many waves, had been completed long before 450 BC.

31. As Professor K. M. Kolobova points out, the language commonly known as 'Assyrian' is in fact identical with Accadian.

32. This song, and also Miriam's song, are possibly as early as the thirteenth century BC.

33. Professor K. M. Kolobova insists that this connection is very difficult to contest, and it is certainly true that the Semitic, ancient Egyptian, and Libyco-Berber languages have in common certain very significant phenomena of grammar, and that in addition Semitic and Hamitic numerals are connected with one another. See the summary by F. Lexa 'Philologica', *Journal of Comparative Philology* (1922), pp. 151–77. Professor Pareti's view is perhaps related to that of C. Brockelmann, *Anthropos* (1932), pp. 797 ff., who suggested that the affinities were due only to borrowings by one language from another. But though borrowing could account for the relatively limited number of agreements in vocabulary, it is most difficult to believe that a language would have borrowed grammatical phenomena as fundamental as those illustrated by Lexa: experience shows that the grammar of a language remains unaffected even though it may borrow countless words from another (as English has from Greek). It remains likely therefore that people with Semitic grammar invaded North Africa, probably before the earliest Egyptian historical records (well before 3000 BC) and that the large number of non-Semitic words in later Libyco (or Hamitic) vocabulary was due to complicated sound-changes or to massive borrowings from the language of the substratum in the area.

34. Professor F. W. König emphasizes that this script has not yet been read: all we can say is that two scripts were used in Elamite territory by the side of Sumeric cuneiform.

35. Professor F. W. König points out that the number 113 is that of the characters used in Elamite translations of inscriptions belonging to the period around 500 BC. Before the Achaemenid period the number was doubtless much greater.

36. See *History of Mankind*, vol. I, part 2, p. 658.

37. The view that phonetic characters were unknown during the Yin and only appeared during the Chou is a highly debatable one. Yin inscriptions have enabled specialists (Hu Hou-hsuan) to make out several phonetic characters among Yin signs. (L. S. Vasilyev.)

38. The oldest Hebrew alphabet was a variant of the Phoenician alphabet. (K. M. Kolobova).

39. But see above, p. 53, note 14.

40. See especially *Studien zur Geschichte des griechischen Alphabets* (Gütersloh, 1887), pp. 119 ff.

41. *The Prae-Italic Dialects of Italy*, II (Oxford, 1933), pp. 531 ff.

42. Gabii treaty, Dion. Hal., IV, 58, 4; Spartan *scutalē*, Thucydides, I, 131, 1 with scholiast's comment.

CHAPTER III

TECHNOLOGY; TRADE; SCIENCE

I. THE MAJOR TECHNIQUES[1]

SOME people, fortunate in their circumstances and helped by their own efforts, reach a superior level of civilization in technical development, in commercial enterprises, and in spiritual and artistic life. When they have reached this level they fulfil the task of spreading their own culture to the neighbouring people with whom they come in contact. They establish an advance guard for human development and, as the history of their generation dictates, one after another pass on the torch of knowledge.

Then there are the people who form an intermediate group. Such vitality as their way of life permits is derived from the first group; and their rate of progress, often very slow, depends on the strength and regularity of these influences from outside.

Finally there will be others, the rear-guard, peripheral people living for millennia in almost unchanged and static conditions. They repeat, without apparent development, their activities according to primeval systems thousands of years old. There will even be cases of people who go backwards as a result of worsening conditions around them, as happened to the Bushmen when they became impoverished.

The chance nature of archaeological finds, especially in the more backward areas of civilization, and the still often insuperable difficulty in fixing synchronisms in development, naturally oblige us often to content ourselves with approximate data. But for the greater part of the 'rear-guard' people, even without archaeological data, we can accept the general assumption that they must have been at a level no higher—perhaps even lower—than that attained today or in periods near our time.

So the inhabitants of vast zones were living then, as later, in a 'primitive' manner by hunting, fishing, and gathering the fruits of the earth; for a long period they ate these in their natural state, and then gradually learnt methods to improve conservation and assimilation of their food (milling, dry-curing, cooking, etc.). Gathering fruits must have been the rule, for example, for the inhabitants of the equatorial forests of central Africa, Ceylon, Malacca, Sumatra, and Brazil. On the other hand in the temperate zones, in the more or less deserted steppes of South Africa, Australia, or northern Eurasia, hunting must have predominated, with pits, traps, arrows, or spears; with temporary halts in such periods and places as the 'one-way traffic' of game dictates. Again, along the beaches and the banks of the rivers, especially in the sub-Arctic area, the basis of life must have been fishing. Finally in the

Arctic zone man is forced to regulate his existence by the only means that nature offers, namely by hunting reindeer, and capturing whales and seals: in these regions life must always have been the same at all times.

Among a number of peoples, however, hunting and fishing would be mainly carried on by the men and the gathering of fruits by the women, provided climate and the ratio between the sexes allowed: in this way the two types of occupation would be complementary. Moreover gathering must have been made easier by the use of certain tools: a rod for knocking down fruit; and a pointed pole and a hoe, either all wood or ending in a smoothed stone, for drawing roots and tubers from the ground.

The people who even to this day live chiefly from hunting, fishing, and gathering were undoubtedly nomadic or even simple wanderers, although the scope and regularity of their wanderings varied with their numbers and their environment. Increase in population would lead to excessive exploitation of an area and force major displacements upon its inhabitants; and climatic change would modify the characteristics of its flora and fauna. Human movement on the steppes and prairies of the temperate zones must have normally been wide and irregular, for game there tends to be abundant but very mobile. In the wet and wooded country of the tropics game is scarcer but more stationary, and human movement is likely to have ranged less far. In the polar and sub-polar regions life is seasonal, and therefore only partly nomadic; for in the winter months the fauna emigrate and fishing too becomes less easy.

Where human groups became thicker, and were not constantly fighting each other, each tribe or clan came to possess territory of its own, vast but with definite boundaries, inside which they would move around as occasion demanded. This state of affairs, however, was upset every time one of the groups wanted to break the conventional barriers and seek its own advantage by raiding and the use of force.

The nomadism of the people who already used domesticated animals had assumed peculiar aspects. In the temperate or sub-polar zones in which they mainly raised herbivorous and gregarious animals (cows, sheep, goats, horses, reindeer), opportunities for grazing depended on the varying supplies of vegetation on the steppes, mountain, or tundra; and these supplies in turn depended on the mean temperature of the country at various seasons, and upon its latitude and height. This compelled the herdsmen and their flocks to move about in search of food according to the weather. On the other hand in the deserts and steppes movements could only take place in the rainy periods; in the dry seasons they had to settle where there were permanent sources of water, such as oases and pools. These people, then, became only partly nomadic.

Nomadic movement could of course for incidental reasons such as war, pressure from foreign migrations, or meteorological catastrophes, turn into a regular migration to completely new geographical surroundings. This might decisively influence the general conditions of a people, quickening their development, or entirely changing their habits and customs: for example, inhabitants of the steppes might become forest-dwellers, mountain people plainsmen, men from the interior coastal-dwellers; or people accustomed to mild climates might find themselves in extreme ones or the other way round.

But man's environment, and with it his food, his lodging, and his social life, decisively change when instead of remaining 'nature's parasite' he decides to overcome the natural conditions around him, securing his food, whatever those conditions may be, by appropriate means invented by his brain. In this way domestication of animals and agricultural technique were born, both probably originating in temperate regions.

Very probably there was no fixed or logical connection between the origins of agriculture and of domestication. Different peoples may have taken up the two institutions with varying degrees of vigour, since each responds to distinct motives and needs; in any case the one was initially the concern mainly of women, the other mainly of men.

Primitive people got their food by gathering wild vegetables, which they might (or might not) put into store. Agriculture was born when certain peoples thought of making collection easier by controlling crops within definite areas through operations at appropriate seasons. Domestication of animals, on the other hand, came about in two ways. Hunters, instead of trusting to chance to find their prey, used the right kind of animal to help them in the chase; and secondly men saw that they could guarantee themselves supplies of food and other useful animal products at all seasons and weathers by keeping at their side other types of animals, which provided meat and produce of various kinds.

Later on close links naturally developed between the two occupations, agriculture and pasturage, which as time went on were both taken over by the male sex, except (in the main) for horticulture and the use of the hoe. Human existence and the growth of population were both decisively affected thereby.

There were undoubtedly regions, such as China, Egypt, Mesopotamia, Asia Minor, Greece, the colonies of Phoenicia and Carthage, Etruria, and Rome, from which successive advances in agriculture were communicated to other peoples.[2] But the problem of the birthplace of agriculture itself is not our direct concern.[3] Rather, however, than accept the proposition of a single zone from which it spread to others we are inclined to believe in polygenesis: for example it appears certain that soft grains were first cultivated in south-west Asia, hard grains in the eastern hills of Africa, and husked grains in the eastern Mediterranean.

Even in the periods with which we are dealing there must still have been people who did not know more than the first steps in agriculture. Either they pushed live roots or the seeds of food-bearing plants into the soil with a stick; or they cleared the ground with an axe and drained the marshland, to grow cereals, vegetables, and roots; or they used a sickle to cut fodder from the meadows for their beasts. They would move periodically from ground that seemed to be exhausted. Other people, however, used casual manure from wandering animals, and then, later, a regular supply from cattle which had been enclosed; this, together with the first simple irrigation systems, succeeded in making the land more consistently fertile; and they eventually attained a more advanced and intensive system of horticulture. Still others, perceiving the possibility of using animals for draught, had transformed the primitive rake or hoe into a plough which could be drawn. Ploughing, even in its simplest forms, made it possible to cultivate increasingly large areas and grow the cereals needed to feed the higher populations resulting from more settled existence. From then on were established those links of affection between man and the land he occupies. They led to one of the highest concepts, that of patriotism.

Naturally the phases just described had been surpassed for a long time in the more civilized areas. But these were always different from one another; each had typical products and typical systems of cultivation.

In Egypt, where the fertility of the soil was helped by soil-irrigation and by human labour, cereal production (wheat, barley, and millet) was such as to allow exports; at the same time there were also remarkable results in hemp, flax, and vegetables.

In the coastal districts of Syria, which were mountainous and less adapted to cereals, the great developments had been in gardening, fruit-growing (cedars, vines, olives), and in the systematic use of conifer woods from which the materials for constructing ships and buildings were derived; so skilful were the Phoenicians, and their Punic colonies,4 at agriculture that they produced early didactic treatises on the subject, such as that by Mago, in the third century BC, and they gave marked importance to agricultural products and timber in their complex maritime trade. In the plains of the Syrian interior, on the other hand, they cultivated barley, vines, olives, and figs, and in the less fertile regions they raised stock. In the Mesopotamian area, much of the country was irrigated by canals, the holdings were very much spread out, and the inhabitants were proud of their grains; but arboriculture was rare and the olive practically non-existent. In Persia gardening, the cultivation of cereals, and pasturing of animals flourished at the same time. In India the scale of agricultural production was even more extensive: it included rice, wheat, barley, vegetables, citrus fruits, cotton, sugar cane, coco, and spice plants.

Greece had above all a population of fishermen and cattle-breeders; and although many attempts were made to expand the cultivable upland areas by terracing, the land was too barren to support a heavy population by agriculture. For this reason it had soon to import foodstuffs, giving in exchange wine, oil, and the products of its manufacturers and artists. None the less agriculture was considered the 'mother and nurse of all the arts' even in the more industrial areas such as Attica and Samos, and it was still the most respected occupation, while land-owning was regarded as the basis for citizenship, and for belonging to the highest social class. For this reason didactic writing interested itself at an early stage in agricultural life, as is shown by Hesiod's *Works and Days*. Technically there was no great progress because the small holdings, except in Thessaly and in Macedonia, were worked superficially with wooden ploughs, which gradually received iron ploughshares, and were mainly sown with barley and emmer. Wheat was confined to the more fertile regions with a primitive system of crop rotation. But the products of its olives and vineyards were fundamental to Greece.

The Greek colonies in Magna Graecia gave an impetus to cereal culture in the flatter areas, from Tarentum to Thurii and in Campania; to viticulture and olive-growing in all the more hilly zones; to forestry and pasturage in the mountain regions. Sicily under Greek colonization early became a famous exporter of cereals; but was concerned also with viticulture and olive-growing, and with the livestock produce attested by its export of cheese and skins.

In the Po valley and in the central districts of Italy the greatest advances in agricultural techniques were made by the Etruscans. Having lived earlier, according to our view, in *palafitte* and *terramare*,5 among the lakes and in artificial lake-type stations planted in alluvial zones, they became experts in dam building, in canal cutting, and in reclaiming land both by drainage and by underground tunnels; the latter they used extensively in Latium, which was marshy in the period of their domination. From the time they lived in the *palafitte* they cultivated emmer, barley, and wheat. They had knowledge of the vine; and as breeders they took care of their pasture land.

Among the other peoples of Italian type, the high population of the Latins, who lived in a large number of villages, on soil not richly endowed by nature, shows the development their agriculture had attained. It is true that the marshland of Latium was not yet malarial and that the Etruscans, who became its overlords, worked at reclaiming these lands; moreover the woods were much thicker so that the tufa of the plain was better covered by humus and was not washed away by rain; and the hills of volcanic origin were suitable for vines. That animal-rearing and agriculture were equally cared for was brought about by many factors. The most usual products were emmer, barley, and (later) wheat as well as beans, garlic, onions, figs, olives, and grapes. The ground was cultivated with a primitive type of plough and with the spade.

It is well known that domestication normally affects animals of gregarious habits, and those which are relatively trustful of men. These animals were used for their flesh, milk, hides, and horns; and also for the help they gave to men's work, in drawing, carrying, and performing various agricultural tasks. With domestication men began to limit their freedom. Their feeding habits were altered and regulated, their reproduction was supervised and directed. But much of the harshness of their struggle for existence was removed.

Domestication of several animal species, such as dogs, sheep, cattle, and goats, was probably invented and organized in many countries, without one depending on another. These species were wild in many parts of the world; and there were many tribes which had attained, especially through agriculture with the hoe, the degree of sedentary life which suggests that their movements were confined to the narrow radius required by domesticated flocks and herds.

Later every people, either through their own initiative or through the influence of others, developed methods to suit themselves, increasing the number of domesticated animals in accordance with their needs. Some remained tied to a few types and to an archaic system; others, more advanced in civilization, evolved more complex forms. The first animal to be domesticated (sometimes perhaps self-domesticated) seems to have been the dog: at the outset perhaps from affection, and then as a help to hunters and as a guardian of flocks. But there must have been peripheral people, like the Tasmanians in recent times, who were quite ignorant of even this form of domestication.

The breeding of cattle, which had reached a high stage of development at the beginning of the Bronze Age, must have undergone some setback at its end, when, for example, the domesticated buffalo disappeared among the Assyrians.

Pig-breeding spread from Asia to Europe, accompanied by the mating of sows from Asia with the local wild boars. The horse, little adapted to marshland and wooded areas, must originally have been domesticated in the Eurasian steppes. From there the Indo-Europeans (whose languages show that they knew the horse before they dispersed) brought the animal to both Europe and Asia; the Turkish peoples were also responsible for its diffusion. Local breeds were domesticated in every region afterwards, even those too small to be used for riding (cf. Herodotus, V, 9). Bones found in the *palafitte* sites make it very likely that in early times the horse was used for its meat and for its by-products. Then it became a transport animal, as is shown by the bits for small horses discovered also in the *palafitte*, and also by a pre-Mycenaean relief on silver from the island of Syros in the Aegean; at the same time hunting and raiding and warrior people found in the horse a rapid means of transport when they used it as a mount. The use of horses spread when the Hyksos, Hittites, Cimmerians, and Scyths used them in their raids; they are domesticated in Babylonia from the twelfth century at latest, and in Assyria at latest from the ninth; but mules were already made use of here during the third millennium.[6]

In other zones and climates there were domestic animals comparable to the horse. Reindeer were used in the western parts of northern Eurasia, at least from about 900 BC; and the Asiatic elephant was used in India for agriculture, though only later for war. The inhabitants of Africa proved incapable of domesticating the local elephant; the Atlantic sub-species was tamed at a relatively late period by the Carthaginians.

At various periods the domestic camel of Bactria spread through the surrounding areas, while the dromedary had its first home in Africa and Arabia. In the Andes the llama and alpaca were domesticated; in Mexico the guinea pig. Poultry breeding was found everywhere, based sometimes on local species and sometimes on imported breeds; and bees were kept in many areas for both their honey and their wax.[7]

We may now review rapidly countries which progressed fastest. In Egypt dogs were bred for hunting; oxen, both of northern and of southern breed, for meat and other products and as draught animals; sheep, both local and Asiatic were also bred; asses were used as beasts of burden and for threshing. Regular use of the camel was earlier than that of the dromedary; the horse was employed in battle at the time of the Hyksos rule, but only came into normal use as a beast of burden later. The domestic goose was widely known but later became, perhaps, less common.[8]

The Assyrians made marked progress in the domestication of the dog, apparently a type of bull-dog which originated in Tibet. We may note also their domestication of the ox (still more the buffalo), the fat-tailed Asiatic sheep, and the horse. At least from the ninth century they were using camels which spread from there to Asia Minor (Archilochus speaks of them) and to Syria. The Hebrew people showed strong attachment to pastoral life; and they regarded agricultural work as punishment inflicted by a wrathful god.

Use of the horse in warfare was considerably extended by the Persian hegemony; and the Persians used camels as early as in the battle of Sardis in 546. Camels were also widely used throughout arid Arabia, because of their resistance to thirst. Horses in battle are attested for the Lydians and Lycians in the seventh century; but they were already known in the Graeco-Mycenaean world. In Asia horses were used for drawing war chariots, as they were later to be used by the Etruscans; and cavalry must have been used throughout the Celtic and German worlds from early times.

a. *Architecture*

Within the populations who had acquired pastoral habits a part must have lived a relatively sedentary existence; this was probably also true of peoples whose principal means of life lay in gathering fruits, or in hunting or fishing. The gathering might be woman's work; and both that and fishing normally require less movement than hunting. In addition agriculture was beginning; and even in its simplest forms this dictates settlement in one place, at any rate during the seasons of sowing and of harvest. The settlement was relative, for it lasted only as long as a tribe remained in a particular area. But it now became the rule that a people occupied the same stations and shelters, even though they might leave them for a time and return to them later. For even the existence of genuine nomads implies, from very early times, the use of shelters, and of more or less temporary dwellings built with the materials provided by the country: these were needed as a protection against the elements and against wild beasts and other men.

These shelters and huts were of very varied kinds. In the more civilized countries they gradually became stronger and more complicated: in other areas the more primitive and simple forms survived. Even today, particularly in backward countries, dwellings of a type which has been in use for thousands of years are found side by side with others of more recent type. Less civilized peoples, especially in cold climates, were able to protect themselves against the weather in shelters under rocks, or in natural caves; the favourite type had a narrow entrance, sometimes reinforced with piles of rubble, which made them easy to defend. Yet even peoples of advanced civilization made use of dwellings in caves dug by man, which were both cool and strong. Diversity in dwellings was also brought about by climatic differences. In warm regions and on the steppes primitive man would protect himself from the squalls of wind and rain with improvised screens of branches laced together with bark. In tropical countries he set up walls to make a shed and held them in a sloping position by means of props. Two screens or two sheds joined together were the origin of the simple sloping hut, which was open on two sides.

Various forms of circular huts are known, with their foundations sunk some distance in the ground to afford better resistance to excessive cold or heat. The simplest form consists of logs planted in the soil and joined together at the top, the whole being covered with boughs or leaves or straw. Another type involved securing the logs at both ends, and yet another consisted of tree trunks arranged in a conical formation, sometimes of beehive or of cupola shape, and sometimes with the skeleton of logs covered by branches or clay or stone chippings, like the 'trulli' of modern Puglie in Italy. In sub-polar or high mountain regions the cupola was formed of packed snow. From all these early types were derived the circular stone huts with real or sham vaulted roofs, which are found in countries of more developed civilization.

The simple type of house of all later times had its prototype in the rectangular hut with walls composed of beams laid one on top of another and with a sloping roof made of branches and straw. In later days these huts were made more impervious to moisture by constructing their lower portions of packed clay or unbaked bricks or stone and using wood only for the upper portions near the cornice, and for the roof. Such simple houses could be increased in size at will, and could be divided into different sections for the human inhabitants, for animals, and for storage of commodities.

Lastly, the early tree-top shelters led in wooded areas to hanging houses, and in marshland to pile-dwellings (*palafitte*). In mountain country they gave place to houses of half-pile type, in which the slope of the hill was compensated in order to attain a level floor.

At this stage various kinds of dwelling might be found in the same country. Moreover in many regions it was common to alternate existence between two kinds of house: in the colder months men lived in fairly stable houses built together to form a village, while during their agricultural labours they slept in improvised huts in the open country.

We can now survey broadly the features of the various dwellings used in the more civilized areas, where relatively reliable evidence exists for our period.

In China one commonly finds a reception hall, flanked by two sheds with the living rooms inside them; a peculiar characteristic of the Chou dwelling were the walls of beaten earth covered with wooden planks. In India huts made of wood or unbaked brick were the normal form, and terraces were greatly favoured, as in all civilized countries of the East. In the Early Vedic period houses (*harmya*) were made of wood, with bamboo roofs. Building methods are not made clear by our texts, but it seems that houses rested on four pillars, strengthened by posters butting against them. The wooden walls were finished up with rush-mats and turf. The building of a house was by itself a sacred act, and as such was governed by rules in the handbooks on ritual. There were no temples, only sacred areas with altars in the open air.

In the regions which had been Babylonian and in those where the Assyrians ruled there were grand palaces made of massive unbaked brick, faced in places with rectangular blocks of stone, with clearly separated apartments for men and their guests, for women and children, and for servants. But there were also ordinary houses, which were always built of baked or unbaked brick with a coating of straw. Here too terraces are a characteristic feature; and like Syria and Egypt these regions used windows which helped to keep down excessive heat. In the Persian empire, where both Assyrian and Indian influences were felt, terraces are again found, opening from large rooms with columns. In Egypt there was a marked contrast between the houses of the upper classes, which were large and complex, and the tiny dwellings of the common people, packed together in their appointed quarters: the latter sometimes had upper floors and terraces, but were throughout constructed of unbaked brick coated with straw. The Phoenicians used many-storied houses crowded into small areas on very narrow streets, with terraces and open courtyards.

We now come to the Mediterranean part of Europe. The Minoan palaces had been destroyed[9] by the Greek invaders and gave place to the palaces of the Mycenaeans: but they too were abandoned when the monarchies fell. The houses of the aristocratic families were divided into rooms, and there were separate halls (*megara*) for men and women, with at least a corridor between: the houses also opened on to courtyards and terraces, and sometimes there was an upper floor for the slaves. But these houses were surrounded by the simple and modest dwellings of humble people. The latter were still of rounded shape with a conical roof and oval base; they had partitions inside to provide more than one room; and they were normally built of stone, brick and wood. In Italy in the earliest periods of the Iron Age it was common to find round or oval huts, like those discovered on the Palatine and depicted in the shape of early Latian urns: these urns, however, are also often modelled on the rectangular type of hut with sloping roof. In Sicily the native one-roomed houses, round, oval, or rectangular, were often built principally of rubble. But we also find remains there of much larger houses of rectangular shape with at least two rooms, which were probably the homes of the rulers; near by are sometimes groups of huts used by clients.

In the North Etruscan region some lake settlements survived, also some of the *terramare* dwellings on the characteristic pile foundations, with platforms and wooden huts. In the Etruscan area proper the round hut was superseded by the four-sided type with one or more rooms, of which we have examples at Veii, Tarquinia, Vetulonia, Chiusi, and Marzabotto. Reliefs on rock tombs, and the sculpted interiors of certain tombs at Caere, tell us precisely how these houses were constructed and divided into rooms, and how they were decorated and furnished. Other tombs copied the early stages in Etruscan house construction of the classical period, with rooms on the sides opening on a half-covered *atrium* and *impluvium*, and with the main body of the building at the back.

The cave and the hut, then, were normally in ancient times the home (*domus*) of the single family. But when related families gradually grew up side by side, and at least for a time were conscious of a common ancestry, the result was the village (*vicus*), sometimes large and sometimes small, which came into being at various stages in a people's development. Several *vici*, open villages inhabited by people of kindred families, would later acquire a common stronghold (*castellum*), which became the centre of a settled population and of its cults and marketing. This was the origin of the *pagi*, which either developed from pre-existing fortified *vici* or else were built by the inhabitants of an area acting in co-operation. The territory of a *pagus* was therefore the normal unit into which ethnic groups (the *nomina populorum*) were divided. Where, at a later stage, a *pagus* with a fortified citadel extended its political power over the other *pagi*, it was assuming the character of the leader of a league; to keep to the language of the Italic world, it was becoming an imperial *oppidum*.

b. *Agriculture*

The different activities developed by man produced a corresponding, though varied, increase in the instruments he used to help him. Our brief

treatment of these may be prefaced by remarking how the peoples whose
cultural development was slow were conservative in retaining older kinds of
object and in their methods of using what they possessed. The advanced
peoples developed many new kinds and took them to a higher stage of
evolution.

The axe, an instrument for carpentry or stone-cutting, is a good example.
Even lately it was unknown to the Tasmanians or pygmies (for example),
whereas it was developed rapidly among other peoples. The earliest materials
used for making it among hunting races were splintered or polished stone
(of a hard variety) or copper or bronze or iron. Its shape became gradually
more complicated. It could be flat or have raised edges; it could have a
sloping blade or projecting ends; it might have a hole for its handle; and its
metal could be plain or carved. Later varieties include the double-edged axe
(*bipennis*), the square or circular shaft, the use of perforation, the adze, and
so on.

We do not propose to examine the various forms assumed in particular
districts and periods by arrows, bows, and spears, which were another
invention of the warrior and hunter peoples. We may equally pass over the
hooks and harpoons invented by fishermen (the harpoon was, of course, also
used for hunting).

We should, however, mention certain later instruments which were less
widely used and which imply that animals had been domesticated and were
used for carrying and drawing: bits and yokes are examples. Bits were of two
basic types, according to whether their bars were taut or supple; and they
are often dug up in pairs, which mean that the carts were drawn by two
animals. They have been found as far back as the Bronze Age strata of the
palafitte, and then in the 'Villanovan' settlements of the Early Iron Age.
Farther east they appear in excavations of Mycenaean palaces and in similar
buildings in Assyrian and Babylonian areas. Double yokes, for horses or for
oxen, and for ploughing or drawing carts, were widely used in our period in
all the districts where the progress of civilization was rapid; but even in
periods near our own they seem to have been unknown in the more peripheral
zones, for instance among the Bushmen, or in Siberia, Australia, and certain
districts of America.

The domestication of animals, the beginnings of agriculture and cooking,
and comparative stability in living conditions, were followed by the manufacture of wooden vessels, and later of vessels in clay. Once again we find
that archaic types and processes endured for indefinite periods among the
peripheral peoples, whereas the more advanced races continually developed
more satisfactory forms. Clay was baked in ovens instead of in the sun; and
shape was achieved by using the potter's wheel, attested as early as the Old
Kingdom of Egypt, the second stratum of Troy and Middle Minoan palaces
(cf. also *Iliad*, XVIII, 600); it is also found in China of the twelfth century B C.
Moreover attention was paid to the purity of clays and to the choice of

colour; and there were advances in decoration, whether painted, in relief, or incised.

Many of the more backward peoples still retained the older implements invented by man for pulling roots and tubers from the ground, namely a straight or pointed stick, or a stick with a hook on the end. In periods near our own some peoples remained faithful to a tool derived from the other instrument known at the dawn of agriculture: this was the hoe, now used chiefly for garden work.

Conditions were very different in the area occupied by the more civilized peoples, in Europe, in Africa, north of Ethiopia and the Sahara, and in Asia outside its north-eastern districts. There the hooked stick and the hoe early gave place to the two basic types of plough, in one of which the stock was horizontal, in the other sloping. Of these the first had its origin in the north-eastern part of Africa, particularly Egypt: the second was brought from western Asia by the so-called 'Painted Vase' peoples. Later the areas into which the two types spread began to overlap; on account of traders, of Greek and Phoenician colonists, and of the Etruscan and Roman empires. Moreover both types spread still farther abroad, and reached northern Europe, the Caucasus and beyond. Still later both types were improved by the addition of wheels to cope with soils which were too heavy or too compact, and, near 900–800, by iron ploughshares, which permitted the working of the fertile heavy soils.[10]

Invention of the plough brought many innovations in working the land. A still wider gap was created between higher and backward civilizations, since the larger agricultural output gained from the plough not only encouraged a growth in population but also allowed the formation of reserves over and above the quantities absorbed in local consumption. The reserves were available for export and the promotion of trade, which led to a general increase in wealth and to a higher standard of life.

All this explains the growth of mythical figures and religious ideas which bear the imprint of cereal cultivation, for instance Demeter in Greece or Ceres at Rome, and Isis in Egypt.

Generally speaking the cereals cultivated in different districts were those which grew there in a wild state or those which answered best the tastes of the native peoples. Barley, for example, was grown in Gaul and Spain; the Po valley produced millet and panic, and some was also grown in Gaul and in the Euxine; Etruria grew the husked grain (*far* or *semen adoreum*), which was also common in Latium and was therefore used in archaic religious rites, such as *confarreatio*, although naked wheat (*frumentum*) also spread to the area; Thrace and Macedonia grew oats; Greece oats and barley.[11] Rice cultivation was limited to eastern Asia, but spread at an early date from China to India.

Ploughing and sowing caused the introduction of a number of primary and subsidiary operations. There was, for example, the system called 'debbio' by the people of modern Liguria, which involved transforming undergrowth into cultivated land for several years by burning it and so turning it into ashes used for manure. The ancients also used 'rotation of crops': land was sown one year with cereals, the next year put under roots, then turned over by the plough and left fallow in the third year for pasture or hay. Our earliest documentary evidence comes from Greece after 400 BC, but rotation probably was invented during the Early Iron Age.[12]

In some areas, Latium for example, as many as three ploughings preceded sowing; but the earliest process was manuring (believed to be under the supervision of the god Stercutius), the materials being straw from the stables, vegetable stalks from the ground, rotten branches or leaves, and burnt stubble. Later on came harrowing and weeding; and the last operation was the harvest, conducted with scythes. The earliest forms of sickle are still in use among the most primitive peoples today: they are made of wood, or of the jawbones of animals, or of wood pointed with sharpened flint. Other peoples continued to use improved types which had spread abroad in the Bronze Age. The more civilized countries had scythes of sizes and shapes which varied with the uses to which they needed to put them; and in certain areas they were adapted for military purposes, as siege weapons or to fix on war chariots and make them more frightening.

Until they were needed for consumption cereals were preserved in pits dug in the ground. They were then reduced to flour in mills which in the more civilized areas were continually improved. The peripheral countries retained the primitive hand mill consisting of two stones, one fixed and the other revolving, or the straightforward mortar and pestle. More civilized countries used a larger mill, shaped like an hour-glass and sometimes turned by animals.[13]

But farmers were not only concerned with cereals and vegetables. On suitable soil they would plant trees for timber and fruit, growing them in nurseries and then transplanting them. They learned how to graft both on the trunk and also with buds; and an entirely special technique was required to clear the ground for planting vines and olives, to harvest fruit, and to crush olives and press grapes. Wine and oil presses originally consisted of two columns, two cross-bars, and a windlass.

The way in which country operations were conducted in the early centuries of Rome can be seen from Fabius Pictor's list of the no less than twelve 'dei Momentanei', who watched over the various stages in turn.[14]

Material life in Vedic and post-Vedic India is known almost solely from literary sources; and they refer only to the Aryan population. In the first Vedic period the main type of existence was cattle-raising; and livestock were consequently the main form of wealth. The most important animals were cattle, and from the end of the Rigvedic period we find signs of the tendency which later made the cow the sacred animal *par excellence*. Nevertheless throughout the Vedic period beef still forms an essential part of the diet of the Aryan tribes, and is even the chief and irreplaceable dish at royal banquets. Cattle were not wild, but were kept in stables; the cow was milked three times a day. In later Vedic texts knowledge about cattle can be seen to have been more complete and accurate; and there are technical terms for various breeds, for various ages in each sex, and for different physiological conditions. In these texts too the cow has already become so far sacred, that to kill one outside the sacrificial area was punishable by death.

Hunting and fishing were of little consequence: they were pastimes rather than means of securing a livelihood. Agriculture was at first of secondary importance, but it made continuous progress. From their origin the Indo-Iranic peoples knew the wooden plough and metal sickle: in the *Atharvaveda* texts the plough is shown as a characteristically Aryan implement, one not used by the non-Aryan populations.

The Vedic peoples had some knowledge of artificial irrigation: the Vedic texts speak of irrigatory canals (*Kulyā*) and of artificial wells.

The principal crops were cereals, and especially barley (if the word *yava* in its origin bore the sense of barley that it has today). Rice (*vrīhi*) seems to have been at first unknown; but it rapidly came into use and was already familiar in the *Atharvaveda* period. In the middle of the first millennium BC rice and barley were the normal food of the Aryan populations, so much so that in time they had to be offered on the domestic hearth (*grhya*) every morning and evening. At the end of this period it is generally true to say that agriculture had become more important than cattle-raising. It early took on a religious character, and every act in the farmer's life was invariably accompanied by the performance of a domestic rite.

The population was sedentary: there are no significant traces of nomad life. The fortified cities known to the Indus civilization had disappeared: the Aryans lived in scattered dwellings and in small unwalled villages, surrounded at the most by a thorn hedge for defence.

Irrigation. From the time when man settled more permanently on one piece of ground and tilled it with the hoe, he felt the need to control so far as possible the distribution of water and to render it independent of the weather. For periods of drought he wanted to have stores to distribute to humans and domestic animals, and to irrigate the cultivated ground; on the other hand it was desirable to remove surplus water and so drain the soil and save the crops. At different times and in different places we find various devices, of varying degrees of efficiency. There were wells, captured springs, and aqueducts; major and minor canals, drawn off from rivers and lakes; embankments and dams round valleys and reservoirs; and terracing of the soil, to hold the water and prevent the *humus* from being washed away. For the opposite task, to deal with surplus water, we find drainage in open ditches or in pipes below ground (*cunicoli*), banking, drainage canals, cuttings in hills, and the trapping of rivers. At the same time some people living, as did the North Etruscans, in lakeland or country subject to floods protected their homes by adopting the system of *palafitte* or *terramare*: these were pile-dwellings, the former on water, the latter houses built on dry land with embankments. The most primitive of these devices were invented when the ground was still tilled with the hoe: they were preserved unchanged into recent times in the peripheral areas like Oceania, America (Mexico and the Andes), and east Africa, where this method of agriculture still went on. The more complicated and improved devices were brought about by people who used the plough. In the Far East of Asia rice cultivation, first in China and later in Indonesia and India too, compelled the invention of methods for irrigating the areas which had been sown.

In China irrigation and the need to control the great rivers led early to the rise of a typically Chinese science, that of hydraulic engineering. It was indeed determined by the hydrographic structure of the central core of ancient China, in which loess can be fertile only if adequately irrigated, and where the Yellow River carries an enormous quantity of sediments and is subject to disastrous floods. The first dykes on the Huang-ho were built by Duke Huan of Ch'i in the first half of the seventh century BC. Since that period, canals and tanks were dug in various feudal states, both for purposes of irrigation and for military aims (artificial flooding of enemy country). The first great irrigation tank seems to have been the Ssu-ssu-pei or Shao-pei (today An-fêng-t'ang) of about 100 km in circuit, to the south of Shou in northern Anhwei; it was built by Sun Shu-ao, a minister of Duke Chuang of Ch'u, during the nominal reign of the Chou king Ting (606–586 BC). However, the great works of hydraulic engineering begin with the following period, mainly because they went beyond the possibilities of small feudal states and required a strong central power.

c. *Metallurgy: Iron*

Iron had been used sporadically from the thirteenth century at latest in Hittite countries and, more sporadically, in Egypt; and from there it spread to Crete and into the Aegean basin at the end of the Mycenaean Age (which we have seen came later than traditional chronology records). But its use on a large scale for arms, utensils and so on is the characteristic feature of metal-working in the period later than *c*.1000 BC. Yet it did not replace other metals entirely: they continued to be used alongside of iron and indeed the hard iron hammers enabled other metals to be worked into sheets more effectively than before. Large-scale use of iron had been delayed for a number of reasons. It was difficult to recover (cf. the term *polykmētos* in Homer); it required furnaces at fairly high temperature,[15] which had therefore to be provided with elaborate means of ventilation dependent on the bellows; moreover its colour was not very attractive, and it easily oxidized and rusted. In the continents which concern us iron could be found in many districts: India, the Urals, the Crimea and Ukraine, Swedish Lapland, the British Isles,

Lorraine and Luxemburg, Normandy and Brittany, southern Westphalia and the district east of Prague, ancient Noricum and the Styrian Alps, the western Lombardic and the Carnic Alps, the island of Elba and the Apuan mountains, Campiglia and Massa Marittima, La Tolfa and Le Allumiere in Tuscany, La Méta in the Liris valley, Sardinia, and the Bilbao district of Spain. But there is no direct relation between the whereabouts of iron deposit and the dates at which countries started to use the metal: one may remember that America, though so rich in iron, knew nothing of its' working before Columbus.

On the other hand it is not unlikely that iron-working was invented on many occasions in different places, and that each time the invention came casually during the fusing of other metals. One such place was probably Pontus in Asia Minor. But from these primary centres the process spread to others, in districts which also turned out to be rich in iron. One example is provided by the Etruscans. In the Po valley they must have learned to work iron through contacts across the Adriatic or the eastern Alps; then when they crossed south of the Apennines and found themselves in lands rich in ferrous metals, they too became famous inventors and workmen. The new methods in Greek lands were kept secret by clubs of initiate artisans, who gave rise to the legends about mythical iron-working races like the Chalybes in Anatolia[16] or the Dactyloi in Phrygia and Crete.

In antiquity an enormous part of the world used no iron, for instance north-east Asia, Indonesia, the whole area of Polynesia and Australasia, South Africa, and the American continent.

There were four stages in the history of all metalworking. First it was hammered (copper), then fused in furnaces ventilated by chimneys, then metals were alloyed together (bronze), and finally molten iron was fused by means of the bellows. These stages were not reached at the same time in all districts: the process went ahead of the average in the earliest civilizations, behind it in the peripheral areas.

To keep up the heat for recovering and working metals, the earliest devices used the fan: this was relatively unsatisfactory, and later on a blowing tube was inserted, the precursor of the bellows. There were various kinds of bellows: leather varieties of different regional types developed into the instrument marked by a single or double bellows. It must be emphasized again that without some system of blowing the extraction and working of metals would have remained most laborious.[17]

The most ancient method of securing gold consisted in washing the gold-bearing sand of river-beds. Rudimentary instruments were employed: the water was collected in wooden bowls and conveyed in canals on an incline. This method was still widespread: but in the seventh or sixth century the inhabitants of Thasos must already have been mining gold from the deposits in Mt Pangaeus (see Part II).

Mercury must have been extracted from cinnabar before the end of our period by the Etruscans (who got their raw material from Mt Amiata) and by the Carthaginians in Spain. The methods later found in use for this purpose were the crushing of cinnabar in vinegar, and heating it in iron vases with pottery lids. A deposit of liquid mercury belonging to the ninth century has been found at Al Mina.

d. *Textiles*

There were various stages in the historical development of spinning, weaving, manufacture of clothes, and dyeing of materials: and once again all these stages are to be found simultaneously in the ancient world, one in the peripheral or barbarian areas, another in the more civilized countries.

Three conditions are needed if weaving is to be possible:

(1) knowledge how to make matting, baskets, trays, or jars by the simple plaiting of string or wicker, with or without clay plastering;

(2) invention of methods for twisting together short fibres of textile material into a continuous thread;

(3) discovery of the earliest forms of loom, so that the warp could be fixed and have the threads of the weft inserted into it.

All these three discoveries were probably made independently in several parts of the world: and all three can be shown by archaeological finds, and also by the existence of common terms in the different Indo-European languages, to go back to very ancient times. The invention of spinning was often attributed to some divine being (Isis, Athena, etc.) or to very early personages such as the Emperor Yao in China or Mama Oello in Peru. Besides wool, which was little used for this purpose in Egypt, the raw material for spinning was commonly flax. Cotton, like hemp, was used in India, but very little in the classical world: the first evidence for it comes from Herodotus. Fragments of woollen cloth have been discovered in the prehistoric tombs of Scandinavia; and pieces of linen have appeared not only in Egypt but in the Swiss pile-dwellings. Herodotus records a famous tunic given as a present by King Amasis and made of linen with gold thread. A kind of silk could be obtained by processing the so-called sea-wool, for which the inhabitants of Cos became famous.

Antiquity kept to two methods of spinning. Either the fibres were twisted by hand on the knee; or a spindle (made of wood, bone, gold, bronze, or ivory) was used to twist fibres held in a distaff. The running operation of the spindle was made more regular by adding one or more wheels, made of bone, stone, clay, ivory or other material. The Egyptians knew two types of primitive loom, the vertical and the horizontal; and the Greeks too must have had these two types, although because of difficulties of perspective their monuments show us only the first. There were very small looms, worked perhaps with the needle, for the manufacture of articles such as handkerchiefs; and very big ones for making curtains and cloaks. Because there were no cylinders on which to wrap continuous cloths, the ancients still made cloth only to the exact measurements required by the article of manufacture. The threads in the warp were held alternately taut and open for the weaving process by means of weights; but very often the shuttle, or movable regulator, was used to insert the weft. Subsidiary instruments attested by archaeology include needles, carding-combs, and scissors—the last found as early as the Swiss pile-dwellings. Spinning and weaving constituted one of the basic industries inside the household: this is true even when, as already in the *Odyssey*, we have evidence of work-rooms with several female slaves and a woman to supervise them.

Antiquity knew nothing of patterned textiles made in the loom: instead the work was done with the needle, as for modern tapestries, and of such work we have the evidence of tradition extending from Homer to Pliny. In civilized areas, however, there was a varied and colourful output of luxury clothing, of which an example among the Hebrews is given in *Isaiah* iii. 18–23.

For dyeing cloth the usual materials were of organic origin. There were indigo and saffron; purple extracted from a mollusc (the murex), a discovery attributed to the Phoenicians; red derived from an insect (*Coccus ilicis*); yellow from lotus roots; brown from bark and roots of trees; and berries, stalks, and flowers of various other plants. The dyers were clever in their mixtures of juices and infusions; and sometimes they dipped the material several times, for instance in the production of purple.

e. *Pottery, Glass, and Enamel*

At the beginning of our period the potter's art had already made great progress in the more civilized areas, but in the more backward and primitive countries very ancient and imperfect methods still prevailed. In some areas the art itself was completely unknown, for instance in Australia and in some regions of America (outside the Mexican and Andean districts). Other countries continued to use pots of raw *impasto* modelled by hand: at the best they had not yet attained appreciable results in baking, turning, or decoration. It must be remembered, however, that even in the more civilized countries relatively undeveloped methods of manufacture are found, in the same place and in the same period, beside methods involving a high degree of perfection: in serving humble clients the potter would content himself (or herself, for the potter was perhaps a woman) with cheap materials and with methods which did not occupy much time.

The gradual improvement in ceramic art took account of four factors. The first was chemical composition; use was made of more refined clay with the grease removed. In Greece limestone was added, and in Egypt flinty materials, in order to obtain a surface varnish which was not scratched through having a different coefficient of expansion from that of the clay. In China on the other hand they added feldspar, which does have a different expansion coefficient, and so obtained cracks in the varnish for artistic purposes. Secondly, the modelling was improved: in early days it was done with a simple disk lying on a pivot turned with the hand, but later a wheel was used to increase the speed and the regularity of the process. Thirdly, firing was done in kilns more suited for the purpose than primitive types had been: there was a fireplace in front and a furnace beneath, and the kiln was regulated to achieve slower burning over a longer period. Fourthly, attention was paid to shape and decoration, which are the features contributing most to artistic differentiation between the various regions and periods and schools of pottery.

In the Greek world the highest levels of technical perfection were attained in the following period (see Part II). But legend had it that the invention of the 'potter's wheel' went back to the mythical Daedalus (Diodorus, IV, 76); and the difficulty of working kilns had attracted enough attention to inspire a short pseudo-Homeric poem entitled 'Kaminos' (the kiln). Already in our period the various local fabrics, especially Proto-Corinthian and Corinthian, were trying to outdo one another in the selection of clays with the best colour, elasticity, appearance, and evenness of composition. They competed for superior elegance of shapes; to obtain uniformity and regularity in firing, without traces of smoke; and to achieve artistic merit in their decoration, carried out on surfaces prepared at the right moment, with better and better varnishes. During the sixth century the typical fabric is Attic, with silhouettes in black figures executed on the red ground of the pot, and completed with incision on the black varnish to bring out features inside the silhouettes. Pottery pieces of the highest quality required work by several artists, some for modelling and others for decoration, as we see by their signatures on the masterpieces in question. This matter will be treated more fully in the chapter on pictorial art (see p. 298).

In Egypt enamel coverings for paste or steatite objects (jewellery, plates, amulets, statuettes, scarabs, and vases) go back to remote antiquity. In our period a type of cloisonné work had been practised for some centuries, with glass pastes in compartments divided by small partitions. But this Egyptian technique was also found in Cyprus, the Aegean areas, and in Asia Minor; and it later spread north to Scythia and west to Etruria, where it was the precursor of the cloisonné of the Middle Ages. In the East enamelled terracottas had been used from ancient times as architectural dressing and for decoration, for instance on the Ištar gate at Babylon in Nebuchadnezzar's time; these were inherited by the Persians and used in such buildings as the palace of Darius I at Susa.

In the production of glass, properly so called, three methods may be distinguished. The earliest is the manufacture of coloured glass paste, to some extent identical with the enamelling mentioned above. In Egypt it can be shown to have been already known in the sixteenth century; and its surface was often coated with scaly ornamentation, incised with a *stilus* during the cooling process while the vitreous material was still viscous. In the Mycenaean world this material probably corresponds with Homer's *Kuanos*, though this is the name given by Theophrastus to a natural material (lapis lazuli) as well as to an artificial composition. From Greece the process spread to the northern countries of the Mediterranean; and exquisite objects were made from it, especially in Etruria.

Transparent plate glass, according to Pliny (xxxvi, 65), was invented by chance in Phoenicia when blocks of saltpetre were being burned in contact with sand on the shore. In Lucian's time the Phoenicians were undoubtedly still famous for this transparent glass: there is, however, evidence of it very early in the Egyptian excavations at Tell el Amarna; and already in the eighth century its use is attested for ointment boxes, of which one bears the name of King Sargon. In China it was manufactured already about 550 BC, and some remnants have come to light in old tombs at Lo-yang. Greek writers from Pindar onward call it *hyalos*, and the Latins *vitrum*. The production of it was not normally as perfect as that attained in Phoenicia, not even in Campania where the sands of Volturnum seemed most suitable for it. Campanian output in fact is more greenish in colour, like that from the independent factories in Spain and Gaul.

In our period the third process, which produced blown or moulded glass, was not in being.

f. *Gold and Precious Stones*

The Middle East, including Egypt and the Aegean area, had from the beginning of our period been long accustomed to make great display of gold for decorating furniture, buildings, clothes, and vessels, and also to make ornaments in leaf and inlay for personal adornment, such as bracelets, rings, and amulets. Tradition assigned special skill in this field to the Phoenicians, who according to the Hebrew *Book of Kings* were expert goldsmiths. After the fall of the Mycenaean world and the temporary slackening in relations between the Aegean and the East, the use of worked gold in Greek lands suffered a setback. Later, however, contacts between the Greek colonists of Asia and the Asianic peoples, especially the Lydians, were reinforced; and Ionian trade developed throughout the Mediterranean basin. So the taste for gold work returned, and gold jewellery of oriental type spread from centres at Ephesus and Phocaea, and later also Rhodes. In the Italian peninsula at the same time there was a real profusion of gold work of 'orientalizing' type, which was later promoted by Carthaginian exports and by the Carthaginians themselves in Spain, Sardinia, and Sicily. This flourishing period of the goldsmith's art was reflected in the Hallstatt civilization of the north-west, and in Scythian culture to the north-east.

'Semi-precious' stones were sought for their rarity, their colours, and also for the magical properties attributed to them. Their use goes fairly far back in Middle Eastern cultures and in the Minoan and Mycenaean world, and

it was further developed in the first half of the first millennium BC. Small
stones were worked in relief or incised; and others formed part of ornamental
plaques, some of which were placed on buildings. In incision there were
famous artificers, such as those of Samos and certain Etruscans.

'Precious' stones, which were valued because of their size or colour and
were often pierced to make necklaces, were still sought and treated much
as they had been in the previous period, the Middle East being the main
area of use. They were normally, however, not cut; the only process was
the polishing of their natural surfaces.

The history of amber manufacture underwent a significant modication,
which also affected the areas in which different types of amber were used.
Originally amber was worked in the areas where it was found and in adjacent
districts: the northern countries used the yellow amber of the Baltic and
North Sea, and Mediterranean countries the reddish-brown variety found in
Syria, Sicily, the extreme south of Italy, and in France. The latter is probably
mentioned in the *Odyssey* (XVIII, 293). Later, however, the two types were
found in competition in the same districts, such as the Po valley of Italy.
The Baltic and North Sea amber was then acknowledged to be superior
and was sought after by the inhabitants of Mediterranean countries too.
Acquaintance with it must have been due to the Phocaean sailors, who at
one time frequented the northern Adriatic and the western Mediterranean.[18]
The first man to describe a voyage to the amber countries of the North was
Pytheas of Massilia (about 300 BC), who supplemented the allusions to the
amber route in Herodotus and later writers. The district of Italy which
showed most taste for large objects made of amber was Picenum.

Coral working is not mentioned by written sources before the Hellenistic
age, but archaeological discoveries at Felsina (the modern Bologna), Este,
Arne and other places show that it had been used for ornaments several
centuries earlier. Discovery of coral may have happened casually.[19] The
story was that coral grew hard when exposed to the air; and this started the
myth that drops fell into the sea from the Gorgon's blood and there became
petrified.

g. *Scents and Cosmetics*

The discovery and use of perfumes imply a marked advance in the standard
of human comfort. Pliny tells us that their cradle lay in the East, and this is a
reasonable view. The East was the region where the appropriate ingredients,
both vegetable and mineral, were most abundant; its peoples were fond of
luxury; and Egyptian methods of embalming were probably a further factor
in promoting production. Perfumes were often used for incense in propitiatory
ceremonies. But their usage spread because anointment was considered
healthy and because, in the absence of soap, scent baths and massage were
the main way of caring for the human body.

Together with scents and ointments, cosmetics and paints were used to animate the face, heighten its shades, and conceal defects in the skin. Dyes were also used to give artificial colour to the hair. In all these departments the Egyptians were expert from ancient times. The Hebrews, who had guilds of scent-makers, obtained their scents from southern Arabia and had what may be called a hymn to scent in the 'Song of Songs'. The Persians, too, liked to anoint themselves with bistre and belladonna, as we know from the famous incident between the young Cyrus and his grandfather Astyages. The Phoenicians were great traders in scents and similar commodities, and the Etruscans were great consumers. In Greece and Magna Graecia there were workmen who specialized in scent manufacture.

2. TRADE

a. *Routes of Communication*

In our period and in the two which followed most land communications were primitive and hardly better than footpaths. In flat country they were very numerous, and also shifting; in the mountains there would be a single fixed route dictated by the essential points of transit. All such routes allowed travel by pedestrians and by people carrying baggage. But in more populous and civilized districts, when carriage came to be done by pack animals, mule tracks were constructed; and although their surfaces were not laid by hand, passage along them was made easier when transport by carts became more common.

In India transportation was chiefly by pack animals and by cart. In the Late Vedic period the goods cart (*anas*) drawn mostly by oxen was carefully distinguished from the war or race chariot (*ratha*) drawn by horses. Horses served equally for driving and for riding. Elephants, then as later, were employed almost only for war and ceremonies. Camels seem to have been in use, but it is doubtful whether the word *uṣṭra* in Vedic texts means camel or buffalo.

The cart was typical of the ancient world, though unknown in America before Columbus. Its invention was made possible with the invention of the wheel; and the solid wheel which carried its axle round with it later gave place to the spoked wheel, of a variety of shapes, which rotated round an axle.[20] Carts, or chariots, had many functions, in war, in agriculture, and for commercial transport. They came to be divided into two main types; the light two-wheeled chariot drawn by horses, used in war and racing; and the heavier carriage drawn by oxen for journeys and for transport of goods. The various forms which were current in different countries and periods need not be dealt with here (see Part II).

The use of carriages gradually brought about the construction of carriage roads on a more level surface. At the outset these were ill-defined and had a number of separate carriage tracks alongside one another. Later firm roads were built, respecting the property of the agricultural owners along their route, and taking advantage, at difficult points, of artificial methods such as cuttings, fords, and levelling operations. In marshy country dykes were also constructed; and every use was made of existing carriage tracks, which made running easier especially in rocky districts.

Permanent paving of roads was used originally only in certain sections, and then only in highly civilized countries such as certain parts of Mesopotamia and one or two Minoan centres. Generally paving was confined to the interior of towns, but town streets, too, underwent complicated modifications. Particular centres such as those inhabited by pile-dwellers, where streets intersected at right angles from the very beginning, were obviously exceptional. Elsewhere streets formed an irregular network, chiefly dictated by the varied nature of the ground in different towns and also by the tendency to pack the houses inside definite areas such as the acropolis or *agorā*. Urban streets of this kind were only paved in exceptional circumstances. Herodotus tells us of paving in Mesopotamia (I, 180); and we know of it from excavations both at Nimrūd and at Minoan and Mycenaean cities in the Aegean, such as Troy, Knossos, and Gournia.

The Persians, if not the later Assyrians, were first to create a permanent system of roads and to provide regular maintenance for their track routes. They constructed artificial works, such as bridges, embankments, and cuttings; and they erected stations at convenient stages for the service of the post, in which lodging and refreshment were also provided for travellers. Herodotus and Xenophon's *Anabasis* and *Cyropaedia* tell us about these Persian roads, with particular reference to the so-called 'Royal Road' from Sardes to Susa, which had 111 stations and was 450 parasangs long ('sang' means stone, and must have meant the 'bornes' indicating the stage reached in the journey, measured in time rather than distance).

The Greek world, however, suffered what was almost a setback in comparison with the Minoan period. It continued with the ancient footpaths and with carriage roads on natural soil; moreover streets inside cities were narrow and irregular, without any use of pavements. The Etruscans, too, when they passed south of the Apennines and were living in hill country very different from the plain of the Po, had to give up the regular systems of rectangular street intersections which they had employed in the *palafitte* and *terramare*.[21] For the most part they went in for networks of narrow and irregular city streets adapted to the contours of the ground: of these we can see an example at Vetulonia, though there the principal street is flanked by a footpath running above the sewer. But at the end of the sixth century the Etruscans reconquered part of the Po valley; and when they came to construct the city which has now been excavated at Marzabotto in Emilia they appear to have been influenced by their older *terramare* models. They therefore built a central street 15 metres wide with lesser streets intersecting it at right angles. In the middle this central street has a 5-metre strip for vehicles: and the two 5-metre strips on each side have stone surfaces for pedestrians.

Both before and during the Etruscan domination the urban centre of Rome must have had an irregular system of streets. But the city acquired commercial importance through lying on the road leading from Etruria to Campania, and through her early domination of Latium. She cannot have been slow in attending to the upkeep of communications outside the city along the roads of varying size which radiated traffic towards Ardea, Gabii, Praeneste, Labicum, Collatia and other places.

b. *Navigation and Ships*

Navigation in the less progressive and peripheral areas was doubtless still carried on by the primitive methods which the ethnologist can show us operating in 'barbarian' countries in times very near to our own. Moreover there were still certainly some seaboard peoples who were ignorant of the art of sailing, either because the waters round them were too difficult for navigation, or because they had no ship-building materials, or because they had no need for trade and other communications with the outside world.

One of the most ancient methods of river transport was to float leather bags and round vessels made of skins, which were carried with their cargoes by the stream: Herodotus (I, 194) describes this practice on the Tigris and Euphrates. (Pl. 1, a.) Another possibility was to float flat or rounded tree trunks, or several trunks tied together into rafts.

A further stage was reached by the peoples who built coracles, either of a single piece of curved bark or of several pieces linked together, or even of the hollowed-out trunk of a tree. These vessels were sometimes weighted to achieve stability: alternatively two trunks could be placed alongside one another.

To hold the wind many shapes of sail were used, and many means of suspending and holding them. A type which became permanent in China was the square ribbed sail, designed to stop undue billowing from a wind blowing down on the vessel.

The type of craft used in the more civilized countries was normally of more advanced technique. Yet regional features are noticeable, resulting partly from the materials available in each country but often from gradual evolution. In Egypt navigation of the Nile was carried on with two basic kinds of craft. One was the low-hulled barque of crescent shape, built of strips of papyrus stalk joined together. The other was a heavier craft of short planks from trees of the country, fastened by nails; but these craft too were of shallow draught designed to avoid mud banks. The sails were square and the oars free; large rudder oars were used in the stern: and sometimes there was a cabin. But sea-going ships, used in war, were more robust and straighter; their oars had rowlocks, and their rudders were fixed. Like the state vessels, which were decorated throughout, these warships were built of tall trunks from Lebanon.

The Assyrians and Babylonians used for river navigation the old type of rounded barque of which we have been speaking. For sea navigation in the eastern Mediterranean, their agents were the Phoenicians, whose powerful trading vessels, the short, stout *gauloi*, were built of timber from the tall conifers of Lebanon: they had keels and ribs and raised decks. Assyrian and Karatepe reliefs of these ships are very instructive. (Pl. 1, b.)

The Hellenes of the Aegean basin, and the Greek colonists abroad wherever they took themselves, used two types of ship, the man-of-war and the merchant vessel. For both types there is some evidence in the Minoan and Mycenaean periods. In Hellenic time the merchant vessel was fairly broad in the beam, more rounded than the warship, with raised decks; it carried a single sail, had wheels fore and aft and a mast fixed into the keel; the steering gear consisted of a large oar projecting each side of the stern; and from the sixth century onwards an anchor was carried. Ships were generally caulked black with pitch, and the hulls were sometimes painted with vermilion. The warship was lighter, and the prow of the long keel ended in a bronze ram; there was a quarterdeck and forecastle, benches for the rowers, and a bridge above them from which the marines could fight. A type which became standardized early was the *dieres*, or ship with two banks of rowers, normally fifty rowers in all (*penteconters*). Later, near 650 BC,[22] the *trireme* was invented to increase speed and the power behind a charge. This was a ship with three banks of seventy rowers arranged in various ways; including the fighting men it carried a crew of 200 in all. Between 110 and 120 feet long and little more than about 17 feet broad, *triremes* were light and consequently required plenty of ballast. Being fragile and easily damaged, they were mainly used during day-time in a calm sea and for actions near inshore.

Warships were seldom at sea for long, and the distance they covered was about 50 miles a day. They would go from port to port to collect food and water: and the ships would be hauled on land or drawn into harbour in case of heavy seas or storms. Merchantmen could trust to the winds, and were therefore less dependent on short cruises along the coasts. But steering by the stars was only possible part of the year, so navigation had to be suspended during the winter months. But the proud deeds of these daring sailors are attested not only by legends, such as those of the Argonauts or Odysseus, but by the colonial ventures in so much of the Mediterranean from the tenth century onwards: the Phocaean colonizers and merchants reached the northern Adriatic and the coasts of Spain and Tunisia. No less impressive enterprises were achieved by other peoples, for instance the circumnavigation of Africa by certain daring Phoenicians on orders from Pharaoh Necho (*c.* 600).[23] *Periploi* or works written to aid navigation, like the Italian 'portolani' of the Middle Ages, must have begun to appear in relatively early times:

they indicated the whereabouts of harbours and the time needed to go from one to another. The average speed of navigation in a fair sea was between 4 and 6 knots.

c. *The Growth of Trade*

One may assume that the less civilized parts of the ancient world acquired goods from abroad in one of the ways illustrated by the evolution of commerce in primitive countries in modern times. The stages in this evolution were roughly as follows: (1) entire isolation of one group of human beings from others; (2) plunder at the expense of one's neighbours; (3) gifts of friendship exchanged between host and guest, in measure unrelated to the concrete value of the goods, a stage familiar (for example) in the Homeric poems; (4) silent barter of the kind described by Herodotus (IV, 196) in speaking of the Carthaginians and the Libyan tribes of the extreme west; (5) voluntary barter, not dependent on a treaty; (6) barter conducted according to treaty; (7) payment for merchandise with valuable objects measured by their weight.

On periods for which we get no help from written tradition and have to depend solely on the evidence of archaeology our information is incomplete. It takes account only of non-perishable objects, such as stone, wood, bone, metal, amber, glass, and pottery, whereas things such as agricultural produce, livestock, skins, cloth, scents, and slaves have disappeared. Yet the Latin word *pecunia* reminds us that livestock were often the main constituent of trade.[24] For the earlier periods we can only state which were the normal exporting and importing countries for objects which have survived: we cannot be sure what was given in exchange. For example yellow amber came from the west coast of the Baltic, tin from Spain and Britain, gold from Nubia and Asia Minor, Thrace, Transylvania; silver from Iran, Asia Minor, the Balkan countries, Greece, Spain, and the Alps, copper from Spain and Cyprus. Trade of this kind often came by river or by land and depended on various points at the intersection of main routes which acted as depots, like the Balkan peninsula and the Po valley. Both routes and depots, however, were changed as time went on, particularly when widespread use of iron became common and when new mines of gold, silver, copper and other metals began to be worked.

After the introduction of iron, the pattern of trade was influenced by Phoenician colonization on the south coast of the Mediterranean and by Greek colonization on the northern coasts, down to the time when the two peoples came into conflict in Spain and Sicily.[25] In fact most of the accepted channels of trade passed through one of these two peoples.

A survey of trade by regions may start from India. As a profession, commerce had a very early origin there and is already mentioned in the hymns of the *Rigveda*. Later the trader (*vanij*) found his social place in the *vaiśya* caste. The profession was often hereditary and was both widespread and respected. A whole hymn of the *Atharvaveda* is dedicated to obtaining commercial success through cleverness in haggling. Trade was essentially by land routes; the sea is mentioned late in the texts and for a long time played little if any role.

In Egypt trade was largely a monopoly of the Pharaoh. By river or caravan the principal imports were gold from Nubia, silver from the Middle East, perfumes and precious stones from south Arabia, ivory from Libya and the Sudan, skins, ebony and scents from tropical Africa, and copper from Sinai. By sea came timber from Lebanon, and miscellaneous products and manufactures from the Aegean islands and Libya. In exchange Egypt's main exports were manufactured linen goods and cereals, glass, and papyrus.

Palestine and Syria lay along the trade route between the Mediterranean countries, Mesopotamia, Egypt, and Anatolia. From this transit trade they made handsome profits, and they were also able to enlarge its orbit by bringing in the western Mediterranean area. They contributed little of their own, apart from manufactures copied from eastern wares, together with amulets, toys, clothing, timber, oil, and honey. Yet another profitable form of trade was that in slaves: the Phoenicians were sometimes very clever in making their captures, as the *Odyssey* tells when recounting the way Eumaeus was seized.

Mesopotamia imported gold from south Arabia and Nubia, silver from the Taurus mountains, copper from Cyprus, Crete, and even the region round Lake Van, spices from Arabia, timber from Lebanon and the region round Lake Van (the region called 'Urartu'), and ivory from Africa and India. Exports provided in exchange were agricultural products, wool, oil; and manufactured goods, especially metalwork and ivories.

Greek trade acquired its greatest development from colonization, which gave the Greeks the means to provide the mother cities and the colonies themselves with foodstuffs and raw materials from all the countries which were now opened up. These included the Black Sea and Sea of Marmora, Thrace, Asia Minor, the Aegean, Egypt, Cyrenaica, Magna Graecia and Sicily, the Adriatic, Tunisia, and the northern Mediterranean from the Gulf of Genoa to eastern Spain.

In return all these countries and their hinterlands were markets for the manufactured goods which the Greeks wanted to export against these imports. Sometimes, however, their trade was based on more complicated arrangements, known as early as Homer and described in the *Odyssey*, under which traders bought up the surpluses of a number of countries and sold or exchanged them elsewhere: their voyages might be of very long duration. In the artistic field this form of economy had the effect of spreading abroad not only typically Greek designs and conceptions but also those originating in the various countries from which articles of trade were derived. For example, the so-called 'orientalizing' art of central Italy is copied from a mixture of models drawn from widely different areas, such as Egypt, Syria, Anatolia, Cyprus, and Crete. This was because the Phocaeans traded with both the Tyrrhenian and the Adriatic coast; and they brought their Italian clients products acquired in all the countries they had frequented in their complicated voyages. One must remember that the eastern Mediterranean markets, such as Al Mina, were receiving wares from very distant countries by sea as well as land: the Arabians helped to carry cargoes. The Greek cities, which rapidly grew out of their primitive economy based on agriculture, were most favourably suited for producing manufactures for export. They included the Ionian colonies such as Miletus, Ephesus, Chios, and Phocaea, and the Dorian colonies such as Rhodes; in the Greek homeland there were Chalcis, Aegina, Megara, Corinth, and later Athens; overseas Byzantium; and in the West Syracuse, Tarentum, Cumae, and Massilia.[26]

A later step of decisive significance in developing trade was the invention of coinage in precious metal with value guaranteed by the various states: this is dealt with later.

The basis of Etruscan trade lay in the surplus of metals mined in the Tuscan mountains and on Elba; in the early growth of navies in the cities near the Tyrrhenian seaboard; and in the extension of their sea-borne traffic to take in Campania and the Po valley at the time of their imperialist expansion in the seventh and sixth centuries. The Etruscan pirates and traders, who in the eighth century were already controlling the sea as far as the Straits of Messina, now enlarged the area of their exports and therefore of their imports too. In particular they acquired, from places as far as Spain, the metals needed for bronze manufacture in alloy with what they themselves produced: and in the seventh and sixth centuries they divided control of the Tyrrhenian Sea with Carthage and Massilia, who usually were at war with one another.

Carthage indeed, after the dismemberment of Tyre's colonial empire in the West and her own succession to the position of mother city, became in the sixth century the greatest commercial power in the western Mediterranean and maintained her strength for centuries to come. She organized her sister colonies as if they were her own, and planted a series of Punic outposts in north-west Africa and southern Spain. In the following generations the Carthaginians sent out daring explorers of their own to secure useful produce, as far afield as the North Sea under Himilco and the west African coast under Hanno. These ventures had their zenith in the period covered by Part II. In general the goods most important to Carthage were gold, oil (before olives were planted in Africa), pottery, and bronze; and her traders offered the precious metals of Spain and more distant countries, together with slaves and other commodities. She also conducted transit trade in central African goods, such as gold, skins, and ivory, which reached the Punic colonies by means of caravan. The commercial class at Carthage was so powerful that it often acquired control of the city's political affairs.

One of the greatest obstacles to the peaceful development of sea-borne commerce, though in some periods more than in others, was piracy, just as brigandage and raiding impeded trade by land. Ancient peoples treated every race other than their own as an enemy, unless the people in question was linked to them by special ties. They therefore regarded piracy and raiding as normal activities, which could even bring honour on their authors in proportion to the boldness they had shown and the success they had achieved. This applied not only to piratical enterprises by small groups of daring men but to mass expeditions like those of the 'Peoples of the Sea' on Egypt, the Cimmerian raiders of Anatolia, the Etruscans in the seas round Sicily, or the Greek colonists themselves—for they too took lands by force and reduced the natives to serfdom. In the *Iliad* Achilles and Odysseus boast of having laid waste and sacked twenty-three cities of the Troad; the *Odyssey* describes expeditions, half-piratical and half-commercial, by Menelaus and Odysseus in the East and by the Phoenicians in the island of Ortygia; Assyrian documents tell us of isolated attacks made by Greek pirates on the Syrian coasts in the eighth and seventh centuries. In Greek epic it came naturally to people to ask whether those they met were pirates or not. Tradition and an inscription speak of the savage acts of piracy by the great lord of Samos, Polycrates, and by his older relatives; and in Solonian Athens it was normal to form clubs for 'piracy' as well as for ordinary commerce.

This state of affairs was still fully operative in the fifth century and was well known to Thucydides, who analyses it (I, 4) with great precision and insight. It was responsible for the fact that so many maritime cities had their centre of habitation some way inland, on a hill which provided better defence. Moreover from the seventh or sixth century onward efforts were made to build navies consisting of light but powerful ships, which could be used exceptionally for war, but which were normally intended to keep down piracy and protect merchant shipping. It seems that Corinth gave the lead in this. As always happens in war, however, piratical action continued to be one of the main ways of engaging and doing harm to the enemy: his fields were ravaged, his houses burnt, and his people reduced to slavery.

d. *Trading Posts and Markets. Commercial Treaties*

In the history of foreign trade special interest attaches to the permission sometimes granted to a number of states to set up warehouses for trading purposes in appropriate quarters of foreign territory. This arrangement was in force in the seventh century at Naucratis in Egypt, and at Al Mina. It was also found in certain cities of western Sicily, such as Motya. In Etruscan areas there were Greek stations on the beaches of Caere, and at Alsium and Pyrgi, and a Carthaginian station at Punicum.

All through the ancient world one of the basic functions of a city was to act as a market town for all the territory or state around it. In Greece from the earliest days after the Mycenaean age every city had a large square or *agorā* which served as a meeting place for the people. In this, besides the public buildings and a number of temples, there were built permanent shops; and above all there would be stalls for the retailers, whose transactions were supervised by the *agorānomoi*, with *metronomoi* to check the weights. Normally each commodity had its own section. At some central point were the bankers (*trapezitai*); and all around, in allotted areas, there assembled the countrymen from each district to conduct their business. Aristotle tells us that at Athens, as later at such places as Priene, the food market and the market for manufactured goods were kept distinct.[27]

The Greek concept of the *agorā* had its Italian counterpart in the *fora* or *comitiā*, which had existed in the pile cities of the North Etruscans. But at Rome there were a number of stages in their development. In the earliest period the 'forum' was the place where travelling traders put up for the night, fed and watered their horses, and then sold their wares. In later times permanent markets for each type of produce began to make their appearance outside the central area: the *fora* called *boarium, olitorium, piscarium, suarium, vinarium, cuppedinis* (i.e. for beef, vegetables, fish, pork, wine, and pottery). The name *macellum* came into common use for food markets, where the principal items on sale were meat and sliced fish.

In the country centres outside Rome temporary markets were arranged at stated periods, normally every eight days (*nundinae*).

When one people, e.g. the Carthaginians, became overlord of another, it was able to keep trade exclusively in its own hands and control its extent. In principle independent states looked on one another as enemies. But in so far as free commerce between them implied a condition of peace and friendship it needed to be regulated by conventions, concessions, and prohibitions. Bilateral treaties of this kind might contain positive clauses allowing trade, and also negative clauses defining areas of monopoly and other restrictive elements. Later on we find precise rules about customs, excise tolls, and immunities. Customs benefited the state and excise duties the individual city. The two are clearly distinguishable in large states with a number of urban communities, but they are of course identical in Greek and other city states.

e. *Precious Metals as a Medium of Trade*

Barter implies that the two parties have a reciprocal need for merchandise, the value of which was determined by the extent of their demand. Eventually, however, metal became a third commodity of determinate value within each transaction. It was the easiest commodity to sell, being accepted by everyone; it was divisible with precision into any fractions one wished; it could be conserved without difficulty and was of limited weight. Here too many systems gradually evolved, more or less independently of one another. But one of the first stages consisted in fixing the weight and quantity of metal required for the purchase of a commodity, whether in gold, electrum, silver, or bronze.

This process started early in India, but was slow in progressing. Already the hymns of the *Ṛigveda* recognize some units of exchange. One of them is the cow. Another seems to have been a gold chain called *niṣka*. Later Vedic texts mention lenders (*kusīdin*) and loans, but no coins proper came as yet into use; the nearest approach to it was the quasi-monetary employ by merchants of the *śatamāna*, a piece of gold weighing 100 *māna* or *kṛṣṇāla*.

Written evidence like the Homeric poems agree with archaeology in showing that merchandise was often exchanged against metal instruments, which were either of given weight or weighed at the time of sale. The instruments in question included axes, anchors, cauldrons, tripods, and spits. Sheets of bronze, or lumps of iron (Sparta) were used for the same purpose; and other peoples employed gold and silver manufactured articles, or gold leaf of any weight which was desired.

Finally a genuine system of coinage was attained. This meant metal disks of a defined weight, content, and value, guaranteed by the particular state which struck them. (Pl. 2.) Inevitably the supply of metals used for coinage, and the difficulties of acquiring them, led to fluctuation in the relative value of coins made of different metals.

The Anatolian world, Lydia in particular, where gold was plentiful, started in the sixth century with gold coins, which provided a standard for the evaluation of coins in other metals. The same was true of the Greek colonies on the Asiatic coast from at least the beginning of the sixth century. Electrum also, an alloy of gold and silver, was frequently used for coinage; but the alloy, whether natural or artificial, varied within so wide limits that the value of the coins was too uncertain, and its use was early abandoned. At this period in Asia Minor the ratio of gold to silver was normally 1:20.[28]

In the Greek homeland a silver standard was preferred; and the bronze coins used for smaller denominations had values fixed in terms of silver. One guarantee of the purity of metal in the coinage and of the accuracy of its weight was the competition between trade rivals in its production. Nonetheless in this early period we are told of the serious fraud in this field perpetrated by Polycrates, tyrant of Samos, who paid the Spartans in counterfeit coins made of gilded lead.

The Greeks devised a number of systems, some similar to one another, some different, for calculating the weights of multiples and fractions of their basic coin. There was first the Aeginetan system with a silver 'stater' of two drachmae which weighed between 12·21 and 13·41 gm.: the drachma was divided into six obols, and 70 or 73 drachmae made up a mina.[29] This was the system used at Athens before Solon.[30] Secondly, there was the Euboic system, which Athens used after Solon. This had a stater weighing from 8·25 to 8·74 gm., and the mina consisted of 100 drachmae. Thirdly, there was the Corinthian system: this differed from the Euboic in that the mina consisted of 150 drachmae, and the stater weighed three drachmae instead of two.

The first extant Greek coins probably go back to the first half of the sixth century BC. Yet Aristotle's generation of Greeks still thought of coined money as a genuine article of exchange whose value had to be equivalent to that of the goods it bought. Only in later periods (fourth century) shall we find some development of the conception of forced currency and fiduciary money.

In other countries, including Italy, precious metals were in short supply. Instead of them bronze either in large sheets or in disks was the main basis of coinage, and only in the third century was silver struck. Rome is an example of this line of development.

f. *Artisans and Light Industry*

In different places and periods, and at different levels of civilization, we find various stages in the history of industry, which is a response to man's demand for the adaptation and transformation of natural products.

In some peripheral areas, and in the earliest periods of other countries, domestic industry continued to be the regular system. All that was needed for the unit of population was produced in a ruler's court, or in the buildings adjoining a temple, or in the house of a single family—if necessary with the help of slaves directed by an overseer, as we see in the *Iliad*. One unit, however, would sometimes exchange its manufactures with another unit, and so meet the needs of its various dependent parts. Ancient tradition records a marked development of this phase in Egypt, where temple organizations tended to monopolize such commodities as textiles and papyrus, and overcome all competitors in the production of these articles.

The second phase was production by artisans, which acquired a firm position in the Greek world from early times. It was based on groups of specialist workmen who were, in principle, part of the system of household economy. With the help of a few free workmen or slaves the craftsman would work to complete his orders either in his own factory or in the homes of his customers: sometimes the materials were supplied by the customers, sometimes he used his own. At this stage specialization was attained through a long apprenticeship. Moreover the secrets of a trade, and the magic formulae considered necessary for its profitable exercise, were handed down by master craftsmen from father to son. The extent to which a particular group of artisans became famous would depend on where it worked, on the availability of raw materials, on the length of tradition behind it, and on the nature of its customers: but some of them undoubtedly exported products over wide areas. Yet they manufactured only enough to meet their orders and were therefore not liable to crises caused by overproduction. They were more likely to be hit by underproduction, mainly the result of war which interfered with the supply of materials or the delivery of the goods once they had been made. In the Greek world of the seventh and sixth centuries the products of certain workshops were famous. The cities mainly concerned were Miletus and Phocaea, Chios and Samos, Crete and Rhodes, Corinth and Aegina, Athens and Chalcis, Syracuse and Massilia.

The third stage, which we may call the stage of light or medium industry, developed in the Greek world early in the ensuing period (see Part II). Its features are a larger number of workmen, increased specialization and improvement in technique, and heavier investment of capital. This was industry in the fullest sense, and the factors promoting it came into being naturally. The use of money as a medium of exchange offered greater possibilities for capital investment; slave labour often reduced production costs;[31] the wider export markets resulting from the spread of colonization put up the demand for manufactured goods; and there was generally a more intense concentration on trading prospects. But the artisan character of the production process was maintained throughout and even a slave could often have an existence very similar to that of the free workman, paying a rent to his patron and living with his family, on the proceeds of his work.

As far as we can tell the story was much the same in the Etruscan and Carthaginian worlds; and at Rome one feature of artisan labour from the Regal period onwards was the organization of corporative bodies called 'collegia'. Plutarch (*Numa*, 17) states that in Regal Rome several regular colleges of artisans had been formed and recognized by the state: they were probably modelled on the priestly colleges. The trades mentioned are carpenters, potters, leather-workers, shoemakers, dyers, coppersmiths, goldsmiths, and flute players. In other respects the economy of the self-sufficient household probably still continued.

Artisans in ancient India are incidentally mentioned in the Vedic hymns, but their organization is not clearly established by the relevant texts. Clearly, however, no social stigma attached in the *Rigveda* period to what were later to be regarded as unclean trades, for example tanning.

g. *The Extension of Markets*

When handicrafts and light industry developed in areas well provided with raw materials, or alternatively with merchant navies for the import of such materials and the re-export of manufactured goods, important consequences might follow. A number of Phoenician, Greek, Etruscan, and Carthaginian cities either erected trading stations for the sale of their wares, or stimulated their colonies, founded it may be for purely agricultural purposes, to take on the appropriate form of commercial activity. The result was that colonies often felt themselves bound to their mother countries by the complementary nature of their economies, in industry and commerce, even more than by ties of blood and affection. At the same time produce from the mother countries, together with manufactured goods from the colonies themselves, made its way to the surrounding native populations: this led to borrowings by one local culture from another, and often caused a region to acquire the cultural stamp of hybrid origin which is normally called a *koiné*. Siculans and Greeks mixed in this way in Sicily, Italians, Greeks and Etruscans in central Italy, Greeks and Celts in Provence, Iberians, Greeks, Carthaginians, and Celts in Spain. In north-west Africa there was a union between Carthaginians, Greeks, and Numidians, and in Cyrenaica between Greeks and Libyans.

In some cases links of this kind were always confined to the economic and cultural spheres, that is mainly to commerce and religion. This was the normal relationship between mother cities in Greece and their western colonies, but there was sometimes more. The Greek cities of Athens, Syracuse, and Massilia, for example, and the Punic city of Carthage, used their periods of hegemony to unite their colonies within the framework of relatively permanent political organisms. The influence thus exerted was a further factor in extending and intensifying the fields of common culture and in promoting trade.

3. THE DEVELOPMENT OF SCIENCE

In primitive stages of civilization all natural phenomena are normally explained in childish and fantastic ways. Their origins are ascribed to magical or miraculous actions; and they become the subject of myths, often described in poetry. But as observation becames keener and experience more mature, the making of myth gives way to reason. The Greek *logos* which took the place of *mythos* is equivalent to empirical science; and the gradual passage from the fantastic and poetical to the rational and concrete leads gradually to what we call Natural Science, knowledge of which was growing all the time.

But after establishing the existence of particulars men turned from them to universal concepts, to what Plato called 'ideas'. Here they went back on their tracks, and introduced a metaphysical element into their empirical knowledge. This was what happened in our period among the Greeks, who were the keenest observers of the material world and also the most acute and tireless of theoretical thinkers.

a. *Geography*

In examining the history of the different ideas of science we will start with Geography, which reached its highest results among the Greeks. In the early centuries of the first millennium BC the Greeks still had exact knowledge only of the eastern Mediterranean lands nearest their own homes. We can see this clearly in the Second Book of the *Iliad*, by comparing the much more precise catalogue of the Greek allies with that of the more distant allies of the Trojans. In their trading enterprises they might have visited more distant countries, at any rate those along the coasts; but they still tended to view them under a veil of legend and miracles, and a veil even thicker and more impenetrable covered those distant lands from which news came to them at second-hand and in scarcely recognizable form. This explains such beliefs as that the flat circle of the Earth was surrounded by the stream of Oceanus, the parent of the great rivers which flowed into the 'Middle Sea', and that on the shores of Oceanus lived the least known and most fabulous peoples of the world.

As commercial and colonial enterprise, aided by genuine exploration, widened Greek knowledge of the world and made it more exact, it naturally followed that the radius of the Earth's circle became gradually longer and the circumference formed by Oceanus was pushed farther away from the centre.

Of exploration proper before about 500 BC we have few examples, whether by Greeks or by Carthaginians. Among Greeks may be mentioned Colaeus of Samos, whom Herodotus records as visiting the deserted trading posts in Spain; and there was Scylax of Caryanda, whom the Persian king Darius (521–485) sent to explore the southern coasts of Asia. Among Carthaginians we must notice Hanno and Himilco, who both lived at the time of Carthage's greatest development (c. 550–480):[32] the former explored the Atlantic coast of Africa and the latter some northern shores of Europe. Both these wrote treatises, which were later translated into Greek. Of Hanno's we have actual fragments, and Himilco's is known through the adaptations of it in Avienus' *Ora Maritima*.

This greater knowledge of the world provided material for the conclusions of Anaximander of Miletus in the second half of the sixth century and of Hecataeus of the same city a few decades later. Anaximander tried to construct a map of the Earth's circle, surrounded by Oceanus and divided into two halves by the 'Middle Sea'. Hecataeus drew up a *pinax* or new type of geographical chart, and illustrated it with a descriptive work (*gēs periodos*) on peoples and their countries. Herodotus (V, 49) tells us that Aristagoras, tyrant of this city of Miletus about 500, possessed a bronze tablet on which lands and seas were depicted.

But following closely on Anaximander another great scholar, Pythagoras of Samos, had reached the concept of the Earth as a sphere. His belief was taken up by his pupils and later by others, and the reasons for it were expounded not only by the Pythagorean school but by Parmenides of Elea.

b. *Astronomy*

Not only in older periods but even among the higher civilizations astronomy —which studies celestial bodies to learn their fixed natural laws and also the nature of the stars—has been often closely linked and confused with astrology —which attempts to study the influence which the stars through their move- ment and changing positions exert on our world on Earth, and more par- ticularly on states and individual men. Astrology thus tries to explain the past and foretell the future.

The progress of astronomy led to continued developments in astrology, which thus became perhaps the chief method of using natural phenomena for purposes of divination. As is well known, the ancient world used many other methods too. Signs given by the weather, such as clouds, hurricanes, and thunderbolts, were studied, so too were the movements of animals, especially the flight of birds, the characteristics of human hands (chiromancy), the rustling of leaves (as at Dodona), monstrous births, dreams (oneiromancy) and many other things. To them must be added the indications obtained by human action, such as casting lots, mixing liquids, and kindling fire to watch the shape of the flame or smoke. They also paid attention to necromancy, to divine judgements, and to the appearance of the entrails of animals in sacrifice.

From the earliest times astronomy was of exceptional importance in China, since it grew out of a religion of a 'cosmic' type and was always regarded as an official science, whose care was a well-defined state duty. The Department of Astronomy in the imperial palace was always one of the essential organs in the central government of China. It is described as such in the *Chou-li*, a compilation of the second century BC which seems to reflect the principles of the Chou state after they had become rigid and had been reduced to a system by later theorists.

According to the *Shu-ching*, the mythical emperor Yao gave official standing to the astronomers Hsi and Ho. The portion of the text containing this brief passage may go back to the eighth or seventh century BC, and is the first mention in history of Chinese astronomy. In fact, however, the Hsi-Ho pair represent the mythical being who is sometimes the mother and sometimes the charioteer of the sun, according to Maspero's view. Astronomy was the secret science of the Chou priest-kings. But we have no precise record of the Chou period, except what can be deduced from the speculations of the period which follows. All that can be said is that the observation of eclipses, especially eclipses of the moon, was of a purely empirical nature and went back to very ancient times. The first certain observation is that recorded in the *Shih-ching*, and its date is 734 BC; but others earlier were mentioned on Shang divination bones, with dates in the fourteenth and thirteenth centuries.

In India of the Early and Late Vedic periods science is of a sacral and ritual nature and is always connected, directly or indirectly, with the proper execution of a sacrifice or with the sacred texts. We cannot properly speak of systematic empirical observations.

We can get a very vague idea of Vedic astronomy from scattered passages of the *Veda*, particularly the *Brāhmana* of the *Yajurveda*. In Late Vedic times, perhaps much later, the traditional conceptions of astronomy got codified in a very short treatise called the *Jyotiṣa-Vedāṅga*, of which there were two recensions, one with 43 verses and the other 36. This work is eminently practical in character; it provides instruction for calculating the auspicious days and hours for sacrifices. Towards the end of this period some Babylonian influences seem to have penetrated into India through the Achaemenid empire, but of this we shall say something in Part II. Indian astronomy was established to meet the needs of the calendar and for the knowledge of cosmic movements, which Brahmanic liturgy had meant for a long time to appropriate as its own.[33] The Vedic year was luni-solar, being divided into 360 days with 12 months: it comprised first 3 and later 6 seasons. To correct the discrepancy arising from the solar and lunar elements use was made of a 5-year cycle (*yuga*), during which 2 months were intercalated according to the methods left undefined by the *Vedāṅga*. Already in the Vedic age the main characteristic of Indian astronomy is represented by the 27 *naksatra* or mansions of the moon, the main purpose of which was to determine the relations between full moon and the sun.

The Babylonians, and indeed the Mesopotamian peoples in general, applied themselves from very early times to empirical observation and measurement of cosmic phenomena in order to formulate regular laws and forecast future occurrences, for instance eclipses. At least as early as the eighth century Chaldean priests had observatories from which they ceaselessly watched the course of the sun, the earth, and the planets, in relation to the fixed constellations. They gradually attained the conception of the Zodiac, which after continuous improvements was given the most precise expression by astronomers of the Persian period of Babylonia, about 538. They expounded theories about solstices and equinoxes, estimated the duration of days and nights at the various seasons, and made similar calculations. But an inevitable result of this very precise knowledge of the time relationships affecting cosmic processes was that in the state service of these countries astronomy became confused with astrology; yet the link between the two provided fresh impulse to the perfection of observation and calculation. The documents of King Ashur-banipal (669–630) are the high watermark in the history of the astronomical and astrological studies which had been going on in the previous centuries. It is to the Babylonians that Herodotus (II, 109) ascribes the invention of the astronomical instruments which later passed to the Greeks. But the whole question of the 'Syrian year', so far as chronology is concerned, is much in debate among modern scholars.

The Egyptians made little progress in astronomical studies after the end of the previous epoch. They had already by empirical methods established the relation between the 'Sotiac' year, which contained 365¼ days and was presumably used by the priests, and the 'approximate' year of 365 or 366 days. The relation was based essentially on observation of the times of Nile floods, on the intervals between the dawn rising of Sirius, and on the passage of the sun through the ecliptic.

In Greece astronomical observation was still in its infancy during the early centuries of the first millennium BC. The only constellations mentioned in the Homeric poems (*Iliad*, XVIII, 486) are the Pleiades, the Hyades, and the Great Bear, which was used to guide seamen; and Hesiod's attention to the most complex celestial phenomena is given only for their local significance in relation to work in the country. But from the first half of the sixth century astronomical notions began to gain ground. They came partly from direct observation, partly from learning derived from contacts with the peoples of Anatolia, Syria, Phoenicia, and Egypt, but most of all from philosophical and dialectical speculations by the Greeks themselves. Theories to explain their observations multiplied unceasingly. The 'Ionian' philosophers attempted to formulate Laws of Nature, even before they had adequate information about the phenomena these Laws were meant to govern. At the same time the Pythagoreans, though equally lacking solid data, sought to explain the world through abstruse and secret formulae related to the theory of numbers.

When Thales of Miletus in the early sixth century supposedly predicted[34] the eclipse of the sun on 28 May 585, he must undoubtedly have made use (having served on campaigns in Lydia) of learning derived from the East, where they knew of the 223 lunations between two successive eclipses. Eastern learning probably also accounts for his affirmation that the angles subtended at the eye by the diameters of sun and moon are each 1/720 of a full circle. It may be the Phoenicians who taught him that sailing should be guided not by the Great Bear but by the Lesser. It is doubtful whether he in fact anticipated Pythagoras in contending that the earth is round.

About the same time, or slightly later, Pherecydes of Leros constructed a sun-dial or 'gnomon' on the island of Leros to observe the sun's movements. His contemporary Anaximander of Miletus is also credited with this discovery, though here too Babylonia was probably the source. Anaximander later observed how the point at which the midday sun is vertical continually shifts with a spiral movement from tropic to tropic; and he affirmed that the earth is poised at the centre of the universe without any support.

A step backward was taken by Anaximenes of Miletus (died *c.* 528–524) who maintained that the earth was flat and supported on air, that the planets are to be distinguished from the fixed stars, being nearer to the sun, but that the sun, the moon, and the stars all took their origin from the earth.

Finally Pythagoras of Samos (died *c.* 497), who had, as we know from his disciples, travelled in Egypt and Babylonia and learned there many secrets in astronomy and mathematics, maintained that the earth is round and is isolated in space. To his astronomy he applied his theories about number and harmony.

c. *Mathematics and Geometry*

The Chinese word for mathematics, *suan*, is not older than Confucius: the character in question may originally have represented the counting-board. From the start Chinese arithmetic was associated with divination. The figures normally used today are already found on divination bones and tortoise-shells of the Shang period and on Chou period bronzes and coins.

From the very beginning the numerical system was decimal and multi-plicative ('300' for example is expressed by characters for 'three' and 'hundred'); it is not cumulative like Latin, which wrote CCC. Only the lower multiples of ten (20, 30, 40) show signs of cumulative principles; with these exceptions the Chinese repeated all the nine original numbers with the addition of a place-value component, the latter not being itself a numeral: thus was laid the foundation of the positional system. Nevertheless the essential pivot was lacking, for there was no zero digit. The character *ling*, which indicates zero today, originally (in the *Shih-ching*) meant the rain-drop, clinging to some object; later it came to mean 'remainder'; but it was not used in the sense of 'zero' before the fifteenth century A D. All these features, and still more the strict decimal notation, make the Chinese numerical system completely independent of that used in Meso-potamia.

There is apparently no long tradition behind mathematics in India: it seems impossible to discover anything of a mathematical nature in the *Rigveda*. The *Yajurveda*, however, already shows knowledge of a set of special terms for the higher powers of ten (up to 10^{12}); and the *Brāhmaṇa* (especially *Śatapatha Brāhmaṇa*) went even further in this direction. The geometry of the *Śulvasūtra* concerns the construction of the Vedic altar; but this text probably belongs to the second half of the first century B C, and will be dealt with later on.

As regards Egypt the secrecy maintained by the priests and their scribes has meant that we have more knowledge of the practical application of mathematics than of the procedure and methods that were followed. But in general two things can be said. First, our period saw little more than a continuation of the methods invented in earlier generations: in many respects there was actual decadence. Secondly, there was still a tendency to use mathematics and geometry to resolve everyday practical problems, such as dividing food rations between groups of men or animals, apportioning tax payments in relation to the precise size of estates, and calculating the number of bricks needed for a building or the number of men required to transport an obelisk or remove a sand-hill in an exact period of time. The Egyptians showed no tendency to construct or even to simplify the methods which had come down to them. Even if antiquated and cumbrous these methods were considered adequate; for example the actual writing of the decimal system numerals required a very large number of signs in the traditional hieroglyphic; and arithmetical operations were carried out by simple count-ing, lengthy though it was.

The same may be said of their primitive reckoning of fractions, normally with the numerator 1. This did not prevent them, however, from reaching the solution of problems with two unknowns, or from understanding many of the properties of plane figures: the latter were necessary for their measure-ments. Herodotus (II, 109) records how Sesostris (i.e. perhaps Ramses II,

I   NAVIGATION I

(a) *Models of Babylonian skin vessels, c. 700 BC*

(b) *Plan of a Phoenician war galley, seventh century BC*

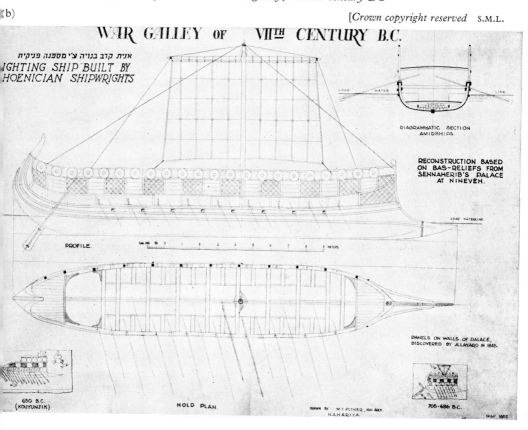

2 ANCIENT COINAGE I

Syracuse, Decadrachm of Cimon, late fifth century BC

[M.G.

3 *Ritual wine vessel, Middle Chou. Paris, Musée Guimet*

4   *Egyptian sculpture, Twenty-sixth Dynasty: head of a priest*

(b) *Ashur banipal on his chariot; bas-relief from Nineveh. Paris, Louvre*

[*photo Chuzeville*]

(a)

[*photo Chuzeville*]

6. Khorsabad palace: the officers: eighth century B.C.

7 (a) *Persepolis, the 'Hall of Xerxes'*, c. 518–460 *BC*
  (b) *Pasargadae, the tomb of Cyrus the Great*, c. 529 *BC*

8 *Anthropoid Punic sarcophagus, fifth century BC, from La Cannita, Sicily*

9 THE EVOLUTION OF ANCIENT CERAMICS, I

(a) *Geometric pictorial decoration on a vase. London, British Museum*

(b) *Dipylon funerary urn: the exhibition of the body and mourners' procession, middle eighth century BC. Paris, Louvre*

(a)   [B.M.

(b)   [*photo Chauseville*

(a)   *[photo Chauseville*

10   THE EVOLUTION OF ANCIENT CERAMICS, II

(a) *Corinthian school: Heracles guest of Eurytius, early sixth century BC. Paris, Louvre*

(b) *Kylix depicting Arcesilas of Cyrene, Laconian ware from Vulci, Etruria, c. 550 BC. Paris, Bibliothèque Nationale*

(b)   [B.N.P.

(a)

[Alinari

II THE EVOLUTION OF ANCIENT
CERAMICS, III

(a) *Black figure Attic Vase, the
'François vase', by Ergoti-
mus and Clitias, c. 570 BC.
Florence, Archaeological
Museum*

(b) *Black figure Attic vase,
by the Priam Painter, c.
510–500 BC.*

[B.M.

12 THE EVOLUTION OF ANCIE
    CERAMICS, IV

   (a) *Black figure Attic va*
      Heracles fighting
      lion; detail showing
      technique of the artis

   (b) *Panathenaic ampho*
      young men racing. (Ro
      Vatican Museum)

[B.F.M.

[A

(a) *'La Dame d'Auxerre', Cretan style archaic statuette, second half of the seventh century BC* (0·65 m.) *Paris, Louvre*

(b) *Statue of Hera from the temple of Hera at Samos, sixth century BC* (1·92 m.). *Paris, Louvre*

(a)

(b)

[photo Chuzeville   *[photo Chuzeville*

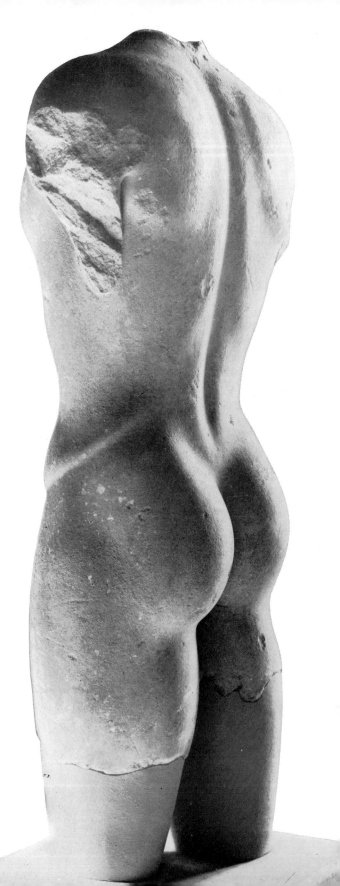

14   ARCHAIC SCULPTURE, II

Torso of a young man from Leontini, Sicily, sixth century BC

[von Matt

15   ARCHAIC SCULPTURE, III
   'The Rape of Europa', c. 550 BC. Metope from a temple, Selinus, Sicily

16 ARCHAIC SCULPTURE, IV

(a) *The Nike of Delos. Athens National Museum*

(b) *Korai, votive statue,* c. 540 *BC. Athens National Museum*

(a)   [Hellenic

(b)   [Hell

1292–1234 B C) had all Egypt divided into a number of quadrilaterals of equal area, in order to obtain uniform tribute from the population, and how he also gave each owner plots of land which exactly corresponded with those ruined by the floods: in this way, Herodotus says, geometry was born among the Egyptians, and it was later transmitted to the Greeks. The measurement of solid figures—pyramids, cubes and spheres—was very probably done by experimental means rather than by calculation.

The same phenomenon of methods discovered much earlier being preserved by tradition in our period is noticeable in the Mesopotamian countries, where the once flourishing culture of the Babylonians was now being maintained and transmitted by the Assyrians, but at a lower pitch. In the past they had undoubtedly attained most remarkable results, including the formulation of what we call Pythagoras' theorem and the solution of quadratic equations with two unknowns.

But the greatest discoveries of mathematical and geometrical truths were due to the Greeks, who were, having learned much from Eastern science, predestined to these studies by their lively intelligence and their invincible desire to understand causes and effects, to find rational explanations, and to engage in abstract thought.[35] With the Greeks the world passed from attempts to solve practical problems of mathematics and geometry to the construction of the most daring and successful theoretical structures. They showed later centuries the methods of research, and actually created the terminology which was later adopted throughout the world.[36]

The ancients affirm that Thales, whose activity belongs to the first half of the sixth century, learned his geometry in Egypt: this should probably be taken to mean that it was in Egypt that he saw diagrams illustrating measurements and sought to draw general conclusions from them. He is credited with the enunciation of certain theorems: that a diameter divides the circle into two equal parts; that opposite angles formed by the intersection of two straight lines are equal; that triangles with three equal angles and an equal side are congruent; and that the angle inscribed in a semicircle is a right angle. By the use of triangles he propounded formulae for determining the height of a building or the distance away of a ship on the sea.

But the really outstanding discoveries in mathematics and geometry were those made in the last decades of our period by Pythagoras and his disciples. They were concerned not only with odd and even, or prime and compound numbers, but with prime numbers related to figures, that is to say with numbers which were imagined to represent the points of a plane figure (triangular, square, pentagonal, hexagonal numbers, etc.) or of a three-dimensional figure (pyramidal, cubic, parallelopiped, etc.). The Pythagoreans were responsible for the theory of proportions and the theory of musical intervals proportionate to the length of a chord at constant tension. Pythagorean arithmetic is illustrated by the work of Nicomachus and Theon of Smyrna in the first century A D and of Iamblichus in the third. It includes the theory of 'perfect' numbers, and of 'side' and 'diameter' numbers; and it was the first to define incommensurate numbers and surds.

In geometry, besides the famous theorem which bears his name, Pythagoras was credited with thorough study of such matters as the five regular solids, the relation between areas of one plane figure and another, the properties of parallel lines, and the proposition that the angles of a triangle are equal to two right angles.

It is very difficult, often impossible, to distinguish what really goes back to Pythagoras, who left no written work, from the additions to the Pythagorean *corpus* made by his many faithful disciples, often exceedingly able men, in the century which takes us to the time of Philolaus, a contemporary of Socrates. The school was also influenced from outside by the modifications and criticisms suggested by Eleatic philosophers like Parmenides and Zeno, especially on the theory of incommensurate numbers.

Another matter which goes back to the Pythagoreans is the classification of the sciences of the so-called 'quadrivium', arithmetic, music, plane geometry (*geodesia* and solid geometry (related to astronomy). One may add, in passing, that the people of central America seem to have shown a special tendency to appreciate abstract numbers.

d. *Medicine*

The legendary founder of Chinese medicine is the equally legendary emperor Shên-nung. In actual fact the evidence for the development of medicine before Confucius' time is exceedingly scanty. The *Chou-li*, a compilation of the second century B C, describes the medical administration in the Chou palace with the rigid schematism characteristic of Confucian theorists, but seems to be founded on a core of genuine fact. There were five departments: general supervision including the health of the emperor; health of the people; ulcers and septic treatment; supervision of the imperial dietary; and veterinary service. The first certain item of a medical nature in historical records appears under the year 540 B C in the *Tso-chuan*, which was probably compiled in the third century B C: it speaks of an illness of the duke of Chin being recognized as due to a failure of *yang* (the male principle —see Part II). And that is about all the evidence for this period.

In India medicine appears as a profession as early as the native hymns of the *Rigveda*: the Aśvin twins are called 'doctors'. Medicine and magic are of course still indistinguishable. From various hymns in the *Atharvaveda* we can see that treatment consisted mainly in the use of herbs, water, and magic formulae. Knowledge of pathology was quite elementary, although the *Atharvaveda* gives the names of a large number of diseases and symptoms without precisely relating the latter to the former. Anatomical knowledge, thanks to the technique used in sacrifices, did make some progress, and the vocabulary in this field is comparatively rich. Moreover the physiological speculation found in the *Upaniṣad*, in the form it takes towards the end of this period, may be connected with medicine, since in some sense it provides its theoretical premises. This is a pneumatic theory of physiology, based on the five kinds of breath (*prāṇa*) which are supposed to give life to the body. On the one hand these breaths are identical with the forces of nature, on the other they correspond with the five organs of the human body, vision, hearing, speech, thought, and touch. The *prāṇa* of the human microcosm are linked with the macrocosm outside by a body of defined relationships.

Medicine in the Mesopotamian areas during the Assyrian period came to a standstill for a time, though the knowledge obtained in the preceding generations was substantially maintained. Men still believed in the importance of a patient's dreams to determine the nature of his illness, in diseases caused by devils or cast on the sufferer by sorcerers, and in 'possessed' persons who made the world around them unclean. Many primitive methods of a magical character were still employed to deal with disease. As time went on, however, some use at any rate was made of suggestion to influence recovery; and it was accompanied at intervals by dietetic remedies and hygienic prescriptions, and by the administration of genuine medicines which had been proved useful by experience. Water, the element of the goddess Ea, mother of Marduk, was of fundamental importance in effecting cures—by baths, washings, compresses and the like—and the doctor was called A-su, the man learned in water. The other element which was at the root of all healing was fire, applied mainly from small torches: fire was dependent on the god Gibil. Appropriate measures were taken against devils and witchcraft: cords and knots to imprison the devils, and exorcism by means of amulets, imprecations, curses, mysterious magical formulae, and similar symbolism.

The heart was still believed to be the seat of the intellect, the blood was the source of life, and the liver the origin of its circulation. Surgical operations had been known for centuries. They must throughout have involved a heavy responsibility for the men performing them; but anatomical knowledge progressed as a result of the operations themselves and of the dissection of animals.

Hebrew monotheism had been preceded by polytheistic ideas, which had not been completely abandoned. There always remained some form of struggle between the idea of God, who was the source of health and punished the wicked with diseases infecting all around them, and the idea of the malignant devil corrupting mankind, who was pictured in the form of a serpent. Medicine was normally practised by the priests, but there were also empirical practitioners; and the embalmers were a profession on their own. In epidemics the Hebrews had recourse to isolation. There were hygienic rules about baths and diet, and some of the characteristic rites, such as circumcision, were perhaps a further measure directed to health.

In Egypt medicine was the science belonging to the god Imhotep. Its practice by the priests now came to be extended to private doctors, who were trained in schools annexed to the temples. A general feature in Egypt was the tendency towards practical knowledge rather than theoretical. We have a number of texts about medicine from papyri of the period between the Thirteenth Dynasty and the tenth century B C. Every one of them is concerned with clinical experience and diagnosis; and they provide an enormous number of prescriptions for drugs and for magical or astrological practices, as well as recommending surgical treatments and rules of hygiene. The witch-doctor in Egypt was still convinced that any abnormal or unknown condition in illness resulted from malevolent influence exercised by evil spirits; and his first task was to use magical action to chase away such spirits before they took hold. So we get formulae, amulets, and all the elements of exorcism. But just because the magician became a doctor he was likely, when his magic had been tried, to have recourse to alternative cures like drugs, and gradually to try out their efficacy.

But though medicine allowed this system of trial and error, and was almost working in the dark, the case of surgery was different. Direct knowledge of the cause of the trouble made surgeons more confident, and cleared their path of the survivals from magical practices. In fact anatomy and comparative physiology had made great progress through the embalming of human beings and animals at the hands of specialists: the progress is shown by the fullness of anatomical vocabulary. The beating of the heart and pulses had long ago brought understanding of the fact that the heart is connected by channels with all parts of the body; but dissection of the dead (and not the living) had left men doubtful as to what flowed in these channels, air or water or mucus or some other substance. They had succeeded in establishing the correspondence between particular movements of the brain and particular activities of the body; but they went on to postulate a curious relation between the ear and the pulmonary system. Hygienic prescriptions had made remarkable progress in recommending bodily cleanliness, physical exercise, abstention from meat unless its condition was assured, and circumcision. Just as a father was forbidden to expose his children, so the doctor was not allowed to assist abortion. From the time of the Homeric poems (see *Odyssey*, IV, 220) to that of Herodotus (II, 84)—and indeed as late as the composition of the works used by Diodorus (I, 82)—the Greeks were generally convinced that the best medical specialists were to be found in Egypt; and the Persians, too, had held this view. In the course of centuries starting in the Minoan and Mycenaean periods Greece was vitally affected by medical science coming from Egypt, as also from Anatolia, Syria, and the Mesopotamian lands. The influence was greatly strengthened when Hellenic colonies were planted in the East and when Greeks began to travel in these parts.

From Minoan and Mycenaean times the Aegean world possessed a remarkable amount of medical knowledge. We know this not only from the discovery of advanced systems of hygiene in the palaces of Crete, with their conduits, drains, baths, and latrines, but from the high qualifications assumed to exist among Homeric doctors like Podalirios the physician or Machaon the surgeon, both of them secular practitioners and highly specialized. In mythology, too, there are many divinities connected with medicine: some, like Apollo, Athena, and Hygieia, were common to all the Greeks; others like Chiron and Asclepius were localized, and were regarded as heroes by those who did not worship them as gods. The cult of Asclepius, however, gradually gained ground,[37] and he became a god to the whole Greek world; temples were erected to him, and their priests became the most distinguished doctors of Greece. The shrines in question were originally placed near sacred springs, with groves near by for the pilgrims and the sick people; later they were equipped with proper rooms for lodging and treatment, at which point we reach the first stages of clinics and hospitals.

In early days treatment was largely of a magical character, based on the interpretation of patients' dreams. Cures were regarded as miraculous, and are described as such on ex-voto tablets which were hung in the rooms of the Asclepiaeum.

Later regular schools of genuine doctors gradually came into being, drawing some of their members from the laity. In these the magical element gave way more and more to actual clinical observation. The school of Cnidus, which began in the seventh century, relied primarily on diagnosis, by means of the symptoms recognized as belonging to each classified disease. The Cos school, which had come into being by the sixth century, mainly paid attention to prognosis and to the way each disease took its course. In later times medical schools were founded independently of the Asclepius temples, for example the one at Croton in Magna Graecia where the Pythagoreans gave instruction. Very soon two types of practitioner existed side by side: the traditionalist, who still employed magic, and the man who liked to be called a 'physician' because he was an observer of human nature in relation to its environment.

Pythagoras, for example, believed that human action emanated from 'universal' action, and supposed a relationship between microcosm and macrocosm of a kind that was later taken up by Plato and the neo-Platonists. The Pythagoreans of the fifth century, Alcmaeon and his disciples Acron and Pausanias, made use of dissection of animals to achieve various anatomical discoveries, such as the optic nerve and the 'Eustacian tube'. In general they believed that health depended on harmony between the elements constituting the body: disharmony brought disease.

Empedocles on the other hand was a follower of Anaximenes (died c. 528–524), who had maintained that air was the primordial element of nature, embracing the universe and constituting the soul which supported the human body. Empedocles himself (died 430) believed that *pneuma*—air, breath, the spirit that rises trembling from sacrificial victims—was the element which runs warm round the heart and veins and which gives life. In this way he was responsible for the development of a 'pneumatic' school, which was advanced further by the fifth-century philosopher Diogenes of Apollonia. For the rest, however, Empedocles was still an exponent of the tendency to combine magic and miracles with genuine observation of nature: yet his own observation was particularly acute, and it eventually led him to discover that respiration takes place through the pores of the skin.

Among Italian peoples the earliest and least derivative advances in medicine were clearly due to the Etruscans, whose Lucumones, according to the Greeks, were descended from Circe, the enchantress skilled in drugs and incantations. It was from Etruria that the rudiments of medicine must have penetrated to Rome. There the earliest ideas on the subject were theistic, as we know from hearing of goddesses of particular diseases such as Febris, Mephitis, and Fessonia, or protectors of particular parts of the body like Uterina, or deities concerned with particular physiological functions like Lucina (the goddess of childbirth). At the head of all was Salus, later worshipped in a temple on the Quirinal. Cato, the Censor, used to say that Rome had lived 'without doctors, but never without medicine'; and in his day diseases in men and animals were still largely treated by magic and ritual, to the accompaniment of mysterious formulae, while health-giving virtues of a general kind were ascribed to certain herbs and to other vegetables such as cabbage. Tradition required every family to preserve the prescriptions and formulae which the *pater familias* was accustomed himself to use.

Pharmacology. The number of substances believed to have healing properties gradually grew as discoveries were made empirically by various peoples in very different parts of the world. One people told another about their virtues, which became better and better understood. At the same time many methods of preparing and administering these substances were invented and became more widely known. Some, it is true, could be swallowed in their natural state, but others had to be crushed or cooked or cleaned; and later they might have to be processed into extracts, pills, or other readily assimilable form, or manufactured into ointment for use in plasters, massage and the like, or even made suitable for administration in inhalations, suppositories, or enemas.

Examples of the materials employed in the earliest times and explanations of their use are provided chiefly by the medical papyri of the Egyptians, who made use of all kinds of substances, animal, vegetable, and mineral. Animal substances included meat, but more particularly fat—from cattle, asses, hippopotamuses, lions, mice, bats, and lizards. The scrapings from horns or tortoise-shells were other ingredients; also portions of skin, bones, and talons, calcified and ground.

Vegetables, prepared by specialists, were sometimes useful in their entirety. Sometimes only the roots, stalks, flowers, fruit, seeds, marrow, or juice would be employed. Many types had proved their worth as medicaments, like poppy, aloe, mint, pomegranate, or henbane. Solutions were usually made in milk, honey, wine, or beer: ointments were based on honey or goose-fat. Special closets and containers were available for keeping medicines. Comparatively sensitive scales were employed to weigh doses which had been precisely prescribed.

Most of these specialized usages and devices passed from the Egyptians and other oriental peoples to the Greeks, and from them on to the Romans.

e. *The Origins of the World*

An account of the theological explanations provided of the origins of the world may be postponed until we reach the history of Greek philosophy. In this chapter on science we need say nothing further about Pherecydes, or about the Ionian 'physiocrats' from Thales onwards with their explanations in terms of single elements, or about Anaximander's theory of the transformation of organic entities from one substance to another.

Serious study of particulars in animal, vegetable, and mineral nature began in the fourth century BC. But the foundations had been laid in the keen observation of nature which had been going on for centuries, especially at the hands of poets and artists. One has only to number the figures of animals and plants, sometimes represented realistically and sometimes stylized, in sculpture, murals, and vase-painting beginning in Minoan and Mycenaean times; the descriptions and similes drawn from domestic animals and from plants in the poets from Homer downwards; and the references to work in the country in Hesiod's *Works and Days*. Theophrastus tells us of early writers on botany and agronomy. As to minerals, the evidence of metal-work, architecture, jewellery, sculpture, and carpentry shows how every type was known and understood.

f. *The Beginnings of Philology*

In the Greek world philology did not develop as a science till the fourth century (see Part II), but some of the earlier attempts made in this direction by eastern countries are worth remembering. The biblical etymologies of proper names are an example; so are the various glossaries and the documents written in more than one language, of which we spoke in the chapter on 'Language and Writing'. These include bilingual texts in Assyrian and Sumerian, in Chaldean and Assyrian, and in Hittite and Phoenician (the Karatepe texts); and trilingual texts in Persian, Elamite, and Babylonian. Their main purpose, however, was to clarify the significance of cuneiform.

In India the fact that the *Veda* were sacred writings, unborn and undying, inevitably led to jealous care to preserve the purity of their text. This gave rise to whole series of post-Vedic writings, which were classified as one of the six *Vedāṅga* (ancillary sciences of the *Veda*). They were given the name of *Śiksa-Vedāṅga* and were concerned with the correct pronunciation and accentuation of the *Veda*.

The earliest manuals of this kind have the general name of *prātiśākhya* and are in prose. More highly favoured later on were the *sūtra*, collections of pithy mnemonic verses, which could be fully understood only with the aid of oral instruction. Very soon the texts began to be examined from the grammatical standpoint; grammar (*vyākaraṇa*) was another of the six *Vedāṅga*. No grammatical writing of the Vedic period has been preserved, unless one classifies under this head the *Uṇādisūtras*, which deal with the derivations of nouns from the roots, or the *Phitsūtra*, which are concerned with accentuation. Both these works, at any rate in their earliest form, refer to the Vedic language and not to Sanskrit. Etymological speculation, another of the six *Vedāṅga*, is represented only by the *Nirukta* of *Yāska*, a series of etymological analyses of Vedic words which had been collected in an earlier work, the *Nighaṇṭu*; the introduction to the *Nirukta* does constitute a genuine small treatise on general grammar.

NOTES TO CHAPTER III

1. Some of this material is excellently treated by Jacquetta Hawkes and Sir Leonard Woolley, *History of Mankind*, Volume I-1, Chapter XI, and Volume I-2, Chapters IV, V, and VI.

2. In the early period of their history the Phoenician and Carthaginian colonies were not agricultural, and so could not serve as centres for the diffusion of agriculture. In North Africa, as in other areas of Phoenician colonization, agriculture developed without the aid of the Phoenicians. (K. M. Kolobova.)

3. See Jacquetta Hawkes, *History of Mankind*, Volume I-1, Chapters VIII and X.

4. In Carthage agriculture was still in its infancy in the fifth century. Mago's work relates to a later period, and cannot be cited in this context. During this period there was indeed highly developed agriculture in Syria and Phoenicia, but we know relatively little about it. (K. M. Kolobova.)

5. See Appendix, Chapter I, pp. 49 ff.

6. On domestication of animals see also Jacquetta Hawkes and Sir Leonard Woolley, *History of Mankind*, I, pp. 279 ff., 519 ff.

7. In Professor F. M. Heichelheim's view bee-keeping goes back to Mesolithic times. He adds that the cat was domesticated in Egypt, and the pigeon (very probably) in Babylonia.

8. Professor H. Michell questions whether there is evidence for any such decline. See the discussion in his book *The Economics of Ancient Greece* (Cambridge, 1940), p. 76.

9. The Minoan palaces in Crete were destroyed twice—about 1600 and about 1500 BC. In the first case they were all restored and enlarged. In the second case the Palace of Knossos survived, although it underwent reconstruction in connection with the appearance of the 'Throne Room'. (K. M. Kolobova.)

10. Dr A. G. Drachmann calls attention to the great improvement made to the early plough when a mould-board was added.

11. Professor H. Michell doubts whether oats were cultivated in ancient Greece: the word *bromos* means the wild oat, which was regarded as a weed. See also A. Jardé, *Les Céréales dans l'antiquité grecque* (Paris, 1925), p. 4.

12. For discussion of the ancient evidence about crop rotation, which leaves one in some doubt about the extent of Greek knowledge of the subject, see H. Michell, *op. cit.*, p. 57.

13. L. A. Moritz, *Grain-mills and Flour in Classical Antiquity* (Oxford, 1958), has now established a strong case for believing that the rotary mill was not invented before *c*. 200 BC, and that consequently before this time the use of animals was impossible. If he is right this is a most interesting example of the unevenness of technological advance in ancient times.

14. Fabius Pictor, the Roman senator and historian, fought in the Second Punic War (late third century BC).

15. Professor H. Michell (see *The Economics of Ancient Greece*, p. 192) shows that furnaces were not hot enough to produce pig iron: they produced wrought iron, which requires only 700° C.

16. The Chalybes were a real tribe, though most of the stories about them were pure legends.

17. Professor F. M. Heichelheim notes that for profitable iron-working it was also essential to have a supply of cheap charcoal.

18. Perhaps also, as Professor F. M. Heichelheim suggests, the Celtic warriors in southern France and northern Italy may have helped here.

19. Coral came to Mediterranean countries from the Red Sea and the Indian Ocean.

20. Dr A. G. Drachmann points out that a solid wheel, too, could rotate round an axle.

21. See Appendix, Chapter I, pp. 49 ff.

22. Thucydides (I, 13) appears to put this invention as early as 700. See, however, J. A. Davison, *Classical Quarterly* (1947), p. 18, who adduces arguments for a much later date (late sixth century).

23. Professor F. M. Heichelheim recalls also the much earlier 'Ophir' expeditions from Elath on the Red Sea to (probably) east Africa, carried out on orders of King Solomon.

24. Professor H. Michell objects that *pecunia* derives from the 'ox-standard' of value, mentioned often in Homer, and that it is unlikely that livestock—generally speaking—were a main constituent of trade. Especially not, one would think, of trade by sea.

25. At the end of the second and the beginning of the first millennia the Phoenicians carried on an extensive trade as intermediaries. They played an important part not only in the slave trade but also in the development of production for the market in the Mediterranean lands. (K. M. Kolobova.)

26. The importance of Croton and Sybaris must not be overlooked, the latter (until her destruction *c*. 510) being Miletus' main source of raw wool.

27. The lay-out described in this paragraph naturally came about only by degrees. In particular the bankers' offices would not have been seen before the late sixth century BC.

28. For the probability that the earliest Greek (silver) coinage was struck in Ionia *c*. 620 BC, see above, p. 53, n. 22. The earliest gold coinage probably appeared in Lydia and Ionia under Croesus (*c*. 560–546). The ratio of gold to silver probably fluctuated widely: Herodotus (III, 95) appears to give a ratio of 1:13 in the Persian empire.

29. A weights and measures table which prescribed 73 drachmae to the mina is hardly conceivable. The figure is probably due to a manuscript corruption in Plutarch, *Solon*, 15.

30. Many scholars now, however, believe that there was no Athenian coinage before Solon, and that what Athens did was first (under Solon) to join the Euboic *metric* system, and then (later) to coin on this system.

31. Professor H. Michell (see also *op. cit.*, pp. 162 ff.) doubts the profitability of slave labour. But for a much more favourable estimate (akin to Professor Pareti's) of the returns accruing to owners, both from the use and from the hiring-out of slaves, see A. H. M. Jones, *Economic History Review* (1956), pp. 187 ff.

32. Professor P. Bosch-Gimpera would place both these explorations about 450 BC. For argument in support of Professor Pareti's date see M. Cary and E. Warmington, *The Ancient Explorers* (London, 1929), pp. 47 ff.

33. It should be pointed out that the beginnings of Indian astronomy do not show that observation of the heavens was used for astrological ends, and that the astronomical

phenomena (as well as the meteorological phenomena which they noticed, such as the monsoon from the south-west) appear to have given rise to a general conception of a natural cosmic order (ṛta, see Chapter V, p. 226, later dharma). The concept of such an order as demonstrating truth and justice appears in any case common to the Iranians and Indians; the ancient Persians knew it under the name of arta (as well as arta brazmaniya or 'Brahmanic order'), and in the Avesta under the name aša.

The Vedic system (Yajurveda and Atharvaveda) of nakṣatra allows the marking of positions of the sun in relation to the full moon and also in regard to the nakṣatra themselves; the sun being in diametrical opposition with the nakṣatra passing the meridian at midnight. The determinations reached by this system are more precise than those of the zodiac which has only twelve divisions and uses the less precise observations based on heliacal risings and settings.

34. It was generally believed in antiquity that Thales made this prediction. But O. Neugebauer (The Exact Sciences in Antiquity [Copenhagen, 1957], p. 142) argues cogently that he could have done no such thing.

35. Professor K. M. Kolobova would rather emphasize the requirements of Greek society, their socio-economic system, and also the fact that Greek scientists in many instances proceed from the achievements of scientists in the ancient East.

36. As Professor Ch. Th. Saricakis points out, the most fundamental contribution of the early Greek mathematicians was the discovery of mathematical proof.

37. Although its greatest advance probably comes in the period covered by Part II, i.e. in the fourth century BC.

CHAPTER IV

POLITICAL ORGANIZATION AND SOCIAL LIFE

I. POLITICAL ORGANIZATION

THE rate of political and social progress in the ancient world was as uneven as that made in other directions. Primitive ideas and institutions of which only traces remained among the leading peoples were still active among others, the precise development of the latter depending on the nature of their contacts with the leaders. A good example can be seen in the small family groups[1] which got established in independent states, each one working on its own with its own permanent or temporary headquarters. The leader might be a priest-magician, or the mightiest man of war, or the oldest and wisest head of a family. This 'tribal' organization continued to be the basis of life among the peripheral peoples, especially in mountainous districts or in steppe and semi-desert country; at the most such regions might achieve federation between a set of tribes, often because they had some of their more important cults in common. But among more civilized peoples the ancient tribal divisions tended to lose their independent status as the total population and its territory grew in size. They were converted into regional divisions used for administrative convenience and for the military levy.

a. *Early Forms of Monarchy*

In archaic times the more progressive peoples were mostly ruled by a king, whose nature and attributes depended on the particular historical background. Especially in the East the king was conceived to be the living personification of a god, or the divine descendant of the dynasty's divine founder, a conception stubbornly preserved when the monarchy ran into trouble, or when assaults were made on its power. When for example in Egypt the priesthood, especially the priests of Ammon, god of Thebes, grew politically and economically powerful, and successfully challenged the rule of the Pharaohs, the new sovereign would still identify himself with a god, both in his lifetime and after his death; and the same happened when the native dynasties gave place to foreigners, Libyans or Nubians. The conception was still maintained even after the conquest by the Persian king: he too had become successor to the Pharaohs, and took care to secure his divine investiture. The Egyptian king's position in matters of religion, war, and justice was not in any doubt.

Less ambitious ties linked the Assyrian royal house with Ashur, the god who protected the capital city of their empire. Amid the high-sounding boasts which accompany the royal titulature from the days of Tiglath-Pileser I, who founded the empire in the eleventh century, to those of his last descendant, the seventh-century Ashur-banipal, we have to scan the inscriptions carefully for phrases defining the relation between king and god. We find words like 'desire of the heart of the gods', the 'exalted priest', who reigns 'by command of Ashur of Shamash and Marduck': he is 'procreation of Ashur and Beltu'; 'Ashur and Sin have called him to the Kingdom in days long past, appointing him even in his mother's womb to pastoral duty over the realm of Ashur'; 'Shamash, Addu, and Ishtar have bidden him wield the royal power'; 'he walks in awe under the word of the gods, to possess their sanctuaries and thrones, to execute their bidding, and to placate their hearts'; and he is their 'priest who implores their help, and with it he has vanquished all his enemies'. Admittedly, then, the Assyrian ruler is theocratic, owing his position to the god whose priest and vicar and governor he is. But he does not fully and directly identify himself with the god.

Of the Medes, Herodotus tells us (I, 96 ff.) that Deioces was chosen king because he administered justice better than any other. If the story is well founded, we may suppose that judicial functions were what mattered most in the king's power; and later the Magi, with their Zoroastrian doctrines, said Deioces behaved in this way because he knew that 'the unjust is enemy of the just'. The Achaemenid Persian rulers, who had initially been vassals of the Medes, were regarded as 'chosen' of the gods: at first of Bel and Nabu, then of Ahura-Mazda. They were raised to more than human stature as fathers of their peoples; they were supermen with whom no mortal might dares to stand compare (Herodotus, III, 160). This exalted position found reflection in the concept that their empire must extend to all quarters of the world. But the tolerance they accorded to the religions of conquered peoples allowed them, when they became sovereigns elsewhere, to be identified also with the gods of whom the rulers they had defeated were regarded as incarnations.

The Hebrews were used to nomadic life in tribes which were separate, or at best united into confederacies by sacred ties around a common temple. They were ruled by local chieftains (Judges), who were chosen by the grace of their god Yahweh for their military, political, or religious deeds. But when the whole nation, at that time in a state of social and economic evolution, had to engage in war against the Philistines, who were powerfully organized because a single monarchy ruled over them, then they too belatedly adopted a monarchic form.[2] An intermediate step was the combination of religious and political power in the hands of Samuel, priest of the shrine at Shiloh (tribe of Ephraim), who first made his influence felt by religious means, and then with the aid of his sons established a recognized position as a Judge. But later he conferred the dignity of King, first secretly and then openly, upon Saul. Samuel kept the religious power in his own hands, but very soon the dualism between king and priests broke up and he was compelled to withdraw from active life. Under David and Solomon the monarchy became unified and dynastic, but under Solomon's son tribal differences and religious dissension caused the nation to split into the two kingdoms of Judah and Israel.

The archaic period of Greek monarchy is revealed in two phases, the earlier attested by the archaeological evidence of the Mycenaean palaces, the latter by the literary evidence of the Homeric poems. The king based his power on descent from a god worshipped by his subjects, and was therefore regarded as a demi-god or hero. His power was transmitted by a combination of election and heredity; and he was at once chief priest, supreme arbiter in lawsuits of first instance and on appeal, and military leader. He controlled his people's goods[3] to the best advantage of the state, and the life of the state was entirely centred in him. Lord of large domains, he lived in a rich and massive palace, surrounded by the eldest and most experienced heads of families; and from the moment of his accession he was recognized as legitimate ruler. He was splendid in his pomp and valiant in war, bestowing some of the booty on the most deserving of his 'hetairoi' or *amici*; and as the owner of slaves, horses and chariots and powerful weapons of war he was feared by his almost unarmed subjects. He was called the *Wanax*, the *Basileus*, the 'shepherd of people', the bravest and richest of men, hero or demi-god; his exploits in peace and war brought him glory; and after his death he merited divine honours.[4]

The Italic peoples, too, those of both the first and the second migration, had from the first, in common with the Celts, the concept of King. We find it among the Siculans (*resos*), and among the Itali at the tip of the peninsula (Rhegium), in Latium (*rex*), among the predecessors of the Etruscans in Tuscany (Regisvilla), among the Oscans ('Diuvei regaturei' on inscriptions of Agnone in Campania), and among the Celts and peoples related to them (*rix*). In Latium a more primitive story of kings who were priests or almost magicians still survived in historical times in the *rex Nemorensis*, who had to yield his place to any stranger who could overcome him. The monarchy at Rome, however, had a relatively recent origin. It grew up afresh in the eighth century, when the inhabitants of the primitive villages, probably by peaceful accord among themselves, established 'Roma Quadrata', sometimes called 'Romulea'. There was no previous dynastic tradition to allow the king to rule by right of divine investiture. He was first and foremost the 'delegate' of the people who chose him, and to him men condemned by the popular assembly could appeal. The elective nature of the Roman kingship is shown by the way kings were drawn from different families; and it also explains the continuous control exercised over the kings by the body of *patres* or heads of families.

These conditions were profoundly altered with the Tarquins, who came as princes of the Etruscan conquerors: they were dynastic in their claims, and their religious attributes were more marked. All religious features connected with the Roman kings can be shown to be of Etruscan origin—the triumph, crown, procession, *fasces*, and lictors, and the tabernacle for taking the auspices.

Yet each of the Etruscan kings, until they began their conquests beyond Tuscany, held sway over a narrow country, in one of the cities belonging to the religious federation round the temple of Voltumna in the territory of Volsinii.

Indian society in this period has practically lost all its semi-nomadic features. Despite the prevalence of cattle-raising at the outset, the general picture we get from the Early and Late Vedic texts is one of a sedentary society, with its roots now firmly in the soil.

In India monarchy is the normal form of government. In the Vedic period the monarch is regarded mainly as a war chief, like the *Herzog* of the Germans. His title to kingship is first and foremost his ability as an army leader, displayed in the position of *vi′pati* or *viśāmpati* or chief of a tribe. The monarchy developed in an atmosphere which was purely patriarchal. The Vedic texts are conspicuously religious in outlook, but the king never appears in them as a divine personage nor even as a 'hero' in the Western sense of that term. Only in the Late Vedic period did features begin to appear, still in outline and with no general acceptance, which later became the basis of the idea of divine kingship, or rather of the divine quality of the dignity, not the person, of the king.

It is still a problem whether the oldest Indian monarchies were hereditary or elective. Some Vedic passages (*Ṛigveda*, X, 124, 8; *Atharvaveda*, III, 4, 2) seem to allude to a process of election by the elders or chiefs of the clans (*kulapati* and *viśpati*). But already in the Early Vedic period this seems to have been a pure formality of confirmation or acceptance; succession by heredity is the normal condition from the start. The position of the king varied in different periods. In the small Vedic tribal state the king's position is not an exalted one, nor are his powers absolute. Often he is merely the senior member in a council of clan chiefs; or at any rate there is a council (*samiti*) which controls his conduct of affairs. When the state grows bigger and possesses a regular territory, the position and privileges of the king naturally increase. It is to be noted that in no case did the king in India have sacerdotal functions; in the organization of later times, which was based on the caste system, the king is always a *Kṣattriya*. He has the duty of seeing to the execution of the great royal sacrifices; but he does no more than give the orders and provide the means, the rites themselves being exclusively the province of the Brahmans. Thus the monarchy is purely secular. Moreover, the king is in no way a legislator: his task is to be guardian and observer of the *dharma*, that moral and social law which has divine origin and is completely independent of the king, being based on the solid nexus of customs and tradition. The king is servant of the law, not its master.

Chinese civilization in the Chou period is entirely sedentary, without the smallest trace of nomadic or semi-nomadic ways. The Chou kings took their ancestry back to the mythical Hou Chi (the Millet Ruler), who was miraculously conceived when his mother stepped on the footmark left by a god (*Shih-ching*). But this does not make the sovereign a being of divine essence. The Chou king reigns through his own power and the power of his ancestors, who are a single bloc with the reigning sovereign, their combined power being the basis of the dynasty's fortunes. The monarchy is strictly hereditary; there is no sign of an elective system. The dynasty acquired its claim to legitimacy through divine mandate (*t'ien-ming*), the 'trusteeship' put in the hands of the dynasty's founder by the Celestial Sovereign (the national god of the Chou). This mandate was made manifest in the founder's success in defeating the last representatives of the preceding dynasty; it lasts till the new dynasty becomes unworthy of it, and then it passes to others. In other words the king is not divine, but he rules by divine commission.

The character of the Chou monarchy is very different from what the Shang had been. The Shang kings were heads of a patriarchal state, in which their authority was limited only by the difficulty of communications; on the periphery it melted into a vague suzerainty over Neolithic tribes. The Chou rule was the result of armed conquest by a people largely foreign to Shang civilization, and its nature, as finally settled after the consolidation of the conquest, was feudal through and through. In the organization designed by the Duke of Chou, the real founder of the state, the centre was the king, who was above all else a sacral head, being the sole repository of the great state cult. In theory the king was the absolute master, the fountain-head of all culture, but in practice he had no economic or military power of his own, and had to depend on the loyalty and good faith of the feudal lords. The lords came to be divided into five classes: *kung, hou, po, tzu,* and *nan,* often translated by our titles of duke, marquess, earl, viscount, and baron.[5] These styles originally denoted degrees of relationship or rank of tribal chiefs, and were only later transferred to the rulers of the feudal states. The latter were originally commanders of garrisons planted by the Chou kings in Shang territory to hold it down. These commanders had been members of the royal house, or its faithful supporters; alternatively they were allies (chiefs of kindred races), or even sometimes representatives of the conquered people who had joined the conqueror. They had full civil and military powers in their fiefs, and were linked to the king only by religious ties and by a general duty to give him aid and assistance: these ties were soon relaxed, and their loosening led from the eighth century onwards to the disintegration of the Chinese feudal monarchy. Tradition, with enough historical probability, depicts the Chinese feudal system in the shape of a small territory (*chung-kuo*) governed directly by the king, surrounded by a fluid and variegated complex of outer states (*wai-kuo*) under feudal princes. Later the significance of the two terms was modified: *chung-kuo* comes to mean the bloc composed of the small royal dominion and the original fiefs which had been granted in the eleventh century, and *wai-kuo* now means the fiefs added later on the periphery, by conquest or voluntary accession, or by breaking away from the older ones. In the feudal states the dominant class was a hereditary and closed aristocracy, which was jealous of its prerogatives; outsiders found it most difficult to gain admission. Its economic basis lay in landed property, as did the reason for its social superiority. Apart from the five orders of feudal nobles listed above, the mass of the dominant class consisted of gentlemen (*shih*), who were specialists in the use of arms (above all the bow) and in handling chariots of war; they were much like the knights of medieval Europe. Their way of life and outlook were largely different from those of the lower orders. Courtesy, respect for ceremonial, and the art of the right social relations were their chief characteristics; but above all their ability to read and write, and so to create a flourishing literature, was an inheritance they alone enjoyed.

b. *From Monarchy to Republic*

The primitive king in Greece was mainly concerned with the life of the state,[6] and only secondarily with his individual subjects. When they were able to have recourse to their sovereign as arbiter of their private disputes, they invariably had to secure support from members of their own families to compel the culprit to pay the arbiter's fine. Even in war an individual soldier, although army units on a territorial or tribal basis did exist, was left on his own, for there was no proper tactical organization; any man might reasonably fear that he would be left alone during an attack, or be abandoned on the field of battle, wounded or dead. The king's subjects gradually made good these obvious defects in the monarchy's functions by uniting themselves into voluntary associations for mutual support in peace and war. These were the *Hetairiai*[7] and *Phratriai*; later the union of several phratries produced *Phylai* or tribes.

In time the state began to use these private societies as administrative units; and at this point the magistrates of phratries and tribes became magistrates of the state, completing—and often replacing—the functions performed by the kings. This point in evolution[8] is illustrated by the counsel given to Agamemnon by Nestor (*Iliad*, II, 362 ff.), 'Agamemnon, divide your men into phratries and tribes, so that phratry may give help to phratry and tribe to tribe'.

But clearly this development must have been a powerful factor in weakening the royal power. The king had for long required helpers in peace and war, because the state had grown bigger; but he was now accompanied by a set of official magistrates in every field where he had originally been sovereign—in religion, in the administration of justice, and in the organization and leadership of the army. His own presence, especially when policy was at stake, came eventually to be regarded as unnecessary or even harmful.

Meanwhile another political force was growing at the expense of the monarchy—the power of the nobles. For various reasons the division of agricultural land had become uneven, and large estates had become concentrated in the hands of a few. Such men had gained importance from undertaking duties on behalf of the king, and they came to retain many clients and slaves, who were ready to do them bold service. Often they were themselves descended from ancient families of kings who had lost their political power but not their wealth, or one of them might secure prestige as hereditary priest of some family cult which gained public recognition. For these and many other reasons a certain number of noble families (genē), which boasted of being able to exhibit their family trees, assumed social standing alongside that of the kings and eventually claimed political equality. Nobles of this kind had endless opportunities to challenge the ruler's will, to form coalitions against him, and to assault some or all of his prerogatives. There might be struggles for the royal succession; the king might be a minor, or sick, or away; there might be discontent or troubles on account of war or famine; risky enterprises of a military or political kind might be provoking nervousness; and there were the occasions when colonial expeditions were being prepared. The nobles, too, had more resources for arming themselves from the moment that arms were made of iron, a metal now in plentiful supply; so they, the great landlords supported by their clients, acquired even greater material power. In general the two anti-monarchical forces, represented by the nobles and the popular magistrates, tended to coincide, since the nobles were able to acquire the magistracies with all their other successes.

For a time the monarch, though he was reduced to becoming *primus inter pares*, was able to withstand the opposition with support from the common people (*dēmos*). But between the ninth and seventh centuries BC, except in outlying areas like Macedonia and Epirus, monarchy declined and fell fairly quickly. In some states it was ended by a *coup d'état*, in others it slowly lost its prerogatives one by one. Sometimes the ancient king retained only his religious functions, like the *Archon Basileus* at Athens. A peculiar development can be seen at Sparta, where an early period of sole monarchy appears to have been succeeded by aristocratic government in the hands of the three heads of tribes (belonging by heredity to the three families of Agiads, Eurypontids, and Aigeidai), supported by a college consisting of twenty-seven heads of phratries (a council numbering thirty in all).[9] But the heads of tribes in the capital proclaimed themselves kings, one alongside the other; the third head, representing the Aigeidai who lived in the country districts, was added to the number of elders or chiefs of phratries, and so the senate numbered twenty-eight apart from the kings.

While monarchy generally tended to survive in the East, it disappeared fairly quickly among Western non-Indo-European peoples, such as Etruscans and Carthaginians, as well as among the Greeks we have already described.

At Rome the phenomenon occurred at the end of the sixth century, when two fundamental causes were operating at the same time. The supporters and delegates of the king had become state magistrates, and eventually, as in other areas, made the king appear almost an unnecessary encumbrance. And secondly, the kingly power was made odious by the accession of foreign rulers, the Etruscan house, who were imposed by force and did not adjust their power to meet the will of the patriciate of native landowners. Yet the Roman monarchy was not completely abolished. Its military and judicial powers were removed, but its religious authority, in part at least, was left to it; for with this the nobles did not dare to tamper, for fear of bringing divine wrath upon themselves. So even after the fall of the kings Rome, like other Latin cities such as Tusculum and Lanuvium, had a *rex sacrificulus* or *rex sacrorum*; and though the *pontifices* took away almost all his functions, and eventually his residence (*regia*) as well, so that he was confined to another building, he always in theory retained the first position among the priests.

In India one cannot speak of an aristocracy in the European sense, although the *kṣattriya* came fairly near it since in theory as well as in practice they had a monopoly of political power and the use of arms. But in northern India (Punjab, Uttar Pradesh, and Bihar) there grew up, at much the same time as in Greece, a number of state formations (*gaṇa*) which may perhaps be defined as aristocratic republics. They exist side by side with monarchy, which, as we have already seen, was always the normal form of government in India. Very often these republics had a tribal form (the Mālava, Yaudheya, etc.); others governed definite territories or cities. They were oligarchic states in which political power was confined to a narrow aristocratic class. In some of them the members of the aristocracy were called *rājā*, a title which in this instance is practically synonymous with *kṣattriya*;[10] and the rest of the population had no political rights. The origin of these republics may probably be found in the evolution, in an oligarchic direction, of those assemblies (*samiti*) of local chiefs (*viśpati*) which we have already encountered as counsellors and electors (in a formal sense) of the Indian king. The king had gradually sunk to be no more than a president, and was merged into the assembly. It is curious that Dravidian India never developed republican constitutions, despite its long tradition of village self-government, which was much stronger there than in the north. On the internal working of these republics our sources are fragmentary and relate to diverse periods; they allow us no more than an outline of certain basic principles. Public life was carried on in an assembly hall (*santhāgāra*) in the capital, where most of the aristocracy lived. The larger republics were divided into provinces under governors chosen from within the ruling class, but the cities formed autonomous units under assemblies of their own. Sovereignty was vested in a General Assembly comprising all the nobles, though naturally only a small proportion took an effective part in meetings. The Assembly elected officials and military leaders. Its chairman was a president (*saṅghamukhya*) whose functions were like those of a head of state. Meetings normally lasted until agreement was reached, but if this proved impossible the decision was taken by a majority of votes. Executive power was in the hands of a small council (nine members in the Licchavi state, four in the Malla) with the *sanghamukhya* in the chair. In this kind of aristocracy there was a natural tendency for offices to become hereditary, but it does not appear that this principle was ever fully accepted.

The Tyrannies. Greek economy was originally based almost entirely on agriculture and pasturage; yet the amount of grain produced by the land was limited, and opportunities for extending the area under pasture were small. So a growth in the population led quickly to the appearance of many persons who possessed little or no land. Moreover in some districts estates were being carved up into smaller and smaller plots to provide for a number of sons, while in others younger sons were being made into disinherited cadets, only eldest sons having the right of succession. All the time there was a natural tendency for large properties to grow at the expense of weaker neighbours; and the victorious patricians would confiscate the lands of small owners who had supported the fallen kings.

To the expansion of the poorer population two main remedies were applied. In some areas the poor, on account of debt, were tied to the soil in something like serfdom,[11] in others they were despatched as emigrants to distant colonies, where the land was initially divided into equal lots.

But in the colonies too the available land would get used up, and the population would reach saturation point. So there too would appear new companies of landless men, who had to become either wage-labourers or beggars. Moreover in both the colonies and the mother cities political power, the administration of justice, and all positions of importance were in the hands of the landed aristocracy, which managed things in a party spirit to suit their own interests.

In time, however, there came a change. A middle class was formed, whose wealth was in movable goods instead of land, and of them the *gamoroi* or landed proprietors had to take serious account. For the growth of shipping, piracy, trade, artisan work, and small industry had put sufficient and even ample means into the hands of many people who had had no economic status before. The introduction and spread of coinage made trade simpler, and removed the need for laborious and complicated barter of merchandise; it both promoted and accelerated the economic changes of this period. In this way too some of the *dēmos*, who had managed to get hold of some money, secured a position in which they could acquire arms and take part in military service, especially as the progress in metal-working had made arms less expensive. In the outcome the owners of movable goods became conscious of their new-found economic and material power and of their own importance in the life and defence of the *polis*. They began to make claims of a political and social nature, to force the landed nobles to grant them a share in political power.

The challenge came more quickly in some states than in others, but practically everywhere it was accompanied by a succession of incidents and by severe stress. The first stage was normally a codification of the laws, in writing and therefore in public; this removed the distortions due to oral tradition, and put an end to the exclusive legal knowledge possessed by a small number of nobles, who were able to apply them for party advantage. So we get the earliest codes of law, which all could consult: the Spartan attributed to Lycurgus, the codes of various cities in Crete, the Draconian and Solonian laws of Athens, and the codes of Zaleucus at Locri, Diocles at Syracuse, Charondas at Catana, and Pittacus at Mitylene.

Then the new rich would seek to participate in political power as well, and the nobles, with a selfish traditionalist outlook, would continue to claim their monopoly. The resulting struggles were often violent and bloody, ending usually in the massacre and exile of the defeated *gamoroi*, whose property was confiscated and in part redistributed.

These struggles gave an opportunity to a number of men, often of exceptional ability, who made their first appearance in the seventh and sixth centuries. Either they were concerned with social justice, or they wanted dictatorial power for themselves: sometimes the power was transmitted to a family dynasty. They made themselves leaders and champions of the people, or rather of the newly enriched bourgeois class which had gained prosperity in the struggle with the landed nobility; they used the armed force this class provided, and later enrolled mercenaries as well, to occupy strategic points and increase their control. They also formed bodyguards for their personal protection. The power of these new rulers might to some extent be concealed, and they evoked varying degrees of support and opposition; their position was an improvisation, and they were given the name of 'tyrannoi', which originally meant that they governed not by hereditary right but through having seized *de facto* power.

In the period of which we are speaking (i.e. in the seventh and sixth centuries) they first appeared, accompanied by a certain amount of political disturbance, in the states where the economic crisis had come soonest and where members of the *dēmos* had most rapidly and decisively gained wealth. In these states, in Asia Minor, especially Mitylene and Miletus, Euboea, Athens, the cities of the isthmus and the Argolid, and in Sicily, the consequent social conflicts had broken out earlier than elsewhere. But it was at the beginning of the next period that tyranny developed most.

The tyrants secured sovereign power and inflicted a mortal blow upon the aristocratic classes. In some cities these classes were destroyed, in others they were deprived of their political supremacy. Normally they took steps to open the magistracies to the people; and in order to break down the predominance which the nobles possessed in the old 'gentile' tribes, they would create new tribes on a purely territorial basis. But above all they promoted the acquisition of wealth by men outside the nobility; for they developed sea-power, opened opportunities for trade, made conquests on land, and constructed great public works (harbours, canals, drainage, roads, temples, city walls, and so on) to expand employment and improve the conditions of their country.

The tyrants, especially in the following period, had importance in other ways. They successfully encouraged literature, and took great pride in the use they made of artistic works. They established and extended hegemonies of which their states were the centres; and they organized constitutions on semi-democratic lines, which normally continued after the fall of the tyrants themselves. The parts of Greece where tyrants were unknown remained in general much more backward, and continued to be subject to selfish oligarchies of nobles.

c. Militarist States

Certain states organized on a military basis deserve separate mention. These had few aims beyond conquest and its exploitation. In the Middle East a prominent example is Assyria, a country of agriculturists, shepherds and soldiers, of diplomats and greedy administrators, whose main qualities were violence and unscrupulous cruelty. During their fluctuating periods of power they valued nothing but the right of the strongest. The wars they waged in the name of their god Ashur were fierce and knew no quarter. Cities and crops were destroyed, canals were diverted, and prisoners-of-war were treated with savagery: the most fortunate were enslaved, the rest were impaled, flayed, mutilated, kept in dungeons, or dragged around with hooks in their mouths. It was rare that their victories were followed by a settlement designed in any way to amalgamate the conquered people with the conquerors. So the history of Assyria is a catalogue of continuous wars, the periods of hegemony being punctuated by withdrawal when they could not hold their own against coalitions of their enemies. In the end they collapsed because, one by one, they had lost their vast dominions.

The fact was that the Assyrian numbers were too small in proportion to the numbers they ruled; and they had increased the disparity and made it more dangerous by transplanting hundreds of thousands of conquered people into their own homeland. Moreover in their weaker periods they had allowed hordes of immigrants, mainly Arameans, to invade this district, so that in the end their own Assyrian language was submerged by the newcomers. The Assyrians therefore wore down their own forces with continual wars, and took no thought to replace the depleted areas by planting them with new citizens; meanwhile they had to put garrisons on the frontiers to hold down by force the recalcitrant areas they had newly conquered. In this way they weakened the defences at the centre of their empire and made it more difficult to deal with revolts; but their soldiers at the same time became too greedy for plunder, and lost the iron discipline which had been the source of their power. They did have kings who cared for art and culture, but in those fields too the Assyrians were undoubtedly inferior to their Babylonian predecessors.

The militarist organization of Greek Lacedaemon (or Sparta) went to nothing like the same extreme lengths. This little state was originally limited to the Eurotas valley, but it then achieved the conquest of all Laconia and most of Messenia. At this point the conquerors found their numbers very small in comparison with those they had subdued; and to avoid the risk of being absorbed or overcome, a risk made obvious by the Messenian revolts, they reduced the civil powers of one group of subjects and the personal liberty of another. The ruling group, who called themselves Spartiates, became what amounted to a camp, an army quartered in the confiscated territory. The previous landowners became Helots, serfs compelled to work the lands which were once theirs but were now divided into lots assigned to the Spartiates; and every year they were compelled to hand to their masters an amount of produce proportionate to the average harvest obtained in the year in question. The rest of the territory was left to the Perioeci, who retained their personal freedom and title to their lands, but who had to pay tribute, surrender their political independence, and contribute auxiliary forces to the Spartan army.

The Spartans were now greatly outnumbered; and to maintain their position of dominance and be always ready to put down revolts they organized themselves into a permanent army. Every citizen was a soldier and must not be distracted from his military duties by the need to secure a living. So the state assigned each family a plot of land which had belonged to the Helots, but was now worked by the Helots for their masters. It was partly because these plots were of uniform value that the full citizens were called *Homoioi* or Equals. Each of them contributed part of the produce he received from his lot to the *Syssitia*, public military messes, in which they had to take at least one meal a day. Anyone who lost his economic status also lost his prerogatives as a full citizen; and no Spartiate could engage in agriculture, industry, or trade to the detriment of his military obligations. This militarist régime broke up the unity of the family. Selected children, after those with physical defects had been put away, were educated by the state in barracks, after which they entered the army at the age of 17 and left it at 60. The family lot was inherited by the rules of primogeniture, that is to say by the eldest male child, and families tended therefore to limit the number of sons.[12] Women were kept apart from their husbands, at any rate while the husbands were relatively young, and were regarded mainly as mothers and nurses. Ultimately, all Spartans were compelled by law to dress alike. Because he was a soldier, a Spartan could not leave the country without the government's permission.

d. *The Magistrates under Republican Constitutions*

We have explained earlier how magistrates had already begun to find a place in most areas while kingship was still in being. With the expansion of the state's territory, the king, who could not be everywhere at once, required men to help him exercise his prerogative. Then when monarchies fell, either by slow evolution or by revolution, power normally passed to such magistrates, now elected by the people. Some continued to hold the positions they had enjoyed when delegates of the king; others were fresh creations intended to carry out the functions previously discharged by the king or new functions which had not previously been performed.

At Sparta, for example, where the revolution against the monarchy had probably caused the creation first of a triad of tribal chiefs, then of a new dual kingship, the earliest magistracy was the Ephorate. There was one Ephor for each of the five territorial tribes[13] into which the state was divided; and his functions were civil and censorial. The consultative assembly of the kings, which had previously been composed of the older heads of families (*gerontes*), was now restricted to comprise only twenty-eight people.

At Athens the king gradually lost his functions, which passed to persons nominated every year. The Eponymous Archon was in charge of jurisdiction, the Polemarch commanded the army, the *Archon Basileus* (also elected annually) retained the religious duties; and this college of new republican magistrates finally contained six other members, the Thesmothetae, who superintended the administration of the laws. Besides this college of nine Archons there was the Areopagus, replacing the King's Council; and of this all ex-Archons became members. The Areopagus judged cases of homicide, was guardian of the laws, and scrutinized the credentials of men chosen for the Archontate.

In some Latin cities the king was replaced by an annual dictator. But at Velitrae there were three pairs of magistrates, so the magistracies were assuming a collegiate character. Again the single praetor of the Alban League gave place to two; but at Rome, where collegiate power was instituted under two praetors (later called consuls), it was customary in times of emergency to fall back on a dictator, who held power for six months and was assisted by a *magister equitum*. Initially these two praetors were not on terms of equality, and the relationship of one colleague to the other was like that of the dictator to his assistant.[14] The *praetor maximus* normally commanded the troops, the *praetor minor* dealt with jurisdiction. Magistrates of lower rank had to be added to fill army commands and to assist in both civil and criminal cases; and alongside the *rex sacrorum* (survivor of the king) more priesthoods were developed, some of them going back to the Regal period, others new.

We now pass to public administration in India and China. It is difficult to describe the main features of the Indian state in this period, since it is very dangerous to project backwards the ideal constructions of later manuals like the *Arthaśāstra*. But it is clear that in the Vedic state the king's power was limited by local councils (*sabhā*) and by the central assembly (*samiti*) in the capital, organs which were apparently aristocratic in character and possessed very ill-defined but mainly consultative functions. In the Late Vedic period, the *samiti* disappears altogether. The older type of *sabhā* also disappears; we find a new organ also called *sabhā*, which is a kind of state council with mainly judicial functions. The *Yajurveda* and *Brāhmaṇas* have preserved some of the titles given to ministers and high officials: *senānī* (commander-in-chief), *sūtra* (commander of the chariots), *grāmaṇī* (perhaps representative of the village chiefs), *saṃgrahītṛ* (treasurer), *bhāgadugha* (minister of finance), and (most important of all) the *purohita* (royal chaplain). These officials, together with the king's relations and the principal courtiers, formed a group of counsellors called *ratnin*.

The central structure of the Chou state at its height is fairly well known from classical texts (admittedly very late ones) like the *Chou-li* and *Li-chi*. But it is hard to say how much of this structure is real and how much is an idealization due to compilers of the Han period. It must again be emphasized that we are here concerned with the central structure—with institutions of the court and the executive offices of the sovereign; provincial institutions are comprised in the feudal organization described above. At the top of the administration, we are told, there were six ministries: of Heaven, under the *chung-tsai*, to keep a general watch on affairs; of Earth, under the *ta ssu-t'u*, for moral and cultural advancement of the people; of Spring, under the *ta tsung-po*, for religion; of Summer, under the *ta ssu-ma*, for war; of Autumn, under the *ta ssu-kou*, for punishment of offenders; and of Winter, under the *ta ssu k'ung*, for public works. At the head of each ministry was a president (*ch'ing*) and two vice-presidents. In addition the king was directly assisted by a Private Council of six high dignitaries, the three *kung* and the three *ku*. There is a strong cosmico-ethical element in all this, with hints of magic, which underlines the artificial character of the whole construction. Of the duties of the *pa* or prince-president something was said in the introductory chapter: the office was too intermittent to acquire precise features.

The administration of the Persian empire was laid down by Darius. He was able to take account of the innovations of his predecessors, and above all of Cyrus, for example the regional governments in the north-west, each under a satrap; and he had before him the example set by the great Eastern states, especially Egypt. He divided his huge empire into twenty satrapies, ethnic and geographical departments which also provided a basis for the distribution of commands, and for the organization of defence and tribute. The satraps were normally members of the imperial family or of the high Median and Persian nobility.

Darius created a successful balance between feudal and autonomist forces on the one hand and centralizing forces on the other. The independent chiefs of earlier days, after their subjection, gradually became officials of the Great King. Competence was left with them in all matters affecting the life of their particular regions (roads, public works, feeding of the army, with some judicial work), and they were in charge of local levies and of tribute collection. But at every key strategic point were stationed troops depending directly on the king; and it was he who fixed the total tribute to come from the various satrapies, on principles which were worked out as occasion seemed to demand.

Darius was also wise enough to respect local religions, and to allow the legal forms of particular regions to continue once he had had them codified by competent assemblies: however it was probably he who appointed the judges. His fragmented country was only brought into a unified system by means of a powerful bureaucracy, radiating from the centre to the periphery. Scribes of Aramaic speech were entrusted with chanceries which controlled the correspondence between the central government and individual satrapies.

e. *Political Power and Religious Power*

Although in the Greek cities and at Rome there were only sporadic quarrels between the political and religious powers, in other parts of the world this struggle was most active, and it had important historical results. During the Twenty-first Dynasty (1090–?947) upper Egypt, nominally vassal to the Tanis Pharaohs, was led by Herihor, High Priest of Ammon at Thebes, into separation from lower Egypt; and a fruitless struggle for political predominance followed, while the whole country fell into disorder and decay. It was eventually reunited when Libyan princes (Twenty-second Dynasty) gained control and gave the High Priesthood at Thebes to the younger sons of the reigning house. But this was not the end of the struggle between the two powers. Some priests of Ammon were unwilling to submit to the Libyan dynasty and removed out of the country to Nubia, which they organized and ran as a theocratic state, holding its king under their control. Only eventually did the Nubian Pianckhi move over to the conquest of Egypt, or rather, as he put it himself, to its restoration (Twenty-third Dynasty). But the power of the Egyptian priests in their relations, for good or ill, with the sovereign is still evident from their hostility towards the Persian conqueror Cambyses, and then the favour they showed in contrast to his more dexterous successor Darius.

Farther east the Hebrews were more sensible of the dualism between political and religious authority from the time when Samuel, priest of the temple at Shiloh, invested Saul first secretly and then openly with the dignity of kingship. Samuel retained for himself the religious power. During the united kingdom which followed, the 'prophets' made themselves felt in opposition to the kings, the people, and even the priesthood. When the monarchy split into the two kingdoms of Israel and Judah, the former was in trouble from the opposition offered by the priests to the syncretist religious policies of the kings; but in Judah too there was some conflict between the two parties.

In the neo-Babylonian empire one has only to remember the quarrel between King Nabunidus and the priests of Marduk. The King was a pious builder and rebuilder of temples, himself the son of a priest and the father of a priestess, but he was accused of showing too little respect towards the gods. This quarrel helped the Persians to victory.

In Assyria the kings certainly met with religious difficulties as when Sennacherib in 705 failed to follow the procession of Marduk at Babylon; and the country was full of religious diviners. But the organization of the monarchy was too strong, and the conviction that the king was God's elect too firmly based, for the dualism to become significant.

The same is true of the Persian empire. Its kings were faithful to Zoroastrianism,[15] but they also showed a wise toleration of the religions of their subjects. Foreign gods were brought within the system of the Supreme God which is the essence of Zoroastrianism. Yet the priests disapproved of these syncretisms, and their intolerance led to the usurpation in 522 of the Magus Gaumata, under whose orders a large number of temples of local gods were destroyed.

In India the relation between political and religious power was very close, especially in the Vedic and post-Vedic periods. Sacrifice is one of the most important state activities: only by sacrifice can one win victories over one's enemies, reap a good harvest, or achieve peace at home. So the priestly class had great importance in public life, and the king had to turn to it in almost every instance. Socially the Brahmans were not dependent on the king; besides, the royal chaplain (*purohita*) was a revered and influential member of the king's Council. On the other hand in the caste system there gradually developed a rigid definition of powers and functions, which prevented the priestly class from overstepping the mark. So tradition and social law placed the religious and the civil power in positions which made it possible for them to be fully interdependent and yet removed all possibilities of a clash.

In China from the earliest times there was never any dualism between the religious and political powers. In the first place Chinese religious feeling went much less deep than did Indian. But above all there was no state religion, only a state cult of a mainly civil nature like the Roman. The king was the supreme sacral power, the high priest, the one and only executant of the most important acts in the official cult. Very soon we meet with the theory that the Son of Heaven is head of family, state, and universe, unique as the sun is unique in the sky—a rigid monist conception which excludes the religious concerns of the individual and centres in the king both cult and administration —both Church and State. In this sense O. Franke has been able to speak of a Chinese theocracy.

2. THE DEVELOPMENT OF CITIES

a. *The Far East*

We know little of Indian cities in this period. The great urban civilization of Harappā has vanished;[16] and the *Ārya* of the *Ṛigveda* did not know regular cities—only villages and hamlets of small size and little importance.

Nor did this situation alter much in the post-Vedic period. In the sixth and fifth centuries, however, some significance begins to attach to certain agglomerations of buildings in the shape of cities, fortified with walls, ditches, and sometimes thorn hedges. We are not well informed about the reasons for their growth, but they were partly religious and partly economic. Examples are Benares, a holy city from the start; Girivrāja and later Rājagṛha, the capital of Magadha (southern Bihar); Ayodhyā, capital of Korśala (eastern Uttar Pradesh): and Ujjayinī, capital of Mālava (Madhya Pradesh). About their appearance, planning, and functions in this period nothing can be said: archaeology is silent, and written evidence, which is almost entirely religious in character, provides very little about the subject.[17] Taken all in all the cities of ancient India had little importance in the general picture of political life.

In China we know a fair amount about Shang cities thanks to the Anyang excavations, but as with contemporary India we have little direct information from archaeology about the cities of the Chou period. But one can easily see that the city in feudal China had no importance in any way comparable with that possessed by the city of the Near East or the Mediterranean: there was no town life and no urban class. As far as we can tell from classical texts, the ancient Chinese city was very small. It was in principle a fortress town (*ch'êng*), inhabited mainly by the feudal lord and his retainers; but later on a market area (*shih*) arose under its walls as a sort of commercial suburb. The capitals (*tu*) of the various principalities were distinguished from the royal cities or from those of the feudal lords (*i*) simply by the presence in them of the temple of the prince's ancestors. Regular inhabitants were few. The cities were agricultural and military, permanent camps built to serve as residences for the warriors and to shelter, in case of need, the entire working population (Granet). But these cities of refuge, surrounded by a double circuit of walls, were made by the commercial suburbs into economic centres. Its very nature, of course, deprived the ancient Chinese city of any autonomous existence. The country is everything: urban life is still in the future.

b. *The Middle East*

The origin of cities in the Middle East is treated in Volume I, and we can confine ourselves to certain general postulates. In the first place, cities grew up both independently and by imitation. At the outset many peoples could independently arrive, for a number of reasons, at the concept of a city, and even devise cities of similar kinds; but later, when those peoples established mutual contact, these various systems influenced one another. In several districts there were villages which grew gradually with an increase in population among the people which built them. Alternatively there might be special features: they might be useful for royal palaces or great temples or other sacred buildings; they might lie on particularly salubrious soil, or on sites favourable for agriculture, seafaring, or relatively easy defence against foreign dangers. Then again in every region there were centres founded by a single deliberate act after a conquest or an invasion or a colonial enterprise: some prince might need one as his citadel; or they might lie at the crossing of important routes.

Sometimes if a city grew slowly its development was irregular and chaotic, with either no plan at all or at best with streets radiating outwards along the lines of the roads. When, however, a city was founded all at once, it might have a regular plan from the start and tend towards a rectilinear pattern or squared network. This was true of the lake-dwellings and *terramare*, and also of Roman colonies, the degree of regularity depending on the contours of the land. Some cities were always open: others were fortified either from the outset or in the light of later developments. Among inhabited centres there was generally a sort of hierarchy which came about spontaneously. The early Latins, for example, had *vici* consisting of a few rural families living in a single group; *pagi* or larger villages; and *oppida*, sites made more easily defensible by nature or by man. The *oppida* gave refuge to the populations of several *vici* and *pagi* in time of danger, and around them the earliest attempts at hegemony were made. In them were situated the organs of government and the temples of the common cult.

In Egypt newly created cities were still planned on chessboard lines, with wide processional streets flanked by trees and by statues of sphinxes, rams, and other figures. These were intersected by lesser roads; and the perimeter was circular or rectangular, sometimes with a wall. This was a layout prompted by the nature of the country, which is flat, with one axis lying along the river and the line of the hills and the other along the transverse canals. The plan was known at least as early as the Twelfth Dynasty, and may have spread towards Syria, where it had to meet the challenge of other schemes invented elsewhere. For in Mesopotamia rectangular cities with squared streets were in use by 2000 BC (Babylon), and survived in the eighth century (the El Merkez of Dur Sarrukim). Another method became popular in Anatolia (Troy) and in Syria (Zengirli, Quadesh, Carchemish): one or more circular walls would enclose streets leading from a central acropolis provided with its own defences, as we still find at Ashur in Assyria in the seventh century. Because they delighted in war, the Assyrians took trouble over their defences: they not only surrounded their towns with external and internal walls, but they dug canals from which the ground could be flooded in time of need, and made their temples and palaces in the form of lofty fortresses. None the less we can see at Nineveh the attention paid to city services such as aqueducts, paved streets, and banking along the navigable rivers.

The fortified palace and quadrilateral city was a system continued by the Persians when they built their great capital cities of Susa, Ecbatana, Persepolis, and Babylon.

c. *Cities of the West*

Archaic Greece retained the Mycenaean system of open cities, consisting mainly of little huts and alleys surrounding a fortified acropolis. The arrangement of Mycenae, Tiryns, and Phylacopi is still to be found at Sardis in Asia Minor; and it can be seen at Athens to the south and north of the Acropolis. Sometimes, however, walls surrounded the whole city, as on the island of Gha in Lake Copais, where the circuit is a little under 2 miles round. An acropolis might be a long way from the residential area, and its defences were strengthened by artificial means, as with the ascents from the Pelargicon and the Enneapylos at Athens.[18] But cities newly founded in hilly country, such as Elis, continued without fortifications even in the fifth century. Fortifications began to be common from the end of the sixth, when wars for supremacy were growing sharper.

The Greek colonies on the other hand had been founded at a single point of time in foreign territory and therefore needed defensive measures from the start. The only exceptions were those like Naucratis in Egypt which were merely a collection of trading-stations belonging to several competing Greek cities under licence of the country whose guests they were: the plan was a set of tiny houses facing narrow streets laid out like a chessboard. When a nucleus of regular colonists built its new home on land taken from native inhabitants, operations were performed of the kind attributed to the Phaeacian king in the *Odyssey* (IV, 7 ff.), who 'surrounded the city with a wall, made temples for the gods, and divided the land'. Under those conditions, unless the walls had to follow inescapable natural features, they would obviously be regular in shape; inside the city there would be an acropolis (or more than one) with still stronger defences; and where possible the houses would be laid out in a standard plan. Aerial photography makes this guess into a certainty for the earliest periods of the Sicilian cities, such as Acragas, Selinus, Solus, and Heraclea Minoa. The same was true of Miletus, every time it was reconstructed, and also of Cyrene.

The Italians had a natural tendency towards regular planning which was also inspired by the ancient example set by the earliest Etruscans in their *palafitte* and *terramare*, the regularity of which has been exaggerated but later underestimated in modern times. Another model was provided by the earliest Greek colonies. It was probably not so much in the Italian *oppida*, those towns which dominated their neighbours and served as a refuge in time of war, where a regular shape was designed, as in the low-lying and open cities at the meeting-places of important roads. The *oppida* were built on steep hills, provided always that there was a supply of water; and their natural defences were reinforced with cuttings, ditches, mounds, ramparts, palisades, and sections of wall. Their roads could not be otherwise than twisted and irregular, of the type found at Vetulonia.

The influence of Hippodamus of Miletus[19] has been exaggerated. Even before his work in the second half of the fifth century there are undoubted examples of cities with regular plans, such as the earliest part of Pompeii and the Etruscan city of Marzabotto, both certainly earlier than the end of the sixth. About the same time as we can see from the 'Servian' walls of Rome and the circuit at Norba, the system of walled perimeters was becoming common. It derives partly from the wars for supremacy, partly from the movement of invaders, and partly from the Celtic raids which were beginning at precisely this time.

In all districts the cities had an important and complex function to perform. They drew the population inwards, and contained the king's palace, the magistrates, the assemblies, and the law courts: they became the essential arteries of political and administrative life. In them were erected the most famous temples, and they were the seat of those priestly colleges which mattered most to the state cult. They provided most of the army, and with their fortifications formed the state's strategic centre. The wealth and labour needed for trade, artisan work, and industry were also concentrated inside the cities; and this made them the scenes of most of the social struggles between the classes. Ultimately the cities became the home of literature and art, and it was in them that language developed and took on refinements; they became the focus of culture, of its growth, its borrowings, and its power to influence others, at a time when in the country districts archaic conditions of life were largely persistent. Everywhere there was opposition between town and country: its severity might vary, but it could never be wholly removed.

The Greek Polis. The Greek city had its own characteristic form of development (though analogies can be found in other parts of the world). The primitive population of Hellas had lived off pasturage, agriculture, or fishing, and had been scattered over the hills, the plains, and the coasts in huts and villages (*dēmoi*); but the political life of every little state had its being in the strong palace of the king, which was surrounded by groups of buildings for the soldiers, courtiers, and craftsmen. This palace, which was large and well defended, could also, like the Latin *oppidum*, serve as a refuge for men and cattle in time of danger. But when the noble families destroyed the king, they demolished his palace: any portion which survived would be turned into a temple. It then became necessary for the mass of the population, under its oligarchy, to find some place—it might be the same as that which the king had chosen—to be a refuge for all in time of war. This would also be a centre for foreign and internal trade, to which merchants could come by land and sea; and it would house the magistrates, assemblies, and law courts, with those common cults which were held in greatest honour.

The idea of the *polis* admittedly owed something to the grouping of houses round the Mycenaean palaces. But the precise form taken by the new foundations depended on the example of the regular cities which the Greeks were getting to know in Anatolia, the cities against which their wars were fought. These were first a model for the Greek colonies on the Asiatic seaboard, then for the more distant coastal settlements in the north-east and in the west, all of these being areas where the Greeks were isolated amid foreigners and enemies and had to keep themselves firmly united in large and powerful centres of habitation, ready for any turn of events.

Part of the population, it is true, might still be scattered in isolated cottages or in country villages over the city's ancient territory, or on some new land which had been acquired. Agriculture, pasturage, and fishing could more conveniently be carried on in this way, and some people might be dispersed deliberately, perhaps on colonial ventures. But it was in the *polis* that politics, administration, law, and religion were centred. Later even more families were drawn in from the territory outside. The nobles could live in greater splendour in the city than was possible on their country estates; the traders wanted to be near the ports and markets; and the artisans and unemployed came in search of work. So once it had become the centre of attraction to all the population, and was housing the majority of citizens as well as being the heart of the state's existence, it gave its name of *polis* to the whole state whose activities were summarized within its walls.

The wealth of the *polis* in men and money, and the efficiency of its organization, made it a nucleus round which a country might unite. Smaller city-states in the neighbourhood, of their own accord or after conquest, would become absorbed politically, or even move their people bodily inside the larger centre (*synoecismus*). Conquered peoples sometimes received the citizenship of the *polis* where they made their homes or to which they resorted for the exercise of civil rights. But in other cases they were reduced to the status of subjects. They might retain their freedom but lack full citizenship, or they might be serfs compelled to work, on some kind of forced *métayage*, the lands their overlords had seized.

Between two or more adjacent *poleis* there was not always a state of war or struggle for hegemony. Often federal states were created with the precedent of the old sacred federations in mind.

The *poleis* or city-states were normally of small territorial dimensions, so that all the inhabitants could easily congregate in the centre, following the irresistible urge which impels all Greeks to take a concrete part in the exercise of their citizen rights. The city was normally a closed political organism, recognizing only the rights of its own members. But although foreigners could not acquire these rights, they were allowed temporary residence as time went on, if a citizen (*prostates*) took responsibility for them; and on payment of an appropriate tax they might even be allowed a permanent home.

But these institutions concerning foreigners do not seem to be those which obtained in archaic times: they can, however, be detected in the colonies where it was normal practice to admit immigrants of various origins. Later on, one remembers how Solon conceived the idea of bringing to Athens as citizens the exiles of other states, and also metics who would take up their homes in the country and work there; Cleisthenes too granted citizenship to many foreigners domiciled in Attica. Even more characteristic, some decades after this period, were the actions of Gelon of Syracuse, who transplanted people from other Siceliote cities and made them Syracusans.

The *polis* was composed of all the free inhabitants of its territory, who contributed to its defence and provided their own weapons. The *politai* or citizens ruled the state directly, without any delegation of powers, since they could and did come together in the popular assemblies and decide on the spot by speech and vote the issues of domestic and foreign policy. They could choose some of their number as magistrates and give them instructions; they could control their magistrates' actions and bring them to book if necessary; they could set up smaller assemblies to give the magistrates advice; and they could modify the laws. The counterpart of this full recognition of the citizens' right to govern was that individuals had to obey such laws as were laid down by the majority and accept the duty of defending the city with arms and money.

This civil organization was the main obstacle to the formation of larger political units in the Greek world. For except when (as in Attica) a whole region came together voluntarily into a single *polis*, the extension of one city's power meant the extinction by force of the sovereign power of the others (see Part II.).

3. SOCIAL INSTITUTIONS

a. *Property and Ownership in the Ancient World*

It may be useful to preface this section by saying that in our view both history and ethnography rule out the doctrine that in origin all property was collective, and also the doctrine that it was all individual. At all times and in all places two or more principal types of property must have existed simultaneously, the property of the king, the family, the individual, and the community.

In Egypt there existed the ancient, and to some extent self-contradictory, conception that the king had a divine mission to administer the country as his personal possession. Everything, the land, employment, trade, and movable goods were at least in theory his, but this formula got modified in practice. Eventually in fact some measure of personal ownership was recognized, and we must examine some of the more important causes of this development. The great dignitaries and royal officers, together with the king's relations, favourites, and friends, had received presents from him, and to land acquired in this way they would add other areas on which they had been able to lay their hands. Even greater were the gifts made to temples and priests, who had collected very large estates in this way and had engaged bands of slaves and artisans to work them, independently of the king and with immunity from taxation. Moreover, in addition to state commerce, private trade had started with foreigners, especially in the Delta, and new units of movable property had come into being. Other such property had originated in gifts made to mercenaries, and even in the essential needs of peasant life. The peasants might work lands for the state and provide their corvées, but they came in the end to possess animals, agricultural implements, and produce of their own. Finally from the eighth century onwards Greek merchants were allowed to found trading-stations, especially at Naucratis; and they had to be allowed to live according to their own laws, including the laws governing private property.

The old customs about property were still accepted in our period by the various overlords of Mesopotamia, and therefore by the Assyrians; indeed there was at times an actual reversion to the past. So we find landed property privately owned by both individuals and families, and estates being freely broken up. The state contented itself with keeping a watchful eye and making a land-register. There was also private property of a movable kind.

On the other hand there were also public or state properties, largely confiscated from foreign enemies. They were often distributed as private lots to men who had rendered service to the state, the origin of military colonies. Other properties belonged collectively to groups of families or to tribes. The sovereign possessed very large territorial domains and vast movable wealth, which made him the greatest capitalist in the empire. The temples too had land and treasures, which enabled them to maintain companies of workmen, although labour was also often hired by private persons. Finally we should notice the part played in commerce by groups of foreign merchants, especially Greeks and Arameans. It was partly this that brought more and more Aramean invaders into Mesopotamia.

The Persian kings, too, were owners of vast properties: palaces in several capitals, estates and gardens ('paradises'), slaves, presents, and revenues from taxes, from all of which they built exceptionally large hoards of treasure. But landed and movable wealth, often of colossal size, was also in the possession of temples, of the king's friends and relations, and in general of noblemen, who were employed as officials and satraps, or who served as cavalry commanders in the army. Then there were the Iranian and non-Iranian farmers, professional men, and artisans, men of moderate means whose standard of living was unchanged from that obtaining under earlier empires in this enormous area. Later, as a result of the peripheral wars, the king came to dispose of new land confiscated from defeated peoples, who were often

transplanted away from their homes. On these lands, mainly in Egypt and
Asia Minor, he was able to found military colonies.

At the close of the Mycenaean Age, and in the archaic period which
followed, Greece partly retained and partly improved the methods of earlier
ages. The large Minoan houses in Crete, often containing twenty rooms, had
been suited to huge families, of almost patriarchal kind, while the smaller
houses of the Mycenaean Age seem to betoken less sizeable family units.

Archaeology and the Homeric poems tell us of the financial power of the
latest kings, when their pomp and the riches of their palaces and tombs were
on the wane. We also hear of the mounting wealth of the nobles who despoiled
these kings and took their places. Yet none of the evidence disproves the
ownership of all kinds of property by the lower classes. Landed property,
including livestock and produce, must normally have belonged to the family:
single individuals could dispose freely only of goods they had acquired in
war, piracy, or trade. In militarist countries like Sparta every family had,
so far as possible, to pass on its lot (*kleros*) intact without division. But with
these exceptions properties could be divided or even alienated. Non-citizens
could not own land unless with explicit leave from the state. A few public
properties still existed, like the mining district of Laurium belonging to
the Attic tyrants and then to Athens.[20] In addition there was the continual
passage into private hands of territory confiscated from the enemy: some
went to individual members of the victorious state, other plots were left to
citizens of the defeated city (in cases where they were not reduced to serfdom).

The absolute ownership of real estate was conditioned by regulations.
which were constantly being improved, to meet the rights of neighbours,
These affected new buildings, excavations, planting of trees, fixing of
boundaries, payment of tolls, use of wells, flow of water-courses, and similar
matters.

The supposed traces of collective property present a special problem. The
example generally given is that of the Cnidian colonists who settled at Lipara
about 580 B C. The conditions, however, were practically military in character,
of the kind which must necessarily attend the early phases of colonization
when a party of entirely male emigrants settle in a country after having been
engaged together for a long time in maritime expeditions and in conquest.
The islands of the Lipara archipelago have very little cultivable land, and
the Cnidian settlers had no immediate chance of raising families by marriage
with native women. Compelled to make a living from fishing and piracy,
and at the same time to engage in continuous war with the Etruscan pirates,
they had no alternative in the early stages to a complete break with tradition
and the organization of a collective system of property. So they cultivated
in common the small available land on the largest island, and continued to
take their meals at one table. Later they developed ordinary family life, and
parcelled out the land in individual lots, first on the largest island, and then

on the others, which had not been inhabited hitherto. Economic inequality, however, would have been fatal in a country which could not be expanded; so they repeated the process of division at intervals, making the lots smaller as the population grew.

Property questions affecting Rome are postponed to the next period, when our evidence becomes reasonably adequate.

Our knowledge of property rights and economic life in Early and Late Vedic India is remarkably scanty, and almost exclusively concerns landed property. Under Late Vedic legislation ownership of land could be attested by documents, witnesses, or simple possession. It appears that family owner-ship of homestead and arable lands was the rule, probably along with communal ownership of pastures. The Indian family in the widest sense, the *gens*, had a rock-like solidarity, which is reflected in its undivided owner-ship of land. The legal representative of this property was the *pater familias*. His powers were limited only by the inevitable dispersion of a *gens* which became too large, requiring the formation of new estates. Thus the *Rigveda* mentions division of *daya* (paternal wealth) and there are repeated instances in Late Vedic literature of patrimonies being divided before the father's death (e.g., *Taittiriya Samhitā*, III, i, 9, 4), but they appear to have concerned movable property rather than land. From this division before death was derived the institution of inheritance, though it is still lacking in form and definition. Women were in any event excluded from division and inheritance: neither women nor *śūdra* could hold property on any terms.

We have already described the way in which the Indian monarchy came into being, and it implies that there can be no trace in this period of royal ownership of state land. Indeed there is a famous anecdote (*Aitareya Brāhmaṇa*, VIII, 21, 8; *Śatapatha Brāhmaṇa*, XIII, 7, 1, 15) of King Visvakarman offering the earth (presumably some estates) to his priest; and the earth 'refused to be given away'; meaning (one imagines) that the donation was a breach of the law. It is likely that the 'gifts' of estates made by ancient Indian kings to their followers concerned the rents and taxation derivable from the land, rather than its outright possession. Nevertheless among royal privileges was included the title to treasure without an owner which might be found on the state's territory.

Economic life was still very primitive, being based on the village, which was a fully self-contained unit and the smallest component part of the state. A noticeable feature is that artisans in the village received a fixed sum from the peasants as a retainer to make them stay in the village; individual jobs were paid for in addition. Some trace of industrial organization can be found as early as the Vedic texts, but our evidence about Indian guilds refers to a later period.

In Chou China land was everything, the basis of all power, wealth, and social position. In theory all land belonged to the king. The earliest Chou rulers divided the soil between members of their family and supporters. So by a kind of delegation all feudatories became owners of their land and could distribute it in their turn. Gifts of land by kings and feudal chiefs gave rise to two types of property—the 'state' (*kuo*) of the feudal chief, and the 'estate' (*i* or *t'ien*) of the individual noble. In both cases the peasant (*chung*) had no legal right of any kind over the soil he tilled, and soon became much like a serf: his person, that is to say, was an integral part of the estate. The proprietor, whose holding was a conditional one, owned the land and those who tilled it, but was also responsible for any offence committed within his area. If he resided at court or was for some other reason an absentee, he administered the land through a bailiff chosen by and responsible to himself.[21]

Later theorists like Mencius describe in detail an ideal system of ancient land tenure (*ching*), under which the country was divided into square sections, each further subdivided in chessboard pattern into nine equal parts. Eight of these parts were allotted to the same number of families to cultivate. The ninth part, in the centre (*kung t'ien*), was cultivated by the eight families in common; and its produce constituted the rent due to the feudal owner, that is to the state. Of this system epigraphy and the earliest literature have no knowledge. It must have been largely an arbitrary construction made by Confucian philosophers, although it seems also to preserve a vague memory of the communal cultivation which was in force in the earliest days of Chinese civilization. It did not imply permanent cultivation of any particular plots: it was carried out by groups of peasants who set fire to the undergrowth to recover pieces of land, worked them for four or five years, and then abandoned them once they were exhausted. This was eminently a co-operative type of working: later, however, the custom was lost, although the theorists may have preserved some record of it. Whatever the truth, the *ching* theory had great significance during all the attempts at pseudo-reform (or return to antiquity) during later centuries.

In the feudal society of the Chou period all economic life was in the last analysis (there being no urban life) based on the serf-cultivator, who had practically no rights, and through him on the pyramid of small and large feudatories living on the produce of the land. Of artisans we know practically nothing. They lived in close contact with the nobility near their seats (i.e. in the towns); we cannot tell whether the work they did for the aristocracy was remunerated at piece-rates or by a regular maintenance. The units of exchange were shells (*kauri*), and to some extent objects of bronze. There was no metal coinage, and therefore there is no question of loans, interest, or the like: such things are not mentioned in the sources.

Organization of Labour; Economic and Social Differences The theories of government current in some countries led to state organization of labour. In Egypt, for example, the Pharaoh was regarded as lord of the land and its inhabitants; and while his normal revenues were ensured by his secular and religious administration, he also had to take it on himself to guarantee employment and means of existence to all his subjects. Hence censuses of the people, of the land, and of livestock; registration of gifts and sales for inheritance purposes: meticulous organization of agricultural work and artisan production; and prescription of corvées for the indispensable maintenance of public works—dykes, canals, roads, conveyances—and for the construction and maintenance of public buildings.

At Sparta, where a handful of conquerors introduced an iron constitution to enable them to rule their subjects in security, we find another kind of state organization, which guaranteed this handful their livelihood though exempting them from agricultural, industrial, and commercial work. The way the Spartiates lived was by dividing part of the conquered territory into equal lots, one for each family of the *Homoioi* (Equals), and requiring these lots to be tilled by the former owners—now reduced to serfdom. Meanwhile the population living in the rest of the territory, those *Perioeci* who were free but deprived of political rights, provided for other needs of the state by paying tribute and serving as auxiliaries in the army.

Even under these static conditions there were always many ways in which individuals could change their standard of life and political rights, especially in a downwards direction. But in countries where state control was less tight, economic differences between the inhabitants were of course even easier and commoner. This was true of Assyria, where control of labour by the king and the priests was much less marked than in Egypt. It is true that the state often fixed wages and prices, provided for regular corvées, and legislated on the relations between landlords and tenants, and on matters related to the hiring of boats and other transport. But there were many other factors favouring the creation of fortunes which were not dependent on landed property and were therefore more subject to fluctuations in size. Trade was on the increase, especially in the hands of foreigners such as Arameans and Greeks; loans at interest were becoming common, though some rates were controlled (for instance those on loans to the poor and the sick); weighed metal, including lead, was being used to make transactions easier, and the relative values of such metals were being realistically laid down. There were thus many new causes which could not but lead to economic inequalities, quite apart from those always associated with landed property—partition, multiple inheritance, destruction by war and cataclysm, and so on.

The Phoenician economy was built on a threefold system, trade by sea and caravan, foundation of trading-posts, mining districts, and colonies, and the organization of industrial craftsmen (though landed property also played its part). Movable property and liquid wealth thus developed early in their history, and economic inequality became natural. Phoenician talents were more commercial than artistic, and their manufactured goods are largely imitated.

For Greece after the Mycenaean period we can give a more detailed account of economic and social developments. On the one hand agrarian conditions were commonly leading to pauperism as the population increased. In some areas properties were ground down to insignificant size by being divided among the growing number of descendants; in others, where succession was limited to the first-born, there would be the problem of the disinherited younger sons. Later the phenomenon was aggravated by the struggle between monarchies and aristocracies, the former supported by the common people. On the other hand commerce, piracy, and artisan production were providing new means of acquiring a livelihood and even a large fortune. There was early development of an export trade in artistic goods to Asia Minor, Cyprus, the Syrian coast, Egypt, south Italy, Sicily, and as far as the smaller islands in the south of the western Mediterranean. In the early days colonization had allowed the disinherited to create a new life for themselves, in which they once more became landowners with holdings of uniform size. But the land became inadequate as lots got divided again and new immigrants began to arrive. There was inequality once more, and the newcomers had to be content with land which was too small and unproductive. Later they might be forced to give up landowning entirely and put up with earning a wage for working the land of another or exploring other means of existence. One may remember Hesiod's advice to the insolvent peasant, to take to a life on the sea.

So we gradually find new legal forms to deal with loans, in goods or precious metal, taken up by men who wanted capital to expand their output: mortgages and 'redemption sales' on real estate, the conditions being regular payment of interest and amortization, defaulters being liable to distraint on their property and even seizure of their persons. Solon's legislation at Athens was a reaction against measures which were too injurious to the liberty of individuals or which threatened to remove from them the minimum resources needed to sustain life. Appointed in 594–3 as a peacemaker, Solon by his *Seisachtheia* (Shaking off Burdens) cancelled all debts which seemed outrageous, together with the pledges into which debtors had entered to secure their loans; and he also tried to bring back debtors who had become bankrupt and had been sold as slaves outside Attica. The whole organization of loans was of course tidied up and made much easier after the introduction of coinage, since citizens with accumulated wealth could now form private banking houses. Interest rates were very varied: from the fifth century the norm was 12 per cent on loans for trade by land and 30 per cent for trade by sea; but no actual maximum was fixed.

At an earlier period the administration of royal and temple treasuries had provided a primitive system of banking. Herodotus (II, 150) says that Ashurbanipal in the seventh century kept his vast treasures hidden in underground vaults at Nineveh. Treasures were also kept by temples in the Assyrian, neo-Babylonian, and Hebrew kingdoms, and private resources could be deposited in their vaults as need arose, the depositor being then able to draw on them to make loans. Proportionately smaller treasures were owned by the early kings and later by cities in archaic Greece, who used to store them safely under divine protection in the temples. There too, as for instance in the Artemisium at Ephesus, private individuals could deposit their savings and later use them for their own transactions.

b. *The Organization of the Family*

This is not the place for a survey of the great controversies about the origin of family organization. Like the state, the family meets human needs which are primitive, profound, and independent of other circumstances, namely the needs of the individual and the needs of a collective unit. Here we need only record our conviction that theories which make the family a precondition and pattern of the state are to be rejected equally with those which suppose the state to have created the family.

The Vedic family was strictly patriarchal and monogamous, and these two factors are fundamental in the Aryan family of India to this day. The *patria potestas* was complete, and, at least in origin, unlimited, passing to the eldest son on the death of a father. The family remained undivided until it reached really large proportions, comparable with those of a *gens*. It was a unit for religious purposes, and domestic ritual was extremely complex and highly developed: about the end of this period it was codified in the *Gṛhyasūtras*. As was shown earlier, the normal state of affairs was the 'joint family', presided over and represented by its oldest male married member. When a son left his family, a new family came into being, a creation symbolized by the kindling of a new domestic fire.

On the other hand the family of Dravidian India, though documentary evidence about it is late, seems originally to have been to some extent at least matriarchal, and this is reflected in the typically southern cult of the Great Mother.[22] In parts of the south polyandry was in force, and even in our own time it has survived in certain districts on the Malabar coast.

The Chinese family was always the core and basic unit of Chinese society. Indeed it was its model, for the Confucian scholars maintained that the state should be ruled like a great family, with the emperor as its father. Its constitution was not unlike that of the Aryan family. The matriarchal features of the Shang family have disappeared or been absorbed so that the family of the Chou period was strongly patriarchal, in a form which lasted down to the reforms introduced by the Communist régime. The father was an absolute master, with the power even of life and death over his sons, limited in practice by the necessity of obtaining the emperor's consent before a son was put to death. The mother's position was correspondingly influential second only to that of the father, her authority over daughters-in-law and marriageable daughters being absolute. Filial piety (*hsiao*) always remained the strongest link in Chinese society, and was matched by brotherly loyalty. These two bonds implied the duty of mutual assistance, including the blood vendetta, which was widely practised in China. On the other hand the unbreakable cohesion of the Chinese family bred the institution of its collective responsibility for offences by one of its members.[23]

Monogamy was the general practice, but concubinage grew up before long and was made regular and legal at an early date. The favourite concubine obtained a position little short of becoming a secondary wife. Sometimes a father would make a concubine's son his heir to the detriment of a son born to his wife, but these were exceptional cases proving the rule that sons of a regular marriage took precedence. In any case maternal authority always belonged to the regular wife only.

In Egypt polygamy and concubinage were allowed to a man, but a woman according to tradition could have only one husband. She had a privileged position as mistress of the house, and as head of the family during widowhood. There is a separate problem whether marriages between brother and sister occurred outside the Pharaonic family, where they were modelled on the myth of Isis and Osiris: the texts which suggest that it was common practice are perhaps to be understood metaphorically. The country's wealth combined with the state's controlled system of labour to free families from the cruellest consequences of poverty, namely exposure of children and the exclusive rights of the first-born. Births had to be scrupulously registered in order that adequate means of maintenance could be provided. It is true that infant mortality must have been heavy in the poor conditions of sanitation.

Assyria was a contrast. There the position of women went down in comparison with the advance made earlier by the Babylonians. A woman had an inferior status at law, and only in later times could she make contracts, even then being unable to control loans on her own account. She had to put up with her husband having other wives and concubines, and it was easy for him to put her away. If she became a widow, she was normally compelled to re-marry with a relation of her husband.

The Hebrews had a very lofty conception of the family, for in this part of social life, as in others, they sought to give practical application to their religious ideas. Marriage was the appropriate means of propagating the human race because there was a precise divine ordinance to that effect; and it was on the family that the Chosen People was founded and from which, as an essential institution, its power was derived.

When a family was established there was a religious ceremony to consecrate its permanence; and various laws laid down the degrees within which marriages were permitted, the duties of spouses, and other rules affecting family rights. In relation to her husband the wife was almost a slave, but it was his duty to show her affection. Polygamy was practised, but unions with foreigners were forbidden, though after a time mixed marriages became common. A characteristic Hebrew practice (one not unparalleled elsewhere) was Levirate, under which, if a man died without sons, his brother or other near relative married his widow. Wives had no right of inheritance; and in general the same applied to daughters if there was male issue. Divorce could not be initiated by wives, but for husbands it was relatively easy, though some justification was necessary and it entailed restriction of the dowry. Adultery, sexual perversion, and prostitution were firmly prohibited and punished by heavy penalties, but certain contraceptive methods were allowed within limits.

Children were regarded as a gift from God, and a large family was a sign of blessing from heaven: infanticide, except for sacrifices to Baal, and also exposures of children, so common among other peoples, were unknown. Children were carefully educated, and were taught to show respect for their parents, both father and mother, a fact which shows that the woman who became a mother was held in great honour. The first-born received a double inheritance; and the sons of concubines enjoyed certain rights.

In Persia, as in India and generally among Indo-European peoples, the family was closely knit, and their religion made of marriage an institution designed to secure the permanence of the race. Genealogies were handed down, and various grades of relationship were classified, for instance at times of mourning. All Persians longed for children, and there were precise rules about inheritance, adoption, and guardians. Polygamy and marriage between close relatives occurred, but were probably the result of foreign influence.

Much the same is true of the Greek family in the archaic period, which is illustrated by Greek epic. We should take the polygamy of Priam, the marriage of Zeus and Hera, the marriages between the sons and daughters of Aeolus, and similar stories to be evidence of non-Greek usages. The normal practice was monogamy, although concubinage was tolerated. Wives were acquired by purchase; yet the woman of good family was not shut up with the female servants in the gyneceum, but took part with her husband in ceremonies and looked after the management of the household during his long and frequent absences. This usage survived in Asiatic Greece, as we know from Simonides and other writers; but in the rest of Greece local customs grew up, the general tendency being to require women to live more segregated lives. A special type of family was imposed on the Spartiates by their exclusively military organization. Conjugal life among young married persons was reduced to a minimum, and only one meal was taken at home. Indeed wives were actually chosen in the dark[24] if our source is correct, and sons once weaned were taken from their parents and brought up by the state.

We need not go into the legal discussions, largely arbitrary and theoretical, about the original structure of the Roman family. The form was undoubtedly patriarchal, the *pater familias* having power not only over his wife and children but also over the families of his sons. On his death, however, the power got divided, since a number of independent families had become established;

yet these could continue to associate closely and carry on the father's line. A man without sons could adopt one and make him his heir. But if he died without having done so, and without a will, his property passed to his near relatives, and in default to the *gens*.

c. *Slavery*

Slavery is certainly not a general phenomenon of all the ancient world and of that world alone.[25] It cannot be shown to have extended to all ancient peoples, and in some places it continued after ancient times. Among the various peoples it may have arisen for a number of reasons, which need not always have operated together. The most usual cause was undoubtedly war, when enemies surrendered or were made prisoner, as individuals or in large groups, and were made slaves as an alternative to death. Ransom, however, was often permitted, or the less inhuman status of serfdom could replace that of outright slavery. Akin to this was the enslavement of foreigners captured by pirates and sold as human merchandise capable of providing labour; or a conquered people might deliver men to their conquerors as a war indemnity. Much less common was the enslavement of a faction by its victorious compatriots; when it does happen, it means that the political struggle has become so bitter that instead of being able to retire into exile the defeated party have to stay in the country, where they are deprived of their liberty and put to forced labour. In many countries those guilty of grave crimes, like adultery, murder, or theft, might lose their liberty and be abandoned to the will of the injured party. In other cases an insolvent debtor might be compelled to work for his creditor until he paid off the debt; or he might have to stay for ever as a serf on the land which he once owned, and have the obligation of delivering an agreed part of the produce to the new proprietor.

About slavery in Egypt we are not well informed. Slaves there must have been almost exclusively prisoners-of-war, tribute paid by subject peoples, or men sold by pirates. It is improbable that the country had slaves of Egyptian origin; and even if a name looks Egyptian it may be a new name given after the slave arrived. Since the main owner was the Pharaoh, slaves usually worked in the palace, or as scribes, especially to deal with foreign languages, or as labourers in the quarries, mines, and other royal possessions. It was not uncommon, however, for the Pharaoh to leave part of the captives as booty to his guards or as a present to high dignitaries. We hear of slaves running away and being recaptured, but we are also told about enfranchisement and of ex-slaves being taken into the army as mercenaries.

In Assyria slavery was very harsh and generally originated from captures made in war. The Phoenicians, as we know from the story of the kidnapping of Eumaeus in the *Odyssey*, were notorious as pirates, who captured free men and sold them.

Although slaves were included in the scope of the Hebrew family, they were never numerous and were extremely well treated. They were usually bankrupt debtors, but whatever the cause of their slavery they regained freedom after seven or fifty years. Even if foreigners became slaves, by right of war perhaps or by purchase, they still enjoyed certain safeguards: for instance they must not be put to death or mutilated, and they must have rest on the Sabbath. There were also paid servitors, with a higher status than that of slaves, including the special class of foreign serving-men, who might or might not be admitted, without full rights, to the Hebrew tribes.

Herodotus (VI, 137) claims that slavery was once unknown in the Greek cities. Yet it certainly spread to Greece in time, and there was a period when Greeks treated their slaves with some barbarity.

In the Homeric poems slaves taken in war or sold by pirates are shown, together with their children, as faithful allies of their patron, who treats them kindly inside his patriarchal domain. Nor do they seem to have been numerous, although in the fourth *Iliad* we hear already of small craftsmen in the household and a certain number of weaving women directed by a female superintendent. In the seventh and sixth centuries the numbers of slaves were continually increasing, first at Asiatic Greek cities like Chios and Miletus (where Hipponax speaks of Phrygian slaves), and then on the mainland, especially at Corinth and Athens. We are told that Cleisthenes of Athens gave citizenship to a number of ex-slaves.

But besides these individual slaves and the gangs employed by industrialists there were whole populations reduced to serfdom on the land: the Helots serving the Laconian state, the Penestai in Thessaly, the Mnoiti in Crete, and other classes attested at Syracuse and in Etruria. As we have already said, the treatment of slaves in Greece got gradually harsher, despite the general rise in moral standards. The difference recognized between Greek and barbarian was becoming sharper. Physical work was increasingly looked down on, and the number of slaves exposed for sale in the markets was growing. Yet for these very reasons, at any rate in the more civilized parts of Greece, it seemed more and more unthinkable that Greeks should be reduced to slavery. One consequence was that enslavement for debt came to be forbidden, Solon's laws being the first example: others were the ease with which prisoners-of-war could be ransomed, and the severity with which attempts to kidnap free-born Greeks were punished.

Slavery certainly came to the Italic world, as will be explained in Part II.

From the outset slavery was an integral part of the feudal Chou society in China. It has two origins, prisoners-of-war and punishment.[26] Gifts of slaves (normally not individuals but whole families) are repeatedly mentioned in our texts, although apparently only one document (a vase inscription of about 900 BC) mentions a purchase and sale of slaves.

d. *Castes and Societies*

The most important feature of the Indian social system is caste. Its origin is not yet entirely clear; according to most scholars it may have resulted from the racial difference between the ruling Aryan invaders and the defeated Dasyu over whom they ruled: the use of the Sanskrit word for 'colour' (*varṇa*) to mean 'caste' indicates an origin of this kind.[27] Development was naturally very slow and gradual, the situation at the outset being a very long way from what later became the rigid caste system. According to the theory of Late Vedic texts, the Brahmans were born free from the Creator's head, the *kṣattriya* from his chest, the *vaiśya* from his thighs, and the *śūdra* from his feet. In its essential lines this theory is already found, with some difference in mental attitude, in a late *Ṛigveda* hymn, the *Purusasukta* (*Ṛigveda*, X, 90), but this is an isolated piece of evidence. In the Early Vedic period Aryan society seems not to have been divided into castes, but into social classes of a mainly professional, but not hereditary, nature. The continual state of war against the non-Aryan natives, one may suppose, caused the formation of a class of professional warriors, while the rest of the Aryan population, feeling themselves secure behind this bulwark, abandoned the use of arms and confined themselves to agriculture and artisan production. This would account for the *kṣattriya* and *vaiśya*. As for the Brahmans, their caste came into being as a direct consequence of the growing complication of ritual. In early times ritual was simple enough to be performed personally by the head of a family or by the prince. But it gradually became so involved that it required the employment of a specialist, i.e. of a professional priest. The *śūdra* in the *Ṛigveda* period seem to have been aboriginal prisoners, or the inhabitants of whole non-Aryan villages compelled to recognize the sovereignty of the conquerors.

Gradually these social classes, which in origin were fluid and open, with complete freedom of relations with each other, began to crystallize in response to a new spirit. This was probably the non-Aryan spirit, with which the Aryan society in its new Indian home was all the time becoming insensibly pervaded. In the Late Vedic period *varṇa* definitely meant 'caste'. The system tended to grow and to take on complications when sub-castes and mixed groups came into being, especially among the *vaiśya*. In theory this was entirely due to mixed marriages, though it should be noted that in this period marriage between a higher-caste man and a lower-caste woman (*anuloma*) was still permitted, where one between a lower-caste man and a higher-caste woman (*pratiloma*) was not. But in practice marriage was only one of the factors which contributed to this phenomenon: perhaps more important was the exclusive rigid attitude adopted by groups who followed defined professions and trades. In later times *conubium* between different castes tends to be excluded altogether, although at the same time the strictest rules of exogamy were being laid down. At the end of this process of development a man may only marry a woman of his own caste, but she must belong to a different *gens* (*gotra*). The rights and duties of each caste, especially from the point of view of ritual, were accurately and minutely described in the *Brāhmaṇas*. A functional division became thus a hierarchic division, with the *vaiśya* superior to the *śūdra* and the *brāhmaṇa* and *kṣattriya* to the *vaiśya*. The two top castes were approximately on equal terms, the *kṣattriya* being superior in political matters and the Brahman in religious. But even then the castes had not become completely rigid; and their principal characteristics, heredity, and the prohibitions on members of different classes intermarrying or inter-dining had not yet been firmly established. This process reached its conclusion, however, in the time of the *Upaniṣads*, which saw a progressive worsening in the conditions of the *vaiśya* and *śūdra*. In the *Gṛhyasūtras* the caste system receives detailed codification. A young man takes on the full rights and duties of his caste at a ceremony of initiation (*upanayana*), held at different ages for the different castes, but confined to members of the first three. In it they receive their second or spiritual birth (thus becoming twice-born, *dvija*), together with the exclusive right to study the *Veda*. The outward sign of this initiation is the ritual thread (*yajñopavⁱta*), which the *dvija* (normally only the Brahman) carries on his shoulder and across his chest for the rest of his life. The system was made completely rigid when the theory of untouchability was introduced—and symptoms of it can be seen at the end of this period. Under this theory contact with a man who by birth or violation of his duties is excluded from the system of caste causes a grave pollution. In the same way, at the end of this period caste differentiation makes itself apparent in the criminal and civil law, where penalties, capacity to act as a witness, and the like are varied from caste to caste.

In Egypt caste divisions, though less rigid than in India, were the natural result of a static organization, in which living standards, professions, and technical skills were handed down from father to son. Herodotus (II, 164) lists seven castes—priests, soldiers, peasants, swineherds or shepherds, merchants, interpreters, and pilots; and to these must be added the artisans.

Members of the priestly class had to undergo special training in the king's palaces and in the temples, in each of which the senior post was that of prophet or chief priest, a post reserved for men of the highest family. Of the soldiers we shall speak in a moment, but it may be said at once that officer posts, apart from those held by foreign captains of mercenaries, were confined to certain families, that the condition of entry was an appropriate course of training, and that their holders were rewarded with a share in the booty, and with decorations, lands, and slaves. Peasants and shepherds, whose life is described variously in our documents as idyllic or as on the verge of ruin, would possess a cottage with a small garden and some livestock; but they were in fact tied to the land, the fortunes of which they would follow with passivity, without the possibility that any of them would escape their lot. They were also subjected to corvées and to the risk of abnormal requisitions.

The artisans who worked in the palace, in the temples, and on their own account, were reasonably sure of their food and clothing, and some of them could even become prosperous, although in certain circumstances their conditions could be so hard as to prompt attempts at revolt. The scribes led a more comfortable existence and were exempt from corvées; their work was of an administrative kind, which required the use of their brains more than of their hands, and included accounting, writing, editing, and translating.

Hebrew society had no very clear class divisions because the tenor of its life was simple, the prevailing occupations being pasturage and agriculture with very little development of commerce. Respect for one's neighbour—his person, his family, and his property—was keenly felt, and it was one's strict duty to pay any wage or price which had been agreed. Slander and any form of attack on another's honour, together with the denunciation of one's neighbour in times of persecution, were grave offences. The keen sense of national solidarity meant that one must give help to the needy, who were part of one's own people.

In the earliest Greek periods very particular importance attached to the private and personal associations called phratries and tribes.[28] To fill the gap left by the state its subjects would organize themselves into societies for mutual assistance in peace and war. The more closely knit of these societies were called *Hetairiai* (companies of friends) or phratries (companies of brothers), while the union between several phratries was the origin of a tribe or phyle. These private societies were hereditary, with their own cults and their own magistrates. In time of peace they looked after the administration of justice to see that verdicts were carried out, and dealt with matters such as the distribution of tax burdens: in war they formed units in which their members served. To remain outside the phratries and tribes by now meant that a man was isolated and undefended and that his life was intolerable; so eventually these societies comprised the whole population. At this point the state recognized their importance, and made them permanent and compulsory, using them as administrative units in civil life, and also for tribute collection, military levies, and regimental divisions in the field.[29]

The caste system of the Spartan state also deserves a mention. The full citizens of *Homoioi* (Equals), who possessed lots, were differentiated from other groups whose status was inferior economically and therefore also politically. These included the *Hypomeiones* (Inferiors), the *Neodamodeis* (new citizens), and the *Perioeci*, these last being the free inhabitants of certain conquered districts, with no political rights.

Religious societies will be dealt with in their proper context.

In Roman history the division into patricians and plebeians is an example of caste.[30] In the writer's view the difference between the two was initially similar to that between the Spartiates and *Perioeci*. The patricians must have been the families of the ruling *oppidum*, Roma Quadrata, from which the *patres* forming the senate were derived, having originally been chosen counsellors of the king; the plebeians were the families of the villages and surrounding country, over which the *oppidum* ruled. But later on, when inequalities of wealth developed, only the richer families remained patrician. Then, in the pride which their wealth had brought them, they began to talk of their ancestors and family trees, to assume 'gentile' names, and to adopt traditions, customs, and cults which distinguished them from the other families. They held assemblies of their *gentiles*, and were followed by trains of plebeian supporters, who were ready to obey them (*cluere*) as their 'clients'. At this stage to be a patrician meant not only to belong to the ruling group, which reserved to itself the principal political rights, but also to be one of the richest and most powerful citizens.

The thirty *curiae* and the three Roman tribes did not, in our view, originate in a way similar to that in which the ancient phratries and personal tribes in Greece took shape. They were a relatively late institution, which resulted from a single act like that which created the later territorial (or state) Greek tribes, being based on the topographical divisions of the Roman city, which by now united the several primitive villages in a single habitation.

e. *A Note on Games*

Even the most primitive peoples knew many kinds of games and competitions: athletic or dramatic or pure pastimes; games of skill or thinking or chance; or simply children's play. A curious popular etymology of classical antiquity attributed *ludi* (games) to the Lydians; but they are clearly customs which were common to all peoples at all times and required no unique origin. Athletic games reached their highest form of expression in Greece, where the writer of the *Iliad* assumed that the heroes would not hesitate to compete in Patroclus' funeral games. The most famous personages of Greece, including its colonial world, were proud to take part in the panhellenic games, which took place every four years and where the victors received semi-divine honours; and the whole education of the Spartans was founded on athleticism of a militarist kind. The Etruscan games, in part at least, were modelled on the Greek; and during the Etruscan domination of Rome the Romans too copied the custom. Games, of one new type after another, were henceforth their passion; games to propitiate the gods or render thanks, games at funerals or the circus or at gladiatorial shows, games accompanied by drama or music, or any other kind.

In every part of the classical period children's and adults' games were developed. For these the continuous mass of literary evidence is supplemented by pictorial representations.

4. INTER-GROUP RELATIONS

a. *Treatment and Assimilation of Conquered Peoples*

On the treatment of conquered people in Vedic India we have no direct evidence. It seems generally that their property and way of life were not greatly upset, their only obligation being the payment of tribute (*bali*) to their conqueror. In the long run they were absorbed into the social system of these conquerors as inferior beings, that is to say as *śūdra* (or sometimes *vaiśya*). The most extreme case was when a defeated enemy was made a *dāsa* (fem. *dāsī*) or servant for life: such people were practically slaves, but it was always household slavery, very mild in both theory and practice. At the end of this period domestic slaves apparently became hereditary.

The treatment of conquered peoples in the everlasting wars between the feudal Chinese states grew worse as time went on. Ultimately victory was measured by the number of severed heads of one's enemy. There are examples, too, of conquered peoples being transplanted, for a peasant was increasingly becoming a rare and precious commodity.

Mesopotamia still retained countless survivals from that early stage of the city-state which had been the point of departure of the great empires. But the Assyrian kings, following the example of the rulers who preceded them, aspired to build a great political organism, in which they would be 'Kings of the four quarters', that is to say that their power would extend in every direction, from Lower to Upper Sea. Indeed they aimed at becoming outright rulers of the whole known world, a dream which in the days of the Sargonids did not any longer seem a complete impossibility. But their empire, like those before it, was like a see-saw, with periods of irresistible expansion followed by counter-thrusts and periods of stagnation; and the causes are many and obvious. Their wars of conquest were conducted with immense effort, their attacks being repeatedly pressed home. But after they had shown extreme cruelty, taking terrible vengeance on their enemies and ruthlessly destroying their property, they took no thought to follow a war with a period of pacification and reconstruction, in which victors and vanquished would co-operate. So none of their enemies, Elamites, Urartu, Chaldeans, and the rest ever let slip a favourable moment for a rebellion in which they might regain their freedom, especially after they saw the ruling race declining in numbers on account of their continuous wars. Other difficulties need only be enumerated briefly. The peoples of the mountains and steppes were repeatedly trying to invade; there was the subtle and dangerous infiltration of the Arameans; there were continual dynastic crises; the people of their empire, who were widely different in race, aspirations, and customs, had an incorrigible tendency to seek autonomy and decentralization; and apart from the Assyrian regiments the imperial army showed little firmness and cohesion. That despite everything the empire survived for so many centuries was mainly due to the inability of its rebellious subjects to organize compact coalitions against it.

The subject peoples were now accustomed to subjection, and it was their same lack of cohesion and their inability to act together which allowed the even wider empire of the Medes and Persians to take shape. This profited from the experience of its predecessors, but it was the genius of the new Indo-European ruling race to be able to couple its ambition for universal dominion with an unusual sense of moderation, tolerance, and humanity. The same race produced the powers which tried next, the Macedonians and the Romans; and they continued and improved the methods laid down by the Persians. Although there was no attempt to press the culture of the subject peoples into a common form the Persians achieved a step forward by promoting a uniformity which came spontaneously. It resulted from their centripetal organization of taxation, law, and military service, which allowed all peoples to retain their own characteristic institutions, but encouraged them to imitate their overlords. Along with the indigenous languages Aramaic now spread widely as the common speech. As regards race, there was decided cultural significance in the fact that parties of Iranians were settled here and there among the subject peoples for purposes of defence. In religion, too, cohesion was promoted by the Persian policy of not persecuting the practices of other peoples: indeed the Great King tried, even in the religious field, to take the place of the dynasts he had deposed and to make direct contact with the cults of conquered peoples. Another unifying factor was the abolition of those internal barriers which impeded trade, with the improvement in communications which resulted from the construction of the great roads. The king maintained a number of the ancient capitals and resided at each in turn; the satrapies, which might each contain more than one racial element, were sometimes directed by local dynasts and noblemen. But more than by any other agent unity was promoted by the clear effort which was being made to ensure peace, prosperity, and justice so far as a government can bring them.

Yet though the Persian empire in its fundamental conceptions was vastly superior to its Middle Eastern predecessors it had vices and weaknesses which hastened its downfall. The levelling of culture, language, and religion came too slowly, among other things because the desert areas broke up the country and destroyed the compactness of its population. Moreover rulers and ruled were too disproportionate in their numbers. Nor was the government's financial policy free from blame. The tendency to hoard precious metals withdrew too much from circulation, and damaged trade, while the use of gold as a means of diplomacy was an easy but dangerous way of maintaining the empire's power. Finally there were the court intrigues, which often led to conspiracy or assassination.

In comparison with these Eastern empires, whose systems though imperfect were obviously being improved, the contemporary Western world was still at the earliest stage of political organization. Tribes were being split up, and city-states were forming. There were small religious federations of little political significance, and minute hegemonies which did not normally extend beyond a single geographical area.

During the late Mycenaean period the Greeks had occupied the whole Aegaean basin, not only the Greek mainland but the islands and the coast of Asia Minor. Tradition and archaeology show that from the first this world was divided into independent city-states. But as early as the period between the ninth and seventh centuries, when the Homeric epics were composed and took shape, some of these cities began to exercise hegemony over the adjoining regions, the smaller and weaker states around them being absorbed either by force or of their own accord.[31] There was often an intermediate stage, attested by the *Iliad* and other traditions, and also by later survivals, in which several city-states came together in federations. Though sometimes political in origin, these were more commonly religious unions promoting the common cult of some deity, and only later became political when one or more cities gained the upper hand. The rivalries which brought about such changes are reflected in the life and foreign relations of the leagues in question.

There were probably many such leagues, but in Asiatic Greece the most famous are those of the Ionic cities around the temple of Poseidon Heliconius on the Mycale promontory and of the Doric cities around the sanctuary of Apollo Triopius at Cnidus. On the Aegean islands the main Amphictionic centre was Apollo's temple at Delos, and the Argolic cities united at the temple of Poseidon on the island of Calauria. But the three sacred leagues or Amphictionies which became most famous in the rest of Greece were those centred on the temples of Zeus at Olympia and Dodona and of Apollo at Thermopylae. The last later moved to Delphi in Phocis.

In the course of its continual struggle to secure Peloponnesian hegemony and support oligarchies against the tyrants, Sparta secured control over the Olympic games. This enabled it to create the largest federal organization known in Greece before 500 BC, the Peloponnesian League—or the alliance of 'Lacedaemonians and their allies', as it was officially called. The individual states made a close pact of federation with Sparta, under which they preserved their autonomy—in the sense that they were not garrisoned by Spartan troops—and decided their own policies, provided that these were not contrary to the policy of the league. The only common organ was a federal assembly, composed of delegates from each allied state, though there were no league magistrates. The Spartan government, supported by the governments of the most loyal among the allies, would convoke the assembly; Sparta had command of the army, which was composed of contingents from all the allies. In this way the Lacedaemonians controlled a coalition of all the Peloponnesian cities except Argos.

Certain parts of Greece, especially in the north-west, must still have remained in archaic conditions, with political life conducted on a tribal basis.

Their organization must have been much like that which was common in the West, where the Italic peoples had started the system of strong centres containing part of the population, with the rest in villages of one kind or another. The Etruscans, who in this, as in other things, were the heirs of the *palafitticoli* and *terramaricoli*, created city-states relatively early. Later, partly of their own accord and partly in imitation of the Greek *dodecapoleis* and similar organizations, they arrived at the stage in which leagues were created. Of these the largest were three in number: one in Etruria proper, which in classical times had its capital at Volsinii; the other two in Campania and the Po valley, where from the seventh century onwards the Etruscans had established an empire outside Tuscany. But these leagues, at any rate in our period, did not promote political unity; for the cities continued to conduct their own policies, and to divide themselves into rival groups.

In the earliest times, about 1000 BC, the normal organization of all the other peoples of ancient Italy, Indo-European and pre-Indo-European, was undoubtedly tribal. But in the first half of the first millennium they must have developed the religious leagues which assumed political significance later on. In Latium we hear of the Albenses, controlled from Alba Longa and then from Rome; the league of Diana Nemorensis, of which Tusculum was in command; and the league of Caput Aquae Ferentinae, the centre of Latin/resistance to the extension of Roman hegemony. There were more leagues north and south of the Tiber, such as that based on the temple of Venus between Laurentum and Ardea. Other Italic peoples, such as the Hernici and Samnites, also had religious federations which often developed into political leagues, and the same was true of the Celts and Iberians beyond the Alps.

Hegemonies of wider dimensions were established in the Greek colonial world, but they were generally short-lived because of the rivalries which developed and because the distances between mother cities and colonies were so great. The relation between Corinth and its colonies is a good example, with the colonies on the Ionian sea remaining more closely linked to their mother city, while those on the west coast of Italy broke away. Similarly Megara Hyblaea broke with Selinus, and Gela with Acragas. After the loss of Corsica detached the Phocaean colonies north of that island from the rest, Massilia was able to reunite the northern group in a small empire of its own.

We find a similar phenomenon among the Phoenician colonies in North Africa, Spain, and the islands of the western Mediterranean. They were originally dependent on Tyre; but when Tyre lost its own independence, and communications with Phoenicia were broken, they were reorganized into a unified empire by Carthage.

b. *International Relations*

We have a certain amount of evidence about political alliances made in our period, either at the conclusion of wars, or to form coalitions, or to lay down relative spheres of action on land and sea. Here is a summary list of the more important:[32]

(1) treaties of friendship, peace, and agreement between the kings of Assyria and their neighbours, concluded *c.*1100, 900, and 860–853;

(2) close coalition against Shalmaneser II made in 854 by the kings of Damascus, Hamath, and the Hittite country, together with the Phoenician states, Israel, the Ammonites, and Egypt;

(3) pact of alliance for the division of Assyria made in 608 between the neo-Babylonian king Nabopolassar and Cyaxares of Media, with conclusion of ties of marriage;

(4) agreement on reciprocal military aid, dated *c.*600, between Alyattes of Lydia and the Asiatic Greek cities of Miletus, Colophon, and Priene;

(5) peace of 585 between the kings Alyattes of Lydia and Cyaxares of Media after an indecisive war;

(6) agreement of 569 between Amasis of Egypt and the Greek city of Cyrene;

(7) understandings made by Croesus of Lydia between 555 and 550 with Ephesus, Nabuna'id of Babylonia, Amasis of Egypt, and Sparta;

(8) alliance of 545–540 between Cyrus of Persia and Miletus;

(9) agreement of 533–532 between Amasis of Egypt and Polycrates of Samos;

(10) pact of 526 between the Persian Cambyses and the Arabians of Sinai.

We also know of the following treaties between Greek cities:

(1) the acceptance by Eleusis of subjection to Athens in *c.*650;

(2) conclusion of the Lelantine war between Chalcis and Eretria in *c.*650;

(3) coalition *c.*625 between Messenians, Argives, Arcadians, and Pisatans against Sparta and Elis;

(4) peace, by arbitration of Periander, between Mitylene and Athens, 610–595;

(5) alliance for 100 years between Elis and Heraia, concluded between 588 and 572;

(6) agreement *c.*555, between Peisistratus and the Thessalians;

(7) agreement for 30 years between Anaia and the Metapii;

(8) agreement between the Spartans and Tegeates against the Messenians, *c.*550;

(9) pact between Athens and Plataea in 519.

In the West there are also recorded:

(1) the treaty of *c.*540 between the Carthaginians and Etruscans against the Phocaeans of Corsica;

(2) subsequent peace between the defeated Carthaginians and the Massiliotes;

(3) first naval treaty between Rome and Carthage, of 508 or slightly earlier. (Under this the Romans were allowed to trade freely in Sicily, and with reservations in Sardinia and Libya, but not beyond the Fair Cape [Cape Farina]; the Carthaginians could trade on the coast of Latium, provided they did not commit acts of piracy or war and provided they did not erect fortified bases there.)

5. PUBLIC INSTITUTIONS

a. Legislation

There was no legislative power in ancient India. According to the theory found in later texts, the sources of law, in order of importance, were first the *Veda*, then tradition (*Smṛti*), and thirdly practices of those versed in the *Vedas*—in other words, the sacred texts and the interpretation gathering around them. In later days various collections of legal texts were produced (the *Dharmaśāstra*), but their validity depended on tacit and spontaneous acceptance by the governing classes and by the people, and it therefore varied at different times and in different places.

The term gradually employed was *dharma*, which had many shades of meaning—moral law, duty, good conduct. But *dharma* after the Late Vedic period was not the same for everyone: each caste, each social status, and each profession had its particular *dharma*. The *dharma* of the soldier was not that of the farmer, that of a woman was not that of a man. A rich complexity, therefore, but also great adaptability: it was round these differences that one of the most exalted texts in India, the *Bhagavadgītā*, was constructed. The king and his counsellors were subject to *dharma* like anyone else, and had no way of making any modification in it. This could only be done by time and by changes in public opinion within the priestly order, which was the chief (but not the only) interpreter of *dharma*.

In the Vedic period the king had the power to punish his subjects, but as yet there was no legal administration or law courts to back this power. From Vedic writings we get some light on offences and their punishment. The worst form of murder, indeed the only form which was regarded as fully coming under this head, was that perpetrated on a Brahman; but in the Vedic period this could still be expiated by the sacrifice of a horse (*aśvamedha*); this was difficult and extremely expensive. A blood vendetta by relations of the murdered man was permitted, but this institution came to be softened by the system of blood-money (*vairadeya*): one text mentions blood-money of a hundred cows paid for the killing of a man. For theft penalties ranged from death at the stake to cutting off a hand and the pillory, according to the gravity of the offence. Cases of minor importance in the villages were left to the decision of rural arbiters (*grāmyavādin*). In criminal procedure witnesses were of primary importance, but recourse was often had to the ordeal, for instance the grasping of a red-hot iron (cf. *Chāndogya Upaniṣad*, VI, 16, 1–2). As regards civil law in the Vedic periods we know only some outlines of the law of patrimony and succession, to which there are several references. Civil procedure made frequent use of the good offices of a referee (*praśna-vivāka*).

The legal situation in the *Upaniṣad* period is reflected in the various *Dharmasūtras*, which were composed in the second half of the first millennium BC, though using ancient materials. *Dharma* extended its efficacy so as to embrace not only civil and criminal law, but every religious act and still more every action affecting society. Consequently religious punishments (penances) and social punishments (loss of caste) frequently took the place of definite legal penalties (usually very severe) for every sort of offence however grave. The king exercised full judicial power, and decided the lawsuits (*vyavahāra*) brought before him. His power of criminal jurisdiction was symbolized by the *daṇḍa* or wand which gives it its name. The king could delegate this jurisdiction to his officials (*adhyakṣa*) or to his council (*pariṣad*). Punishments were corporal or alternatively exile, although pecuniary penalties (in the etymological sense of the Latin word) were beginning to be recognized. In this period punishments were already graded according to caste, robbery with violence by a *śūdra* being punished by death and confiscation of property, but the penalty for the same crime by a Brahman being blinding. Blood-money was still allowed, but this too was graded by caste: the killing of a Brahman was now declared a crime beyond expiation: that of a *kṣattriya* could be compensated by a thousand cows, that of a *vaiśya* by a hundred cows, and that of a *śūdra* by ten cows. In the law of succession women were generally debarred from inheriting, although this principle was somewhat modified at the end of this period, as we shall see later. Precedence in succession was given to male relations up to the sixth degree (*sapinda*), and only then to anyone more distant (*sakulya*). There was no will and its place was taken by the distribution of property made in the owner's lifetime. All the same the dispositions of the oldest relevant texts are imprecise and often self-contradictory, and it was local and family custom which reigned supreme.

The foundation of Hebrew law was the statute (*Thora*), and its essential core, summarizing all statutes, was the Ten Commandments (the Decalogue).

The traditional story of the way this Law was given by the God of the Hebrews shows us at once how dependent it was on revelation. We see the deeply religious character of the Hebrew code, and the intimate bond which has always existed for them between the precepts of religion and the statutes of their law. There is something of this kind among other Eastern peoples but among the Hebrews the religious aspect is so much more emphasized that it is ultimately the characteristic feature of their nation.

The purpose behind every statute was from first to last the religious and transcendent one of glorifying God and promoting his Kingdom. This meant that every breach of the law was regarded as a sin or profanation, requiring a sacrifice to expiate it. The guiding principle of all Hebrew legislation was a precise calculation of giving and receiving, a rigid mathematical criterion which measured every action to assign it a proportionate retribution. In this way human actions were all valued in terms of reward or punishment in this world; every man gets classified according to his deserts among the just or among the wicked.

This ethical and religious colouring was reflected fairly obviously in the particular statutes adopted. On the one hand they may be found to reflect a spirit of strict justice rather than an attitude of piety; but on the other hand one meets precepts and ordinances of a very high moral standard, such as those on protection of widows and orphans, the suppression of usury, or the regulation of property. Yet we cannot say exactly how far these rules were applied in practice. The lofty protests of the prophets may imply frequent disregard of the code which had been laid down, and a low standard of respect for law.

Besides the written Law, preserved in detail in various books of the Bible, there was also oral Law, which served to interpret the written code and adapt it to particular situations which might be encountered during the changes and chances of life. The written Law, being God's word, was sacred and could not be altered: the oral Law proceeded from expositions by the rabbis, and in time became more oppressive and meticulous, until it was enunciated under 613 heads, 248 positive and 365 negative, in Talmudic times. As a result Hebrew scholars, as we have already seen, devoted much time and attention to study of the Law.

We explained above that retribution was almost the guiding principle of Hebrew legislation. The law of 'talion' was continually made more explicit in the criminal code, and not only the individual but his whole family were involved in the assessment of responsibility. Sometimes money compensation was allowed instead of the strict payment of 'an eye for an eye'; on other occasions the guilty party could gain asylum in one of certain recognized holy places. Capital punishment was usually carried out by stoning: prison as a punishment was unknown.

Moses, and then in their turn the kings, had acted as judges, but judicial functions were ordinarily entrusted to elders and heads of tribes—and in later days to the Levites. These judges would sit in front of city gates. After hearing the parties, together with at least two witnesses to guarantee the truth of the deposition, they would pronounce sentence, and if possible see that the sentence was carried out immediately.

Our summing-up must be that Hebrew law-giving was pervaded by lofty ideals of morality, its aim being on the whole to protect the poor, help the needy, and prevent injustice. In comparison with other Eastern legal codes it is clearly superior, though Hebrew history records many examples of infraction of their laws.

In Egypt the primitive idea was that the Pharaoh's divine will as expressed in his orders must be carried into effect even if it was prompted by malice. The effects of this were tempered in time, because kings would stay their hand when they remembered what harm had been caused by some of their predecessors' regulations. For these reasons didactic handbooks got written, such as the 'Lessons of a Pharaoh to his Sons' accompanied by collections of illustrative stories.

At the same time the decisions made by Pharaohs on particular occasions led on to written sets of rules, drawn up on general principles but also anticipating individual happenings. These rules have not come down to us. The king always remained the highest judge of appeals. Diodorus (I, 74 ff.) lists five law-giving Pharaohs before the Persian conquest, and on the fourth of them, Bocchoris, he pauses (*ib.* 79) to record some of his laws on commerce, loans, and contracts, asserting that many of this Pharaoh's regulations survived to his own time (meaning the time of his source).

The Greek world was divided into city-states, each of which had its own laws. Yet they are all very similar to one another, because they were inspired by common legal concepts and because inter-city leagues and treaties encouraged uniformity. Originally law emanated from the kings, with guidance from their Council of Elders or Senators. The kings were then succeeded by oligarchies, whose governing organs now made laws and applied customs in a way which suited their partisan interests. Finally a *nomothetes* or law-giver in each city would be appointed on the request of the people to draft a fixed code, based partly on ancient custom and partly on innovation. To secure its permanence the law-givers (especially the earliest ones) sometimes invented a myth and presented their work as divinely inspired.33 Alterations, which were of course inevitable in time, were decided by assemblies of the whole people, or of some part of them, on a proposal made by magistrates.

Family rights were by custom the province of heads of family, whose power was in origin absolute but became milder and more restricted as time went on. They could still ordain the exposure of newly born children or the banishment of an unworthy son, but a son's right of inheritance tended to pass out of a father's control when the son had entered on his eighteenth year. Guardianship over the legal acts of a woman also became less rigid, and the guardian of a widow was only concerned to help her in her affairs. It became common practice for the guardian of a minor to entrust his ward's funds to the management of some citizen who would pay an agreed sum by way of interest. It was regarded as normal that a son should succeed his father, and an adopted son his adoptive father. A woman who had received a dowry was normally excluded from her father's will, but special regulations governed the case of heiresses. The city's laws protected in the first instance those males of eighteen years and over who possessed the requirements for full citizenship. But they also gave specific forms of assistance to classes in the population who did not enjoy such citizenship: for instance to ex-foreigners who had obtained a form of citizenship through domicile and possession of property, and to foreigners who were only allowed domicile under protection of a patron. There were special laws governing the passage from slavery to freedom. From archaic times recognition was given to the legal capacity of certain societies and colleges, both public and private.

There were definite rules about various forms of property, classified into visibles (such as premises, livestock, or slaves) and invisibles, which as such might escape taxation. Legal as well as contractual forms of easement were recognized. The sale of real estate had to be preceded by specific forms of public notice and required registration; moreover there were rules about the moment at which ownership passed from seller to buyer and about the deposit which the buyer might have to make. Every city would also have regulations about terms of credit, related either to agreements made in money, for the discharge of fines, or to loans with definite arrangements for repayment and penalties for default. As regards damage to persons, customary criminal law originally assented to the practice of a vendetta conducted by the injured party's family. Later, compensation was fixed by referees selected by the state, and the state's judicial machinery took the place of the vendetta, although the family's right to interfere was always implicit in the procedure. Accidental homicide, originally not distinguished from deliberate, now had a different penalty (exile instead of death), at any rate under the Draconian code at Athens. A similar distinction was made between thieves caught in the act and other thieves. The laws were also severe on wounding, grave slander, and adultery.

Offences against the state, originally within the king's jurisdiction, were generally tried by the accepted machinery, which in an oligarchic régime meant the senate and magistrates rather than the whole people. But in more serious cases of impiety, desertion, treachery, and peculation there might be information laid in approved form and tried by some form of popular assembly.

We have very little concrete information about the development of law in the Regal period at Rome. The natural heads of families and tribes must have laid down rules on matters which concerned their own members, and seen to their execution, following the *mos maiorum*, while matters of concern to the state were dealt with by the king assisted by the senate. Tradition speaks of *leges regiae*, and it is reasonable to think that such laws existed, whatever value we set on those that are actually recorded. The king undoubtedly presided over a court of final appeal. The college of pontiffs, although they were neither judges nor law-givers, played an important part in litigation, since, as keepers of the secret archives and directors of the *sacra* which affected private and public life alike, they were in a position to give appropriate counsel and responses. In the law of the family these pontifical responses were decisive, when questions were at issue about transmission

of the *sacra* or about the validity of marriages, adoptions, and wills. The
pontiffs, moreover, were the experts on sacred and public canons, who
determined how the ancestral gods should be conducted. They were the
regular 'jurisconsults' who alone possessed all the secrets and could advise
which of the many possible procedures a litigant should adopt. So without an
authentic interpretation from them the laws could not be applied.

b. *Finance and Taxation*

In ancient India tribute (*bali*), which was at first voluntary but later
compulsory, is mentioned as early as the *Ṛigveda* period (I, 70, 9; V, 1, 10,
etc.). The king is described as the 'devourer of the people', i.e. as living and
performing his task on the tribute the people give him. To collect and bring
in this tribute he employed officials (*bhāgadugha, saṃgrahītṛ*), who were at the
same time members of the royal council. Taxes (*sulka*) were in kind, fixed
as percentages ($\frac{1}{16}$ according to *Atharvaveda* III, 29) of the crops or livestock
produce. It appears that from very ancient times members of the royal family
and *Kṣattriya* generally (the class dominant in politics), together with the
Brahmans (the class dominant in religion), were exempt from taxation.
Since *śūdra* on the other hand had no right of property, the whole burden
fell on the *vaiśya*.

In the Late Vedic period taxation was better defined and organized, but
given the date of the relevant texts it is wiser to deal with this matter in Part II.

In Egypt the Pharaoh had to meet huge expenses for his sumptuous court,
for the costs of administration and the official cult, and for the army, especially
its mercenary section. But he also had very large funds to meet these expenses,
partly produce stored in granaries, partly precious metals in his treasuries.
Besides the returns from his vast domains, the main sources of income were
as follows. There was a poll tax and a tax on each head of livestock; a per-
centage was due to the state on all crops, including the produce of gardens
and orchards; and a levy was made on manufacturers and professional men.
To this should be added the yield from state trading and the duties imposed
on private trade, the booty from war, and the tribute and presents received
from vassal states. At the same time large savings were made possible by the
imposition of every kind of corvée on the king's subjects.

In Assyria, too, expenses were fairly heavy. There was the magnificence
displayed by the king and his household, the construction and maintenance
of the palace and temples, the management of royal domains, the cost of
sacrifices, the administrative system with its system of controls, and above all
there was an army continuously engaged in fighting. On the other hand the
enormous size of the domains and of the returns they brought in, together
with the lack of any distinction between state and royal treasuries, gave the
king unfettered control over provincial revenues, taxes, dues, and corvées, as
well as over booty and over presents and tribute (regular and extraordinary)

from vassal peoples. This wealth he stored and hoarded, some of it being occasionally used to make loans or to engage in profitable operations.

Hoarding was also possible for smaller peoples, since they could pay for war out of war itself. And in fact large hoards are recorded, for instance Solomon's famous treasure, which was valued at a thousand talents of gold and a thousand of silver.

For Persia Herodotus (III, 88–96) has given us the figures for the tribute imposed by Darius on each of his twenty satrapies. The lowest are 170 Babylonian talents of silver for the seventh satrapy, and 200 each for the eleventh and eighteenth: the highest are 360 talents of gold dust (equivalent to 4,680 Euboic silver talents) for the twentieth satrapy (India), 1,000 silver talents for the ninth satrapy (Babylonia), and 700 for the sixth (Egypt). Herodotus calculates the total annual revenue at 14,560 Euboic silver talents. Each satrapy had to make other contributions, too: for instance the fourth satrapy (Cilicia) had to provide 360 white horses each year, and the ninth 500 castrated youths, while the sixth (Egypt) was made to deliver the fish caught in Lake Moeris.

In such circumstances we can easily see how Alexander the Great was said to have found 380,000 silver talents in the treasury of Ecbatana. The size of the tribute was undoubtedly out of all proportion to what was spent on the satrapies themselves. We know that out of 500 Euboic silver talents paid by the fourth satrapy only 140 remained at the disposal of the satrap while 360 went to Darius. Moreover since the normal contributions did not exclude the possibility of abnormal exactions, and since the normal levy could be regularly increased, the system was undoubtedly one of the main causes of revolts, especially in Babylonia.

In Greece of the Mycenaean Age and during the centuries when the oldest Homeric poems were written the king possessed the returns from his own domains and in addition the booty from war and the presents made him by his subjects, who also contributed to the expenses of sacrifices, hecatombs, and banquets. Other expenses were relatively small. In war, for example, fighting men had to look after their own maintenance and equipment. The state continued to enjoy these favourable conditions in the early part of the ensuing oligarchic period, when magistrates were still unpaid. But state expenses were already increasing—for naval construction, missions abroad, public sacrifices, and festivals—while the income to meet them was still confined to the revenues from public (previously royal) lands, supplemented by voluntary contributions (*epidoseis*) made by citizens, especially for equipping the navy. In Solon's time the state had very little additional income, such as that from court fees, fines, or the sale of skins of sacrificial victims. Expenses then mounted heavily during the age of tyranny, to provide for their courts, public works, gifts to temples, fleets, and mercenaries; and corresponding provision was made to increase state revenues. The Cypselids at Corinth, for example, are said to have taxed sales. Most tyrants imposed harbour dues, and Peisistratus was first responsible for the Athenian tax of 5 per cent on the produce of the soil.

c. *War and the Organization of the Military*

War technique in feudal China during the first half of the first millennium BC was based on the chariot, carrying a noble warrior with his charioteer and shieldbearer. Around him were massed his vassals fighting on foot, but they were of little military value. So in the Chou period there is an increasingly ceremonial and artificial character about war, which is reduced to a rigid schematism, eventually rather like the ballet, with a very complicated knightly code. The leader in war, as in all social life of this period, was the aristocrat or *chün-tzu*. But when, in the course of these unending wars, the number of feudal states declined and larger units took shape, as happened at the end of this period, the traditional type of fighting tended to change and to assume features more related to reality. For example in 540 BC the state of Chin won an important victory over the mountain people called Jung by using infantry instead of chariots, despite keen opposition by the nobles.

The arms were mainly the mace (pre-Chou), lance, and spear, with points first of bronze and only later (*c.* 500 BC) of iron. The Chinese bow from the start was composite (i.e. made of different materials), and reflex (i.e. it changed its direction of curvature, as contrasted with the almost perfect half-ellipse of the long bow). The typical Chinese bow was made of a horn element applied on the bamboo stave in the 'belly' or convexity of the bow. The carefully treated sinew, soaked in glue and laid with the same substance, was always applied to the back, and was often protected by a layer of supple tree-bark, such as birch. The whole 'leaf-spring' assembly was then lacquered or painted externally, for protection against the weather. The third-century BC *Chou-li*, which reflects earlier traditions, has a long chapter on the bow in its section entitled *K'ao-kung-chi* (Artificers' Record).

The Vedic writings give us some idea of the methods of war in the earliest period of India. The king and the *Kṣattriya* fought from chariots, with such of the commons as took part in war accompanying them on foot. We find certain words for military units (*gaṇa*, *śardha*, *vrāta*), but their precise meaning cannot be defined. The principal arms were bow and arrows, with points of metal or horn, though lance, sword, axe, and sling were also used as offensive weapons. There was defensive armour, but we have no particulars. Siege warfare was still very primitive, although the *Ṛigveda* already show knowledge of a 'mobile fortress' for attacking the Dasyu strongholds. The people of this period must have been able to ride horses, but they did not do so in war.

The art of war became increasingly specialized in the hands of the *Kṣattriya*, who were soldiers by profession, with the result that definite rules were laid down, such as a prohibition on the use of poisoned weapons and on the killing of a foe who surrendered. War became to some extent ceremonial; and although there were no further important developments in this direction, this period did much to create something which was most charactetistic of all Indian military history, namely that their machinery of war got enslaved to tradition and was antiquated in comparison with that used by their neighbours and invaders.

As described in Indian epic, war is not very different from the war of the Homeric poems. Armies were composed of vassal or allied chiefs and their supporters. There was no standing army, although the *Kṣattriya* as a caste had some of the characteristics of professionals. A battle centred round decisive duels between the chiefs and principal warriors, against a background of confused and indecisive fighting between the masses on each side. Later on the art of war became, like other things, the subject of theorizing. At the end of our period we get the theory of the complete ideal army in four sections (*aṅga*)—chariots, cavalry, elephants, and infantry—called therefore *caturaṅga*.

In Egypt we find two forces pulling in opposite directions. The people was by nature peace-loving, since for centuries it had been secure in the geographical isolation of the country: but defensive measures were necessarily imposed in time by the invasions of nomads from beyond the frontiers and by the struggles for supremacy against other empires which had advanced to the Egyptian border. Yet Pharaohs and people continued to regard war as a transient rather than a permanent state of affairs, which did not require any military organization to continue in times of peace. Recruiting was therefore difficult and required special measures when emergencies arose; and a soldier had little prestige in society. Eventually the lack of military preparedness led the government to recruit professional mercenaries to meet particular occasions—Nubians, Asiatics, Libyans, and Greeks. This had its usual results in heavy expenditure, friction between mercenaries and native population, and an army that was doubtfully loyal. Mercenary chieftains would try to usurp the royal power; certain Libyans and Nubians actually succeeded. The solution devised was to transform the mercenaries in peace-time into peasants, giving each a plot of land, so as to have a permanent force of peasant soldiers. But this was not particularly valuable, because in periods when the central power was weak the mercenaries tended to cast off their military obligations and become simply agricultural proprietors.

The Assyrians, conquerors and warlords *par excellence*, naturally put a special force behind their army and its operations. In this department the great organizer was Ashur-nasipal II (883–859), but it was almost a constant characteristic of Assyrian kings to be brave and experienced generals. The army was put together by regular conscription of substantial quotas from the ruling population, each class providing appropriate types of unit and armament, backed up by contributions from the various subject peoples.

A rich and powerful Assyrian fought in one of two ways. Either he rode in a chariot drawn by two horses, with room for a charioteer, for the warrior himself, and for a servant holding a shield. Or alternatively he fought on horseback (without stirrups and with a coverlet serving as a saddle). In early days a rider was accompanied by grooms, but later he fought alone with his horse caparisoned and protected by armour.

The lower classes, vassals, and mercenaries were infantry and specialist forces, such as archers, slingers, and engineers (to deal with bridges, fords, and roads). They also looked after the baggage train and siege operations, employing ladders, rams, and parapets, and it was from these classes that the navy was drawn.

Intensive use of cavalry is also a feature of the Persian army. The satrapies, as well as being administrative units, served as regimental bases. Each included very varied races, cultures, methods of warfare, and fighting material, which made their levies difficult to combine with one another. It was not obvious that all were inspired by patriotism: indeed many were longing to regain their liberty. The forces on which the government could count were the Iranian levies, which formed the core of the army, the king's bodyguard (his chosen corps of 'Immortals'), and the garrisons of fortresses: and with them could be reckoned certain classes of mercenaries, especially the Greeks. The latter could be ready for any emergency, but the enrolment, training, and mobilization of the regional forces took a quite excessively long time, even though the construction of roads had made it possible to quicken their marches and improve their commissariat.

In the Mycenaean Age, and during the following centuries which are reflected in Homer, we can trace various phases in the history of Greek armies and the Greek art of war. Initially the power of the army was concentrated in the persons of the king and his powerful companions, who possessed chariots, horses, and shieldbearers. They were clothed in full armour, with very large shields of wood and hide, which later gave place to smaller ones made of bronze. Their subjects followed them as ill-armed foot-soldiers, whose confused encounters were only the background to the main action, the combats between the princes, fighting from their chariots or on foot. The next phase came when the masses were first given tactical organization, being distributed into phratries and tribes which they had spontaneously created (*Iliad*, II, 362). We find a reflection of this kind of organization in the five Myrmidon battalions of 500 men each (*ib.* II, 168 ff.). In battle there were three lines, first the chariots, then the inferior infantry, and in the third the infantry of better quality (*ib.* IV, 297 ff.). The last phase is described by the *Iliad* (XIII, 130 ff.; XVI, 212 ff.) in a way which exactly fits Tyrtaeus' verses on Spartan battles:34 there is a compact phalanx of hoplites in a leather and metal armour, with lance and shield, whose power consisted in the weight behind the unbroken line they could fling at their enemy in a charge.

In contrast with the popularity and success of the phalanx, cavalry tended to lose importance in most of the Greek world once war chariots had disappeared. Mounted men were now used simply for advanced reconnaissance: otherwise they dismounted and fought on foot. Hoplite forces were divided into regiments which corresponded at first to the 'personal' tribes, and later to the local tribes created by the state (five at Sparta, ten at Athens).

At Rome the first military organization of which we have any detailed knowledge is that based on thirty centuries of infantry provided by thirty *curiae*, together with three squadrons of *celeres* or cavalry. This made up the 'legion' of 3,000 foot and 300 horse (1,000 + 100 from each tribe). Tradition ascribed this system to Romulus, but it clearly presupposes the existence of the state tribes on a local basis; and those are to be attributed to Servius Tullius, in whose time the main hills of Rome were united into a single 'urbs'. Servius divided the inhabitants into three sections, which were not entirely new, called Ramnes (the Romans of Roma Quadrata), Titienses (or Quirites of the Quirinal and Capitoline), and Luceres (of the Coelian, Esquiline, and Velia).

But at the end of the Regal period and in early Republican days the infantry were already 6,000 in six battalions, and the cavalry 600 also in six regiments, so that each praetor commanded a legion of 3,000 plus 300. This means that each of the three tribes had been doubled in size, by the addition of 'second' Ramnes, Titienses, and Luceres. All these soldiers still continued to be drawn from the propertied classes, in groups of *gentiles* supported by their clients. In the period of the Etruscan kings there would certainly also have been non-Roman troops, brought by the kings from Etruria as a personal bodyguard.

NOTES TO CHAPTER IV

1. These groups were collections of what would now be called 'families'; and they owned, in commonalty, the means of production, i.e. herds, cattle, and even the land. The Greeks called them *genē*, and the Romans *gentes*.

   As Dr P. Oliva points out, the individual family, as the basis of social relations, did not originate until relatively late; but of course from early times the family kept house independently, and thus promoted the decomposition of the tribe. In the Homeric poems the soil is owned collectively (by groups of families), but the *basileis* receive the best lots 'as a present from the people'.

2. The authors do not understand sufficiently clearly the origin and social function of the state, and they fail to show that it came into being as the result of certain changes in the social and economic structure. (K. M. Kolobova.)

3. It is of course implied that the goods were in theory regarded as the property of the people.

4. Yet the Greek king was of course nothing like an oriental or Hellenistic monarch. He headed a confederacy of tribes, and was responsible to the council of the oldest heads of families—or even (see *Iliad*, II, 207 ff.) to the Assembly of the people.

5. Many Soviet historians consider it totally incorrect to identify the ancient Chinese titles *kung, hou, po, tzu*, and *nan* with the European terms duke, marquess, earl, viscount, and baron (see, for example, L. V. Simonovskaya, 'Voprosy periodizatsii drevney istorii

Kitaya' [Problems of Periodization in Ancient Chinese History], *Vestnik drevney istorii*, 1950, no. 1).

Apart from this, even if it were possible to accept such an identification, it would be valid only for the middle of the first millennium BC, and under no circumstances for the beginning of that millennium. During the early Chou these terms still denoted relations of kinship (*po*—uncle, *tzu*—son), or else referred to tribal chiefs (*kung*) and their aides and followers (*hou*). It was only from the ninth and eighth centuries BC onwards that these terms came to be transformed into titles of rulers of individual kingdoms and 'fiefs'. (L. S. Vasilyev.)

6. Dr P. Oliva objects to the use of such a word about the Homeric period. All Professor Pareti means, however, is that the king was concerned with the organization of which he was the head, and not with individuals' rights.

7. As Dr P. Oliva notes, this word is perhaps anachronistic for so early a period.

8. Professor K. M. Kolobova maintains that Nestor, so far from recommending an innovation, was appealing to his own longevity and counselling a return to the past. The *Iliad* (II, 655) suggests that the division into tribes was already recognized, and it is arguable that other ancient evidence (e.g. Aristotle's *Constitution of Athens*) attests tribal divisions in Mycenaean times.

9. Professor Pareti's arguments for this view of early Spartan constitutional development are given in *Storia di Sparta arcaica* (Florence, 1920), esp. I, 177. It has been strongly contested, and it must be admitted that a period of 'sole monarchy' has no support in ancient sources. But the suggestion that it was the heads of twenty-seven phratries (the number which celebrated the festival called Carneia) *plus* the two kings *plus* the head of a third house (the Aegeidae) which built up the number thirty of the Spartan Council is substantially accepted by G. L. Huxley, *Early Sparta* (London, 1962), p. 48, and has great attractiveness. Whatever the truth on these points, however, the Spartan kings continued to be two, not three. The other important early developments (see also below, p. 169) were the institution of the five Ephors (attributed to King Theopompus, perhaps c.700 BC), and that of the Council of Thirty, apparently a reform for which religious sanction was sought from Delphi. Both the latter institutions were attributed by early tradition to the law-giver Lycurgus; see above, p. 27, note 23.

10. The term *rājā* (*rājan*) does not seem to be a synonym for *kṣattriya*: in principle the *rājan* is a *kṣattriya*, but all *kṣattriya* are not *rājan*, they are *rājanya*.

11. The 'Hectemors' of early Athens may have had a status of this kind, tied to their plots and rendering a sixth part to their lords. But Professor Pareti's statement is valid in relation to the generality of Greek states.

12. This is a possible reason for the decline in Spartan population, which so much impressed itself on Greeks of the classical period (e.g. Aristotle, *Politics*, 1270 a 20). But the event from which the Spartans never recovered was the earthquake of 464 BC; before this they are not known to have had any population problem. Later the state tried desperately to remedy matters, by penalizing celibacy and by giving privileges to fathers of three sons. See H. Michell, *Sparta* (Cambridge, 1952), p. 248.

13. Or perhaps rather the villages or obes, which were probably five in number at the time (c.700 BC) when the Ephorate was created.

14. In his account of early Rome Professor Pareti follows closely the views of G. de Sanctis (on this point see *Storia dei Romani* [Turin, 1907], I, 399 ff.). It must be said, however, that the Romans themselves were confident that the two collegiate magistrates who succeeded the kings were on terms of equality with one another. The term *praetor maximus* is more usually taken to derive from a later period (perhaps the mid-fifth century) when *two* further praetors were added; so there were two *praetores maximi*, who later became called *consules*, and their two junior colleagues remained as *praetores*.

15. But see p. 55, note 43.

16. See Sir Leonard Woolley, *History of Mankind*, I-2, pp. 451 ff.

17. The recent excavations carried out by the University of Allahabad at Kausambi now provide direct archaeological data. See also p. 286 (Rājagṛha).

18. The classic fortifications of Athens were built after the Persian wars (479–478 BC), but strong defences had gradually been erected at various earlier dates. See Ida Hill, *The Ancient City of Athens* (London, 1953), esp. pp. 8 ff.

19. The main authority for regarding Hippodamus' regular town-planning as the work of a pioneer is Aristotle, *Politics*, 1267a. It does indeed seem likely that he greatly influenced the development of Greek (as distinct from Italian) cities from the late fifth century onwards. In his own area the lay-out of Priene, with straight streets though the town is on a hillside, is remarkable.

20. The view that the Laurium mines at one time belonged to the Pisistratid tyrants is the basis of a fascinating theory advanced by P. N. Ure, *The Origin of Tyranny* (Cambridge, 1922). It unfortunately rests on no very precise ancient evidence, though it is probable that Athens worked the mines as early as the sixth century.

21. It should be noted that the character of land ownership and tenure in China underwent an important evolution during the first centuries of the Chou. In brief it can be summarized as follows:

After the Yin conquest there came into existence the right of supreme property over all the conquered territory. This was invested in the Chou *wang*, who in the name of the Chous made rich grants of landed 'fiefs' to his relatives and supporters on the basis of conditional tenure. Only the territory inhabited by the Chous themselves ('the domain of the *wang*', as it is sometimes called) were not at first turned into granted land, but were *de facto* the property of the collective (commune) of the victorious Chous. As the power of the *wang* weakened, some of the former 'fiefs' turned into independent kingdoms. Their new rulers came to exercise rights of supreme proprietorship over the territory of their kingdoms, and in turn began to grant it to their relatives and retainers on conditional tenure. In the *wang*'s 'domain' a similar process occurred. Having lost the income that had previously come from what were now independent kingdoms, the *wang* was obliged to exercise his right of supreme proprietorship over the lands of the Chous. The free commune of Chous was deprived of its *de facto* right of ownership, and the lands were taken by the *wang* to enable him to make grants to his retainers and officials on terms of conditional tenure. In this way, by the eighth century BC or thereabouts, the picture was as follows: supreme suzerainty of the Chou *wang*, which was just a formality, a historical relic; right of supreme proprietorship exercised by the rulers of the large independent kingdoms; right of conditional tenure invested in the nobility; right of land used by the communes.

See L. S. Vasilyev, *Agrarnie otnosheniya i obshchina v Drevnem Kitae* [*Agrarian Relations and Community in Ancient China*] (Moscow, 1961). (L. S. Vasilyev.)

22. The existence of polyandry in a limited region of Dravidian India, and without any ancient attestation, is not enough to establish that the Dravidian family was to any extent matriarchal. The cult of the Great Mother cannot be regarded as typically southern: the earliest sources (Tamil literature, said to be by Sangam) make no reference to it. The first allusions to such a cult are relatively late, and concern not only the 'Mother' but the god Murugan (Kumāra) as well and even primarily. In later literature and in temples the cult of the 'Mother' has no greater attestation than in the north.

23. The process whereby the large Chinese peasant families disintegrated into small isolated families, each farming on its own account, coincided with the disintegration of the communal collective economy. The existence of such small isolated families is registered already in the later songs of the *Shih Ching* (section Kuo feng). With them there also developed the system of individual plots, from about the eighth–seventh centuries BC onwards. (L. S. Vasilyev.)

24. This story has only the authority of the Athenian fifth-century comic poet Hermippus, and is perhaps not to be taken too seriously.

25. Dr P. Oliva insists that slavery was none the less a very typical phenomenon of the ancient world, and Professor K. M. Kolobova regrets the limitations of this section. She considers that the author should have indicated the connection between slavery and a

particular stage of social and economic development. This omission would suggest to Professor Kolobova that the author is not fully aware of the class structure of ancient society, in which the dominating mode of production was that of slave-owning.

26. Enslavement as punishment for crime was not a common source of slavery in China during the first half of the first millennium BC: this relates in the main to later periods. See V. A. Rubin, 'Rabovladenie v drevnem Kitaye v 7–5 vv. do n. e.' (Slave-owning in Ancient China, seventh–fifth centuries BC), *Vestnik drevney istorii*, 1959, no 3. (L. S. Vasilyev.)

27. Professor J. Filliozat disputes the validity of this argument from the word *varṇa*, on the ground that the colour in question is not that of the skin. He maintains also that the late *Ṛigveda* (X, 90, cited below) applies the four-class division to all mankind, not to Indian society only; furthermore that the *śūdra*, who equally with the other classes are drawn from the body of cosmic man, are not regarded as a different race. See also his article 'Les classes sociales de l'Inde' in G. Olivier, *Anthropologie des Tamouls de l'Inde du Sud* (Paris, 1961).

28. Though in one sense these were private associations, Dr P. Oliva points out that they were recognized units of the tribal society, which then continued their existence after the state organization had taken shape. What Professor Pareti goes on to say suggests that he would have assented to some such formulation.

29. See Nestor's advice to Agamemnon (*Iliad*, II, 362, quoted above, p. 162).

30. For a concise summary of the various views which have been held on the origins of this division (racial, social, or economic), see H. Scullard, *A History of the Roman World, 753–146 B.C.* (2nd ed., London, 1951), pp. 39–41. There is practically no ancient testimony on the point.

31. On the reduction of certain conquered populations to serfdom see above, p. 189.

32. Since Professor Pareti wrote, evidence has been discovered of a further set of seventh-century treaties, made by Esarhaddon of Assyria. See *Iraq*, 1958, pp. 1 ff.

33. Sometimes also later generations, to give the sanction of antiquity to their institutions, attributed the bulk of them arbitrarily to a single law-giver. Many scholars have held that Lycurgus the Spartan was a fiction of this kind.

34. Tyrtaeus (*floruit c.*660–640) is describing the contemporary war against Messenia, the 'Second Messenian War'. We have similar evidence about the mercenary infantry of Gyges of Lydia, slightly earlier in the century; and paintings on early seventh-century vases also depict hoplite formations.

CHAPTER V

RELIGION AND THE BEGINNINGS
OF PHILOSOPHY

I. THE MAIN RELIGIONS, 1200–500 BC

a. *China*

The background to Chinese religion in the Chou period was that typical of an agricultural people. In a closed and feudal society, where the gens (or clan) was the basic unit, where older matriarchal customs had now given place to patriarchy, and where agriculture with the changes in the seasons hung over everything in life, fundamental beliefs were inevitably connected with the soil and the family. Hence the great festivals which the *Shih-ching* describes, orgiastic as a propitiation to secure a good harvest, and orgiastic again because they were occasions when the sexes came together and when marriages were concluded. The calendar dominated these festivals like an inexorable law. The guiding principle in the religious system was a dualistic concept which went very deep in the Chinese mind, that of *yin* and *yang*. These were two concrete categories and at the same time two active forces. *Yang* corresponds to male, heavens, bright, and light; *yin* to female, earth, dark, and heavy. The two principles are opposed, but also complementary to and inseparable from one another: in their equilibrium lies the prime condition for all well-being and permanence. In their continual interplay they symbolize the relation between the macrocosm and the microcosm. Space is made out of their opposition, time out of their alternation.

From this pair of opposing forces were elaborated certain ideas of semi-divine forces and beings, such as Earth, the mother of the family, and the family's ancestors. With them went a simple farmer's mythology, but this was never more than a background. Chinese religion was always rational and was not given to mystical impulses. It was matter-of-fact and prosaic, somewhat like Roman religion.

Above the religion of the peasants there was the family cult of the great aristocratic houses, whose organization and ideals were different from those of their vassals. In this feudal religion the highest place belonged to the Sovereign above, the August Heaven (Huang-t'ien Shang-ti). He ordained the seasons, and as such his worship came near to the farmer's cult. But he was also the supreme regulator of order in nature (not the creator, a being unknown to Chinese religion): so from him all constituted authority descended. He bore the title *tien-wang*, king (by grace) of heaven: indeed he was *T'ien-tzu*, son of heaven, holding his power by virtue of *t'ien-ming*, celestial mandate. Political order, in principle at least, was only a reflection

on earth of cosmic order. Besides the worship of heaven the feudal lord
practised a cult of earth; and this had two aspects. There was a soil god of the
country and of its capital, and a god of the patrimonial lands of the lord
himself. Another important cult was that of the ancestors, who were regarded
as part of the family as if they were still alive; it was from them that the family
drew its force and power. The ancestor cult was also a projection into the
next world of the filial piety shown in this one: 'filial piety creates in his
lifetime the majesty of the ancestor-to-be' (Granet). This religion too had its
mythology, which was of a Euhemerist kind. Many priestly hymns in the
Shih-ching are intended to glorify the dynastic heroes.

The aristocracy's cult reached perfection and united all its essential features
in the royal cult, which was exclusively entrusted to the Chou dynasty. This
cult was the essential feature of sovereignty: the conventional way of saying
that a state had become extinct was to say that its sacrifices had come to an
end. The majesty of the Chou kings was symbolized by nine large tripods
of bronze. When it fell the tripods were lost, giving rise to various legends
and beliefs about their origin and significance.

b. *Assyria and Neo-Babylonia*

The Assyrians brought few new features to earlier religion. In the main
they preserved what they had taken over from the Babylonians, just as the
Babylonians had carried on Sumerian cults. Even the names of Assyrian
gods are of Sumerian origin, just like the religious and mythological literature
which the Babylonians, and the Assyrians after them, translated and adapted
for transmission from one generation to another. So the Assyrians took over
the Babylonian pantheon almost as it stood, with its deification of natural
forces and heavenly powers. Each god had been given a genealogy, on
principles which were both logical and historical, and they were conceived of
anthropomorphically, without any noticeable tendency to monotheism or
pantheism. Naturally some purely Assyrian gods could be added, some of
the old divinities could gain in popularity, and some attributes, together
with the related myths, might be altered up to a point.

The main innovation was the introduction and importance of the cult of
Ashur, the tribal god who protected Ashur city and was made, above all by
the Sargonids, into the supreme god of the whole vast empire. Originally
Ashur was a solar deity, as his pictures still show, especially that of the god
radiate spreading his two hands. But when he became the chief god he was
called self-procreate, father of the gods, king of heaven and earth, and
creator of mankind. As such he took the place of Anum, and of the Babylonian
Marduk, as we see from the Assyrian edition of the ancient 'poem of creation'.
Ashur is the god who proclaims wars, and in them leads the Assyrians to
victory. The arms are his, and to him belongs part of the booty.

The goddess Ishtar, to whom a precious hymn is preserved, was greatly
honoured by the Assyrians, less as the goddess of love than as the warrior

goddess. They also worshipped Adud, the god of storms, who seemed a symbol of their own tempestuous inroads. The gods Sin-Luna and Nabu, protector of scribes, were made popular by the neo-Babylonian kings, later especially by Nabuna'id.

The Assyrians retained the ethical and religious notions of their predecessors, though they gave them fuller content. They showed fear rather than love to their gods, and life after death was regarded as dismal and pale. Since there was no clear relation between the treatment accorded to a soul and the man's deserts, they used to pray their gods to give them long life rather than reward in another world. This produced a fatalistic attitude, and the Assyrians showed no particular interest in the dead or their tombs. They believed in demons, who were regarded as the authors of disease and whom they tried to chase away by cathartic rites.

The official religion gave important scope for magical spells and incantations, for divination in the most diverse forms, and for astrology, although astral divinities never became pre-eminent. All three tendencies continued after the fall of Assyria, and attained exaggerated heights under the Chaldeans.

The Assyrians also followed Babylonian ideas in the construction of complicated classes of priesthoods and in the erection of temples as homes for their gods, although they replaced the older wooden altars with more durable altars made of stone.

c. *The Hebrews*

The exodus of the Hebrew tribes from Egypt under their commander and law-giver Moses had led to the conquest of the 'Promised Land', when they invaded Palestine after crossing the desert and outflanking the region east of Jordan.

Being tribes of nomadic shepherds (the Bible mentions thirteen tribes) they settled in the country districts. But some cities were also occupied, and the episode of the capture of Jericho by Joshua, one of Moses' successors in the leadership, has been made famous, though it has still to be confirmed by archaeology. The enemies were the Canaanites, whose conquest was first followed by massacre but later by progressive assimilation. Compromise was impossible, because the dominant principle of the victors was to keep Yahvistic monotheism safe at all costs, and to preserve their faith, to them the most precious and characteristic feature of their race, free from all danger of contamination by heathen cults. If success attended Hebrew arms, it was regarded as a sign of divine blessing. Israel's triumph was converted into the glorification of God, for this people regarded everything they did in life as carrying out the pact of absolute dedication they had made with Yahweh.

The whole political and social order of the Hebrews was deliberately related to their religion. Indeed at this time political and religious functions were not yet separate; in the unique community life of the Chosen People there was no room for differences between the two aspects. The only source of authority was the will of God, and the only motive for war was religion. In any case the Hebrews never sought to obtain empire, but only to defend the territory they had occupied from the frequent incursions and insistent threats of their powerful neighbours. At times of greatest danger all power was entrusted to 'Judges', who extended their jurisdiction from the civil to the military sphere. But the power of these men was always limited and occasional, and it was always exercised in virtue of divine grace or election.

The first and most famous judge was the Joshua mentioned above, who carried out the conquest of Canaan in the second half of the thirteenth century. He undoubtedly played a notable part in this period of Hebrew history, even though literary tradition later invested his exploits with epic features and also attributed some actions to him which were the work of other men. Also worthy of mention are the judge Aod (Ehud), who freed the Israelite tribes from a Moabite attempt to subject them in the twelfth century; the judge Gideon, who acquired his position after a special divine vision, and rescued the children of Israel from raiders coming from the Syrian desert; Samson, whose semi-legendary exploits are known to all for their heroic nature; and finally Samuel, who was the link between the 'charismatic' age and the age of monarchy.

The stories about the *Judges* come from an *Old Testament* book of that name, which tells of six judges at length and more briefly of another six. As always, the historical information is neither complete nor orderly, but serves as a background for a theological doctrine of the time of the later kings along the lines of the motif which constantly recurs in the Bible, namely that Israel's fortunes depend on its behaviour towards the Lord God and on its observance of the Law: political success is the result of obedience to God. There are well-known difficulties about the date of this book's composition, as well as about the interpretation of certain delicate matters such as the vow of the judge Jephthah, which probably was a quite straightforward case of human sacrifice. The story of Samuel is contained in another book, which bears his name though he was not of course its author. It covers the period from about 1075 (Samuel's birth) to 975, falling in the reign of David. We must assume that both these books represent older works which were recast at the end of the eighth century, or possibly later: the text of *Samuel* is a very difficult one, because the Greek version offers a number of variant readings and there are many problems of interpretation as well.

The monarchy was created at the end of the second millennium BC. It originated as an attempt by the Hebrews to unify their country and centralize its government in order to offer more effective resistance to foreign pressure, especially to the Philistines, a 'people of the sea' who lived in the coastal district south of Palestine and had erected a powerful federation of cities. The monarchy was later able to take advantage of a particularly favourable moment in international politics, when the neighbouring empires in Egypt and Mesopotamia were weak and a strong state could come into being in between. The old order of tribes and clans, together with the traditional particularism, was now a thing of the past. At the same time the fact that the king was directly chosen by God and then anointed and consecrated in a religious ceremony gave him an exceptional prestige. His investiture had more than human sanction.

But the new constitution brought its problems. The incorrigibly individualistic and tribal tradition of the Hebrew people was ill adapted to the standardization of life which monarchy brought, and there was active rivalry between the tribes of the South (Judah) and those of the North (Israel). But this was not all. The most important source of trouble was that the monarchy posed for the first time the problem of relations between the authority of the priests and the civil power. Saul, as is well known, was ruined because of quarrels with the priests; and though David and Solomon, in an able political manœuvre, tried to overcome the dualism by attaching the priests themselves to the court, they eventually created greater difficulties than before. For the established religion was challenged by a popular form which emerged spontaneously and broke away from all authoritarian rules.

Such was the origin of the prophets, who attempted to recall Israel to the pure tradition of monotheism, and to proclaim the rights of personal religion and the most elementary claims of justice against any arbitrary dictation by the king (representing the state) and against all opportunist compromises. In the pages of the Bible there are many examples of clashes between prophets and kings. Some were due to prophetic warnings, to threats of disaster brought on the country and its ruling house by the arbitrary and unjust use of supreme power. Others resulted from reprisals by the kings, who regarded the prophets as a disruptive force in the national structure, supporters of public disorder and instigators of civil disobedience.

We need not spend time on a full list of the strictly political achievements of the Hebrew kings. It is enough to say that the regal period was one of great economic prosperity, since trade flourished and expansion became possible, while the mineral wealth was exploited and important public works were carried out. But court life in the same period was a continuous series of rebellions and settlements, caused not so much by any political or personal forces as by the incessant threat which in the background hung over the Mosaic tradition: for the introduction of idolatry became probable whenever a king, for opportunist political reasons, was inclined to accept foreign cults. Certain examples are well known. Jeroboam I revived an ancient worship, similar to that introduced by Aaron, when he erected at Bethel and Dan figures of calves to symbolize the invisible presence of Yahweh. Manasseh (687–642) put into practice the magic and divination widely used in contemporary Assyria. And in 842 a bloodthirsty queen named Athaliah, daughter of King Ahab and the Phoenician princess Jezebel, worshipped Baal and tried to exterminate all the house of David. On the other hand Josiah (d. 609) undertook a radical purification of Hebrew cult, assisted by the discovery during his reign of a codex which is very probably the *Book of Deuteronomy*, and which naturally provoked great enthusiasm among his people.

Our information about the regal period is plentiful on the rise and government of David, since he was later looked on as a symbol of the most glorious period of Hebrew history, his name being synonymous with peace, prosperity, and piety. But on the divided kingdoms evidence is much more scanty. The compilers of the *Books of Kings* and *Chronicles* (the latter a comparatively late version from the period after the Captivity) probably belonged to the priestly class, and were concerned less with historical facts than with religious considerations. Their aim was to enunciate once more the familiar concept that disobedience to God's word brought tribulation, in political as well as in other fields.

Later developments in the political situation aggravated the struggle all the time. The decline of Israel was seen as a sign of God's displeasure at his people's betrayals. Not only was it a betrayal to worship idols or to commit one or another form of moral iniquity. Even worse was to trust to human means of obtaining some end, to believe that one could achieve results by the same weapons of diplomacy as other nations used. The Hebrews had to remember their duty of trusting only in God, of achieving only through him their individual and collective salvation. All human and temporal success must be despised if it meant descending to compromise in religion and disloyalty to the people's Covenant with God.

So the prophets lifted their voices ever more loudly against all constituted authority,[1] if it started to depart from the observance of the law of God. Their views found a large following, as is shown in the formation of sects and groups who detached themselves from society and were often hostile to it. For them Yahweh's Law was the one perfect justice, and only through its observance could a community prosper: anyone who did not conform to the Law would be punished. But from this conclusion it was easy to take a further step and say that foreigners might be a valuable instrument in God's hands for summoning obstinate people back to obedience. So a teleological justification was provided for Israel's political decline, and a meaning was recognized even in terrible happenings such as loss of liberty, deportation, and exile among people who worshipped idols. Even more important was the reversal of the attitude adopted toward government policy some centuries earlier, when material success was considered to be God's just reward for a faithful people. Now the prophets' preaching led to the conclusion that for Yahweh's will to be done and his promises to be fulfilled it was necessary that Israel's temporal power be ruined. Only after such a catastrophe could the new story of God's true people begin.

The prophets' teaching is a typical expression of the Hebrews' religious mind, and it is futile to try to explain it in terms of related phenomena found among other peoples. Even more misleading is the view that it was a vulgar way of imposing on men's credulity. If we make due allowance for pseudo-prophetic activity by professional soothsayers who made their own claims to divine missions, there remains no doubt that there was a numerous and reputable group of men 'called by God'.[2] By a sudden unexpected action of heaven (charisma) they were turned from their normal activities to become criers of a message, which they could not avoid delivering at those moments when they were under the divine influence. Moreover, even if they were not as individuals men of superior intelligence and wide culture (none the less they were all men of exemplary character and followed an ascetic life, some-times of the most rigid kind), they enunciated certain great ideas, which have become part of the common inheritance of mankind. They made use of the language which they found most familiar, employing images and sentiments which would evoke a response from those around them, but they were not afraid to say things which were disagreeable or even apparently absurd. At first they confined themselves to speaking and preaching; on rare occasions, to be more effective, they employed symbolic actions too, and explained their significance. But later they wrote or dictated, and gave the world works of the most exalted poetry, with truth far beyond the particular content and situation which inspired it.

In a broad sense even Abraham and Moses can be considered prophets, but the golden age of Hebrew prophecy lasted from the eighth to the sixth centuries, when the ancient religion of Yahweh was undergoing transforma-tion because Canaanite cult was being assimilated to it. It was therefore necessary to oppose the inclusion of observances which did not conform to the primitive Hebrew conception of religion, and to continue the religious tradition in its purest form. So on the one hand we find the prophets protest-ing against the orders of authority and expressing contempt for the growth of corruption: on the other hand we meet their insistent call for justice and humility of heart, their specific claims about the value of cult observances, and their strict warnings to respect the Covenant. But in this revival of primitive ways we already find—as so often in such movements—all the conditions needed for an advance forward; and in fact Hebrew religion after the exile was clearly much changed. Prophecies had revealed God's plans for his people, elucidating the true meaning of the Covenant between the Lord and the 'remnant' of Israel, and had even begun to speak of Him 'that should come' to found a Kingdom. Their material was valuable prepara-tion for the new developments; and although it was full of rebukes and went on threatening heavy chastisements, it ended with a word of hope and gave a glimpse of a better world.

The work of the prophets lasted almost without interruption from Samuel in the eleventh century to Malachi in the fifth, but it is only from the eighth century that direct (i.e. primary) evidence about these 'charismatics' begins and provides us with a relative abundance of detailed knowledge. Without getting lost in long lists of names, we may mention some of the greater prophets of the early period. In the ninth century lived Elijah ('Yahweh is my God'), a heroic ascetic who set himself against Queen Jezebel and the false priests of Baal and was accorded various visible and miraculous signs of God's good will; his successor was Elisha, who saw the end of the wicked house of Omri and the abolition of the Phoenician cult at the hands of the general Jehu. After these so-called 'prophets of action', in the middle of the eighth century, came the 'rhapsodes' or declaimers, who (as their name implies) warned the people by word of mouth and by writing to remain faithful to the Lord. These, in chronological order, were Amos and Hosea in the kingdom of Samaria, and Micah in the kingdom of Judah. Contemporary with Micah was Isaiah, born of aristocratic parentage at Jerusalem and called to his ministry in 738; he died, perhaps a martyr, in the days of the evil King Manasseh.

We may pass over some of the Minor Prophets, although the name is sometimes given only on account of the brevity of their surviving writings rather than because they were of little account in politics and religion. Mention must be made, however, of the great and humane Jeremiah, who was born near Jerusalem and elected prophet in 626. In the last phase of the tempestuous history of Judah he played a part3 which won him the reputation of being a defeatist and an enemy to his country, but after the catastrophe he was practically the only man who still tried to save what could be saved. He died, perhaps at the hands of his own countrymen, in Egypt, where he had continued his duties as prophet amid incomprehension and ridicule, supported only by his faithful secretary Baruch, a prophet like himself. With Ezekiel—who prophesied from 593 to about 570 in a Jewish colony of exiles in Babylonia we reach a new period, in which the so-called Deutero-Isaiah also belongs. Its features are an all-embracing monotheism, the concept of purification, insistence on the responsibility of individuals rather than of the community alone, and a movement towards personal religion, although at the same time the priesthood gained notably in power and prestige.

The last great prophet of the period of Exile was the semi-legendary Daniel, who enjoyed great favour at the Babylonian court and died in 536. After the Hebrews returned to their country the prophets' work was continued by Haggai, Zechariah, Joel, Obadiah, and Malachi.

In a work like this it is impossible to tackle the numerous and difficult problems arising from a close examination of the prophetic books of the *Old Testament*, on which various theories have been advanced, most of them markedly different from the beliefs of religious tradition. The sayings of the prophets were presumably put into writing, at least in part, by themselves or their disciples; but the compositions to which their names are given are largely collections drawn up later on certain definite principles. They are not an organic whole, and their transmission has produced significant differences between the Hebrew text and the Greek. Nevertheless nearly all these books are very lofty works of poetry which can be taken and read with great spiritual pleasure. Interest never flags, and does not depend on the particular content or on references to events which were the contingent cause of the writing.

The *Book of Isaiah* excels in sublimity of doctrine, and contains Messianic prophecies of an impressive clarity. *Jeremiah* is richer in ethics and psychology, and has great historical value for the history of the last kings of Judah. The *Book of Lamentations* is a work on its own. But whoever was its author, it bears witness to a life of deep sorrow, which even in the midst of disillusioning happenings did not lose an unshakable faith in divine justice. The most serious problems of history, language, and interpretation are connected with the *Book of Daniel*, but a solution has been reached which steers a course between the extreme views of older scholars. The work in its present form, we may believe, was composed by an unknown author about 300 BC, collecting older documents some of which may even go back to Daniel himself.

Some of the Minor Prophets are hard to date precisely, and it is an open question whether some of the exploits attributed to them, such as Hosea's marriage or Jonah's adventures, are history or literary fiction. Significant in all of them, however, are the clear references to salvation by a Messiah and the frank advocacy of social justice, nor are they lacking in valuable references to historical events. Once again their pages enunciate the fundamental principles of Hebrew religion, such as loyalty to the Lord and the duty of observing his commands.

The idea of divinity which was Israel's own and which always characterized her people, was that of a single God, personal, eternal, and ever-present, who created the world. This is a conception different from that formed by any other people and it had decisive importance for all later religious history over a wide part of mankind. For their belief in a single God the Hebrews did not offer weighty philosophical proofs, partly because they were little drawn towards speculation, partly because their belief was an axiom from which they drew many conclusions in the field of morality and social life. Instead they took pleasure in criticizing polytheism and laughing at idolaters. They exalted the majesty and unapproachable grandeur of their God, but at the same time his contacts with man and his interest in his people. So, though they could not even say their God's name, they yet spoke of him with anthropomorphic imagery and attributed actions and feelings to him of an excessively human kind (though it is clear that these expressions ought to be given a metaphorical meaning and purpose, being designed to make men feel that God was near and to look on him as provident and good).

Among the various attributes of divinity that which most befits the Hebrew God is to be a just God: everything else must be set below the triumph of God's justice. History is the great field when God was at work, and in it we can see the struggle not only between the God of the Hebrews and the powers of evil, but also between God and his people, who were unceasingly forgetful of the favours he had shown, or were attempting to follow idols. It was true that contact with Canaanite civilization had allowed some syncretist elements to creep into Hebrew religion. Yet the opposition only served to strengthen the idea of God's uniqueness; and it was the great achievement of the prophets in history to recall Israel to the purer monotheistic tradition, securing the continuity of the religion of Yahweh amid all surrounding dangers. But it was in this period of the prophets that the conception of divinity became much more spiritual, that ideas of life after death were formulated more clearly, and above all that a new great principle of Hebrew religion took shape and rapidly became more active, the idea of the Messiah with all the consequences it brought to so many branches of thought and action.

Since Yahweh is the true king and his Law is the supreme ordinance, the perfect state is one derived from God, which is governed according to the Lord's spirit and looks to the accomplishment of his kingdom. But at this point was posed a question. Who personified and interpreted God's will? Who had received an investiture which put him in a position to discharge a duty which was religious as well as political? In Israel there were two schools of thought from the period of the prophets onward. One wanted monarchy as an institution, believing it advantageous for the salvation of the Hebrew people. This school aimed to make the monarchy hereditary in order to give it stability and increase its power: the term used for this type of king is *melék*. The other school regarded such an institution as an attack on the absolute sovereignty of Yahweh, and continued to favour a *magid*, a 'charismatic' leader raised up by the divine spirit at the right moment to deal with a given situation.

The two schools went through periods of sharp dissension with intervals of tacit understanding. On the whole the great prophets were hostile to political powers and sometimes even launched most violent denunciations at the ruling house. Their reason was always the same: they became suspicious when faced with 'diplomatic' methods and with all the excessively worldly and temporal attitude characteristic of politicians, which they found lacking in confidence towards the Lord and in surrender to his will. Moreover the prophets were not troubled by the material ruin of Israel, since they saw in it a providential type of punishment and a recall to the 'rule of things of the spirit'.

As to the Hebrew monarchy, it had characteristics very like those seen in the kings of Babylonia.⁴ In neither institution was the sovereign regarded as a god, though he was invested with divine authority to carry out his functions. If anyone tried to be deified outright, he was immediately treated as a usurper. The king was not even chief priest: indeed the distinction between the two orders—civil and ecclesiastical—was most carefully maintained. Yet in certain circumstances the king would discharge cult tasks, and on very solemn occasions his position carried with it the duties of the priesthood (so David bore the ark to Jerusalem and Solomon consecrated the temple). The priests looked after ordinary cult acts.

One characteristic of Hebrew religion was undoubtedly its collective outlook. Its chief task, that is to say, was to watch over the behaviour of an entire people towards the God who was its own God. The relation between man and the superior being was something public, resting on a definite fact, namely the covenant 'I am your God and you are my people'. In its turn the whole nation was regarded as a living organism, one might almost say as a person, sometimes falling away and being deservedly punished, at other times earning reward for its loyalty. In other words it was the community which principally benefited or suffered from the effect of divine plans for good or ill.

But is this the whole story? Was there no place in Hebrew religion for another more particular relationship, that between Yahweh and individual men? Perhaps some forms of intimate and personal piety were recognized as well.[5] Some scholars have supposed a radical opposition between the two outlooks and imagined that the advent of individual religion in the time of the prophets, especially Jeremiah and Ezekiel, signified the end of community religion, since the new form contradicted the basic principle contained in 'I am the Lord your God'. This is not so. It is abundantly true that the personal side of religion is little developed in the biblical texts (i.e. in the *Pentateuch*, *Judges*, and *Kings*), because they had other purposes and concerns. But from them and other sources it is possible to discover various pointers to the place assigned to the individual in the general plan of salvation; they deal with his moral duties and duties of worship, and kindred matters.

Above all we can see that Hebrew monotheism included a specifically moral outlook, in the sense that belief in the existence of a single God—a personal and living Being who was creator and judge, holy and benign— implied a series of ethical conclusions, which found their codification in the Decalogue or in other sets of rules recurring throughout the Bible. The latter vary in number and content, but always express substantially the same principles. Hebrew ethic rested on justice and pity; and as Jesus later reminded the world in his own time, the commandment to love God and to love one's neighbour represented the whole conclusion of the Law and the Prophets together. Yet something which might seem to be a duty of charity was in substance no more than an act of justice, since what one gave to others was, according to God's commandment, what they had a right to have. We can now understand the legal tone which governed and pervaded all Hebrew morality, its best-known manifestation being the vast number of precepts, to which new rules of increasing minuteness were being added all the time. Once the 'Book of the Law' (perhaps *Deuteronomy*) was discovered in a cupboard of the temple by the priest Hilkiah in King Josiah's time (637–608), all religious life both public and private was regulated by this all-important text.

As in any religious system, the notion of retribution is found among the

Hebrews, being attested clearly by passages of the *Old Testament*. Yet its significance changed markedly as time went on, and it is fair to claim that we can witness a genuine development, which eventually revealed the fundamental concept of distributive justice. This was due to the fact that other ideas were changing too, ideas about the nature of the soul, eternal happiness, and life after death. For centuries the Hebrews had no notion of a future life and no belief in retribution beyond the grave: the just man survived no differently from the unjust, the faithful no differently from the sinner. Reward and punishment were given by God on earth, in the shape of happiness or misfortune, in accordance with rigid consistency and strict justice: 'the fathers have eaten a sour grape and the children's teeth are set on edge.' (*Jeremiah*, xxxi. 29; *Ezekiel*, xviii. 2). This was another reason, it may be said in passing, why all ascetic mysticism was foreign to Hebrew mentality: to enjoy the blessings created by God, and within limits to satisfy man's natural instincts, was the logical consequence of the principle that success was a sign of divine approval.

The above quotation and many other passages which may easily come to mind show that in this matter too collective religion was the dominant form. The sanction applied was a common sanction, rewards and punishments being awarded not for the behaviour of individuals but for that of the community. Personal recompense, given for the failings or merits of the individual, was only taken into account much later; and even when a concept of that kind was formulated, it was confined at first to recompense in this world along strict principles of retaliation. But then there was too easy an objection. In the majority of cases it could be seen that on earth the just man suffered and the unjust man rejoiced: good was often vanquished and evil triumphed. Though this rule might be proved wrong within the complete picture of a people's history, it was unfortunately true practically without exception if only the limited existence of individuals was considered. So fresh and vast views were opened for reflection by Hebrew thinkers and prophets, and at this stage new ideas found a place in their thought, although they held firm to the concept of Yahweh's absolute and infinite justice, so firmly rooted in the Hebrew people. The new ideas[6] were individual retribution beyond the grave and the resurrection of the body. All humanity could thus participate in a new state of life, which was the fruit of actions body and soul had committed together during their first existence.

But we must not forget another strand which runs through all Hebrew thinking about problems of religion and ethics, although it has something of mystery about it. This is the doctrine of sin, original and personal, and the connected doctrines of atonement and forgiveness. From reading the Bible one certainly sees that its various authors were conscious, however vaguely, of the existence of sin, and tended to derive it either from intervention by superhuman powers of evil or from individual free will. To recreate the equilibrium which sin has destroyed, or (if we look at the matter in the terms considered so far) to renew the Covenant between Israel and Yahweh, it was originally enough to make a sacrifice of atonement. But here too an attitude of greater intimacy tended to prevail in later times, and it was seen that repentance was necessary to obtain God's forgiveness, and that what mattered most was the new spirit in which the various actions of individuals were now performed.

Phoenician religion will be considered with Punic (see pp. 242 ff.).

d. *Egypt*

For the general ideas of Egyptian religion and an outline of its history we refer the reader back to Volume I.7 But we may note here that from the Twentieth Dynasty onwards its very complex features still remained after thousands of years of development, deriving as they did from the amalgamation of pantheons originally conceived in a variety of regions. The later syncretisms took account of divine forms and attributes which were often misleading; and the theogonies with their systematic hierarchies and family trees were too numerous and superficial to make matters any simpler. The intention had been to establish links and identities between divinities of a standard type, such as material objects (fetishes, animals, and plants), gods in human form, cosmic elements, or abstract concepts (sentiments, and personifications of events or places). But many of these divine figures were independent of one another, and the differences between them were the product of different regional origins.

In our period certain tendencies should be noted, some of them of spontaneous growth in Egypt, others due to the influence of traders, mercenaries, and subject peoples. In the official cult the attempt to reconcile the restored religion of Ammon with an opposition centred on the Pharaohs, who worshipped Ra, Ptah, and Set, led men to regard divinity as something unknowable, mysterious, and not to be personified. As in their literature, art, and other activities of the spirit, the Egyptians of this period display much greater directness of expression in their religion. There is a feeling towards mysticism and passion, an attempt to get closer to the mysterious god who works in all things, and really to live one's religion: we find this attitude even among lower classes. By imagining a divinity who was perfect, and who consequently was patient with imperfect men, one could find a deeper communion with one's god. The dramatic and mysterious myth of Osiris and Isis, which was re-enacted by the initiate's symbolic death, his journey to the lower world, and his resurrection, took such hold on men's minds that it soon attracted the attention of Greek thinkers (and later of Romans): in the fifth century Herodotus (II, 87) claimed that the Egyptians were the most religious people in the world. Meanwhile the worship of animals had a quaint revival, giving rise later to the probably fictitious story of the Persian conqueror Cambyses committing outrage when he killed the god Apis. There was also an exceptional growth of astrology, magic, fortune-telling,

superstition, and legends about gods on earth. Demotic literature bristles
with magic formulae. They gave a new theme to the 'Books of the Dead',
though these books retained so much that was traditional. The dead man
is shown the prescription for magical responses which will enable him to
escape the consequences of the 'weight on his soul'; for when it enters the
kingdom of Osiris the soul will have to evade the unfavourable verdicts of
forty-two judges on his sins.

The priesthood of Ammon at Thebes was ambitious of power and its
rivalry with the various dynasties is a vital element in the history of the
country. Under the Twentieth Dynasty an understanding was reached
between the priests and the Delta rulers, under which the queen, as well as
the chief priest's wife, became 'adorer of the god'. Under the Twenty-first
Dynasty, which was formed by a priest of Thebes, the duties of Pharaoh and
priest tended to accumulate within a single family. Later the support of the
Theban priests was what decided the fate of the Libyan and Nubian Pharaohs.
The dissension began again under the Saites, but was healed once more
when Psammetichus I (663–609) had the title of 'adorer of the god' conferred
on his own daughter.

e. The religion of the Indo-Europeans: India

The only Indian religion known to us in this period is the Vedic. We have
no direct acquaintance with those Munda, Dravidian, and other non-Aryan
cults which profoundly affected Aryan religion and contributed to its
transformation into Brahmanism and later into Hinduism, since they in
turn disappeared before the expansion of the larger religion (or at least
pursued a wretched existence as popular creeds in small areas).

Vedic religion is known to us through its sacred writings, the four *Veda*,
rounded off by the earliest exegetic literature (especially the *Brāhmaṇas*).
It is essentially a ritualistic religion, with little ethical content, designed to
obtain earthly happiness and prosperity by means of invocation and propitiation of the various deities, above all by sacrifice (*yajña*).

Ṛigvedic mythology was naturalistic, but not purely so. Natural phenomena
were always personified, and sometimes at least the reverse seems to happen,
i.e., the myth of a divinity was modelled on natural phenomena. The gods
were usually imagined in human form, though there were endless ways
of doing this.[8] No attempt to classify the amorphous pantheon received
general recognition, the number of thirty-three major gods being a later
conception. The best-known classification is that into gods of earth, air, and
heaven made in *Ṛigveda*, I, 139, 11. Features common to these gods are
anthropomorphism, immortality, benign nature (except Rudra, to some
extent), and a certain absence of clear-cut individuality and distinct characteristics. The main celestial deities were as follows. Varuṇa was originally the
god of the vault of the sky covering and embracing all things, guardian of
the moral and cosmic order (*ṛta*) and ethical king of the world; but he was

always connected with the waters and the ocean, and this aspect was more firmly emphasized as time went on. Then there were Sūrya, god of the sun; Savitṛ, the golden god, often confused with Sūrya; Uṣas, the dawn; the twin gods called Asvin or Nāsatya, gods of the morning, whose aid was invoked in time of need and who were therefore also gods of medicine; and among minor divinities we already find Viṣṇu, perhaps the symbol of the apparent motions of the sun. Of the gods of air the most important was Indra, the main Rigvedic god, who let loose the cosmic waters but was above all the god of war, a great warrior and a great devourer, depicted as a cheerful and blustering giant with features which are often grotesque. There were also the Maruts, gods of storms; Vāyu, the wind; Parjanya, the cloud heavy with rain; and among secondary gods there was Rudra, the terrific god. The principal gods of earth were two personifications of ingredients essential in sacrifice, Agni, the fire (especially in its ritual aspect), and Soma, the sacrificial juice of the plant called by that name. Over against the gods stood their eternal enemies, the demons, of whom the Asuras were foremost.

For cosmological ideas see pp. 245 ff. below.

Ideas of an after-life are still crude. The dead man enters the kingdom of Yama, god of the other world, as if into a kind of paradise of milk and honey mainly material in conception, which is attainable by correct ritual. Some hymns seem to refer to a kind of hell. But in fact these were problems of little interest to Vedic bards. The Rigvedic man thought mainly about this world, was pleased to be alive and enjoyed his life, and cared only for happiness on earth, a long life, health, riches, many sons, victory over his enemies, and so on.

So his religion was utilitarian, a contract in the form *do ut des* in which man offered sacrifice to god to obtain material prosperity.

Another very different side of Vedic religion is found in the *Atharvaveda*. This collection, although it was compiled after the earlier *Veda* and added to them, contains some material which is not later than the *Rigveda*, but belongs to a different religious world. In it the magical and popular aspects of Vedism are emphasized. The ruling mentality is that of the popular magician or miracle-worker, and the hymns are mainly magic formulae designed to secure the reciter's wishes by means of the power they contain. So the gods take a lower place, the scope of Atharvanic formulae being to pacify demons, bless one's friends, and curse one's enemies.

The philosophic content of the *Atharvaveda* is by no means negligible, and it is interesting to observe a monotheistic streak when Prajāpati is accepted as the supreme creator of the universe. But taken as a whole the *Atharvaveda* hymns do not move in the direction of the philosophical advances of later ages, but carry us down to the amorphous mass of popular superstitions and beliefs.

In the other two *Veda* (*Yajurveda* and *Samaveda*) ritualism reigns supreme. The rite acquires an increasing importance because it has the power to compel the god to grant the favour requested. So precise execution of the rite is more important than the moods and will of the god himself. Rite commands and the god obeys. This ritual grew increasingly advanced and complicated, until it became necessary for anyone wanting to perform a rite (*yajamāna*) to employ a professional priest, who alone was capable of executing all the minute particulars correctly. This applies to domestic rites (*gṛhya*), but above all to the major sacrifices (*śrauta*), in which fire was the chief element. The texts recited at the sacrifice are collected in these two *Veda*, and the ritual is codified in the vast though arid literature of the *Brāhmaṇa*. It is enough to say that the priests were divided into four categories. One was led by the *hotṛ*, who chose the hymns to be sung during the sacrifice and invoked the gods to be present at it. The second was under the *udgatṛ* or singer, who chanted or sang the hymns. The third leader was the *adhvaryu* or executant, who carried out the physical actions and murmured the sacred formulae in prose. And the fourth was the Brahman, who surveyed the whole performance to prevent mistakes, and recited formulae to protect the sacrificial act and atone for such mistakes if they were committed. In fact the smallest mistake invalidated the rite and could bring ruin instead of prosperity on the *yajamāna*. The sacrifice could be bloodless, in which case the holy liquor *soma* played the chief part in it; or it was accompanied by blood, on some occasions going as far as human sacrifice (*puruṣamedha*). Prajāpati appears as the chief divinity, lord of creation and god of sacrifice, but beside him is Rudra, the terrific god who accepts the material offering made. The cosmology of the *Brāhmaṇas* divided the universe into three zones, earth, intermediate space (*antarikṣa*), and sky. The earth was circular and rested on the ocean, which covered all space. Among philosophical advances that most pregnant for the future was the theory that a virtuous man after his death is born again in a place of delight and an evil man in a place of torment, as the automatic result of actions committed during their lives. In addition the idea took shape that these rewards and punishments were not eternal, but came to an end when the effect of the actions had been exhausted. So in embryo we have the theory of *karman* (action as an automatic cause of retribution in after-life) and *saṃsāra*, the unceasing cycle of births and deaths, the alternating phases being due to *karman* and to the exhaustion of its effects.

So into the orbit of the ancient, optimistic, and naturalistic paganism of the Aryans there entered an outside speculative element; for its origin was probably non-Aryan.[9] This element gradually penetrated deeply into Vedic religion. Although it left its forms, its pantheon, and its ritual intact, it deprived them of their content and substituted one which was completely different, being speculative and pessimistic. This process of penetration is the very essence in the history of early Indian thought. Aryan religion was hollowed out, and its shell was refilled with a new and non-Aryan fruit. The eventual result was Brahmanism, and after it Hinduism.

Very soon the excessive ritualism of the *Brāhmaṇas*, with its aridity and the power it conferred on the religious class, inevitably led to movements of protest and reaction. Two of these, Buddhism and Jainism, started new religions and will be dealt with in later chapters. Others stayed within the fold of the old religion, helped by its extreme adaptability and capacity for compromise.

The malcontents were mainly to be found among the *kṣattriya*, although there were Brahmans too. From their speculations was born the great philosophical school of the *Upaniṣad*, so called from the name given to their writings. *Upaniṣad* thought is absolute monism, contained in the recognition of unity between the individual principle (*ātman*) with the cosmic principle or essence of the universe (*brahman*). As the *Chāndogya Upaniṣad* (VI, 8–16) puts it in sublimely pithy terms, 'tat tvam asi', meaning 'thou art that' (i.e. the All). Other basic concepts are *prāṇa* (later fivefold), meaning breathing as the external manifestation of *ātman*; *māyā*, not in the later sense of illusion, but meaning the force which prevents *ātman* from recognizing its true nature; and *karman* as the source and regulator of rewards and punishments. Moreover the idea of *saṃsārā* was taken farther, and a corollary was evolved that even in the periods of paradise which *saṃsārā* could confer it was itself an evil: the only true, ultimate, and supreme happiness consisted in liberation from it (*mokṣa*). So the *Upaniṣad* contain abstract speculations, but also a practical method of salvation, namely the way of securing *mokṣa*. This is possible only through knowledge, through the recognition of the unity between *brahman* and *ātman*. Ascetic practices could help, but knowledge is the one true way, and sacrifice is no good. The path of knowledge (*jñāñāmārga*) diverges utterly and deliberately from that of the sacrificial act (*karmamārga*).

Yet by the side of Upanisadic thought the old ritualistic strain was for a long time continued in the *Sūtras*, brief texts which are condensed and laconic almost to the point of being unintelligible and which were intended to be mnemonic aids for oral teaching. In them the trend revealed by the *Brāhmaṇas* is carried to its logical conclusion: the deity almost vanishes, and sacrifice becomes an infallible magical means of obtaining one's desires.

f. *The Iranians*

Just as the monotheistic religion of Moses was a reaction against an earlier polytheism, so Zoroastrian dualism was preceded and also accompanied by polytheistic ideas which eventually pervaded it. Herodotus (I, 131) understood the position when he spoke of Persian polytheism. It must in its early stages have been very like the Indian religion found in the *Veda*.

The reformer was called Zarathustra ('the man of the old camels'), a name drawn from the pastoral life from which he sprang: compare his father's name Pourosapsa ('the man of the grey horses'). Parsee tradition puts him 300 years before Alexander, about 640 BC in round figures; but Xanthus of Lydia, an historian of the mid-fifth century BC, puts him 600 years before

Xerxes (486–465), which would take him back to the eleventh century. The latter date is certainly too early, but it ill accords with the attempt of some modern scholars to date him as late as the sixth or fifth century, which is in any case refuted by the archaic language of the *Gātha*. So the prince Vistaspa who favoured him is unlikely to have been either Hystaspes, father of Darius I, or Astyages, who reigned from 585 to 550, but was more probably the Persian Teipses, who was king from c.675 to 640. The seventeen hymns of the *Gātha*, said by the *Avesta* to have been composed by Zarathustra, only give us summary notes on his life. His early preaching, as priest of the family of Spitames, had little effect owing to the resistance of priests of the ancient cults; he had few disciples apart from his own son and uncle, and also met with opposition from the court. The dialect of the *Gātha* would suggest that he came from central Asiatic north-east Iran, though some scholars say north-west. Tradition, however, says he was born at Ramay near Teheran, in Media: and it was in fact there that he found supporters in the 'Magi', whether this name originally denotes a tribe, like the Hebrew tribe of Levi, or whether they were a special priesthood among the Medes.

Zarathustra created a religious, philosophical, and ethical system designed to bring man and the world to salvation. It ordained belief in a single god, Ahura Mazdah ('the lord who knows'), in all probability an ancient god whom the polytheistic period had regarded as supreme deity of the heavens. Zarathustra made him the one founder and guide of the universe, the good spirit from whom six abstract entities (the Sacred Immortals) emanate. The six are truth (or right thought), good will and holy piety, chosen sovereignty, meekness (or perfect law), integrity, and immortality; and they fight by Ahura Mazdah's side against the anti-god or evil spirit, Ahriman. This enemy was aided by the *Daeva* (the ancient gods debased to become demons): evil thought, lies, misgovernment, rebellion, infirmity, and death. All the world pivots round the struggle between the good and the evil spirit—the moral and the practical world alike: for example the conflict between peaceful farmers and the robbers who lay waste their fields is an emanation of the great struggle. So we get a series of prohibitions laid on all actions through which the spirit of evil might gain the victory (for example on killing animals, using them as sacrificial victims, or failing to care for them), together with injunctions to do good works and fight the allies of the evil spirit, such as robbers, animals of prey, or poisonous plants. The ultimate goal of this hard struggle was the triumph of the good, with reward of the virtuous and punishment of the wicked. The new cult also brought a reduction in ancient Indo-Aryan ceremonies and ritual, together with the exclusion of stimulating drink (*haoma*) and of sacrifices attended by blood. The rites of the purifying fire persisted: it was kept continually burning in the 'room of fire' under surveillance by the priests, and had to be kept far away from any possible impurity.

In the *Avesta*, a work drawn up by the Magi in the Achaemenid period, we

find a later phase of Zoroastrianism, which after it had been adopted by the
Achaemenid Darius I[10] and his successors was transformed into Mazdaism.
The innovations stand out fairly clearly. The most obvious is that in the
divine plan reflected in the *Avesta* a number of figures from the old polytheistic pantheon reappear by the side of Ahura Mazdah. These are either
'venerable' good spirits, like the sun-god Mithras, the spirit of fertility
Anāhitā, the heavenly bodies (sun, moon, and Sirius), the elements (water
and wind), and the protecting spirits of ancestors (Fravasi); or they are
Daeva, evil spirits, like Indra, Saurva, or Nanhaithya. This probably resulted
from a reaction against the new religion from popular beliefs still preserved
in regions to which Zoroastrianism had spread; and a further cause was the
religious toleration practised by the Achaemenid kings, despite such purist
opposition from the Magi as we find in Gaumata's revolt. A remarkable
instance of the new development is found on Darius I's official documents,
where as well as of Ahura Mazdah mention is made of the 'other gods we
possess' (Mithras and Anāhitā), without even any reference to Zarathustra.
At the same time emphasis was placed on the division of the real world into
the two categories of Goods (oxen, dogs, plants, and metals) and Bads
(wolves, serpents, and so on): man stands in the middle, being free to choose
evil or to follow good according to divine precepts. All the eschatological
ideas of Mazdaic religion were given shape in the Mithraic mystery rites of
initiation. Three days after death the human soul, with special protection
in the case of initiates, must present himself at the bridge Cinvat ('the divider')
for judgement by Mithras, Sraosa, and Rasnu; the souls of the good succeed
in crossing the bridge to enter the heavens of Ahura Mazdah (paradise),
while those of the wicked find the bridge shrinking to become just a thread,
and so fall into the abyss (hell). But the states of souls after judgement are
not eternal, since all will be brought to an end by a mighty purification
started by a great fire, and then men will rise again to immortal life.

Ritual, too, was becoming complicated once more. For instance, the spirit
of the stimulant drink *haoma* was admitted as a good spirit again, and the
rites of the purifying fire became more intricate. The number of priesthoods
was increased to deal with these rites, and priesthoods were made hereditary.
Moreover to avoid impurities harming either the fire or the earth, a definite
prohibition was placed on cremation as well as on burial of the dead. Bodies
had to be exposed in the 'towers of silence' until their flesh had worn away, and
then the skeletons were placed in ossuaries near by.

g. *Greeks*

Primitive Greek religion was established in the Hellenic peninsula by the
first invasions of the Chalcolithic period, crossed to the Aegean and the
Asiatic coast in the Mycenaean Age, and entered the colonial areas in the
period *c*. 800–500 BC. It involved the worship of divinities of the most diverse
origin. Like other Indo-European peoples the Greeks, before they reached

their final homes, were venerating various objects: inanimate things, animals and plants, phenomena on earth (seas, rivers, springs, woods, volcanoes, and caves), cosmic phenomena (sun, moon, the starry firmament, day, and night), and meteoric phenomena (such as winds, eclipses, and rain). They would also regard as divine any object or action which seemed miraculous or animated by some inward power (Lat. *anima*). Clearly, however, many of these divine beings, if they appeared to have no universal character, were destined to be forgotten even before the migration was over, or perhaps to be replaced by others more appropriate to their new homes. So there are few Greek gods which should be reckoned as palaeo-Hellenic, dating back to the early days of the invasion of the peninsula: they include Zeus, Gē-meter, Poseidon, Hermes, Helios, Ares, Eos, and Hestia. The other divinities venerated in historical times are for the most part of different origin. Many quite certainly derive from the earlier inhabitants of the country, both gods responding to primitive ideas of worship paid to animals, plants, and inanimate objects, and the more advanced anthropomorphic type of god. This can be proved either by names of non-Greek etymology or by corresponding types of cult existing in the Minoan Age: an example of the former is Hyakinthos, examples of the latter are Athena, Dictynna, Britomartis, and Persephone. The same phenomenon naturally recurred in the colonies of Asia Minor, Thrace, and other areas, where the Greeks took over such gods as Apollo, Aphrodite, Hephaistos, Bacchos, and Sabazios.

But many other divinities were creations of the Greeks themselves in their new homes, and for the most part had local significance only, representing natural phenomena, objects or concepts peculiar to these places, such as streams, caverns, or springs. Sometimes an isolated epithet would give rise to a new divinity. In the end the pantheon presented different peculiarities in each region, even in each city and small settlement.

This period of differentiation and regionalism may perhaps have lasted more than a thousand years, but it was followed by a converse period, one of syncretism, identification, and selection. The first impulse came when the politico-religious leagues were formed in Greece and Asia Minor, and when the more powerful cities began to extend their hegemonies, since this presented an opportunity for comparing the divinities of one area with those of another with which it had come in contact. It was then found that deities representing the self-same concepts were being worshipped in several places under names which were wholly or partly different—deities of the firmament, the sun, moon, sea, fertility of crops, and so on. Eventually these figures would be syncretized into one single divinity comprising all the variations. This procedure is found, for example, in the so-called 'Homeric Hymn to Apollo'.

Factors contributing to the selection of a definite number of major gods who would be common to all were the Homeric epic, the great sanctuaries which attracted Greeks from every country to their ceremonies, and the sacred leagues formed round famous places of worship. The Homeric poems had their birth in Asia Minor, where federations of the kind which encouraged syncretism came earlier than elsewhere; and they were directed at the polished aristocracies all over the Greek world, who came to regard Homer as 'the Book' and had little interest in ruder cults of a popular kind or in divine figures which lacked human form and had no life. These men liked to see the major gods united as they were themselves, in a family with a clearly drawn genealogy and a hierarchy. The sacred *genos* of the immortals in Hesiod's *Theogony* is illustrative.

Some of these major divinities also owed their establishment to the worship paid them by members of the sacred leagues, and to celebrations at their most famous sanctuaries during the great festivals. These were held at regular intervals for games and religious purposes, and they drew Greeks even from the most distant parts. The festival of Zeus at Olympia was celebrated at least as early as 776 BC; and there were regular festivals to Zeus in the Nemea valley near Phlius, to Poseidon at Corinth, to Apollo at Delphi,[11] and others besides (the operation of the oracular cult is discussed later).

In contrast to this small number of great gods who were recognized by all Greeks there were still very many other divine beings with local cults, whose worship and divinity were not acknowledged outside a narrow area. This was the position with heroes and demi-gods, or with the sons and relatives of gods, who were believed to have lived on earth in bygone days. There was in point of fact a kind of theological consideration which differentiated them from gods. One could indicate the tombs of many of them, precisely because they went back to very ancient times, when the idea of a dying god was generally accepted, or because they were gods of the underworld connected with some cavern; sometimes there was even a skeleton, though generally this arose from childish confusion with the fossilized bones of some large animal. Yet for the Greeks of more advanced civilization a mortal god had become an absurdity, so these deities were classified down to become heroes. Naturally in epic, heroes deriving from fallen divinities mingle with kings who have attained divinity by their deeds and their sovereignty, but also with fictitious personages created by the poet's fancy. Yet the former class, the one which concerns us at present, can easily be picked out by the fact that all its members, in an area sometimes large and sometimes relatively small, were still regarded as gods and received a cult. As to some of the older naturalistic cults of animals, plants, and so on, their deities when they attained human shape gave rise to curious myths about metamorphoses: the actual passage from inanimate to animate being was turned upside down, and it was made to seem that a being in human shape had been turned to stone or into an animal or plant.

Another dualism can be detected in Greek religion, at any rate after the monarchical period: the relation between public and private cults, even though they were often amalgamated and intertwined. In general the official cult of a city was concerned with the dozen or so major deities of 'poliad' or

Homeric status, while private cults could more easily be directed to those minor deities who had sunk to hero status in other parts of Greece. The specific links between groups of people and particular divinities were of various origins. As a rule a family might claim to have had one or more divine personages as its founders, and would therefore look on them as its special protectors. Sometimes a phratry or 'personal' tribe or *genos* had taken a divine being as its patron. Again one or more private individuals might seek guidance from a prophetic god and place their fate in his hands. Or lastly an unofficial party of people might be initiated into the secret rites of a god.

We have already noticed the importance of oracles in promoting the cult of certain gods. The divine predictions of oracles, an exalted kind of divination, had a very early history in the Greek world as elsewhere; but they appealed mainly to the common people, and consequently the Homeric poems, which were addressed to the aristocratic élites, say practically nothing about them. There is some mention of diviners, and the oracles of Pytho (Delphi) get an incidental reference in *Iliad* IX and *Odyssey* VIII, while there are allusions to these answers in the Homeric Hymns to Apollo Delius and Apollo Pythius. In contrast the responses were valued greatly by the many emigrants who consulted them about colonization projects in the eighth, seventh, and sixth centuries, and by such people as sailors and traders—private citizens of every kind rather than states. So there were oracles served by their own colleges of priests: these existed to some extent in every part of Greece, both in Asia Minor where there were inspired prophets, and in the peninsula, where prophetesses were commoner. They were connected with the cult of Zeus at Dodona and Olympia, and with the cults of Hera, Aphrodite, Amphiaraus, Athena, Dionysus, Heracles, Asclepius, Pluton (Hades), Poseidon, Trophonius, and so on. But Apollo was the god chiefly concerned, for besides his famous shrines at Delphi, Delos, and Claros near Colophon we know of at least twenty-six other oracular temples.

Some cities, such as Athens and Sparta, had special interpreters of Delphic oracles; but there were also 'exegetes' (Chresmologoi), who interpreted oracles on request, a famous example being the Athenian Onomacritus in Peisistratid times. They were responsible also for various collections of oracles, some true, some bogus, which they attributed to ancient prophets of both history and legend. The poets now began to compose 'lives' of these gods in human shape and to suggest syncretisms between the god of one place and that of another. The more success they had, the more men longed to probe deeply into the shape of their gods, and to understand their precise pedigrees and successions, which hitherto had been treated in episodes and fragments with endless inconsistencies. It was essential, too, to understand the references to them in epic and religious poetry, to strengthen the links between gods and demi-gods, and between both of them and the traditional founders of great families. All this sprang from a desire to get the genealogies clear, but it had political and historical importance too. We find the first examples in Epic. *Iliad* VI lists the descendants of Sisyphus, *Iliad* II the successive holders of the sceptre of Agamemnon, and *Odyssey* XI the famous women. The *Titanomachia* and the *Epigonoi* provide other instances. But a fuller attempt at a catalogue comes first in the didactic works ascribed to Hesiod. The *Theogony*, a work of rather over a thousand lines many times revised by later hands, begins with a long list of gods, of which the first are the three primeval divinities, Chaos, Gaia, and Eros, all arranged in their order of time and put into genealogical trees. This list, which follows an organic plan, is interspersed with 'medallions' constructed in greater detail —the birth of Aphrodite, the episode of the Styx, the hymn to Hecate, the Prometheus myth, the Titanomachia, and stories about Zeus.

The last lines of the *Theogony* tell of heroes born of unions between goddesses and mortals; and their logical sequel is provided in the so-called 'Hesiodic catalogues', part of which is a list of mortal women loved by gods. These catalogues are really lists of heroes, regarded as founders of noble Greek families, who are provided with their ancestries on both the divine and the mortal side, a sort of Panhellenic Almanach de Gotha for the various clans.

All primitive peoples, provided they had learned to till the soil, were struck by the phenomenon of Nature, which 'dies' every winter, and every spring is 'born anew'. Perhaps no other cult has occurred independently to so many different people, though the ways in which the myth is told and the order of its ceremonies have been altered by contacts between one people and another. The cult of Mother Earth, including the marvellous re-creation of Nature, existed among Indo-Europeans before they dispersed: compare the Greek Demeter with the Latin Ceres, the Siculan Gereatis, the Celtic and British goddesses who were later syncretized with Demeter and Korē (Strabo, IV, p. 198), and similar conceptions among the Germans. Fresh impulse was given to these very ancient cults among the Greeks when the rustic peasant class, who had naturally preserved them, acquired greater importance with the development of social life.

On the other hand belief in a human soul, the 'vital' breath which survives after it has been separated from the body, and the conviction that the soul exists in a life beyond the grave, are also very ancient concepts, as is proved by the funeral rites of various peoples. With the development of moral ideas of right and wrong it became possible to believe that there was more than one form of life after death. Not all men had a pale existence less desirable than their life on earth, but the man who had led a just life passed into happiness when he died and had his after-life crowned by the supreme reward of resurrection. As early as *Odyssey* XI we have a list of those punished in the nether world, and the list has a moral background. The analogy eventually became clear between the death and subsequent resurrection of the gods of vegetation on the one hand and on the other the fate the human soul desired in another world.

A third element, the mystery ceremonies, taught men ways of removing the stains on the soul, in order to free it from the influence of demons, conquer fate, and in the end procure happiness in another world and the prize of resurrection. This knowledge came from a divine and secret revelation, given by the lords of the underworld, fashioners of the miracle of rebirth in nature, to their faithful people, who were gradually initiated to receive it. Here too the ideas were born independently in many regions; for it is equally impossible to prove that the Greeks took them wholesale from other people, such as the Egyptians, as it is to show that they themselves originated them and passed them on. Yet there may have been syncretism, such as that probably created by the Greek colonists at Naucratis between Greek Demeter and Egyptian Isis.

On the one side, then, the cult of the underworld gods was connected with the miracle of death and rebirth in vegetation, on the other with the world of human souls beyond the grave. At some point in the history of ideas the two elements united, revealing the secret links which the miracle of nature had with the problem of the human soul's salvation. So were invented the rites of initiation into various grades, whereby the initiate learned mystic secrets which he undertook to reveal to no one, on pain of terrible profanation. Initiates had to undergo symbolically the sequence of death, journey to the underworld, and resurrection to a new life. In the second phase of this sequence they attained to knowledge of hidden truths, being shown sacred representations of the divine myth, seeing and touching sacred objects, and partaking of sacrificial food, all under the influence of intoxicating drink or during a trance.

Some of these cults were concerned with the process of generation and evolved the new mystery ideas along lines of their own, without coming under any exotic influences. This was true of the mysteries of Demeter and Korē, who at Eleusis, originally a Neolithic cult site, were joined with other divinities (Pluton, Hecate, Triptolemus, and Iacchus). The first reference to this cult is in the Homeric Hymn to Demeter (line 476). The mysteries of Hecate at Aegina, of Demeter Hagne at Andania in Messenia, and of Lycon in Arcadia were probably on similar lines. Others again were the result of syncretism between Greek and non-Greek concepts. Examples are the Cabeiric mysteries at Erythrae, where Demeter and Korē, Hades and Hermes, were joined with the Kyrbantes; the mysteries of Zeus Idaeus in Crete; or those of Cybele, Attis, and the Magna Mater in Phrygia and neighbouring parts.

The mystery cult of Dionysus must have arisen spontaneously in Greece, as one can see from such evidence as the name Dionysus Mystes at Tegea in Arcadia.[12] But when Greek colonies were founded on the coast of Thrace there was syncretism with the crude, fierce, exciting legends current among the natives—the myths of Zagreus, devoured by the Titans, and Sabazios. The sacred representations of the complex Dionysiac story, with its alternation of sorrow and joy in his death and rebirth, were later of great importance in the evolution of dramatic literature (see Chapter VI).

In the age of tyranny a reaction set in, or perhaps one should rather call it an improvement of the wild Dionysiac cult. This was brought about by 'Orphism', the origin of which is placed far back in time by certain spurious sources, but should probably be brought down to the last half of the sixth century and connected with the colonial policy of the Peisistratids.[13] The Orphic theogony, which in part follows but in part diverges from that of Hesiod, derives mankind from the Titans and by this means explains the inheritance of sin and guilt which it possesses. But the Orphics sought to satisfy their inward aspiration to climb higher, to purify themselves, and get free from the great struggle, so that they might live their religion both spiritually and morally. They wanted to be different from the rude followers of Dionysus, according to the saying 'Those who bear the thyrsus are many, but those who are inspired are few'. They longed to free the soul from its prison in the body, and hoped that their communion rites would help to make them one with Zagreus, the god of sorrow who was torn in pieces by the Titans. So by abstaining from meat, and by purity and faith, they might attain that health which the soul can reach after three successive existences in the bodies of men and animals, and after that take their seats among the gods, while the souls of non-initiates go to Hades and there lie in the mud. The funeral rites of Orphics also became more spiritual. The souls of the dead need no tombs with rich furnishing, but only a tablet inscribed with the dead man's name, and a prayer that he be well received in Hades, together with some topographical information to enable him to find his way.

This theory of man's salvation had its prophets, singers, sorcerers, ascetics, preachers, and men who published oracles in verse. The last produced both genuine and spurious work. Examples are Onomacritus, the friend of the Peisistratids who composed poems attributed to Musaeus, and Epimenides, who is said by Plato to have visited Athens in 500 B C.[14]

Many Orphic ideas were later taken up by the Pythagoreans (see pp. 147, 249 ff.).

h. *Romans*

Roman religion is much more primitive than that in contemporary Greece, because it developed more slowly and was therefore still close to the religion of the Indo-Europeans at the time of their dispersion. We know more about it than about that of other Italic peoples of the same racial family, but they too remained at the same level as the Romans before all of them came under the influence of Greek, Etruscan, and Punic cults.

Their main concern, to some extent a remarkable one, was with countless *numina* affecting particular moments of man's life (*indigitamenta*), each of which had a limited field of activity and showed itself in an isolated phenomenon, a single action, or a definite object in nature. There were *numina* concerned with particular operations in farming, particular moments in the process of giving milk to babies, and so on. Others, for example, protected the gates or gateposts. There were sacred stones, such as meteorites, thunderbolts, the 'lapis manalis' and other components of amulets, or boundary-marks; and reverence was also given to certain columns, spears, and shields. There were *numina*, too, in animals which were considered to be ancestors of particular portions of mankind or which were venerated on account of their supposed good or ill will towards man, such as wolves and woodpeckers; and there were *numina* in healing or poisonous plants, such as figs, mountain ash, lotus, and beech; and also in trees struck by lightning. *Numina* belonged to harmful phenomena, under names such as Lua, Robigo, Febris, Pavor, Pallor. The majority were identified with the actual object in which they were involved, or with the action they provoked. They were obscure forces, with little or no personality or descriptive background, venerated because their effects had been felt. If their cult was neglected, or if they were roused by magic, they could become unfriendly, and it was therefore essential to placate them by all possible means.

But besides these innumerable forces which operated within narrow limits there were others called *praecipuae*, which seemed more important because connected with phenomena of wide effect. They acquired personalities from the scope of their activities, and also from characteristics which clearly linked them with other divinities belonging to distinct natural phenomena. Examples are Juppiter (Iovis), god of the sky in day-time, lord of the thunderbolt, who fertilizes the earth with rain and takes special care of the cultivation of upland districts, such as vineyards; Juno, goddess of the night sky, of new moons and procreation; Diana, the moon goddess, guardian of childbirth and guide of fugitives; Vulcanus, god of fire; and Neptunus, god of water. There were principal divinities for agriculture, husbandry, and pasturage, such as Mars and Ceres, both related to the renewal of nature year by year; Mars became the defender of the fields, both from pestilence and from foreign invaders, and Ceres was the giver of harvests. Besides there were Saturnus, god of sown soil and the treasures beneath it; Lua, who brings but also heals the diseases of plants; Consus, god of the harvest of all crops; Ops, who sees to the harvest's abundance; and Maia, who makes the fruit grow. Then there were divinities of the family, like Mater Matuta, Liber or Libera, and the Penates (who were originally protectors of the store-room); and there were divinities of the underworld, such as Vediovis, Orcus, and the others who were later eclipsed by the Greek Persephone (with the names Mania, Furina, and Larenta).

As Rome met peoples of different civilizations, with gods of their own, two parallel movements started in Roman religion, the adoption of foreign cults, and a syncretism between such cults and those it already possessed. It believed, too, that if it adopted the gods who protected enemy cities it would deprive those cities of their divine aid; moreover it was natural for it to allow the subjects it had won by conquest to retain their own cults, and equally natural for these cults to grow. Finally as it learned more about the religion of other peoples it came to recognize that some cults were already common to victors and vanquished ('divi quorum est potestas nostrorum hostiumque'), and that the similarities were such as to suggest the possibility of syncretism.

Naturally its first borrowings in religion were from the Italic cities nearest to it: Iuturna and Fortuna from the Latin cities of Lavinium and Praeneste, Feronia and Vacuna from the Sabine country. Then in the period of Etruscan domination began the large-scale invasion by Etruscan cults (Nortia, Manturna, Laverna, Voltumna), and assimilations between Roman and Etruscan divinities (Juppiter= Tinia) and between Roman gods and gods borrowed by the Etruscans from Italic peoples (Juno= Uni). At much the same time syncretisms between Roman and Greek cults were growing more numerous, together with some wholesale adoptions of Greek cults. This happened either through contact between Romans and sailors from the Chalcidic cities of Campania, or through the Phocaean trading-post at the mouth of the Tiber, or through the Etruscans acting as intermediaries. Other factors were the diffusion of Greek pottery painted with mythical scenes, and consultation of the Sibylline Books.

According to the early Romans divine good will had to be secured by following a meticulous magic ritual, by pronouncing without the smallest mistake formulae which in time had become incomprehensible, and by offering the gods what was believed to please them (food, sacrifices of animals, and originally human sacrifices too) on condition that they consented in advance to listen to prayer. The gods, it was believed, made their views known through phenomena of varying abnormality; and their displeasure had to be placated by offerings and lustral ceremonies to remove the effects of acts of impurity and of wrong-doing. Originally altars were erected to the gods on the tops of mountains, or in grottoes communicating with the underworld, or in mysterious woods, the areas or *templa* being marked out with sacred rites. Later they were placed in temple buildings, of which the earliest recorded by tradition go back to the time of the Etruscan kings—the temple of Diana on the Aventine, and the temples with three *cellae* on the Quirinal and Capitoline hills.

The systems of cremation which became common in Latium through influence of the invading Second Italici were one of the reasons why early Romans had little interest in their dead, whose ashes or graves were placed in isolated spots, even though they might be accompanied by appropriate furnishings. On fixed days it was the custom to open the approach to the lower world where the spirits congregated, and give access both to the good spirits (Manes and Lares) and to those who brought danger (Lemures); but for all the rest of the year the approach was closed by the stone of the 'mundus'.

At Rome as elsewhere the king was the religious head of the state, and as such he was the founder, in fairly early days, of the various priestly orders needed to help him or to act as delegates for particular duties. He still remained as *rex sacrificulus* in Republican times, and it was due to him and the sacerdotal colleges that the new magistrates did not add religious duties to their other functions. In their turn the priests did not achieve a direct and complete control over the magistrates.

Perhaps the oldest priesthood, in one view dating back in some form to a period before the Indo-European dispersion, is that of the *flamines*, of etymology believed to be akin to that of the Indian *Brāhmaṇa*. They are later found in two groups, the older being the threefold college of Flamen Dialis, Martialis, and Quirinalis, the later one attached to the twelve gods. The Salii, on the other hand, who had archaic rites connected with inanimate objects, were of early Latin origin, and turn up again at Laurentum, Lavinium, Aricia, Tusculum, Tibur, and Anagnia. The Vestals must at first have been priestesses of the ancient goddess of fire, Caca, who was later identified with Vesta. The colleges of Augures and Fetiales, used in relations with foreign states, seem to be of later origin, but the most important college was undoubtedly that of the Pontifices, which tradition dates back to the time of Numa. After the beginning of the Republic the pontiffs succeeded in making themselves independent of the *rex sacrorum*, and replaced him in the direction of sacred affairs. Their duties included regulation of the calendar and drawing up the 'tabulae dealbatae', on which the principal doings of each year were recorded. Later on patrician families had their private priesthoods, like the Luperci Fabiani and Luperci Quintiales.

i. *Etruscans*

The Etruscans are one of the few western peoples whose religion and rituals we are in a position to reconstruct during this period. They are known to us in two ways. One is direct and contemporary, through pictures on monuments and through inscriptions; the other comes indirectly through the evidence of Greek and Latin writers, both pagan and Christian, and is normally fairly late—from the end of the Republic and still more from imperial times. The latter evidence naturally does not often tell us about conditions and ideas belonging to earlier periods, but deals with later and contemporary conditions, when Etruscan religion had undergone contamination and distortion. It did in fact draw new features from every quarter. Contact with the Greeks and their philosophical and religious writings was important, but still more the propaganda of the itinerant Chaldeans, mainly easterners, who infected Etruscan religion by the production of quite arbitrary interpretations and supposed likenesses, particularly based on the traditional origin of the Etruscans from the East (which the present writer regards as fictitious). No modern reconstruction which is essentially based on this late and tendentious evidence can possibly give a genuine picture of Etruscan religion in its early stages. Serious anachronism would be inescapable.

Every example we can verify suggests that Etruscan religion, in very ancient times, was continually undergoing modification, and that its pantheon too was by no means constant. There was an early stage when pre-anthropomorphic cults still persisted and worship was paid to stones, armour, rivers, and the like; but even then there were also anthropomorphic gods whose power of action was sometimes wide and sometimes narrow, and their antiquity is guaranteed by pure Etruscan names, although very soon they lent themselves to syncretism with gods from abroad. Illustrative names are Tinia, Fufluns, Setlans, Turms, Turan, Tin, Vertumnus or Voltumnus (round whose shrine one of the Etruscan leagues had its being), Mantus, Mania, Catha, Northia, Tages, Vegonia and the tutelary god of cities, Tarchu. There were as many others whose power may have been more limited, such as Cilens, Cvalp, Ethausva, Letham, Tecum, Thuftha, Tluscu, Letha, Laran, and many others whose forms are depicted on Etruscan mirrors.

Other divinities can be shown to have originated among Indo-European peoples, and more specifically the Italici alongside whom the Etruscans lived for centuries. These include Ani (Janus), Nethuns (Neptunus), Selvans (Silvanus), Usil (Ausosa, Aurora), Vetis (Vedius, Vediovis), Catra (Saturnus), Mae (Maia), and all the gods of the famous triad—Uni (Juno), Maris (Mars, evidently replacing a similar native divinity), and Mnrva (Minerva).

There are also divinities whose origin was clearly Greek though the names are sometimes distorted, and who must be derived from contacts with the Hellenic colonies in Italy. There was Aplu (Apollo), Artume or Aritimi (Artemis), Hercle (Heracles), Aite (Hades), and Persipnai (Persephone, related to the native deities Mantus and Mania). But normally it seemed enough to establish syncretisms between Etruscan and Greek, or Etruscan and Italian gods: Tinia with Juppiter and Zeus; Fufluns with Bacchus and Dionysus; Setlans with Vulcanus and Hephaestus; Turms with Mercurius and Hermes; Turan with Venus and Aphrodite; Tin with Diana/Luna and Selene; and the Etrusco-Italic Mnrva (Minerva) with the Greek Athene.

Along with the shapes and attributes of so many Greek gods there travelled from Greece to Etruria a number of myths, sometimes in their entirety. Vase-painting shows how they were shortened, contaminated, misunderstood, and 'Etruscized' generally. There was also much passage of Greek ritual and methods of cult.

The concept of life after death underwent a complete cycle of change brought about by the history of the native population combined with Greek influence. Three main stages can be defined. Long before their invading parties crossed into Tuscany the North Etruscan tribes had practised cremation, their purpose being to destroy the dead bodies. This probably corresponds to the dominant idea of very early days, that of preventing the dead man from appearing again as a ghost to disturb the life of the living. The next stage follows closely on the introduction of inhumation, due to

THE ANCIENT WORLD

contact with the Italici, and was also caused by the influence of Greek ideas on the relations between life on earth and life in the next world. The Etruscans, especially their upper classes, attained a more serene conception of life after death, in which the human spirit was carried away by a winged demon, and arrived in the underworld in a chariot or on horseback or on foot, accompanied by a Lasa reciting a roll which described the life the man had led on earth. The third stage came mainly in the period of Part II, starting in the fifth century when cultural relations between Greece and Etruria were broken. Pictures in tombs then show the Etruscans returning once again to a more sombre, sad, and fearful conception of life after death.

Etruscan religion was exceptionally formalized, and was rich in the details of ritual in magic formulae and prescriptions which had to be followed scrupulously in all public and private actions. Traditional ideas of religion dictated the construction of city walls, the lay-out of temples, and the form of sacrifices and of banquets held on characteristic occasions of life. All this built up a science known to the priests, the Etruscan 'disciplina', which was certainly not unchanging, but was constantly being modified like every other product of the human mind. The priests were expert at ways of learning the will of the gods, which was made known not so much through oracles as through direct signs and portents, requiring correct interpretation, such as the characteristics of thunderbolts, the flight of birds, and the shape of entrails of sacrificial victims—especially their livers (the science of hepatoscopy). As is well known, such methods have made their appearance independently among primitive races of every period and place, without it being possible to deduce direct influence by one upon another of the kind some modern scholars have wanted to establish between Asia Minor, Greece, and Etruria. This rich and constantly developing ritual naturally gave rise to the compilation of written formularies, and probably these too were periodically revised; for the material for them, the rites themselves and still more their interpretation, was continually being altered in a way that was secret and difficult to control. The period of greatest innovation came when the Etruscan priests had close and frequent contacts with the itinerant Chaldeans. The literature includes the *Libri Tagetici* (or *Haruspicini*), in which the rules are set out in the form of a dialogue between the heroic figures Tages and Tarchna, the *Libri Vegonici*, ascribed to the nymph Vegonia, and books called *fulgurales*, *rituales*, *fatales*, and *Acheruntici* (this last a Greek name).

j. *Phoenician and Punic religion*

Before coming to Punic religion we must say a word about the religion of Phoenicia and Canaan, from which it was derived.

From fragments of a Greek version made by Philon of Byblos in the first or second century AD, we know something of the Phoenician religious system as it was supposed to have been drawn up in the time of Solomon by a priest called Sankhuniaton. But in fact the picture is one of earlier conditions, which moreover were clearly recast in the post-Hellenistic period, particularly with the addition of a kind of astrological superstructure.

We get more genuine, or at any rate less controversial, information by taking as our point of departure the sacred texts of Ugarit (c. 1400 BC) the data provided by the Old Testament, and the evidence of epigraphy and archaeology. These show us that the tribes of Canaan originally preserved their archaic worship of inanimate and naturalistic objects in the fields— stones, poles, and sacred trees. In time they came to venerate divine beings called Baālim and Baalat: these are names for the male and female forms respectively, sometimes used for single divinities, sometimes for pairs or triads, both by the whole people and by individual cities, for their particular gods. At the outset they had little personality or myths attaching to them, and sometimes no proper names of their own. Only in time, under the influence of foreign contacts, were myths evolved and embellished.

One pair of supreme divinities was composed of El (The God), creator of the world and lord of the gods, and his consort Asherāh; and there was a triad consisting of Baal (The Lord), a god of the storm and lightning similar to the Mesopotamian Hadad, his wife Astarte, and the boy Adonis, who dies and is resurrected, symbolizing nature's death and rebirth. Adonis had his counterpart in Alian Ba'al, found in wells and underground springs, and in Mot, the god of harvests and fruits: another comparison is with Dagon, god of corn. At Tyre the god most revered was Melqart (King of the City), who was first a sun god and later also a god of the sea: eventually with Dagon of the sea-coast and with Resef he was identified with Apollo. Sidon worshipped Esmun, later made equivalent to Asclepius. The priests of Ugarit and the later Phoenicians and Carthaginians were called 'Kōhen' like the Hebrew priests, and were organized in colleges; prophets too had an important role, as we see from I *Kings* xviii. Archaeology and the *Old Testament* show that sacrificial ritual was most meticulous and that a significant part was played by human sacrifices, expecially those offered to Malik, god of first-born sons (the Moloch of the Bible), for instance when a foundation stone was being laid for a house. Other ancient rites were sacred prostitution and circumcision. The god revealed himself especially in cult places, marked by a pillar or a pair of pillars in the open air, and later by regular shrines of which there was already one at Ugarit. Much care was given to tombs, and in very early times, perhaps under influence from Babylon and Egypt, the theory was evolved that life on earth affected the way the soul was treated after death.

The human personalities eventually given to Phoenician deities were largely owed to syncretism with the gods of other peoples. But the syncretism was often very superficial, based on incidental resemblances, such as those between Tyrian Ba'alat and Egyptian Hathor, between Melqart and the Greek Heracles, Eshmun and Asclepius, and Astarte and Aphrodite.

The Phoenician colonies of the West, later organized by Carthage into an empire of its own, were separated from Phoenicia by a long distance, and by a breakdown in direct communications after the fall of Tyre. So Punic religion took on a peculiar character, and a number of syncretisms were evolved. Many of these are attested by the Punico-Macedonian treaty between Hannibal and Philip V (Polybius, VII, 9), where we also find evidence that nature cults of 'rivers, plants, and waters' and the familiar grouping of divinities in triads still went on. The two basic Punic divinities were El's successor Baal Hammon, who was identified with the Greek Zeus and with the Latin Saturnus (rather than Juppiter), as the god who creates and destroys, and his wife Tanit, successor to Astarte, identified with Cybele and with Juno Caelestis. Melqart was also important; so was Eshmun, identified with Asclepius and worship on the hill of Byrsa. Pictures of divine figures on coins of the Punic colonies in Sicily show how syncretisms had been established between Punic gods and almost all the main Greek divinities. From native Sicily, too, Carthage took various Hellenized divinities like Demeter and Korē, who later spread to the Numidian hinterland, together with the goddess of Mount Eryx who was later identified with Astarte, Aphrodite, and Venus. It may be assumed that there were also syncretisms with native and Hellenized divinities of North Africa, Spain, and Sardinia.

We are told of Punic priestly colleges (*mirzah*), high priests (*rab kohānim*) and priestesses, generally chosen from leading families. Greek writers said that religious feeling among the Carthaginians was in proportion to their fear of dangers. Archaeological evidence shows exaggerated use of amulets, and the lives of great Carthaginians, like Hannibal, show how superstitious they were. Excavations of the great Carthaginian metropolis, relating to a period beginning with the eighth century, have confirmed the frightful usage of Moloch sacrifices of first-born sons to Baal Hammon and Tanit, but Sicilian excavations show that there the inhumanity was abandoned and small animals were used instead. Yet the appalling sacrificial slaughter at the taking of Himera in 409 proves that the prohibition on human sacrifices made by Gelon (and in another part of the world by Darius I) had no validity for the Carthaginians.

There was sporadic use of cremation in the seventh century, but the Carthaginians normally buried their dead, as we can see from archaeological evidence rather than having to rely on Timaeus (Justin, XIX, I, II). They employed death masks in human shape (two examples have been found at La Cannita near Palermo). The theory that deserts during life governed a soul's treatment in the underworld had a normal development similar to that found among the Hebrews.

2. COSMOGONIES AMONG VARIOUS PEOPLES

All ancient peoples of whom we have adequate knowledge to form a judgement tried early in their history to picture the origin of the world (*cosmogonia*). Their naïve speculations normally start from the concept of a creator; some people supposed him to have created from nothing, others that he gave order to elements which at the outset were confused in chaos or immersed in the ocean.

The Chinese, using the image of a tortoise-shell, made the creator plant at the four corners of the earth four great claws of a tortoise to hold the sky, which was a fusion of stones of many colours. Then he freed the world from the black dragon, created banks for the rivers, and so forth.

Vedic cosmogony is still vague, but with it are connected the beginnings of Indian philosophical thought. Some hymns of the tenth *maṇḍala* of the *Rigveda* already have a semi-philosophical character and contain the gist of certain views which belong to the thought of later ages, monism for example. Hymn I, 164, 46 makes undifferentiated being (*sat*) the primeval principle at the origin of the world. It is presented as usual as the moral or cosmic order (*ṛta*) mentioned earlier in this chapter, and is manifested by the regularity of astronomical phenomena. Later this primeval principle got personified as a creator deity (Hiraṇyagarbha or Viśvakarman). The primordial element from which all others issued was water. But the so-called philosophical hymns go further, and *Rigveda*, X, 129 already speaks of an absolute which is prior to the distinction between existence (*sat*) and non-existence (*asat*) and can only be defined negatively. Being becomes such through heat (*tapas*), and desire (*kāma*) is the link uniting *sat* with *asat*. Yet the expressions and mentality behind all this are based on contingent empiricism and have not yet risen to monist and idealist speculation.

The Assyrians, like the Babylonians before them, retained the theories about the 'Creation of the World' (Enuma Elish = when in the heavens), which the Sumerians had introduced into Mesopotamia long ago. Among the relatively few modifications was the substitution of their national god Ashur as the creator.

In Egypt, too, ideas on this matter, explained in Volume I, remained unchanged.

The first Persian theories of cosmogony probably go back to the time of Zarathustra although apart from one precious and eloquent reference in the fourth-century Greek historian Theopompus none of our evidence is earlier than the Sassanid period, and most of it is found in writings of the ninth century AD (*Bundahishn*). World history was divided into four periods, each of 3,000 years. In the first period Ahura Mazdah, living on high, created the celestial powers; in the second Ahriman, living in darkness down below, set up his demons in opposition, while Ahura Mazdah proceeded with the creation of the world, the land, vegetation, animals, and men. In the third period began the strife between the two powers, with alternating phases of deaths and rebirths, down to the appearance of the first great kings and of Zarathustra. In the fourth period will come the decisive victory of Ahura Mazdah.

The earliest source for Phoenician cosmogony seems to be contained in the work of Sankhuniaton (eleventh century BC), which was edited by Philon of Byblos in the second century AD (see p. 242). From the union of Chaos with the Spirit there was born the cosmic egg Mot, which split in two and created the sky and the earth. Then followed the creation of the stars, wind, clouds, and rain; and of gods, giants and men, and so of all human activities, especially religion and worship.

As to Hebrew cosmogony the current doctrine is that in the earliest chapters of *Genesis* we have two stories, one older than the other, which originated from different documents. The editor who has given the book its present form has taken the general scheme of the later story as the basis of his narrative, but has inserted certain matter from the earlier one without minding about the resulting contradictions; for they affected the manner and ideal scheme of his exposition and never the reality of the story he was telling. Of course one should not take every expression as an assertion of objective reality. The facts under discussion must be distinguished from the literary genre or manner used to express them, which conforms to the artistic and didactic standards of the editor's time, and meets the needs of the public to which the story was directed and the capacity of this public to understand.

The basic document is now normally called 'Priestly', since its features suggest that it derived from a circle of priests and highly educated people, whereas the older document (normally called J. or Yahwist, because God is normally indicated by the name he had among the Hebrews) is more anthropomorphic in outlook. In the one the picture is wider, embracing the general problem of the origin of the Universe, while in the other the horizon is restricted to man and the question of his duties, his purpose, and so on. Moreover the cosmogony in the Priestly account is dominated by the element of Water, regarded as something hostile to man, to the point at which conquest of cultivable soil consists in redeeming it from Water. But in the Yahwist version the dominant feature is a desert which has to be made fertile by rain and springs, even though these waters too must be regulated by man before they can take proper effect.

What we have said so far may help in identifying the provenance of the two accounts, the older of which may be placed in Syria and Arabia, the later in Mesopotamia. As to the date, the Yahwist version may be ninth or eighth century BC, the later version belongs to the late seventh or early sixth, but the data on which its priestly writers worked are distinctly earlier. Links with the cosmogony of other eastern Semitic peoples are many and obvious. It could not be otherwise; yet the biblical author shows a higher conception of God, insisting on his oneness and admitting no one outside him or against him, or at any rate picturing the primordial state (that which was antecedent to God's ordering), as one on which God works by the power of his Word rather than as an obstacle which must be overcome by means of a struggle. In this way the Hebrew story acquires, as a noble piece of moral and religious teaching, a value lacking in parallel Sumerian and Egyptian accounts. We may regard the undoubted similarities in terminology as due to the author's deliberate adoption of words which could be understood by all. It was not simply that he depended on the origins accepted by other people.

The story of the creation of the world and of man was undoubtedly presented in the way which could most easily express in a simple style the succeeding phases of God's work, which had had complete freedom to plan the best possible state for man, with the good as a goal. Yet man had to feel both his absolute dependence on his Lord and his duty to mark his difference from the beasts (in other countries sexual relations with animals were allowed, although the purpose was simply to encourage their fertility.) The author however uses naïve conceptions, in the picturesque manner to which he has accustomed us, to emphasize in his narrative the close relation between man and woman, since he wants to bring out the lofty significance of their union, the purpose of which is to multiply creation. Moreover the whole complex narrative is fitted into a scheme (six days of labour and one of rest) which has a clearly didactic purpose; it follows a recurring formula of Semitic literature, which makes events on earth a replica of what happens in heaven. In any case the editor of *Genesis* did not mean every single detail, any more than the complete account, to be taken as objective fact. The details were expressed in conventional terms which conformed to the outlook of his race and the society of his time. They were intended to enunciate, in unescapable terms, certain great truths which were fundamental for human existence.

As regards Greek thought, the ideas of cosmogony which prevailed when the Homeric epic was compiled are known to us from *Iliad* XIV, 200 ff. From Earth (Thetis) and Ocean was born Rhea, the wife of Cronos and mother of Zeus and Hera. In the Hesiodic Age which followed, the *Theogony*, which later became a fundamental work to the Greeks, laid down the system which gained general diffusion until the *physiologoi* started their philosophies. According to Hesiod the age of Chaos came first, then there appeared Earth (Gea), Darkness (Tartaros), and the god of Love (Eros). From Chaos were born the Eclipse (Erebos) and Night (Nyx); from Earth came the Heavens (Ouranos), the mountains, and the Sea (Pontos). From the union of these first elements were derived the abstract forces (Themis, Thanatos, Nikē, Nemesis) and the first legendary people (Cyclopes, Erinnyes, Moirai, Gorgones). As well as these Cronos, Nereus, and Cerberus were born; and there followed the second generation of Cronos, and the third generation of Zeus.

Pherecydes of Syros (first half of sixth century), who is known as a pupil of the 'Wise Man' Pittacus and teacher of Pythagoras, made a greater effort to

distinguish within this theoretical and mythical cosmogony the elements of
the world. He thus established a kind of primordial physics, in which interest
in ethics is also visible. In his work *Pentamychos* (the cavern of five chambers)
he maintained that initially there was Chaos, whom he identified with Oceanus;
next came Zeus, who disposed the moral order and took on also the duties
of Eros, with Chronos (or Cronos) the primordial essence of Time, and
Earth. From the seed of Chronos were born Fire, Air, and Water, and so
we have the gods in each of the five chambers of the cavern. The order of the
world derived from the strife between the gods, those who were beaten
being cast down into Oceanus.

There are similar ethical conclusions in the cosmogony of the Orphics
and in Pythagoreanism.

3. THE FIRST STEPS IN GREEK PHILOSOPHY

In this section it seems inappropriate to collect the earliest references to
philosophy among other peoples; and in any case enough has been said of
this in connection with their science, religion, and cosmogony.

The same pre-eminence which the Greeks achieved in pure science they
were destined to obtain in their conquest of philosophical thought, owing to
their remarkable capacity for moving from empirical study of facts and
phenomena on to rational and abstract study of the essential nature of these
facts. Through their voyages and colonization the Greeks came to know all
the coasts of the three continents facing the Mediterranean and its connecting
seas, with the peoples and cultures to be found in these lands; and they
themselves had a wealth of political and social experience in these periods,
under kings, aristocracies, tyrannies, and democracies. Moreover they had
attained early an advanced stage of ethical speculation, illustrated by the
opinions of the 'Seven Wise Men', by their 'gnomic' poetry, and by the
balances shown in their codes of laws. They were not held back by any
religious castes which had taken control of science and philosophy; so as
these fields opened before their minds, they enjoyed freedom of ideas and an
individualism which allowed the most daring thoughts. Being logical by
nature and carried easily towards the development of reasoning and towards
the creation of logical systems, they were less fond of scientific study for its
practical applications (though they did learn and improve these applications
under all scientific heads) than for its theoretical refinement, which enabled
them to explain things and phenomena as a rational whole.

The earliest Greek philosophers directed themselves along two separate
paths. In the search for a principle governing the real world, one school
attached predominant importance to the material from which things are made
and given life, the other to the forms which make things different from one
another. In our period the former method was represented by the so-called
physiologoi of Ionia.

Thales of Miletus (*c.* 625–585) through his travels was enabled to learn the practical geometry of the Egyptians, from which he established some new general theorems, and also some astronomical notions of Babylonian origin, which allowed him to predict the eclipse of the sun on May 28, 585. But he wanted to explain the origin of the world without repeating the myths of old cosmogonies, which supposed that the elements had been distinct from the start. For him Water was the primary substance, ageless and imperishable, divine in character; and from it the other elements were derived—Earth, the solid element, and Air, the gaseous element.

His pupil Anaximander (*c.*610–546), a Milesian like himself, and also a geographer and astronomer, saw the difficulties involved in trying to derive all elements from one of their own number. He supposed that to the Infinite (*apeiron*), an indefinable entity which recalls the Chaos of the cosmogonies, differentiation was introduced by cold and heat, dry and wet, and so on; and that in this way were born Earth, Water, Air, and Fire. In addition his reflections about organic beings led him to derive one kind from another, for example man from fish.

His pupil Anaximenes (*c.*585–528 or 524) returned to the theory of a definite primordial element, but applied his master's propositions about the two opposite phenomena of rarefaction and condensation. He maintained therefore that the air or gaseous state, the element which to him was primordial and embraced the Universe and the human soul, generated fire by rarefaction, and water (the fluid state) and earth (the solid state) by intermediate stages of condensation illustrated by the wind and the clouds.

Pythagoras of Samos (570–497) settled after long journeys at Croton, gained control of its aristocracy, and in 532 founded there a famous society of ascetic bent, which studied philosophy, politics, and science. He became master of the city until he was turned out by the *demos* and went to Metapontum. The prime idea behind all his researches and discoveries in astronomy, physics, and mathematics (see p. 147 f.), an idea developed later in every possible direction by his pupils, was that matter was measurable and countable, and that in every real thing a mathematical relation existed as its basis. For him the objects in nature were not to be unified as the result of any substantial oneness of matter, as they were for the Milesian *physiologoi*; but there was a common basis in number, which determined nature's variety. Another of the fundamental themes later developed on a broad front by the Pythagorean school was that of the oppositions: between infinite and finite, even and odd, and so on. Pythagoras was a convinced believer in the religious doctrines of the Orphics; and for him scientific study and a life devoted to higher theoretical research were the most effective means of redeeming and purifying the soul, freeing it from the passions during its various existences within a body. Yet it is clear that not all his followers could understand and support both sides of his teaching, and that therefore many of them built their lives only round the mystical and ethical side, though they might admit the scientific and philosophical side as a sort of dogma which was not comprehensible in the same way.

Xenophanes of Colophon (c. 580–480), a wandering singer of his own religious epics, settled in the new colony of Elea (Velia) which the Phocaeans founded in southern Italy, and established there a religious and philosophical school which was markedly hostile to the prevailing ideas to be found in the Homeric and Hesiodic poems. In opposition to the 'areté' of those works the new school set up 'sophia', the wisdom which sees, contemplates, and so comes to know and understand, its conclusion being both monotheism and monophysism. The one all-powerful divinity, despite his diverse ways of showing himself, must not be conceived in anthropomorphic terms, with a human face and human habits, sometimes wicked and immoral. Eternal and unchanging, this god could not be seen or heard or known by man, from whom he was altogether dissimilar. Without needing to move he still saw and controlled everything, while his thought was automatically turned into reality. Xenophanes made no attempt to provide a clear and confident opinion about the origin of the world. He rejected the ancient myths, attempting to replace them by naturalistic and empirical interpretations of phenomena. His belief was that the fundamental elements were the earth and the sea, from which by a natural process were derived the clouds (for example he thought Iris only a cloud), together with the winds, the rain, and the streams.

In the development of the Eleatic school a much greater figure than Xenophanes was his 'pupil' Parmenides of Elea, whose *floruit* is put at 504–501 BC (sixty-ninth Olympiad). Under him the monotheist beliefs of the school genuinely blended with monophysism. In his view in order to achieve knowledge 'according to truth' one must avail oneself of logical investigation, reason, and intelligence. One must master the problems of Being and Not-Being, of positive and negative, and of substantive and predicate. Only by means of the intellect could man intuit the truest truth, the substantive being, which neither was born nor dies, and was compact, unmovable, unchangeable. Over against this absolute reality stood a reality 'according to the opinion of mortals', that is to say reality according to the senses; and in this everything appeared in a definite way, partly because it did not appear as other things appear. From this derived the antithesis between Being and Not-Being, an antinomy which Parmenides refused to accept. For this reason he was convinced that the only reality was logical reality, the reality obtained by the senses being illusory.

His contemporary Heraclitus of Ephesus, who also flourished in the sixty-ninth Olympiad, produced an almost diametrically opposite conception. For him it was precisely the opposition and contradiction between things which constituted the proof of their reality, since nothing abided, everything was changing and becoming. War, opposition, distinction, and contrast were the basis of the world, the 'discordant concord' which ruled over the life of nature and of man, according to the immanent divine law (approached by initiates) which had its response in all existence, and from which human law derives. All elements, water, air, and earth, were in a continual process of becoming by the operation of fire. It was fire which was related to the moments at which matter was changed, and which initiated the perpetual becoming.[15]

NOTES TO CHAPTER V

1. Professor Martin McGuire suggests that this gives an exaggerated impression. In his view there was no real conflict between prophets and priests over matters of orthodoxy.

2. This is a possible etymological rendering of one of the Hebrew words used for 'prophets'; but others interpret it as 'seers' or 'speakers in place of . . .'. The relevant terminology is very variable, and still gives rise to the most lively controversies.

3. Jeremiah in effect preached non-violence.

4. Also, as Professor F. M. Heichelheim points out, in those of Assyria, and of the Phoenician and Syrian principalities.

5. This is clearly indicated in some of the early Psalms.

6. These ideas are first found in the decades before the Captivity.

7. *History of Mankind*, I–2, Chapter I, pp. 380–4; Chapter VIII, pp. 714–18.

8. They are not represented, to our knowledge, in material images, and the allusions which are made in the hymns to them and to their actions are not always compatible with an imaginative evocation of them in human form. Agni, e.g., is represented as a bull, a horse, a bird, etc. Cf. full references in A. Bergaigne, *La religion védique d'après les hymnes du Rig-veda* (Paris, 1878), t. I, pp. 142 ff. *passim*.

9. The hypothesis which considers that the origin of the speculative element was non-Aryan gratuitously supposes that Aryan society was incapable of creative work.
    The classic and ancient theory that Buddhism and Jainism were movements of protest and reaction against the excessive ritualism of the *Brāhmaṇa* and the power it gave the religious class, fails to realize that these two movements were essentially concerned with liberation from existence and not with struggling against social servitudes. They are addressed as much to the privileged of the world as to others. It was the fact that they were directed at material prosperity which made the Brahmanical religion, philosophies, and techniques for salvation of their time seem insufficient to them. The Buddha defeated the heretics but converted the Brahmans.

10. See Chapter I, note 43.

11. The Delphic festival, known as the Pythia, was reorganized under the Amphictionic Council in 582 BC and was thenceforth, like the Olympian festival, held every four years. The Corinthian ('Isthmian') and Nemean festivals, each held every other year, were placed on a regular footing about the same time.

12. Professor Pareti has unfortunately not made it clear why this shrine (Pausanias, VIII, 5, 4) proves an indigenous origin for Dionysus. Ancient Greek tradition uniformly supposed Dionysus to be a foreigner, Thracian or Phrygian (and the Phrygians were of Thracian origin); and it is held by most scholars that ecstasy accompanied the cult from the first. More difficult are the questions when and how Dionysus became a god of vegetation, and especially of the vine, and how his cult (e.g. in the Ionian festival of the Anthesteria) came to be associated with the dead. The classic discussion by Jane Harrison, *Prolegomena to the Study of Greek Religion* (3rd edition, Cambridge, 1922), pp. 364 ff., is still of great value; see also M. P. Nilsson, *Geschichte d. griech. Religion* (Munich, 1941), I, pp. 532 ff.

13. Here too one must regret that Professor Pareti was unable to develop his interesting reference to the *colonial* policy of the Peisistratids. Certainly Onomacritus, the oracle-monger who as a close friend of Peisistratus' sons (see Herodotus, VII. 6) was responsible for composing much of the earliest 'Orphic' writing; see W. K. C. Guthrie, *Orpheus and Greek Religion* (London, 1935), pp. 13 ff., pp. 107 ff. But though a sixth-century Attic origin for Orphism has much to commend it, the close relations between Orphic ideas and those of Pythagoreanism (see below pp. 249) must not be ignored; and indeed tradition associates Onomacritus with certain western Greek sages; see Guthrie, *op. cit.*, pp. 216 ff.

14. Epimenides the Cretan was a seer of whom many legendary tales are told stretching over a period as long as the great age with which he was credited (on one view he lived 299 years). One well-known action was his purification of Athens from the pollution resulting from the murder of Cylon's followers by the Alcmaeonids. The murder occurred *c.* 630 BC, and the purification is dated by Plutarch to Solon's time (*c.* 595). But it is just possible that the story in Plato (*Laws*, 642 D) is right, and that Epimenides purified Athens after the Alcmaeonid Cleisthenes, who legislated in 508, had been brought back from exile.

15. Dr P. Oliva comments that he would have preferred this paragraph on Heraclitus to follow closely on those concerning the Milesian *physiologoi* and to precede any reference to the Eleatics. It is true that the date given by Professor Pareti for Parmenides' *floruit* (provided by the chronographer Apollodorus) may well be too early (Plato, *Parmenides*, 127 B, and in other passages makes him talk to Socrates in Athens as late as *c.* 450 BC); and it is clear that Heraclitus, who knew nothing of the Eleatics, was in the Ionian tradition, particularly in his theory of 'opposites' which goes back to Anaximander. But Heraclitus, who included his older contemporary Xenophanes in his contempt for earlier writers, cannot be dissociated from Xenophanes, since both mark the beginnings of the great period of Greek rationalism. Heraclitus above all is the inaugurator of a new method in philosophy, with his emphasis on *Logos*.

CHAPTER VI

LITERATURE AND ART, 1200–600 BC

I. LITERATURE

a. *China*

At the beginning of Chinese literature orthodox Confucian tradition places the so-called 'Five Classics', among which three occupy a position of pre-eminence, *I-ching*, *Shu-ching*, and *Shih-ching*. There has been much discussion about their date and authenticity. They may be taken to be the compilation in a written form (carried out in the middle of the first millennium BC) of a body of legends, traditions, poems, songs, etc., going back to the early Chou period.

The *I-ching* (Book of Changes), attributed to the mythical emperor Fu-hsi, probably had its origin in a collection of peasant omen texts: it accumulates a mass of material used in the practices of divination. It centres round the eight trigrams (*pa-kua*) and sixty-four hexagrams, which represent the possible combinations of three and six parallel sections of a line, each section being either whole or broken in two. Each of them is followed by an explanatory phrase attributed to Wên-wang (the first Chou king) and by six phrases of commentary attributed to the Duke of Chou. Then there are ten appendices (*shih-i*), which in the twelfth century AD served as the basis of the neo-Confucian philosophy of Chu Hsi. The date of this highly respected book has been the subject of much controversy. Kuo Mo-jo, for example, would put the bulk of it in the fourth and third centuries BC, with additions of the Han period. More plausible is the view of Li Ching-ch'ih, who traces the basic core of the work to an augural compilation of the eighth or seventh centuries BC, but would place its modern form no earlier than the fourth century BC.

The *Shu-ching* (Book of Documents) is a collection of various kinds of document, discourse, and oration, attributed by tradition to the earliest Chou period. Only certain pieces, however, are earlier than the eighth century, the bulk being a patchwork made up with pieces of very varying date.

The *Shih-ching* (Book of Odes) is a collection of ancient songs, the discovery and assembly of which are attributed to Confucius. In fact it may well be earlier. In any event the *Shih-ching* contains a large genuine core of ancient popular and rustic verse, belonging to the first half of the first millennium BC.

The influence of these texts on later thought was immense, especially that of the *I-ching*. Later commentators treated it as a store-house of abstract concepts, to which every event or idea could be traced and in which all future progress was foreshadowed.

b. *India*

Vedic literature is entirely anonymous. This despite the traditions which make the mythical bard Vyāsa the composer of the *Veda*, and despite the groups of hymns which got attributed to little-known priestly families. This literature, concentrated as it is upon ritual and sacrifice, has an exclusively religious or—to put it more precisely—a priestly character. None of the secular strains or infiltrations which recur in the *Upaniṣad* are yet visible in the Vedic texts. We have, therefore, an enormous mass of poetry, and somewhat later of prose, which was collected or composed by generation after generation of unknown priests.

The *Veda* were sacred, and were regarded as having existed from eternity without creation. This accounts for the enormous importance attached to the establishment of their text and the meticulous care devoted to their correct pronunciation. Various methods were employed, chief among which was the *Padapathas*, that is to say the Vedic text transcribed word for word without any attention to the rules of euphonic composition (*sandhi*). Of the phonetic manuals (*prātiśākhya*) something will be said in Part II. But the main point is that the sacred text was transmitted orally over dozens of generations. Every manuscript existing today is very late, not only because the materials used were perishable, but because it was forbidden to entrust the revealed word to writing. Oral tradition, though it has become very feeble, has never been interrupted to this day. At Benares, as well as in the south, masters make their pupils memorize passages of sacred text which may be quite long and even comprise a whole *Veda*, just as they did three thousand years ago. Nevertheless the text has been preserved very pure.

Of the four *Veda*, the first is the *Rigveda*, which is presupposed by all the other Vedic texts but itself presupposes none of them. This relative chronology is difficult to tie on to an absolute one. Extreme dates have been proposed (Jacobi suggested 4000 BC, Tilak 6000). But it can broadly be said that the central core of the Ṛigvedic hymns (not the *Ṛigveda* as a collection) is contemporary with the Aryan migration into India and can therefore be dated about the middle of the second millennium BC. The *Ṛigveda* contains the strophes (*ṛk*) recited in the course of sacrifice. It is divided into ten *maṇḍala*, the primitive nucleus being those numbered II to VII inclusive, each of which is attributed to a priestly family; VIII contains a fair number of interpolations; IX seems to be very early material which has entered the collection later; I is partly ancient, partly late. Finally there is X, sharply to be distinguished from all the others and decidedly late; it contains the main hymns of philosophical type. This vast anthology comprises hymns on the world's origins and history, panegyrics praising the gods, liturgical poems describing rites, and every other kind of hymn. Although later tradition tells of several Rigvedic schools, only one recension, that of the Śākala school, is preserved. The very numerous citations of Ṛigvedic hymns in other texts betray marked variants, but these only serve to confirm the validity of the vulgate text.

The *Yajurveda* is the assembly of sacrificial formulae (*yajus*). Of this there are five recensions or collections (*samhita*), four (*Kāṭhaka*, *Kapiṣṭhala*, *Maitrāyaṇī*, and *Taittirīya*) representing the so-called 'black' *Yajurveda* with the sacred formulae interspersed with glosses in prose, and the fifth (*Vājasa-neyi* with its two sub-recensions) being the 'white' *Yajurveda* whose text is free from contamination by glosses. As a literary document the *Yajurveda* is certainly inferior to the *Ṛigveda*. Its original elements, in contrast with the composition of its elder sister, are represented precisely by the *yajus*, which are mainly in prose and are arid formulae without any marked character.

The *Samaveda* is the collection of *saman* or melodies, and is therefore a manual of sacred song. There are three extant recensions of it (*Kauthuma*, *Jaiminīya*, and *Rāṇayanīya*); the songs are mostly lifted from the *Ṛigveda*, and the choice has been made mainly from a practical musical standpoint; in other words verses have been selected which could serve as the base (*yoni*) of a melody. The original musical notation has, however, disappeared; we shall have something further to say of the later notation preserved by the commentators.

The *Atharvaveda* is a collection of magical formulae and is markedly different from the other three *Veda*, both in religious outlook and in literary form. It is preserved in two recensions (*Śaunaka* and *Paippalāda*) which show significant divergences from one another; the text has come down to us much less pure than that of the *Ṛigveda*. Most interesting from the religious and ethnological standpoints, this collection is much less so on stylistic grounds. Yet it has been fairly observed that although the language is distinctly later than that of the *Ṛigveda*, the style, with its alliterations, repetitions, and assonances, gives an impression of being more archaic than that of the other text. In this way its chronology can be deduced: the formulae are very ancient, mainly contemporary with the *Ṛigveda*, but they have been modernized and collected at a much later date.

Attached to the four sacred *Veda* is a vast mass of literature varying from straightforward exegesis to very special studies of a theoretical kind, which can only by an effort be related to the *Veda*—and then simply in a formal sense. Among this Late Vedic literature, which until we reach the *Upaniṣad* is exclusively sacerdotal and anonymous, the earliest productions are the *Brāhmaṇas*, liturgies mixed with liturgical exegesis, all written in prose. A substantial number of these are extant, divided into four groups in accordance with the connection between each text and one of the four Vedic *samhita*. The most important is the *Śatapatha Brāhmaṇa* (formally linked with the white *Yajurveda*), which contains speculation and myth of a remarkable kind. The style of the *Brāhmaṇas* is dry and exceptionally monotonous. These explanations of the significance and order of sacrifice are abstruse and often tortuous; they offer little possibility for any style not purely didactic and scholastic. Once again the chronology of the *Brāhmaṇas* can only be relative, but it is a reasonable hypothesis that the bulk of these works goes back to the first quarter of the first millennium BC.

The *Brāhmanas* are followed by the *Āranyakas*, mixtures of Vedic formulae and commentaries of a kind similar to that found in the *Brāhmanas*. Their content is very uneven, and their importance in the history of Indian literature is secondary.

With the *Upaniṣad* we have already emerged from the Vedic field, even though tradition wants to impose an artificial connection which by now has lost all meaning. The *Upaniṣad* are mainly short texts of a philosophical or semi-philosophical nature, with less emphasis on the religious element. They do not actually entail a complete break with the past, since some parts of the *Śatapatha Brāhmaṇa* are already pointing to the trend of thought they contain. The principal *Upaniṣad* are fourteen in number. The oldest among them are relatively long, written in prose interspersed with pieces of verse: instances are the *Bṛhadāraṇyaka* and the *Chāndogya*, which are closely connected with the *Brāhmaṇas*. Slightly later and much shorter is the *Aitareya*, and then a group comprising the *Kauṣītaki*, the *Kena*, and the *Taittirīya*. Their pithy style, packed with thought and also rich in lofty images and vivid comparisons, is one of the finest to be found in Indian literature. To a markedly different group, generally of later date, belong the *Upaniṣad* in verse, the language of which is by now far enough removed from that of the Vedic to be classed as a pre-classical Sanskrit. But in style the poetry of this group lacks unity, sequence, and homogeneity. The main texts are the *Kāṭhaka*, *Śvetāśvatara*, *Muṇḍaka*, and *Praśna*; and to them is attached a small, slightly later group, written in prose, the *Māṇḍūkya* and the *Maitrāyaṇīya*. Here too the chronology is difficult to tie down. The oldest *Upaniṣad* are certainly pre-Buddhist, but with the group of the verse *Upaniṣad* we reach a period and a society not far away from the Buddhists which takes us to about 500 BC. The most striking feature of this literature is something we have already mentioned, namely that it is not exclusively Brahmanic, written by Brahmans and addressed to the same class. All of it—but particularly the verse *Upaniṣad* —is sharply distinguishable from Vedic literature, and comes from circles in which the *Kṣattriya* were concerning themselves with religious questions and in which the Brahmans themselves were taking account of new problems and not simply of ritual. The audience was much wider than the Brahmanic conventicles and liturgical schools. Perhaps the direct contribution of the *Kṣattriya*, in contrast to what we may call the liberal Brahmans, should not be overestimated; all we can say with certainty is that the Brahmanic monopoly has been broken by the appearance of new ideas, a new style, and almost beyond new men. Whatever the exact story, these thinkers unquestionably mark a step forward, not only in religion but in literature too, on the road leading to a modification of Aryan traditions by the autochthonous substratum of India.

c. *Formation of the Old Testament*

There are two essential problems about the formation of the Old Testament, one concerned with the composition of the different books, the other with their transmission. To take the latter and more restricted subject first, it is enough to note that, apart from the manuscripts recently discovered in the Judah desert, we have no very early documents which have preserved the primitive redactions of the various texts. Consequently we can get no farther back than the Massoretic recension, which (as is generally known) takes us to a period between the sixth and eleventh centuries AD and was concerned with establishing the traditional pronunciation by inserting vowels in the text and adding certain notes and variant readings. Collation with brief passages preserved in patristic writings throws some degree of light on the early versions, but such opportunities are few. Another valuable point of comparison is offered by the Greek and Syriac translations of the Hebrew books, which were undoubtedly made from texts different from the Massoretic, although our knowledge of them is inadequate to allow us to reconstruct what is lost.

Yet other difficulties arise when we ask how the various books were transcribed in the period immediately following their composition, before we get to the point at which the text has clearly attained a uniform pattern and been fixed in the shape which (apart from variations due to accident) was later stereotyped by the Massoretic editors: this latter stage was reached in the second century AD. We can start with the period when the Temple and Jerusalem were destroyed by Nebuchadnezzar II, a period which followed some time after that of Manasseh's reign during which Yahwist religion suffered unparalleled contamination from syncretism with foreign cults. On occasions such as these a portion of the sacred books got lost, and the textual tradition became very complicated and obscure. To Ezra, whose activity began probably in 398 BC, belongs the credit for the laborious task, carried out along with his restoration of the cult, of seeing that order was restored to the sacred writings and that correct readings were inserted. Tradition ascribed to him many later achievements which were not his doing, but it is certain that intense work was carried out on the texts during this period and in that which followed, with the object of reassembling and rescuing the ancient cultural heritage of the nation. Such alterations, transpositions, and additions as can be shown to have taken place in the intervening years did not modify the substance of the earlier biblical stories, nor did they introduce any mistakes which were either serious or irreparable.

Which, however, were the books already composed by that time, and which were added later to make up the officially recognized 'canon' of the *Old Testament*? This is where our inquiry shifts to the former of the two problems outlined above.

We know that today the books of the Bible are arranged practically in the order corresponding to the chronology of the events they narrate. The sources of information vary in character and in volume, but in general they were such as to provide an agreed reconstruction of the various phases of Hebrew history in a sufficiently detailed and precise form. The question, however, is whether these writings were composed in the order in which they are now found. This is of particular interest in relation to the *Pentateuch*, which concerns the earliest and most obscure period of Hebrew life, dealing rapidly with the various patriarchs and then dwelling at length on the figure of Moses and the vicissitudes of the people down to the point at which they stood on the threshold of the Promised Land. The theory of G. Wellhausen, which has dominated criticism on this point for a long time past, tended to bring down sharply the date at which these books were compiled, and to regard them as a heap of heterogeneous elements, different in language, conception, and tone, and derived from a multiplicity of sources, which biblical scholars have tracked down with great erudition and acumen. Today, however, many of the assumptions behind this school of criticism have been seriously upset by the wealth of archaeological finds and by a wider knowledge of the adjacent countries, making it possible to establish successful comparisons with the writings and traditions of other peoples. These have irrefutably proved the truth of many statements in the *Pentateuch* which had hitherto been rejected or doubted, and the logical implication has been that the composition of the *Pentateuch* text was a much earlier and more highly organized affair than was previously supposed.

This is not to say that the compilation is to be attributed to Moses in person. Not only can we securely show the existence and employment of earlier sources, but we can also prove later modifications and additions; in the legislative section, for example, and in the historical narrative, too, we can see a progressive development due to the social and religious conditions of later times. It remains true, however, that at the time when Israel first became a people—a moment at which the figure of Moses, as organizer and leader, was undoubtedly dominating the stage—there was formed the nucleus and the substance of the traditions which later came together in the *Pentateuch*. The work can therefore be called Mosaic in origin, even if it will always be futile to attempt precision about the extent of the original version or to determine how the various traditions and collections of laws found their way into the form in which the text exists today. Under the impact of new needs and of new circumstances in their life and culture, the Hebrews made many advances from the religious position established in the Mosaic period, but for all of them the ancient Hebrew leader can be called responsible, for his personality had made an indelible mark on his people. It may be that a middle position of this kind will enable the various schools of criticism to find common ground on which can be undertaken new and fruitful work of exegesis on these writings, which have been the spiritual food of so large a section of mankind.

What we have so far called the *Pentateuch*—a word literally meaning five 'cases', and indicating the way in which the book-rolls read at meetings were kept—was called by the Hebrews 'the Law' *par excellence*. It formed the first and more important part of their biblical canon, and the Law was sometimes used to indicate the whole corpus of inspired books. The second part comprises 'the Prophets', divided into earlier (*Joshua, Judges, Samuel* and *Kings*[1]) and later (*Isaiah, Jeremiah, Ezekiel*, and twelve minor prophets included in a single book). The assembly of this material was slower and on the whole later than the compilation of the Law; and though some prophets looked after the arrangement of their own writings, the work of others certainly underwent revision at a later date. In addition the transmission of the text has been complicated, since some portions have come down only in the Greek translation, in which additions were not seldom inserted.

The last part of the Hebrew Bible comprises the 'Writings' or 'Hagiographies', namely *Psalms, Proverbs, Job, Ruth*, the *Song of Songs, Ecclesiastes, Lamentations, Esther, Daniel, Ezra* and *Nehemiah*, and *Chronicles* (Books I and II of the *Paralipomena*). Since Hebrew orthodoxy held that the Bible canon had been definitely closed at the time of Ezra (see above), there was no place in it for certain later works written in Greek, such as *Tobit, Judith, Wisdom, Ecclesiastes, Ecclesiasticus, Baruch, Maccabees*, and some chapters of *Esther* and *Daniel*, although these are accepted by Catholics. Moreover the distribution of the material is different in the two canons, and the order of the books varies considerably. There has been prolonged controversy about these works—called deutero-canonical—but it does not concern our question. We should, however, mention the numerous 'apocryphal' writings which had a particular vogue in the closing days of Judaism and which have been important historically; they have revealed much about the environment which produced them and have had great influence upon later literature.

Hebrew historiography has been entirely dominated by a religious ideal. In telling the story of their nation its writers were moved neither by scholarly interest nor by the desire to praise one or another ruler. The objectives always before them were twofold. First and foremost they aimed to show the will of God in these events, to reveal the providential design which made a unity of them, to exalt the glories of the Lord, and to make clear the power he wielded against any enemy who came against him. Secondly they wanted to admonish their co-religionists, to teach them their duty, and to make them understand present events in the light of their knowledge of what had happened in the past.

Consequently their theory of history was not, as among other peoples, based upon cycles, in which things perennially recurred without advance or progress. It was an open and confident theory, whose upholders believed in the action of God and of Man, and had unquestioning faith in the victory of the good. But from these premises was derived also a tendency which is very evident among Hebrew historical writers, that of raising their work to the level at which it became a philosophy of history, in fact ultimately a teleological theory, since everything was viewed in religious terms and explained on the strength of divine revelation.

The Hebrews made history an important element in their belief, since only in history was their God made manifest. To put it another way, historical events allowed them to demonstrate—or so they thought—the truth of their convictions about their people's mission, and the certainty of their Lord's power. This was their bank of proofs, without which Hebrew religion would have lacked solidity and shape for the future.

The keen desire to possess their own account of their own history, in the fullest detail, led the Hebrews in time to collect abundant material, which they preserved, amplified, and transmitted to succeeding generations. So there was created a heritage of chronicles and other stories, which constitute a valuable source of information although it naturally has to be used with caution. Above all the reader must separate off the sections which are simply additions or pictures designed to highlight the religious aspect, the intervention of Yahweh, and so on; in addition he must bear in mind the particular artistic form used in these writings, together with such features as mnemonic devices, rhetorical ornaments, and poetical expression.

The Hebrew historian was much less concerned to reproduce past events with scrupulous accuracy than to draw a moral from these events, and therefore to dramatize a fact in order to achieve greater effect upon the reader. This accounts for the large gaps, the inconsistencies in chronology, the metaphors and stylistic tricks, all of which form part of a conscious literary process.

Writings of the 'wisdom' type are undoubtedly found in all Eastern literature, but in Israel they reached their highest point of development only in the period after the Exile. They are an epilogue in the evolution of biblical thought: indeed some of them are not even accepted into the Hebrew canon because they were composed so late and are very markedly influenced by the ideas of societies outside Palestine. Their recurrent theme, which they went on enunciating with relentless emphasis, was the meaning of man's existence and the duty required of him to live a good life, despite the suffering and passion to which he is subject. The objective of these works is therefore ethical rather than intellectual, and their portrait of the wise man is not so much of a man of learning as of a person who knows how to behave rightly, in the fear of God. In addition great importance necessarily attaches to the problem of pain and punishment; moreover an attempt is often made to personify Wisdom itself, regarded as the chief among all the attributes of God, and language is used which is unfamiliar in the other Old Testament books.

It is easy to find didactic passages in all biblical literature, but this branch of letters is most clearly represented by *Proverbs*, *Job*, *Ecclesiastes*, *Ecclesiasticus*, and *Wisdom*. The fundamental feature of the genre is its use of parallelism to express moral maxims, but often the whole story is spun out into a parable or allegory, in order to pose—and sometimes to offer a solution of—grave speculative or ethical questions.

Probably only a small portion of the large collection called the 'Proverbs of Solomon' goes back to that king, who in Hebrew tradition was regarded as the wise and just man *par excellence*. The remainder is the work of later but unknown authors, and the book is now composed of nine sets of gnomic sayings and sentences, which are unduly influenced by Egyptian thought (especially the writing of Amenhotep described below) and set forth an excessively utilitarian ethic, essentially directed to the attainment of happiness and earthly success. Yet wise counsels are not wholly lacking, and there are many fine pages, such as the warm eulogy of the virtuous and industrious woman. Owing to the multiplicity of separate sections which go to compose the text, there is marked variety between the different editions; and there are quite a number of differences between the original Hebrew and the Greek version of the Seventy.

The *Book of Job* is a literary masterpiece even when judged by world standards. In poetry of the most exalted kind it attempts to answer the eternal question why the just man suffers without having sinned, if it be not that God, the source and measure of all justice, bears responsibility. The problem is not solved, but the interesting points are the narrative movement of the composition and the large number of detailed considerations which are handled. Historically it is of some importance that we find connections with Accadian wisdom literature, and that the leading figure is presented not as a Hebrew but as an Arab sheik. Views about the date of composition vary between the period of the Captivity and 400 BC, and it is not impossible that the closing chapters are a later addition.

There is some resemblance to *Job* in *Ecclesiastes*—the Greek name used to translate the Hebrew term for a chairman of a public meeting. Unlike *Job*, however, the latter work is not a dialogue, but a collection of observations with no one logical thread running through them, all of them tinged with a vein of deep scepticism, not entirely free from a form of hedonism. By a very common literary fiction the author presents himself as a son of David, and has therefore been identified with Solomon; but internal and stylistic grounds make this identification quite impossible, given that the book was composed about the end of the third century BC by a 'wise man' who knew of the currents of thought being evolved at that time in non-Hebrew circles.

The title *Ecclesiasticus* is given in the Vulgate to a work which in Hebrew may have been a second book called Proverbs and in Greek was entitled 'Wisdom of Jesus son of Sirach'. In the course of his writing the author provides various autobiographical information, from which it appears that he was an inhabitant of Jerusalem, cultivated and well-to-do, who composed his book in the first two decades of the second century BC. He presents a panorama of Israelitish moral and religious duties and also develops his historical theme, the so-called Praise of the ancient patriarchs designed to exalt *Old Testament* heroes. But his main purpose was to inculcate fidelity to the Law. A large portion of the Hebrew text was discovered at the end of the last century on manuscripts preserved in the storehouse belonging to the Cairo synagogue; and this proves that the book, even if not accepted by the Hebrews of Palestine, was none the less recognized by those in Egypt. But for this work too the problems raised by the editorship and the relations between the various versions are extremely complex.

The latest canonical book in the *Old Testament* is *Wisdom*, written in Greek by a Hellenized Hebrew who lived in Egypt in the first century BC. By the well-known literary fiction the author put out his work under the name of Solomon, but he makes no pretence that he is really to be regarded as such. His purpose was to rescue his co-religionists from the perils of idolatry and to comfort them in their difficulties. Terms belonging to Greek culture are found in abundance, but the lines of thought are in conformity with biblical tradition: of especial note is the advance made in the doctrine of an after-life.

Among the various types of poetry which undoubtedly flourished among the Hebrews from the earliest times, the only ones preserved in the Bible are those linked most closely with the teaching of religion or forms of worship, and those of a lyrical or 'wisdom' character—the last two types cannot be firmly distinguished because there is continual overlapping between them. But what we have is already more than adequate to allow appreciation of Hebrew poetry and a description of the characteristic patterns, although many problems still remain open to discussion and may be insoluble in the present state of our knowledge. It is certain that an essential element was the so-called Law of Parallelism, implying the enunciation of an idea through various parallel concepts, generally forming a couplet in which the two lines composing a verse corresponded one to the other. Either the idea was repeated in similar words (synonymous parallelism); or it was made clearer by a contrasting sentence (antithetic parallelism, the commonest form); or again it was developed by dependent propositions (synthetic or progressive parallelism). A similar scheme can be found in the literatures of other Semitic peoples.

What we cannot yet understand is what technique of rhythm regulated Hebrew poetry, other than the logical technique just explained. We do not know whether the harmony of the verse was provided by the length or quantity of the syllables, or by the number of stresses or accents; and the system of strophes, which must have existed, is entirely obscure. This is sad, but it is easily understandable when we remember the vicissitudes undergone by these texts before they attained their present form, and also the various methods followed to transcribe them phonetically. Earlier paragraphs have described the prophetic and didactic books, in which the poetical sections are substantial and important. Other specimens of Hebrew poetry include blessings (for instance of wives and mothers), warlike exhortations (the victory song of Deborah in *Judges* v is full of fine epic phrases),[2] elegies (lamentations), and songs of thanksgiving. But mention must above all be made of the *Psalms* (or Book of Praise) and the *Song of Songs* (the superlative title given to the most sublime song of all).

The *Psalms* are a collection of about 150 hymns which were sung with musical accompaniment (whence the Greek word *psalmos*). In all of them religious sentiment is extremely keen, but there is considerable variation in the themes, which has allowed later scholars to construct regular systems of classification, often excessively complicated. The psalter as we have it was undoubtedly composed over a long period; and though some portions may go back to very early times, it only achieved a definite form after the days of Ezra and Nehemiah. But it is an exaggerated view which treats almost all the psalms as post-Captivity or really late, although some certainly refer to events of the period of the Maccabees. A fair number may reasonably be attributed to King David, since the general reorganization of the cult which he certainly promoted was favourable to the development of music and of songs composed for collective prayer and other liturgical uses; but if we trusted the titles prefixed to each psalm, which are ancient enough to carry weight though they are not actually authentic, we should have a number varying (according to the different versions) from 70 to 85, and this is too high. We need not dwell on the diverse systems of numbering and the various divisions of the collection which have been put forward from ancient to quite modern times; and there is no help to be gained from the names of authors indicated in the titles mentioned a moment ago (they may well be the names of persons who compiled the first incomplete collections).

The simplest in structure are the hymns about God and about his works in nature and in history; they have little psychological interest, but are rich in lyric poetry, and from the religious standpoint they are the least committed. Apart from these, a fair number of psalms are devoted to lamentations both individual and public, and an equal number to thanksgiving, expressing joy for the realization of something which had been requested in imploring language in the opening verses. Some psalms are relatively didactic in character, others again have a prophetic or eschatological tone, sometimes with quite explicit references to the Messiah. In all these poems we meet precise rules of composition corresponding to the literary genre which has been followed. Apart from their artistic merit, which is remarkable and can easily be recognized by any reader, the *Psalms* contain thought which reflects the most widely accepted Hebrew ideas about the justice of God, retribution for human actions, the destiny of the Chosen People, the many ways of backsliding into irreligion, and the like.

The *Song of Songs* does not fit into any of the usual classifications of literary genres, and this may be the reason why there have been so many interpretations of its content—collections of love songs, pastoral drama, praise of marriage, a close pact between God and the Hebrews, and so on. But what matters is that this short composition is a work of the highest poetry and of stupendous literary beauty, written just before the Captivity or perhaps just after it (linguistic grounds make the latter hypothesis more likely, while the loftiness of inspiration suggests the former). It is in dialogue form, which reminds one of the 'Disputes of Lovers', well known in the literature of so many peoples.

d. *Egypt*

Literary activity in Egypt was principally concerned in our period with the production of religious texts, including some in demotic. These included hymns to the gods, lamentations of Isis over the corpse of Osiris, funeral liturgies pregnant with magical formulae, and glosses, the meaning of which is not always clear to us, on the *Book of the Dead* or the *Book of Breathing*. In epic genre we have fragments of the cycle known as the *Petubastic Saga*, recording the wars between Egypt and Assyria with heroic episodes and heroic style.

Stories of a mixed variety, neither purely historical nor definitely imaginary and romantic, have been found on a text full of lacunae, in which the Theban Wenamūn (Twenty-first Dynasty) tells his adventures after he had been sent to Syria on a Phoenician ship to get timber for the barque of Ammon. Before he landed at Byblos his goods were plundered, but he restored his fortunes by robbing the native inhabitants; for this he was in danger of not being received by the king of the city, until a courtier who was a catechumen of Ammon interceded on his behalf. By playing up the importance of Ammon and providing guarantees he succeeded with difficulty in obtaining the timber he wanted. But when he left the harbour he was attacked by the people he had robbed, and was only saved by a storm, which cast him up on Cyprus. The work breaks off in the middle of a dialogue with a Cypriot queen.

Two other works of fiction have as their chief figures Khaemwēse, the fabulous magician who was the son of Ramses II, and Khaemwēse's son who was a magician too. The father had managed to procure a book enabling him to understand the speech of animals and to see the gods; the son was engaged in conflict with magicians throughout his various reincarnations, which allowed him to visit the underworld and see the rewards and punishments given to the souls of the dead.

A new group of 'silent sages', content with their lot and living a life apart from the world, are found in the various collections of maxims, of which the teaching of Amenhotep (Twentieth and Twenty-first Dynasties) is an example. These contain a series of didactic proverbs, teaching one not to oppress the poor, make friends with hot-tempered men, remove boundary stones, aspire to riches, and so on. The analogy with Hebrew precepts, for instance *Proverbs* 22–3, is extremely curious, and too close to be accidental.

For various reasons the Hebrew work is more likely to derive from the Egyptian than the Egyptian from the Hebrew.

Among lyrical works certain inspired love poems are worthy of note, together with a hymn in praise of death, and a number of funerary epigrams in verse.

e. Assyria

The greatest period of Assyrian literary culture was probably reached under Ashur-banipal (669–626 BC). By good fortune a large part of his library has been found collected in the palaces of Nineveh; in it the king had brought together everything surviving from Mesopotamian literature back to the earliest Sumerian times, and had told his scribes to make transcriptions of documents from every source. These works were copied on to innumerable terracotta tablets, with a mark to indicate the tablet number belonging to the original work, and others showing whence it came and to what literary genre it belonged. Other texts have come down to us on metal plates and on flat pieces of stone. Like the other departments of their life, including their science, which had practical rather than theoretical aims, Mesopotamian literature was traditionalist and static, and the same sort of thing got reproduced over thousands of years. Assyrian texts derive not only from the Babylonian period, but even from Sumerian prototypes. The scribes in the temple schools, who transcribed or translated the texts, allowed themselves little freedom: some change of wording, a few glosses, and an occasional note of 'ul idi' (I don't know) on illegible passages. It is rarely that, as on historical inscriptions, Assyrian work assumes any features which are original or peculiar.

So the Assyrian still handed down mythological poems which went back to the Sumerians, such as the Poem of Creation (*Enuna Eliah*) in seven cantos of rhythmic verse rich in alliteration; and there were half-mythical epics like the poem of Gilgamesh, twelve rhythmic cantos in praise of the beings known as the 'Mesopotamian Dioscuri'.

They also transcribed and sometimes imitated the ancient Sumerian or Accadian Hymns to the Gods, which often contained fine poetry like the *Hymn to the Sun*. They had 'penitential psalms' like those of the Hebrews in which the writer, often the king, would confess his sins and his moral misery. Then there were the 'purificatory prayers', of which the *Lamentations of King Ashur-banipal to the Goddess Ninlil* are outstanding examples.

There are many oracular texts, some of which derive from Kings Esarhaddon and Ashur-banipal. Among them we may note requests to the god for counsel about military expeditions, sieges, the choice of magistrates, and so on, with the divine answers attached to each. There are quite a few ritual writings for use by the priests in every kind of rite and ceremony; and there are countless augural texts, especially for use in hepatoscopy (these are sometimes inscribed on a model of a liver), which show what might happen if the particular features indicated were encountered in the entrails of the sacrificial animal.

Other types of writing include incantations, which show first the ill afflicting the author and the demon causing it, then the rites he must perform, and finally the curse he must utter. With these go 'liftings of hands', which are prayers in misfortune (*shú-íla*); 'kindlings', or rites designed to destroy witchcraft by fire; and other utterances directed against fevers, headaches, and so on.

In writings of the chronicle or semi-historical type there is a clear contrast between the Assyrian period and those which preceded it. In earlier days the inscriptions of kings, if they were not limited to the king's name and some mention of his ancestry, were normally concerned with the construction of temples, canals, and the like, rather than with war. Under the Assyrian kings the long inscriptions on cylinders or prisms are intended more as boastful propaganda than as historical evidence. Year after year they tell of military exploits, with grandiloquent and cruel details of slaughter, often no doubt including exaggeration about Assyrian victories and other peoples' defeats. Sometimes the record is divided into different areas of action; sometimes it tells also of building works. A few texts of Ashur-banipal have real literary merit. Some inscriptions, generally called the Synchronous History, and mainly composed on the occasion of a treaty with foreign peoples to deal with boundary questions, give lists of warlike operations and earlier treaties; others preserve lists of kings with their genealogies, providing chronological data together with information about a king's death and place of burial, or sometimes lists of eponymous officials.

There is, of course, no literary value in the legal and economic texts, including the laws themselves. Of varying merit are the numerous public and private letters, a few fables, and occasional collections of proverbs and moral maxims. Then there is a considerable output, mainly unoriginal, on science, or rather on the practical application of various sciences, including philology, grammar, mathematics, geometry, geography, medicine, chemistry, botany, and zoology. Of these mention has been made in Chapter III.

f. *Phoenician and Carthaginian Literature*

Practically no Phoenician literature survives from this period, since the religious poems and poems of creation found at Ugarit are considerably earlier. All we have amounts to a few annalistic fragments, and an occasional inscription, generally short: even on law and economics we possess too little evidence. The view of V. Bérard that there was a periegetic work illustrating the Mediterranean coast, which he conceived to be a source of information for the Homeric epic, is pure hypothesis, and we cannot accept it.

Again, we know very little about literary output at Carthage. Our knowledge is limited to two works on travels both written between 550 and 480 (see p. 142, and Pliny, *N.H.*, II, 169, '*Carthaginis potentia florente*'), by Hanno who explored the Atlantic coast of Africa, and Himilco who did the same on the coast of Europe. We possess Hanno's work in a Greek translation which appears to belong to the fourth century BC; a Greek translation of Himilco also existed, perhaps written about 400, and was used very much later by Avienus for his *Ora Maritima*.

There is no reason to think that any significant number of the works found in the library at Carthage by the Romans in 146 BC (Pliny, XVIII, 22) went back to the period before 500 BC, rather than being writings of the fifth to second centuries. We shall deal later with Mago's famous book on agriculture.

g. *Persia*

Only two kinds of Persian text have come down to us, commemorative inscriptions and religious writings; but it may be presumed that other kinds existed. Athenaeus, for example (XIII, 25), records a graceful story about Odati and Zariadre; and scientific writing can hardly have been lacking.

Commemorative inscriptions must have been fairly numerous; and indirectly they were certainly a source for the information about Medo-Persian kings provided by Greek writers, such as Herodotus, Ctesias, and Chares. A short inscription in three languages was found in the palace of Cyrus (558–529) at Pasargadae; and Strabo, XV, p. 730, tells of another on Cyrus' tomb. On the other hand the texts on two gold plates which purport to derive from the parents of Cyrus the Great are forgeries, probably of the time of Artaxerxes II. The most noteworthy inscriptions concern Darius I (521–486), in the first place a relatively long one accompanied by reliefs, which can be admired on a crag at Bīsutūn. This must surely have had religious rather than propaganda purposes, because from 300 feet below it is practically impossible to read. It has two versions, composed in a variety of Persian, Accadian, and Elamite languages; and in epic tones it first recounts the events of the struggle against the usurper Gaumata, which brought Darius to the throne, then lists the king's military achievements, and concludes with a prayer to later generations to treat the inscription with respect (as they did down to the last war). Another inscription of Darius is cut on the rock tomb of Naqsh-i-Rustem, on which the king starts with his profession of faith, and then lists the countries he had conquered while the monument was being presented to its readers. The palace at Susa has another commemorative inscription, enumerating the materials used by artists of various nations in its construction, and there is yet another recording the canal dug between the Red Sea and the Mediterranean.

In the *Avesta* are preserved certain documents of a religious nature. Parts of them indeed, the *Yašt*, may go back to ancient cults before the introduction of Zoroastrianism. The *Gātha* are written in archaic language, and may preserve poetical summaries of Zarathustra's soliloquies, or possibly pieces which were inserted from the start between the narrative sections; their tone is lofty, but they are not easy to interpret. The remainder of the *Avesta* is a single section of a large work originally comprising twenty-one *nask* (pages), put together by the priestly class and bearing on liturgy and ritual. The language is of later date than that used in the *Gātha*. In the present writer's view this whole work, in all its parts, was transmitted by word of mouth over centuries and was only written down in an authoritative version in Parthian times. At the best there can have been a series of versions, each one containing revisions of the last.

h. *Greek Literature*

The Epic. In the Greek world religious songs and epic first evolved at the same time. The religious songs created the myths and made them known, some of them being naïve rationalizations, others subtle allegories, others again fantastic inventions with a romantic background. All such myths contributed markedly to the humanization of the gods, who were conceived in the guise of princes on earth; and the myths also promoted syncretism of a kind which gave more flesh and blood to all the major deities.

The Homeric poems constantly allude to prayers, vows, and hymns to the gods and to the dead; also to mythical stories, known to the readers, about the Amazons, the Argonauts, the Centaurs, and the Lapiths. Moreover in *Odyssey* VIII the very human episode of the loves of Ares and Aphrodite is given full rein. The thirty-four surviving 'Homeric Hymns' may give us some idea of this religious literature. It seems clear, however, that from the start there existed regular cycles of religious poems: for instance about the struggle of the Danaoi, spirits of clouds, against the Lukioi, spirits of light; or the rape of Helen (Selene, the Moon) by a divine lover (the New Moon), and her rescue by a couple of young gods; only later were these two stories localized on earth, and then merged into the epic lays about the conquest of Troy.

For parallel with the religious songs there were growing up poems which were genuinely epic, and which preserved a record in verse of adventurous enterprises, accomplished in a period of history which was regarded as paramountly the epic period. It was in fact the time when, under assault by bold parties of Greeks, the fortresses and cities of pre-Greek peoples had fallen one after another into the invader's hands: the Minoan cities of Crete, the Cycladic in the Aegean islands, the Anatolian cities facing the Aegean Sea from Aeolis to Doris and farther east as far as Pamphylia, Cyprus, and the coast of Syria. Moreover the exploits of the new cities, which had to form federations to combat the original inhabitants, seemed so important that they were recorded not only in Greek writings but in works written by foreigners. There is no doubting the evidence that an ancient epic of genuine Greek origin was in existence before the Homeric poems. Examination of the *Iliad* shows accomplished rules of metre, virtuosity of style, a hybrid language of literary type corresponding to no dialect that was actually spoken, and the use of concepts and terms which had become fossilized in the language and were no longer understood. Every one of these factors seems to make it certain that this particular literary genre had already undergone a long process of development. The same is indicated by the assumption in the poem that its audience knew, without being told, both the personages of the action and the events of the ten years of war, although the poem itself deals only with a short period in the tenth year. Indeed in the *Iliad*, the *Odyssey*, and the cyclic poems we find evidence that a story in an earlier epic is presupposed. In this two heroes from north-east Greece, Achilles and Odysseus, were leaders in the conquest of twelve maritime and eleven inland cities (Troy being simply the twelfth of the latter); and all were in the area of the later Aeolic colonies, which were precisely divided into groups of twelve and settled from north-east Greece.

Yet the *Iliad* as we have it was composed in Ionia, and is no longer a straightforward epic of the kind its Aeolic model must have been. Instead it is a mixture of epic and romance, and is concerned not with the conquest of a country but with the fictitious recovery of a woman. This is because epic subjects have been fused with the mythical topics of which we spoke just now, and the fusion has created a new kind of poem. In fact while epic originally aimed at glorifying real persons who had been deified, the mythical poems were concerned with gods who had been brought down to the level of heroes, and who behaved accordingly. The deeds of heroic mortals, aided by the divinities whose progeny they were said to be, were mingled with humanized gods; and in the outcome a poet would sing at one and the same time of great kings of old, divine 'shepherds of peoples', of local heroes, and of gods in human shape, all three being mixed together in the same story.

We know something of the life of the bards, for references to them in the *Odyssey* are clear enough: they seem to have been markedly different from the 'rhapsodes' who followed them, and from the medieval troubadours. Each had a permanent position at one of the many courts, so clearly they could only give pleasure to their audiences if they added continually to their repertoires, which came to comprise both familiar stories and also novelties. A bard would recite songs he had heard, and add others of his own composition; he would repeat old stories if his audience asked for them, and also follow his own fancy in singing of new ones. In a single performance the bard Demodocus is said in *Odyssey* VIII to have sung in turn of the quarrel between Odysseus and Achilles, the loves of Aphrodite and Ares, and the stratagem of the wooden horse.

Clearly then every bard would inherit something from his predecessors, introduce changes of his own, and make additions. The transmission from bard to bard was partly through word of mouth and partly (from the eighth century onwards) in writing; it may be that there came into being written summaries or skeletons, which each singer could fill out in his own way. In one place (*Odyssey*, VIII, 481) the poem represents the bards as being joined together by mutual ties—a band of men beloved of the Muses—and naturally the repertoire of a singer would pass from father to son and from master to pupil. Our sources tell us of a *genos* on the island of Chios who called themselves Homeridai: they were said to be descendants of Homer and handed down songs from generation to generation. It is on these lines that we must look for the most probable explanation of the way all the Homeric poems took shape; for without losing their organic conception they reflect in their different portions a great diversity of periods and ideas, or perhaps one should rather describe them as reflecting a whole process of evolution.

The way in which the poems took on repeated elaborations and additions becomes obvious if we look at the episodic character of both *Iliad* and *Odyssey* and at the continual breaks in the main stories. In the *Iliad* certain portions stand out as the most perfect and noble; their forms, artistic methods, and means of achieving effect all display similar features; and together they constitute a complete and logical series of basic episodes. These are the wrath of Achilles (I), the unsuccessful attempt of Agamemnon to fight without him (XI), the death of Patroclus (XVI), the reconciliation of Achilles with Agamemnon (beginning of XVII), and the death of Hector (XXII). These may be attributed to 'Homer', or at any rate to the founder of the Homeridai, the greatest of them all. All the rest is composed of episodes which have been inserted or added, some of them linked together in a chain, and most of them slowing up the action as it was conceived by the first bard. Here then there have been later revisions and more than one general plan: we can tell that from the plot, the style, the artistic technique, and the reminiscences of the earlier lays, reminiscences which sometimes become regular refrains. Similarly the *Odyssey* was certainly not conceived at a single time. There are too many subsidiary sections retarding the action; more-over the *Telemachia* (I–IV) was quite obviously an addition, and the second *Nekyia* (XXIV) is clearly late and derivative. If we disregard interpolations and minor traces of touching up by later hands, we get the broad impression that the poem was created at three main periods: from the first we have the story of Odysseus' adventurous journeys; in the second was added his arrival in Ithaca and the revenge taken on the Suitors; and lastly the *Tele-machia* reflects a later desire to give the 'Return' of Odysseus its place among the Returns of the other Greek heroes. But even the section which appears to be earliest, that dealing with the hero's journeys, shows clearly a sudden switch from the Black Sea to the waters round Sicily and Italy; and there are other signs of addition and revision.

As a whole the *Iliad* and *Odyssey* are trying to depict two periods of Greek colonization which were far apart in time: the period when the Greeks established themselves on the seaboard of Asia Minor in the fourteenth to tenth centuries BC after they had destroyed the native cities, and the period of the pre-colonial voyages in the farthest parts of the north-east and north-west, the voyages which gave rise to the eighth-century foundations. But in particular sections the contradictions are immense; and they are not just the product of fiction, since they correspond to different actual points in the history of culture and events. For example Ilium in the earliest passages is a small city near the sea (compare the excavations at Hissarlik), whose attackers are few in number and its defenders equally so: but in the latest sections it is imagined to be vast, lofty, and far from the sea, defended by the whole barbarian world against an attack by all the Greeks. The historical geography of the *Iliad* and *Odyssey*, in its placing of the various Greek and barbarian states, shows sharp contrasts between different sections; this too is a reflection of actual conditions obtaining in different periods and is not the product of fancy.

The contradictions caused by these earlier and later backgrounds are so marked that if we set out the data of the poems in the right way we can follow all the phases in the cycle of political change—from kingship to the rise to power of the aristocratic landowners, and from the resulting oligarchies to the first struggles preceding the third phase, when wealth had been accumulated mainly by means of piracy and commerce. The poems testify to the early fear of the dangers, real or exaggerated, arising from voyages in distant seas, designed sometimes to barter Greek wares against foodstuffs and raw materials, at other times to engage in raiding and the capture of slaves. Yet we also find references to the successive phases of colonization, the Phaeacians being one example. In contrasting passages of epic we can follow the evolution of religious thought. First a list of principal divinities is grouped around Zeus in a deliberate hierarchy, a process tending in the direction of monotheism. Later there is an attempt to rebut criticism of the excessive humanization of the gods by insistence on their moral nature. A place is found for freedom of the human will, for the beginnings of ethical ideas, and for the birth of philosophical thinking.

The institution of the family, as it evolved over several centuries, is shown us in all its workings—marriage, birth, death, dowries, wills, and so on. Slavery appears in the form both of servants living in the household and of workmen engaged on primitive industries. We can trace the rise of magistracies, tribunals, and the earliest conceptions of law. In warfare, we find the different types of defensive armour which were used in different periods, the large shields giving place to the small round variety; and there are different types of offensive weapons. The fighting by chieftains from chariots in open array against a background of amorphous masses of troops is succeeded by cavalry with the common soldiers grouped in tactical units, and eventually by the phalanx of hoplites found in Tyrtaeus, and with Gyges. For navigation flat-bottomed boats give place to ships with over a hundred rowers.

The changing tastes of the bards' audiences can be seen in a change in the favourite kinds of story. At one time they were bloodthirsty tales of war, then we find adventure stories, then again poems containing dialogues full of human character and finally the main features are highly lyrical passages provoking intimacy of emotion.

In the earliest stages only copper and bronze are used: then we pass to a period in which iron starts as a rarity but soon becomes the dominant metal, although bronze still maintains its use for the more artistic and durable objects. There are sections from which we can deduce the relative value of the precious metals, both to one another and to other goods; and a few passages tell us of the beginning of textile, dyeing, and metalworking operations.

In the contrasting data we can also see passing before our eyes the phases in the development of palaces, houses, walls, shrines (and later of temples with their statues), and finally of irrigation and agricultural works. Funeral rites are shown, first of one kind and then of another. We can see the origin of the Panhellenic games, and the successive stages in the history of dress, furniture, carving, and the goldsmith's art. To say therefore that the *Iliad* and *Odyssey* in their various sections reflect the diversity in the phases of Greek life from *c.*900 to *c.*650 BC is simply to state an incontrovertible fact which should be more widely recognized.

The Rhapsodes: The Epic Cycle and other 'Homeric' Works. When the monarchies fell and after them the possessions of the great aristocratic houses got broken up, the bard who in earlier days had his permanent abode in a palace had to become a 'rhapsode' or wandering singer. He addressed himself to an increasingly varied and numerous public, including more and more of the common people, in the open spaces of cities, at markets and at feasts. It was to the work of these men, and also to the transmission of written texts, that Greece owed the dissemination of the Homeric epic over all the mainland and the colonies as well, partly for the pleasure it gave and partly to give instruction about the past. Its text, now practically established, was like a permanent inheritance in the Greek world, and it provided a perpetual source of evidence for historians and dramatists, as well as for Greek religion and above all for Greek literary language.

The texts of the two poems were now settled, on account of the more elaborate revision which had been devoted to them and because they had a greater reputation and were more perfect than other epics. What remained for the last bards and then for the rhapsodes was the opportunity to take the two great poems as models and so to repeat, recast, and expand all the other lays. Some of these were about Troy, on the first nine years of the war and on the events after the death of Hector; others were on different subjects, starting with the 'Returns' of the heroes, parts of which had been published in earlier times but had been left incomplete and fragmentary, without being made into an organic whole. The events before those treated in the *Iliad* gave material for the *Cypria*, attributed to Hegesias or Stasinus; those after Hector's death were the theme of the *Aethiopis* and the *Iliou Persis* (*Sack of Troy*), attributed to Arctinus, and of the *Little Iliad*, of which Lesches of Mitylene was said to be the author. In the *Nostoi* or *Returns*, on the other hand, Agias of Troezen dealt with the adventurous homecomings of the heroes (apart from Odysseus) from the Trojan War; and in the *Telegonia* Eugammon of Cyrene collected the legends about the deaths of Odysseus and his descendants.

But these poems, better called fictional chronicles in verse, were the works of relatively second-rate artists, and never had a popularity comparable with that of the Homeric poems, although they were used as a source by scholars and artists in later times. The same was true of the similar works which developed other cycles of legends—the *Titanomachia, Oedipodea, Thebais, Amphiarai Exelasis, Epigoni, Alcmaeonis, Minyas, Oechaliae Halosis, Heracleis*, and so on.[3]

But around the Homeric poems there also grew up other types of literature. First there were the 'Homeric Hymns', originally preludes or invocations to the gods, which singers would preface to their recitations. Of these we possess thirty-four, of very varying date and merit.[4] Secondly the ever-growing contrast between men's actual environment and the heroic world idealized by the bards led to parodies of the Homeric poems—the *Margites* (*Simple Simon*), the *Batrachomyomachia* (*Battle of Frogs and Mice*), the *Lawsuit* between Zeus and Hera, and many more.

The Hesiodic didactic poetry. The newly-educated public of Greece, both hearers and readers, found in the new epic forms a way of satisfying its nascent desire to learn about history. At the same time scientific curiosity was beginning; and this was satisfied by didactic writing, which as a result became very common. We may call the new fashion 'Hesiodic', though it is already to be seen in some later passages of the 'Homeric' epic. The Catalogue of Ships in the second book of the *Iliad* is really a piece of early work on historical geography; the list of Famous Women in the eleventh *Odyssey* is very like the *Ehoiai*[5] attributed to Hesiod; the list of those suffering punishments, in the same book, is already in the genre of moralizing treatises; and some of the lists of heroes and explanations of their pedigrees (*Iliad*, VI, 154; II, 100 ff.) foreshadow the *Theogony*.

Epic and sacred hymns provided information about gods and heroes, but it was episodic, fragmentary, and inconsistent. The Greeks wanted to know clearly the relationship of these beings both to one another and also to the noble clans and families who claimed descent from them. They therefore asked for works which could offer a harmonious picture of this kind, both on a Panhellenic and on a local scale.

Tradition ascribes to Hesiod (although a reference in the exordium in fact rules him out)[6] the poem of rather more than a thousand lines called the *Theogony*. This gives a fairly systematic list of divinities arranged in time periods and generations. The list is much less monotonous than it might have been, partly because the poet has inserted six detailed descriptions of the gods' more important doings; these are artistic pieces conceived at a later date.

The last lines of the *Theogony* speak of heroes born from unions between goddesses and mortals. The *Ehoiai* and the *Catalogues*, also attributed to Hesiod, are merely complementary pieces, the former enumerating the women who were loved by gods, the latter establishing the relationships between hero ancestors of illustrious families on the one hand and both gods and mortals on the other.

Similar types of poem were the *Descent of Theseus to Hades*, which gave a list of great heroes of the past, and the *Melampodia*, which told of the famous seers. There were also genealogical works confined to particular cities and particular clans.

The Hesiodic didactic works so far mentioned were the precursors of historical writing. There is another work which is allied less with history than with philosophy, exact science, and personal lyric, possessing sections in each one of these genres. This is the *Works and Days*, a short poem genuinely attributable to Hesiod, though obvious additions and later hands have left it in a very disordered condition. It comprises an exhortation to toil accompanied by a large collection of myths, allegories, moral precepts, proverbs, and also lyrical passages. Advice is provided for each season of the farmer's year, lessons of a technical kind being interspersed with enthusiastic descriptions of country life. There is also advice on navigation, for the farmers who had to take to the sea to sell their produce; there is moral counsel; and finally there is a section on the calendar of lucky and unlucky days.

Learned tradition has concentrated most didactic poetry upon the name of Hesiod (just as most epic was centred round that of Homer). But the references to their author made by the poems themselves are contradictory and ambiguous: it is hard to say whether he was really a Boeotian or a native of Asiatic Cumae, or perhaps a man who had lived in Boeotia but remained essentially Asiatic. This casts doubt on the commonly accepted view that epic is a product of Asia Minor but didactic poetry a product of the Greek mainland. As regards the date of composition there is no value in the traditional evidence about Hesiod's supposed life, which is related to the equally fictitious life of Homer. The environment depicted in the *Works and Days* undoubtedly corresponds to that of the seventh century, although some of the added sections take us down to an even later period.[7]

Elegiac and Iambic lyrical poetry. Quite a few of the cultivated lyric genres, which under the influence of a keener individualism began to take shape from the seventh century onwards, had their origins in the preceding period. Indeed this was recognized by tradition, which provides lists of many ancient singers, real or fictitious; and the Homeric epic frequently refers to

(a)   [Alinari

17   ETRUSCAN ART, I
    (a) *Etruscan 'hut' type urn, seventh century BC*
    (b) *Ploughman with his team, from Arezzo, fourth century BC.*
    Rome, Museum of the Villa Giuglia

(b)   [S.A.E.M.

18   ETRUSCAN ART, II

   (a) *'Buccheri' vases. Rome, Gregorian Etruscan Museum*
   (b) *Clay mouldings, antifixes from a temple. Rome, Museum of the Villa Giuglia*

Sarcophagus, sixth cen-
tury BC, from Caere.
Museum of the Villa
Giuglia, Rome

[Alinari]

[Alinari

20　*Etruscan style terra-cotta head of Jupiter, from the temple of Mater
Matuta at Satricum, Latium (now Conca), early fifth century BC.
Height* 0·25 *m. (Rome, Museum of the Villa Giuglia)*

21

(a) *Aerial view of Dzanbas-kala, on the right bank of the Amu Darya, Uzbekistan. The area covered is 200 ms. × 170 ms.*

(b) *Ordos, bronze finial, two ibexes with turquoise inlay in the nostrils, height 0·12 ms.*

(b)   [O.M.

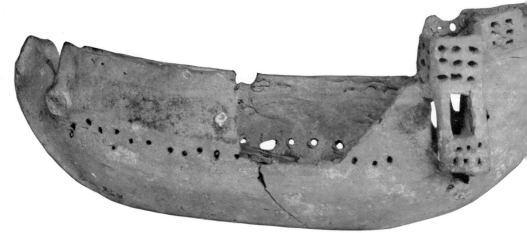

22   NAVIGATION, II

    (a) *Terra-cotta model of a boat from Amathus,* c. 500 BC

    (b) *Model of a Greek galley, fourth century BC, broadside*

(a) *Silver denarius: oath of the Italian Allies during the Social Wars*

(b) *Coin of the 'gens hostilia' with presumed head of Vercingetorix*

(c) *80 drachms, copper coin with head of Cleopatra, 45–30 BC*

(a)   [M.C.

(b)   [M.C.

(c)   [Berlin

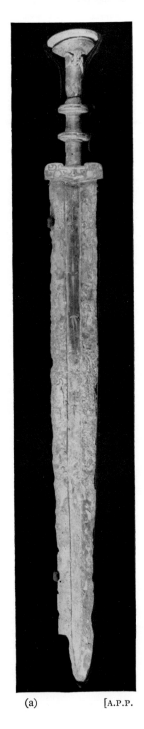

(a) [A.P.P.

(b) [M.G.

24 (a) *Bronze sword from Li-yü'in Shansi, Warring States period*
    (b) *Crossbow of the Han dynasty*

songs sung at dances, weddings, victory celebrations, and funerals, as also to poems of both lamentation and invective. Moreover examples of popular songs and of ditties sung at work have actually come down to us. Similarly certain musical instruments go back to remote antiquity. Already in the Mycenaean Age there was a stringed instrument, of varying shape and a varying number of strings, and a wind instrument which we call the flute; and besides strictly instrumental music the epic poets know of music associated with solo and choral singing, and also with the dance.

The lyre, which made it possible for the same person to sing and play at once, had been used by the bards to accompany their recitals, which were made in clear and descriptive hexameters. But the faster and more sprightly metres required either instruments with many strings or else accompaniment by a musician playing the flute (*aulos*). The development of flute technique permitted gradations of tones to suit the sentiments which had to be expressed. Finally the use of zither and flute together encouraged the growth of new forms and new metres, for choral as well as for solo singing, until we finally reach the 'antiphonal' choruses in which male, female, and child voices were all combined.

Dactylic metre, a heavy and solemn measure in four-time with the beat at the beginning of each foot, had hitherto been employed for epic, religious, didactic, and moral poems. Now when flute accompaniment made two performers combine, the metre took on syncopated forms as well; and from these was derived the distich of elegy, which could express pain and pleasure, love, friendship, counsel, and rebuke, in a dignified manner without any violence or jerkiness. The earliest elegists lived in the earlier part of the seventh century, the most notable being Callinus of Ephesus, whose fragments allude to the Cimmerian inroads on Lydia and the Greek colonies of Asia Minor. The songs (exhortations) of the Spartan Tyrtaeus in the third quarter of the seventh century (the days of the Second Messenian War) were very similar in purpose; and Tyrtaeus was also the author of a short poem called *Eunomia* to allay the quarrels among his fellow-citizens by reminding them of the good order which had prevailed in the city under the constitution issued by the Delphic oracle. In addition he wrote 'embateria', in anapaestic verse; these were songs to be chanted by soldiers at the moment of an attack.

Another author of political and patriotic elegy, though more famous for his melancholy and exquisite elegies of love, was Mimnermus of Colophon, an early sixth-century poet (one fragment alludes to the eclipse of the sun in 585).[8] A contemporary of his was the Athenian poet and politician Solon (whose reforms belong to 594 or 592 BC), the author of political, gnomic, and religious elegies. The value of these consists in the conciliatory nature of his moral and political arguments and in the fineness of his religious thinking.

Moralizing elegiacs were also written by Phocylides of Miletus (*floruit c.* 540 BC), the authentic fragments of whose work (an actual poem attributed to him is a late forgery) are reflections on ethical ideas distilled into short sentences of a kind easy to remember.

In the period when elegy was reaching its acme and beginning to decline, the epigram, often in dactylic couplets but sometimes in iambic trimeters, was beginning to come into its own. It was first used in the sixth century by anonymous authors of inscriptions on tombs and monuments, and then reached its noblest form in the writings of Simonides of Ceos.

As well as dactylic rhythm more nimble and lively metres in three-time came to be used. One was the flexible trochee, used for love songs, another the vigorous iambic, for invective and comic verse. Both these metres moved in a way which was close to normal speech when affected by tears or laughter. The first poet to achieve dazzling effects from them was Archilochus, who was born at Paros, the bastard of a nobleman and a slave girl, and lived in the first half of the seventh century. He was crossed in love, heavily involved in political party strife, and went as a colonist to Thasos at a time when the Thracians were menacing the island: then he became a mercenary soldier and died while still young. His most famous genre was iambic satire, which he used with remarkable facility for changes in expression. This proletarian with an aristocratic education can be idealistic or impudent, ferocious or graceful, violent or ironical, bitter or genial; and his work is full of graphic pictures, or profound reflections, and of fables and digressions in which we even find animals in human guise. Archilochus' reputation as a poet made him worthy to be classed with Homer.

An approximate contemporary of Archilochus was Semonides of Samos, who took part in the colonization of Amorgos. Besides his elegiac verse, which includes a *History of Samos*, he wrote iambics, not personal invective, but satire of a general and almost gnomic kind. The best-known are a fragment on human misery and the so-called *Censure of Women*: the latter divides women into ten species, seven derived from vicious types of animal, two from earth and sea, and one from the useful hard-working bee.

At the end of the sixth century Hipponax of Ephesus, who lived in exile at Clazomenae, marks a last rude stage in the decline of iambic. This was a mendicant poet, both violent and trivial, who wrote fierce invectives and also touching descriptions of misery and despair. But the metre which he had refined was left as a heritage to two other genres, comedy (see pp. 281 f.) and the animal fable. The origins of the latter form of story-telling are certainly fairly ancient: there are already examples in Hesiod, Archilochus, and the *Batrachomyomachia*. Its subjects passed from one city to another, being handed on by word of mouth between traders, travellers, mercenaries, and slaves, until the repertories possessed by different people often became inextricably mixed up. Tradition tells us of a half-legendary figure called Aesopus, a wit and comedian, who may have lived at the end of the sixth century but about whose history there is no general agreement. To him is attributed a collection of animal fables in prose, though it is sometimes cited in verse and was continually being re-edited.

Monodic lyric. Particular gods, and above all Apollo, were honoured by the composition of 'nomoi', liturgical hymns sung by soloists to accompaniment of the zither (*nomos citharodicos*) or of the flute (*nomos aulodicos*); or sometimes they would consist only of a musical passage played on the flute (*nomos auleticos*). The supposed inventor of the *nomos citharodicos* was Terpander of Antissa in Lesbos, who migrated to Sparta and is alleged to have there been victorious in the Carnean contest of 676 BC; his songs were accompanied by a zither of seven strings and were composed in various metres. His successor was Clonas, possibly a native of Tegea in Arcadia, who brought in the *nomos aulodicos*, especially for use in processions.

At the same time in the island of Lesbos another development was taking place. This was the personal lyric, or 'melic', which had as its basic subjects love, wine, and politics. Its songs were intimate and melodious, and were accompanied by instruments with up to twenty strings (the *barbitos*, *magadis*, or *pectis*), which could play both very high and very low notes. The metres varied, and attention was given to construction of strophes. The two earliest and best known melic poets were Alcaeus and Sappho, contemporaries of one another: tradition dates them to the turn of the seventh and sixth centuries, but they were still alive about the middle of the sixth, since we are told that Alcaeus fought against Athens for possession of Sigeum in Peisistratus' time.[9] Alcaeus was an aristocrat of Mitylene on Lesbos, though exiled to distant lands on account of his enmity with the tyrants and also with Pittacus, and he wrote in an Aeolic literary dialect. Some of his poems are eloquent and forceful utterances on political topics; others are fresh and lively banqueting songs, in praise of wine; others again are in praise of Apollo or Hermes or Athena. But the most beautiful, sensual, and delicate of his works are love poems, for boys (*epheboi*) like Lykos or for Sappho. His metres show great variety.

Sappho too was an aristocrat of Lesbos, born at Eresus, and her life was that of the class to which she belonged. After a period of exile in Sicily she returned to her country and there kept a girls' school, where music, singing dancing, and elegant manners were taught, but (so it appears from the fragments) there was also instruction in moral behaviour. She was attacked by the Attic comedians, who accused her of immorality and introduced childish anachronisms into their charges. But this is probably all legend, due partly to malicious invention and partly to misunderstanding of feminine customs which were freer than those current at Athens. The charge is refuted not only by the majority of her poems, but by the regard in which she was held by her fellow-citizens, who had her head engraved on their coins in Hellenistic-Roman times.

Her poems were in Aeolic dialect and used many metres: ancient editors collected them into nine books. There are songs of passionate love, tender, pathetic, and sometimes angry; there are epithalamia of marked spontaneity and freshness, full of tasteful wit; and there are hymns to the gods. With her exquisite choice of language and her ear for melody went directness of emotion, deep understanding of human feeling, daring imagery, and a keen appreciation of nature. All combined to make Sappho a poetess of the highest rank.

The example of these two Lesbian lyric poets was followed in the second half of the sixth century by many other writers. They included three poetesses, the Boeotians Corinna and Myrtis, and the Dorian Erinna from Argos; as well as Anacreon, the great Ionian poet from Teos, who first settled at Abdera and later wandered from court to court. Anacreon, who wrote in Ionic dialect, came under many influences—the personal invective of the iambic writers, Mimnermus' hedonism, and the lyrical, metrical, and musical forms employed by the melic poets of Lesbos. The content of his poems is slight: they are mostly devoted to wine and free love, without either political passion or philosophical interests. For centuries to come they were admired and imitated, but they mark the exhaustion and consequent decline of Greek melic poetry as an important art form. After Anacreon came the great rise of different genres, the choral lyrics and the poetry of drama.

Choral Lyric in the Peloponnese, Italy, and Ionia. Alcman was a native of Sparta, of respectable family. He composed songs (the ancient world possessed six books of them) in which the Parthenoi or maidens played a great part, and which were sung by choirs of girls taking part at the festivals called Gymnopaedia, assisted by young athletes and by dancers of both sexes. They begin with mythical narrative, and follow it with a passage about real events. Alcman's fancy was calm and joyful: his poetry is supple and animated, while at the same time concise with rapid transitions. He also composed hymns, paeans, banqueting songs, hyporchemes (choral songs to Apollo), love songs, and marriage celebrations: he used a variety of metres, including some very complicated systems of rhythm. Tradition puts his *floruit* variously at about 672, 657, and 612 BC, but various considerations suggest that he was still active after 600.[10]

The story was that Arion of Methymna was one of Alcman's pupils, and that he migrated to Corinth to the court of Periander (627–585 BC?), thence proceeding on to Sparta, where he won contests at the Carnean festival. But the whole account of Arion's life is a tissue of legends. He is supposed to have given literary status to an ancient kind of choral song, called dithyramb, and to have made it a regular artistic form: this was a song full of swift and emotional movement, dedicated in early days to a number of divinities, to Adrastus for example at Sicyon, but soon (as we can already see in fragments of Archilochus) to Dionysus. No genuine fragments of Arion's dithyrambs have come down to us, and it is not clear what a famous statement, traceable back to Solon, is precisely attributing to him. It may actually mean the dithyrambs from which scholars used to believe that tragedy was derived; or it may imply that he invented 'tragic choruses' (the phrase meaning either songs of worshippers disguised as goats, or alternatively songs by boys who have reached the age of puberty), choruses which are themselves connected by some scholars with the origins of tragedy.

Perhaps half a century after Arion, Lasus of Hermione, the teacher of Pindar and Simonides, developed the dithyramb further and gave it its permanent form, namely a chorus accompanied by complicated orchestration played by the flute. He is said to have composed a dithyramb called *The Centaurs*, in which there was a curious avoidance of the letter sigma on the ground that its pronunciation was too harsh.

Choral poetry also made its mark in the Italiote colonies, which in our period produced the man we call Stesichorus I and also Ibycus. Learned tradition made two poets of the same name Stesichorus into one: the first came from Matauros in Magna Graecia and lived at the time of the battle of Sagra and the eclipse of 557 BC; the second was a native of Himera in Sicily and was still alive after 485–484. It is not too late to undo this confusion.[11] The earlier writer, called Tisias, was a singer of 'citharodic' choruses, and gained his name Stesichorus thereby. Simonides compared him with Homer, and it is to him that the 'Stesichorean' invention of the strophic triad is ascribed. He was undoubtedly the author of the ode attacking Helen and also the 'palinodia', which relates to the battle of Sagra. Probably he was also the author of a paean, a hymn to Athena, an epithalamium for Helen, some love songs, and the story of the chaste maiden Calica and of Rhadine, victim of a Corinthian tyrant (possibly Cypselus).

Ibycus of Rhegium, according to ancient accounts, flourished about 568 or 548 BC, and was entertained by Polycrates of Samos. Seven books of his poems existed in Hellenistic times, but only a few fragments have survived. Yet we can see in them the fineness and calm serenity of his genius, with the inspiration he drew from Alcman, Sappho, and Stesichorus I. The types of poem displayed are hymns sung by choirs of youths, in praise of the beauty of particular men or to depict the love stories of the gods.

Choral lyric in Ionic, at the point of transition between our period and that which follows, is chiefly represented by Simonides of Ceos, who passed his life travelling from city to city, from one contest to another. He was entertained by Hipparchus at Athens down to 514, then in Thessaly by Scopas of Crannon and the Aleuadae at Larissa, then he visited Athens again and passed on to Acragas and finally to Syracuse, where he died about 470. His poems related a large number of myths, and his total output was vast, comprising hymns, paeans, dithyrambs, encomia, celebrations of victories in the national games, dirges following deaths of famous men, hyporchemes or songs for dances, elegies, and epigrams. In the last genre he attained enormous success. He made the writing of poetry his profession, and Pindar said he lived not for himself but for other men: as such he praised the victories and lamented the suffering of others, with moral principles which were utilitarian rather than unbending, lukewarm religious opinions, considerable adaptability in politics, and little insistence on insight into character. He was not exuberant as an artist; yet his technique was exquisite, his style full of colour and his language carefully chosen, whether he was writing elegies in Ionic, melic poetry in Doric, or his epigrams in a variety of dialects.

The Origins of the Forms of the Greek Theatre. It was long believed that tragedy, satyric drama, and comedy at Athens were all derived from Dionysiac rites, but their origins are now regarded by modern scholars as having been much more complicated and obscure. Tragedy, for example, has been connected in turn with the dramatic ceremonies in the Eleusinian mysteries, with vegetation rites, with the cults of the dead or of heroes, and with festivals for the resurgent spirit of the year.

Tragedy, to be sure, was not born at one moment, but came into being by slow evolution and by combination between a number of pre-existing factors. Various Greek cults of an orgiastic and pathetic type, connected with mysteries of resurrection or the like, lent themselves to the creation of dramatic forms. Archaeological evidence, especially from Sparta, shows that the use of masks to represent gods and heroes was very ancient; archaic too is the custom, derived from early rituals of animal-type divinities, of having men disguised at sacred ceremonies, in the form of lions, goats, bears, stags, horses, and so on. Early Greece also knew of many dances and sacred songs full of rapid movement, such as those performed by the Dactyli, Telchini, Cercopes, Cabeiri, and Corybantes. Finally there were many heroes, whose deeds were regarded in classical times as historical actions performed on earth—indeed the presence of a *didascalus* or teacher was a natural accompaniment of their representation: yet originally these things had been legends about local deities, to imitate whose activities was consequently a ritual matter.

All this must be admitted, and yet it seems clear that the vital step came when an actor-poet tried to represent the deeds and words of a god or hero before a chorus with whom he conducted a dialogue. From that moment tragedy came into being, and would have done so even without the Dionysiac cult at Athens. In fact we are told of ancient dramas outside Athens, and of themes which were not Dionysiac.

Moreover since the dithyramb itself was initially based on a single singer and a chorus, there is no objection to the view that the earliest form of tragedy was precisely the dithyramb, connected with epic so far as subjects are concerned and as regards form with the choral lyric.

But later at Athens, although a large number of subjects were treated, ragedy in its earliest stages came to be associated chiefly with Bacchic celebrations; and this happened all the more when a satyric drama, with its straightforward incantation to Dionysus, was put on at the end of a tragedy.

We may mention some of the early Attic tragedians, down to the first decades of the fifth century, who are all recorded as having taken part in Dionysiac contests at Athens.

The tragedies of Thespis, of the deme of Ikaria, are completely lost, but it seems that, besides a chorus, they contained a prologue and a story, both recited by a masked actor. They were performed in the villages of Attica by the poet himself, who carried his equipment with him on a cart; but eventually he established himself in Athens, and there at the wish of Peisistratus tragic contests were now initiated during the festivals of Dionysus. The next name is that of Choerilus, an Athenian famous for his satirical tone, of whom 160 plays and 16 victories were recorded, the first in 524–520 though he was still competing in 484–480 BC. Then Pratinas of Phlius, who is said to have brought the satyric drama to Athens, is credited with 50 plays including 32 of satyric type (we possess a hyporcheme which he wrote); he is known to have competed in 499–496 and to have died before 467, in which year his *Combatants* was performed as a posthumous work. At the appropriate time we shall continue the list with Phrynichus, Thespis' pupil. A recently discovered papyrus records a fragment from a pre-Aeschylean tragedy about Gyges.

Satyric drama was something intermediate between tragedy and comedy, a 'tragedy with a happy ending', well suited to Dionysiac cult and probably derived from the Bacchic dithyramb. A principal part was played by satyrs in costume, who danced the 'sikinnis' and were led by old Silenus. When the sequence of three tragedies became the standard form in Athenian contests at the festivals of Dionysus, we can well understand why it was arranged that the trilogy on sad and violent themes should be followed by a satyric play which constituted a joyful, Bacchic, drama of its own. It contained rapid dialogue, crude and even obscene language, and a grotesque plot, with characters who were bizarre, unexpected, and fantastic.

Jests and jibes and satire were surely as old as the Greek people itself. Iambic poetry was based on them, and after that came comedy, a genre for which undoubtedly many precedents prepared the way. There had been processions accompanied by wild songs in honour of Phales and other divinities of fertility. There had also been caricatures of deformed or grotesque individuals; and above all, as the name comedy implies, there had been *komoi* by people in masks, who toured the villages and pilloried the first person they met, putting about gossip and scandal. Every time one of these charades turned into dialogue form around a plot, a comedy may be said to have been composed. This is precisely why comedy became a literary form in several districts at the same time. At Sparta clowns called Dikelistai played funny scenes in which the performers were deformed or ridiculous. At Sicyon the masked Phallophoroi would first sing in chorus and perform queer actions and would then put on a scene; and something similar took place at the festivals of Damia and Auxesia at Aegina. At Megara, where there was an

attempt to connect the word 'comedy' with the word *komai* (villages), implying that comedies were country farces, Maison and Susarion after the establishment of the democracy gave satyric performances a political tone; and this
subsequently, in 581 or 562 BC, became the fashion in Athens. Another
Athenian poet was Myllos, who though deaf knew every kind of swear-word.
The Italiote colonies too were fond of coarse, obscene farces called *phlyaces*,
lisodiai, and *magodiai*; and they were paralleled among the Siceliotes, where
Epicharmus had more than one precursor.

For prophecy, in both its political and religious aspects, see pp. 234 ff.

Prose: History and Geography. We are concerned once again with the earliest
Greek writings on philosophy and science. It has already been explained how
one of the objectives of epic writing of genealogical or didactic type was to
satisfy the growing Greek desire for historical and geographical knowledge.
They wanted to learn the story of peoples, cities, and heroes of ancient days,
and the more or less marvellous characteristics of distant lands and nations.

Once this need for history and geography had been felt, it continued to
grow. Men wanted to know not only legendary deeds of early days, but more
likely facts about very recent periods; and they were concerned to tell posterity
about the doings of their own times. At this point they directed their attention
beyond the purely marvellous on to concrete evidence about the features of
countries, and about the customs, characters, and racial composition of foreign
nations. These new kinds of narrative were no longer written in verse, but in
prose. With the decline in illiteracy there was now a relatively large number of
possible readers, as distinct from hearers, and it was no longer necessary to
write in verse in order to attract attention and assist the audience's memory.
The desire for knowledge became more important than the need to please.
It was the Ionians who, on their repeated commercial and colonial voyages,
had most frequent occasion to see different lands and learn about different
nations and political institutions; and it was therefore in Ionia that historical
and geographical writing was born.

At the same time there was a growing desire to make public documents
generally known—such texts as laws, treaties, pedigrees, annalistic lists of
magistrates, commemorative and autobiographical records, or the observations of the priests. This led to an increase in the number of inscriptions; and
historians, who paid some degree of attention to such material, were able to
widen their range of evidence.

The newly established science of geography has its earliest document (see
p. 142) in the middle of the sixth century BC, when Anaximander of Miletus
used information brought by sailors to describe the form of the earth with an
accompanying plan.

The earliest historians (*logographoi*, or *orographoi* as they were later called)
gathered their information partly from written and partly from oral sources,
sometimes adding evidence which had come to them through personal ac-

quaintance with the relevant facts and places. The written sources included epic and genealogical poetry, lists of priests and magistrates, and public inscriptions. Different authors pieced all this evidence together with innumerable rival hypotheses, of varying degrees of logical consistency; some were ingenious deductions from real or supposed affinities between the place-names, customs, or cults of different regions, others were based on rationalization of myths and an attempt to translate them into human terms.

The most famous and perhaps the earliest of these logographers was Hecataeus of Miletus, who lived at the turn of the sixth and fifth centuries. He was a personage of importance in his city in 499, and was alive at least as late as 479. His historical work (later divided into four books) was called *Genealogies*, partly because it propounded a chronological scheme based on generations of forty years. It contained propositions of a methodical nature, such as 'I write these things in the way that seems to me true, since the stories of the Hellenes, so it appears to me, are many and absurd'. This important statement reveals the beginnings of historical criticism, even though in fact Hecataeus' reconstruction of Greek origins remained in so many places very far from the truth. In another work, the *Ges Periodos*, Hecataeus made good use of the direct knowledge of certain countries which he had acquired during his life. Naturally his book is better informed about coastal than about inland areas, and about countries adjacent to Greek colonies rather than those outside the orbit of Greek culture.

If we could believe tradition, Cadmus of Miletus, an Ionian like Hecataeus, would figure as an even earlier writer. But the story of his life has a mythical appearance (he is called the son of the Athenian king Pandion), and the work on the origins of Miletus which is attributed to him was already believed by some ancients to be a forgery.

We have already mentioned the genuine work on exploration by Scylax of Caryanda, written in the time of Darius. The same author is credited with an historical monograph on Heracleides, lord of Mylasa.

i. *Etruscan and primitive Roman literature*

Writing came early to Etruria, as is shown by the model Greek alphabets and by the oldest native inscriptions, the latter dating from the beginning of the seventh century. More than 10,000 inscriptions in all have come down to us, suggesting that a people so fond of writing is likely to have been well to the fore in producing a literature. We know particularly of the large output on cult and religion, and on other matters in the didactic or liturgical genre (see above p. 242), because it aroused the interest of the Romans. But there is no doubt that other literary forms came early to Etruria. Epic poems are suggested by paintings from Vulci about the deeds of the brothers Vibenna and of Mastarna, and by monuments at Bologna (for example) depicting episodes in the fighting between Etruscans and Celts. They are confirmed by the evidence of Dionysius of Halicarnassus (I, 21) about the national songs of Falerii and the songs of Veii on Aleso.

There must have been other stories and poems about the myths of hybrid Etruscan and Greek origin which we find represented on monuments. Besides this, Varro quotes from 'historiae Tuscae', which Cato used for his *Origines* and the emperor Claudius for his *Tyrrhenica*; and we are told of Etruscan works, of uncertain date, about hydraulics and medicine. The actual Latin words *histrio* and *lanista*, *scaena* and *persona*, being derived directly or indirectly (through Greek) from Etruscan, show that Rome got not a few of its concepts about the theatre from Etruria. The same is true about games, which Roman tradition likewise maintained were imported to the city from Etruria, giving the date 364 BC.

Rome too must have produced a popular epic at an early date, nor is this surprising in view of the epic happenings in its history. Cicero (Brutus, 19, 75) complains of the loss of these ancient poems about illustrious individuals which were in existence many centuries before Cato. The loss can be explained by the fact that from the third century onwards the earliest artistic poems (those of Naevius and Ennius), and the earliest annalists, took over everything they contained and provided an adequate replacement.

Nevertheless these verses, of which the poetical content is still the basis of the earlier narrative of Livy, had provided material for the pontiffs in the fourth century BC. At that time they were issuing their first edition of the *Annales Maximi* and reconstructing their annual tables, which had been compiled since the beginning of the Republic but had been burnt in the Gallic capture of Rome. They appended a brief summary of the history of the Regal period, and to compose it they collected not only the evidence of oral tradition or that still available from their own tables, but also the evidence of official documents, which at Rome were drawn up at least as early as the seventh century.

Nor is there doubt that documents were written in Rome and Latium as early as this date: it is proved by surviving texts, and also by the existence in antiquity of a large number of others now lost. They included regal laws, treaties, religious ordinances, formularies, pontifical responses and decrees, lists of magistrates and priests, catalogues of prodigies, and calendars with rules about intercalation. One such document, of immense historical value, is the first treaty between Rome and Carthage, preserved by Polybius, and probably first put into writing at a time when the Etruscans were still ruling Rome.

2. ART

a. *China*

Chou art continues that of the preceding Shang period, but there are very marked differences, amounting to a halt, or even in some fields a setback, to the progress made hitherto. It was in fact a reflection of the essential characteristics of the rough Chou conquerors, who came from the same stock as the Shang people they subdued, but who belonged to the fringe of Sinic civilization and were therefore culturally backward in comparison with the relatively advanced Shang.

Free-standing sculpture disappears for practically a thousand years. The artistic work which has come down to us is therefore mostly confined to bronzes, although marble and jade objects are not wanting. The great Shang tradition continued to govern the art forms used for sacred bronze vessels, the style being first that which is normally called 'transitional Yin-Chou' (c. 1030–950), and then the Middle Chou (c. 950–650). (Pl. 3.) Ritual vases, most notably those discovered in the tombs of Chou princes at Hsün-hsien, are still made in the classical forms characteristic of the best bronze age, the most widespread type being the tripod (ting). But more typical of this period are the tsun (with a bell-shaped base, wide middle section, and a long neck like a chalice), and the kuei (a deep urn with round or square foot and handles which are generally in the shape of animals). In the Middle Chou period we find the i, a kind of sauce-boat representing a bull: the lip is often like a bull's head, there are four feet of bovine type, and the handle is carved like an animal of prey gripping the bull's back. Decoration declines in elegance and becomes more simple and severe, although it retains a restraint of great power and an energy which is almost brutal. In particular the t'ao-t'ieh mask, so dominant in the Shang period, first dwindled in size and underwent alterations then became less common, and finally disappeared altogether. Instead we find motifs of a heavy and rigid geometric type. Even the technique altered, as alt-relief disappeared and gave place to a simple form of flat relief. The general impression is one of static and ponderous rigidity, combined with a drying-up of artistic imagination. From the middle of the seventh century, and even more clearly in the middle of the sixth, a change set in with the rise of the Huai style, with which we deal later.

Side by side with the art of Chinese bronzes proper, which means those connected with the Chou dynasty and the fiefs in the Huang-ho basin there existed a southern style in the kingdom of Ch'u, very like the Chou style but showing features of even more marked simplicity.

Chinese pottery of the Chou period excelled in the manufacture of high-fire vitrified wares. But alongside them there was in common use a grey ware of coarser make and less skilled workmanship, which continued in use for most of the first millennium BC.

b. *Northern Asia*

In the great metal working basin of Minusinsk on the upper Yenisei the civilization of Karasuk was at its zenith between 1200 and 700. Its bronzes are clearly influenced by those of Anyang, but there is a marked time-lag; the influence was certainly not in the opposite direction, as was believed until the fundamental work of Kiselev. The essential characteristic is representation of animals; and the bronze knives and other weapons, as well as the carved stonework, reveal a style which is still rough and ponderous, though it foreshadows the magnificent Steppe art of the succeeding period.

Karasuk was followed by the Tagar culture (700–100), which was still centred in the Minusinsk basin and may be attributed to Hsiung-nu clans. There are bronzes from its earliest period (700–400) which show the heavy Karasuk style giving place to quick, light movement of a dynamic and elastic type. In its splendid naturalistic renderings of animals—tigers, lynxes, bears, wild boars, stags, and so on—there is already a trend toward stylization, in which heraldic features predominate. It is an extraordinarily rich form of art, and in the ensuing period we shall find its influence extending from China to the Ukraine.

c. India

In this period there is a large gap in our knowledge about Indian art. A thousand years of almost complete darkness exists between the end of the urban and commercial civilization of Harappā and the earliest stages of the court art of the Mauryas. The Aryans destroyed the art that went before them, without being capable, for a very long time, of replacing it with something new. We learn little or nothing from written evidence; at the best we can derive some interest from the rules laid down for constructing a sacrificial altar in the *Śulvasūtras*, writings which belong to the next period but reflect post-Vedic theory. In any case the relics of any art from this period are exceedingly few. Architecture was in wood or bamboo, and no building has survived. Nevertheless we know that in this period architectonic forms were evolved for wooden material and subsequently imitated (or even copied) in stone; examples are the monastic room (*caitya*) and the doorway of a sacred enclosure (*toraṇa*). At the same date there was evolved the theoretical lay-out of an Indian village as it is described in later treatises— a rectangle intersected by two cross-roads leading to four gates.

About the end of this period stone began to appear as a building material, and in particular, for obvious reasons, replaced wood in the construction of city walls. The one example which still exists in part is to be found in the remains of the walls of Rājagṛha, attributable to the sixth century. Of funerary architecture the main instances are the enormous burial mounds of Lauriya Nandangarh, which are prototypes of the *stūpa* of the succeeding period. In the south, at Mennapuram and Calicut, tombs have been found cut in the rock, in a manner possible only before inhumation was completely replaced by cremation. They take the form of roofed rooms with a monolithic stone in the centre: in other words, they are stone reproductions of the Vedic but normally made of wood or matting. Another similar structure, interpreted by some as a fire-temple, has been found at Bangala Motta Paramba.

Indian pottery of this period is interesting from the archaeological point of view only; as a rule, it is strictly utilitarian and of little artistic merit.

The most representative ceramic is the Painted Grey ware (eighth–fifth centuries BC), occurring mainly in northern India.[12] It is made of fine clay, wheel-turned, rather thin, well fired and with a grey or greyish-brown surface. The painted ornament is usually black and consists of linear and dotted patterns, spirals, concentric circles, etc. (Fig. I.)

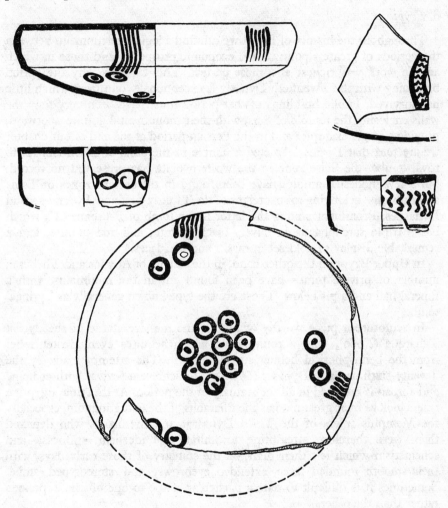

FIG. I.   Painted Grey ware from Ahicchatrā (after M. Wheeler).

Some sculpture survives, but it is hardly representative of the period as a whole. The best-known piece is a gold figurine in relief, found in one of the Lauriya Nandangarh tombs, which its discoverer interpreted as depicting a Vedic goddess (Pṛthivī, the Earth): more probably it represents the common type of Magna Mater which we find so often in practically all parts of Asia.

In style it seems to mark a transition between the plastic art of Harappā and the Mauryas. Various sorts of terracottas, especially of the Magna Mater, have been uncovered in a number of places. Some of them, found at Mathura, come from the same school as the Lauriya Nandangarh figurine.

d. *Egypt*

Throughout the history of Egypt we can find a logical relationship between the periods of greatest political and economic prosperity and those in which artistic work was richest and most perfect. This explains why the period beginning with the Twentieth Dynasty is exceptionally one from which little has survived. Public buildings of that period must have been very few: the walls enclosing the temple of Sais, with their monumental granite doorways, provide a single example; and in the Persian period at the end of our chapter we are told that Darius I erected a temple in the oasis of El Hibeh. As to royal tombs, the Saite zone in the western delta has preserved no record, but a few modest examples have been found in the eastern zones of Tanis and Bubastis, belonging to sovereigns of the Twenty-first and Twenty-second Dynasties. Prominent among the latter is the tomb of Psusennes II, which has a triple sarcophagus in silver, black granite, and red granite, and a remarkable display of gold set in masks and necklaces.

In Upper Egypt on the other hand, in the district of Abydos and Thebes, a number of private tombs have been found cut in the mountains, with a funeral hall and a pit below. Those are the type known generally as 'syringa' tombs.

In sculpture a piece worthy of note is the massive statue of the dynast Taharqua (*c*. 660), with a round head which acquires even greater relief from the hemispherical helmet surrounding it. The attempt made by the Twenty-sixth or Saite Dynasty (663–525) to achieve a revival both at home and abroad is reflected in all the statuary of the period. At that time Egyptian rulers took as their great models the Pharaohs of the Old Kingdom, especially the Memphis rulers of the Third Dynasty; and the artists who depicted them were therefore attempting to imitate the idealism, stiffness, and schematism which left their mark on the statuary of those early days, with their smooth rounded faces, extended eyebrows, and stereotyped smile. Sometimes it is difficult to date a particular statue to one of these periods rather than the other.

Statues of priests on the other hand, which were not executed on these archaizing principles, show a remarkable power of portraiture. One may mention a famous head in green now in the Berlin Museum, which is expressive and realistic in the highest degree, for example in the characteristic fleshy treatment of the ears. It was during the Saite period that Greek traders from Naucratis, and after them Greek mercenaries, were able to acquaint their fellow-countrymen with the main features of Egyptian statuary, which therefore, as we shall see (p. 299), came to exercise an important influence on Greek sculpture. (Pl. 4.)

e. Assyria

In art as in all other forms of culture Assyria was traditionalist and conservative. With few innovations or even logical developments, the Assyrians retained and perpetuated methods which had been the rule for thousands of years in Mesopotamia, even in fields where Assyrian environment was different. For example, although Assyria was relatively well provided with solid building materials in both stone and timber, they still employed the Babylonian form of construction in clay bricks, generally sun-baked and bound together with bitumen, reeds, and straw: only for foundations or in exceptional cases did they use stone or bricks baked in the oven. This compelled them to construct buildings resembling mountains of earth, with high blank walls. There was practically no opening to let in light; the rooms were small and dark; very occasionally there would be a false cupola at the top, but generally the roof would be made of short timber and would provide a terrace. Arches were used only for certain doorways; moreover though the column was known to the Assyrians, they used it simply as a decorative element, and not to give support. The great royal palaces, and buildings of a public and religious nature, were constructed on high plateau land to give protection from floods; but the military character of Assyrian life made each one of these buildings into a fortress, with turreted outer walls, few gates giving access to the outside, and battlements on the roofs. Practically every king constructed a royal palace with a temple attached: the most famous (with ruins surviving) are Ashur-nazirpal II's at Nimrod, Sargon II's palace at Dur-Sharrukin (the modern Khorsabad), and Ashur-banipal's at Nineveh. The second of these was built on an artificial terrace, 50 feet in average height and about 25 acres in area. The interior was divided into a number of separate courts, and comprised about 200 very narrow rooms; these were set in three main groups, one the seraglio, the second the rooms adjoining it, and the third a collection of six shrines, while at the side was the temple with its *ziggurat* and gardens with aqueducts to water them. The outer walls of the palace had uniform surfaces, the monotony of which was broken by buttresses, towers, and decorated sections, but by practically no windows at all; the rooms were cool, as the country's climate demands, but they were fairly dark, obtaining their light only through doors and small openings on to the courts. The temples too were surrounded by walls and possessed a number of rooms for lodging, offices, stores, and treasures, besides those devoted to cult purposes. The famous towers with between four and seven storeys of gradually decreasing size set one upon another, which were grouped round a massive central platform (*ziggurat*), ended, so Herodotus tells us, in a sanctuary: this therefore came to be a 'High Place' of an artificial nature, and was also useful as an astronomical observatory.

The figurative arts in Assyria have one tendency in common. They normally present human figures in a decorative manner, symbolist and abstract. These figures are stiff and rigid, lacking any expression of sentiment and emotion, showing a passion for symmetry and characteristic devices of stylization: for instance the eyes, beard, and upper part of the bust face forward, even when the rest of the figure is in profile (Pl. 6). Extreme care is taken over drapery, stylized curls in the beard, and women's hair. Women and nudes are depicted only rarely, and landscape backgrounds are of a uniform type. On the other hand realism of the starkest kind is almost absolute when they come to depict any kind of animal, real or imaginary— winged bulls (Pl. 5, a), lions with crinkled hair, dogs, horses, antelopes, wild asses, boars, birds, or fishes. A curious feature in their technique lay in giving quadrupeds a fifth leg, so that one can always see four whether the animal is full face or foreshortened.

Everything said so far applies not only to regular free-standing sculpture (like the marvellous statue of Ashur-banipal found at Nimrod and now in the British Museum), but even more to the countless scenes depicted in relief. These are sometimes mythical, like that of Gilgamesh strangling a lion, or the winged bulls with human heads: or they can be scenes of human life, hunting, battles, massacres, processions of prisoners, sacrifices, or banquets of kings and queens in their gardens. These scenes, mainly bas-reliefs cut on some soft stone such as chalk or alabaster, or possibly enamels, cover enormous surfaces on the smooth walls of buildings; for instance in the palace of Khorsabad they take up nearly 60,000 square feet, often in a series of pictures devoted to events succeeding one another in time. But such reliefs are also to be found on *stelae* and obelisks, for instance the black obelisk of Shalmaneser III, and also on bronze tablets, such as those used to decorate doors. A characteristic piece of naïveté is used to deal with perspective: scenes designed to show more than one plane have files of figures of equal proportions, one above the other, with a dividing line between them. (Pl. 5, b).

Instead of using reliefs the Assyrians sometimes covered their mural surfaces with gesso and painted them with ornamental designs or with scenes of men and animals. Besides white and black they employed red, blue, green, and yellow.

Among lesser arts the carving of seals and amulets deserves special mention. The finer ones were made of precious stones, such as lapis lazuli, cornelian, serpentine, and hematite; but there were cheaper articles of varying shape (flat, conical, hemispherical, but above all cylindrical), which contained symmetrical scenes, often of mythological topics.

f. *Persia*

Persian art was in essence a court art, ceremonial in character and designed to render the King of Kings the homage that was due to him. It found outlet particularly in architectural constructions and the decoration of their walls. The Persian religion did not need great temples: it was content with altars, as is shown (for example) by the finds at Naqsh-i-Rustem. It was a manifestation of the dynasty, and owed its origin largely to the greatest architect of the Achaemenid empire, Darius I. Precisely for this reason it is a composite art, drawing inspiration from various sources: materials and artists were drawn from every part of the empire, and each artist worked along his own traditional lines, though he was assisted by sound and original guidance derived from the taste of his patron.

The great inscription on the palace at Susa describes the way in which the palace itself was built, and provides interesting details. 'The Babylonians worked at excavating the site, covering it with gravel, and manufacturing the bricks; the cedarwood was brought from a mountain called Libanus ... the oakwood from Gandhāra and Carmania. From Sardis and Bactria came the gold, which was then worked on the site; from Sogdiana came the stone (lapis lazuli and serpentine) also worked here, as was the hematite from Khorasmia; the silver and copper came from Egypt. The decoration on the wall is from Ionia; the ivory from Ethiopia, India, and Arachosia. The stone for the columns, which were made on the spot, came from Aphrodisia in Lydia, and the chisels to cut it were Ionian and Sardian. The workmen for the platform were Median and Egyptian; the cutters of precious stones were Sardian and Egyptian; the brickmakers were Ionian and Babylonian; the builders of the walls were Median and Egyptian.'

In Persia the great palaces of Pasargadae and Persepolis (Pl. 7, a) (1,650 ×1,000 ft), and in Mesopotamia the palace of Susa, all built with great care despite the enormous complexity of their planning, show features derived (with appropriate modifications) from the different cultural areas which had become parts of this vast empire. Assyrian influence, for example, is visible in various ways. There is the great raised foundation structure, artificial in whole or in part, the object of which was to exalt the level of the palace rather than to protect it from floods; there are the battlements on the buildings and at Susa the smooth facing of bricks; and the outer walls and staircases are covered with tablets carved in bas-relief, often accompanied by historical inscriptions and containing several subjects which also betoken Assyrian origin. Nevertheless the reliefs do not normally, as they did among the Assyrians, depict war scenes; and in later times they are enlivened by colouring, and by precious stones and gold.

Yet unlike the Assyrian palaces, but in imitation and improvement of those in Egypt and of the earliest Greek temples, the main portion of the Persian palace was composed of the great throne-room (*apadana*), with a thin ceiling of cedarwood supported by high slender columns. These were set at some distance from one another, and were sometimes smooth, sometimes fluted; they were often bell-shaped at the base with leaf ornament, and at the top, where they held up the architrave, they had a characteristic type of capital with a couple of heads of bulls or horses. In the slender columns we can see the Ionian Greek influence, which is also found in the way the bas-reliefs are modelled, and in the very careful drapery of the figures (which are always male).

The royal tombs in the days of Cyrus the Great (Pl. 7, b) were still modelled on whatever type of mausoleum was favoured by the region in question. But from Darius' time they were simplified, and were based on the underground tombs of Egypt.

Apart from decorated court architecture we can say little about Persian art, because discoveries have been so few. Of their sculpture we can only instance a single silver statuette, a bronze lion, and a gold chest with figured decoration. As to carving, a seal of Darius I, comparable with Assyrian and Anatolian art, is worthy of note, as is also the coining of the earliest gold 'darics', which carry a figure on one side only, that of the king in armour. In these coins we can see the influence of Lydia and Greece, which can also be discerned in the legend 'basileus' appearing on some later issues by the satraps.

g. *Phoenician and Carthaginian Art*

Phoenician art has very little individuality. The country lay where lines of communication intersected, and its people, though given over to trade (and especially sea-borne trade), were devoid of artistic inspiration. Their art, therefore, is full of elements derived from other countries, chiefly Egypt, Greece, and Assyria/Mesopotamia: yet these elements were haphazard and ill organized, for they were not given new life in any manner that was original, despite the medley of styles and techniques. The same lack of firm character is evident in the products they exported. Sometimes they simply collected objects of art from various countries in the course of their voyages, and then proceeded to re-sell them indiscriminately (the hybrid features of the Orientalizing period of Greek art owed much to this practice); or alternatively they would export cheap imitations from their own factories, reproducing other peoples' work in completely haphazard fashion. Some clay models of their palaces and temples survive: they were relatively small in size, and show Mesopotamian influence, although the Phoenicians made greater use of stone; when we reach the period of the Ugarit models, showing an open space with an altar, and behind it corridors and a *cella*, we can see the influence of Mycenaean Greece as well. In sculpture Egyptian inspiration is evident in the characteristic stone sarcophagi with half-human figures found at Sidon, and in the thirteenth-century tomb of King Ahiram at Byblos: the form of the clothing, and the sphinxes at the sides, point the same way. The numerous small objects which are a special feature of archaeological finds in Syria, and which therefore show the commercial importance of the country from an early date, are a further proof of the hybrid character of Phoenician art. Either they are straightforward foreign products, such as

Assyrian seals, Egyptian scarabs, or Mycenaean ivories, or they are cheap local imitations. The bronzes and glass-work are worthy of some attention.

The artistic habits of the Phoenicians did not change in their western colonies, which later became united under the leadership of Carthage. Indeed when these Punic colonies were cut off from their mother country they too came under foreign and especially Greek influence: most specifically was this true of the influence exerted by the Ionian Greeks who in the seventh and sixth centuries established themselves on the actual Punic coasts at Kybos and near by, and also by the Phocaean and Massiliote settlements clustered along the shore from eastern Spain to the Gulf of Lions. Another powerful force came from the Etruscans, who for a long time held joint maritime supremacy with the Carthaginians, and who themselves were highly Hellenized.

The root and branch destruction of Carthage by Rome has almost wholly deprived us of evidence about their monuments and large-size statues. Yet the material from their burial sites still shows how Greek stylistic methods were continually adapted to Punic tastes and ideas. Clearly therefore the Greek artists of North Africa, who succeeded in adapting their styles and models to these very different Punic tastes, must have been men of fundamental importance in artistic history. A typical feature is the horizontal position of human figures on tombs, which are looked at as if they were vertical statues. (Pl. 8.)

h. Greek Art

The end of Mycenaean types and the Transition to Geometric. Mycenaean art had arisen in court circles, the product of non-Greek Minoan ideas and forms uniting with Hellenic tastes and techniques. It began to alter with the Greek conquest of the islands and eastern coast of the Aegean when the natives lost their liberty, and consequently the fruitful cultural collaboration between Greeks and pre-Greeks slackened or disappeared. At the same time the sharp decline of the Egyptian empire under the Twenty-first Dynasty, and of the Hittite empire in the last centuries of the second millennium, coupled with the repeated set-backs to the Assyrian empire between the twelfth and tenth centuries, all reduced trade between the vast ancient countries of the East and the Aegean world; and the spasmodic or even non-existent relations of this period were reflected in the cultural and artistic spheres. There was also a consequent decline in the economic prosperity of potential buyers in Greece and the Aegean: so the standard of production went down, in respect both of artistic quality and of the fineness and value of the materials employed. This process was intensified by the fact that the largest exports were now directed at countries where culture had as yet made little progress, the areas where Hellenic colonization was soon to develop.

In any case it was natural that Mycenaean art should exhaust itself after centuries of growth and that an innovating movement should make itself felt amid the sterility of Mycenaean methods and rules. In some fields too a movement of this kind was promoted by the complete revolution in metal-working which resulted from the availability of large supplies of iron. But the decisive reason for the decline of Mycenaean art, this courtly product, was the fall of most Greek monarchies, one after the other; in the ensuing period the vast riches which had belonged to these rulers and which had been needed to adorn their houses and tombs with art treasures were no longer concentrated in a few hands. The houses of the nobles who took the kings' places, but who were engaged in continual struggles among themselves with consequent expenditure of money, were in no position to give permanent employment to numerous crowds of specialized artists. The next age was one of political turmoil and social conflict; the population was increasing and large fortunes were therefore being split up; there was a bitter struggle for existence and men rendered landless were undertaking those commercial enterprises which prepared the way for and later accompanied the new great emigration of colonists. In this Iron Age, which looked back with longing to the ancient 'Age of Gold', the man who could operate with profit and security was no longer the delicate artist making expensive articles, but the artisan. For by now only the few could seek out *chefs d'œuvres* made from fine materials: what was needed everywhere was a large quantity of modest industrial goods, both for use at home and also for export to distant countries, where they were exchanged for base metals and foodstuffs offered by the native in-habitants.

So gradually men turned to a 'geometric' style. This was a style much favoured on account of its simplicity and spontaneity by the reformers of the day, and it was one to which the increasingly emphatic stylization of Minoan-Mycenaean products was already tending. Something like it had in any case always existed in the western and northern parts of the Greek world, where Mycenaean civilization had made little mark, and also in south-eastern districts for the coarse articles used by the poorer classes. It was completely dominant in the Balkans and Italy, the destination first of traders seeking metals, amber, and the like, and later of colonial emigrants. The designs of certain textiles imported from the East were another factor favouring the new style.

The passage from Mycenaean to Geometric was slower in some areas than in others; and it was marked in particular localities by distinguishable phases of transition, which are normally called Sub-Mycenaean. Mycenaean must have been still common in some parts of Greece when the earliest sailors were taking its products as far as the island of Ischia, and even when the first Laconian colonists settled at Tarentum. But a few decades earlier, in the first half of the eighth century, it had been superseded in the homeland of the 'Achaean' colonists of south Italy and the Chalcidian colonists in Sicily.

The Geometric period was for a long while called the 'Greek Middle Ages', as if it had been a cultural decline caused by admixtures with peoples of different civilization. In fact, however, the adoption of the new style had nothing to do with the ethnic changes brought about by the much earlier Dorian migration: on the contrary it was the Mycenaean style which had been due to admixtures, and this style was now abandoned in order to return to spontaneous methods which came naturally to the indigenous populations. Moreover even if it is legitimate to speak of a decline in the figured arts, this was heavily compensated by the rapid progress made in other departments of human activity, metalworking, navigation, colonization, political organization and ordering of legal codes, religion, customs of life, and morals. Add to this the new methods of alphabetic writing, and literature which included the dazzling Homeric epic and the didactic poetry of Hesiod; nor was the least achievement one to be found in artistic production itself, namely the invention of temple architecture.

Architecture. Temples and Shrines. Too few remains of archaic Greek architecture have been excavated, and many buildings, made in relatively perishable material, have been destroyed. But what little we know of archaic architecture is important, since it reveals a continuous process of evolution from the Mycenaean to the Classical period. The portion of a Mycenaean palace devoted to the gods, and containing shrines, sacred areas, and idols, was small: but this is true only in appearance, because the royal palace itself was the house of a person of divine origin, namely the king, and it was consequently built for the gods whose descendant and high priest he was. So it need cause no surprise if it was often on the ruins of the Mycenaean royal palaces that the archaic temples were built, as houses for the anthropomorphic gods, their high priests being sometimes the ancient kings with their other functions removed; it is natural too that the earliest form of temple was modelled on the megaron, the great festive hall of the Mycenaean palace. Later this was copied in the construction of other temples where no regular palaces had existed. There was, for instance, the so-called 'Temple A of Primias' in Crete, with a cella 31 × 19 ft, a pronaos with two entrance doors between quadrangular pilasters, and a frieze on the architrave. Mention may be made too of the 'Pythion of Gortyna' and of the lay-out of the temple of 'Artemis Orthia' at Sparta, the latter with two naves like those in some rooms in prehistoric Troy.

But in addition to isolated temples there was a marked growth in the eighth and seventh centuries of a certain form of sanctuary. These with their oracles, festivals, gymnastic games, and contests in poetry and music, became the meeting-place of pilgrims and of athletes, and also of artists, poets, and musicians. They were the homes of culture and the sources of its diffusion. First place among them belongs to the sanctuary of Olympia in the sacred grove of Zeus, the Altis, on the right bank of the Alpheus beneath Mt Cronion, where villages had existed from the end of the Stone Age. Its games are traced back to the eighth century, and there were important edifices erected here in every period—temples (the Heraeum belongs to the seventh century), public and decorative buildings, altars, scattered votive monuments, and the famous 'thesauroi': the last were small buildings shaped like temples, and each was intended to house the more valuable of the votive offerings which came in from a particular district of Greece.

The oracular responses from the sanctuary of Pytho at Delphi were already famous in the eighth century. This lay beneath the Phaedriad rocks close to the Castalian spring; and its centre was Apollo's temple where stood the *omphalos,* the navel of the world, a sacred stone said to be the tomb of the python which the god had killed. Gradually other temples grew up, with treasuries, commemorative and votive monuments, and decorative buildings of various kinds.

The Earliest Architectural Orders. At the same time the form of temples was growing more elaborate. Originally consisting of a single *cella* or two naves, with or without a porch in front, their rows of columns now became gradually more imposing. These columns were constructed according to one of two architectural systems or 'Orders', originally devised in two different areas, but later to be found more or less indiscriminately in the whole Greek world. One of them, perhaps the more ancient, is generally called Doric, though 'Argolic' would be a better name. It was compact and solemn, with massive proportions, and of the two Orders this one retained more traces of the timber construction which was common in early days. This was especially true of the columns, which grew narrower towards the top and of which the bases fitted directly on to the floor of the temple; they had shallow acute-angled fluting, and their capitals were composed of a curved cushion below a square flag-stone which supported the architrave; this last was decorated with reliefs in the metopes and pediments, and was painted in many colours, particularly in the upper portions. (Fig. 2, a.)

The other Order is usually called Ionic, but a better name might be 'Ionico-Aeolic' or 'Asiatic': it shows eastern influence, and tended to divide into a number of sub-species. Its slender column rests on a base, has deep fluting with semi-circular interstices and blunt angles on the outside, and is surmounted by a capital with floral and plant designs. Instead of metopes and triglyphs the architrave has a fillet or frieze sculpted in relief. The building was adorned with many colours and other sculptured portions. (Fig. 2, b.)

Geometric Pictorial Decoration. Geometric art found its outlet mainly in painting (to some extent also in sculpture); and we know enough about its history to be able to determine its general features. For decoration an artist used primarily geometric elements—points, lines, zig-zag, lozenges, or patterns of network, chessboard, herringbone, or maze varieties, all painted with clear black varnish and often arranged to make a complete, elegant, and harmonious whole (Pl. 9, a). But in addition he would fill the portions most easily visible with figures of animals and human beings, one behind another in stylized manner; and later we find scenes of everyday life and episodes taken from Epic. Such pictures are clearly derived from designs used in the weaving of rugs and embroidery (on canvas), a process about which we have information

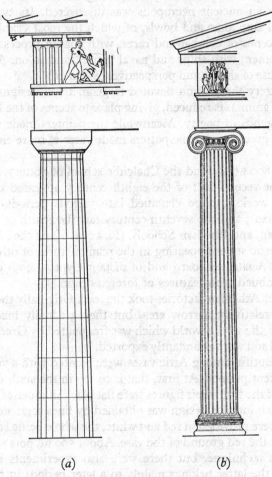

(a)   (b)

FIG. 2.   The classical Orders.
(a) Doric, (b) Ionic.

from the *Iliad* (III, 125 ff.). We can tell this from the stylized and angular shapes of the figures with their flat colours, and from the way they are arranged in horizontal and vertical lines to satisfy a taste which 'abhors a vacuum'. Decorated vases in this style are made in the most diverse shapes and sizes, ranging from very small pots to funeral amphorae over 6 feet high. Sometimes the painting, especially on lids, is accompanied by plastic decoration as well.

Geometric pottery can be classified by local styles, by the degree of stylization in reminiscence of Mycenaean, and by the extent of foreign (and particularly Oriental) influence, this last growing all the time.

The most ancient (tenth century onwards) and also the most spontaneous
school was perhaps the Athenian style of pottery known as Dipylon—from the
place in which an ancient necropolis was discovered. Its typical products
are the colossal amphorae and bowls, of which the most visible portions are
painted with scenes of combat and races, with chariot processions and lines
of men and women, with ships and naval battles, and so on. All is curiously
stylized in the use of shapes and perspective. (Pl. 9, b.)

On later pottery the portion devoted to geometrical designs and to strips
decorated with animals is reduced, giving place to scenes of the lives of heroes,
drawn from legends in poetry. Meanwhile the painters made the decoration
finer and more graceful, and the potters made vases of more elegant and perfect shapes.

From about 800 BC we find the Chalcidic school of pottery, with offshoots
in Sicily; in the second half of the eighth century appeared the Corinthian
school, whose works can be classified into various periods, starting with
'Proto-Corinthian'; and the seventh century saw the zenith of the Laconico-
Cyrenaic, Cretan, and Rhodian Schools. (Pl. 10, a, b.) At the same time there
were characteristic styles appearing in the manufactures of other cities, such
as those of the Asiatic seaboard and of distant Cyprus, both of which were
more deeply imbued with features of foreign origin.[13]

Soon however Athenian factories took the lead. Originally their wares were
known over a relatively narrow area, but they gradually made themselves
recognized over the whole world which was frequented by Greeks. They were
in avid demand and were abundantly exported.

The most beautiful among Attic vases were painted with a variety of techniques in different periods. At first, that is to say in the sixth century and at
the beginning of the fifth, their figures were flat black silhouettes (Pls. 11, a, b,;
12, a, b) in which interior design was obtained by lines scratched with a tool:
other touches were provided in red and white, the whole being set as a separate
element against the red ground of the vase. About 500 BC pots were still being
made with this technique, but there were also experiments in a new one.
The history of the latter belongs mainly to a later period: in contrast to the
earlier style it used a background covered with black colour and left the figures
in the red of the clay, interior design consisting of black lines which were
added by pencil. In the earlier technique the most famous painters known to
us are Ergotimus (aided by the potter Clitias) (Pl. 11, a), Execias, and Nicos-
thenes. But we possess other monuments of archaic painting besides those on
vases: painted metopes have been discovered in the temple of Apollo at
Thermos in Aetolia; there are some votive tablets (pinaces) from Athens;
and at Clazomenae have been found about seventy sarcophagi, on some of
which the Black Figure and Red Figure techniques are combined. Finally

there is the magnificent architectural use of many-coloured pottery on temples, as a covering for the portions built in timber.

Archaic Greek Sculpture. Diodorus (IV, 76) tells us that before Daedalus all human figures in regular sculpture were represented with half-closed eyes and with arms clinging to the body; but that this great artist discovered how to sculpt figures in which the eyes could seem to look at something, the legs could seem to walk, and the arms could stretch. These two kinds of statuary are in fact identifiable. The earliest examples of pre-Daedalic sculpture belong to the eighth century, and mainly suggest models drawn from trunks or branches of trees; certain ivory statuettes of a nude goddess found at Athens provide an instance, and there are other examples in Crete and Sicily. The Boeotian pottery figurines, with their wide bell-shaped dress, covered with geometric and animal designs, are very comparable.

A second phase, which still finds expression in cylindrical or flattened statuary made of wood from tree-trunks or planks, makes an effort to show movement, and is marked by care in the representation of drapery. (Pl. 13, a.) Examples are the seventh-century statue dedicated by Nicander at Delos and that offered to Hera by Cheramyes at Samos. (Pl. 13, b.) In its early stages this sculpture used a very small number of almost standard types of gods and of heroes in human form—or rather of idealized human beings. (Pl. 14.) There were female figures standing or seated and clothed; naked male figures standing erect; men running or on horseback or wrestling; figures of Hermes or Silenus, together with Centaurs, sphinxes, lions, and winged victories. Over many generations artists repeated these types and improved on their conception, their proportions, their anatomy, movement, and drapery, until complete excellence was achieved. Even when imitating foreign models Greek artists were able to assimilate and transform them, thinking them out anew: naturalism was confined to certain portions of their work; the rest was idealized. Among foreign influences the most obvious is the statuary of Egypt, knowledge of which came through the colonies and mercenaries settled in the Nile delta: it is particularly evident in their hair style, the pose of hands, and the advance of the left foot. But other influences, resulting from increasing trade relations, came from Cyprus, Syria, and Anatolia. These were responsible for the complexity of types found in the 'Orientalizing' Art of the seventh century.

Beyond doubt archaic Greek sculpture had many centres, but two basic genres can be discovered: the two schools seem to correspond to two different ideals of life. One predominated in Dorian countries, such as the Peloponnese, Crete, and Rhodes; the other in the Ionian colonies of Asia Minor. We can see the difference in statues both draped and nude, and also in architectural and funerary reliefs.

The former school, attested by finds at Sparta, Sicyon, Argos, Delphi, Corcyra, and other places, was engaged in representing, with increasing success, the spiritual qualities of humanity in a form that was grave, harmonious, and serene. Their statues were forceful but heavy; and though they made continual advances in technique and ideas, they always retained an archaic outlook, which is shown in the rigidity of their figures and in the simple flat surfaces of their draperies. Examples are the colossal, diademed, head of Hera found at Olympia, and the series of metopes at Selinus. (Pl. 15.) The latter are of increasing excellence as time goes on, the earliest ones being parts of a shrine, the others belonging to temples C. and F. and to the monuments associated with them.

The second school, the Ionic, produced representations of a more varied and gayer though more artificial type of beauty. It attached importance to ornamentation—to hair style, delicate pleating of dress, sinuous lines, elegance and affectation in the representation of detail and movement, and charm of expression in the face. Examples are the seated statues of divinities adorning the road from Didyma to Miletus (first half of sixth century), the Apollo of Tenea, the Naxian sphinx (mid-sixth century), the Moscophorus of Rhombos (an ex-voto of the late sixth century), and the Nikē of Delos. (Pl. 16, a.) Among reliefs may be mentioned a sepulchral *stele* now at the Villa Albani at Rome (*c.* 550), and the pediment and eastern frieze of the Siphnians' treasury at Delphi.

At Athens we find some kind of fusion between the canons of the two schools. The firm bodies and nobility of aspect found in Athenian statues was often combined with delicacy of drapery and other details; and important examples of the result can be seen in the seventy or so votive statues painted with many colours which have been found on the Acropolis, depicting Korai. (Pl. 16, b.) Among reliefs of this Attic type we may mention the coloured 'Typhon' group, a work of the mid-sixth century which belonged to the pediment of the Hecatompedon at Athens.

These various styles were reflected in the cutting of gems and on archaic coins, both of which help us to understand the tastes of the different regions of Greece and the technique which prevailed in each. (Pl. 2.)

i. *Italic Civilization. Originality of Etruscan Art*

In the last centuries of the Bronze Age and the first of the Iron Age (the transition must have occurred about the tenth century BC) a number of foreign styles and techniques were imported into Italy. The first were Mycenaean, derived from the objects traded by Greek merchants with the natives as far west as Ischia, or manufactured in their new homes by the pioneers of Greek colonization in Italy, that is to say by the people of Tarentum. Later there arrived Geometric wares, brought to Italy by Illyrian immigrants who settled on the Adriatic and Ionian coasts, or by Greeks reinforcing their colonizing movement into Italy and Sicily. The latter embellished and established more firmly the Geometric style they had brought from their various and distant homes.

When iron became known it of course did not eclipse the use of bronze, especially in early days when bronze was still valued highly enough to be used for inlays. Indeed the new iron hammers and anvils made it possible to construct bronze in sheets and to work reliefs on bronze armour, vessels, and ornaments.

From this large number of centres the radiation of Greek civilization was increasing all the time. First there were the colonies and their offshoots, spreading over south Italy and Sicily; then came the extension of the great network of Phocaean trade, with the stations planted on the Adriatic and Tyrrhenian coasts as far as the Gulf of Lions, and on the east coast of Spain. Moreover in the course of the seventh century Carthaginian trade was beginning, and they too imported foreign wares. As we have already explained, this whole process started the 'Orientalizing' period in the art of many Italian coastal districts.

The people who profited earliest and most intensively from these foreign borrowings were that portion of the Etruscans who had crossed the Apennines about 1000 BC and had gradually occupied Tuscany, from which they proceeded to extend their empire southwards as far as the territory of Salerno. In the marshy country of the Po valley this section of proto-Etruscans had, in the opinion of the present author, been compelled to build the lake stations (*palafitte*) and later the *terramare*. But when they left this country and its floods behind them and settled in the hilly lands of Tuscany, they gave up the laborious building systems of their past history: all they retained were the defensive terraces and (where possible) the regular and rectangular lay-out of their roads. Meanwhile, even before they came under direct influence from Greek and Oriental cultures, they were able to show their skill and artistic sense by originating their own types of architecture. The lines they marked out for themselves here were spontaneous, and Greek influence intervened only in the later stages. Graves gave place to funeral vaults, earth-mounds of the *terramare* kind to the earliest city-walls, and the regular plans of the *terramare* settlements to cities with a *cardo* and *decumanus*; instead too of the crude spherical vases used as ossuaries we find the two-horned Villanovan cups, the 'canopi' of Chiusi (vases shaped in human form), and eventually the 'busta' made from sheeted bronze.

In the process of civilizing Italy the importance of the Etruscans was quite fundamental, on account both of their own virtues and also of the things which they absorbed from Greek culture and then passed on to other people. Etruscan civilization was far from being a pale copy of Hellenic, and there was no systematic borrowing; moreover we cannot simply credit Greek residents with all the manufactured objects found in Etruria which reveal any deep or original artistic quality. If Etruria over the course of centuries was capable of this wide, profound, and continuous assimilation of Greek art and myths, and later of Greek literature and techniques—to the point at which indigenous and imported ideas became blended into a single whole, the latter being given a new life and, in the archaic age at least, sometimes actually surpassing the excellence they had attained in their previous homes—all this implies that the Etruscan and Greek peoples were exceedingly amenable one to the other. It is true that the Etruscan products known to us, which are generally industrial goods manufactured for private use, are often inferior to Greek products, which not infrequently are solemn dedications made by cities. Yet the Etruscan works have their own individuality; and whole departments of artistic production can be regarded as the creation of the Etruscan mind, seeing that for these types no foreign models were in existence. Furthermore the variation between the art of different districts, which had no political unity, is an obvious proof of Etruscan independence.

Cities, Houses, Tombs, and Temples. When the Etruscans came down into Tuscany, they lived mainly either in small rural centres which consisted of an assembly of huts and cottages, or alternatively in dwellings scattered over the agricultural areas. These were accompanied by a few *oppida* in strong positions, which served as refuges in time of need. Only later, when some centres acquired political domination over others, and when 'Lucumones'[14] were formed and started their series of feuds, did some of these *oppida* obtain decisive supremacy. In later times the need was felt to give these Lucumones stronger centres, which had therefore to receive regular fortifications: the reason was still foreign dangers, the Gauls advancing in the north, and in the south the anti-Etruscan reaction by the Italici. It was then, for example, that on the hills opposite the older city in the plain of modern Florence was built the fortification of Faesulae. In those *oppida* the contours of the country did not of course allow, at Populonia for instance, any wholesale application of the normal Etruscan plan of regular streets, in the way in which it became possible to adapt it in the fifth century at Marzabotto. To defend relatively low-lying centres use had to be made of terraces or earthworks like those in the villages of ancient Rome; but on higher sites the earliest defences consisted simply of the folds in the ground, whether tufa or rock, with some artificial improvement, of the kind found at Orvieto, Chiusi, Veii, and Falerii. Only later, from the sixth century onwards, were stone walls erected on the Greek model, as at Volaterrae, Faesulae, Saturnia, Perusia, or brick walls as at Arretium. The skill of the Etruscans as builders and hydraulic engineers can also be seen in their construction of roads, bridges, cuttings in the hill country, and drainage works in the plain, the last being accompanied by canals or underground tunnels (*cunicoli*).

Such Etruscan houses as have been found in excavation were generally small and simple. They often contained only one room, and differed little from the original Villanovan huts, which were constructed in wood or unbaked bricks, or were wattled with a covering of clay. They got quickly destroyed, but their shapes are reproduced for future generations in the funerary urns of the so-called 'Hut' type. (Pl. 17, a.) More considerable and complex dwellings are also known to us from vase paintings, from tombs with several rooms which are modelled on the houses of the living, and also from notices in Greek writings. The Greeks derived their word 'Tursenoi' from the solidity and strength of the Etruscan 'turseis'. Roman writers regarded their own type of house as being of Etruscan origin, the house with an *atrium* (a non-Latin word) and *tablinum*, in which a partly covered court, with a roof sloping forwards and backwards, gave access to one or more rooms. From this evidence it is clear that the more important Etruscan houses became fairly complicated as time went on, and that they were of a regular type. Of the *atrium* archaeologists give various explanations: some derive it from the primitive hut round which habitable rooms were added, others from the *megaron* of the Graeco-Mycenaean house, others think it was the *tablinum* which originated from the hut and that the *atrium* was the surrounding enclosure.

The same progressive development which is evident in their types of dwellings can be demonstrated in their tombs, which are found in clusters or else in great cemeteries outside the inhabited centres. The earliest cemeteries after the Etruscan descent into Tuscany contain cremation and inhumation graves side by side with identical kinds of furnishing: this undoubtedly resulted from the association of the cremation traditionally practised by the Villanovan Etruscans with the inhumation of the pre-existing inhabitants of the country. These inhabitants were now absorbed by the newcomers, who to some extent adopted their rites. The two systems continued and became amalgamated, so that we cannot with any precision attribute the inhumation graves with their rectangular ditches to the natives and the circular pits always to the Etruscans. New features were then added to these early types, and gradually there evolved those monumental tombs which are found from later periods, with a quadrilateral base and either a sham ogival vault or dome (*tholos*), or a flat roof sometimes with undulating surface. Both types, whether built inside an artificial *tumulus* or cut as underground chambers in the rock or tufa, could be of very large dimensions (one *tumulus* at Populonia is nearly 90 ft in diameter) and extremely complex, with secondary rooms or cells adjoining the main one. The François tomb at Vulci has seven cells and an *atrium*; and other examples are the Isis tomb (also at Vulci), the Campana tomb at Veii, the tomb of the 'seven seats' at Caere (with three parallel naves and an *atrium*), and the tomb of the Volumnii at Perugia. At the same time the construction work was being ornamented with ceilings, pilasters, columns, reliefs, inlay, and painting; and some Streets of the Dead had carefully aligned façades, with attention paid to the exterior architecture.

These pseudo-arches and sham vaults or cupolas were primitive shapes invented by the Etruscans in the course of their experiments in slantwise building, which involved them in placing blocks on top of one another, each projecting farther than the last. From these beginnings they attained in relatively late times to the construction of genuine arches and regular wedge vaulting. Moreover these successive forms of architecture spread outside Etruria, particularly into Latium: Rome was the main area where they were assimilated and improved.

In its earliest phases the Etruscan temple was affected by Greek influences: later it preserved its archaizing style. Down to late times it was built mainly of timber and terracotta. The plinths were normally stone, the room-walls of brick, but the frequent columns, with the ceilings and roof, were of wood. But the interior walls, roof, and gutters (these were narrow at first but were later given very broad dimensions) were still covered with tiles and tablets; they were also ornamented with coloured terracotta antefixes. There was generally a façade at one end only, the wall at the opposite end being closed; and the triangular pediment commonly remained open, unadorned with statues or reliefs. Temples originally had a long and a short side: but both in temples with a single *cella*, and in those with three *cellae* for the divine triads, the length in later times was generally little greater than the breadth. Of the tripartite type remains have been found at Marzabotto, Florence, Fiesole, Orvieto, and Civita Castellana in Etruria, and at Rome, Segni, and other places in the parts of Latium where the Etruscans once ruled. Vitruvius (*archit.*, IV, 77) tells us of the normal proportions of an Etruscan temple, but he is undoubtedly dealing with a fourth-century example rather than with one from the early days of the fifth.

Sculpture and Painting. The earliest Etruscan sculptors were excellent moulders and carvers who made use of both clay and bronze. Varro (in Pliny, *N.H.*, XXXV, 157) speaks of a famous sculptor of Veii called Vulca, the author of terracotta statues of Jupiter Capitolinus and Hercules which were erected at Rome; and Plutarch records a clay chariot executed by this artist, placed on top of the Capitoline temple. Archaeological finds have shown the skill possessed by these moulders of clay in various districts and periods, beginning from their very first efforts in the craft. Examples are the group which ornaments a Geometric vase from Montescudaio near Volaterrae, the tablets and antefixes provided as temple decorations (Pl. 18, b), and the so-called *canopi* from Chiusi: these last were originally cinerary urns, but the lids were then fashioned as human heads and the handles as human arms, and they became regular statues depicting the dead men whose ashes they contained. But the most perfect examples of this moulding in clay are the sixth-century statues of gods, Apollo and others, found at Vulca's home town of Veii, and forming part of a group of statuary of which other fragments survive. Comparable are the coloured sixth-century sarcophagi from Caere (Pl. 19), with a dead man and his wife lying banqueting at a table as on their funeral bier; note also the coloured pottery decoration from a temple at Falerii.

Equal skill and progress was manifested by Etruscan sculptors who used bronze with various techniques of casting, relief moulding, and incision, the earliest examples being crude bronze-cast statuettes like those found at Broglio. The small Etruscan bronzes (*Tyrrhena sigilla*) used to ornament houses and tombs were famous in all ages: they included statuettes (Pl. 17, b), candelabra, lamp-stands, tripods, vases, mirrors, armour, and parts of war-chariots. We also however possess some great examples from the archaic period, such as the Capitoline She-Wolf (late sixth century), a bust of a woman from Vulci, and a number of 'canopi' from Chiusi.

For works which required no particular polish or elaboration of plastic detail the Etruscan sculptors learned to use alabaster, sandstone, and volcanic stone from their own country ('nenfro' and 'pietra fetida'). In various periods all these materials were used to carve urns, busts, reliefs on *stelae* and cippi, sphinxes, and figured sarcophagi.

In all this plastic work there is no denying the influence of Greek art, which was recognized in ancient times (Pliny, *N.H.*, XXXV, 152). It is evident in the models, the style, the myths which were represented, and the treatment of the drapery. Yet it is clear that Etruscan artists also introduced new systems, such as those used for their great statuary in clay; and that new styles of an exclusively native kind were exhibited in their realistic treatment of the face and other details of the body. Their liking for portrait busts, and their skill in constructing them, can be seen from examples which are older than any coming from Greek countries, such as (once more) the *canopi* of Chiusi, and a seventh-century statuette found at Montalto di Castro. Both finds and tradition (Pliny, *N.H.*, XXXIV, 34) show the liking which the cities of Etruria, especially those in the south, had for plastic work. The Etruscan people also had a marked fondness for all small artistic objects of a light-hearted kind— such as gold jewellery, incised or carved ivories, inlay in metal, painted vases, or pottery modelled in imitation of bronzework with the black translucent colour of bronze (the *buccheri* vases). (Pl. 18, a.) The tombs and houses of Etruria, above all in the Orientalizing period, were consequently full of *objets d'art* of native and foreign manufacture, the imported goods coming through Greek (especially Phocaean) and Punic merchants.

These vases, plates, and coloured statues in clay, together with the tempera frescoes in tombs, make it possible to trace the gradual development of archaic Etruscan painting and to compare it with that of the painted objects imported from the Italiote colonies and from the Greek East.

Etruscan pottery was originally of the Villanovan Geometric type, made by the methods the invaders brought from the Po valley. But gradually a change set in, especially in the southern districts, as the Etruscans became familiar with the Greek wares imported from Magna Graecia, and later with those which originated from a wider range of Greek lands and were brought by Phocaean traders. Indeed Etruria, especially its seaboard and southern portions, was inundated with painted imported pottery, not only Italian Geometric from Magna Graecia, but Chalcidian, Ionian, Rhodian, Cretan, Cypriot, Corinthian, Laconico-Cyrenaic, and finally Attic (Pl. 11, b). These imports later inspired a whole range of local imitations, cheap on the whole, but not devoid of originality in type as well as in decoration. Yet all the while the native production of *buccheri* still went on.

In the period of hybrid and Orientalizing art, which coincided with the high watermark of Phocaean trade at the end of the seventh and beginning of the sixth centuries, we also find in Etruria the familiar pottery plates painted in vivid reds, blacks, browns, and yellows against a white ground. These depict sphinxes, and also scenes in this and the next world, with groups of figures engaged in discussion, procession, sacrifice, taking auspices, and many other activities. The subjects chosen attest not only Greek influence but also the Etruscan fondness for reproducing native usages, rites, cults, and dress, together with realistic faces and expressions.

Another feature of the Orientalizing period is the appearance, in Etruria south of Chiusi, of tomb-paintings in extremely vivid colours, designed to relieve the gloom of the tomb. Their excellence is clear testimony, *a fortiori*, to what must have been the fineness and power of Etruscan painting on houses and temples, which were both executed and looked at in reasonable light. These paintings were mainly in tempera, but were sometimes frescoes or painted directly on the tufa: in early days only a few colours were employed. They represent, in increasingly realistic and decisive manner, scenes of hunting and fishing, athletic and gladiatorial contests, banquets, chariot races, jugglers, funerals, and scenes of domestic life and of life in the next world. Gaudy and luxurious dresses are depicted with minute attention; the colouring is vivid; there is alert realism over pictures of animals and flowers; and a seeking after elegance is everywhere obvious. This all betokens artists with strong personality, even though they increasingly show the influence of the various techniques and types found in Greek painting with each of which they gradually became familiar.

j. *The Features of Latin Civilization—Creation of a Triple Koiné*

Rome lay at the centre of many peoples in cultural ferment, on the banks of a large navigable river, and on lines of communication between Etruria and Campania (the most civilized districts of proto-historic Italy); in its own territory too there was trade in early times. From the first, therefore, its civilization and art were of a mixed type, its own tendencies being blended with those which came from abroad; what it imported was given a Roman colouring, the new style then spreading to more backward populations outside. The story of the rough manners and semi-barbarism of Rome in the Regal period, found sometimes in ancient writers, is pure legend; and equally legend, though this time semi-erudite, is the view of certain modern scholars, who deny the Romans any instinct or capacity for art, regarding them as slavish imitators from the start. The truth is rather that Rome, whose population was continually being swollen by the incorporation of other peoples it had conquered, drew from early times on a number of different components of culture, but recreated them and gave them continuous and spontaneous evolution in accordance with its own conception of civilization.

The evidence from Roman and Latian cemeteries show the complexity which underlay the culture of Latium from the earliest historical period. We can clearly see the persistence of features going back to the First Italici, who had lived in the country from the end of the Copper Age: inhumation is one example, and the shapes, decoration, and general conception of Latin tombs are another. At the beginning of the Iron Age we find new features added, some brought by the Second Italici who filtered into the region (e.g. cremation, and instruments like trays, knives, and brooches, which had been used by the *terramaricoli*), others due to the first Roman contacts with the Etruscans (the use of defensive ramparts and palisades, and the concepts of the *pomerium* and the sacrificial *mundus*).

This complexity never grew less: it was actually enhanced by the events of the seventh and sixth centuries BC. The historical explanation of the magnificent cultural *koiné* which can be found over the whole area from southern Etruria to Campania is intricate. The causes include the Etruscan dominion, chaotic and interrupted though it was, over Rome, Latium, and part of Campania; for about a century (*c*.630–540) there was keen trade with the Phocaeans, who frequented the coasts of Latium and settled a number of craftsmen there; meanwhile the Chalcidians of Cumae kept up their commercial contacts, and the Romans were beginning to take to the sea. For more than a century the three races, Italic, Etruscan, and Greek, were living together in daily contact. They reacted one upon another, and in the whole of this vast area they created a superior form of civilization which to outward appearance was fairly homogeneous. The fusion of its elements was harmonious, though it remained a hybrid culture on account of its three-fold racial origin. For the moment we can confine ourselves to the phenomenon as it was presented in Latium, at Rome, Praeneste, Aricia, and similar towns. In the second Regal period Rome was given stone walls like the early or contemporary walls built on the Greek model in a number of cities of Etruria; the flow of water in the lower parts of the city was controlled by the construction of drains (e.g. the *cloaca maxima*); and the engineering efficiency of the Etruscan princes was shown in the drainage of entire areas in the plain of Latium, by means of underground tunnels. This was the period when the Carcer Mamertinus was built, with its original duty of constituting a water reserve; and tripartite temples with three *cellae*, on the Etruscan model, were erected first on the Quirinal and then on the Capitol. For these last buildings we are told by tradition that Tarquinius Superbus caused a number of artists and workmen to come to Rome; and it was from this period that artisans in the city became numerous, and were organized into colleges.

The earliest substantial buildings in wood and stone, temples, offices of magistrates (*regia, curia*, etc.) and the like, were frequently in this period embellished with mural ornament and with decoration in clay (Pl. 18, b); and this was directly due to Etruscan influence. Archaeological confirmation comes from the Capitoline temple and from other temples on the Esquiline and Palatine, while Pliny speaks of the well-known Veientine artist Vulca who beyond doubt drew his ultimate inspiration from Greek statuary (Pl. 20.).

According to Varro, archaic Roman statuary started in the time of Servius Tullius, and examples are found in succeeding centuries, including a statue in the Forum Boarium which is supposed to represent that king. There were also a statue of Diana from her temple on the Aventine, allegedly of Ephesian or Massiliote type, which was probably imported by the Phocaeans; statues of Juppiter Capitolinus and of Hercules, of which Vulca of Veii was supposed to be the author; and (probably of the same period) the statues which were said to represent Horatius Cocles and Cloelia. We still possess clay fragments such as the friezes in the Boston Museum; also the famous Capitoline She-Wolf; and a number of smaller statuettes, like the one depicting a king which was found in the Forum.

The *chefs d'œuvres* of the Orientalizing period are works of jewellery, bronze and ivory carving, and vases. They were the result of collaboration between Greek, Etruscan, and Italic artists and of the availability of models drawn from every country in the Mediterranean, mainly those in Greece and the Orient. Examples have been found in the country round Caere, once proto-Latin but now Etruscan; in purely Etruscan cemeteries such as Tarquinia, Vulci, Vetulonia, and Marsigliana; in the Latin town of Praeneste, which by now was also ruled by Etruscan princes; and finally in Greek Cumae. The most magnificent works from this composite artistic school were spread over Latium in the houses of the more powerful families, and in the tombs of the *primores*; meanwhile the lower classes continued to use instruments made of less costly material, mainly modelled on local types. Yet even behind this less important work we can see to some extent the influence of eastern models; clay objects, for instance, imitated luxury ware in metal; and local pottery copied Greek.

From Latium we possess no great mural paintings like the late seventh- and sixth-century murals found in southern Etruscan tombs. Yet in Pliny's day (*N.H.*, XXXV, 17) it seems that paintings of this kind were preserved not only in Etruscan Caere, but also at Ardea and Lanuvium. Quintilian (*Inst.*, I, 4, 16) copied the names inscribed on them in ancient writing; and if we trust his evidence, they depicted the same Greek mythological scenes which the import of painted Greek pottery had already made familiar in Etruria and Latium. In any case we are told that actual Hellenic painters had provided examples of their work in Etruria, like the Damophilus and Gorgasus who (according to Pliny, *N.H.*, XXXV, 154) decorated the temple of Ceres at Rome.

3. MUSIC

From primitive times man felt the need of song to amplify the sounds he made under the influence of emotion, and to give them emphasis and exaltation. He also wanted to accentuate the rhythm of other activities, such as the march and the dance, with sounds produced by clapping the hands or by playing instruments of a fairly rudimentary nature: these instruments were probably 'invented' independently by various peoples, that is to say through polygenesis. Men were led to create them empirically by the noises they obtained, sometimes quite casually, through percussion, or shaking, or quick rotary movement, or rubbing, or plucking at resonant and vibrant objects, or blowing at reeds and similar hollow tubes. Vibration caused by pressure gave rise to hurdy-gurdies, cymbals, castanets, and the like; percussion on resonant sticks or hollow tree-trunks or tablets or taut membranes led to the various kinds of xylophone and to drums or timpani; rapid rotation in the air made people invent peals of bells, sirens, and their variants; the emission of sounds by shaking suggested the sistrum and the rattle; the simplest methods of friction (on notched sticks or toothed bows or 'clappers') produced instruments consisting of taut, sounding strings to which a bow was applied; and the plucking of reeds or bark or similar substances led to the various instruments based on the plectrum (the zither, guitar, harp, and so on).

At the same time wind instruments were invented and developed. Some required continuous blowing on one or more reeds, which could be open or closed, and which might or might not have holes to be shut down with the finger. On others the blowing was intermittent, the sound being obtained by the vibration either of the mouthpiece (as with horns or trumpets) or again of some type of reed (as with the oboe, the Greek *aulos*, or the like).

The execution of music, both singing and instrumental playing, was originally free and spontaneous, whether it was carried out individually or collectively. But it began to be controlled and to follow a regular form when performances began to take place on relatively solemn occasions before an audience, as at sacred ceremonies or at funerals or on the field of battle. Eventually it acquired traditional and 'scholastic' rules.

In varying degree we have certain types of evidence for music among ancient peoples. There are monuments figuring scenes of singers, dancers, and players; some ancient musical instruments have survived; there are allusions in literature; and sometimes there are even musical scores in the poetic texts as they have been transmitted to us.

India. Nothing is known of early Indian music, except in so far as it was connected with the Vedic sacrifice. The Vedic hymns (*sāman* from the musical point of view) were sung or chanted according to fixed rules, which formed the object of a special manual, the *Ṛgprātiśākhya*. The tradition of

Vedic chanting has lasted down to these days, more or less faithfully preserved. Four song-books (*Gāna*) are employed for study or practice. They are technical works of very late age, connected with the *Samaveda*. They give the Vedic texts in their chanted form, i.e., with the insertion of additional syllables or whole words (*stobha*), mostly meaningless and intended to make the verses agree rhythmically with the melody. Musical notation is of a primitive kind. On this basis a reconstruction of Vedic hymn-singing of 3,000 years ago has been attempted; but of course this contains an all-too-strong element of surmise and hypothesis.

Egypt. On monuments showing processions, retinues, and armies on the march both singers and players are represented. Of the latter some have vertical flutes with as many as eleven stops, and sometimes double flutes; others have harps, with up to twenty strings; others have lyres, drums, or rattles.

Assyria preserved and improved the types of musical activity which had been current in the Middle East since Sumerian times. Here too monuments show scenes of singers and musicians taking part in temple rites, funeral ceremonies, processions, and military operations. The instruments are generally either harps, lyres, and lutes; or double flutes and trumpets; or tambourines, timpani, and cymbals.

For the *Hebrews* we have the evidence of the Bible showing that music was used to accompany songs, both individual lyrics and choral chants, at consecration ceremonies and at public addresses. We also find it used in the recital of the sacred prose writings, which were intoned against the background of melodious compositions following prescribed rules. The Hebrews therefore used both wind instruments such as the horn and also strings (the guitar, lyre, and harp) to accompany their choral songs, for which the Temple employed extensive choirs.

In the *Greek world* monuments as early as the Mycenaean age attest the presence of singers and the use of musical instruments—the sistrum, the zither, and the flute. Zithers, which perhaps derived from Egypt or Asia Minor, were of various kinds, their size, shape, and the number of strings (from seven to eleven) depending on the nature of the piece to be played. Among wind instruments the *aulos* or oboe (made of wood, bone, or metal) had various ranges of pitch (known as *parthenoi, paidikoi, teleioi,* and *hyperteleioi*); and the double flute, played with both hands, had one reed for the song and the other for its accompaniment (*krousis*). Sometimes use was made of the horizontal flute. The ancient *syrinx*, the shepherd's pipe, had between seven and nine reeds of the same length but of different diameters; but when used for artistic music it developed into an instrument in which the lengths of reed and their diameters were both different. Trumpets were of various proportions and had various depths of tone. Percussion instruments included wooden rattles (castanets), cymbals of various sizes, and timpani.

From Mycenaean times there were two distinct types of musical accompaniment for poetry. One became especially popular in Ionia, and was used in the solo recital or declamation of epic verse. The sound came from the lyre (*phorminx*), which was for the most part played by the singer himself; and the same technique was later employed in reciting didactic ('Hesiodic') poetry, and also elegy and iambus. The other type of accompaniment was used to provide the tune for lyric poetry, both in solo recitals and in choral performances.

The *Iliad* has many references to music, for instance to the singing of paeans (*I*, 472; XXII, 391). Moreover in the Eighteenth Book, describing the scenes on the shield made by Hephaestus, the poet tells of the dances, songs, and notes from *auloi* and *phorminges* which accompanied a wedding. There are the shepherds playing the *syrinx*, the maidens singing to the sound of the lute, the harvesters dancing and yelling, and a piazza where young men and girls do their dance.

In later times recitation of poetry was accompanied less and less by music, and eventually without it altogether. But lyric accompaniments grew in importance and became increasingly varied. On the one hand we find musical 'arias', purely instrumental pieces without any singing: these were sometimes for the pipe and sometimes for strings, one example being the *nomoi* addressed to the gods at public ceremonies. On the other hand there were *nomoi* on both pipe and string with liturgical song to accompany them. Clonas was renowned for *nomoi* on the pipe, the 'aulodic' genre, and Terpander of Lesbos for the 'citharodic' *nomos*. The sections of the liturgical hymn grew in number from three to seven.

It was in Lesbos too that the personal lyric reached its zenith, with wide variety of rhythm, metre, and strophes: the musical accompaniment was executed on instruments with as many as twenty strings (on the *barbitos*, *magadis*, or *pectis*), which enabled extremely low and extremely high notes to be played. In the work of Alcaeus, Sappho, and Anacreon this musical element, so far as we can judge, corresponded precisely to the sung verses, with their marvellous use of varied metre and rhythm, but eventually it was the music which gained the upper hand (see pp. 277 f.).

At the same time in Dorian lands the choral song was revived to express lyric sentiments, both for solo voices and for choirs. It was performed in dialogue by young men and girls, by athletes and dancers, and at weddings, in the strophic arrangement characteristic of Alcman. Dithyrambs too were composed, in honour of the gods, with dance and song alternating between the poet and his choirs, all to the sound of the flute: the works of Arion and Lasus are notable examples. Then there were choral songs of a type midway between epic and lyric, accompanied by the sound of the zither, such as Stesichorus I composed; and lastly Ibycus' choral hymns of praise, and the works of Simonides of Ceos written in honour of victories in war and at the games.

Meanwhile Pythagoras and his pupils worked at the study of acoustics and mathematics in relation to music. We need say no more here than that they enunciated the relation between musical intervals and the length of strings.

Monuments show how the Etruscans too were devoted to music and dancing and how they made use of both on public occasions, at games, and at funerals. The instruments in most common use were the lyre, the flute, and the *subulus* (or double flute), the bronze trumpet with curving mouthpiece (*lituus*), and the circular horn. We do not know what their musical compositions were like, but they must have drawn heavily upon Greek models. In execution we can see from monuments that it was common practice to let two players accompany each other, one on strings and one on the double flute.

NOTES TO CHAPTER VI

1. The two books of Samuel are sometimes described as *Kings* I and II, with the two books of *Kings* becoming III and IV.

2. The song of Deborah, like the song in *Exodus* xv, was almost certainly composed in the second millennium BC.

3. Allusions in Greek art show that many of these legends had developed as early as the eighth century BC.

4. The Hymn to Demeter is certainly seventh century or earlier, the Hymn to Pan is probably fifth century at the earliest, and the Hymn to Dionysus may be a work of the fourth century or later.

5. In this work the tale of each woman began with the words ἢ οἵη ('or like her who').

6. Line 22 of the *Theogony* mentions the name Hesiod as that of a poet already well known. But many scholars take this to be Hesiod's way of signing his authorship of the poem.

7. There is no decisive evidence about Hesiod's date but Professor Pareti brings him distinctly later than do most modern scholars. Herodotus indeed (II, 53) put Hesiod (with Homer) into the ninth century, and this date was supported, with ingenious argument, by T. W. Allen, *Homer, Origins and Transmission* (Oxford, 1924), pp. 78 ff. More probable seems a late eighth-century date, for Hesiod tells us (*Works and Days*, pp. 654 ff.) that he attended the funeral games of King Amphidamas of Chalcis, who fought in the 'Lelantine War', probably *c.* 705 BC. Professor Pareti may be too sceptical about the stories of Hesiod's life, about which the poet tells us quite a bit; and it is surely certain that his father migrated to Boeotia from Aeolic Cumae (*Works and Days*, 635–6).

8. The traditional date for Mimnermus' *floruit* is 630 BC, and many scholars suppose the eclipse to be that of 648 BC. Among Mimnermus' themes was the war between Smyrna and Gyges, in the first half of the seventh century, though this, like his account of the founding of Smyrna from his native Colophon, may relate to generations earlier than his own.

9. Here Professor Pareti follows once more the chronology propounded by K. J. Beloch, *Griechische Geschichte*, I, 2 (2nd edition, Strassburg, 1912), pp. 314 ff., pp. 357 ff. A passage in Herodotus (V, 94) appears to associate Alcaeus both with the Corinthian tyrant Periander (whose reign is traditionally dated 625–585) and with a son of the Athenian tyrant Peisistratus (this son being born of a marriage contracted after 560). Beloch tried to solve this and other difficulties by dating the Corinthian tyrants at least a generation later than does the tradition, by extending the lives of the Lesbian poets, and by redating various other events in the sixth century. Recent scholars have usually felt that his chronology

creates more problems than it solves. For a discussion of the Lesbian evidence, which in other respects is self-consistent on the whole and puts the *floruit* of Alcaeus and Sappho *c.* 610–580, see D. L. Page, *Sappho and Alcaeus* (Oxford, 1955), esp. pp. 149 ff.

10. Apart from the long life generally ascribed to Alcman, there is no strong evidence for this view. See D. L. Page, *Alcman, the Partheneion* (Oxford, 1951), p. 164.

11. This solution was first propounded by U. von Wilamowitz-Moellendorff, *Sappho und Simonides* (Berlin, 1913), pp. 233 ff. For counter-arguments see C. M. Bowra, *Greek Lyric Poetry* (Oxford, 1936), pp. 77 ff.

12. See Volume I, Part 2, p. 411, note 37.

13. This period of Greek painting, especially on Proto-Corinthian and Corinthian pottery, has great fascination. The 'Orientalizing' artists produced a riot of decoration, in which the motifs were sometimes fanciful (griffins, lions, and other monsters) and sometimes realistic (lines of hoplites, real animals, or flowers), all accompanied by daring experiments in outline drawing, colour, and incision. It is interesting to find a fairly constant time-lag between the manifestations of this art in mainland Greece and the periods of its models: it seems likely that Rhodian and other East Greek intermediaries stood between the Eastern origins and the great artists of Corinth. For a brief but vivid description see A. R. Burn, *The Lyric Age of Greece* (London, 1960), pp. 61–2, pp. 85–7.

14. These were the kings of the cities which were gradually established in Etruria. Lars Porsenna of Clusium, who captured Rome for a short time after the expulsion of the Tarquins, is the most familiar example.

PART TWO

MANKIND FROM ABOUT 500 BC TO THE CHRISTIAN ERA

CHAPTER VII

WORLD HISTORY:
500 BC TO THE CHRISTIAN ERA

I. THE FAR EAST

a. *China*

THE states which formed the political constellation of China were now no longer feudal, and the struggle between them took on substantially different features during the period traditionally called the 'Warring States' (*ch'an-kuo*, 481–221 BC). (Map VI.) Such will to federalism as survived grew gradually weaker, and it finally vanished with the failure and eventual disappearance of the office of hegemon (*pa*). The tendency now was not to federate with one's neighbour but to obliterate him, a tendency towards conquest pure and simple. In these struggles the old tribal aristocracy bled to death. The new methods of warfare had removed its pre-eminence in the art of war; the appearance of iron, the development of irrigation and agriculture, the flourishing of crafts and the spreading of brisk trade had sapped its economic basis. In its place a new, different type of landed nobility arose, and at the same time there was a growing trend toward consolidation of the central power within the single states. Among the various philosophical and political schools increasing importance in public affairs was assumed by the 'Legalists' (*fa-chia*), whose ideas were harsh and militarist, favouring a centralized and almost totalitarian constitution. They provided the theoretical background for a unified state; and in the principality of Ch'in they provided both the pattern for the later bureaucratic empire and the nucleus round which it was formed.

The beginning of this period is marked by the last efforts at federal organization. Two of the three states which had dominated the scene in the preceding period, Ch'in in the upper and middle valley of the Wei and Ch'u on the middle Yangtze-kiang, still maintained their position, though somewhat weakened. But the third, Chin in the middle valley of the Huang-ho, disappeared in the course of the fifth century; it gradually splintered into three successor states, Wei, Han, and Chao. For a moment a new factor came on the scene, the state of Wu in the lower valley of the Yangtze, a state whose racial basis was only partly Chinese. In 482 it attempted to obtain recognition as the leading power; but its fall was as meteoric as its rise, and in 473 it was destroyed. Most of its lands were annexed by another southern state, this time almost wholly non-Sinic in language and race, Yüeh in the coastal provinces south of the Yangtze. Kouchien of Yüeh tried to wield the position of *pa*

after 473, but his inept successors could not maintain themselves at the level
of their founder; and in 333 the state was destroyed by Ch'u.

Meanwhile in the far north the Chinese peasantry, who were the backbone
chiefly of the principalities of Wei and Chao, spread their advanced form of
agriculture as far as natural conditions allowed, that is to say as far as irrigation was possible. Some of the backward populations of the frontier strip
were assimilated; others were driven towards the steppe and the desert,

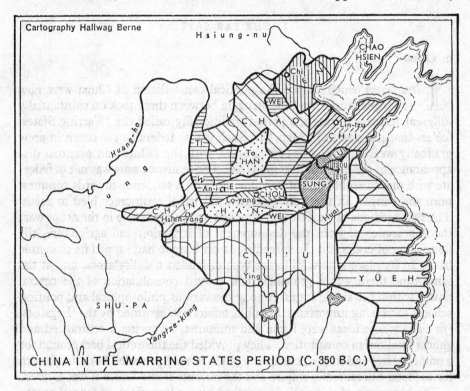

CHINA IN THE WARRING STATES PERIOD (C. 350 B.C.)

MAP VI

where they developed a new form of life completely antithetic to sedentary
agriculture, namely pastoral nomadism. Chao in particular added to its power
during this process of expansion, both by increasing its population and
economic potential, and also by building a formidable army on the new model
which gradually came into being when cavalry took the place of war chariots.

Ch'in remained in obscurity during the fifth century, but after 419 it
began to exert a strong pressure towards the east and south. Duke Hsiao
(361–338), aided by his great minister Shang Yang, reorganized the state on
'Legalistic' principles, constructed a new capital, Hsien-yang (near the
present Sian-fu), and in 343 secured election by the chiefs to the office of *pa*:
this election was confirmed by the fainéant Chou king. But the dignity had

lost all significance: the original conception behind it was played out, now that in these years every prince, one after the other, had assumed the royal title. The final success of Ch'in was assured by the conquest of Ho-hsi (on the banks of the middle Huang-ho) in 330, and by the annexation and settlement of the rich region of Shu and Pa (the modern Szechwan) in 316. Against the constant pressure from Ch'in and Ch'u (and to some extent Ch'i) the other states tried to defend themselves by allying both among themselves and with one or another of the larger states in a regular system of alternance, called by historians the 'vertical and transverse' alliances (*tsung-hêng*).

In its broad outline the political problem was now more simple. The feudal system had broken down, and the fiefs had merged into three major units together with a few minor ones. Now that all attempt at confederation was at an end, these units had become real independent states; and the one political factor they had in common was a complicated game of alliances and wars. From the ethnic standpoint they included a number of non-Sinic elements, though these were gradually being Sinized.

The interminable struggle reached its end in the years following 256. The Chou dynasty was formally deposed. King Chêng of Ch'in (reigning from 247), with the aid of his chief minister Li Ssŭ, ended the work with the conquest of the remaining states, including Ch'u in 223 and Ch'i in 221.

Chêng ruled over a state of which the essential constituents were the basins of the Huang-ho and the Yangtze-kiang. The long war had completely wiped out Chou feudalism in this huge area, and Chêng and Li Ssŭ applied to it the centralizing and authoritarian principles of the Legalistic School, which had represented the moving spirit and the strength of the Ch'in state. The country was divided into thirty-six provinces under governors sent out by the central power. This constructive work amounted to the creation of a new order: to give it outward significance, Chêng in 221 took the title of emperor (*huang-ti*), and posterity therefore knew him as Ch'in Shih-huang-ti. With him begins the history of the Chinese empire which lasted until 1912. The first emperor reigned for only eleven years; but the work accomplished in that time—largely due to Li Ssŭ—was immense, and it left an indelible mark on the country. A powerful effort towards uniformity, excessive in its rigidity but a natural reaction to centuries of turmoil, seized in its grip the whole Chinese people. Writing was standardized, and local variations eliminated; weights, measures, and also coinage, were unified. An attempt was even made to impose uniformity of thought. Every memory of the past was attacked. In order to obliterate all material which might be used for hostile propaganda the government proceeded to confiscate and destroy most of the existing literature, particularly the Confucian writings. The adherents of Confucianism, who had increased continuously in numbers and influence during the preceding century, were persecuted. A further policy was the promotion of conquest and colonization in the far south, which till this time was practically unknown territory. The occupation of modern Kuangtung opened the way for Chinese colonization of the south, though its political integration was only made definitive a century later, and its Sinization was a slow process; in the south-west it is not fully accomplished even today. A corollary of this very slow development was that the far south was regarded as colonial or half-colonial territory, almost to the end of the period covered by this volume.

The founder of the empire and his minister carried their work to its conclusion. But their iron harshness imposed such sufferings on the people that rebellions broke out. They were partly led by the remnants of the old aristocracy, but for another part they represented a spontaneous rising of the farmers, the first hint of those peasant revolutions that were a recurring feature of Chinese history during periods of decay. The dynasty fell only three years after Shih-huang-ti's death in 210; Ch'in with the policy it stood for became anathema in historical writing. There followed five years of civil war, till Liu Chi, a rebel chief of peasant origin, defeated all his rivals and founded the Han dynasty (202). He built a new capital, Ch'ang-an (Figs 3 & 4), at some distance from the Ch'in capital of Hsien-yang in the Wei valley, which had been sacked and destroyed.

During the civil war feudalism had revived, and the founder of the Han dynasty had to take account of the change.[1] At first in the new Chinese state, provinces and fiefs co-existed side by side. But then the fiefs lost all political and administrative significance, and became simply titles granted to great lords who were government pensioners. The structure of government and the administrative system of the Ch'in rulers, the work of the Legalistic School, were preserved in substance, but there were important modifications and concessions. Above all the spiritual outlook was completely altered when Confucianism was accepted as the political philosophy and theoretical foundation of the state, as it gradually came to be in the course of the second century BC. There now came into existence a characteristic figure, who more or less dominated public life in China down to the early twentieth century. This was the gentleman-official, highly educated, well versed in Confucian writings, and generally the owner of fairly wide landed estates. In theory he was chosen for his post among the best men in China, by methods which later developed into a regular system of state examinations. But in practice the combination of bureaucrats, literati, and landowners, with their monopoly of the difficult system of writing and the refined administrative technique, became eventually a semi-closed caste.

Till now China had concentrated on its own problems, but under Wu-ti (141–87) it turned outwards and began its first phase of imperial expansion. The far south of China, northern Vietnam, and parts of Korea, were formally annexed, all of them territories which after centuries of integration with China absorbed a full measure of Chinese thought and civilization. The struggle with the first great empire of the Steppes, the Hsiung-nu in modern Mongolia, began about 200 BC and was carried to a conclusion with bravery and incredible tenacity. From that moment the problem of the northern frontier, which means the problem of the nomads, became one of the basic factors in Chinese history; and it remained so for nineteen centuries. It was in the context of this struggle that Chang Ch'ien carried out his adventurous mission into central Asia between 138 and 125: this opened up for China the caravan routes across the Tarim basin, and put it into direct contact with the western countries, i.e., with the eastern outposts of the Iranic world. Not only were the foundations of geographical knowledge immensely enlarged, but a variety of artistic and religious concepts reached China by these routes and contributed in some measure to shaping Chinese culture.

Wu-ti's successors reaped the harvest of his breadth of vision and his tenacity. By the middle of the first century BC the Hsiung-nu could be considered subdued; and at the same time the whole Tarim basin passed under Chinese domination and was given a special administration of colonial type. But by now the dynasty was in decline. The political position of the emperor had been weakened to the advantage of the Confucian literati, but still more to that of influences working through the female side of the court, i.e. brothers, cousins, and other relatives of the various empresses. By the end of the first century all effective power was in the hands of the Wang family; and its head Wang Mang took the final step when he deposed the Han dynasty and proclaimed himself emperor.

b. *Central and North Asia*

The darkness of prehistory begins to lift over central and northern Asia in this period, but for the earlier part of it we are entirely dependent on archaeology for evidence. It tells us of the metalworking centre of Minusinsk on the upper Yenisei, the products of which between the fifth and first centuries belong to the Tagar II culture and are characterized by the use of iron. The Scytho-Sarmatian element was still dominant at the beginning of the period, but from the beginning of the third century the Indo-Europeans yielded their position to the Altaic peoples. Before that happened, however, this great civilization of the Steppe flowered for the last time in the magnificent culture of Pazyryk in the Altai mountains. The Kurgans (funeral mounds) of Upper Altai, frozen deep in the ground, have preserved under particularly favourable conditions the remains of a fine art and of the luxurious life enjoyed by these great nomad princes. The influence of Achaemenid Persia was strongly felt, even after the fall of that empire; it was the decisive element in the civilization of these regions, and provides the first example of that posthumous expansion of Iranic culture which will often meet us again. There were many occasions on which Iranic light flashed eastward after it had been extinguished in the country which originally kindled it.

On the frontiers of China meanwhile the Chinese peasantry were pressing relentlessly northwards in search of new lands. No name is associated with this resolute advance, but it pushed the less civilized peoples of the border country, the Ti and the Jung, back towards the steppe and the desert. Its limit was reached only when the Chinese could no longer find conditions permitting the artificial irrigation required by their intensive form of agriculture. On the other side the amorphous populations which retired northwards were compelled to change their mixed economy for one based on nomadism and pasturage. The non-differentiated frontier belt was now replaced by a sharply marked border-line, even though its position fluctuated from time to time; it was the frontier between agriculture and cattle-raising between sedentary people and the nomads, between two opposite and irreconcilable worlds. We have seen already how the problem of the nomads became one of the basic factors in China's history. But later a similar process began outside the northern frontiers, largely as a reaction and as a legitimate defence against Chinese aggression, when China became organized and unified into a centralized empire at the end of the third century. This was the origin of the first empire of the Steppes, the empire of the people whom the Chinese called Hsiung-nu and who are certainly identical in name, and perhaps also to some extent in race, with the Huns who appear in the history of Europe. The founder of the new state was T'ou-man (the names of these rulers are known only through their Chinese transcriptions): he died in 210/209, and is thus a contemporary of Shih-huang-ti, the founder of the Chinese empire. The Hsiung-nu empire reached its zenith with Mao-tun (209–174). China, several times invaded, made great efforts to defend itself by arms and by diplomacy; but its heavy and slow-moving armies could not prevent continuous devastation of the frontier districts at the hands of the horsemen from the steppes.

The most important result of Hsiung-nu expansion was a large movement of populations with consequences felt over all Asia. Practically the whole effort of T'ou-man and Mao-tun was concentrated on the people called Yüeh-chih, originally settled in the modern Chinese province of Kansu. Lao-shang (174–161) completed the work of his father Mao-tun when he defeated and killed the enemy king, made his skull into a drinking cup, and drove out the Yüeh-chih. The latter, deprived of their ancestral lands, migrated westwards. Their attempt to settle in the Ili valley was frustrated by the Wu-sun, a red-bearded people with blue eyes, who were perhaps Indo-Europeans. The Yüeh-chih then moved into territory which is today included in the Soviet Republic of the Kirghiz; and there they found a temporary home by turning out the previous inhabitants, the Sacae, in about 150 BC. In their turn the Sacae launched themselves on the Greek kingdom of Bactria, which collapsed under their attacks, and then passed on into Iran, and beyond it into India. Shortly after this (perhaps about 125) the Yüeh-chih resumed their advance and settled in Bactria: a century later the Kuṣāṇa organized them into a powerful state, which extended across the Hindu Kush into India.

South of the steppe belt extended a desert region, sprinkled with oases of

varying size. Where these oases were relatively large a state based on agricultural economy would come into being, like Sogdiana and Khwarezm
(Fig. 3) at the end of the sixth century: Soviet excavations, particularly those
by Tolstov, have brought to light in that region a rich and manifold culture.
In small oases city-states grew up (Pl. 21a), *poleis* whose economy was partly
agricultural but even more commercial. The oases on the northern and
southern fringes of the arid desert of Takla-Makan were of this type: their

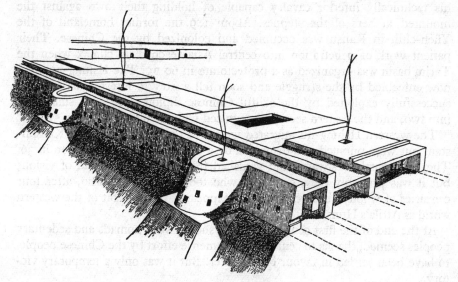

FIG. 3. Reconstruction of the wall of an early Khwarezmian citadel
(after S. P. Tolstov).

position determined the direction of the two caravan routes between West
and East, called by the Chinese *pei-lu* and *nan-lu* (the northern and the southern route). The wealth of these states combined with their political and
military weakness and with their commercial and strategic importance, to
make them for many years a coveted prey for their neighbours, the nomads on
one side, the Chinese on the other. Between 135 and 127 Chang Ch'ien was
sent as Chinese ambassador to propose to the Yüeh-chih that they resume war
against the Hsiung-nu. His diplomatic mission failed, for the Yüeh-chih
refused; but a result of the mission was that the Chinese gained knowledge
of the roads to central Asia and the countries of the West. A gateway was
thus opened, which was never closed again. Through it was passed throughout the centuries a traffic as fruitful in ideas and culture as any that history
has seen. Central Asia became the meeting ground of the movements started
by all the great civilizations of the time, Iranic, Hellenistic Greek, Indian,
and Chinese. In turn they inspired one another, but it was not only the countries on the border of Asia to which this trade brought new ideas and

invigorating force; in the end a new civilization, highly original in its eclectic outlook, was created in the heart of central Asia itself.

In the political field the struggle between Hsiung-nu and Chinese influence continued for several decades, until China eventually prevailed. The decisive war had been begun by the emperor Wu-ti. He attacked the Hsiung-nu in the heart of the Gobi desert, and for this purpose he sought as far as Ferghana the large and robust horses of central Asia, the only breed which could make his technically inferior cavalry capable of holding their own against the mounted archers of the steppes. About 119 the former homeland of the Yüeh-chih in Kansu was occupied and colonized by the Chinese. Their patient work of penetration into central Asia reached its climax when the Tarim basin was organized as a protectorate in 60 BC. The Hsiung-nu were now enfeebled by the struggle and soon fell a prey to internal dissensions, successfully exploited by the skilful Chinese diplomacy. Their state split into two, and the eastern section recognized Chinese overlordship in 51.

The western Hsiung-nu migrated westward on to the steppes of Kazakhstan, but were pursued and dispersed by a daring Chinese expedition in 36. They fled north-westwards and vanished from the Chinese field of vision; but it was probably they, or others who took their name, who, after four centuries of wholly obscure existence reappeared in the orbit of the western world as Attila's Huns.

At the end of the first century BC the issue between nomads and sedentary peoples seemed, thanks to centuries of immense effort by the Chinese people, to have been settled in favour of the latter. But it was only a temporary victory.

c. Japan

The scene of the last phases of neolithic 'Jōmon' culture was mainly northern and eastern Japan. Its features are pottery which, though technically backward, was of serious artistic merit, with manufactured goods of a high order though entirely made of stone. Metals were still completely unknown. Later the predominance of Jōmon began to be challenged by the 'Yayoi' culture, attested in the first century BC in Kyushu and datable from Chinese bronzes found in the same tombs; its name derives from a ward of Tokyo where its earliest remains were found. Nevertheless Jōmon still maintained its position in the north in prehistoric and historical times. Meanwhile the Japanese took shape as the people which we know today. The first bearers of the Jōmon culture were the Ainu, a Caucasian people, but they were later pushed back to the north of the main island (and later into Hokkaido) and gave place to a people of mixed proto-Malayan and Mongoloid elements. The latter seem to have acquired their leading features rather early; for the Yayoi culture presents remarkable homogeneity and uniformity.

2. INDIA

About 500 BC a centre of some importance began to exert political influence in northern India, namely the Magadha kingdom in what is today southern Bihar. Under Bimbisāra and Ajātaśatru, both contemporaries and patrons of Buddha, Magadha influence extended over neighbouring districts, especially after the opposition of the Vaiśālī kingdom had been broken. For the first time a centripetal and unifying force disturbed the equilibrium of the north. It will meet us again at irregular intervals in the course of history, though it finds resistance in the difficulties of communication over these enormous distances and in the political looseness inherent in Indian society.[2] The latter factor may seem paradoxical, but is in fact a logical result of the subdivision of society into castes which despite apparent social harmony have no political consistence. The history of the Indian sub-continent throughout the Hindu period is that of the alternating expansion and contraction of a great power in the Ganges basin. The greatest period of expansion, under the Mauryas in the fourth and third centuries BC actually embraced all India. Later empires were on an ever-decreasing scale, until after the seventh century AD the process ceased entirely and gave place to a system of zonal equilibrium. This, though precarious, was destined to endure: in fact it lasted till the Muslim conquest in the twelfth–fourteenth centuries.

The Bimbisāra dynasty was succeeded in Magadha by the Nanda (c. 370–320) who had their capital at Pāṭaliputra (modern Patna), the principal city of northern India for about a millennium. At the same time Persian rule survived in the Punjab, being exercised through the two satraps of India and Gandhāra. Iranic influence grew weaker during the fourth century and to all appearance it was eliminated by the bold expedition of Alexander the Great. But Alexander in fact was a restorer: he conceived and carried out his expedition to recover the Indian boundaries of the Achaemenid empire, of which he felt himself to be the legitimate successor. Hence the mutiny of the armies of Macedonia and the Greek League at the Hyphasis: they had reached the theoretical limits of the empire they had set out to conquer.

Alexander organized the Indus valley as something between a province and a protectorate, but the system crumbled as soon as he was dead. His passage into India had been an event of very little importance, to judge from the complete absence of his name in Indian tradition.[3]

In the anarchy which followed Alexander's death an adventurer of genius named Chandragupta came to the fore. He became known during the struggle against the Macedonian officers, and with the prestige he had acquired he made his way into Magadha. There with the aid of his minister, a great statesman named Cāṇakya or Kauṭilya, he dethroned the Nandas and founded the new dynasty of the Mauryas (c. 320–187), quickly extending his rule to cover all northern India, including the districts which had been Macedonian. (Map VII.) Seleucus' expedition to the borders of India in 305–4 ended with a

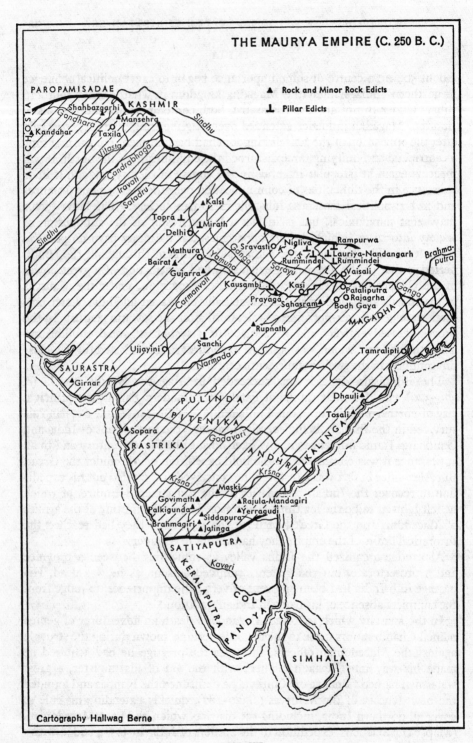

THE MAURYA EMPIRE (C. 250 B. C.)

▲ Rock and Minor Rock Edicts
⊥ Pillar Edicts

PAROPAMISADAE

ARACHOSIA

KASHMIR

Shahbazgarhi
Gandhara
Kandahar
Taxila
Mansehra

Sindhu

Vitasta
Candrabhaga
Iravati
Satadru

Sindhu

Kalsi
Topra ⊥
⊥ Mirath
Delhi

Sravasti
Nigliva
Rampurwa
⊥ ⊥
Lauriya-Nandangarh
⊥ Rummindei

Mathura
Bairat ▲
Gujarra

Ganga
Yamuna
Rummindei
Sarayu

KOŚALA

Vaisali

Brahmaputra

Carmanvati

Kausambi
Prayaga
Sahasram ▲
Kasi

Pataliputra
Rajagrha
Bodh Gaya

Ganga

MAGADHA

Rupnath ▲

Ujjayini

⊥ Sanchi

Narmada

Tamralipti

SAURASTRA

Girnar

PULINDA

PITENIKA

Dhauli ▲

Tosali

Sopara

RASTRIKA

Godavari

ANDHRA

KALINGA

Krsna

Krsna

Maski ▲

Govimath ▲
Palkigunda
Brahmagiri ▲

Rajula-Mandagiri ▲
Yerragudi ▲
Siddapura ▲
Jatinga ▲

SATIYAPUTRA

KERALAPUTRA

Kaveri

COLA

PANDYA

SIMHALA

Cartography Hallwag Berne

MAP VII

treaty recognizing Chandragupta as ruler not only of India but of Aria, Arachosia, and the Paropamisadae. Normal diplomatic relations were started, and we have fragments of a valuable description of the country given by Megasthenes, the ambassador of Seleucus to Pāṭaliputra.

Chandragupta and his son Bindusāra extended the Maurya empire over the whole of India, with the exception of the southern tip. Bindusāra's successor Aśoka (c. 273–236) is a figure of the first rank in Indian history. Indian epigraphy really starts with him; and he was responsible for the active propagation of Buddhism within India and outside it. With Aśoka Buddhism ceased to be a small local sect of Magadha, and became an all-Indian religion, looking forward to becoming an all-Asian religion. Aśoka's inscriptions reveal his pacifist convictions, the care he showed for his subjects, and his burning zeal for *dharma* (the moral law). From a strictly political standpoint, however, this period saw a standstill to imperial expansion, followed immediately afterwards by a precipitous decline. Meanwhile the international contacts of the Maurya rulers extended to Ceylon, to the Iranic peoples on the border, and to the contemporary Hellenistic kings: the last included Aṃtiyoka (Antiochus I), Turamāya (Ptolemy II), Aṃtekina (Antigonus Gonatas), Māga (ruler of Cyrene), and Alikasudara (Alexander of Epirus).

The end of the 3rd century saw the rapid decline of the Mauryas, and also the futile expedition to the borders of India launched in 206 by Antiochus III. About 187 the Mauryas, now rulers of little more than Magadha itself, were deposed by Puṣyamitra, the representative of a reaction in favour of the old religion. His dynasty, the Śuṅga (c. 187–75), was purely brahmanic, but (as is so often the way in India) this entailed no kind of persecution of Buddhism. The Śuṅgas successfully resisted Greek invasion; but their resistance was purely passive, and counter-attack was out of the question. Under their successors, the fainéant dynasty called Kāṇva (c. 75–30), Magadha had for the time being come to the end of its position as a unifying force; and for several centuries it disappears again into obscurity.

The North-West (modern West Pakistan), with its Iranic associations, had secured independence of the Mauryas even before the arrival of Antiochus III. Some decades later it again saw a Greek army on its own soil. One of the Greek kings of Bactria (Demetrius according to some, Menander according to others) invaded India and pushed as far as Pāṭaliputra, to which he laid siege. The venture failed,[4] but at least the Punjab and parts of Sind remained in Greek hands. About 130 BC the Bactrian kingdom collapsed under the attacks of the Yüeh-chih, and the last Greek rulers took refuge in Afghanistan. About 100 BC the Greek territories in India were divided among various kings, who are known only from their coins. Of these rulers the most important was Menander (second century BC): he clearly symbolizes the cultural union of Indians and Greeks, and is the chief figure in the Buddhist dialogue called *Milindapañha* (Menander's Questions). Nevertheless one must emphasize the strangeness of the phenomenon by which Hellenism apparently began to exert cultural and artistic influence in India only after the Graeco-Indian kingdoms had come to an end.

The Sacae meanwhile, after occupying Bactria, had penetrated into Iran, where they failed to break the Parthian barrier, but settled in the country which from them took its name of Śakastan (the modern Seistan). From there they made their way through the deserts of Gedrosia and poured into India, crossed the Indus, and took the Indian Greeks in the rear, driving a wedge into their territory by the occupation of Taxila. The Greek kingdom of eastern Punjab was overcome and soon disappeared from existence; the western kingdom kept up a feeble resistance in the mountain fastness of the Kabul valley. The Śaka introduced into the Indus valley a somewhat loose feudalism, under which the various *kṣatrapa* (satraps) recognized the overlordship of the Śaka king of Drangiana, and later had their own 'King of Kings' in the Indus valley; but this central authority was always very weak. Amid the feudal anarchy of the Śaka, the last effort at Greek resistance, and the eclipse of Magadha, north India at the beginning of our era was shattered into very small fragments.

The history of the peninsula south of the Vindhya mountains is almost unknown. In Orissa a great ruler appeared for a moment in Khāravela (first century BC); but he is an isolated figure, and Orissa never again played a significant part in Indian history. Further west the Sātavāhana kingdom was created by Śimuka in the second half of the first century, and had a great future in the period which follows.

When the curtain of history rises on the Dravidian south, it is found divided into three solid and lasting political formations, which contrast with the alternance of empires and fragmentation of petty states in northern India. The three states are the Cola on the Coromandel coast, the Pāṇḍya at the tip of the peninsula, and Cera, or Kerala, on the south-west coast. All three kingdoms are political creations of the Tamil people (and also of the Malayalam, whose language branched off from Tamil relatively late).

The island of Ceylon was colonized by Aryans, at a date not precisely determined but probably as late as the fifth or fourth century BC. From the outset the invaders were organized into a kingdom, and in the second half of the third century they were converted to Buddhism by Aśoka's brother Mahinda. From that time Ceylon remained a strong outpost of Buddhism in the south.

3. THE PERSIAN KINGDOM

In 512 the Persian king Darius had made an expedition to the Danube and beyond it, against the Thracians, Getae, and Scythians.[5] When he returned to Sardis he left officers in the Balkans, Megabazus and his successor Otanes, who established a bridgehead in Europe, taking possession of Perinthus, Byzantium, part of the Thracian Chersonese, and the islands of Lemnos and Imbros. These extensions of the Persian empire were followed by treaties designed to win over the king of Macedon and then by an attack on Naxos; at the same time commercial privileges were granted to Egypt and Phoenicia. The result was a violent revolt of the Ionian colonies, who remembered the flourishing trade they had once enjoyed and saw it damaged by their new masters. The insurgents were quickly joined by Aristagoras, tyrant of Miletus,[6] and by the dynasts of Caria and Cyprus; moreover an appeal was made to the Greeks of the homeland, who were also threatened by the Persian advance. Sparta, however, made no move, and several states preferred to make sure of friendship with Persia; Athens and Eretria gave help, but the few ships they sent were withdrawn after the rebels failed to take the acropolis of Sardis in 498. Meanwhile Persian punitive measures were beginning. Cyprus, Caria, and the Hellespont were occupied, and the Ionian navy was defeated at Lade; finally in 494 Miletus was subdued with great slaughter, and much of its population was transplanted.

Darius now decided to resume his European conquests. In 492 he extended his occupation of Thrace and Macedonia; and in 490, after destroying Samos and receiving the submission of the Cyclades, the Persian forces burned Eretria and landed in the Bay of Marathon, north of Athens. His objective was to punish Athens and restore its tyrant Hippias, who had taken refuge at his court. The Spartan allies of Athens sent no help, but the Athenians succeeded in defeating the Persians and subsequently prevented the fleet from landing off Athens itself.

In 486 Egypt revolted against excessive tribute and Darius was unable to launch a quick counter-attack against the Greeks. He was succeeded in 486 by his son Xerxes, who put down the revolt in Egypt and another in Babylonia, and then completed his father's preparations in the west. The new Persian expedition consisted of enormous forces on both land and sea. It started in the spring of 480, was victorious at Thermopylae, and invaded Attica. But it then suffered three defeats, first on sea at Salamis, then on land at Plataea in 479, and thirdly in another sea battle at Mycale on the Asiatic coast. Ten years or so later the Persian squadrons were again beaten at the mouth of the Eurymedon in Pamphylia.

Shortly afterwards Xerxes and his eldest son were assassinated, and the throne passed to his second son Artaxerxes I. This king was immediately occupied in putting down a Bactrian revolt supported by his brother; and he then had to contend with Inaros of Egypt, who attempted, with Athenian aid, to liberate his country from Persian domination. The war lasted six years and ended with the reconquest of Egypt by Persia and the conclusion of a treaty with Athens. The latter fixed the harbour of Phaselis as the limit for operations by the Greek and Persian fleets, on the west and east respectively.

Yet the decline of Persian power was continually manifested by court tragedies and by the rebellions and political quarrels of the satraps. On the death of Artaxerxes in 424, for example, his son Darius II had to get rid of two of his brothers before he secured the throne; and his reign (423–404) saw repeated revolts by satraps, the most serious being that of Pissuthnes in Lydia in 414. The king wanted the two Greek coalitions, headed by Athens and Sparta, to wear one another out, but his satraps favoured first one city then the other; and he finally replaced one of them by his own son Cyrus the Younger. Meanwhile Egypt regained its liberty and kept it for sixty years.

These difficulties were repeated under the new king Artaxerxes II (404–358). He started with open rivalry with his brother Cyrus the Younger, who fell at Cunaxa in 401 after waging war on the king; and he had to put down his wife and three of his sons who were aspiring to the succession. He was then engaged in war with Sparta in Asia Minor from 401 to 394. In this war, it is true, the Spartan navy was destroyed at Cnidus: and in the 'Corinthian' war which followed a Greek coalition was organized against Sparta, permitting the revival of Athens under the leadership of Conon. But this did not prevent the Spartans from achieving a revised political settlement, under which they recognized Persian domination over the Greek cities of Asia but secured Persian support for the Spartan hegemony in Greece (386).

The next king, Artaxerxes III (358–338), rid himself of all possible contenders for the throne, and ruthlessly suppressed rebellions in the empire with the aid of Greek mercenaries. But his harsh treatment of the Asiatic Greeks began to attract the attention of Philip II of Macedonia, whose expedition in 336 was designed to help them. The expedition ended in the same year, when Philip was assassinated; but a few months later Artaxerxes too was murdered, and after a brief reign by his younger son Arses (who was quickly eliminated) the throne passed to Darius III (335–330). This king, however, was defeated by Alexander the Great at Issus and Gaugamela; after the fall of Persepolis he fled to the eastern satrapies, where in 330 he was put to death by Bessus, satrap of Bactria. His murderer usurped the Persian throne under the name of Artaxerxes IV, but he was brought to book by Alexander, who entered Bactria after his occupation of Hyrcania and Drangiana. The conqueror then took Sogdiana on his way to India (327). By now all the Persian possessions had passed to the Macedonian; he took over the rights of sovereignty and used the seals of the kings he had put down.

4. THE HEBREWS AND THE DIASPORA

The Hebrews who had been transplanted into Babylonia fairly quickly learned how to adapt themselves to their new situation. Many of them achieved so satisfactory a position in life that they refused to return to their country when the time came. Yet longing for the lost home country remained keen, partly because the prophets and priests kept it alive. The years of waiting were ended by a rapid and unexpected solution, when the various victories won by the Persian king Cyrus brought about the fall of the Chaldean kingdom in the middle of the sixth century. Since he had shown tolerance to other conquered peoples who had been subdued by his enemies, the Hebrews too sought to return home; and permission was immediately granted, conforming as it did with Cyrus' political principles. The decree appears in *Ezra* 1. 2-4, but may be only a résumé of the original. It was for these reasons that Cyrus figured in later Jewish tradition as the 'Anointed', chosen by God to give freedom to his Chosen People.

Those who decided to leave moved in the spring of 537. Lists of their old homes had already been prepared, and they proceeded to take them over on arrival: but they met with many difficulties. The miscellaneous people who had remained behind under the government of Babylonian officials viewed the newcomers with a jealous eye; and the hostility of their Samaritan neighbours was supported by the Persian governors of the district. We know very little about Cambyses' reign; he undoubtedly passed through Palestine on his way to Egypt, but there is no evidence of dealings with the inhabitants. Under Darius an important event occurred. When the prophet Haggai persuaded the Hebrews to start rebuilding the Temple they incurred suspicion from the local satrap, who inspected the work and reported to the king. But Darius, who discovered Cyrus' edict in the central archives, not only gave his consent but bestowed a number of favours. So between 520 and 515 the Temple was set up.

For the ensuing period we are unfortunately without evidence. It appears that the Samaritans offered new opposition to the attempt to rebuild the walls of Jerusalem and prevailed on Artaxerxes to have the work stopped: perhaps even what had been erected had to be pulled down. But Artaxerxes II in 398 started a new series of generous concessions by the Persian kings to the Hebrews. Meanwhile the relations between the small Jewish state and its powerful neighbours became less important than internal Jewish politics, and this remained true till Alexander's conquest.

The period of Alexander, who took possession of Palestine in 332, passed off fairly quietly for the Hebrews. Their troubles came during the struggle between the Diadochi, since both the Seleucids and the Ptolemies coveted southern Syria and it only finally became a possession of the former in 195. Another cause of grave disturbances lay in the plan of Antiochus IV to Hellenize Palestine by prohibiting the practice of Hebrew religion and turning the Temple into a heathen shrine. In the subsequent rebellion, supported by Rome, Judas Maccabaeus reoccupied Jerusalem in 165, and together with his brothers asserted the independence of the country. This was recognized in 142 when the Hasmonaean princes were given the official title of 'High Priests and Princes of the Jews'. They vigorously defended this independence against the Syrian kings, and in the period of Syrian dissolution they extended the area of their state, especially under John Hyrcanus. Soon after this, however, the internal peace of the country was disturbed by the quarrels of the two factions, Pharisees and Sadducees, which became marked in the reign of Alexander Jannaeus; and affairs were made worse by the rivalry between his sons Aristobulus and Hyrcanus II. The latter was supported by Pompey, who besieged and took Jerusalem in 63. Hyrcanus was left in charge with the title 'ethnarch', but had to pay tribute to Rome.

Aristobulus' son Alexander attempted rebellion, but the proconsul Gabinius (57) replied by dividing Judaea into five districts, each under separate administration. Hyrcanus II remained pro-Roman throughout and continued as High Priest, later supporting Caesar in the Civil War and giving him assistance in his Egyptian campaign. He was rewarded by receiving his principality and title of ethnarch once more; and his power was extended to cover the Jews of the Diaspora.

When Cassius was in charge of the East after Caesar's death he imposed a heavy war-tax on the Jews and sold part of the population as slaves. This weakened the power of Hyrcanus at a time when he was also being challenged by the pro-Parthian faction: Judaea lost many of its territories and several leading men were murdered during the struggles of the court. After the battle of Philippi (42) Antonius confirmed the position of Hyrcanus, but conditions remained so bad that various embassies invited Antonius to abolish the principality and annex Judaea to the province of Syria.

The Parthian invasion of Syria (40) saw Hyrcanus deposed and the pro-Parthian Antigonus put in his place; but the latter was beheaded when Herod recovered Jerusalem with Roman assistance. Earlier, as a refugee in Rome, Herod had been made king, and at his death his possessions were divided between his three sons; in AD 6, however, Judaea was once more directly taken over by Rome and became a province.

The Hebrews of Palestine remained markedly hostile to the ideas and practices which had grown up among other peoples. Their resistance to the introduction of Gentile rites and customs into Jerusalem was the background of many famous scenes in their rebellion. Meanwhile all their writings in the last centuries of the Old Testament period emphasize their firm resolve to defend their traditions jealously and to keep their people apart from the world around them.

For a long time, however, the phenomenon known as the 'Diaspora' had been in progress, and Jews were scattered in the principal centres of the Mediterranean basin, sometimes even in cities farther afield. Not only had there been numerous forced deportations, but there was no room in the small mother country for all its sons; and the more enterprising among them planned to gain a better position by settling in commercial and business centres. We have a wealth of evidence about these Hebrew colonies, but much of it has reached us by pure chance, such as that relating to the important post of Elephantine on the southern frontier of Egypt: very probably there were many other colonies of which we know nothing. The various local rulers generally tolerated or even encouraged these Jewish groups, on condition that they did not disturb public order and that they respected the fundamental laws of the state they were in. A decree of the Roman senate in 138 shows concern for the Hebrews scattered from Egypt to Cappadocia, and from Pergamum to the Greek islands. The foundation of Alexandria in Egypt made a strong appeal to the Jews. They had ancient links with the country; and Alexander, who was anxious to populate his new city, made their conditions of residence attractive. They had a quarter of their own, and in time the Hebrew population of Alexandria exceeded that of Jerusalem; it has been estimated at 100,000 in the middle of the first century BC, and in Philo's day there were a million Jews in Egypt as a whole. Similar development can be seen at Antioch in Syria. The Jewish communities of the Diaspora kept up close relations with one another, and exchanged letters. At the head of each was a college of magistrates for administrative and judicial affairs: there were various officials, and the archisynagogus presided over religious meetings. Although they had close relations with the Gentiles among whom they lived, and often spoke their languages, even the Jews of the Diaspora undoubtedly kept themselves substantially apart from the world around them. They remained faithful to God's Law, and retained that national religious outlook which is the main feature of Hebrew history throughout antiquity. Yet it was in these foreign surroundings—at Alexandria above all—that an event took place which had vast importance for the cultural and spiritual history of a large part of mankind. This was the translation of the Bible into Greek, involving the adaptation by one mentality of the expressions and ideas framed by a mentality which was very different. This development was not regarded favourably by strict Jews, even in later times. But for the Jews of the Diaspora it was a necessity, for they no longer understood their original language and yet were unwilling to give up their sacred texts. The work was started at the beginning of the third century, and by the middle of the second all the ancient books had been translated. The legend was invented of the Seventy translators (72 to be precise) who finished the work with great speed; but in fact there were many and occasionally competing authors at various dates and of varying merit. For a long time the 'Septuagint' was given exclusive official recognition, but later other translations appeared; and beside them a complete literature was written by the Hellenistic Jews to defend the tenets of Hebrew religion among non-believers (as time went on proselytism among the Gentiles was by no means rare). Some books which entered the Old Testament were written in Greek from the start, *Maccabees* and *Wisdom*, for example: the latter book, with six others, is not in the Hebrew Bible, but Catholics regard it as 'deuterocanonical'. But these too show the same sharp divergence from Hellenistic thought, being severe in their condemnation of all idolatry and in their rejection of syncretistic views. None the less a process of dilution inevitably set in as well, leaving marked traces and valuable results.

5. THE DEVELOPMENT OF GREECE

a. *Local Hegemonies*

In the years immediately following the Greek victories over Persia the Spartan Pausanias, victor of Plataea, tried to retain command of the confederate Greek fleet. He began the liberation of the Hellenic colonies on the Asiatic coast; but he lost the support both of his government and of his crews, and in 478 he gave up his command. Leadership of the island states, and of the seaboard cities on the far side of the Aegean, now passed to Athens, whose statesmen were at first united in the policy of forming an alliance against Persia: in this matter Themistocles, the democratic victor of Salamis, was at one with his old rival Aristides, the actual creator of the 'Delio-Attic' League which was formed in 478 to pursue the war of liberation. Each participant city made a contribution, some in ships and crews, others in money. But the Athenian politicians soon split: the conservatives wanted, while fighting Persia, to retain Spartan friendship, but the democrats were anxious for the dissolution of Sparta's Peloponnesian League. The influence of the former, led by Cimon, made possible a resounding naval victory over the Persians at the Eurymedon (c. 469), while Sparta was reinforcing her league. But then came a lull in the war with Persia; the allies grew discontented, and reluctant to pay tribute; and the rivalry between Athens and Sparta grew more marked. In 464 Sparta's Helots revolted, and Cimon led an Athenian army to Sparta's aid; but Sparta suspected the anti-oligarchic sentiments of the Athenian troops, and curtly dismissed them. Power at Athens consequently passed to the democrats, above all to Pericles, whose programme was Athenian hegemony, to be obtained by all possible means. War with Persia was carried on by aiding an Egyptian revolt (c. 460–455); an attempt was made to break Sparta's confederacy (460–446); and Athens tried to become leader of a unified Western Greece against the Sabellian invasions of Magna Graecia and against the predominance of Syracuse in Sicily. But this ambitious programme was too much for Athenian strength; it came to grief in all three fields. Cimon momentarily returned to power, but after his death in Cyprus Athens made peace with Persia in 449. A peace with Sparta, intended to last thirty years, followed in 445.

When he returned to power Pericles attempted a more restricted programme. Action against Persia was stopped; and the allies were reduced to subjects, since their tribute was no longer needed for the Persian war but went to make Athens a splendid metropolis and build its economic strength. The 'mirage' of the West was still in view: the Athenians founded Thurii in Magna Graecia and gave help to the Elymians and Chalcidians in Sicily. But the chief aim was to resume action against Sparta and Corinth. This new programme evoked opposition to Pericles within Athens itself, and several of his friends were put on trial. But in 434 Athens allied itself with Corinth's colony Corcyra, the second naval power in Greece; and the provocation offered to Corinth eventually led to an ultimatum being delivered to Athens from the Peloponnesian League, and so to the long struggle known as the Peloponnesian War, which began in 431. Pericles saw only its beginning, for he died of the plague in 429; after his death the struggle between democrats and conservative pacifists still went on at Athens. The first phase of the war (431–421) brought no concrete results: Athens, powerful at sea, attacked the Peloponnesian coasts and captured Pylos in Messenia; Sparta with its land power ravaged Attica, destroyed Plataea, and occupied Heraclea in Trachis and Amphipolis in the 'Thraceward' area. Athenian action in the West was once more unsuccessful. Yet in the peace of 421 Athens was able to retain maritime hegemony.

Soon, however, the war parties at both Athens and Sparta gained the upper hand, and the war was renewed, made wider and more complex when a third coalition headed by Argos came into being and played the other two off against each other. But now Athens suffered a series of disasters. The Spartans permanently occupied Decelea and prevented all cultivation in Attica; a powerful expedition to Sicily came to unrelieved failure in 413; the Athenian exile Alcibiades crossed over to the enemy, and enabled the Spartans to build a fleet by obtaining for them Persian gold; and a large number of subject allies revolted.

These reversals of fortune brought about an oligarchic revolution at Athens in 411. Later, it is true, democracy was restored, Alcibiades was recalled from exile, and the war at sea improved; there was even hope of economic aid from Persia. This was not to be. Shortly afterwards Alcibiades was exiled again, and Sparta formed an alliance with Persia; despite several heroic actions in the war the Athenian position became desperate. Finally they were defeated at Aegospotami, deserted by their allies, and blockaded by Spartan forces. They were compelled to recognize the political supremacy of their enemy, to pull down their walls, and to adopt an oligarchic constitution once more (404).

The domination of the Greek world by Sparta in the next generation meant domination by the 2,000 full citizens who alone composed the narrow oligarchy in that city. The acquisition of hegemony made the 'Lycurgan' constitution out of date; but the struggles between the royal houses and the Ephorate were still a hampering factor, and Sparta's army and navy had not shared in the technical progress attained by other Greeks. Moreover Sparta was doing nothing to retain the sympathy of the allies it had won from its rival. They began to realize that they had only changed masters, compelled as they were to adopt oligarchies, pay tribute, and maintain Spartan garrisons; often they were at the mercy of terrorist governments formed by returned exiles thirsting for revenge. Revolts and revolutions followed, put down with equal violence; the case of Athens, which is best known to us, is typical. For some time they were forced to adopt an oligarchic régime. Political rights were confined to 3,000 persons with 30 delegates at their head; and the whole was supervised by 700 Spartan soldiers and by the board of police known as the Eleven. From this Athens was liberated by a group of exiles, and the democratic government which they restored took on the hard task of rebuilding their city after its disasters. But the restoration was intransigent, and the philosopher Socrates, the greatest citizen whom Athens could boast in the moral and spiritual fields, fell a victim to its narrow outlook (399).

In 401 Sparta incurred the anger of Artaxerxes II for having sent help to his defeated brother Cyrus. The charge that Sparta had received foreign gold to maintain its position was admitted to be groundless, but it became involved in a war in Asia Minor against the Persian satrap Pharnabazus. In his turn the king distributed money among Sparta's enemies, and built up a coalition against it which began the so-called Corinthian War. In Greece the Spartans were victorious, but they were defeated at sea near Cnidus by a fleet under command of the Athenian Conon (394): this enabled him, still with the help of Persian gold, to rebuild the walls of Athens, which took part in the last phase of the Corinthian War and still had dreams of maritime hegemony. Sparta was saved by the peace of 386. It recognized that the Greek cities of Asia Minor, together with Clazomenae and Cyprus, belonged to the Great King; and he in his turn put the Spartans in a position to make all the cities of Greece autonomous, and thus to dissolve the political league to which they belonged and to impose oligarchies and tribute upon them. The immediate cause of the end of Spartan hegemony and the beginning of the Theban came when a Spartan garrison seized by force the citadel of Thebes. A party of Theban democrats under Epaminondas and Pelopidas replied by expelling the Spartan garrison and overturning the Theban oligarchy. Thebes recovered its hegemony in Boeotia (379) and made an alliance with Athens. The Athenians in 377 once more became the centre of a maritime league of seventy cities; the Thebans pressed on with their war against Sparta until they defeated it decisively at Leuctra in 371.

The new hegemony met with resistance as soon as it began: a coalition was made between Athens, Sparta, the Isthmiac states, and Thessaly. Epaminondas replied by invoking diplomatic help from Persia and by military action. Pelopidas fell in a victorious action in Thessaly, and the war was carried into the Peloponnese where Epaminondas was also killed in a victory at Mantinea (362). With the death of the two great Thebans the democratically based hegemony of Boeotia fell rapidly apart. It had been no more careful than its predecessors of the legitimate aspirations of its allies; and it was incapable of holding its own against Macedon, which had a more powerful army than its own.

Macedon, a large and populous area with important agricultural and mineral wealth, had found in its Argead dynasty a force which gave it a marked measure of Hellenization. King Philip II, who came to the throne in 359, was an excellent strategist with admirable lieutenants. After strengthening and reorganizing the army, he used war and his family connections to extend his dominions, both in the Balkan hinterland and on the Aegean coast, where he occupied the gold mines of Mount Pangaeus.

Thebes now tried to deprive the Phocians of their seat on the Amphictiony. When the Phocians, supported by Athens, Pherae, and Sparta, offered resistance, Philip intervened in favour of the Thessalians, who became his subjects and elected him their chief magistrate. He next occupied and destroyed Olynthus, to which Athens sent help too late (348). Returning to central Greece, he took and garrisoned Delphi, where he assumed the presidency of the Pythian Games (346); then he besieged Byzantium, but that city appealed to Athens and he was unsuccessful in forestalling Athenian reinforcements (340). A new coalition of Greek cities was now formed to counter him, but he moved quickly and routed their forces at Chaeroneia (338). Soon after this representatives of all the Greek states except Sparta met at Corinth and created a federation of free cities in alliance with Philip; the king assumed command of the League army and navy, to resume the war against Persia.

b. *The Conquests of Philip II and of Alexander*

The political progamme of Greek union against Persia, proclaimed since the first twenty years of the fourth century by Gorgias, Lysias, and Isocrates, was finally put into action by the influence of Philip II of Macedon. The Graeco-Macedonian League furnished troops and ships in adequate numbers to free the Greeks of Asia from overlords whose weakness had long ago been shown in face of the 10,000 Greek mercenaries at Cunaxa in 401, and who could only count on Greek and Phoenician mercenaries to man their fleet. War was declared when the Persians intervened in Europe on behalf of Perinthus, contrary to the peace of 386; and in 336 a first corps of 10,000 Macedonians crossed into Asia Minor. But the assassination of Philip and the succession of his twenty-year-old son Alexander put off the actual operations for two years. During this time the new king, who had been proclaimed general of the Panhellenic League, carried out a series of operations in the Balkan peninsula, on the Danube, in Illyria, and in Greece itself (where he besieged and destroyed his enemy Thebes). He thus removed opposition and danger from his rear before becoming engaged in the East.

The first objective of the great enterprise was to take from the Great King all Asia Minor, Syria, and Phoenicia, with the naval bases on the Mediterranean. This was achieved by the victory at the Granicus, the capitulation of Sardis, and the taking of Miletus, in 334, by the battle of Issus in the following year, and by the fall of Tyre in 332. After this Alexander occupied Egypt, which acclaimed him as liberator and 'Pharaoh', and to which he gave its new capital of Alexandria. (Map VIII.)

In the spring of 331 he returned to Asia, crossed the Euphrates and Tigris, and defeated Darius at Gaugamela. Darius took refuge in Media, and his conqueror occupied, one by one, the places he had used as capitals, Susa, Persepolis, and Ecbatana. Receiving news that Bessus, satrap of Bactria, had captured and executed Darius and usurped his throne, Alexander occupied Hyrcania, Drangiana, and Bactria, and had Bessus condemned to death. He then took possession of Sogdiana, and finally penetrated into India as far as the Hyphasis (326). At this point he had to meet the longing of his soldiers for an end to their labours; and he needed to put the conquered lands

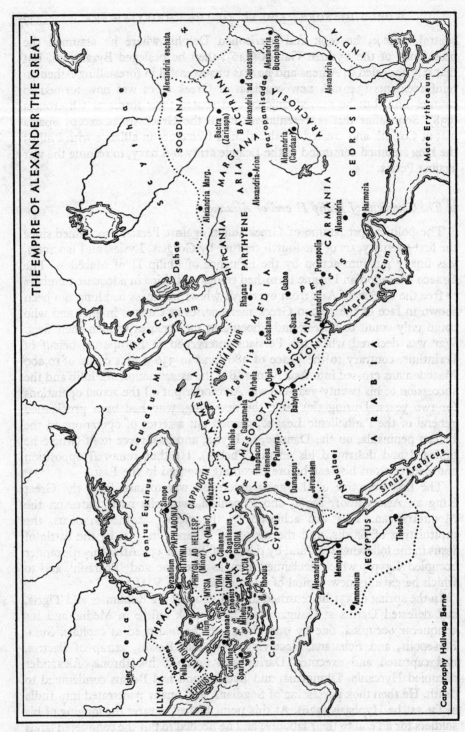

THE EMPIRE OF ALEXANDER THE GREAT

MAP VIII

Cartography Hallwag Berne

in order. He therefore returned to Susa, where he was recognized not only as king of the Macedonians and general of the Greek League, but as king of Asia, Pharaoh of Egypt, and King of Kings of the Persian lands. He put the conquered Persians on a level with the Macedonians, and employed them together in the army and in the administrative services, as well as permitting fusion of religions and mixed marriages. He founded a number of cities in the Persian districts, settling both veterans and immigrants from Macedonia and Greece; and he developed trade between the different regions of the new vast empire, in which he made Babylon the capital but Greek the official language. At the moment of his death he was preparing and even equipping new expeditions of conquest and exploration, designed to make him master of a still larger empire, a world empire embracing the Caucasus regions, Arabia, and the central and western Mediterranean. But in 323, at the age of 33, he died.

c. *The Hellenistic Empires*

The main obstacles to the preservation of Alexander's work and schemes were the separatism existing in several satrapies, the desire of the Greeks to regain their autonomy, and the hostility between the Macedonian conquerors and the Persians whom Alexander had raised to their level.[7] For a brief time the political unity of the vast new empire was maintained because the troops were loyal, and because Perdiccas, aided by Craterus, was supreme among the 'Diadochi' or surviving generals. At this stage the worst difficulties were encountered by Antipater, who had to meet a Greek rebellion, instigated mainly by Demosthenes (d. 322).

Meanwhile the Diadochi were gradually turning the areas they governed into personal domains, and forming coalitions to carry on their feuds. At each temporary peace a new distribution of territory was made. One such settlement was made at Triparadeisus in 321, another in 311 when five clearly demarcated states were distinguished, each under its separate king. The settlement after the battle of Ipsus in 301 recognized four major states and two minor ones, as follows: (1) Macedonia and Greece, (2) Thrace and Western Anatolia, (3) Syria and Mesopotamia, (4) Egypt and Libya, (5) Cyprus, (6) Caria and Cilicia. After a complicated sequence of events Antigonus Gonatas succeeded in imposing his rule on Thrace as well as on Macedonia and Greece; and thus for about a century following 276 the empire was divided into three main parts, with three 'Hellenistic' dynasties descended from Alexander's generals. The Antigonids had Macedonia and the other Balkan regions: the Seleucids in Syria and Asia were regarded as successors of the Achaemenid kings of Persia; the Ptolemaic dynasty in Egypt was successor to the Pharaohs. (Map IX.)

Of these three the richest and most populous was the Seleucid kingdom, more extensive on the east than the Persian empire, though smaller on the

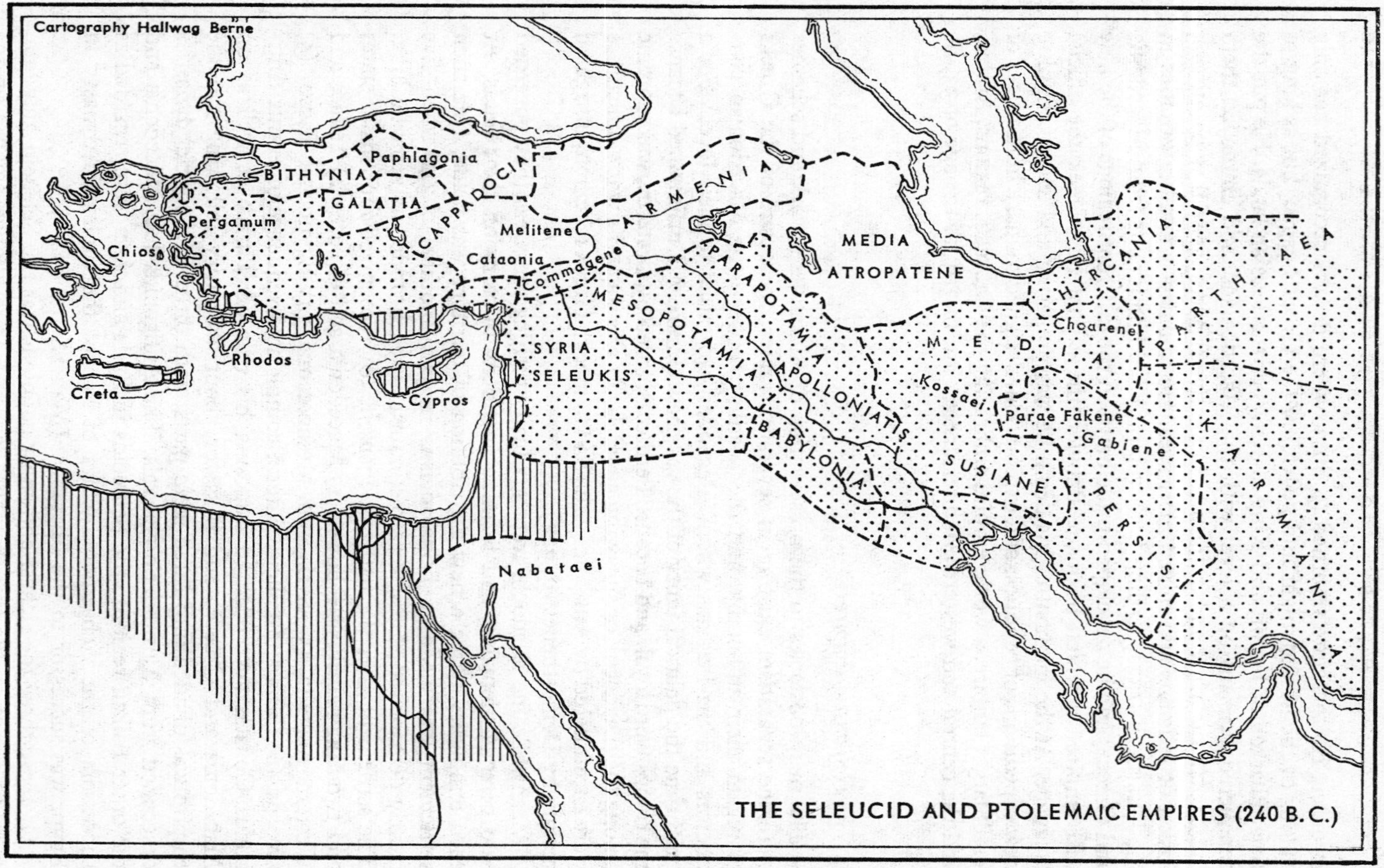
Cartography Hallwag Berne
THE SELEUCID AND PTOLEMAIC EMPIRES (240 B.C.)
Paphlagonia
BITHYNIA
GALATIA
CAPPADOCIA
ARMENIA
Pergamum
Chios
Melitene
MEDIA
ATROPATENE
Cataonia
Commagene
PARAPOTAMIA
MESOPOTAMIA
HYRCANIA
PARTHAEA
Rhodos
Creta
Cypros
SYRIA
SELEUKIS
Choarene
MEDIA
Kossaei
APOLLONIATIS
Parae Fakene
Gabiene
BABYLONIA
SUSIANE
PERSIS
KARMANIA
Nabataei

MAP IX

west because Egypt was excluded. Yet its many races were too various, and were often separated from one another by deserts; centrifugal tendencies appeared in the peripheral districts. Moreover the barbarian Celtic tribes called Galatae drove a wedge between the Iranic culture of eastern Asia Minor and the Greek culture of the western zone. But the worst disadvantage from which this political formation suffered was that commodities carried from eastern districts to the Syrian coast and Egypt depended on Egyptian vessels to find their markets. For long periods Egypt dominated the two areas of sea, for it controlled Cyprus and very often the Aegean islands, and at some periods the Cilician, Lycian, and Carian coasts as well.

The Ptolemaic kingdom was the smallest of the three. But being compact and thickly populated it was always ready to expand its power, especially as it had an effective fleet in Mediterranean waters.

The least populous and the poorest of the three was the kingdom of Macedon, and its history was the most troubled. It had to contend not only with the Balkan tribes and the Celtic invaders, but with the difficulties caused by dissensions and disorders among the Greeks. All Greeks wanted freedom, but each city in turn would aspire to exercise a hegemony of its own.

Within the Seleucid sphere a growing number of states were gradually attaining independence, not only in the East but also such kingdoms as Pergamum, Bithynia, Pontus, Cappadocia, Galatia, and Pisidia, in the western areas. But the main rival of the Seleucid kingdom was always the Ptolemaic empire, which in a series of wars (as was mentioned above) tried repeatedly to establish at least temporary occupation of the coasts of Syria and Asia Minor and of the adjacent islands. The main problem of the Macedonian kingdom, on the other hand, was its continuous struggle with the Greeks, who were longing for independence. This is the theme of the Chremonidean War, which began against Antigonus Gonatas in 267 and in which Ptolemy II gave Athens and Sparta support in an unsuccessful attack on Macedon; and also of the wars of Aratus of Sicyon, the moving spirit of the Achaean League, against Gonatas and his successors Demetrius II and Antigonus Doson. In 226, however, the Achaean League was defeated at Megalopolis by Sparta, which had come into prominence after the social reforms of Agis IV and Cleomenes III. To hold their own the league sought support from their recent enemy, Antigonus Doson, and the Spartans in their turn were defeated at Sellasia in 222. Antigonus now succeeded in uniting all Greece (except Athens, Elis, Messenia, and the Aetolian League) in a more stable alliance with Macedon. But an anti-Macedonian coalition was formed against his successor Philip V, with Athens and the Aetolian League at its head, and the war was only ended in 217 by the Peace of Naupactus, which Philip concluded to free his hands for measures of protection against the danger of Roman penetration into the Adriatic.

d. *The Struggle for Hegemony in Western Greece*

While the Greeks of the East, in the first decades of the fifth century, were menaced by Persia, their compatriots in the West had to face the threat of Etruria and Carthage combined. The Etruscans still maintained some control in Campania and were hostile to Cumae. The Carthaginians with their foothold in Sicily prevented any fresh Greek foundation in the western part of the island; and they gathered to their side some of the native population, together with those Greek colonies which were opposed to Syracuse and Acragas, the dominant powers. For some time the Etruscans and Carthaginians had been in actual alliance to control the Tyrrhenian Sea and frustrate the Greeks.

But in 480–479 the two great tyrants, Gelon of Syracuse (who started as tyrant of Gela) and Theron of Acragas, routed the Carthaginians at Himera and removed any hope of a counter-attack for three-quarters of a century. The Etruscans were equally crushed. They moved to attack Cumae on the death of its tyrant Aristodemus, but were decisively defeated at sea before the city by the intervention of Hieron, the new tyrant of Syracuse, who put an end to their empire in Campania (473). For some time Greek civilization in the West seemed secure; and under the Deinomenidae (Gelon and Hieron) and under Theron of Acragas, Sicily enjoyed a period of great power and cultural splendour.

In time the two cities lost their hold on their respective confederacies; and the resulting wars between the towns which had been subject to them, and between parties of mercenaries who had lost their employment, allowed the native Sicels and Elymians to throw off the yoke of their Greek overlords for a time. These events encouraged the Athenians to think that they too might gain a foothold in Sicily; and on two occasions, about 454 and in the years following 433–432, they showed what they had in mind. At the same time they entertained the possibility of establishing their hegemony in Magna Graecia, but this too came to nothing. At this time Magna Graecia, after its liberation from the Etruscans, was being menaced by the expansion of the Iapygians, from modern Puglie, and by the gradual descent of the Sabellian immigrants into Samnium, Campania, Lucania, and Bruttium. The dissensions among the Greek colonies made it easier for these tribes to defeat them one by one and gradually to reduce them to subjection.

The first check to Athenian dreams of Western hegemony came in Magna Graecia, where the new colony of Thurii, founded in 446, quickly passed from their control. The Siceliotes too gave them an awakening in 424 by holding a peace congress and showing the Athenians the door. In 416 new struggles broke out, between Segesta and Selinus and between the Chalcidian cities and Syracuse. The Athenians sent very powerful fleets and armies to Sicily to support their friends, but their expedition ended disastrously under the walls of Syracuse, which was reinforced by the Spartan Gylippus after a fruitless siege (415–413).

Neither the Chalcidians nor the Elymians had been able to achieve their freedom through Athenian intervention; but a few years later the Elymians sought aid from Carthage. So, after seventy years of inactivity in the island, the Carthaginians came back to enlarge their base and to take revenge on Syracuse and Acragas. Selinus and Himera were taken and destroyed by their army in 409, and Acragas in 406. In 405 Dionysius I failed to rescue Gela, though shortly afterwards he became master of Syracuse; and at the peace which followed Carthage emerged mistress of three-fifths of Sicily. Dionysius however turned to large-scale military preparations on his own account. After reinforcing the defence of his capital and making an alliance with Sparta, he reunited eastern Sicily under his rule. This empire, though small, had a splendid cultural history, and Dionysius increased his power in three directions. Between 397 and 368 he four times resumed war with the Carthaginians and pushed them back beyond 'Platani' (southern Himera). Secondly, in alliance with Rhegium and the Lucanians, he took the field against the Italiote League and occupied modern Calabria as far as the isthmus of Catanzaro. Finally he broke with the Lucanians and defeated them in battle; and he then proceeded to plundering raids, followed by colonial enterprises, in the upper Tyrrhenian Sea and northern Adriatic.

But the empire of Dionysius I was already beginning to dissolve under his successor Dionysius II, who acceded in 367. His reign was disturbed by the continual attempts to supplant him made, with varying success, by his maternal uncle Dion, the philosophizing friend of Plato. Later, when Dionysius II returned to power in 347, Syracuse's mother city Corinth sent Timoleon against him. This statesman, who died in 336, exiled the tyrant, established a moderate oligarchy at Syracuse, and freed it from Carthaginian pressure. He put an end to the petty tyrants who had established themselves in the various cities and to the raiding hoards of mercenaries who were roaming round their territories.

About twenty years later Agathocles (317–289) became master of Syracuse. His programme was twofold. He first formed a league of Siceliote Greeks to turn the Carthaginians out of the island, and he even ventured on an expedition to Africa to fight them there (310–306). Then he tried to reunite Magna Graecia as well under his hegemony; after the death of Dionysius I this country, deprived of protection from the Siceliotes, was gradually subjected to Sabellian and Iapygian pressure, and one after another the Greek cities were losing their independence. Tarentum had received help from Sparta under King Archidamus (342–338), from Epirus under King Alexander 'the Molossian' (336-331), and again from Sparta under Cleonymus (beginning in 303); but these rescue operations had had little effect, and the dangers were growing all the time. At last Agathocles began the task of establishing a hegemony from outside in Magna Graecia, and he took his conquests farther: he occupied not only Croton but Corcyra. But his death in 289 broke his empire, which split up into a number of tiny states under tyrants or mercenary armies (Messana for example); and the Sabellians on the one side resumed their advance in Italy, the Carthaginians on the other their occupation of Sicily. In 285 Thurii, and in 282 Locri and Rhegium, appealed to Rome for help against the Sabellians: Rome put a garrison in these cities, and made an alliance with Croton. But in 280 a quarrel between Tarentum and Rome occasioned the last intervention in Magna Graecia and Sicily by a Greek adventurer who tried to create an empire for himself by assuming the protection of the Western Greek world; this was Pyrrhus, king of Epirus. But Pyrrhus was unsuccessful in both fields of operation. In Italy Rome defeated him, and in Sicily the independent spirit of the Greek colonies and of the natives was too strong.

6. ITALY AND ROMAN DEVELOPMENT

At this point we must say something about events in the rest of Italy and of the rising hegemony of Rome. At the turn of the sixth to fifth centuries the aristocracy of the 'gentes', which had overcome the foreign rule of the Etruscans and set up the republic, established its ascendancy at Rome. The ruling Etruscan power, however, had been responsible for Rome's hegemony over Latium; with their fall the hegemony collapsed, and had to be rebuilt step by step. At the same time Rome had to face an economic and social upset, which was caused by the fall of the Etruscan kings and made more severe by the patricians' monopoly of power. When the plebeians aspired to improvement of their social and political conditions, the resulting struggles between them and the patricians led gradually to a more even balance of power, the main steps being the Laws of the Twelve Tables (451–450), the Leges Valeriae Horatiae, and the Leges Canuleiae. Meanwhile the Latins had attempted to separate from Rome; but they were defeated at Lake Regillus, and in 493 Rome contracted an alliance with them on equal terms, into which the Hernici were later admitted. The Romans were thus enabled to confront the Volsci and the Aequi in the south, in wars which lasted over a century between 497 and 393. At the same time they were engaged against the Sabines and the southern cities of Etruria on their northern front; they became masters of the territories of Fidenae, Veii (taken in 396), and Capena (in the following year). Eventually they secured the fortresses of Sutrium and Nepete, and made an alliance with Caere.

Once again, however, the hegemony of Rome was overtaken by catastrophe. From the end of the sixth century[8] the movement of the Celts from Gaul to the Danube valley had been accompanied by a penetration of these peoples into northern Italy, where they wiped out part of the Ligurian and Etruscan tribes and accelerated the southward progress of the Oscans and Umbrians. At the beginning of the fourth century, the Celts began a series of raiding expeditions with horse-shoed cavalry into central Italy; and one of these (the chroniclers synchronize it with Greek events in 386) pushed down as far as Latium, defeated Roman resistance on the river Allia, and entered the city of Rome, putting it to fire and sword. These disasters had serious consequences: the Latins and Hernici left the Roman alliance, the colonies of Velitrae, Satricum, and Circeii revolted, and the Etruscans, Volsci, and Aequi resumed hostilities. The collapse was almost complete, but Rome reacted energetically. After strengthening its walls and reinforcing its treaties with the few cities which had remained loyal, it engaged for a generation in wars of reconquest against the Latins, Hernici, Volsci, Aequi, and Etruscans. In the outcome Rome's hegemony, by the middle of the fourth century, again extended to Circeii and Terracina on the south, and to Caere, Sutrium, and Nepete on the north. The new hegemony was recognized in 348 when a fresh maritime treaty between Rome and Carthage was signed; and its internal strength seemed guaranteed by the new method of treating the conquered states, whereby each was given a distinct status varying with the services or hostility it had shown to Rome. To the most loyal among them Rome was ready to bestow its own citizenship. Meanwhile a greater measure of social equality was established at home. Generous concessions were made to the *plebs*, the constitution was reorganized, and a further set of reforms strengthened the Roman army and made it more compact.[9]

It was now clearly necessary to attend to the movements of the Sabellian tribes. These were showing a tendency to expand from the mountain country and to dominate the plains below; indeed part of the plain country was already occupied by tribes of like race, who had acquired civilization through contact with Greeks and Etruscans. The first skirmishes were concerned with possession of the Liris valley. For a time Rome and the Samnites were allies, but the alliance was broken when in 343 the Campanians asked Rome for aid against Samnium. This first war (343-341) was short and of little consequence; the Samnites were engaged against Tarentum, to the help of which had come Archidamus of Sparta and later Alexander of Epirus; and the Romans were held up by a concerted revolt of the Latins, Volsci, Aurunci, Sidicini, and Campanians, which occupied them until 334. But the war which broke out in 327-326 between Rome and Neapolis, the Roman advance towards the Adriatic and Apulia (Arpi became an ally and Luceria a Latin colony in 325), and its attempted alliance with Lucania, all gave the Samnites the impression that they were being encircled. So began the Second Samnite War (c. 324-305), fought at first with varying fortunes in Samnium, Apulia, and Campania, and even at the southern gateway to Latium; later Rome faced a revolt among the Apennine peoples, and the Etruscans entered the war against it. Finally however it obtained victory on all fronts. In the north its system of alliances was extended to new districts of Etruria and Umbria; in the south it cleared the route to the Adriatic, put down the revolts, and reoccupied part of Apulia. The Samnites were thus decisively beaten, and the new status of the Roman League was recognized by a third treaty between Rome and Carthage in 306.

But a few years later, about 300, a new and still larger coalition came into being against Rome. It eventually comprised the Samnites, certain Apennine tribes, some of the Sabines, Umbrians, and Etruscans, and also the Gallic tribe of the Senones. Its formation was reported to Rome by the people of Picenum and Lucania, and so began the Third Samnite War (299–290). The hardest-fought battle was at Sentinum (295). This split the coalition apart, and Rome was able to subdue each member in isolation from the rest, by campaigns in Umbria, Etruria, Apulia, Samnium, and the central Apennines. In the next decade the Senones were defeated; and the Gallic tribe of the Boii, who had intervened in Etruria, were crushed at Lake Vadimon. The conquest of Etruria was now complete. At the same time Rome rescued the Greek city of Thurii from attacks by the Lucanians, Bruttians, and certain Samnites; garrisons were also planted at Rhegium, Locri, and other Italiote cities. All the harbours of Italy, from Pisa to Thurii and from Apulia to Ariminum, were now in Roman hands.

Yet an ancient treaty with Tarentum, made when conditions were very different, prevented Roman ships from sailing north of the Lacinian promontory. Believing that this was a dead letter, Rome sent a small fleet to cruise in the direction of its Adriatic possessions (282); and this led to war with Tarentum. After trying to embroil Rome with the Samnites, Lucanians, Apulians, and Bruttians, the Tarentines appealed for help to Pyrrhus, king of Epirus (280). In the early operations Pyrrhus succeeded in gaining control of southern Italy, from the country of the Hirpini to the straits; but he could not break through Rome's defence along the line Venusia–Beneventum–Neapolis. When he resumed his action after an unsuccessful expedition to Sicily, Pyrrhus was defeated at Beneventum and retired to Epirus (275). Tarentum was left to its fate, and soon fell into Roman hands.

It was in these same years that Rome brought the conquest of northern Etruria and the maremme to its conclusion, while in the south it recovered what it had lost in Magna Graecia and completed its conquest of that area. At the same time it entered into friendly relations not only with tribes across the Adriatic but with the distant Ptolemaic kingdom of Egypt.[10] It helped to put an end to Seleucid dreams of obtaining mastery both in Egypt and in the areas occupied by Ptolemaic forces in the Syrian and Aegean Seas.

a. *The Romanization of the Peninsula*

About 264, therefore, of the whole peninsula from Pisa and Rimini to the Straits of Messina, one quarter was covered by the Roman state, one tenth by the Latins and Latin colonies, and the remainder by the organism known as the *socii*, the allies of Rome. The size of this residue clearly marks a slowing-down, almost to a complete halt, of the 'ladder' system whereby the allies received Roman citizenship and were admitted into new 'rustic' tribes. There were doubtless selfish motives for this change in policy, but it was also in part justified by the entry into the Roman League of new races, whose assimilation came slowly and with difficulty, and whose desire for autonomy, together with their distance from Rome, made them less conscious of the benefit of Roman citizenship. For the time being, then, they were not very anxious for the grant; and Rome thought it better, while orientating the different peoples of Italy upon itself as their leader and co-ordinator, to strike various types of alliance with them, some favourable, some less so. These treaties broke up the pre-existing political ties and, as previously, graded separate sections of the conquered populations at different levels.

In this way the slow process of cultural and administrative unification went on. It had already been attempted in some parts of the peninsula by other imperialist powers; but though some of the geographical, racial, and historical factors were favourable, others were certainly not. Rome was the only power which successfully completed the process. From the outset a feature of its civilization was its power to take everything capable of assimilation which was offered by the races with which it came into contact or alliance, especially the Etruscans, Greeks and Italians—whether their contribution was indigenous or imported—and then to weld the result into a coherent whole. It lay in the midst of many peoples whose evolution was in its critical stage, at the centre of various streams of trade and culture; the racial amalgam of its population, though complex, had solidity; and it was thus able to absorb the civilization of its neighbours and to blend it with its own. The result was a new Italo-Roman culture, capable of being transmitted to other peoples: we find it in language and customs, in cults and ritual, in art and techniques, and in the genres and sentiments of Latin literature. In this way the more the city accepted new citizens from various parts, and the farther it travelled from the restricted Latin basis of its foundation, the more firmly it established itself as a union of racial and cultural elements from every region of the peninsula.

Yet while Rome became Italianized, Italy was also being Romanized. There were Romans and Latins in the colonies, in the rural tribes, on land distributed to individuals, and in garrisons abroad. Citizens and allies served together in the armies; and the process was also aided by the development of trunk roads for trade and communication. Moreover Romanization never involved suppressing or doing violence to the natural features of particular regions. The old political leagues were dissolved; but once this had been done the indigenous population of each region continued to be in a majority, and retained its old dialects and literary languages, its own municipal administration, its special usages and customs, and the legal traditions peculiar to the area. Sometimes it might eventually forget such things of its own accord in face of Roman importations, but more often the indigenous and imported would mix. We have already seen how these developments can be traced not only in linguistic phenomena but in the history of society, law, religion, literature, and art.[11]

b. *Conflict with Carthage*

Although the treaty between Rome and Carthage had been renewed in 278, Carthage during the war with Pyrrhus had shown a clear desire to assert its position in Italy, and on the other side Rome in 270 entered on relations with Hieron II, tyrant of Syracuse. Together with the Carthaginian eparchy and the Mamertine state at Messana, Hieron was master of one of the three main political formations in Sicily; and it was through his doing that the Mamertine state in these years had gradually lost power, until it had to seek help from both Rome and Carthage. The Carthaginians put a garrison in Messana, but their strategic position there was too grave a threat to Italy. Rome was driven to assist the Mamertines, while Hieron veered towards Carthage. In the First Punic War (264–241) Hieron quickly withdrew from the struggle. The Romans in the early stages were supported by the natives in the island, and became involved in increasingly severe actions on land and sea, including a disastrous expedition to Africa. In the end they defeated the Carthaginians decisively at the Aegates Insulae (241).

Three-quarters of Sicily remained in the hands of the Romans and they were now allied with Hieron as well as Messana, who between them occupied the other quarter. But the island only became a 'province' in 227, when Rome imposed the same status on Sardinia and Corsica, both of which had been permanently occupied between 238 and 230.

In the years following the First Punic War Rome led an expedition to defend the northern Etruscan cities and also Massilia against the Ligurians, whose territory was now in part occupied. Two further campaigns were designed to exact retaliation from the Adriatic pirates and to give support to the Greek colonies against the Illyrians: the result was the annexation of Histria. Rome then strengthened the alliance with the Ptolemies and made contact with the Seleucids, and also with several Greek cities, particularly Athens. It had once again to take action against the Gallic advances into central Italy: the Gauls were defeated at Telamon (225); and Rome followed this with victories in the Gallic lands of the Po valley, and founded the colonies of Placentia and Cremona. Finally they secured themselves against the progress of the Carthaginians, who had occupied all southern Spain and were giving assistance to the anti-Roman activity of the Gauls. They imposed a *diktat* that the Carthaginians should not cross the Ebro, and they made an alliance with the powerful Iberian city of Saguntum.

The Carthaginian general Hannibal replied by besieging and taking Saguntum, which led to a rupture between Rome and Carthage, and to the outbreak of the Second Punic War (218–202). Hannibal invaded Italy, and in the early part of the struggle won a series of victories, which led to revolts by several Roman allies over southern Italy. The next phase was a war of attrition in this part of Italy, combined with the revolt of Syracuse from Rome (213) and an alliance between Hannibal and Philip V of Macedon (215). Rome then counter-attacked. In the First Macedonian War a number of Greek powers gave it support; and the successful sieges of Syracuse and Acragas brought it to complete occupation of Sicily. It conquered practically the whole of Punic Spain; and the last stage was the expedition to Africa of Publius Scipio, later called Africanus the Elder. Hannibal followed him, but he was decisively defeated at Zama in 202. The possessions of Carthage in Africa were then overcome, the Numidians receiving independence; and the Roman possessions in Italy were reorganized. The revolted peoples were punished, and colonies were settled in their territories; the Ligurian and Gallic territories to the north of Pisa and Ariminum were conquered once again, with the foundation of strong colonies on both sides of the Po. Sardinia and Corsica were pacified; and Rome's allies the Veneti were freed on their eastern border from attacks by the Carni and Histri, the Latin colony of Aquileia being founded as an advanced watch post.

Meanwhile the equilibrium in the eastern Mediterranean between the Hellenistic powers, and also between the Greek states, was being upset. In 203 Philip V of Macedon and Antiochus III made a compact to extend their respective empires, the former in Greece and Asia Minor, the latter at the expense of the Ptolemies in Phoenicia and Judaea. When the Greek states which were harmed by this compact appealed to Rome, its first act was to request that the Hellenes be respected; when Philip attacked Athens and the Greek cities in Thrace, Rome fought the Second Macedonian War (200–196), in which the factions in the Greek cities took part, some on Philip's side, some on Rome's. Philip was decisively beaten at Cynoscephalae in 197; and next year the Roman senate, under the influence of Scipio Africanus, the great statesman who had willed the preservation of defeated Carthage, compelled Philip to evacuate Greece. The Greek cities were made allies of Rome and were solemnly declared by Titus Flamininus to be free. But Philip was left independent; and he too was made an ally. Rome found him of use as a defender of the Mediterranean countries against the barbarian peoples in the north of the Balkan peninsula.

All this time Antiochus III was asserting his power at the expense of the Greek cities and other states of Asia Minor, especially Pergamum and Rhodes; he was threatening the Ptolemaic possessions, and also aimed to occupy the Thracian Chersonese. He was urged on by his guest, the exiled Hannibal, who proposed an invasion of Italy from the Balkans, and he was supported by the anti-Roman cities in Greece. But when the Seleucid forces began action with a landing in Greece, they were defeated at Thermopylae by Manius Acilius Glabrio in 191 and had to give up all further operations outside Asia. In 190 the war was resumed in Asia. In a short time Antiochus was irrevocably defeated at Magnesia on the Hermus by L. Cornelius Scipio, who during the campaign (but not at the final battle) was aided by his brother the great Africanus. Peace followed at Apamea in 188. Antiochus lost his possessions north of the Taurus chain, but he remained independent and kept everything south of that line. Most of the Greek cities of Asia Minor were made free, and the states of Pergamum and Rhodes increased their territories. So the network of Roman alliances was extended. Rome still adhered to the policy of Africanus: it wanted no direct possessions in the East, but simply the enlargement of its system of alliances to preserve the balance of power.

But Africanus and the section of the governing class which shared his views had their opponents, not only over foreign policy, but over their domestic programme of eliminating class conflict, improving the lot of the poor, and gradually conceding citizenship to the conquered peoples. By degrees the opposing policy gained ground. Its chief supporter was M. Porcius Cato; and since it identified the interests of the state with those of the 'nobilitas' its principles included the enslavement of conquered peoples, a check to all concessions to the lower orders, no extension of citizenship, and keeping the provincial areas in a subject status.[12]

These new policies were disagreeable to the Greek world, which was already torn apart, almost to the point of anarchy, by the struggle for hegemony. They were also disagreeable to Macedon, both to Philip V who had always wanted to rebuild his power, and to his son Perseus who succeeded him on the throne in 179. The latter tried to organize against Rome a movement of the popular classes in Greece; the result was the Third Macedonian War, which completely overturned the earlier settlement made by Rome in Greece, in the Balkans, and in Asia Minor. After the victory of L. Aemilius Paullus at Pydna (168) the Roman senate adopted the line of naked imperialism.[13] Macedonia was divided into four republics which were subjected to tribute; Greek cities which had revolted were punished and made to give hostages; and in Asia Minor the republic of Rhodes and the kingdom of Pergamum lost both territory and importance, on the ostensible ground that their attitude to the war had been ambiguous, though their main crime in fact was that they had grown too strong.

At this point the war mentality and imperialist outlook of Rome found their chief exponent in Cornelius Scipio Aemilianus. The stage was set for a series of conflicts; for on their side Rome's allies, both in the East and in Africa, were dissatisfied with their kings and with their pro-Roman governing classes, while the provincial territories were disturbed by rebellious movements. The result was the ruthless destruction of cities such as Corinth, Carthage, and Numantia, and the creation of new provincial areas, in place of allied states, in Greece, Africa, and Spain.

For a decade (164–155) the Roman government had tried to involve itself as little as possible in Greek local quarrels and in the dynastic struggles of Asia and Egypt. But it then took the side of Ptolemy Euergetes of Egypt against his brother Philometor; and in Syria Rome supported Alexander Balas against Demetrius I, being not opposed to the gradual collapse of Seleucid power in its eastern territories. Meanwhile it had to take up arms against a certain Andriscus, who was attempting to restore the Macedonian monarchy after its destruction in the partition of 168. In 148–147 Macedonia, including the Illyrian and Epirote districts, was reduced to the status of a province. But at the same time the ambitions of the Achaean League had created a condition of perpetual disorder in Greece, especially in the Peloponnese, so the Roman government decided to reduce the league to its original proportions. L. Mummius defeated the Achaeans at Leucopetra; and in 146 he destroyed Corinth, enslaved its population, and made its territory into *ager publicus*. The revolted Greek cities were annexed to the province of Macedonia; the remaining cities, including Athens, were left as allies of Rome.

At the same moment in Africa the peaceful coexistence of Carthage and the Numidian kingdom of Masinissa broke down. Masinissa was anxious to extend his territory, and Carthage, receiving no help from arbitration by Rome, was forced to take up arms in its defence. It was defeated, but Cato maintained that its recent revival constituted a danger which must be destroyed. Under his continual prompting Rome mobilized, demanding that Carthage should be pulled down and its population transplanted ten Roman miles from the sea. When the Carthaginians offered resistance, their city was besieged, taken, and destroyed (146). The destruction of lesser Punic cities followed, and the Carthaginian territory was made into a province with the name of Africa.

Part of the Iberian peninsula had already been made into two provinces, called Hispania Citerior and Ulterior. Here too Rome, whose military forces were thin, was slow to enlarge its conquests, and even had to deal with a series of revolts and native attacks, especially from the Celtiberians and Lusitanians. The cautious policy of Ti. Sempronius Gracchus secured peace for a quarter of a century (179–154); but then disorder started again when independently of one another the Lusitanians and Celtiberians revolted. The conciliatory action of M. Claudius Marcellus seemed to have restored the situation, but Rome then despatched to the front new generals, whose policy was imperialistic and whose methods were those of terrorism—L. Licinius Lucullus, his legate Scipio Aemilianus, and the praetor Servius Sulpicius Galba. Their behaviour prompted a new outbreak of the Lusitanian revolt under the leadership of Viriathus between 147 and 139; and between 143 and 133 the Celtiberians also rebelled again, formed strongholds around Termantia and Numantia, and inflicted repeated losses on the Roman commanders. Finally in 134 Scipio Aemilianus laid siege to Numantia, and next year he succeeded in taking and destroying it, selling the survivors into slavery. The violent methods of imperialism shown in the destruction of these three cities, Corinth, Carthage, and Numantia, brought new strength to Rome's empire. But they had reactions in Rome as well as in its dominions, and were in part responsible for the series of crises which characterized the last days of the Republic.

c. *Political and Social History from the Gracchan Age to Caesar*

The great conquests had transformed the economic picture of Italy. It was once based on smallholdings, but the way was now open for the creation of *latifundia* for pasturage and arboriculture; slave labour was generally adopted; and the small proprietors and free workmen were ruined. Some enlightened men, who were trying to halt the excessive power of the *optimates*, saw and denounced the danger, but conditions became continually more serious. Some evidence is given by the slave revolts, often supported by the country pro-letariats. They were at first sporadic throughout Italy (139–132) and then came to a head in the First Servile War (136–131), which was accompanied by similar movements in Greece and Asia Minor.

It was against this background that the two brothers, Tiberius and Gaius Sempronius Gracchus, made their largely unsuccessful attempts to find a remedy for the social and political evils. Tiberius tried to rebuild the peasant class by reviving an old law which set a limit on the amount of *ager publicus*[14] allowed for tenure by a single family; he could then redistribute what was over. He also attempted to break down the political power usurped by the senate and restore it to the people, which in his view had the right to dispose of the property and lands of Attalus III, king of Pergamum, since the king had left the Roman people as his heir. One result was a revolt by a pretender to the Pergamene throne named Aristonicus, who was supported by the lower orders and the slaves of the country; but the Pergamene kingdom was made into the province of Asia. Gaius Gracchus continued the agrarian policy of his brother, but also sought support from the knights against the *optimates*; he promoted the foundation of colonies outside as well as inside Italy, and the relief of the allies by granting Roman citizenship.[15] The reaction to the Gracchan pro-gramme strengthened the imperialist policies of the nobles, who were now led by the Metelli and had reached an understanding with the knights. One concrete result of this was the creation of new provinces in Asia (mentioned above) and in Narbonese Gaul. But the knights broke with the senate and once more allied with the popular party; and the responsibility for this lay with a former colleague of Metellus named Gaius Marius.

Marius had the good fortune to have deserved the credit for two great victories. He overcame Jugurtha, grandson of Masinissa, who had occupied all Numidia and murdered his cousin the Roman nominee Adherbal; the long and eventful Jugurthine War (111–106) ended with the partition of these territories into two kingdoms allied with Rome. Then in Narbonese Gaul and in the Po valley Marius defeated the Cimbri and Teutones (104–101), the advanced guard of a German migration, who had penetrated into Roman territory and defeated the legions several times. On top of the military effort needed to achieve these successes came the Second Servile War in Sicily (104–101), and M. Antonius' action against the pirates in 102, which led to the formation of the provinces of Cilicia and Pamphylia. But meanwhile Mithradates VI Eupator, king of Pontus, was organizing a large anti-Roman coalition in the East. He overran the Crimea, partitioned Paphlagonia and Galatia with Nicomedes II of Bithynia (104-103), and engineered a scheme to win Cappadocia. When it became known that Marius was meditating a war of reprisal the coalition remained inactive, and the danger had been averted for the present. Yet Marius had now been discredited in the eyes of every party. After allying himself in 103 with the democratic leaders Saturninus and Glaucia, during his consulship in 100 he allowed them to be murdered, so the nobles gained the upper hand again, and Marius withdrew from politics. M. Livius Drusus made a disinterested but utopian effort to reconcile the parties and to reach agreement on the various issues of the day by securing concessions from each side. But the scheme failed, and the way was open for the armed conflict (90-88) between Rome and the Italians. The Roman government would not grant the citizenship the Italians sought: instead they fought and won, and then felt bound to grant it after all.

Meanwhile the fortune of politics was passing to L. Cornelius Sulla, formerly legate to Marius and the actual conqueror of Jugurtha. In 88 war broke out with the anti-Roman coalition organized round the king of Pontus; and for this, the victorious First Mithradatic War, Sulla obtained the command over the heads of the Marians. Marius was driven into exile, but he later returned with force at his back,[16] and became master of Rome in alliance with Cinna. But after indulging in the most ruthless massacre of his opponents he died a few days after entering on his seventh consulship; and the brief and bloody dictatorship of the popular leaders Cinna and Carbo (86-83) was no more fortunate. Sulla returned in triumph from the East, routed the Marians with C. Marius' son of the same name at their head, and entered Rome. There he assumed a dictatorship for any period he might think necessary to prepare a new constitution. The senate remained the chief organ of government, but it was a senate greatly diluted by the introduction of large numbers of knights. The aim was a balance between classes and a levelling of living standards. Large distributions of land were made to veterans. The magistracies were reorganized, the civil power of the urban magistracies being separated from the power of the pro-magistrates—the generals and provincial governors. At the beginning of 79, when Sulla judged his task complete, he resigned the dictatorship and retired into private life until his death in 78.

After the death of Sulla the struggle between *optimates* and democrats (or Marians) broke out afresh.[17] Two of the latter, Sertorius and Perperna, crossed to Spain and tried to make it a base for the war against the nobles by organizing the native population. But the feature of the period was the rise of the military glory of Cn. Pompeius and then his attainment of political power. He conquered Sertorius and settled Spain (77-72); then he came in at the death to destroy the last bands of rebel slaves under Spartacus,[18] who had already been decisively defeated by Licinius Crassus (73-71); he became consul with Crassus in 70; in 67 he defeated and exterminated the pirates who were infesting the Mediterranean. In that year he succeeded L. Licinius Lucullus, who had conducted the second war against Mithradates and Tigranes between 74 and 67. Tigranes was compelled to surrender, after pressure had been put on his father-in-law Phraates III of Parthia, and Mithradates was pursued by Pompey into the Caucasus. Pompey created three new provinces, Pontus-Bithynia, Crete with Cyrenaica, and Syria; and he organized a number of vassal states, including Jerusalem, which was left in the hands of the Hasmonaeans after its siege and capture in 63. He then returned to Rome in the winter of 63/2. But while these events were occurring in Pompey's orbit, the star of C. Iulius Caesar was rising at Rome. An unsuccessful attempt was made to involve him in Catiline's conspiracy on behalf of the proletariat against the oligarchic government in 63. In the next year he was praetor, and in 61 he was pro-praetor in Spain. From there he returned to obtain the consulate for 59. But first he had made a secret pact with Pompey and Crassus, known as the First Triumvirate, which was renewed at a conference at Luca in 56.

In 58 Caesar, with extraordinary powers for five years, took up his command in Cisalpine Gaul, in Transalpine Gaul (Narbonensis), and in Illyricum. His first action in Gaul was to check migration by the Helvetii; he then threw back the German Ariovistus and crushed the power of the Germanized tribes of Belgica; then he took action to stop fresh intervention by Germans from beyond the Rhine, and by Britons from their island. His plan was to create friendly federations in Gaul, centred on the tribes which for some time past had favoured Rome. But just when his project was nearing completion, the bases for understanding between the triumvirs began to crumble. Julia, daughter to Caesar and wife to Pompey, died; and Crassus was killed, in an expedition undertaken against the Parthians in 54 and 53. Pompey, who ought to have taken over the proconsulate of Spain for five years in 54, stayed in Rome as the real arbiter of the state. News of the decline in Caesar's political position reached the Gauls, and was the part cause of a general revolt under Vercingetorix in 53 and 52, the embers of which were still smouldering in 51 and 50. The revolt was crushed; but it compelled Caesar to change his plan, and to give the conquered country a much less liberal settlement in the shape of a province.

Although Caesar made many efforts to reach a settlement with Pompey and the senate, their schemes to take away his command before the date that had been fixed brought on the Civil War. This saw the Roman world divided between the two triumvirs, and the soldiers supporting each were locked in armed conflict.

The war began in Italy, but later passed over to the Balkans. In 48 Pompey was crushed at Pharsalus, and was then put to death on the Egyptian coast by the guardians of Ptolemy XIV. In consequence Caesar as victor occupied Egypt, and settled it as a vassal kingdom, after which he crossed to Asia

Minor and defeated Mithradates' son Pharnaces at Zela. He then made himself master of Africa, which had been in the hands of the younger Cato; and Spain was won from other Pompeian survivors by his victory at Munda in 45.

He now returned to Rome; and in the last months of 45 and in early 44 he reformed the state to make it the imperial power he desired. The faction fights were to be ended: Caesar (and his successors after him) was to be dictator and ruler of the state for life; and the members of the state were to be increased by grants of citizenship to provincials. The provinces, now governed by responsible officers, were gradually to rise to the level of Italy; and Rome would have become the metropolis of a bilingual world, creating a harmony between the Greek and Latin civilizations. But in March 44 Caesar had decided to launch a last great military expedition, to conquer the Parthians who had killed Crassus and then to return to Rome with a vast demonstration of power through the Caucasus, Scythia, the Danubian and Rhine areas, and Gaul. Before this colossal expedition could set out Caesar was murdered by a group of senators on 15 March, 44 B C.[19]

d. From Triumvirate to Empire

Power was successfully taken over by the consul Marcus Antonius, who had been a loyal collaborator with Caesar and was supported by the people and by the veterans. For a brief moment he was ready to negotiate with Caesar's murderers, but only to give him time to rouse the mass of the people against them; and the two leaders of the conspiracy, M. Iunius Brutus and C. Cassius, left Rome and crossed to the East. But Antonius' leadership of the Caesarians was now challenged by the young C. Octavius, known as C. Caesar Octavianus because he had been adopted by Caesar. After some delay he arrived from Epirus, collected forces of his own, secured support from a group of senators, and made an alliance with another of Caesar's murderers, Decimus Brutus. He attacked and defeated Antonius' army, and claimed the consulate; then in November, 43, he reached agreement with Antonius and Lepidus, and formed a triumvirate which the senate were compelled to recognize. The triumviral programme was to avenge Caesar and to preserve the principles of his imperial ideas. After removing their opponents by bloody proscriptions they moved to attack Brutus and Cassius, who had made themselves masters of the East. These two were defeated in two battles at Philippi (42) and forced to suicide. The triumvirs now made a division of the areas they were to rule, though they were hampered by the continued existence of anti-Caesarian forces in the pirate fleet commanded by Sextus Pompeius, son of Pompey the Great. Antonius in the East planned a war on the Parthians and Armenians: against the latter he was successful, but against the Parthians he failed. He combined with Cleopatra, queen of Egypt, to found an empire of the Hellenistic and Oriental type. Octavian meanwhile removed Sextus Pompeius and Lepidus (36), and thus became sole master of the Western world. The struggle between the two surviving triumvirs grew progressively more acute and finally developed into war. This was ended by the battle of Actium, after which Octavian in 30 took possession of Egypt, and Antonius with Cleopatra committed suicide.

Octavian remained sole ruler. He refused the dictatorship, but retained his supreme command of all armed forces and his complete control of finance. He made the senate his ally: it was now convinced that one man must rule, and it gradually conferred all power on him by spontaneous and official grants, embraced generally by the title Augustus which was accorded in 27. For one period of ten years after another Augustus was made proconsul of his provinces; he had sanctity through the full tribunician power conferred in 23; and in 12 B C he became Pontifex Maximus.

The senate was radically overhauled, the chief change being that it was now bound to ratify the conclusions of a 'consilium principis' composed of persons in Augustus' confidence. A new bureaucracy drawn from among the knights was entrusted with the government of certain imperial provinces and with the discharge of a number of other tasks. The provinces were divided into senatorial and imperial, the former being the pacified areas, the latter those where units of the army were needed. A slowing-up is noticeable in the process of transforming the provinces by grants of citizenship; but meanwhile colonies were founded, and large public works were carried out in Rome, Italy, and the provinces. Apart from the troops needed to protect the emperor's person and to garrison Rome and Italy, the armies came to be stationed on the frontiers of the empire, their total size (excluding contributions from allied states) being reduced to about 300,000 men. Attention was given to the regular financial arrangements, and an imperial treasury was created as well. The conquest of Syria was completed; in the Alps Rome's territories were expanded; the defence systems on the Euphrates and the Danube were improved; and an attempt was made, but later abandoned, to occupy Germany as far as the Elbe. If we add the care taken to secure a trained successor with many years of tutelage behind him, we now have the main features of the Augustan empire, whose principles included the maintenance of Italy's superiority over the provinces, though the government ensured that the Italians should show themselves worthy of this preferential treatment.

7. THE TRANSFORMATION OF THE GREEK EAST

During the empire of Alexander and the Diadochi, and under the Seleucids after 301, there was a process of close fusion between Greek and Oriental civilizations in the parts of the East which the Macedonians had conquered. Even in the Far-Eastern provinces, especially Bactria, this reached very high levels, being largely responsible for the cultural exchange between the Hellenized world and foreign parts. It was precisely in Bactria, however, that we also find the first moves towards independence among the Seleucid provinces;

and this led gradually to the formation of the Parthian power under the Arsacid kings. In the middle of the third century, with the help of the local Greek cities, the satrap Diodotus of Bactria created an independent state under Greek rulers. After a few successors of Diodotus' line Euthydemus of Magnesia usurped the throne, but the Greeks governed the country for a century, down to 140 BC. They extended their territory to take in Arachosia and the areas of the Punjab and Sind, and accomplished a considerable task in promoting exchanges between the cultures of the Greek and Indian worlds. The middle of the third century, which saw the rise of the Bactrian kingdom, was also the period in which the Scythian Arsaces murdered the Seleucid satrap of Parthia and became master of his territory. He declared its independence and founded what became the nucleus of the Arsacid empire, an amalgam between Scyths and Iranian Parthians. Arsaces was succeeded in 248/247 (the Parthian era begins on 14th April 247) by his brother Tiridates, who used Bactrian aid to annex Hyrcania and Comisene; his successor Artabanus I (214–196) added Coarene. The renewal of Seleucid expansion under Antiochus III meant a setback for the Parthian empire. But after the discomfiture of Antiochus by the Romans at Magnesia (189) a revival occurred under Phraates I, who occupied the country as far as the 'Caspian Gates' and thus opened the way to Media and Persis, both of which countries were soon afterwards annexed by his successor Mithradates I (c. 171–138). This king also took over Elimias (Susiana), Babylonia, Adiabene, and Seleucia (141–140), and adopted the seal of the Achaemenids together with their ancient title, 'King of Kings'. He was ruler from the Caspian to the Persian Gulf, and the Seleucid Demitrius II, who tried in vain to check his progress, was defeated and taken prisoner. Arsacid history in fact consists of an unceasing struggle to defend their western frontiers against the Seleucids and later the Romans, and their north-eastern frontiers against nomad invasions. As early as 155 the Sacae had occupied Śakastan (modern Seistan), which bears their name.

The next king, Phraates II, lost certain territory to Antiochus Sidetes, but recovered it when he defeated and killed the Seleucid king. He in his turn fell fighting against the Sacae, who under pressure from the Yüeh-chih had destroyed the Bactrian kingdom and become masters of Sogdiana, Hyrcania, Comisene, and finally Adiabene. His successor, Artabanus II, thrust the Sacae back, but he too was killed in battle in 124.

The first act of Mithradates II (c. 124–88) was the recovery of Babylonia and Caracene, which had become independent in 126. Then in the east he seized western Bactria from the Sacae as far as the plain of Merv, and in the north-west took possession of certain Armenian territories. By taking advantage of the new caravan routes to China he was able to expand the trade of his subjects in both directions, thus establishing Parthia's first political contact with the Roman world in an embassy sent to Sulla when he was praetor in Cilicia in 92. But the last years of his reign, and the twenty years which followed, saw another setback, caused by endless internal disturbances, as a result of which the territories lately won from Armenia were lost and in 77 Sanatruces, a king imposed by the Sacae, secured the Parthian throne.

The power, however, passed to Phraates III (c. 69–c. 57). This king refused an alliance against Armenia offered by the Roman commander Lucullus, who promised the disputed territories as his reward. An alliance on the same terms with Pompey was accepted; but after Phraates had taken a lukewarm part in the war his hopes were frustrated, and after lengthy negotiations he had to be content with the cession of Adiabene.

Phraates III was murdered by his two sons, Orodes II who secured the throne in 57, and Mithradates III who was engaged in continuous war with his brother until he himself was removed in 54. Meanwhile the Roman triumvir Crassus was starting the campaign against Parthia which ended with his disastrous defeat at Carrhae in the following year. The result of this was that Orodes not only reconquered Mesopotamia but was able to cast his eye on the Syrian and Anatolian lands, although in 50 a counter-attack by Cassius Longinus pushed the frontier back to the Euphrates. It was crossed by both powers in the years which followed. After the death of Cassius at Philippi the Parthians invaded, but Orodes in person was defeated by the legions at Gindarus in 38, and his successor Phraates IV (37–2 BC) had to meet a severe threat from the triumvir Antonius, who prepared an expedition as the avenger of Crassus. But the Roman invasion passed off without inflicting harm, and indeed caused a breach between the Romans and Artavasdes I of Armenia. During the civil war between Octavian and Antonius, Phraates IV tried to pursue his policy of expansion by securing Armenia, but his dreams were ended when Augustus united the Roman power. In 20 BC he had to agree to restore the standards and prisoners taken at Carrhae to the emperor's stepson Tiberius, and to accept a policy of friendship with Rome, to which he sent four of his sons as pupils. At the beginning of our era he was succeeded by Phraates or Phraataces (2 BC–AD 4), his son by an Italian woman named Musa.

8. ARMENIA

Armenia was inhabited by people of the old Urartic stock who had mixed with 'Armenoid' and Indo-European immigrants. As a semi-independent satrapy under the Persians, it had been loyal to their kings but had been governed by two dynasties of its own, in Armenia Maior and Armenia Minor. It was then occupied by Alexander the Great, but on his death the satrap Orontes declared the country's independence, which was maintained, despite the threat offered by Eumenes of Cardia, in face of all the successors. It was only much later that Antiochus III succeeded in obtaining suzerainty over this large area, still divided into the two satrapies of Greater and Lesser Armenia, one east and the other west of the Euphrates. But the country regained its independence after Antiochus' defeat at Magnesia in 189, with Artaxias ruling in Greater Armenia and Zariadres in Lesser. The decades that followed were marked by the rise to power of the Parthians, whom the Armenian kingdom had to recognize as overlords; but in the subsequent period of Parthian weakness Tigranes II, the new and active ruler of Armenia Maior, was able to put an end to this state of affairs. The king now annexed Armenia Minor, extended his territory on the south at the expense of the Parthians in Upper Mesopotamia, and took Cappadocia from its king Ariobarzanes. When the latter fled to Rome in 93, Tigranes made an alliance with King Mithradates Eupator of Pontus and invaded Cilicia and Syria, sealing his new power by taking the title 'King of Kings' and by founding a fresh capital at Tigranocerta. But by these means he had provoked the opposition of Rome. As its enemy in the Mithradatic Wars he first lost Cappadocia, given back to Ariobarzanes by Sulla; and in 69 the campaign of Lucullus deprived him of all his Western conquests, though by a desperate resistance in 68 and 66 he halted his enemy in Lesser Armenia.

When Pompey succeeded Lucullus, however, the Romans entered Artaxata, and Tigranes was forced to give up Syria and Armenia Minor, and to recognize Roman suzerainty. The victory of the Parthians over the legions of Crassus in 53 brought Armenia, under its new king Artavasdes, into the Parthian system, but it was recovered for Rome by Antonius. Though Artavasdes once more tried to escape from dependence on Rome, he was held responsible by Antonius for the failure of his Parthian expedition and severely punished: Artaxata was taken, Artavasdes made prisoner, and Armenia made a fief for Alexander the son of Antonius and Cleopatra. During the civil war between Octavian and Antonius the legions were withdrawn, and under its new king Artaxes Armenia reverted to Parthia; but on the king's death in 20 BC, Augustus now being master of the empire, Tiberius his stepson put on the Armenian throne a new king, Tigranes III, who accepted Roman suzerainty. After later rebellions Rome found other kings, the Median Ariobarzanes (imposed by Gaius Caesar in 1 BC), Artavasdes II, and finally Tigranes IV.

NOTES TO CHAPTER VII

1. The view that there was feudalism during the Han is supported by many Marxist historians, and in particular by the overwhelming majority of contemporary Chinese historians.

However, they see the existence of this feudalism not only and not primarily in the fact that Liu Pang revived the institution of land grants to the aristocracy, but in the fact that the entire system of social and economic (and in particular agrarian) relations during the Han was based on principles characteristic of the feudal mode of production (see, e.g., L. I. Duman, 'O sotsialnoekonomicheskom stroye Kitaya v 3 v. do n. e.—1 v. n. e.' [On the Social and Economic Structure of China from the third century BC to the first century AD], *Voprosy istorii*, 1957, no. 2).

The institutions introduced by the Ch'in, which the authors think limited 'feudalism', in fact did not stand in the slightest contradiction to the feudal mode of production, but were merely a characteristic, specific feature of it. (L. S. Vasilyev.)

2. The history of India that we are reconstructing is summary and condensed: it enumerates successive invasions and struggles which are brought together in the account, but which in reality were spread over a very long period in time and across a vast area. Peaceful periods and regions were not lacking but historians ordinarily abandon the study of their products, which prove their existence, to philologists and archaeologists. The frequency of conflicts is in reality no greater in India than in other countries of the world. Even the political anarchy of the eighteenth century, which led to the British conquest of India and contributed to a belief in the congenital propensity of India to anarchy, had as its counterpart the European wars which had repercussions in India and helped to unsettle it.

One does not see why the division of society into classes should have necessarily removed political stability from the time when it represented the normal structure and not an occasional situation. At any rate a demonstration of the assertion would be useful. Struggles took place between classes but mainly between peoples through invasions or rivalry among princes. The classes took part in the struggles as a group but not always in a direction leading to anarchy; it was the Brahmans who most fiercely opposed Alexander's invasion, so Arrian tells us (*Anabasis*, *VI*, 2). The classes who took political action were not always those in the *varṇa* social scale. The Buddhists supported invaders on several occasions, although they themselves recruited from all classes without distinction.

In any case the multiple dynastic changes (frequently separated by long periods in time) did not always introduce many modifications into a society which was culturally unaffected by these changes.

3. Except, as Professor J. Filliozat notes, that Alexander's invasion had lessened Persian power without substituting a comparable Greek power. So the Oriental empire could regain the satrapies conquered by the Persians in the sixth century BC.

4. The failure was largely due to Seleucid interference.

5. In this expedition Darius first secured the submission of the tribes of Thrace, then crossed the Danube and led his army through the regions which are now Moldavia and Bessarabia, the natives retiring before him. The Transdanuvian campaign was fruitless, and its motives are obscure: possibly Darius was concerned to obtain further information about the tribes Persia had encountered on its Caspian frontier.

6. Aristagoras, if not the architect of this revolt, was at least an early convert, and lost his life fighting for the Thracian mines coveted by Miletus. If commercial pressures were all-important in causing the rising (and the question is most obscure), it seems likely that Milesian interests were prominent: there may have been distress resulting from the loss of their main source of raw wool when Sybaris in Italy was destroyed *c.* 510. But a further cause must have been the rise of 'democratic' elements (i.e. of a citizen class jealous of the families which, often with Persian support, had been dominant hitherto): this factor was recognized by the Persians after the revolt, when they established 'democracies' instead of tyrannies in the cities. The revolt cannot therefore be explained wholly on commercial or nationalist lines.

7. Professor C. Danov considers that more weight should have been given to the ethnic and economic forces, as distinct from the political and military events, which led to the dissolution of Alexander's empire. Some of the economic factors are treated in Chapter IX.

8. For the chronology see above, p. 78 with note 29.

9. The Roman *plebs* obtained equal rights with the patricians not as a result of 'generosity' on the part of the latter, but as a result of a bitter and protracted struggle. (E. M. Shtaerman.)

10. Professor Ch. Th. Saricakis maintains that such relations are most improbable in the early third century BC. But though the treaty with Egypt, dated by Livy to 273, may not have had any serious significance, by the later part of the century Rome was undoubtedly a power which no Mediterranean monarchy could fail to recognize as a competitor for hegemony. On this whole subject the views of M. Holleaux, *Rome, la Grèce et les monarchies hellénistiques* (Paris, 1921) have found wide acceptance: on the Egyptian treaty see his pp. 46 ff.

11. Professor C. Danov considers this account of Roman imperialism to be far too favourable. To him the fundamental policy of Rome was expressed in their maxim 'divide et impera', and he regards it as misleading to speak of the conquest of the peninsula as bringing about the Romanization of Italy and the Italianization of Rome. Professor Pareti's view, however, is reinforced, not only by the story of Italian loyalty during the Second Punic War, but by the development of Romano-Italian religion, literature, and art (see Chapters XI and XII).

12. Although these were doubtless the views of certain second-century senators, it is questionable whether Cato held them. Though brutal in his attitude to slaves, Cato is not known to have favoured harshness to the Roman *plebs* or to the provincials (apart from his hostility to Carthage): the salient feature of his foreign policy was his anti-Hellenism, which led him actually to oppose any annexations in Greek lands, while at home he advocated reconstruction and reform on traditionalist lines and was active in promoting public works. For a brief sketch see A. H. McDonald in *Oxford Classical Dictionary* (1946), s.v. 'Cato'. Another reason for the differences between second-century Roman statesmen over foreign policy was the division of the senate into groups, each with political and economic interests in particular areas; this phenomenon has been attractively analysed by E. Badian, *Foreign Clientelae* (Oxford, 1958).

13. Professor C. Danov insists that Rome aimed at outright conquest as early as the First Punic War. Far-sighted Greeks certainly feared the 'cloud in the West' long before the battle of Pydna, cf. Polybius, V. 104, 10. Yet the motives of Rome's foreign policy in the late third and early second centuries are highly controversial: M. Holleaux, *Rome, La Grèce et les monarchies hellénistiques* (Paris, 1921) argued for self-defence; G. de Sanctis, *Storia dei Romani*, IV (Turin, 1923) for aggressive militarism; E. Badian, *op. cit.*, pp. 62 ff., for fear combined with desire for revenge.

14. This was land to which the Romans acquired title after a conquest, but which they had allowed squatters to occupy. See below, p. 488.

15. The grievances of the allies, which C. Gracchus sought to remove by grants of citizenship, had been fanned by the Gracchi themselves; for the 'public land' which Tiberius' law redistributed was often in the hands of allied proprietors.

16. It was actually Sulla in 88 who was the first to march on Rome with armed force.

17. For fuller analysis of the political and constitutional struggles of this period see Chapter X. After the land confiscations which Sulla effected in 81 the social discontent in the Italian countryside was severe. Catiline's conspiracy (see below) was based on genuine distress, whether or not the motives of its leader were sincere.

18. For this rebellion, the most terrible of all the Servile Wars, see below p. 487 and p. 497

19. For the features in Caesar's rule which led to his murder see below, p. 502.

CHAPTER VIII

THE DEVELOPMENT OF LANGUAGE
AND WRITING TO THE CHRISTIAN ERA

I. LANGUAGE

a. *Chinese and Its Diffusion*

IN the history of Chinese it is essential, though difficult, to distinguish the factors affecting speech from those affecting writing. In regard to the former, the chronological picture is very hazy, and the grammatical development of classical Chinese is scarcely perceptible. Thanks, however, to Karlgren's work, the phonetic development, at least in the great northern capitals, is better known, though we know very little about other Chinese dialects.

In 213 BC occurred the great reform of the script imposed by Li Ssŭ, which we shall discuss later on. An official list of standard characters was set up and promulgated; and this helped to settle the form of the written language. But the most decisive factor was the conscious and unconscious imitation of ancient authors by the writers of the Han Dynasty. The Chinese literary language was then fixed in the form which it preserved down to the twentieth century. Meanwhile its use spread gradually as the result of colonization and cultural assimilation during the period of the Warring States.

The language of the Li Ssŭ period (the end of the third century BC) was approximately what modern sinologues (Karlgren, Simon, Forrest) call Archaic Chinese, which began about 500 BC. The Proto-Chinese of the *Shih-ching*, described in Part I, underwent in this period its most rapid and profound changes. Above all, the majority of the 'Phonetic Compounds' were fixed at this time. Some of the final occlusives of Proto-Chinese now vanished: the consonantal clusters at the beginning of words, which were one of the salient features of the previous phonetic period, were simplified. These phonetic changes seem connected with the fact that, with the breakdown of feudalism and the coming of the unifying central government of the Ch'in, supremacy was won by linguistic forms belonging not only to other areas but to social levels different from those of the nearly extinct aristocracy.

From the point of view of vocabulary the Chinese language continued to develop almost without resorting to borrowings from other languages; it found in itself sufficient resources to indicate new ideas and new material objects as soon as the need presented itself. The autochthonous character and independent vocabulary of Chinese is one of its fundamental features at all times. Chinese is, and has always been, one of the few languages which have not applied to foreign tongues for the creation of technical and philosophic neologisms.

b. *Languages in India*

In this period the linguistic geography of India shows a progressive, though very slow, spread of Aryan speech southward, as far as the present-day confines of the Dravidic languages.

Classical Sanskrit ceases to be a spoken language and becomes finally fixed, in all its richness and complexity, in Pāṇini's great grammatical work.

The Prakrit dialects continued their development and became in this period the official languages of administration in the great Indian states. The earliest Indian inscriptions are those of Aśoka (third century BC) and they are all in Prakrit, slightly differentiated in four dialects according to the regions in which they were inscribed. This Aśokan Prakrit is particularly interesting as it is presumably very close, though not identical, to the spoken language of the north Indian ruling classes of that time. Even after Aśoka too it was used officially and it was employed in all the rare inscriptions of this period.

There is no direct evidence for literary Prakrit in this period. It is reasonable to assume that the oral teaching of the new religions, Buddhism and Jainism, used some Prakrit dialect; but it was only fixed as a written form in the following period.

c. *Iranic*

The official language of the Achaemenid conquerors, Old Persian, never succeeded in becoming either the common language or the language of administration (which used Aramaic). It was rarely used and rapidly declined, and this is proved by Artaxerxes' documents. Parts of the epigraphic monuments of Darius and of Xerxes were written in this language in our period.

Alexander's conquest removed it from circulation except as a dialect, and it was used as such in Persis, in south-western Iran, its birthplace, during the centuries which followed. Although there is no literary evidence, the eastern Iranic dialects survived into the Hellenistic period and the succeeding centuries and were never eclipsed by the use of Greek. This is particularly true of Sogdian, which did not develop until relatively late.

Naturally as soon as the eastern satrapies detached themselves from the Seleucid empire, Greek, which had been adopted there, slowly gave ground to a revival of the earlier languages, and to the growth of Aramaic as a common cultural language.

We shall complete the story of Middle Iranic in its two groups in Part III, although their first phases of development must certainly have occurred before the Christian era.

d. *Semitic*

The Semitic languages, and particularly those of the north-west, have several general features. They continued to be used in the Asiatic and Egyptian areas, but their use was less common, since they were supplanted in the East by Aramaic, which was also a Semitic language, and in the western Mediterranean by Punic, which was derived from Phoenician. We shall return to Punic later.

From the fifth to the third century we have a great many, though usually short and uniform, Phoenician inscriptions, but by the first century Phoenician had been supplanted by Aramaic. Similarly Hebrew, which had been used in the fifth–fourth centuries for writing the ancient religious and legal texts, was gradually infiltrated by Aramaic. By Alexander's time Aramaic had been substituted for common use even though scholars and nationalists continued to write in pure Hebrew until about 100.

In Egypt however the Hebrews became accustomed to Greek. This led to the Septuagint translation of the Bible, and to the preference for Greek shown by oriental Christendom.

During this period Aramaic had spread over a very wide area and replaced the old tongues such as Accadian, Phoenician, and Hebrew. We have tablets, written in Aramaic in Babylonia during the Persian domination in the fifth century and parchments which are specimens of the Aramaic of the Achaemenid empire administration. Later evidence of it is found in Cappadocia, in the Caucasus, and in India. It reached its greatest extension from about 300 BC onwards, with many autonomous regional developments. A Palestinian Aramaic can be distinguished, and also a form of Biblical Aramaic with continually increasing Aramaic features used for the transmission of certain biblical texts: for example in the books of *Ezra* and of *Daniel*, which spread as far as the Jewish colony of Elephantine in Egypt, founded in the fifth century. The Nabataeans, given their racial background, produced an Aramaic with Arabian overtones, but in Palmyra, although it was dominated for a long time by Arabian elements, from 43 BC onwards we find documents in a language similar to the Palestinian Aramaic of the next century.

In Babylonia Aramaic appears from the seventh century onwards, and from the Persian period there are the sixth- and fifth-century tablets mentioned above. From other easterly areas there are some 'Syriac' inscriptions of Edessa.

Phoenician, as we have said, had its own colonial development, with few regional differences, in Punic. The documents which have come down to us are mainly from the fourth century BC onwards, and have been found not only in Africa, but in Spain, Sardinia, and Sicily. At the end of the third century BC Plautus in his *Poenulus* has given us ten Punic verses in a Latinized form of vocalization, and the manuscripts also contain a version in Libyan Punic. A mutilated form of Punic, called Neo-Punic, is attested in inscriptions from the time the Punic zone came under Roman domination, and some of these are bilingual, in Neo-Punic and Latin. Punic spread through the neighbouring peoples and was used as a commercial language by the Berbers and Numidians of northern Africa.

The southern Semitic languages, those of an Arabian type, can be divided into three zones. One lay more to the north, to which we can assign the people stationed along the great caravan routes from Syria towards the Persian Gulf and the Yemen. On the first of these routes states had centred round the oases of el Giof and Taimā; on the second, round the oases of Lilyān near Dedan, and Tamūd, near the Gulf of Aqaba. The written texts can be dated from the second century BC to the sixth century AD.

The central Arabian district was inhabited by nomads, and has left no written documents before the Christian era. However in the southern region —in the Yemen and in the oases north of Hedjaz—the agricultural and sedentary life favoured the growth of an early civilization and state system. In our period these peoples, speaking a number of kindred dialects, were dominated from about the third century onwards by the Sabaei who had gradually assumed control of the area. From about 500 the southern Arabian dialects crossed over to Ethiopia on the African continent to the region later known as Abyssinia. There the natives added Cushite features to them. When a unified state arose in the first century BC the dialects assumed a more homogeneous form.

e. *Greek Dialects and Idioms*

The Greek dialects imported into the colonies suffered for various reasons. The colonists themselves were mixed in race, for a number of different stocks would take part in these foundations, and later foreigners would be brought in. Moreover over the centuries the colonists lived in increasing intimacy with the natives, who became Hellenized, but in their turn influenced the Hellenes. This is clearly shown in Sicily where there were mixed Ionic-Doric colonies, such as Himera; at Syracuse too there was heavy Aeolic penetration into the Doric tongue, and the Syracusan poets Epicharmus and Theocritus constantly use terms which are Siculan in origin. It can be seen too in the diverse peoples with whom they came into contact in the colonies, where, especially in popular speech, new sub-species of Greek dialects were formed: for example, in the colonies of Italy, and in such areas as Provence, Catalonia, the Adriatic, the Pontus, Cyrenaica, etc.

This development certainly had its effect upon literary Greek. But here there was a tendency in authors to copy the use of other dialects than their own—either because the dialect in question had been used successfully in the literary genre being attempted, or because the people who spoke it were politically or culturally dominant. As a result three different literary languages were in use from the end of the sixth century and the beginning of the fifth.

The first one was basically Ionic, and was used, for example, by the first prose writers up to Herodotus; the other two were fundamentally Doric—one used in Greece (cf. Pindar and Bacchylides), the other in the West (cf. the two Stesichori, Epicharmus, and later Archimedes). It must be understood, however, that each of these authors altered, modified, or mutilated the adopted model to suit his own tastes.

At the end of the fifth century, however, Attic became the common language partly because of Athenian cultural supremacy and also because the Sophistic movement was creating a uniform intellectual atmosphere. Gorgias, a Sicilian Greek, was one of the earliest to write in Attic. A new prose was shaped at Athens: one that no longer shifted from form to form, but, free from poetic conventions, was dominated by logic and rationalism. It loved to talk of mankind, the city and concrete reality, and, therefore, of history, science, morals, and politics. It took varied forms with different authors, but in all of them it was sober, precise, measured, as subtle as could be, capable of expressing irony, and of making a point understood by barely alluding to it.

Alexander's conquests had a decisive influence on the use of Greek as the official language of the Macedonian empire: not only in areas such as Aegean Asia where it had been spoken for centuries by the Greek colonists, and, side by side with Aramaic which had spread with the Persian empire, by the indigenous people. It was used also in the predominantly Iranic areas such as Pontus and Cappadocia; in Syrian and Mesopotamian zones where the Semitic languages, especially Aramaic, were dominant; in Egypt; and as far distant as India. It is true that after a few decades the following three countries broke away politically: India in 316 and again near 100, Bactria about 246 and again in 188, and Parthia (with the Arsacids) in 247 and 188. But in less distant parts of these areas Greek lasted as the language of the upper classes, of the well-educated, and of the people in the Greek cities, against the earlier languages and dialects used by the commoners and country people.

This Greek, the Attic koiné, was used everywhere in the Hellenistic world. It penetrated into Macedonia and was taken by the Macedonian conquerors throughout their vast empire through court channels and by the Graeco-Macedonian colonies. It was an Attic different enough from the genuine one spoken at Athens; while it had lost some of its own peculiarities it had been influenced by the other Greek dialects, especially Ionic, and by the acceptance of some barbarian neologisms. A common language of this kind is quite well known to us through Egyptian papyri and the translation of the Bible by the 'Seventy'. All the other dialects spoken in the Aegean Greek world gave way before its slow advance.

Much the same thing happened later to the Doric literary languages, and especially to those of the Peloponnese which were mainly Corinthian in origin, but had also spread in the Graeco-Italian world through the dominance of Syracuse and were current in north-western Greece. Even if the dialects persisted in popular usage, they were no longer employed in literature, except in a few areas such as Laconia. A tidy version of the vulgate tongue, with its Attic base, came to be used by the non-Athenian Hellenistic prose writers: they all expressed themselves clearly but their manner tended to be heavy, abstract, monotonous, and without elegance. The poets continued to use the traditional dialects for particular genres but their work is mostly an erudite and painstaking mosaic.

It is worth our reviewing briefly the various qualities and types of Greek civilization which succeeded in imposing themselves on the Hellenistic world. In the parts of Asia Minor nearest the Aegean, where for centuries Greek colonies had clustered on the shores and their language had penetrated the interior, many new Greek cities had been founded by the Diadochi, the Seleucids, and the lords of Pergamum, Bithynia, and Pontus. At least fifty of these cities formed a sort of ethnic girdle behind the coastal zone. As inscriptions show, the spread of Greek language and culture was massive although, especially in the east and centre, the indigenous languages were not completely obliterated; they were confined to country areas. The most famous Greek centres for literary production were Cos, Samos, Ephesus, Rhodes, Lampsacus, Byzantium, Chalcedon, Pergamum, Perge, and Nicomedia.

In Cilicia there already existed old Greek colonies such as Soloi and Mallus, and the Diadochi and the Seleucids had formed others by settling Macedonian veterans and Greek colonists. Here Greek penetration went fairly deep. The court of the Seleucids gathered together writers and philosophers from all over Greece, and they set up their schools there. The Hellenization of southern Syria was less strong, but always marked: they had already had phil-hellene dynasts, such as Strato of Sidon about 370; the Diadochi founded a Graeco-Macedonian 'dodecapolis' in Transjordan; and the Seleucids, later followed by Pompey, stationed a number of new Greek colonies there. But the political discontent and persistence of indigenous cultures, especially that of the Hebrews, worked against Hellenization.

In heavily populated Mesopotamia, the seat of a thousand-year-old civilization, the few Greek cities founded by Alexander, the Diadochi, and the Seleucids were more centres for absorbing Oriental culture than for the diffusion of Greek values. However they did not lack indigenous writers who used Greek, such as Berosus, Diogenes, and Seleucus of Seleucia.

The Greek sites founded by Alexander and the Seleucids farther to the east were quickly paralysed when the areas in which they lay broke away politically, even when their new dynasts wanted to adopt Greek ways.

Finally in Egypt where Alexander had added Alexandria to the old trading stations at Naucratis, and the Ptolemies had founded Ptolemais and several outposts on the Red Sea, the Greeks spread as colonists even in the country districts; and for long periods Mediterranean regions with ancient Greek civilizations, such as the Cyclades and Cyrenaica, depended politically on Egypt.

These Egyptian Greeks preserved their own language and succeeded in converting to its use the educated portion of the Semitic element in the country, namely the Jews, who, especially in Alexandria, constituted one of the fundamental elements of the population. But though many of these Greeks became the dominant cultural element at the court and in the country, so much so that Egypt became one of the great Greek literary centres—they never succeeded in eclipsing the indigenous language and culture of Egypt although they won over some of the better-educated people such as Manetho.

In any case the establishment of the Hellenistic *koiné* was not entirely uniform, even in language. The accurate observer will notice perceptible differences in the Greek manifestations in different areas: each one reveals its own tendencies in taste, customs, and literary production.

When Rome gradually extended its dominion in the Asiatic and most of the Oriental world, it did not attempt the impossible task of substituting Latin for Greek as the cultivated language. Aware of the revival that was taking place, except in a few areas, of earlier languages and civilizations with Iranic, Semitic, Syrian, and Egyptian roots, Rome was content to protect the Greek culture of the upper classes. This was achieved by supporting Greek teachers of Grammar, and by the creation of more Greek colonies especially in the more inland Anatolian areas and also in Syria, even though sometimes there were competing Latin elements in these colonies. Even though the Arsacids of Parthia, and other dynasts outside the confines of the empire, indulged in the knowledge and diffusion of Greek language and culture, Rome was not able to stop the reappearance of Aramaic and Arabian speech in Syria and Mesopotamia, nor of the Iranic languages in Pontus and Cappadocia.

f. *Italic Languages*

In the last centuries of the ancient world the production of inscriptions by the various peoples of diverse races who had inhabited Italy before and after the Roman conquest slowed down. The greater part of the Etruscan inscriptions, from Etruria proper, and those from the short-lived Tyrrhenian empire—to the south, east, north-west, and in part of the Po valley to the north—come from the fifth to the third centuries, which period must have seen the *floruit* of Etruscan literature. The Po valley has revealed a variety of inscriptions. There are several groups attributable to the North Etruscans, and conceivably a few texts founded on Ligurian: later on we shall have something to say about the Celtic texts. But there are also about 200 Venetic inscriptions of Illyrian type, comparable to some extent with the 200 or so Messapian inscriptions of the fourth century and later from Puglie. At many places on the coasts of Magna Graecia and Sicily Greek dialects continued to be spoken and written. In inland Sicily the Siculans and Sicanians cut inscriptions of a 'First Italic' type; and from the extreme west of the island we have coin legends inscribed by the Elymians, and some texts from the Punic colonists. Similar Punic inscriptions are found also in Sardinia, though there they were still using primitive pre-Indo-European dialects.

We have yet to speak of the 'Italic' languages of the continent. The areas where 'First Italic' dialects were spoken got modified because of the movements of the Oscan and Umbrian 'Second Italic' speaking peoples; both dialect groups were also affected by Latinization. Of the three most important linguistic events in Italy in the second half of the first millennium BC we shall discuss later the consequences of the Celtic migration. The others were the Sabellic migration and the Roman conquest with the Latinization it brought about.

Between the sixth and fourth centuries the Oscan and Umbrian peoples were on the move, and to some extent became superimposed on each other. The consequence was a linguistic change over much of the Italian peninsula, from the central districts to the extreme south. This affected the peoples of European speech, the First Italici, and also the Iapygians and Greek colonists: it also affected the survivors of pre-Indo-European speakers on the coasts of the Adriatic and Etruria. The displacement of these people carried a southward movement by Umbrians, Oscans, and the Volsci—a mixture of the two; this wedged itself between the Latins and the Ausones and Aurunci as far as Antium.

The southward migration of these Oscan bands had various results. Their first movement founded the Picentes, Praetuttii, Vestini, Paeligni, Marrucini, Marsi, and Frentani. The second founded the Samnites (Hirpini, Penti, Caudini, and Carecini), who submerged the Ausones and Opici but also created the Campanians. The third created the Lucanians, from whom the Bruttii were a later offshoot; and this time the Oenotrian Italici were submerged, and the very existence of the Greek colonies in southern Italy was imperilled. Naturally, the differences between the various Oscan dialects are largely due to fusions with earlier peoples. The inscriptions show evidence of hybrid language, for example the mixture of Etruscan and Campanian which followed the expansion of Etruscan power.

The advance of Oscan speech was not halted even at the Straits of Messina, because the Siculans employed strong bands of Oscan mercenaries, especially Campanians and Samnites, in the fifth and fourth centuries. The Oscan penetration, either as new citizens or as conquerors, in both Greek and non-Greek cities, had the effect of introducing a marked Oscan element into the island. This was denounced as a grave danger in the letters attributed to Plato, and is borne out on inscriptions and coins.

Romanization of Italy. Generally speaking, Romanization did not make the ancient pre-Roman languages of Italy disappear. But it gradually substituted Latin for literary and administrative use and in the exchanges between educated people. At the same time vulgar usage in the cities, and even more in the country, declined into dialects heavily larded with Latin. Just as in modern Italy there are both a literary language and a number of dialects, so in ancient times too there was a form of bilingualism between Latin and local dialects.

The penetration of Latin as the educated language had various and diverse phases. At the beginning it was spread by the Roman and Latin colonists planted in territories of foreign speech; individual Latins were enrolled in rustic tribes; and the Roman armies were temporarily stationed in the various regions. Trade, too, was made easier by new methods of communication. Later on, in every part occupied by Rome, in the Marsic country and in Umbria, in Apulia and Picenum, hybrid blends of Roman and indigenous peoples were formed, as we see from inscriptions.

With the system inaugurated at the beginning of the fourth century, of granting Roman citizenship which they could exercise in Rome, to the inhabitants of allied cities, Latin spreadi n the *municipia*; but at the same time some of the new citizens migrated to Rome and brought their foreign speech to the city. But from then on educated people in the cities became systematically and spontaneously bilingual, speaking Latin and a local dialect at the same time. This explains, for example, the request from the Cumaeans in 180 to Rome for permission to use Latin in their forum (Livy, XI, 42). It explains too why, from the beginning of the second half of the third century, so many of the most famous writers of Latin did not come from Latium. Naevius came from Campania; Livius Andronicus from Tarentum; Pacuvius from Brundisium; Ennius from the country of the Sallentini; Plautus from Umbria; Accius from Picenum. The temporary flood of imported slaves of widely different origins no more than mildly upset the balance of this development.

Let us repeat that it was only gradually that the various Italic languages ceased to be written. They were preserved in everyday speech and were the distant base of the modern dialects, the mixture of Latin and native languages spoken in every part of Italy. This is why Oscan was still written in the first century of the empire at Pompeii; why, at the time of Strabo, a few kilometres from Rome the Falisci spoke a different language from the Latins; why Dionysius of Halicarnassus says in the time of Augustus that Etruscan still existed. According to Arrian, Rhaetian and Celtic were still spoken in Hadrian's time: about AD 175 Oscan, Greek, Etruscan, and Celtic were spoken, according to Aulus Gellius. Apuleius says that the Sicilians were trilingual: they spoke Siculan, Latin, and Greek.

The persistence of the ancient pre-Roman languages existing in a Latinized form side by side with the Latin of the educated classes, and the influence they had on each other, explain the regional quality of the Latin used even by great writers if born outside Latium (cf. Livy's *Patavinitas*). This is all the more true of the Latin used by educated people in particular areas (according to Cicero, *Brutus*, 171, in the Celticized zones). It also explains hybrid constructions of names of persons and places.

We can also understand in this way the persistence in modern Italian dialects, and through them in literary Italian, of ancient word-formations and of phonetic phenomena derived from Ligurian, Sardinian, Corsican, Greek, Etruscan, Celtic, Oscan, Umbrian, or Venetic. We can see the reason for the differences and the frontiers between the dialects: they conform in general with those of the ancient pre-Roman languages. Compare, for example, the area of Celtic dialects in modern Italy with the part of the Po valley occupied in ancient times by the Celts. Compare also the neighbouring dialects, Ligurian, Venetic, and Middle-Italic, with the old areas of the Ligurians, Veneti and Italici.

Romanization of the Provinces. What we have said about the Romanization of Italy was repeated on a much larger scale in the western and northern Roman world. In general the rest of the world was left to its Greek culture, except in the east where Greek lost ground in the revival of native languages. We shall return to this argument in Part III, and shall only consider it briefly here. At the end of the third century and in the first decades of the second century BC power and policies pivoted round Scipio Africanus the Elder, and his belief was that the conquered countries, Carthage, Macedonia, and the Seleucid territories, having become allies, should, in collaboration with Rome, undertake the task of civilizing the neighbouring barbarian world. In the Mediterranean world there should be three areas: one Latinized, one Greek, and the third Punicized: this triple division lasted for some time. But the allied states became subjects towards the middle of the second century, and one of the three areas, the Punic, gradually lost its function. It lay between the Latin and Greek areas and was encroached upon, and so reduced in size, by both of them. At first Punic literary works were translated into Greek (Hanno, Himilco and Mago); then Greek was used by Carthaginian writers, such as Hannibal, for his books on strategy, and later by the Numidian king Juba II. Finally Punic scholars migrated to Greek countries—Hasdrubal, known as Clitomachus, is an example; he was an academic teacher in Athens from 127 to 110.

At the same time Numidian scholars stopped writing in Punic and began to write in Latin. There are many examples: Hiempsal II, cited by Sallust; the comic writer Terence; and the naturalist, Turanius Gracilis. Meanwhile the classic works of Punic culture, like those of Mago, were translated into Latin as well as Greek.

From then on the Mediterranean world, and in general the Roman-dominated world, split into two dominant linguistic zones, Greek and Latin. There were a few temporary interruptions. Greek entered the Western world through Sicily and the area round Massilia; and Latin entered the East in parts of Asia Minor and Syria where Roman colonies were wedged between

Greek and Aramaic and other native spheres of influence. This led to a
Syriac literature written in Latin, of which Publilius Syrus the writer of
mimes is a prototype as early as the first century BC.[1]

Rome had no illusions that it could supplant Greek culture in the Hellenic
and Hellenistic countries. On the contrary it supported it against the revival
of pre-Alexandrian Oriental languages. It created two concepts, which were
vigorously asserted and realized by Caesar. As educated people knew the
two languages, all scholarly works produced throughout the empire could
remain bilingual in Greek and Latin; in the metropolis, Rome, this bilingualism was almost universal. The second concept was that Latinization should
be the only process in the western, non-Hellenized section of the empire:
in the former Carthaginian Africa, Spain, Gaul and its adjacent areas in
Italy, and in the central Balkans north of the Hellenized regions.

In all these areas Romanization was much slower than it had been in Italy;
this was partly because of the different ethnic background, and also because
of the slow rate of colonization and of grants of Roman citizenship. As a
result the linguistic assimilation, and the more far-reaching mergers and
hybridization, were hindered. In each of these provincial zones the original
language flourished in everyday speech; the indigenous Iberian and Celtic
languages while continuing to be universally used in ordinary life were slowly
transformed into a local Latin 'patois', which served as the base for the later
languages.[2] See for example the surviving Celto-Iberian inscriptions from the
second century AD. By the first century BC we find Latin writers of Spanish
origin, such as the two Hygini; and from Narbonese Gaul came the grammarian M. Antonius Gnipho, the two poets Cornelius Gallus and Terentius
Varro Atacinus, and slightly later the historian Pompeius Trogus.

In the Hellenized East, Rome had been unable to stop the ethnic regional
differences from having a profound influence on both spoken language and
literature. This phenomenon became even more noticeable in the area which
got slowly Latinized. In these there not only developed several distinct, and
distinguishable, kinds of vulgar Latin, but also several forms of the literary
language, each giving a fairly clear stamp to the literature of a particular region.

Evolution of Roman Speech. All this was important in the development of
the spoken language in the city of Rome. Its ethnic structure was being
completely transformed by the influx of *cives Romani* who came from widely
different subject countries, and also by the complex origin of the slaves
and freedmen who congregated there. This state of affairs was to be more
marked during the Imperial period, but could already be seen in the early
days of grants of citizenship, which started with Camillus in the fourth
century BC. Numerous neologisms, with grammatical and phonetic features
of a non-Latin type, thus could enter Rome from the Oscan, Umbrian,
Etruscan, and Greek countries. At the same time various forms of literature
gradually made their way to the capital. From the Oscan country came the

Fabulae Atellanae, masked plays, both in the original and in translation. From Caere, where the fourth-century Romans sent their sons to school (Livy, IX, 36), and from other deeply Hellenized Etruscan towns, came writings on history, religion, and augury, together with didactic and poetical works, the products of those Tyrrhenians who had once been masters of Rome. Some of these were in translation, such as Tarquitius Priscus' works. Falerii introduced the Fescennine verses: and from the Hellenic country, where the Sibylline Books had come in the sixth century from Cumae, Rome received the translation of the *Odyssey* by Livius Andronicus. Meanwhile the Messapian Ennius translated the 'Sacred History' of Euhemerus into Latin; and the first Roman historians, before Cato's day, were writing their annals in Greek.

g. *Celtic Languages*

According to Caesar there were special ties between the Goidelic-speaking Belgae who entered Gaul in the Hallstatt period in the first Celtic migration, and the Armoricans, maritime people who lived between the mouths of the Seine and Loire; and it is certainly the case that the two peoples acted together during Caesar's campaigns. From archaeological evidence one may believe that the split occurred about the fifth century. At the same time Caesar himself, and he is confirmed in this by Pliny and Ptolemy, asserts that the Celts in Britain derived from the Belgae and Armoricans; and he cites as evidence their linguistic affinities and the racial names they have in common, as well as the co-operation they gave to the people across the channel. Archaeological evidence confirms that up to the fifth century BC Britain was occupied by pre-Celtic, and, consequently pre-Indo-European, peoples, who slowly accepted Celtic civilization from the coast of Gaul opposite;[3] this continued when these territories were invaded by the second wave of Celts, commonly called 'Cymric'.

Tradition recognizes Celtiberi in the Iberian peninsula, and history tells of the struggle Rome had with a people of this name in the third century. The presence of Celtic elements, mixed in various ways with the pre-Celtic population, is attested by inscriptions, coin-legends, and place-names; between these and the Goidelic dialects there are fairly certain affinities,[4] but with the Cymric dialects affinities are less common. This may be the result of the number of superimposed invasions, and of forms of hybridism which were certainly different, and possibly more complete, than those found in Gaul.

From the sixth century onwards we find a third area of Celtic civilization in the Danube valley, and this view is confirmed by tradition. It was due to conquest by the Celts of Gaul, or rather to their partial return to countries where they had lived in earlier times,[5] and where they had closely intermingled with Illyrian elements.

The fourth Celtic invasion, that into the valley of the Po, is better known from tradition, written texts, and archaeology. Here the Celts entered the western and central zones before they moved into the south-east. And where they merged with the Ligurians and North Etruscans they created a linguistic and ethnic mixture. Tradition recognized this hybridism and was uncertain whether certain peoples should be called Ligurians or Celts; it is supported by the language found on the so-called Lepontine inscriptions which are written in a mixture of Celtic and Ligurian. On the other hand the inscriptions of the so-called North Etruscans in the eastern area are a mixture between Celtic and Etruscan. It is only in the Apennine mountain regions that the Ligurian element remains pure as we see in the inscribed *menhir* of Luna.

The fifth and farthest Celtic expansion was towards the east, and is proved by the ethnic wedge of 'Galatic' people who settled in the middle of Anatolia during the third century. They divided the Hellenized western area from the eastern zone in which Iranic culture revived. The Galatians gradually contaminated their Celtic dialect, as is shown by their personal and place-names, with predominantly Greek admixtures, which led to the Romans describing them as the Gallo-Graeci; their dialect also acquired Phrygian features from the population they had supplanted.

The other Celtic languages were Latinized in varying degrees: a phenomenon which in our period was well advanced in the Po valley, Narbonensis, and Celtiberia. The block grants of Latin and later of Roman citizenship given by Pompey and by Caesar, first to the Cispadani and then to the Transpadani, made a great contribution to Latinization in the Po valley. The most obvious result of this rapid Romanization, which did not kill the Celtic dialects but transformed them into a Celtic-Latin patois, is provided by the Latin literature written by men born in the Celtic part of the Po valley. As early as the first half of the second century BC the Insubrian Caecilius Statius was writing his plays; in later periods we have Valerius Cato, Cinna of Brixia, Bibaculus from Cremona, and also Cornelius Nepos, Catius and Albucius Silo. They prove that the Celtic zone was not slower in Romanization than either the Venetic, where Catullus, Aemilius Macer, Vitruvius, and Livy had their homes, or the Etruscan area north of the Apennines, which produced Virgil of Mantua.

We have already mentioned Narbonensis. In Spain the Latin inscriptions allow us to put the fusion of Latin and Celtic in the Celtiberian region back to a period earlier than the Christian era. In general the languages of southern Spain seem to have disappeared earlier than those of Celtiberia and of the north and west.

h. *German Languages*

The first expansions of Germanic populations outside present-day north-western Germany, which had been their temporary home, were probably those beyond the Rhine into Belgica. At the same time, or possibly earlier, the Celtic Belgae may have reached this region. In any case it is probable that it was the expansion of the Germans towards the south and the west that caused the Celts to move into the homes they occupied in historical times. The Helvetians, for example, still remembered having once occupied the region between the Hercynian forest, the Rhine, and the Main (Tacitus, *Germ.*, 28).

In Caesar's time[6] the majority of the inhabitants of Belgica, that is to say all those outside 'Belgium' (which was the term he used to describe the purely Celtic area), were mixed with Germans from beyond the Rhine. These Germans formed the greater part of the population even though they had quickly adopted Celtic language and customs because of the higher level of civilization among the Belgae. How this came about is clear: it was not only that the Germans wanted conquest but also that the Celts, who needed help in their own internal struggles, invited them in. Groups of Germans and Germanized Belgae then crossed over from Belgica to Britain at the end of the previous period and at the beginning of our own. In Britain we find Menapic and Caledonian Germans (Tacitus, *Agricola*, 11) and Tacitus himself asserts linguistic similarities between some of the Britons and the German Oestii.

The first mention of German soldiers penetrating into Italy in an expedition against the Romans is given in the *Fasti Triumphales*, under 222 BC, which include a triumph over the Germans. These Germans were 'Gaesates', that is mercenaries of the Celts armed with the *gaesum*.

A century later we hear of the great expedition of Cimbrians and Teutons, which first succeeded and then came to grief with great slaughter. They roamed round the Roman provinces and the non-Roman areas of south-western Europe in their search for land in which to settle. Because of their constant movements and the disastrous result they could not modify language in any perceptible way. The first real contact between Rome and the German world occurred with Caesar, whose campaign in Gaul had three main aims: to save Helvetia from the Germans; to prevent the hordes under Ariovistus, whom he chased out, establishing themselves permanently in Gaul and bringing in other Germans from beyond the Rhine; and thirdly so to weaken the Germanized tribes of the Belgae that he discouraged Germans from crossing the Rhine to reinforce them. Augustus later was to carry the same policy east of the Rhine, but with impermanent results. The work of Romanization in this region falls in the period following the one we are now describing.

2. WRITING

a. *Chinese*

In the field of Chinese writing the important event of this period is the reform, better described as a codification or standardization, carried out in

213 BC by Li Ssŭ, the great minister of the first emperor of China. It was in the main a unifying measure, which resulted in a list of about 3,300 characters being compiled. For this purpose Li Ssŭ made use of a system which had already existed for some time, the system of 'radicals'; this he codified, and gave it official sanction. Most Chinese characters belong in fact to the class in which a radical and a phonetic are compounded, the sixth (hsing-shêng) of the classes mentioned in Part I. The importance of this act was immense: it assured the uniformity of the written language, in whatever spoken dialect a written passage might be read aloud. From this time on there were no changes in the internal structure of the Chinese characters. All that happened was an enormous increase in their number during the course of centuries, partly to answer new needs, but partly also because they got invented arbitrarily without any real necessity for them. The form of the characters was initially still the Seal form: in the earliest period, that of the Warring States, the Great Seal script was used (ta-ch'uan), but later the Little Seal script (hsiao-ch'uan). In the official script (li-shu) adopted by the Ch'in chancery, and inherited later by the Han, a step had already been taken in the direction of more cursive forms. From that script was derived the formal style of writing (ch'iai-shu) used under the Han dynasty, and this corresponds in almost every respect to the modern form. The adoption of the writing brush, mentioned below, meant that a finer and more artistic ductus, with elegant curves, came into fashion, a flowing and continuous script instead of the angular scribbling produced by the old reed pen. The Chinese ideogram in this way could become a work of art; and in fact calligraphy reached the level of one of the great arts in China, often being appreciated as highly as painting.

Writing material was revolutionized by the invention of the brush pen, ascribed by tradition to Meng T'ien, a Ch'in general, about 215 BC. But we have already seen in Part I that the brush pen was in existence almost a thousand years earlier: it seems that Meng T'ien's service consisted mainly in perfecting its construction and popularizing its use.

For a long time writing was still on tablets of wood and bamboo: but in addition silk came into increasing use, especially after the brush had completely ousted the reed pen.

b. *Indian*

The first records of the new Indian scripts are the inscriptions of Aśoka in the third century BC. These presuppose a considerable previous history, but at present we cannot determine what that history was.

Common to all Indian writings are their syllabic nature and their very strict and precise adherence to the facts of the language. The unit in writing is the *akṣara*, which indicates a simple or compound syllabic sound, which always ends in a vowel. Short a is always inherent in the consonant, while the other vowels and diphthongs are indicated by special signs placed above, below, or alongside the *akṣara*.

The alphabets used on Aśokan inscriptions are two in number, Brahmī and Kharoṣṭhī. The former, which spread all over the sub-continent and is the parent of all modern Indian scripts, is *par excellence* the alphabet of India. It has thirty-nine simple (i.e. uncompounded) letters and is written from left to right. In Part I we have already discussed its possible origin. A southern variety of Brahmī seemingly isolated is the script of the stūpa of Bhattiprolu.

The history of Kharoṣṭhī writing, on the other hand, is very clear. This is a script written from right to left, confined to the extreme north-west in India, but employed also in the Indian trading colonies of central Asia. It is evidently an adaptation of the Aramaic script to meet the needs of a Prakrit dialect. Aramaic was the official alphabet of the Achaemenid government, and had consequently been known for centuries in the old Persian satrapy of India when this area, which now forms part of Afghanistan and of Pakistan, passed under Maurya domination about 300 BC (we have inscriptions of Aśoka in Aramaic). To produce Kharoṣṭhī, the Aramaic script was probably recast with the Brahmī script as a model. This we may suppose not only from the form of several letters but from the fact that the governing phonetic principle is the same in the two scripts, which are both of syllabic type and adhere closely to the actual sounds. Kharoṣṭhī writing, though always confined to a very narrow area, remained in use until the end of our next period; then it became extinct. It left no survivals either in India or elsewhere, and must therefore be regarded as a phenomenon which was isolated in time and space and had no consequences for the history of writing.

c. *Aramaic and its Derivatives*

From the moment in the sixth century when Aramaic suddenly attained a wide expansion and was taken up as the language of trade and administration between the various parts of the Persian empire to the west of the Tigris, there was a practically corresponding growth in the use of the Aramaic alphabet even where earlier systems survived.

The Hebrew zone is an instance. From the time of the Maccabean kingdom (second century BC) to its final subjection by Hadrian (second century AD) coins prove the persistence of a revised form of Old Hebrew in nationalistic circles. At the same time, by a fusion between Aramaic and Old Hebrew writing, a new form, the 'Square Hebrew Alphabet', became established: its earliest known document is dated 176 BC. This new system later became common, but for the first centuries of its use we have only sparse evidence on ossuaries, sepulchral inscriptions, and papyri (the earliest is from the beginning of the second century AD); only much later is it found used for biblical texts.

The Palmyra script is fairly close to Square Hebrew, and its earliest documents go back to the last decades of the first century BC, but it is attested with several hundred texts up to the fall of Palmyra in AD 274, from Palmyra itself and in different parts of the ancient world where Palmyrenes happened to be living. It is found in two forms, monumental and cursive (sometimes vertical) with a few ligatures between letters.

Aramaic alphabets that penetrated farther south underwent more rapid diversification, with a predominance of cursive forms. Nabataean was one of these, attested from the third century BC, and from it neo-Sinaitic was derived; but for the latter we have evidence only from the Christian era (see Part III).

Farther east Aramaic spread on a very wide scale, to some extent in the period with which we are dealing. This was true of the Iranic zone: in the north-east of Iran they used the so-called Arsacid Pehlevīk script, and in the south-west Sassanid Pehlevīk or *pārsīk*, both of them derived from Aramaic towards the end of the third or in the second century BC. Only the cursive forms have come down to us, most of them rather late, but we have a Pehlevīk document on parchment from the first century found in Persian Kurdistan.

For southern Arabian alphabets, see Part III, Chapter XIV.

d. *Ethiopian*

The Ethiopian zone, and Nubia in general, officially used the Egyptian language and script for a long time, even after the country had made itself independent of Egypt. But about 200 BC the local language gained supremacy; and a new system of writing was created for it, of which the oldest documents date from the second and first centuries BC. They are in two forms. The first one was hieroglyphic but with twenty-three signs (including vowels), almost all of them alphabetic. They differed from Egyptian in phonetic value, form, and direction. The second was cursive and it is subject to argument whether its characters were a simplification of Egyptian demotic, or a derivation from the southern Arabian alphabets. The evidence is discussed in Part III.

e. *Punic Scripts*

In the Carthaginian area the Punic script was converted from the second century onwards into the neo-Punic. This had both a lapidary and a cursive form. It carried frequent ligatures, had a number of local variations, and showed clearly the influence of Latin writing. It lasted for half a millennium, and was also used in Sardinia, where neo-Punic inscriptions are found from about 200 BC.

A derivative of Punic script, with some modifications and the addition of some old characters peculiar to the region, is the Libyo-Berber writing, which in its older form is sometimes called Numidian. Some of the evidence for it comes from bilingual inscriptions, in Libyan and Punic, Libyan and neo-Punic, or Libyan and Latin. There must also be a relationship between the Punic and Iberian scripts, of which there were three main types, Turdeta-nian (or Andaluso-Turdetanian), the writing of southern Hispania Citerior, and the writing of northern Citerior. The evidence for these Iberian systems consists of coin-legends and short inscriptions on a variety of objects, going back to the fourth or third century BC and forward into the Roman imperial period. All of them probably possess the same Punic substratum, but local differences have been increased by the addition of certain characters and the modification of others. Various causes brought about these modifications. There was intrusion by old pre-Punic characters, peculiar to the districts in question and sometimes perhaps akin to Berber signs; new elements were drawn from the scripts of newer civilized peoples, Greeks and later Romans, with whom the Iberians came into contact; and Celtic features entered Spain when the Celtiberian people took shape.

f. Greek Alphabets

In the period after 500 BC the Greek alphabets continued to spread from the Hellenic colonial areas to the neighbouring countries of foreign speech. But sometimes alphabets of different colonies converged on the same spot; and in other Greek districts hybrid systems of writing resulted from the action of an imperial power within the region, or from the mixture of races in a single colony. The Etruscan alphabet, which derived from Cumae, is an example. At first we find two distinct types, one in Southern Etruria the other in Northern, but during the sixth and fifth centuries these became a single alphabet, with some letters modified from the originals, others abandoned, and one or two more invented (like the sign 8 used for f.). On the other hand when the Etruscans appeared as conquerors in Campania, and Etrusco-Campanian inscriptions began to be cut, we notice a new influence, coming directly from the Chalcidian Greek alphabets. Similarly when the Etruscans also extended their empire to certain parts of the Po valley they took their own alphabet with them, an alphabet distinct from the one of North Etruscan type which the country had previously used.

But meanwhile the Greek alphabets continued to have their effect, direct or indirect, on all the systems of writing which existed in the Mediterranean lands. They entered the Iberian peninsula through the Phocaean settlements, and came to the Sicans and Sicels of Sicily by way of various colonies, of which the chief were Selinus, Gela, Syracuse, Zancle, and Himera. In the Italian peninsula the Umbrians and Oscans got their Greek type of writing through the intermediary of the Etruscans, modifying and adding to it to suit their own idioms; but there are also Oscan inscriptions written in a straightforward Greek alphabet.

In Greece itself in 403 BC the Athenians decided to adopt the Ionic alphabet officially, though it did not come into general use for many years after this date. Within a few decades this had become the alphabet used generally by all Greeks, and the various systems of the previous centuries were forgotten. Meanwhile both the uncial and cursive scripts grew up by the side of the lapidary form and were used for manuscripts. From the time of Alexander the Great onwards changes in Greek cursive writing can be used to date Greek documents to a generation, if not a decade. Other alterations in the signs were made for calligraphic reasons, such as the addition of apices and other forms of ornamentation, and the use of ligatures, 'sigle', and other abbreviations. Accents and other phonetical signs were invented about 200 BC.

g. Latin

Our present period is that into which, with a few early exceptions, all the archaic monuments of Latin script fall, and even they are rare before the end of the third century. The script originally had twenty letters, but it had no aspirated sounds and therefore no letters to correspond with them. In the third century Z was dropped and G was added; in the first century Z was adopted again, and Y was added in the transcriptions of Greek words.

The progressive penetration of the Latin language into the Western countries conquered by Rome brought with it the spread of the Latin alphabet. It reached its farthest extension in the imperial period.

Latin inscriptions use ligatures to join two or three letters, especially at the ends of lines. Characteristic features are the standard systems evolved for abbreviations, and the way in which a point, or a number of points above one another, were used to separate words.

NOTES TO CHAPTER VIII

1. Professor A. Lesky points out, however, that Publilius (though probably born at Antioch) was educated in Rome.
2. Professor A. Tovar notes that although Strabo (III, p. 151), drawing on Artemidorus, implies that the Romanization of much of southern Spain was accomplished in the second century BC, yet there are Celto-Iberic inscriptions from this area three centuries later.
3. For the strongly held view, supported by Professor P. Bosch-Gimpera, that Celts crossed to Britain long before 500 BC, see above, Part I, p. 106, note 28.
4. Professor A. Tovar expresses confidence that the Celto-Iberic dialect is closer to Goidelic than to any other form of Celtic spoken in Gaul or Britain.
5. Dr P. Oliva calls attention to the mingling of these Danuvian Celts with peoples of Illyrian stock, exemplified by the Eravisci who lived near Aquincum (Buda) in Roman imperial days.
6. Professor F. M. Heichelheim notes that we have only Caesar's own word for this view—though there is no good reason for rejecting it.

CHAPTER IX

THE DEVELOPMENT OF TECHNIQUES, TRADE, AND SCIENTIFIC LIFE

I. CONTACTS BETWEEN THE GREEK AND MIDDLE EASTERN WORLDS

THE period from 500 BC to the beginning of our era saw a gradual extension of contacts and cultural exchanges between the Greek colonies dotted round the Mediterranean on the one hand and the Eastern countries on the other. Moreover wider and more distant areas were becoming involved in both directions. The initial cultural relations of the previous period had been limited to the Aegean world, western Anatolia, Syria, and Egypt; and there had been alternating phases of intensity. Relations were highly developed in the Minoan and Mycenaean Ages, declined in the Geometric period which followed, then recovered again in the seventh and sixth centuries, and were finally weakened again after the conquests which made the Persians masters of south-west Asia and Egypt.

At the beginning of our period the Greek world had come near to destruction at the hands of the Persians and of the other barbarians who assailed it simultaneously in the West.[1] The victories of 480 and 479 put an end to their enemies' hopes. In the eastern Mediterranean there followed a period of sporadic warfare and armed vigilance, until half-way through the fifth century the Greeks made peace with the Persians, to free their own hands for their fruitless domestic struggles for hegemony in Hellas. This gave Persia the chance of greater intervention in Greek affairs in the period when Sparta was succeeding Athens, and Thebes Sparta, as the leading state in Greece. The Persians contributed money to help in extending these conflicts, since through them alone could the Great King exercise control of the Greek states amid the shifting balance of power. The culmination of this phase of history was reached with the Peace of Antalcidas in 387–386. Persia's *de facto* supremacy in the last decade of the fifth century and at various periods of the fourth was of decisive importance in intensifying cultural relations between Greece and the East, though it is very difficult, if not impossible, to be clear whether Greece had greater influence on the Middle East in these years or the Middle East on Greece. All the countries which had been Persian, and others beyond them, were then conquered in the war begun by Philip of Macedon and completed by Alexander. But so far from interrupting the complicated pattern of give-and-take the conquest actually promoted it, though in some areas the Greek element came clearly to the fore. It emerged as the predominant force in the large cities, both old and new, in which the

Greek population was concentrated; and this was especially true of the great *metropoleis*, where cultural foundations pursued scientific work according to the canons laid down by Aristotle and his school.

The resulting synthesis of Greek and Oriental cultures was a far-reaching phenomenon which lasted for many centuries, although the areas affected and their political masters were often changing. The first to get detached from the Hellenistic kingdoms were the areas farthest east, where Hellenic ways survived up to a point, but were gradually reinforced by native forms; of these the Parthian kingdom is an example. Then one by one the Hellenistic powers gave place to Rome. But instead of attempting to Romanize its eastern possessions, Rome encouraged the growth of Greek culture, or rather of the combined Hellenic and Oriental culture which was already dominant in the East. This had marked influence on every other part of its great Mediterranean empire. At the same moment new routes and new trade relations were taking shape between that empire and the Far East, carrying western commerce as far as China.

The advent of the Roman empire entailed therefore a vast increase in the cultural relations between East and West. Every country felt the effect, from India and China to Spain and Gaul. The next stage is to examine the process under various heads—production, manufacturing methods, commercial techniques, and scientific advance—whether single peoples were responsible for them, or a number of people combining or borrowing from one another as a result of the unity of their cultures. We may start with agriculture.

2. MAJOR TECHNIQUES

a. *Agricultural Advances*

Conditions in the Far East. Water control in China was mostly a concern of the central government. It was indeed one of its major duties and responsibilities in a country where intensive agriculture (which meant its whole economic life) depended so much on flood-control and artificial irrigation: a strong, authoritarian central government was best qualified for commandeering and co-ordinating the huge mass of labourers required. This function of the government is much more important in China than in the West, and it has been regarded as the main characteristic of Oriental despotism (theory of K. A. Wittfogel); an extreme view which does not seem to be supported by the historical facts.

It is in any case true that the power of Ch'in in the third century BC (and the ensuing foundation of the Chinese empire) was based to a large extent on great irrigation works in the Wei valley and on the possibility of sending grain supplies to the fighting troops.

From the point of view of the state, canals served a double purpose: first for the transport of taxes, i.e. for navigation; secondly for irrigation and flood-control. The same applied to the great rivers, though with them the second purpose was more important. The problem of the Yellow river, of the enormous quantity of silt it carries and of its ruinous floods, is the central one in the history of Chinese hydraulic engineering.

Canal building began when the rise of private land ownership, and the simplification and consolidation of Chou feudalism into a few large-size regional states, made available both the manpower and the managerial organization necessary for the purpose. It coincided also more or less with the recognition of the fertilizing qualities of the loess slime carried by the western rivers. The first canal was perhaps the Hung-kou, which joined the Huang-ho, near K'ai-feng, with the Pien-ho (afterwards integrated in the Grand Canal); it was probably dug at the beginning of the fifth century BC. The great wars of the period saw several large enterprises inspired by military purposes, such as the digging of the Hai-kou, connecting the Huai with the Yangtze-kiang. It was ordered by Fu Ch'ai, ruler of Wu, in order to ensure supplies for his troops. Shao Hsin-ch'u (381–334) dug the Ch'ien-lu Pei in southern Honan, by a barrage on a northern tributary of the Han river.

Ch'in rule is marked by three great enterprises. They are: (1) The canal built by the engineer Chêng Kuo for the princes of Ch'in and Han. It diverted the Ching river along the foot of the northern hills, discharging it into the Lo river. The result was an irrigation canal of more than 100 miles, which was finished in 246 BC. It was repaired and renewed several times, and remains today one of the greatest hydraulic works of China.

(2) The Kuan-hsien canal in Szechwan. The governor Li Ping started it after 250 BC, and it was finished after his death about 230. The Min river is divided by a stone jutting into two channels. The eastern one is an irrigation canal and is led through a cutting about 100 feet high. Both are then sub-divided in lateral (526) and sublateral (c. 22,000) canals, all of which discharge into the Yangtze-kiang below Chiating. The maximum level is reached in June–July, the minimum in December–March. For more than two thousand years the local people have followed the advice of Li Ping, 'to clear out the beds and to keep the dykes low'; this is done by large annual works of dredging and repairs.

(3) In contrast the Ling-ch'u canal is intended for transportation. It joins two rivers in Kuang-hsi, i.e. between the Tung-t'ing lake and Canton. It seems to be the work of the first emperor Shih-huang-ti, built for supplying the army which was sent to the conquest of Yüeh (south China) in 219 BC. It involves a diversion of part of the Hsiang waters by means of a stone nose into an artificial canal on the hill slopes; and the canal goes to join the Kuei river.

Sluice gates appear at the end of the first century BC; but the greatest step towards a regulated internal navigation, i.e. the invention of lock-gates (double sluices), was not to come before the T'ang period.

Agriculture in China was the basis of economic life, and thus of paramount importance. This is reflected in an old ritual, the ceremonial hand-ploughing of a furrow in the precincts of the Temple of Heaven; it was done personally by the emperor on New Year's day, i.e. in the first half of February, and indicated the beginning of the agricultural year. It was one of the most sacred and cherished imperial privileges.

Agricultural technique varied according to the regions, but in the core of the Chinese lands (the lower Huang-ho) tilling was intensive and the procedure was very careful, almost equivalent to horticulture. The tools of this period are known only from the form of ideographs, from the shape of coins, and from scanty literary references. Foremost among agricultural implements was the *lei*, a digging fork, originating from the old Shang territory; and the *ssŭ*, a sort of hoe either of wood or of metal, probably originating from the Western territories. The plough was a late comer. Oxen were at first only employed for drawing carts. Some scholars maintain that ox-ploughing came into use between the fifth and the third centuries BC; but it appears that there is no literary evidence for it earlier than a passage of the *Han-shu* referring to *c.* 90 BC. Of course, with the coming of the plough the *lei* and the *ssŭ* became mere supplementary tools; they did not, however, disappear; it was simply that their form underwent evolution.

What we know about Indian agriculture in this period derives only from stray references in Buddhist texts and from the somewhat schematized body of rules and prescriptions given in the *Arthaśāstra*; the latter, however, concerns more the administrative and fiscal aspects of farming. Agriculture centred round the village (*grāma*), surrounded by its arable lands (*grāma-kṣetra*). Smallholding was the rule, and cultivation was done directly by the owner. Landless labourers were despised and occupied a low place in society. Large estates were rare but did exist, usually in the hands of Brahmans. Village cattle were entrusted to a common herdsman (*gopālaka*); cattle-breeding was still important, although the gradual increase in cultivated land was reducing the amount of pasture. Cattle-lifting was a common evil and is mentioned fairly frequently in the epics. Village lands ended in wild jungle of which the products were exploited to a small extent in order to supplement agriculture. Of the technical side of farming we know next to nothing.[2]

In the Mediterranean Zone. With the growth of population in the Greek homeland it became increasingly necessary to increase cereal imports. This could be done partly by direct increase in home production, and partly through action by the Greek colonies scattered along the shores of the Mediterranean.[3] Grain, often in the form of tribute, was acquired from the native populations, who would accept in return Greek manufactured goods, both common ware and works of artistic merit. But at the same time Greece itself was making use of intensive methods of cultivation, fostered by the propaganda of didactic writers on the subject, such as Charmantides of Paros, Apollodorus of Lemnos, and Androtion of Athens. In this connection certain pages of Xenophon's *Oeconomicus* are of interest, as are also parts of the Theophrastus' *Historia Plantarum*. The rotation of crops was improved, the two-field system of grain alternating with fallow giving place to a three-field rotation of winter grain, summer grain, and fallow; and for the fallow year there was usually substituted a sowing of vegetables or fodder, the latter including lucerne, the 'Median' herb introduced from Persia. Many areas too had vineyards, oliveyards, and orchards of figs between the arable fields, and in some areas cereals actually gave way before these other products.

Except in places like Athens, where Solon's laws favoured the smallholders, and Sparta, where egalitarian methods prevailed, the land both of Greece and of the colonial world was at the beginning of our period still mainly in the hands of large owners or *gāmoroi*. But in many cities, such as Syracuse and Megara Hyblaea, the progress of democratic ideas led to revolution and the distribution of land among the lower classes, while in other places the liquid capital that was accumulating found an investment in land and promoted the formation of agricultural properties of medium size. In the next centuries the indebtedness of smallholders and the abundance of slave labour were factors favouring large estates, but there was a continual counter-movement in the direction of smaller properties; and these ups and downs were linked throughout with the struggle between farmers and capitalists for political power. The condition of the smallholders was later made worse by the use of slave labour. They were dispossessed of their lands and reduced to the status of a starving country proletariat, and all the while with the development of agricultural methods pasturage and arboriculture gained at the expense of cereal cultivation.

Before the Romans became masters of Italy Etruscan agriculture had reached a high level of prosperity. During their imperialist period they made known advanced methods of land reclamation and drainage, enabling the cultivation of areas which had earlier been fenland or ruined by floods. Their vast underground canals or tunnels in Latium are a memorable example. Conditions in the colonies of Magna Graecia were also flourishing until the region was seriously affected by the spread of malaria. Sicily made considerable strides towards becoming a granary for the export of cereals; but with the continuous growth of large fortunes there the *latifundia* based on pasturage and arboriculture made their appearance again, and the island turned instead to the export of wine, oil, and livestock products, such as hides and cheese.

When Etruscan rule in Latium ended, the large estates of the previous lords were divided into small plots for the native population, but these plots could not be exploited to provide all the food required. This was mainly on account of the deforestation carried out to enlarge the arable area, which increased the amount of flooding and made the abnormally shallow humus more easily washed away. While the older lands were turned to pasture it was continually necessary to find new ones, and this was one of the main reasons for the spread of Roman conquests. It also meant that after conquests had been won part of the population of Latium would be settled as members of the rural tribes in colonies, moving farther afield as time went on; and it was also responsible for the practice of regarding one third of conquered territory as *ager publicus* at the disposal of Rome. The converse process is also noticeable: many of the wars in central Italy resulted from the need felt by various hill peoples to move their flocks down in winter and consequently to contend with peoples already in occupation for possession of the plain country below.

In the third and second centuries BC individual assignations of land and colonial foundations continued. The social policy of Scipio Africanus the Elder tended also to favour smallholdings, and then came the Gracchan distributions, plots being taken from *latifundia* which had been created by arbitrary squatting on public land. With the smallholdings resulting from these and other factors came a revival of Italian grain production. But factors working in the opposite direction made this revival precarious. War devastations, and the ruin of smallholders who were conscripted for military service and lost their land through debt and mortgages, were accompanied by the intolerable competition which slave working presented to the older, patriarchal, types of agriculture. Moreover the owners of *latifundia*, who possessed the means needed for converting the soil, gave preference to cattle-breeding or the growing of vines and olives, while Italian corn was subjected to ruinous competition from provincial imports, either obtained as tribute or purchased at cut prices.

Yet the defects inherent in large estates run by slave labour were quickly apparent both in Italy and in the provinces, especially in Sicily. Although slave labour required a larger working force, it perpetuated primitive techniques in such processes as cutting, threshing, and sifting. Moreover the cultivation of cereals tended to be abandoned entirely, being given sixth place by Cato among the profitable operations of the country, after wine-growing, horticulture, willow plantations, olive-growing, and pasture. The spread of *latifundia* in the provinces not only led, in Sicily above all, to the frightful Servile Wars, with the country populations giving help to the slaves, but they made it harder for Rome to get the grain imports it needed for the *frumentatio*, the corn it distributed to the *plebs* in the city. So by a slow but perceptible process the Roman government began to break up the big Sicilian estates and increase cereal cultivation in the island, generally by means of tenants who each worked a small plot.

Meanwhile in Italy too the *latifundia* were continually reviving, and we find the free labourers joining the slave revolt of Spartacus. When to this were added new wars and the depredations of the pirates in the Mediterranean, it became clear that Italy must at all costs be made self-supporting in agricultural production. To this programme the settlement of veterans by the triumvirs and others made some contribution; but under pressure of the new danger revealed when the younger Pompeius occupied Sicily, and the grain ships failed to arrive, Augustus made the revival of agriculture one of the fixed points in his policies. He secured the co-operation of poets and agricultural writers to put out his propaganda.

Whereas therefore Cato's agricultural work in the second century, like Mago's book translated from the Carthaginian, gives us a picture of large and medium-sized Italian farms worked by slaves, in Varro, Hyginus, and Virgil we return to the patriarchal ideal of moderate or even small under-takings, run by a family with the help of free labourers.[4]

b. *Mining and Metallurgy*

Theophrastus tells us that in 415 BC the Athenian Callias acquired a fortune by working Spanish cinnabar (from Almaden). In later times the Spanish mines passed into Roman hands and were heavily exploited, the raw material, according to Pliny, being carried to Rome. The method of producing mercury from cinnabar is described by Theophrastus, and later by Dio-scorides and Pliny.

Scientific working of the gold-bearing deposits of Mt Pangaeus in eastern Macedonia was of great importance to Greek economy. Legend ascribed their discovery to Cadmus, but they were known to the native Thracians (the Edonians) at least as early as the seventh century. These natives, who exploited them in a rough and ready way, later resisted attempts made first by Darius and then, after the Persian Wars, by the Athenians, to take possession of them. The proximity of these mines explains the foundation of the Athenian colony of Amphipolis in 437, the capture of the city by Spartan Brasidas in 424, and the occupation of the place by Philip II in 358. Philip, who set great store by these mines, founded the city of Philippi to the north of Pangaeus to keep watch over them, and at the same time exploited the other veins of gold in Chalcidice near by.

Pliny in later times speaks of two additions made to the old washing technique for the recovery of gold from the sands of river beds, and probably both were invented in our period. One, practised in Spain, was the use of hydraulic pressure to break up the lumps containing gold; the other involved reconstituting the gold-dust by means of mercury, which was later removed by filtering and distillation.

c. *Textiles and Silk*

Silk was the most important textile of China, one of the main products of its economy and its chief item of export; it is also the only one of which remnants from this period have been preserved. It was produced in China from the very earliest times; cocoons have appeared among remains of the Yang-shao period, and actual fragments of silk were found encrusted on the patina of a bronze axe of the Shang period. Silk fabric was recovered from the

Ch'ang-sha mounds (fourth–third centuries BC). Woven silk was discovered in the Korean tombs at Lo-lang (c. 825 BC–AD 100) in watch towers along the Chinese *limes* on the Etsingol river (100 BC–AD 100), and at Pazyryk in the Altai (some centuries BC). Han green taffeta was found as far west as Palmyra. We know also from the classical authors that Han silks (*Sericae vestes*) freely reached the Roman empire in the first centuries of our era and created a considerable effect there; they were often re-woven in other patterns. As is pointed out elsewhere, silk played such an outstanding role in the economy that in the period 200–600 it served as currency for larger transactions.

In the Greek and Italian worlds wool was still the fabric chiefly used. For some centuries linen cloth was still imported from the East, especially from Egypt, and was used for luxury goods. Later on flax was grown in the Aegean at Amorgus, in the Po valley near the Ticino confluence, in Spain, and in other districts, all of which were thus able to manufacture all kinds of linen, from the finest (*byssus*) to the cheapest varieties.

The first Greek mention of cotton is found in Assyrian cuneiform texts, and later in Herodotus and Ctesias; its use spread after Alexander's expedition to India. We are told that his Macedonian soldiers used it mainly to cover pillows and saddles. The earliest factories grew up at Antinopolis, Tralles, and Damascus, where light, delicate muslins or cambrics were made, and also coloured materials. Later on imitation fabrics came into use, manufactured from fibres grown locally, for instance in Cappadocia, Cilicia, Judaea, and Elis, though they were always regarded as a form of linen.

Aristotle tells us that silk from cocoons of larvae was invented at Cos by a woman named Pamphile. Other silken materials were used at Amorgus and Tarentum in the manufacture of sails: and at the latter town they spun the *pinna*, a secretion of the mollusc.

Later on, from the first century BC, Chinese silk became known. But the stuffs imported from China were exceedingly expensive and were also thought to be too stiff and heavy, so they were often unpicked and then woven again with an admixture of woollen, linen, or cotton threads. This probably took place in industrial cities, on the Sinai peninsula and at Cos.

There is evidence of sporadic employment of certain other fibres, such as hemp, mallow, or amianthus.

d. *Pottery*

Chinese ceramic in this period is more uniform than that of Shang or early Chou. Production, however, was still highly decentralized. The main centres were Chin-ts'un (near Lo-yang), Hai-an, and Hui-hsien in northern Honan. Chou pottery may be classified as follows: (1) Grey ware (the overwhelming bulk); (2) red ware; (3) black ware (found at Hui-hsien only). The last-named is highly refined and represents the non plus ultra of Chou ceramics. The forms were mostly *li* tripods and round-bottom jars, for the greater part inspired by contemporary bronzes. A new technique of ornament, that of painting, was gaining acceptance by the side of the older ones.

During the Warring States and Early Han periods the main producing sites were Shou-chou in An-hwei (the capital of the state of Ch'u where the earliest examples of Chinese stoneware have been found) and Shao-hsing in Chekiang (the capital of Yüeh). Slightly later are the centres of Hsi-an and of Ch'ang-sha, the latter with some peculiar pieces covered with a tin sheet in imitation of bronze. Hellenistic influence, such as decoration with 'Cupids' and vine-leaves, is noticeable in Chinese pottery of the Han period.

Japanese pottery of this time belongs to the late Jōmon period (neolithic). It is characterized by a decoration impressed on the surface of vessels by means of tressed cords, called Jōmon. The forms were varied, but mostly utilitarian. Decoration, although on a high level of aesthetic refinement, was based on simple geometric patterns, without any tendency toward animal forms or the imitation of nature. The potter's wheel was still unknown.

Indian pottery was always intended for daily use rather than for ornament; and thus it remained always a village industry and hardly ever reached a real artistic level.

The Painted Grey ware was followed in northern and also in central India by the Northern Black Polished ware (fifth to second centuries BC), which is characteristic of the Iron Age in India; it was the pottery in common use in the Mauryan period, being found at Pāṭaliputra, Sarnath, Rajghat and above all at Ahicchatrā. It is wheel-made and thin, with a highly lustrous surface; the colour is usually grey, sometimes ranging to black, and has a steel-like appearance (Fig. 4). On the whole its technical level is very high. In the south of India a Black and Red ware is fairly common throughout the first millennium BC.

In the fifth and fourth centuries BC Greek pottery reached its highest level of perfection from every standpoint—purity of the impasto, lightness combined with durability, faultless firing, delicate shapes, artistic decoration, and transparent though brilliant varnish. These requirements were constant, but they were attained with such wealth of variety and individuality of inspiration that pottery, even in fragments, is often enough to determine precisely the date and particular provenance of the objects found in an excavation, and also of their setting.

The finest of the Greek pottery traditions was to be found in the workshops of Attica. Their products were at first decorated with black silhouettes on the red ground of the vase; but later the figures were drawn in outline on the red clay and the ground between them was covered in black. Both styles were liberally imitated outside Attica, and sometimes the figures were enlivened by painting some features in other colours. (Pls 11 and 12.)

Other techniques used locally include (*a*) encaustic decoration on a whitened ground, found for example at Canusium in Apulia and Centuripae in Sicily; (*b*) the use of red varnish to brighten the surface of the vase, found at Samos, Arretium, and other places; and (*c*) the *bucchero* style of Etruria. (Pl. 46.)

Decoration in relief was another novelty of this period. It was achieved by moulding fresh, unfired clay with a tool, or impressing it with a stamp (which was sometimes a coin or medal); and very often metal vases were

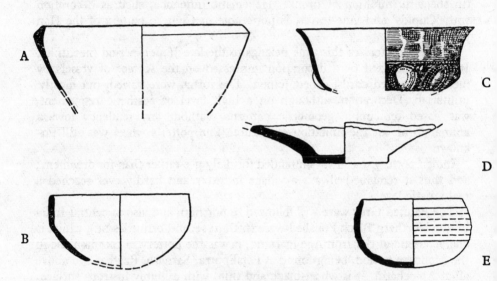

FIG. 4. Northern Black Polished Ware. A, B.: from Rupar; C: from Taxila; D: from Hastināpura; E: from Ahicchatrā; (after M. Wheeler).

taken as a model. The subjects were very varied, including not only architectural design but the representation of flowers, animals, and human beings. Another technique was the *barbotine*, in which the vase was covered with a clay slip which was then modelled and either varnished or painted.

The large number of different shapes included large jars, amphorae, pitchers (*hydriae*), oil-flasks (*lekythoi*), mixing-bowls (*craters*), saucer-shaped cups (*phialai*), drinking-vessels, lamps and so on. They had different purposes, but also corresponded to variations in local and personal tastes.

e. *Glass, goldsmith's work, and scent*

A number of relatively simple processes for glass manufacture were evolved during this period. Plain cast glass, sometimes moulded, was employed instead of metal or pottery for objects in common use, like jars, bottles, plates, amphorae, and cups. Ptolemaic Egypt had complicated techniques for blowing, turning, and spinning glass, and for painting it in many colours; sometimes coloured pins of glass were worked into a mosaic. An example of painted glass from the second century BC, probably from the school of Tarentum, has been found at Varafodio in Calabria. In the *vicus vitrarius* at Rome many kinds of glass were made—not only window-panes, urns, and scent-containers, but also ornamentation for buildings, of which a well-known example is the theatre of Scaurus.

The goldsmith's art in China is first known in the gold and silver inlays on Shang and Chou bronzes; inlay grows still more abundant in the Huai period and remains for centuries the most important branch of this art. Its technique was probably imported from the West, but perfected in China. Objects cast in pure gold are known from the Huai period; among the earliest are the Hsin-chêng gold sheets (*c.* 575 BC), with geometrical designs and a pattern of interlaced serpent-dragons. Later we have chiefly sword-mountings, dress ornaments, dress hooks mounted with jade, and jewellery. They were rare at first, but became more common when contact with the West grew closer, in the fourth–second centuries. The general forms however remained the same; the technique also, both in casting and for inlay, did not essentially change. The gold plaques from the Ordos region, like the same region's bronzes, show strong influence from the animal style of Steppe art. Cast silver cups and toilet boxes also appear in this period.

Han gold work is marked by the appearance of granulation, shown for example on dragons from the Lo-lang tombs in northern Korea. This technique is doubtless influenced by Indo-Persian art. Jewellery proper is, however, rare and consists only of hair ornaments, finger rings, and bracelets.

Indian jewellery has a very ancient tradition, as is shown by the finds at Mohenjo-daro and Harappā. The craft is also repeatedly mentioned in Buddhist texts. But actual specimens of this period are very rare. The remains found at Pātaliputra are an example, and help us in reconstructing the technique of this art by providing the tools used, finished and unfinished products, and evidence concerning every stage of the process. But in the main we are still limited to reproductions of jewels and ornaments on terracotta figurines (e.g. Ahicchatrā) and stone reliefs (e.g. Bharhut and Sanchi). The only exception is beads, made of shell, gold, bronze, copper, and chiefly of glass, which are abundant at Taxila in the north and at Brahmagiri in the south, as they were at Harappā and Mohenjo-daro.

Some of the peculiarities of the jewellery made in Mediterranean lands are worth attention. The most delicate jewels are those made in various countries in imitation of Greek models: extremely heavy and clumsy work was produced when Greek influence faded or disappeared. This is markedly the case with Etruscan work from the fifth century onwards, when cultural contact between Etruria and Greece became isolated and tenuous. Some types of jewellery spread widely, such as the 'set' pearls, which were probably made first in Syria but are later found in Egypt and Etruria, and also in China.

There was a considerable advance in the working of semi-precious stones in the Hellenistic period,5 both in Greek countries and in those which borrowed their technique. The process reached a high level of artistic achievement, and we know the names of famous masters, such as Pyrgoteles in Alexander's time and Satyreios in the reign of Ptolemy I. The same period saw the first appearance of genuine cameos, made especially for princes at Antioch and Alexandria. They were used in many ways, sometimes worked into vases or musical instruments, sometimes sewn onto fabrics, strung on necklaces, or set in rings; and they frequently depicted the features of some high personage. They were regarded as jewels of exquisite merit, and were sought after by every potentate as far as the Crimea.

Precious stones were also much in use at Hellenistic courts, in jewellery and in other objects of value, such as diadems, cups, and goblets.

People of elegance in Greece were using scent and cosmetics freely well before the Hellenistic age began. Most of them were of Eastern origin. The scents used by Aspasia and by Crito were actually made the subject of treatises; and in the fourth century the comic poet Antiphanes gave a detailed analysis of the scent used by a courtesan. In his *Historia Plantarum* (Book IX) Theophrastus describes the substances which went to make scents, cosmetics, and hair-dyes. That Greeks in the second century BC commonly painted their faces we know from Plautus' *Mostellaria*, which was based on a Greek original.

f. *The Development of Small-Scale Industry*

Information on industrial organization in India is scanty and wholly limited to literary sources. The *Jātaka* refer to a standard number of eighteen handicrafts (wood-workers, smiths, leather-workers, painters, ivory-carvers, weavers, jewellers, etc.). On a lower level there were the debased crafts, which inflicted the stigma of social inferiority on those who practised them; for example the hunters, fishermen, butchers, tanners, snake-charmers, dancers, musicians.

Localization of crafts and industries appears at a very early stage. This localization could be by street, by quarter and even by village, each unit consisting wholly or mainly of craftsmen of the same trade. Industry was free and the state did not control prices, except for its own purchases through official valuers.

From the very beginning craftsmen are found organized in strongly built and closely knit guilds (*śreṇī*) which even cut across the boundaries of caste. The *Jātaka* again give the number of eighteen for them; but this of course is wholly conventional. Membership was mostly hereditary, as indeed was the occupation itself. The guild was governed by a headman called (in Pali) *jeṭṭhaka* or *pamukha*. Within the guild apprenticeship meant a welcome loosening of the rigidities of heredity; master and pupil (*ācariyo* and *antevāsi*) are often mentioned in the Pali texts. According to the later law books (e.g. the *Nārada-smṛti*), it appears that apprenticeship was in practice akin to domestic slavery.

Besides their economic functions, corporations held complete judicial authority over their own members. Guild bye-laws were considered as fully valid; and the royal government not only upheld them, but had to take them into account in framing its own regulations. Relations with the court were therefore rather close, and the more important guilds kept representatives of their own there. The common and most dreaded penalty for infractions of the guild laws was expulsion.

The *Kauṭṭilīya Arthaśāstra*, which may be taken to illustrate conditions in the post-Maurya age, gives increased importance to the guilds; they now served also as banks, receiving deposits at interest (at least for religious purposes). They even undertook some military tasks, in so far as the wealthiest of them kept bodies of troops, which could be summoned by the king. There was even a tendency towards a federation of trade unions under heads called *bhaṇḍāgarika*. But state control in the society depicted by the *Arthaśāstra* was much closer than in the times of the Buddha. Some handicrafts were state monopolies, such as mines, pearl-fishing, salt, coinage, manufacture of arms and of ships. The state also controlled and licensed the manufacture of liquor.

Moreover the state itself was active in the industrial field, with cotton, oil, and sugar factories. Convict labour was partly employed for the purpose. The same applied to the state spinning-houses, which yielded a steady output of textiles and clothes.

In fifth- and fourth-century Greece small and medium-sized industrial undertakings were beginning to develop at the side of artisan workshops at Athens and a few other centres, such as Corinth, Delos, Miletus, Samos, and at Syracuse and Massilia in the West. They were run by citizens or resident aliens (metics), who used slaves as well as free labour. These centres of production were few in relation to the vast area over which their manufactures were exported and profits were correspondingly high; moreover the competition between a large number of craftsmen was a constant encouragement to specialization and to improvement in production. Specialization on these lines is recommended by Plato and Xenophon, and it is attested in the pottery workshops, where modellers, painters, and stokers were working side by side.

All kinds of workshops and so-called *ergasteria* existed at Athens. They made metal goods in iron, copper, and bronze, such as arms, lamps, and miscellaneous utensils; they manufactured the leather which was produced at home or imported from the Pontus; they employed craftsmen, carvers and turners, to make jewellery out of precious metals or semi-precious stones or ivory; they wove cloth; and they produced painted vases. It was through the export of these manufactures that Athens was able to import not only raw materials, but also its grain and other essential supplies of food.

In the Hellenistic age the leading centres of artisan and industrial production moved eastward. In some of the older Greek colonial centres it was intensified, such as Ephesus with its marble, metals, woollens, and carpets, Smyrna with its marble and clay, or the industrial production of Rhodes. But in all the new countries, the Seleucid and Ptolemaic empires above all, industrial output was a feature; there was a multiplicity of factories at Alexandria, which could draw raw materials of all kinds from Asia and Africa. But this large number of new centres of manufacture and export, when added to the old ones, meant that each had normally to operate in a narrower field and adapt itself more closely to local tastes. Profits were more modest, especially in view of the tax-collectors' demands. Yet on the other side of the balance sheet there were larger home orders, to execute the great public works favoured by all Hellenistic rulers.

Nevertheless conditions were not the same in all areas. In Egypt, for example, the Greek dynasty took over the monopolistic system which went back to the days of the New Kingdom. Here practically the only producer, seller, buyer, and exporter was the state, which fixed the prices and selling margins both for agricultural products (oil, beer, etc.) and for linens, woollens, papyrus, unguents, and the rest.

In other countries the free workmen, son following father, were organized in corporations which transmitted the secret of certain crafts; and the state imposed a tax on their operations, even for the smallest and most humble undertakings.

We have a fairly good knowledge of the organization of Carthaginian production between the fifth and second centuries. They specialized in the standardized type of manufactures, which were easy to sell. Their factories excelled in naval construction, in metalwork, and in the working of gold, semi-precious stones, ivory, and glass. Some of these operations were in the hands of monopolies, others were freely carried out by artisans.

Italy came to be ruled by Rome, and the first Western provinces, which were founded by the end of our present period, were gradually being Latinized. But in all this area small industry continued, with roughly the same local markets as had been fixed in the pre-Roman period.

Rome's economy was mainly based on the city itself and the surrounding countryside. Its main output came from its kilns, from its metalworking, textile, and pottery factories, and from its goldsmiths on the Via Sacra. But there were corresponding developments of artisan working and small industry with regional significance at Ostia (mainly naval construction, as also at Ravenna and Misenum), at Sulmo, Pompeii, and Puteoli (iron and vases), at Capua (bronzes, scents, and pottery), at Cumae, the island of Aenaria, Tarentum, Canusium, Comum, Bergomum, Aquileia, and many other towns.

Rome did nothing to organize and protect the export of Italian manufactured goods to the provinces, but this did not prevent local centres from developing artisan and industrial operations with a very wide market.

We are told that the *collegia opificum*, the corporations of artisans, were preserved when the other corporations, which had degenerated into political clubs, were suppressed first by Caesar and then by Augustus.

3. THE DEVELOPMENT OF TRADE

Trade in India in the age of the Buddha was already highly developed, and we hear of merchant princes such as Anāthapiṇḍika, who was a generous benefactor of the young Buddhist community. In the towns trade centred in the bazaars, where shops (*āpaṇa*) and store-rooms (*antarāpaṇa*) were to be found. An exception was trade in perishable foodstuffs; this was carried out in markets situated outside the town gates.

Trade was partly by barter (on the lower level), and partly by money payment ('for fees, pensions, fines, loans, hoarded treasure, and income'). Finance had already gone beyond the cruder stage, for we hear of loans 'given on security of gold such as a ring' or a debtor's personal guarantee. We read of wives or children being pledged or sold for debt, and of IOUs or schedules of debt. Loans carried interest, called *vṛddhi*. Money-lending was approved as an honest calling along with tillage, harvesting, and trade.

Traders were organized, like the craftsmen, in guilds (*śreṇi*) led by headmen called *śreṣṭhins*. Anāthapiṇḍika was a *mahāśreṣṭhin*, i.e. the head of a union of merchant guilds.

The normal means of transport in India were bullock carts and pack animals (horses, oxen and buffaloes, camels in the north-west). Water transport also played a role.

The Buddhist texts allow us to infer the existence of several commercial routes, radiating from Śravasti to Rājagṭha, to Paithan and towards Sindhṛ and to the sea. Later on Megasthenes describes the Royal Road from Pāṭaliputra to the north-western frontier, the forerunner of the Grand Trunk Road, for a distance of about ten thousand stades (Strabo XVII, 2). The Maurya government did much to improve communications, and Aśoka's inscriptions are witness to the care he took over the security of the roads and amenities for travellers (by the planting of trees along the route, etc.).

In the time of the *Arthaśāstra* the carrying of goods was usually organized, for reasons of security, in convoys or caravans under a leader called *sārthavāha*, who was responsible both for the safety of goods and travellers and also for the success of the journey. Transit must have been much impeded by a suspicious police control (passes were required), but above all by fiscalism. Foreign merchants had to pay transit duties (*vartanī*) and tolls (*śulka*) at the frontier. But even in the interior of the kingdoms taxes were levied at several points on the roads, and octrois had always to be paid at the gates, which were strictly controlled by customs officers; the customs houses even contained detention rooms for merchants caught violating octroi rules. The only relieving feature of this ruthless fiscalism was that there was a government guarantee for losses in transit, which had to be made up by the local authorities concerned.

Greek commerce was considerably promoted by the circulation of coinage and by the invention of bottomry loans (capital lent by private individuals to merchants). But although till the end of the sixth century and also in part of the fifth the profession of merchant was regarded as respectable, in the ensuing period it was pursued by non-citizens or members of the lower orders of society and was therefore less highly esteemed. Moreover merchants did not have their own corporations and were not even a single recognized class. They were divided into wholesalers, retailers, and shippers, the last of whom sometimes had their own ship and sometimes a ship on charter.

Merchants also had to encounter many obstacles in their travels. Goods had to pass through the territories or the waters of several states, and duties were imposed on entry and exit. The continual wars, domestic and foreign, subjected trade to great risks. Laws varied greatly from state to state, though they were generally severe on debtors. State hoarding would often withdraw liquid capital from circulation, and there were frequent embargoes of a protectionist kind on both export and import.

In the Hellenistic period the merchants' field of action was substantially enlarged, at least in theory, by the opening of new territories through Alexander's conquests and by the fresh creation of large towns which served as markets for the sale and exchange of their wares.[6] The size of the new states was another advantage, since it reduced the number of frontiers. Moreover a considerable amount of precious metal previously stored in the Great King's coffers was now circulating in the form of money; and communications by land, river, and sea were being improved. It was true, as we have already pointed out, that the proliferation of industry in all big towns tended to limit the market for manufactured goods to the immediately surrounding areas. But it still remained essential to seek out the raw materials for industry in distant producing countries, if necessary with the aid of middlemen; and also to arrange for a regular trade in manufactured goods against foodstuffs and other prime commodities.[7] The main producing areas of these commodities were very much scattered. Cereals came from the Pontus and from Cyrenaica; timber from the Caucasus, Anatolia, and Lebanon, iron from the northern area of Anatolia near Sinope; gold from Colchis and Armenia; silver from Carmania; tin from Drangiana; copper from Cyprus; and bronze from Corinth, Delos, Chios, and Samos. Egypt (and certain other areas) had abundant supplies of salt; Lydia, Egypt, and Armenia of soda (nitrum); Palestine of asphalt; and Assyria, Babylonia, and Susiana of rock-oil (naphtha). The best-known producers of flax were Syria, Phoenicia, Cilicia, Babylonia, Egypt, and Amorgus; of wool, Cyprus, Phrygia, Galatia, Lydia, Ionia, and Achaea; of silk, Cos and Phoenicia; of cotton, Babylonia, Egypt and Phoenicia; of papyrus, Egypt, but Ptolemaic control on its export promoted the trade in parchment from Pergamum. Among the manufactures derived from these materials special reputation was enjoyed by Egyptian, Damascene, and Phoenician carpets and hangings; by Phoenician and Palestinian purple goods; by the dyes of Hierapolis, by Greek pottery; by Phoenician and Egyptian glass; by oriental perfumes (these were distributed through Cyzicus and Cyrene); and by the arms manufactured at Pergamum, Cyzicus, and Rhodes.

Some areas, however, had become less favourable to trade and business operations, mainland Greece being one example. There were still some cities of great importance, but the country grew more and more disturbed and impoverished by its wars; it was also ravaged by Galatian raids, and depopulated by the movements of emigration to the new cities inside the Hellenistic empires.

In Egypt we learn of many obstacles to trade. There were heavy customs duties on imported goods, as well as tolls, harbour and canal dues, and taxes on business. Monopolies or semi-monopolies controlled trade in salt, wine, oil, precious stones, ivory, papyrus, textiles, scents, and spices.

After the fall of the Tarquins, and once again after the Gauls had burnt the city in 386, Rome gradually extended its possessions, until after the expedition of Pyrrhus they comprised the whole peninsula of Italy. *Pari passu* with these conquests it extended the exercise of its rights over the adjoining seas. We can see this from a comparison between the various maritime treaties it made with Carthage between 509 and 278 BC. They show how Rome gradually acquired greater freedom for its trade, especially through Ostia, Misenum, and the other sea-board cities of Italy which had come into its hands.[8]

The conquest of Italy was followed by that of the western Mediterranean islands, Spain, north-west Africa, the Balkans, and the areas which earlier formed part of the Hellenistic empires. This political unification led to a growing unity of the Mediterranean in the economic sphere. But from these vast territories and from those beyond the frontiers, Rome under the Republic drew only such merchandise as was needed by its own city and by the Italian peninsula. This merchandise included grain from Sicily, Sardinia, Corsica, Spain, and Africa; salt fish and cheese from Spain, Gaul, and the Pontus; spices from Arabia; metals, wool, and hides from Spain and Gaul; timber from the Pontus, Asia, and Syria; ivory and various luxury objects from Arabia, Phoenicia, Syria, and Egypt; and slaves from Gaul, Germany, and the East.

These imports were systematically making Italy into a pauper country, living on the money it drew as tribute. Rome made no effort to balance them by guaranteeing monopolies for the export of industrial products from the city and the peninsula. It is true that some conquered cities, like Corinth and Carthage, were for a time destroyed. But in general the peoples and cities who became Rome's subjects were freely allowed to develop their commerce as they wished, and to build industries, serving more or less localized markets.

Such Italian goods as were exported came more from Etruria, Campania, and the Po valley than from Rome and Latium. A further feature of the period was that the competition of imported grain drove the Italian farmers to develop vine- and olive-growing, and also pasturage, at the expense of the cultivation of cereals.

The small industries of Latium and other parts of Italy had earlier been run by corporations of free artisans. These now generally became undertakings employing slave labour, although artisan working did not entirely disappear.

a. Main Roads

The history of commerce implies attention to the conditions of road and sea transport. For various reasons, including the number of their colonies, the Greeks were more accustomed to travel by sea than by land; and so far as roads were concerned, they took more trouble, especially in pre-Hellenistic times, with communications inside individual cities than with inter-city traffic. We have plenty of information about city streets in the period of the fifth and fourth centuries when the regular planning begun by Hippodamus of Miletus was being put into effect. This system is later found in many places in Miletus and other cities of Asia Minor, in the Piraeus at Athens, at Thurii, and at Selinus; and in the Hellenistic period it was copied at Megalopolis, Alexandria, Nicaea, Cnidus, and Priene. The streets were normally still fairly narrow; only in a few cases were they as much as 50 feet wide. Roads between cities, on the other hand, still very often lacked artificial bedding, and were more suitable for traffic by pack-animals than for carriages.

But in the Persian empire, and in the Hellenistic kingdoms which succeeded it, things were different. The great roads which the Persians had built for their armies and traders, and for the service of the post, were kept up by the Hellenistic rulers and extended on the lines the Persians had laid down. We can see this from a papyrus of 255 BC, of the time of Ptolemy II Philadelphus, which preserves a fragment of a 'post-book' recording despatches exchanged between the king and his minister of finance.

Roman roads were of largely artificial construction. The beds were of pommelled gravel sometimes covered with concrete; and the surfaces were paved with polygonal blocks to secure maximum life and minimum cost of maintenance. The technique began with the construction of part of the Via Appia in 312 BC, and was then extended rapidly as Roman conquests increased and the conquered areas became Romanized. These roads almost always formed part of a permanent scheme of planning based on pre-existing routes, which had come into being naturally through the movement of baggage animals and travellers on foot. They therefore followed lines dictated by the contours and by the need to avoid country subject to flooding. Daring bridges, cuttings, escarpments, and even short tunnels were built to ensure the uninterrupted course of these roads. Often they would encounter steep gradients in climbing the ridges of hills, and whenever possible they would drive in a straight line over part of their course. The carriage-way was normally between 8 and 13 feet wide, with a footpath running on a natural bed at each side. Posting stations were provided, and branch roads ran in every direction to the smaller towns. These great roads became one of the foundations of Rome's empire, ensuring the free movement of its armies and the regular development of its trade, communications, and postal service. They were maintained partly out of the receipts from tolls and partly at the expense of the towns through which they passed. The continually increasing number of itineraries were recorded in guide-books, and distances along the ground were marked by milestones. In Augustus' time we are told that an up-to-date catalogue was made on the 'golden milestone', which was placed in the Temple of Saturn at Rome in 20 BC. (Map XV.)

In respect of our present period it is sufficient to mention the following roads of the Italian network: (1) The *Appia*, started in 312 BC and built in sections in succeeding years, ran from Rome to Brundisium. (2) The *Flaminia* was started in 220, and went as far as Ariminum. (3) The *Valeria* ran towards the Adriatic Sea through the valley of the Aternus, then along the coast northwards to join the Flaminia at Fanum. (4) The *Salaria* ran along the valley of the Truentus and then south along the coast, as far as Brundisium. (5) The *Aurelia* coasted the Tyrrhenian Sea as far as Pisa and beyond. (6) The *Cassia* of the interior ran to Volsinii and Florentia, whence it branched off to Pisa and Bononia. (7) The *Aemilia* ran from Ariminum to Placentia and beyond. (8) The *Postumia*, started in 176 BC, ran from Genua to Placentia and then north of the Po to Aquileia. (9) The *Popilia* ran across Magna Graecia towards the straits.

China too took care to see that its main lines of communication were in order, for example the two roads across the Great Wall which allowed trade with the West, at any rate between the end of the third century BC and the beginning of the third century AD. These roads, like the Roman ones, were divided into appropriate stretches with a station at the end of each. The silk traders brought an account of their routes to the West, and Ptolemy was later able to make use of them in his work on Geography.

b. *Navigation and Piracy*

The history of the purely commercial vessel is different from the history of the warship, though the two are closely connected. From the fifth century onwards warships were made gradually bigger and stronger, with a corresponding increase in the number of rowers, so that they could carry on board both machines such as catapults and grappling-irons, and also a larger number of marines for fighting. (Pl. 22.) The normal ship consequently had between four and six banks of oars (some had as many as twenty), and it was accompanied by fast light craft and also by transport vessels (*naves onerariae*) to carry landing parties, food, and horses. Commercial ships, on the other hand, were built to much the same moderate-sized tonnage as before. But warships were not only used for naval actions; the threat presented by a fleet on the water was a guarantee of free navigation of the seas; or, conversely, a fleet could often prevent access by foreign ships to waters which a powerful nation wanted to keep for itself. In this context the naval and commercial treaties, dated 509, 348, c. 306, and 278 between Rome and Carthage are of great importance. The presence of navies also made large-scale piracy more difficult, and pirates were in practice confined to areas where navies could not make their strength fully felt. In the Adriatic, for example, pirate ships were helped by the countless natural hiding-places offered them by the islands and the broken coastline of the eastern shore.

In the periods when powerful naval squadrons controlled the Mediterranean destitute men who sought a life of adventure had to find an outlet in mercenary service rather than in piracy. But with the extension of Roman dominion there was gradually less use for mercenary armies, while at the same time less need was felt for maintaining large navies. The result was a revival of piracy.

Meanwhile the limits of the known world, and with them the range of commerce, were growing all the time. For this the famous explorers were largely responsible, especially in the fourth and third centuries B C. Pytheas of Massilia voyaged in the Atlantic, and reached the British Isles and the coast of Germany; Nearchus travelled in the country between the mouths of the Euphrates and Indus; Androsthenes sailed between Arabia and India, and Eudoxus along the coast of Africa. There were others of the same kind. Constant efforts were also made, by means of harbour works and lighthouses, to make it easier for ships to put into land; the best-known examples are the Piraeus and the fourth-century Pharos of Alexandria.

During periods of war between great naval powers piracy took on a special function, because the combatant fleets themselves carried out piratical enterprises to harm their enemies, and on the fringe of operations there would be established nests of genuine pirates acting on their own, who were ready to take advantage of any favourable situation. We find this for instance during the struggle between Greece and Persia in the first decades of the fifth century, when the Delio-Attic league, after its victory over the Persians, had to clear the seas of pirates. During the wars of the Greek cities for hegemony in the fifth and fourth centuries pirate enterprises again appeared on the fringes of the zones of action.

Alexander's unification of political power subdued the pirates for a time, but they revived during the continuous struggles between the dynasties which divided up his empire. Indeed there were now pirate squadrons acting under orders of the Hellenistic rulers, just as they made use of mercenary armies. Their most notorious lairs were in Cilicia, Crete, and Aetolia.9 At the end of the third century and during part of the second the eastern Mediterranean pirates grew weaker on account of the naval strength acquired by the Ptolemies, with their bases in Egypt and Rhodes. They revived later, especially when Rome was fighting Mithradates, who had organized bands of pirates to help him. In this way the whole Mediterranean was thrown into confusion. The pirates ravaged the coastal districts, interfered with regular trade, and paralysed the food supplies not only of the armed forces but of civilian populations. Rome's war against the pirates lasted for many years and was eventually completed by Pompey the Great in 67 BC. At this stage Pompey tried to prevent any recurrence of the scourge by giving the pirates land and trying to turn them into peasants. But his own son Sextus was responsible for the resurgence of piracy for a number of years during the wars of the Second Triumvirate. After this action was ended the pirates were exterminated.

In very early times the most famous pirates of the western Mediterranean were the Etruscans and Carthaginians. But pirate squadrons were also active in these seas in the fifth and fourth centuries, their chief enemies being the Syracusans who wanted to protect their trade. From the third century Rome's expansion encountered an obstacle in the piratical activities of the Illyrian peoples, and regular military action had to be taken against them at various intervals between 229 BC and the time of Augustus.

c. Coinage

Chinese coinage had its precursors, as in many other countries, in the use of cowrie shells, their imitations, and the 'ant nose money' (i-pi ch'ien), which appears to have been a degenerate form of imitation cowrie. Actual minting began under the Chou dynasty and copper became for about a thousand years the means for ordinary transactions. The first actual coins were the bronze or copper spade coins (pu); originally they were actual agricultural tools, which then degenerated into toys too small for practical use, and then into legend-bearing coins, of which there were four main varieties. Their dating is still doubtful, and their origin may go back as far as the beginning of the Chou period; but their use became general only after about 500 BC. In their latest forms they circulated till the end of the anarchy and the unification of China by the Ch'in. The spades were a regional currency, and 187 mint names are known, mostly from states on the banks of the Huang-ho. Minting was at first free and coins were merely a commodity for barter. The principle of state monopoly for minting and of standardization of the issues appeared rather late, perhaps for the first time in the state of Ch'in at the time of its reform by Shang-chün along legalist lines. For a long time Ch'in was alone in having a state currency.

Along with the spades, the knife coinage (tao) came into use, chiefly in the rich mercantile state of Ch'i and other states on the Shantung peninsula, in the seventh century BC or even earlier. At first they bore much resemblance to the real tool ('early knives'), but then they spread toward the north and

north-west, taking the place of the spades in that region and losing the
characteristics of a tool to assume those of a currency ('late knives'). Two
main types are extant. The Ch'i knives were guaranteed (even if not actually
minted) by the state, and bore a stamp indicating them as such.

The south, including above all its largest state Ch'u, had a quite different
coinage of its own, consisting of a gold currency (*ying-huan*).

Spades and knives yielded to the round coins (*ch'ien*), having a square
hole for tying them together in strings (the first 'cash'). This happened toward
the end of the Chou period. But with characteristic conservatism in the former
'knives' territory the 'cash' maintained the monetary unit of the old Ch'i
currency, the *huo* (denominations of 1, 2, 4 and 6 *huo*); while the ex-'spade'
territory had as its unit the *chin*. The new round copper coin was the normal
circulating medium for all ordinary purposes during the Former Han dynasty; for large transactions gold in *catties* was used.

During the short-lived Ch'in dynasty the round coin was called *pan-liang*
and weighed probably 12 *shu*, i.e. half an ounce. Han Kao-tsu (202–195)
abolished it as being too heavy and relaxed also the state monopoly of
coinage, as being too closely connected with the totalitarian principles of the
fallen dynasty; private minting was allowed and coins sharply decreased in
weight. Shortly afterwards various measures had to be taken in order to
increase the weight of coins; in 175 BC Wên-ti issued a *pan-liang* coin of
4 *shu*. The heavy expenditure for the Hsiung-nu wars necessitated other
arrangements and in 118 a coin of 5 *shu* was issued, the legend of which also
indicated its actual weight. After 113 minting became once more a government monopoly and this state coin proved to be very practical in use. The
new currency was stable and lasted in use till the end of the dynasty and
beyond.

We must not, however, lose sight of a general characteristic of Chinese
coinage: its use did not go much beyond commercial transactions and failed
to dominate public economy until the Ming period. State finance was
reckoned in terms of money, but taxation in this period was mostly in kind,
and so was public expenditure.

For Indian coinage we have to take into account the rules concerning
weight and denomination set down by the *Dharmaśāstras*, but above all the
coins themselves. The lists of weights and coins found e.g. in the code of
Manu (VIII, 132 ff.) go to great detail, although a great part of it is mere
theorizing without factual importance. The basis is always the *rati* (weight
of a gunja berry: 0·118 g). The standard piece of gold is the *suvarṇa* of 80
ratis. The most important silver piece is said to be the *purāṇa* or *dharana*,
of 32 *ratis*, and the copper piece is the *kārṣāpaṇa*, of 80 *ratis*. Each of them
has various multiples and subdivisions. But actual use, as reflected in the
Buddhist texts, seems to have known only one standard piece, the silver
āpaṇa; it seems that when afterwards it went out of use it was called by the
legal texts *purāṇa*, 'the old one'. The standard copper coin was really the

māsaka, of which sixteen went to a *kārṣāpaṇa*. As can be seen the ratio
1 rupee = 16 annas is very ancient.

The earliest Indian coins seem to go back to the sixth century at the
earliest. They were purely Indian in weight and execution; and this coinage
went on with little change for several centuries. No gold was minted, but
silver and copper coins are extant in great numbers. Most of them are rather
crude pieces of any shape (round, square, rectangular, etc.), stamped with a
great number of devices (over 300 are known including the sun and various
animals and symbols); they are called by the clumsy name of 'punch-marked'
coins. Generally speaking, they are tribal in origin. Most of the silver coins
correspond in weight to the *kārṣāpaṇa*; but there are numerous examples
of double, half and quarter *kārṣāpaṇas*; only a very few minute silver coins
correspond to the *kṛṣṇāla*, i.e. one-sixteenth of a *kārṣāpaṇa*. Copper coins
cannot at present be reduced to a single standard, as their variety of weight
is bewildering.

The punch-marked coins were the coinage actually current in the Maurya
empire. But even before its rise, and chiefly after its disappearance, Iranian
and then Greek influence began to be felt in what is now West Pakistan.
The first coins of this type are thick, slightly bent bars of silver, stamped with
wheel or sun-like designs, double on the large denominations and single on
others. They go back to the last years of Achaemenid rule in the Indus
valley, and are struck on the Persian standard (*siglos*, 5·601 gm), showing
double, half, and quarter *sigloi*. The Athenian *drachms* too reached India,
in the wake of the brisk commerce through the Persian empire; they were
even imitated locally.

Slightly later north-western India felt the influence of the splendid Graeco-
Bactrian coinage, which of course is a part (perhaps the most beautiful one)
of Hellenistic coinage and not of Indian. Indo-Greek coins were at first
purely Hellenistic in character and were struck on the Attic standard (mostly
hemidrachms). But with some of the last Greek rulers the legends became
bilingual and the Attic standard faded away, replaced by the earlier Achaemenid standard. In one way and another, Greek influence wrought a complete
change in the form and metrology of coinage in the Indus valley.

A particular phenomenon of Greek coinage is noticeable in cities which
lived under the political influence of Persia. Originally the gold and silver
of Croesus was used for the empire of Cyrus and Cambyses. Darius I was
the first to issue Persian gold and silver as a world currency. An official
relationship was established between Greek silver coins of regular weight
and composition on the one hand and Persian gold coins on the other. The
latter, however, were part of a managed currency, containing metal of
intrinsic weight lower than the value fixed officially by the government. So
the Greek silver disappeared, and the Greek districts accepted a local invasion
by depreciated Persian gold.

Mainland Greece and the Greek colonies, like the Roman world, were in

fact on a silver standard, and even when gold was struck the basis of calculation was still related to silver. Bronze coins in Italy, Egypt, and Carthage
retained the weight and composition which corresponded to their values
(Pl. 23). In other places such coinage represented defined fractions of a given
unit, and had a legal fiduciary value higher than that of the metal they contained.[10]

In fairly early times, especially at moments of crisis, tricks were played
with the coinage. Sometimes the government was speculating, sometimes
(as in the case of Persia) it wanted to stop melting by operators who made a
corner in coins, or to check the drain of gold to foreign parts. The state could
gain practical benefit from expedients of this kind when they were used
exceptionally and unexpectedly; otherwise they produced inflation of prices,
equivalent to a fall in the value of money, since the state was not in a position
to impose an artificial value as a permanency. Perdiccas III of Macedon
resorted to a debased currency to pay his army in time of war; so did Athens
in the long war against Sparta. The Ptolemies in Egypt followed their
example. The Roman government did the same during the Hannibalic war,
and again in 91 BC and during Sulla's dictatorship.

d. *Business Practices*

In Greek towns the central square or *Agorā* was not only the normal
meeting-place of the popular assembly, round which public buildings and
the principal temples were erected, but it also served as a market-place
where shops and movable counters were usually grouped according to the
type of commodity offered for sale. The quality of goods on the counters
was supervised by the *agorānomoi*, and the weighing of them by the *metronomoi*. The *Agorā* was also the place where the *trapezitai* or money-changers
congregated; and in various adjacent parts, embellished with porticoes,
fountains and the like, were the meeting-places of the countrymen who came
to sell or exchange their wares. As the citizen population grew, and with it
the number who would come in from the country and from other cities,
every city developed a number of specialized markets for the different types
of produce, especially for foodstuffs.

The same thing happened at Rome and the cities which Rome founded.
The central market split into a number of smaller ones, which specialized
in particular commodities, such as cattle, pigs, fish, oil, or wine. More
important sales, which brought together larger numbers of traders and a
greater volume of goods, were often organized in special parts of the market-
place, even in small towns; the dates for these were fixed in the calendar,
like the *nundinae* held every eight days in Latin communities. Often again
the towns lying along the main roads would provide quarters furnished with
wells and drinking-troughs, in which beasts of burden, and even flocks and
herds, could be stalled, as they had been in early times in the *Forum Romanum*.

In other respects transport of goods by land (though less so by sea or river) was made difficult at the outset by the fact that each state was so small. At every stage tolls could be exacted, or customs and excise duties on both imports and exports. Things became easier when the area of the average state increased. (Customs and excise were often the same thing in the earliest days of city-states, but they were differentiated later as empires grew bigger.) Yet even in these larger states freedom of trade could encounter obstacles and not only those imposed by transit and import duties (called *portoria* when exacted at harbours). The import of certain goods was limited or prevented by protectionist restrictions, or by monopolies which made the state or the priesthood (as in Egypt) the sole trader in a large number of commodities.

Individual states wanted to extend their own trade and impede that of rival or enemy cities. Naturally, therefore, the trade between two or more contracting states was governed by fixed rules. Although the absence of any unifying political organization made it impossible to arrive at any common 'commercial code', convention and community of standards brought into being a number of formulae applied to commerce on both land and sea.

The ancient world, we must remember, generally believed that foreigners and enemies were identical. It is therefore clear, even when we have no particular evidence, that the operation of trade over a wide area implies the existence of a number of rules about permits, safe-conducts, reciprocal benefits, and compensation when needed. These rules could be positive in the sense of allowing concessions based on definite treaties, but they might be restrictive, or even negative, as when entry or trade in particular commodities was prohibited in certain areas. Agreements of this kind were often the result of wars, when the victors at the time of signing peace would get guarantees of certain rights or privileges or monopolies or favours. Typical examples of commercial treaties are those made between Athens and certain allies, or between Rome and Carthage at various moments of their relationship, from which we can see the reciprocal concessions and prohibitions being gradually modified.

In the days of its expansion Rome was never an upholder of monopolies in sea-borne trade. All it did from time to time was to fix general rules governing access to its territories and harbours, and it was broadly speaking friendly to the freedom of the seas. It is true that with the extension of its possessions to all shores of the Mediterranean international rules became superfluous or fell into disuse.

In the period when slavery, and correspondingly also piracy, were at their height, the slave trade tended to concentrate on large ports, especially those like Delos which were regarded as free.

The port in antiquity can in fact be regarded as an entity almost distinct from the city it served. It could have its own magistrates, and it sometimes therefore acquired all the features of a free port. This is what happened to **Delos under Roman protection.**

e. *The Social Impact of Trade and Industry*

The growth of industry and commerce naturally bore a close relation to other historical conditions obtaining in different parts of the world, some of which were favourable and others not. During the Graeco-Persian struggles, for example, the political position of the Greek cities in Asia declined generally; and for a time their economic prosperity fell away too, to the advantage of the leading cities of the Greek mainland, such as Athens and Corinth.

At the same time victory over Carthage and Etruria put the Sicilian Greek colonies into the limelight, especially Syracuse and Acragas, and the prosperity of Syracuse mounted to greater heights with the creation of the empire of Dionysius I. A century later we find the situation profoundly altered. The great Hellenistic cities had taken the lead in the East at the expense of the mother country, and in the West the world power of Rome had entered the field.

But the growth of industry and commerce, which encouraged the formation of large fortunes in liquid wealth, had the additional result of altering radically the relations between the social classes. At the expense of the old landed aristocracy new elements rising from the middle classes were coming to power. Since a large part of the available wealth was in their hands, they were forming an aristocracy of money over against that based on landed estates, and were gradually detaching themselves from the class from which they were drawn. The rest of the middle class was moving progressively downwards to join the proletariat.

This phenomenon was general, and is found on the Greek mainland no less than in the colonies. At Carthage too history over centuries is based on the struggle between the land-owning class, who wanted peace, and the industrialists, arms manufacturers, and merchants, who wanted war as a means of enriching themselves by supplying armaments and by enlarging the city's empire and therefore its trade. In Athens Aristophanes informs us about similar trends for the decades of the Peloponnesian War.

The same development can be seen in the plebeian class at Rome. A minority of wealthy knights broke away, to share power with the nobles and even to swamp them: these knights had no interest in common with the impoverished residue of the middle class from which they sprang. In their hands was all the industry, commerce, and tax-farming; and often also the military commands with the booty they brought. In the end they used part of their wealth to acquire land, and became owners of large estates themselves.

4. SCIENCE

a. *Indian Beginnings*

Indian speculative thought reached the border of science, but crossed it only in a few cases. It can be maintained that some of the *śāstra* (treatises or manuals) in Indian literature show a scientifico-technological character, although a theoretical and abstract one. The *śāstra* literature is formally connected with the *Vedas* and consists almost entirely of commentaries, elucidating some ancient and brief text (mostly lost). They aim at giving the means for easier and more perfect execution of religious practices in their various aspects. Thus we have texts referring to every branch of knowledge: medicine, astronomy, mathematics, drama, grammar, lexicography, hippology, jewellery, and even theft. The problem of dating the single works is a formidable and hardly soluble one. Most of them belong (at least in their present shape) to a period later than the limits set to the present volume. We shall therefore mention only those which go back, at least with some probability, to the Gupta age or earlier. The *śāstras* of the major sciences (medicine, mathematics, astronomy) will be dealt with in their proper place. Of the minor sciences, we may list here the texts on archery (*Dhanurveda*), all of them late; hippology (*Aśvaśāstra*), of which several treatises of unknown date are extant; jewellery (*Ratnaśāstra*), etc.

b. *Astrology and Astronomy*

Before the coming of Greek influences post-Vedic astronomy is very little known. The influence chiefly felt was that of the *Jyotiṣa Vedāṅga*, which, moreover, was put into writing only during this period. The material underlying a Jain work called *Sūriyapaṇṇatti* (but not the work's compilation) may belong to the last centuries BC. In this the astronomy is still Vedic, but its cosmology is akin to that of the *Purāṇa*, with Mt Meru in the centre surrounded by seven stories; the central story is divided into four parts, of which the southerly one is *Bharatavarṣa* or India. One of the most famous astronomers was Garga, but the work attributed to him is a late compilation. From all this it is practically impossible to reconstruct the main lines of the history of Indian astronomy. Probably, however, one can speak of some degree of Babylonian influence, which came in through the Achaemenid provinces of the Indus valley.[11] This would be the origin of the concept and calculation of the Great Periods of stellar revolution, which appear in astronomical writings of the following period.

China has no real astronomical literature in this period. The main evidence about the extent of knowledge of this subject comes in the chapters on astronomy, the calendar, and celestial phenomena in the dynastic histories and other works.

One of the most famous texts is the *Hsia-hsiao-chiêng*, a farmer's calendar for the 12 lunations, of the mid-fourth century BC; at the beginning of our era this was incorporated into chapter 47 of the *Ta-tai Li-chi*. Of the same period or somewhat later are the earliest stellar catalogues, compiled by Shih-Shên, Kan Tê, and Wu Hsien: all three are lost. But from a work written in the eighth century AD, the *K'ai-yüan-chang-ching* of Ch'ü-t'an-Hsi-ta, we know that observations made in the fourth century BC had led to the construction of a catalogue of 1,464 stars divided into 284 constellations. The principal document still preserved is the chapter on astronomy (*t'ien-kuan*) in the *Shih-chi* of Ssu-ma Ch'ien (*c.*90 BC); it contains a list of the constellations, describes celestial movements and conjunctions, and offers interpretations of unusual phenomena. Astronomy, as always in Chinese history, was a state affair, closely connected with the rites of the great imperial cult.

As to the general principles, there was an ancient theory, enunciated for example in the *Shan-shu-wei-k'ao-ling-yao* of the first century BC, according to which the earth moves 30,000 *li* to the west after the winter solstice and 30,000 *li* to the east after the summer solstice; only at the equinoxes is it still. This meant that the earth is continually moving, but that man is unaware of the movement; so one might as well base one's assumptions on an earth which did not move. In the later phases of its development Chinese astronomy diverged completely from Greek. Greek was 'ecliptic, angular, true, and annual'; Chinese was 'equatorial, hourly, mean, and diurnal'. The Chinese did not observe 'the heliac passage of the star on the ecliptic', but they determined 'culmination and lower transits (i.e. meridian passages) of the circumpolar stars'.

'Just as the influence of the Son of Heaven on earth radiated to all directions so the hour-circles radiated from the pole'. In this period the Chinese constructed a complete system of equatorial divisions, defined by the points of intersection between the equator and these hour-circles. These divisions were the *hsiu*, which must be conceived as slices of an orange labelled by names of constellations, normally those of small magnitude; when the constellations are invisible, the *hsiu* are fixed by means of the circumpolar stars belonging to the slice in question. This solved the sidereal-solar problem, since the full moon is exactly opposite to the sun and therefore the sidereal position of the moon is opposite that of the sun. The 28 *hsiu* are grouped in the four celestial palaces (with the same names as the four seasons), to which was added a fifth (the Emperor, corresponding to the Pole Star). The core of this system goes back to the Shang astronomers, but we first find it complete in the period of Shih-Shên and Kan Tê. Its similarity to the 27 or 28 Indian *nakṣatra* is obvious, though it is hard to say whether this is a case of borrowing or of independent creation. A common origin in Babylonia has been suggested, but there is no certainty.

Some simple astronomical instruments were already known. One was the gnomon, a plain stick held in a perfectly vertical position, the length of which was in early times fixed at 8 feet. It is mentioned in the *Chou-li* (*c.*175 BC), which attributes the first observation of the summer solstice to the Duke of Chou in the ninth century BC. By a simple alteration, namely by inclining the stick in the direction of the pole, the gnomon is converted into a sundial. This appears to be a fourth-century invention, though its first mention is in the *Shih-chi* under the date 104 BC.

The calendar was fixed by purely empirical methods, but quite soon certain principles got established. The division of the year into 12 months was for a long time connected with the cycle of 12 animals, which was common in all eastern Asia. Later the Chinese discovered the period after which a tropic year and a lunar month coincide again; this is the Chang cycle of 19 tropic years corresponding to approximately 235 lunations, and is therefore identical with Meton's cycle; various other cycles were determined as multiples of this one. At the end of this period a beginning was made with the recording of conjunctions and occultations of stars.

The observation of eclipses continued. The true cause of eclipses of the sun seems to have been known as early as the fourth century BC, and is certainly mentioned in the *Wu-ching-t'ung-i* of Liu Hsiang (*c.* 20 BC). Predictions could be made on the basis of a cycle (*chiao-shih-chou*) of 135 months containing 23 eclipses. This was invented in the first century and we find an example of its use by Liu Hsin in the *San-t'ung* calendar of 7 BC.

Observations of novae and supernovae were made from early times with remarkable accuracy. The list of Ma Tuan-lin (thirteenth century AD) starts with the same nova of 134 BC which led Hipparchus to begin his stellar catalogue. We find the chroniclers normally noting the time, duration, exact position, brightness, and colour of these phenomena. Later the comets are described with great care, and the catalogue made of them in Chinese sources is the most complete which exists today.

Finally it is worth observing that the Chinese gave close attention to meteorology. Systematic records, especially of rainfall, were kept as early as the Shang period. The meteorological cycle—clouds, rain, evaporation—has already been mentioned in the *Chi-ni-tzŭ* of the late fourth century BC. We also have long lists of floods and droughts.

Astrological and astronomical science in Babylonia established new propositions, and improved on the formulation of those which had been enunciated in the preceding period. Greek and Latin writers speak of a famous Babylonian astronomer called Cidenas (Kidinim), who calculated the movements of the sun and moon; and there is no doubt that this period saw an advance in knowledge about the relations between the movements of these two bodies. It was claimed that they were in the same position relatively to one another every eight years; later the theory was improved by positing a cycle of 19 years and 235 lunations. Furthermore the correspondence between the 360 degrees of the earth's circumference and the subdivision of the solar day was now established (4 minutes = 1 degree); the constellations were reduced to geometric shapes; observation was made of the sidereal years based on the passage of the sun between the constellations, as well as of the tropic year resulting from the succession of equinoxes and solstices; and, among other things, the Babylonians enunciated the varying rate of the sun's passage over the ecliptic, due to the eccentricity of its orbit. Parallel with these discoveries went the development of astrological doctrines.

These concern the influence on human actions of the movements of the heavenly bodies and of their positions relative to one another; knowledge of the way these complex movements are going to succeed one another is thought to make it possible to predict the future. At the same time the Chaldean seers used other methods of divination. They drew a man's horoscope at the moment of his birth, and revealed the future destiny of every man alive. We find this in the *Anaphoricos*, a Greek work inspired by Chaldean sources, which was compiled about 100 BC and wrongly attributed to Hypsicles of Alexandria. This proves the spread of those theories in the Mediterranean world.

In Greek lands the progress already made by Thales and Pythagoras had also owed much to oriental influence. In the fifth century BC Greece had some outstanding astronomical scholars. Anaxagoras (*c.* 500–428), who was put on trial for heresy because he deduced from the fall of a meteor that the sun was mineral, had several discoveries to his credit. He established that the moon shone with reflected light, and explained the moon's phases, the causes of eclipses, and the stellar composition of the Milky Way. Oenopides, who is always called the discoverer of the oblique ecliptic, calculated the Great (Luni-solar) Year of 59 years of $365\frac{22}{59}$ days each, which gives an error of only 3 hours each year. Meton then posited the cycle of 19 years containing 235 months, which we have seen may have been derived from the Babylonians; 12 of the years had 12 months and 7 had 13, while of the months 125 had 30 days and 110 had 29; here the error is reduced to half an hour a year. Empedocles tried to establish the relative distances from the earth of the sun and moon. The Pythagorean Philolaus maintained that in the cosmic sphere, besides the earth, the main heavenly bodies, and the other fixed stars, there was a central fire, distant in a geometrical ratio from the orbits of these bodies and facing an uninhabited side of the earth.

In the fourth century Plato changed his ideas in the course of his thought. His system was at first geocentric, but he ended as a heliocentric thinker believing that the earth went round the sun.[12] Eudoxus, who had learned the results of astronomical observations made by the priests at Heliopolis, imagined the planets to be fixed in 27 ideal concentric spheres, all revolving round a fixed earth and each with its axis pivoting upon another sphere. This theory was taken up by Callippus, who increased the number of spheres to 34, and by Polemarchus and others, who increased them again to 56. It was accepted by Aristotle, who expressed it in material terms, substituting a mechanical basis for the geometrical one. On the other hand the two Syracusans Hicetas and Ecphantus maintained that the earth was the one moving body amid the fixed stars, and that there was a fire at the centre of the universe. This theory was similar to an early view put forward by Heraclides Ponticus, that around an earth rotating on its own axis revolved the sun, and around the sun Mercury and Venus; later however he maintained that Mars, Jupiter, and Saturn also revolved round the sun, a view taken to its proper heliocentric conclusion later by Aristarchus, and endorsed by Seleucus. In Sicily Pheidias and his son Archimedes treated of the relative sizes and distances of the heavenly bodies; and Eratosthenes of Cyrene devoted his *katasterismoi* to astronomical studies on the constellations, of a semi-mythological kind.

In the second century BC Apollonius Pergaeus, instead of using the theory of rotating spheres to represent the movement of the planets, invented the theory of epicycles, according to which each star revolved round an ideal point. This was developed by Hipparchus, who with the aid of appropriate instruments was able to identify 850 stars, of six different magnitudes, and to give each its celestial co-ordinates. He enunciated the inclination of the plane of the ecliptic (the precession of the equinoxes), and brought into being what was later known as the Ptolemaic system of the circulating bodies, each with a path related to that of another. He calculated the distance and size of the moon with an error of 1/10. He also believed in the scientific value of astrology, which had undergone a period of great development in all the Hellenistic world through the spread of the old Babylonian theories, propagated by 'Chaldeans' who wandered from city to city.

An example of this development is the way in which these Chaldeans' ideas became amalgamated with others which various countries already possessed, especially on the subject of divination. We can see this in Etruscan religion, which in its later development seems to have been deeply tainted by recently imported oriental features (these are often wrongly held to be ancient and are connected with the problem of the origin of the Etruscans).

Another source for the import of oriental ideas into Italy lay in the Stoic philosophers, for their school had Hellenized discoveries which had originally been made in the ancient East. At Rome we find a certain degree of astronomical knowledge by the second century BC. For instance in 191 Acilius Glabrio perceived the defects in the system of intercalating in the calendar; and C. Sulpicius Galba foresaw an eclipse of the moon before the battle of Pydna. Here too the spread of the treatise *Anaphoricos* (mentioned earlier) made an important contribution; so did the astrological propaganda of the Stoics, and we may remember the judgement of St Augustine on the Stoic Posidonius, 'fatalium siderum adsertor'. In quite early times, indeed, the activity of these prophets was considered dangerous, and they were frequently expelled, for instance in 139. Although he was a pupil of Posidonius, M. Tullius Cicero was hostile to astral theories. But it was in his day that theories of this kind were spread abroad by Nigidius Figulus (d. 45), the Magus and astrologer who wrote his *Sphaera Graecanica* to show that the great heroes were metamorphosed into stars. This work had not a little to do with the fact that C. Iulius Caesar (who himself was expert in astronomy and astrology, wrote a *De Astris*, and reformed the Roman calendar with the aid of Sosigenes) was believed after his death to have been changed into a star.

c. *Mathematics and Geometry*

Chinese numeral notation, as described in Part I, was already finally settled. Starting from the first century BC we find also more complicated forms to express the numerals from 1 to 9, the so-called 'accountants' forms' (*ta-hsieh-tzŭ*), which were designed to make fraudulent alterations more difficult.

Chinese mathematical literature has its origins in a classic text, the *Chou-pei-suan-ching*, 'Arithmetical Classic of the Gnomon and the circular paths of Heaven', the first part of which may go back to the fourth century BC, though the second part is three or four centuries later. In the first part the properties of the right-angled triangle are already known, and Pythagoras' theorem is propounded but not demonstrated. The text shows also a knowledge of the use of the gnomon, of the circle and of several astronomic-solar principles. It makes practical use of fractions and of their multiplication and division, and even of square roots. Already at that early time Chinese mathematics clearly displays its arithmetico-algebraic and anti-geometrical outlook. Geometric properties depend on the number, and no interest is shown in abstract algebra; the Chinese never developed an algebraic notation. The text is remarkably free of mystical and magical elements.

The Chinese have always recognized the four basic arithmetical operations alone. It appears from a passage of the *Kuan-tzŭ* that the Pythagoraic table was not unknown. As a mechanical aid to arithmetic ·the counting rods (*ch'ou* or *ts'ê*) were used, and they are mentioned already in the fourth and third centuries BC.

Chinese metrology at first made use of variable measures, partly based on the human body. Later the decimal system became common, its chief champion being Mo-ti (*c.*330 BC); in 170 BC a memorial submitted to the throne already proposed the adoption of the decimal system for all measures; but for the time being the proposal was not accepted.

Some seeds of theoretical geometry are contained in the text of Mo-ti, but they were not developed; and geometry remained unknown. This serious gap represents the weakest point in Chinese mathematics.

Indian chronology is so incorrigibly fluid that it is extremely uncertain what stage mathematics (*gaṇita*) had reached during this period. Nevertheless we know that these centuries saw the birth of the positional arithmetic which is the foundation of all future advance. From the start the Indian system of numbers was strictly decimal. The earliest digits had no positional value; they are already found on Aśoka's inscriptions (third century BC), although the complete series is not attested in epigraphy before the second century BC. But the essential feature was already there, and it appears that the manual on metric called *Chandraḥ Sūtra*, attributed to Pingala (200 BC) implies a knowledge of the zero, though the latter is not actually named.

Our information about geometry is less vague. There have survived a series of manuals called *Śulvasūtra*, which give practical rules for the rite of *agnicayana*, the construction of an altar for Vedic sacrifice. The *Śulvasūtra* are a part of the *Kalpasūtras*, or more precisely of the *Śrautasūtras*, very condensed summaries of Vedic lore for use in schools. Seven of them have come down to us. The practical rules they contain presuppose knowledge of various geometrical operations, although the latter are not enunciated and discussed. There must, for instance, have been a practical knowledge of Pythagoras' theorem, of the transformation of areas, and of the doubling of squares. This last implies taking the square root of 2, the value of which is taken in the *Śulvasūtra* as $1 \cdot 4142156$ ($1 \cdot 414213$ is the correct approximation).

The problems in advanced geometry which most interested the Greeks after 450 BC were the trisection of angles, the squaring of the circle, and the duplication of the cube. Hippias of Elis invented a curve, which he used not only for trisection of angles but later also for squaring the circle, and which was therefore known as *quadratrix*. Hippocrates of Chios, author about 450 of an early treatise on mathematics, although he failed to square the circle or to duplicate the cube, achieved notable results, for instance about the relation between the circle and the square on its diameter. Democritus of Abdera (460–370?), among his many works, wrote treatises on mathematics, though we know of them little more than their titles: he was concerned with surds, in connection with parallel sections of a cone, and also with the volume of cones and pyramids. The Pythagorean Archytas in his work on mathematics successfully solved the problem of doubling the cube; and Theodorus, the teacher of Plato and Theatetus, gave a definition of surds and of their main properties, which were later expounded in the tenth book of Euclid.

Plato (427–347) made no new discoveries or applications, but from the technical standpoint he attached enormous importance to geometry and arithmetic, and wanted statesmen to contemplate the nature of number and to study geometry out of pure love of knowledge. He preached the need for mathematical analysis, and his theories of classes and forms also contributed to throw light on the subject. Eudoxus of Chios (408–355) had two claims to fame, his theory of proportions, which could be applied to commensurable and incommensurable magnitudes alike (see Euclid, Book V), and the method of 'exhaustion', which proves by *reductio ad absurdum* the equivalence of two magnitudes between which no difference can be shown. A pupil of his, called Menaichmus, took up the study of conic sections.

About the end of the fourth century the *Elementa* of Euclid appeared in thirteen books, which because of the clarity of their exposition had a great future in all subsequent treatment of mathematics in schools, and were the continuous subject of commentaries. Euclid naturally made use of the propositions of his predecessors, expounding and improving them systematically. Books I–VI deal with plane geometry and the general theory of magnitudes, Books VII–IX with arithmetic, Book X with surds and in-commensurables, Books XI–XIII with solid geometry. Other works by Euclid have come down to us, treating of elementary and higher geometry and of applied mathematics (Phenomena, Optics, and the Elements of Music).

Aristarchus of Samos (310–c.230) intensified the application of geometrical processes and trigonometrical ratios to astronomy. Archimedes of Syracuse (287–212), who also studied in Alexandria, was remarkable for the breadth of his interests and investigations. He was an astronomer, a student of hydrostatics who discovered the Law of Floating Bodies, a mechanic who invented such things as engines of war and hydraulic tubes for pumps (water snails), but above all a mathematician. In geometry he did distinguished work in the measurement of curvilinear figures and solids. He was devoted to pure theory as much as to the practical application of mathematics, and wrote a large number of specialized treatises, several of which survive.

Eratosthenes of Cyrene (275–195), whom we mentioned earlier as an astronomer, was a friend of Archimedes and like him a scholar whose learning ranged over every field. Among other things he invented an apparatus with which he obtained results in duplication of cubes; and in his *Platonicus* he expounded the relations between philosophy and the science of numbers. Nicomedes invented the 'conoid' or 'cocloid', and Diocles the 'cissoid' curves for determining duplication of cubes and trisection of angles.

With Apollonius of Perge (d. 170) geometry attained the highest point which was possible before the use of algebra. His great work on conic sections has survived partly in Greek and partly in Arabic: of his many other writings, which formed part of the *Treasury of Analysis*, no trace remains.

The great astronomer Hipparchus of Nicaea (160–125) developed the methods of trigonometry. To the end of our period belong a number of specialist scholars: Hypsicles, who added a XIVth Book, on regular solids, to the work of Euclid; Persaeus, who studied spiral sections; Zenodotus, who analysed 'isometric' figures, planes and solids with equal perimeters and areas; and Theodosius of Bithynia, who examined the properties of the sphere.

We must also mention the Stoic philosopher Posidonius of Apamea (135–51), one of whose many writings dealt with definitions in elementary geometry, for instance the definition of parallels. His pupil Geminus of Rhodes wrote a general work on mathematical and geometrical disciplines.

d. *Geography*

The basic idea of Chinese geography is the earth considered as a square or nearly square plate, surrounded by the sea on every side, with the half-sphere of the sky above it. The whole is subject to the fundamental Chinese idea of a close correspondence between heaven and earth, between the movement of the celestial bodies and the development of mankind. A sort of *axis mundi* connects the whole and is represented by the emperor. Therefore China is the centre of the world; in earlier times it was even accepted as the world.

The oldest geographical text is the *Yü-kung* chapter of the *Shu-ching;* it purports to be a description of the dominions of the legendary emperor Yao, compiled by his minister Yü in order to show the proper places for digging canals and regulating the waters. Its main interest is therefore hydraulic and economic. In reality the text goes back to the fifth century BC and covers more or less the lands on the middle and lower Huang-ho. Being a section of a canonical text, the *Yü-kung* enjoyed widespread authority, but was soon overwhelmed by a still more famous text: the *Shan-hai-ching* (Classic of mountains and seas). The latter is an unequal compilation, where elements of positive geography are inextricably mixed with tales of fabulous monsters and of legendary populations. It is interesting to note that many of these fabulous beings are closely similar to those described by Herodotus, Strabo, and Pliny; their common origin seems to lie in India or Iran, perhaps even in Mesopotamia. According to Karlgren, the text belongs to the Han period, and in some portions even to the Later Han; but a good deal of its material seems to go back to the times, and perhaps to the school, of Tsou Yen (end of the fourth century BC). Geographical material is also found scattered in the fourth chapter of the *Huai-nan-tzǔ*, a collection of essays by various authors of the mid-second century BC. Another class of geographical writing, that of tales of travel, is opened by the *Mu-t'ien-tzǔ-chuan*, the partly legendary account of the journey of the Chou king Mu to the fairy Hsi-wang-mu in the Western countries. It was discovered in AD 281 in the tomb of a prince who had died in 296 BC; it therefore goes back to the fourth century BC.

Knowledge of geography became more and more a recognized part of science. Beginning with the *Shih-chi* of Ssǔ-ma Ch'ien all the dynastic histories include a section (*Ti-li-chih*) on the geography of the empire; often also some accounts of foreign countries are placed at the end of the biographical sections. The latter had their true beginning with the fateful missions of Chang Ch'ien (138–125 BC), who opened up the West to Chinese explorers, mostly envoys and merchants; and soon a vast literature arose on the subject. Hydrography too, after its first beginnings in the *Yü-kung*, took on definite shape with the original *Shui-ching* (Water Classic) of Sang Ch'in (first century BC), though this was soon afterwards lost.

Chinese cartography existed from an early age; the *Chou-li* refers to officials preparing maps of feudal principalities. The first mention of a map of a district incised on wood appears in 227 BC, in connection with an attempt at murdering the king of Ch'in. All extant maps were shortly afterwards collected by order of the first emperor Shih-huang-ti; they continued in existence for a long time after the fall of Ch'in. In Han times too maps are mentioned, e.g. on the occasion of investitures of feudal princes (117 BC) or of Li Ling's campaign against the Hsiung-nu (99 BC). In 35 BC an imperial general, on returning from crushing the Hsiung-nu chief Chih-chih in the far west, showed the harem ladies maps or paintings of his campaign (*t'u-shu*; the term is ambiguous).

In the fifth and fourth centuries the Pythagorean theory of the earth's sphericity was used to effect in explaining climatic phenomena and seasonal cycles. In the third century Dicaearchus and Eratosthenes gave attention to measurements of the earth and to construction of maps.[13] In this period historians and geographers, because of their journeys, were fond of including geographical or ethnographical digressions in their works: Herodotus did this, and after him Ctesias of Cnidus, Ephorus of Cyme, and among later writers Timaeus in the third century, Polybius in the second, and Posidonius in the first. For similar reasons the reports of the sixth-century Carthaginian explorers, Himilco and Hanno, were translated into Greek.

Alexander the Great took with him on his expedition a number of historians and geometers, such as Beton, Diognetus, and Amyntas. The result was a remarkable development in exploration, and similar journeys were undertaken under the Hellenistic rulers who followed Alexander. Part of the Indian ocean was explored by Nearchus, and later described by Simias and Agatharcides (second century); Androsthenes of Thasos explored Arabia, Dasius and Simonides the Nile basin, Patroclus the Caspian, Demodemus the regions of Scythia, and Megasthenes India.

The expedition against Carthage by Agathocles of Syracuse enlarged Greek knowledge of North Africa; the journeys of Pytheas of Massilia discovered eastern Britain, and also western Germany as far as the Elbe; about 120–115 Eudoxus of Cyzicus sailed along the coasts of Africa; in 95 Publius Crassus reached the Cassiterides islands; and finally the conquests of C. Iulius Caesar brought close knowledge of all western Europe.

All this gave great impetus to the production of the guide-books known as *periploi* and *periegeseis*. The one wrongly attributed to Scylax was composed about 340–330; and others were written by Timosthenes of Rhodes, Cleon and Nymphodorus of Syracuse, Demetrius of Callatis, Mnaseas of Patrae, the pseudo-Scymnus, Artemidorus of Miletus, and Alexander Polyhistor (with separate monographs on particular parts of the world). King Juba II of Mauretania wrote a treatise on Libya and Africa; and Menippus of Pergamum was the author of a *Periplus Maris Interni*.

The growth of geographical knowledge was also responsible, at the end of our period and the beginning of the next, for the production of two great works designed to make known all the world which was then in Roman hands. One was the *Geography* of Strabo of Amasia (60 BC–AD 25). The second was the *Commentarii* of M. Vipsanius Agrippa, based on a series of researches on the ground by Isidore of Charax and others, and leading to the construction of a great map of the empire set up by Augustus in Rome.

e. *Medicine, Anatomy, and Pharmacopoeia*

In ancient Chinese thought medicine is closely integrated with the other pre-scientific disciplines: cosmology, astrology, geomancy. The first medical text (apart from one famous passage in the *Tso-ch'uan*) is the 'Yellow Emperor's classic of internal medicine' (*Huang-ti nei-ching*). It is attributed to hoary antiquity, but goes back probably to the fourth century and is connected with Taoist speculation. It is divided into two parts (*Su-wên* and *Ling-ch'u*), both heavily interpolated in the Han period. According to this text, health is due to the harmony of *yin* and *yang*; illness is due to its disturbance. It gives prominence to acupuncture (perhaps the outstanding original feature of Chinese medicine) and rejects the incantations of the priest-doctor. It accepts the mysticism of numbers, but rejects religions. A very minute description of symptoms is given, but they are not distinguished from disease. Much emphasis is placed on the constitution of the individual and on environment; diet is given considerable attention, and this discloses the knowledge of some elements of dietetics. Knowledge of the pulse is well developed and diagnosis is usually made thereby.

The first treatise on Chinese pharmacology is the *Pên-ts'ao-ching*, attributed to the mythical emperor Shên-nung but probably belonging to the first century BC. It describes 365 types of drugs and shows a considerable knowledge of emetics, purgatives, and antipyretics.

The only real document on the practical working of Chinese medicine in this period is contained in a passage of the *Shih-chi* concerning the physician Ch'un Yü-i (fl. 167 BC). Upon his dismissal he submitted to the government a curriculum vitae followed by twenty-five medical observations and eight questions and replies on teaching, as it was then practised by oral transmission from teacher to pupil. He knew the five inner organs (heart, liver, lungs, spleen, kidneys), and there is a position of the pulse for diagnosis on each organ. The breath-power (*ch-i*) circulates through meridians (*ching*), sorts of force-lines which communicate between themselves by means of the vessels (*lo*). This pneumatic theory is completed by the influence of *yin* and *yang*, whose dominance and equilibrium follow the seasons. They must influence the patient without penetrating too deep. Therapeutics are eclectic; mineral and vegetable drugs in pills, decoction or infusion; physiotherapy, massage, acupuncture, and *moxas* on fixed points. Numerous diseases are known by name.

As everywhere else, Indian medicine has its origins in curative magic: several medical spells are preserved in the *Atharvaveda*, and their ritual use is explained in the *Kauṣikasūtra*. Pathology is characterized by a close relation between illness and sin. The latter results in consumption or organic waste (*yakṣma*). The *Atharvaveda* has a fair knowledge of the various kinds of fevers; but symptoms are not yet properly separated from illness, and most of the pathological terms apply to external phenomena. Cure was mostly by spells and incantations, although a crude therapy by herbs was not unknown; but even the herbs were employed chiefly because of their magical power. The Vedic doctor had, a considerable knowledge of anatomy (even of the inner organs) and of physiology. The central theme of their lore was a close correspondence between the body and its several parts, and the cosmos and its divisions. Thus breath corresponds to the wind, the eye to the sun, etc. A pneumatic theory was developing, which reached its final shape with the classical texts of Indian medicine in the next period. One at least of the Late Vedic medical works, the *Bhelasaṃhitā*, is preserved; it appears to go back to the last centuries B C. A comparison of the *Bhelasaṃhitā* with the (later) *Carakasaṃhitā* makes possible a reconstruction of the original doctrines and knowledge which both texts trace back to Ātreya. The elements of their physiology are those of the *Yajurveda* and *Atharvaveda*. The pneumatic theory has its Hellenistic counterpart in the treatise *Peri Physeon* in the Hippocratic Corpus. Besides, the fundamental theory of the three elements of the body and the universe, which belongs to classical Indian medicine, finds its counterpart in the theory of Plato's *Timaeus*; and the connection between Indian and Greek medicine at the time of Plato and of the Hippocratic Corpus is attested by the references in the latter to Indian remedies and medical recipes, about which see later (Part III, Chapter XV).

Medicine in Greece of the late sixth century had made such advances that about 520 Democedes became the doctor of highest renown at the Persian court of Darius I. Again in the mid-fifth century Onesilus of Cyprus had a great reputation in the Oriental world, and at the beginning of the fourth century Ctesias of Cnidus was doctor to Artaxerxes II. At Croton, Rhodes, Cyrene, Cos, and Cnidus schools of medicine competed with one another for primacy; and empirical observation freed itself more and more from the practice of magic, though the latter was still important to Empedocles of Acragas. Among the Crotoniate school must be noticed Alcmaeon (early fifth century), who is credited with discovering the Eustachian tube and the optic nerves and was a pioneer in the important Greek studies on the working of the brain. Empedocles expounded theories on the derivation of blood from the heart,[14] on the importance of the pores in sensation and respiration, on the structure of the eye, and on the morphology which is common to hair and feathers. At the end of the fifth century Diogenes of Apollonia had a considerable reputation: he dissected corpses to study the vessels of the blood, and evolved the so-called 'pneumatic' theory.

The collection of writings which have most value for the study of Greek medicine in the fifth and fourth centuries is that attributed, for the most part with justice,[15] to Hippocrates of Cos. He had pupils throughout Greece, and was a man of great cultivation, discretion, and precision, considerate and humane towards his patients, as can be seen from the oath which he exacted from his pupils about the way in which they should pursue their profession. Hippocratic medicine was based on the premises that health depends on the harmony of the human body, on the proper distribution and balance of the elements which compose it. These elements were earth, air, water, and fire, each with its own characteristics—dryness, cold, moisture, and heat, and with its respective 'humours'—blood, phlegm, black bile, and yellow bile.[16] Hippocrates' work started from facts ascertained by direct observation, mainly by auscultation, from symptoms ('clinical signs'), and from the progress of diseases and the way epidemics spread. In this way he was able to formulate a number of clinical studies, of which more than forty are known to us, and to indicate the remedies needed to overcome the various types of disharmony between the elements and humours. In many cases he assisted the patient to reach and pass the 'crisis', leading on to recovery by means of appropriate diet, rest, baths, bleeding, or limited use of drugs. Many of his aphorisms have become a vital part of the wisdom of mankind.

The lack of systematic experiment in physiology, pathology, and anatomy prevented Hippocrates from reaching results in surgery as decisive as those he reached in medicine. He could do no more than give careful attention to wounds, fractures, and dislocations, as well as studying skeletons and the dissection of animals, especially during sacrifices and the taking of omens. The means at his disposal were certainly inadequate, but he brought meticulous preparation, and all the preparatory thinking one could wish, to bear on quite difficult operations, such as opening the chest for empyema, or trepanning the head.

At the beginning of the third century the most famous head of a medical school was Herophilus of Chalcedon, who practised at Alexandria and wrote a work on anatomy. This book won a great reputation on account of its general observations on dissection methods and also because of its descriptions of particular workings of the human body—nerves, eyes, the vascular system (Herophilus saw the relation between the heart, the circulation of the blood, and the rhythm of the pulse), glands, digestion and liver, reproduction, and bone structure.

A younger contemporary of Herophilus, also working at Alexandria about 258, was Erasistratus of Ceos, known mainly through Galen's criticisms. From these we learn that he in part followed traditional ideas, such as the pneumatic theory and the use of diet as the main element in cures, but that he also had progressive notions based on his various experiments. He studied the epiglottis, the lymphatic ducts, the anatomy of the brain and blood, and the action of the motor muscles and sensory nerves.

Another head of a school was Philinus of Cos, a pupil of Herophilus, who practised in the Serapeum about 240. He was an empiricist in outlook, but was disposed to over-value drugs and considered the cause of diseases, like anatomy, to be of secondary interest. The same tendency was shown by Heracleides of Tarentum (c. 100) and by Asclepiades of Prusa (130–40 BC), a follower of Epicurus who spent much of his life at Rome. The latter was an enthusiastic atomist, an orator and psychologist, and an inventor of

remedies. He wrote a number of works on medicine, and had a close understanding of certain diseases, including dropsy, tetanus, and malaria. He
attacked the theory of 'humours', but strongly believed in the efficacy of
physical education. He used to describe perfect cures with the saying 'Cito,
tuto, iucunde' ('with speed, safety, and comfort').

It had been the presence of Greek doctors which started the rational
practice of medicine at Rome. The earliest was Arcagathus in 219 BC, who
earned the title 'carnifex' ('butcher') for his audacious surgery. Medicine
was regarded as a profession beneath the dignity of a Roman, so it was
predominantly practised at Rome by foreigners, mainly freedmen of Greek
origin: they were responsible for great advances, although they were opposed
by traditional politicians like Cato and his followers. At the same time,
however, the Romans showed strong interest in the practice of hygiene:
this went back to the time when the *cloaca maxima*, and the first aqueducts
and baths, were constructed, and when the corn supply and purifying of
water were brought under control. The Twelve Tables already laid down
that graves must lie outside inhabited areas; and the earliest drainage operations aimed at reducing the malarial districts. A series of laws regulated and
supervised the conduct of doctors, being directed particularly against
abortion, poisoning, and negligence towards patients.

Caesar set store by genuine doctors, and in his day any foreign student or
practitioner who took up residence in Rome enjoyed privileges and concessions, even Roman citizenship. Medical schools could come into being,
and in the next generation a well-known doctor was Augustus' physician
Antonius Musa, who cured him of a serious illness in 23 BC, and compiled
works about medicinal herbs.

The advance of medicine was accompanied, as we saw in the cases of
Philinus, Heraclides, and Asclepiades, by progress in pharmacology, which
is frequently mentioned in our sources. We are told of about 300 ingredients
which were made up in powders, pills, infusions, decoctions, tisanes, ointments, and so on. They could be administered by the mouth, or in packs,
frictions, massages, baths, gargles, inhalations, or enemas. They included
purges, emetics, diuretics, and drugs to induce perspiration or sleep; or they
might be generally designed to rid the body of 'humours' which had gone
wrong.

f. *The Natural Sciences and the Origins of the World*

The Greek world gradually extended its knowledge of zoology and botany
as observation became closer, the known world grew larger, and the element
of fancy and story-telling got progressively discarded. Yet this last element
was slow to disappear: we must remember the fantastic animals described by
Ctesias about 400, and later by Megasthenes, and later still in the 'Paradoxical
Stories' of Antigonus of Carystus (born *c.*295–290). But all the time the

habits of particular types of animal were undergoing observation, as we see in Xenophon's work on hunting; and ideas were collected about the young of animals in the work written by Polybius about 380 BC. Considerable progress in zoology was made by Aristotle (384–322), particularly on account of his systematic approach. He catalogued about fifty species in his ten books *De Historia Animalium*; he then wrote a further five books on the reproduction of animals, and a further five on the parts of their bodies. He put marine animals in a class by themselves, paying special attention to their description, and gave similar treatment to insects and their metamorphoses.

Next in time should be mentioned the observations of Callimachus on birds and of Nicander on bees. Bees were also the subject of the *De Apibus* of C. Ilius Hyginus (37 BC), and of Virgil in his *Georgics*. About 20 BC Trogus Pompeius wrote on animals and plants, and he was followed by Juba II on various phenomena in nature, by the African Turanius Gracilis on zoology and botany, and by Trebius Niger on fish and other marine animals.

Meanwhile the study of botany had been markedly advanced, mainly by Aristotle's pupil Theophrastus of Eresus (372–287), who wrote an *Historia Plantarum* in nine books, with systematic description of various vegetables, particularly those related to agriculture. Other Greek writers were Phainias of Eresus, another pupil of Aristotle; Dicaearchus of Messana; and Nicander of Colophon, who wrote *Georgics*. Rome was influenced by the Carthaginian works on agriculture, for instance Mago's book, translated into both Greek and Latin. The Latin output included Cato's *De Agricultura* (he died in 149 BC), the three books of Varro's *De Re Rustica*, the *De Agricultura* of Hyginus published in 37 BC, and the *Georgics* of Virgil. Then the Sisennae (father and son) wrote on agriculture, and were followed by C. Tremellius Scrofa and Manilius Sura; Juba II wrote on euphorbia and the Etruscan Tarquitius Priscus produced a work on the flowering and colouring of plants.

Researches into nature gave a new impetus to speculation about the origins of the world. Bearing in mind the materialist monism of the Ionian philosophers and the spiritual outlook of the Eleatics, Empedocles of Acragas (490–430) advanced a new rationalist and mechanical explanation of the world. The four elements, or roots of the material world, were brought together by love or alternatively separated by hate; and so birth and death came to being. Anaxagoras of Clazomenae (c. 500–428) came to believe in dualism of a teleological kind. He held that there existed an infinite quantity of tiny elements, the seeds of things; that from their union or disunion birth and death were derived; and that the finest and purest of these elements constituted Mind, which gathered the world from the primeval mass of seeds by sending matter round in rotatory motion and so separating the various elements from one another. A third explanation was given by the Atomists, Leucippus of Miletus and Democritus of Abdera (460–370). Democritus supposed a Void, and thought it was moving Matter, composed of an infinite number of indivisible atoms, homogeneous in substance but variable in weight and size. In the eternal movement of atoms those of equal weight tried to unite with another to form various bodies, but when struck by others of different velocity they started to revolve and so created 'phenomena'.

Plato, above all in his *Timaeus*, gives an explanation which is a mixture of realism and poetry; it is largely enigmatic and is based on Pythagorean ideas. The Creator or Demiurge, the boundless and unchanging principle of the God, had in his work of creation to take account of three factors, Necessity, Reason, and Disorder (with the movement that Disorder brings). He created the spirit of the world, bringing the Cosmos, or organized world, out of chaos, and bringing rule and order from that which lacked both. This is the macrocosm, inscribed in a harmony of celestial spheres; and the microcosm or man is in its image, with his head a sphere, containing the brain in which his thoughts go round. The power of vision given by light and fire, and the power of touch given by the earth, are directly related to the other two elements, air and water. These elements can be conceived as geometrical shapes, earth as a cube, fire as a pyramid, air as an octahedron, and water as an eicosahedron; all can then be reduced to a set of triangles, and are interchangeable one with the other.

With Epicurus of Samos (341–271) we return to Atomism, and it had now developed more fully. Matter and the Void exist, and Matter is composed of atoms, simple particles of the smallest size, countless and indivisible. They are continually uniting and dividing; and where they fall into the Void with a swerving movement they collide, combine, and so form bodies, which later dissolve again into atoms. In the cosmic Void, which is infinite and incommensurable, there exist countless worlds, but of these we know but one, which is isolated from this Void around it. The worlds are born and move about without end, and in the vortex of these successive experiments nature has made our own world and man as he exists today. The soul consists of the lightest atoms. It cannot live without the body, nor the body without it: when the body dies, the soul dies too. Every body gives off images of itself, again composed of very light atoms, which impact on our senses and there form impressions. Sometimes these images combine, and it is then that errors of the senses and concepts of the unreal arise.

The theories of Epicurus were later modified in the works of pupils belonging to his school, for instance Asclepiades (130–40), who maintained that atoms could be divided. In the Roman world the greatest exponent of Epicureanism was the poet Lucretius (*c.*95–50 BC). Of his poem *De Rerum Natura* in six books, the first two books deal with cosmogony, the third with the theory of the soul, the fourth with perception, and the last two with the origin and history of nature and man.

g. *Philology*

Chinese lexicography had its beginnings in the works of commentators on the classics. Their collections of rare and obscure terms were the earliest examples of vocabularies. The first work of this kind is the *Êrh-ya*, attributed to Tzŭ Hsia, a pupil of Confucius, but really belonging to the second or first century BC. This glossary of terms in the classics is divided by subjects, the items being grouped together in nineteen sections.

Another incentive to lexicography came from quite another direction, the official reorganization of writing under the Ch'in emperors. Li Ssŭ's list of standard characters, the *San-ts'ang* (now lost), was also in itself a sort of dictionary, which aimed at completeness rather than at explaining difficult terms.

After the beginning of our era dictionaries and glossaries (and later encyclopaedias) took two main forms: either they were classified by subjects, on the model of the *Êrh-ya*; or they were arranged by 'characteristics' or 'radicals' of the character to be explained (later also by rhymes). The latter class was inaugurated by an etymological dictionary, the *Shuo-wên chieh-tzŭ* of Hsü Shen (c. AD 120). It is organized according to a system of 540 radicals and contains 9,353 characters, plus 1,163 doubles, i.e. 10,516 items in all. It is the ancestor of all the later dictionaries arranged on a key system, down to the famous *K'ang-hsi tzŭ-tien* of the early thirteenth century.

A place by itself was occupied by a dialect dictionary, the *Fang-yen*, compiled in the first two centuries of our era, but lost long ago.

Indian grammar (*vyākaraṇa*) has a long tradition. Its origin goes back to the post-Vedic treatises concerning the proper recitation and understanding of the sacred texts. Hence the particular care given to it, and the very high place that grammatical studies always occupied in the literary life of India.

The first treatise preserved and the most authoritative one is the *Astā-dhyāyī* of Pāṇini, belonging probably to the fourth century BC. As the name implies, it is divided into eight sections (*adhyāya*) and contains about 4,000 rules (*sūtra*). The first two sections set forth definitions and general principles; sections 3, 4 and 5 deal with nominal derivation; sections 6 and 7 give phonetic rules concerning junction (*sandhi*) of composites and derivative formations, with a sub-section on accent (*svara*). The last *adhyāya* deals with the *sandhi* of sentences. Pāṇini's rules are couched in the shortest and pithiest mode of expression possible: a few words only for each. The work is practically a series of algebraic formulae, very precise and exact in their meaning. They were meant of course only as a mnemonic help to oral teaching, which alone could vivify the obscure text.

The work of Pāṇini represents a landmark in the development of grammatical studies. It caught the language in the process of transition from Vedic to classical Sanskrit and dealt with all its minutiae, thus decisively contributing to fix it in that rigid and invariable shape which is peculiar to dead languages. The mentality which inspires it is thoroughly scientific, to a degree rare in India. Thus it was a revelation to the early European philologists, who adopted several of its leading ideas and some of its happiest technical terms.

Of course Pāṇini, in spite of his immense authority, did not say the last word on Sanskrit grammar. His great work was either too general or too short or too obscure on several minor points. Therefore a large body of commentaries arose. Pāṇini's foremost successor Kātyāyana is known only by name. But we have a work by Patañjali (not identical with the Yoga philosopher), the *Mahābhāsya*, i.e. the great commentary on Pāṇini. It may be placed in the second century BC and is a discussion on the single *vārttikas* (elements of interpretation) of Kātyāyana. It is thus an interesting example not only of grammatical science, but also of dialectic discussion as practised in the Indian schools of that time.

The process of interpreting the ancient poets, especially the Homeric cycle, made the Greeks of quite early times want to explain words of particularly obscure meaning. They formulated 'glosses' on a wide variety of topics, ranging from straightforward formal grammar to analysis of philosophical doctrine. About 500 BC they came up against the problem of the origin of language. Heraclitus of Ephesus, followed later by the Stoics, thought language developed naturally (φύσει) while the Eleatics, followed by the Atomists, derived it from a convention among mankind (νόμῳ, θέσει). Etymology and similar-sounding place-names were used by historians from Hecataeus onwards as evidence for reconstructing historical events.

Grammar and correct use of words may be said to have started with the observations of Protagoras of Abdera (c.480–410). To him goes back the recognition of the three genders, the formulation of precise rules about the appropriate moods of verbs to use in particular forms of sentence (imperative for command, optative for request, interrogative for a question, affirmative for reply), and the identification of irregularities in inflection of verbs. Synonymous words were studied by Prodicus of Ceos (c.470–400), and style together with phonetics by Hippias of Elis. Investigations of this kind, and also comparisons between the dialects, soon became of general interest, as we see, for example, from the frequent mention of them in Herodotus' *History*.

In the fourth century the problems went deeper. For instance Plato examined the origins of poetry, aesthetic criticism, and exegesis; he also analysed the parts of speech, substantives and verbs, and made a study of such matters as the origin of language and etymology. The *Cratylus* is our main source on the latter topic: Plato derives words from expressive-sounding elements which developed by convention.

Aristotle too devoted thought to the origins of poetry and other types of literature. He also analysed parts of speech, letters, syllables, conjunctions, nouns, verbs, inflection, and prepositions. But his work may be called the end of general philological studies with a theoretical basis, which gave place in the Hellenistic age to a number of distinct types of grammatical investigation. These included linguistic and literary phenomena, the various types of style, the lives of writers, and the history of literature. Athens and the older centres of culture had in this period the aid of the great libraries, above all those at Alexandria and Pergamum. But while at Athens the favourite field of study was on critical editions of early authors, especially Homer, and at Cos Philetas was writing on miscellaneous problems (*Atakta*), Philetas' pupil Zenodotus of Ephesus (325–260) was starting the series of complicated studies centred on the library at Alexandria, of which he became the first librarian in 282. Alexandrian work was based on analysis of the language and style of particular authors. With this they prepared editions designed to get rid of alterations to the text; and believing that language originated by convention, they studied the various dialects, the etymologies of the words they used, and the exact way in which they were written. To reconstruct texts they freely used the criteria of analogy, harmony, and proportion, and produced general lexicons as well as volumes on particular authors and dialects.

In the linguistic field the main works of the Alexandrian librarians were as follows: Zenodotus produced a Homeric lexicon; Callimachus composed a history of literature (the *Pinakes*) and a number of 'glosses' on place-names; Aristophanes of Byzantium, who invented both the theory of 'analogy' (on which inflection is held to follow rational rules) and also the 'diacritic' signs used in editions, edited a dictionary which took account of dialect variations; and Aristarchus of Samothrace wrote on parts of speech and on the value of analogy.

Meanwhile the Stoics, starting with Chrysippus of Soloi (280–206) had a line of their own. They still believed in the natural origin of language, and with the aid of phonetic symbolism they worked on the possibilities of onomatopoeic or direct imitation, on likenesses and contrasts, on the theory of grammatical forms, and on etymology. But the laws they formulated were capricious, and were severely criticized by the Alexandrians.

Another school was working at the same time at Pergamum. The principle of Crates of Mallus, who wrote a famous Attic lexicon about 168, was the theory of anomaly, or grammatical irregularity. An age-long argument, with exaggeration on both sides, resulted between Analogists and Anomalists, ending with the creation of a definitive theory of grammar which took account of the concrete data accumulated by the advocates of both theories. The dispute later found its way to Rome when the Stoic Panaetius (180–110), a member of the Scipionic circle, took up residence there.

The first effort to reconcile the Pergamenes and Alexandrians was made about the middle of the second century in the etymological researches of Apollodorus of Athens. An attempt was also made to reconcile the theories of the Stoics and Pergamenes when Dionysius Thrax, a pupil of Aristarchus born at Alexandria, founded the school of Rhodes. Dionysius wrote a famous school-book on grammar, which was continually re-edited and remained the standard work for a thousand years, though the paradigms it offered were sometimes arbitrary. It was divided into six parts, reading, etymology, analogy, exegesis of poetical writings (images, glosses, and content), criticism, and judgement.

There were certain later modifications to Dionysius' scheme. Asclepiades of Myrleia (150–50), who came to Rome from Alexandria with Pompey, reduced the treatment of the subject to three parts: linguistic technique, history, and criticism (or exegesis). His pupil Tyrannio of Amisus (100–26 BC), who also came to Rome, had four divisions: reading, textual criticism, exegesis, and criticism of the subject matter. The arrival of these grammarians in Rome had a most important effect on the beginnings of Roman study of philology, although the foundation of this had been very different, seeing that it was concerned with Latin language and literature rather than with Greek. A number of Latin writers on philology deserve mention. The tragedian Accius (170–c. 90) gave attention to the orthography of long vowels and the transcription of Greek terminations. The Lanuvian Stoic L. Aelius Stilo Praeconinus (150–90), who lived first at Rhodes and taught both Cicero and Varro, supported the natural origin of language and placed great importance on syntax. M. Antonius Gnipho, the Celtic tutor of C. Iulius Caesar, wrote a work *De Sermone Latino*. Stilo's pupil M. Terentius Varro (116–26), the author of many works on grammar, was an eclectic between the Analogist and Anomalist schools, since he believed that the artist might depart from traditional rules: we possess his twenty-five books *De Lingua Latina*, published after 25 BC, which start with an introduction and then proceed to etymology, inflections, constructions, and syntax. Nigidius Figulus (d. 45 BC) wrote a work called *Commentarii Grammatici*; Santra about 50 BC published *De Antiquitate Verborum*; and L. Ateius Praetextatus (died after 29 BC) produced collections of glosses. Nor should we forget Caesar's own philological writings.

In later times the Alexandrians gave attention to Latin by the side of Greek. Tryphon in Augustus' day was mainly concerned with syntax; and he was followed by Didymus (65 BC–AD 10), by Philoxenus of Alexandria, who studied the roots of words, and by Juba II, who made etymological comparisons between Greek and Latin.

NOTES TO CHAPTER IX

1. Dr P. Oliva emphasizes, however, that Greek culture survived Persian conquest in Asia Minor, and that we may therefore doubt whether it was really in danger of being destroyed, even if the Persians had been strong enough to conquer mainland Greece.

2. Except, Professor F. M. Heichelheim notes, that we can recognize the influence of Hellenistic techniques.

3. Professor C. Danov maintains that the exploitation of slave labour was a primary factor in the development of Greek agriculture from the end of the fifth or beginning of the fourth century B C, as it was also in contemporary China. For the view that the use of slaves in agriculture has been underestimated throughout Greek history see M. Finley, *Slavery in Classical Antiquity* (Cambridge, 1960), pp. 53 ff.: *contra*, A. H. M. Jones, *ibid.*, p. 3. It is very doubtful, however, whether slave labour was productive of technological developments, which are the subject of Professor Pareti's present section.

4. In his *Georgics* Virgil does not touch upon the labour force at all. Varro's treatise indicates that the purely slave-owning farms had made considerable progress since the days of Cato. According to the latter, the basic nucleus of workers on the villa consists of slaves, but there are also various categories of free workers, and the relationship between them and the landowners (e.g., share-cropping) apparently still has many features of the patriarchal relationship of the dependent client to his patron. According to Varro slaves play a fairly important part. Free landless labourers and artisans are employed on small farms, and traces of the old relationships (e.g., the exploitation of enslaved debtors) have been preserved, in his words, only in the provinces. It is only simple peasants, he says, who work the land themselves. (E. M. Shtaerman.)

5. The same period saw considerable achievement in the carving of gold. Professor C. Danov calls attention to the treasure recently discovered at Panaghiuriște (in the region of Plovdiv), for which see D. Končev, *Neue Denkmaler antiker Toreutik* (Prague, 1956), p. 717.

6. As Professor C. Danov points out, the main centres in the Hellenistic period were in the East—Alexandria, Seleuceia, Antioch, with Rhodes also playing an important role. The centre of gravity of commerce no longer lay in mainland Greece and the Balkan area: see below, Chapter X, pp. 468 ff.

7. The pseudo-Xenophontine *Constitution of Athens* has a fascinating passage (II, 7) on the variety of Athenian imports during the late fifth century B C.

8. But there are scant signs of any Roman mercantilist policies throughout the Republican period: see H. H. Scullard, *A History of the Roman World 753–146 BC* (second edition, London, 1951), pp. 218 ff., pp. 244 ff. There was an advance in Italian industry in the late fourth and third centuries, and it was Italian, rather than Roman, merchants who led the way in promoting commerce with the East in the period of the great Roman conquests. See also Part III, pp. 737 ff.

9. In the Black Sea too, as Professor C. Danov emphasizes, pirates were a constant menace to the corn trade.

10. Athens about 450 imposed a uniform system of weights and measures on its empire, and Athenian 'owls' became the recognized coinage (though some other issues continued). Professor F. M Heichelheim also notes the establishment of 'world-wide' currencies at various points in this period, such as the 'Attic' coinage under Alexander and the Successors, the 'Phoenician' coinage of the Ptolemies, and the more or less 'Attic' Roman *denarius* of the second century B C.

11. Cf. O. Neugebauer, *The Exact Sciences in Antiquity* (second edition, Copenhagen, 1957), p. 166.

12. Professor Pareti had no opportunity to set out the evidence for this view. The *Timaeus*, a late dialogue, has no passage which unmistakably supports it. The heliocentric doctrine is generally thought to have been first advanced by Aristarchus of Samos (third century B C). See p. 414.

13. Eratosthenes (*c.*275–194) was the first systematic geographer. Though his system was of course erroneous, and indeed was much criticized in antiquity, he made fairly accurate computations of the earth's circumference and of its distance from the sun and moon.

14. The true nature of the circulation of the blood was of course not discovered in ancient times.

15. The view that a substantial part of the 'Hippocratic Corpus' is the work of Hippocrates himself is strongly contested by Professor A. Lesky and by many other scholars: see C. Singer in *Oxford Classical Dictionary* (1946), s.v. 'Anatomy and Physiology', 'Hippocratic Corpus', and 'Medicine'. The inconsistencies between different sections of the Corpus are indeed very marked.

16. The classic treatise on the 'humours' was that attributed to Polybus, supposedly Hippocrates' son-in-law. Both this and also Polybus' *Sacred Disease* had influence on medical theory and practice until well into the nineteenth century, and even now are responsible for much medical terminology.

CHAPTER X

PUBLIC ADMINISTRATION, POLITICS, AND SOCIAL CONDITIONS

I. CHINA

a. *Political Theory to the third Century* BC

Chinese polity was to a large extent influenced by philosophical thought, its currents and controversies. Conversely, Chinese philosophy since its very beginning in the sixth–fifth centuries BC was strongly conditioned by sociological preoccupations and was mainly political in its aims and problems. Thus it is difficult to separate politics from philosophy, and we cannot avoid a certain amount of repetition in dealing with Chinese thought both in this and in the following chapter. We may, however, simplify matters by leaving to our account of Chinese philosophy the description of those political theories which exerted no considerable influence on the history of the country or on the development of its institutions. We therefore deal in this chapter with two systems only: Confucianism (*ju-chia*) and Legalism (*fa-chia*).

At the foundation of Confucius' thought (551–479) was society as it existed in his times, i.e., the feudal structure as it had developed during the decadence of the Chou kingdom; the men to whom he addressed himself were the gentlemen (*chün-tzŭ*). He accepted this society and within its frame tried to build up a conservative polity based on a high moral standard. Man ought to act in society not for any profit, but only because he thinks it right and proper, and therefore morally obligatory, to act in a given manner, even if his action cannot be crowned by success. It follows from this that righteousness is the leading idea of the political man. The school of Confucius, and foremost among them Mencius, worked out these simple principles into a coherent system. Humanity should be regulated by the five relationships: affection between father and son, respect between ruler and subject, love between husband and wife, affection between elder and younger brother, loyalty between friends. This is what differentiated man from birds and beasts. No universal love, but a graduated scale of affection and respect. The state is based upon it and represents a moral entity. It follows that the ruler ought to be a moral man and to act only according to a strict standard of morality. It is a fundamental postulate of Confucian political theory, never demonstrated but always asserted, that the moral conduct of the ruler and the example he sets imply a material power of their own, which compels his subjects to follow his lead and to behave according to morality, i.e. according to Confucian rules and precedents. A properly constructed state needs no actual laws, no police, no tribunals; the moral example set by the ruler is sufficient for all practical purposes. If violence and crime prevail, the fault lies usually with the ruler, whose example is not lofty and compelling enough. And if the ruler is utterly bad, he morally ceases to be a ruler, and the people has the right to rebel and to depose him. Hence a sharply drawn distinction between legitimate ruler (*wang*) and tyrant (*pa*).

Another aspect of Confucianism is that the political·ideal is sought for in the hoariest past, in the golden times of the mythical rulers Yao and Shun. Thus Confucianism is not exactly a conservative theory; it is a revolutionary one of a peculiar kind, viz. one which tries to abandon the present and the near past and to work back to remote antiquity; the latter in itself is largely fictitious, being but an ideal reconstruction by the Confucians, thrown back into the past.

In the field of sociology and economics, the main conception of Confucianism is the *ching* (square field) system, which has been described above; although petrified in an absurdly rigid and schematic form, it may really go back to a hazy recollection of collective soil-ownership in the Shang period.

Of course these principles too often clashed with the stern reality of the terrible suffering, bloodshed, and crime of the Warring States period. Some adaptation to actual conditions was attempted even within the Confucian school. This was chiefly the work of Hsün-tzŭ (third century BC) who, starting from the postulate (diametrically opposed to Mencius) that man's nature is intrinsically and potentially evil, asserted the necessity of rules of conduct (*li*). This conception of *li* (ceremonies, rites, customary rules of living and of social intercourse) became afterwards an all-important element in the practice of Confucian life. Although their need is postulated from a purely utilitarian point of view, the *li* are no positive laws; they are merely a code of moral and social behaviour, compliance with which is compelled by moral feeling, the example of the ruler, and public opinion, but never by penal sanctions. That was a step which Confucianism, even in its most rationalist wing, never took.

But another school arose, which took its stand exclusively upon the actual conditions of the time, without any thought for abstract morality or for the examples of the past. They reflected the changing society of the Warring States, in which the gentleman class was slowly killing itself off in unceasing warfare, and two political elements only were left to face one another: the rulers and the peasantry (towns and town life practically counted for nothing). Those harsh times required a high degree of organization and of military or quasi-military discipline, if a state was to survive at all. Therefore the Legalist school, whose last and greatest theoretician was Han-fei-tzŭ (third century BC), held that man's nature is intrinsically bad and that he cannot be expected to act socially if not under the spur of reward and the threat of punishment. Antiquity and its tradition have no practical importance. 'As conditions in the world change, different principles are practised' (*Shang-tzŭ* II, 7). The state must be governed by a clear, precise, and severe set of laws (*fa*), which must explain in detail to the subjects what ought to be done, and the reward and punishment for doing or not doing it. The ruler has the power and authority (*shih*) to punish and reward. He is under no necessity to be nearly superhuman, as the Confucians would have him; he merely needs the statecraft (*shu*) necessary for finding and handling an efficient staff to carry out his orders. In a word, the Legalist ideal is that of a despotic, authoritarian, and even totalitarian state. The conflict between Confucianism and Legalism was a fundamental one; it was a clash of idealism and realism, of feudalism and absolutism, of ethics and practice, of optimism and pessimism.

The first serious instance of putting Legalist theories, indeed any political theory at all, into practice, was in the fourth century BC in the north-western state of Ch'in. There Shang Yang (d. 338), being appointed minister, re-organized the machinery of the state strictly according to Legalist ideas. He set down the principle of mutual responsibility, by which the people was organized into groups of families who were responsible for the good behaviour of any of their members and suffered collective punishment in case of a crime or transgression. Agricultural labour was compulsory. On the other side, collective land-ownership began to be broken up and private property was favoured. Economy was subjected to a sort of state planning. The aristocracy was greatly diminished in power and practically disappeared as a class. Severe, even cruel, laws regulated every activity of the people. The army was reorganized. The territory of the Ch'in state was divided into thirty-one districts (*hsien*), ruled by governors appointed by the king and removable at will. In other words a military authoritarian state was built up, which in the long run proved to be the strongest of all. Its victory was accompanied as a matter of course by the victory of the political theory that had shaped it.

Thus it came about that the new Chinese empire founded by the ruler of Ch'in in 221 BC was built upon Legalist principles. Indeed, it was but the extension to the whole of Chinese territory of that organization which had been the peculiarity of Ch'in for more than a century and had given it victory over all its rivals.

b. *The Organization of the New Empire*

Yet in the position of the head of the state there was something that went far beyond the strictly utilitarian tenets of the Legalists. The new emperor was the heir of the Chou kings and of their sacred paramountcy. His very title (*huang-ti*) went back to the legendary emperors of high antiquity. He held the mandate of heaven (*t'ien-ming*) to rule the earth and was the head of the state cult (at least potentially, because Shih-huang-ti did not stress overmuch this aspect of his power). Thus a ruler conceived according to tradition was the head of a novel form of state. This traditional conception of the supreme position of the emperor became one of the strongest permanent elements in Chinese society. The emperor held his authority directly from heaven. Later on it came to be accepted that his mandate was not irrevocable; but if the emperor was weak or bad heaven could withdraw it and transfer it to another dynasty. The symptom of the changed will of heaven was the success of a new pretender to the throne; the actual transfer of the mandate was later formally expressed by a religious ceremony by which the last representative of the old dynasty handed over the insignia to the founder of the new one. This was a convenient theory for explaining and justifying usurpation; it also acted within certain limits as a corrective to the sacral conception of the emperor. In some aspects the latter's authority extended even to heaven, inasmuch as he could and did confer titles, and promote or demote lesser gods; the Chinese extended to heaven the bureaucratic régime of their own country. The emperor could only be one: 'as there is only one sun in the sky, so there is only one ruler on earth'. He was at the centre of the cosmogonic conception of the world (All Under Heaven, *t'ien-hsia*), and conceived foreign countries only as an outer ring of 'barbarians' of less than human status. The emperor thus came to be regarded as a real *axis mundi*, and the Chinese heaven-willed state assumed some of the formal aspects of a theocracy.

Feudalism was wholly abolished, and so were local autonomies. The aristocracy, or whatever was left of it after centuries of war and the first emperor's wholesale deportations, lost all power. The new state was divided into thirty-six (later forty) provinces (*chün*). These were governed by prefects (*shou*); but the local levies were commanded by a general (*wei*) directly dependent upon the central government. The latter was highly centralized; its proper functioning took a heavy toll of the ruler's capacities for work. The ministers were only his executives and did not form a cabinet. Foremost among them were the two state ministers (*ch'êng-hsiang*), the Commander-in-chief (*kuo-wei*), the Chief Judge (*t'ing-wei*), and the Chief Inspector (*yü-shih ta-fu*). A powerful unifying drive led to far-reaching changes. Weights, measures, the laws, and writing were made uniform throughout the empire. The triumph of the Legalist school was complete and the Confucians were cruelly persecuted; their writings, and indeed all books except those treating of technical matters, were banned and destroyed. Although trade was beginning to flourish with the cessation of wars and of insecurity along the roads, the economic policy of the Ch'in government followed the principle of favouring agriculture and repressing trade. Whatever its merits and demerits, this policy was followed with greater or lesser consistency throughout Chinese history down to the nineteenth century.

The reaction of almost all classes of the population against the iron rule and the exasperated centralism of the Ch'in swept away that short-lived dynasty and marked a step back on the path hitherto followed. The Legalist system was rejected, and the stigma attaching to it as a result of its association with the hated régime prevented any serious recovery; the *fachia* lingered on obscurely and died out in the course of the second century. But the Legalist collapse did not give victory to Confucianism, and the reign of the first Han emperors was the triumph of empiricism over doctrinaire political theory.

c. *Politics under the Han*

Feudalism had revived during the civil war of 207–202. It represented not so much a *revanche* of the old ruling class, as a revival of the traditions of local autonomy. The new Han dynasty accepted the fact, but saw to it that this dangerous return of feudalism was gradually emptied of any threat to the unity of the empire. They divided the fiefs into small units, granting the larger ones to members of the imperial family, and enjoining the division of the inheritance among all heirs; and lastly they withdrew from the princes the actual administration of their territories, placing it in charge of imperial officials who merely paid the revenues to the titular incumbents. At first the empire appeared as a motley and irrational mosaic, consisting partly of provinces under direct rule, partly of feudal states. But by the time of Wu-ti (141–87), the last revolts having been suppressed, the provincial bureaucratic administration covered the whole country; political feudalism (i.e. feudalism in the proper meaning of the word) died a natural death, to be revived for a short time and in different circumstances only about the middle of the seventeenth century.

The empire was now ruled by officials who could be promoted, dismissed, and transferred at will by the government; that is, by a bureaucracy. The only rivals they found were the families of the empresses, the Lü in the early second and the Wang in the late first centuries B C. The new ruling class owed their positions not to noble birth, but to ability, patronage, or both. The fact that high officialdom was at times nearly hereditary in one family was marginal and not essential to the new system. Its recruiting had its basis in the famous edict of 196 B C. This enjoined on governors and local officials to send young people of promising talents to the capital, to be educated there with a view to further employment. Step by step upon this basis a scheme was built, which eventually resulted in the Chinese state examinations, whereby access to administration was by means of public competitions on literary subjects. After the middle of the second century B C Confucianism triumphed at court, and in 140 it secured an edict excluding from public service the followers of the most important rival schools, and above all of Legalism. This meant that only men trained in the Confucian lore of the classics could accede to high office. The bureaucracy, and with it the whole state, became Confucianized. This was at first a rather peculiar Confucianism, as we shall see later. But Chinese tradition and the Chinese state (in so far as it was national, not dominated by foreigners) never swerved from this path until the beginning of the twentieth century. In this way a characteristic figure came into being: the literatus, an official Confucian scholar, who was usually at the same time a land-holder on a fairly large scale; his landed property belonged to him partly as member of a family belonging to the ruling class and partly as a normal reward of high office. Ch'in legislation was abrogated and the principle of mutual responsibility was formally abolished.

But in spite of everything the victory of Confucianism was more apparent than real. Confucian morals were paramount, but the administration of the empire was not brought back to the feudalism of the early Chou times (the classical antiquity of the Confucian school); it went on the path traced for it by Shang Yang, Li Ssŭ, and the other Legalist statesmen. The result was a harmonious blend of morality and practice—a Legalist organism directed by Confucians in a Confucian spirit. Legalism was dead, but its great creation, the centralized bureaucratic empire, was adopted by the rival school and with its help lasted for two thousand years.

Han administration was mainly a development of Ch'in. The emperor was theoretically absolute. Gradually, however, a convention developed by which the emperor did not usually take the initiative in issuing an order, but merely expressed his approval or disapproval of measures proposed to him by his chief ministers or other high officials. This considerably lightened the burden on the ruler, while safeguarding his control of state affairs if he was strong enough to exercise it; otherwise power tended to slip into the hands of the bureaucracy.

The emperor was flanked by an advisory council (t'ien-i), modelled on the legendary institutions of antiquity and including the Three Dukes (san-kung), the Nine Ministers (chiu-ch'ing), and other advisers summoned from time to time. Central administration was conducted by the twelve above-mentioned officials. The Three Dukes were the Counsellor (ch'êng-hsiang), the Commander-in-chief (t'ai-wei—the post was mostly vacant), and the Chief Supervisor (yü-shih ta-fu). The last office became the nucleus of that highly influential and beneficent institution, the censorate; it supervised all the branches of the administration and had the privilege of submitting memorials directly to the emperor. The Nine Ministers included a mixture of political and court officials. The only ones among them who were entrusted with general administrative duties were the t'ai-ch'ang, in charge of relations with the tributary barbarians; the ta-li or t'ing-wei, chief judge; the ta-ssŭ-nung, general tax collector; and the shao-fu, in charge of the Privy Treasury of the emperor. Each minister had at his disposal an assistant (ch'êng) and several subordinate officers (ts'ao). Official correspondence soon increased to such a bulk that the emperor Wu-ti had to organize four secretariats for coping with it. The Chief Secretary (shang-shu ling) was normally an official of lesser rank; but he was in closest attendance on the emperor and was usually the actual medium through which the latter shaped his policy. His importance therefore increased rapidly and excited the jealousy of the bureaucracy.

The empire was divided into provinces (chün). Their number went on increasing, by conquest of new territories or by the partition of unduly large units; at the end of the dynasty they numbered more than a hundred. The governors (t'ai-shou) held full administrative, judicial, and military powers, and exercised them through six offices (ts'ao), modelled upon those of the central government. A good road network and an efficient postal system (t'ing) ensured regular communications between centre and provinces.

Taxation was chiefly in kind, and only secondarily in money; officials received half of their salary in kind and half in cash. The basis of all revenue was the land tax, which was proportionate to the cultivated area, the unit being the *mou* (piece of land yielding about 30 litres of grain). The grain was stored and sold, or otherwise employed locally, and only a portion was sent to the capital. Money taxation included a personal tax (*suan-fu*) on every male adult; a military tax for any conscripts not called out; and revenue from the salt, iron, and strong liquor monopolies. When these were not sufficient, the sale of office was widely resorted to. The Privy Treasury of the emperor was supported by its own system of taxation (on markets and shops, on children, on princes *per capita* of their subjects; also revenues of the private estates of the emperor). It was a rigid and unwieldy system, in which the only taxpayer of any importance was the peasant.

The art of war was the foremost occupation of the Chinese nobility in early Chou times (Pl. 24, a), and it soon became the subject of theoretical treatises. The earliest extant is the *Sun-tzŭ-ping-fa* (Master Sun's Art of War), written in the state of Wu by a contemporary of Confucius, about 500 BC. It is precise and matter-of-fact, but is concerned with strategy and tactics only, and not with technique. Slightly later (beginning in the fourth century BC) is the *Wu-tzŭ*, written by Wu Ch'i of the Wei state. Other manuals were composed in the Han period.

The early Han period saw remarkable developments: the introduction of the crossbow (Pl. 24, b) and the perfecting of siege warfare. The crossbow (*nu*) was an import from northern Eurasia. Although wall crossbows and cavalry crossbows were not unknown, it was a typical infantry weapon, whose use entailed a change in infantry tactics. The disciplined bodies of crossbowmen, formed in three lines, offered an insuperable resistance to the nomad mounted archers, whose weapons they heavily outranged. The crossbow was a standard weapon with a most ingenious release mechanism of fused iron, consisting of three parts pivoting on two axes. It was usually cocked by the foot. We possess several originals of the Han era and a substantial number of good copies of the Ming period. Its use appears to go back to the fourth and even fifth century BC, and by the second it was in common use; an important memorial by Ch'ao Ts'o dated 169 BC concerns the utilization of crossbows and crossbowmen. The Tun-huang documents show that the crossbows were preserved in special magazines and classified according to the weight necessary for cocking them.

Heavier machines of war were *arcubalistae*, cocked by means of a winch; multiple-bolt *arcubalistae* are mentioned in the last year of Shih-huang-ti (210 BC) and were perfected by Chu-ko Liang (*c.*225 AD). Trebuchets (worked by a heavy counter-weight) are mentioned. *Petrariae* existed since the time of the Warring States and were much in use under the Ch'in, the Han, and afterwards.

The Han army was in principle based on a militia system; but actually few recruits were called out and its core became the Imperial Guards, organized in two 'armies' and consisting mainly of professional soldiers. In case of war on the frontier, the Guard was not usually sent there, but levies were raised locally or in the neighbouring provinces. It was a slow and inefficient system, which was unable to keep the barbarians outside the Great Wall. The standard weapon of the Han infantry was, as we said above, the crossbow. Such was the superiority it conferred on the imperial troops that for a certain period export of the trigger mechanism was severely prohibited. In case of offensive expeditions into the steppe the main arm was cavalry, organized in companies of 100 men (*tui*) and regiments of 1,000 men commanded by colonels (*hsiao-wei*). The commissariat was primitive and badly organized, and the hardships caused to the peasants in collecting grain and transporting it to the field army were always the source of much oppression and discontent, and sometimes of revolt. For this reason stable garrisons were supposed to grow their own food, on land specially granted to them and tilled by squads of soldiers. This is the origin of the military colonies (*t'un-t'ien*), fairly akin in nature and organization to the Roman ones. Their first beginnings go back to the conquest of Kansu in 121 BC. Their complete and typical form is due to Chao Ch'ung-kao (*c.* 60 BC).

d. *Social conditions*

Chinese society at the beginning of this period was still a purely feudal one in the political and economic meaning of the word. It included three main classes: aristocracy, peasants, and slaves. The main concerns of the nobles were sacrificial ceremonies and warfare. The land belonged to them, but of course the princes of the several feudal states claimed rent and corvée from their aristocracy. The peasants were hereditary tenants of the fields they tilled; this tenancy could not be sold nor transferred to others. They had to pay dues to the aristocracy in grain, cloth, and labour. Actually their life was not far better than that of the slaves. The latter were mostly prisoners of war or their descendants; they had two main functions, household work and the tilling of the fields (although there are some doubts on this second point). But the intensive farming of northern China, with its horticultural aspects, was not conducive to a real slave economy, like that developed in Italy in late republican times.

The wars of the fifth–third centuries BC caused a progressive impoverishment and decay of the aristocracy, as well as a considerable diminution of the hereditary slaves. Aristocracy as such ceased to exist and their lands passed into the possession of new social elements, rich peasants and merchants. Land was and remained for a long time the only effective form of investment. Thus people disposing of large amounts of cash invested it in land; and not being able or willing to cultivate such large areas themselves, they let it out to tenants at a high rent. The owners kept on their estate some members of the family to supervise their tenants, but themselves usually lived in the nearest town. Lesser cultivators became clients and protégés of the big landowners. The latter enjoyed not only the prestige and influence conferred upon them by their wealth, but even functioned *de facto* as tax collectors. These wealthy proprietors became gradually the centre of all social, political, and educational life; bureaucracy was mostly drawn from their ranks, since only men of substance could afford the means for imparting to their sons the education and training needed for passing the state examinations successfully. Thus Han society revolved around the two poles of the rich land-owners and of the mass of the tenants.

Landless labourers always had the possibility of migrating to less inhabited regions; and indeed the Han period witnessed a most intense colonization of the southern Chinese space by northerners. Social pressure resulted thus in the expansion of the Chinese people southward.

The tenants were always living nearly on starvation level, and being without reserves were at the mercy of any natural calamity or increase of taxation, easily fell into debt to the town merchants, and sank deeper till their lot became unbearable. The result was then one of those peasant revolts which so often characterize periods of social stress throughout Chinese history.

Slavery in the Han period still existed, but mainly as a household institution. The origin of slaves was now mainly from convicted prisoners (who became state slaves) and from peasant children sold by their starving parents in times of distress. Slaves imported from abroad were merely a luxury in the houses of the richest. But on the whole it is calculated that slaves accounted for less than 1 per cent of the whole population during Han times.

The market towns (*shih-i*) and townspeople played an increasingly important role in economy, but not in politics. They were strictly under the control of the government, and no beginning of corporate life or of administrative autonomy was apparent. There was no industry on any large scale, but craftsmen were supported by the government. The most important elements in the towns were the merchants. They acquired an increasing economic influence, being favoured by the expansion of territory, by the betterment of communications, and by the resulting increase in trade. Their wealth and their usurious exploitation of the peasants' indebtedness made them exceedingly unpopular, and they usually became the first target of any peasant revolt. But also Han Confucianism considered them as enemies of the cultivator, as social drones, as responsible for monetary devaluation and for the subversion of rural economy. Thus they were regarded with suspicion by the government, and repressive laws were passed against them from the very beginning of the dynasty, by means of heavy taxation, exclusion from office, and sumptuary regulations, but the effects of these laws on the strength and compactness of this class were scanty. Other means for curbing the merchants' activities were the state monopolies and the so-called Equalizing Granaries (*p'ing-ts'ang*), introduced by the Han and later perfected and enhanced by Wang Mang. The monopolies were attacked on moral grounds by the Confucianists, but were defended on the ground of expediency by the greatest economist in

Chinese antiquity, Sang Hung-yang. The proceedings (*Yen-tieh-lun*, Discourses on Salt and Iron) of this famous debate, held about 86–81 BC, are one of our major sources for the economic history of this period.

2. THE NOMAD SOCIETIES OF THE STEPPES

Steppe society is historically linked with nomadism. But recent research has shown that nomadism, at least in the case of north-eastern Asia, is a secondary development due to ever-increasing differentiation between two forms of agriculture: a full-time one on fairly fertile soil with a sufficient water supply, and a marginal one on a meagre soil with little water, which with its ever-diminishing returns eventually compels the local tribes 'to neglect the use of agricultural resources and to develop as an alternative the use of pastoral resources. It was only when this diverging specialization had been carried to a certain point that the marginal steppe society ceased to be marginal and committed itself definitely to the steppe. Having reached that point it was ready to take advantage of a steppe technique of horse usage in order to increase the efficiency of life within the steppe environment' (O. Lattimore, *Inner Asian Frontiers of China*, p. 59). The early Chinese were not in contact with horsemen; these begin to be mentioned only after *c.* 500 BC. The process sketched above thus attained maturity about that time.

The main features of the new society were indeed the paramount importance of the horse, and of cattle as the main source of subsistence. Agriculture became a part-time operation (mostly left to women), to be used only in order to gain some fresh vegetables as a supplement to meat and milk. Later even this limited agriculture was abandoned, and the necessary products were gained by bartering with or raiding the cultivators on the border. This was the stage of pure nomadism.

In nomad society the land has no importance, with the exception of the grazing rights on it. Wealth is measured in terms of cattle. On this economic basis a society grew up, whose pattern is uniform throughout the steppe areas. It has been defined by Vladimirtsov as nomad feudalism, although the term is not a very happy one. Its structure is aristocratic. A hereditary ruling class of cattle-owners is at the top, with their private retainers specially bound to them by contract; then the free men, i.e. the mass of the nomads, bound to the nobility by ties of blood and of economic dependence; lastly the slaves, usually prisoners-of-war from the sedentary peoples. No higher political organization is normally developed, and the clan, or at the most the tribe, is the highest unit. Only in times of stress a tribal confederacy may come into life under some outstanding chieftain, and this may give origin to what Grousset aptly called an 'empire of the steppes'. The normal course of events is then a series of victories over the sedentaries, going as far as the conquest of a more or less substantial portion of their lands. In this case the nomad aristocracy move into the conquered territory and live on the fat of the land, gradually allowing themselves to be assimilated by the superior culture of their subjects. They lose contact with their own poorer tribesmen, who have remained in the steppe. Then the political band snaps or becomes obliterated and the confederacy dissolves in a sort of social dust. Then, after a more or less long period of disintegration and of relative peace and inactivity, the same cycle can start all over again. As seen from the point of view of the cultivators in the fertile lands to the south, the result is a series of cataclysms, of eruptions from the steppe at irregular intervals of centuries, with masses of nomad horsemen overwhelming the frontier defences with dire consequences for the agricultural states which bear the brunt.

The first important nomad state in Asia, or at least the first one about which we have sufficient information, was that of the Hsiung-nu. Its rise was contemporary with the unification of China and the foundation of the empire, and probably there was some socio-economic connection between the two events. The political structure of the Hsiung-nu is known from the Chinese sources. The latter gave to their chief the title of *shan-yü* (a word of uncertain meaning) or *ch'êng-li ku-t'u shan-yü* (the first four characters seem to transcribe a proto-Turkic term *tengri-qut*, majesty of heaven). Under him were the Wise Kings *t'u-ch'i* (proto-Turkic *doqri*), of the right and of the left, that of the left being in principle the heir-apparent. Below them were two *ku-li*, kings of the left and of the right, the two great generals (as above), the two great governors (as above), the two great *tang-hu* (as above), the two great *ku-tu* (as above), the chiefs of 1,000, of 100, and of 10 men. It was a politico-military organization which reproduced the form of an army drawn up for battle, facing south. This pattern is met with in most of the later empires of the steppes. The same can be said of the dichotomy of the people into two wings or halves, which was usually the starting point for a growing political estrangement and for the dissolution of the state into two rival ones.

The religion of the Hsiung-nu was shamanism, in which the foremost place was occupied by the cult of Tengri, heaven. Their way of life was that of the nomads, with limited semi-annual migrations between summer and winter pastures. Their formidable military power was represented by the masses of horse archers, wielding the composite bow; and their skill of born and bred hunters and cattlemen was more than a match for any regular army of the sedentary peoples. Their favourite tactic was the sudden attack and nimble retreat, without committing themselves to hand-to-hand fighting before the adversary was exhausted by the rain of arrows and was manœuvred into unfavourable positions, where he could be ridden down without difficulty. This military supremacy of the nomad over the armies of the southern and western agricultural countries became a truism to be experienced again and again, till the coming of fire-arms spelt the end not only of the supremacy, but even of the military importance of the mounted archers.

3. INDIA

a. *Administration and Politics*

India had no unitary tradition, no systematically selected bureaucracy, no state organization independent of and more lasting than the dynasty. Thus we cannot speak of a linear development of Indian administrative institutions. There was no continuity. Every founder of a kingdom created a new organization of his own. Of course this was usually done on the traditional pattern; novelties were eschewed and the influence of political and legal thought was always strong. But the fact remains that no administrative structure was permanent and none lasted after the collapse of the dynasty to which it belonged. This makes the history of Indian institutions something quite different from that of Rome, China, and even of Egypt and Assyria-Babylonia. The lack of a historical literature is also a great hindrance; inscriptions are a poor substitute, and the fairly numerous works on political and legal theory, however important, fail to give us a really satisfactory picture of the historical development of the various institutions.

The first authentic account of the working of the administration in a large Indian state is found in the fragments of Megasthenes, the ambassador of Seleucus I at the court of Chandragupta Maurya. It is a rather one-sided description, not free from misunderstandings, but it has the all-important advantage of describing what was the actual practice, and not the theoretical organization prescribed by the *śāstras*. The king was not only the titular head of the state, but also the chief of the government, which he directed personally. Because of this his daily routine was very heavy and he had to attend to business even while having himself combed and massaged. He was the centre of a magnificent and large court and appeared in public only in great state and with rich pomp. But his rule was based on systematic suspicion; not only did he employ an army of spies, as was always the tradition in India, but he was always surrounded by a bodyguard of armed women, who watched the access to his inner apartments and accompanied him when he appeared in public. The chief executives under him were a body of counsellors and assessors, who had the main responsibility for choosing subordinate officials.

Pāṭaliputra, the seat of Chandragupta's government, was a large city, with a length of 80 stades and a breadth of 15; its walls had 64 gates and 570 towers. Its administration was placed under a sort of municipal board consisting of six committees of five members each (*astynomoi*). These committees took care respectively of the artisans; of foreigners; of birth and death registration; of trade, weights, and measures; of the municipal manufactures; and of the sales tax (10 per cent). Some subjects were reserved for the united body of all the six committees. Such were the upkeep of public buildings, regulation of prices, and the care of markets, harbours, and temples. Of course, this administration was a strictly authoritarian one. As in China, so too in the

Mauryan empire, there was no local autonomy. The capital and the other cities too were under the rule of the king's officials; and no local bodies, not even the merchants' guilds (*śreṇī*), played any role in it. Generally speaking, town life was of but little importance. During this period there were in India but two cities that held a high rank and played any substantial role in history. They were Pāṭaliputra, the capital of the kingdom of Magadha and of the Mauryan empire; and Takṣaśilā (Taxila), the chief centre (but by no means the only one) of the successive foreign dominations in north-western India. Another town of importance, but only on a regional scale, was Ujjayinī. Not only is it well known from the literary texts, but recent excavations have brought to light a part of the ancient city, with its strong clay walls reinforced by iron beams. Other ancient cities that have been excavated are Kauśāmbī and Ahicchatrā, both in Uttar Pradesh.

Provincial administration in the Mauryan empire was directed by a regular hierarchy of functionaries, beginning with the governors (mostly princes of the blood) of the few large units into which it was divided. The districts were entrusted to officials (*agoranómoi*, probably a mistake for *agronómoi*), whose main concern was with land measurement, and with irrigation and the distribution of canal waters. Other supervisors were in charge of agriculture, forestry, timber works, foundries, mines, and roads. Of the army we shall speak later. The country seems to have been flourishing and happy, and the soil of northern India, being less exhausted than today, gave bountiful crops, with two harvests per year. Famine was practically unknown. Wars made no great difference, since (according to Megasthenes) the cultivator was considered 'neutral and inviolable', and was strictly left alone by marching and fighting armies. Trade was very brisk and was carefully protected by government. Economy was under a measure of state supervision; at least government was actively participating in it by conducting manufactures of its own and by keeping in its pay as state servants the merchant sailors on the rivers.

To a slightly later stage of the Mauryan empire belongs the information that can be gleaned from the inscriptions of Aśoka and Buddhist literary sources relating to that period. The huge empire, covering the whole of India with the exception of the southernmost tip, included some autonomous states (mostly in backward areas) but was as a whole still directly ruled by the king. It appears that he was assisted by a sub-king (*uparāja*; his brother Tissa) and by the heir-apparent (*yuvarāja*). There was also a chief minister (*agrāmātya*) and a council (*pariṣad*). The territory was divided into a few great viceroyalties, ruled by princes of the blood; we know the names of four of them: Taxila, Ujjain, Tosali (Orissa), and Suvarṇagiri (central India). Under the viceroys were the provincial governors (*prādeśika*). Farther below there were three groups of officials: district prefects with chiefly judicial powers (*rājūka*), district finance directors (*yuta*), and officers in charge of town administration and of reviewing the administration of justice (*mahāmātra*). Among the latter were the superintendents of religious and moral affairs (*dharma-mahāmātra*), and of women (*strī-adhyakṣa-mahāmātra*). Cities were governed no longer by committees, but by a single *mahāmātra*; provincial capitals were under the joint administration of the prince-viceroys and of *mahāmātras*. The local judiciary was entrusted to town judges (*nagara-vyavahāraka*). There was a sort of diplomatic service, i.e., a body of envoys (*dūta*). And, last but not least, there were the all-important and always present informers of the police (*prativedaka*). A good deal of care was bestowed on public works and chiefly on the water supply (*kūpa, udapāna*), the gardens (*udyāna*), and the botanical gardens. They were under the general charge of a *vrajabhūmika*. The smooth working of the huge machinery was ensured by quinquennial and triennial circuits of inspection (*anusaṃyāna*), conducted by the three above-mentioned classes of officials. The main concern of Aśoka's administrative policy seems to have been that of ensuring a continuous and intimate contact between the government and the subjects. In this as well as in his religious policy Aśoka stood quite isolated, and Indian governments of later days were content with a much smaller degree of interference with the way of life and opinions of their subjects.

The system of administration of the Śuṅga dynasty was a continuation of that of the Mauryas, with a much looser organization. Provinces were ruled by prince-viceroys who bore the same simple title of *rājan* as the king. Feudatory families had the right of issuing coins at the principal cities.

The foremost theoretical work on politics is the *Arthaśāstra* traditionally attributed to Kauṭilya or Cāṇakya, the minister of Chandragupta and the real founder of the Mauryan empire (an interesting parallel case to Chin Shih-huang-ti and Li Ssŭ). The authorship of Kauṭilya has been challenged by many scholars and the date of composition of the *Arthaśāstra* has been pulled as far down as the fourth century A D, although everybody agrees that the materials on which it is based may be much earlier. In any case it seems safer not to take the *Arthaśāstra* as a manual of Maurya administration. The political system to which it refers is a constellation of smaller or larger states, not one huge empire. We can assume therefore that it represents the political theories current in post-Mauryan times, i.e., in the last two centuries B C.

The form of government described in the *Arthaśāstra* is absolute monarchy. The king's authority is full and unchecked by the necessities of expediency and custom. He is, however, advised by a council (*pariṣad*) of the highest officials (*mantrin*). These had at the same time executive functions, being each in charge of a department of government. Under them work the *sannidhātṛ* (treasurer) and the *samāhartṛ* (collector-general). Under the ministers stood the directors of departments, or superintendents (*adhyakṣa*). Government kept in touch with and controlled public opinion through a well-organized system of spies and secret agents (*gūḍapuruṣa*). The basic element of the state was the village, whose economic and social life was to follow fixed rules laid down and enforced by the government. For survey and land-revenue purposes five or ten villages were grouped together under a revenue and police officer (*gopa*). These were in their turn supervised by the provincial finance officers (*sthanīya*).

Bureaucratic work was to a large extent carried out in writing, and the *Arthaśāstra* gives rules both for account-keeping and letter-writing. Finance was based on the land-tax, consisting in a fixed share of the produce, plus varying additional demands; various devices are prescribed for raising additional revenue in times of stress. Officials are paid by the exchequer according to a fixed scale.

As was pointed out above, the state is not conceived as an all-embracing unity as in China, but as an element of a political constellation, with the would-be conqueror (*vijigiṣu*) at the centre surrounded by a circle of actual or potential allies and enemies. Politics was strictly a practical statecraft on a power basis and with no element of morality in it except the material welfare of the state, or of the king (which was the same thing). War seems to be the normal condition of international relations, and peace in its several varieties is only a means of escaping conquest or of preparing for it.

The question how far the precepts of the *Arthaśāstra* were followed in actual practice is a moot point; but some influence at least on the administrative titles of later times cannot be gainsaid.

Lastly, it should be noticed that republics and republican states have little place in the *Arthaśāstra*; as a matter of fact the republic was but a minor form of polity. It was limited to some well-defined areas on the north and north-west and seems to have been slowly decaying, although republics continued to exist at least till Gupta times.

The ideal figure of the sovereign in Indian literature requires some comment. There was no conception like the Mandate of Heaven in China. The highest ideal was that of the *cakravartin*, the conqueror of the universe, who finds his moral justification only in the way in which he discharges his duties. He is bound to uphold moral and civil justice (*dharma*), to be beneficent and pious, and to rule for the welfare of his subjects only. But he remains an idealized and isolated figure, deeply individualistic like everything Indian. The very concept of dynasty is strange to Indian thought (but not to the semi-historical lore of the *Purāṇas*); so is also the state as an entity transcending the king who rules it.

b. *Political and Social Theory*

Religious and social law (*dharma*), as distinguished from administration and politics (*artha*), is the subject of a special class of literature, the *Dharmaśāstra*. Several texts are extant but, as usual, it is difficult to determine which of them were compiled during this period. The only one of which this can be assumed with some degree of likelihood is the *Manava-Dharmaśāstra* or *Manu-smṛti*; its authorship is attributed to Manu, the first man. This work exerted an enormous influence not only on later legal thought, but on the institutions and social life of the Indian people at large.

The *Manu-smṛti* recognizes four sources of law: the sacred scriptures (the *Vedas*), the legal books (*smṛti*), the customs of holy men and the inner feeling of man about what is just and unjust. It is interesting to note that Kauṭilya, possibly in conscious opposition, places the royal edicts uppermost, followed in order by custom, contract, and sacred law. But for Manu too the power of punishment (*daṇḍa*) of the king is the supreme guarantee of the law. Criminal law is based on the gradation of punishment not only according to the gravity of the fault, but also according to the caste of the offender; Brahmans are always let off more lightly and are in no case subject to the death penalty, however heinous their offence. The caste system is by now well established and the *Manu-smṛti* gives it the full weight of its sanctity. The scale of punishment is harsh, death in various forms (some of them outrageously cruel) being imposed even for minor offences. Mutilation is often resorted to. The role of the witness in both civil and military law is all-important, but as a rule women and the men of the several castes should give evidence only on behalf of people of the same class. In serious cases, however, and when other evidence was lacking, any witness was accepted in court, or else there was trial by ordeal. The tribunals were to be presided over by the king himself, or in his absence by a learned Brahman appointed by him, assisted by three counsellors who were normally Brahmans versed in the *Vedas*.

As can be seen, the Brahman is everything in Manu's society; he is teacher, priest, judge, minister; he is also a member of the *dharma-pariṣad*, the body appointed by the king as a standing legislative commission. Manu's rules for the *śūdras* are very harsh and they are treated little better than slaves. Still, the system has not yet complete rigidity, since Manu admits inter-marriage between males of higher and females of lower castes (*anuloma*) without loss of status for their progeny; the opposite case (*pratiloma*) is forbidden, and if it occurs, any issue goes to form a special caste. The whole caste system was in this period undergoing a twofold process, of a growing rigidity and seclusion between the castes and of a large increase in the number of mixed castes. Manu explains the latter as due firstly to marriage between different castes, and secondly to members of the upper castes being degraded on account of not fulfilling their sacred duties (*vrātya*). This is of course but a convenient convention for explaining the ever-increasing number of sub-castes, arising specially from guild-like associations of people following similar arts and crafts. It served also the useful purpose of incorporating into Hindu society foreigners (traders or conquerors) and the primitive jungle tribes; and this has remained one of the features of modern Hinduism.

Caste was as a matter of principle disregarded in the Buddhist and Jain communities; even where they are mentioned, the *kṣattriyas* invariably take precedence over the Brahmans.

Alongside the caste system there ran the broader distinction between free men and slaves. Slavery in India existed since the earliest period. In Vedic times prisoners-of-war of both sexes belonging to non-Aryan peoples were reduced to slavery, and their very name (*Dāsa*) came to indicate the slaves (like Slavs in Europe). In the time of the Buddha (*c.* 500 BC) slavery was diffused in the north Indian monarchies. But although several large estates were partially tilled by slave labour, this type of economy seems never to have played any substantial role in Indian agriculture. Most of the slaves were employed in household work. It also appears that even the Buddhist monasteries owned slaves, who were employed in menial duties for the community. Slaves were such by birth, by sale (mostly by indigent parents), by capture in war, or by penal sentence. At a later time, Kauṭilya dedicated a whole chapter (III, 13) to them. Besides life slaves, he knows of a new category, that of slaves for a definite term. The rules he sets down are on the whole slightly more humane, chiefly over protection of slave girls. It appears that the institution of slavery, through economic causes, went into a slow decay after the break-up of the Mauryan empire.

Another social subdivision was that of the four *āśramas*, or patterns of material, religious, and spiritual life, conceived as successive stages in human existence. They make their appearance in this period and play a great role in the *Dharmaśāstras*. They are: (1) *brāhmacārin*, the young student who goes to live in the home of a teacher in order to learn from him the sacred texts; (2) *gṛhastha*, the grown-up married man and head of a family, who conducts the domestic ritual; (3) *vanaprastha* or *bhikṣu*, the elderly man, who lessens, though he does not entirely interrupt, his sacrifices and his family ties, and retires to the forest to lead a life of restraint and self-denial and to meditate on the significance of the sacrifices; (4) *sannyāsin*, who renounces his family, his sacrifices, the world, and his caste and leads a life of absolute austerity as a wandering ascetic, in order to meditate on the absolute. This last *āśrama* was a later addition to the first three and was always the chosen refuge of thinkers who felt dissatisfied with the Brahmanic ritual. Of course, the *āśramas* were purely voluntary, and as such were on a quite different plane from the castes, which were inborn and therefore inescapable.

c. *Warfare and Military Institutions*

One particular but important aspect of life in ancient India (as elsewhere) was war. As a matter of principle, war was the duty and privilege of the *kṣattriya* caste; it formed their religious obligation (*dharma*) and no other caste was supposed to take part in it, although in actual practice this rule was not strictly observed, chiefly in the case of infantry. Being reserved to a professional hereditary class, warfare soon became an elaborate art, with conventions and rules to be observed by every warrior. It tended thus to assume a ceremonial character, although the presence of foreigners on Indian soil, who were not bound to observe the rules, prevented its growing into a rite like that found in Aztec Mexico. Still, the result was a general trend toward obsolescence in military technique, and this goes to explain why nearly every foreign invasion of Hindu India was successful in its first impact.

An Indian army was traditionally composed of four arms (*caturaṅga*): chariots, elephants, cavalry, infantry. It is noteworthy that out of an old Indian war game our modern game of chess was developed; its European terminology mostly comes from Persian, but its Persian name, *śatranj*, is merely a transcription of *caturaṅga*. According to Megasthenes, the armed forces of the Mauryan empire were supervised by six committees of five members each: one for each arm, plus one for the commissariat and one for the navy (i.e. river craft, mainly used for transport only). The total force was 600,000 infantry, 30,000 cavalry, 9,000 elephants; the number of chariots is not stated.

Chariots were the foremost arm for the Aryan warrior of Vedic times, and the Mahābhārata war was principally a fight between charioteers. The Vedic chariot was a simple wooden structure with two wheels on a wooden axle, drawn by two horses (rarely four) attached on either side of the pole. It carried usually two persons only, the fighter and the driver. Later the vehicle became larger, heavier, and slower. It still formed a conspicuous part of Porus' army in his fight against Alexander; his chariots accommodated six men (two shield-bearers, two archers, two driver-fighters). In the Mauryan army they carried two men-at-arms and one charioteer. But chariotry had already become insignificant as a war weapon; and it gradually went out of use (as everywhere in Asia) during this period, except for ceremonial purposes.

The elephants formed the shock element of an Indian army till the end of the Middle Ages. They were the typically Indian contribution to the history of warfare. From India they were taken over by Alexander's successors, in whose time the possession of elephants was a decisive element of military potential; and thence they came into the Carthaginian army. An elephant carried usually three archers beside the driver. Their great drawback was that, if wounded, they would be seized by panic, and carry confusion and destruction into their own ranks.

Cavalry was comparatively a late-comer, in India as everywhere else. It was hardly known in the Vedic and Epic period, and seems to have been introduced in India chiefly through contact with Achaemenid Iran on the Indus. It became all-important after the wars with the Śaka and Parthians in the decades before and after the beginning of our era, and then became the backbone of the army. In Mauryan times cavalry technique was rather primitive, neither stirrup nor saddle nor bit being known. But then it rapidly improved: saddle and stirrups appear in the Sanchi reliefs (end of this period), with an anticipation of about 500 years over the rest of Eurasia. The main weapon of the horseman was the spear; horse archery of the central Asian type was not popular in India, and this was another element of weakness as against nomad invaders.

Infantry were enrolled in large masses but had little training and discipline. Their status went on deteriorating after the Vedic age and they were no match for the chariots in early days, and for cavalry later. Their chief weapons were the bow and the lance.

The Mauryan army was a standing and professional one. It received regular pay from the government, and its only duty was to fight. The army depicted by the *Arthaśāstra* was rather different, including troops bound by hereditary loyalty (*maula*), mercenary troops (*bhṛta*), soldiers of the guilds (*śreṇibala*), allied troops (*mitrabala*), deserters or contingents exacted from a defeated enemy (*amitrabala*), and forest tribes (*āṭāvi*; chiefly as scouts). There was even a sort of medical corps.

Indian tactics seem to be mainly characterized by the importance of forts. Siege warfare plays a great role in Indian history along with pitched battles. Alexander's campaign on the north-western frontier is an instance in point; also the *Arthaśāstra* deals with the subject in some detail. Simple war machines such as large stone-throwers are mentioned, but the battering-ram appears to have been unknown.

The queen of Indian weapons was the long-bow, made of bamboo, horn, or metal, shooting arrows of reeds and iron. Archery was the chief accomplishment of the warrior and of the king. Defensive armour was worn from an early period; its chief forms were mail and the long and narrow infantry shield.

4. PERSIA

After the reign of Darius I, who had given the Persian empire its greatest extension and laid the foundations for making it into a concrete whole, his successors could not find a way to prevent its deterioration and decline; indeed they often, though unwittingly, accelerated their empire's fall by their own behaviour. By making themselves into absolute rulers of the oriental type they became estranged from their subjects; they were kept aloof in their palaces by a rigorous system of etiquette, making it difficult even for their own wives to approach them and impossible for anyone to see them except when the people prostrated itself before them at great ceremonies. This state of affairs fostered court intrigues, conspiracies, and outbreaks of violence. Official inscriptions show us how the absolute power of the sovereign was justified. The appeal was to his race (he was a Persian and an Aryan), to his family (he was an Achaemenid and descendant of Achaemenids), to his outstanding position as King of Kings, and to the extent and populousness of his dominions, which included countless peoples of many races.

But the Achaemenids were unable to overcome the irresistible dualism which divided the Iranian and Zoroastrian portion of their empire from the rest. They could not quell it by religious intolerance along lines dictated by the Iranian policy of theocracy favoured by the Magi, which increased the discontent of the subject peoples. Tolerance, on the other hand, antagonized the priesthood of the Iranian nation. In any case there were racial considerations preventing cohesion: the dominant Iranian race was too small numerically in comparison with the mass of other peoples in the empire. From the time of Xerxes (486–465) there were many periods of intolerance, accompanied by great harshness towards subjects either guilty or suspected of back-sliding, such as the Egyptians and Babylonians: one example is the severity shown to the admirals of the Phoenician fleet after their defeat by the Greeks at Salamis. This, however, does not exhaust the reasons why Cyprus, Caria, parts of Anatolia, Egypt, and other peripheral areas tried to break away. A further source of trouble was the formation of centrifugal groups among the fiefs, which controlled their own armies, mainly consisting of mercenaries; it was easy for satraps to revolt, given the amount of military and adminis-trative power they possessed. Moreover the whole history of the Achaemenid empire, from the 'Persian Wars' to Alexander's conquest, proves the weakness of its gigantic but ill-organized army: defeated again and again by the Greeks between 480 and 469, it was shattered at Cunaxa in 401 by 10,000 Hellenic mercenaries, who were then able to return to their homeland almost without loss; and Alexander was able to confront it in confidence, though at the outset he possessed only 40,000 men and 160 ships. The fact was that as early as the fifth century the most solid force in the Persian army consisted of Greek mercenaries, just as the core of the fleet was composed of Phoenician vessels; but the latter were in practice no more effective than they had been in 480. In 469, for instance, they refused battle at the Eurymedon.

Under Xerxes and his three successors the kings of Persia were already giving up boasting of their warlike enterprises on their sepulchral inscrip-tions. They preferred diplomatic to military intervention; to be more exact, their policy was to divide, and so to weaken, rival nations by financing one faction against another in a way which would further their own interests. The careers of Alcibiades, the Spartan Lysander, Conon, Evagoras of Salamis, and Epaminondas, together with the history of the Corinthian War, contain abundant elements to support this account of Persian policy; and another telling point is Alexander's accusation that the Great King had suborned murderers to cause the death of his father Philip.

The Achaemenid dynasty showed remarkably little interest in intellectual or scientific developments or in unifying the culture of their empire.[1] The sporadic achievements in this field were due to the priests (for example the completion of calculations about the calendar) or to single individuals. Simi-larly no concrete or deliberate initiative by the government was in the main responsible for the cultural relations which existed between Iran and India on the one side, and Greece on the other. These were mainly caused by spon-taneous forces reacting on one another in the countries on each side of the borders of the empire; and a further factor was the existence of mercenaries and other Greeks, who lived for extensive periods as individuals or as parts of communities in Persian countries (apart of course from those in the Greek territories under the control of the Great King). As regards artistic borrowings the essential cause was employment by the Achaemenid kings of Greek work-men, who transplanted their methods into Persia and later made Persian methods familiar to their own countrymen. Scientific and cultural borrowings took place through the intermediary of individual Greeks, above all the doctors, like Ctesias, who lived in Persia in the service of the king or his satraps—these last had not infrequently married Greek wives. In this way they also made contact with India, whose cures and other branches of medical science were already known to them. At the same time religious and philosophical ideas passed between Greece and Persia, not least because there were Persian students at the school of Plato.

After his conquest of the Persian empire Alexander, followed by his successors, attempted to build on to the foundations of Greek culture, although he also drew suggestions and instructions from Achaemenid methods when evolving his own. Yet he was not successful in laying bases on which Greek and Persian civilizations could be blended into a single and lasting whole. One reason was that he and the Successors found themselves facing two markedly different worlds, one in the borderlands where the Persians had previously been overlords, the other in the Iranian homeland from which the overlords had sprung. Hellenization was relatively easy in the western portions which in later times were firmly held by the Seleucids and Ptolemies, and in the intermediate areas of Babylonia and Mesopotamia, where civilization had prevailed from ancient times; it was also possible in Bactria (in the extreme north-east) where Greek culture lasted for two whole centuries after the country's separation from the Seleucid empire by Diodotus about 246 BC, and was brought to an end only when the land was captured by the Scythian hordes. But Hellenization penetrated much less deeply in the Iranian areas which lay between these two extremes. Achaemenid traditions and institutions were too strong, and these were combined with resistance from Zoroastrian religion and the Magi. Moreover the races of this region remained separate from 'Outer Iran', that is to say from Iranian peoples such as the Scyths and Sacae of the areas round the Caspian, who were always ready to invade. To them was due the formation of the new independent state of Parthia, created by Arsaces the Scyth.

This new kingdom in the process of its continual expansion became the heir to the Persian empire three-quarters of a century after that empire had disappeared. It never succeeded in reaching the old Achaemenid frontiers; but it attained such success that it became not only a barrier against nomad attacks but was the one formidable enemy of Rome, which was trying its best to rescue and promote Greek culture in the East and to impede Parthia's westward advance. At the end of the first round of contests between these powers, which falls within the period of this present chapter, Rome under its general Crassus was defeated at Carrhae in 53 BC; and even Augustus, who later set himself the task of salvaging everything possible in Greek civilization in the East, did not feel confident enough to take decisive vengeance. Yet even at this period the quarrels between the kings, princes, and nobles of Parthia were a great aid to Roman diplomacy, which took strenuous action to intensify these conflicts and make use of them in the interests of Rome.

5. THE GREEK WORLD

a. *Evolution of Politics after 500 BC*

Two tendencies, antithetic to each other, were common to all Greeks; and both were an important cause of the exhaustion of Greek vigour as well as preventing any lasting success attending any attempt at national unity. One tendency was shown in the efforts made by individual cities to establish empire over others: the second is marked by the desire of every *polis* for freedom undiluted and unqualified, making it resist every attempt to dominate it from outside. These tendencies gave rise to a third, which is also found throughout Greek history, namely a rigid and uncompromising attitude towards political ideas; and this frequently exacerbated the internal affairs of the different cities. There were therefore frequent wars between the Greeks, both in the mother country and in portions of the colonial areas where they had acquired supremacy over the natives; and these wars were exhausting to Greek populations and economic resources.

It is true that methods of warfare in those days limited the number of casualties in land actions. Cavalry were little used, the main reliance being placed on the heavily armoured and slow-moving hoplite; pursuit was very difficult, and siege operations were slow. Even so we hear of bloody battles such as Delium, Leuctra, and Chaeroneia. Moreover losses in naval campaigns were normally very high: in Athenian history one has only to remember the Egyptian expedition in the days of Pericles and the Syracusan expedition in the days of Alcibiades, as well as the battles of Arginusae and Aegospotami. In any case the disastrous effect of wars was not felt only in the numbers of killed, or of heavily wounded who were rendered unfit for work, or even of prisoners or displaced persons. One has also to reckon with the cost of war to individuals and to cities, especially in the provision of naval equipment; and also with the destruction of crops and trees, the abandonment of the fields, and the famines that resulted. There were many epidemics; the farmers and middle classes, who served at their own expense, were gradually impoverished; people were exiled in lands far from their homes; and sieges were pressed ruthlessly to the point at which the population starved. Three tendencies were becoming more serious all the time, each of them draining the life-blood of the population and retarding social progress. The first was a growth in the number of mercenaries; the second a revival of colonial emigration, due (as was mercenary service) to poverty and unemployment; the third was the enslavement of large bodies of Greeks who had been made prisoners, though it is true that their servitude was normally only temporary owing to the great efforts made for their redemption and the willingness of purchasers to accept ransom.

But the passion for freedom and the continual effort to build an empire over other cities, these two inborn characteristics of the Greeks, can be seen even better in the failure of every attempt at any lasting political union. One or two efforts did succeed, at least momentarily, in bringing larger political organisms into being. But they were precarious and incomplete; and each one owed its origin to the threat of foreign domination—by Persians or Carthaginians, Etruscans or Sabellians, Macedonians or Romans. Against the Persians, for instance, we find the Ionians of Asia Minor uniting under the leadership of Aristagoras of Miletus; the Athenians receiving support from the Peloponnesians; later the two Attic leagues; the Theban league of Epaminondas' time; and then the confederate Greek leagues formed by the Macedonians Philip II and Alexander. All these are successive phases of the same effort at unity which was imposed on mainland Greece by the Persian danger; and all were led by men who were actually or nominally in the position of tyrants. In the same way many of the Siceliotes came together under the leadership of Gelon and Theron against the Carthaginians, and we find the same phenomenon in the days of Dionysius I, Timoleon, Agathocles, and Pyrrhus. Many of the Italiotes too, came together to resist the Lucanians and Iapyges, and also the Sicilian threat from Dionysius I and Agathocles; they sought a unifier from abroad to help them in their task, Archidamus or Cleonymus, and Alexander or Pyrrhus from Epirus.

But union never lasted longer than the continuance of the danger, and was sometimes dissolved before the danger was over. Every time the irresistible particularism of Greek politics reasserted itself. After this sort of thing had happened again and again—and every attempt at unity had failed—many of the most representative figures in Greece came even more firmly to regard a small city as being the inevitable model on which the Greek political unit should be based. Plato thought the right size was about 5,000 citizens, Aristotle put it at not more than 10,000. Yet Aristotle was the teacher of Alexander, who achieved political union, short-lived though it was, in so great a part of the civilized world.

The same particularist forces were responsible eventually for weakening the Amphictionic Leagues. Every imperialist power which belonged to one of these would conceive the idea of making itself the sole director, and would gain support from groups of subordinate powers. So the struggle to acquire a majority of votes on the Amphictionic council led to continual wars and provided a field for the most bitter political propaganda. The Amphictionic Leagues therefore never carried out for any length of time even the main task for which they had been formed, namely that of avoiding wars between league members. We hear, for example, of three 'Sacred Wars' fought for the control of Delphi.

It goes without saying that the stability of leagues whose basis was more purely political (the *Koinai*) was for the most part even more precarious. More than the religious leagues they were at the mercy of the ups and downs of political events, and there were continual jealousies and struggles connected with attempts by one state after another to acquire hegemony within the alliance. As time went on individual member-cities, which had originally enjoyed equality of status, would react against the most powerful member of the alliance if it was trying to reduce them to subjection. The history of the Delio-Attic League provides an example.

The most lasting leagues in early times were the Thessalian, Peloponnesian, Boeotian, and the two Athenian confederacies; and in later times there were the Achaean and Aetolian Leagues. But all had a troubled history and an erratic process of development, since despite their frequently sincere intention of acting in concert, they all had to recognize that unity was an ideal practically unobtainable by part of the Greek race. We see this very clearly in connection with peace treaties concluded at the end of a conflict between great powers. They would swear oaths to remain at peace for ever, or at any rate for 100 (or 50 or 30) years; but they were then almost invariably ready to break the compact, sometimes after a very short interval, rather than attempt to iron out any unexpected difficulties or submit to any loss of what they considered to be their rights.

b. *The Poleis: Basic Constitutional Elements*

Almost every Greek city-state had three basic constitutional elements, the Popular Assembly, the body known as the Boulé, and the magistrates. But in each state these institutions possessed peculiar features and were organized in an individual way.

The Assembly of the people had much less part to play in oligarchic cities, where it was convened relatively seldom: the direction of affairs was entrusted almost wholly to the other two organs of government—and of course also to the royal power, if this still existed in any form. In any case the 'people' was reduced to small dimensions in cities of this kind, since persons under a fairly mature age, or who did not possess a given census, or who belonged to certain supposedly unworthy professions, would all be excluded. Moreover in order to exercise his right to speak a man had to obey very exact rules of precedence. In democratic cities almost completely opposite assumptions prevailed. There the theory was that every adult citizen could take part and speak at any of the frequent meetings of the fully sovereign Popular Assembly, though in practice it was true that the less well-to-do people who lived on land at a distance from the city were not always in a position to exercise their full rights.

The Council (Boulé), Senate (Gerousia), or other smaller assembly had of course more importance relatively to the Popular Assembly in oligarchic states than in democratic. In oligarchies the *primores* who exercised power tended to form a small senate (only twenty-eight members at Sparta), with a long term of office, membership being sometimes for life. Consequently their policies were stable, being dictated by tradition and by the overriding interests of the class to which the members belonged; and their powers, especially in judicial matters, were very wide. Democratic cities, on the other hand, made their Councils large, kept down the duration of membership (normally limited to a single year), and restricted the Council's powers.

The fundamental differences in the position of magistrates in the two types of régime were less striking, though here too there were variations in the way magistrates came into being and in the names and particular functions they were assigned. Certain features were general: magistrates were annual, collegiate, and responsible, and were therefore liable to render account of what they had done; they were not arbitrary officers, but were there to execute the duties laid on them by the assemblies.

It is, of course, impossible to give an account of all the idiosyncrasies found in the changing political organizations found in so vast a number of *poleis*, which varied from the closest and most restrictive oligarchy of *gamoroi*, through moderate oligarchies and democracies, to the most unbridled form of demagogy. The histories of these cities were too different for any definite rules to be laid down, and the most diverse distribution of landed and movable property prevailed among them. Moreover, we must reckon with the strong individualism of the Greeks, who could not be persuaded for long to respect a régime imposed from above or to surrender the particular experience of politics they had acquired in their own right. So there were great variations. In some oligarchic cities, such as Sparta, the number of families of *homoioi*, who had at the outset possessed equal allotments of land, grew disastrously smaller in the course of time: the original 8,000 Spartan citizens with full rights had become, by stages, 2,000 in the early fourth century, 1,000 in the time of Aristotle, and 700 in 241, thus justifying the revolution of Cleomenes, who brought the number back to 4,000. Other cities, though equally conservative in their outlook and so equally insistent on minimum ages and census qualifications for the exercise of political rights (both active and passive), none the less took account of movable as well as of landed property in calculating the census. In them, therefore, power was not confined to the landed nobility, but was a prerogative of the rich in general.

In democracies every citizen had *isonomia*, full equality of rights both active and passive. So everyone could speak in the assemblies, and could become a counsellor or magistrate (though a minimum census was sometimes retained for treasury officials, and military experience was demanded of generals). To make all this possible for the less well-to-do, pay was instituted for magistrates and members of the Boulé (*misthophora*), just as the provision of free equipment to the army had made it possible to recruit from the poorer classes. But in places and periods in which democracy descended to demagogy, greater extremes were reached. Magistrates were selected by lot, a ticket entitling pay was issued to those who took part in assemblies and juries, and the poor were recompensed for judging and attendance at public spectacles, so that they could interrupt their work without suffering personal loss.

We have explained earlier how archaic Greece, and later still more the Greek colonies, allowed foreigners not only to reside but to obtain citizenship.

The consequences of this could be extremely significant when special tribes or other units were created for the new citizens (*Neopolitai*), for instance when one city received a large influx of persons who had previously lived elsewhere. In the classical period this situation was even more variously handled than before. In Sparta, for instance, xenophobia was the ruling force: but at Athens the number of resident aliens (*metoikoi*) was growing all the time. There were merchants, artisans and industrial workmen, political refugees, artists and men of letters, and pupils of various schools; moreover people engaged in definite branches of commerce and industry could settle in the city to the point at which they became a substantial element in the population when measured in terms of economic potential, labour, or productive output. They paid taxes and performed military service for the city whose guests they were, in the same way as citizens; and like citizens again, they were protected by the courts and could take part in cult acts and attend schools. But they were usually prohibited from owning land, and they could not exercise either active or passive political rights. We are told that a law of Pericles, which later worked against its own author on account of his union with Aspasia of Miletus and the son she bore him, declared that only the son of two Athenian parents could be regarded as a citizen. Moreover only in rare cases was citizenship granted to *metoikoi*.

At one moment régimes of an oligarchic tendency would be in the ascendancy, at another those of democratic outlook; and the main reasons for this short-lived predominance lay in the more important historical events, such as wars (especially national Greek wars) or the rise and fall of tyrannies and of imperial cities. In the Greek peninsula before the Persian Wars the supremacy of the Peloponnesian League had set its mark on a period in which oligarchic ideals were triumphant. But after the victory at Salamis, Athens, the main author of that victory, came to the fore, having already taken important steps in the direction of democratic concepts; and in the period which followed, the successes of the maritime and imperial policies of Themistocles and Pericles, combined with the formation of the Delio-Attic League with its national anti-Persian programme (at least at its outset), were a fundamental cause of the development and spread of democracy.

When it became obvious that Athens was being defeated in its thirty-years war with Sparta, there were repeated attempts at oligarchic restoration in the cities of the empire; and these were carried to a conclusion after the decisive defeat in 404. But the oligarchies imposed by the Spartan Lysander also collapsed with the decline of Spartan power, while democratic ideas were once more spread by Athens and by the city which had destroyed Spartan hegemony, namely Thebes.[2]

c. *The Individual and the State: Tyrannies*

It would be a great mistake to attempt to establish a direct relationship in Greece between oligarchies and over-emphasis on the individual, and between democracies and under-emphasis. In no city was it perhaps so difficult to set up a single man as ruler as in oligarchic Sparta, where there prevailed the myth of equality and equilibrium between the *homoioi*; in no city was it so dangerous for anyone to make the attempt and in none was it so rare that an attempt was successful. In democracies, on the other hand, and in cities where the *demos* was seeking to free itself from control by cliques of nobles, tyranny would find a fruitful field because the masses were bound to seek for leaders. Social conflict indeed is one of the commonest backgrounds against which the tyrants of the fifth and fourth centuries came into being. At the same time these tyrants, open or disguised, were adept at showing they could interpret and realize the peoples' longing to free themselves from the power of their enemies or to accomplish some dream of imperialist expansion.

On the other hand, imperialism permitted the formation of great fortunes, and through these new men would come to power. They would combine with military leaders in opposition to the tyrant and would intrigue against a smooth succession, which might be already difficult to achieve owing to the existence of rival claimants. In this way tyranny would be overthrown; and the same would happen if a tyrant risked a war to consolidate his power and reputation, and then was unsuccessful. Even if the price of liberation might be the loss of the city's imperial power, many citizens would be concerned to see that tyranny, once overthrown, could never revive. Various means were adopted to this end, such as propaganda designed to demolish the myth of the man of genius, by asserting that his successes were due not to himself but to his people; or the deliberate and simultaneous elevation of personages who were all remarkable but in a single field only, one being an eloquent politician, another a competent general, and a third an invaluable financial expert. A less logical, and therefore less efficient, means was the institution known at Athens as ostracism and at Syracuse as petalism. Ostracism consisted in a vote in the Popular Assembly, at which every voter wrote on a potsherd the name of the politician he considered most dangerous; the man who received most votes had to go into exile for ten years. In fact this system finally enabled the most skilful aspirants to power to eliminate their most threatening rivals. We are told that in 417 Hyperbolus asked for a vote of ostracism in order to break the power of Nicias and Alcibiades, but that in the outcome he was himself removed, while the other two were elected generals.

The complete eradication of tyranny was always difficult. If an empire created by a tyrant collapsed, it was often followed (as happened in Sicily) by the rise of a number of lesser tyrannies in the cities which had been liberated. Similarly the fall of a tyranny did not render the city in question immune from this form of government later, since tyrants arose whenever there was an appropriate situation and a suitable man: once again there is the case of Syracuse, where the rule of the Deinomenids was followed, after some interval of time, by Dionysius I and his son, and later by Agathocles. Two cities of completely different outlook, Sparta and Thebes, after the magnificent successes achieved by Lysander and by Epaminondas and Pelopidas, were prepared to regard those commanders as supermen who merited divinity.[3]

But there are a number of other ways in which a study of the relationship between state and individual in the fourth century, and of the obvious consequences of this relationship, will help us to understand the radical changes which converted the world of *poleis* into the world of monarchies.

During the fifth century most of democratic Greece followed the example of Athens in setting the interests of the state above those of individuals. But after the fall of Athens and of its political ideals the centralizing force of the *polis* suffered a progressive decline, and the individual came to enjoy a greater measure of freedom. This meant that he was inclined to concern himself largely with his own well-being and with ways of increasing it, and to take as little interest as possible in the problems and needs of the community. It is true that the state had to obtain money, among other things for the payment of citizens who were beginning to show reluctance to take part in public duties; taxation, tolls, and customs duties were all heavily increased, and besides this the rich had to pay contributions towards the liturgies (which included the trierarchy for the construction and equipment of warships, the choregia and gymnasiarchy for the upkeep of dramatic and gymnastic festivals, as well as the provision of torch-races, public banquets, and sacred embassies). But just because they were not interested in public office and preferred to attend to their lands, their commerce, and their industries, most rich men did not feel themselves aggrieved by these payments: they were finding it fairly easy to make large profits. In addition the state came to the assistance of those citizens whose individualist attitude made them reluctant to be distracted from the pursuit of their own undertakings by the performance of military service. Large numbers could be exempted by the increasing employment of mercenaries, which was also the simplest means—now that colonization was no longer available—of ensuring a livelihood to unemployed persons, exiles, and the like.

There are other clear consequences of this general decline of the state and of the lack of enthusiasm to assist the *polis*. Public duties were not performed even when pay was granted; assemblies were increasingly smaller, being attended only by the unemployed and by persons of little account; there was less philanthropy; and there was a falling-off in the number of marriages and births. Not a few philosophers met this situation by working out a panacea in the form of novel and ideal constitutions, full of unpractical logic and abstract ideas which made it impossible to put them into effect. More practical minds, like those of Xenophon (*Hieron* and *Cyropaedia*) and Isocrates (*Ad Nicoclem*) took the view that a strong form of government was needed, of the kind that could only be provided by a monarchy or tyranny. And in fact there was a fairly general resurgence of tyranny, rather like the rise which had occurred two centuries earlier. We know of about 130 tyrants in this period: they are found in the western colonies, in Thessaly, at Corinth and

Sicyon, at Pellene in Achaea, at Lesbos, in Cyprus, in the Pontic cities, and many other places. This was one of the preludes to the transition which was soon to be made from the age of city-states to the age of the Hellenistic monarchies.

d. *Hegemonies*

Cities. We shall now attempt a brief and generalized history of the great hegemonies which appeared one after another in Greece, calling attention to the imperialist outlook which was their common failing. Western Greece we shall pass over, but there too the same story was true.

Pausanias the Spartan had attempted to exploit the victories over Persia, to which his city had made a powerful contribution, by building a Spartan empire outside the Peloponnese while proceeding to liberate further Greek areas from foreign rule. But he had neither support from his government nor co-operation from the allied navies. From 478 the direction of the fleet, and the same programme of liberation, was taken over by Athens; the credit for this belongs mainly to Aristides, who created the Delio-Attic League with its centre and treasury at Delos, its operations depending on the provision by the allies of either naval squadrons or money contributions for common purposes. Then, however, imperialist aims, which had not been diminished by the fall of the Peisistratids, divided the Athenian leaders, together with the factions supporting them in their alternating periods of power, into two groups. Aristides and later Cimon wanted war to the death against Persia and friendship with Sparta: Themistocles, Ephialtes, and later Pericles (after the disastrous failure of his first plan of simultaneous action against Persia and the Spartan League) preferred to come to terms with Persia. And in fact peace with Persia was concluded in 449, to prepare the way for the contest against Sparta for hegemony over all Greeks, including the Greeks of the West.

But this latter policy altered the basis of the Delio-Attic League, because the allied contributions, which had been fixed in relation to the continuance of the Persian War, were now, after peace had been made, put into a reserve fund, or else used to embellish Athens and provide it with the means to fight its rival. The pretext was that Athens was really protecting the allies against dangers of every kind. Naturally not all the allies, especially the stronger cities or those in a position to revolt, were sympathetic to Athenian pretensions; but when Samos revolted in 440/439, it received no outside help, and was therefore defeated and disarmed. The allies were gradually transformed into subjects; the Athenians, though ruled democratically at home, used oligarchic methods abroad.[4] The annual contributions from the allies, now converted into tribute impositions, were paid to Athena in its Parthenon; and law-courts for the allies were set up in Athens to guarantee the loyalty of its new subjects. For 'defensive' purposes 'cleruchies' of Athenian citizen-soldiers were sent out to allied territory; and all the time the empire was being enlarged by new conquests, while Athens did its best to intervene in the affairs of western Greece and to detach allies from Sparta and generally weaken its power. But after twenty-seven years of almost continuous war Athens fell, ruined by the bloody defeat inflicted on it beneath the walls of Syracuse, by the revolts of its subjects, and by the offensive carried on by the Spartan Lysander with the help of Persian gold. For the next thirty years a new hegemony was established under Sparta, this time of oligarchic rather than democratic sympathies.

But this hegemony, too, though it was a source of admiration and interest to many politicians, historians, and philosophers (including some Athenians like Xenophon) was to prove short-lived. The former subjects of Athens, who had helped to bring it into being, expected that they would really receive the freedom which the Spartans had promised; but they then found that they had simply changed one master for another, and therefore were anxious to dissolve the hegemony and follow their own devices. But this was not the only factor. Sparta was culturally incapable of leading Greece, and at this particular moment it also seemed unworthy to do so, because it had won with the help of Persian gold. Moreover it had emerged from the war with its internal structure seriously dislocated, since the conquest of an empire had made it impossible to preserve the 'Lycurgean' ordinances unchanged. The Spartan state had to procure economic means of a kind to which it was not accustomed, in order to maintain the fleet needed to rule the seas. Equality between the *homoioi* had now become a plain lie; some had grown extremely rich, while others had lost their lots and with them their rights of full citizenship. The struggle between Ephors and kings, and between the two royal houses, impeded every action; the Spartan armies were not developing techniques which could match those being perfected elsewhere; and without Persian aid the Spartan navy, so far from growing stronger, could not even act as an adequate defensive force. When Lysander was seen to be preparing a revision of the constitution, which might have brought some relief, he was sent abroad in what amounted to exile, and his attempt was frustrated.

But above all Sparta did nothing to retain the sympathy and loyalty of its new allies (or subjects), to whom it had promised autonomy and freedom from Persia. Instead of granting autonomy it laid claim to a tribute of 1,000 talents; and in every city, as well as imposing the rule of oligarchic factions, which inaugurated a reign of terror in their greed for vengeance, it stationed a Spartan garrison under a 'harmost'. As to its second promise, it is true that, to prevent the dissolution of the hegemony, it did renew the war against Persia; but the Great King financed the rebels who fought at Coronea in 394, the same year in which, also assisted by Persia, the Athenian fleet built by Conon defeated the Spartans at Cnidus. So in 387/6 the Spartan Antalcidas, to check the growing power of Sparta's Theban and Athenian adversaries, made peace with the Persian king, recognizing his ownership of all the cities of Asia Minor and Cyprus. Sparta undertook to get this Diktat accepted by all cities of the peninsula, which were by yet another show of empty words declared to be autonomous, and in which Sparta once again installed oligarchic factions and stationed, by force, garrisons of its own troops.

All this led to the breakdown of the Spartan hegemony. A revolt by the Thebans against Spartan occupation of the Cadmea was the beginning of the next hegemony, that of Thebes, which in 379 assumed once more the leadership of Boeotia. It then made an alliance with the naval power of Athens,[5] and with Jason, the strong ruler of Pherae in Thessaly. The victory of Leuctra in 371 enabled it to turn all the Spartan garrisons out of central Greece, to invade the Peloponnese, and to detach large areas away from Sparta by giving assistance to the movement in favour of democracy. But it proved impossible to carry on this new Theban hegemony after the deaths of the two great men who had created it, Epaminondas and Pelopidas: so it too collapsed quickly. Although the régimes it imposed were democratic and not oligarchic, it worked always through force and the promotion of faction; and when one of its two great founders tried to give a definite measure of autonomy to the cities, his plan was frustrated. Theban dominion had come into being through the victories of its two great generals and their armies; and when these two disappeared from the scene, the cohesive force behind the régime, which did not consist in any ties of a moral kind, was gone. Meanwhile another army, the Macedonian, seized the chance of making itself more powerful than the Theban, by improving on the reforms of Pelopidas. Revolts multiplied, but the most decisive was that of the Phocians, who occupied the temple of Delphi: the ensuing Sacred War (356–346) provided Philip II with his opportunity to intervene; and so began a new hegemony in Greece, and one of fundamental importance in history.

Philip of Macedon. Philip had created a strong army by bringing to perfection a combination of light-armed peltasts and heavy-armed phalangites. He annexed Epirus and Illyria to his empire, captured the Greek cities of Amphipolis, Potidaea, and Methone as bases for his fleet, and occupied the gold mines of Pangaeus. During the Sacred War he took the side of the Thebans, Locrians, and Thessalians against the Phocians, Athenians, and Spartans; and after defeating his opponents he occupied Delphi and rearranged the Amphictiony to suit himself. Then, after many other achievements which there is no need to list here, and after overcoming the final resistance of his enemies at Chaeroneia in Boeotia in 338, he was elected general of a new 'Koinon synedrion' of the Hellenes at a Panhellenic congress held at Corinth. In this new league all cities preserved their internal institutions, but each provided forces proportionate to its size for the war by land and sea which was the proposed aim of the league, and which was in fact begun in 336, though it was then interrupted by the king's death. This war against Persia had been broken off by the Athenians when they were in control in 449: Sparta had resumed it to no effect between 400 and 394; and Gorgias, Lysias, and

Isocrates had proclaimed it at the great Olympic meetings of 392, 388, and 380, but their appeals had found no response. It was a great task in the national interest; it justified the new league's existence, and its leadership by the most powerful Greek state of the day. But it was not the only thing that Philip's league was intended to achieve. Macedonian hegemony gave concrete effect to the internal autonomy of the cities, which up till then had been promised at the outset of every hegemony, only to be disavowed very quickly thereafter. It was this same autonomy which Demosthenes prized with so exact an assessment in his political programme, at the time when, in desperation and already too late, he prepared to organize a 'free confederacy of Greek states'.

e. Characteristics of the Hellenistic monarchies

Alexander's empire, and the collection of Hellenistic states which carried it on, extended over wider areas and over peoples more numerous and varied than the Persian empire which preceded it and to some extent prepared the ground: in its turn it opened the way for the Roman empire, which in both area and population was larger still. In the unified form achieved by Alexander this was a much shorter-lived empire than its predecessor or its successor; but its importance for history and civilization was immense, on account of the prolonged influence exercised by the Hellenistic political organisms which it generated.

It was essentially due to the differences in method of the Successors, and to their personal ambitions, that Alexander's great empire split up. But in addition the states into which it split went on disintegrating, because the many little cells represented by the autonomous Greek cities could only with difficulty be controlled by the state on to which they were grafted; furthermore there were dissensions between Greeks and natives, and several regions were inclined to separatism. So foreign invasions and the Roman conquest can be regarded as the logical effect of the collapse rather than its operative cause.

One of the main features of Alexander's system, to some extent carried on by the Hellenistic dynasts too, was to transplant large numbers of Greeks to the East, as well as promoting the exchange of commodities and cultural ideas between the Greek and Oriental sections of the lands he had conquered. The result was an impressive phenomenon, a koiné between the two races and cultures, though one in which Hellenization of the eastern peoples was generally more marked than was Orientalization of the Greeks. [6]

Something has been said already of the inevitable revival of the monarchical ideal among fourth-century Greeks. Of this ideal Philip II was the incarnation, as leader of a powerful army and as the man who proclaimed a Panhellenic enterprise against Persia. The first period after Alexander's death was one of adjustment, in which the desire to preserve the great founder's legacy in a united form was in conflict with the tendency of the Successors to build up dominions of their own. [7] From this period emerged three major states, those of the Lagids in Egypt, the Seleucids in Asia, and the Antigonids in Macedonia; but, particularly inside the second of these, smaller dynasties arose at different times, such as those of Pergamum, Bithynia, and Pontus; and others, such as the Parthian kingdom, were created when areas once Seleucid got detached. In this last type of case the ruling elements were Hellenized orientals: otherwise the basis of all these monarchies was Graeco-Macedonian, with some oriental influence.

Meanwhile monarchy persisted in the Balkan peninsula, not only in Macedonia, but in peripheral regions such as Epirus, Illyria, and Thrace; and in Sicily the new group of tyrants like Agathocles and Hieron II assumed the title of 'King', with the consent of their subjects.

Here we must pause to consider some of the features of these monarchies which derived from Alexander's empire. The king, beloved of the gods, is an expert and brave soldier, the true and legitimate leader of his army, credited with a many-sided virtue (*areté*) which makes him a sublime and heroic figure. He is the only law-giver, directing and protecting the life of his state in full awareness of the weight of his duties, and looked to as lord and benefactor of his subjects. Usually his eldest son succeeds him, but he has the right to prefer another member of his family, using his own unfettered judgement on the point; and he can associate his successor as co-regent with himself to prepare him for full succession. Although originally these kings did not favour undue personal parade, and liked wearing Macedonian dress, their dignity could only be shown to the world if they also wore a diadem. They were surrounded by their faithful friends and courtiers, and also by their generals: all of these became their counsellors (and at times they had to put up with their intrigues), as well as serving as a class from which major dignitaries such as military commanders, ambassadors, and ministers were drawn. Although they used native personnel in local administration and to some extent preserved the pattern of the former satrapies, for all higher and more delicate jobs they employed Greeks, at least alongside the natives; and these were an organized bureaucracy, who were commonly fairly leisurely in the performance of their tasks.

In every country the king owned vast domains of every kind, which were largely worked by masses of slaves, serfs, or dependent labour. To the income from their rents he added the yield from taxation, the main element in which was the annual *phoros* imposed on every inhabited centre; and eventually there was a poll tax on every human being and head of livestock, a tax on the produce of the land, and customs duties, excise, and corvées. From this revenue the king had to meet the expenses of his court and officials of his army and donatives, and of his patronage of artists, writers, and so on.

The difficulties of administering these vast multi-racial states were later increased by the existence of regions which were under special government and required peculiar treatment. These included peoples retaining their traditional kings, who were in fact vassals and whose 'gifts' were really no better than tribute; secondly peoples of minor importance ruled by dynasts;

thirdly supposedly autonomous peoples, who sometimes still preserved a tribal organization; and lastly the Greek cities.

Alexander had founded Graeco-Macedonian colonies in various parts of his new empire.[8] These were independent states, whose task was to provide the government with fortresses at strategic points and commercial centres, as well as to spread Greek culture and language, and to give land and a livelihood to large numbers of impoverished and vagabond Greeks who had left their own cities. These colonies, with their defensive walls, their temples dedicated to Greek gods, their democratic institutions and magistracies of Greek type (including tribes, demes, popular assemblies, councils and so on), and their autonomous administration, were so many islands of the Greek race amid alien territory. They paid a modest tribute to the king; they accepted a garrison and sometimes control by an *epistatēs*; and if they became capitals of the new Hellenistic states they were the seats of the king's court, though naturally they did not concern themselves with foreign policy.

These colonies were later multiplied in number by individual Hellenistic rulers. Sometimes they were set down in existing native 'cities', whose populations lived together with the Greek settlers under conditions similar to those of *metoikoi* in Greek cities (the same was true of natives permitted to reside in colonies founded where no city had existed before). The status of many of these natives, whose origin was semi-servile, was improved in time, as their economic position and their degree of Hellenization increased, and as they gradually contracted ties of marriage with the colonists: eventually they could obtain access to the citizenship of the *polis*. This situation was of obvious importance in promoting Hellenization within the empire, a process which we have already seen to have been more significant than the effect of Eastern influence on the Greek population.

The army of a Hellenistic state consisted normally of a permanent core of paid Greek and Macedonian soldiers, who provided the king's bodyguard and the garrison troops. These could constitute the hoplite phalanx, now relatively lightly armed, and the squadrons of heavy cavalry. To meet emergencies native troops could be mobilized, in which case their civil status was enhanced; and in addition use was made of Greeks scattered over the king's territories in military colonies, or of mercenaries either recruited individually or offering their service in regular units under their *condottieri*. In general the Hellenistic states did much to promote military technique, for instance in organizing a strong and fast-moving cavalry arm, in their employment of elephants acquired from India and of artillery machines both in the field and for siege operations, and in their building of large warships. (Pl. 22, b.)

When the chequered period of the Hellenistic monarchs is viewed as a whole, down to the time when the most easterly regions got detached and Rome gradually conquered the remainder, it appears as above all a period of peace, which worked to the distinct material advantage of the countries concerned. In some the existing development was preserved and advanced, in others a start was made from scratch. Hydraulic works were revived and improved, additions were made to the road system, and harbour services were brought into line with current needs. Care was taken over the cultivation of vines and olives where climate permitted; and there was supervision of grain production and also of afforestation. Though there was no uniform system of standards, more money was put into circulation: and this did much to promote trade, when combined with the network of roads inside the Hellenistic countries, and with the attention paid to the caravan routes connecting these countries with central and east Asia, and to the sea routes starting from the northern parts of the Red Sea and the Persian Gulf. Although these routes were run by foreigners they gave new impetus to Hellenistic economy, by opening new outlets for exports and making possible the import of silk, cotton, ivory, costly woods, pearls and precious stones, spices, scents, and so on. Governments exercised a watchful control over all this trade by laying their hands on large stocks of exportable goods acquired at low prices, even if this meant keeping the standard of living of the natives at an unduly low level.

f. *The Areas of Seleucid Rule*

Conditions in the various Hellenistic states were rendered different by geographical and racial factors, by divergent theories of government, and by the relative importance of the Greek element in the population and the degree of Hellenization that had been achieved. In broad outline, therefore, we must take each of the larger areas in turn, starting with the Seleucid countries in Asia.

The Seleucid kings owned very large domains, cultivated by serfs, and paid a great deal of attention to all aspects of their administration. They were not, however, excessively concerned to centralize the government of their very numerous and diverse subjects, and did not impose heavy taxes upon them. This very large territory with its many races did not lend itself to uniform methods; and the returns from taxation were high enough without any need to make its rate particularly onerous.

The sole founder of this dynasty was Seleucus, a man who had shown himself not averse from Alexander's ideas of fusion between Graeco-Macedonians and natives: he had not copied the other generals after their leader's death in at once renouncing his marriage, and had kept the Syrian Apama as his wife. Moreover his successors had continued his policy of founding Greek cities with characteristically democratic constitutions; he himself had founded at least fifty-nine. Yet little was done to combine these cities in a single whole with the multi-racial native towns; the latter were governed by oligarchies and were reduced to poverty as well as being deprived of their legal liberties. It was to the Greek *poleis*, together with the Greek soldiers and officials, that the general level of culture and the prevalence of Hellenism were due. The racial admixture of the non-Greeks with one another was only in small measure the result of rural settlements formed by the transplantation of peoples such as Hebrews, Persians, Mysians, Galatians, or Carduchi.

On the coast of Asia Minor as far east as Pontus and Cilicia there had been clusters of Greek colonies before Alexander's time, and from them Greek culture and language had penetrated the interior to Mylasa, Pergamum, Tralles, and Sardis. Under the Successors new cities came into being at Antigoneia (later called Nicaea), Docimium, and Synnada. Then the Seleucids refounded Celaenae with the name of Apamea, and established settlements at Laodicea on the Lycus, Themisonium, Antioch on the Maeander, Seleucia and Antioch on the borders between Phrygia and Pisidia, and several other places; meanwhile veteran colonies grew up at Peltae, Thyateira, Nacrasa, Blaundus, and Magnesia by Sipylus, and Lysimachus founded Lysimacheia on the neck of the Chersonnese.

The autonomous states of the region were equally active in their colonization. In Bithynia we find Zipoetium and Nicomedia; as well the kings of Pergamum built Philetaireia, Attalia, Gergitha, and Eumenia, and at times taxed all their colonies severely. In the third century no less than fifty of these Graeco-Macedonian settlements in Asia Minor can be counted: they completed the early ring of Hellenic colonies, and were for the most part placed in the hills just inland from the coastal districts. One can easily see how important the whole chain of Greek cities was in furthering the spread of Greek ideas, language, religion, and trade: goods were exchanged above all through the flourishing cities of Ephesus, Miletus, Magnesia, Smyrna, Pergamum, and Rhodes; and the results of the whole process are attested by Greek inscriptions throughout the region, by syncretism between Greek and native cults, and by archaeology. Yet native languages, though they were driven out into country districts, still survived; and the cult of the ancient gods was still carried on, especially in central and eastern districts, where Hellenism made marked progress only in Roman times. To judge from literature, the most important cultural centres were still those in the older Greek lands. Cos was the home not only of a flourishing school of medicine, but also of poets and philologists of the school of Philetas; Samos was the birthplace of Duris, Asclepiades, Aristarchus, Conon, and Epicurus; and other poets and scholars came from Ephesus (Zenodotus), Rhodes (Antagoras, Apollonius, Hieronymus), Lampsacus (many Epicureans), Byzantium (Moero and others), Perge (Apollonius), and so on.

In the two sections of Syria Hellenism progressed at very different rates. It went ahead far more rapidly in the north, where the Seleucids had their seat of government; in the south, a region most of which in any case was controlled by the Ptolemies for about a century, progress was relatively slow. In northern Syria the old Greek colonies attained some cultural importance, for instance Soli (the home of Aratus, Chrysippus, Crantor, and Philemon) and Mallus (which produced Dionysiades); but there was additional colonization by Macedonian veterans and Greek immigrants as early as the Succession period, when Antigoneia, Apamea on the Orontes (first called Pella), and Alexandria on the Issus were founded. Under the Seleucids the region became virtually a Greek country, and local place-names were replaced by Greek: it was then that the capital Antioch, with its port Seleucia, was founded, and later came Laodicea, Seleucia, Apamea, Europus and Amphipolis on the Euphrates, Cyrrhus, Beroea, Chalcis, Arethusa, Maronea, Larissa, Leucas, and other cities. This was a land richly endowed by nature, and the Hellenistic rulers endeavoured to increase its production of cereals, oil, and wine, to develop its orchards, and to build roads for the promotion of trade. The religion and art of the country, and still more its literature, reveal an impressive admixture of cultures. The court of Antioch attracted a collection of scholars and philosophers from all over the Greek world, such as Aratus, Hegesianax, Euphorion, Erasistratus, and Lycon. Members of the royal family, such as Stratonice, daughter of Antiochus Soter, were patrons of literature; and the town, with its great library, became a most important centre of Greek civilization, showing all the peculiar features of Hellenism in its materialist, sceptical, and cosmopolitan outlook, including a great delight in novels and fanciful romances. Strabo compared it as a cultural centre with Athens and Alexandria. Scholars of local origin, such as Posidonius of Apamea, were not lacking; and it was here, too, that in later days the apostle Paul came to make the teaching of Christ accessible to the Hellenistic world.

The Hellenization of southern Syria, though less deep, was still significant. Greek influence had been felt before Alexander's day, and can be seen in the philhellenism of Strato II, king of Sidon from 373 to 362. The Successors founded here a Graeco-Macedonian Dodecapolis, of which Gadara, Dion, and Pella (Berenice) were the best-known members. Tyre was repopulated by Alexander himself after its siege, and he also sent settlers to Gaza. The Seleucids colonized Samaria; and the Ptolemies during their occupation of the country founded Philadelphia, Philetaireia, Arsinoe, and Berenice, making use to some extent of the peculiar methods of government which they employed in Egypt. In the Jordan valley there existed a Greek Dodecapolis in Pompey's time, and there was a Tripolis on the sea-coast. But the process of Hellenization was hampered by political disaffection, combined with the peculiarities of the indigenous Semitic culture, especially that of the Hebrews; and the intrusion of Ptolemaic methods was a further complicating factor.

In Mesopotamia, Babylonia, and Susiana, where civilization had flourished for thousands of years and where the population was high, it would be natural to think that there was little room for colonies and small chance of Hellenization succeeding. Nevertheless the Alexandria founded by Alexander at the mouth of the Tigris and the Macedonian settlement at Carrhae (Harran) in 312 were followed by a number of Seleucid cities. Seleucia-on-the-Tigris was their new capital, and they also founded Anthemusia, Antioch Arabis, Antioch in Mygdonia, Apollonia east of the Tigris, Edessa, and Ichnae, as well as the Euphrates cities mentioned above. In this area it may be that Hellenism received more from the civilizations of antiquity than it gave—in religion, for example, and in the sciences, astronomy and astrology: yet we find works written in Greek by scholars who were born in Mesopotamia and neighbouring countries, such as Berosus of Babylonia or Diogenes and Seleucus of Seleucia.

In these countries, too, as in all districts of the Seleucid empire (including those farthest to the east) parties of Greeks were allowed to settle outside the regular *poleis*. They often travelled, traded, and acquired land in organized groups, which made a significant contribution to the spread of culture and to economic and intellectual progress.

Indeed even beyond the Choaspes, in the most easterly districts he had conquered, Alexander founded several stations along the caravan routes and garrison posts on the frontiers, for example the five cities which bore his name (in Margiana, Sogdiana, Areia, Bactria, and Arachosia). The Seleucids founded, or refounded, several more: Europus (Rhagae) and Ecbatana in Media; Antioch in Persis; Achaia, Charis, Calliope, Hecatompylus, and Soteria in Parthia; Antioch in Margiana; and others besides. It is true that these farthest districts, as has been stated earlier, were soon separated off from the Seleucid domains, but the process of Hellenization left its mark there, and in Bactria it was revived by the new dynasty over the century 246–150 (*circa*). Even the Parthians did not show themselves hostile to Hellenism: at the time of their victory over Crassus they still liked to recite Greek plays at their festivals.

g. *Egypt, Macedonia, Western Greece*

The greater part of the Nile valley, which unlike the Seleucid dominions had a homogeneous native population, belonged to the royal domains. It was let out in plots, but the farmers were left no freedom: they were obliged to till given areas and raise certain crops, and their produce was impounded until the next year's seed together with their rent and taxes had been withdrawn from it, which left a very small amount for the labourers to live on. In the rest of the country too there was a rigid state economy with an infinite number of controls, in order to ensure that the country produced export goods (cereals, wine, and oil) in the maximum quantity and at the minimum cost. The state monopolies laid down rules of production: for instance oil must not be extracted in privately owned presses, and must be handed over to officials at a price fixed by the state. The principal industries were also monopolies.

For a long time past Egypt had had the Greek trading station of Naucratis: Alexander added the Greek *polis* of Alexandria, by the side of which the Ptolemies built Ptolemais, as well as several commercial factories on the Red Sea coast. One cannot, however, speak of any large-scale foundation of Greek colonies comparable with that in certain Seleucid countries. The creation of *poleis* would have diminished the absolute powers of the kings in a part of their territory. But if the Lagids were reluctant for this, they were at great pains to preserve the racial integrity of the ruling house and never fully learned the

25

(a) *Winged horse and birds, clay tile from a tomb. Early Han, third to second century BC*

(b) *Cervide figure from Pazyryk in the Altai. Leningrad Hermitage Museum*

(a)

(b)

[I.O.

26 *Bharhut: three Yakshinis*

[*photo Josephine Powell*   (a) II   [D.A.I.

27   *Sanchi, India: The North Gate*

     (a) (i) *Ensemble view from the interior;* (ii) *East pillar, inside top panel: the musicians*

     (b) *Façade of the Bhaja caitya, India*

(b)   [D.A.I.

(a)

[Alinar

28 *Athens: The Acropolis*
   (a) *General view with the Parthenon*
   (b) *The Propylaea seen from the West, 437–432 BC*

(b)

[Alinar

(a)   [Alinari

29   *Athens:*
  (a) *The Theseum, c. 449–444 BC*
  (b) *The Erechtheum, c. 421–405 BC:*
       (i) *North portico,* (ii) *Caryatid porch*

(b) I   [Alinari

(b) II ·   [Alinari

(a)

30   DORIC TEMPLES I

(a) *Sunium, temple of Poseidon, 444–440 BC*

(b) *Agrigento (Acragas), Sicily, temple of Hera Lacinia,* c. 460 BC

(b)

(a)   [B.F.M.

31   DORIC TEMPLES II

(a) *Segesta, Sicily*, c. 424–416 *BC*

(b) *Paestum, temple of Poseidon*, c. 460 *BC*

(b)   [B.F.M.

(a)

32 (a) *Epidaurus, the Greek theatre*, c. 350 *BC*
    (b) *Phlyakes masque, Taranto, National Museum*

(b)

(a)   [Alinari

33   *The 'Ludovisi Throne', mid-fifth century BC, Rome, Terme Museum*

    (a) *The birth of Venus*

    (b) *Woman burning incense*

    (c) *Flute player*

b)   [Alinari   (c)   [Alinari

34   GREEK SCULPTURE

(a) *The charioteer, bronze, c. 474, Delphi Museum*

(b) *Pallas Athena, after Myron*

(c) *The Athena Lemnia by Pheidias, Dresden Museum (the original head is at the Municip Museum, Bologna)*

(a)   [Alinari

Olympia, Temple of Zeus, Olympia Museum

(a) *Eastern pediment, Zeus presiding over the sacrifices before the competition between Pelops and Oenomaus,* c. 457 BC

(b) *Western pediment, Apollo,* c. 457 BC

(b)   [B.F.M.

36 *Athens, the Parthenon, scenes from the Panathenaic procession,* c. 435 *BC.* [B.M.
   London, British Museum

37 *Scopas, Greeks and Amazons, detail from the frieze of the Mausoleum at Halicarnassus,*
    c. 350 BC. London, British Museum

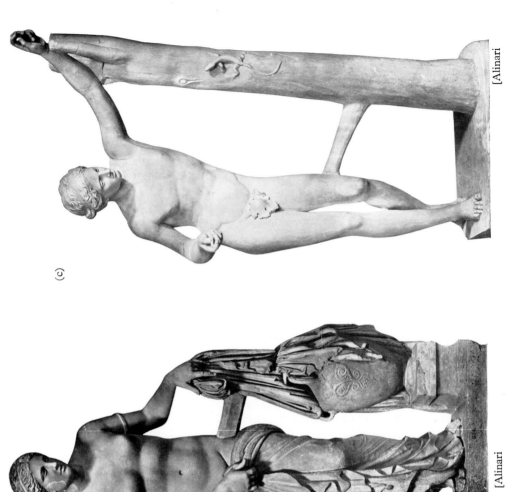

(a)

(b)

38   GREEK SCULPTURE

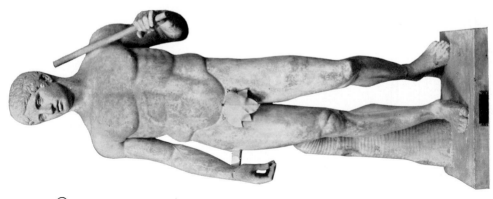

(c)

39

(a) *After Lysippus, Mars at Rest.*
    Rome, Terme Museum

(b) *'The Pugilist', third century BC.*
    Rome, Terme Museum

(a)   [Alinari

(b)   [Alinari

40   *The Victory of Samothrace, second century BC. Paris, Louvre*

native language; this may explain their readiness to grant a privileged status to Greek settlers, both in the cities and elsewhere.

Greeks in the cities lived on free and autonomous territory. But Alexandria contained the royal abode, and from the first allowed 'metic' inhabitants, particularly the native population of the pre-existing settlement of Rhacotis and also the Hebrew community. These all took on a wide measure of Hellenization: an effort was made to impede mixed marriages, but some degree of infiltration proved inevitable. A number of natives obtained the citizenship, though a more frequent outcome was discord and rioting. But many Greeks lived in other places than the three cities, either on their own or in groups. They might be state officials, or traders in other towns, or possibly *cleruchs* settled as soldiers on the land, which became their private property although their heirs were tied to it for the future. The Greek settlers in Egypt were the party of order, from which the officials were drawn. They provided the regular and essential establishment for the army, which in time of war was expanded to include Greek mercenaries: native recruits were employed only on menial tasks. In the course of time, however, the various classes of soldiers became less distinct, as was inevitable in view of the small number of Greeks and the high native population. Moreover in the light of these proportions it is not surprising that native cults and language survived, nor that the Hellenization of other races (represented, for instance, by the Greek writings of the Egyptian Manetho, or the Greek translation of the Bible for use by local Hebrews) was fairly often accompanied by the opposite phenomenon, namely the absorption of Greek elements by the natives. The centre of Greek intellectual life, recognized of course also by the Ptolemaic possessions outside Egypt in the Cyclades, Cyrenaica, and the semi-Greek areas of Cyprus and southern Syria, was Alexandria; and there were built the vast and famous Library, the second library in the temple of Sarapis, and the 'Museum' with its arrangements for salaried artists. At the court of the Ptolemies, who were often enthusiastic patrons of literature, there was always a large circle of scholars and artists drawn from countries inside the Ptolemaic empire and from all other parts of the Greek world. Under the first Lagids there were Theodorus and Hegesias from Cyrene, Demetrius of Phalerum, Hecataeus of Abdera, Zenodotus of Ephesus, Straton of Lampsacus, Philetas of Cos, Euclides of Alexandria with his mathematical school, and Herophilus of Chalcedon with a school of medicine. In the time of Ptolemy Philadelphus (258–247) Alexandria was the home of a large group of poets, some belonging to the 'Pleiad', such as Alexander of Pleuron, Callimachus of Cyrene, Dionysiades, Philiscus, Lycophron, and Sosiphanes. Under Ptolemy Euergetes (246–221) the list included Apollonius of Perge, Apollonius of Rhodes, Conon of Samos, Dositheus of Pelusium, Dioscorides, and Eratosthenes and Lacydes of Cyrene.

Macedonia was of Hellenic origin and was fairly well in unison with the spiritual and literary movements going on in the Greek peninsula. There were naturally only a few Hellenistic Greek colonies in the area, such as

Cassander's foundation at Antipatreia in his southern Illyrian dominions, and
that made by Antigonus Gonatas at Antigoneia in Paeonia. Greek influence
received a severe setback on the coast of Thrace, where several colonies were
overwhelmed by the Celtic invasion of 279. The artistic and literary centre of
the Macedonian empire was of course at its court; and for some time under
Antigonus Gonatas there was a circle of scholars and artists: these included the
poets Alexander of Pleuron, Antagoras of Rhodes, Aratus, and Nicander, the
philosophers Bion, Menedemus, and Persaeus, and the historian Hieronymus
of Cardia.

At this period the Greek elements in Magna Graecia were in continuous
retreat before the Sabellians, and until the time of the Roman conquest it
was only foreign aid that preserved them. These then were clearly not times
in which art and thought could prosper as in previous generations. It is
believed that at the beginning of the fourth century Croton, the second Greek
city of the district after Tarentum, could put only 2,000 citizens under arms.

In the Greek part of Sicily the situation was much less disastrous than in
Italy. Indeed the Sicilian Greeks enjoyed a new period of prosperity under the
empire of Agathocles, which extended at some moments over practically the
whole island. Equally beneficial, though confined to a portion of eastern
Sicily, was the long and peaceful reign of Hieron II. Under his rule the climate
was clearly favourable to science and the arts: whereas before his day there
was a continual exodus of intellectuals from the West—such as Leonidas of
Tarentum, Lydus of Rhegium, Timaeus of Tauromenium, Boeotus and Theocritus of Syracuse—in Hieron's time we find some of them, like Timaeus and
Theocritus, coming back again. Moreover Syracuse in these years could take
pride in the genius of its citizen Archimedes; and once again it became one
of the greatest cities of the Greek world, not only as an intellectual centre but
as a home of riches and trade.

h. *The Greek Peninsula*

Meanwhile the little *poleis* and the federations in the Greek peninsula still
continued with their republican institutions inside a world of monarchies
both great and small. They were kept in political subjection, although they
were always ready to start abortive and short-lived revolts. Their social and
economic conditions, together with their population levels and military potential, were worsening all the time.

The decline in commerce came about because the task once performed for
Mediterranean trade by the ports in the peninsula had now been taken over by
those in Egypt and Asia Minor. The actual Aegean trade tended to be monopolized by Rhodes and Delos, and the mainland cities did not own sufficient
tonnage to overcome this competition. Moreover the routes of navigation had
changed, leading now to the great new ports, which soon included Rome. The
industries of older Greece were still on a small scale, resembling artisanship,

and could not stand up to the competition of the large factories built in the Hellenistic countries. The prices at which wine and oil could be bought in these empires were so low that production for export from Greece often became futile; but it was increasingly necessary to import grain, and this had to be bought at high prices. In this way famine, unemployment, and major economic disasters became frequent; and even social revolution was a common phenomenon (the most serious example indeed was seen in traditionalist Sparta), made easier by the abolition of pay for officials, which restored *de facto* power in democratic cities to the well-to-do bourgeoisie. As the only means of escaping such upheavals men would leave their homes in Greece to become members of the rising *poleis* in the East or to enrol as mercenaries in the service of the new empires. But this of course led, when combined with other results of poverty (such as a decline in marriages, exposure of children, or an increased death rate), to gradual depopulation of the country. Another partial remedy was devised in the constitution of new federations on a larger scale, avoiding the main defects found in the older leagues: the two new leagues we have chiefly in mind are the Aetolian and the Achaean. They were the only organizations large enough to be able to put a significant army in the field, given the immense forces belonging to the new empires. Their main feature was genuine autonomy of the individual member-states in their internal policy and the discarding of all possible imperialist ambitions: external policy was co-ordinated by the decisions of a central council with a general at its head, and the members of this, in numbers proportionate to the importance of each member-state, were appointed each year by the General Assembly of all citizens. This assembly met at fixed intervals in cities which were chosen for each occasion.

But from the cultural standpoint the centre of peninsular Greece remained at Athens. Indeed during the half-century lasting from the death of Alexander to the imposition of more severe Macedonian rule, and particularly under the government of Demetrius of Phalerum (317–307), Athens was still the centre of the whole Greek world. During those fifty years philosophers of almost every school were teaching there: the Peripatetics from Theophrastus to Straton; the Cynics under Crates; the Stoics under Zeno; Epicurus in person; and the Academy under Xenocrates and Polemo. There were orators like Demetrius, Deinarchus, Demochares, Stratocles, and Philiscus; historians such as Diyllus, Demochares, Timaeus, and Philochares; and writers on the history of art like Xenocrates. Meanwhile Menander, Philemon, Diphilus, Philippides, Apollodorus, and Posidippus were writing for the theatre; and there were epic poets such as Antagoras and Aratus, not to mention a number of tragedians belonging to the so-called 'Pleiad'.

Later, however, while the great Greek cities of the East were attracting more people to their courts and their learning, Athens in the period of its subjection (263–228) withdrew more into itself. This was the result of the philosophy prevalent at the time, which was largely sceptical and pessimistic;

and the habit persisted even after the city recovered its freedom. Yet the
language of Athens was becoming the Hellenistic language: it spread far
enough to become the officially recognized language of half the known world.

It is commonly said that in contrast to the *polites* of earlier times the Hellenistic age provides us above all with the 'cosmopolites'. But these concepts
need precise definition. The Greeks, it is true, had been divided into a large
number of cities down to the time of Philip and Alexander: but the same is
true, in broad terms, of the Greek peninsula and part of western Greece
down to the Roman conquest, and even later. When Aristotle wrote his
Politics, at the height of Alexander's conquests, his ideal was still the small
polis of Greek tradition; and when the Greeks and Macedonians became
masters of the world, each of the colonies they founded in the East was still
given the old municipal constitution of the *poleis*.

As to cosmopolitanism, though some philosophers arrived at the concept
that all men are naturally equal, that was not the normal way of thinking of
the Greeks and Macedonians who conquered the East. One proof is the fact
that Alexander's plan for fusion of Greeks with natives died with him: the
conquerors always regarded themselves as a privileged people. The Ptolemies,
for instance, according to Plutarch, were never prepared to speak the Egyptian
tongue. So Greek cosmopolitanism of the Hellenistic period must certainly
in general be understood in a different sense. Greeks of all regions had for
long been accustomed to get involved in the politics of empires, in commercial
enterprises, and in warfare (particularly as mercenary soldiers). After the conquests and colonization achieved by Alexander and his successors they found
themselves even more heavily involved, and were adopting other peoples'
ways of life, at the same time as they were feeling themselves to be 'citizens
of the world' because the whole world belonged to them. A 'cosmopolites'
for this generation simply betokened a member of the 'Greek world'. Anyone
who spoke no Greek, even if he was a subject of a Greek state, remained in
Greek eyes a 'barbarian'.

So there was no very great process of levelling between Greeks and non-
Greeks. Even the levelling among Greeks themselves was neither complete
nor real, since they were still separated into a multiplicity of autonomous
poleis. In addition the profound and subtle differences of outlook between the
various Greek areas still persisted. The Greeks of the peninsula and the West
were still a turbulent people, always in the throes of political strife and the
problems of defending their own cities: their feelings and tastes are in contrast with those of the Greek world in the great Hellenistic states, where
politics revolved round the king's government, and where the artist became
once more a part of the court, as he had been in times long past. There was
always an essential difference between Athens, where philosophers of all
schools and outlooks met and argued, and Alexandria or Pergamum, where
the scholar or scientist predominated; between Athens again, where 'New
Comedy' was born, or the Sicily which produced Theocritus, and on the other

hand Alexandria the home of libraries, where patient philologists and biblio-
philes catalogued, collated, annotated, and published the various ancient texts.

6. THE ROMAN WORLD

a. *The Republican Constitution and Social Conditions to 390 BC*

We have already spoken of the causes and history of the fall of regal power
at Rome; as well as of the earliest collegiate magistracies, a 'praetor maximus'
and a 'praetor minor' (from *prae-ire*, i.e. 'leaders'), which were supported by
lesser offices. In times of exceptional crisis power was given, for the duration
of a campaign or for six months, to a dictator, aided by a 'magister equitum'.
The fall of the foreign kings had grave results in the economic and social
fields. Hegemony over Latium, which the monarchy had been responsible for
establishing, was now lost; and agriculture deteriorated because it became
impossible to maintain the expensive drainage works built by the Etruscan
princes. The people were compressed into a narrow area of land which had
to be carved up into lots so small that starvation levels were common; both
sea-borne commerce and the transit trade across Latium were brought to a
standstill, with the result that there was a shortage of gold and also of raw
materials for the nascent industries. The patriciate, however, had formed itself
into a closed caste, and was able to assert itself. Its power came from the
possession of large landed estates and of clients attached to each individual
and family; moreover it had all the magistracies, priesthoods, law-courts, and
army commands in its own hands.

The *plebs* gradually got divided into two sections, which sometimes collaborated but at other times did not. One consisted of the richer plebeians,
often clients or retainers of the patricians; and this section wanted political
equality, that is to say parity in voting and eligibility for all offices. The other
section were the owners of inadequate plots of land, together with men who
were entirely landless and unemployed, whose claims were essentially economic and social. These two factions carried on the battle; but the first, although
they could always count on support from the second, were sometimes careless
of the interests of their allies.

The first armed secession of the *plebs* in 494 led to the creation of 'tribuni
plebis', two in number, who were private magistrates of the plebeians and took
on the protection of their order. They were declared 'sacrosanct', in that the
plebeians bound themselves with an oath to defend their inviolability with all
force at their command; and to them were added as treasurers two plebeian
'aediles' known as Ceriales. The tribunes presided at assemblies of those
plebeians who were enrolled in tribes (the later *Comitia Tributa*), and in 492
this assembly obtained allowances of corn from the government in order to
meet a famine. One of the most pressing demands, resulting from the recurrent land-hunger, was for division among the plebeians of the unnecessarily

large plots of *ager publicus* occupied by the patricians. This the patricians resisted to the death, and executed in 486 the praetor Spurius Cassius who had declared himself in favour of a redistribution.

Between 482 and 471 a new system of 'centuries' was introduced, in the effort to detach the rich plebeians sharply from the poor.[9] The population was divided into centuries, grouped by census qualifications into five 'classes', outside of which were the centuries of the 'Knights' drawn from the 'primores urbis'. The system was so arranged that in the *Comitia Centuriata* the centuries of the knights and those of the first class (in which the rich plebeians were enrolled) comprised more than half the total voting units. In reaction to this the number of tribunes was raised in 471[10] to five and in 457 to ten, the numbers corresponding to the number of classes, with each one of which, since they differed in census and in aims, a tribune or tribunes were to be linked: but this move had little result. In 456 the plebeians successfully carried a plebiscite redistributing the public land on the Aventine, with compensation for the dispossessed patricians. For many years, beginning in 462, the patricians conducted resistance to a proposal to appoint *Decemviri* to produce a written code of laws; and such a board was finally appointed in 451, all other magistracies being suspended for a year. When at the end of the year only ten tables had been drawn up it was agreed to appoint a second college for 450, this time with half its members plebeians; but after they had drafted two further tables they ran into opposition from both patricians and plebeians (for opposing reasons), and their operations were interrupted by violence. The result of this work was a set of laws befitting the archaic conditions of a people engaged in a backward type of agriculture and possessing very severe conceptions of law and morals. Yet they achieved the passage of a law preventing a capital sentence on any citizen without a judgement by the people, a principle reaffirmed in 449 by one of the laws passed by the praetors Valerius and Horatius to the effect that no magistrate could pronounce sentence of death without the possibility of 'provocatio' (appeal to the people). Another law of these praetors declared anyone who inflicted injury on a tribune or any other plebeian magistrate to be 'outside the law'.

In 445 C. Canuleius proposed to abolish the prohibition on marriages between patricians and plebeians, and after heated debate the proposal was carried. Another proposal was for the election of one patrician and one plebeian praetor every year; but decision on this was postponed until the end of the war then in progress, and in the next year (444) the election of praetors[11] was suspended. Instead their power was given to 'tribuni militum', whose numbers (3, 4, 6 or 8) varied from year to year according to the needs of the wars simultaneously being carried on against many foreign states; these were chosen for their technical abilities from among the patricians, but from the end of the century plebeians were elected too. Meanwhile, to avoid irregularities in the assessment of census qualifications, which affected enrolment of the classes and the determination of fiscal and military obligations, the patricians instituted new officials called 'censors', who had to take census every four or five years. In 421 plebeians were included among the *quaestores aerarii*, who kept the state treasury; and in 406 the military *stipendium* was fixed at a rate which allowed the poorer plebeians to provide their own arms and to avoid complete ruin in the long and frequent wars of the period.

A word may here be said about Rome's foreign relations and the methods it used to maintain the new hegemony it established in central Italy in the fifth century. After the Latin Coalition had been defeated, Rome in 493 made a defensive alliance with the Latins on terms of equality (the *foedus Cassianum*), but with the command reserved for Roman generals. This meant that Rome's conquests to south and east were common to the two parties to the alliance; and from this originated the concept of 'Latin colonies', and also the form taken by these colonies, in which the two peoples took part with equal shares. The Hernici, with whom a further *foedus* was concluded in 486, were admitted as a third party. But later, when Rome had to defend itself unaided against the Sabines and Etruscans, and then passed over to conquer Sabine and Etruscan territory, it was natural that purely Roman colonies should be founded, with settlers enrolled in Rome's 'rustic tribes'. So the new hegemony was uneven: Rome's power was absolute in Etruria and the Sabine country, but in the south it held a condominium with other peoples.

b. *Constitutional and Imperial Changes to the First Punic War*

The siege and sack of Rome by the Gauls in 390 (Roman chronology; the Greeks said 387/386) not only involved the loss of most of its army and the burning of its streets, but was followed by the revolt of many allies. These included both the Etruscan, Volscian, and Aequian towns with the colonies which held guard over them, and also many of the Latins and Hernici. These people, who had begun to be afraid of their powerful ally and were anxious to forestall the danger of being transformed into satellites, thought the sudden collapse of Rome's prestige provided a good moment for breaking away and revising their treaties. It was Rome's good fortune that a certain number of cities and colonies remained loyal, for these not only formed a defensive ring but erected barriers which broke the territorial continuity of its enemies.

So Rome took up again with vigour its work of imperialist conquest, and after half a century, about 325, it possessed, directly or indirectly, the whole of central Italy. Its dominion ran on the Tyrrhenian side from Sutri and Nepet in the north to Nuceria in the south, on the Adriatic side from the Aternus valley to northern Apulia. It was the achievement of men like L. Furius Camillus, and of the others who assisted and carried on his work, to conceive a vast new system of organization, in which all older methods of treating allies and defeated enemies, hitherto used empirically and without discrimination by the Romans, were employed together on well-defined principles. It was essential to prevent cities which had been brought into Rome's orbit from rebuilding political or military coalitions against the mother city. At the same time it was important to relate the treatment of each individual city to the services or harm it had done to Rome, and to make each realize that its legal and material position was not fixed for ever but could be changed for better or for worse, depending on the city's future behaviour. So the various forms of status were arranged like the rungs of a ladder, which one could go up but also go down. It was also desirable to interpose regions of one type between those of another, so as to encourage emulation and frustrate hostile combinations; and the Roman citizens who had been settled individually ('viritim') in conquered areas had to be given security by the foundation, alongside them, of compact colonies, which were ready to defend their neighbours and safeguard Rome's possession of the territories in question. But the most important task was to bind conquered peoples to Rome by ever stronger ties, and to enlarge the actual nucleus represented by the dominant element, in proportion to the size of its dominions. This problem Rome handled in the most liberal and humane manner possible.[12] The peoples who showed themselves most friendly and who were most akin to Rome in race were gradually admitted to full Roman citizenship; but for loyal peoples of relatively different race a new experimental method was devised, under which their autonomy was in part respected and they acquired a sort of half-citizenship. This latter method did not infringe the structure of the ruling power, which preserved full initiative in the political and military spheres. These various forms of status must now be examined in greater detail.

The first grant of Roman citizenship to an ally was that made by Camillus to Tusculum: the first settlement of Romans on conquered territory in the first sixteen *tribus rusticae* probably goes back to 495, and in 318 the twenty-seventh such tribe was formed. In these tribes there were also enrolled the inhabitants of any existing communities (such as Tusculum, Aricia, or Lanuvium) which had been granted Roman citizenship. In *tribus rusticae* which possessed no town, and in areas where the nearest town was too far away, Rome established villages where meetings, markets, and religious ceremonies could be held. These were called 'conciliabula', and to them were added 'fora' along the main roads. Both types of foundation were often the nuclei from which new towns came into being.

Along with the tribes there was a new set of colonies, both Roman and Latin. The former were originally situated inland as well as on the coasts, but in later times they were generally maritime. They were composed of Roman citizens, settled sometimes in places where a previous community had existed and sometimes on fresh sites; in return for the duties of defence undertaken by their citizens they were excused ordinary military service. These citizens, though always regarded as part of the Roman people, enjoyed some measure of autonomy; and they had their own magistrates, modelled on those of Rome, with limited functions in the administrative, financial, and judicial spheres. The name of 'Latin colony', in contrast, was given to a town formed of non-Romans, or of Romans who elected to take part in it. The latter was possible in early days, since Latin colonies enjoyed greater autonomy, and this seemed to imply a more favoured status at a time when full citizenship did not, as it did later, include a mass of advantages and privileges. The condition of these colonies, therefore, was analogous to that of the 'cives sine suffragio' mentioned below. For to the most friendly cities Rome would not send colonies but would give a reward for their services; and of these, though all were called 'municipia', some had full citizen rights and others were made 'sine suffragio', implying that their inhabitants could not vote at Rome or become Roman magistrates. They were autonomous, with their own magistrates and councils, and to a large extent their own judicial arrangements; and they had rights of *conubium* and *commercium* with Rome (*ius Latii*). It was only later that this favoured status became in practice a diminution of rights.

The peoples who remained as *socii* were bound to Rome by treaty. Some had 'foedera aequa', treaties made on the basis of equality, with defensive obligations but with the right to make peace and war on their own, although they were bound to give passage through their countries to Roman armies. The peoples in question were few in number, and were for the most part far away from Rome. Some had to provide assistance in agreed quotas, on land and sea. But most *foedera* were 'iniqua', unilateral instruments devised in Rome's interest without any attempt at equality. These allies were obliged to furnish military contingents brigaded as auxiliary troops under Roman *praefecti*; they were not allowed to make war or new alliances; and they were bound to accept Roman arbitration if they were involved in disputes. Apart from the *socii* there were peoples bound by *indutiae* or voluntary truces; and there were others standing in the general relationship of *amicitia* (friendship). The permanence of the latter relationship varied, but it normally included the obligation not to help Rome's enemies.

We now turn to the domestic reorganization which Rome underwent during this half-century. The Gallic disaster had reopened the struggle for a definition of the respective powers and functions of patricians and plebeians, with the plebeians reviving their assault on the patrician monopoly of magistracies and high offices. Their demands were from the first acceptable to enlightened patricians like Camillus, and they formed the background to the attempt at tyranny made by M. Manlius Capitolinus. After the tribunes had pressed them with fervour over a period of ten years, they at last resulted in the passage of the Leges Liciniae Sextiae in 367. These reduced debts, limited to 500 *iugera* the amount of public land which a single family could hold, and brought to an end the *imperium* of the *tribuni militum*. Once again two annual chief magistrates were appointed on the lines of the earlier praetors; but there were significant modifications, and it was now possible for plebeians to hold the office. The new magistrates, who were called 'consules', were a regular college, in which each member had equal rights with the other and could veto his colleague's action (*intercessio*); each was empowered to summon the senate or the people in order to get guidance; and both could be absent from Rome in the conduct of war, since the administration of justice in the city was entrusted to a new officer, the *praetor urbanus*. At first, it is true, the patricians by mobilizing their clients and creating riots were able to prevent any plebeian being elected for a number of years after 366. But in 356 we find the first plebeian dictator, and in 351 the first plebeian censor; and plebeians and patricians held office in alternate years as *aediles ceriales*, deputies of the consuls for policing the city, supervising markets, guarding the treasury, and so on. This drew the plebeian *aediles* into the regular state machinery, and gradually the tribunes were incorporated as one of the organizations of the state proper. They were allowed to summon the senate, and to speak and make formal proposals at its meetings; later on plebiscites ratified by the senate were recognized as equivalent to state laws.

Camillus is also credited with the reorganization of the army, in which the phalanx was replaced by the more flexible 'manipular' order of battle. This was a criss-cross formation in three lines, each provided with different types of weapon suitable to the men's age and the task they had to perform. Technical considerations instead of wealth determined a man's place in the field.

The wealthy plebeians, it is true, were concerned with obtaining equality with the patricians inside a constitution which remained an oligarchic stronghold of the rich, nobles and plebeians alike. Yet some measures were also taken to help the lower classes. In 357 the interest on loans was lowered, and in 352 debtors who had fallen into arrears were given advances from state funds. It was all too little for the people who were engaged in fighting Rome's wars for the possession of central Italy, with their own livelihood disappearing in the process. After the failure of an army rebellion designed to seize the Campanian lands a series of plebiscites were passed in the same year (326). According to Livy these laid down 'that loans at interest were prohibited, that no one could hold the same office until ten years had elapsed, that one man could not hold two magistracies in the same year, and that both consuls could be plebeians'. The same author declares that this year 'was for the Roman *plebs* like a second beginning of liberty, because imprisonment for debt was brought to an end'.

Meanwhile the progress of conquest led to constitutional change. The assembly of the people in their centuries was becoming less representative of the will of all citizens, because many of them lived far away from the city. At the same time the consuls were often out of Rome for long periods on campaigns. It was therefore inevitable that direction of public affairs should be centred on the senate, a body which was composed of the best men from all factions, chosen conscientiously by the censors, and which was in a position to ensure stability and continuity of policy. Senators were mainly drawn from the richest and most illustrious patrician and plebeian families, those which produced generals and diplomats, law-givers and administrators. Yet the hardening of tradition tended to produce a uniform type among their members, and there came into being a governing oligarchy grouped round a small number of families. This frustrated the initiative of individuals and put a curb on any move in the direction of dictatorship, but it also weakened the power of the magistrates, who were already too few in number to cope with the growth of business and the new tasks that were constantly arising.

For the increase in political problems was accompanied by new problems of an economic kind. Deforestation, with the resulting erosion of the top-soil, was changing the character of the districts nearest to Rome from arable land to pasture, and it became essential to conquer new lands for the production of cereals. At the same time bronze coinage was circulating more widely, and with it the standard of well-to-do living was rising but the poorer classes were encountering higher prices and mounting debts. This last was in part compensated by the outlets for employment opened by the revival of transit trade and of small industry.

At the turn of the fourth century the political struggle had revealed three main parties at Rome. The first, which at this time had its typical representative in Q. Fabius Maximus Rullianus, was narrowly patrician and intransigently conservative, opposing all fresh concessions to the *plebs*. The second, a moderate party represented by Appius Claudius, favoured an outright census qualification for the exercise of political and civil rights, and was therefore prepared to grant a place among the privileged classes (at this time composed in the main of landed proprietors, both patrician and plebeian) to newly rich men who had made fortunes in commerce and industry: for traditional reasons, however, religious offices were to be confined to the old nobility. The third party was composed of illustrious plebeians like Q. Decius Mus. It aimed at using the plebeians, of whatever social standing, to break the *optimates*, and was prepared to uphold the claims of the humblest among the *plebs*.

During the censorship of Appius Claudius, and during his consulship later, the social position of the poorer classes was significantly improved by their employment on the construction of the Via Appia and the Appian aqueduct. Moreover the better-to-do members of the *plebs*, who because they had no landed property had been confined to the lowest census class and were not enrolled in tribes, now secured enrolment in the tribe of their choice and in the census group which corresponded to their actual economic status in society. This enabled the state to tax them proportionately, and it was a measure particularly favourable to sons of freedmen; many of these were foreigners of good family who had served as slaves in the noblest and richest houses in Rome, and they were therefore the best-educated and most active section of the plebeians.

The aristocrats led by Rullianus, who was censor in 304, managed to limit the influence of these new citizens by confining them to the urban tribes, the argument being that such persons were essentially residents of the city. This enabled the aristocrats to preserve their freedom of manoeuvre in the use of their clients in the rural tribes. Yet it did not prevent a certain amount of new recruitment to the governing class, as we see from the career of Cn. Flavius (son of a freedman called Annius), who was successfully elected to various magistracies and became a senator in reward for his services as a *scriba* of Appius Claudius. He had drawn up a list, for all to consult, of the *dies fasti* on which justice could be obtained; and he had produced a pamphlet containing the *actiones* or procedural rules for legal suits, which had hitherto been the secret property of the pontiffs and had been employed by them as they pleased.

The power of the people and their *comitia* to limit the arbitrary decisions of magistrates went on growing, as did the penetration of the plebeians into the various offices. From 362 some of the *tribuni militum* in the legions had been appointed by popular vote: in 321 the number was raised to twelve, and in 311 to sixteen, out of the twenty-four tribunes in the four legions. In the same year, 311, the *duoviri navales* were also chosen by the people. In 300 the tribune Q. Ogulnius and his brother Gnaeus secured the opening of religious offices to the plebeian order: the colleges of pontiffs and augurs were each raised to nine members, of whom four pontiffs and five augurs were plebeians. Also in 300 a *Lex Valeria* prohibited the flogging or execution of a citizen without appeal to the people.

Yet these reforms were not enough to make the constitution democratic. It was essentially the rich plebeians—the new nobility of wealth, including men serving in the cavalry at their own expense—who secured election to military commands, wrested offices and privileges from the nobility of birth, and won support at the *comitia*. These *comitia*, because the citizen body was so scattered over territories far from Rome and because the ordinary citizen had no right to propose measures or even to speak, became increasingly less representative of the broad interests of the masses. It would be wrong to regard the last struggles between patricians and plebeians before the First Punic War as phases in a class conflict between rich and poor: such a conflict did exist, as we have shown, but it has left little definite mark on history. In reality the patricians and plebeians who were contending for power were both members of the richer classes; and the outcome was not a victory by one section over the other, but the formation of a dual power composed of the senate, where the old nobility still had the upper hand, and the *comitia*, dominated by the most powerful among the plebeian families. By and large the Roman state was now a plutocracy, whether its rich rulers were nobles or plebeians.

The poorest classes in the *plebs* were increasingly forgotten, and were left to fight their own battles. Their hardships must have reached extreme heights if despite state intervention to relieve the famine of 299 and the plagues of 295 and 293, and despite fines and other penalties imposed on usurers, the struggle broke out again with such violence that in 287 the *plebs* seceded. Q. Hortensius succeeded in placating them by securing that the senate would give its preliminary ratification to all *plebiscita*, which thus assumed the force of laws. The first plebiscite which automatically became law in this way was one in the interests of the poorer classes, cancelling certain debts and reducing others. But the future operation of Hortensius' measure mainly favoured the rich plebeians, the class which in 280 succeeded in getting the first plebeian censor elected.

The rise to power of this new nobility of wealth had its effect on the economy in general, and it contributed to the constructive effort which put Rome on the same level as the greatest powers in the Mediterranean, now that it was mistress of the Italian peninsula. One indication of this rapid development was the appearance of silver coinage from the Roman mint in 269.[13] Other effects were seen in the constitutional field, such as the growing estrangement of the chief magistrates from the senate. Now that wars were being fought over long periods at a great distance from Rome the practice was started of prolonging commands beyond the period of a year; and this made the magistrates increasingly independent of the senate, though it also enabled the senate to saddle them with the blame for any defeats. At the same time the senate was more effectively than ever becoming the motive power in the state. It was the only organ capable of exercising some continuity in policy and overcoming the consequences of the annual rotation of consuls and *praetors*. It was also the great repository of technical experience, gained through the variety of fields in which its members had commanded or otherwise operated. In the end the senate claimed the credit for every victory and every achievement, and thus enhanced both the measure and the permanence of its own prestige.

Meanwhile Rome's methods of exercising dominion were undergoing a gradual change. When in 264 the great political organism of the Roman state and its allies covered the whole peninsula from Pisa and Ariminum to the Straits of Messina, only about a quarter of this area comprised citizen territory and land directly owned by Romans, one-tenth belonged to Latins and to Latin colonies, and all the remainder (a territory three times that of the *ager Romanus*) was in the hands of 'allies'. This undoubtedly indicates an alteration in the 'ladder' system. Grants of Roman citizenship and the creation of *tribus rusticae* had been halted; Roman colonies were becoming less frequent; and there was an increase both in the amount of territory confiscated to become *ager publicus* and in the number of treaties of alliance. In part at least the change was due to three things. Different races, whose assimilation would be a slower and more difficult process, were entering the great political organization; certain peoples desired a wider measure of autonomy; and many of the newcomers lived so far from Rome that the benefits of Roman citizenship would for them have been negligible in practice. The new policy was to orientate the diverse and distant peoples of Italy upon Rome by making use of existing treaties of alliance and by breaking up the old political leagues. So began the cultural and political unity of the peninsula described in Chapter VII.

c. *The Punic Wars*

From the start of the campaign in Sicily the cities of that island which had joined Rome either voluntarily or under compulsion were made to provide regular supplies and troops for the war. They were in any case already accustomed to paying tribute to the dominant power, which before the Roman intervention was in most cases Carthage, though some cities were tributary to the Mamertines and others to Syracuse. When, therefore, both during the war and after the peace of 241, Rome made a provisional settlement of the conquered portions of the island, which were administered by one of the *quaestores classici*, it deliberately placed the cities on a lower footing and avoided any policy which might have tended to equate victors with vanquished, such as founding colonies, granting citizenship either wholesale or selectively, or employing Sicilians in the army. On the principle that cities were to be treated in a way which reflected their conduct during the war, some remained in a treaty relationship and were exempt from tribute, a second class were 'liberae et immunes', though obliged to furnish a tenth of their produce, and a third class, called 'decumanae', were made to provide the tenth free and further 'tenths' against payment. Finally, on the land confiscated from cities which had revolted, since Rome was unwilling for the present to allow Roman citizens to settle there, plots of land were relet for rent to the former owners, the cities in question being called 'censoriae'.

These arrangements could be varied in detail, and were so on many occasions. The first was in 227, when after conquering parts of Sardinia and Corsica and dividing them up into only two categories of community (*decumanae* and *censoriae*), Rome made a definitive settlement of all three islands as 'provinciae'. To the four praetors with *imperium* existing at that time (two urban and two *peregrini*) a further two were added, one for Sicily and the other for Sardinia/Corsica; and the district in which they exercised command was called a 'provincia', because that word denoted each magistrate's specific sphere of power. But the new praetors had exceptional powers in comparison with the old. They combined the military functions of a consul with the judicial functions of a praetor; they were exempt from collegiate restraint, since there was only one for each province; and they had absolute control over property and persons, there being no tribunician veto, no *intercessio*, no *provocatio*. So Rome had renounced any policy of uniting the people of the two large islands with the Italian nation. Instead of following the generous plan laid down by Camillus it was applying to its conquests outside the peninsula the methods of the Carthaginian 'eparchies'.

The long and hazardous course of the First Punic War, fought so far from home, did much to alter the lives and aspirations of Rome's subjects. For many years the armies were in contact with civilized peoples of a different culture, learning to speculate, to spend their money, to use their leisure, and to purchase possessions: all these new habits were making their characters different and more refined. The bolder among the small proprietors, when they returned to find their holdings untilled or mortgaged or sold, were not prepared to become peasants again and perhaps fall to the status of day-labourers: they embarked on a more adventurous existence as travelling *negotiatores*, or as something like pirate sailors. The great landed proprietors, for their part, once they had swallowed up these smallholdings by fore-closure or purchase and had arbitrarily taken possession of large tracts of *ager publicus*, became the owners of vast *latifundia*; and these they preferred to use for pasturage or arboriculture, employing for this purpose the slaves acquired as the result of war and piracy. Meanwhile the rich plebeians—and also such nobles as possessed liquid assets—not only found occasion to increase their stake in commerce and light industry, but also took up such occupations as piracy, money-lending, tax-farming, army services, trade in distant countries, and traffic in slaves.

The *comitia* of the people acquired unexpected importance in the course of these years. In 264, for example, in alliance with the consul Appius Claudius Caudex, they pressed for the despatch of assistance to the Mamertines; in 241 they insisted on reopening the discussion about peace terms; and similar activity can be seen later, in 223, when they allowed C. Flaminius the honour of a triumph refused him by the senate. On the other hand the selfish policy of the senate must have been in the ascendant during much of this period. Only thus can we explain Rome's failure to make extensive grants of citizen-ship to its allies, who were contributing with so much of their life-blood to its wars and conquests—and its application of so illiberal a method of govern-ment to its provinces, which became the 'praedia populi Romani'.

Even when its conquests on both sides of the Po left it, inside the peninsula itself, with very large areas of public land for disposal, the official policy was not to distribute it in individual assignments to needy citizens, but to get money for the treasury by letting it out to the native inhabitants, as had been done with the lands of *censoriae civitates* in the provinces. In 232 this policy was violently opposed by C. Flaminius Nepos, who carried a plebiscite dividing among members of the Roman *plebs* the lands south of Ariminum which had been taken from the Senones and Picentes. About fifteen years later the same Flaminius passed another plebiscite forbidding senators to possess ships larger than were needed to carry produce from their own estates, 'for all traffic by senators was regarded as unworthy'.

A new spirit is evident in Roman politics during the quarter of a century when Publius Cornelius Scipio (Africanus maior) and the senatorial faction supporting him were normally in power. It is visible in 202, when terms were dictated to Carthage after its defeat. No new provinces were created in Africa, and Scipio refused to accept the proposal of his counsellors to destroy the city of Carthage and demand the surrender of Hannibal. Instead Rome established a balance of power between the small state, which was all that was left to Carthage, and the Numidian kingdom of Masinissa, enlarged to its original dimensions, both of them recognizing the alliance and protection of Rome. So we get a return to the old ideology, an extension of supremacy through alliances with states recognizing Rome as the head. It was not only a more generous conception than that of direct rule of provincial territory (or of colonies, to use modern terms): it also avoided the military effort involved by the latter policy of holding down conquered countries by armed occupation, and it allowed former enemies the opportunity to collaborate with Rome in the cultural field and to defend their own countries from barbarians invading from remoter zones. The same policy was followed, under the leadership of Africanus and his friends, when in 196, after the defeat of Philip V, Macedonia was allowed to remain as an allied and independent state, reduced to its original position in relation to Greece, but able to fulfil its function of civilizing and perhaps even annexing the countries of the northern Balkans. The programme corollary to this was one of giving freedom to the Greeks and recognizing their freedom for the future. It is true that this was regarded by many Romans as a means of preventing the formation of great powers in the Balkan area which might challenge Rome itself, and of promoting instead the development of a large number of tiny Hellenistic states with a balance of power, all friendly and looking towards Rome. Yet Rome was in no way aiming at direct rule of a provincial kind, nor at a protectorate in which it would be automatically involved. In the minds of T. Quinctius Flamininus and his supporters it was a disinterested policy and a moral one. Moreover the same principles were applied when the Seleucid kingdom was defeated and dismembered, for here too Rome made no effort to impose direct rule.

But Africanus also showed himself conscious of other unresolved problems in the political and social organization of Rome. One was that of the citizen proletariate, who may be said to have lost their natural protectors, the tribunes of the *plebs*, from the time when the senate succeeded in attaching these officers to itself. The poverty of this proletariate was in strong contrast with the wealth of the state, and with that of the senatorial aristocracy and equestrian bourgeoisie. Africanus promoted a number of corn distributions, and dispensed land to his veterans in Spain, Sicily, Sardinia, and Africa. He also carried laws for large-scale individual assignations of land in Bruttium, Lucania, and Apulia, confiscated from allies who had revolted during the Hannibalic War; and he settled other groups of landless men in new Latin colonies, or as reinforcements to older foundations, or in a large group of new citizen colonies on the coasts of Italy. In addition he tried to meet the complaints of those richer citizens (knights and freedmen) who felt that their political status was unequal to their census qualification and that their businesses were suffering because they were not given adequate public recognition. The senate under his guidance allowed well-to-do freedmen enrolment in any tribe they chose, and granted the knights reserved places at public shows. He also gave attention to the fundamental problem of the Latins and other Italian allies. Their complaints concerned first the halt in grants of Roman citizenship to their cities and peoples; secondly, the Roman monopoly of military commands, provincial governorships, and ambassadorships; and thirdly their own inability to share in tithes, customs revenues, and other provincial taxes, or even (to any significant extent) in war-booty, which was not divided among the soldiers but went to the treasury at Rome. To these Scipio made some answer. He founded a large number of Latin colonies, into which Italian allies were admitted; he granted Roman citizenship to the inhabitants of Formiae, Fundi, and Arpinum; he allowed the Campanians to be enrolled as Roman citizens once more, a privilege they had lost in 211; and he made no resistance to the settlement in Rome of 12,000 Latin families who secured Roman citizenship thereby, nor (probably) to Latin families sharing in Roman colonies.

d. The Age of Cato

The appearance in politics of a strong individual line like that of Africanus was repugnant to the rigid senatorial oligarchy and to its interests. His philhellenism and his idea of achieving a Roman empire by means of alliances and by a synthesis between the Italians and other Mediterranean peoples appeared a mistaken view of politics both to these oligarchs and to 'new men' like Cato[14] who had been incorporated into the oligarchy and became its most intransigent defenders. To such men the 'Graeculi' of that day were the people really responsible for the moral decline of their Roman imitators, being the prototypes of 'levitas', with all manner of vices elegantly blended in their characters. The Scipionic policy seemed to sacrifice all the permanent advantages which Rome's victories might have secured for the state and for its business classes. Lastly, the oligarchs were not willing to allow one family group among them to become dominant, and for the individual at the head of this group to be regarded as a man out of the ordinary, an arbiter who imposed his own judgement on the rest. The method adopted to bring about Scipio's fall was the same as that employed against Pericles at Athens. First they accused his most loyal supporters, and then his own brother Lucius, of various irregularities; finally in 184 their great opponent left Rome in anger and retired to one of his villas.

In the next decades a number of factions contended for power and carried on the broad process of constitutional development. They were personal and family groupings without settled programmes, subject to sudden changes of direction in the course of their temporary alliances and arbitrary blends of policy. In broad terms there were three main groups, the Scipionians, the Catonians, and a middle party, though each was constantly evolving. But the real embodiment of this period was Cato, and it was he who was most responsible for everything that followed. His influence on events was especially felt in the early and most decisive years, namely the decade 180–170, but it continued right down to his death in 149.

Cato made no real effort to solve any of the problems which had confronted Africanus. He was concerned only to undo Africanus' work, even though this might make some of the problems more serious than before. He punished with great severity several thousand people for being members of religious conventicles where the Bacchanalia were celebrated, on the ground that they were conspiring against the state; and he brought to trial and execution another unfortunate group of persons who were accused of causing a plague by spreading poison. He thought he could improve the people's morals by doubling the taxes on luxury goods. Moreover he purged the senate, removing from it seven of his political opponents, and excluded from the equestrian order anyone who was prevented by physical disabilities from riding a horse. Yet at the same time he was using gangs of slaves to till his estates and was calling attention to the value of slave labour in his writings, as if there were no hosts of unemployed free men. In addition he opposed every grant of citizenship to the allies.

This period saw the beginnings of the harsh imperialism which drove the provinces to their first revolts, put down with bloodshed. The new set of allies were treated without any consideration, in the firm conviction that it was far more convenient and more profitable for the state and its ruling oligarchy to reduce them to the status of provinces.

To achieve greater stability and loyalty among the new allies Africanus had arranged to give power inside republican states to oligarchic factions, and had seen to it that in monarchies the rulers should be men on whose pro-Roman outlook one could rely, because they had lived at Rome and been in contact with the more powerful families there. But putting this system into practice required statesmanship of the kind Roman politicians neither possessed nor desired. It meant avoiding entanglement in an endless series of crises, each more violent than the last, in the course of the struggles between the pro-Roman oligarchs and their democratic opponents, the latter always ready to give support to anti-Roman powers. It meant taking care to see that kings, like Masinissa and Eumenes II, could not indulge their dreams of expansion in a way which upset the balance of power desired by Rome. It was also essential to keep an eye on each dynasty at the moment of a succession, since a new ruler might bring great changes.

A fresh Macedonian war broke out when King Perseus gave support to the democratic movements and popularist factions in Greece. After he had been finally defeated at Pydna, his conqueror, L. Aemilius Paullus, in the consequent settlement of the country, was made to apply a principle which derived from a compromise between the parties in the senate. The monarchy in Macedonia and Illyria was brought to an end, and the two countries were dismembered politically and economically. Cato's ideas were put into effect in that a *vectigal* was imposed as if the territories were being annexed; but Rome avoided the responsibility and burden of provincial occupation, and the military and administrative duties this would have implied. In this way

Macedonia was divided into four republics, with an absurd prohibition on intermarriage and the purchase and sale of land between members of one republic and another: trade in salt and shipbuilding materials was also forbidden. The inhabitants of Illyria too were divided into tributary and nontributary states, the former being further subdivided into three distinct groups. In the Greek districts, loyal allies received additions of land, but the territories of the remainder were still further reduced by the formation of small autonomous states between them and their neighbours. The Achaean League was compelled to send a number of suspect persons to Rome as hostages. Finally, fierce reprisals were taken in Epirus, where many cities were sacked and razed, the inhabitants being reduced to slavery.

The war had also had repercussions in Asia, and the consequent measures taken by Rome reveal the same harsh spirit of imperialism. Rhodes and Pergamum were deprived of territory, while Rome gave help to states wanting to attack them: and humiliations were heaped on them, as when Eumenes II at Sardis was compelled to hear his enemies accuse him of every sort of crime in the presence of a Roman legate.

For about 25 years (180–155) this imperialist policy could still be checked, and sometimes reversed, at the hands of Africanus' party and the moderates. But the latter were tending to concern themselves more with detail than with major changes of principle; and after the death of Ti. Sempronius Gracchus, who had been the most energetic supporter of pacification, the younger generation, accustomed now to elegant living, but freed from all inhibitions, found a very young leader in P. Cornelius Scipio Aemilianus. These new Romans, used to the bowing and presents, the prayers and laments, of Greek and Eastern kings and ambassadors, suddenly found themselves heavily engaged with peoples who were ready to defend their liberties at any cost and any sacrifice. This unexpected revival of enemy opposition, which the Romans quite underrated, was the more wounding to their pride in that each new war began with severe and bloody defeats of their legions; and it was undoubtedly one of the main reasons for the violent action now taken by Roman generals. More than at any other time in Rome's history they showed an absence of all humanity in putting down revolts, making use in their diplomacy of the kind of trickery and perfidy which is all too often shown by conquerors conscious of their overwhelming power and of their destiny to rule.

The most important results of this imperialism are too well known to require attention here. In 148/7 Macedonia was unified territorially again but reduced to provincial status, being obliged to pay tribute and furnish mineral and agricultural supplies to Rome. In 146 Greece saw its great port and industrial city of Corinth—an object of jealousy to Roman business men and a centre of democratic influences—sacked and completely destroyed, the population being sold as slaves and the territory made into *ager publicus*. Other Greek cities received various forms of treatment related to their behaviour during the 'Achaean War'. Some districts were attached to the

province of Macedonia; several cities became tributary with oligarchic constitutions and a ban on the reconstitution of the leagues Rome had dissolved;
others were made 'liberae et immunes' with various types of treaty, of which
that with Athens was the only one on terms of equality.

The same thing happened in Africa. Rome had failed to give Carthage
proper protection against the growing claims of Masinissa, and Cato carried
on his obstinate campaign against the danger of a supposed Punic revival.
After a heroic defence the city was taken and destroyed, amid scenes of
barbaric massacre and rapine; and curses were pronounced over its area
against anyone who should try to inhabit it again. Its territory, up to the 'fossa
regia', became a province.

But the growing severity of Roman imperial methods had its most tragic
results in the older provinces. We must briefly recount what happened in
Spain and Sicily. When Scipio (later Africanus) relinquished his command
in Spain, having completed the work of his father and uncle, the two provinces established in the country were given a 'ladder system' with communities of different status like those in Sicily and Sardinia (*civitates foederatae*,
liberae, and *stipendiariae*, together with Roman domains). In general, however,
conditions were more generous than those in Sicily, mainly because the number of cities in the more privileged categories was quite high. There were also
already several *vici* in Spain inhabited by Italians, which like Roman colonies
were available to Romanize the country and to raise its communities gradually
to the upper rungs of the 'ladder' on the Italian model. A further point was
that Scipio had intended Roman commands in Spain to be held for long terms,
in order to promote friendly relations with a native population which was
proud and devoted to its liberties. But the senate in fear of providing opportunity for a possible dictator adopted the system of annual commands, and
also reduced the occupation troops below the level of safety. So the changing
policies of governors, the conflict between the desire for expansion and the
small forces available to effect it, and the lack of contact between rulers and
ruled, all led to discontent and rebellion. The first revolts were largely quelled
in 179 by the wise action of Ti. Sempronius Gracchus, who bound the population by treaties so clear that future governors could not misinterpret them,
and also distributed presents and land in generous measure to the poorer
classes, to the extent of founding mixed towns of Romans, Italians, and
Iberians. After his day peace lasted for a quarter of a century, but then increased severity led to further revolts. In vain M. Claudius Marcellus laboured
to restore order: in 151 the despatch of L. Licinius Lucullus, with the young
Scipio Aemilianus as his assistant, signified the whole-hearted application of
Rome's methods of terror and exploitation. So the war with Viriathus blazed
into fury, ending with the terrible punitive expedition into Lusitania and
neighbouring areas in 138/7; and after heroic resistance Numantia capitulated
at discretion to Aemilianus in 133, any inhabitants who had not committed
suicide being sold as slaves, and the town like others being razed to the ground.

Its policy of imperialism undoubtedly gave Rome the direct rule of most of the world, but in the end it provoked, in Italy as well as outside it, the series of crises which mark the closing period of Republican history.

e. *Political and Social Problems under the Gracchans*[15]

The ease with which slaves could be acquired at low prices in the period of conquests, and the small cost of their upkeep, led the owners of *latifundia* and of medium-sized estates to prefer slave to free labour. On the other hand the unbearable conditions of slavery caused its unfortunate victims, especially those who were born free, to dream of liberty and plan revenge. They were regarded purely as tools, and were the property of their masters, who had rights of life and death over them and who could exercise any form of cruelty without intervention by the law: and a master was entitled to compensation if a third party did harm to his slaves. In general they were treated brutally, packed into *ergastula* in chains, branded like beasts, fed on inadequate food of the cheapest kind, and kept half-naked. When they became old or infirm they were sold again. Beaten almost to death, they were made savage by seeing the rich and luxurious lives of their masters, whose avarice made them shut their eyes when slaves provided themselves with food and clothing by robbing another's property. Many of these slaves remembered being free and even powerful, but they despaired of acquiring the *peculium* needed to redeem their liberty. Yet when herded together in gangs they became conscious of their power, and as the only tillers of the soil they knew what advantages their masters derived from their labour. In the harshest periods of imperialism there must have been constant revolts here and there, although our sources allude to them rarely and then only in the briefest terms. At the beginning of the second century we hear of a revolt at Setia in 198, another in Etruria in 196, and a third in Apulia in 185. In 139 the praetor P. Popillius Laenas had to attend to trouble of this kind, and between 142 and 138 some revolted slaves on estates in Bruttium carried out a series of murders. All the time that Roman forces were kept occupied by the great revolt in Sicily, from 136 to 132, there were lesser risings in Rome itself, and at Minturnae, Sinuessa, in the mines of Attica, and at Delos; and in Asia Aristonicus used rebel slaves to lay waste the country far and wide.

In these convulsive outbreaks against land-owners the slaves often found natural allies in other outcasts of society, who, although they too were victims of the *latifondisti*, might well have been regarded as enemies of the slaves. These were the small countrymen, now landless, men whose estates had been swallowed up by the *latifundia*: the slaves were the principal obstacle to their leading at least the life of wage-earners on the land, and were therefore looked on as the ill-omened instrument by which *latifundia* were further developed. Yet a common misery and despair united slaves and rural proletariate in their resistance; and they must often have supported one another in the way we find them operating together later in the Servile Wars in Sicily and in

Spartacus' rebellion.[16] In this way a social rising against the rich took on also an anti-Roman political aspect, its authors regarding the Roman conquerors as responsible for all their misfortunes.

The *Lex Rupilia* of 131, passed after the bloody and ruinous First Servile War, attempted to put Sicily on a new footing. The *latifundia* were to be broken up, new lands were to be brought under cereal cultivation, the volume of slaves was to be reduced, and limits were to be set to the numbers of landless men. Lastly the natives were to be granted a measure of autonomy, especially in judicial matters, in order to allay the hostility towards Rome. The effects of the more enduring portion of Ti. Sempronius Gracchus' work were already being felt, even though it was in the very year of his legislation that he fell— a victim to his own mission.

The first step taken by Tiberius was in the field of agrarian reform. His bill as first drafted aimed at the re-enactment of an ancient limitation (never abrogated) on the amount of *ager publicus* which could be occupied by an individual, and at the recovery, and subsequent distribution to the needy, of amounts occupied illegally or in excess of the quota. Generous provisions were offered in addition: for example, amounts over and above the 500 *iugera* could be claimed in respect of grown-up sons, compensation was given to ex-owners for any improvements they had carried out, and occupied land once reduced to its proper dimensions was to be held in full ownership. The proposal could not, of course, be agreeable to the diehards: they lost property thereby, and part of the proletariate on which they counted for their electoral manoeuvres would disappear from the city. But in its essence the reform, which benefited Italian allies as well as Roman citizens,[17] might have been carried out (as indeed it was, even after Tiberius' death) without any violent convulsions, if the *optimates*, relying on the distortion which had taken place in the tribunate's function, had not obtained another tribune, M. Octavius, to interpose his veto. Tiberius reacted by having Octavius deposed by the *comitia* and another tribune elected in his place. He was accused of violating the sanctity of tribunes and of aiming at tyranny; the attacks grew in strength, and eventually led to his destruction, when he presented himself for re-election to the tribunate in the following year with an enlarged programme of a frankly political kind. In the debate about the use of the property and land left to Rome by Attalus III of Pergamum, Tiberius proposed that the decision should be taken by the people, thus reclaiming for the people and the magistrates functions which the senate had usurped. He furthermore intended to propose an extension of *provocatio* and the introduction of knights to the jury-courts. In this crisis the senators established an entirely illegal procedure, used by them on many occasions later to get rid of an opponent without recourse to regular trial. Tiberius was declared a public enemy ('hostis'), and the senate constituted itself a court-martial which pronounced the 'senatus consultum ultimum'.

The second Gracchus, Gaius, had started with a political plan designed to give himself the support of a coalition containing other malcontents, namely the knights and the Italian allies, besides the urban *plebs*. In 125 his ally, the consul M. Fulvius Flaccus, proposed a law to grant citizenship to the Latins and allies: though rejected by the senate this provoked lively agitation among the Italians, and an increase in the numbers of *peregrini* registered in the census had to be allowed. After securing a law permitting tribunes of the people to be re-elected, he was himself elected tribune for the first time for 123. His legislation opened with two plebiscites, one excluding any deposed magistrate from holding office during the remainder of his life, the other prohibiting condemnation without appeal to the people. Then he went on to a number of *leges*. One was a *Lex Agraria*, restoring full powers to the triumviral commission, which now resumed the recovery and assignation of *ager publicus*. Then there was a *Lex Frumentaria* for the benefit of the urban *plebs*, and thirdly a *Lex de Comitiis* governing the drawing of lots to decide which centuries should vote first. For the equestrian class he secured reserved seats at theatre performances, compensation for *publicani* who failed to gather the tribute which the state had farmed to them against advance payments, and the reorganization of provincial statutes (*Leges de provinciis*) in a manner which suited equestrian interests, with the addition of a *Lex de Asia*. Meanwhile Gaius opposed the cession of Phrygia to Pontus, and supported the extension of Roman conquests in Gaul in order to increase the areas in which Roman businessmen could operate. Gaius was then re-elected for 122, and proceeded, at the expense of the senate, to secure the passage of a *Lex Iudiciaria* putting knights as well as senators on the courts for cases of extortion (*quaestiones repetundarum*); a number of less important laws were also passed about these courts. At the same time he caused a colleague to propose a law for the foundation of colonies overseas, on provincial soil, starting with one called Iunonia at Carthage; other colonies were founded at Tarentum and Capua, and Gracchus constructed roads, warehouses, and markets. But while he was in Africa attending to the foundation of Iunonia, the *optimates* counter-attacked by denouncing him as sacrilegious for including in his new colony lands which Scipio Aemilianus had placed under a curse. They also tried to deprive Gaius of his support from the Italian allies by causing the tribune M. Livius Drusus (the Elder) to propose laws in the allied interest. Meanwhile the knights, who had got what they wanted from Gaius, were already tending to make common cause with their old opponents.

Gaius met this attack by attempting to prove that there was no sacrilege, and also by proposing Roman citizenship for the Latins and Latin franchise for the Italians. But his opponents convinced the urban *plebs*, and the citizen body in general, that they would suffer greatly from the passage of such a bill. In the outcome Gaius was not re-elected tribune for 121, and the consul L. Opimius proposed the abrogation of all Gracchan laws. Gaius now surrounded himself with armed bands, and could not prevent one of his opponents from being killed during a public meeting: the result was the passage of the *senatus consultum ultimum* against him, his own death, and the execution of 3,000 of his followers. So the Gracchan reforms perished in bloodshed. Yet the grave problems his legislation had been designed to solve—the problems of the proletariate, the allies, the provincials, and the slaves—remained wide open, and the danger was great.

f. *The Democratic Revival*

The quarrel between the two sections of the governing class, senate and knights, broke out again on many occasions, though it would then be composed when the interests of the two bodies coincided once more. The most characteristic instance of the process began in 111, when war was declared on Jugurtha to punish him for the massacre of Italians who had contributed to the defence of Cirta; and it was necessary to put the economy on an emergency footing. One expression of this moment of concord was a new *Lex Agraria*, bringing together all earlier provisions, and attempting to reconcile divergent interests by arranging for the sale of the remaining *ager publicus* to any bidder. This closed the agrarian question for the time being. But the Jugurthine war revived the quarrel between knights and senate in an even more venomous form. The former wanted to conquer tracts of Numidia in order to enlarge the field for business interests, while the *nobilitas* were accused by their opponents of carrying on the war too half-heartedly because Jugurtha had bribed them. The friction grew gradually more serious, and it was then successfully exploited by the plebeian C. Marius, legate of the victorious new general Q. Caecilius Metellus (later Numidicus). Marius claimed the successes won as his own, attacked Metellus for not having allowed him leave to return to Rome at the proper time to present his candidature for the consulship, and then, with support from the knights and the people, obtained both the consulate for 107 and the command in the war, which was still not decided. In the ensuing action Marius found an able and impartial collaborator, especially in diplomatic matters, in a noble called L. Cornelius Sulla (later Felix), who was his quaestor; and the war ended with the capture of Jugurtha and the partition of Numidia, on the Scipionic model, into two states allied to Rome, a solution avoiding any increase in Rome's military burdens. But in the course of the war Marius began to use a new recruiting system of his own devising, which allowed proletarians to volunteer and receive pay. This absorbed practically the whole force of landless men of military age, and was therefore a long step in the direction of solving that particular social problem; it also made possible the creation of a standing army, with well-trained and competent soldiers serving for long terms. The new army admittedly tended to attach itself to those of its generals who had won most glory and who offered them the best prospects, rather than carrying out policies which were best in the interests of the state. It therefore provided a foundation for the gradual growth in extraordinary commands by dictators and commanders (*imperatores*).

The Jugurthine war was hardly over when Marius, after winning a second consulate for 104, obtained the command against the Cimbri, Teutones, and Ambrones. In the years 104–101 he defeated these tribes several times and annihilated their main forces, securing in the process new areas for commercial development and enormous hordes of slaves for the landed proprietors. Meanwhile his association with Appuleius Saturninus, tribune in 103, helped him to renew his consulates year after year and to secure lands for his veterans.

But the military effort required to meet the barbarians had brought internal stresses which complicated a situation already acute. Recruiting needs had led the government to order the manumission of all slaves who had once been free allies; and this brought a flood of requests from slaves and also protests from such land-owners as were affected. So in some areas the order was not carried out; and there followed slave revolts at Nuceria, Capua, and above all in Sicily, where Rome had to face a regular war (the second Servile War, 104–101). After it was over the victorious commander M'. Aquillius took care to break up the *latifundia* and to transform landless men into peasant proprietors, an operation which led to the prosperity and high levels of agricultural production found by C. Verres during his governorship of the island in 73–71. At the same time as the Servile War there was a campaign against the pirates, whose refuges were mainly in Crete and Cilicia; and this resulted in the formation of two new provincial areas, Cilicia and Pamphylia.

Meanwhile Marius, as we have said, had since 103 been in alliance with that year's tribune Appuleius Saturninus, enabling the latter to launch a large-scale attack on the senate and to lay before the people a programme of laws in this sense: an example is his *Lex de Maiestate*, a regular Sword of Damocles hanging over the head of every Roman citizen in that it punished with death anyone who had offended the majesty of the Roman people. Another law, proposed by the tribune Atinius, gave tribunes the right of proposing *sententiae* in the senate, and consequently of sitting in that body. Saturninus was now allied with C. Servilius Glaucia, who some years earlier had carried as tribune a *Lex Servilia Repetundarum*. Their combined authority was such that even when Saturninus was a private citizen in 102 the censor Q. Caecilius Metellus Numidicus could not expel them from the senate against the opposition of his censorial colleague, who was afraid of the people's reaction. In the next year (100) Saturninus secured another tribunate, while Glaucia obtained the praetorship and Marius his sixth consulate. This enabled Marius to carry the provisions he needed to reward his veterans. One such provision he simply assumed arbitrarily, when he granted Roman citizenship to 1,000 veterans from Camerinum for their services in the field. A plebiscite put forward by Saturninus was opposed not only by certain senators (despite the fact that any who did not swear to observe its provisions were threatened with expulsion from the senate and a fine), but also by many of the people, who maintained that only the allies would benefit from it. Nevertheless he obtained the required majority for it by bringing to Rome a mass of country voters in the rural tribes, who did not refrain from violence. The bill gave Marius' veterans lands in Sicily, Achaea, Macedonia, Corsica (where there was a 'Colonia Mariana'), and in the Po valley where the Cimbri had been defeated and where the Latin colony of Eporedia was now founded. Money was voted for the recovery and purchase of the land; and Marius was allowed to create a given number of Roman citizens in each colony.

But the price Marius had to pay for this assistance was dear. He was asked to support Saturninus' candidature for a third tribunate in 99 and Glaucia's candidature for a consulate in the same year. At the consular elections the popular party murdered an opponent of Glaucia, after which Saturninus and Glaucia together with the voters from the rural tribes occupied the Capitol. The senate passed the *senatus consultum ultimum*, calling on the consuls, of whom Marius was one, to take appropriate measures. The position of Marius was very delicate: he disapproved of the illegalities and violence of his supporters, but he wanted them to be brought to book by legal means and not by the procedure involved in the *senatus consultum ultimum*, which was no less violent and illegal than their own behaviour, and which would make him appear to be the executioner of his own friends. While he was seeking a way to gain time, the opposing party shut Saturninus and his supporters into the senate house and there put them to death. So Marius became a scapegoat, attacked no less by the popular party than by the patricians. He had been a great soldier, but he was not born for politics and was quickly ruined when he tried to engage in them. For the time being he went into retirement, leaving the city for a 'legatio libera' in Galatia.

After the popular leaders had been killed and Marius had retired into private life outside Rome, the immediate step taken by the senate was to invalidate Saturninus' laws, including that assigning lands to Marius' veterans. A strict control was imposed on the behaviour of the knights in the provinces, and the creation of new provinces, which would have favoured equestrian interests, was avoided: for instance no action was taken to annex Cyrenaica, left to Rome by Ptolemy Apion. New restrictions were placed on the grant of citizenship to the Latins and Italians, and those whose claims were doubtful were excluded by a law of 95.

Then in 91 came an important event, namely the attempt of the tribune M. Livius Drusus (the Younger) to achieve reform not through the victory of a single party but by agreement among all interested classes to bring about a general improvement in conditions. The government and the jury-courts in extortion cases were once more to be in the hands of senators only, but in return the senate would at one blow admit into its own ranks the best among the *equites*. They would also surrender all *ager publicus* occupied in excess of the legal amounts so as to ensure a livelihood, in Italy as well as overseas, to the mass of proletarians who could be made smallholders once more. Drusus thought it right that the most deserving and honourable of the knights should become senators and share in the government and the courts, but they in turn would have to sever their duties and aims from those of the businessmen. The landless citizens had little chance, during the period of peace through which Rome was passing, of finding a solution to their economic problems through recruitment in the army; and Drusus maintained that they should be given immediate relief by distributions of food, and more permanent support by land assignations. Their contribution to the settlement must be to give up their opposition to the grant of citizenship to the Italian allies, who were all the time giving their lives for Rome in the field, but whose franchise rights, recognized as early as Camillus' day, had been disputed and whittled down over two centuries. On the other hand the richer Italians would have to resign themselves to surrendering excessive and illegally held portions of *ager publicus*, in order to solve the proletarian problem. To carry this plan into effect Drusus proposed all the necessary laws and other provisions. Naturally every class showed itself ready to take what favoured its interests, but each rejected what it was asked to concede. The diehard senators and the equestrian class as a whole, together with their respective clients among the *plebs*, broke with Drusus, and suspected him of aiming at tyranny. In the autumn of 91 he was attacked by the consul L. Marcius Philippus and defended by the orator L. Licinius Crassus: subsequently, on the pretext of unfavourable auspices, his laws were annulled. After he had retired to his house he was assassinated by an unknown hand, and the senate instituted no inquiry.

Drusus naturally had close relations with the Italians, but it is certainly false to accuse him of responsibility for the Social War that followed. War had been preparing for a long time, and it was not his proposals but their abrogation which clearly provided the occasion. There followed, even during the war, a number of other measures against anyone who favoured allied claims; and children of unions between Romans and Italians were to be made in all circumstances non-Roman. But already during the year 90 the senate, with a furious conflict on its hands, began to revise its attitude. First they passed a *Lex Calpurnia* which enabled citizenship, in two new tribes, to be given to deserving veterans and soldiers in the field; we know that Cn. Pompeius Strabo made use of this law to give Roman citizenship to thirty Spanish cavalrymen. A block grant of citizenship was then made to the people of Tuder; and finally by a *Lex Iulia* the number of tribes in which loyal Italian allies or deserving soldiers could be enrolled was increased to ten. In 89 Pompeius Strabo gave Latin rights to the Transpadani; and then laws under the names Plautia Papiria gave citizenship to the Cispadani between the Rubicon and the Cottian Alps, and to all Italians south of the Rubicon who had remained loyal and 'who made a request for the grant within sixty days'. (Pl. 23, a.) The Italians were defeated in the field but were in fact victorious, for they had obtained what they sought. Yet the war had cost 300,000 lives, and the army emerged from it disorganized and disordered. In consequence new agrarian measures became necessary, as well as action of a financial kind, such as a reduction in the weight of the *as*.

The new citizens, however, were relegated to the last tribes, which in practice were never called on to vote. P. Sulpicius Rufus now passed a bill distributing them among all the tribes, and this enabled him to bring a mass of new citizens back to Rome and persuade them to vote, amid scenes of violence, for another bill transferring the command of the Mithradatic War from Sulla (to whom it had originally been assigned) to Marius. There followed Sulla's march on Rome and Marius' flight to Carthage; he and eleven of his supporters were declared *hostes*, and arrangements of a summary kind were made to restore the constitution. Sulpicius' measures were rescinded, and with them the provision that plebiscites must be given automatic approval by the senate in advance. The *comitia tributa* lost all importance, their function passing to the *comitia centuriata*. It was agreed to introduce 300 knights into the senate, to diminish the power of the tribunes, and to grant a remission of debts.

As consuls for 87 Sulla left at home two men whom he hoped would prove evenly balanced, the moderate optimate Cn. Octavius and the anti-senatorial L. Cornelius Cinna. But they quickly moved in opposite directions, Cinna carrying on the work of Sulpicius and preparing the way for the return of Marius with support from the new citizens, Octavius defending the rights of the senate with support from the original citizens and from certain tribunes. Cinna, who wanted Sulla to be put on trial for condemning the Marians without allowing them *provocatio*, was expelled from the city. But forming a coalition of new citizens, townsmen in Latium, and the garrison troops in Campania, he joined the returning Marians, and with these forces captured Rome. Diodorus says that when they became masters of the city Marius and Cinna, with their supporters, decided to put their enemies to death so that their own rule could be peaceful. So began vendettas and purges; homes were ruined, and men put to death without trial; revolutionary courts were indeed held, but with the inevitable accompaniment of delation and inquisition. Sulla's laws were abrogated, his houses were destroyed, and the senate was made to declare him a *hostis* along with such followers of his as were still alive. Companies of freed slaves committed such outrages that it was found necessary to massacre them. For the next year (86) Marius and Cinna were consuls, but within a few days Marius died and so Cinna was in effect left master of Rome, to nominate himself consul for both 85 and 84. But he revealed no complete or rational plan. Revenge continued, and the support of the knights and people was canvassed by the repeal of certain laws. Monetary measures were passed of a type which, in Sallust's words, mean that 'copper was paid out instead of silver'. Cinna was then stoned to death by his soldiers in their refusal to embark on an expedition against Sulla.

Sulla now returned victorious from the East, defeated the Marians, and entered Rome with the city's destinies in his control. His first act was a wholesale massacre of the conquered soldiers together with the proscription (in an initial list) of 40 senators and 1,600 knights. Then, on the proposal of the *princeps senatus*, L. Valerius Flaccus, he was nominated dictator 'for as long as he wished'. This was not the type of dictatorship which had fallen into dis-use at the end of the Second Punic War, nor was it modelled on Greek tyran-nies or Hellenistic monarchies. It looked back to the ancient Roman concept of elective kings, and specifically to the example of Servius Tullius, who according to tradition had actually given Rome the idea of a republic and had later expressed his intention of abdicating. Moreover Sulla's momentary evocation of that monarchy establishes a logical connection between it and the later conception of the *imperator*, no matter what political formula was used to justify a Roman emperor's rule.

The senate, which had now become the preserve of a few dozen families, both patrician and plebeian, and which in fact consisted of only about a hundred members,[18] was to be made the central guiding force in the state, providing the supreme courts of justice and controlling all legislation. But it was radically overhauled. Five hundred knights from the army and the professions (but excluding businessmen) were admitted, and its members were ensured for the future by granting membership not only to persons elected to the higher magistracies, but also to ex-quaestors. Having thus secured a permanent place in the senate for 'the better' among the Equites, Sulla showed no favour to the greedy class of speculators who formed the main body of the equestrian order. He put a stop to their excesses in the collection of tribute, excluded them from serving on the courts, and forbade them to exercise privilege betokening their dignity. The lot of the people Sulla tried to improve, not by expensive and degrading distributions of corn, but by giving employment on great public works, by fixing maximum prices, by reducing debts and regulating interest rates, and finally by granting land to 120,000 veterans. He also allowed the people the satisfaction of electing the consuls, but he put an end to the distortion of the tribunician power. The tribunes lost their rights of veto, their position in the *cursus honorum*, and the powers of summoning the senate or of presenting proposals to the people which had not received prior senatorial approval. They became simply defenders and patrons of the people, and in this way Sulla frustrated any attempt to establish dual control by his new senate and by the people.

From the allies who had newly become citizens he took away neither their citizenship nor their voting rights. But he was harsh in his treatment of any who had assisted the Marians, their lands being confiscated for distribution to his veterans along with such *ager publicus* as was available to him from other sources. He increased the number of magistrates, the quaestors from eight to twenty and the praetors from six to eight; but he raised the minimum age for holding each post, and set an interval of ten years before a man could hold a second consulate.[19] He also suppressed the censorship; but his major measure in this field was a *Lex Cornelia de provinciis ordinandis* which firmly distinguished the purely civil powers of consuls and praetors during their year of office in Italy from the military commands they were to hold outside Italy as proconsuls or pro-praetors in the ensuing year.[20]

Finally, he attempted by a large range of laws to check the moral and political corruption he was convinced was affecting the life of his day. These laws were severe and detailed, amounting to a complete revision of the criminal code. Sulla also avoided military operations abroad as far as possible, kept a check on any of his supporters who might subvert the constitution, and carried out important public works. Then, without transmitting his power to any successor, he voluntarily abdicated (February, 79, is a likely date), and retired into private life.[21]

g. *Caesar's Consulate—the Ascendancy of Pompey*

Sulla's retirement left his constitution at the mercy of events, and of party struggles and individual ambitions. The first signs of a breakdown came when Cn. Pompeius Magnus, now in alliance with the powerful family of the Metelli, secured a triumph which Sulla had refused him. The Metelli were among the supporters of Sextus Roscius, falsely accused by Sulla's treacherous freedman Chrysogonus and defended by the young M. Tullius Cicero, whose success was a signal event.

Of the two consuls for 79 Q. Lutatius Catulus was a Sullan and a friend of the senate: the other, M. Aemilius Lepidus, was a Marian who had crossed to Sulla but had then resumed his old allegiance. Lepidus went round haranguing the mob with promises to recall the proscribed and to wrest land away from the veterans in order to give it back to the dispossessed owners. Naturally the latter were induced to revolt, and trouble broke out on the land at Faesulae. Lepidus, his consulate now over, united the rebels together with certain scattered leaders of the Marian party, and sent an ultimatum to the senate. That body at last decided on resistance, declared Lepidus a *hostis*, and pronounced the *senatus consultum ultimum* against him. They found it a simple matter to tear up the Sullan constitution and give the young Pompeius an extraordinary *imperium* in Italy. The defeated rebels crossed to Sardinia, where Lepidus died: then under the command of Perperna they passed on into Spain to join hands with another Marian who had established himself there, namely Q. Sertorius.

By making a treaty with the continually rebellious Lusitani and then extending his activities to Celtiberia and the Nearer province, Sertorius had built in Spain a fortress for the Marian movement, with an organization which followed in the footsteps of the elder Scipio Africanus, Ti. Sempronius Gracchus, and M. Claudius Marcellus. His halo of greatness, fearlessness, and moderation brought him the support of the 'sacred societies', and he was able to organize, on the Roman model, a powerful army of natives with Italian commanders and subordinate officers. Among the natives, whom he governed through Italian magistrates, he spread the conception of democracy, aiming at the voluntary Romanization of the entire population in a single whole with the Italian settlers, with both groups on the same political and social level. This could be made to serve as the fulcrum of a new organization in the Roman world, taking the place of the plutocracy which was in persistent charge of Rome. The Italian nucleus was now reinforced by the arrival of Perperna's forces, and Sertorius created a senate to advise the magistrates, and not a degenerate body like the senate at Rome. At the same time, in order to prepare the native chiefs for their new role he opened a school of Graeco-Latin culture for them at Osca (Huesca). Pompeius Magnus was now sent against him with exceptional proconsular power, but with scanty means. By threats and other forms of pressure he obtained from Rome the necessary reinforcements, and Sertorian resistance was broken by military attack, promises of an amnesty, and Perperna's treachery, the last leading to Sertorius' murder. Sertorius' organization collapsed, but his work endured: in Caesar's words 'Pompey reaped what Sertorius had sown'. Pompey continued the measures of relief in Spain and its Romanization, with a charter of freedom to Osca, the foundation of Pompaelo, grants of citizenship to loyalists, and many other measures. To this was due the loyalty of the country and its rapid adoption of Roman ways.

Meanwhile at Rome, despite the trouble-making of individual politicians, there was a gradual movement towards conciliation, aiming at restoring the tribunician powers removed by Sulla. The recent entry of 500 knights to the senate had made its policy less rigid; and it was also felt that by making the tribunate once more a step in the *cursus honorum* one could prevent any excessive combination between the tribunes and the poorer sections of the *plebs*. Moreover by now everyone was conscious of the losses Rome was incurring, and the grave peril it was in, from the continuance of political and social struggles. Of the latter there was now an example in the rising of Spartacus. Although this was not supported by slaves from the towns, the rural proletariate (especially that resulting from Sulla's confiscations) broke into revolt at the same time and made common cause with the rebellious slaves.[22] Italy had to suffer a devastating war, which lasted three years (73–71) before it was put down by M. Licinius Crassus.

But at the last moment Crassus found part of his credit snatched from him by the arrival from Spain of the victorious Pompey, who routed a band of Spartacist survivors. The two generals with their armies, keeping close watch on each other, marched as far as the line of Rome's *pomerium*, where they agreed to form a kind of 'duumvirate' and demanded the consulate for 70. When this had been granted, they proceeded to revise the constitution in a manner which favoured the equestrian class, to which both had originally belonged, at the expense of the senate. Probably aided by the propaganda of their future colleague in the triumvirate, C. Iulius Caesar, who was then simply a *tribunus militum*, they restored the tribunate of the *plebs* to its former position and also had censors elected once more: the latter revived the *lectio* of the senate (expelling sixty-four members) and of the knights, and also completed the first census since the extension of the citizenship. Particular problems of a controversial nature were once again reviewed. The

Sullan system of exclusively senatorial juries, since the senators had abused it, was brought to an end, and the jurors were now to be one-third senators, one-third *equites*, and one-third *tribuni aerarii* (mainly younger members of the senatorial families). Persons convicted of electoral corruption were debarred from office for ten years. The consuls announced that, to use Pompey's words, 'the provinces were ruined and plundered'; so the system of farming tithe-collection at Rome was revived. Meanwhile the embezzlement case against the member of the nobility who had governed Sicily from 73 to 71 was ably prosecuted by M. Tullius Cicero (who undoubtedly exaggerated), and it gave convincing proof of the need for reform. Even though immediately thereafter the new juries showed partiality in favour of an embezzler from the equestrian class, it was clear that under Pompey's leadership the breakdown of the Sullan system had brought social equilibrium. The knights were the basis of the new system, but the democrats from the people were satisfied and the senate had not lost all its power. Subsequent events make it impossible to suppose that Pompey aimed at an out-and-out dictatorship.

The victorious Eastern campaign of L. Licinius Lucullus resulted in a temporary ascendancy of the conservatives at Rome. Then, however, the news arrived of the mutiny of his troops, corrupted by democratic propaganda, and of the inevitable renunciation of his plans for further conquests. A reaction in favour of the anti-senatorial party began, and it was given powerful impetus by the return of C. Iulius Caesar from Spain, where he had been pro-quaestor. Caesar supported in the senate a series of popularist bills which certain tribunes were putting forward in the interests of the people: and he himself made propaganda in favour of granting full citizenship to the Transpadani, who at the time had only Latin rights. The tribunician proposals, which were strongly opposed by the conservatives, had a fourfold aim. Loans to foreign ambassadors in Rome were prohibited: a bribery law was directed not only at candidates at elections but at their lackeys (the *divisores*); the senate was forbidden to grant dispensations from the laws unless 200 voters were present, the people's right to intervene being still preserved; and governors were obliged to publish, at the outset of their tenure of office, the *edictum perpetuum* containing the rules by which they would be bound.

But Caesar's main support was reserved for a number of proposals by A. Gabinius. These included such matters as prohibition of exorbitant rates of interest; but the most important concerned the command in the war against the pirates, and led to a decision based on a scheme prepared in 100 BC by Marius but never put into action. The senate designated Pompey as commander, and gave him *imperium maius* for three years over all the seas and adjoining coasts, with 25 legates, 500 ships, up to 20 legions, and the use of the funds controlled by the quaestors at Rome and of the societies concerned with collection of provincial tribute. Once again Pompey showed no ambition to become dictator, but completed his task in three months instead of three years.

The result was that in 66, while Pompey was still in Cilicia attending to the settlement of the defeated pirates as peasants, the tribune C. Manilius Crispus proposed that he should be given 'imperium extra ordinem' without limit of time, to finish the war with Mithradates and to have the right to make war and peace at his will or to declare peoples enemies or allies of Rome. The majority of the *patres*, though they had not the courage to act in accordance with their views, were hostile to this *imperium*, which by its enormity in time, in space, and in powers seemed like a straightforward dictatorship—or at any rate could prepare the way for one. Cicero was then urban praetor, and he opposed the timid senators in his speech *De Imperio Cn. Pompei*: he maintained that the generalissimo would become a constitutional figure again once his task was accomplished, and cited the names of four illustrious statesmen who were standing ready to support his case. But Cicero was not alone. The bill was supported also by Caesar, who had less reason than any man to favour the dictatorial aims of another, since he was in secret preparing the way to dictatorship for himself. Pompey, although his work in organizing conquered or newly allied territories had the most important historical consequences, was above all proud of his military abilities, having always had the good fortune to overcome enemies who had already been weakened by his predecessors in command. He was often in a position to make himself dictator and seize the reins of government, but this pride made him regard the exceptional powers with which he had been invested as simply giving him a military task to accomplish and as lapsing once the task was done. For a few years Cicero thought he might become the 'princeps' guiding the state in alliance with the senate. But much more realistic were those senators who saw in him as a young man, and still again as an old man, the sword that was needed to free them from their dangerous adversaries.

h. *The Implementation of Caesar's Programme*

After Pompey's departure for the East the *equites* lost their leader, and the popular party had a period of revival, marked in the elections for 65. Two *populares* were successful for the consulate, Caesar for the aedileship, and Crassus for the post of censor. But the *optimates* ousted the two consuls-designate by accusing them of bribery, and there ensued a popularist conspiracy about which, since it never came to fruition, our evidence is tenuous and self-contradictory. The most probable reconstruction of Caesar's plan is that Crassus was to assume the dictatorship with Caesar as his *magister equitum*, and that when senatorial resistance had been broken the two deprived consuls-designate would be restored to their positions, while in the Transpadana, Spain, Mauretania, and Egypt partisan groups would have been supporting revolutionary action aimed at changing the constitution. When the conspiracy failed, the popularist leaders tried to salvage everything possible. The tribunes proposed unsuccessfully that Caesar should be sent to give Egypt, which had been left to Rome as an inheritance, its provincial organization; and Crassus was equally unsuccessful with a proposal to grant full citizenship to the Transpadani. Meanwhile Caesar as aedile kept himself in the public eye by spending heavily on great shows to delight the *plebs*. Then having made sure of his support, he committed acts of audacity such as the restoration of Marius' trophies, which the Sullan party had overthrown, and the prosecution under the *Lex de Sicariis* of some of the most notorious agents of the Sullan persecutions.

In 63 it was undoubtedly Caesar who inspired another unsuccessful proposal, a new agrarian bill put forward by the tribune P. Servilius Rullus, under which practically all existing *ager publicus* was to be requisitioned to provide a stable livelihood for the landless population and relieve congestion in the city. At this point Caesar obtained the dignity of *pontifex maximus*. His next move was to prompt the tribune T. Labienus to accuse of *perduellio* certain senators who had carried out *senatus consulta ultima*, decrees which in Caesar's view were illegal. Here too there was no practical result, but Caesar achieved a moral victory by getting the *optimates* put on their defence.

It was about this time that L. Sergius Catilina struck out a political line of his own, pressing his candidature for the consulate, which was to serve him as a jumping-off ground for a dictatorship. He was assisted by some of the conspirators of 65, but no longer had support from Crassus and Caesar. His programme involved the exclusion of the oligarchs from offices and priesthoods, the remission of debts in Italy, the revision of the judicial system, and the redistribution of wealth, as well as financial measures, sumptuary legislation, and other such matters. But when his third attempt on the consulate failed, he gave up legal methods and attempted to put his programme into effect by force. Cicero, consul for 63, succeeded in having the *senatus consultum ultimum* passed against the conspirators; and as a result those who had been imprisoned were strangled, and an army took the field and annihilated those who had left Rome. Caesar, who had been designated praetor for 62, naturally took the view that the procedure was illegal in that no citizen could be condemned without a proper trial, involving an appeal to the people. But no one at the time succeeded in proving that Caesar was privy to the conspiracy. Cicero did not even try to do so, and no value can be attached to the story which he tried to put about later, after Caesar's murder.

As praetor in 62 Caesar continued the battle with the *optimates*, often without carrying his actions to a conclusion but being satisfied if he could damage them in the face of public opinion. Naturally they counter-attacked. He was accused of participating in a riot and suspended from his office, but he was then reinstated since he was clearly not guilty. He was then accused of complicity with the Catilinarians; but he was acquitted once he had appealed to Cicero's own evidence in his favour, and he then took legal proceedings against his false accusers. Crassus had meanwhile retired to Macedonia in nervousness at the news of Pompey's homecoming (though this was subsequently postponed); and Caesar was left as sole leader of the popular factions.

When Pompey finally returned to Italy in January 61, he disbanded his army, thus justifying the view of Caesar who had denied that Pompey wanted to become dictator. Caesar persuaded Crassus to come back and make his peace with Pompey. Then he proceeded very late to a governorship in Spain, but in a few months succeeded in improving the administration and extending Rome's dominions.

While he was away the difficulties between Pompey and the senate grew sharper. Pompey was closely linked with the equestrian order: the senate's suspicions were played on by L. Licinius Lucullus, who felt slighted on account of his replacement by Pompey in the conduct of the Mithradatic War. Pompey failed to obtain either land for his veterans or the ratification *en bloc* of the decisions he had taken in Asia. Consequently when Caesar returned from Spain in 60 and found both Crassus and Pompey in political low water, it was a simple matter to bring about a complete reconciliation between the two and to become himself the third and most influential member of a secret coalition (the so-called First Triumvirate), with the object of exercising all possible force to overcome the nobility. With the support of his two allies Caesar secured the consulate for 59: and this enabled him, with the co-operation of tribunes and other magistrates, to unfold the first parts of the combined plan, while his consular colleague Bibulus retired, at least in appearance, into contemptuous inactivity. When the senate refused to entertain his proposals, Caesar had them passed by the people, the most important in the early period being a *Lex Iulia de Repetundis* to improve the moral standard of provincial government, with heavy penalties for violation, and two agrarian laws. The latter distributed to veterans (who were not allowed to sell their allotments for twenty years) the surviving portions of *ager publicus*, certain other lands purchased by the state, and the *Ager Stellatis* and *Ager Campanus*, these last confiscated from the nobles who were occupying them. In addition Caesar had Pompey's Eastern settlements ratified, and arranged for the *publicani* to recover sums equivalent to the amount they were out of pocket over their payments for farming the taxes. At the same time he tried unsuccessfully to win over Cicero, who since 64–63 had crossed to the optimate party and was now deploring the activity of Pompey, now linked to the popular side by family and other ties. By a proposal of the tribune Vatinius, who was taking his lead from the triennial command conferred some years earlier on Pompey, Caesar was given the government of Illyricum and later of Gaul for five years; and at the beginning of 58 he began his proconsulate, while political strife and intrigue continued to be rife at Rome. In April 56 the triumvirs, at a conference held at Luca, decided that Crassus and Pompey, after holding the consulate in 55, should be proconsuls for five years, while Caesar's extraordinary power was pro-longed to the same terminal date as that of the other two. In this way he hoped to get his two allies out of Rome and prevent their acquiring an advantage over himself; but though he succeeded with Crassus, who was subsequently killed at Carrhae in 53, it was otherwise with Pompey, who remained in Italy at the head of his army and became free of his family ties through the death of his wife Julia, Caesar's daughter. With Crassus' death the triumvirate became a duumvirate, and Pompey began to follow a line of his own, seeking a concordat between *equites* and senate under his own domination. The senate now granted him a prolongation of his five-year *imperium*; and this, if implemented, would have made it possible for him to become arbiter of the state, and to eliminate Caesar as a political force when the latter returned as a private citizen.

There is no need here to dwell on the events of the Civil War, or on Pompey's death and the destruction of his party. But we must say something about the way in which Caesar gradually established his power and put his constitution into effect during his brief periods of residence at Rome. He was there first in 49 after having, in absence, been elected dictator for the first time; then again in 47; then in 46, when he was sole consul for five years (later extended for ten years more in 45); and finally during the last months of 45 and the first months of 44, being elected dictator and perpetual censor on 4 February of the latter year. Several times he refused to alter the character of this dictatorship by assuming the title of king, though his enemies spoke of his 'adfectatio regni'. Yet there is no evidence that he intended, like Sulla, to bring his power to an end; indeed, though he was in no hurry about the particular steps to be taken in the matter, he was preparing to make his sister's grandson, C. Octavius, his successor, and secretly adopted him by a will drawn up on 13 September 45.

Once he had become head of the state instead of head of a party, Caesar did not desire the ascendancy of any faction, whether noble senators or rich knights or lower classes; nor did he want the struggle between factions to continue, for he had made himself the arbiter between them. With this in mind he reduced the powers of the senate, altered its composition, even opened its doors to a few provincials, and regarded *patres* and *equites* as equals so far as the dignity derived from their census qualifications was concerned. Yet he would not have knights outnumbering senators on the juries, and he was anxious to prevent the wealth of the knights from becoming inordinately large. Moreover, although in every way he met the fair demands of the *plebs* in the economic sphere, he prevented them from forming associations which might open the way to conspiracies, riots, and divisions within the state; and he imposed a rigorous control on the numbers of poor people who had a prescriptive right to state relief and bounties. Reviving the application of the 'ladder' system, he wanted provincials, by stages, to become Roman citizens; and meanwhile there was to be greater justice in provincial government by the transformation of the old type of military governors into responsible officials. The position of Italy became less privileged; it was made into a single nation, with all its communities receiving the same status, but the provinces were to be raised gradually to the Italian level. He gave preference neither to the East, where he tried to strengthen Hellenization, nor to the West, where he wanted to accelerate Latinization. He conceived that the two civilizations, Greek and Latin, were capable of being welded together into a higher synthesis among the classes of highest culture and in the capital city of Rome, and that this capital could become a majestic and monumental metropolis where the cultivated people resided and spoke both languages. Greek and Roman civilization must then be harmonized and blended in the artistic field as well.

i. The Imperial Conceptions of M. Antonius and of Augustus

As early as the archaic period the Romans had regarded their first king, Romulus, as the son of Mars, received into heaven as the god Quirinus, and their second king, Numa, as inspired in his legislation by the nymph (or Camena) Egeria. When exceptional individuals began to appear, men like Scipio Africanus, Sempronius Gracchus, Marius, or Sertorius, whom foreigners were readily prepared to regard as divine beings superior to the ordinary run of men, it was natural that many of them, like Sulla, should believe their actions to have been assisted by divine agreement, attested by predictions, prodigies, dreams, and the like; and that others, like Caesar, should attach special importance to the legendary traditions linking their families with gods —in Caesar's own case with Venus Genetrix. But though even Cicero was ready, in his *pro Marcello*, to declare that Caesar was 'deo simillimus', and the senate erected a statue to him with the dedication 'Caesari semidio', Caesar never claimed recognition as a god in his lifetime. His apotheosis came only after his death through the wish of the Second Triumvirate, who by this means pointed the way which his designated heir was to follow. The way marked out by Marcus Antonius was very different.

Antonius was a loyal supporter of Caesar's conceptions of dictatorship, and had a contempt not only for the republic but for all compromise forms of constitution. He was convinced that ruling the empire required an iron hand; he had no more confidence in the traditional system of dictatorship than in the imprecise concept of a 'princeps' formulated by Cicero. In the East, moreover, he was no longer in daily relations with the senate and people of Rome. These were the factors which first impelled him to adopt a more personal concept of the ruler, one conflicting with traditional Roman ideas, but later on he was even more decisively influenced by the Eastern environment in which he lived. He was in contact with peoples who from the distant past had been accustomed to be ruled by all-powerful princes, whose subjects looked to them as veritable gods on earth and were permanently in a relationship which implied servile veneration and obedience. Antony came from a family boasting descent from Hercules and had physical characteristics which Cicero described as 'gladiatorial'. In 41, when he landed at

Ephesus at the moment of the Dionysiac festival, he was greeted as the 'New Dionysus'. But the real turning-point in his policy came about through the bold action of a remarkable Egyptian queen, Cleopatra, who prevailed on him to make a 'hierogamia', a divine marriage between herself, identified with Isis and Aphrodite, and Antony, identified with Dionysus-Osiris. The divine marriage took on very human features later, with the birth of three children who were set alongside the son which Cleopatra claimed she had borne to Caesar. In a famous ceremony at Alexandria Antony, who had already rounded off Cleopatra's possessions with lands belonging to Rome, announced the territories of which the four children of Cleopatra would become rulers under their mother's protection; and it is certain that at this moment the triumvir had been plainly converted into an absolute ruler of half the Roman empire, and was ready to become 'dominus' of the whole in the event of his victory over Octavian. He was bound by 'personal' ties to the Alexandrian 'Queen of Kings': and she, by means of the children she had borne him, was ruler of another autonomous and allied empire, to which were assigned Roman provinces and states once allied to Rome. This was not the Caesarian idea, but a complex new conception half-Roman and half-Pharaonic.

Before he became Augustus in 27 BC, Octavian's policy was made up of a series of contingent struggles, and there is no need to recall its evolution in detail. At the outset he was the rival and enemy of Antony who had seized the leadership of the *populares* and was putting obstacles in the way of his obtaining the adoption and inheritance left him by Caesar. At one moment Antony tried to crush him, at another to put him in a subordinate position. In the next stage we find Octavian raising his own army, reaching agreement with the Caesaricide D. Brutus (who, like Cicero, saw in him the 'princeps' ready to draw his sword in defence of their rights), and taking the field against Antony, who had now been declared a *hostis*. But the accord with the senate was short-lived. Octavian soon concluded a new triumvirate with the Caesarians Antony and Lepidus, after having entered Rome with an army and secured the consulate by force. Once the 'imperia maiora' which the triumvirs had assigned to themselves had been confirmed by law, Octavian was associated in the bloody proscriptions and sentences carried out against anti-Caesarian elements (Cicero included), and in securing Caesar's deification; then he took part in the war which overcame M. Brutus and Cassius, the two most powerful murderers of Caesar. A number of fresh partitions of the area under triumviral control were arranged, in partnership with Antony and Lepidus, and later with Sex. Pompeius. But the elimination of first Lepidus and then Sextus led to a duumvirate and so to the decisive struggle for sole mastery between the two survivors. So we come to Antony's fall, to Octavian's reorganization of the East, and to the final triumph he celebrated in 29.

For a year and a half, from the later part of 29 to the beginning of 27, although he abolished the office of triumvir and assumed that of consul, Octavian still held absolute power 'per consensum universorum . . . rerum omnium'. He was *imperator* for life; he held the position of *princeps senatus* and in virtue of it called himself 'princeps' in the Ciceronian sense of chief citizen; and he possessed the *ius auxilii* in addition to the inviolability of a tribune. In this period he provided for his veterans, and held a *lectio senatus*, expelling 168 members and introducing fresh blood, which was of use in the future. On 10 January 27 he resigned all his abnormal positions: 'I transferred the state from my own power into that of the senate and people of Rome'. But on 13 January he received the name 'Augustus', a word of religious significance indicating his sanctity; and in the outcome, to use his own words once more, 'I was superior to all in *auctoritas*, but I had no greater power than those others who were my colleagues in the magistracies'.

In fact his outstanding *auctoritas* depended on his accumulation of offices, on the fact that those offices were repeated over many years or even for life, on the extended functions of office which were granted to him and not to other holders, and on the positions of dignity reserved for him alone. In this way the whole life of the state passed under his guardianship, control, and direction; and it was always open to him to take on new functions or to modify, even radically, his earlier settlements and definitions of his position.

He was clever enough to induce the senate and people of Rome to restore to him piece by piece all the extraordinary powers he had formally resigned, and to do so officially and of their own free will. The senate and people were under the illusion that all the power of the *princeps* was legal, because it had been conferred by themselves in accordance with republican practice. They imagined too that they retained for the future the unfettered right to impose a new settlement at the death of this particular ruler, although in fact they lacked the military or economic means which would eventually be needed if they were to offer opposition either to the present or to future *principes*. Augustus was consul down to 23: but his power was nothing like that of an ordinary consul either in its duration or in the authority he wielded, seeing that he commanded all the armies and possessed the right to choose his own colleagues. In 27 the empire was divided into imperial provinces, in principle those which required substantial military forces, and senatorial provinces, mainly those which were peaceful and prosperous. This left Augustus in almost exclusive control of all operations in the provinces containing legions, but he also secured the right to intervene at his discretion in those provinces which in theory were entrusted to the senate (and through them to proconsuls). When finally in 23 he replaced the consulate by a proconsulate, his power was not comparable with that of the normal proconsuls who governed provinces for a single year. He received, for one ten-year period after another, exclusive and complete rights over military, civil, and judicial matters in all the imperial provinces; and he also had discretionary rights of a general nature in Rome, Italy, and the senatorial provinces, which last could be transformed into military provinces if he wished it. In the same year 23 the senate conferred on him, in place of the partial attributes of a tribune which he had acquired earlier, the full tribunician authority, thus guaranteeing the sanctity of his position. But he had little to do with the ordinary annual tribunes, who were subjected to the veto of their colleagues and whose activity was limited to Rome: Augustus' tribunician power lasted until his death, was immune from veto, and gave him the right to oppose any decision of the senate and magistrates throughout the whole empire. Add to this accumulation of magistracies with extended powers that in 22 Augustus was given charge of the corn supply; that in 21 he was enabled to superintend the fire services; and that in 12 BC, on the death of Lepidus, he acquired the office of *pontifex maximus*, giving him control of all religion. It becomes clear that he had gradually concentrated unlimited power within his grasp, with each element in the power being delegated to him by separate conferments originating with the senate and people.

Moreover in his time the republican magistracies and institutions were transformed to the point at which they retained nothing from the past but their names. Though at first the *comitia* of the people still elected some categories of magistrate, many candidates for the higher offices were suggested by Augustus, whose wish was tantamount to a command. Later the prerogatives of the people were cut down, and a lead at elections was conferred on an assembly consisting of senators and knights, who cast their votes first. The senate itself, several times purged in order to get rid of Augustus' opponents as well as of unworthy members, was gradually reduced in number to 600, with its composition arranged according to Augustus' principles. Furthermore its work was gradually confined simply to the ratification of decisions already taken by a kind of junta, the 'consilium principis', composed of members of the imperial family, certain faithful friends, and a few senators and knights of proved loyalty.

Down to this time most of the important officers had been drawn from the senatorial class, and had not been paid. But to govern a few of the imperial provinces (including the vital province of Egypt) and look after some of the services he directed, Augustus chose officials from a new bureaucracy drawn from the equestrian order, with titles such as *praefecti*, *procuratores*, or *praesides*. All were paid a stipend related to their duties, and they became responsible to the *princeps* for what they were doing. The house of Augustus, containing his confidential servants, became the seat of government, and it also was the meeting-place of the *consilium principis*. (Other aspects of Augustus' reforms are considered in Part III, in relation to the way in which they were later developed.)

NOTES TO CHAPTER X

1. But the administration of their empire was entrusted to a body of civil servants who used the Aramaic language and writing and were established wherever the Achaemenid dynasty was in power. It is this which explains so much of the cultural relations between the Hellenic, Babylonian, Indian, and Iranian countries. The use of the Aramaic language and culture, and the cultural exchanges, are attested particularly in India by the development of Kharoṣṭhī writing (see Chapter VIII, p. 377) which presupposes the adaptation of the Aramaic alphabet to an exact phonetic analysis of language, an analysis which characterizes ancient Indian philology. These exchanges are again attested by the use among the Persians of a Babylonian medical manual, and the obvious influence of similar works on a part of Indian medical tradition independent of their classic rational doctrine. (*Journal Asiatique*, 1952, pp. 299 etc.).

2. Soviet historians consider the events of Greek history in the late fifth and fourth centuries BC as the result of a crisis in the Greek city-states. The development of slave-owning relations in the more advanced of these city-states accentuated sharply the contradictions between various groups of free men as well. The internal social struggle was closely linked with the foreign wars. Moreover, it is precisely at this time that areas hitherto backward began to develop. But their course of development had specific features in view of the crisis in the city-state system. All this had a significant effect upon the complex interaction of events at that time, the intensity in the relationship between different social groups, which found expression in the existence of various philosophical schools. (E. M. Shtaerman.)

3. Professor C. Danov considers that a sharp distinction should be made between the earlier and the later Greek tyrannies. Professor Pareti is of course distinguishing between the seventh- and sixth-century tyrannies, the largely economic causes of which are outlined in Part I, pp. 300 ff., and those which began with the early fifth-century Deinomenids at Syracuse. It is an entirely tenable view that all the Syracusan tyrants—Gelon *c.*500, Dionysius I *c.*400, and Agathocles *c.*300—came into power for similar reasons.

4. Professor Pareti means, of course, not that Athens ruled its subjects through oligarchies (in fact the norm, if not the rule, was that its cities were governed by democracies), but that Athens did not use democratic means to determine league policies. Yet it is arguable that the democratic elements in the cities were contented with Athenian rule: see G. E. M. de Ste Croix, *Historia*, 1954–5, pp. 1 ff.

5. Between 377 and 355 Athens had constituted a new confederacy of maritime states.

6. The author does not touch at all upon the problem of the social roots of Hellenism, or the degree to which slave-owning of the type found in antiquity was diffused in the various Hellenistic countries, or the relationship between this and the forms of exploitation that prevailed in the East. In Soviet historiography the problem of the relationship between social-economic and cultural 'Hellenization' (as later with 'Romanization') is considered very important and has frequently been the topic of specific discussions. See *Vsemirnaya istoriya* (*World History*), Vol. II, Moscow, 1956, pp. 231–5. (E. M. Shtaerman.)

7. There were many such attempts. One rather more permanent than the rest was the kingdom established in Thrace and north-western Anatolia by the thorough though harsh administrator Lysimachus. He was defeated and killed by Seleucus I in 281, but most of his dominions were incorporated into Macedonia rather than Syria: the Chersonnese (Gallipoli) fell temporarily to the Ptolemies.

8. Already his father Philip had colonized extensively after his conquests in Thrace, Philippopolis (near Sofia) being one of the most permanent of his foundations.

9. Roman tradition, in the main, ascribed the establishment of the centuries to Servius Tullius, king in the mid-sixth century. But both the date and the motive for their establishment are highly controversial, and it is unlikely that further light will ever be thrown on the question. For a summary of conflicting views see H. H. Scullard, *A History of the Roman World, 753–146 BC* (second edition, London, 1951), Appendix 3.

10. These and other dates in the early republic are for the most part those given by Livy.

11. Tradition anachronistically calls the praetors 'consuls', using the name adopted in 366; and for the same reason the succeeding *tribuni militum* are said to be 'consulari potestate'.

12. Professor Ch. Th. Saricakis protests against the use of words such as these (cf. 'moral', p. 482 below) to describe Roman foreign policy. He cites E. Täubler, *Imperium Romanum*, (Leipzig, 1913, esp. p. 239) for the view that Rome was purely selfish throughout. He is right to emphasize that from the late third century onwards Rome showed a brutality which shocked contemporary Greeks (cf. Polybius, XI, 5, 6) and an unscrupulousness in diplomacy which has shocked most later generations. Yet its earlier policy in Italy, though doubtless conceived in its own interests and consequently amoral, was remarkably far-sighted: it was not unreasonable (see the words attributed to the emperor Claudius by Tacitus, *Annals*, XI, 24) to claim that its liberal treatment of conquered tribes and cities, in its early period at least, was the foundation of its long-lived dominion.

13. In a classic paper H. Mattingly and E. S. G. Robinson, *Proceedings of the British Academy*, *1933*, argued that the regular Roman *denarius* did not appear till 187. But Dr Mattingly subsequently (*Journal of Roman Studies*, 1945, pp. 65 ff.), showed that the date given by Professor Pareti is that of the first silver (*drachmae*) issued by the Roman mint.

14. For the particular views of Cato, which are perhaps here made too egoistic, see above, p. 361, note 12.

15. In connection with the reforms of the Gracchi, the author mentions the importance of the development of slavery, but after this no attention at all is paid to its role in social history, which determined the course of political history as well. Yet it is sufficient to compare the data of Cato and Varro to observe that during the last centuries of the republic the share of slave labour increased *vis-à-vis* that of other forms of exploitation (employment of landless labourers, share-croppers, etc.), although the latter (particularly the exploitation of clients, debtors, and small tenants) continued to exist, especially in the larger agricultural—but not cattle-breeding—estates. Their role varied in different parts of Italy. (E. M. Shtaerman.)

16. This is argued more fully by Professor Pareti in *Storia di Roma*, III, pp. 295, 492, 694. Professor Ch. Th. Saricakis calls attention to the criticisms recently made by J. Vogt, *Abhandl. Mainz.*, 1957, p. 54.

17. This is a controversial point. Professor Pareti follows the account of our main source (Appian, *de Bello Civili*, I), but there is reason to doubt whether any but Romans were offered allotments (see E. Badian, *Foreign Clientelae* (Oxford, 1958), pp. 169 ff.). In any case, non-Roman proprietors complained that their land was being seized by the Gracchan commissioners.

18. The normal number of senators before Sulla was 300, but it may be that civil war and proscriptions had heavily reduced this number by 81 BC.

19. Professor Ch. Th. Saricakis points out that here Sulla was only reiterating an ancient law (Livy, VII, 42, 2—342 BC).

20. This was the view of Mommsen and of most historians before recent times, but it has little ancient authority: see J. P. V. D. Balsdon, *Journal of Roman Studies*, 1939, pp. 57 ff. It is certain, however, that Sulla imposed stringent rules about the conduct (as distinct from the tenure) of provincial commands.

21. Professor C. Danov contends that Professor Pareti gives too favourable an account of Sulla and minimizes his 'reactionary' tendencies. Sulla's main aim, we may agree, was to restore the 'authority' of the senate, both against the *plebs* and the tribunes who courted them, and against ambitious senatorial generals; and this was a traditionalist aim. Yet the measures Sulla used to attain it were novel; and his economic measures, though rigid and perhaps unimaginative, were far from pleasing to the rich. So little so that J. Carcopino, *Sylla ou la monarchie manquée* (Paris, 1931), was able to maintain (probably wrongly) that Sulla was hostile to the senate and simply concerned to perpetuate his own régime.

22. See above, p. 361, note 17.

CHAPTER XI

RELIGION AND THE EVOLUTION
OF PHILOSOPHY

1. CONFUCIANISM AND TAOISM

CHINESE religious life in this period is mainly a continuation of that of the feudal period. But with the consolidation of regional states, and still more with the formation of the empire, religious life, or at least its formal expression in the cult, assumed an increasingly official character; and it became, in the words of Granet, an administrative religion. The state cult itself grew more and more formalized. It lost the larger part of its religious content and became a highly developed ceremonial with strict rules; the countryman's everyday religious life, on the other hand, concerned as it was with agriculture and with ancestor worship, never ascended to a higher level. These conditions were not conducive to any sort of philosophical thought. When the latter took place about 500 BC, it came from quite another direction, and played a much more significant role in China than religion could ever have done. It has been rightly said that 'the place which philosophy has occupied in Chinese civilization has been comparable to that of religion in other civilizations' (Fêng Yu-lan).

From its inception, and ever after, Chinese thought was chiefly moral and political in its aims, with a sociological undertone; metaphysics and formal logic were not an original component and never played an outstanding role. This is the main characteristic of ancient Chinese philosophy, the period of the 'Hundred Philosophers' (c. 500–200 BC). It was a magnificent flowering of philosophic thought, one of those god-graced periods in the history of a nation, in which suffering, and political and economic chaos, is matched by the brilliance of spiritual achievement. The principal schools, according to the classical list proposed by Ssŭ-ma T'an (second century BC) and modernized by Fêng Yu-lan, were the following six:

(1) The school of the literati (ju-chia), descended from K'ung-tzŭ (Confucius, 551–479 BC). A man of high birth, Confucius passed his life as a travelling adviser to the feudal princes, and then as the head of a flourishing private school of ethics. His teaching career was long and influential, but nothing in it seems to justify the enormous success enjoyed by his teaching after his death. It seems that no actual writing by Confucius is extant, with the exception, perhaps, of his share as editor in the Ch'un-ch'iu annals of the Lu state. His thought is best known from the Lun-yü (Analects): a collection of his utterances compiled by some immediate or mediate disciples. His

cultural basis was the Classics (*I-ching*, *Shih-ching*, *Shu-ching*), of which
he was the first expounder and which for him were the root of all knowledge
and rule of life. He conceived himself solely as an interpreter of this old
traditional role, 'a transmitter, not an originator' (*Lun-yü*, VII, 1). This was
true from many points of view, but in several other respects it was only a
cover for the introduction of a new, severely ethical ideology. Of his political
philosophy we have already spoken. He had a highly moral, but none the
less aristocratic conception of social relations. He was aware, of course, that
actual practice was very different from ancient theory, and this is the reason
why he and his followers insisted upon the need for making things and
functions correspond to the ideals attached to them by their names; this they
called the 'rectification of names' (*Lun-yü*, XIII, 3). Individual morals are
based on the idea that man ought to act rightly because this is a categorical
imperative (*i*) and not because of the hope of any advantage (*li*). The consequence is that man must act, but without any thought for success or failure.
The value of doing what he ought to do lies in the doing itself, and not in the
external result. Only fate (*ming*) can decide the issue. The all-important
thing is to be aware of the existence of fate, or of the decree of heaven (as
Confucius himself seems to have understood the term) and to act accordingly.
For him the inner law (*tao*) of the phenomenal world was a moral one.

The school of Confucius did not come into the limelight during the first
century or so after the death of its founder. It lived in obscurity and received
its real impetus only from the work of Mencius (Meng-tzŭ 371–289 BC).
Mencius represents the idealistic trend in Confucianism. Starting from the
postulate that human nature is intrinsically good, he maintains that man has
in himself the four beginnings (humanity, righteousness, propriety, wisdom)
and that he is capable, and therefore bound, to develop them. He fought
bitterly against both the hedonism of the early Taoists and the indiscriminate
love of Mo-ti, which he maintained was something artificial and imposed
from without, while Confucius' graded relationship meant a human good-
heartedness that developed naturally from within man's nature. Hence also
the all-important imperative of Mencius' political theory: the state exists in
its own right and is a moral institution, carrying out a moral task.

The realistic wing of the Confucian school was represented by Hsün-tzŭ
(*c.*298–238). In contrast with Mencius, he held that human nature is originally
and intrinsically evil, and that everything that is good comes only from man's
conscious effort against his tendencies and towards culture. Social relations
are based mainly on two particular aspects of the old conception of customary
ceremonies toward the ancestors; these are the *li*, as a norm of social behaviour,
and music as a means of furthering social harmony. Up to a certain point,
Hsün-tzŭ's ideas move on lines that are parallel with Legalism; and it is
noteworthy that the chief exponents of Legalism, Han-fei-tzŭ (theory)
and Li Ssŭ (practice), were both disciples of Hsün-tzŭ.

(2) The second main philosophical school was that of Mo-ti or Mo-tzŭ,

who probably lived in the second half of the fifth century BC. His thought is opposed to that of Confucius in so far as Mo-ti denied the validity of tradition-al lore and its usefulness. His own background was not the aristocracy of the gentlemen-scholars, but the warrior class (*yu-hsieh*). His anti-Confucian criticism lies mainly in the field of practical ethics: he maintains that Con-fucian morality is harmful to society and to mankind, and above all he rejects the Confucian idea of the six graded relations as the basis of all society, and substitutes for them the conception of all-embracing love, an idea that was but an extension of the professional ethics of the knight class to which he himself belonged. It is, however, characteristic of the general Chinese 'this-world' attitude that this lofty principle is upheld mainly on utilitarian grounds, in view of the good ensuing from it for society at large. It is not an emotional love, but a purely intellectual one. In contrast with Confucius' agnosticism, Mo-ti upheld the existence of a supreme god—who loves all men and whose will is that all men should love each other. These tenets were expanded further by the later Moists, who introduced a large element of dialectic and went far towards creating a system of logic and epistemology.

(3) Another philosophical school was the one which we usually call Taoism. A sharp distinction must be drawn between Taoism as a philosophy (which is theoretical and early) and the Taoistic religion which is quite practical in outlook and aims and arose much later. Taoist thought is mainly a form of escapism; a philosophy of men who recognized human society as bad and therefore abandoned it and its struggles, and turned to seclusion in mountains or in other natural solitudes.

The earliest thinker of this school was Yang Chu (perhaps fourth century BC). His theory is a sort of egotistical hedonism: 'though he might have profited the whole world by plucking out a single hair, he would not have done it'. It was each man for himself. This, the earliest phase of Taoism, was limited to a desire to preserve life and avoid injury, and was later followed by a second one in which, escape not being always possible, an attempt was made to reach at the inner laws according to which things develop and change in this world.

A later stage is represented by the most puzzling and much discussed work of Chinese philosophical literature, the *Tao-tê-ching*. It is attributed by tradition to Lao-tzŭ, an older contemporary of Confucius. But the evanes-cent figure of Lao-tzŭ is, in all likelihood, unhistorical, and the book may date from the beginning of the third century BC. It is mainly a discussion about the *tao*, conceived as the unnameable, the ultimate principle that lies beyond shapes and features and is the beginning of heaven and earth. It is the absolute underlying principle, beyond good and evil, not amoral but super-moral. The *tao* includes the invariable law of nature, according to which when a thing reaches one extreme, it reverts from it to become its opposite. Man should know the laws of nature and act according to them. 'If one intends to achieve something, he starts with its opposite, and if he wants to retain anything he admits in it something of its opposite.' The other main conception is *tê* (power or virtue). *Tao* being the origin of all things, each thing obtains something from the universal *tao*, and this something is called *tê*. The *tê* of a thing is what it naturally is. Life should abandon itself to *tao* and *tê* and activity should be much reduced (non-action, *wu-wei*), avoiding all over-doing and unnatural strain. The resulting political theory is that 'the empire is gained by remaining constantly in non-action. As soon as one becomes active, one is unable to gain the empire. How do I know that this is so? By this: the more taboos and prohibitions there are in the empire, the poorer the people will be. The more useful implements the people have, the more state and dynasty will be in confusion. The more cunning craftsmen there are, the more bizarre contrivances will spring up. The more laws and ordinances are promulgated, the more thieves and robbers will there be.' (*Tao-tê-ching*, 57; trans. Duyvendak.) This means anti-statalism; it is a theory reminiscent of Max Stirner and anarchism.

About the same epoch, these theories were brought to their logical con-clusion by the composite work traditionally attributed to Chuang-tzŭ (*c.*369–286 BC). Man's chief purpose is the achievement of happiness. A relative kind of happiness can be reached by the free development of our nature through the use of our inborn ability (*tê*). Natures are not uniform, and every attempt to make them so conduces only to grief, and therefore Chuang-tzŭ is utterly against any formal government and maintains that the best way to govern is by letting people strictly alone (by non-government). But there is another, higher happiness, which comes only from recognizing the relativity of the nature of things and identifying man with the Whole. Thus knowledge alone leads to ultimate happiness, and only the true sage, the spiritual man, can be perfectly happy. This can be achieved by the gradual recognition of all distinctions as mere conventions, which from the viewpoint of the *tao* are relative and not absolute. This is true also of the greatest distinction of all, that between life and death. The sage merely needs to be one with the Great One, which is unthinkable and unspeakable. The end of knowledge is its own abolition, it is no-knowledge. The practice can be summarized in the two words: do nothing (*wu-wei*); in the sense of acting wholly spontaneously and naturally, without any conscious effort. 'By doing nothing there is nothing that is not done' (*Tao-tê-ching*, 48). The perfect man does nothing and the great sage originates nothing—they merely contemplate the universe. Taoist thought at this stage is therefore a mystical scepticism with a strong anarchical element.

(4) The so-called School of Names (*ming-chia*) was composed of logicians, often misnamed sophists. The Chinese language is constitutionally not adapted to organic logic of the Aristotelian type. Still the problem of the relation between the name (*ming*) and the reality implied by it (*shih*) led to subtle, and sometimes even captious, disputes of a quasi-logical character. The foremost teachers of this school were Hui Shih (*c.*350–260 BC); and

Kung-sun Lung (*c.* 284–259 BC). The latter, by emphasizing that names are absolute and permanent, developed an epistemology which came very near to the Platonic universals.

(5) With the *yin-yang* school we are moving into another field. It hails from the para-technical circles of occultists (*fang-shih*) and geomancers, whose main purpose was the practical one of finding or causing a favourable combination of natural forces for any enterprise. The meanings of the two opposite and complementary terms *yin* and *yang* have been explained in Part I. The theory built around them was a line of thought that later merged with a similar one, that of the Five Elements (*wu-hsing*: water, fire, wood, metal, earth), into what can be considered as a single school. Its main representative was Tsou Yen (third century BC). It gave a well-balanced cosmology and a series of practical precepts meant to place man's behaviour in harmony with nature, as the only possible path to success and happiness. Later on the theory of *yin* and *yang* was connected with the hexagrams of the Book of Changes (*I-ching*), probably an old diviner's handbook. Its influence in court life and even in the conduct of state affairs was at times very large, but of course this semi-magical lore can hardly be called a philosophy.

(6) Legalism (*fa-chia*) was mainly a school of political thought, and as such has been chiefly dealt with in the preceding chapter. Its chief theoretician, its synthetizer though not its founder, was Han-fei-tzŭ (d. 233 BC). We may recall that the Legalist philosophy of history was the only one which did not regard the past as the precedent and model for present behaviour.

This luxuriant expansion of philosophical thought underwent a process of simplification, but also of impoverishment, with the events that led to the foundation of the empire by the Ch'in and its final organization by the Han. Legalism met with disaster and was practically suppressed. Moism and the School of Names petered out. The *yin-yang* school ceased to lead an independent life and at first merged (at least to a great extent) with Confucianism. This left Confucianism and Taoism alone in the field. While the latter, being anti-statal, soon became a philosophy for disgruntled officials and retired politicians, Confucianism after several vicissitudes became the official ideology of the Han state. Its victory was complete by the second half of the second century BC.

But Han Confucianism was something very different from the teaching of the old sage, and it also differed from the later developments of the school. Its chief representative was Tung Chung-shu (179–104 BC). He was the theorist of the Han empire and also a great statesman; the first beginnings of the Chinese state-examinations system owed a great deal to him. His cosmology is a blend of Confucianism and of the *yin-yang* theories; according to him, the universe consists of ten constituents: heaven, earth, *yin* and *yang*, the Five Elements, and man. The waxing and waning of *yin* and *yang* are at the basis of all processes of nature and also of changes within the social order. Politics and the action of government should be modelled on the pattern of the four seasons. History itself is brought into this system, the changes of dynasties being influenced by the movements of a cycle of three colours: black, white, and red. It was also Tung Chung-shu who gave a final form to the theory of the mandate of heaven (*t'ien-ming*) and incorporated it into his philosophical system. He stressed the superhuman position of the emperor, thus supporting the authoritarian trend of the institutions. At the same time the circles around Tung Chung-shu introduced into Confucianism a great quantity of pseudo-scientific and even magical practices.

It can thus be seen that the rich variety of thought of the Warring States period gave way, if not to a synthesis, to a form of eclecticism. Tung Chung-shu was essentially an eclectic. The unknown authors of the interpolated chapters of Chuang-tzŭ and Hsün-tzŭ, which probably go back to the Early Han, were also eclectics. The best representative of this trend of thought is perhaps the *Huai-nan-tzŭ*, a collective work with a strong leaning toward Taoism.

The religious content of Chinese philosophy in general and of Confucianism in particular is very low by our standard. Under the Han the official cult was a state religion, one of the main concerns of government, urban in character and under the tutorship of the literati. Religion itself became bureaucratized. The emperor could and did prescribe a cult for new deities and demote gods to a lesser rank for state ceremonies. The state's bureaucratic system projected itself into heaven. The official cult of the ancient agrarian gods of the earth and of the crops, which had fallen into oblivion during the Warring States period, was restored by the Han; but the gods lost all reality. The various earth deities were synthetized into a single one, the Sovereign Earth, while the August Heaven (*huang-t'ien*) was dismembered by the Ch'in into several figures: the Green, Yellow, Red, and White rulers. To these the Han added the Black ruler, thus completing the number five as a counterpart to the Five Elements. This cult was more and more localized on five sacred mountains, of which the T'ai-shan in Shantung was the most famous. The imperial sacrifice on the T'ai-shan became the most august, elaborate, and costly rite of the official religion, and only six rulers in Chinese history were able to perform it. The foremost practical aspect of the state religion was perhaps the calendar, and determining it was one of the most jealously guarded imperial prerogatives.

In the private religion of the upper and lower classes the cult of the ancestors took such a place that it became the real mainstay of Chinese religious life. But in the official practice this too became a dematerialized, symbolic, abstract rite; a simple commemoration without any feeling of personal communication.

All this was not enough for the religious needs of the people at large.[1] Although the average Chinese is utterly 'this-worldly', there was still a natural yearning for some emotional uplift of the soul, for something that could give consolation to the simple man, for that heartfelt solace which the dry as dust state-cult or the cold moral norm of the Confucianists could not give. This was particularly true in times of anarchy, economic depression, and civil war, when the farmer turned from his present hopeless conditions toward something which could give him at least a glimmer of hope beyond this life. The only element of mysticism in this period was supplied by Taoism; not by the philosophy of Lao-tzŭ and Chuang-tzŭ, but by the mass of popular beliefs and superstitions that go under the same name. But these trends lived an underground life, and it was only during the Later Han period that they took the shape of sectarian movements, through which they ended by becoming a true religion. For the rest, Chinese everyday spiritual life was to a more or less extent dominated by the belief in spirits (*kuei*), sometimes beneficent but more often impish or even malignant, and by the all-present need of taking into due account the underground currents of supernatural forces, i.e. geomancy (*feng-shui*).

2. RELIGION AND PHILOSOPHY IN INDIA

While in China the philosophic values ignore or exclude the religious ones, in India philosophy starts from religion[2] and for a long time is intimately connected with it. While in China philosophy is 'this-worldly' and centres around society, the state, and their inter-relations, in India it is metaphysical and individualistic. The innermost natures of the two great Asiatic civilizations, partly conditioned by climate and environment, are therefore quite different.

About 500 BC religious life in India had not yet gone far from the Vedic stage. The Vedic ritual was more or less followed by the Brahmans, sole performers of its complicated sacrifices. Thus we have evidence that the highest rite of all, the horse sacrifice (*aśvamedha*), reserved for a great king and conqueror, was occasionally performed and in any case highly regarded. In keeping with the spirit of the sacred texts, there were no temples as yet, but only open-air altars. But, apart from the reform movements of which we shall speak presently, the practice of religion and above all the mythology as a living belief came to be gradually modified by the non-Aryan substrata of Indian society; and this process grew stronger as it kept pace with the advance of Aryan civilization southward. The libation (*yajña*) of the Aryans, usually of *soma* into fire, was slowly supplanted by the offering (*pūjā*), originally consisting in the anointing of the image and in any case including a strong element of ritual purification.

Thus the priestly and naturalistic Vedic religion underwent an insensible change. The old deities, too indefinite and too closely connected with natural phenomena, were replaced in popular favour by the earth gods, often theriomorphic and with a dominance of feminine deities. Varuṇa, Agni and the rest vanished out of the horizon of practical worship. Only Viṣṇu and Indra remained. To Viṣṇu local heroes like Kṛṣṇa and Vāsudeva and local gods like Nārāyaṇa were assimilated. The cycle of Kṛṣṇa is already a major factor in the great epics; even more so is Rāma, the central figure of the *Rāmāyaṇa*, another hero of northern India who was later equated with Viṣṇu. On the other side the terrific aspects in southern religiosity came to be typified in Śiva, the god of destruction, while the numerous Mother Goddesses merged into Durgā or Kālī or Pārvatī, the feminine counterpart of Śiva. With the epics, i.e. during the last few centuries of this period, the fusion between Aryan and non-Aryan elements is complete. The *Vedas* are still regarded as sacred texts, but the living religion is something new; it is Brahmanism.

Secular thought went on building on the base laid by the early *Upaniṣads*. The later *Upaniṣads* develop still further the ideas of *karman* as the human act that automatically produces its own retribution in the next life; of *ātman*, the individual principle, and of its essential identity with *brāhmaṇ*, the world soul, the essence of the universe. But a shifting of emphasis comes in with the introduction of a strong deistic element, i.e. the exaltation of Viṣṇu or of Śiva (usually called Rudra) and with the beginnings of an emotional devotion (*bhakti*). Some hints of early philosophical conceptions of the Sāṅkhya type are not lacking. Typical in this respect is the *Śvetāśvatara Upaniṣad*, which has been said to usher in Hinduism. These elements increase with time, and the modern *Upaniṣads* (some have been compiled as late as the sixteenth century) are but a very secondary appendage to devotional literature.

Philosophical thought in the *Mahābhārata* is difficult to date, since that huge encyclopaedia grew slowly in piecemeal fashion in the course of centuries. By far the most important text is the *Bhagavadgītā* (Mhbh. VI, 23–40). It is a short poem of 700 *ślokas* in eighteen chapters, in which Kṛṣṇa assuages the doubts of the hero Arjuna, who cannot bring himself to fight against his friends and relatives on the opposite side. What Kṛṣṇa sets forth is a philosophy of action. Man must act according to his law or duty (*dharma*); but he must consider neither success nor failure nor reward; his action must be completely desireless. Salvation is obtained by three paths. The first two are the path of action (*karmamārga*) and the path of knowledge (*jñānamārga*). By the desireless act man enters the way of knowledge. But the latter is completely obtained only by meditation, and meditation is efficacious only through its special technique (*yoga*). Through *yoga* man reaches the highest of the three paths, that of emotional devotion (*bhaktimārga*). Many developments of later thought are included *in nuce* in this short beautiful poem: early *Sāṅkhya*, *Yoga*, the devotion to Kṛṣṇa. But above all the historical importance of the *Bhagavadgītā* is enormous; it became, and still is, the most popular and most commented-upon text of Hinduism, taking the place of the sacred *Vedas* in living religion. By its very vagueness and composite content, it is admirably suited to the introduction of new trends of thought by means of commentaries.

This leads us to the origins of classical Hindu philosophy. As always in India, the historian is handicapped by the utter uncertainty of chronology (even of a relative one) and by the anonymity of the texts. Later tradition distinguishes six philosophical systems (*darśana*), coupled two by two: *Vendānta* and *Mīmāṃsā, Saṅkhya* and *Yoga, Nyāya* and *Vaiśeṣika*. Of these, only *Vendānta* and *Sāṅkhya* are philosophies in the complete sense of the word, the other four relating to partial problems or to techniques. Making all due allowance for the impossibility of fixing even approximate dates, we may perhaps assume with some reason that *Sāṅkhya* and *Yoga* had their beginnings in this period. The case of *Vedānta* lies on another plane; it is mainly the linear descendant of Upanisadic thought, and the problem is one of drawing the frontier between the two. But in any case it will be safer and sounder to give a connected account of the six *darśanas* in Part III, because it appears that by the end of the Gupta period they were already fixed in their main outlines.

The main test of orthodoxy is the recognition of the sacred character of the *Vedas*. Beyond this pale, we are outside Hinduism. The first currents we meet with, as a sort of borderline case, are the sceptical and materialistic trends, which are one of the inborn ingredients of human thought. They did not much come to the fore in India. Still, some disjointed schools of this sort did exist, though they are known mostly from quotations in polemical writings of other schools. Such were the Ajñānikas or agnostics, who denied the possibility of knowledge itself. Then there were the Cārvākas or Lokāyatas, materialists who maintained the complete dissolution of man after death into the five elements, and the identity of the *ātman* with the body; they denied the existence of God, the sanctity of the *Vedas*, the law of *karman*; for them, therefore, there is nothing to be released from, and the only aim in life must be its enjoyment. There were also the Ājīvikas or fatalists, founded by Makkhali Gosāla, a contemporary of the Buddha. He maintained that the world exists because of the cohesion of the five elements (earth, water, fire, air, and life), and this meld is determined not by *karman* but entirely by blind fate (*niyati*). The cycle of deaths and rebirths (*saṃsārā*) is therefore predestined, and nothing that man does can influence it. Release is not elimination, but the non-manifestation of the eternal *saṃsārā*; it is, therefore, impermanent.

The arid formalism of Vedic religion, as we have said, provoked reactions from several quarters. In the case of the *Upaniṣads*, this reaction managed to keep within the very elastic bounds of orthodoxy and it merely contributed another spiritual facet within the old frame. But with the two reformers who lived about 500 BC, this reaction broke all bounds and resulted in the foundation of two new religions: Jainism and Buddhism.

a. *Jainism*

According to tradition Jainism was derived from a long line of teachers (*tīrthakara*), of whom the last but one, Pārśva (eighth or seventh century BC?), may have been a historical person. This was certainly the case with the last

of the series, Vardhamāna, later called Mahāvīra (Great Hero) and Jina
(Victorious One)—he died *c*.477 BC. Unlike the Buddha, therefore, he was
no originator but the continuer of a tradition, to which he added much, but
not over-much, of his own. The Jain religion, to which he gave shape, is
essentially an ascetic one. It reposes on a theory which denies the absolute
validity of knowledge and recognizes solely its probability (*syādvāda*, the
theory of 'may be', i.e. of looking from some point of view). There are two
correlative and eternally independent categories, the conscious (*jīva*) and the
unconscious (*ajīva*). The conscious corresponds almost to an individual soul.
The unconscious is all the remaining things: matter (*pudgala*), space, time,
qualities, etc. The innumerable *jīvas* are by their own nature eternal, omnis-
cient, untroubled; but their junction with *pudgala* in the shape of action
(*karman*) troubles this purity. The only way to restore this purity and to
attain isolation (*kaivalya*), which means salvation, is through a life of utmost
rigorous asceticism. In this the prohibition of taking life in any form plays
an outstanding role. The main external feature of Jainism is the monastic
order, a flexible and yet closely-knit institution that has allowed the Jain
religion to continue in existence to this day; it is supported by the community
of 'hearers' (*śrāvaka*), who, by a virtuous life, prepare for a future re-birth
in which they may enter the strenuous career of the ascetic. No God is
recognized: the Hindu deities are considered as impermanent and can be
released from *saṃsāra* only if they are re-born as men and turn ascetic. In
Jainism as well as in Buddhism man stands alone—he is the only shaper of
his destiny and release can come only from his own efforts.

Jainism possessed a body of traditional lore, which had grown up in the
course of centuries: it was sanctioned and fixed (according to tradition) in a
council said to have been held in the third century BC at Pāṭaliputra under the
presidency of Sthūlabhadra. But the Jain canon was only put into writing
much later. Jainism never became a faith of the masses because of the terrible
severity of its life, its conservatism, and also because it found no Aśoka;
it was limited to definite circles (mostly wealthy traders) and, although it
spread throughout India, it never went beyond its frontiers.

b. *Buddhism*

According to most modern scholars Gautama Siddhartha lived *c*. 563–
483 BC. Born at Kapilavastu in the aristocratic republic of the Śākya in
northern Bihar, he lived the luxurious life of a young nobleman until he
felt impelled to abandon it to seek a means of release from *saṃsāra*. After
he had forsaken as useless the terrible austerities which he had tried in the
first place, he later, meditating under a tree at Bodh Gaya, found illumination
(*bodhi*) at last. He preached the Law (*dharma*) for the first time at Sarnath
near Benares; and henceforward the Illuminate (*buddha*), as he was called,
taught and lived his doctrine until he died at the age of eighty at Kuśīnāgara.
As far as we can reconstruct his teaching (he never wrote a line), it is based

on the following essentials: there are four Noble Truths: (1) existence (the *saṃsāra*) is misery; (2) attachment (*tṛṣṇa:* thirst) the cause of existence; (3) misery can be ended by the elimination of attachment; (4) there is a path to the destruction of attachment: this is the Eightfold Path of right faith, speech, action, livelihood, mind, meditation, resolution, and view. In investigating things, the smallest unit we can reach is the *dharma* (properly the 'law' whereby their nature and condition are regulated), which is an irreducible factor of existence. The *dharmas*, and therefore the phenomenal world, have no existence, nor does a soul or individual principle (*ātman*) exist. Buddhism is also atheistic, in the sense that the gods of the *Veda* are impermanent and bound to the *saṃsāra* (as in Jainism) and can anyhow be of no help in obtaining release. Salvation means the attainment of *nirvāṇa*—a condition which can only be defined negatively; it is the absolute state where all distinctions of life and death, good, evil, knowledge and non-knowledge, cease to exist.

The main external feature of the Buddha's teaching was the institution of a monastic community, ruled by severe rules, living on alms and supported by lay believers. Every monk and nun, and they alone, could strive towards the attainment of *nirvāṇa* by the path shown by the Master. Thus the triad, the Buddha, the Law (*dharma*), and the Community (*saṅgha*) is the mainstay of the new religion.

After the death of the founder his community developed slowly, as just one sect among many similar ones in north-eastern India. The utterances of the Buddha were collected by his disciples and their descendants and were first put into some shape at the so-called first council, in the first half of the fifth century BC. A second council was held at Vaiśālī, in the early fourth century BC, but their account is untrustworthy, and the historicity of the event itself is not beyond doubt. It was during this council that the first split occurred between the Elders (Sanskrit *sthavira*, Pali *thera*), who claimed to be the authorized depositories of the tradition, and the Western monks, who seceded and convened a rival council; hence the name *Theravāda* for the first school and *Mahāsāṅghika* for the second. The conflict was mainly on points of discipline; but later doctrinal differences arose as well, and the number of schools went on increasing. Tradition mentions eighteen schools, but this is a sacred and therefore fictitious number. Anyhow, the schisms did not impede the decisive expansion of Buddhism from a local sect into a pan-Indian religion, thanks to the enthusiastic support of Aśoka. Not only did the king become a devout Buddhist, but he took serious and efficient steps to spread his faith throughout the whole of India and even outside it; his bilingual Greek-Aramaic inscription, recently found at Kandahar, is perhaps the most eloquent sign of his zeal for morality and orderliness. One mission, headed by his brother Mahinda, was sent to Ceylon, which was soon completely converted and became the stronghold of Buddhism in the south.

The Pali recension of the Buddhist canon, which tradition ascribes to a

legendary third council convened by Aśoka, was introduced into Ceylon
and received its final shape there in the last years before our era. It is written
in Pali (a dialect which may have been spoken in Magadha), and is divided
into three 'baskets' (*pitaka*): *Sutta* (Sanskr. *sūtra*), containing the word
of the Master, i.e. his speeches and teachings; *Vinaya*, the monastic rules;
Abhidhamma (Sanskr. *abhidharma*), a miscellaneous section of apparently
later origin, which came to contain most of the philosophical doctrines. Of
course this huge collection contains material of various origin, reflecting the
opinions of the Buddha's disciples and their successors, and the discussions
that took place in later generations. The Pali canon is that of the *Theravāda*
school; but the missionaries were not particular about language; they put
their texts into the tongue of the country in which they were preaching, and
thus we also have fragments of canonical writings (chiefly *Vinaya*) in Sanskrit,
Prakrit, and in an Indian dialect that underwent a thorough process of
Sanskritization, and is known as Hybrid Sanskrit. But most of the non-
Theravāda literature is now preserved only in Chinese and Tibetan translations.

Although the Śūṅga dynasty, which succeeded the Maurya, returned to
Brahmanic orthodoxy and did not favour (though it did not hinder) Buddhism,
about the beginning of our era Buddhist monasteries and monks were fairly
widely spread throughout India. There was never, however, a central
organization: not only was every monastery independent of the others, but
the superior in each place had no authority beyond the administrative sphere.
There was hardly any doctrinal control, and the only disciplinary court
competent to judge a monk was the community of his brethren.

3. RELIGIOUS AND PHILOSOPHIC IDEAS IN PERSIA

In the fifth and fourth centuries the Zoroastrian religion lost its exclusively
dualistic character. This was because the old gods (and in particular the
western ones—Mithras, Anahitā, Verethreghae and Vayū), which had been
preserved in popular worship, gradually recovered their importance and
extended their influence at the expense of Ahura Mazda, who had been
imposed by Zarathustra. However, the opposition between the powers of
the Spirit of Good and the Spirit of Evil was accentuated, while the Magi
supported the pessimistic conception of 'Zervanism': this made Zervan the
Supreme Being, while Ahura Mazda and Ahra Mainyu are his two sons
working against each other, with Mithras acting as a moderator between
them. Herodotus was familiar with the Persian cults and sacrifices of his
own day, offered to the sun, moon, earth, fire, water, and wind; just as he
also knows of bloody sacrifices which had been forbidden by Zoroastrianism.
Other ancient rites, which had already been outlawed, also returned, such
as the use of the intoxicant 'haoma', though it had now been made less
noxious; moreover the funeral rites of Zoroastrianism began to lose some of
their rigidity.

The religious policy of the Achaemenid kings sometimes underwent sharp changes, such as the time Xerxes (486–465), in his anger against the revolt of Babylonia, forbade the cult of Marduk. But it tended in the main to religious tolerance, of which the Persian attitude to the Jews is an example. They allowed the Zervanism of the Magi, the Mithraic mysteries, the Anahitā cult (authenticated under Artaxerxes II, 404–358), and the use of sacred images.³ At the same time they were discovering the ancient myths on early man, on the primordial king, the fights between heroes and dragons, and so on. In philosophy the influence of Greece on Persia and of Persia on Greece is apparent in the time of Plato, who had Persians among the pupils at his school; from them he was able to get greater information about Zoroastrian dualism.

Graeco-Persian religious syncretisms were of course at their fullest development when Alexander and his successors were ruling the Iranian countries. Nor did things change sensibly when certain lands about 247 got detached from the Seleucid empire, and were formed into the Parthian kingdom of the Arsacids (cf. Part III). These syncretistic ideas persisted into the Mithradatic kingdom of Pontus even when it was ruled by Mithradates Eupator, the great enemy of Rome, whom apocalyptic prophecy identified with Mithras, come down to earth to combat Ahriman—probably the beginnings of the Hellenized Mithras mysteries. (For the development of the *Avesta* cf. Parts I and III.)

4. THE HEBREWS

The first example of a 'diaspora' or dispersion of the Hebrew people took place, as we have seen, with the transplanting of conquered Jews into the countries of their conquerors. This happened in 732 under Tiglath-Pileser III, in 722 under Sargon II, in *c.* 700 under Sennacherib, and in 597 and 586 under Nebuchadnezzar: the Jews were transplanted to agricultural colonies on the Lower Euphrates and to the city of Babylon, from which 50,000 survivors were repatriated in 539 by Cyrus the Great. But real Diasporai, following one after another, occurred above all in the time of Alexander the Great's successors. In this period the Hebrews were scattered in vast numbers throughout the Mediterranean basin; the movement was both voluntary and under compulsion, and is recorded by various writers who were conscious of this phenomenon. One of the countries to which they made their way (or in which they were forcibly settled) was Egypt, where indeed they had already taken roots under Jeremiah in the sixth and in Elephantine in the fifth and fourth centuries. The Diaspora was most marked during the vicissitudes of Palestine under Antiochus IV (Epiphanes) and Pompey, just as we find it repeated later under the Flavians and Hadrian. When the Romans, in the middle of the second century BC, supported the independence of Judaea, a Judaean (*Oracula Sibyll.*, III, 271) boasted that his compatriots were scattered throughout the world, on land and on sea. The places to which the Jews went from choice were, naturally, the great ports and commercial centres: in some places they lived in their own quarters, in others they were dispersed. In Alexandria, where the Jewish colony was always very numerous and particularly so during the period when the Ptolemies occupied Palestine, the figure of 100,000 Hebrews is given. However it is not impossible that there were a million Jews in Egypt, since Jewish emigrants may well have outnumbered those who had remained in Palestine. If we take into account their spirit of kinship, ability in affairs, and the distance which they kept between themselves and other people, it is easy to understand the strength which these people represented to the ancient world.

The political and legal position of these Hebrews was very uncertain. In some respects, undoubtedly, they were given various privileges, but from another standpoint they were there on sufferance, regarded with suspicion, and sometimes the victims of riots and persecutions. Violent popular manifestations of anti-Semitic hatred, followed by a reaction from the Hebrews, often brought sharp intervention by the government; but in other places and times we find a kind of fashion for Jewish usages, accompanied by a tendency on the part of the Gentiles to accept Jewish customs and faiths. Governments, however, were not always tolerant of this proselytizing.

The use of Greek (see below) by large groups of Jews in the Diaspora facilitated proselytizing, which was pursued with tenacity and skill among people of all ranks and achieved success in all districts. The majority of the new disciples remained, however, at the level of sympathizers, perhaps because circumcision, which was indispensable for becoming fully Jewish, was a distinct obstacle for pagans. In any case, the difficulties for pagan followers of Judaism were great because of the irreconcilable conflict between the exclusively monotheistic conception of the Hebrews and the polytheistic state-cults. These differences were already serious for relations between the Jews and the cities which sheltered them, despite their recognition of Jewish national religion; they were much more so when they affected the family and public life of catechumens, who were full citizens of their respective cities. We see this trouble beginning in 139 BC, when the Jews were first expelled from Rome for making converts there.

Caesar showed particular benevolence towards the Jews, and created a special legal status for them which survived in its broad outlines into later times. The Hebrew 'ethnos' was considered similar to a corporation, with an ethnarch, protected by Rome, at its head; members of the Diaspora were allowed to belong to it and to preserve the national religion. The Roman state dispensed them from military service, and from attending tribunals on the sabbath; and they were allowed to administer their own property. It is certain that the Hebrews of the Diaspora, from all their main centres, maintained most active relations with Jerusalem on religious matters. All Hebrews sought to go to the temple at Jerusalem on great occasions as it was considered the one true place of worship, although of course each local community had synagogues with its own leaders and men who had accepted a religious calling. The Hebrew community in Rome was very large. It is calculated that there could not have been less than 30,000 Jews at the time of Christ: there were several communities independent of one another, each provided with an autonomous council, and with meeting places for prayer. The attempt by the high priest Onias IV to erect a new temple at Leontopolis in Egypt was exceptional; it lasted a short time and the attempt was not repeated.

While the Hebrews in Palestine were subject in turn to the influences of Seleucid, Ptolemaic, and Roman domination, the scribes were giving their religion a new direction. These men had become interpreters, teachers, and preachers. They were devotees of the Law in its most meticulous applications, adhering both to its letter and to its allegorical meanings, stubbornly holding themselves aloof, 'separated' (Pharisee), from idolatrous Hellenistic thought. They pushed to its extreme the theory of the transcendent and unknowable God; and they developed the conception of celestial mediators, the various categories of angels who shielded God from any contact with the world, though He had always been ready to intervene to preserve the faithful and would always do so in the future. These ideas were mostly developed in the second century BC before, during, and after the period of the Maccabees, in the *Books of Esther, Judith,* and *Tobias*; at the same time poetic psalms celebrated the greatness, goodness, and justice of God, which would make Israel rule the world. Other works of apocalyptic type, such as the *Book of Daniel,* prepared the way for the advent of the Messiah who would found an empire, an empire ruled by the Almighty and no longer by alien races. The *Books of Enoch* (first century BC) belong to the same period and order of ideas. The attempt to maintain the purity of the tradition and the Law was, however, easier in Palestine than in any of the areas of the Diaspora. There, at least among the more educated classes, there was bound to be much give-and-take with native ideas; comparisons and syncretisms were made between the Hebrew religion and other religions. This happened very early and on a large scale in two areas.

In Asia Minor and in pre-Maccabean Palestine the meeting with local cults was almost inevitable. They had in common the use of the epithet the 'Highest' (*Hypsistos*), a name applied to the indigenous Attis; there was Sabazios whose name evoked the Sabbath; there were similar rituals for purification, and an analogous conception of a guardian angel who would guide its own charge to the seat of the blessed after his death.

If we leave out Parthia, the second area where an important meeting of religions took place was Egypt, and in particular Alexandria. There the Greek language was in such common use among Hebrews that for the understanding of their own Sacred Books they preferred to use the Greek translation, the earliest parts of which appear to go back to the times of Ptolemy Philadelphus. Later, when the inaccuracies of this translation were noticed (they are easily explained by the difficulty of transferring the peculiar Hebrew conceptions and forms of expression into a language such as the Alexandrian Greek *koiné*, which has a completely different structure), this version was gradually removed and no fewer than three other translations were substituted in the Imperial period.

The blending of religious ideas was natural enough in such surroundings; and there was an obvious likeness between the ideas of the Prophets and the 'Scriptures' in general on the one hand, and those of the philosophers and of Greek 'mystery' works on the other—although the Jews were wedded to the belief that the latter derived from the Hebrew. Such a tendency was naturally opposed by a party whom we may call 'particularists'; but the resulting arguments ended by provoking the formation of several Jewish-Pagan sects who were strongly at variance with one another. The comparisons and syncretisms were not without strong support in the Hebrew camp, for instance in the work attributed to 'Rabbi Qoheleth' (*c.*200 BC) or in the 'explanation of the Mosaic laws' (at the beginning of the second century) by Aristobulus, who was both a Jew and a peripatetic philosopher, or in the 'Book of Wisdom' by the pseudo-Solomon. But we find this tendency above all in the writings of Philo (*c.*30 BC—*c.* AD 40) whose clarity and influence on later works caused him to be known as the Jewish Plato. Philo, an expert on the Bible and also on Greek philosophy, wrote works expounding the *Pentateuch*, defending Judaism (*Moses*, and *An Apologia for the Jews*), setting forth a religious philosophy (*On the Contemplative Life*, *On the Liberty of the Sages*, *Treatises on Providence*, etc.), and other works of a historical type (*The Embassy to Caligula*, the *Contra Flaccum*). His theories were of great importance in creating an atmosphere in which the Christian idea could develop. They mark an intermediate stage between Plato, the Bible, and the Fathers of the Church: these last continued to use his works which, though clear and frequently enlivened by imaginative and creative lyricism, are long-winded and weighed down by a parade of technical terminology. His greatest aim was to attract pagans to Judaism because, according to him, the revelations of Moses, by explaining the creed, had made it possible to attain the true philosophy which Pythagoras, Plato, and Aristotle had drawn from Judaism. His thought is not always consistent, either on the nature of the matter with which God eschews all relationship, or on that of the beings intermediate between God and this matter. The word (*logos*) used by God to create the world coincides with the neo-Pythagorean word *logos*, and Philo deals at great length with this great mediator with God. According to him the conflict between the spirit and the flesh is fundamental: morality consists in destroying sin, but as in Platonic ethics, there is no true virtue without faith and the intention of serving God. Biblical history is dissolved into allegories and becomes a series of myths. Philo's idea of science is Platonic. Fundamental Jewish ideas, such as the Messiah, do not interest him much.

It is clear that the proselytizing of the Palestinian Pharisaic Judaism and that of the Hellenistic Hebrew gnosticism led towards different lives, but both developed because both found minds and hearts quick to accept them. Jewish propaganda was not regarded favourably by frivolous people because the austerity of its rites, its simplicity of dogma, and the purity of its ethics were not designed for ordinary people. Yet the fervour of their propaganda for the unity of God, and the virtuous nature of their lives, drew supporters. But the Hebraic gnosticism of Alexandria had many more followers since it did not demand that pagans should abandon their traditional culture; indeed this culture was actually essential to it.

So we can conclude that the most important consequence of the Jewish Diaspora was to effect some breach in the exclusive national religion which had been the fundamental characteristic of the old Israel, and so to make easier the transition to the universal Christianity of later years.

5. GREECE

a. *The Rise of Scepticism*

The political separatism of the Greeks, even after their common adoption of the Homeric-Olympian élite divinities, steadfastly retained the original variety of religious ideas and pantheon from region to region. In every colony religious practice was altered and diversified through the adoption of local cults or syncretism with them; and cities which came under the hegemony of another were affected by the cults of the ruling power. Mythology was continually modified by the unrestrained licence of poets; and the gods of one people became heroes among other people, and changed their genealogies. The lack of a powerful priestly class common to all Greeks made it impossible to control these variations, while the contrast between the refined conception of divinity maintained by philosophy and the banal, often immoral, 'lives' of the gods, humanized by the poets, was too strong. All this and a gradually increasing individualism helped to diminish the various state-religions in the minds of the more educated, while the misfortunes of wars loosened the hold of the traditional gods, who had been vaunted as defenders of the cities (*poliad*), on the minds of the poorer classes. The educated classes shocked the ordinary people by paying attention to the theories of an Anaxagoras (according to whom the sun was nothing but 'one huge incandescent stone') or to the atheistic ideas of some sophists; or by tolerating the dramatists' parodies of certain myths; and, on occasions, perpetrating acts of sacrilege such as those blamed on Alcibiades' circles, the mutilation of the Hermae and the parodies of the Eleusinian mysteries. On the other hand the rough and primitive religious attitude of the common people, teeming with superstitions and fatuous magic practices, irritated the more educated classes. We are able to follow the development of this complex phenomenon particularly at Athens and in the period of the long war to the death with Sparta (431–404 BC).[4]

The outbreak of the war was bad enough; but when it was followed by the early disappointments, and then by anti-democratic moves which were still unavailing to avert the final collapse, it may have seemed to the Athenians that the disasters they had suffered were a punishment inflicted by outraged divinities. So a sharp and violent reaction in the field of religion was inevitable. Then the lack of interest and scepticism which the ruling classes showed towards the old religion of their fathers, the contempt and the parodies, the irreverent confiscation of sacred treasures, the obvious agnosticism of Protagoras, the astonishing claims of Anaxagoras, the atheism of Diagoras of Melos, the parodies and criticisms in Euripides, greatly aroused the anger of the people. Trials and sentences followed against the unbelievers: Anaxagoras (432), Alcibiades (415), Protagoras (411), Diagoras (411). Euripides also ran into trouble.

In the meantime the religious feelings of the mob also found an outlet and satisfaction in the introduction of pathetic, orgiastic, and violent new cults derived from Phrygia (Cybele, the Great Mother, Sabazius), from Cyprus (Aphrodite and Adonis), from Egypt (Ammon), from Thrace (Cotytto and Bendis). Initiation into the Orphic and Pythagorean secrets or to Demeter's mysteries at Eleusis, or to those of the great Cabeiroi on Samothrace, became commoner than ever.

Faced by this revival of religious feeling and the tendency towards new superstitions, the upper classes, though scornful of these excesses and in private indifferent to them, adopted in public an attitude of recognition: sometimes they were attracted by the charm of the Dionysiac cult, like Euripides in the *Bacchae*, his last tragedy.5 Between these two trends, the scepticism of the upper classes and the superstitions of the *demos*, stood Socrates, the man who dealt the heaviest blows against the Sophistic movement, and whose thought inspired all later generations of Greeks. Of his religious beliefs and martyrdom we shall speak later.

b. *The Greek Religion and Hellenistic Conquests*

The conquests of Alexander the Great in the East, and the subsequent creation of a number of new Greek states, did not bring chaotic consequences. In general the oriental cults and their temples underwent no great vicissitudes. There were some disagreements between the Egyptian priests and the ruling Ptolemies, under Ptolemy I, IV, and VIII; the Seleucid attempts to confiscate the temple treasures in 210 and 187 provoked reactions; and there were the inevitable difficulties with the monotheistic Hebrews, particularly when Antiochus IV determined to Hellenize their cults. But on more than one occasion Alexander had found himself defending the local religions and priests against real or alleged abuses by the ruling Persians; and from that time on the cults of the Eastern peoples were generally respected and their temples enriched.

For the Greeks themselves direct contact with so many exotic cults did not seem to create great difficulties. It was easy to invent or deduce new identifications between many such cults and the Hellenistic pantheon; for others the way was open for their introduction into Greece, where the list of divinities became like a book without end.

Never did the Hellenic cults, at any rate in Eastern countries, appear more splendid in their works of art, their temples, their votive offerings, and their festivals; for they helped to glorify the new Greek cities which were being founded in those lands. Nevertheless, believers felt that the traditional religion of *poliad* (protecting *polis*) divinities was not able to fulfil the more refined service that was now demanded of it—of satisfying human feeling and guaranteeing happiness after death. Intimate forms of worship were gradually confined to a few of the more cherished figures such as Zeus, Dionysus, and Asclepius; and to these was added Tyche (Fortune), to whom Aristotle and thereafter the Epicureans had already given recognition.

The new practice of deifying Hellenistic sovereigns, which took different forms according to areas and habits, ended by weakening still further the concept of gods in human form. Various essential factors brought about the new practice: the revival in Greece of the hero-cult to include 'men of distinction' and 'founders'; the example of Egypt, the only oriental dynasty whose divine nature was a dogma; and the admiration and adulation given to the great benevolent rulers. From these emerged the bold theories of Euhemerus, who in his 'Sacred History' held that even the traditional divinities were in general only great human figures, the kings of old who had been deified.

Everything appeared to push the educated people towards new concepts of divinity—loftier, more monotheistic, more intellectual—and so to lead them to take refuge in syncretistic movements.

c. *Religious and Philosophic Syncretism*

While, as we shall see, ancient Greece remained to the fore in philosophic progress, religious changes were pioneered by the new Greek lands of the East. Religious feeling, even if it was unsatisfied, was not dead among the Greeks: neither among the philosophers, who argued about a single god, a *nous* or a pure act which gave movement to the world, a being beyond imagining, a governor of the Universe; nor among the people, who in the depths of their superstition had recourse to fortune-tellers, questioned the oracles, were initiated at the Mysteries, and frequented foreigners' temples.

On this state of affairs were superimposed the new syncretistic trends from the East, both from Egypt, where the government had sponsored a flourishing cult of universal character based on native traditions, and from Syria and Chaldea, where what seemed vague ideas evolved by Greek philosophers were given embodiment in the astrological theories of those countries.

In Egypt Ptolemy Soter, in order to give religious unity to his Greek and Egyptian subjects, transferred the cult of Osiris Apis (or Serapis, as the Greeks called him) from the old native capital of Memphis to the new capital of Alexandria, where Isis was already being worshipped. Serapis was a miracle-working god, who had revealed himself to the king. He procured the salvation of the faithful after their deaths; and he alone dominated the whole world—in the heavens, the earth, the sea, and in hell. He embraced the whole of humanity. He was a god who contained in himself all the Greek and Egyptian gods so that none could supersede him; he could place them all in a great subordinate pantheon; and he allowed himself to be worshipped by the priests of all peoples. Linked with the belief in after-life and with the doctrine of the Mysteries of Demeter which had been taken to Alexandria and called Isiac (by the syncretism of Demeter with Isis) the Serapis cult spread in Egypt and beyond it wherever the Nile merchants went.

The syncretism which spread to the ancient Greek world from the Seleucid zones was in contrast astral in base. For some time in Greece there had been a tendency, indirectly influenced as well by the East, towards coalition between astronomical and philosophical studies, leading to a pantheistic astral doctrine within which the Greek divinities were identified with the stars worshipped by the Syrians and Chaldeans. From Pythagoras and Plato down to Aristotle the tendency to identify the stars with divinities became ever sharper; and for the first time, in the *Epinomis* attributed to Plato, the planets take the names of the traditional gods. Later, when Alexander had conquered the Syrian and Mesopotamian world, Syrian and Chaldean astrologers began to tour Greek lands; and the Babylonian priest Berosus, for example, set up a school of astrology at Cos. So it is not surprising that in Stoic theory, evolved first by Eastern philosophers, like Zeno, who had migrated to Greece,[6] a pantheistic concept of the universe predominates. Stoicism combines all that the Greeks succeeded in evolving on their own account with what the East had taught them. It was a spiritual religious doctrine, according to which worship could consist only in understanding of the divine nature.

Not all minds of course were able to reach the heights of Stoic theory. The Greek populace were content to see the astrologers, particularly the charlatans who had come from the East, as magicians, and in their dazzling theories to fall ever deeper into vulgar superstition.

In the meantime genuine Pythagoreanism, which had been dying for centuries, still existed in some form in the Orphic-Pythagorean Mysteries, and in the so-called 'Pythagorean life' of asceticism. These ideas, linked with others borrowed from Plato, Aristotle, and the Stoics, were developed until they formed the creed of a neo-Pythagorean school at Alexandria. This school maintained that, while corruptible matter is governed by necessity, God is transcendent and unknowable, and that the intermediary between God and man is formed by the *logos*. The relation between the gods of the past and the one God lay in the fact that they were particular and local expressions of Him. The neo-Pythagorean faith was spread by regular missionaries, preachers, and comforters, many of whom came from among the Cynics. They assisted in teaching the young to live; they prepared men for death; they sought to give all men an assurance that their hopes were firmly grounded in a just future after death, the other life being an appropriate reward for a man's deserts in this one; and they set themselves to satisfy the religious feeling of mankind. The actual ceremonies of these cults were striking and attractive: they resorted to fortune-telling, magical manifestations, music, the recitation of mysterious and incomprehensible phrases, acts of purification and expiation, and public confessions with declarations made in writing. According to these neo-Pythagoreans the soul is subjected in hell to various purifications, and, depending on the degree of purity achieved, returns to earth in the form of a plant, an animal, or another human being; life is a brief second and should be lived in purity.

Of another syncretistic trend—the Hebrew-Hellenistic—we have spoken earlier.

d. *Systems of Cosmogony*

We have seen (Chapter IX) how in the course of the fifth century in Greece, and particularly after the successful result of the 'Persian Wars', there was a lively development in scientific research; in mathematics and astronomy, in biology and medicine.[7] From these researches sprang a keen new impulse to study the origins of the world; Empedocles of Acragas (*c.* 490–430), was said to be a pupil of the Pythagoreans, as well as of Parmenides and Anaxagoras. He was of noble birth and took an active part in the political life of his city before withdrawing to the new foundation of Thurii and then going on to the Peloponnese and to Athens. He was a highly religious mystic, famous as a worker of miracles, a pioneer in many kinds of literature and science, and regarded as the founder of Sicilian rhetoric. He wrote an historical poem and, perhaps, a medical treatise; he was an expert on meteorology and hydraulics; but his fame rested above all on two philosophic poems which indicated his attitude towards scientific experiment, towards the materialistic Monism of the Ionians, and towards the spiritualism of the Eleatics. In the first poem of about 2,000 lines 'On the Nature of Things' he gives a new rational and mechanical explanation of the world. The four elements, which he calls 'the roots of things' are fire, light, earth, and water. These can never die, but they are variously blended by love which tends to unite them in the 'Sphere'; and at this point the cosmic cycle enters a stage of calm and of not-being in the perceptible world. Hate, on the other hand, tends to divide the elements and when it succeeds they are no longer compounded in any particular object. The being of things is therefore given by the antithesis between love and hate, and endures in the cosmic periods intermediate between those in which one or other of these forces is temporarily dominant. In the other poem, 'The Purifications', he propounds the mystico-religious aim of showing men the fundamental aspirations of the human soul, overflowing (like Xenophanes) all anthropomorphic and polytheistic concept of divinity, and believing (like Pythagoras) in the immortality of the soul and its purification in metempsychosis through successive human and non-human existences. From this belief it followed that man must purify himself, and must respect the beings, plant and animal, which marked the stages in the progressive rise of the souls they entertained, souls which were indestructible and of divine origin.

For Anaxagoras of Clazomenae, Leucippus, and Democritus, see above, pp. 421 f.

e. *The Sophists—Socrates*

Faced with the irreconcilable contradictoriness of the various systems put forward to account for the world which surrounded them, the Greeks were assailed by the doubt, already advanced by Parmenides, whether the senses could give more than subjective truth; and Heraclitus even questioned human reason. So some men tried to attain a form of cognition surer than that provided by the senses: others adopted a scepticism of a more or less absolute kind, or reconciled themselves to a truth which was relative. Indeed this relativism which was apparently established in cognition seemed to make itself evident in many other fields as well. In religion, for instance, anthropomorphism had been overthrown by Xenophanes; and his polytheism gave place to the idea, admittedly tenuous as yet,[8] of a single divinity, like the *nous* of Anaxagoras, though some people began to demand proofs of the very existence of any divine power. The same tendency is found in ethics and in law. It was now established that every people was governed by different laws and customs. Some thinkers therefore set up as superior to all else a common natural law, the law of the strongest and the weakest; others disputed this, and insisted on the distinction between man as a social being and animals. Finally what was one to make of dialectic, when every day one could see, in assemblies and law-courts, how oratorical skill, by the process of suggestion, could overthrow justice?

So the Sophists grew up, at first identical with the orators, but assuming decisive importance in the evolution of Greek thought and writing. They attracted to themselves the young men who were eager for advancement, and who were captivated by the audacity of the new propositions and the sparkling character of the dialectical debates. The speakers were grandiloquently called 'sophistai' or wise men (experts); but after Socrates and his diatribes this name acquired the derogatory meaning of 'tricksters', just as a fallacious or specious piece of reasoning was called a 'sophisma'. Even now, when so many centuries have intervened, many people repeat the view taken by their contemporary detractors that the Sophists misdirected Greek thought and made it sceptical, empty, formal, and amoral.

This judgement contains something of the truth, but it is greatly exaggerated. There were great and small Sophists, some harmful, some harmless; and there was never one general sophistic theory, but rather a number of Sophists of differing views possessing certain features in common. These features included contempt for the metaphysics of earlier days, confidence in their own power of reasoning, a desire for novelty which was sometimes exaggerated and arrogant, and (to some extent at least) a significant tinge of scepticism. Yet the Sophists were not always harmful, and in any case they had other qualities. They toured the country, and for a fairly modest fee would give young Greeks of the better families a kind of instruction which had never been provided before, teaching them to express themselves and defend their theses and opinions. They made known the doctrines of philosophers and the discoveries of scientists, and they opened men's minds to the finer issues of philosophy, ethics, logic, and aesthetics. It was in the sophistic movement that the mind of Pericles, the drama of Euripides, and the scientific history of Thucydides were fashioned; and it was this movement which evoked the thinking of Socrates, promoted study of language and grammar, and spread abroad an interest in the exposition of ancient texts and in the history of their transmission.

The sophistic movement started simultaneously among the East Greeks (those of the Hellespont and Asia Minor) and among the Greeks of Sicily. It acquired a close connection with the new ideas in Rhetoric, and so made its way to mainland Greece and Athens, where, like the Encyclopaedism of the eighteenth century, it acted as a leavening influence on all thought and literature. Two of the greatest Sophists deserve a mention.[9] Protagoras of Abdera (480–410) lived his life journeying round the Greek lands, especially to Sicily, to Thurii, where he drew up the legal code, and to Athens, from which he was probably banished during the oligarchic reaction of 411. He made large profits from his teaching, and wrote discourses, such as the 'Case for a Salary', together with various treatises. But his main philosophical work was entitled *Truth*, and it contained his two famous maxims: that on the relativity of knowledge ('Man is the measure of all things, of being in so far as it exists and of not-being in so far as it does not exist'); and the maxim about the impossibility of proving divine existence ('About the gods I can say nothing, neither that they exist nor that they do not; many things prevent one from knowing, such as the obscurity of the problem and the shortness of human life'). Protagoras was accused of having taught his pupils to 'make the worse cause appear the better', and it seems true that his oratory attempted to convince his hearers of the conclusion he set out to prove, even when this conclusion was unfair. Yet it remains the case that he imparted ethical instruction to his pupils, and did so lavishly. He taught by giving examples, some allegorical, others evidential or explanatory; he was effective in making his hearers commit pieces to memory; and he supervised debates in which one side would contradict the other.[10]

Prodicus of Iulis on Ceos (*c.*470–400) came to Athens as an ambassador and took up residence there. He liked to study the precise value of terms and the validity of synonyms, and Plato mimicked this passion of his. In ethics he upheld the old traditional ideas, in his *Horae* he told the pleasant story of Heracles at the cross-roads, giving exhortations to domestic and public virtues in so orthodox a fashion that Socrates used to call him Master.

Simultaneously with the anti-democratic reaction which engaged many young Athenians of noble family in 411 and 404 there was a reaction against all the characteristic culture of the democracy, and especially against sophism —which had been this culture's pivot. The uneducated masses too were ready to regard sophism as the cause of all corruption and of all their ills, and consequently to strike at its most vulnerable flank, namely its religious scepticism. The symbol of this crucial phase in the struggle of thought was Socrates, who had personally involved himself amid the various currents of opinion in a way from which there was no drawing back.

Socrates (470–399), the son of a sculptor and a midwife, had been given some small education, but was deeply devout, especially in respect to the god of Delphi. He had given up his father's craft and was content with the very modest standard of life allowed him by his tiny patrimony. He devoted himself wholly to the mission to which, since his boyhood, he had been drawn by divine inspiration—by a voice (*daimon*) within him which urged him on[11] at every stage. This mission consisted in teaching about what was truly good and in improving men who were like himself. He had no organic system; and he was not a Sophist in the sense in which the word was then used; for he ran no regular courses and claimed no pay from his hearers. He used to stop and discuss in any place with anyone who willed, from the noblest Athenians down to the sons of slaves; and the argument about 'what each thing really is', conducted with great dialectical skill, inevitably led his interlocutor to confess his ignorance, at which point the process of rational reconstruction would begin.

We have no direct acquaintance with Socrates' doctrines, which he did not leave behind him in written form. We know them through the statements of his pupils, who often dressed them up in various ways. Xenophon weakened their force and Plato heightened it, as befitted these two men's intellectual powers and personal views. In general one can at least regard as Socratic that of which we have agreed testimony from pupils whose outlook was different.

Socrates did not concern himself with problems of natural science. He was interested in man as a rational being, a being whose good consists in knowledge. But to achieve knowledge one must not rest, as the Sophists did, on opinions derived from sensations, which are changeable, relative, and conflicting. Rather one must, by means of argument, eliminate from the data of the senses everything that is contingent and individual, so as to reach a definition of the essence of each thing—to discover its universal 'concept',[12] which is the truth acceptable by all men and not by an individual alone. This is the inductive process by which an examination of many just things, or many beautiful things, or many trees, leads one to define what is 'just', what is 'beautiful', what is 'a tree'.

Applying this principle of cognition to the Good, Socrates asserted that the Good consisted in Knowledge, in organizing one's behaviour and directing one's search for happiness in a rational manner, rising above impulses and opinions to be guided by the 'concepts'. The greatest ill afflicting humanity is ignorance. We must act well because to do so is useful (and some pupils, like Xenophon, stopped at this proposition because their mentality did not allow them to go further), and still more because it is pleasing to the gods, the intelligent authors of an ordered world and of ethical concepts with divine and absolute value, concepts useful to mankind. These are the old concepts which have been handed down. In this way human morality consisted for Socrates in obedience to divinity and in living with divinity; and it was this that constituted the loftiest and most lasting part of his teaching.

But there was also a part which was more of an innovation and which tended to supersede the traditional religion. Although he never disowned the ordinary furniture of mythology, and even declared he was a worshipper of the sun and the moon, Socrates was in fact subverting the religious ideas of the city. The 'daimon' to which he continually alluded, and which may have been, as Plato implies, simply conscience, was, in the end, partly because of the exaggerated language of some of his pupils, believed by outsiders to be a new independent divinity, introduced by the philosopher without the permission of the people. There began an obtuse opposition, of which as early as 423 Aristophanes was a mouthpiece in his *Clouds*; yet for another quarter of a century the philosopher was able to continue his discussions and mode of life undisturbed. But when the new democracy was established after the overthrow of the oligarchic 'tyrants', accusations and hatred were poured on Socrates as the teacher of Alcibiades, Critias, and many other young aristocrats to whom the country's ruin was ascribed. With the agreement, in all good faith, of a citizen named Anytus, a man who wanted Athens to have concord at home, Socrates was in 399 accused of corrupting the youth, of not believing in his country's gods, and of introducing new divinities. It was thought that he would defend himself, but he declared that he was innocent and that he deserved to be maintained at public expense in the Prytaneum; moreover he affirmed that he had no fear of death, because his disciples would carry on his work. He was condemned to death by a small majority. It was thought that he would make his escape from the prison, which was not well guarded; but he would not do so, and instead drank the hemlock. His voluntary martyrdom brought sublimation to his doctrines. Within a few years all Greece was filled with Socratics; and Plato, Xenophon, and the rest were competing with one another to give clear exposition of their master's thought and to glorify his martyr's death.

No less than five schools appeared as off-shoots of Socrates' teaching and propounded their own systems. A few words may first be said about four of them, which were of minor importance and linked Socrates with pre-Socratic features: longer treatment will be reserved for the fifth school.

The Megarian school and the very closely related school of Elis developed the Socratic dialectic of the Concept, combining it with certain propositions of Parmenides, and using Zeno's method to put forward a general thesis and refute objections. To Euclides of Megara the only reality lay in changeless and incorporeal entities, and the world of sense was illusory. Good was unchangeable: it was reason, and God, and the only concept which had existence.

The Cynics were led by Antisthenes of Athens (c. 440–360), a pupil of Gorgias and Socrates, and later by Diogenes of Sinope (d. 323), who was known as the 'mad Socrates'. They maintained, against Socrates, that cognition consisted in sensation, that there were no definable general concepts, and that only the individual was real and possessed an existence which could be intuited. Virtue was the one Good, making us like to God: all the rest, art and science, pleasures and pains, were indifferent matters. Man, they thought, must renounce all forms of culture which did not conduce to virtue. He must return to the state of nature, abolish social distinctions, and reduce his material needs, thus making happiness consist in misery. These theories were upheld not only with words and writings but by the practical example set by Cynics who lived squalid and miserable lives, and appear to have influenced proletarian and social revolutionary movements during the following centuries.

Directly opposed to the Cynics were the Cyrenaics or hedonists, who were indifferent to the religious problem and concerned themselves only with ethics. They maintained that the true good of man consisted in the mental and physical pleasure generated by sensations. But although man must savour this pleasure he must keep such freedom as enabled him to possess pleasure and not be possessed by it.

But these lesser schools, which largely differed from Socrates, remained for some time isolated and smothered on account of the overwhelming success of Plato and Aristotle. Only later, as we shall see, did they develop and expand under new forms.

f. *Plato and the Academy*

Aristocles, called Plato (428–347), was of noble Athenian family and had learned to write poetry as a boy. He always remained a poet at heart, but later was taught by Cratylus and, from 407, by Socrates, the latter of whom he loved as if he had been his son. After Socrates' death he stayed in Megara, perhaps then in Egypt, and then in southern Italy, where he was friendly with the Pythagorean Archytas and others. He then spent some time in Syracuse. His political career in democratic Athens had been brought to an end on account of the oligarchic views of his family,[13] and he thought he might be able to bring to reality at Syracuse his perfect constitution, which may be an idealization of the constitution of Sparta. But he was unable to convince the Syracusan ruler Dionysius I. So he returned to Athens and opened a school in the gymnasium of the Academy, where he taught first mathematics and later on philosophy. Pupils came from every part of Greece, and his discussions with them enlarged his knowledge on various matters, including the ideas of scholars in distant lands; these pupils were very numerous, drawn mostly from influential families. After two more fruitless attempts to impose his 'constitution', now brought up to date, on the Syracusans, he returned to his Athenian school until the time of his death.

Plato was a man of very great culture, learned in the various philosophical systems of his own day and of the past, and he possessed notable artistic ability in both speaking and writing. He had enormous success in carrying the Socratic doctrines to perfection. The theory of 'concepts', which Socrates had confined almost entirely to ethical thought, was extended by Plato to the whole world and was transformed, with essential features drawn from other schools, into the Theory of 'Ideas'.[14] This meant that for him there were so many universal ideas, incorporeal, eternal, and intelligible, which corresponded to the various types of object. They were conceived by the divine worker (*demiourgos*) as single entities in a hierarchic system, and were given actuality by Him within the formless matter of the original chaos, this being the way in which He created the world of perceptible nature, which consists of a number of copies of the ideas. The human soul, the higher element in which, namely reason, is the work of God, once upon a time had direct knowledge of the ideas. But when it was united with a body it forgot them, and only with great labour, through the experience of the senses, can it remember them, subject to limitless possibilities of error.

Plato agreed with Socrates that knowledge led to virtue and to happiness. But accepting Orphic and Pythagorean views of life after death, he added that the whole process must serve as a preparation for the after-life, because the soul, after a series of more or less painful reincarnations, is able to return to its earliest state and to its divine home. The ethical ideal consists in harmony between body and soul: more specifically it involves justice, wisdom, fortitude, and temperance.

In his last years Plato came increasingly under the influence of the mystical and numerical theories of the Pythagoreans, and established a reconciliation between them and his own Theory of Ideas, the result being pictured in mathematical figures and relationships. He also concerned himself, as we said above, with the constitution of the ideal state; and in an early design for it, set out in his *Republic*, he idealized and completed the constitution of the city which had at that time become famous through its victory and its hegemony, namely Sparta.[15] He propounded a state consisting of three parts: the philosophers, educated in mathematics and dialectic, represented Reason, and were therefore at the head of the government; the warriors defended the state and advanced its gymnastic and musical education; and finally there were the peasants and merchants, who had no part in politics. The main task of this state was to advance under discipline towards justice,[16] and as a consequence all particular interests, such as the family and private property, had to be eliminated. Later, when his attempts to give his Republic reality at Syracuse had failed and when the Spartan hegemony had fallen,[17] Plato in his *Laws* made a new constitutional design, taking more account of the actual political and social conditions of the Greek world.

Plato's literary output was immense. In the main he wrote short dialogues in which he applied the Socratic dialectic and set out to defend his master's theories and his own by confuting the Sophists and representatives of other schools. In these the characters are drawn with great artistry in their real features. They engage in lively discussion in a language of the purest Attic; the style is harmonious and controlled, capable of becoming stirring or tense, ironical or lyrical, as occasion demands. In some passages too one can feel the poet in Plato, and it is not surprising that some of his works, in the enthusiasm of his dialectical triumph, actually end with mythical sections.

Apart from the poetical fragments, the ancient corpus of Plato included forty-two dialogues, thirteen letters, and a certain number of 'definitions'. But the ancients already recognized that seven of the dialogues were spurious, and some modern scholars have shown good ground (in my view at least) for supposing the same for many letters and the definitions. The authorship of some of the remaining thirty-five dialogues is also in doubt.

The school founded by Plato had a long life and was directed by a long succession of heads. Its history, to which we shall return later, is normally divided into three periods, called the Older, Middle, and New Academies.

g. *Aristotle and the Peripatetics*

Yet Aristotle, the greatest of Plato's pupils (384–322), founded a school of his own. He was born at Stagirus in Chalcidice of a family of doctors, and his own early education,[18] which had an important influence on his philosophical studies, was concerned with medicine and natural science. In 367 he came to Athens and stayed there for twenty years: though a very faithful pupil of Plato he also came under the influence of Isocrates' teaching. When Plato died in 347, Aristotle went to Asia Minor and on to Mitylene; then in 343/2 he was made the tutor of the young Alexander of Macedon; then when Alexander took Athens in 335/4, Aristotle settled there with his friend Theophrastus, opened a school in the Lyceum, and taught there for twelve years. The scholars of the school were known as Peripatetics because their master used to teach while walking up and down the avenues. Finally Aristotle was attacked as a friend of Alexander and prosecuted for impiety. He gave charge of the school to Theophrastus and left Athens in 323. Shortly afterwards he died.

Aristotle's output was enormous; one should perhaps rather say the output of his school, since his pupils collaborated with him and the works which have come down to us are often drafts for his lectures or notes and versions made by pupils. Diogenes Laertius tells us that Aristotle wrote 146 works in 400 books (others speak of 1,000 books), a total of 445,270 lines. His scientific curiosity, sustained by a rich library, was universal and encyclopaedic. He concerned himself with everything that could be known, and had so vast an acquaintance with all philosophical schools that he can also, with reason, be called the first historian of Greek philosophy.

Many of his works are lost, for instance a few dialogues of the Platonic type and some popularizing writings. The collection which has come down to us was derived from a copy of the Aristotelian corpus brought to Rome in 84 BC after having been hidden away for a long period.

With his *Organon*, the collection of works on logic and the theory of knowledge, Aristotle was the founder of knowledge through syllogisms, that is to say the understanding of causes by means of reasoning. In this process one either passes from general premises to particular deductions or from particular premises to general inductions. Experience leads to knowledge, by means of the senses, of individual substances which have real existence; and from experience one proceeds, by means of thought, to intellectual understanding of being or intelligible form.

The work called 'First Philosophy' is devoted to metaphysics, and in it Aristotle rejects Plato's Theory of Ideas.[19] The live individual or organism is a union of two basic elements, one potential, the other actual. It consists, in other words, first of indeterminate matter, possessing no form but capable of assuming form, a potential element able to become something and be made perfect; and secondly of form, the actuality which determines its nature, the perfect 'idea' of the species it represents. Beings are arranged in a hierarchy with two heads, God and crude matter. Every intermediate being is matter or potentiality in relation to the being immediately above it. One being only is entirely pure actuality and unchanging form: that is God, who gave the first impulse to universal movement and life.

On the natural sciences or 'physics' Aristotle wrote his *Physics, De Caelo, Meteorologica, Historia Animalium, De Generatione et Corruptione, De Generatione Animalium,* and other works. Many lesser writings on kindred topics seem to be spurious. There are for him two opposing worlds: the heavens full of unalterable, unchanging ether, moving in circular motion; and the earth, on which everything is composed of the four elements, moving vertically and continually being transformed. The earth is fixed and spherical, surrounded by the moving planetary spheres, besides which there are the fixed stars and the ethereal sky. On the earth there exist inorganic beings, composed of elements but lacking soul, and also living organisms possessing soul. Plants have only a vegetative soul; animals have a sensitive soul as well; only in man is there a third soul, the intellectual. Aristotle's studies on the behaviour and psychology of animals, on anatomy, and on physiology are most remarkable, and his classifications of being in a scale of nature are still fundamental.

The treatises *De Anima* and the so-called *Parva Naturalia* are concerned with psychology, dealing with such subjects as perception, memory, length of life, sleep, and death. The soul, which is form and act, is the principle of life, being joined to the body, which is potentiality and matter. The philosopher also examines the various moments when human cognition becomes actual, when sense-perception (*anima sensitiva*) and intellectual (*anima intellectiva*) are acting together. He goes on to study the senses, the operation of the intellect, and other matters.

His works on morals are the *Nicomachean Ethics*, the *Eudemian Ethics*, and the *Magna Moralia*.[20] The supreme good of man is happiness, consisting not only in riches and pleasure, or in friendship and health, but essentially in reason or virtue. Moral virtue is to keep the just mean between too much and too little: and intellectual virtues include intelligence, science, and wisdom.

On political and allied questions he wrote the *Politics*, and there are fragments of some of 158 short works on constitutions, among which we possess on a papyrus the *Constitution of Athens*. The *Economicus* also exists, though with substantial re-editing and rearrangement. Man in these works is regarded as a social being by nature, and individual happiness can only be attained within social organization, which from the primitive bond of the family evolves towards its most perfect form in the state. Yet it is strange that Aristotle, who lived in the days of the great state organisms like that of Macedonia, still conceives his ideal state, with the exception of some remarks on kingship, in terms of the tiny size of the ancient Greek *poleis*. In order to write his work on politics he wanted to be acquainted with individual constitutions, and his school accordingly collected material on the history of 158 Greek constitutions, together with those of Carthage and Lycia, although some (the *Athenian Constitution* for example) were written after the *Politics* had been completed. In his view no constitution was wholly good or wholly bad, since much depended on the temper of the people concerned. He laid down three superior forms of government, monarchy, aristocracy, and republic; and three inferior forms, tyranny, oligarchy, and democracy. His preference was for a constitution in which all had equal rights in law but in which the rulers were the older members of the middle class, the best men, the aristocracy of intellect and virtue rather than the aristocracy of birth and wealth. He also devoted his inquiries to the method of apportioning the powers into which sovereignty of the state can be divided; the deliberative powers, the executive, and the judiciary.

The *Poetics*, an incomplete work, and the *Rhetoric* are concerned with literary theory. Art in Aristotle's view depended on the spirit of imitation and tries to purify the emotions. It allowed one to overcome the failings of nature by drawing one nearer to the universal. Beauty consisted in order, grandeur, and morality.

The breadth of his knowledge and scientific insight, the rigour of his researches, and the results he achieved made Aristotle the greatest among Greek philosophers and scientists. Philosophy with him was contemptuous of any stylistic dressing and literary artifices. It became a genuine science, and was expounded in a style which was precise and simple, although sometimes unduly monotonous and dry. We must not forget, however, that his works are often not books of his own, but 'notes' taken from scientific lectures.[21]

h. *The Stoics*

In the Hellenistic age it is generally true that philosophy mainly developed in the older Greek world, to which even people born in eastern parts migrated if they wanted to be philosophers; but that progress in science was chiefly the product of the new colonial lands in the East.

In Athens when Aristotle departed the direction of the Peripatetic school fell to Theophrastus of Eresus (*c.* 372–287), who had once been a pupil of Plato and was later Aristotle's most faithful follower. Although he never made great advances in ideas, he worked in every field where his master had sown, especially in natural scientific research; and he made a powerful contribution to the school's reputation. He wrote 240 works, and also organized the school in a manner which served as a model to the Museum of Alexandria. We have already spoken about his scientific works. There survives, in a very heavily edited and corrupt text, a short work on 'Characters', comprising a description of thirty defects common to all mankind. They are described and analysed with great liveliness and polish, his style being simple, clear, and reasonably elegant.

The culture and output of Aristotle and Theophrastus were so enormous that one is not surprised to find pupils of theirs in every branch of knowledge. But most of these ignore the scientific side, to which their masters had devoted so much attention, and concern themselves rather with ethics, metaphysics, and so on.

The new school of the Stoics was in its origins connected with that of the Cynics. Zeno of Kition on the island of Cyprus (*c.* 334–262) was an Easterner like the last group of Cynics; indeed he was actually of Semitic blood, the son of a merchant. About 313 he took up residence in Athens, and attended the schools of Crates the Cynic, Stilpo the Megarian, and Polemo of the Academy. Later he founded his own school, and this was given the name of the Stoa because it was located in the portico painted by Polygnotus (*stoa poikile*). It quickly acquired a throng of young men, including the later king of Macedonia, Antigonus Gonatas, the son of Demetrius Poliorcetes, but its master continued to live a life of poverty in the Cynic style. For his teaching he used an Attic which was terse and epigrammatic, though perhaps not of the purest; and gradually he evolved his whole system. At the age of 72 he died by his own hand, leaving a number of works of which we possess only the titles and a few fragments: they included a *Politicus*, written from the communistic standpoint.

His successor at the head of the school in 262 was Cleanthes of Assos in the Troad (331–232). He lived in extreme poverty, for a long time exercising himself as an athlete and in later days watering his garden, replying to the mockery of his companions with wit and good temper. He continued to develop Stoic theories in a number of works on logic, rhetoric, physics, and theology. His *Hymn to Zeus*, which has survived, lays down the essential pantheistic principle of Stoicism. Cleanthes finally starved himself to death.

The next head after Cleanthes, from 232 onwards, was Chrysippus of Soloi in Cilicia (280–206), who before becoming a Stoic had belonged to the Academy. A tireless worker, formidable dialectician, and possessing an astonishing capacity for absorbing knowledge, he left behind him an imposing collection of writings in 705 books, which, though their style is careless and hurried, constitute a complete summary of Stoic theory. Numerous fragments remain.

With these first three heads of the school Stoicism completed the evolution of its doctrine. For them philosophy was wisdom in matters human and divine, and this wisdom led to virtue of thought (logic), virtue of under-standing (physics), and moral virtue (ethics). Logic was the science of thought and discourse (it therefore comprised grammar and rhetoric as well), and the Stoics took pains to establish every possible form of syllogism. Knowledge came from sensations imprinted on the virgin human soul; the soul remem-bered them, and then from the multitude of similar images attained, by means of reason, to general notions. True representations were distinguished from false ones (phantasms) by their clarity, which compels belief in them.

Physics was the true science of everything material, that is everything that was real, namely nature, man, the principles of the universe, and God. Bodies had two principles, the passive one given by matter, and the active one which gives life to matter. The human soul, which resided in the heart and regulated the senses, speech, reproduction, and the principle of direction, was itself matter and destructible. God was the immanent soul of the world; and the old mythology was interpreted allegorically and rationalistically, since the gods were simply the forces of nature. The cosmic fire was the essence which gave life to nature, and from which the soul was formed. This fire changed chaos into air; from air came water, and from water earth; and after a Great Year (12,945 natural years) all would return to chaos. The world was governed by cause; all was linked together in a chain of cause and effect.

There was Good and Evil, but even from Evil Good could come; and the free man was he who lived according to the rules of Fate, which moved in accordance with reason. The end of life was happiness, which consisted in the Stoic virtue of living according to nature; for man this meant living according to reason, human reason being a part of universal or cosmic reason. Man must be self-sufficient; but just because his reason was part of universal reason he must live in society according to law, and all men must be considered equal in relation to nature.

This is pre-eminently a dogmatic and theological system of philosophy. It sprang from the minds not of true Greeks, but from those of Semites and Hellenizing Easterners. After these founders of Stoicism the school expanded and prospered down to late imperial times. Mention may be made here of Panaetius and Posidonius, who were 'eclectics' rather than orthodox members of the school.

Panaetius of Rhodes (180–110) studied at Pergamum with the grammarian Crates of Mallus and then at Athens with the Stoics Diogenes and Antipater. Later he lived for a long time at Rome in the Scipionic circle, was a friend of Polybius, and became the founder of Roman Stoicism. From 129 he was head of the Athenian school and published a number of works, especially on ethics, including *Duty* (drawn on by Cicero in his *De Officiis*), *Providence*, and *Politics*. He did not believe in divination or astrology; and he modified Stoic doctrines by contaminating them with whatever he found to be good in the works of Plato, Aristotle, Xenocrates, Theophrastus, Demetrius of Phalerum, and others.

Among Panaetius' pupils was Posidonius of Apamea (135–51), a man of encyclopaedic culture, who came to Rome in the course of his travels and conceived much affection for it. He later founded a school at Rhodes, which was attended by Cicero. Though a Stoic, he had eclectic views, verging towards mysticism: he believed in divining and in the immortality of the soul. Like Panaetius he wrote a work *On Duty*.

i. The Epicureans

Epicurus (341–271) was born at Samos, the son of an Athenian cleruch who had become a teacher. He began his studies at Samos, did military service at Athens in 324/3, and after teaching for a while at Mitylene and Lampsacus opened a school in a garden at Athens in 306. Three hundred books of his writings, of which 37 were *On Nature*, were current in antiquity. But his doctrine was also published in summaries of varying length, of which the most concise edition is that which has come down to us from Diogenes Laertius. In addition we possess substantial fragments of the work *On Nature*, together with some letters and some sayings. Moreover the ideas of Epicurus inspired the work of Lucretius, Philodemus, and Seneca, and are also quoted by opponents like Cicero and Plutarch.

According to Epicurus the objective of philosophy is a happy life, and therefore any science which does not conduce to that end is futile. The sole purpose of getting to understand nature is to free man from fear and superstition. Our senses do not deceive us, but our hypotheses about the causes of facts can often be erroneous. There certainly exist bodies formed of matter, for the senses tell us this: and reason adds that void exists as well. Matter is composed of atoms, innumerable, tiny, indivisible bodies of a simple kind, which are constantly uniting and separating. They fall in the void with a slant: so they strike one another, combine, and form bodies, and the bodies then dissolve again into atoms. In the measureless infinite void of the *cosmos* there exist, separately from the void itself, a vast number of worlds, though we have acquaintance with only one of them. These worlds are born and move without any purpose. By dint of successive experiments nature has made the world we live in, and man as we know him.

The soul is composed of the lightest kind of atoms. It cannot live without the body nor the body without it: when the body dies, the soul dies too. So it is absurd to fear death. All bodies emit images of themselves, composed of very light atoms which make their way to our senses and leave an impression there. Sometimes these images combine, this being the source of errors of the senses and concepts of the unreal. Epicurus was opposed to religion and to accepted forms of worship, but he was not an atheist. He believed that there were gods, since we have the concept of gods. But in his view they were blessed and immortal beings who did not concern themselves with mankind, living in the spaces between the worlds, an area where there existed only ether and where there was no movement of atoms. Accepted religion was born of fear, and its practices were wholly useless. Providence did not exist.[22]

In ethics Epicurus came under the influence of Cyrenaic theories. By nature man seeks pleasure and avoids pain, but happiness consists not in isolated and desultory pleasure but in *eudaimonia*, pleasure which was moderate, lasting, and serene. It is then that the body is without pain and the spirit free from cares. So happiness consists in a life which follows moderation, reason, and virtue.

j. *The Sceptics and the New Academy*

The philosophers of the Megarian school, who were affected also by Cynic ideas, were inclined towards scepticism, both in religious questions and in their theories of knowledge. This scepticism was developed into a regular system by Pyrrhon (*c.* 360–270), who drew negative conclusions from the disagreement between the ideas of different philosophers. Pyrrhon was born in Elis, and always resided there. He was a pupil of the Democritean philosopher Anaxarchus, and was heavily influenced by the Megarians: it is not impossible that he drew something from the idea of *ataraxia* put forward by the Indian ascetics, with some of whom he was personally acquainted. His sceptic doctrine can be roughly summarized as follows. Nothing exists in real truth; good and evil are only conventions; reason cannot construct anything, nor can it attain knowledge of what is real; all hypothesis is futile; there can be no science; so the ideal of happiness is to remain indifferent to everything, and not to speak (*aphasia*) or to make a judgement. The life of this original philosopher became a tissue of legend. His theories, preached rather than written, quickly reached a ready public, and were then inherited by Timon of Phlius (320–230), another pupil of Stilpon and a wandering philosopher-sophist. Timon wrote tragedies, satyric dramas, iambics, and such-like; but there is special interest in three books of *Silloi*, of which fairly extensive fragments survive. In a parody of the Homeric Nekyia the poet pretended he was descending to the lower world among the philosophers and carrying on discussions with them, particularly with Xenophanes. In this way he was able to criticize and caricature all the characters he depicted.

The Sceptics did not create a regular school. After the earliest period of their preaching (the Early Scepticism) their theories were largely taken over by the Academicians, starting with Arcesilaus of Pitane in Aeolis (315–241), who was head of the Academy from 264 to his death. His philosophy was a compound of Academic, Megarian, and Sceptic doctrines, markedly opposed to Stoicism. He wrote little and what he did write was generally in verse; but he had a magnificent reputation as a dialectician and controversialist. He maintained that the human spirit could not grasp the truth, because what was false presented itself just as irresistibly as what was true; a wise man should remain doubtful or 'moderate' in relation to the truth, contenting himself with what was probable.

Arcesilaus brought about a revival in the Academy, which now became gradually more eclectic. Carneades of Cyrene (215–129), a great dialectician and orator, maintained that there were three degrees of probability, but that objective truth was unknowable and unattainable, since human beings could know only appearance. When, on an embassy to Rome in 156, he gave two discourses, the first to prove the existence of justice and the second to disprove it, he shocked the virtuous public of Rome profoundly by his sophistries.

6. ROME

a. *Forms of Religious Observance*

'Sua cuique civitati religio est.' This trite observation of Cicero (*pro Flacco*, 28) reflects the varied condition of religion among the diverse groups of people, in city and country, within the parts of the world which had been made Roman. To some extent at least, local cults were preserved in all regions, either in their original state or in forms resulting from syncretism with the Graeco-Roman pantheon. We can prove this from literary evidence, but still more from epigraphy and monuments derived from the various regions.

The phenomenon was most noticeable among the poorer members of the *populus* and among the countryfolk, who were shocked at what to them were incomprehensible and heretical deviations on the part of the upper classes. In all districts they attached themselves tenaciously to such primitive native cults as had survived, in other words to a small number of beloved and kindly deities whom they felt were always near them in their families and houses, in the streets or fields, or at their work, and to whom there was an age-long tradition of sacrifice on the domestic altars, or at the cross-roads and in little shrines. The most traditionally-minded people were of course the countrymen, the *pagani*. This situation was grounded in the original differences of race, culture, and religion between Rome and the conquered peoples which came into political unity with it. It was a situation perpetuated by the almost complete freedom of thought which Rome allowed to its subjects.

But meanwhile soldiers, traders, and other persons of moderate education were more and more apt to find themselves quartered in the provinces, especially the provinces of the East. There were also educated slaves and other immigrants from various parts of the East who were domiciled in Rome and the Western provinces. All these classes contributed to a rapid spread of particular Eastern cults in the West. The Magna Mater of Pessinus was identified with Cybele and her cult was installed on the Palatine in 204 BC. Isis and Serapis were introduced in Sulla's time, and four separate attempts to prohibit the cult between 58 and 48 came to nothing. Mithras was taken over by the pirates and then brought to Rome by Pompey and his veterans.

Finally, there was the attitude of the most highly educated classes. Not only were they quite blankly incredulous of the mythology of the Greek poets, which had been grafted on to the native Roman cults, but they showed no interest in the cults themselves and were eventually quite ignorant about them. Although certain cults survived, their observance was now a mechanical affair carried out by the priests without evoking feeling or even attendance on the part of devotees. Although in Rome itself the *pontifices* sometimes took radical steps to defend the ancient cults, Varro predicted that many of them would die through the *incuria* of Roman citizens.

In 249 BC P. Claudius Pulcher was put on trial for impiety when he cast the haruspical chickens into the sea because they refused to drink. But less than three-quarters of a century later Ennius could translate the atheistical Sacred History of Euhemerus for a Roman public; and Plautus in the *Amphitruo* (I, 126) and in the *Pseudolus* (III, 2, 50) was making telling parodies of sacred figures, in which he was followed by other writers of comedy and mime and by the poets in general. Pomponius caricatured the *haruspices* and the augurs, and a saying attributed to Cato the censor, to the effect that *haruspices* could hardly meet each other without laughing, showed a similar attitude. Lucilius (*Sat.* XV, 2) ridiculed the frightening religious devices ascribed to Numa Pompilius. Varro's laments have been mentioned above, 'the gods are dying, not at the hands of our enemies but because our citizens do not care'. It may be added that some of the priestly offices were for a long time left unfilled, that of *rex sacrorum* from the second century, and that of *flamen Dialis* from 87 to 11 BC.

The fact was that the old myths and ritual had often become incomprehensible, and could no longer be articles of faith with educated and cultured people. Sceptics had by now eaten their way into the old speculative proofs of 'being' and had made men tired of the constructions of Greek dialectic with its endless assertions and denials. Moreover the general development of moral and social ideas had led to a change and a sublimation in the outlook and purpose of religion: men now tended to put their faith and trust in the suggestions made, however obscurely, by the consciences within them. So it was not to atheism that they had recourse: one can prove this by the failure of the Epicurean doctrine so passionately upheld by Lucretius, which was designed to show that religion was born of fear of death and of the gods and was the cause of all ills. The movement was instead towards the triumph of 'religious sentiment'.

We reach the same conclusion if we remember the great interest in religious problems shown in the writings of Varro and Tarquitius Priscus. When Rome conquered the Mediterranean world it ordered it on new and more up-to-date principles, and so many social, moral, and legal ideas had been renovated that there was inevitably going to be an attempt to revolutionize religion too. Provision therefore had to be made for a religion of 'sentiment' by taking account of other movements of a spiritual kind. For a small group of men the yearning for a moral law was satisfied by the study of philosophy, but by now it was becoming obvious that Stoic teaching could not provide the means for a definite social reform of the population as a whole. The remainder of mankind, whose religious aspirations were stronger than those of this small group, embraced syncretistic cults of Eastern origin, even though they were not genuinely Eastern but a jumble of heterogeneous elements brought together quite arbitrarily.

b. *Diffusion of Religion and Philosophy*

These new syncretistic ideas were indeed spreading fast, especially those of a neo-Pythagorean and Hellenistico-Jewish variety. Juba II, the learned king of Numidia, made a collection of neo-Pythagorean writings. At Rome they found a ready audience, since Roman scholars much enjoyed spending time on religious problems. The first effects can be seen in the *Rudens* of Plautus;[23] the first reactions in the other direction came as early as 181 BC, in connection with the books ascribed to Numa Pompilius.

As was indicated earlier, the attention given to religious problems by Varro in his *Antiquitatum rerum humanarum et divinarum libri* is a characteristic example of Roman treatment of the subject. For instance he maintained that there were three different conceptions of divinity, the poetical, the political, and the philosophical (here he was drawing on the Stoics, and in particular on Posidonius). The work was pervaded throughout by philo-sophical speculation, popular belief, and a fondness for evolving syncretisms between various religions on very much the same principles as Caesar used. We are told that Varro was buried with neo-Pythagorean rites (Pliny, *N.H.*, XXXV, 160). The same tendencies are displayed in the study of various foreign religions, for instance in the *De Disciplina Etrusca* of Tarquitius Priscus; and they are the reason why Rome was invaded by Eastern syn-cretistic cults of an astral nature, exemplified in the apotheosis of Julius Caesar as a star. Eastern Messianic conceptions and neo-Pythagorean purificatory doctrines find an echo in Virgil's IVth *Eclogue* and in the descent of Aeneas to Elysium described in the *Aeneid*. Even Cicero is writing under the influence of some version of these new ideas in the passage called *Somnium Scipionis* which closes his *De Republica* and in which he asserts that good works open the road to heaven; and in another passage he writes that the prayers of the Vestals secure pardon from the gods. Sallust too declares that the gods watch over the good and evil acts of men. The movement found its greatest exponent in Nigidius Figulus (98–45), whom Rome regarded as a magician and astrologer. He was a neo-Pythagorean, and in his *Sphaera Graecanica* and *Sphaera Barbarica* gave explanations of the heavens and of the metamorphoses of men into stars.

All this new type of feeling towards religious atmosphere, this longing for mysticism, does something to explain Augustus' conception of a religious revival. It also accounts for some of the conditions which somewhat later favoured the spread of Christian ideas, despite all earlier Roman legislation and despite the new imperial cult.

c. *Foreign Cults*

In the fourth century BC Rome under Camillus' leadership resumed the advance to hegemony and at the same time instituted the system of making gradual concessions to the conquered peoples, enabling many of them to migrate to Rome. This threatened the ancestral religion with extinction, and it must have been at this time that Rome passed a law which was the basis of its religious policy in later times. It is recorded by Cicero in the *De Legibus* (II, 8, 1; 10, 25), and runs 'no citizen may worship special gods, either new or foreign, unless they have first been accepted publicly by the state; and in private only the gods of our fathers may be worshipped'. So in law gods not accepted by the state could not be worshipped by citizens even in private. On the other hand non-citizens, either in their own countries, or in private at Rome if they resided there, could worship their own ancestral gods—which might or might not be syncretized with those of Rome—once an appropriate decree of the senate had sanctioned them.

The law to which Cicero refers was never repealed, but in practice it was rigorously enforced only at periods of crisis. Generally it was employed leniently and then only at occasional moments; for instance in 242 when the *sortes Praenestinae*[24] were banned. So in the course of the fourth and third centuries almost all the major divinities of the peninsula found their way into the Roman pantheon for practical purposes, either directly or in syncretism with other gods; and the state did not seriously interfere.

The matter became more complex and worrying when the Roman empire began gradually to include territories outside the peninsula, with peoples to whom Rome had no intention of granting citizenship and cults which were obviously very different from its own. It was at this point that a more rigid line began to be taken, for instance when foreign cults were prohibited in 213. Later, however, partly as the result of the alternating dominance of phil-Hellenism and anti-Hellenism at Rome, the educated classes were first attracted by the fantasies of Greek mythology and then began to see how inconsistent it all was. A whole flood of mystery cults and of oriental doctrines about the after-life then proceeded to invade Italy by various paths, the state neither giving them an enthusiastic welcome nor being able or willing to offer any effective opposition. After a time, however, the *pontifices* and the anti-Hellenist members of the senate, who believed that in Greek cults and in Hellenic influence in general they could detect the main causes of the corruption of Roman *mores*, were successful in organizing a reactionary policy of intolerance and religious persecution. Their leader was M. Porcius Cato, and their policy was undoubtedly based on the illegality involved in introducing such cults and on the danger of moral and political decline they were supposed to bring. In this atmosphere there was held, over a period of five years, the famous inquiry into the *Bacchanalia*, in which 7,000 persons were implicated; and another manifestation of the reaction can be seen in 181, when the 'Pythagorean books' ascribed to King Numa were burnt by the public executioner. All this led naturally to suppression of any innovation which seemed to be a corrupting influence, one consequence being the expulsion of philosophers and rhetoricians in 161.

Certain general propositions were in this way reaffirmed. First, that a new cult might not be practised without the state's consent; secondly that cults which were tolerated for non-citizens and foreigners might not proselytize among Romans without incurring grave danger; and thirdly that all religious practices which could be shown to be morally objectionable must be uprooted. For this reason the Chaldean diviners were banished in 139, and the early Jewish conventicles, then engaged in promoting worship of their God (wrongly identified by contemporary Romans with the Phrygian Sabazios), were made illegal.

But no law, especially one applied spasmodically and within a society which was in part opposed to it and in part indifferent, could check the spontaneous growth of a new culture. It crept in through countless channels which were scarcely visible, and it brought with it new ideas in religion to meet men's hopes and longings.

So although there was still vigilant opposition, illustrated in the four decrees against the resurgent Isis cult which were mentioned earlier, none the less new cults and foreign rites, especially those reflecting the prevalent syncretism of the East, continued to make their way more or less secretly into Rome. They were still brought in by Easterners living in the West, by slaves of diverse origin, by Italians who had been initiated during their residence in the East, and by Chaldeans wandering round the world. The most difficult problem was to prevent such people proselytizing among the Italians, although it was a problem which worried only the conservative elements in politics.

d. *Religious and Political Difficulties with the Jews*

One reason for the dispersion of Jews about the Roman world had been the assistance given by Rome to the Hasmoneans (the Maccabees) against the Seleucid attempt to Hellenize Judaea. From 165 BC there was a pro-Roman party in Judaea, but this did not prevent a wholesale expulsion of Jews from Rome in 139 when the first Jewish communities there were indulging in organized efforts to make proselytes. Relations were again strained during the Mithradatic War, when one Jewish party, the Sadducees, still supported Parthia, and the other, the Pharisees, retained their philhellenic policy. The next decisive events were the victory of Pompey over Mithradates VI and the reduction of Judaea to a vassal state under the leadership of Hyrcanus II with Pharisaic support, though the anti-Roman and pro-Parthian party was still in opposition. The assistance offered by Hyrcanus to Caesar for his Egyptian campaign in 47 had beneficial results not only for him personally but for the Jewish settlements scattered throughout the Roman world. They were allowed to live in peace, still paying their 'di-drachm' to the Temple at Jerusalem, and Rome allowed them to possess 'collegia'. But throughout the civil wars the anti-Roman factions could continue to hope for the ruin of their overlord. After Caesar's death they supported the Caesaricide C. Cassius Longinus, who had established himself in Syria and entered on an alliance with Parthia. When M. Antonius became master of Syria the pro-Roman party was restored to power. But stability was still threatened, first by the Parthian invasions of Syria, and secondly by Antonius' assignment of much of Palestine to the Pharaonic domain of Cleopatra.

The victory of Octavian over Antony and his accord with Herod, much resented by the anti-Roman party, made peaceful co-existence between Jews and Romans possible once more. Then, however, new difficulties appeared. In 4 BC Herod died, and his possessions were divided among his three sons, whose kingdoms were in a state of discord. There was increasing dependence on Roman procurators, who had little knowledge of local conditions. But the chief trouble was the compulsory imposition by Augustus of the cult of Dea Roma and of the deified emperors. The difficulties were in part surmounted by the able dispositions of Augustus, but they again became acute in the time of his successor.

e. *Augustan Religion*

In 27 BC, after assuming the title 'Augustus', the first emperor began his reconstruction of the Roman world. He at once showed himself markedly hostile to foreign cults, and he also created new factors which made it still more difficult for Rome to come to terms with the monotheists among its subjects. Once he had put Italy in a position of political and economic superiority to the provinces, he wanted Italy to show itself morally worthy of the mission he had entrusted to it. Cassius Dio (LIII, 36) asserts that Maecenas gave the young Octavian the following advice: 'do you yourself worship the divine power everywhere by every means, in accordance with the tradition of our fathers, and compel others to honour it too. Hate and punish all who try to introduce innovations in this regard, not only for the sake of the gods ... but because those who introduce new divinities persuade many to change their thoughts and practices; and from this there spring up conspiracies, revolts, and factions. ... Do not tolerate atheists or magicians ... and keep your eye on philosophers too'. Augustus seems to have had a fair measure of superstition himself and to have been attracted by neo-Pythagorean doctrines, but he undoubtedly thought religion was indispensable both on account of his personal feelings and also for political reasons. Yet his general plan for the state demanded that his religion, for Italians, should still be the ancient Roman system. He wanted Italians to return to the cults of their fathers and be deflected from the supposedly subversive propaganda which accompanied foreign cults, though he inevitably deceived himself in thinking that this return, being forced and made in the face of history, could ever be an intimate affair rather than remaining purely external. So he restored eighty-two temples, had altars to the Lares erected at the cross-roads in every *vicus*, revived forgotten festivals such as the Lupercalia, celebrated the Secular Games with solemnity, and had the Sibylline Books put into order once more, at the same time consigning hundreds of false oracles and works on ritual to the flames.

Much more important for Rome's relations with religions of mono-theistic type was Augustus' new conception of a cult of Dea Roma and of emperors who were deified after their deaths, a cult which was to be obligatory throughout the empire. It was intended to be something above all national religions, cementing political and spiritual cohesion and ensuring the loyalty of the provinces. In actual fact the origins of this conception lay far in the past, and were not Roman but Italiote and Hellenistic. Since the third century BC the Greeks, who were fond of personifying abstract concepts, had imagined a Dea Roma, whom we find depicted on 'Romano-Campanian' coins and also given temples in Greece and Asia Minor from 196 and 195, although this goddess was not yet worshipped in Rome. Likewise the Hellenistic East, which was accustomed to worship living rulers, quickly paid divine honours to Roman personages of regal bearing. In this way

Caesar was a god as Alexander had been, and after him there was Antonius, the neo-Dionysus. Augustus himself after Actium was portrayed on statues as a god, his hair curled and bound with a fillet inlaid with jewels, or wearing a radiate crown. He too, even in his lifetime, was worshipped as a god, not at Rome, except by colleges of freedmen, but in Asia, Spain, Gaul, and eventually Germany. In Rome he did not yet dare to institute such a practice, but people already spoke of the Caesar's protecting genius.

Yet the compulsory adoption throughout the empire, including Italy, of the cult of Dea Roma and of the emperors deified after their deaths was definitely willed by Augustus, who was responsible for the deification of Caesar; and when Augustus died, he too was deified, and the first temple to him as *divus* was set up on the Palatine at Rome by his widow Livia. Later on Caligula was the first of a discontinuous series of emperors who, copying Antonius, desired to be worshipped as gods, in Rome and Italy, during their actual lifetimes.

This new imperial religion, like the previous enforcement of a return to the forgotten gods of Italy, did not move the minds of the masses by any poetical myths or philosophical theology. It therefore left a void in men's hearts, which they more than ever sought to fill with the new faiths imported from abroad. Yet it was regarded as essential for the life of the state, since, as Virgil and Horace maintained, the permanence of the empire depended on religion. In time, however, it came to be a formidable obstacle to the existence and growth of monotheistic religions, such as Judaism and later Christianity, among Roman citizens; and these two faiths in any case made things more difficult on their own account, owing to their uncompromising denial of all other gods. But for the moment Augustus attempted to overcome friction with the Jews by confirming and extending the measures taken by Pompey and Caesar. He allowed Jews of the Diaspora to meet for Sabbath observance and to send the traditional two drachmas to the Temple at Jerusalem. Their only obligation, seeing that they were not willing to sacrifice to the gods of Rome, was to make sacrifice to Yahweh for the emperor's good fortune and to send the emperor a donative.

f. *Eclecticism and Philosophy (Marcus Tullius Cicero)*

Amid the great flood of philosophical doctrines, all claiming to set forth the absolute truth, and with controversies sometimes raging no less fiercely in that they were directed to disinterested questions of the spirit, it was natural for the general tone of philosophical studies to be lowered, a consequence which would have in any case followed from the heresies and schisms within the various schools. Inevitably men tried to find agreement through contaminating different doctrines, in other words through 'eclecticism', one of the features of late Hellenistic philosophy. We find, from time to time, contamination between all kinds of doctrine, Cynic and Cyrenaic, Academic and Sceptic, Academic and Stoic, and so on. We should not forget that many schools were in agreement on basic points and were at variance mainly on particular questions. The tendency towards eclecticism grew stronger all the time and became the prevailing mood in the Roman period.

From the outset there had never been real philosophers at Rome. There were orators, historians, and jurists who came under the influence of Greek philosophers, the Stoics appealing mainly to the jurists and the Academicians to the orators. Cicero says that before his time Rome possessed practically no philosophical work except from the Epicurean school. From them he cites three Latin writers, Amafinius, Catius and Rabirius; and of course we must add the great Lucretius.

But Greek philosophers were finding Rome a suitable soil for their teaching and writing from Panaetius' time. This meant that when Roman philosophy made its appearance with Cicero it had the general features of the eclectic Stoicism professed by Panaetius and Posidonius, and the same interest as they had in moral and political, rather than in metaphysical, problems. Rome's additional contribution was an aversion from the endless inconclusive disputes of dialectic.

Cicero's first effort at philosophical writing was made in a letter to his brother Quintus in 60 BC and was concerned with provincial government, in other words with political philosophy. His earliest philosophical treatises, the *De Re Publica* of 54–51 and the *De Legibus*, have the same theme. Of these the former, of which we possess only a part, is a dialogue imagined to have taken place in 129 between persons of the circle of Scipio Aemilianus. It upholds the need for a mixed form of government, with a temporary 'princeps' at its head. The *De Legibus*, which has survived with a gap in Book III, is concerned to redraft the laws on the principles of natural right. Later Cicero sought consolation for his political and private troubles by writing a series of works of philosophical type, which succeeded one another rapidly in 45 and 44, so rapidly indeed that some have held the exaggerated view that they were simply translations or refurbishings of Greek texts. In 45 he published the following: a *consolatio* for the death of his daughter; the *Hortensius*, an exhortation to philosophy; the *Academica*, designed to expound the various Greek schools by setting one against another; the *De Finibus Bonorum et Malorum*, where he shows that Sceptic and Stoic views on the *summum bonum* and *summum malum* came to the same thing; a translation of Plato's *Timaeus*, now almost entirely lost; and his five books of *Tusculan Disputations*, in which he takes the Stoic view. In 44 he wrote a lifeless compilation entitled *De Divinatione*, and his *De Fato*; later on a number of works of genuine feeling, mainly derived from the Stoics, the *Cato Maior* (or *De Senectute*), the *Laelius* (or *De Amicitia*), and the *De Officiis*; and finally the *De Auguriis* and *De Gloria*, both of which have perished.

This hurried set of philosophical writings by Cicero has certainly no originality. It is a blend between Sceptic Academism where 'pure reason' is concerned and eclectic Stoicism where he is dealing with 'practical reason'. But Cicero can take credit for a number of things. He gave the Romans a clear picture of the opposing Greek theories, which are upheld by the various characters in his dialogues. To some extent he created a philosophical terminology in Latin. And finally he caused the treatment of philosophy to assume once more the graceful form it had practically lost in Greece since Plato's day.

g. *T. Lucretius Carus*: *Epicureanism*

Before Lucretius a number of didactic writers of Latin verse had addressed themselves to philosophical argument. T. Albucius, an Epicurean enthusiast for things Greek, had put the theory of Epicurus into verse; C. Sallustius had composed his *Empedoclea*, which Cicero considered unreadable; and Varro, among all his other works, had written a philosophic poem mentioned by Quintilian.

We have very little biographical information about T. Lucretius Carus (99/94–55/50 BC). His *cognomen* and certain allusions in the poem have made some scholars believe, without adequate foundation, that he was a Celt and the son of a freedman. Jerome states that he was driven mad by a love philtre, but had lucid intervals during which he composed 'aliquot libros', and later committed suicide. It has indeed been thought that evidence of his *insania* can be found in certain passages where with great liveliness he describes nightmares and the madness of love and the agitation of the soul. However all this may be, he left behind him a poem *De Rerum Natura* in six books, complete but not revised, and later published on Cicero's advice. The latter was unwilling to alter it. He left abrupt transitions and preliminary arrangements of the poet's material, especially in the last book.

Although Lucretius played no part in public life, he had suffered like others from the ills which tormented his generation and had witnessed riots and massacres. He wanted to offer his contemporaries a means of salvation, a word of truth in which he believed with all his heart. This was the theory of Epicurus.

In Lucretius' view nothing is born of nothing, and nothing returns to nothing. The universe is a matter from eternity, and consists in an infinity of immortal atoms, which are falling without any pause in infinite space. These atoms meet, and so create bodies: they separate, and so dissolve the bodies, all in accord with absolute laws. The soul too is formed of slender atoms composed of wind, heat, air, and a fourth very fine element. The soul is diffused throughout the body, and both the instincts of animals and the characters of men depend on the varying blends between the four components. When the body dissolves, the soul dissolves too. From the surface of objects there move off thin tissues, which stimulate our senses, even during sleep. In perception it is not the senses which err, but the reason in the process of interpreting them; for human judgement is misled by passions, which it is our duty to avoid. The poet describes the origins of the world—of the earth, and of plants, animals, and men, begotten and made fruitful by the earth herself. Primitive men, through the work of heroes, gradually made life less harsh. They created the family, the state, and language; they made technical and artistic discoveries; and they were governed by monarchies. But there followed a general upheaval, and the thrones began to fall. Then things returned to order with the institution of laws, magistrates, and punishments; and religion was invented, because man was ignorant of the true causes of cataclysms (which the poet digresses to describe) and attributed such things to the wrath of the gods.

It is not the power behind his reconstruction of Epicurean science which makes Lucretius' poem so magnificent. The science is often *simpliste*, and the system contains too many flaws and internal contradictions to be admired for its coherence. Even the happiness which he so longs to achieve is not depicted without some lack of clarity. The poet's greatness lies rather in the granite faith with which he believes he can attain truth by reason. This gives him the boldness and burning light of a prophet, and he shows an eager and passionate longing to propound a new ideal and a new truth to a sceptical and disorientated world. There is greatness too in the boundless admiration shown for his master, Epicurus, and in the enthusiasm with which he attacks his task, though it may be that here we can detect the influence of the pathos of Empedocles or even a certain hypersensitiveness in the poet's make-up. But it is certain that Lucretius' enthusiasm and tenacity, which contrast so strongly with the litigious arguments of his Greek contemporaries, are no isolated phenomenon in the Latin world, where conviction became an absolute rule of life.

NOTES TO CHAPTER XI

1. The authors attribute the development and diffusion of Taoism in China, with its mysticism, gigantic pantheon, etc., to the fact that the local and state cults of heaven, earth and ancestors were insufficient to satisfy the people's religious needs, and that the people yearned for 'some emotional uplift of the soul'. In fact it was not the people who called into being a religion that could satisfy their 'religious needs' but, on the contrary, all the age-old popular beliefs in gods, holy spirits, werewolves, etc., as well as everyday superstitions, beliefs in mystical reincarnation, and so on—all of which in the course of time came to be embraced within the framework of a religious teaching, based on a particular religious treatment of the philosophical concept *tao*. (L. S. Vasilyev.)

2. It is questionable whether Indian philosophy has its origin in religion. It is never produced quite simply from changes in cults or religious ideas. More account should be taken of the efforts at rational cosmological explanations of the world and the human condition, the existence of which is particularly attested in the ancient Buddhist texts (*Dīghanikāya*) denouncing them as erroneous (an allusion is made to them on p. 829).

3. It would be interesting to recall here that among the religious policies of the Achaemenids was the installation of the *arta brazmaniya*, 'Brahmanic good order' (ancient Persian *arta*, or Vedic ṛta), which reveals another case of probable contact or an original relationship between Iranian and Indian doctrines.

4. The various philosophical schools that contended with one another in Greece during the fifth and fourth centuries BC were closely connected with the bitter social struggle going on at that time in the Greek city-states. The problems of the structure of society and the state, and their possible reconstruction, of the duties and tasks of the individual and the citizen, and his relationships with his native *polis* and the human race in general —all these questions were hotly debated by the broadest social circles, were discussed by orators at public debates, and were taken as the themes of comedies and tragedies staged before crowds of spectators. One might also say that there are few periods of history when one can see more clearly that the struggle between ideologies stemmed from the struggle between social classes. (E. M. Shtaerman.)

5. Most scholars have now abandoned this view of the *Bacchae*. Professor B. A. van Groningen, for example, writes 'All we can assert is that, at the end of his life, Euripides' artistic soul felt with great intensity the charm of the passionate Dionysiac cult. But his soul was the soul of an artist, and that is hardly the same thing as the soul of a believer.' See above all E. R. Dodds' edition of the play (Oxford, 1944).

6. See above, p. 469, although Professor A. Lesky maintains that Professor Pareti has exaggerated the oriental origins of Stoicism, and Professor B. A. van Groningen points out that Zeno was the only Easterner among the founders of the school.

7. See also Part I, pp. 248 ff. As has been emphasized by Dr P. Oliva and Professor C. Danov, the origins of Greek philosophy, which are discussed in the following paragraphs, are intimately linked with the all-important Greek work on physics and cosmogony, from Thales to Anaxagoras and Democritus; and one must remember the materialist strain in this thought, not least in the last-named thinker.

8. Yet the idea is found in two older contemporaries of Anaxagoras, of very different outlook from each other, namely the poets Aeschylus and Pindar.

9. Another famous Sophist was Gorgias of Leontini (c. 483–376), who wrote a treatise to prove the impossibility of positive knowledge, and then devoted himself to showing his contemporaries the power of words and to the evolution of a prose style. He was said in antiquity to have influenced both Thucydides and Isocrates.

10. As Professor A. Lesky shows, Protagoras too must have made a notable contribution to political thought. The Platonic dialogue bearing his name shows him upholding that virtue, both social and political, is teachable, a doctrine which disturbed Socrates. For an attempt to reconcile the doctrine with Protagoras' alleged subjectivism (for which the evidence comes from Plato's *Theaetetus*) see A. Levi, *Mind*, 1940, pp. 284 ff.

11. The *daimon*, as Professor A. Lesky points out, was more a warning than a motive force.

12. *Translator's Note.* In the sections on Socratico-Platonic philosophy the Italian words 'concetto' and 'idea' have been directly transliterated since no other translation would be free from controversy. But the reader should be warned that the history of philosophy has dealt differently with these two words in Italian and English.

13. Still more responsible, perhaps, were his own anti-democratic convictions, formed in the latter part of the Peloponnesian War and strengthened by the fate of Socrates.

14. See Note 12 above. (*Translator*.)

15. Professor Pareti's view that the *Republic* was an idealization of the Spartan constitution needs qualification. No doubt he was extremely interested in Sparta, but there are revolutionary, and entirely un-Spartan, elements in his ideal state; and some of these are described in Professor Pareti's next sentences.

16. With the help of an elaborate system of education, which, as Professor F. M. Heichelheim notes, was not far removed from the modern division into 'primary, higher, and University' education.

17. Here too, as Professor B. A. van Groningen points out, it may be unwise to regard the contemporary history of Sparta as an important force in turning Plato towards the more rigorous system propounded in the *Laws*.

18. In particular Aristotle was greatly influenced by Democritus (see above, pp. 421).

19. For a brilliant short summary of Aristotle's relationship to Plato, both in epistemology and in ethics, see W. D. Ross, *Oxford Classical Dictionary* (1946), s.v. 'Aristotle'.

20. This work is often regarded as spurious.

21. Alternatively his own notes for his lectures, which notes he may have revised at various times during his life.

22. Dr P. Oliva, adding to Professor Pareti's analysis the fact that Epicurus denied life after death, considers that the materialistic strain in Epicureanism is under-emphasized.

23. This play is modelled on a Greek original by Diphilus (fourth century BC), and it is therefore not quite safe to assume that the neo-Pythagorean elements are due to Plautus.

24. One of the many Italian forms of divination, probably a simple drawing of inscribed lots (Polybius, VI, 11). It was later greatly in vogue among the higher classes, including the imperial family, during the first century AD.

CHAPTER XII

LITERATURE AND ART: 500 BC TO AD 1

I. THE DEVELOPMENT OF LITERATURE

a. *China*

Chinese literature in the Warring States period (fifth to third centuries BC.) is concerned on the one hand with the development of philosophical thought; this is mainly prose and has been dealt with in the preceding chapter. It should be remembered that the Discourses of Confucius (*Lun-yü*) seem to employ the spoken language of the time and are an outstanding example of fresh, unsophisticated prose, full of idioms and supple phrases. Poetry, on the other hand, is less connected with philosophy, although the style of the *Tao-te-ching* is very often near to poetry. The poetical production of the Western Chou had been a strictly official, court-sponsored, and impersonal body of writing. It was only much later that a quite novel note was struck. This happened about 300 BC in the Ch'u kingdom in the Yangtze-kiang valley. This new poetry was produced by an originally non-Chinese society, in which the common people was still 'barbarian' and only the cultural élite spoke and wrote Chinese. The 'elegies of Ch'u' (*Ch'u-tz'ŭ*) are thus something quite different from the tradition of the 'Book of Odes'. Their background is mainly magical, and this is true even for its longest composition, the *Li-sao* (meaning probably 'Sorrows of banishment'). Its author Ch'ü Yüan complains of his disgrace and his inability to serve his sovereign. He expresses himself in a rather stilted and unpoetic language full of allegories, invocations, and mystical allusions, not devoid of real eloquence. This luxuriant poetry is magical and religious in character, and not political like the Chou Odes with their sober and chaste style. The metre of the Ch'u poetry is based on a verse of six syllables (as against the Odes' four). From this, in the course of the Han period, there arose the *fu*, a sort of unfettered recitative, bound only to a strong rhythm, but also making use of rhyme. The contents of the *fu* were usually descriptions of cities, palaces, gardens, etc., in a highly strung language that tended often to fall into ornate but rather empty rhetoric. The chief representatives of this poetry were Chia I (201–169) and Ssŭ-ma Hsiang-ju (179–117).

Chinese history writing goes as far back as that venerable document, the 'Spring and Autumn' (*Ch'un-ch'iu*), i.e. the Annals, whose compilation, or at least revision, is traditionally attributed to Confucius. They cover the period 722–481 and are a dry-as-dust chronological register of events centring

---

* The passages within square brackets were contributed by Professor Pierre Grimal, to supplement the original text, after the death of Professor Pareti.

round the principality of Lu, Confucius' home country. Only slightly later (fourth century) is the *Tso-chuan*, a real attempt at writing history. It is highly impersonal, the author disappearing behind the events he relates; his opinion is reflected, at the most, in the choice of the event to be registered. In its impassive style it still succeeds in giving a quite lively and colourful picture of Chinese life at that time.

Afterwards the taste of the reading circles leaned rather toward the *bon mot*, the anecdote, the dramatic effect, as evidenced chiefly by true or supposed political speeches. These are the main contents of such works as the 'Discourses of the States' (*Kuo-yü*) and the 'Politics of the Warring States' (*Chan-kuo-ts'ê*). From these writings one reaches nearly fictional works, and historical novels such as the travelogue *Mu-t'ien-tzŭ-chuan* 'Biography of the Son of Heaven called Mu'). Much of this literature was destroyed on the occasion of the 'burning of the books' ordered by Ch'in Shih-huang-ti, and even more when the Imperial Library in Hsien-yang was ravaged by fire during the civil war following the fall of the Ch'in; but a not inconsiderable body has survived to this day.

All this is not yet true history. Yet it showed the path for the future, and set down once and for all two of the foremost characteristics of Chinese historiography—impersonality, and love for detail. The father of Chinese historical writing, the 'Herodotus of China', was Ssŭ-ma Ch'ien (*c.* 135–87). His work, the 'Historical Memoirs' (*Shih-chi*), a private undertaking, was finished about 90 BC, but was published only after the death of its author. Its terse and pithy style, and its well thought out structure, served as a model for all the later dynastic histories, which were written by imperial command, each dynasty as a rule undertaking to compile the history of the preceding one. This enormous collection contains today twenty-six dynastic histories and carries the history down to 1912. The normal pattern, as set down by Ssŭ-ma Ch'ien and by Pan Ku, the author of the second history, provides for four separate sections: (1) basic annals (*pên-chi*), a rather jejune chronological list of court events and of imperial mandates; (2) monographs (*chih*) on special subjects, such as astronomy and calendar, geography, economy, administration, rites, bibliography, music, etc.; (3) tables (*piao*) of imperial genealogies, lists of officials, etc.; (4) biographies (*lieh-chuan*) of the most outstanding personages of the period; this forms the bulk of the work, both for size and importance of the contents. This pattern lent itself to rigid and mechanical imitation, but Ssŭ-ma Ch'ien was a highly original and talented writer, whose personality shines through the apparently impassive and cold array of facts and information in his huge work.

We notice also that the need to recover, sort, and settle the classical texts after the storm of the Ch'in persecution gave rise, thanks to the labours of Liu Hsiang (79–8 BC) and of his son Liu Hsin (died AD 23) to a highly refined technique of philological criticism, which was far in advance of anything else in Asia and finds its counterpart only in the Alexandrian schools.

b. *India*

Indian (Sanskrit) secular literature may be said to begin with the stories and ballads of an epic character found in the later Vedic texts; such as the *Cycle of Suparṇa*. In the later and artificial classification of Sanskrit literature, epics (*itihāsa*) are placed after the *Atharvaveda*, to which they are said to be closely related. The authors, transmitters, and preservers of this heroic poetry were professional singers (*sūta*), who lived at court and recited their songs at great festivals in honour of their protectors. They also followed the king in battle, in order to be able to sing of his heroic deeds from their own observations. This form of poetry seems to have been widely diffused, but all the early poems are lost and only two great epic cycles have come down to us: that of the Bhārata war, and that of Rāma.

The *Mahābhārata* has been defined as not one poetic production, but rather a whole literature, a repertory of the whole of the old bardic poetry (Winternitz). This enormous poem of about 100,000 *śloka* in eighteen sections (*parvan*) plus a supplement (the *Harivaṃsa*, which is really a *purāṇa*) centres round the family feud of the two branches of the Bhārata family in northern India, the Kaurava and the Pāṇḍava. A long, bitter, and bloody war ensues, in which all the Indian heroes (including Kṛṣṇa) take sides for one or other family. The war ends with the complete destruction of the Kauravas, but also with the withdrawal from worldly life of the few Pāṇḍavas left. The poem, it appears, grew around an original nucleus that was favourable to the Kauravas, and was later modified in a pro-Pāṇḍava sense. It is not the work of one poet, although tradition attributes it to the mythical sage Vyāsa; it grew over the course of centuries, chiefly through a luxuriant efflorescence of side-themes, episodes, and digressions, until it reached its present unwieldy bulk. In the process its character as an essentially secular poetical work was modified, as the Brahmans, and chiefly the court priests (*purohita*), introduced into it more and more mythical and didactic matter, of a clearly Vishnuite character. Even philosophical and ascetic portions are not missing, and we need only recall in this connection the *Bhagavadgītā*. Prose-pieces, too, have found their way into the *Mahābhārata*, which, as we have it now, may be best defined as an encyclopaedia of ancient Indian lore. All this process was long drawn out and may be taken to have occupied seven or eight centuries, from about the fourth BC to fourth AD. By the Gupta period it was already settled in its final form, substantially the one we know today.

The other great poem is the *Rāmāyaṇa*. It is an account of the youth of Rāma, his feats, and of his winning Sītā as his wife. Sītā is carried away by the demon Rāvaṇa, who brings her to Laṅkā (Ceylon). Rāma collects an army, wins the help of the monkey-king Sugriva, overruns Laṅkā, slays Rāvaṇa, and liberates Sītā. The story of their further destinies is a later accretion. The poem is divided into seven *kāṇḍa* and consists of about 24,000 *ślokas*. It is preserved in three recensions, with fairly serious differences. It is, however, much more of a unit than the *Mahābhārata* and responds more closely to our ideas of what an epic poem should be. It is traditionally attributed to the sage and seer Valmiki, and it may indeed be probable that at least its nucleus (substantially *kāṇḍas* 2–6) is the work of one poet, or at least of one poetical school. Its style is more polished and more advanced, and it already contains the first beginnings of ornate art poetry (*kāvya*). As Winternitz said, 'while we found in the *Mahābhārata* a mixture of popular epic and theological didactic poetry (*purāṇa*), the *Rāmāyaṇa* appears to us as a work that is popular epic and ornate poetry at the same time'. The core of the *Rāmāyaṇa* is more archaic in appearance than the earliest portion of the *Mahābhārata*. Thus Rāma is only a hero and the Vedic Indra is the supreme god. We are still on Late Vedic ground, and only the later portions (first and seventh *kāṇḍas*), which are strikingly similar to the *Mahābhārata* in character, make Rāma a god and identify him with Viṣṇu. The chronology of the *Rāmāyaṇa* may be best defined as follows. In its present form it is older by about a couple of centuries than the *Mahābhārata* we have now. On the other hand the legend of Rāma appears to be of later origin than that of the Bhārata war; its atmosphere is more polished and gentle than the cruder one of the *Mahābhārata*, so full of passion and hatred. The period during which the *Rāmāyaṇa* grew appears, therefore, to lie encompassed within the longer period of the *Mahābhārata*: we may suggest about the third century BC to the second century AD.

Something can also be said about localization: the larger poem belongs to north-western India, mainly to the zone around Delhi, while the theatre of the *Rāmāyaṇa* is mainly northern India, in the western portions of Uttar Pradesh.

Both the great poems became very popular, in the sense that their core became part and parcel of Indian life of all ages. Over and above this the *Rāmāyaṇa*, chiefly as recast in modern Indian dialects (the most famous is the Hindi *Rām-carit-manas* of Tulsī Dās) became a true devotional book, which exerted a deep influence on the spiritual life of the masses in India.

c. *Hebrew Historiography*

Given the complexity of the problem of creation and chronology for each part of the Persian *Avesta*, with the exception of the *Gāthā* which is its earliest section and which was discussed in Part I, it is preferable to assemble the data in Part III.

We have also preferred to treat the books of the Hebrew Bible as a whole, though indicating which are the latest sections—the fifth century for *Chronicles* and *Job*, the fourth for *Ezra* and (conceivably) *Daniel*, third for *Ecclesiastes*, the second and first for the *Works of Wisdom*, etc. Here we would like to deal only with Hebrew historiography after 500.

After the end of the exile and in the succeeding centuries the historical genre was much in vogue among the Hebrews, but a fundamental distinction made itself felt within this branch of literature, since some writers of the period write genuine historical books and others edifying monographs. Among the latter it is possible to pick out the stories of Esther, Judith, Tobias, and Jonah—the stories themselves give very little information but they are important as literature; some parts of the *Book of Job* should be added to this catalogue; the dating of *Ruth*, however, remains difficult. The *Chronicles*, the *Book of Ezra*, the *Book of Nehemiah*, and the *Maccabees* excel among the historical works; names and brief fragments alone remain of the various other authors.

We need not modify the observations made earlier on the character of Hebrew historiography. It deals always with 'sacred history' in which religious purpose predominates in the most obvious way; and the preoccupation with drawing a moral and a lesson from the narrative facts is constant. Yet it should be explained that in the monographs listed above it is impossible to draw a precise line between the historical event from which it begins and the embellishments added for various reasons (sentiment, liturgy, reason, as well as legitimate artistic requirements, which imposed the need for effects, the use of parallelism, etc.). However, there is no need to talk about pure legend, nor to give an exclusively allegorical interpretation to their story. One must simply recognize that these compositions resulted from the elaboration of certain facts which really existed, although they are mostly unidentifiable now.

The historical books, like the others, are always supporting a thesis, and therefore the selection and presentation of facts do not respond to the needs of pure erudition; however these works are of considerable importance because they have made use of varied sources (often in a rather free way), and have adapted documents and oral traditions, of which we would have very little knowledge without these echoes. The first *Book of the Maccabees*, the most important of them all, tells the history of the Palestinian Hebrews from 175 to 135 BC, and shows the struggle they maintained in defence of their faith: the objectivity is absolute, though coupled with a genuine poetic sentiment, even in the bare description. The studied aim of the author is achieved better by the simple recollection of facts than by the pressure of personal considerations. The original Hebrew has been lost, but the text exists in a Greek translation: one can believe that it was composed in the last decade of the second century BC.

The first *Book of the Maccabees* mentions a chronicle on the life of the priest John Hyrcanus, but this has been lost; so also has been a vast work in five books, written by Jason of Cyrene, a learned Hebrew, who, shortly after 161, described the events of 175, having collected contemporary accounts of that year: however the second *Book of the Maccabees* is simply a recapitulation of Jason, as the author explicitly explains. Therefore the two *Books of the Maccabees* have a chronological period in common, but the tone of the two accounts is very different, and they use different evidence even where they deal with the same fact; from the historical point of view the first Book is in every case the respected authority; on the other hand the second Book is more theological, being based upon a profound conviction of the working of Providence in human historical events. From the end of the third century BC many Hellenistic Jews wrote several books to exalt the glory of their people, and to defend their co-religionists from the accusations current among the pagans. The names remain of Demetrius, Eupolemus, Artapanus, Aristeas, Cleodemus; Alexander Polistor made an important collection of their writings, and from there some fragments found their way into Christian works, and were inserted in their books.

d. Greek and Roman Literature

Epic Poetry. [Greek thinkers of every period regarded the Homeric epics as the source of all literature. Homer haunted the poet's imagination long after the end of what we call the *epic age* (once the Homeric poems had settled into their final form, at the end of the sixth century BC); but his lessons were applied in different ways, according to individual judgement.

Some poets tried to imitate the historical aspect of his compositions (for the *Iliad* was regarded as an account of historic events, substantially true in spite of its mythological 'embellishments').] The result was that instead of creative works of art inspired by specific great events, Epic gradually became history in verse. Examples include *The Foundation of Colophon* and *The Foundation of Elea* by Xenophanes of Colophon (see p. 250). [Other poets set themselves to amplify certain themes which they thought Homer had dealt with too cursorily.] This alternative was short episodic or biographical poems of a partly lyrical, partly epic form. The best-known poet of the latter type was the second of those known as Stesichorus (see p. 279): he was the son of Eucleides from Himera in Sicily, who had prevented Gelon from taking possession of his city; then he migrated to Greece in 485, and later returned to his own country after the defeat of the Carthaginians in 479 near Himera. One of his undoubted aims in his *Geryonis*, which deals with the adventures of Heracles in the West (including western Sicily), is to justify the recent enterprise of the 'Heraclid' Dorieus to appropriate the area of Mount Eryx. *Iliou Persis*, the *Orestiad*, the *Hunting of Wild Boars*, and the *Nostoi* must certainly all be attributed to him. [The *Iliou Persis* and the *Nostoi* claimed to supplement Homer's poems. The former gave an uninterrupted, consecutive account of the episodes that culminated in the fall of Troy,[1] while the latter described the heroes' adventures on their way back to their respective countries, and was thus an 'expansion' of the *Odyssey*.[2]]

[Again, some poets tried to transpose Homer's method to cycles of legend not included in the classical epics.] Thus, the ancient mythical material was further expanded in the *Thebaid* by Antimachus of Colophon (died in 404) which was variously evaluated in the ancient world. At the same time the events of the recent Persian Wars provided the argument of the *Perseid* by Choerilus of Samos, who was still alive in 404; he was also the author of *Samiaca*.

The poets of the Hellenistic age still considered that the epic represented the highest form of poetry, with the result that many epic poets of the Hellenistic era wrote poems of varying length, some on mythical stories, others on recent events. These were primarily philologists, filled with great love for Homer, but not always equipped with the capacity to write epics. The most famous of them was Callimachus of Cyrene (*c.* 310–235) an erudite and prolific poet [whose influence spread far beyond the Alexandrian court circle in which he lived, not only as a court poet, but as a highly reputed philologist; after his death, this influence became supreme in Rome from the middle of the first century B C. Catullus, writing about 55 B C, and shortly after him Propertius, strove to be 'the Roman Callimachus'. The chief concern of Callimachus himself was to arrive at poetic beauty through absolute perfection of style. He therefore sometimes rejected the Homeric model—not out of contempt, but from a feeling that times had changed since the heroic age and that 'modern' poetry should take a new turn.] Callimachus is the author of the *Coma Berenices*, in which a lock of Queen Berenice's hair, transformed into a newly discovered constellation, tells its own story; it is a slight plot overloaded with astronomical erudition and reflections on love and marriage. [The poem is written for a particular occasion, and is a delicate allegory drawing upon oriental beliefs which connected certain divinities with particular stars—beliefs which the Ptolemies, like other dynasties founded when the Alexandrian empire was dismembered, had taken over as mystical appendages of the royal house. Religious inspiration plays a leading part in the work of Callimachus, who lived in a profoundly religious, even mystical period. He treats the ancient classical Greek myths in the light of the new sentiments, so that they emerge as legends to be approached ironically, in the certitude that religion, the divine reality, is on quite a different plane.] His six surviving hymns were in part supposed, like the ancient *Nomoi*, to be the central theme of sacred celebrations: they sing the praises of the gods and relate legends about them. To the modern reader it may seem that the praise is made up of tepid enthusiasm, rhetorical flights, and learned pieces of fiction; the story is told not by a true believer, but by a scholar in search of romantic tales and marvellous transformations. [This is an opinion frequently expressed, but it by no means does justice to these pieces, many of them extremely subtle and packed with meanings which are difficult to interpret.]

Callimachus' great poem the *Aetia* ('On the Origins', i.e., 'on the reasons for things'—explaining certain rites, etc.)—considerable fragments of which have been recovered in papyrus—is in four books of the epico-mythological type: there are gathered together, in many episodes, what the Muses 'have told him' about the origins of a number of historical events, geographical facts, curious customs, and stories of love affairs. It is therefore a sort of erudite encyclopaedia of mythology, history, and folklore, in which he uses great precision in quoting sources and a wide range of learning. [In this part of his work Callimachus is inspired not so much by the Homeric spirit as by Hesiod, whom he takes up and modernizes.]

Callimachus was convinced that a literary work should be short to be appreciated. Stung by the challenge of his opponent Apollonius (the objective of his poem the *Ibis*, a ferocious invective of which we get some idea from the imitation written by Ovid) he composed a short poem of about 500 verses, *The Hecale*, which, in his view, was to be the model of a new epic. This short poem took its name from an old country-woman who entertained Theseus before his struggle with the bull of Marathon and passed the time by recounting old legends, all done in the most meticulous detail.[3]

Apollonius 'Rhodius' (295–215), the pupil and rival of Callimachus, was a devotee of Homer and set himself as a young man to compose the *Argonautica*, which appeared eventually as four books of about 6,000 verses. He wanted to reconcile the acceptable part of traditional mythology with what he thought was required by the tastes of his own time: in other words he had to include information about geography, etymology, and the customs of barbarians. He also wanted to introduce love, an important factor in poetry. The resulting poem was of very varied merit and appeal. The part which describes heroic deeds is smothered by oppressive erudition, and the epic practically becomes prose. On the other hand in the love passages, the figure of Medea is wonderfully outlined, with an analysis of passion and feeling which no other ancient author knew how to give. Apollonius indulged the taste of his own period by also composing brief poems concerning the beginning and the history of the two areas known to him. Alexandria, Naucratis, and Canopus were one; the other was Rhodes, with Cnidus and Caunus.

Among the historical epics of the Alexandrian period the *Messeniaca* by Rhianus of Bene in Crete should be mentioned: this describes the Messenian Wars in an anti-Spartan spirit.

In the Greek world, where life now seemed hardly heroic, Epic was dying. [In central Italy the spirit of the heroic era seems to have survived for some considerable time, thanks to the Etruscans, who drew extensively on Homer's tales in their art and (perhaps) in their literature. It is also possible that the Roman national traditions were embodied in literary form—passed on in some cases by word of mouth—and thus paved the way for Roman epic poetry.] But the great events during their rising hegemony gave the Romans inexhaustible subjects which, together with the material from their ancient folk-songs, were transformed into great artistic poems once the Homeric models were known. [The earliest surviving epic poem in the Latin tongue was composed by a Greek from Tarentum, Andronicus, a freedman of the *gens Livia*, who went by the name of L. Livius Andronicus.] It is thought that, taken to Rome as a slave in 272, he made these Homeric models known to the Romans; he wanted them to appreciate the superb beauty of the Homeric epic. Rome in 272 had already become the ruler of the Italiote area, and was becoming so in Siceliote territory. Before he died about 204, Androni-cus in fact wrote in rough and uninteresting Latin an 'Odyssey', a free translation of the great poem of the same name, composed in Saturnian verses, after substituting Latin ideas for Greek ones; his work was successful enough to be used as a text in some schools even in Horace's day.[4]

[It may be wondered why Rome felt the need to develop a literature, and why it was so late in doing so. Incidentally, the first Latin writers were not Romans but southern Italians, either from Tarentum (like Livius Andronicus) or from Campania (like Naevius and Ennius); in other words from regions where the Greek influence of the former Hellenic colonies (Tarentum, Naples, etc.) had been grafted on the old Italic stock and brought it to fresh flowering. But it is remarkable, too, that these earliest works were written in Latin rather than in one of the southern tongues, such as Oscan, the national language of Campania. This shows that the influence of Rome had also been important, even, perhaps, decisive. The emergence of a Roman state, with a sense of community and national pride, was required before the need for a literature could be felt and the means develop; and that literature was 'Roman' from the outset. The forms with which it began, epic and drama, have a social function to fulfil—the former commemorating the glories of history, the latter connected with religious festivals. Roman literature came to birth in the Rome that had defeated Carthage, after the First Punic War; not until the beginning of the third century, after routing Pyrrhus and unifying almost the whole peninsula in confrontation with Grecian Sicily and the power of Carthage, did Rome begin to regard itself as a national community and therefore to feel the need of literary expression. But the Romans were already acquainted with Greek culture, to some extent at least; it was not a revelation opened up for them by their first writers. The more modest task of those early authors was to adapt Hellenism to the demands of a Rome just awakening to an interest in the Muses and in the kind of immortality—and spiritual development—they can bestow.]

Shortly after Andronicus, about 235, the Campanian Cn. Naevius, who had taken part in the First Punic War, started his prolific literary output in Rome; this was interrupted by his exile to Utica in 201, and he died about 194. Naevius too used Homer as his model and aimed at writing a form of Latin *Iliad* in which the legends linking Rome with Troy would be blended with those glories of the 'cives Romani' which had reached their greatest fulfilment in the victories over Carthage. But only the last five cantos of his poem refer to that war: the first two were devoted to the great mythological antecedents of these conflicts, in fact the origins of Rome and Carthage, tragically united by the adventures of Dido and Aeneas. With Naevius the anonymous Roman epic poetry became an artistic genre with new characteristics. It had a Roman subject and a Greek form; it glorified facts which were in part ancient and mythical but in part recent and historical. But even in the form of the poetry there was a survival of native Roman practice in the use of the ancient 'Saturnian' metre, though he made it more supple and stirring, a less unpolished instrument than that employed by Andronicus.[5]

Q. Ennius, almost a compatriot of Andronicus, had been born in Messapian Rudiae (239–*c*. 169), and came to Rome in 204, where he displayed his knowledge of three languages (Greek, Latin, and Oscan). [Like his two predecessors, he was both a dramatic and an epic poet. He had begun his career as a centurion in an army corps in his own country. During the Second Punic War he served in Sardinia, where he attracted the attention of Cato (the Censor). Cato sent for him to Rome and gave him the semi-official post of *poeta*, in which he succeeded Naevius. Ennius began to write his epic in the atmosphere of fiery patriotism prevailing at that time, when Rome's whole strength was banded against Hannibal, shortly after it had seemed in danger of destruction.] Ennius named his poem the *Annales*: it was an epic containing the whole of Roman history, from the beginning to the recent events seen by the poet himself. [He is much more 'modern' than either of his predecessors, and reveals the influence of contemporary Hellenism much more strongly. He shows certain characteristics in common with the Alexandrian poets (a taste for virtuosity, a bold tendency towards verbal innovation, and a leaning towards didactic verse, in which he even included such an unexpected subject as gastronomy, dealt with in his *Hedyphagetica*). He is the least deeply Italic of the ancient Latin poets, full of disdain for the 'barbarous' style of Andronicus and Naevius.]

A great admirer of Homer, whose soul he proudly believed he had inherited by metamorphosis, he wanted to be the Roman Homer: he was the first to introduce to the Latin world the famous metre of the Greek Epic, the dactylic hexameter. This involved him in great linguistic difficulties but he braved them, not without some noticeable strain in scansion and in his use of the caesura, syncope, and the like. He was the true creator of the noble and lofty language of Roman Epic and Tragedy, a language which when compared with that of Andronicus and Naevius demonstrates the great cultural and aesthetic progress accomplished in Roman letters between the First Punic War and the end of the Second. The great poem to which he applied himself for many years was divided into books, which may have been published either in groups or one by one. The treatment grows in breadth as it descends in time: ancient myths are unfolded in the first books; in the others the epic tone is maintained by heroic stories in lofty style and pure language (although it is a little artificial because of the numerous alliterations). Everything betrays a great love for the Roman world and its heroes. He drew on every source for their adventures—the ancient epic folk poems, the *Annales Maximi*, Naevius, the Greek Timaeus, and the first Roman annalist Fabius Pictor. Only small fragments of this great work, about 600 badly mutilated lines, have survived.

[The Romans considered Ennius as the founder of their literature. This, though unfair to Andronicus and Naevius, is true inasmuch as he was the first to achieve the transposition of Greek writing and the Greek spirit which, generally speaking, constitutes Latin literature. They gave him the title of *Pater*, which he thus shared with Juppiter, Mars, Janus, and others of the greatest, most benevolent, and venerated gods; and both Virgil and Lucretius borrowed heavily from him. In that sense he is really the Father.]

P. Vergilius Maro (79–c. 19 BC) of Andes near Mantua, perhaps the school friend and later in his life protégé of Octavian, was already experimenting with a type of Hellenistic lyric and with his *Bucolica* and *Georgics* (see below p. 588, and also p. 572 on the *Catalepton*). Towards 30 BC he began the great epic poem, the *Aeneid*, which was to eclipse all the work preceding Roman epic writers, and in which he proposed to glorify the predestined rule of Rome and of its ruler Augustus. [In embarking upon his epic poem, Virgil was faithful to the Roman concept of the *epos* as a nationalistic poem expressing the requirements of patriotism and setting up a common ideal for the citizens. Maecenas, and the political leaders of the new régime, would have liked a poet to extol Octavian's military exploits and compare him, after his defeat of Antony, to the great heroes of ancient times. But Virgil had the happy idea of imitating Naevius and Ennius, rather than writing a rigidly historical poem. Better still, he gave his theme a legendary setting, thus conferring upon it an extra dimension, a depth in which it seems to be the channel of Destiny. In so doing he recaptured an essential feature of Homeric poetry; for the *Iliad*, too, is a poem that reverts to those 'origins' whose nobility, glory, etc., illuminate the present day. By going deliberately back to Homer, Virgil remains faithful to the spirit of the Greek *epos*, regarded as the touchstone of national culture. Thanks to him, Rome is seen more clearly than ever as the cultural heir of Hellenism (in the widest sense). This intention was in keeping with the policy of Augustus, who was anxious to 'reconcile' the two halves of the empire, the Hellenized East and the Romanized West, and to create a single, syncretic culture, shared by Rome and Greece.]

The wanderings of Aeneas and his conquest of Latium are like a compendium of a new *Odyssey* and a new *Iliad*; and in fact the Homeric poems were always present to the mind of Virgil, who draws inspiration from them in many episodes which rival the models he was imitating. The Roman poem differs widely from the *Iliad* in that it sets the stage for a duel between two peoples (Rome and Carthage) not for a woman but for the dominion of the world; and the work of Aeneas is not an end in itself, but the task of a man predestined by fate to pass through human events and sorrows and achieve something of superhuman importance for the history of the world. The *Aeneid* is the celebration of Italy, both its history and natural beauties, which pass before our eyes throughout the various books. But at the same time it is an acknowledgement of the beauty of the whole Mediterranean world, which Rome had united; it shows sympathy therefore towards the Asian peoples, from whom came the hero who put ashore in Latium, and similarly for the Africans of the afflicted Dido, where Augustus had revived the flourishing and powerful *Colonia Iunonia* of Carthage.

The *Aeneid* is also a poem of religious feeling, pious and profound, the feeling which Augustus counted on being able to revive in order to achieve his restoration of Italy. The Penates of Troy are the same as those of the empire. Aeneas is guided step by step by the divine will; sanctified by his superhuman knowledge of the mysteries of Elysium, he begins with his undertakings the foundation of Destiny's preordained history of Rome. In this poem Virgil, who had already moved from his early Epicureanism to Stoicism, climbed another rung and reached an almost Neoplatonic mysticism; this is at its most impressive in the episode of the descent into Hell in the sixth Book, which is connected with rediscovered Hellenistic epic fragments, and where we see the purification of souls liberated from bodies, with the reincarnation of those who were not yet sufficiently purified, and the final liberation of others into Elysium.

Originally a 'Poeta novus' (new poet) of the Alexandrian type, in his last two great poems Virgil left the school for ever; he maintained the technique he had acquired, but he gave his didactic and heroic works a loftier and nobler content. He combined passionate devotion to polished workmanship with the spontaneous lyrical power which springs from his deep sympathy with his themes. He thus achieved great dignity and restraint of style, with a remarkable facility for concise utterance. His diction is in general modern, [but he draws extensively upon the vocabulary of Ennius and Lucretius, who thus appear as his forerunners. Virgil established a definite 'poetic language' in Latin; it was used after his time, but of course to less effect, for while with him it was a creative process, his imitators were using it as an academic exercise. Virgil achieves a great and apparently effortless variety of tone; sometimes he is epic, in the Homeric style, at other times he writes simply, almost like a folk poet; and he is also capable of tremendously vivid description and tragic intensity. Some of his imagery has remained famous and even shapes our present-day imagination—such as the '*Ibant obscuri sola sub nocte, per umbram* . . .' by which he describes Aeneas' descent into Hell, accompanied by the Sybil, drawing a picture the subtlety of which is enhanced by its sober restraint. Virgil's style is that of a 'classic';] he preserves a healthy equilibrium between this modernity and the restrained use of archaisms and verses from early poets. The flow of his hexameters is well-nigh perfect, each line often corresponding to the complete expression of an idea.[6]

Elegy, Lyric, and Epigram. With the first decades of the fifth century BC we reach in Theognis the last of the great Greek elegists. He has been regarded as a native of Megara Nisaea in Greece, living about 540 BC; but in our opinion this is incorrect since there is evidence that he was a Siceliote Greek, born at Megara Hyblaea, and that he flourished in the early part of the fifth century.7 The manuscript tradition ascribes to him a collection of poems in two books, one of 1,230 the other of 159 lines. He came from a rich and noble family and with other nobles became involved in a struggle against the *demos*. Eventually he was overpowered in a riot, deprived of his property, and reduced to the most squalid poverty. When his city was taken by the tyrant Gelon in 482 (and shortly afterwards destroyed), he retired to Megara Nisaea in Greece, where in 480–479 he mourned the dangers which his new country was encountering from the Persians, though soon afterwards he was celebrating their liberation after the battle of Plataea. Theognis composed many detached elegies, but what has come down to us is only a collection or anthology, compiled about 400 BC, in which extracts from various poems, divorced from their contexts, are juxtaposed, contaminated, and subjected to interpolation by fragments of various other poets. Sometimes the non-Theognidean elements can be identified, and in this way distinguished from about eighty definitely authentic poems among the collection of 370. Theognis was sober, realistic, and restrained in his ideas: flights of lyric fancy were not his way. Unassuming in his constructions and prone to abstraction, he showed himself an experienced thinker, one who knew the human heart and was also passionate, bitter, and easily roused over matters of politics: in this last he was very far removed from Solon, despite the great resemblances between the two poets as dialecticians and moralists. As to morals, Theognis was clear and moderate: following the views of conservative thinkers of his day he believed that the foundations of virtue lay in right judgement, tranquillity, and balance. He also showed himself reverent towards his god, whom he regarded as a being free from human passions.

During the fifth and fourth centuries elegy and epigram were used occasionally by all the great writers of the time (Aeschylus, Sophocles, Euripides, Thucydides, Plato, etc.). They were the favourite genre for certain lesser poets, such as Euenus of Paros (460–390) who wrote elegant and pithy aphorisms, or Critias, or Antimachus, the author of an epic-elegiac poem on ancient heroes crossed in love.

In addition certain forms of iambic composition were still to be found. Cercidas of Megalopolis with his *Meliambi* anticipated the Horatian spirit; and the militant Cynic philosopher Crates of Thebes, who flourished about 325, wrote *Iambi* directed at improving men's behaviour. There was also an output of parodies of ancient myths.

The form of lyric which survived with greatest vitality was the choral poem. [In Greece in the late sixth and early fifth century, this was the dominant form of poetic expression, having succeeded the epic and not being yet ousted by the tragic form. Choral poetry at this time was already scenic, for it constituted a complete performance, comprising the movements of a chorus, with chanting, recitative and music. It is difficult for us today to imagine what such a performance can have been like, for the words alone have come down to us, without their accompanying melody. We even find it difficult to reconstruct the rhythm, with its complex pattern, its repetition of symmetrical triads (strophe, antistrophe, epode), and can only form an abstract idea of it. These choral poems were splendidly spectacular, for they were songs of praise, extolling the glorious deeds of past heroes and above all those of the chief heroes of Greece in their day, the victors in the great Games.]

The first and most important name in this period is that of Pindar the Boeotian (about 522-446), whose earliest datable ode is in 498 and the latest 446. His fame as a panhellenic poet was such that, although his praises were never servile, all the nobles in the Greek world sought to receive them and have him as their guest, so that his life was a peregrination from court to court. Of his seventeen books of choral songs of all types all that has survived —apart from various fragments—are the four sets of *Epinikia* for victories in the Olympian, Pythian, Nemean, and Isthmian games. His poems are in a stately metre, in a dialect derived from that of earlier lyricists, tending both towards Doric and towards Aeolic. The style is almost inimitable, imaginative and sensitive. The odes were sung to the accompaniment of a flute or lyre, or of both instruments together. They celebrate not so much the actual victors as their cities (Pindar preferred aristocratic or tyrannic régimes, provided that they were moderate). With them he celebrates the cities' gods, his conception of whom is based on profound religious feeling, influenced by Orphic and Pythagorean theories; he therefore corrects his legends to suit the dictates of morality.

Thirteen odes to victory, elegant and polished rather than gay, together with fragments, have survived from Bacchylides of Ceos (late-sixth to mid-fifth century). He too wrote many types of poems: they show analytical, narrative, colourful, and decorative talent, but have no overriding conception of a religious, political, or moral kind. They must have lost a good deal of their original attraction from the loss of the music which accompanied them.

During the Attic period there were great developments in the lyric field, in dithyramb and other forms,[8] which reached their highest point at the beginning of the fourth century.

The use of more complicated musical instruments, and the new polyphonic conceptions, both allowed and required that the lyrical and dramatic compositions to be set to music should be long, yet not monotonous. At the same time prose was being used for arguments of a moral or didactic nature; and the flowering and the fame of the dramatic style were concentrating the taste of the Greek public on 'pathetic' poetry (by which the Greeks meant sensuous forms or those which arouse passion). All this meant that from the fifth century onwards Greek lyric was normally limited to two forms, the dithyramb and the *nomos*.[9] Both forms were heavily dramatized, with choral sections, while other parts were sung and presented by actors. In this way the musical element became more important than the poetry and ideas, and the two forms were eventually very similar. Their poetical sections, which were often reduced to a mere 'libretto' of an affecting and imaginative kind, are known to us by the fragments which have survived. But they have lost the musical portions which were their very being, and it is therefore impossible to get an adequate idea of the artistic value and interest of this form of literature.

For these lyrical, dramatic, and musical compositions, many of which we know only from comments by playwrights, there were regular competitions at a number of annual festivals at Athens from the end of 508 BC; and about 440 Pericles constructed a covered theatre called the Odeion to be used for this purpose.

We also possess some fragments of the 'soft' dithyrambs of Melanippides of Melos (died before 413). We are told too of comic poets who were immoral, obscure, vacuous, and pretentious, such as the Athenian Cinesias; and of effeminate poets such as the Mytilenean Phrynis, the winner of a competition in 412. Philoxenus of Cythera (435–380) was the author of twenty-four dithyrambs, and in one of them, the *Cyclops*, a bucolic piece dramatizing the love-affair of Polyphemus with Galatea, he revenges himself by tart allusions to the Syracusan tyrant Dionysius I who had imprisoned him.

The ancient world possessed eighteen books of lyrics by Timotheus of Miletus (*c.* 450–360); we can judge the value of the poetry, but not fully that of the rather revolutionary music, from various fragments and also from part of a *nomos* called *The Persians* (much admired by Hellenistic scholars for its music), which was discovered on an Egyptian papyrus. In this work he describes the victory of Salamis in an extravagant and bizarre style, rather like the libretto of a melodrama, and reduces historical truth to an absurd level. An opera by Timotheus sings of the pains of *Semele's Delivery*; others were dedicated to Scylla, Niobe, and Odysseus.

Greek lyric poetry in the Hellenistic period[10] was not addressed to the populace; it was poetry well stocked and heavy with erudition, which could be enjoyed only by a suitably restricted circle of connoisseurs. Refined in style, chiselled in its phrases, accomplished in the choice of its vocabulary, it did not gush from the heart but from the brain. The favourite subject was love, and its metre the hexameter. The mode was either elegy, normally of a sad and sentimental tone, or epigram, the brief vivacious composition designed to express wit and 'ideas'.

The first representative of this new artistic tendency was Philetas of Cos (*c.* 340–280) a grammarian who lived surrounded by a circle of friends. His most famous work was a series of elegies of love praising his Bittis, all of which poems were certainly inspired by Antimachus' *Lydia*. We know too of his other poetic works on Telephus, Hermes, and Demeter. Theocritus recognized him as his master, and Propertius considered him as a poet of the highest order; it is clear that he must have provided them with new models for elegies on love and mythology, and for the well-chiselled epigram.

At the same time the epigram, in the form that was common in the peninsula and in the western colonies, inspired by the contemplation of nature and by a longing for peace of soul, found talented expression in the work of two poetesses, Anyte of Tegea and Nossis of Locri. Another Asiatic form of the epigram, full of erotic passion, was launched at the same time by a great poet, Asclepiades of Samos: in his brief odes, written in new metres which have taken their name from him, he confesses his love-pangs, exalts the beauty of his beloved, and describes the impassioned life of the city with a fineness and vigour that are truly exquisite.

Leonidas of Tarentum (about 300–270), a poor wandering poet, lived by writing epigrams for tombs, offerings to the gods by humble people, inscriptions on statues, and the like. Only about a hundred have survived, but they show him to be a true poet, capable of moving us and of being moved, neither banal nor stuffed with erudition.

Later Meleager of Gadara (100 BC), the pupil of the Cynic Menippus, was a famous epigrammatist, whose love-poetry is veiled by a moving melancholy. He also helped to publish his predecessor's works, and collected them in an anthology which he called the *Garland* (*Corolla*).

While the Greek world was producing a rather decadent lyric form which was seldom of true worth, Latin lyric, at first based on the Hellenistic model but later following other paths, was gradually asserting its place. About most of the works written between 150 and 60 BC, when the school of 'new' poets became prominent, we have only poor and fragmentary information.

But it was approximately between 60 and 50 BC that the school of the 'new poets', whom Cicero in derision called the *cantores Euphorionis*, established themselves at Rome. Lovers of form above all, they preferred brief but polished poems, metrically rich in spondees and a vocabulary of neologisms. They were a closed circle far from the common world; some of them were even cut off from any public career. In this way they led frivolous and fastidious lives amid their pleasures and their loves. They adored the foreign women, the courtesans from the East, who were flocking into Rome: and with them they loved those Roman women who competed with the foreigners in fastidiousness of culture, in freedom of attire, and in political intrigues. Their natural tendencies were developed by their literary contacts with Greek poets of the same temperament who were then living at Rome, particularly Parthenius and Philodemus.

But though Greek in form and tastes, the best of them were none the less true lyricists, who based their poems on the sentimental episodes of their own lives. The passion which they describe is Roman, often violent, often generous. In general their poetic worth, precisely because they were more sincere and more inspired, was better than that of their Greek friends, among whom there was no Catullus.

The earliest among these new poets (or 'Neoterics') were quickly eclipsed by their greatest pupil (C.) Catullus, a Veronese of noble birth who came to

Rome and lived in its poetic circle among both many friends and many enemies. [Although we have lost almost all the short lyrical poems (epigrams and short pieces after the manner of Meleager of Gadara) written by Catullus' Roman contemporaries, everything he himself wrote has come down to us. It is a variegated collection. It includes 'occasional' verses, most of them satirical, alluding to leading citizens and events at Verona, and others which refer to Caesar and his friends, at a time when Catullus and his own friends were 'members of the opposition' and ranked with the conservatives. These pieces are cruel, sometimes coarse, and contrast sharply with those in the other two groups—the love-poems and the great 'Alexandrine' poems.

Catullus relates in some detail the story of his love for a certain Lesbia—a pseudonym for Clodia, a sister of the demagogue P. Clodius Pulcher, Cicero's enemy. The choice of pseudonym is not accidental, for Lesbia is intended as an allusion to Sappho, and Catullus is the disciple of the Aeolian lyrical poets. Like Sappho, he strives to express the joys and fears of the lover.] This part of his work consists of sincere poems, even though the form follows the school; they deal with true passion, now sweet and gentle, now violent and vulgar, and even repugnant in their crudity. At times the passion of love reaches the utmost limits of feeling and is expressed with indescribable freshness and spontaneity even in passages where the poet has paraphrased Sappho and other Greek lyricists. They are impressionist poems which reflect fleeting moments of the heart: love and happiness, unrestrained sensuality, anger, hate, sad resignation, hopelessness of a hypersensitive sentimental mind.

[The third section of his work, comprising the great Alexandrine poems, is of more difficult interpretation. Catullus is trying here to paint sweeping pictures in the style of Callimachus, combining a sense of composition with great perfection of detail. He has been attracted by religious sensibility in its most extreme forms of expression. His *Attis* (an evocation of the worship of the Phrygian Great Mother, with its orgiastic, bloodthirsty, and sensual rites)] represents a violent movement and feeling—turbulence, noise, murmuring, and despair—and therefore employs the characteristic 'Galliambic' metre. [Even in the quieter pieces (such as the *Epithalamium* of Thetis and Peleus which, with its 408 lines, is the longest of all the poems) the religious spirit is always present; the tale is always pervaded by moral considerations. They are written] in hexameters, or sometimes elegiac metre. We find an imitation (rather than a translation) of Callimachus' *Lock of Berenice*; a marvellous lament for the death of his brother and his own sorrow; the story of the marriage of Peleus and Thetis; and with this the episode of the pitiful weeping of Ariadne when Theseus abandoned her.

Virgil had composed his *Catalepton* when still a youth of hardly sixteen. These are short pieces of poetry, together with a narrative poem, the *Culex*, which imitates Alexandria in its subject and style. A mosquito stings a sleeping shepherd, saving him from a serpent's bite; squashed by him the mosquito reappears in a dream, describing the inhabitants of the underworld. The shepherd raises to the insect an altar bedecked with flowers.[11]

[The work of Horace stands out from the rest of Roman lyrical poetry, if only through its metric form. In his *Epodes*, and subsequently in his *Odes* (*Carmina*), Horace set himself to imitate the Aeolian poets. For the *Epodes*, many of which are violently satirical, he usually takes Archilochus as his model, while in the *Odes* he chiefly follows Sappho. The first three books of *Odes* were published together, in the year 23 BC, and it is often very difficult, or even impossible, to ascribe a date to a particular poem. Thus, any attempt to trace the chronological development of Horace's ideas must be largely conjectural. It is rash to assert, for instance, that Horace's admiration for Augustus' achievements only began after the victory at Actium. For since the spring of the year 38 BC, at latest, Horace belonged to the group surrounding Maecenas, who was devoted to Augustus. He was not merely a fair-weather friend, but remained faithful through the dark days, and by the year 38 he was already convinced that Octavian's party alone could restore peace in Rome and in the outside world. It is quite plausible that he may have collaborated with Virgil in framing Augustus' future programme, though not always in complete agreement with the policy of the *Princeps*. For instance, he repeatedly calls for war in the East, against the Parthians, as a revenge for their routing of Crassus in 53; but Octavian always firmly refuses. It is also an error to ignore everything except the political aspect of Horace's lyrical writings, for that is only one side of the moral, gnomic character inseparable from the lyrical poetry of classical antiquity. The *Odes* reflect a philosophical attitude towards everyday life which at first is Epicurean (delight in the passing hour, as a protection against melancholy and the thought of death), but which gradually takes a more virile turn (praise of freedom in all its forms, outward and inward, liberation from wealth, from the passions, from pleasure itself). Horace's feeling for nature, one of his chief sources of inspiration, is inseparable from thoughts of death, and provides a starting-point for meditation on man's place in the creation. This concentration on thoughts, which are more important to Horace than perfection of style, sets him clearly apart from the Alexandrian spirit and that of the *Neoteroi* from whom, like Virgil, he originally set out. In this respect Horace is profoundly 'Roman'—even his most playful and charming poems are marked by an undeniable *gravitas*.]

The Latin poets seem to have invented the erotic personal elegy once more and carried it to the highest levels of artistic development, in their technique of couplets or groups of couplets covering a single theme. [In point of fact, the circumstances attending this 'invention' are by no means clear. The Roman elegists took as their model, to some extent, the series of poems in the elegiac metre composed by certain Alexandrian poets and dedicated to the woman they loved (see above). But the latter used another style as well, that of the love-epigram in the manner of Meleager of Gadara. The Roman love-elegy combines the narrative elegy and the erotic epigram, accentuating one or the other aspect as the mood suggests. This explains why the *Elegies* of Tibullus and Propertius include poems of very different character, some of them inspired by love, while others come much closer to the *Aetia* of Callimachus (see above). The Roman love-elegy developed slowly, during the generation from 60 to 20 BC.] The first examples had already been produced by Catullus, but the acknowledged master of the school was Cornelius Gallus, a poet, the friend of Virgil and another member of the 'Alexandrine' group then flourishing in Cisalpine Gaul; his highly praised *Lycoris* (about 40 BC) contained the four books of his love-elegies.

His greatest follower was Albius Tibullus (*c.*59–19 BC) a Roman knight and a friend of Horace. Afflicted by ill-health, economic disasters, and unlucky love-affairs, he lived a mainly retired life in his villa at Pedum, dying while quite young. Tibullus' unhappy love for Delia and for Nemesis are given fanciful expression in his elegies. These have a deliberate plot in which memories and personal feelings are entangled, in a nimble and smooth flowing verse which fascinates the reader, with philosophical thoughts and moral hints, but above all with flights of fancy about bygone days of legend. [The most characteristic feature of Tibullus' poetry is his feeling for nature— his love of the countryside and of peace, his horror of war. He is torn between two sentiments which the Roman soul generally managed to bring into harmony—love of the soil, of peasant life, and admiration for military valour. Tibullus was intended for an active career; his patron, Valerius Messalla, summoned him to take part in Octavius' eastern campaigns; but he accepted reluctantly and was delighted, in his secret heart, when illness prevented him from following his comrades-in-arms and compelled him to return to Rome. There, at least, was Delia, the woman he loved. He longed to take her to live with him on his family estate, so that he could concentrate on farming. Unfortunately, Delia—a courtesan—was only happy in Rome, living in luxury amid male admiration. So Tibullus suffered deeply. No poet excels him in describing the charms of rustic paganism, with its family divinities and picturesque ceremonies. In this respect he comes very close to the Virgil of the *Georgics*. To the mythological evocations favoured by the Alexandrine poets, he preferred more measured phrases,] given us without any straining for erudition in a series of eposodic pictures; and the whole work is as though it were covered by a thin veil of gentle melancholy, of romantic sadness, which again and again brings the poet back to images of sorrow and of death.

Sextus Propertius of Asisium (*c.*50–15 BC) possessed greater vigour, learning, and fancy. He had come to Rome to devote himself to politics, but was carried away by an unlucky love for a girl he called by the pseudonym Cynthia.[12] The first book of the *Elegies* takes us back to the period of this love-affair, [or rather to the beginning of this adventure, which filled Propertius' whole life and provided him with the essence of his poetical inspiration.

This first book is significantly entitled *Cynthia Monobiblos*; for Cynthia is to the poet an 'Iliad' in herself, a universe he never quite finished exploring. This is an important milestone in the history of human sentiments, the beginning of the 'worship of women' which is not always recognized as having originated in Rome. This book includes some 'epigrams' in the traditional style, and the love-poems are already more concerned with mythology than were the elegies of Tibullus. In this respect Propertius comes closer than Tibullus to their Alexandrian forerunners, especially Callimachus, whose influence is even more evident in his later work (Book IV). But he does not use mythology for purely ornamental purposes; with him it is a way of thought, an expression of sensibility, sometimes a channel for religious feeling. Propertius realizes the religious value of love—and here he is faithful to a certain Roman tradition. For him, love has mystical connotations, it opens the door of eternity to the soul. This Platonic strain in Propertius finds vent in his recourse to myths—the power of love makes Cynthia the equal of the heroines of ancient times, she becomes their companion in the other world.

Propertius is also the poet of unhappy love. Cynthia is not faithful to him —quite naturally, for she was not his wife, but a courtesan, free to lead her own life—and this makes him wretched. The contrast between what he had expected from love and what love brings him—between *Dichtung* and *Wahrheit*—which had torn cries of rage from Catullus, induces Propertius to study his own feelings and to realize the fatal character of a passion which is not amenable to reason. This analysis of unhappy love takes up most of the two following books (II and III), though into these he was already also incorporating mythological, social, and political themes.

Book IV, which was published after his death, deals almost entirely with a new source of inspiration—the Roman legends, treated in the manner of Callimachus. Propertius, the friend of Virgil and a member of the group which had Maecenas as its patron, plays an active part in extolling the Roman past and the religious and moral works of the new régime.]

Publius Ovidius Naso (Ovid) (43 BC–AD 17) who came from a well-to-do family of Sulmo, never wished to be anything but a poet, and lived until the age of fifty as an idle gentleman. But in AD 8 Augustus, in an unexpected decree, exiled him as a corrupter of morals to Tomi on the Black Sea, and he never succeeded in getting recalled. Ovid himself separates his work before the exile into light and serious writings. The *Heroides*, supposed letters written about their loves by women, both mythological and real, belong to the first category, so do *Amores* in which he speaks of his facile, frivolous, numerous, and passing relationships. There is also a group of pseudo-instructive works: *De medicamine faciei*, *Ars amatoria*, and *Remedia amoris*. To the second, 'serious', group belong the *Fasti*, descriptions of the calendar to extol Augustus' religious policy; and the *Metamorphoses*, mythical stories of the transformation of human beings into plants, animals, and inanimate bodies, for which he had collected 250 legends and bound them together into a lightly connected history. He was not interested in the myths apart from the romantic element, the story; and he was unconcerned when he produced doublets or even triplets of the same episode. They are a series of vignettes, of which the most eloquent illustration is given by Hellenistic reliefs and paintings, since poetry and visual art lived in a continuing alliance and were constantly borrowing from one another.

His exile provided the background for the last Ovidian writings. The *Tristia* and the *Epistulae ex Ponto* are lyrical letters from the poet to his friends, his songs of exile. They are no longer art for art's sake, but sincere personal poetry, full of truth and melancholy, human even though tiresomely circling the same ideas. They offer a defence for his poetry, regret for all that he has lost in his homeland, contempt for the country and conditions in which he lives, and hatred for his critics and the friends who have betrayed him.

A facile poet, spontaneous, but for the most part an improviser and a fertile rhetorician, Ovid as an 'impressionist' passed from image to image, picture to picture, and love to love, without pause. All too frequently his work lacks depth, restraint, and finish: at times it even lacks adequate learning. Too often he is satisfied, like an able Alexandrian versifier, with his fancy and a general feeling for beauty.[13]

Tragedy and Comedy. In the fifth century tragedy, particularly at Athens, assumed, aesthetically and didactically, very great religious and moral importance; religion, history, rhetoric, and ethics were focused and taught by its means. The tragic performances became a form of cult, prepared for solemn festivals. This happened at Athens during the various Dionysiac festivals; and also at Syracuse, Epidaurus, Argos, and gradually in all the cities which had developed real theatres out of the primitive open space on a slope or an area with a flight of steps. The characters (originally one but they finally grew to three and exceptionally to four), their faces covered by a mask, obtained their scenic effects by voice and mimicry alone; they had a choral retinue of twelve, later fifteen, with a leader supported by a flautist and, in monodies, by a lutanist. The themes were those of heroic history, and therefore in general the heroes of mythology; but they also included the most important and stirring deeds of contemporary history, such as the *Sack of Miletus* by Phrynichus, and the *Persae* by Aeschylus, as well as purely imaginary themes such as the *Anthos* by Agathon. Originally the choral sections, with their songs and lyrics, had predominated over the recited passages, but later the balance was the other way. Three great tragic poets stand out in fifth-century Greek literature, Aeschylus, Sophocles, and Euripides.

Aeschylus of Eleusis (*c.*525–456/5) was an actor and an author; twenty-eight times winner of tragic contests, he wrote about ninety tragedies and satyric dramas. Apart from many references in authors and especially extensive fragments on papyrus, we have seven of his tragedies, of which four are independent, and three form part of the same tetralogy.[14] Simple in plot, they are developed around a moving heroic or historic event, using characters with superhuman features hieratically drawn in the grand manner. But the sentiments are deeply analysed, and the tragedies are dominated by lofty religious and moral concepts in the mythological tradition. Certain guiding ideas are put forward throughout. There is the destiny which hangs over human life; the intervention of the gods on behalf of their adherents, and their jealousy of excessive human glory;[15] the hereditary taint which is derived from sin and from the curses to which it gives rise; the inferiority of brute force over spiritual strength; the superiority of the laws of civilized peoples; and there are the claims of love.

Sophocles (c. 500–406/5) was born at Athens, and lived almost all his life in that city where he was the idol of the mob. One hundred and twenty-three of his dramatic works are recorded, often repeating themes treated by Aeschylus and others; and seven tragedies have come down to us. Profoundly persuaded that the world is governed by a divinity of inscrutable wisdom, and an independent-minded critic of the theories of the philosophers and sophists, he presents characters who are still a little stylized, but yet are deeply human because of their will, their feelings, and their weaknesses. He captivates the audience with the lively struggles between these characters, with the nobility and drama of his dialogue, with the ease with which he unravels his plots, and with his analysis of character and feeling (particularly of women).

Euripides (c. 485–406) was not very popular with the people because of his religious and moral audacity, which stemmed from his passionate participation in the sophistic movement. We know of ninety-two tragedies of various types of which only seventeen authentic ones (apart from a spurious work) and extensive papyrus fragments have come down to us. As a rule they are indifferent to dramatic unity, and include a succession of episodes brought on by theatrical expedients, the connection between them lying outside the play. The main intention is to portray the development of feelings, even at the cost of having to explain the plot to the audience either by anticipating its outline in the prologue or by summarizing it in the final scenes. The whole artistic power of the tragedy appears in the monologues. The choral sections meanwhile have lost part of their importance and tend to become lyrico-melodic 'intermissions'. Their words were a vehicle for the accompanying music, of which we unfortunately know nothing.

Euripides was not really a true philosopher, though he had an open mind about the many moral, philosophical, and cosmogonic theories which excited learned men from Heraclitus to Socrates. Some of these are reflected here and there, often in a contradictory form, in his dialogues, and in the subtle and sometimes paradoxical discussions between his characters and the chorus.

He was inclined to scepticism, and did not scruple to bring forward his criticisms of established beliefs and opinions, both religious and moral. His characters are neither supermen, nor stylized humans, but real men and women, individuals whom the poet had observed in the world around him, whose instincts, passions, feelings, and intrigues he reproduced with maximum effect. From them he acquired material for satirizing the public and private habits of society, especially of women, and thus opened the way to the satires on behaviour which became the fundamental theme of New Comedy.

Chance has preserved part of the work of these three great tragedians, but they had competitors who were also writers of great power. We know the names of another 140 such plays, while it is calculated that in the fifth century at the Great Dionysia of Athens alone 1,200 tragedies and satyric dramas were presented, written by the most brilliant minds in Greece. As had already been the case with epic and philosophy, there were families and clans of dramatic authors, who handed down works and teachings to one another, as well as taking charge of recitations and bringing the old tragedies up to date.

Tragedy, however, slowly declined. The same overworked themes had been put too often into competitions by the artists; they had lost the original deeply religious purpose; too much attention had to be paid to public taste which was hostile to certain characters and took exaggerated account of the actors' ability. Moreover tragedy became saturated with rhetoric, philosophy, and dialectical virtuosity, and abused the employment of unlikely shifts of fortune and theatrical scenic effects (which gave rise to parodies such as those by Diogenes of Sinope and Crates of Thebes). At the same time it had to meet competition from lyrical compositions set to music. It is true that Ptolemy Philadelphus about 284–281 tried to imitate Athens by instituting tragic contests at Alexandria; eventually he selected from among the best competitors a list of the seven greatest and compared them with the seven stars of the 'Pleiades'. But these writers, like their competitors, were no longer genuine tragedians. They were learned philologists, who attempted in a curious fashion to restore drama to its original form (at least in theory). Thus Sositheus tried to reproduce the earliest dithyrambs, and Philiscus brought historical characters like Themistocles on to the stage. They were unsuccessful in producing anything vital, writing dramas which had to be read with learned commentaries, while real tragedy as a creative genre remained silent; and the dramas of Euripides continued to triumph even though they were abbreviated and deprived of their choral passages. From the authors of the *Pleias* there has survived a most peculiar work, the *Alexandra*, which made the reputation of its author Lycophron of Chalcis in the first half of the third century. Its 1,474 iambic trimeters describe how Cassandra, a prisoner in a tower, predicts the history of Greece up to the time of the author. In this composition, which lacks any breath of poetry, and is full of undigested learning, there is a continuous effort to enhance the tragic style by obscurity, pedantic eccentricity, and the use of foolish meta-phors. This hotch-potch of almost incomprehensible phrases is indeed far from the flights of Pindar or the pathos of Aeschylus.

The nature of Roman tragedy was complex because it was a Greek plant growing on Latin soil. Its earliest subjects, as well as the actual genre, were derived from the Greek tragedians, above all the themes from the Trojan cycle, which became Roman by adoption. But plots were altered, ideas were Romanized, and subjects were contaminated. The Roman custom (perhaps originally Etruscan) of giving the senators and magistrates places in the orchestra limited the space and the action, and consequently the importance of the chorus.[16] Tragedy came to Rome through the medium of Etruria, the home of the *Histriones*; and this, as well as the adoption of motifs and innovations on the Roman model, was probably responsible for some of the differences from Greek plays. In fact probably from its first appearance Latin tragedy presented plots concerned with national myth and history. These are found in the *fabulae praetextatae*, which at least in their content are entirely indigenous.

L. Livius Andronicus, the Tarentine who wrote an abridged *Odyssey*, is known as the first tragedian, from about 240 BC onwards. He produced and acted his plays and was the first organizer of recitations, which later were regularly incorporated in both tragedy and comedy. His tragedies dealt with Greek themes, but we know nothing of his sources or the extent of his debt to them.

From Cn. Naevius, on the other hand, we are told not only of several tragedies abridged from Greek, which sometimes amalgamate more than one model, but also of two *praetextatae* with genuine Roman plots, the *Clastidium* and the *Romulus*. The same can be said of Q. Ennius from whom we possess twenty-two certain titles of tragedies with Greek subjects, and also the titles of two *praetextatae*, *Sabinae* and *Ambracia*. The Ennian fragments show that though he sometimes translated literally from his Greek source, yet he would often revise both story and text, rearrange the chronology of events, and use more than one model. Moreover we can see in his work great pathos and sententiousness; his plays are full of moral maxims, philosophic motifs and dialectical terms; there are dashing descriptions of wars, and songs of high lyric quality. In fact we can appreciate all the virtues which, combined with the variety of his metres, enabled his tragedies to dominate the Roman stage for two centuries.

M. Pacuvius, from Brundisium, a nephew of Ennius, was a painter as well as a poet (220–132). We know the titles of thirteen tragedies with Greek themes, most of them corrupted by the insertion of material adapted to Roman taste; and he also wrote the *Paulus*, a play with a native background. He knew how to fascinate his public and his actors with emotional parts; he had a wonderful power of description; he could utter serious maxims, and was also bold in style and in the use of imagery. Cicero, though he criticized his language, thought him the greatest tragedian; and it is certain that his plays were still alive at the end of the Republic, when the recitation of his poem on Ajax dying (from the *Armorum Iudicium* in imitation of a play by Aeschylus) served to excite the people against the murderers of Caesar.

L. Accius of Pisaurum (179–90), succeeded Pacuvius, and for half a century dominated the Roman tragic stage. He wrote numerous tragedies on Greek subjects and inspired by Greek models, and also some *praetextatae*, of which the *Brutus* and *Aeneadae* (or *Decius*) are recorded. His works were accorded a very favourable judgement by later men of letters. The fragments show him as sceptical about religious questions, vivid in narrative, sententious, fond of moving oratory, and convincing in his dialectic.

This tendency to oratory and declamation in Roman tragedy was accentuated, and reached its height in Seneca. The reduction of the choral part, and the custom of reciting tragic monologues in halls of recitation, contributed to this trend.

The origin of comedy lay to some extent in the work of Epicharmus (c. 540–457) in Syracuse. Of his thirty-five recorded comedies nineteen provide caricatures of the mythological traditions about gods and heroes; a dozen are of the descriptive type with very little plot, forerunners of the 'mimes' which put typical human beings on the stage, imitating and exploiting their gay and amusing angles; and three are 'controversies' (e.g. does Land or Sea give greater blessing to man?). His comedies did not set out to be didactic satire, nor to attack individual political characters; they are good-humoured and popular caricatures and parodies of human life. The dialect he uses is also a popular one (a hybrid Syracusan); the plot is schematic; there is frequent play on words and utterances which can be taken either seriously or in jest. They even formed the material for a 'book of maxims', to which spurious material was added. Epicharmus enjoyed such a reputation that Plato put him on a level with Homer.

In Sicily in the fifth century there were other comedians, such as Phormis, his son Deinolochus, and Meson of Megara. But comedy ended by setting off a new literary genre, the 'mime'; and this enjoyed wide popularity. It consisted at this period of a short scene drawn from life, with either a monologue or a dialogue between two people, composed in rhythmic prose and in Doric dialect with much use of native Siculan terminology. It was performed at banquets and at public contests as an interlude, and an essential part of it was the imitation of behaviour and typical characters.

Sophron of Syracuse, who lived 'at the time of Xerxes and Euripides', wrote many mimes full of jokes, sometimes decorous, sometimes vulgar. Some were called 'masculine' (*The Fishermen in the Country*, *The Fisher of Tunny*, *Prometheus*, etc.); others were 'feminine' (*The Woman Doctor*, *The Sorceresses making the Goddess Appear*, *The Spectators at the Isthmian Games*, *The Lady's Maid*, *The Mother-in-law*, etc.). Plato read these mimes for pleasure; and their vivid realism and supple dialogue technique seem to have influenced the composition of his own dialogues.

Sophron's son Xenarchus, on orders from Dionysius I, is known to have composed a mime in which he burlesqued the cowardice of the people of Rhegium, comparing them to fleeing hares.

Rhinthon, who was famous for 'phlyacic' comedies, was a native of Syracuse, but later moved to Tarentum, where he was living at the end of the fourth century. It is not clear whether 'phlyax' means 'chatterbox', 'buffoon', or specifically 'demon, imp of fertility'. It is certain that these 'phlyacic' comedies, which were widespread throughout Magna Graecia as far as Campania (where they were called *Atellanae*), and which were recited by actors, clumsily and indecently disguised, were fairly coarse parodies and farces. Often they parodied divine figures and the myths depicted in tragedies, being also called *Hilarotragodiae*. We know something of the contents of the *phlyakes* not only from fragments but from scenes represented in pictures and reliefs.

At the same time as Sicilian and in part under its influence, Attic 'Old Comedy' established itself on similar lines to tragedy in the half-century before the Peloponnesian War. At first it was performed in the 'demes' and city suburbs; but at least from 488 the Athenian government created a contest for it, which was inserted in the plan of the Dionysiac competitions. The comedian was not governed by the limits of time or space; for the more improbable the situation, the more it made the audience laugh. The characters of comedy were shameless and rascally buffoons; the chorus sang, danced, did mimicry and acrobatics, chattered, interrupted one another, and passed judgement. Even the gods were not spared; and clouds, wasps, birds, frogs, Attic demes, and islands were put on the stage. Born of the iambics composed by men in their cups, and developed in a free democratic atmosphere, Attic Old Comedy remained a comic fable, an irreverent satire, an extravagant carnival revelry. It was illogical and disorganized, but ready to pierce like a steel knife, and to fight for its own basic ideals. Being handled by skilful fencers it was a potent weapon; the state had to take account of it, and in 440 and 416 passed laws which prohibited comedians from making personal allusions. But the genre pleased the Athenians and was greatly cultivated: it is enough to say that we possess the names of 170 comic writers and the titles of almost 1,500 comedies.

The Athenian Aristophanes (*c.*446–385) is the only author of Old Comedy whom we know well and directly; and with Eupolis and Cratinus (of whom we have extensive fragments on papyrus) he was also the most famous. There have survived eleven out of his forty comedies, the earliest of which were presented under pseudonyms. He had inexhaustible invention, dazzling, malicious, and impudent, with an unsurpassed repertoire of jokes and contrivances. He was skilful in devising lively plots to support his allegory and satire, for the most part grouping his scenes into two parts, the intrigue and then its consequences. For his attacks on people he was content with

the slenderest factual basis and some remote resemblance to the person to
be shot at: to these he added features to make the whole thing absurd,
including slander, gossip, and invention. In this fashion he assailed and caricatured with incredible audacity all the powerful and eminent figures, and
also institutions; no literary, artistic, musical, moral, religious, political,
or social innovation escaped his lash. He has the mentality of the critic and
caricaturist which sees the comic side of everything; but also of the sceptic
who scorns to seem to have been taken in.

It is not surprising therefore that, though a defender of the old religion,
he frequently burlesques the gods in front of a people who rigorously
observed the national religion; though a supporter of morals, he is shameless
in his allusions; though the enemy of rhetoricians, he relies on logic and
frequently on sophistry; though a detractor of Euripides, he shows signs of
his influence. His imaginative, comical songs, full of double meanings, were
the delight of the people, who learnt them by heart; his works dominated
the Athenian comic theatre for forty years.

The latest Aristophanic comedies, sometimes without a chorus or *parabasis*
(the verses in which the poet, through the chorus, had addressed his audience
on topical themes), and directed to social themes or parodies, already take
comedy into its second phase, which then underwent a great development
and is called the Middle Comedy (*c.*400–338). Many changes in environment
and in taste combined to modify the literary genre. Athens had been defeated
and subjected by Sparta; then, after its internal quarrels had been ended with
an amnesty, it with great difficulty managed to make some headway towards
redeeming its independence. It was no longer possible to want a satirical
comedy full of incidental allusions, which would wound individuals and
rekindle the old hatreds. By this time refined taste had turned away from the
obscene language of earlier times, and the spread of reflective thought had
killed enjoyment of illogical flights of fancy. Finally the exhaustion of public
finances and the reduction of individual fortunes had compelled the cutting-
down of expense on stage representations.

For all these reasons, and for others as well, comedy had to do without
the traditional use of a *parabasis* and regular chorus,[17] and also to change its
tone. Personal attacks were excluded, speech became more refined, plots
were made less illogical, and the obscene costumes of actors were abolished.
As to subjects, there was still a fondness for parody of the myths which were
dramatized in tragedy; but the trend was towards bringing everyday life,
with all its natural humour, upon the stage, and to substitute the representation of types for that of individuals.

We therefore find comedies which display such features of particular
trades as could be made the subject of satire. We have the cook, the peasant,
the painter, the slave-dealer, the braggart soldier, or the gardener. There
are people from various countries and various social levels (the parasite,
the philosopher, the doctor, the poet). Plots were now based on human

impulses (depicting, say, an enemy of villains, or a crime), or on casual combinations (such as twins, or homonyms).

Middle Comedy was therefore more reflective, less popular, less vivacious, and profoundly influenced by the Sophists and rhetoricians. Tradition preserves the names of no less than fifty-seven poets and 607 titles of Middle Comedy: but our knowledge of them is entirely from fragments. We can get a better idea of works of this type from the Latin comedies which probably derived from them, such as Plautus' *Amphitruo* and *Persa*.

What we call New Comedy flourished at Athens in the period between Alexander and the city's loss of its liberty. It never took root outside Athens, although many tried to make it do so. It is no longer a mirror of political life, of parties in the *polis*, but of universal humanity. It is no longer a parody of exceptional and ridiculous types. For although it still makes use of stock figures (parasite, braggart soldier, intriguing slave, pimp, etc.), it represents the life and normal habits of ordinary people excited by common human passions; and the commonest passion is love, into which fathers, young men, women, harlots are drawn across a thousand intrigues, contretemps, surprises, and catastrophes. For each category of person comedy created a particular type, which the public soon recognized from the special masks used by the actors; for each hitch in the plot it had an artificial device ready to untie it; each character is given a form of speech suited to his state of mind; in every discourse reflections of common experience are inserted. Although not banal these last are sometimes ridiculous, but they made people think. New Comedy, now so different from Old, perfectly reflects Greek Hellenistic civilization with its taste, its eloquence, its spiritual Epicureanism, and its vivacity.

The most famous of these comedians was the Athenian Menander (343/2–292/1), who so loved his city that he would not leave it for Alexandria, and had a superb understanding of the society he put on the stage. His finesse in presenting types, the perfection of his language and its adaptation to his characters and their feelings, the nobility of his moral maxims and his ability to give fresh life to trite themes and traditional forces, all these were qualities not always appreciated by the Athenian public. Many of them preferred Philemon, but Menander has gained the admiration of posterity. He was the author of 108 comedies, of which very extensive fragments have been rediscovered on papyrus.[18]

In the meantime mime had spread from Sicily. Syracuse had had a new practitioner in Boeotus; and now Phoenix of Colophon and Herodas, perhaps of Cos, who lived about 250, distinguished themselves; seven mimes by the latter have been found on papyri, and also one fragment. He presented, with great fidelity, probably earlier than Theocritus, scenes from daily life in temples, law-courts, schools, shops, and so on. They are rapid dialogues between two or three people, sometimes monologues, in which persons of all sorts of quality and moral talent are presented. They are sketches cleverly drawn; the characters spring to life without disguise, and we are given insight into their souls. The metre is choliambic (i.e. iambic with a final long foot); the language is Ionic with Attic and Doric infiltrations.

Much later, though it still engaged authors of worth such as Philistion, Greek mime declined, reducing itself to mime 'hypotheses' (situations or plots suitable to mimes) with a stage setting. These are a set of canvases to be developed under the direction of an 'archimimus'.

Latin comedy was more natural and indigenous in its origins than tragedy, because of the bantering tendency (the 'Italum acetum' of Horace) of the Italian people. In the rural festivals of grain, wine, etc., and at marriages, this mockery was made the occasion for piquant poetic contexts, which in one small Faliscan town named Fescennium developed into regular farces improvised by masked peasants (*Fescennina carmina*). In this form they were transplanted to Rome. But the licentiousness of these Fescennines was such, and the attacks which men made on their neighbours were so unrestrained, that a curb was put on them in a law of the XII Tables.

Livy, noting that in 364 the first 'ludi scaenici' were registered, says that in that year some Etruscan jugglers (*histri*) came to Rome and danced to the music of the flute. The young Romans, who were already producing improvised Fescennines, now added music and dance to them; and from this was derived the *Satura*, an elaborate dramatic text presented by comic actors. Since, however, a more likely etymology for the name 'satura' would be from satyrs, it is more probable that it was derived, via the Etruscans (or Etruscanized Campania), from the Greek satyr drama and from its Italiote form the phlyax-plays and 'Rhinthonic' farces. It also corresponds to them in its content.

To the two types of Fescennines, the native type and the Graeco-Etruscan *Satura*, can be added the Oscan *Atellana* (from Atella in Campania, influenced by the *phlyakes*) which continued to be used by some of those who spoke the Oscan dialect. These *Atellanae* were transferred to Rome; and though at first they were produced in a popular manner with amateur actors they eventually reached the dignity of an art, and were recited by professional actors. Like the satyr dramas in Greece, they were used as an *exodium* after the performance of tragedies. They were short farces about some form of entanglement; the themes were drawn from the life of the people and countryside, full of obscenity and crude jokes, and founded on a few fixed types. There was Maccus, the young peasant, greedy, and boorish; Pappus, the miserly and stupid old man; Bucco, the young glutton and braggart; and Dossennus, the hunchback and astute swindler.

Finally there was added the translation or the re-fashioning of Greek comedies and the Siceliote *Hilarotragodiai*; and these were called *palliatae* because the actors wore Greek dress. Some of them used subjects from Old Comedy which lent themselves to personal satire; but most subjects were drawn from Middle and above all from New Comedy, and therefore revolved round an almost standard series of stock types. After Naevius' period Greek comedies were often contaminated; in fact the plots of one or more authors were amalgamated. But the Greek plots were only the form into which Roman writers placed what, for them and for their audience, were in fact the essentials: the comedy of the situations, gay fantasy, the continuous cracking jests, the implications, the double meanings, the parody of noble style, the medley of ideas in newly composed words, and mock scenes of stateliness; in fact the whole of typical Roman comedy which we know from Plautus' inexhaustible vein. The themes of indigenous characters soon attracted the attention of the writers of *palliatae*, and it developed in the following fashion: through the strong influence of the *palliatae*, 'togata' comedy, which placed the Roman world and characters on the stage, drew from them as much value as from the Greeks, and divided them into appropriate social types representative of their class.

As a writer of comedy we know little of L. Livius Andronicus other than that he wrote three comedies entitled *Gladiolus*, *Ludius*, and *Virgus* or *Verpus*. In contrast there are titles and fragments of thirty-three comedies by Cn. Naevius, some of which seem to be *togatae* of the 'taverna' type, and others of the Atellane farces.

The greatest Latin comedy-writer, T. Maccius Plautus, who was born at Sarsina in Umbria (*c*.254–180), was a little younger than Naevius. A businessman, he lost all his property, and so he went to Rome where he earned his living, so it is said, turning the grinding-stone in a flour-mill. He put together three comedies, slowly recovered his financial position, and from then on wrote comedies in the years that followed (130 pieces according to Varro, 100 according to Gellius: many of them are spurious). The stage direcions show that there was an early corpus of twenty-one authentic comedies, and they have survived completely except that the *Vidularia* is fragmentary.[19]

The prologues and allusions in the text in a good many of these comedies inform us that in ten cases Plautus availed himself of one or more Greek comedies. But what of the other eleven? Though he may have used Greek sources and often takes us to Greek cities and the life of Hellenistic people, Plautus knew how to give his comedies the sharp stamp of originality as well as Romanization.[20] And this is not only a matter of form, in which there is evidence of many innovations, but even more so one of substance. There are whole comedies for which it is not possible to indicate either the Greek source or plausibly to show its existence; in them all, and even in those in which the original Greek is certainly employed, we find new Roman types inserted, and representations of surroundings and habits which are frankly contemporary and Roman; there is clear Romanization of Greek myths, and new uses for old comic expedients. But where Plautus' comedy is most Roman and original is in all his expression, line after line: he uses the genuine language of daily life, and varies the mode of speech according to the mentality and class of his characters, who are contrasted in the dialogues with wonderful spontaneity. There is continual brilliance in the humour of his witticisms and double meanings: there is turbulent vivacity in his discussions and altercations; and the fluency of his verse is obtained in so wonderful and skilful a fashion that the ancient grammarians eventually claimed that it was not verse but prose.

Between Plautus and Terence there was a whole series of *palliatae* and *togatae* which have been lost, one reason probably being that they were unable to stand up to the two great authors.

It is not possible to give precise dates for P. Terentius Afer's short life, but in any event it was between 200 and 160. Born at Carthage and probably a Libyan by origin, he was taken as a slave to Rome, but was later manumitted, and became the friend of distinguished people. In each of his six surviving comedies half the play is entirely based on a Greek model, and the other half is influenced by one or more authors. Recitation and dialogue in these comedies are less than are to be found in Plautus. Their originality is revealed particularly in the characteristics of the people, who seem particularly to conform to Roman types and tastes; there is a tendency to idealize (virtuous, reasonable, and submissive matrons, courtesans capable of generosity, modest and loving fathers, polite children, servants who are fond of their masters). In addition a wonderful effect is produced by the original style. Living at a time when Roman comedy was very advanced, and when many of his contemporaries had great knowledge and respect for Greek models, Terence was a target for severe criticism, against which he defended himself more or less openly in the prologues to the comedies. Like his predecessors he was accused of contaminating the Greek comedies which were much admired, and of having secret collaborators, a charge for which evidence was brought. His fame was in every sense greater and more lasting after his death.[21]

The Greek-inspired *palliatae* comedies had no more famous authors after Terence, though the *togatae* with their Roman themes took new forms. L. Afranius, who was writing about 94 BC, produced about forty-four, which deal with familiar themes, individual characters, and types from the professions and trades; they resemble fairly closely the plots and developments of the *palliatae*, putting forward Greek comic models as well as Roman. A clever psychologist, he gave great importance to both feminine and regional types, and as a moralist he drew close to Terence. Of T. Quinctius Atta, who died in 78 BC, we know the titles of twelve *togatae* and a few fragments; the scenes of the latter take place during feasts, or are reproductions of daily life and familiar happenings. He too seems to have given great importance to women.

At the same time, in Sulla's period, we find a new form of art, the popular Atellanes; these gradually came to resemble the 'fabula togata tabernaria', a more humble type of art, and were ultimately merged with them. Atellanes by Novius, and those by Pomponius (who was born at Bononia and flourished about 89), present various innovations on the earlier versions: they were written by educated men, presented by professional actors, and written in Latin, with the Oscan dialect reserved for particular characters. Both these two authors were prolific writers. They brought on to the stage not only the four fundamental characters of the Atellane, but country-people, personifications of vice and misery, important or mythical people in parody, fantastic beings, and talking animals, all in a continuous passage from comedy to farce, parody, and fable.

Meanwhile the mime, a genre very similar to comedy and Atellane, had been transferred to Rome, and developed an even stronger resemblance to the other genres because of the poetical form in which it was clothed (cf. the *mimiambi*). At times it took on the characteristics of satire. The best-known Latin writer of mimes was Decimus Laberius, a knight, who was forced by Caesar in 46 to go on the stage, as a mimic, in a contest in which he was defeated by Publilius Syrus. The latter was an ex-slave of Syrian origin who was famous for his witty maxims which were gathered into collections. A place apart belongs to the *mimiambi* or comic iambics, with their life-like scenes and wit. The fragments which were written by Cn. Matius provide excellent justification for Gellius' great praise for him as a writer.

Bucolic and Didactic Poetry. Theocritus was considered the last of the great creators of Greek literary genres, his invention being bucolic poetry. A Syracusan (about 300–250), he lived for a long time on the island of Cos, then for some years at Alexandria; then he returned to Cos, and in the end went back to Sicily. The surviving collection of 'small compositions' (*Idylls*) or of 'selected compositions' (*Eclogues*) have certainly been altered. They contain poems of varied moods and of different types. The bucolic poems are the most characteristic type, in which the poet made the traditional poetic duels between the shepherds of his land into a form of art. They sing against a joyful background of rustic life, in the middle of gentle, smiling nature, among the animals who love them: they are ingenuous creatures, superstitious and true to life, although greatly idealized. There are other, related poems which record mythical legends about shepherds: but in the collection there have also been included real mimes, some short poems which are half-lyric and half-epic, two elegies for great lords, and twenty-six beautiful epigrams.

Theocritus is a lyric poet of exquisite sensibility, whose senses always respond to the stimulus of nature, as well as a vigorous dramatist who knows how to create and animate living characters. He is a realist who depicts the most delicate shades of feeling, but an idealist too who enhances the more poetical and idyllic sides of his characters. He is finally a scholar of good taste who knows how to conceal his erudition. A poetic innovator, he uses the dactylic hexameter in all types of poems, is musical in his style, and writes in a lively though moderate language without pedantic affectation. His shepherds speak a Syracusan dialect which is a little unrefined; speech in the mimes has some Ionic influence. Other dialects are used in other forms of poems.

In the Greek world Theocritus had annotators and imitators such as Bion and Moschus, but his only worthy rival and successor was a Roman, Virgil.

Virgil's *Bucolica* (which he too called 'Eclogae', probably because the ten published poems were a selection) mainly differ from the Theocritean poems in that their material is drawn from literary sources rather than from contact with the rustic world: they thus have an artificial aspect for which the model was the genre of poetry called 'Arcadian'. From this literary inspiration stem in part the most outstanding characteristics: the imprecise contours of the unreal landscapes; the ill-defined characters who preserve their names, but change appearances and types; the continuous contradictions in the plot. But the fact that the poet, generalizing a system sometimes used by Theocritus, has given an allegorical significance to some of his Eclogues, hinting at episodes from his own life, and identifying himself time and again with his characters, so that they seem to have double lives, contributes to all this confusion. Nor are some of these allegories easy to understand, and attempts to interpret them, both in ancient and in modern times, have been sometimes grotesque[22].

Didactic poetry too, in the period in question, had more able devotees in the Latin world than in the Greek. The names of Aratus and Nicander stand out in the Greek world. Aratus of Soloi (about 315–240 BC) was a philosopher, a mathematician, and a poet. In his work, called *Phainomena*, he popularized the astronomical and meteorological teachings of Eudoxus of Cnidus, in very competent verse, but in a somewhat heavy style. Nicander is credited with poems on poisons, on antidotes, on bees, and on *Georgics*. *The Wonders of Italy* of Heliodorus, the *Chronology* of Apollodorus, and the *periegesis* of the pseudo-Scymnus are compositions with a purely mnemonic purpose.

In Latin the heights of poetry were reached by Lucretius with his *De rerum natura*, of which we spoke earlier on, by Virgil with his *Georgics*, by Horace with his *Ars poetica*, and by some works of Ovid.

Virgil was inspired to write the *Georgics* by one of the canons of the great programme of restoration of Augustus by which Italy would regain its prosperity through the rebirth of agriculture and love for the land.[23] Virgil devoted seven years to this work (37 to 30 BC) although it consisted of little more than 2,000 verses. The *Georgics* consist of four books which deal in turn with agriculture (the working of the land, seeds, and the periods and signs of the zodiac); with arboriculture; with the breeding of animals; and with bee-keeping. Although Virgil was the son of a peasant family and had early on shown himself in the *Bucolica* to be a lover of nature and of the land, he devoted a long time to studying the specialists beginning with Hesiod's *Works and Days*, in order to become a specialist too. The writings of these two poets agree in the conception that work is a duty imposed upon men and that sweat cannot be avoided on the path to virtue. It must not be forgotten, however, that Virgil held the view that work was the essence of the successful history of Rome (let us remember the motto of Aeneas to his son: 'my son, learn from me virtue and true work; others will teach you happiness') and in any event the *Georgics* dealt with Italy and not with Greece. This poem also demonstrates the stage in Virgil's philosophical thought when he was absorbed by the Stoic theory of immanence which led him to perceive divinity in every small particle of the universe. Yet he did not succeed in freeing himself entirely from Epicurean deterministic conceptions: they come out in the *Georgics* here and there. The main characteristics of the work are first a deep awareness and love of nature and of animals and plants, which are described by the poet with sincere and vibrating lyricism; secondly its novel ideas on the blending of tradition with a direct sensation of reality. A love of nature is combined with the glorification of the anonymous work of millions of workers who collaborated with Augustus in the rebirth of Italy.

Horace's *Ars Poetica* is the last of the *Epistulae* of the second book, and was soon published as a short poem on its own. It consists of 476 verses which the poet based upon a work by Neoptolemus of Parium. Contrary to the episodic production of the Alexandrines, Horace requires unity of conception in a work of art. He then speaks of expression, by which he means language; of metre and literary form; and finally of characters and plot. He dwells upon the theatre, insisting upon the rule of five acts and four actors, and he criticizes the abuse of choral and musical parts. He maintains that poetry does not depend only upon inspiration, but also upon technique, and that, as it must 'delight' and 'profit', it cannot be either pure art or amoral.

There are also several works of Ovid which can be described as didactic. The *Ars Amatoria* consists of three books which teach men how to conquer and dominate women; but in the last book Ovid suggests to women the means to defend themselves against men. All this work is pervaded by a subtle sense of humour and is full of salacious anecdotes. The *Medicamina Faciei* deals with the ways of keeping the skin white, smooth, and without blemish. The *Remedia Amoris* teaches desperate lovers how to avoid suicide. The *Fasti* was conceived to glorify the religious policies of Augustus: it was designed as a description of the calendar in twelve books, one for each month, which illustrated with episodes and suitable scenes those days which were auspicious or ill-omened, and days when the *comitia* were permitted or forbidden. Ovid's description is enlivened by a series of vivacious and graceful pictures, where the gods are made to have an outlook very similar to that of the capricious mortals of the Hellenistic age. The *Fasti*, however, lacks any sense of religion and any harmony with Augustus' strict and pious work of reform.[24]

There were at least four different types of Roman satire, although all of them had more or less fundamental characteristics in common. We have already spoken of the first type, which is the dramatic theatrical satire. The second type was also burlesque and moralizing, but consisted of books on all kinds of subjects written partly in prose and partly in verse of various metres. The works of Ennius were of this type. They comprised general 'saturae' and also other satires with their own titles which were probably part of the major general work. There was a *Dialogue between Life and Death*, an *Epicharmus*, and an *Euhemerus* with a translation of the *Historia Sacra* by that author.

The work of Lucilius of Suessa Aurunca (about 180–103 BC) belongs to the third type of satire. He wrote thirty books from which 1,375 verses are still in existence. His satire was influenced by Iambic writers and Old Comedy, by philosophical and burlesque polemics, and by the *silloi* of Timon and his imitators, including Clitomachus who was a friend of Lucilius. In his first composition Lucilius used a most colourful variety of metres, but later on he preferred a monometric verse of the kind used by his great successors, namely the hexameter.

His satires describe every kind of person around him, portraying their different types, recording anecdotes and dialogues, drawing caricatures and making hints. His accent varies from the clearest epic tone to the completely vulgar and scurrilous. He lashes the new rich, the people who were mad about anything Greek, and also women. He hits at political opponents, and on occasion the whole Roman people, tribe by tribe.

He wrote gentle satire against writers and literary works, tragedies in particular, and against the taste of Romans (whom he put last after the people of Tarentum, of Cosa, and of Sicily); he wrote philosophical satire, against the doctrine of perfection of the Stoics in particular, although he preferred philosophy to inventive poetry, even that of Homer.

A fourth type of satire found its origins in the works of Menippus of Gadara, and because of this Varro called it 'Saturae Menippeae'.

We are told that M. Terentius Varro of Reate (116–26 BC) produced 74 works in 620 books. The works which concern us in the field of satire are: four books of *Saturae* which were probably of the same type as those of Lucilius; six books of *Pseudotragoediae* or *Hilarotragoediae*, which consisted of humorous criticism of tragic characters set out in dialogue form; and, of particular interest, the *Saturae Menippeae*, from which we know 96 titles and 600 fragments. Varro in these satires uses a variety of metres and also follows Menippus in that he joins parts written in prose to those in verse and interposes Greek in the Latin. The content of his satires was extremely diversified. There were attacks on personal enemies; criticism of Epicureans and Stoics in defence of an eclectic philosophy; criticisms of the customs of the time; literary, grammatical, and historical criticism; spirited anecdotes; humorous explanations of mottoes and proverbs; a sort of 'code of table manners'; and a burlesque treatment of myths. The style of Varro was imaginative and descriptive, as in his other works. Yet it lacked conciseness and agility; it was fond of classifications, archaisms, and obscure hints; and often it was artificial, with a long series of adjectives and diminutives.

The satirical works of Q. Horatius Flaccus (65–8 BC) can be divided into two groups with largely different characteristics. The first group was written between the years 45 and 30 BC and the second from 23 to about 13 BC.

The first group belongs to the period before the imperial domination of Augustus and consists of Horace's aggressive and personal writings in iambics. To this period belong the seventeen *Epodes*, which remind us of Archilochus; and also eighteen satires, which recall Aristophanes and Lucilius, in the first two books of the *Saturae*. The poet had an irritable temper and was embittered by life, and although wanting to find 'the happy mean' he preferred to give vent to bitter invective and personal criticism of the Stoics and their hypocritical followers, literary men of various schools, 'neoteric' poets, Lucilius, and politicians.

After the victory of Actium, however, and during the rule of Augustus, Roman society changed deeply. So when Horace, then a mature man, went back to writing satire his mordacity gave way to humour, and the *iambus* to a calm criticism of customs and tendencies. He rightly said that he was, at that time, nearer to Terence than to Aristophanes. The satires of this new type which are contained in the first book of the *Epistles* tend to be philosophical. Horace was an Epicurean, who took life in a happy way, but his eclecticism made it possible for him to accept the precepts on moderation and on the 'aurea mediocritas' proclaimed by the Cyrenaics and by Aristippus.

The contents of the second book of the *Epistles* are mostly literary. In the *Epistles* the poet turns to Augustus and makes a subtle criticism of the archaic tendency of a new taste which had begun to prevail; he criticizes ancient poetry and hopes for the rebirth of the theatre and of epic; he apologizes for doing so little work, for, he says, the torment of artistic production tires him. He puts forward his *Ars Poetica* (of which we have already spoken).[25]

Prose: The Greek Historians. Perhaps in no other field, except in tragedy, is the strong influence of the Sophists felt so much as in historical literature. The same difference which divides Euripides and Sophocles can also be seen between Thucydides and Herodotus, although there are barely twenty years between the two. Only a few fragments are left to tell us anything of the works of the later *logographoi* such as Hellanicus of Mitylene, the author of works on local history, on mythical stories, and on chronology. Fragments remain of the work of Damastes of Sigeum and Antiochus of Syracuse, author of a history of Sicily up to the year 424 BC and of a history of Italy. The works of Herodotus have survived complete.

Herodotus (about 484–425 BC) was born in Halicarnassus. He took part in the colonization of Thurii, but both before and after this time he travelled to Athens and in the Greek peninsula, and to Asia Minor, Persia, Egypt, Cyrene, Magna Graecia, and Sicily. His history was written in Ionic and was later divided into nine books. The purpose of the writings of Herodotus was to recount the long fighting between the Greeks and the barbarians of Asia, a struggle which started in mythical times. The part which deals with more recent times describes the wars between the Lydians and the Greek settlers, and between the Greeks and Persians. It seems that he wrote each single section of his work separately and then fitted them together into a pre-established framework. Characteristics of his work are the long geographical and ethnographical digressions inspired by his travels; it is not very clear, however, how much information Herodotus drew from traditional stories which he heard locally and how much from the Greek writers of before his time.

The mind of Herodotus wavers where mythology and religion are concerned, for he does not know how to choose between or reconcile the various tendencies. Sometimes he rationalizes like Hecataeus, at other times, he refers to myths and oracles with respect. There are moments in which he seems to echo the criticism against the pantheon and the traditional gods; but for the most part he repeats the common ideas of his time, such as the belief that envy moves the gods to oppose human actions. He thinks that, apart from occasional divine interventions, historical events depend as a rule on the actions and the free will of men. But when it comes to great historical figures he does not succeed in co-ordinating the conflicting traditions; and there are many apparent contradictions in his work, for example in his portrayal of Miltiades and Themistocles. Herodotus is faithful to a Homeric model and does not try to get to know the concrete causes of events, or to teach politically, or to improve morally. He wants to please with his artistic narrative, the events of which are well chosen and well arranged; he writes in a form which is simple, ingenuous, fascinating, and suitable for public readings. He transformed history into a work of art and because of this he became the 'father of history'.[26]

Time had already greatly altered the contents of tradition, and Herodotus, while usually omitting the precise sources of it, elaborated upon it artistically and not critically. (He said that he recounted what he believed without always being fully convinced of it.) When speaking of tradition he resorted to fantasy: he invented dialogues, conversations, and anecdotes. There are many errors in his narrative because of the scant knowledge he had of military and political matters, and because he was uncritical of his sources of information. He is a decided partisan of Athens and of the democratic cities against the others. He is partisan against Themistocles and in favour of the family of the Alcmaeonids: for the latter were related to a man he esteemed very greatly, namely Pericles.

Thucydides (about 465/460–395 BC) was the son of Olorus, a name associated with Thrace.[27] He was a friend of the Sophists, and was general at Athens in 424. Luck was not on his side, however, and in that year he was banished from Athens for twenty years. He wrote an incomplete history later divided into eight books, which dealt with the contemporary events of the Peloponnesian War, and had a preface on the preceding period of fifty years. He obtained his information from the stories of eye-witnesses which he weighed in the light of his own experience. For chronological precision he divided the events into years and seasons and according to areas of activity.

There is a gulf between the poetic and religious sense of Herodotus and the natural interpretation of Thucydides. Thucydides never speaks of divine intervention, though on some occasions he speaks of *Tyche* (luck). When mentioning the oracles he does not hide his scepticism; and he is sometimes sarcastic. All phenomena are brought back to natural causes; and according to him historical events depend upon a conflict of forces and upon the ability of men. For this reason, he says that the death of Pericles influenced the course of the war, for it was entrusted to successors, demagogues, who were far inferior. Thucydides was very skilled in outlining military events. He did not deal directly with the internal struggles of political parties,[28] though he gave some information about them in the form of conversations which he invented and put into the mouth of his characters. This method he used for the purpose of clarifying different points of view which were in contrast. It was ideas more than men which counted with Thucydides, but his characters became alive and real from their magnificent and learned Antiphontean speeches and their dramatic debates, in a way which was far better and could not have been achieved by any description. He also made indirect use of speeches to insert his opinions, for his greatest aim was that of remaining impartial. Thucydides never had a great interest in economic, commercial, or financial problems; and he was not infallible, for there are a few errors and gaps due both to erroneous information and to lack of revision of his work. He did not like digressions, but he had to use them when he wanted to rectify the stories of his predecessors or to teach. When he speaks of ancient history his critical sense is occasionally faulty, but he is capable of acute deductions from the archaeological evidence at his disposal.

The writings of Thucydides are a typical example of the works of prose and science which were produced in Attica at the time of the Sophists. The language is sometimes too affected, as in Gorgias, with a large number of new terms and new meanings; the style is forceful although at times it is laborious and mannered. All this, however, is proof of a gigantic struggle between thought and form, and it does not prevent us from considering Thucydides as the founder of scientific history, in which he has left us a masterpiece never surpassed in ancient times.[29]

The works of Herodotus had rivals in the *History of the Medes* written by Ctesias of Cnidus, physician to Artaxerxes, and the *Persica* by Deinon of Colophon which finishes with the year 340 BC. Thucydides too had various imitators, as for example Philistus of Syracuse, author of *Sicelica*; and Cratippus, Xenophon, and Theopompus wrote sequels to his work. The scant information we had of the Athenian Cratippus has now been completed by the discovery of large fragments, which almost certainly are his work, and from which it is apparent that he dealt with the events of the period between the years 415 and 393 BC and perhaps until the year 386 BC. In politics he appears to be moderate, averse from the demagogues, anxious for agreement between the Greeks and for a war against Persia. As a historian he carefully ascertained facts: he searched for their causes and thought that the actions of individuals were important. He kept psychological analysis within moderate limits, and preferred to deal with military events. As a stylist, although in part he followed Isocrates, he wrote in a manner which was clear but unpolished, avoiding any tendency towards fancy and romance, or towards rhetorical declamation, or even towards moralizing. It is due to the lack of rhetoric that his works were supplanted by those of later rhetorical historians, who made great use of his work as a source. Polybius is the great Greek historian who resembles him most.

Xenophon (about 430–354 BC) was an Athenian aristocrat. He started as an opponent of the democrats in his own city; then he enlisted as a mercenary together with the 10,000 who supported Cyrus the Younger against his brother. In the *Anabasis*, which he published under a false name, he described the events of that expedition, and the difficulties met by the Greek survivors who elected him their leader during their return to their homeland; in all this he was not averse from exaggerating his own merits. The *Anabasis* is not a true historical work outlining the grave consequences which fell upon Greece for having taken part in Cyrus' attempt; it is a diary with clear descriptions of feats of arms and the life of a mercenary army. It is written in pure Attic language and is a literary masterpiece of the new type of post-Sophist prose.

In the year 400 BC war broke out between Sparta and Persia, and Xenophon enrolled in the Spartan army. Later, in the year 394 BC, he fought on the side of Agesilaus of Sparta against the Athenians, and after having been banished from his country spent the rest of his life in places which were under the sway of Sparta. His major historical work is the *Hellenica*, which consists of seven books covering the period between the years 411 and 362 BC. The nucleus of this work is the hegemony of Sparta; and whereas in the first part he follows the outline of Thucydides and is under his influence, in the other parts he does not write a complete 'Greek History' but a narrative of the things which he has seen personally without regard to the rest. His partisanship is great even if achieved by silence and not by direct distortion. In other respects Xenophon is an honest narrator, well informed, and an expert on military and political facts. He never poses general problems to himself, and it is therefore useless to seek from him the explanation of the establishment and dissolution of the Greek hegemonies of which he writes.

Of historical character also is the praise of Agesilaus, written in the years 361–360 BC, to be found in the manuscript of the *Hellenica*. The *Constitution of Sparta*, *Hieron*, and *Cyropaedia* are different, being semi-historical and

[von Matt

41 HELLENISTIC STATUARY

    (a) *Head of Medusa, from
        Acrae, Sicily*

    (b) *Fisherman, from the
        Esquiline. Rome, Palazzo
        dei Conservatori*

(b)　　　　　　　　　　[Alinari

42   *The battle of Alexander and Cyrus; mosaic from Pompeii. Naples, National Museum*

[Alinari]

(a)

43　MOSAICS

    (a) *from Utica depicting a hunting scene. London, British Museum*

    (b) *from Ostia depicting tritons and marine deities. Ostia, the Thermae*

(b)

(a)

[Alinari

44

(a) *Volterra, the 'arch gate'*, c. 300 BC

(b) *Rome, the aqueduct of Claudius completed AD 52 and the Appian way*

(b)

[Alinari

45 Etruscan sarcophagus so-called 'Del Magnate'. Tarquinia Museum

(a)   [G.F.N.

46   ETRUSCAN PAINTING

    (a) *Mastarna or Servius Tullius;*
        detail from the fresco of the
        so-called 'François tomb' at
        Vulci. Rome, Torlonia Museum

    (b) *Episode from the Roman-Samnite*
        wars, fresco on a tomb on the
        Esquiline

(b)   [Alinari

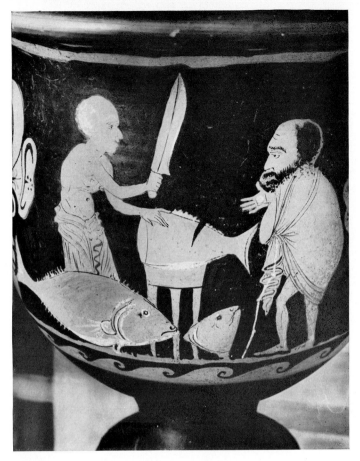

47   (a) *Hellenistic vase from Sicily depicting a fishmonger* (*detail*)
     (b) *Campanian plate depicting a war elephant*

(b)   S.A.E.M.

(a)

[Alinari

48 The so-called 'Ficoroni' casket,
    fourth century BC. Rome, Museum
    of the Villa Giuglia
    (a) Front view
    (b) Detail of the lid

(b)

[Alinari

[Ward Perkins (b) [Ward Perkins

49 *Roman building techniques:*

(a) opus incertum, *with quoins of dressed stone. Temple of Juppiter Anxur, Terracina*

(b) *opus reticulatum, used with brick courses and relieving arches, Villa of Hadrian, near Tivoli*

(c) opus latericium, *showing that the brick is only a facing to the core of rubble concrete. Villa of the Gordians beside Via Praenestina, Rome*

[Ward Perkins

[Alinari

(a)

50

(a)

Susa, Piedmont, the arc of Augustus, 8 BC

(b)

Aosta (Augusta Praetoria) Piedmont: the praetoria gate and the propugnaculum

[Alinari

(b)

(a)   [Alinari

51   *Roman tombs:*
    (a) *of Caecilia Metalla, c. 20 BC, on the Appian way*
    (b) *of Marcus Virgilius Eurisaces (the Baker), in Rome*

       (b)   [Alinari

(a)   [Alinari

52 *Roman sculpture*
   (a) *after Arcesilaus, 'Venus Genetrix'.*
       Rome, Terme Museum

   (b) *Augustus as* Pontifex. *Rome, Vatican*
       Museum

(b)   [Alinari

53 (a) *Arretine Vase in* terra sigillata. *London, British Museum*
    (b) *Detail of stucco work from the Thermae Stabianae, Pompeii*

(a)

54 (a) *The 'Ara Pacis'*, Saturnia Tellus, *first century BC*
(b) *Tiberius conqueror of the Pannonians, cameo attributed to Dioscurides. Vienna, National Museum*

(b)

55

ROMAN PAINTING I
*Detail from 'The
Aldobrandini
Marriage'. Rome,
Vatican Museum*

[Alinari

[Alinari

56   ROMAN PAINTING II

(a) *Rome, the Palatine, Villa of Livia, detail of the frescoes showing the main characteristics of the second style of Roman painting*

(b) *Pompeii, House of Amandus, the Fall of Icarus, wall painting*

[Alinari

political; and the last of these is stylistically the most perfect work that Xenophon ever wrote. It is a kind of imaginary constitution for a monarchy according to his ideals. The famous semi-legendary king of Persia, Cyrus I, is the main character; and the place in which he was brought up is not the real Persian capital but an ideal city in which the system of education is partly Spartan and partly a Xenophontine version of Socratic teaching.

There is another group of works by Xenophon which deals with Socratic subjects. This group includes the *Memorabilia* (*Apomnemoneumata*) of Socrates, which is a dialogue; the *Symposium*; the *Apology of Socrates*, a defence of that philosopher; and the *Oeconomicus*, which also deals with agriculture. These works show how the teaching of Socrates had been understood and transformed in the mind of Xenophon.

In matters of religion, this pupil of the enemy of the Sophists does not go back to the Herodotean conception of divinity. His opinion is that the gods do not take sides but punish those who violate the moral law.

The work of Xenophon must be judged as a whole. He was an honest and prolific writer, a lover of justice, and an enthusiast.[30] He was rather superficial in matters of history, philosophy, and politics, but an expert in military matters. Finally he was an excellent stylist with great literary talent, and he wrote the purest and most charming Attic prose of the post-Sophist epoch.

Up to this time Greek historical literature was of monographic character, for even the historical works of Herodotus were not really universal. However, when a great part of the Hellenic nation was united into a political system by Philip II, and when Alexander enlarged this system into an almost universal empire, there was need for comprehensive general history. It was then that the pupils of the two rival schools of Isocrates and Polycrates competed to satisfy this need, the first school represented by Ephorus and Theopompus and the second by Zoilus and Anaximenes.[31] Here we shall only mention that Zoilus of Amphipolis (about 400–330 BC) wrote a *History from the Theogonia to the death of Philip*, and Anaximenes of Lampsacus (380–320 BC) the *Hellenica*, the *Philippica*, and the *Deeds of Alexander*.

Ephorus was born in Kyme of Aeolis probably between the years 408 and 405 BC. He was a pupil of Isocrates and did not busy himself with politics: indeed he was perhaps the first Greek historian who lived only amongst his books. This was a great advantage to his impartiality of judgement, but it became a disadvantage to his understanding of the facts. His historical work was simply called *Historiae*, and was divided by him into twenty-seven books. It dealt with the period from the return of the Heracleidae to the years 367–366 BC and it was continued by his son Damophilus with a further three books dealing with the period down to the years 341–340 BC. The subject of his writings was Greek and Western history, but it excluded the history of the barbarians. When Ephorus dealt with the history of ancient times he followed the system of Hecataeus in that he rationalized myths. Further he maintained that summarized sources of information were enough for this kind of history, whereas more detailed sources were necessary for writing the history of recent times. He liked rhetorical embellishments and was very fond of moralizing judgements. He praised and regretted the passing of the hegemony of Thebes; he was a friend of Athens, and an enemy of Sparta.

Theopompus of Chios (about 377–300) was born of an aristocratic family and suffered many political vicissitudes because of repeated banishments. His first work was a summary in two books of the works of Herodotus. He then wrote twelve books of *Hellenica,* in which he continued the work of Thucydides and dealt with the years between 411 and 394 BC. Lastly he compiled the lengthy *Philippica* in fifty-eight books which came out about the year 320 BC. He was a fierce enemy of Athens, but a great friend of Macedonia, of Sparta, and of Agesilaus; severe and impetuous in his judgements, a fanatical oligarch, ignorant of military matters, inclined to moralizing, and capable of psychological analysis. A profound rhetorician, he filled his works with orations, dialogues, endless digressions, and mythical tales.

The deeds of Alexander were the subject of a work by Callisthenes of Olynthus, author of other historical writings; of fabulous tales by Onesicritus of Astypalaea; of a bombastic and fanciful *History of Alexander* by Cleitarchus of Colophon; and of serious memoirs by Ptolemy, son of Lagus, Aristobulus, and Nearchus. In the fourth century BC there was a series of flattering works devoted to the hegemonies which in turn followed one another, those of Athens, Sparta, Thebes, and Macedonia.

After the conquest of the Eastern world the Hellenes were anxious to learn the histories of the peoples they had vanquished. It would have been natural for them therefore to have collected, with the help of the natives, genuine historical documents. Yet for the most part they did nothing of the kind; and after the death of Alexander they continued to talk about the history of the East with much the same imperfect foundations of knowledge as had Herodotus and Ctesias.

Works of greater historical value were written in Greek by Eastern authors. Berosus, for example, who was a priest of Bel in Babylon and later an astrologer in Cos, wrote his work between the years 281 and 261 BC. This was less a history than a chronology of kings (*Babyloniaca*) in three books. He dealt also with astronomy and astrology. There are only a few fragments of his work extant and his works did not influence the Alexandrian chronographers. Another Eastern author was Manetho (first half of the third century). He was a priest in Heliopolis and wrote three books on the thirty-one Egyptian dynasties, from their origin to the time of Alexander. This work was written with the aim of acquainting the conquerors with the history of Egypt; and although it was based on authentic documents it was not free from serious errors because of the author's lack of criticism. There remain, however, some very useful fragments.

We shall omit a number of authors of the fourth and third centuries BC, who tried their skill on general and regional history and on biography; here we shall speak only of Duris and of other major authors who dealt also with the West, such as Timaeus, Polybius, and Poseidonius. Duris of Samos (340–270 BC) was the prototype of the new rhetorical and learned tendencies, and was a pupil of both Theophrastus and the rhetoricians. He wrote at least twenty-three books of history divided into two parts—*Hellenica* and *Macedonica*—which covered the period from the beginning of the Theban hegemony up to the final constitution of the Hellenic states. His work was very learned but deeply rhetorical, and it aimed at gaining the interest of the reader by vivid descriptions of events, presented with picturesque details and in anecdotal form (*mimesis*). Duris, however, found some difficulty in recounting his anecdotes without lingering on descriptions of the dresses of his characters or on the sound of the trumpets in battle. It was said of him by some of the ancients that he lied even when there was no occasion to do so. Yet his work, which we can know from many fragments, was learned: it was much appreciated, and had a great effect on later writers.

The historical work on the West which supplanted all its predecessors was written by Timaeus of Tauromenium (about 345–250 BC) who was exiled by Agathocles and for half a century lived in Athens, where he was engaged solely on rhetorical studies. He was exclusively a man of science, and during his long exile he gathered much information on the history of Greece and of the barbarians of the West. He wrote a great historical work which told the history of the Italiotes and Siceliotes from their origins until 264 BC—the year which marked the beginning of the First Punic War. He made use of the writings of all the authors who had gone before him and added the findings of his own very careful research into the field of chronology and constitutional history. When he recounted recent events he was uncommonly tendentious in favour of friends such as Timoleon to the prejudice of enemies such as Agathocles and the tyrants in general. He was so bitter against his predecessors that he earned the nickname of *Epitimaeus* (the slanderer). He was rhetorical in style, superstitious in thought, and everywhere saw the work of divine providence revealed through miracles. His work became the acknowledged classic on the history of the West.

The historical works of Timaeus were continued by Polybius (210/8–128/6 BC) of Megalopolis in Arcadia. After Pydna he was one of the thousand Achaeans deported to various Italian towns, where he remained for seventeen years, although he was given permission to visit Magna Graecia, Sicily, and Spain.[32] Meanwhile he had an eye-witness view of how things stood in Rome, became a friend of the younger Scipio Africanus, gradually convinced himself that Rome's hegemony was unavoidable and that it would be wise for the Greeks to submit to it. He was therefore sent home to settle conditions for the Greek towns, and achieved his mission with great satisfaction to both sides.

The work of Polybius deserved the fame it received,[33] for it reveals an author who is learned, diligent, and clear, hostile to rhetorical and romantic writers of history, competent in military and political matters and worthy of standing at the side of Thucydides although inferior to him. It is evident that, so far as his religious opinions are concerned, this historian does not believe in the popular gods and that he follows the line of thought of the Stoic philosophers. He tries, however, to explain human events by human causes if he can do so; and if he cannot do this, as in the case of epidemics, he falls back upon *Tyche*. His work also contains some errors: he was not infallible. Information is sometimes incorrect (especially in respect of more ancient events for which he had to depend upon previous sources of varying worth, such as Fabius Pictor, Philinus, Aratus, Silenus, Sosilus, etc.). There is bias in favour of the Romans,[34] pedantry in his criticism, and a utilitarian conception which excludes any tendency towards idealism.

The work of Polybius was carried on by Poseidonius of Apamea (135–51 BC), whom we already know as a Stoic philosopher. His fifty-two books of *Historiae* were a continuation of the history of Polybius dealing with events beginning in the year 146 BC and ending with the dictatorship of Sulla (82 BC). Only fragments remain of his work, but it is certain that they were the main source for all ancient authors who later dealt with that period of history. Poseidonius was a man of science; he had good literary taste and was an able psychologist who had a deep interest in social questions. But he was no expert in military matters and believed in miracles.

Leaving out the Chroniclers we will pause to consider the Biographers. When Hellenistic scholars were confronted by literary masterpieces of the past they felt they wanted to know their authors; therefore, everything which was known or believed to be known, or which could be deduced from the works themselves, was collected and set out embellished with anecdotes and invented stories. This form of literature can be related to some extent to the *elogeion* used in Greece in the fourth century BC, because the eulogies necessarily contained many biographical facts. It was enough to fit the known facts into a predetermined pattern to achieve a 'bios'. The Hellenistic philological schools, descendants of the Athenian Peripatetic school, gave great impulse to this new form of literature.

Diodorus of Agyrium in Sicily (about 90–30 BC) settled in Rome and lived there for a long time after wide travels which he described with great enthusiasm. He states that he worked for thirty years on his *Library of History*, which consisted of forty books and which covers the period from the beginning of history to the consulate of Caesar. Only part of his work remains, and it is a universal history in that it deals with different peoples, one after the other. It is, however, no pragmatic synthesis, but a juxtaposition of extracts from the works of other authors which were different in value, character, and style, and which Diodorus summarized in such pedestrian form that they still contained allusions which had become absurd or anachronistic in the new work. Yet the practical value of the work from our point of view does lie in the fact that it preserves for us the writings of many authors which might otherwise have been lost. Diodorus followed the chronological pattern provided by the *Chronicle* of Castor of Rhodes. Over long periods of time he normally takes information on all subjects from a single source, without making additions of his own or drawing upon other authors. His work contains obvious contradictions, false emphases in the summings-up, and chronological errors.

Dionysius of Halicarnassus (about 60–5 BC), rhetorician and critic of historians, went to Rome in the year 30 BC. He wanted to write not merely a simple account of wars or of constitutions, but a work rich in political thought and practical philosophy. The period he selected was Roman history before the year 264 BC—an earlier epoch than had been dealt with by either Polybius or Poseidonius. After twenty-two years of research, twenty books of the *Ancient History of Rome* came out in the year 7 BC, but they have come down to us only in part. Dionysius made use of many Roman sources, particularly the more recent and less truthful annalists; he used few Greek sources; and he embodied the whole in a heavy miscellaneous work, which had the pretence of being pragmatic history but which showed no clear understanding of how real history differed from false history or legend. He had no clear notions of the law, though he dealt continuously with constitutions; he was frequently anachronistic, and made use of ornate orations which were tedious and spun out; he had a pedestrian and scholastic style, monotonous and heavy; and he wrote in the full conviction that the writing of history meant the piecing together of miscellaneous evidence to achieve a rhetorical piece of literature.

Strabo of Amasia (about 60 BC–AD 25) was rich and studious; he sat at the feet of many teachers; he made long journeys (in Asia Minor, Armenia, Syria, Egypt, Greece, and Italy); he read widely, and remained faithful to the models of Polybius and Poseidonius. His forty-seven books called *Historical Studies* started with a preface on the conquests of Rome and then dealt with the history of the period beginning in 146 BC. They did not deal with detailed history, for the work was directed at the Greeks and the Romans and tried to extract the experiences of the past from its facts. Strabo dwelt only on the major historical figures and events, enlarging on the more recent ones not dealt with by Poseidonius. He was, in fact, very like Polybius and superior to Poseidonius.

Nicolaus of Damascus, born in 64 BC of a Greek family, was secretary and confidant to Herod the Great, King of Judaea: in that capacity he often went to Rome. His most important work was the *Historiae*, written between the years 16 BC and AD 4 for the purpose of entertaining Herod, and consisting of 144 books. This was a hurried work, similar to that of Diodorus. It included a universal history, which spanned the period from the earliest times to the time of Augustus. The larger part of it dealt with more recent periods, for as much as sixty books were devoted to the last century. Of this work we know the first seven books on primitive Greece fairly well. This hasty piece of writing paraphrased the works of other authors with narrative and moralistic purpose. The average output was five to six books a year, which were to be read as they were published. They lacked originality, particularly in the first part as there had been no research into Eastern history. The value of the account of more recent events must have been greater, as the author had the benefit of his own observation and knowledge although he showed himself to be tendentious.

Timagenes of Alexandria went to Rome as a prisoner in 55 BC; later he became a freedman under the protection of Asinius Pollio. He wrote some books called *About Kings*, which were a history of Mediterranean peoples with frequent descriptions of geographical and ethnographical character, and were written with deep personal anti-Roman feeling. If we note the common aversion from Rome, the similarity of pattern, and the almost literal dependence of Timagenes' fragments and Justin's summary of them upon the *Philippic Stories* of Trogus Pompeius, it seems possible that Timagenes was translated into Latin by Trogus and this author summarized by Justin.[35]

Early Roman Prose Writing. Roman literature seems to have been acquainted with poetry (in the widest sense) before prose. At all events, poetic expression was the first to rise to literary value and to have a social function, for it is essentially the vehicle of sacred matters. The requirements of religion and of political and judicial life led to the use of a language different from that of every day. Thus it is that, going back to the sources, we find *Carmina* before any prose writing existed. The surviving fragments of the law of the Twelve Tables and of the hymns used in the liturgy have a rhythmic form, if they are not metrical in the strict sense. Prose may be assumed to have originated when the laws began to be put into writing and reports issued on the proceedings in the senate; another early example may well have been the *Annales* of the pontiffs, which recorded any daily events deemed to be noteworthy. Early Latin prose is preoccupied not with art but with clarity; there must not be the slightest ambiguity in the text. This accounts for certain fundamental features of this Latin prose, which were to be retained for a long time—a taste for tautology, for the *copia verborum* (verbal prolixity) to which Cicero resorted systematically; the care with which statements were differentiated (to make a clear distinction between an objective statement and one influenced by the opinion of the speaker or of some other person); the insistence on establishing absolutely definite connexions by repeating the theme, etc. Prose of this nature, governed by such requirements, could not rapidly produce literary works. But when political changes made it necessary to throw open certain subjects for public debate, the great leaders were compelled to invent eloquence and discover the art of persuasion.

The earliest Roman orator whose name has come down to posterity was the old censor, Appius Claudius the Blind. Cicero records some of the arguments he put forward in the senate against the party which was inclined to favour Pyrrhus. But it was not until the period of the Punic Wars that eloquence began to develop into an art in Rome. Parallel with it was another 'style', that of the funeral orations, which Cicero tells us had some influence on the earliest Roman historical writings. (He adds that the influence was disastrous, because the orations were so biased.) These speeches of praise were delivered at funerals by some close relative of the defunct (usually his eldest son) and no doubt described his past achievements. We may suppose them to have been fairly short, but we do not know exactly when they came into general fashion.

Such were the circumstances in which the earliest Latin prose developed. It had not yet reached maturity at the time of the Second Punic War, for the first annals, dating from that period, were written in Greek.]

The Roman Annalists and Historians. The reason why the first Roman annalists, from Q. Fabius Pictor to C. Acilius and A. Postumius Albinus, wrote in Greek is controversial. Was it because there was not yet a true Roman prose form? Was it because of a love of the Hellenes? Or was it done in order to spread the glories of Rome outside the Latin world?[36] It is possible that all these reasons played their part. The very number of the first annalists and the Latin translations of at least two of their works (of Fabius Pictor and C. Acilius) proves that this new form of literature had success with the public. The contents of these *Annales*, which took as a model the ancient *Annales Maximi* of the pontiffs, must have been for the greater part as arid and disconnected as the pontifical entries. (Every year they carried the names of the supreme magistrates, of victories, of triumphs, of portents, and so on.) Parts of the new *Annales*, however, must have had a very different character, in that some of them either directly, or through oral tradition, or through the *Annales Maximi*, went back to the old epic poems and, in the case of the work of less ancient annalists, also to the new great poems of Naevius and Ennius. Other parts were derived from historians of other nations such as the Greeks (from Greece itself and from the Western colonies), the Oscans, and the Etruscans. These parts must have had different characteristics from the others because of their length, their sentimentality, and the frequent learned hypotheses they contained. Between the various groups of stories, therefore, there must have been a great difference in tone; they must also have been disconnected and of different lengths. On the other hand there was the common feature of a desire to give prominent space to early history, which was rich in myths and legends already well known in the Roman world and also to the period of the authors themselves (because they had at their disposal wider sources of information, whether oral, personal, or documentary). All this was at the expense of the middle period between the fall of the monarchy and the first years of the third century, a period which was dealt with quickly and drily. The typical defect of the annalists, which increased with time, was that of magnifying the real or fictitious glories of their own families. Ancient opinions and fragments show that the form of these works was crude and naïve and that their authors loved brevity without purposeless ornament. Historical criticism was still in its infancy, and it was seldom that attempts were made to choose between contradictory stories, or to pragmatize by inferring from various traditions, or to classify facts on the basis of relations between cause and effect.

The first and most remarkable of the annalists who wrote in Greek was Q. Fabius Pictor, who was born about the middle of the third century and took part in the war against the Gauls in 225 BC. There is also a Latin version of his *Annales*, but it is not known whether it was written by him. His work dealt with the period from the earliest days up to his time. In narrating ancient events he drew his information from every kind of source, but for recent events he drew on his own personal memories and those of his contemporaries. The annalists who followed him, as well as Polybius, Livy, and Dionysius, made use of his text. His work was full of exaggerations, omissions, and errors, but it must have been a very important source of information, even though, like Polybius, he separated his evidence from his judgements.

Fabius Pictor was followed by other annalists who wrote in Greek. They were L. Cincius Alimentus, C. Acilius, A. Postumius Albinus, and others. As a reaction against the foreign language and the system of these authors, M. Porcius Cato (234?–149 BC) wrote his *Origines* and can be considered the father of the art of Latin prose. His life and his multifarious activities made him one of the most outstanding people of the Rome of his time and of the great debates which took place in it. Cato's historical works are two: one, written in 185 BC, was a compendium which had the purpose of teaching his son; the other, the *Origines*, consists of seven books at which he worked for a quarter of a century until his death. The title recalls that of the Greek *Ktiseis* and perhaps also Etruscan and Oscan annalistic literature.

This title is perhaps better suited to the first three books, of which Book One dealt with the origins of Rome, and the two others with the origins of those Italian towns which were gradually coming into contact with Rome. The following four books dealt with the period of the Punic Wars from 264 until 149 BC, the year of his death. He made use of Roman, Greek, Etruscan, and Oscan sources; and he made great changes from the pattern and nature of narration used by the annalists. His interests lay only in the most important events in the life of the Roman people and not in the life of the real or fictitious heroes of the *gentes*. For this reason he omitted almost any mention of specific characters.[37]

National pride in Roman conquests, a religious feeling for the past, a love for learning, the example of the great Latin work by Cato, and a new mine of information to be found in the *Annales Maximi* (published in full in 148 BC by P. Mucius Scaevola), all gave impulse to a great new output of annalistic history by Roman patricians. It will be sufficient to mention the names of C. Calpurnius Frugi, Cassius Hemina, Q. Fabius Maximus Servilianus, C. Fannius, Cn. Gellius, and C. Sempronius Tuditanus.

Meanwhile a new type of historical writings was born. These were inspired by the model set by the great Greek Polybius and perhaps by some indigenous efforts as well. A large number of annalistic works had already been published, and these showed a natural inclination to deal with recent history. Added to which there was the magnitude of pressing events happening all around and the wish to recount things which had been seen by the authors. These new works were in the nature of monographs of pragmatic reconstruction, memorials of witnessed events, autobiographies, and *Commentarii* recording the author's own deeds. There were also some epistolary writings.

L. Coelius Antipater (140–91 BC) was younger than Polybius and wrote at least seven books of *Annales* (or *Bellum Punicum*) which dealt with the war against Hannibal. Besides Polybius, his sources were the Greek writer Silenus[38] and certain Roman annalists; and in his turn he was largely used, along with Polybius, as a source by Livy. Antipater's work was an attempt to produce a pragmatic historical monograph; and, interspersed as it was with long harangues, it was a monument of oratorical style in accordance with the new prevailing taste. It earned him praise from Cicero and Fronto.

Sempronius Asellio (born about 160) wrote the *Historiae* or *Rerum gestarum libri*, and was still working at this when a very old man in the year 91 BC. His style was dull and unpolished, and was a narrative of things he had seen. But it contained attempts at pragmatic explanations in the Polybian manner, of which there is evidence in the fine statements on method preserved in some of the fragments. He argued against annalistic works which were like diaries, and said 'to tell what has happened does not suffice me; I must show the reason which caused the event to happen and the means which were used'; and he criticized savagely the old system: 'id fabulas pueri est narrare, non historias scribere'. Like Polybius he was an expert on military matters.

In the age of Sulla there was yet another group of annalists who retold the whole history of Rome according to the canons of the new rhetorical and artistic methods of historical writing. Sometimes they were content to forget the truth, and none of them shrank from the most blatant falsifications if they would bring glory to their ancestors. It is enough to mention here the names of Q. Claudius Quadrigarius, Valerius Antias, and Licinius Macer. The *Historiae* of L. Cornelius Sisenna, however, were somewhat more austere and truthful.

With M. Terentius Varro (116–26 BC), work on the ancient history of Rome was linked again to the *Origines* of Cato. He also gave play to the new antiquarian tendencies, and spread his studies, with a great love for learning and for Rome, to a whole series of side researches into the public and private life of past centuries. Varro wrote historical investigations into the period of

Roman origins, the primitive conditions of life in the Eternal City, the tribes, topographical matters, and the explanation of customs. He wrote some essays on contemporary history, and also two great works, one on the philosophy of history (*Logistorici*) consisting of seventy-six books, the other on ancient matters, divine and human (*Antiquitatum rerum divinarum et humanarum* in forty-one books). Lastly there was a very complicated biographical work, the *Imagines sive hebdomades* in fifteen books, which related to 700 people who had been famous in different fields. These were divided by him into seven groups of 100 weeks. Each group (kings and generals, orators, prose-writers, scientists, and others) was dealt with in two books, one devoted to seven weeks of Roman figures and the other to seven weeks of non-Romans. The work had a preface on fourteen 'inventores' of different sciences and arts. Some Ciceronian works of similar type have been lost. They consisted of memoirs on his consulate in the year 63 BC written in Greek, and the *De consiliis suis*, edited in 43 BC and containing serious accusations against Caesar, who was recently dead. They must have had little regard for real truth.

The *Commentarii* of C. Iulius Caesar (102–44 BC) have survived entire. Caesar made use of his reports to the senate, of official acts, and of war diaries; and in the winter of 52/51 BC he very rapidly completed the commentaries *De bello Gallico*, which included all events to the end of 52 BC. Later on, after having vanquished the followers of Pompeius, he wrote in the last months of his life, equally quickly and making use of similar sources, the story of the first two years (49 and 48 BC) of the civil war in his *De bello civili*.

Both works are brisk, extraordinarily simple and clear in their naked purity; they bear no traces of outside influence or theories, and they reveal the spontaneous genius of a great author. Some of the ancients, however, for example Asinius Pollio, complained that they were tendentious and inaccurate. It is true that it is easy to point to errors which were intended, to prudent silences, and to a partisan version of the facts; but the faults of this apologetic polemic work must not be exaggerated. They could not have been very great, for they referred to events known to everybody of those days. Indeed Caesar's writings must be greatly valued for the contribution they make to the knowledge we have of great events, of the habits and customs of the barbarians, and of the ingenious military tactics which Caesar employed in his wars.

The *Commentarii* remained incomplete because of the death of Caesar, with gaps covering the years 51–50 and 48–45 BC. Aulus Hirtius, one of Caesar's generals, started to fill those gaps with an eighth book of the *De bello Gallico* and with the *De bello Alexandrino* for the year 47 BC; but he too died, and two other authors carried on his work. One, who must have been an educated person, wrote the *Bellum Africum* on the year 46 BC; and the other, a rough man of arms, wrote the *Bellum Hispaniense* dealing with the year 45.

C. Sallustius Crispus (86–35 BC) was a wealthy plebeian from Amiternum who fought on the side of Caesar and the democrats. He was expelled from the senate in 50 BC, was elected to the office of quaestor in 48 BC, and again became a senator with the help of Caesar and supported his action in the civil war. After his appointment as governor of Africa Nova he was accused of corrupt administration and therefore retired and devoted the last ten years of his life to literary work. In his *De Catilinae coniuratione* he tried to defend Caesar after his death from the accusations of Cicero according to whom Caesar had been in league with Catiline. To achieve his purpose he even went to the length of showing the Catilinarian movement to be of less deep social significance than it was, and of distorting chronology. The work of the senate is shown as centring around Cato, and Sallust belittles Cicero, reducing him to the role of a secondary character (while seldom missing an occasion to mock him). There is no attempt at historical criticism in this short work and Sallust only states his theses to glorify Caesar. The *Bellum Iugur-thinum* gave him the opportunity to show the corrupt and venal behaviour of the Roman aristocracy, which is blamed for the never-ending war. Their conduct is contrasted with the quick and decisive action of C. Marius (who in fact only had to complete the work of the patrician Metellus).

Sallust began to write his *Historiae* as a continuation of those written by Sisenna. They began with the death of Sulla, and there were five books covering the years from 78 to 67 BC. But the work was never finished, and all that survives are some scattered sheets of an otherwise lost manuscript. Sallust tells history in his own way and in the light of his outlook as a demo-crat opposed to the aristocracy. He believes that history is motivated by the action of a few men who follow their 'ingenium'. This belief is the reason why he dwells so greatly upon some characters, and on the description of their nature shown in his biographical and psychological pictures, which from a literary viewpoint are magnificent.

His style is oratorical and he applies it in his work, which is full of orations and deeply moving documents. He believed that in this way he followed the model of Thucydides. But much more successful is the way in which he imitated the style of that great author by launching a beautiful new anti-Ciceronian style, of neo-Attic type. The main characteristics of this style are a nervous conciseness, a truncated and asymmetrical building of sentences, and a refined use of archaic forms.

As the new generations required yet more up-to-date treatments of general history, there appeared two new types of this kind of literature. There were the works of Hyginus and Cornelius Nepos which were very much a collection of biographies, and those of Livy and Trogus Pompeius, greatly different from one another but with a tendency to systematic treatment. Hyginus was a librarian of Spanish origin who lived first in Alexandria and then in Rome. He wrote *De vita rebusque illustrium virorum, Exempla, De familiis Troianis, De origine et situ urbium Italicarum.*

Cornelius Nepos (99–30 BC) was born in the Po valley in Cisalpine Gaul, the land of the Insubrians. He did not take part in political life but concentrated upon works of an historical nature. He wrote a summary of universal history which determined Graeco-Roman synchronisms, including typical Euhemeristic interpretations of myths and a number of fables and literary notes. His *Exemplorum libri* were a collection of anecdotes and of historical, geographical, and ethnographical curiosities. He also wrote a *Life of Cicero* which was full of praise, and a *Life of Cato the Censor*.

The most famous work of Nepos, however, was the *De illustribus viris*, consisting of sixteen books which in couples (one book for the Romans and one for the foreigners) dealt with kings, generals, poets, orators, historians, philosophers, jurists, grammarians, and scientists. This work had a moral purpose in that it set out to tell the 'virtutes' of the characters, who were all equally great and heroic men. The book on foreign generals has survived, together with separate biographies of Cato and of Pomponius Atticus; this provides us with twenty-three fairly short biographies with many errors and confusions, devoid of criticism of facts or sources, but drawn in clear and simple form. Nepos did not produce a work of science, but he did much to spread a taste for biographical literature at Rome.

Titus Livius (59 BC–AD 17) has given us a great annalistic history of Rome, of a type which had gradually developed from the time of Fabius Pictor to the age of Sulla. Livy's was the artistic masterpiece which closed that series at the time in which the greatness of Rome was at its peak. He was born in Patavium and went to Rome before the year 30 BC. He wrote *Ab urbe condita libri CXXXXII*, which covered the time from the origins to the year 9 BC; when he had reached that point death cut short his work. He did not follow the oldest and purest historical works such as the *Annales Maximi*, Fabius Pictor, and Cato, although he was acquainted with them. He based his work on later and less reliable sources such as those of the Sullan age, because they were longer and more rhetorical. It was seldom that Livy intended to draw from tradition a pragmatic reconstruction; for he was satisfied to deduce facts here and there and mostly only to juxtapose contrasting traditions. He never bothered to check or to make use of such ancient documents as still existed in Rome, though they had attracted the attention of foreign authors such as Polybius and Dionysius. It must be added that when he used Greek sources he often misunderstood them or translated them very approximately; that he did not try to have a clear idea of geographical or topographical matters even if they were of basic importance; that he had inadequate knowledge of military art; that his attempts at psychological interpretation were often empty and superficial; and lastly that he did not make sufficient efforts to understand the great social and economic struggles nor the evolution of institutions although he continually spoke about them. Despite all these obvious faults, Livy had several outstanding qualities, which caused his historical work to gain immediate and far-reaching fame in

Rome. It became a classic book, and put all previous *Annales* into the shade, at the same time making it impossible for posterity to try to rival it. His work had the qualities of honesty, of patriotism, of artistic perfection, of moral greatness, and of balanced political tendencies. Livy's history, if not a great work of science, is a great work of art; the poetry of its narrative, the eloquence achieved by the construction of its sentences of Ciceronian type, and the gracefulness of its descriptions are truly great. The language, often poetic and tending towards the archaic, has a fascination that never fails.

Livy, together with Cicero and Plutarch, was an exquisite representative of ancient humanity. In politics he was a moderate, in that he accepted for his world the order of ideas common to his times. There was latent in him, however, a lively passion for the greatness of the old Republic and for oligarchic republican theories. He was, therefore, an aristocrat by inclination, but a moderate in practice. Augustus rightly called him 'Pompeianus', for he loved the Republic without hating the monarchy too much, and he found the realization of his state of mind in the Augustan régime in which the monarchy had come to an agreement with the senate. He was, therefore, in perfect unison with the Restorer of Rome, for he admired the work of the emperor and he praised at the same time the ancient glories of the Republic.

Roughly coeval with the work of Livy, but deeply different in its plan and tendencies, was the historical work of Pompeius Trogus, a Gaul from Narbo. His forty-four books of *Historiae Philippicae*, which were finished about the year AD 9, have survived through a badly proportioned and disorderly epitome by one Justinus who lived in the second or third century. We have already noticed the anti-Roman character of the work of Timagenes. The Augustan era also produced the *Historiae* (from 62 to 42 BC) of Asinius Pollio; the commentaries and the memoirs of M. Valerius Messala Corvinus; and the histories of the civil wars by the Elder Seneca (50 BC–AD 37). Then there were the historical works of Augustus himself: the *rescripta Bruto de Catone* which were a defence of the monarchy; thirteen books *de vita sua*; a *vita Drusi*; and the *Index rerum gestarum* which survives in epigraphic form and consists of thirty-five chapters. This last work tells with extreme simplicity but great efficiency of all the honours and offices which were bestowed upon him, of all the deeds accomplished to improve the Roman world, and of all the works carried out to increase its power and its welfare.

Oratory and Rhetoric. We have spoken already of scientific and philosophical literary production (Chapters IX and X); it remains to speak of oratory. The Greek people was always fond of eloquence; and the epic of Homer is evidence of how important it was for the kings and the 'shepherds of people' to be able to speak 'like gods', often giving examples of speeches and debates. Primitive Greek eloquence had definite characteristics. It dwelt on subjects which were intimate and moving; it relied upon religious principles; and it

made use of demonstrative argument. It was an ingenuous and spontaneous
way of speaking which can still be found in the speeches of the histories of
Herodotus. There were two regions, however, which because of their democratic life made people more alive to oratorical skill than the others. These
were Athens and Syracuse. The Athenian citizen had constant occasion to
try his skill as an orator in front of an intelligent audience which was hard to
please. The assembly of the people, where everyone was free to speak,
became the teaching place of deliberative and political eloquence. The trials
before popular juries trained contenders and logographers (who prepared
speeches and learned them by heart) to act with adroitness in judicial oratory.

Patriotic ceremonies and public days gave opportunities to eminent
people to deliver 'epideictic' speeches (speeches on a set theme). Our sources
give us constant proof of the oratorical ability of the great Athenians of
the fourth century. In Sicily, and particularly in Syracuse, countless trials
followed the fall of the tyrants. It was this that gave rise to an early desire
to theorize and to write books on practical oratorical art (*techne*) which would
teach the people concerned the way to prevail in their cause by being convincing in its formulation. We know of two Syracusans, Korax and his pupil
Teisias, born about 480 BC, who published two books, or two versions of the
same book, on practical rhetoric, and who for payment would teach that art.
In these first schools of rhetoric, which moved from town to town, the
teacher would give some examples, and the pupils would practise by debating
with him. The new teaching had no moral object: its sole purpose was that
the thesis of the orator should prevail. This teaching was connected with
culture, however, because it enlarged literary and legal knowledge. It was
not teaching of a philosophical or artistic nature; but it became so when
oratorical *techne* was combined by Gorgias with sophistry, and when, with
him, these schools went from Syracuse to Athens. With the fusion of rhetoric
and sophistic, Attic oratorical prose reached a perfection, a strength, and a
pathos which can be compared with that attained by historical prose between
Herodotus and Thucydides and by dramatic language between Sophocles
and Euripides.

Antiphon (480–411 BC) of the deme of Rhamnus, can be considered as a
typical representative of this first phase. After the fall of the new régime he
was condemned to death for being one of the promoters of the oligarchic
revolution of 411 BC. Thucydides states that the speech he made in his own
defence at his trial was one of the best ever spoken; and a fragment which
has come down to us shows that it was both scornful and noble. During his
life, Antiphon was essentially a logographer: the ancients knew of rhetorical
treatises published in his name, as well as thirty-five genuine orations,
of which three surviving tetralogies are models of judicial debate.39 They
contain the speeches of the prosecution and those of the defence, the reply
of the prosecution and the counter-reply of the defence; and they concern
capital trials. Antiphon proved to be very able both in dialectic and in the

art of influencing and moving the judges. A further three judicial orations by him have come down to us. They are: *On the murder of Herodes*, *On the choral dancer*, and *On the poisoning charge against a stepmother*. The Athenian Sophist Antiphon, of whom we have recovered in papyrus considerable fragments of his work *On Truth*, and who debated with Socrates, is probably the same person.

Even oratorical prose felt the effect of the anti-sophist reaction, which called for a style which was both strong and graceful. The new rhetoric met with great success and moulded the taste of the whole nation. Although its aim was to achieve pathos, it had to give up many antitheses and symmetries; it had to be graceful and harmonious, moderate, and exquisitely Attic.

Andocides, Lysias, and Isaeus were the three great orators of that time who dealt mainly with judicial oratory. Andocides (born in Athens about the year 440 BC) was the least of the three and his judicial orations concerned him personally; for he led a very eventful life and was continually involved in law cases.[40] His earliest known oration is dated to 408 BC and is entitled *On his return*: this still reflected the style of Gorgias. We have, however, two further orations which are clear and attractive. Their titles are: *On the mysteries* (the best and more convincing) and *On the peace*; both follow in style the new tendency.

Lysias (about 440–380) was the son of a rich Syracusan who had settled in Athens. He studied art in Thurii at the school of Teisias and went back to Athens in the year 413 BC where he looked after his business with his brother Polemarchus. In 404 BC, however, his property was confiscated and his brother killed by the oligarchs. He returned to the city in 403 filled with a desire to avenge his brother, and accused Eratosthenes, whom he considered to be the guilty person, despite the fact that he was protected by an amnesty. The speech he made was a brilliant masterpiece vibrating with passion and sarcasm. He had, however, the bad idea of attacking the memory of Theramenes who was considered a saint by the people, and as a result he not only lost the cause he had pleaded, but his decree of citizenship was annulled. He became a metic again and was reduced to poverty, so he started on the profitable but delicate and difficult profession of logographer. He died in 380 BC. Lysias wrote many things and the ancients knew at least 233 of his speeches. Only thirty-four have come down to us, and not all of these are genuine; some are written for the courts, others are 'epideictic' (rhetorical pieces on a set theme). As an orator he knew how to embody in a speech the style and language suited to his clients and he succeeded admirably in disguising this skill. The dialectic part, however, was disconnected and not always faultless, and the pattern used over and over again led to monotony. His style was very graceful, simple, moderate, and elegant. He used the purest Attic language and was indeed a great artist.

Isaeus was born in Chalcis and later became Athenian. He wrote his orations between the years 390 and 353 BC. It seems that he was a pupil of Lysias and the teacher of Demosthenes. We have his judicial orations on questions of inheritance. The language and style he used were similar to those of Lysias, but his dialectic was much better, his reasoning more compact, his explanations more convincing; and his thought was imparted in a manner which was more authoritative, vigorous, and profound.

At the beginning of the fourth century BC there were several rival and contrasting tendencies both in decorative oratory and in the theory of oratory. Exponents of these theories were Polycrates, Alcidamas and Isocrates.

The main work of Polycrates consisted of examples for teaching; he gave paradoxical theses to his young pupils to make them practise in difficult subjects. Alcidamas, on the other hand, argued the merits of improvised oratory, which he thought should contain poetical forms and rhetorical figures, and be natural, clear, and pleasant.

Isocrates (436–338 BC) was an Athenian and the son of an industrialist. When he was young, he followed Prodicus, Socrates, and Gorgias. After the fall of Athens, however, he was left poor and so he started to work as a logographer. Yet the weakness of his voice, his slow composition, a shyness which he could not overcome, and the competition of Lysias, soon forced him to give it up. Therefore, in the year 388 BC he opened a school of rhetoric and made his fortune: he succeeded in attracting a constant stream of able students from all parts of Greece. He did not influence his pupils, but encouraged them to follow their own tendencies; and he introduced them to all the different fields of literature. Meanwhile he prepared his epideictic orations, which he did not proclaim in front of the general public but published as small pamphlets.[41] In this way cultivated people in all parts of Greece could read them, re-read them, and meditate upon them, especially when he spoke of a Greek federation against Persia. His physical defects prevented him from taking part in political life, but he was nevertheless very keen to talk about politics. By writing his orations he succeeded in making his views known to everybody, whether near or far away, to contemporaries and to posterity. Isocrates used pure Attic language; it was carefully selected like that of Lysias; it had no poetic terms and made careful use of rhetorical figures; but it was constantly rhythmical and scrupulously excluded the hiatus.

He was skilful in the choice of his form, was smooth and polished, and expressed himself in lengthily constructed phrases. Nevertheless this admirable prose leaves us cold, as it merely dazzles without either enrapturing or stimulating.

Political eloquence had its outstanding representatives in Athens during the last decades in which the city fought its final struggles for independence. The greatest men of different political parties fought each other in the assemblies and in court with fiery speeches in which patriotism rose high above personal interests. The tragedy of events and strong party feelings explain the tone, which was aggressive yet full of pathos, of their wonderful oratorical efforts. The greatest of the patriotic speakers was undoubtedly Demosthenes (384–322 BC). He was the son of a rich industrialist and a pupil of Isaeus. While he was a minor his fortune was squandered by his guardians, and he therefore decided to become a logographer and to improve his historical and legal culture; it is said that he also had some pupils. Sixty-five orations are ascribed to him, sixty-one of which have come down to us: many of the latter, however, are of doubtful authenticity, particularly some of the court speeches. These court speeches are less interesting from a literary point of view, for he had to adapt them to the mentality and class of his clients and because the subject was less congenial to his tendency to pathos. But the true Demosthenes is the man who delivered political orations, such as those he started in 351 BC and directed for ten years against Philip of Macedon. They were attacking speeches so long as Demosthenes was a member of the anti-Macedonian opposition. But in the year 346 BC he became the leader of the party which dominated Athens and from then on his orations were delivered in his own defence. The same thing can be said about the speech *On the Crown*, which was aimed against Aeschines, orator for the opposing party. The first political orations of Demosthenes were delivered in a style which was still hard and Thucydidean, though they show evidence of the orator's passion. Later orations, which were deliberative, are unsurpassable masterpieces. Demosthenes was a skilful improviser if the situation required it, but he liked to prepare his speeches very carefully, and he edited them with equal care before he published them as pamphlets which could be read and meditated upon. From Isocrates he learned the art of polishing but he did not abuse it; he wanted not only to achieve literary fame, to please the ear, but still more to defeat the enemy, to win his cause, and to carry away the public with his passion. The art is there, but it is hidden; it can be perceived in the harmony of the rhythm, in the planned absence of the hiatus, and in the placing together of short syllables. It is an art which has no monotony, and which does not impair either spontaneity or enthusiasm. The passion of the orator reveals itself in the style, rich in metaphors and images, in the lively syntax, in transparent feelings of passion. The way of reasoning is superb; the descriptions are concise and wonderful; the language is very simple and pure choice Attic with few poetic terms. It was mostly during the twenty years between 350 and 330 BC that all the great Attic orators fought for their political ideals. Some of them, such as Lycurgus and Hyperides, were for the most part in agreement with Demosthenes; some of them, Aeschines for example, were in the opposite camp.

Lycurgus (about 390–324 BC) was an Athenian of the famous family of the Eteobutadae; he was a pupil of Plato and Isocrates, and a political friend of Demosthenes. When the power of Athens was broken at Chaeronea he became for twelve years the leader of his town and the supporter of its finances. His speeches were mostly accusations made to defend the state from guilty citizens; they were implacable and dominated by an overwhelming passion for his country, but they were full of legal sophistries.

Hyperides (389–322 BC) was an Athenian, a pupil of Isocrates and perhaps of Plato. When young he worked as a logographer (professional writer of speeches for others to deliver); he became rich and he liked to spend his riches. He started to take part in public life from the year 362 BC, and became the accuser of many people. For a long time he collaborated with Demosthenes against the Macedonians, but later he disagreed with him about the affair of Harpalus. The two became reconciled for the Lamian War against Antipater in 323; but they disagreed again later. Antipater ordered Hyperides to be executed. The ancients knew fifty-two of his orations; but only some parts of six of them have come down to us. Four of them are on judicial matters; one is political (*Against Demosthenes*); and one is written to commemorate the dead of the Lamian War (*Epitaphius*). His style was simple and clear like that of Lysias and almost as vigorous as that of Demosthenes.

The greatest opponent of Demosthenes was Aeschines (about 390–320 BC). He came from a simple family and entered political life in 357 BC after having been a clerk and an actor. At the beginning he opposed Philip; later on, after a mission to Macedonia, he went over to the party of peace. This was the starting-point of his relentless battle with Demosthenes, which ended when he was banished from Athens in 323 BC to Rhodes where he started a school. Whatever judgement may be pronounced on Aeschines as a party man, it cannot be denied that artistically he was a great stylist. His style was strong and simple, musical and elegant. He had dialectical ability and emotive power. His language was pure and precise.

After the time of Alexander Greek oratory differed according to the different places from which it came. Whereas in Greece itself there was public oratory in some towns at various periods, in other regions with a monarchic régime oratory had to follow new ways. It had to become more refined and learned for teaching purposes, or it had to be the bombastic substance of a panegyric or gala lecture. After the conquests of Alexander and the end of the works of Lycurgus, Demosthenes, and Hyperides, political and forensic debates went on in Athens for quite a while. Deinarchus, for example, was thirty years later, and other orators later still.

Deinarchus of Corinth took up residence in Athens and was a pupil of Theophrastus. He started his career as a logographer in 336 BC and was very active between the years 322 and 307 BC. He was then banished; but went back to Athens in 292 BC when he was employed in a trial. He wrote about a hundred orations, but only three of them are left, and they concerned the affair of Harpalus. He followed the style of his predecessors and this earned him the nickname of 'The country Demosthenes'.

Meanwhile, in addition to the style of the great orators of the fourth century BC, there was a simpler, though elegant, style which became common in Athens. It was mostly the work of the Peripatetic school of Aristotle and Theophrastus. This was called the 'middle style' and was later transplanted to several Hellenistic cultural centres such as Alexandria and Pergamum, partly through the activity of Demetrius of Phalerum. The ancients considered Demetrius' eloquence elegant but lacking in power. The oratorical art taught in Pergamum by Crates of Mallus had similar qualities but it tended to philosophical speculation. Crates had a deep knowledge of dialectic and encouraged imitation of the old Athenian models.

The oratory favoured at Rhodes was not very different, for here the school of Aeschines had developed a moderate style. The school was directed by Molon when Caesar and Cicero attended it.

All these arts of oratory were more or less similar. Greatly different, on the other hand, was the oratory taught by Hegesias of Magnesia (about 250 BC) in the Greek towns of the Asiatic coast. This was a prolific writer, with a style which was pompous, solemn, affected, metaphorical, tortuous, sententious, and with a broken rhythm. The new system was conceived in the luxurious towns of Asia Minor; but it had some popularity even in the Greek peninsula.

The main tendencies developed by Hellenistic oratory in the third and second centuries BC lasted through the following century as well. There were two types of tendency which were in strong contrast with each other. The 'Asianist' type was pompous, affected, richer in fanciful Eastern images than in logic or dialectic, declamatory, full of mimicry, and sensational. The 'Attic' style was terse, severe and tending to archaism, and was based on Thucydides and on orators of the fourth century BC. Aeschylus of Cnidus and Aeschylus of Miletus were the representatives of the 'Asianist' type; whereas Gorgias was the chief exponent of the 'Attic'. The latter was the teacher of Cicero's son and the author of a work on *The figures of rhetoric* of which a Latin summary was later made by Rutilius Lupus.

The most flourishing schools, however, followed a path between these two contrasting types of oratory. The Rhodian school had great similarity with the Asianists, while the school of Pergamum was nearer to the Atticists. The orators of the Rhodian school wanted to keep the flamboyance of the Asianistic style under control and to approach the style of Hyperides, the richest among Attic orators. As a rule, however, they avoided pre-established patterns and left room for inventive freedom or 'anomaly' (irregularity). The orators of the school of Pergamum required a philosophical culture from their speakers; they modelled themselves on Demosthenes, and from their insistence that the declension of nouns and verbs was capable of regular classification were called 'analogists' (believers in similarity of forms).

Two ardent and active Atticists carried on their profession in Rome at the time of Augustus. They were Dionysius of Halicarnassus and Caecilius of Calacte. They opposed contemporary authors with some success by reacting against the eclecticism of the *koiné*; but they did not demand a pure Atticism as happened later in the second century AD.

Dionysius of Halicarnassus (see above p. 599) had a learned and bookish culture. He dogmatically divided literary men into two groups—those who were infallible and to be idolized, and the reprobates who were to be routed —not because of their passions and their purpose, but because of the style and forms they used. Many of his rhetorical works have come down to us. Archagathus was a Jew of servile origin from Calacte in Sicily. He took the name of Caecilius from his liberator and went to Rome about the year 2 BC where he opened a school. He was an ardent admirer of Demosthenes and of Lysias, but had a low opinion of Plato and of the Asianists. He wrote a significant treatise on oratorical technique, and various critical and historical works.

Oratory had great importance in the formation and establishment of the art of Latin prose.42 In Rome, with the development of public and judicial life, and because of practical needs, it very soon achieved a high degree of excellence. We have little information, however, of orators who lived before the second half of the second century BC until we come to Cato.43 Cato and his followers in vain opposed the establishment of Greek oratorical theories in Rome; despite their efforts Greek schools of rhetoric were opened.44 In Rome these schools found a larger field of expression than they did in Hellenistic capitals, for the orators did not speak only in the schools and before an initiated audience, but in the presence of the general public in the forum and the senate. They did not deal with dead scholastic themes, but with great and vital problems which stirred the city and the world. The theories of the rhetoricians had, therefore, to be adapted to the hard realities of life. (The expulsion of rascally and ignorant orators by the censors in 92 BC should be remembered.) Asian artificiality had to give way to clarity of dialectic, which was indispensable in political debates. Roman orators were men who both led a practical life, and were politicians and thinkers. They welcomed, therefore, the thesis of those Greeks who wanted to end the age-long disagreement between sophistic and philosophy, and between rhetoric and historical experience. They created an oratorical art in which beauty of form was completed by a profound philosophical doctrine about history and law.

Cicero, in his rhetorical works, the *Brutus* particularly, gave long lists of Roman orators with short appraisals of their activity which we can no longer check. All the great public men of Rome are recalled to us.

Fragments show that Roman eloquence started to show the influence of Greece and particularly of the Asian schools with Tiberius Sempronius Gracchus, who was tribune in the year 133 BC and a pupil of Greek rhetoricians and philosophers. The same thing can be said about his brother Gaius Gracchus, who according to Cicero excelled all other orators in oratorical vehemence. He was incapable of speaking without getting excited; and he started his speech by tuning his voice to the sound played by a flute-player.

The group of the Asianists can be completed with the names of Q. Hortensius Hortalus (114–50 BC), who was its greatest champion, and by Marcus Antonius who was one of his successors.

The *Rhetorica ad Herennium*, which most certainly was not written by Cicero, but was very probably used by him, reflects the debates which took place about rhetoric between the years 86 and 82 BC. This work was published in four books (about the orator, his themes, and his elocution) by a Marian democrat who wanted to reduce the mania for things Greek, together with the excessive rules and erudition which were current in oratory. He used Greek ideas and classifications, but his technical terminology is both Latin and precise.

M. Tullius Cicero (106–43 BC) was born in Arpinum, and as a very young man accepted the Asianist theories, which he supported in his *De inventione*, written when he was only twenty. He made use of these theories in his first orations, but after he returned from his travels in the East he became a supporter of the 'middle style' which he had learned at the school of Molon at Rhodes. Cicero was a politician, an orator, a theorist on the subject of eloquence, a philosopher, a geographer, an historian, a letter-writer, and a poet. He was a complex many-sided figure and he embodied the splendour and the weakness of his troubled age. Although he was a literary man and a great master of style his great ambition was to become a politician, and, through his oratory, to be an outstanding figure in a world which was then dominated by the sword.

But he lacked courage and a firm line of conduct, for he was eclectic both in politics and philosophy and he never had a directive 'credo' of life.[45]

There were at least 106 orations, but only 58 of them have come down to us together with 17 fragments and 31 titles. We have no means of judging his speeches as they were delivered, for he often improvised and we know them only in the form in which he published them. Speaking of the *Pro Milone*, Asconius states very clearly that there were great differences between the two drafts of it, both in style and in the facts presented. We can be sure that the same was true of many other Ciceronian orations. All of them, whether judicial, deliberative, or epideictic, have certain common characteristics. They are full of pleading pathos designed to carry away the public; their style shows supreme virtuosity; and there is rhythm in the endings of paragraphs and sentences, which transforms the orations almost into poetry.

But there are faults too. The dialectic was questionable; the violence of the accusations was too great, since it was a habit of the age to make charges which could not be fully proved. Rhetorical tricks often overshadowed and displaced sound oratory, and the style was frequently overloaded.

Cicero also set out to be a theorist on oratorical art. We have already mentioned his *De inventione*, written in the year 86 BC, in which he supported rhetorical eclecticism. In 55 BC he published the *De oratore*, written in the form of dialogue on the Platonic model, in which he imagined a discussion between several orators taking place in the year 91 BC. In this work, some of the orators were shown as maintaining that an orator had to have a wide culture; whereas others contended that he had to rely on inspiration. In 46 BC Cicero wrote another dialogue, entitled *Brutus*, in which he argued against the Atticists and recounted a long history of Roman eloquence. His *Orator ad M. Brutum* written in the same year contains yet another polemic against the Atticists; in it he states that a real orator is a man who knows how to make use of every tone and style, and he dwells on the theory of rhythm. Lastly, in his *De optimo genere oratorum*, which is a preface to a translation of Aeschines and Demosthenes, Cicero attempts to show that they are more like him than like the Atticists. The long and repeated polemics of Cicero prove that the school of the so-called Atticists was very strong and ready to argue for itself. This school made almost the same criticism of him, namely that of pomposity and exaggeration, as he had made of the Asianists. It consisted of a group of young people who desired to achieve a form of spontaneous oratory. They wanted to see Art emerging from an idea, instead of being an embellishment to the idea; and they considered that the fundamentals of an oration should lie in a sincere exposition of the facts and in dialectic. This school had two teachers, the orators C. Licinius Calvus and M. Iunius Brutus (the murderer of Caesar). Both died young. The popularity achieved by anti-Ciceronian styles was due to this school, although such was not the intention of its adherents. It was a popularity already established by C. Iulius Caesar, whose style was very similar to that of Lysias, and by C. Sallustius Crispus who recalled Thucydides.

C. Iulius Caesar had been active all his life as a political and military orator and his orations must have had the same qualities of style as are shown in the *Commentarii*. He also wrote a work, *De analogia*, in which he maintained that the fundamental task of an orator is the choice of words, and that the orator must avoid using irrational terms which are not appropriate to his methods of argument. We know he wrote three collections of witty sayings (*Dicta collectanea*); but their publication was forbidden by Augustus. Sallust's orations are illustrated in his historical works; we also possess his *Invective* against Cicero, which was mentioned by Quintilian.[46]

Ciceronians like Messala, and Atticists like Asinius Pollio and Augustus himself, were still opposed to one another. But it was not long before all polemics quietened down, and the style of oratory became enfeebled. This was because, with the coming of the empire, political debates were restricted and the art of eloquence died. It was once again confined to the courts of law, where it was exhibited in the presence of bureaucrats, or to schools, where it became once again merely an exercise upon banal themes, or to formal performances before specialist audiences. It should be added that very soon the professional teachers of this new rhetoric were generally not Italians but Spaniards; it is easy, therefore, to understand its history down to the Elder Seneca's time.

It became fashionable to declaim—sometimes in a sing-song voice—speeches which consisted of witticisms, of far-fetched ideas, of extravagant metaphors, and of play of words around fictitious themes. This was done following either the form of 'suasoriae' (to persuade some ancient personage to take a certain decision) or the form of 'controversiae' (to support, on the basis of imaginary laws, the two opposite view-points upon a legal controversy). Both were rightly criticized by Petronius, by Quintilian, and by the Elder Seneca. The last-named recounts the plots of these orations, and we therefore know the names of their authors. He himself was L. Annaeus Seneca (50 BC–AD 39), born at Corduba in Spain; and he wrote for his sons (who studied rhetoric about the year AD 37) at least ten books on *Oratorum et rhetorum sententiae, divisiones, colores controversiarum*, and seven on *Sententiae et divisiones Suasoriarum*. He had an exceptional memory and his information came from declamations he had heard in the past. These he could not refrain from criticizing very sharply.

2. ART

a. *China*

The crumbling away of the old feudal state into a feudal confederacy and hence into anarchy pure and simple, coupled with the rise of a few strong regional states, exercised a markedly decentralizing influence on Chinese art. The single centre of attraction represented by the court of the Chou was replaced by half a dozen regional centres, which rivalled one another not only in politics, but also in the display of pomp and splendour, and therefore in art. Hence the Late Chou period shows a courtly and luxurious art with a lavish use of gold, silver, jade, and turquoise. Jade carving now reaches its zenith; but even more important is the fact that, after the decay during the Middle Chou period, bronze-casting improves rapidly and soon once more becomes supreme, its rich variety being due to the blending of several regional styles. Among these the 'Huai style' (a name introduced by the Swedish archaeologists) is dominant. It marks a reawakening of Chinese creative genius after a long period of semi-barrenness. Geometric elements are full of movement and fantasy; the ancient *t'ao-t'ieh* mask fades into a purely ornamental assemblage of curves and lines. A favourite subject is animals, treated with a levity and exuberance of details that contrast deeply with the austerity of Middle Chou. The best products are perhaps those from the tombs of the princes of Han (fifth to third centuries BC)(Pl. 25, a)at Chin-ts'un near Lo-yang. Here for the first time we also meet the bronze mirrors that were to become so characteristic of Han art. They are exquisite objects, ornamented with geometrical designs (T and L patterns); it is noteworthy that the spirit of this decorative style is quite opposite to the animal naturalism of the vases.

Among the latter, those of Li-yü on the northern frontier present a rather close analogy with the Ordos bronzes; Hsiung-nu and Chinese did not merely clash on the battlefield, but exchanged, at least to a certain extent, artistic motifs and ideas. In this particular case it appears that the 'barbarians' were the givers and the Chinese the receivers.

Quite another school, indeed another art, is that of the wooden sculptures and of the lacquer boxes of Ch'ang-sha, in the territory of the ancient state of Ch'u. They include also peculiar funeral figurines, made as substitutes of real people for funeral purposes: the *ming-ch'i*. Their sly archaic smile characterizes them as belonging to another world, to a psychology different from the austere milieu of the north Chinese courts.

Architecture and painting of this period are known only from literary texts and from imitations on vases and (for painting) on lacquer boxes.

Ch'in art was only an appendix to that of the Warring States (or Late Chou). At that time the background of Chinese art changed once more, its main features being the centralized bureaucratic empire and the contacts with the West. This meant that art production under the Han centred again around the imperial capital Ch'ang-an and was exposed to various aesthetic influences introduced from central Asia. The foreign motifs, however, were incorporated into, but did not dominate, the aesthetic rules of Early Han times (202 BC to AD 23).

Little has survived of the sculpture of this period, and this little is mostly associated with burial and tomb construction. The most imposing monument of this period is the tomb of General Ho Ch'ü-ping (d. 117 BC) in Shansi; a stone figure of a horse standing over a fallen warrior (probably a Hsiung-nu) is a quite remarkable piece and a fitting epitaph for the young hero of the Hsiung-nu wars.

Painting of the Early Han is little known. The lacquer finds and the highly interesting painting on silk from Ch'ang-sha have been believed to have originated in the Ch'u territory. As known from the literary texts, this was above all an age of wall-painting, and the Ch'ang-an palaces contained large amounts of it; but nothing has come down to us.

b. *The Art of the Steppes*

In southern Siberia, around the metallurgical centre of the Minusinsk, the culture of Tagar II (*c.*400 to 100 BC) perfected the animal style of the steppe art. The most characteristic motif of this period are the galloping stag and the hunting tiger crushing down a stag. Farther south, the *kurgans* (funeral mounds) of Pazyryk in the Altai, frozen from top to bottom, have miraculously preserved corpses of men and horses, with clothing and accoutrements, in fact the whole funeral furnishing of rich local princes. The art of Pazyryk (*c.* fourth to first centuries BC) is quite clearly influenced by Achaemenid art,—a posthumous influence, being later than the overthrow of the Persian empire by Alexander (Pl. 25, b).

In a more eastern region, the Ordos bronzes (Pl. 21, b), plaques, agrafes, buttons etc. (c. fourth to first centuries BC) derive partly from the art of Tagar, but represent an original development, which in its turn made its impact felt on the Chinese bronzes of the Warring States period. The bearers of this art were, at least in its later phase, the Hsiung-nu. We have direct evidence in the tomb of a Hsiung-nu chief found by Kozlov at Nain Ola near Ulan Bator Khoto, containing beautiful bronzes and strips of woollen cloth woven with motifs of fighting animals. It is datable to the beginning of our era.

c. India

Apart from descriptions of buildings in the epics and in the Buddhist *Jātakas*, no specimen of Indian art after the end of the Harappā civilization and before the fourth century BC has come down to us, with the possible exception of the funeral mounds at Lauriya Nandangarh, already mentioned above. The sculptural remains are so scarce and of so crude a quality, that we have to assume a very substantial hiatus in artistic development from Harappā to the Mauryas.

Indian art of the Maurya period (c. 321–185 BC) is characterized by a strong foreign influence, that of the Achaemenid court, exerting itself after the latter had been wiped out of existence by the conquest of Alexander the Great.[47] Chandragupta's palace at Pāṭaliputra, as known from Megasthenes' descriptions and (to a very small extent) by excavations, consisted mainly of a central audience hall (*apadāna*) supported by eighty huge monolithic columns of sandstone, on the pattern of the royal palaces of Iran. We know nothing of the buildings of Aśoka, except for some of his religious foundations, such as the façade of the Lomasa Rishi cave. It ushers in a long series of Buddhist assembly halls (*caitya*) and monasteries (*sanghārāma*, *vihāra*) hewn into the rock or adapted from already-existing caves, in painstaking imitation of wooden buildings.

Maurya sculpture too is in the main a local development of Achaemenid themes. This is the case above all for the lotus-shaped bell capitals that topped the pillars on which Aśoka inscribed his edicts; they are imitated from the capitals of Persepolis, although their beautiful finish and careful execution make up for their lack of originality. The capital in its turn was usually surmounted by one or more heraldic lions and sometimes also by one or more wheels, symbolizing the 'turning the wheel of the Law', i.e. the preaching of the Buddhist religion. We are thus confronted for the first time with a fact that was to be characteristic of most of the art of north-western India for the next five centuries: the expression of purely local (Buddhist) ideas through foreign stylistic modes. We have at least one statue of the Maurya period (if not earlier): the Yakṣa (semi-god) of Parkham, a squat completely frontal figure of no real aesthetic value. For once it is completely Indian in character and seems to be directly descended from the art of

Harappā. But already the late Mauryan Yakṣa from Patna shows unmistakable reminiscences of Persepolitan art.

Although the fall of the Mauryan empire was accompanied by an anti-Buddhist reaction, and although the Śuṅgas in northern India (c. 185–72) and later also the Andhras in the Deccan were both Hindu dynasties, Buddhism continued to dominate the inspiration and content of Indian art.[48] The Śuṅga period is chiefly represented by the decoration of the railings and gateways that surrounded the *stūpas* of Sanchi and of Bharhut. The *stūpa* was at first a funeral mound covering the relics of the Buddha or of some holy man. Later it became a dome-shaped structure of masonry surmounted by a cube (*harmikā*) from which a mast (*yaṣṭi*) emerged; the whole was meant to symbolize the world with the Heaven of the Thirty-Three Gods above, and the *axis mundi* transversing both. The *stūpas* were usually enclosed by elaborately carved railings. The typical examples of such sculptures from the Śuṅga period (c. 100 BC), representing subjects drawn from the *Jātakas* and from the life of the Buddha, are those of Bharhut, now dispersed in several museums. (Pl. 26.) Achaemenid influence is still present, but now only in faint reminiscences; the reliefs are somewhat archaic in aspect and strictly functional in character, the aim of telling a story or conveying a religious idea predominating over the aesthetic features. The ornamentation of the *stūpa* n. 2 at Sanchi may be slightly earlier (end of the second century BC), (Pl. 27, a) while the railings of the Mahābodhi temple at Bodh Gaya belong to the end of this period.

Śuṅga art is continued by and culminates in (during the so-called 'Early Andhra' period, c. 72–25 BC; a misnomer) the magnificent sculptural decoration of the *stūpa* n. 1 at Sanchi. It is characterized by four huge gateways (*toraṇa*) literally covered with reliefs which are the finest in early Indian art. Nothing can match the sensuous vitality and the fulness of form of the female figures of Sanchi, or the rhythmic and choral effect of some of the great scenes from the life of the Buddha. In all these sculptures the Buddha, however, is never portrayed, but his presence is hinted at by a symbol (the sandals, a parasol, etc.).

As a parallel with Sanchi we find also the first extant relics of Indian painting, those in Cave X at Ajanta (Bombay State), representing the *Saddanta Jātaka*, with their free-moving and naturalistic figures of elephants and other animals in an entirely formalized setting.

The architecture of the last two centuries BC is characterized by several rock-cut cave *caityas*, which developed yet farther the pattern set at Lomasa Rishi. The elaborate imitation of wooden vaults with their rafters led to ever more imposing structures, such as can be seen e.g. at Bhaja (c. 50 BC), where the sculptural decor seems to be connected with the Bharhut school. (Pl. 27, b.)

d. *Greek Art*

Architecture. During the fifth century and the first half of the fourth, a singular phenomenon is to be observed both in art and in literature. Architecture, sculpture, painting, and ceramics had originally progressed faster in several regions of the Greek world than in Athens. The same thing happened in the literary field. After Athens had felt and assimilated this progress, however, it took the lead in the aesthetic movement and produced the most magnificent examples of different artistic styles such as those conceived by Myron, Pheidias, Alcamenes, Polygnotus, Micon, Nicias, Euphronius, Duris, and Meidias.

If we observe the whole Hellenic production of this period in both art and thought, it appears that the arts evolved at different speeds which depended upon the technical progress made in the various fields. The same new tendency, therefore, developed spontaneously at different times in different kinds of artistic and literary productions. It is not therefore anachronistic, from a conceptual point of view, to discover a close link between Pindar, Aeschylus, Polygnotus, and Myron—or between Pheidias, Sophocles, Zeuxis and Parrhasius—even if they were not completely contemporaneous.

That same study of the individual which brings into existence psychology in the philosophical field, and the writing of 'Lives' in literature, is the force which creates the portrait in art. The ideal beauty which inspired Plato and later Epicurus is to be found during the intermediate period, in the pure and serene sculptural creations of Praxiteles; the search of Isocrates for a delicate style finds a counterpart in the supreme delicacy of Lysippus; the study of nature by Aristotle and his first pupils is a fore-runner of the deep and meticulous anatomical studies and the representation of landscape and animals of the Hellenistic age; the idyllic subjects of Theocritus are to be found again in the sculpture and paintings of the age after Alexander; and finally, the frightening realism of tragedy finds, through the statuary of Scopas, its last terrific echo in the *Laocoön*.

Greece enjoyed about half a century of relative calm which lasted from the expulsion of the Persians to the Peloponnesian War, and was particularly peaceful just after the treaties of 449 and 446. For the Greek world of the West, peace followed for a few decades after the victories over the Carthaginians in 479 and over the Etruscans in 473. The improvement in financial resources and the gratitude towards the gods, dispensers of victories, stimulated an understandable desire to have new temples worthy of all the gods. At first, almost all the new temples were built in the Doric style, which had different characteristics according to the period of time and to the places where the temples were built. This style tended to a refinement of the relative proportions of the width and the length of a building, and of the height and diameter of its columns. In later years there developed a taste for hybridism between different styles, so that the elements of one, two, or even three styles were to be found in the same building. Most temples of the period were vast and were very precisely designed, at the cost of great financial outlay. It must be remembered that Pericles spent around 2,000 talents for public buildings in a few years.

The first task of the citizens of Athens was to provide their town with powerful defensive walls and with adequate harbour installations. After the treasure of the League had been taken to the city, both means and leisure were available for a magnificent restoration of the Acropolis, which was still full of the ruins caused by Persian devastation. Between the years 449 and 432 BC Athens built the Parthenon. (Pl. 28, a.) It was the most magnificent temple of its period in all the Greek peninsula, the abode of the protecting goddess to whom the treasure of the League was entrusted. About 70 metres by 31 metres, it was a peripteral (i.e., one completely surrounded by columns) Doric temple with some elements of Ionic style, and was built by the architect Ictinus, who worked under the supervision of Pheidias. It glittered with Pentelic marble, and was decorated with carved pediments, metopes, and friezes; in it was the gold-and-ivory statue carved by Pheidias. Inscriptions give us a day-to-day story of how this great artistic work came to be achieved.

Where the monumental entrance erected by Peisistratus stood at the door of the Acropolis, Mnesicles built (437–432 BC) his magnificent and harmonious *Propylaea*. (Pl. 28, b.) The plan of this construction was complex but well suited to the lay-out of the ground, and it was decorated with pictures and statues.

At the same time as the Parthenon, the Athenians built the so-called Theseum in the lower part of the town near the market. (Pl. 29, a.) It was a peripteral Doric temple (probably the temple of Hephaestus), and was resplendent with white marble. It is well preserved to this day. A few years later, after the peace of 421, many new buildings were erected in Athens. There was a small elegant Ionic temple, surrounded by a balustrade in honour of Athena Nikē; and the Erechtheum, Philocles' reconstruction of the temple of Athena Polias (built again in the fourth century after the fire of 405 BC), which consisted of a fusion of many buildings into one of 23·50 metres by 13 metres. It had two graceful balconies, one of which forms a porch supported by the wonderful statues of six Korai, young maidens of exquisite designs. (Pl. 29, b.)

Of the same period as the Parthenon and the Theseum were the peripteral Doric temples built on the headland of Sunium (Pl. 30, a); the temple of Nemesis in Rhamnus, built in the place of one which had been destroyed by the Persians; and the Telesterion for the celebration of Mysteries, also replacing a sanctuary destroyed by the barbarians. This last temple was the work of the architects Coroebus, Metagenes, and Xenocles, and the general plans were drawn by Ictinus. It was a large building of Doric style, almost square, on two floors. Inside the temple were rich colonnades of seven rows of columns, with forty-two columns in all, to receive the faithful worshippers of the goddesses.

In the Peloponnese, at the *Altis* of Olympia, Lybon erected a great temple (64·10 metres by 27·60 metres) of Doric style, in honour of Zeus. It was built of stuccoed and polychromatic limestone and of marble. The basic structure of the building was finished in 456 BC; it had two large pediments and sculpted metopes and was ready to receive the gigantic chryselephantine

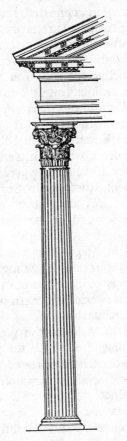

FIG. 5. The Corinthian Order.

statue of the god later executed by Pheidias. The temple of Apollon Epicurius on the slopes of Bassae, near Phigaleia in Arcadia, was a new work by Ictinus (about 430–420). Its style was hybrid in the extreme, for it was Doric but has Ionic columns and Corinthian capitals (the first example of the new Corinthian style). (Fig. 5.) At Mycenae in the Argolid, Eupolemus of Argos built in the year 423 BC a new great temple of Hera in place of an earlier temple which had been destroyed by fire.

In Sicily, some temples were built even earlier. There was the temple of

Demeter and Korē in Syracuse, which was started by Gelon and finished by his successors, and the Athenaeum with its tall columns (today a cathedral). A series of new temples were built at Acragas in the fifth century: they justified the opinion of Pindar, according to whom Acragas was 'the most beautiful city of mortal men'. (Pl. 30, b.) The temples of Heracles and of the Dioscuri were built to celebrate the victory over the Carthaginians in the year 479 BC. After they had been completed Theron started to build a vast temple in honour of Olympian Zeus (121 metres by 55 metres), which had not yet been finished when the town was destroyed in 405 BC. It had the characteristic colonnade closed by huge half-columns and tall 'telamons' (gigantic male figures supporting the roof over 7 metres high) which were probably to support the flat ceilings from the inside. The so-called temples of Athens, of Concord, of Vulcan, of Asclepius, and others were also built at Acragas during the course of that century (Pl. 30, b.); at the same time the so-called temples A., O., and E. were built at Selinus, and E. (the peripteral Doric temple of Hera) contains a wonderful series of metopes. At Himera there was a temple in memory of the victory over the Carthaginians. Because of Greek influence an ancient sanctuary in Segesta was surrounded by a temple-like construction; the lack of grooves in its columns shows that subsequent events in the town and in the island prevented the temple's completion. (Pl. 31, a.)

At Poseidonia (Paestum) in Magna Graecia a peripteral Doric temple, the Poseidonium (Pl. 31, b) (60 metres by 24 metres) was finished about the middle of the century. This is perhaps the most beautiful and harmonious temple of that time built in western Greece. In it archaic styles are blended with a general softening of architectural lines.

As well as the temples, the walls of the great panhellenic sanctuaries enclosed several small buildings erected for the purpose of keeping in safe custody the *ex-voto* offerings of each town, the so-called treasures which were of a variety of types. There was, for example, the extremely beautiful treasure of the Athenians which was kept at Delphi and which was consecrated after the battle of Marathon.

The inhabitants of the Greek peninsula did not build many temples during the fourth century BC. Their finances were not sufficient and even Athens did not build any temple of importance. Building, in those days, sometimes merely consisted of a reconstruction of ancient and ruined buildings, normally with an amalgamation of different styles. It is interesting to notice, however, that temples and votive monuments were sometimes constructed on a circular plan: this revived the old Mycenaean dome (*tholos*) style, which had never fallen wholly into disuse and may have been employed for roofing parts of open-air meeting-places (*skiades*) in sixth-century Sparta. For musical auditions, therefore, temples and votive monuments were sometimes built on a circular plan. The following buildings are the most worthy of notice: a new large temple to Apollo built at Delphi and finished in the year 394 BC; the temple to Athena Alea erected at Tegea in Arcadia after the battle of Leuctra (371 BC) under the supervision of Scopas; and the Asclepieum at Epidaurus, of the first decades of the century, which was the work of Theodorus and had columns in all three orders. Polycletus the Younger built a *tholos* (diameter 21·82 metres) next to it, with a circular colonnade. This type of building was repeated at Olympia in the Philippeion, which was erected by Alexander in memory of his father and endowed with many statues of people of his family. It was copied in Athens as a graceful monument to the choregic victories of Lysicrates (335–334), and the Athenian building has remained almost intact.

In this period the wealth of Ionia revived, and with it came a revival of building activity: the temples were still in ruins after their destruction by the Persians. The new buildings, however, were still in the old local Ionic style. The Branchidae built the Didymeion near Miletus in honour of Apollo. It was started in the year 333 BC by Paeonius and Daphnis and was still not finished in the year 150 BC. It was the largest temple of the Greek world (132 metres by 73 metres) and as it was built very slowly with a double colonnade it clearly reveals all the variations of style of a couple of centuries. Pythius built a peripteral temple to Athena Polias in Priene, which was dedicated to the goddess by Alexander in 334 BC. Vitruvius tells us that about 340 BC Paeonius reconstructed the Artemisium of Ephesus, which had been spared by Xerxes but in 356 was burned by one Herostratus,[49] who wanted to make himself famous. It had very tall columns (18 metres) with reliefs sculpted by Scopas and Praxiteles, and it was immediately regarded as one of the wonders of the world.

Other great buildings were erected during the fifth and fourth centuries. There were covered theatres, such as the semicircular Odeum at Athens, built about 440 BC by Pericles for musical performances. Then there was the open-air stone theatre at Athens, reconstructed in the fourth century by Lycurgus; and similar theatres at the Piraeus, at Thoricus, at Corinth and at Syracuse. This last originally had a trapezoidal arena, constructed by Damocopus at the time of Hiero I, but it was made circular in Dionysius' day. There were many others, such as the exceedingly fine theatre of Epidaurus built in the enclosure of Asclepius by Polycletus II about the middle of the fourth century (Pl. 32, a) (Fig. 6), and the Thersileion of Megalopolis. The latter is named after its architect, who built it in 371 BC: it recaptured the style of the Telesteion of Eleusis, and could seat 6,000 people (66 metres by 52 metres). Its colonnades were situated in such a way that an orator in its centre could be seen by the whole audience.[50]

The *Stadium* for athletic contest and races was built in Athens at the time of Lycurgus. The oldest parts of the stadium of Delphi are of the fifth century.

Harbour installations often had architectural importance, as for example those of the Piraeus and of Syracuse. Also important were the walls of towns, such as those of the linked fortification Athens-Piraeus-Munychia, and those built by Dionysius for the defence of Syracuse, with its vast circle and strong castle. The first doors with a real arch appeared in Acarnania in the fifth century; and architecturally important also are the urban plans of Piraeus, of Selinus, of Rhodes, and of Thurii, all of which are attributed to Hippodamus of Miletus.

When monarchy revived in the Greek East, and in the West imperialistic

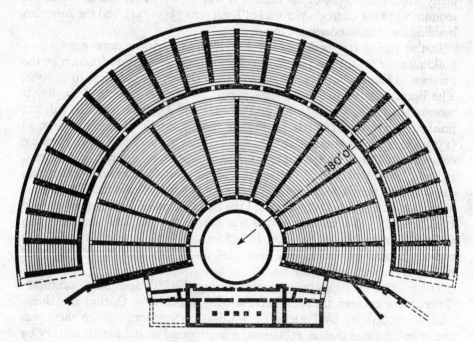

FIG. 6. Epidaurus: Plan of the theatre (after B. Fletcher).

tyrannies obtained repeated successes, there was a rebirth of court architecture appropriate to buildings of a type which had fallen out of use, just as there was a rebirth of a court epic. Royal palaces were built, such as those of Pella in Macedonia, famous for its frescoes by Zeuxis; of Alexandria; of Antioch; of Pergamum; of Syracuse; that of Rhegium built for Dionysius I; and many others. There were tombs for princes such as the Charmylion of Cos: and the Mausoleum which Mausolus, king of Caria (who died in 353 BC), ordered the architect Pythius (with the help of the sculptors Scopas, Timotheus, Bryaxis, and Leochares) to build in Halicarnassus for himself and his wife Artemisia. This Mausoleum was one of the most remarkable buildings of the fourth century. It had a high paved base (66 metres by 77·50 metres) surmounted by a temple-type building of Ionic type. It was crowned by a pyramid of steps with a large four-horsed chariot on top. It was about 46 metres high altogether, and was beautifully decorated with reliefs.

Painting. Our knowledge of Greek painting in the fifth and fourth centuries BC is very incomplete. Classical writers tell us of a large number of artists and works; but their references are too vague and can be interpreted in more than one way, and we have no original paintings which could explain them. Luckily we can deduce some information on paintings of great art, however small and formal, from paintings on ceramics, which were more 'industrialized' and technically simplified, and of which we have many beautiful examples.

During the first half of the fifth century, monumental painting for decoration of interiors established itself first of all in Ionia. Mandrocles of Samos, for example, painted in the Samian temple of Hera a scene depicting the passage of the Persian army into Europe. Later on Ionians like Micon and islanders like Polygnotus of Thasos brought this kind of art to Athens. Micon and Polygnotus, sometimes by themselves, sometimes together, and sometimes with Panaenus, brother of Pheidias (who at first had been a painter), decorated many Athenian buildings with their works. They painted, for example, the decorated porch (*stoa poikilē*) near the market with scenes representing episodes of ancient history (wars of the Amazons, the war of Troy) and of recent history (the battles of Marathon, of Oenophyta, and others). Several other works by Polygnotus were to be seen in temples and buildings in Athens, in Plataea, and in particular in the porch of the Cnidians at Delphi. We know of the existence of many other artists who were either fellow-workers of his (as his brother Aristophon) or pupils (Onasias for example). Although his perspective was faulty and the colours at his disposal very few, his art appears to have been as powerful and great as the tragic art of Aeschylus, who was his contemporary. He painted scenes which were complex and full of groups of people. Each person was represented in a different attitude and movement, and his name was painted at his side. The paintings of Polygnotus depicted mythical and historical episodes, which were pervaded by a deep religious feeling; and the people were shown as superhuman heroes.

The style of the art of Polygnotus and of the painters of his school influenced the art of ceramics. Potters of that time often copied the style of composition of Polygnotus; and like him they chose noble and great subjects and gave 'instantaneous' glimpses of bodies in rapid movement.

During the second half of the fifth century, people discovered the third dimension, perspective, and shadows. (This discovery was probably helped by the art of theatrical painting.) Artists, therefore, were able to produce paintings which were perfect in their conception and with a strong suggestion of suppleness. The masters of this new style were Agatharchus of Samos; Apollodorus of Athens; and, above all, Zeuxis of Heraclea in Italy, and

Parrhasius of Ephesus. These two last painters lived in Athens for a long time and were the masters of what may be called 'flowered' painting. The works of Zeuxis were both monochromes (depicting subjects in chiaroscuro) and polychromes. The picture of Eros crowned with roses is famous for its beauty, and it is said that when he painted his Helen, he did good business by charging money to allow people to see his picture. The most famous work of Parrhasius was a picture of Theseus in brilliant colours. Timanthes of Sicyon, the younger Aglaophon, and Pauson, the caricaturist, worked in a similar style. Some echo of this new technique can be found in a painted *stele* in Thebes and in some paintings of much later date at Herculaneum, Pompeii, and Rome. There are also fourth-century ceramics in which the painting has some 'flowered' characteristics: the graceful, but sometimes affected, work of Meidias is one example. Their imitation of the style of painters brought wide technical changes in the potter's art. This was due to the fact that the simple lines of red colour on a black background were not sufficient: potters, therefore, started to touch up the designs with added colours as in a real picture. This method was applied in many of the loveliest Athenian *lekythoi*.

The most important progress made by Greek painting during the fourth century consisted of the representation of the pathos and spirituality of the figures and of a masterful use of light and shade.

The most famous painters of that time were the following: Aristeides of Thebes of the Attico-Boeotian school, who lived in the age of the hegemony of his town, and who is said to have made fabulous earnings: his son Nicomachus; the Athenian (?) Euphranor who was also well known as a sculptor; his pupil Nicias, famous for his female figures (Io, Andromeda, Calypso and others), and for the skilful use of light and shade.

The school of Sicyon had a similar tendency and took great care to achieve purity of design and beauty of colour. It specialized in the technique of encaustic painting (painting by burning in heated wax), which was very suitable for small paintings and which gave brilliant results. The most famous artists of this school were Eupompus of Sicyon, Pamphilus of Amphipolis, Melanthius, and Pausias of Sicyon, who was a famous painter of flowers, fruit, and scenes of battles in encaustic technique. Apelles of Colophon, who afterwards settled in Pella, and later, at the time of Alexander, in Miletus, attended the school of Sicyon to perfect his work. His best-known painting is the Aphrodite Anadyomene (rising out of the sea), commissioned for the Asclepieum of Cos. He was so renowned as a portrait painter that the town of Ephesus paid him twenty talents to paint the portrait of Alexander. Protogenes of Caunus is also worthy of mention as the famous author of the picture of Ialysus, the eponymous hero of Rhodes, at which it seems that he worked for seven years.

We can get a better idea of Greek painting of that time from works of art painted in far-away lands, such as Etruria and Magna Graecia (Capua and

Poseidonia); or from those painted in later generations (at Pompeii for example), which show Greek influence. Knowledge can also be obtained from the art of painted ceramics which tended more and more to a technique of superimposing one colour on another. The simple technique of a red design on a black background was now used only for the production of commercialized wares which were exported to distant lands, to the north Euxine in particular.

Italiote pottery had a place of its own. It was probably started by potters who had left the Greek peninsula and moved to Italy, and particularly to Tarentum; it spread throughout Magna Graecia, developed its own individual style, and became Italiote. The Italiote potters wanted to achieve a pictorial effect more than a fine design, and they liked to depict scenes drawn from tragedies (including historical tragedies as Aeschylus' *Persae*), from comedies which were parodies of epics, and from the *phlyakes* (see above, p. 581). (Pl. 32, b.) Asteas of Poseidonia was the most famous master of this school, which was later subdivided into at least three schools, in Campania, in Lucania, and in Apulia, each with its own regional tendencies.

Sculpture. By about the time of the Persian Wars, it is already possible to perceive the characteristics of individual masters and of each school of sculpture, for we have copies of works which can be identified with complete certainty (as, for example, the *Tyrannicides* sculpted by the Athenians Critias and Nesiotes). We also have some works which are original, even if we cannot attribute them to any particular sculptors. Finally information about many artists is to be found in the works of ancient authors. We know that Calamis (of Argos?) sculpted the famous statue of Aphrodite Sosandra, which was once kept in the Propylaea on the Acropolis of Athens. We have information of Onatas of Aegina; of Aigias, teacher of Pheidias; of Pythagoras of Rhegium, who worked between 476 and 452 BC, and who was famous for his Philoctetes and for his sculptures of athletes. To try to attribute the works which have come down to us to the individual artists we have mentioned above would be too subjective a piece of research and would lie outside our scope. We shall simply try to define the characteristics of three well-defined schools, all of which developed from foundations laid in an earlier age. The 'Ionic' school continued its preference for gracefulness and has given us some delicate masterpieces, such as the *Birth of Aphrodite*, and the so-called 'Ludovisi throne'. (Pl. 33.) The school of Argos, Aegina, and perhaps Rhegium, has a stronger style tending towards the archaic, and reveals a careful study of anatomy and of the movements of naked bodies. The works of this school, however, show little interest in facial expression; the features are toneless with formalized smiles (see the *Charioteer* of Delphi (Pl. 34, a), and the scenes on the pediments of the temple of Aphaia on Aegina). The Attico-Boeotian school strives to reproduce a perfect anatomy and eurhythmic movements of human bodies, for example in the *Tyrannicides* mentioned above. At the outset this school was incapable of reproducing facial expressions: in later years, however, it made use of simple technical means and succeeded in giving the features of its sculptures a uniformly severe sadness. This school also began to understand the importance of drapery, although in this department its sculptures continued to show a certain archaic rigidity.

The first great artist of the Attico-Boeotian school who gives a glimpse of the tendency of his style and of his personal innovations is Myron of Eleutherae (about 500–450 BC). The ancients praised the naturalness and the boldness of movement of two of his works, which were the statue of an athlete called Ladas, and the statue of a cow. We can still see these characteristics in the copies of his *Discobolus* and of his statuary group of Athena and Marsyas. Myron likes to portray movement which is sudden, violent, and unstable (even if a little hard and contorted), for it allows him to show all his skill in the field of anatomy. He likes the contrast between violent movement and solemn stability. But even this artist did not give much attention to spiritual expression, and he sculpted head-dresses with archaic artificiality. (Pl. 34, b.)

This, then, was an art which had archaic tendencies of style but liked to portray movement and anatomical skilfulness. A reaction against it is seen in the sculptures by an anonymous artist on the temple of Zeus at Olympia (those on the eastern pediment in particular, which portrayed the struggle between Pelops and Oenomaus) (Pl. 35, a). This artist disdained excessive anatomical analysis, and preferred to put into his work only the important elements, even at the cost of producing bodies which were of great solidity. (Pl. 35, b.) He did not like stylized and expressionless faces; they must be alive even if somewhat vulgar. His drapery was natural but stiff; and through the contrast between his figures he searched for unity in the scenes of his groups. He became aware, however, that his reaction had been too strong; and he modified his style in the western pediment of the temple which portrayed a battle of Centaurs.

It seems possible that the author of the impressionistic reaction was an Athenian. He was certainly followed and surpassed by Attic artists who also wanted to improve on archaic methods, but who did it with a noble idealism and not with a rustic realism.

The consummate master of this style was the Athenian Pheidias, son of Charmides (about 500–432 BC), who was the brother of the painter Panaenus. Pheidias began as a painter but later became a sculptor, and he used all kinds of materials (wood, marble, bronze, ivory, and gold). He sculpted in bronze two famous statues of Athena (Promachus and Lemnia) (Pl. 34, c), and about the year 460 he made the statuary group which was sent to Delphi by the Athenians in memory of the battle of Marathon. The huge 'chryselephantine' statue of Zeus (447–440 BC) for the temple of Olympia was his work. He became the adviser of Pericles on all works for the Acropolis; he directed the execution of the Parthenon sculptures (the ninety-eight metopes and the frieze, 160 metres long, which portrayed the Panathenaic procession) (Pl. 36);

and he made the chryselephantine statue of Athena Parthenos (439–434 BC). In the years 433–432 BC he was brought to trial by the Athenians, who during those years tried to strike at all the friends of Pericles; he was condemned for a supposed theft of ivory, and ended his life miserably either in prison or in exile some fifteen years later.

Regrettably we have no means to form a direct and precise opinion of this great sculptor of ancient times, because all that survives from his masterpieces are some bad copies reduced in size. We can get a fair idea of him, however, from the work of his pupils, which is to be found in the sculptures of the pediments, metopes, and friezes of the Parthenon. If we observe the individual statues which make up these sculptures, we can see in them the varying styles and ability of the pupils. The whole work, however, reveals the organic conception of Pheidias' mind. He wanted to portray gods, or superhuman beings who embodied divine beauty and the high ideals of ethics. Their bodies, therefore, so he considered, should be conceived as a synthesis of many individual beauties and not as a copy of just one human model. Their attitude must always be dignified, and their faces a reflection of solemn majesty, of sublime benevolence, of noble grace, of great power, and of Olympian calm. The scenes in which they take part must be worthy of the life of the gods. Given the beauty of these monochrome and rather hurried works of Pheidias' pupils, we can easily imagine the devastating charm and striking greatness of his chryselephantine works (the 'Parthenos' was about 12 metres high). The ancients have described the sensation of wonder, of awe, of mysticism felt in front of those giants of gold and ivory, resplendent in the faint light and reflecting in the surrounding marble—miracles of thought, of shape, and of colour.

The art of Pheidias was unsurpassed throughout all later ages, even if it appeared a bit monotonous because his figures were too perfect and therefore too much alike, and even if his idealization seemed sometimes unreal (for instance in his drapery). We know the names of many pupils of his: Alcamenes, still alive in 403/2, and very skilful with gold and ivory; Cresilas, the author of an idealized portrait of Pericles; Agoracritus; and Pyrrhus. We also know of many late fifth-century sculptures which definitely show the influence of Pheidias. They included reliefs on temples, funeral *stelae*, idealized portraits, and statues of gods and *victories*. Amongst these there was the beautiful work of Paeonius of Mende which the Messenians placed in front of the sanctuary of Olympia in about 425 BC or slightly later. Naturally these pupils and 'epigoni' never succeeded in achieving the virtuosity of their master. They exaggerated his methods, particularly in the drapery which steadily became more broken and transparent; they also came under other influences including that of painting.

Outside Athens, and at the same time as the school of Pheidias, the Argive school had a stamp of its own. (The school of Aegina was absorbed by that of Athens.) The teacher of the Argive school was Polycletus, born between

470 and 460 BC. After 423 BC he created a new chryselephantine statue for the temple of Hera in Argos, and in 405 he placed at Amyclae a memorial monument of the battle of Aegospotami. Like his contemporary artists, Polycletus reacted both against archaism and against an excessively dynamic impressionism; and he idealized human beings. In contrast to Pheidias, who wanted to portray the spirituality of the gods, Polycletus was satisfied if he could portray his ideal in human form, and show athletic beauty or a virile nude without overmuch attention to psychological expression. Polycletus' statues of athletes showed that his anatomical studies had concentrated upon the essential elements of muscular action, and that he had attempted to discover the law of eurhythmic relations and the proportions between different parts of the body. Polycletus wrote about these laws in a treatise or *Canon*. Time and again this master and his pupils reproduced beautiful human bodies in positions of repose and with a serene expression; and they rigorously applied to their work the rule of the *Canon*, even at the cost of being monotonous. Polycletus' statues were generally made of bronze, and the ones which the ancients liked most, as we can tell from the number of copies, were the *Doryphorus* (or lancebearer–Pl. 38, a), and the *Diadumenus* (or athlete wearing his crown of victory). There were many in antiquity who compared Polycletus with Pheidias, and some who held him in greater esteem.

We have already said that the economic conditions of the Greek peninsula in the fourth century were not favourable to the development of its artistic heritage. Schools of sculpture, however, continued to exist in Attica and in the Argolid, although they worked only for the towns and wealthy people of the Greek East. Attic art continued to favour the portrayal of gods and heroes, and Argive art the representation of athletes. But both schools tended to give more importance to the spirit than to the body, and this was in line with ideas developing at the time.

The new artists, therefore, abandoned the beautiful and impassive expressions of Pheidias and Polycletus and tried to put 'pathos' into the faces they created. They knew about the controversies on divinity which were taking place in a world divided into superstitious persons and sceptics. So in portraying the gods they chose deities who seemed to be relatively near to human nature (Aphrodite, Apollo, Dionysus, Asclepius . . .), or demons, or gods who personified human passions. (Pl. 38, b.) When, following this new fashion, these artists created statues of famous men, they idealized their subjects with moderation.

In Attica, the sculptor who broke the tradition set by Pheidias was Scopas. He was born in Paros, and he lived first in the Peloponnese, then in Attica, and later in Caria. Whereas we have ancient descriptions of many of his statues (for example that of a frenzied Maenad) we have only a few works by him or by his pupils and these have come down to us in fragments (for example the temple at Tegea and the Mausoleum). (Pl. 37.) These fragments have made it possible for us to attribute to Scopas and to his school other works which have survived only as late copies (the famous group of the *Niobids* is an instance). His reaction against previous tendencies was strong. He was not content to copy the true expression of feeling on human faces; he distorted his faces and turned them into masks showing pain and sadness. The heads of his statues were big and hanging; the faces were square; the mouths half-open and panting; the eyes tired and sunken; and the foreheads full and powerful.

To Praxiteles this reaction must have seemed to have gone too far. His father Cephisodotus had retained the style of Pheidias, for example in his beautiful group of Eirene and Plutus; yet the son accepted part of Scopas' technique. After 370 BC Praxiteles worked in Mantinea, then at Cnidus and Cos, then at Ephesus on the temple of Artemis, and finally at Athens. Two original works of his survive, the *Apollo and Marsyas* and the *Apollo Sauroctonus*. There are also several probable attributes, together with ancient descriptions of some of his statues and Roman copies of certain masterpieces (in particular the *Apollo Sauroctonus* and the *Aphrodite of Cnidus*). His statues were eurhythmically arranged in a system of inclined planes. Male deities were presented in graceful postures with effeminate bearing, and female deities were sculpted in the nude. Praxiteles mainly used marble, because its qualities of light and softness, shading and smooth planes, provided the best means of reproducing the skin. The colour of skin was in fact imitated, with the aid of the painter Nicias, by painting a thin layer of amber-coloured paint over the statue. The heads were large and had soft hair; and with their smile they gave an indefinable feeling of dreamy softness. (Pl. 38, c.)

There are some minor artists of the Attic school who seem to have kept their own individuality, such as the three artists who assisted Scopas in the building of the Mausoleum and the sculpture of the battle of the Amazons. One of these was Timotheus, who is known to us for his sculpture of the temple of Asclepius at Epidaurus. Leochares is the second, famous for his group representing the *Rape of Ganymede*, which is characterized by the effort of reproducing a complex movement of ascent. The third was Bryaxis, who made the statue of Sarapis at Alexandria. We cannot trace the activity of other individual artists, but there is anonymous work on many reliefs on *stelae* of varying artistic value: these were placed in front of the graves on the side of the roads which radiated from Athens.

The Peloponnesian school of Lysippus of Sicyon reacted against the representation of these frail, tired, dreamy gods of Praxiteles. Lysippus was a self-taught coppersmith, but he acknowledged two masters, Polycletus and nature. He was born probably about 370 BC and was already very famous when he did a bust of Alexander. In 314 BC he was at the court of Cassander; in 306 BC he was working at the statue of King Seleucus; and he died probably at the end of the century. The ancients attributed to him 1,500 statues, chiefly of bronze; we have none of his original work, but there are copies of works certainly attributable to him, such as the *Apollo Apoxyomenus* and the statue of Agias for Delphi, and these have made it possible to ascribe to him other unattributed pieces. Lysippus did not like to portray female figures; for his portrayal of the gods he chose those who had the most virile characteristics (Pl. 39, a), and if his subjects were human he chose athletes. He also created large statuary groups, for example the twenty-five *Companions* of Alexander who died at the battle of Granicus. He represented men 'as they should have been', according to a new rule which required them to be tall and slim, with a small head and soft hair, and with much emphasis given to the muscles and bone structure. They had to be in attitudes of restless repose, in the attitude of a single moment, alert and ready to spring, supple, but of thoughtful appearance. Lysippus liked to reproduce the realities of nature and was a great portraitist, the leader of all who followed him. He was so skilful in his portrayal of *Alexander leaning on a lance*, that the great Macedonian decided that no one else should represent him in sculpture. His skill is also apparent in the statue of Agias.

Lysippus had many pupils at his industrious workshop, such as his sons Boëdas and Euthycrates, and Euthychides of Sicyon, who sculpted a *Tyche* for the town of Antioch (300 BC). It can be rightly said that Alexandrian realism in the art of portraiture derives for the most part from his productive example.

e. *The Hellenistic World and Art*

Architecture. A new area well suited to artistic production was to be found in the Greek world outside the Greek peninsula. In the first place, the conquests of Alexander had led to the formation of rich Hellenistic states, and to the birth of new capital cities and many Graeco-Macedonian colonies scattered around the East. Secondly, Alexander and the Successors, followed in this by all the princes of small states, had shown great love of the arts. Thirdly, powerful federations had come into being in the older Greek world, and they were matched by Agathocles' empire in Sicily. Lastly, commerce had brought great wealth to certain Greek towns and states of the Aegean islands and of the Asiatic coast. This general state of magnificence and well-being in the outer Greek world contrasted sharply with the low economic and political condition of that part of the Greek peninsula which for long had been the mainspring of Hellenic civilization. All this was reflected in artistic production. A brake was put on its evolution in places where art merely confined itself to repeating the ideas of the past with slight variations. At the same time, the inherent sense of balance and moderation, which up to this time had characterized even the most audacious innovations of Greek art, disappeared completely. Architects had a vast field for their activity in the construction of new towns. From the time of Alexander's architect Deinocrates they generally applied the system of Hippodamus, which consisted of great roads dividing the flat areas into rectangles, and the hilly areas into trapezoidal shapes rather like amphitheatres. Public buildings, as well as private houses, were built in these well-planned towns. No innovations were brought to the building of temples, but the Ionic style, with some elements of the Corinthian, was preferred to the Doric order, which was thought to be faulty in its proportions. The new temple of Zeus Olympius in Athens is an example.

More than anything else architects wanted magnificence. Famous amongst them was Hermogenes who built the temple of Artemis Leucophryene at Magnesia on the Maeander. Capitals of Egyptian style are to be seen in some places; at Alexandria and elsewhere there were ornamental obelisks, the tallest of which was in front of the temple of Arsinoe. New types of sacred buildings were erected and the lay-out was dictated by the needs of mystery cults. Samothrace had its temple for the celebration of the mysteries of the Cabiri, built probably in 260 BC; it had a double front porch with Doric columns, a tripartite *cella*, and at the back an apse on a raised plane over a crypt used for sacrifices. Magnificent sacrificial altars were built in many places. That built by Hieron II in Syracuse was 198 metres by 22 metres; there was another, even larger, in Paros; and at Pergamum a square altar (the sides of which were more than 30 metres long) was built by Eumenes II to celebrate his victory over Antiochus the Great.

The magnificent royal palaces with gardens and annexes were small towns in themselves; and vast numbers of architects were engaged on the construction of the rich houses of wealthy people. About these we have no archaeological information, but there are many traces of private houses, for example at Priene and on Delos.

The following architectural details of public buildings are worthy of mention: (1) the large porches—for example the porch of the sanctuary at Delos with bull's-head capitals, and that of the sanctuary of Athena at Pergamum supported by two tiers of colonnades (one Doric and the other Ionic) and by balustrades decorated with war trophies. (2) The *agorā* squares embellished by porticoes. (3) Buildings for meetings of the *boulè*, with internal flights of steps made of marble (at Priene and Miletus for example). (4) Gymnasia, sometimes regarded as *heroa* for benefactors. (5) The octagonal 'Towers of the Winds', which were also used for sundials and water-clocks (one of these still exists in Athens).

Sculpture. Sculpture is the form of Hellenistic art we know best, for we still have many original works. We have no records, however, which make it possible to know the output of each artist. During those centuries, indeed, there appear to have been no great masters (as there had been in earlier times) who made a personal impression upon artistic production as a whole. Instead, there was a general uniformity of types and tendencies which dominated the field of sculpture.

In Athens, the style of Praxiteles was continued until the beginning of the third century by his sons Cephisodotus and Timarchus. So most work of Athenian origin retained the main features of the style of that master. This can be seen in the *Aphrodite of Melos*; in the portrait of Demosthenes made by Polyeuctus in 284/3; and in the *Nikē of Samothrace* with its wonderful movement of drapery blown by the wind, which was commissioned after 306 by Demetrius Poliorcetes. (Pl. 40.)

The style of the school of Sicyon, that is of Lysippus, survived for a long time through his sons and pupils. Chares of Lindus is famous amongst these pupils for his gigantic statue of the sun, made in Rhodes about 290, which was to be a rival of the colossal statue of Zeus made by Lysippus for the people of Tarentum.

These schools of the peninsula, the school of Lysippus in particular, probably have some general connection with the Hellenistic statues of athletes which portrayed professional boxers. These statues depicted brutal faces and exaggerated muscular structure; the athletes were portrayed bleeding; their features were bruised and stupefied by the fight. (Pl. 39, b.)

A peculiar feature of this period was its scant production of statues of important gods: it preferred to portray minor deities and demi-gods (such as Muses, Centaurs, and Satyrs). The few examples of deities which survive come mostly from the mainland-Greek schools, for instance the Sarapis of Bryaxis similar to the Zeus of tradition, which we have already mentioned. The schools of Pergamum and Rhodes preferred great groups of statuary on mythological subjects. (Pl. 41, a.)

The groups of statuary in the Acropolis of Pergamum, both those commemorating the victories of Attalus over the Galatians and the Seleucids, and those on the altar erected by Eumenes II to Zeus, are violent expressions of an overwhelming struggle, and of the terrifying anguish of impending death. The movements displayed in these groups are daring in the extreme, and the features become masks of pain. The mythological sculpture of Rhodes shows similar violent and powerful representations of human pain in its death agony. It is enough to remember famous groups like the *Laocoön* (by Hagesander, Polydorus, and Athenodorus); or the *Menelaus and Patroclus* and the *Execution of Dirce* (by the brothers Apollonius and Tauriscus). Love of artistic realism developed the type of portrait conceived by Lysippus, which made it possible to catch the character of its subjects by depicting flashes of personal expression displayed on its features. Typical portraits of this kind include a sad and old Demosthenes, a contemplative Epicurus, a miserable and deformed Diogenes, a mocking Aesop, a Homer who can see despite his blindness, and a vulgar and violent Euthydemus (I of Bactria).

The Hellenistic age also liked statuary which represented people as types, for example those portraying simple scenes like that of the *Boy strangling a goose*, or the thin and decrepit figure of an old fisherman (Pl. 41, b), or that of a disgusting and drunken old woman.

Reliefs depict the same passion for realism. They often show obvious derivations from painting in their portrayal of excited groups of fighters and complex scenes of hunting. The same derivation can be seen in stuccoed murals (as in the *Terme Stabiane* in Pompeii) and in carving (as in the famous onyx known as *The Farnese Cup*).

Painting and Mosaic. Literary tradition has given us much information about the painters of the Hellenistic age and the subjects they preferred.

From this information we know of Protogenes of Caunus who was a rival of Apelles: of Theon of Samos who liked to depict mythological scenes; of Pausias of Sicyon who liked genre-painting of unimportant subjects; of Peiraicus who reproduced intimate scenes which recalled the Mimes. We can achieve a more adequate knowledge of Greek painting, however, by studying the few original Hellenistic paintings which are still extant, and by considering paintings of a later age which were based on Greek originals. There are mosaics too, both Greek and Roman, which recall earlier models.

Original paintings of the Hellenistic period can be found on the funeral *stelae* discovered at Pagasae, datable between the years 300 and 50 BC. They depict moving scenes which remind one of reliefs on the *stelae* of Attica.

In respect of later paintings, it is not unreasonable to associate the information we have about the historical picture by Aëtion (painted for the marriage of Alexander to Roxane) with the fresco found in Rome which is known as *The Aldobrandini marriage* (Pl. 55.) In the same way we can connect the references to mythical scenes painted in the third century by Athenion of Maronea, and in the second century by Timomachus of Byzantium, with the Pompeian painting called *Achilles discovered among the daughters of Lycomedes* and the painting at Herculaneum entitled *Medea in thought*.

The pretty still-lifes (*rhopographia*), in which the famous Egyptian Antiphilus excelled, and the genre-painting of Alexandria, find their echo in the beautiful series of Pompeian *amoretti* in the House of the Vettii, in the animal parody of *Aeneas and Anchises*, and in the scenes depicting *Fights of cockerels*. The model of these paintings was undoubtedly Alexandrian, for the flora and the fauna on them are those of the Nile.

The same observations can be made about mosaics, a new Hellenistic art originating from Alexandria and Pergamum. Here too the mosaic in the *House of the Faun* at Pompeii (depicting a *Battle of Alexander the Great* with wonderful movement and pathos–Pl. 42) recalls a famous picture which Philoxenus of Eretria painted for Cassander. The scenes which depict animals, or the picture of masked acrobats signed by Dioscurides of Samos, in the villa of Cicero, or the *Cat and the Quail* in another house at Pompeii, recall Hellenistic subjects of the East, as can be seen from the repeated reproduction of details characteristic of Nile scenery.

In this art, which is both pictorial and tessellated, we find the echo of a new artistic taste, which should be connected with naturalistic researches, with bucolic poetry, and with the natural tendencies of Eastern peoples.

It is a taste for plant and animal nature (Pl. 43, a), which recurs continually as the main subject and as ornament in all forms of art. Artists of the Hellenistic age were widely employed by kings and rich men to embellish public and private buildings; but there are clear signs that the new impressionist art, so violently pathetic, made people tired in the long run and turned their thoughts to the past. Scholars started to write the history of ancient artists, and scattered works of art began to be collected. In Pergamum, for example, the rulers started a gallery of sculptures which contained original works and copies of all the most famous artists, from the earliest times until Praxiteles.

Even the houses of rich private citizens tended to become museums of art, and this explains the vast number of surviving copies of statues made in the Hellenistic age.

f. *Art in Italy and in Rome to the Second Century* BC

Architecture. When we dealt with the previous period, we spoke of the huge constructions of city walls (built in some places of polygonal blocks, in others of small rows of rectangular blocks), which had been erected throughout the Etruscan, Italic, and Latin regions. We also mentioned the erection of the Servian walls in Rome, which had been destroyed in the Gallic fire, and which were replaced during our present period.

Meanwhile, first of all in Etruria, and later in Rome, architecture developed a new system of building by introducing the true arch and the true vault. An example of the employment of this new system can be seen and dated in several places. The 'Arch Gate' at Volterra in Etruria belongs to the fourth or third century (Pl. 44, a); the 'Door of Zeus' at Falerii near Rome was reconstructed in a new position by the Romans in 241. The first examples of arches and vaults in Etruscan tombs are to be found in the so-called *Temple of San Manno* at Perugia, in the *Tomb of Pythagoras* at Cortona, and in the *Tomb of the Grand Duke* at Chiusi.

Probably at the same time two other techniques of assistance to architecture were discovered. These were learned and employed to advantage by the Latins; and together with the arch and the vault they became decisive elements of Roman architecture, giving it effective supremacy and a style of its own. These techniques were: (1) The *opus latericium*, which consisted of bricks burned in an oven and joined by mortar: this was much superior to the technique of unburned bricks used in Sicily for the restoration of the walls of Gela and Heraclea Minoa. The Etruscan origin of this technique used in Rome is noted by Vitruvius, and is exemplified in the great brick walls of Arretium. (2) The *opus caementicium*, which consisted in the making of a form of concrete from stone and cement. The place of origin of this technique is not very clear; it is certain, however, that it was to be found in Rome at the end of the second century BC. By using both these techniques of construction, Roman architects were able to solve the problems of roofing large buildings (a problem which the Greeks were never able to overcome); for with these two techniques every stone or brick was tightly joined to the next, like the cells of an organism. It was therefore possible to attempt the construction of wide arches and spacious dome-shaped or vaulted rooms, suitable to magnificent buildings where crowds could gather (like basilicas, temples, baths, or covered theatres). Roman architects became so skilled that their services were asked for, even in Hellenistic regions. Vitruvius relates that as early as 175 BC Antiochus Epiphanes entrusted the erection of the Olympieum at Athens to M. Cossutius who came from Rome.

Links between Latium and Etruria in the designing of temples lasted down to the third century BC, for it was at that time that the type of temple described by Vitruvius became popular. This type of construction was square; the *cella* and columns were made of stone; and there was projecting guttering. The temple had terracotta decorations, consisting especially of free-standing groups of statues, or reliefs, in the pediments. Examples are to be found in the Etruscan zone at Orvieto and Marzabotto and in the Faliscan region (temple of Celle at Falerii).

In Etruria tombs were still constructed as more or less complex underground chambers hollowed out of the tufa with flat or vaulted ceilings. But side by side with these we now find new styles of vaulting, and a further innovation resulting from the use of painted decoration. The tombs of Praeneste in Latium show very clearly the successive influences of Etruscan styles, but they present a difference arising from an increased concern with the destiny of the dead person in the next world. Etruscan influence, both in architecture and in the decorative arts, can be found also farther south: in Campania (Nola, Capua, Cumae), in Lucania (Poseidonia = Paestum), in Samnium (Allifae), and in Iapygia (Ruve and Gnathia). Everywhere we find it combined with local styles.

Athens had had an aqueduct since the end of the sixth century. Others were later built in Samos, in many towns of Asia Minor, in Sicily (particularly at Syracuse, Acragas, and Selinus), and in the dry land of Apulia. No city, however, had such important water-carrying installations as Rome. From 312 the *Aqua Appia* brought water to Rome from 16 kilometres away, by a course which lay largely underground. This aqueduct was followed by the *Anio Vetus* in 272 BC and by the *Aqua Marcia* built between 144 and 140 BC, the latter 92 kilometres long and including 11 kilometres carried on arches. The habit of building aqueducts high above ground increased steadily, and this type of construction achieved real architectural merit. (Pl. 44, b.)

Sculpture. Etruscan sculpture of the period in question shows some outstanding peculiarities. The decoration of temples with terracotta friezes and plaques is enriched by a new range of flowers and plants which are extremely realistic. The *acroteria* and antefixes depict new types of gods, in place of the old groups of Sileni and Maenads. The lovely groups of the 'Temple of the

Scasato' at Falerii are a good example; but originality is shown most of all in isolated statues and sculpted groups placed inside the pediments. These sometimes depict mythical episodes and sometimes historical happenings (such as the battles with Gauls to be found in a pediment at Civitalba). The technique of such works at first shows the Greek influence of Praxiteles, Scopas, and Lysippus (the two heads and the figure of Apollo at the temple of the Scasato, for example). Later, however, it became exaggeratedly full of movement, as can be seen in a pediment at Telamone (*War at Thebes*), in one in Luna (*The massacre of the Niobids*), and even more in the pediment at Civitalba (*Bacchus rediscovering Ariadne*).

Another series of Etruscan sculptures is to be found in several sarcophagi and in a vast number of urns made of terracotta, travertine, alabaster, and peperino. They displayed for the most part mythical scenes with battles and brutal killings, which are based on Greek models but are given an Etruscan interpretation. They are interspersed with local historical and mythical figures. They sometimes constitute real masterpieces as, for example, two sculptured and many-coloured sarcophagi, one at Torre San Severo near Orvieto and the other (*Del Magnate*) at Tarquinia. (Pl. 45.) The covers of sarcophagi generally depicted the features of the dead person or of a dead couple with a sense of realism which was more expressive and faithful and less mannered than the style of Alexandrian portraits.

The most genuine impression of the ability of Etruscan sculptors in portraiture can be gained from statues made of bronze. There are graceful and realistic statues of children; and the statue of the so-called *Haranguer*, which was found near Lake Trasimeno, depicts a certain Aulus Metilius, whose face clearly shows the spiritual effort required to deliver a speech. There were other indigenous schools in central Italy, which reproduced Greek models in their own way. In Umbria for example, a bronze statue of Mars found at Todi reflects the posture of a Greek model, although it was made to look clumsy by the unskilful artist who added a breast-plate which was too rigid. Roman sculpture, and that of Latium also, shows a general Greek influence and a specific Graeco-Etruscan influence. This was due to the presence of Greek and Etruscan artists in Rome and to the vast number of monuments brought back from the regions which had been conquered (Veii, Volsinii, Syracuse, and the towns of Greece).

The following sculptures full of moving pathos show Greek influence: (1) The fragments of a male head found at Antemnae. (2) The statues on the pediment of a temple at the foot of the Capitol. There is, on the other hand, a similarity between the terracotta reliefs of Etruscan temples and the marble relief with a Typhon ending with snakes or the *Campana* plaques of marble about which we shall speak later. Roman sculpture achieved perfection and originality in portraiture much sooner than in other aspects; for besides external influence there was also the stimulus of the native practice of constructing funeral masks of ancestors. Not only the state, but private citizens and sometimes even foreigners, commissioned a large number of sculptured portraits to be made in Rome. These were exhibited either in public places or in private houses. At first they portrayed only people who had deserved well of their country, but in later years poets (beginning from L. Accius) and artists were depicted as well. The works of the age we are dealing with, however, are almost all lost. Moreover it is only for the ensuing period that we have any considerable remains of those commercialized works which are so typical of Rome and Italy. These consisted of marble or bronze copies of ancient Greek statues, and were intended as decoration for houses and villas.

Wall-painting and Ceramics. During the fourth and third centuries the paintings of artistic value in Etruria were to be found in the decorations of tombs. They depicted either scenes from daily life, or scenes of myth and the underworld with horrible and excited figures of demons, or famous historical scenes like those of the *François Tomb* at Vulci. (Pl. 46, a.) Greek influence, with its recent discoveries of foreshortening and chiaroscuro, shows itself very clearly in the technique; it can be seen in the paintings on tombs and on the sarcophagi (as, for example, the famous two at Tarquinia with their scenes of the wars of the Amazons).

As we have already said, these tomb paintings, and the shape of the undergound chambers which contained them, are very like those of Campania, Lucania, and Apulia. In these regions we sometimes find reproductions of battle scenes; and there are figures of soldiers (as at Capua) with their typical gaudy local costumes and with many-coloured trophies taken from the enemy.

Also in Rome, great wall-paintings were made portraying human figures and historical episodes of local character, despite the fact that houses were usually decorated by pictorial masterpieces brought from the conquered regions, or by copies of them. Historical tradition records a picture shown by Manius Valerius Messala on the wall of the Curia Hostilia in memory of his actions against the Carthaginians in 263/2 BC, another shown by the family of the Scipios in memory of victories in Asia, and a third shown to the people by L. Hostilius Mancinus to exalt his successful coup against Carthage in 147. A similar fragment was discovered in a house on the Esquiline, which can be dated to the end of the fourth century or the beginning of the third; it shows the surrender of a fortress by a Samnite called M. Fannius to the Roman Q. Fabius. (Pl. 46, b.) Tradition has also preserved the names of some famous Roman painters of that age, such as C. Fabius Pictor who in 304 decorated the temple of Salus on the Quirinal, and Pacuvius, the tragedian, who after 168 BC painted the temple of Hercules in the Forum Boarium.

For painted ceramics there was at this time a series of factories in southern Italy and in Etruria. They imitated Greek vases, Attic red-figured in particular, the importation of which into Italy was beginning to fall away. (Pl. 47, a.) Yet they used shapes, subjects, and techniques which for the most part had local characteristics; and they made a vast number of copies which were scattered all over the peninsula. The vases which were made in southern Italy generally go under the name of 'Apuli'. It is possible, however, to distinguish between them fairly well, for some were made in Apulia, some in Lucania, some in Campania. Some probably based their style directly on Greek models, whereas others derived it in a roundabout way through the Etruscans.

Amongst other things, the Apulian factories of Ruve and Canosa made huge vases of unusual shapes in an exuberant mass of colours, with a dark-red background and a greenish-black glaze. They were decorated with flowers, with mythical or historical scenes of great verisimilitude and tragic inspiration, or with funeral scenes.

Lucanian vases had a lighter background. The decoration was less exuberant and on a more modest scale, with a coarse design of scenes of comedy and parody (derived from the *phlyakes*).

Campanian pottery seems to have been derived most directly from Greek models. The shape is clumsy and the subjects disconnected: there are single figures, bits of still life, and heads of Sileni and Maenads.

There was another kind of pottery, typical of southern Italy and widely used throughout the Mediterranean world. It was covered by black glaze with ornamental drawings and scenes in superimposed colours (white, yellow, purple-red, and gold). By means of outline drawings and graffito it tried to imitate vases made out of metal. It is usually called 'Etrusco-Campanian' and was probably the product of factories in Campania and Apulia. (Pl. 47, b.)

There were, of course, also factories of purely Etruscan pottery, as for example at Chiusi and Volterra (where they imitated Attic pots), and perhaps also at Volsinii, which made many-coloured vases with decoration in relief (to imitate vases made of metal). Sometimes these vases were even silvered or gilded.

The most famous pottery factory of central Italy, however, was probably that at Falerii before the year 241 BC, when the town was transplanted elsewhere. This factory produced vases which were normally for daily use rather than for burial ornaments; they were simple in shape, decoration, and design; and they imitated Attic vases though they could be distinguished from them by a different form of background and by the use of black varnish of lesser depth. For the most part they depicted mythical scenes (Dionysiac in particular) and naked figures: the latter, in accordance with Hellenistic tendency, were mainly women.

Minor Arts. Even in the previous age, the Etruscans had been renowned engravers; and their works (statuettes, tripods, candelabra, censers, washbasins, arms, and decoration-pieces for furniture or triumphal cars) were widely known. From the sixth century onwards they had specialized in making bronze mirrors; they decorated them with engravings and reliefs, which at the beginning were more faithful to Greek models and mythical subjects, but which later became increasingly commercialized and conformed more to local taste.

During the fifth century and the centuries which followed the factories of Praeneste in Latium became famous for their artistic caskets of bronze. These had a cylindrical shape; they were covered with graffito drawings and surmounted by free-standing circular figures. The technique and subjects of their mythical graffiti recall works not only by Greek sculptors, painters, and potters, but by those of Apulia, the Faliscan territory, and Etruria— showing the large number of artistic currents which met and blended in Latian art of the fourth and third centuries BC. Generally the earliest caskets are the most beautiful, as for example the so-called 'Barberini' casket. It appears that an artist from Campania domiciled in Rome was commissioned to make the so-called 'Ficoroni' casket by someone from Praeneste. (Pl. 48.) This work portrayed admirably the scene of the landing of Jason and his companions in the country of the Bebryci; the artist derived his subject via Magna Graecia from a famous painting of Polygnotus.

From ancient times the Etruscans were also able goldsmiths; their work generally consisted of gold foil which was worked in relief or engraved. This art lasted until the end of the third century and was also carried on at Praeneste and Satricum.

The art of carving precious stones, which the Etruscans imitated and developed from Egyptian scarabs, also survived for some time in Etruria. But it gradually died, and its place was taken by the work of Roman cutters, who worked on small slabs of precious stone or glass paste.

Something should also be said about coins. The second half of the fourth century BC saw the appearance, both in Rome and in the towns of Etruria, of regular money made of a bronze alloy. The coin called *aes* had a fixed weight and was minted by the state. The earliest shape was a large disk, the *aes grave* (in Rome it weighed a pound), which was divided into twelve parts called 'unciae': later the weight was reduced and it became a fiduciary coinage. Meanwhile from the fifth century BC Etruria, following the example of the Italiotes and of the Siceliotes, started to coin silver money, and in rare cases even gold coins. The early minting was poor, but in the fourth century some coins have the imprint of genuine art.

At the end of the fourth century BC, the Romans started to commission the coining of their silver money from Capua; later, from 269 BC according to tradition, they coined their own silver *denarii* themselves.[51]

g. The Celtic Civilization

The Po Valley. The Gauls began to enter the Po valley in the sixth century:[52] from the second half of the third century they were gradually conquered by the military exploits of Rome. About the year 150 therefore their cultural stamp must have been largely pre-Roman. Archaeological evidence proves that the Celtic peoples at first only entered the north-western part of the Po valley; it was only in later years that they succeeded in reaching the regions lying to the east and south of the Po, and in occupying part of the Adriatic coast which lay between the two arms of the delta of that river. (cf. Pseudo-Scylax 16–18.) They penetrated, and mixed with, the Ligurians, Etruscans, and related tribes. Later they carried out frequent expeditions over the Apennines to plunder Italian lands as far as Iapygia; these raids ended, however, with the defeat at Telamo in 225 BC, the year which marks the beginning of the Roman conquest. Polybius, as a contemporary historian, tells about their civilization as it was about 150 BC, and his narrative (II, 17) is confirmed by Diodorus (V, 26–31), who based his information on Poseidonius. Polybius says: 'They lived in villages without walls, and did not know of or use furniture; for they led a primitive life and slept on stacks of grass or straw. For the most part they fed on meat; they devoted their attention solely to wars or agriculture, and had no knowledge of art or science. The wealth of each person consisted of cattle and gold which could be used as currency on all occasions and taken about at will. They valued friendships most of all, because for them the greatest fame and power belonged to the man who was surrounded by many people dependent on his good-will.'

It is obvious, however, that the Gauls achieved an earlier degree of civilization (due partly to a knowledge of writing) in the regions where they kept in closest contact with the Etruscan survivors, and where they became ethnically mixed with them.

[*The Iberians and Celts.** Under Greek influence, one of the most remarkable bodies of art in barbarian Europe developed among the Tartesso-Iberian tribes of Spain and southern France.

The Celts of central Spain, Galicia, and Portugal prolonged the Hallstatt traditions (post-Hallstatt civilization). They built fortified villages similar to the European 'Ringwälle', and in Old Castile they had great burial-grounds in which Antennae swords and daggers, belt-buckles, fibulae, and other objects have been found. They used geometrical patterns for niello work and to decorate their gold and silver torques (Galicia). In the first Iron Age the Celts already had stone *stelae* carved with very primitive designs (war chariots) and groups of small bronze votive figures resembling those found in central Europe (Hallstatt). At the entrance to their fortified villages they set up stone figures of animals ('berracos'), and in Portugal stone figures of warriors have also been found. Finds in central Spain include great numbers of bronze fibulae engraved with figures of horsemen; these were influenced by Iberian art as, probably, was the stone sculpture.

The Tartesso-Iberian civilization established itself in a number of regional

* By Pedro Bosch-Gimpera.

centres in Spain, and in south-east France the Iberian influence was carried as far as the Marseilles area, before the invasion of the Volcae—a Celtic people—about the third century BC.

In south and south-east Spain there were towns, many of them fortified (e.g., Meca, in the province of Albacete), with monuments such as the temple at Cerro de los Santos, containing numerous ex-votos which bear witness to great skill in stone-carving (statues of warriors, and of women whose dress shows Greek influence and who are adorned with jewels). (Pl. 57, a.) At Galera (province of Granada) there were stone-built mortuary chambers with wall paintings. In other towns, shrines were set up in humbler buildings (e.g., La Serreta de Alcoy) and had ex-votos in terracotta, of the same types as the stone statues, while in the caverns of Andalusia there were rural shrines (Castellar de Santisteban and Despeñaperros, in the province of Jaen) where the votive objects included bronze figurines, articles of adornment, and even the reproduction of sets of false teeth. Here, too, the figurines are of the same types as the large sculpture and show the influence of Greek models, particularly of the early epoch. It is difficult to classify them in chronological order, as the same types were repeated until a very late period.

The influence of archaic Greek sculpture is also seen in some stone statues of animals in a deliberately archaic style, including the human-headed bull known as 'la bicha de Balazote', which Heuzeuy considered to be reminiscent of Mesopotamia, lions which recall the Phocaean lion, sphinxes, etc.

Iberian sculpture was influenced by classical models, as may be seen from the stone warrior at Elche and the bronze warriors and ladies in the sanctuary of La Luz (provinces of Murcia). Greek influence continued down to the Hellenistic period.

The theory has been advanced that some of the sculpture may be the work of provincial Greek artists—including, for instance, certain sphinxes and the statue of a woman seated on a throne at Verdolay, which may date from the early fifth century. One outstandingly fine work is a polychrome bust of a richly dressed lady with a veil on her head, held in place by a comb in the manner of the present-day Spanish 'mantilla'; this is the 'Lady of Elche', a unique piece generally believed to be the work of a Greek artist of about 400 BC. (Pl. 57, b.)

At Osuna (province of Seville) there are stone slabs carved with reliefs representing warriors or personages celebrating religious rites, musicians, and acrobats, in a style resembling that of archaic Greek art, but thought to date from the third century BC; the warriors carry bucklers of the La Tène B type.

Painted pottery had made its appearance, in all probability, by the end of the sixth century. The earliest decorative patterns were geometrical, imitated from the simplest Ionian ceramic work (coloured lines, concentric circles, parallel wavy lines, swastikas). (Pl. 58, a.) In Andalusia, these geometrical decorations—the only ones used in the pottery of that region—also show the influence of Phoenician ceramics. In south-eastern Spain the development of geometrical decoration went hand in hand with that of floral and animal designs, soon followed by human figures and scenes from life—as illustrated by urns found in the burial-grounds at Verdolay, Archena, and Oliva, and at the towns of La Serreta de Alcoy and Liria in the province of Valencia. The floral and animal decorations recall those of the latest Greek vases influenced by oriental models, with combinations of spirals ending in stylized flowers, or series of animals (carnivores and birds). This style presumably originated during the sixth century BC, for the oriental-type pottery could not reach Spain at a later date; but it survived for a long time, and its finest period was in the fifth and fourth centuries. During the fifth century the influence of the red-figured pottery produced in Attica resulted in the warrior vase discovered at Archena—the style of which is still somewhat rough—while the fourth-century urns found at Oliva are decorated with friezes of quite realistic horsemen and with a scene showing a fortress under siege. The same lavish decoration, in which floral motives are combined with scenes of warfare or ritual dances showing musicians and richly-dressed women, is to be found in the pottery produced at Liria which flourished for a long time, down to the second century. Here the latest urns, the style of which had notably deteriorated, show fishing scenes or sea-fights.

In the north of the kingdom of Valencia, Lower Aragon, and Catalonia, art included little or no sculpture. This was a peasant civilization, with fortified villages which, as the fourth century proceeded, grew into towns, some of them with strongholds (e.g. San Antonio de Calaceite, in the province of Teruel, and Los Foyos at Lucena del Cid in the province of Castellón). The pottery here repeats the floral and geometrical patterns found in the south-east, and sometimes reveals a strong decorative sense (e.g. Tossal de las Tenalles, at Sidamunt, in the province of Lerida). Ceramics from the kiln at Fontscaldes (province of Tarragona), or from potteries working in the same style, were exported to other villages in Iberian Catalonia, to the south of France (Ensérune, near Béziers) and even to Italy (Ischia). In the Ebro valley in Aragon there was a school of ceramists who used the geometrical motives in an original manner, more especially in some very baroque combinations of spiral lines; this survived down to the first century BC.

Near Tivissa, in Catalonia (province of Tarragona), a shrine in the Iberian village of Le Castellet de Banyoles contained silver-gilt ritual vases decorated with scenes of religious ceremonial by local goldsmiths, together with imported Hellenistic silver vases.

Treasure-hoards found in south-east Spain include some remarkable examples of goldsmiths' work, such as the diadem discovered at Javea, in the province of Alicante; and Andalusia abounds in silver vases (treasures of Perotitos and Mogón, in the province of Jaen). The Greek influence generalized the use of coins, which were minted in several native towns, and of writing, evidenced by letters scratched on vases and by inscriptions engraved on lead, such as the small plaque found at La Serreta de Alcoy and those at La Bastida de Mogente (province of Valencia), the latter constituting something very like a collection of records.

Iberian pottery spread into south-east France (Montlaurés, near Narbonne, Ensérune, near Béziers) and reached the vicinity of Marseilles. In course of time, and more especially after this region was conquered by the Volcae, it made way for Celtic pottery of the La Tène style. Catalonia was influenced by south-east Spain, or imported work from that region, as may be seen from the vase with a battle or hunting scene found at Emporion and from vases decorated with birds in the style of Archena and Elche, also found at Emporion and at L'Aigueta, near Figueras.

Provence developed Celtic sculpture, influenced by Greek art, which has remarkable parallels with Iberian sculpture. There is the same influence of the archaic, shown in the statues of warriors found at Sainte Anastasie and Grézan. This was followed, in the third–second centuries BC, by the Hellenistic influences traceable in the statues of the shrines at Entremont and Roquepertuse. Stone carvings of animals, similar to the 'berracos' of Celtic Spain, have been found in France as well.

The influence of Iberian pottery penetrated into Old Castile, and Iberian geometrical decoration appears on Celtic urns found in burial-grounds in the Jalón Valley (provinces of Soria and Guadalajara), which date from the post-Hallstatt period. At Numantia, where the lowest levels of the town have yielded painted Celtic pottery with scenes of battle and horse-breaking, a school of ceramists developed about the third–second centuries under the influence of Iberian techniques and styles of decoration; this produced curious and extremely original work. During the period preceding its destruction in 133 BC, Numantia grew into a populous city; its circumference still followed the line of the 'Ringwall', but inside this the streets intersected in a chessboard pattern apparently derived from the plan of Emporion, which also influenced the lay-out of the Iberian towns in the Ebro valley. The same combination of the Celtic 'Ringwall' with a symmetrical street-pattern is found in the Celtic towns of northern Portugal (the 'Citania' of Sabroso) and Galicia (Santa Tecla), in this case with stone-built houses erected on a circular ground-plan. A feature of Sabroso is its mortuary chambers which have façades crowned by a pediment adorned with geometrical designs apparently stemming from the Celtic goldsmiths' work which had spread to the north-west of the peninsula (gold torques found in treasure hoards).

In eastern Spain and Andalusia the Iberian traditions survived during the Roman republican period (painted ceramics, heads of warriors and horsemen on Iberian coins, decoration on silver vases). The school of ceramists at Azaila, in the Ebro valley, continued into the first century BC.

(Pl. 58, b.) The Iberian tradition in pottery was still fostered at Numantia, too, after it was rebuilt under the Romans. The Celtic towns clung to their existence in Galicia and Portugal as well, and it took a long time for the indigenous civilizations to be replaced by that of Rome.]

h. *Art in the Roman World from the Second Century* BC

Architecture. One of the fundamental characteristics of classical Roman architecture is the importance of the interiors in comparison with the exteriors of buildings. This was due to an inbred tendency towards the practical. So towns built on the Roman model, though they adhered to a geometrical plan whenever possible, did not offer a vision of monumental unity, with flights of façades and squares at road-crossings, such as the style of Hippodamus of Miletus demanded for new Greek towns. The different aspect of Roman towns was also due to the new technique of masonry which replaced the technique of building with rectangular blocks of stone. (These stone blocks, however, were still used, particularly for the exteriors of monumental buildings, such as the theatre of Marcellus, and later for amphitheatres.) The new techniques were as follows (cf. Pl. 49):

(1) The *opus incertum* which consisted of stones of irregular shape but flat on the outside and tightly cemented together. (It was used particularly from the second century BC to the first century AD.)

(2) The *opus reticulatum* which consisted of small pyramidal stones set in diagonal rows. (Used from the first century BC to the second AD.)

(3) The *opus latericium* which consisted of baked bricks of varying sizes and layers of cement of varying thicknesses. (Used from the age of Augustus on.) Buildings of major importance were lined with marble on the outside and covered with stuccoes on the inside.

Roman constructions were very compactly built because of the conglomerates used; they could be of great heights and contained rooms which were large and bright and covered by vaults or domes. They did not need intermediate lines of support from columns or architraves. The columns, which were tall and slender, were therefore used purely as a decorative element, and the entablatures were just ornamental strips.

The houses became bigger; the atrium was enlarged to take in a peristyle; the rooms increased in number; and buildings tended to become higher. But every effort was directed to beautify the interiors of houses in the great towns and even more so of houses in smaller towns and country villas. Yet exterior walls were normally plain and unadorned except for those which overlooked main roads.

The number of temples increased in both Rome and Latium. In the time of Sulla were built the temples of Fortune at Praeneste, Gabii, and Tibur. Pompey built the temple of Venus Victrix, Caesar that of Venus Genetrix, and others were constructed by Augustus. When these temples were not sited on high ground, they were placed on artificially raised stylobates and dominated surrounding buildings with their size. Tuscan columns were preferred to Greek in temples built on a rectangular plan; *cellae* were enlarged even at the cost of removing lateral colonnades or of encasing the columns in the outside walls. In the building of temples with a circular plan, care was taken to create either a straight approach (of Greek type in the case of grandiose buildings like the Pantheon of Agrippa), or to develop the rooms radially. The types of Roman temples, later listed in the works of Vitruvius, started to spread all over the world beginning at the age of Augustus. It was then that the following temples were erected: the temples of Augustus at Nemausus (Nîmes: the *Maison Carrée*) and at Vienne in Gaul; the octastyle temple at Tarragona in Spain; the temple at Ancyra in Galatia; and so on. Very often these temples had to be built by Italian architects. It was thus that Rome started to dominate and spread its influence even in the field of practical aesthetics.

Roman basilicas, although the word *basilica* is Greek, were very different from the usual porticoed promenades of Hellenistic regions. They were designed to be closed buildings with inside colonnades, and originally they had only one outlook, on one of the shorter sides. The first imperial *Fora*, those of Caesar and Augustus, consisted of wide spaces fenced in by walls with colonnades and shops on the inside. The Romans started to build permanent theatres, both in Rome and outside, at the time of Pompey. (Fig. 7.) If these were not roofed they were built with a deeper *cavea*,[53] and were enclosed by a stage of more than one floor. Roman architects specialized in the construction of theatres as well, and were invited to build them in the East. For example M. and C. Stallius rebuilt the Odeum in Athens after its destruction during the Mithradatic war.

There was a new type of monument which was purely Roman, the triumphal or memorial arch. The first known examples of arches erected by victorious generals, paid for by the booty of war, were built in 196 and in 190 BC. In 121 BC Rome built the first arch under which a victorious army could parade: this was inspired by the *Porta triumphalis* of the so-called Servian walls.

We have much information about the first type and there are many examples: the arch of the Sergii at Pola (31 BC); that of the Gavii at Verona; and that of Marcus Antonius at Aquinum, which is probably older (about 50 BC). Tradition recalls examples of triumphal arches on the Caelian and the Aventine. From the time of Augustus on, however, they were only built for emperors. There were arches erected in honour of Augustus in the Forum at Rome (20 BC), at Ariminum (27 BC), at Augusta Praetoria (25 BC) and at Segusio (Susa, 2 BC). (Pl. 50, a.) Other arches built outside Italy and worthy of mention are those of Glanum (Saint Rémy), Nîmes, Vaison, Orange, Thessalonica (the *Gate of Vardar*, 42 BC), and Ephesus (4/3 BC).

Pompey and Caesar built several monuments to commemorate their deeds in Spain; and there was a monument to Augustus at La Turbie in honour of his Alpine conquests.

Caesar's plan for improving the monumental architecture of the city of Rome was, for the most part, carried out by Augustus. He erected new public buildings; he restored temples, roads, and pavements; and he drew up a town plan in which middle-class districts and villas were moved beyond

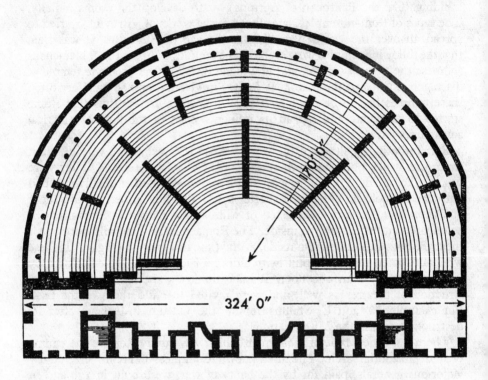

FIG. 7.   Orange: plan of the theatre, restored (after B. Fletcher).

the destroyed Servian walls. Similar great constructions were erected outside Rome for the housing of new colonies.

Both in Italy and throughout the provinces the great ways of communication were increased in number and their actual routes modified and improved (as in the case of the Flaminia). Outside Italy towns started to need a system of aqueducts which often required great and daring works of engineering. Examples can be seen in the imposing ruins of the aqueduct with a triple order of arches, which crosses the river Gard near Nîmes, and in the Augustan aqueducts of Tarraco and Ephesus. Amazing works of excavation were done by the architects of Augustus, by Cocceius in particular. They transformed the Lucrine lake into a gulf; they built underwater tunnels to improve communications; and they constructed water reservoirs, such as the *Piscina mirabilis* of Bacoli, and arsenals such as the so-called *Cento Camerelle* of Misenum.

The baths at Rome became more and more magnificent. Those of Agrippa near the Pantheon (19 BC), besides the usual rooms, had large halls for swimming-pools, changing-rooms, assembly-rooms, and reading-rooms; and their model was copied in the provinces. Several town walls and their doors can be dated to the time of Augustus, such as those at Augusta Praetoria, Augusta Taurinorum, Fanum, Hispellum, Tergeste, and Iader. (Pl. 50, b.) City gates were often complex works of fortification; they had two ways of access, with a courtyard between them (*propugnaculum*), which was guarded by overlooking galleries. The *Porta Palatina* at Turin, in brick, has four arches, of which two are small but the other two have upper storeys with projecting or contained windows; and there are two battlemented towers with sixteen faces.

A simpler type is to be found in the following *Porta Augusta* of Fanum, the construction of which was attributed to Vitruvius and built in 9/10 AD; it had three arches of which the middle one was the highest. That in the walls of Aosta is similar; so is the *Arch of Riccardo* at Tergeste, low and wide, with one arch only, which is flanked by half-pillars with Corinthian capitals.

Roman tombs were of different sizes, and sometimes they had curious architectural shapes. The following are worthy of mention: (1) The tomb of a baker, of the first century BC, adjoining the Porta Maggiore in Rome (Pl. 51, b); this is shaped like an oven with doors, and has a frieze depicting the baking of bread, the cinerary urn for the baker's wife being shaped like a bread-bin. (2) The tomb of the Julii at Glanum (Saint Rémy) built for a family of freedmen of Caesar; it consists of a square platform, decorated with reliefs, which rests on two steps, and is surmounted by a *tetrapylon* with arched windows supporting a domed colonnade of circular shape. (It reminds one of the choregic monument to Lysicrates at Athens.) (3) The tomb of Sestius near the Porta Ostiensis in Rome, built shortly before the year 12 BC; this was an imitation of the Egyptian pyramids and its *cella* was decorated with painted stuccoes. Sometimes architects built tombs with a cylindrical platform surmounted by a dome, by a pinnacle or by a balcony. The Mausoleum of Augustus had a diameter of 95 metres, a front porch, and a pinnacle planted with cypresses which carried the statue of the emperor. The tomb of Caecilia Metella, built for the daughter-in-law of Crassus the triumvir, had a diameter of 28 metres, a square base decorated with a frieze, and a pinnacle on top. (Pl. 51, a.) Whereas the great and the wealthy people had monumental tombs, the middle and poorer classes adopted the custom, from the time of Augustus on, of joining together in brotherhoods to own a *columbarium* of the type found in Egypt in the Ptolemaic era. The *columbarium* consisted of large rooms, mostly underground, which had several recesses (*loculi*) with inscribed tablets, to contain the cinerary urns of the members of the brotherhood. Sometimes they were bare and plain, like that of the *Vigna Codini* on the Appian way; sometimes they were decorated with paintings like that of the Augustan Villa Pamphili.

Sculpture. At first native Roman tendencies of style in the field of sculpture risked being lost because authentic Greek works reached Rome very easily or were copied there by Hellenistic artists and their pupils who had settled in the capital. Even the statue of Caesar in the Forum Iulium derived from the model of a statue of Alexander made by Lysippus, in every detail except the head. Meanwhile, Greek and Italiote artists working in Rome turned to the new trends of the creative activity of Greece, of Athens most of all. This new trend started as a reaction against Alexandrian decadence and reverted to the models and shapes of the sculpture of the fifth and fourth centuries. The style of Praxiteles, therefore, was adopted for the statues of the gods; the style of Polycletus for the statues of athletes; and the Alexandrian style for figures of minor importance. At the same time, the people of Latium and the Italiotes, who commissioned the works, insisted that their tastes should be followed, at least in part; for they were still attracted by the old Etruscan and Italiote production. The result was an eclectic tendency which was typically Roman, though the schools of art were otherwise fairly different.

Arcesilaus, for instance (with the collaboration of a certain Coponius) preferred to draw his inspiration from Hellenistic masterpieces for a group of *amoretti* playing with a lioness. It is probable that his statue of Venus Genetrix, made for the temple which Caesar erected in honour of that goddess, was the prototype for many other works depicting the goddess in a languid lying position with Cupid on her shoulders. (Pl. 52, a.) On the other hand an Italiote called Pasiteles, with his pupil Stephanus and Menelaus the pupil of Stephanus (who as a freedman took the name of M. Cossutius Cerdo), liked to draw their inspiration from the great Greek models of the fifth and fourth centuries, and from the terracotta masterpieces which derived from them (Pliny notes this when speaking of the terracottas made by Pasiteles). Some of the works by Stephanus appear to be inspired by sculptors earlier than Pheidias (as for example the *Ephebe of the Villa Albani* and the *Pan* in the British Museum). The bronze head of the *Doryphorus* by the Athenian Apollonius at Herculaneum recalls the style of Polycletus. A third group of artists was very eclectic, including Salpion, Sosibius, Pontius, and others, to whom are ascribed the Artemis and the *Tyrannicides* in the Museum of Naples, some decorated stone curbs for mouths of wells, and some funerary altars. They used to combine faces of archaic type with draperies of Hellenistic design.

It is certain that these Greek and Italiote artists had local pupils and native workmen to whom they communicated their neo-Atticism, in its essential features at any rate. The pupils in their turn displayed it in every kind of decoration. The following are the better-known types of work: (1) Plaques of polychrome terracotta (the so-called *Lastre Campane*), series of which were used as friezes to decorate halls. Sometimes they depicted simple floral subjects, either realistic or stylized; sometimes they portrayed Bacchic scenes and dancing Corybants, or Satyrs, Maenads, Victories, or winged Genii; sometimes again they showed imaginary landscapes, mostly recalling the Nile. (2) Vases of precious metal, mostly silver, which were to be found in great quantity both in Italy (at Pompeii and particularly at Boscoreale) and outside the peninsula. These were decorated with floral scrolls either stylized in 'arabesque', or realistic; they depicted figures of animals, mythical scenes and allegorical figures. (3) The 'Arretine' pottery made of *terra sigillata* and produced from engraved moulds. These pots have a shiny glaze and slender shapes; the reliefs on them are Muses, Genii, nymphs, love scenes, and sometimes even Roman soldiers. (Pl. 53, a.) They were made by many factories (of Tigranes, of Bardates, of Cerdo). (4) Stuccoes to cover walls and vaults, designed to hide the rough surface of *caementicium* or *latericium*. (Pl. 53, b.) The recurrent types of ornament and figurines which these stuccoes contain were produced by casting; but the central scenes were laid on by individual plasterers with quick but often masterly strokes. Delicate examples of stuccoes of the Augustan era are those of the Villa Farnesina; these decorate three rooms. (5) The reliefs on altars, on the circular stones for wells, on fountains, on monumental vases, and on sarcophagi.

Native taste prevailed in the old Italic and Western centres still more than at Rome. Even at Rome, however, indigenous taste did not forget the Etrusco-Latin tradition, and was markedly felt in two departments of sculpture, namely portraiture and historical reliefs.

There was a first period in which portraiture shows traces either of an excessive native realism (as for example in the funerary relief portraying the family of L. Vibius) or of an excessive idealization attributable to Greek influence (as with the bust of Octavian in the Vatican Museum). But a rational balance between the two tendencies was soon achieved, as can be seen in three statues of Augustus, two showing the *princeps* in armour (Prima Porta and Cherchell), the third (in the Vatican) depicting him as *pontifex* in his toga. (Pl. 52, b.) The heads of these statues portray faithfully the lean but noble features of the emperor, and the proportions of the body are natural. Realism must have been even greater when the original colours survived. Despite this realism, in the statues where he is armed he becomes a hero, whereas when he is *pontifex* we can clearly perceive his spiritual nobility. The reliefs on the breast-plate of the statue at Prima Porta appear to be completely Roman: they glorify the victories of Rome and its emperor over conquered peoples, and portray the scene in which its Parthian enemies hand back the standards they had captured from Crassus. The same magnificent balance of tendencies is to be found in the surviving portraits of Livia, Octavia, Tiberius, Marcellus, Drusus, Antonius, Brutus, and many others. The same characteristics can be seen in coins, on which a few brief lines succeed in giving a wonderful outline of the characters.

Of historical reliefs the earliest example which draws our attention is a monument to Cn. Domitius Ahenobarbus made not much later than 42 BC. It supported a statuary group made by Scopas, which had been brought to Rome; but all that survives is the base, with reliefs depicting a procession of creatures of the sea, and a sacrifice offered by Domitius for the *lustratio* of the army. The *Ara Pacis* (consecrated by the senate in the Campus Martius in 9 BC) has several reliefs, four of which are of great interest as they depict mythical and allegorical subjects (Aeneas, Romulus and Remus, the Dea Roma, and Tellus). (Pl. 54, a.) Its frieze represents the ceremony of a libation to the gods to obtain peace in the world; this portrays the emperor and his family, the priests, magistrates, and senators, and the people with their women and children. The execution is so realistic that every person can be easily distinguished. The same is true of the reliefs on the Basilica Aemilia, of the scenes of the battle of Actium (now in Budapest and in the Vatican), of the reliefs now in San Vitale at Ravenna, and of the decorations on the earliest triumphal arches such as the Arch of Susa.

The same quality is to be found on certain exquisite products of toreutic art, for instance on two silver cups of Boscoreale. One of these depicts homage offered to Augustus by defeated provinces and peoples; the other shows the return of Tiberius from Pannonia, perhaps in AD 11. Glyptic art was also similar, particularly in the making of large and precious cameos. Fine examples include the cameo attributed to Dioscurides which again portrays Tiberius in front of Augustus, probably on his return from Pannonia (Pl. 54, b); or the cameo (now in Boston) representing Augustus as Neptunus after the battle of Actium.

There are some features common to all these reliefs. The mythical element of Greek type has declined, and is often represented only by a single god or hero; in contrast there is great emphasis on the indigenous element, particularly in symbolic personifications such as those of Rome, Italy, or the provinces. Roman manners are reproduced in the dresses; people of all ages, including children, are portrayed; background spaces are filled with crowds, landscapes, or architectural views; and finally there is clear rendering of individual feeling.

Painting and Mosaic. From at least the beginning of the second century BC Italians liked to decorate the interior of their houses with paintings. We have some examples of those in Rome, but many more from Herculaneum and Pompeii. The wealth of specimens makes it possible to perceive the existence of four pictorial styles current between the second century BC and AD 79, the year of the destruction of Pompeii. These can be identified fairly easily, and two of them come within the chronological limits of this chapter.

The first was the 'incrustation' style, which was used between about the years 150 and 50 BC. The walls were decorated with stucco frames containing rectangular painted panels, which at first imitated marble linings and later were painted in colours freely arranged.

The second style depended upon the use of perspective, and dated from about 50 BC to about AD 14. Examples are the *Villa of Fannius* at Boscoreale, the *House of Augustus* on the Palatine, and the *Villa of Livia* ('ad gallinas albas') near Prima Porta. This style was characterized by smooth walls without stucco, painted in brilliant colours, with false skirtings, false columns and slender pillars, and sometimes with porticoes and cornices. All this was painted in perspective and contained landscapes and mythical scenes. (Pl. 56, a.) In the *Villa of Livia* the paintings on the walls of a room convey the idea of being in a garden. The paintings within the frames on the walls, therefore, appear as real pictures which sometimes clearly derive from Greek models: this we noticed earlier in connection with the paintings representing Medea, Achilles amongst the daughters of Lycomedes, and the *Aldobrandini marriage*. (Pl. 55.) Italic technique and taste, however, can also be found in the carelessness of the design of the colouring and in some typical tendencies such as the theatricality of the poses. (Pl. 56, b.) Sometimes these paintings have an Italic subject, Aeneas and Dido, for example, or Aeneas wounded. Sometimes the subject reflects typical local beliefs (as in the wonderful pictures on epic and clearly Orphic subjects in the *triclinium* of the *Villa of Mysteries*).

In painting, too, the Romans were fond of portraiture. This is shown in the anecdote of a certain Arellius who lived in the last years of the republic, and who created a great scandal by portraying the goddesses with the features of his mistresses.

In those days, mosaic was the rival of painting, because of the delicacy achieved by using minute cubes of uniform size and many colours (*tessellae*). Sometimes they reproduced famous pictures of the Hellenistic age, such as *Alexander's battle* in the *House of the Faun* at Pompeii; at other times the subjects were genre or still life, both also to be found in the same Pompeian house. Sometimes they were undoubtedly the work of Greek artists, for example the scene depicting acrobats and signed by Dioscurides of Samos which was found in the *House of Cicero*. In those days wealthy Italians generally liked mosaics which depicted mythical subjects, genre-subjects, scenes of fishing, and borders of floral scrolls—with a certain amount of stylization. (Pl. 43, b.) They used to line columns and niches with minute pieces of either gold or deep-blue colour; and this type of decoration later developed into the admirable art of wall mosaic.

3. MUSIC

Music held an important place in Chinese society, especially after the final victory of Confucianism. The school of Confucius built up a system correlating the musical sounds with the order of the Universe; music was conceived as a transcendent or even magical power, of primary importance for the harmony and proper government of the state. As such, it was a primary concern of the ruler, and under Han Wu-ti (141–87 BC) an Imperial Bureau of Music (*yüeh-fu*) was set up. All this concerned the ritual music, of unitary character throughout the empire, and as such quite different from the tunes and happy songs of the common people with their unending local varieties.

Sonorous stones (*ch'ing*) and globular flutes (*hsün*) were known already in Shang times. The advent of the Chou had brought a great increase in the number and use of musical instruments. Among them, the seven-stringed zither (*ch'in*) soon stood out and became the classical instrument of the cultured classes. Another zither was the *cheng*, with thirteen brass strings.

The original scale was pentatonic (*do, re, mi, soh, la*). But already the first text on musical theory, found in the *Lü-shih Ch'un-ch'iu* of 239 BC, recognized two scales, male and female of six notes each. The *Huai-nan-tzu* (end of second century BC) seems to know a scale of seven notes. In 40 BC Ching Fang increased the 'male' to sixty notes, with which it ceased to be a scale and became a tablature.

As to actual remnants of notated music, no specimen earlier than the T'ang dynasty (618–907) has come down to us. We have only literary descriptions of orchestras and names of songs.

Indian music never had a unitary character like the Chinese ritual music, but embraced a wide field of different phenomena. The classical theory, along with that of acting and dancing, was settled in the *Nāṭyaśāstra* of Bhārata, attributed to the first century BC. It is divided into thirty-six chapters, of which chapters 28–33 deal with music proper. It seems to be a compilation of fragments of different origins. But the fully developed classic theory of music is found only in the much later *Saṅgītiratnakara* (thirteenth century AD) and cannot be dealt with here.

A position by itself is occupied by Bharata's *Gītalamkara*, probably of the first or even second century BC, which gives a different classification of the musical elements (male, female, and derivated modes). It remains outside the main current of classical theory, but it represents a popular tradition which dominated the field in the times of the Moghul empire (sixteenth–eighteenth centuries) and survives to this day.

The instruments were percussion (*ghana*), drums (*avanaddha*), wind instruments (*susira*) and above all stringed instruments (*tata*). Of the latter, the most venerated was the *vīna*, to which mythical origins were attributed. It was originally a fretted plucked instrument, with one gourd attached to each extremity, and with seven strings, of which four served for the melody.

Philo and Heron tell us of a noteworthy advance in the musical instruments of the Greek world, in that the mathematician Ctesibius (third century BC) produced, among his other inventions, a keyboard organ worked by hydraulic power.

Ordinary accompaniment to the recital of poetry, that is to say to epic or the like, gradually fell into disuse and was regarded as superfluous. But music as an accompaniment to choral song gradually gained in quality and variety. We are speaking now of the time of Pindar, the score for whose *First Pythian* is actually known. His victory songs, and those of Bacchylides, were sung, to the accompaniment of the flute or the lyre or of both, by a choir consisting of the companions of the victorious hero as he returned home. A choir-master conducted the performance, which was of great religious solemnity; and the construction of the verses, with their strophes and antistrophes, was highly diversified.

In later times Greek lyric tended to be confined to dithyramb and *nomos*, some portions being choral, others solos which were either sung or recited. The music tended to gain ground markedly at the expense of the poetry and ideas; a good example is the *nomos* called *The Persians*, by Timotheus of Miletus (450–360 BC). in which the *citharoedus* plays a predominant part.

But meanwhile drama (from Phrynichus onwards) established a new and fruitful opportunity for union between music and poetry. The solo parts, themselves accompanied by the zither, were interposed by choruses, intoned by anything from twelve to fifteen singers with a flautist in the background. At the outset the choral passages predominated, but from Sophocles' time the recitative lines were more numerous than the lyric; and in Euripides the lyric sections became just intermezzi, in which the words were nothing more than the occasion for the accompanying music. We see this from a fragment of Euripides' *Orestes* which has survived with musical scoring.

Certain 'Delphic hymns' of the second century have also come down to us with scores. These show that an archaizing tendency was combined with innovations, in that the maximum interval in the melody was extended from an octave to an eleventh and that modulation became more frequent.

Allusions to the theory of music, and some outline of musical history, are to be found among Plato's references to aesthetics, especially in the *Republic*; also in the enquiries into tone made by Eudoxus of Cnidus (390–337), and in some passages of Aristotle (the 'Aristotelian' *Problemata*, a spurious work, will be mentioned in Part III). Then there are the fundamental theories of Aristoxenus of Tarentum, known as the 'Musician' (*floruit* 320–300), who used Pythagorean teaching to good effect, and was followed in this by Euclides about 300. Finally there are the *Pneumatica* of Heron of Alexandria and the *De Musica* of Philodemus of Gadara.

In the Roman world Greek influence may be seen at work twice over. It first reached Rome through the Etruscans; and here we may note that the shapes of Roman musical instruments are Greek, but the words *subulus* and *lituus* are Etruscan. Then later there was direct contact between Rome and the Greeks and the gradual Roman conquest of Greek lands. So the techniques of Greek music passed wholesale to Rome, where musicians were generally Greek slaves or freedmen.

NOTES TO CHAPTER XII

1. Many attempts have been made to reconstruct the principal episodes in this poem with the help of the *Tabula Iliaca*, dating from Nero's period and now in the Capitol Museum in Rome; but the results are very inconclusive. (Pierre Grimal.)

2. In point of fact, Stesichorus was merely following a much more ancient tradition. There was an *Iliou Persis* by Arctinus of Miletus and *Nostoi* (in five cantos) by Hagias of Troezen. There were also *Nostoi* by Eumelus of Corinth, who lived in the eighth century. Useful information on all these problems is given in Jean Bérard's *La colonisation grecque de l'Italie méridionale et de la Sicile dans l'Antiquité* (second edition, Paris 1957), pp. 323 ff. (Pierre Grimal.)

3. Professor Pareti is much less appreciative of this poet than most recent scholars have been, and especially (as Professor Lesky protests) of his lively style and delicate irony. Erudite *par excellence*, Callimachus was none the less a writer of marked versatility and originality; and though much criticized by his contemporaries, he had important influence on several Roman poets, notably Catullus, Propertius, and Ovid.

4. There is a chronological objection to the theory advanced here by Professor Pareti. Livius Andronicus, who was still alive in 204, must have been a mere child when Tarentum was captured in 272. It is difficult to see where he could have obtained a thorough knowledge of Greek culture except at Rome, which suggests that Hellenism was already flourishing in that city before his arrival. His choice of the Odyssey as his theme may well have been due to political considerations, for at that time (about 220) Rome was taking an active interest in the Adriatic. (See my book *Siècle des Scipions*, Paris 1953.) Andronicus' *Odissia* has come down to us only in some scraps which it would be rash to take as the basis of an aesthetic judgement. The fact that this 'translation' was written in a national verse-form (known as 'Saturnian' because Saturn was the outstanding Italic god) implies the existence of an oral epic tradition, if not a written one, in which that metre was familiar. Andronicus was also Rome's earliest tragic poet (see below, p. 579) and must be considered under both these aspects if we are to appreciate his importance in Roman literary history. (Pierre Grimal.)

5. The epic writings of Naevius have been studied and annotated, on the strength of the few surviving fragments, by Marino Barchiesi in his *Nevio Epico*, Padua, 1962 (with the previous bibliography). (Pierre Grimal.)

6. Yet, as Professor A. Lesky points out, Virgil also showed consummate artistry by means of 'enjambement' (the carrying on of sense and sentences over the ends of lines).

7. This opinion which originated with K. J. Beloch, is now almost unanimously rejected. His *floruit* is placed between 548 and 540, and his birthplace at Megara in Greece, not in Sicily (despite Plato, *Laws*, 630a, who is taken up, for saying that Theognis was a Sicilian, by Didymus, *ap. schol. ad loc.*). Theognis was born at Megara in Greece, but may later have become a citizen of the Sicilian town of that name. As to the present state of opinion about Theognis, see R. Burn, *The Lyric Age of Greece* (London, 1960), pp. 247–58. (Pierre Grimal.)

8. For dithyramb see Part I, p. 278.

9. For *nomos* see Part I, p. 277.

10. With this section, and especially with what is said about Philetas, should be read the paragraphs on contemporary Alexandrian epic and *epyllion* (pp. 570 ff. above).

11. These pieces—the epigrams which make up the *Catalepton* (i.e., 'Light Pieces') and the parody-epic of the *Gnat* (*Culex*)—are included in the manuscripts among the works attributed to Virgil. But it is not certain whether he actually wrote them all—the *Culex* for instance, may be an imitation, written later. Some of the epigrams in the *Catalepton* are almost certainly by Virgil; they allude to incidents in his life which are confirmed by what may be regarded as independent sources. But this whole problem is still obscure. In any case, if Virgil did write some of the epigrams in the *Catalepton*, it must have been in his youth (before 44). (Pierre Grimal.)

12. This name, like those of Delia and Lesbia, was chosen with an intention we can easily divine. Lesbia was intended to recall the memory of Sappho (see above, p. 277); Delia and Cynthia belong to the sphere of Apollo, for they are two of the names of the goddess Artemis (born, as we know, on the island of Delos, at the foot of the Cynthe). Tradition has it that Delia's real name was Plania—and 'Delia' might be regarded as a Greek translation of that name (the Greek word *delos* means clear, evident, as does *planus* in Latin). So Tibullus was amusing himself with a play upon words. Cynthia's real name was Hostia, and in this case there is no connection between the two. It is therefore justifiable to assume that Tibullus was the first to choose the name Delia, and that Propertius, imitating him in spirit of courteous rivalry, decided to link his own mistress in name with the youngest and most beautiful of the goddesses. (Pierre Grimal.)

13. Ovid belongs to the second generation of poets of the Augustan Age. He has learnt from the experience of his immediate predecessors and we see a Roman tradition developing in his work, building up an output that includes all the principal aspects of poetry in that era. The epos is represented by the *Metamorphoses*, a tremendous cosmogony inspired by Pythagoras, the love-elegy by the *Amores* and the *Heroides*, Callimachus' elegiac style by the *Fasti*. Ovid also wrote a tragedy, *Medea*, which was famous in its day, but has now vanished.

Ovid is a prolific and skilful poet, adept at handling the verse-forms (hexameter and elegiac distich) already perfected by his forerunners; but many modern critics have censured him for this virtuosity, which enables him to produce a flow of banalities with no depth of feeling. His influence on mediaeval Europe was considerable. (Pierre Grimal.)

14. These three, the *Agamemnon*, the *Choephoroi*, and the *Eumenides* form the *Oresteia* (which the English poet Swinburne called 'the greatest achievement of the human spirit').

15. This doctrine was firmly rejected by Aeschylus (*Agamemnon*, pp. 757 ff.) in favour of the view that it was sin which brought suffering, and so further sin. See E. Fraenkel's *Commentary* (Oxford, 1950) on the passage, against the suggestion that there is any inconsistency with what Aeschylus says elsewhere.

16. This development had already started in the Hellenistic world. There, for instance, the actors had begun to be separated from the *orchestra*, where the chorus went through its part, and the chorus was contributing less and less to the action. There was in fact no break in continuity between the Hellenistic and the Roman theatre. When the audience was allowed to occupy what had formerly been the *orchestra*, it was because the latter was no longer needed; the *pulpitum* (the *proscenion* of the Greek theatre) had expanded, and now allowed for a greater number of performers, among whom were the *choreutes*—singers and musicians. (Pierre Grimal.)

17. The chorus was now limited to the singing of lyrics, almost wholly unconnected with the play.

18. Until recently we knew nothing of the work of Menander except a few fragments and the imitations made by Plautus and Terence. Now, however, it is being restored to us in part, thanks to certain papyri. The most celebrated and complete of these is the Papyrus Bodmer, containing an entire play, the *Dyscolus* (the *Man of Moods*), which was found in 1957 and has since been printed in many editions. This is a comedy, centred on Cnemon, an irascible old man, who has gone to live in the depths of the country, because his wife has left him owing to his bad temper. Cnemon has a daughter, and a young townsman falls in love with her—at the instigation of Pan, who wishes to reward the girl for her piety to the nymphs. Sostrates, the young man, is eager to marry the girl, but her surly father will let no one come near her. As a pretext for coming to the lonely spot where Cnemon lives, Sostrates disguises himself as a peasant and tills the soil. After various ups and downs, in the course of which the misanthropist falls into a well, undergoes a spectacular change of heart and is reconciled to his family, Sostrates is allowed to marry his love, and the whole thing concludes with a banquet, amid noisy festivities. (Pierre Grimal.)

19. Among them the *Menaechmi*, source for Shakespeare's *Comedy of Errors*, and the *Aulularia*, source for Molière's *L'Avare*.

20. For a more conservative view of Plautus' originality over plots and backgrounds, though not, of course, over outlook and style, see E. Fraenkel, *Plautinisches in Plautus* (Berlin, 1922).

21. Although Plautus and Terence both drew upon the same sources—the Greek poets of the New Comedy—there is a great difference between their works. The plots are similar, based on the same situations (the love of a young man for a young girl or a courtesan, the wiles of a slave who manages to get money from the youth's father, with which to buy the girl's favours or win her hand, etc.) and the same stock characters are introduced (the old father, the bright young spark, the astute slave, the grasping courtesan, etc.); but the spirit in which they are used is completely different. Between the generations of the two authors the spirit of Rome had altered, and with it the demands made upon comedy. Plautus is faithful to the old Roman moral standards; he regards love as a dangerous passion, not to be indulged in by a man who intends to remain a good citizen, to hold on to his property, etc., whereas Terence does not entirely blame young people for giving way to their feelings. Terence is the champion of human values—affection, freedom, indulgence, charity almost—as against the harsh, austere moral code of earlier times. Obsessed with the problem of children's upbringing (with which he deals in one of his comedies, *Adelphi*), he maintains that a father should not be too stern, but should make allowance for the feelings natural to youth, and be indulgent to them. This was a problem that Roman educationalists were continually discussing about 160 BC, when the influence of the Greek philosophers was rapidly increasing. The common talk was that Terence was merely the spokesman of the 'philhellene' group, led by his friends Scipio Aemilianus and Laelius, who were accused of helping him to write his plays. Generally speaking Terence's comedies were less popular than those of Plautus—the latter, though far less subtle, being more 'amusing' and closer to the common taste. (Pierre Grimal.)

22. Virgil composed his *Bucolics* approximately between 44 and 39 BC, when still under the influence of his Alexandrine models. He seems to have chosen this form because the others were already in use (the elegy by Cornelius Gallus, etc.), and in his desire to be original, he had to make the best of a style not yet adopted by any other Roman poet. But though Theocritus was his model, he at once began to make innovations. Having grown up in northern Italy amid the peaceful countryside of Cisalpine Gaul, he could not describe nature in the same terms as Theocritus, the Sicilian. So a first touch of originality comes with his choice of scene. Moreover the life he describes, the characters depicted in his little sketches, are those of the Roman countryside, not the Sicilian goatherds and shepherds. They have their own interests and adventures—those of the period, perhaps even, in some instances, those of the poet himself; for it is suggested that under the name of Meliboeus, Virgil was relating the tragedy he had experienced himself, when the Italian peasants were driven from their land in the year 42, to make way for the veterans of the triumvirs. It very soon becomes evident that these little poems are only Greek in the most superficial sense, that they are entirely Roman in content. Virgil is not a writer who can long remain absent from the contemporary scene, and his verses hold many echoes of current events. For example—though this interpretation is sometimes challenged—the *Fifth Eclogue*, which tells of the death and apotheosis of a mysterious Daphnis, is probably an allegorical account of the death and apotheosis of Caesar. And there is no doubt that the *Fourth Eclogue*, dedicated to Pollio, consul for the year 40, is a celebration of the treaty concluded at Brindisi between Octavian and Antony, and expresses the deep satisfaction of all Romans at the idea that peace was at last to be restored. This aspect of Virgil's bucolic poetry, which is quite alien to that style of writing in its original form, led him into increasingly close collaboration with Maecenas and the circle around Octavian. (Pierre Grimal.)

23. This long-standing interpretation must now be given up. For it has been pointed out that when Virgil embarked on his poem—certainly not later than the year 37, and more probably in 38—Octavian could not possibly have had an agricultural policy. Moreover, it is hard to look on the *Georgics* as a practical handbook of agriculture. Nor does Octavian seem to have adopted the agricultural policy thus attributed to him, even at a later date. In the reign of Augustus, the system of land tenure remained as it had been during the

republic, with *latifundia* worked chiefly by slave labour, etc. It was in response to his own feelings on the subject that Virgil began the *Georgics*. Just as he had formerly 'annexed' bucolic poetry, he now proceeded to take over Hesiod's form, that of *Works and Days*, which no one in Rome had imitated until then. At the beginning of Book III he boasts of this, comparing himself to a victorious general, laden with the spoils of a conquered country. In writing his *Bucolics*, he had been led to take an interest in the rustic 'plebs', and had even identified himself with them, in the two characters of the first *Bucolic*, Tityrus and Meliboeus. From this standpoint, the *Georgics* form a sequel to the previous work. Moreover, in its didactical aspect this poem is a successor to Lucretius, and contains many imitations of *De Rerum Natura*. Virgil helped to draw up the imperial ideology and to revive the old rustic traditions of Roman life; but he did it not to order, but merely in response to his own deep-seated urge. (Pierre Grimal.)

24. The *Fasti* are among the most valuable source-material for our knowledge of Roman religion; in this work, Ovid has recorded many details which would otherwise have been forgotten. He was, of course, a man of his own day, and reveals a certain scepticism with regard to the ancient beliefs. Besides, his attitude is that of the poet and artist, eager for picturesque features and fond of descriptions based on Alexandrine models. This may have led to accusations of irreverence, or at least have suggested that he was out of sympathy with the old Roman religion. But in point of fact that religion was no longer accepted in his day; it had already come to be regarded as a venerable but outworn survival from times gone by. Ovid is deeply religious, all the same, but after a more modern fashion. In Book I of the *Fasti*, for example, he gives the reasons why a particular victim was chosen for sacrifice to a particular divinity; but he lets it be clearly understood that his own conscience is revolted by these bloodthirsty ceremonies. Here his Pythagorean beliefs (see above p. 659, note 13) rise to the surface; holding them, he cannot approve of 'murder', not even the slaughter of animals. His own religious feeling has a spirituality which was absent from the ancient national rites. Hence his lack of sympathy for them— something not peculiar to him, but common to all progressive thinkers of his generation. (Pierre Grimal.)

25. No poem in Horace's 'satirical' compositions is actually entitled a 'satire'. The *Epodes* are called *Iambics* and, as already mentioned (see above, p. 573) were imitated from Archilochus. These are the only works by Horace which could be described as satires in the modern sense of the word—that is, as poems attacking a particular person and ridiculing his defects or his manners. These 'iambics', written by Horace from the beginning of his career as a poet (probably originating in 39 BC, with *Epode* XVI) and continuing until about the year 30, are essentially lyrical pieces. In the manuscript tradition, what are usually known as the *Satires* go by the title of *Sermones* (Conversations), which is reminiscent of the *Diatribai* (Discourses) published by the Greek philosophers. The two books of *Sermones* are, in fact, collections of moral discourses, true 'sermons' in which the poet exhorts men to wisdom and urges them to shake off their most serious vices, such as avarice, love of money, the taste for debauchery, etc. He is not mocking his contemporaries, but trying to teach them. The characters he brings in are either dead or fictitious and are only mentioned as illustrations of moral attitudes, for the purpose of edification.

    Horace's other works include two books of *Epistles* which follow the same lines as the *Sermones* but differ from them in being addressed to an individual instead of to the general public. These *Epistles* also deal with moral problems (particularly those of Book I) or literary questions (those of Book II). 'Satire' in the modern sense did not yet exist—it was to be originated by Juvenal. (Pierre Grimal.)

26. Herodotus' claim to be the father of history perhaps rests most on his honest (if ingenuous) search for truth and his determined investigations into the causes of men's actions.

27. The Athenian statesman Cimon (see above, p. 334) had a Thracian grandfather of this name.

28. But Thucydides was keenly conscious of the conflict between oligarchy and democracy: besides his account in Book VIII of the Athenian oligarchic revolution of 411 BC, see his classic analysis of the civil war at Corcyra (III, 82 ff.), which he claimed was typical of conditions in Greek cities during the Peloponnesian War. He himself, though an

ardent admirer of the democrat Pericles and of many of the ideals of Athenian democracy (see the 'Funeral Speech' in Book II), expresses approval of the moderate oligarchy established after the fall of the Four Hundred in 411 (VIII, 97), and was violently hostile to Cleon and other 'demagogues'.

29. Despite this final judgement, Professor Pareti's account of Thucydides must strike many as unsympathetic. Thucydides' chief hope (I, 22) was that his work would be useful for the understanding of future events similar to those in the war he describes, and countless readers have found that he achieved his end. His great virtues are candour, determination, and insight into political life; his methods of research were like those of the medical scientists of his day (and this not only in his careful account of the Athenian plague, II, 48 ff.); and although he was frank about his likes and dislikes (what he most admired was the energy and far-sightedness of a Themistocles, a Pericles, or at times an Alcibiades), he is tireless in his impartial debates on the great problems of politics.

30. For instance in his uncritical admiration for Sparta and its constitution.

31. Until we come to Polybius, none of the works mentioned in this or the following section has survived except for small fragments.

32. Unlike the other Achaean hostages, Polybius obtained permission to settle in Rome, where he lived in the household of Aemilius Paulus who had defeated Perseus. He was the guide and counsellor of the youthful Scipio Aemilianus, and has left us a lively picture of philhellene circles in Rome about the year 160 BC. (Pierre Grimal.)

33. Polybius was the first writer of a 'Universal History', i.e. one of all the Mediterranean lands. His work covered the period 220–145 BC and was in forty books, of which the first five (to 216 BC) survive entire, the rest in fragments.

34. Polybius, as Dr N. I. Golubtsova points out, was a well-to-do Greek. He admired those Roman politicians who were thought to be philhellene, and was intensely interested in those features of Rome's constitution and military organization which had brought it dominion over the whole Mediterranean within a few decades. But he fiercely attacked such earlier historians as he considered to be uncritically biased in Rome's favour, and late in his life he was suspicious of certain democratic forces at Rome.

35. For criticism of this view see O. Seel, *Die Praefatio des Trogus Pompeius* (Erlangen, 1955).

36. The first and last of these factors seem to have been the deciding ones, for the philhellenism of a section of Roman society did not take definite shape until two generations later, at the time of Rome's Eastern conquests. The two reasons reinforce each other: during the Second Punic War, when Hannibal, having concluded an alliance with Philip of Macedon, was trying to stir up Greek opinion against Rome and turn the armies of the Eastern kingdoms against his own enemies, it was very important for the Romans to make a counter-attack. That was no doubt why the senate decided to send an embassy to Delphi, a lively diplomatic centre where the sacred deputations met together and anything said would be carried far and wide. It was hoped that a history of Rome written in Greek would convince the Greek peoples that the Romans were sincere, calling attention to their *fides* and their liberal policy, which had so often supported the Greek cause during the struggle between the Samnites and the Greek colonies in southern Italy. This history, written by Fabius Pictor, was primarily a diplomatic instrument. It would have been pointless to write it in Latin, where the prose style was still immature—and the Romans, long accustomed to use the Greek language, were perfectly aware of its superiority. The earliest Roman historians were thus trained in the Greek school, and it was the example of Greek prose that first impelled them to devise a more artistic vehicle of expression. (Pierre Grimal.)

37. Cato also deserves to be called 'the father of Latin prose' because of another book, likewise of great importance—his treatise *On Agriculture*, which has come down to us and draws a very interesting picture of the Roman rural economy at the beginning of the second century BC. Cato wrote it in imitation of the treatise written in Punic by Mago, of Carthage, because he wanted to give the Romans the benefit of foreign experience. He hoped thus to consolidate the rural, agricultural aspect of Roman society and economic life; for this he regarded as urgent in view of the increase in personal riches and the

expansion of trade resulting from Rome's defeat of Carthage, which brought it into direct contact with the great trading network of the Hellenistic world. Cato was seeking to prove that agriculture could be a source of wealth, that the good *pater familias* who wished to maintain a proper train of life had no need to launch into trade with far-off places (senators were prohibited by law from doing so). *De Agricultura* is written in a language already well established, but with no literary flourishes; in addition to observations concerning crops, and the prayers which should be offered to the gods in order to ensure good harvests, it contains culinary recipes and even old wives' remedies. In the reign of Augustus, Varro was to write three books of *Res Rusticae*, with the same intention as Cato; and a comparison of the two works shows that in the intervening century and a half, Roman agriculture had made considerable progress. (Pierre Grimal.)

38. This was a writer who saw things from the Carthaginian angle.

39. Although the authenticity of these works of Antiphon has been much disputed.

40. Andocides was exiled as a member of, and informer about, the aristocratic gang around Alcibiades who were supposed to have mutilated the Hermae in 415 BC.

41. These political tracts are the most important of Isocrates' surviving works. Already in 380 he wrote the *Panegyricus*, urging Athens and Sparta to compose their quarrels and jointly lead a crusade against Persia; in 368 he appealed similarly to Dionysius I (Letter I), and in 356 to the king of Sparta; finally in 346, with the *Philippus*, he turned to Philip of Macedon, to whom he wrote a congratulatory letter on the victory of Chaeronea, in the last year of his life. Significant in a different way are the *Areopagiticus* (c. 355), glorifying the times of Solon and Cleisthenes in contrast with the Athenian democracy of his own days, and the *Panathenaicus* (c. 340), also a survey of Athens' past greatness. But though Isocrates has received praise for a panhellenism which looked beyond the horizons of the single city-state, it is perhaps not surprising that his somewhat academic rhetoric failed to inspire his contemporaries: for pungent criticism see W. Jaeger, *Demosthenes* (Cambridge, 1938), pp. 17–18. His ideas, as well as his style, owed much to the sophist Gorgias (above, p. 554, note 9): his systematic rhetorical instruction was pregnant with influence on the future.

42. See above, pp. 600 ff.

43. Many characteristic fragments of Cato's speeches have been preserved.

44. The problem of the teaching of rhetoric in Rome, and of the attempts made by conservative Romans to prevent professors of eloquence from setting up as teachers, is a somewhat complex one. Put briefly, the situation was that while no one dreamt of forbidding the Greek rhetoricians to teach young Romans the Greek style of eloquence, many senators thought it dangerous to apply this teaching to the Latin language. Hence, though schools of Greek rhetoric could be opened in Rome, Latin rhetoricians were expelled from the city. The objections raised by the conservatives were the same that had induced Plato to pronounce against rhetoric, on the grounds that it might make the worse appear the better cause, and that those who could make use of it gained dangerous power over men's minds. Cicero, at the beginning of the first century BC, had to fight against prejudice, and that was no doubt one of his reasons for declaring that orators must go through a moral and intellectual training before beginning to practise rhetoric. (Pierre Grimal.)

45. This opinion of Cicero, though backed by tradition, has no foundation in fact. To contrast Cicero's political behaviour with that of Caesar and Pompey is really to compare two completely different things. Caesar, Pompey, and Crassus were trying to deflect the Roman political machinery for their own benefit, whereas Cicero wished to improve the system, for the benefit of a whole social class, that of the knights, an order which was not confined to Rome itself, but spread all over Italy. The former were ambitious men, straining every nerve to consolidate their personal authority, the latter a genuine reformer trying to apply new principles—those for which he pleaded towards the end of his life in his treatise *De Re Publica* (of which fairly ample portions have survived).

Cicero tried to combine action with reflection. Before his time, ideological speculation had been left to the Greek thinkers, more especially to the philosophers, while the Romans concentrated their ambition on military and political activities. Cicero pursued the habitual career in the magistracy (*cursus honorum*) and used his natural eloquence to win him a very prominent position in the state; but at the same time he made no secret of his intention to take that position as a starting-point for practising the theories he had formulated during his philosophical studies.

Cicero had been interested in philosophy ever since he visited Athens as a young man, and declared repeatedly that he would have devoted himself exclusively to the subject had he not been prevented by a life of action. Whenever he had leisure to do so—for instance, when Caesar's *coup d'état* and the defeat of the Republicans reduced him to enforced idleness—he wrote a philosophical treatise. Cicero refused to join any one school. This independence of mind had been inculcated in him by his masters when he was studying at the New Academy at Athens. Most important of all, he realized sooner than anyone else that the discussions of the Greek philosophers, who led a life of study, could not meet the needs of the Romans, who had the practical task of governing the world they had conquered. He did not feel himself called upon to acquaint the Romans with Greek philosophy (they all read Greek and spoke it fluently), so much as to compare Greek ideas, patiently, point by point, with Roman practice. This is what he proceeded to do, not only in treatises such as *De Natura Deorum* and *De Divinatione* but also in his *Tusculans* and *De Finibus*, dialogues in which Roman patricians frankly discuss the traditional views propounded by the different schools. These discussions tend towards a compromise between the Greek and Roman worlds, and instead of speaking of Cicero's 'eclecticism' it would be more accurate to describe this as the birth of a new philosophy, thanks to a revision of the accepted views.

As a writer on the theory of eloquence, and as an orator, Cicero was equally scrupulous in the defence of philosophy, holding virtuosity in speech to be of less importance than the search for truth and the proclamation of it, in all its forms. As a disciple of the Academicians he knew that the concept of truth is multiple, that there is a form of truth in action which can often be equated with probability; and this seems to be the doctrine he strove to put into practice. (See A. Michel, *Rhétorique et Philosophie chez Cicéron*, Paris, 1960.) (Pierre Grimal.)

46. Despite Quintilian's authority the authenticity of this *Invective* is much disputed.

47. The dependence of Maurya art on Achaemenid art appears here to be exaggerated: Persian influence, strong as it was, did not exclude all originality in the little that is known to us and, shortly after the Maurya period, Buddhist Suṅga art developed a vigorous originality.

48. Professor Ch. Th. Saricakis calls attention to the influence exercised by Greek art on India, citing the fundamental work of W. W. Tarn, *The Greeks in Bactria and in India* (Cambridge, 1938), pp. 393 ff.

49. Allegedly a man who aspired to a place in history, even at the cost of doing an infamous act.

50. The normal construction of a Greek theatre allowed for a more than semicircular auditorium (Fig. 6), with a circular space (*orchestra*) inside this for the chorus, side passages (*parodoi*) at each end of the auditorium, and on the other side of these the line of the stage (*scenē*, originally of wood). See D. S. Robertson, *Greek and Roman Architecture* (second edition, 1943), p. 164.

51. But see above, p. 508, note 13. The writers there cited would date the earliest Roman *aes* to the early third rather than to the fourth century.

52. Professor Pareti's views on the Celtic invasion are more fully set out in Part I, Chapters I and II.

53. The Roman theatre, in contrast to the Greek (see above, note 51), had a semicircular auditorium (*cavea*) (Fig. 7). The stage was a wide raised platform, with a wall behind it as the *cavea*: this wall was normally an elaborate structure with columns, niches, and statues.

PART THREE

MANKIND FROM THE BEGINNING OF THE CHRISTIAN ERA TO ABOUT AD 500

CHAPTER XIII

HISTORICAL BACKGROUND: FROM THE BEGINNING OF THE CHRISTIAN ERA TO *c.* AD 500

I. CENTRAL ASIA

THE profound social and political convulsions in China at the end of the Earlier Han dynasty inevitably made their repercussions felt beyond the northern and western frontiers. From AD 16, during Wang Mang's short usurpation, the Protectorate of the Western Countries was abandoned by Chinese troops and officials. The Eastern Hsiung-nu automatically regained their independence; they tried to extend their authority over the most easterly oases in central Asia, and they resumed their unceasing raids on the Chinese frontier. But their military strength was now only a memory of the past. The restored Han dynasty, though it confined military operations to the indispensable minimum, found no difficulty in opposing the renewed danger by means of its cunning diplomacy. In AD 48 eight Hsiung-nu clans submitted to China, and were settled as *foederati* (to use a Roman term) on the borders of Kansu and Shensi, as the Southern Hsiung-nu. Against the remainder (the Northern Hsiung-nu) the Chinese invoked the aid of the Hsien-pei, a proto-Mongol people of western Manchuria. The brief but victorious Chinese campaigns in the Gobi desert (89–91), together with the disaster inflicted on the Hsiung-nu by the Hsien-pei in 93, broke their power for war. The old empire of Mao-tun was brought to an end by the Hsien-pei in 155.

When China reconquered the Tarim basin through the efforts of Pan Ch'ao (73–102), it regained control of the 'cross-roads' of Asia, dominating the caravan routes between East and West and to some extent also those by which Siberian gold came down into India. The political results were remarkable, but still more so the effects upon commerce and art. For practically the whole of the second century the Protectorate General of the Western Countries knit this area together into an administrative structure which was flexible, but sufficiently tight; and this was the Golden Age of the great trade along the silk-route between Lo-yang and Rome.

The period of most active intercourse of all kinds across the steppes and the desert began to flag about AD 200. China was exhausted, and withdrew within its frontiers. It became immersed in the internal struggles which ended by splitting it apart; and this, combined with the simultaneous decay of the Roman empire, caused a slackening in the caravan traffic in the

Tarim basin. The situation in the Gobi desert was not very different, since the Hsien-pei were unable to profit from the disintegration of the Chinese empire. A tribal confederation with scanty capacity for political organization, they could not take up the tradition of the great Hsiung-nu rulers, and their activity spent itself in the territory immediately surrounding them. Weak attempts to penetrate into Chinese territory (156–177) were easily beaten back, and they kept relatively quiet even during the critical period of the Three Kingdoms (220–280). In the second decade of the fourth century the Chinese barrier collapsed; but even then the Hsien-pei showed neither skill in exploiting the situation nor desire to do so. The first people to profit were the Hsiung-nu clans which had been for some time established inside the frontier; and when in the course of the fourth century the Hsien-pei took a part in dividing the spoils, the initiative came from enterprising single clans like the Mu-jung rather than from the tribal confederation. Only when a new people, the Juan-juan, made their appearance (402), did the Steppe kingdom assume a dynamic nature once more.

2. CHINA TO AD 589

The usurper Wang Mang (AD 9–23) plunged headlong into a whole series of agrarian, economic, fiscal, and administrative reforms. His aim was partly to increase the imperial revenue, partly to make the state conform in all respects to a fictitious ideal of classical antiquity, an ideal invented by the *literati* of his time and projected back into the past. Almost every aspect of public life was caught in this storm of reorganization: there was redistribution of land and a limit to the size of estates; creation of state monopolies; revision of the administrative divisions; and reforms in the state cult, in weights and measures, and in coinage. This frantic activity ended by antagonizing every class in society and shaking the very foundations of the state; at the same time China's possessions in central Asia were lost, and the Hsiung-nu threat had reappeared. The social and economic upheaval eventually provoked a rising of the peasants of the Great Plain. This is the so-called revolt of the Red Eyebrows, which is much better known than that of Ch'ên Shêng at the end of the third century BC. These movements are found scattered throughout Chinese history; though generally put down with bloodshed, they are the most notable feature of the decline of the principal Chinese dynasties and herald their falls. All these rebellions fit into a certain pattern: they break out in the overpopulated territory of western Shantung, southern Hopei, and north-western Honan; and their immediate cause is activity by secret societies with a Taoist and magico-religious background. The revolt of the Red Eyebrows was ably exploited by legitimist circles, who succeeded first in bringing about a Han restoration and then in putting down the revolt itself.

The new dynasty of the Eastern (or Later) Han abandoned Ch'ang-an, built by the Western Han, and established themselves at Lo-yang in Honan.

Their policy was one of salutary retrenchment, of peace and reconstruction. At first they gave up any ambition to reconquer the imperial positions which had been lost. Later, when the political and social situation had been stabilized and the wounds of the civil war had been healed and forgotten, the urge to the West reappeared. But this time there was no considered and deliberate policy on the part of the imperial government: the initiative, and the strength of will behind it, were in the hands of the general Pan Ch'ao, the greatest proconsul China had ever sent to its colonial possessions. His labours lasted nearly thirty years (73–102), during which, with scanty means and without any backing from his government, he reconstructed the Chinese empire in central Asia. It was a long and wearying task, but its results were solid enough to cope with the great rebellion which followed Pan Ch'ao's recall and death, and to guarantee China's control of the silk-route practically throughout the second century.

Soon after the middle of the first century occurred the introduction of Buddhism, an event which was destined to have profound effects on the spirit of China and its neighbours. But it spread slowly, the Buddhist communities being at first confined to the lowest classes in the population. Only in the course of the second century were they fully organized by missionaries from India and central Asia.

Very soon the second Han dynasty declined like its predecessors. Once again the malignant disease spread from the feminine milieu of the court; at first from the families of the emperors' wives, and then from the eunuchs of the harem. The court struggle centred on the factions of the eunuchs and of the officials and *literati*, while effective power slipped gradually into the hands of the army commanders in the provinces, who alone possessed effective forces. The familiar features of the dynasty's fall now reappeared with the peasant revolt of the Yellow Turbans (184). This was put down, after a short but terrible war, by a supreme effort of all the political forces of the day— eunuchs, *literati*, army officers—who formed a temporary coalition in the face of social revolution. But then the struggle was transferred to the various army commanders. In 190 power fell into the hands of a rough and violent dictator named Tung Cho. He was murdered in 193, and the conflict now centred round two rivals, neither of whom could obtain decisive mastery, the general Ts'ao Ts'ao and the pretender Liu Pei, a distant cousin of the imperial house of Han. In 220 Ts'ao Ts'ao's son deposed the Han and proclaimed the Wei dynasty, with its capital at Lo-yang.

But Liu Pei took similar action: he established himself in Szechwan, where he founded the Shu Han dynasty. Meanwhile Sun Ch'üan, governor of the South (a region which was still semi-colonial and scantily populated), also had himself proclaimed emperor, founding the Wu dynasty with the capital at Chien-k'ang, the modern Nanking. This was the period of the Three States (*san-kuo*; 220–280), a period of great adventures and warlike deeds. (Map X.) It was the favourite setting for the Chinese novel writers a thousand

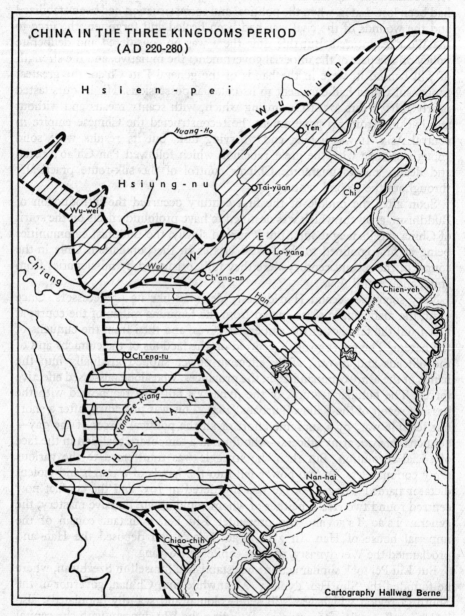

CHINA IN THE THREE KINGDOMS PERIOD
(A D 220-280)

Hsien-pei

Wu-huan

Huang-Ho

Hsiung-nu

Yen

Tai-yüan

Chi

Wu-wei

Ch'iang

Wei

E

W

Lo-yang

Ch'ang-an

Han

Chien-yeh

Yangtze-Kiang

Ch'eng-tu

W

U

Yangtze-Kiang

S H U

Nan-hai

Chiao-chih

Cartography Hallwag Berne

MAP X

years later, but it was also a period of great suffering for China. It saw marked shifts of population: the Chinese migration southward was accelerated, with the support of the new independent government of the South; and on the northern frontiers numerous Hsiung-nu clans came to settle, being brought in as auxiliaries by Ts'ao Ts'ao. In Wei, the strongest of the three states, all power passed into the hands of the Ssŭ-ma family after 239; in 263 this family put an end to the kingdom of Shu Han; and in 265 it ascended the imperial throne as the Chin dynasty. Its conquest of the Wu kingdom in 280 brought a temporary unification of China, under a dynasty remarkably barren in personalities and subject to incurable intestine quarrels.

After this reunification the imperial army was disbanded as a measure of economy. So the real masters of the state were the imperial princes, governors of provinces, and commanders of provincial armies, who contended for the guardianship of the fainéant emperors. A further factor of weakness was the antiquated and disorganized administrative system. In fact the one young and active force lay in the 'federate' Hsiung-nu clans who lived in northern Shensi and Shansi: the aristocracy which governed them was still semi-nomadic, but some of its members had received a cultural and administrative training in the 'School of Young Nobles' (kuo-tsu-hsüeh) at Lo-yang and were therefore strongly influenced by Chinese civilization. Confronted with the obvious impotence of the Chin dynasty, some of these nobles conceived the idea of seizing the imperial crown. In 304 their chief Liu Yüan united the five tribes of the Southern Hsiung-nu into a single state under the name of Han, in an attempt to exploit the glorious memories of the now extinct dynasty. After his early death his son Liu Ts'ung (311–318) realized his father's political programme by seizing Lo-yang in 311 and Ch'ang-an in 317; on both occasions a Chin emperor fell a prisoner to the rebels. But an imperial prince kept up resistance, proclaiming himself emperor at Chien-k'ang, and Chinese unity was once more smashed.

In the period 317–589 China developed along two divergent lines. In the North we find a series of ephemeral states, founded either by barbarian tribes or by individual adventurers of barbarian origin. There was fragmentation of a kaleidoscopic kind and a continuous change of rulers, the only exceptions being Fu Chien's attempt at unification in the fourth century and the more prolonged rule (439–534) by the united empire of the proto-Turkish Tabġač. Beneath this highly disturbed political surface there developed and flourished a civilization which was fundamentally Chinese, though deeply imbued with alien elements of Western origin. The ruling classes were foreigners, and only at the end of the period did the old Confucian bureaucracy succeed in recovering control of the country. In the South, on the other hand, the imperial tradition was preserved, in a single state governed by five successive dynasties all purely Chinese. Culture remained entirely Chinese, and so did the governing class; some of its members were of local origin, but the majority were immigrants from the North. This Southern state brings

Byzantium irresistibly into one's mind: there was the same refinement of manners, the same cold contempt for the 'barbarians', the same proud traditions in administration; and both civilizations underwent a very gradual decadence which in the early stages was accompanied by a remarkable resilience. A feature common to both North and South is the progressive spread of Buddhism. It penetrated the ruling classes and the court in the South; and for political reasons it received strong support from the government and was for some time regarded as a state religion by the barbarians in the North.

The political history both of the North and of the South in this period is complicated. We need to draw attention only to the essential points.

In the North the Hsiung-nu (the Han dynasty, afterwards called Early and Late Chao) were incapable of building a solid state and eventually destroyed one another in a crescendo of savagery and atrocities. Torn by internecine wars and the risings of exasperated peasants the dynasty was exterminated. For a brief time a Hsien-pei family called Mu-jung seemed to have gained the ascendancy from its basis in the North-East; but a few years later the whole of the North fell under the rule of Fu Chien (357–385). He was a Ti (proto-Tibetan) adventurer, kind and generous, a good general but an inept statesman. His empire extended its influence as far as central Asia; but the administration of this hastily-built and heterogeneous state was inefficient; and when a grandiose attempt to conquer the South came to grief in 383 the whole structure collapsed like a house of cards.

The ensuing period saw fragmentation and complete anarchy: Mu-jung, Ti, and Ch'iang (all proto-Tibetans) together with the Hsien-pei and Hsiung-nu, contended with varying fortunes for supremacy in north China, while the Juan-juan nomads were pressing in from the Gobi desert, and the Chinese of the South were attempting to regain their lost capitals. Amid this chaos there gradually came into prominence the proto-Turkish Tabġač, who for some time had ruled over a small state on the steppe on the northern frontiers of Shansi. In 398 they dealt a mortal blow to the Mu-jung. They held the Juan-juan and the southern Chinese in check, and from 418 they gradually unified the North, completing the process in 439.

The Tabġač (as a Chinese dynasty known as Wei) now governed the Northern area for a century; they engaged in many wars with the Southern dynasties, but they never made a serious attempt to conquer the South, perhaps because they remembered the disaster of Fu Chien. They protected Buddhism and fostered the arts: above all they helped to introduce the Western artistic influence which dominates the magnificent sculptures of Yün-kang and Lung-men. This dynasty, which imposed a firm rule on the country, took a long time to forget their own nomad origins, and kept the Turkish aristocracy in the key positions of government. But eventually, when the capital was transferred from northern Shansi to Lo-yang in 494, and when Tabġač language and customs were prohibited at court, they entered frankly upon the path of Sinization. The result was a reaction from the conservative section of the proto-Turkish nobility and a complicated series of internal struggles with a variety of factors at work. The rivalry between the conservatives and the supporters of Chinese culture was resolved in 534 when the state fell apart into two sections: the party leaders, under the nominal cover of two fainéant emperors, took up their headquarters, the one at Yeh in Honan, the other at Ch'ang-an. The Eastern Wei, as the state erected by Kao Huan, leader of the pro-Chinese faction, was called, was the weaker of the two. The last Wei emperors were deposed by Kao Huan's descendants, but the dynasty created by the latter (northern Ch'i, 550–577) was eventually suppressed by the sister kingdom. In the north-west the Yü-wen family, the effective rulers of the western Wei empire, attempted to restore the Tabġač national state, but it was too late, since tribal unity of the Tabġač had by now broken down, and even when the Yü-wen themselves mounted the throne (northern Chou, 557–581), the objective could not be achieved. Although in 577 they succeeded in unifying the North, their dynasty was deposed only four years later by one of their ministers, Yang Chien, a typical bureaucrat of pure Chinese stock, who founded the Sui dynasty. In 589 the new dynasty put an end to the Southern empire, and finally restored Chinese unity after a break lasting more than two centuries and a half.

In the South the Chin, though increasingly feeble and incompetent, maintained themselves from 318 to 420. They owed their survival to the deeply-felt, though undeserved, devotion shown them by their officials and army leaders, who were ready to give their blood for an unworthy dynasty. On two occasions (356 and 416) their armies took the offensive northwards; great, though ephemeral, victories were won, and Lo-yang was for a time reoccupied. It was indeed remarkable what powers of revival still lay hidden in the South. Liu Yü, the victorious general of 416, deposed the Chin and founded the Sung dynasty (420–479), which succeeded in checking the threatening pressure of the Tabġač and under which south China made good progress in the economic field: it was at this time that there were laid the foundations of the fortune of Canton, based on the sea-borne trade with south Asia. The southern Ch'i (479–502) were compelled to give place to a branch of their own family, the Liang (502–555), under whose rule the South enjoyed forty years of peace and prosperity, with Buddhism achieving remarkable advances. But the Liang collapsed in a tremendous civil war, in which the western Wei intervened. The Southern empire emerged from this with considerable loss of territory and of inner strength; the blow had been a mortal one. The last of its dynasties, the Ch'ên (555–589), was able only to prolong the agony of a state which had outlived its own vitality. The historical and practical justification for the existence of a Chinese national state in the South disappeared once the North had been unified by a Chinese dynasty. And when in 589 the Sui forces marched on Chien-k'ang they met with no resistance; the Southern bureaucracy went over to their brethren in the North, and Chinese unity was re-established without a blow being struck.

3. KOREA

Northern Korea (Chin. 'Chao-hsien', Korean 'Chosŏn') had been conquered by the Chinese in 108 BC. It was organized into four districts, and over a period of centuries it felt the influence of Chinese culture, which left an indelible mark upon the country. The excavations at Lo-lang (Korean 'Naknang') have shown how this Chinese province played a full part in the artistic achievement of the Han homeland. At the end of the first century AD Chinese domination was limited to the north-west coast, but in that one area it lasted down to the fourth century. The remainder of Korea, namely the southern section, had for long been divided between three tribal confederacies, the so-called Three Hab. The population here differed in many respects from that of the North: their culture was allied rather to the primitive culture of the south Asiatic countries, although later they too came under the influence of China. In 57 BC (according to the traditional chronology) there arose among them the nucleus of the state of Silla, which was destined to last as late as 935. A little later, in the inaccessible territories of the north-east, was formed the small kingdom of Koguryŏ, which lasted down to 668 and gave its name to the country. Its zenith was reached in the fifth century, when the northern part of the peninsula became united under the Koguryŏ kings, all trace of Chinese domination having by now vanished. Buddhism made its first appearance in 372, and a few years later it also reached the south.

4. JAPAN

In the first centuries of our era Japan slowly emerges from the darkness of prehistory. According to tradition the date of the empire's foundation is 660 BC, when the Emperor Jimmu, who came from the southern part of Kyūshū, established himself in Yamato near Ōsaka. The fact, but above all the date, cannot stand up to criticism. Yet the references to Japan in contemporary dynastic chronicles of China are consistent enough to allow the history of this period to be reconstructed in broad outline. In the first century BC the country appears to have been divided into numerous independent principalities (there were more than 100), one of which in AD 57 received an official seal from the Chinese emperor. There were further exchanges of ambassadors in 239 and 247. In this period the states seem to have been reduced to about thirty in number, under the suzerainty of Yamato (perhaps in the island of Kyūshū), which was governed by a queen. After 269 relations with China ceased, but they were resumed in 421, when Japan appears already united into a single state under the dynasty which rules even today. It seems that the unification should be placed in the first half of the fourth century, and that it was due to Yamato princes, who moved from Kyūshū to Hondō, although they preserved the original name of their state. It could be that one of these princes bore the name of Jimmu Tennō, which the later chronicles (*Kojiki* and *Nihongi*) pushed back a millennium in the past.

To this period probably go back the most important characteristics which are always attributed to the dynasty in later times: its descent from Amaterasu, goddess of the sun, and the three royal symbols—the mirror, the sword, and the jewel. However that may be, the Korean chronicles tell us that in 369 Japan was strong enough to intervene in the affairs of Korea: the expedition then sent seems likely to be the one attributed by Japanese sources to the Empress Jingo Kogo. Through this action a Japanese protectorate was created over the little territory of Mimana (around modern Pusan), and it lasted down to 562.

Across Korea the cultural, social, and religious ideas of the continent began gradually to reach the archipelago. It was probably in the fifth century that the difficult task was first undertaken of adapting Chinese script to a language which was totally different from Chinese. In the fifth century the first Buddhist missionaries began to arrive, and the new religion set foot for the first time in the Japanese empire, which at that time comprised only Kyūshū, Shikoku, and the southern part of Hondō. Very soon Buddhism became the most passionately debated question of the day: it was both touchstone and excuse for the struggles among the great noble houses which were contending for supremacy at court (the Soga, Nakatomi, and Mononobe). In 538 a relic was sent to the capital by the Korean king of Paikche, and from that moment begins the official history of Japanese Buddhism. The obverse of the story is the beginning, slow at first but always gathering momentum, of the movement which later came to a head in the reforms of Shōtoku Taishi and those of the Taikwa period.

5. INDIA

In the first decades of our era the history of northern India seems to have been dominated by movements of 'barbarians'. As a matter of fact, these peoples arrived in India after having undergone a more or less thorough process of Iranization, and this resulted in an increase of the political and cultural influence of Iran. The case of the Śaka is typical; and even more direct was the Iranian influence exercised by the Parthians, whose invasion of India presumably took place in the first years of our era, and was promoted not by the Arsacids but by the turbulent nobility of the frontier districts. The best known of these sovereigns in India is the Gu(n)duvhara of inscriptions, called Gondophernes in the legend of St Thomas the Apostle, whose martyrdom is said to have taken place in this king's reign. The one result of the Parthian inroad was to transform the Śaka aristocracy into an anarchic feudal system run by Śaka and Parthians combined: this extended its influence to Madhya Pradesh and Gujarat. Moreover when the Śaka and Parthians of the Indus valley came under the Kuṣāṇa rule, the Śaka Ksatrapas

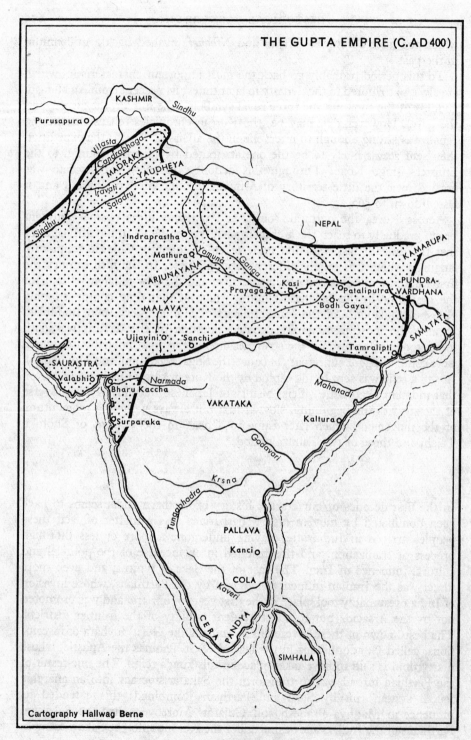

THE GUPTA EMPIRE (C. AD 400)

KASHMIR
Sindhu
Purusapura
Vitasta
Candrabhaga
MADRAKA
Iravati
Satadru
Sindhu
YAUDHEYA
NEPAL
KAMARUPA
Indraprastha
Mathura
Yamuna
Ganga
ARJUNAYANA
Kasi
Prayaga
Pataliputra
PUNDRA-VARDHANA
MALAVA
Bodh Gaya
SAMATATA
Ujjayini
Sanchi
Tamralipti
SAURASTRA
Valabhi
Narmada
Mahanadi
Bharu Kaccha
VAKATAKA
Surparaka
Kaltura
Godavari
Krsna
Tungabhadra
PALLAVA
Kanci
COLA
Kaveri
CERA
PANDYA
SIMHALA

Cartography Hallwag Berne

MAP XI

of Malwa maintained their independence for three centuries; although they were foreigners, they helped to establish Sanskrit as the secular literary language in India. The Kṣatrapa of Ujjain were conquered by the Guptas round about 400.

Meanwhile the Kuṣāṇa, one of the five principalities set up by the Yüeh-chih in Bactria, were acquiring importance under their leader Kujula Kadphises. He not only unified his own people, but conquered Afghanistan and brought to an end the last surviving Greek kingdom in India, that of Hermaeus (c. AD 20).[1] His son Wema Kadphises extended Kuṣāṇa rule all over the Indus basin and as far as the western basin of the Ganges. The two Kadphises were succeeded, probably after some interval, by Kaniṣka, the greatest of the Kuṣāṇa. The question of his date is one of the most complicated, important, and hotly debated in Indian history. Here we can do no more than mention the two main schools that hold the field: one makes him the founder of the so-called Saka era starting in AD 78, the other puts his accession at a date (variously stated by different authors) in the second quarter of the second century. Whichever view one takes, it is clear that the kingdom of the Kuṣāṇa preserved its power for about a century after Kaniṣka's accession. It was a land complex which faced two ways and had two sorts of interest, since it held sway in both Transoxiana and India. By its nature, therefore, it was destined to become a channel for the passage of cultural and religious ideas between India, Iran, and central Asia. In its international atmosphere the Indo-Hellenistic and Indo-Roman art of Gandhāra could develop; Indian deities alternate with Iranian and Greek on the coins; trade flourished; and along the caravan routes and through the colonies of Indian traders in the Tarim basin, Buddhism penetrated into central Asia, and from there on into China, Korea, and Japan. In India the Kuṣāṇa empire seems to have been gradually confined to the Punjab; in the third century the kingdom lost its territories across the Oxus and consequently its power to pursue further its cultural mission. Nevertheless under various dynasties (Kidāra, Little Kuṣāṇa) it continued to perform the task of guarding the frontier against Iran.

The Sassanids made a brief appearance on this frontier in the third century, but their empire seems never to have crossed the limits of present-day Afghanistan, where a peculiar Irano-Buddhist form of art took shape. But in the fifth century the defences on the Indian frontier were broken down by the invasion of the Hephthalites (the Hūna of Indian texts). These barbarians conquered the Afghan country, and then poured into India. Initially they were checked by the Guptas, but they resumed their attack; and about 500 their king Toramāṇa held a considerable dominion in north-west India. It was short-lived, being overcome after a few years by an Indian counter-attack. But the great religious and cultural centres of the north-west, particularly those in present-day Afghanistan, never recovered from the Hephthalite ravages.

After Kuṣāṇa supremacy had declined the Ganges valley remained divided among obscure local dynasties and the surviving aristocratic republics; the latter still existed in Rajasthan and the Punjab, but were beginning to disappear at the end of this period. Then for a time Magadha and Pāṭaliputra resumed their position as a factor of unity in Indian history. Chandragupta I founded the Gupta dynasty (320–c. 550), which achieved its greatest territorial expansion under Samudragupta (c. 335–375) and Chandragupta II (375–414). (Map XI.) Yet the Gupta empire was not remotely comparable with that of the Mauryas: it was confined to northern India, and although it stretched from sea to sea it did not include most of the Indus basin. South of the Vindhya mountains it bordered with the solid kingdom of the Vākāṭaka, which had emerged from the ruins of the Andhra régime and which preserved its independence throughout, keeping on good terms with its larger neighbour to the north. Under the Guptas Indian culture reached its full development and its climax; this is undoubtedly the classic period of Hindu India. Western influences were either eliminated or absorbed; and literature, art, and the various religions achieved a state of balance and internal harmony such as was never surpassed or even equalled in later times. But this Augustan age was short. Skandagupta (455–467) succeeded in repelling the first onslaught of the Hephthalites, but this victorious resistance cost the empire dear. It was weakened to the point of exhaustion, and after a gradual decline it dissolved in the first decades of the sixth century. In its last days the centre was moved towards Madhya Pradesh; and Pāṭaliputra in consequence ceased for all time to be the moral capital of northern India.

In the centre of the peninsula the kingdom of the Sātāvahana, founded at the end of the previous period in the region of Nasik, was for a time pushed south-eastwards by the expansion of the Śaka from Malwa. It was at this time that the Telugu-speaking districts on the east coast were conquered and annexed. The Sātavāhana or Andhra, as they are also called, reached their zenith under Gautamīputra Sātakarṇi (c. 106–130), when they took their revenge on the Śaka and reoccupied their original territory in the north-western Deccan.

The Sātavāhana kingdom, though it dissolved and finally disappeared about 220–230, had been a centre from which Aryan culture expanded among the Dravida of the Deccan. Literary work in Prakrit was strongly encouraged at the Andhra court.

In the south in the first century AD the strongest of the three traditional kingdoms was that of the Cola; then the hegemony passed to the Pāṇḍya. But in these centuries the history of the south is very obscure, and is almost exclusively literary. We know that trade with the Roman empire had assumed great importance in the economic life of the area, and perhaps also influenced artistic taste. Finds at the trading station excavated at Virapattanam (also called Arikamedu; probably the Poducē of Ptolemy) give us a most vivid picture of this traffic.

To the north-east of the Three Kingdoms, in the hinterland of modern Madras, there came into being in the third century the Pallava kingdom at whose capital (Kañcī), Sanskrit literature, Buddhism, and Jainism flourished vigorously. In comparison with the untainted Dravidian culture[2] found in the Three Kingdoms of the far south, the Pallava state became the main centre through which Aryan outlook and culture spread to the foot of the peninsula.

The history of Ceylon in this period has mainly a local interest. It was only later that the island played an all-important role in the diffusion of Buddhist ideas in south-east Asia. During the first centuries AD Ceylon retained its independence, and developed its own civilization without more than relatively limited contact with India. For the time being attempts at infiltration, both warlike and peaceful, by the Tamils of the mainland were held off. The capital at this time was Anuradhapura, the ruins of which are the most impressive memorial of ancient Ceylon.

6. SOUTH-EAST ASIA

At the beginning of our era there are to be seen in south-east Asia the first signs of a massive movement, which eventually allowed these regions to be pervaded by Indian art, religion, and institutions, even to the point of creating a 'Greater India' beyond the Seas.[3] It is a movement to which neither names nor distinct phases can be attached, but it was mainly due to the growth of sea-borne commerce in the hands of Indian merchants. This penetration of ideas and customs did not bring about a political colonization. Instead there came into being a number of native states, whose political and social structure was Indian and who were imbued with Indian culture. Neither now nor later, therefore, was there any hint of dependence upon the Indian kingdoms, even of an indirect or theoretical kind. The governing classes were the local aristocracy, which had a fair measure of Indian blood resulting from inter-marriage with the newcomers: it regarded itself, justly so, as an Indian aristocracy, and followed the religious and social usages of India.

One example is the Pyu kingdom, of proto-Burman speech, which was founded in the middle valley of the Irrawaddy in the third century. Another is the Bhnam kingdom (the Fu-nan of the Chinese) which appeared on the lower Mekong at the outset of the third century: it lasted down to the sixth century, and gave place first to the Chên-la kingdom, and then to the great Khmer empire of Cambodia, perhaps the main centre of Indian civilization in this region. At the same period (late second century) there came into being the Champa kingdom on the sea-board of the South China Sea, in the lands which today form the southern republic of Vietnam: the history of this Hindu state is one of constant struggle against pressure from the Annamites (modern Tonkin was a Chinese province from AD 44), in other words against Chinese civilization pressing down from the north. More scanty is evidence on Indonesia, where inscriptions date back no farther than the early fifth century AD.

7. PARTHIA

a. *The Arsacid Period*

In 20 BC Phraates IV, king of the feudal Parthian state, had restored to Augustus' general Tiberius the standards captured at Carrhae in 53 and such prisoners as survived. He sent his own sons and grandsons to Rome to learn Roman culture, and a brief entente between the two powers ensued. This was especially marked in the reign of Phraates V, whose mother Musa, his co-ruler, had been an Italian slave presented to Phraates IV by Augustus. The policy of his successor, Vonones, was similar, but this king had been educated at Rome and was consequently foreign to his country's ways. He was deposed, his place being taken by Artabanus III (AD 10–40), an Arsacid on his mother's side though born in Iran. In his reign the tension with Rome was renewed; it was due not only to the imperialist ambitions of the two powers, and to the Parthian spirit of nationalism, but to the fact that the two cultures were so different from each other. The Romans supported a pretender, Tiridates III, who had lived in Rome, and later there were several further incidents. Artabanus wanted to secure the Armenian throne for one of his sons, but was opposed by Tiberius; and the Parthian king resumed the attempt in 34, when the Iberians, incited by Rome, made their own king's brother, Mithradates, ruler of Armenia. After the death of Artabanus III the succession was contested between Vardanes, the son of his body, and his adoptive son Gotarzes. Both claimants were anti-Roman, but Rome's prestige in Parthia seemed to revive for just a moment when Gotarzes, though victorious, provoked such discontent among his subjects by his cruelty that they recalled the son of Vonones I (Mihrdat or Meherdates) from Rome. Yet in 49 this prince was put away by Gotarzes, who had him mutilated. Soon afterwards three brothers belonging to the reigning house of Atropatene succeeded each in obtaining a kingdom: Vologaesus I secured the throne of Parthia, Pacorus that of Atropatene, and Tiridates that of Armenia without seeking investiture by Rome. Domitius Corbulo was now sent out by Nero, and in 59–60, aided by the struggle of the Hyrcanians against Parthia, he overran the whole of Armenia. At first Tigranes, great-grandson of Herod of Judaea, was put in as king; but later Corbulo reached an understanding with Tiridates, who in 66 came to Rome to receive his investiture. At this point there began a fresh period of more peaceful relations between Rome and Parthia, the latter taking advantage of the situation to extend its influence towards India.

Armenia was once more a cause of discord in the days of Trajan and Osroes. Trajan invaded and reduced Armenia to the status of a province; he then pushed down into Persia and captured Ctesiphon (?115). But after his death

Hadrian made peace with Osroes, and made Armenia an independent kingdom again. For the same reason again trouble broke out in the time of Marcus Aurelius and Vologaesus III, the latter of whom had turned out the Roman vassal Sohaemus and tried to put his brother Pacorus in Armenia (161). The Roman nominee regained his throne, and the Parthians, defeated at Europus, saw the palace of Ctesiphon destroyed and Seleucia put to flames.

The next period of crisis, in the time of Vologaesus IV and Septimius Severus, had a similar outcome. Severus' objective was the defence of Nisibis and revenge on the Parthian king for the support given to his rival Pescennius Niger. He sacked Ctesiphon, and once more made Armenia a client state of Rome (199). Action was renewed, first by Caracalla and then by Macrinus, against the Arsacid Artabanus V, still on account of Armenia, where the anti-Roman Tiridates had ascended the throne. This time however the war ended with the defeat of the Roman troops near Nisibis, and Rome had to recognize Tiridates as a client king.

b. *The Sassanid Rule*

The southern provinces of the Parthian kingdom had been the cradle of the Achaemenids, and it was in one of these, Persis (Fars), that the national tradition of Iran and the Zoroastrian religion had been preserved most pure and stubborn. From there came Ardashir, who led a revolt against Artabanus V, defeated him in a pitched battle in Susiana (224), and two years later succeeded in taking Ctesiphon (26 September, 226, the beginning of the Sassanid era). Becoming master, King of Kings, of all the Arsacid territories, he was the founder of the Sassanid dynasty, so called from Sāsān, the half-mythical ancestor of his house; and he claimed to be the descendant of the Achaemenid kings. We know this from the 'book of the deeds of Ardashir, son of Papak'; this was published in its present form only in the seventh century, but the fact is confirmed by Sassanid bas-reliefs placed alongside those of the Achaemenidae. The new dynasty at once secured support from the Persian people, whose pride had never allowed them to regard the Arsacids as a dynasty belonging to their own nation; and support also came from the priestly class. Indeed its decided policy of nationalism was the characteristic of this dynasty, which for four centuries withstood every attack from both civilized empires and nomad tribes. Its nationalism was political and cultural alike: it was imbued with fervour for the Zoroastrian creed, which became a regular state religion of the Iranian race and was intolerant of all attempts to import foreign ideas and beliefs.

Ardashir, who according to tradition founded many new cities, was concerned to rid himself of all opposition from the Arsacids, one member of which house, Khosrev, king of Armenia, was claiming the Parthian succession. Ardashir had him murdered, and then tried to take possession of Armenia, even at the cost of attacking the Roman districts. He pushed into Mesopotamia as far as Hatra, and later laid siege to Nisibis and Carrhae; but he was driven back.

The attempt was resumed, this time with success, by his son Shahpuhr I (Sapor: 241–272). Initially he was defeated by Gordian III, in a war lasting from 242 to 244, but in the peace concluded with Philip the Arab, Shahpuhr obtained Armenia. He returned to the attack on Roman territories from 251 to 259, when he took Dura-Europus, attacked Edessa, and in 260 succeeded in capturing the Roman emperor Valerian who had come to the city's help. Valerian's successor Gallienus failed to secure his release, and the Roman prisoners were put to work on the building of aqueducts, bridges, and new cities in Khuzistan: meanwhile the much-vaunted victory was magnified on his bas-reliefs which survive to this day. Nevertheless Shahpuhr failed in an attack on the state of Palmyra, and ended by making an alliance with its queen Zenobia against Rome. Mention will be made later of the support given by Shahpuhr to the preaching of Mani, the founder of the new syncretistic religion called Manichaeism, which combined the doctrines of Christ, Zoroaster, and Buddha. Later the Magi reacted: Mani was crucified, and his doctrines were made illegal (273).

King Bahram II (276–293) fared badly in a new war with Rome. The emperor Aurelius Carus took the field against him, occupied Armenia and northern Mesopotamia, and pushed down as far as Ctesiphon, beneath the walls of which he died in 283. The struggle continued with varying fortunes against Numerian and Carinus in the ensuing months; and in 293 the Persians under their new king Narseh (Narsetes: 293–302) succeeded in recovering Armenia. But they were forced to formal surrender of that district, together with Mesopotamia and the lands east of the Tigris, when Galerius Maximianus mounted a vigorous offensive against them (296–298).

During his long reign (309–379) Shahpuhr II resumed the conflict with Rome, which now took on a religious character. Up till now the Parthians had been tolerant of the Christians, who in escaping the Roman persecutions were entering their dominions in great numbers. But in Constantine's day to be a Christian became synonymous with being a Roman, and furthermore his rival Tiridates of Armenia himself became a Christian. Shahpuhr II in 342 then began to persecute the Christians, having first renewed the struggle against Rome from the outset of the reign of Constantius II and then carried it on practically without a break. In his first attempt, during which he besieged Nisibis, he was not successful: he compelled the king of Armenia to pay tribute, but he could not obtain full possession of Armenia. In 345 he met with still more serious reverses, being defeated at Singara and suffering the loss of his son as a prisoner. A second and a third time (346 and 350) he failed before Nisibis, and in 360 he had to face an attack by the emperor Julian, who was resolved to finish the issue once and for all. But Julian, though he won marked successes, had to abandon the siege of Ctesiphon and vainly sought a pitched battle: on 27 June he died of wounds. With him ended the great Roman offensive against the Parthians, since the new emperor Jovian preferred to make peace, surrendering Nisibis, Armenia, and Georgia. Rome did return to the attack against the later Sassanids; Shahpuhr III, for example, was compelled to conclude a treaty with Theodosius I and surrendered Lesser Armenia. But under his successor Bahram IV (388–399) Armenia was divided into two parts, the larger as a vassal of the Parthians, the smaller a vassal of Rome. Yezdegert (399–420), who showed such tolerance in religion that he was opposed and later probably removed by the clergy, entered upon close relations with Byzantium; and Procopius tells us that Arcadius entrusted him with the guardianship of his family.

A few decades later (outside the scope of this volume) the new Nestorian schism took firm root in the Persian country, where the local Christian Church fully embraced its doctrines.

8. THE ETHIOPIAN REGION

A note may be added here on the Ethiopian region. In the introduction to Part II it was shown how southern Arabian peoples had founded settlements in Ethiopia and how Graeco-Ptolemaic trading posts had been formed by their side. At this time the capital city of those posts was one of the southern Arabian colonies named Axum: it is first mentioned in a source from the first century AD (the *Periplus Maris Erythraei*), but it reached its greatest prosperity in the third century AD when it succeeded in acquiring control even of the south Arabian territory from which the colonists had come. In this period its foreign policy included interest in both the Arabian and the Syrian region, and there is record of an agreement reached with Zenobia.

This Ethiopian state of Axum was on unfriendly terms with its northern neighbours, the Nubians of Meroë, with whom Nero had established a connection. In this direction too the Axumites were able to extend their hegemony, aided by similar aggressive action by the Roman empire from Egypt. Decius' action against the Nubians and Blemmyes is an example of the latter tendency; he was followed by Diocletian, who in 297 attempted to expel the Nubians from the Dodekaschoinos.

During the fourth century Axum under its king Amida and his son Ezana succeeded in suppressing Meroë. Ezana was converted to Christianity by St Frumentius and spread the new religion over the Ethiopian territory. Even after its political collapse, Axum remained the religious capital of the country.

9. THE ROMAN EMPIRE

a. *To AD* 192

The successors of Augustus, Tiberius and the rest, each had his own history and the experience he had thereby acquired; and each was friendly or hostile to particular men and particular classes. But in principle they knew the features of three imperial systems which, like patterns for the future, had been instituted one after another at the dawn of the imperial period. First there was Caesar's system: he had been dictator for life and had concentrated all power and responsibility into his own hands without making the senate his partner; moreover he set himself, without prejudice, to give equality in political status to all parts of the empire. Then there was the system of Augustus, who appeared to express precisely the senate's will, and who exalted Italy above the provinces, as well as showing a preference for the West. Thirdly there had been the régime of Marcus Antonius, a King of Kings on the oriental model, God on earth, and disposer of the provinces in his own autocratic way, a manner almost feudal. It was logical therefore that each ruler should either show decided preference for one of the three types of empire, or, faced with the difficulty of striking a balance between the opposing forces, should attempt to combine the old features in a novel manner and even bring new principles into play.

For the opposing forces existed and could not be ignored. The empire itself (Map XII) was formed out of two parts which were different in tradition and culture, in race, and in aims: one was Greek or Hellenized, the other Italian or in process of Romanization. One or other might be preferred; or the two could be regarded as partners, proceeding towards a joint dominion. Then there was the opposition resulting from the relation between Italy and the provinces. This could either be perpetuated, leaving Italy in a privileged condition and limiting grants of citizenship to the minimum; or one could try to remove the distinction altogether, and be lavish with concessions of this kind. Differences of opinion were also possible on political and social objectives. Some might want a constitution of a definite type, aristocratic or plutocratic, or popular, or mixed (the knights in alliance with one of the other two factions): others on the contrary might attempt to subordinate all class interests to the uniformity imposed by the emperor. Either the organization and forms of the old republican magistracies and constitutional elements could be preserved with the senate at the head; or they could be supplanted by bureaucratic officials and by the Consilium of the Princeps. The armed forces, whether the legions on the frontiers or the praetorian guard stationed in Italy, could either be allowed to take a concrete part in political life, or their interference could be resisted. Again, one could favour a policy of peace and consolidation, or go in for military action to enlarge the bounds of the empire farther and farther afield; and one could aim at rigid economic arrangements which would keep the state's budget in balance and no more, or alternatively seek to build up reserves for special undertakings. Then one could be open and tolerant towards the new religious ideas of the day, or take a rigid stand on the traditional beliefs; one could accept, with some reserve, oriental views of the deification of dead emperors, or lay direct claim to have veneration and cult accorded to emperors in their

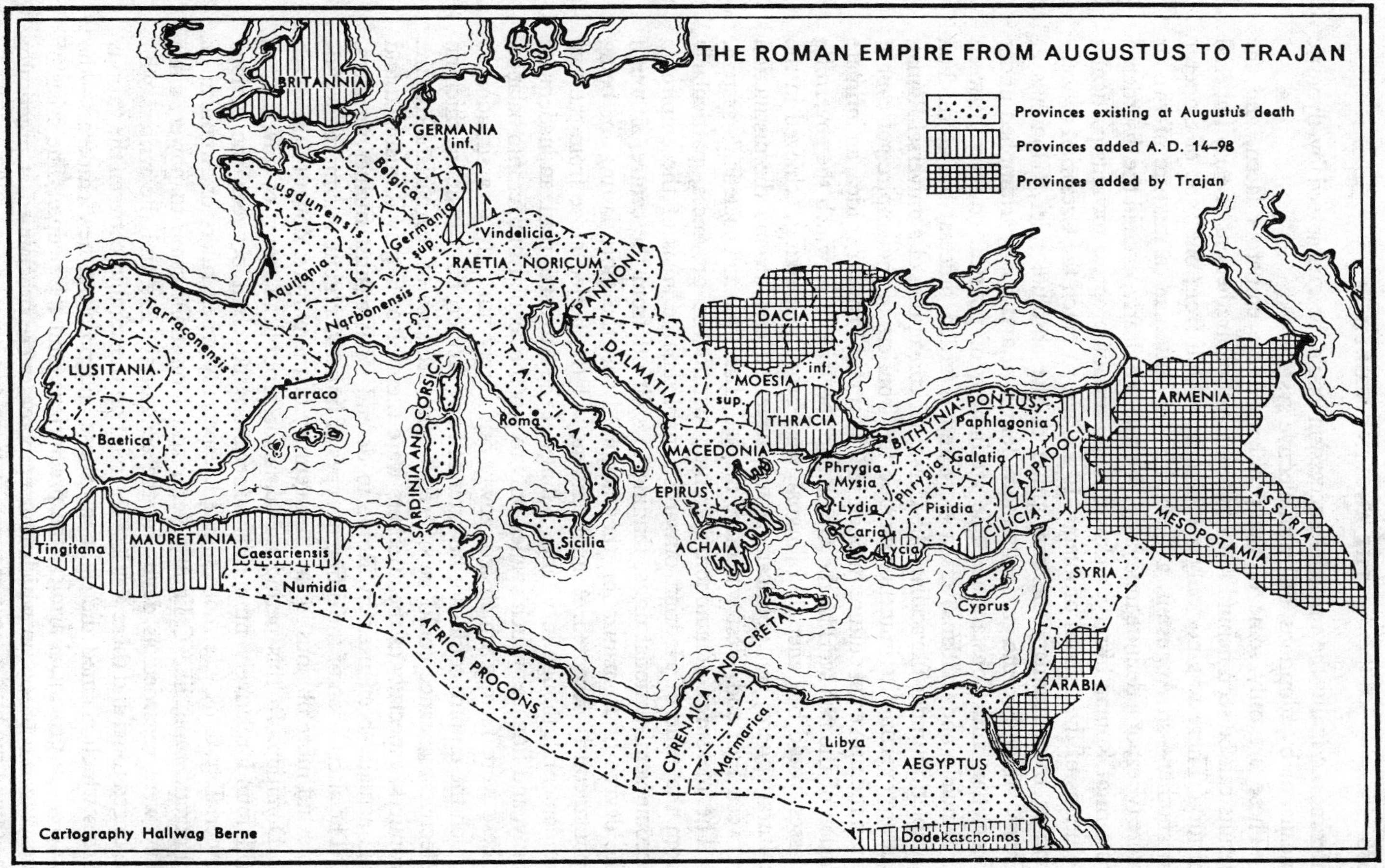

THE ROMAN EMPIRE FROM AUGUSTUS TO TRAJAN

Provinces existing at Augustus death
Provinces added A. D. 14–98
Provinces added by Trajan

BRITANNIA

GERMANIA inf.

Belgica

Lugdunensis

Germ. sup.

Aquitania

Narbonensis

Tarraconensis

LUSITANIA

Baetica

Tingitana

MAURETANIA

Caesariensis

Numidia

AFRICA PROCONS

Tarraco

RAETIA

Vindelicia

NORICUM

PANNONIA

VINONONIA

DALMATIA

I T A L I A

Roma

SARDINIA AND CORSICA

Sicilia

DACIA

MOESIA inf.

MOESIA sup.

THRACIA

MACEDONIA

EPIRUS

ACHAIA

CRETA

BITHYNIA-PONTUS

Paphagonia

Galatia

Phrygia

Mysia

Lydia

Pisidia

Caria

Lycia

CAPPADOCIA

ARMENIA

ASSYRIA

MESOPOTAMIA

SYRIA

CILICIA

Cyprus

ARABIA

AEGYPTUS

Libya

CYRENAICA AND MARMARICA

Marmarica

Dodekaschoinos

MAP XII

Cartography Hallwag Berne

lifetimes. Finally the imperial succession could be guaranteed by dynastic means, or by adoptions, or by an elective system.

These are only some of the problems these emperors faced, and the results can be seen behind the variations and contradictions of early imperial history. There was not only a continual switch from one type of emperor to another—an Augustan, a Caesarian, an Antonian, a mixture of two or more types, or a definite innovator. We also see clearly, even in the disordered pattern of Roman history, a slow but continuous progress towards particular solutions of the various problems. It was not so much the Caesarian conception as the Antonian, the conception of the absolute ruler, 'Dominus et Deus', which became gradually more dominant and finally triumphed under Diocletian and Constantine. The attainment of political equality between provincials and Italians was a slow and retarded process, but it reached completion under Caracalla. The Caesarian conception of a universal Roman culture exerting its influence outside the frontiers of the empire got caught up in the universal culture implicit in Christanity. His other idea, an intimate fusion of the two worlds, the Greek and the Italian, in which the governing classes would be generally bilingual, was, broadly speaking, achieved in the cultural sphere; but politically it was never successful, and the distinction between East and West was more marked than ever in Diocletian's system.

The measures of autonomy granted within the provinces, particularly from the time of Hadrian onwards, enabled large areas of the empire to become semi-national units, tending to split off from the centre, although the degree of Romanization they acquired was the more lasting for being spontaneously accepted. A final tendency of the period arose from the two fundamental, though inevitable, failings of the Augustan plan, an inadequate army, and finances which availed only to put the regular budget into balance. These were factors which led slowly but surely not only to a situation in which the empire could not be extended any farther, but to one in which no effective resistance could be offered to the pressure of 'barbarians' on the frontiers, especially as the attackers were themselves largely Romanized and had actually been used by Rome to defend itself against further invaders.

The alternation of the different types of imperial régime was more formidable and more obvious in the first century of the empire, down to the death of Domitian. In this period nostalgia for republican forms of government still found relatively numerous adherents; the clash between the various imperial systems was more marked, especially when rulers of Antonian or autocratic type, like Caligula, Nero, and Domitian, came to power, since they were regarded as devils by the senatorial class and the writers who belonged to it; and there was less restraint on the conflict between the various forces which claimed the right to choose and proclaim new emperors—the senate, the provincial armies, the praetorians, and the people. The crisis of the years AD 68–69, in which four emperors were proclaimed at practically the same time by different groups of legions and praetorians, is clear evidence of the warlike fury shown by the contending parties; and one may add the open or secret assassination of several emperors, and the use of one method after another to secure the succession. Almost all these emperors indulged in heavy expense on public works, on shows, and on distributions to the people; but all too often they ran into trouble because their finances were insufficient. Moreover the army, though adequate to secure the frontiers in time of peace, had no forces large enough for reserve or manœuvre. It could not push into territory beyond the frontiers: it could not even securely defend the frontiers which were threatened, unless forces from other fronts were withdrawn. An example can be seen as early as Augustus' day, when the unfortunate expedition of Varus between the Rhine and the Elbe compelled the assumption of the defensive policy which Tiberius vigorously maintained. Later stable defence works had to be erected along the whole frontier, the so-called *limes* with its entrenched forts, beginning with Claudius and extended by Vespasian and Domitian. Claudius in fact was the only one of these emperors who achieved noteworthy conquests: he operated on the Danube, in Thrace, and in Britain, in the last of which his conquests were later expanded by Nero and by Vespasian and his sons. The Parthian actions of Caligula and Nero ended with failure to compromise, as did the wars of Domitian against the Dacians. As early as Nero's time we find the first examples of those transplantations of barbarians into Roman territory to defend the frontier (in this case the Danube frontier), which were later to prove so perilous. To all this must be added the birth and development of a religious crisis, brought about by Jewish and Christian propaganda and by the reaction of the Roman state. First apparent in Claudius' time, this crisis led to bloodshed and violence under Nero and Domitian.

The eighty-four years from 96 to 180, from Nerva's election to the death of Marcus Aurelius, are a period of calm in the struggle between the various systems of government. It was not that any one system had prevailed against all the others, but that a more stable equilibrium had now been reached among the claims of the opposing interests, since all the parties wanted to achieve a synthesis in the manner most beneficial to the common good and best adapted to the bent and aims and powers of the empire as a whole. This was also the period in which the work of Romanization, in part of the empire, was made most intense, and that in which the greatest cultural and political harmony was attained between East and West, with all provinces being gradually raised in status as Caesar had originally planned.

It is typical of this period that two emperors, Trajan and Hadrian, were born in Spain, Marcus Aurelius was partly of Spanish origin, and Antoninus Pius of Gallic. Moreover since no emperor from Nerva to Pius had a son to succeed him, each was inevitably forced on to the system of adoption, in contrast to the dynastic system practised by the Flavians. Nevertheless Marcus Aurelius returned to the dynastic principle, when he left his throne to his son Commodus. Foreign policy underwent many phases. Trajan sought to extend the empire in Dacia, Arabia, and Parthia; and Marcus spent seventeen of his nineteen years of rule in war against the Parthians, against barbarian invaders from the north, and against the rebel Avidius Cassius.⁴ Hadrian, on the other hand, followed by Pius, and later by Commodus too, preferred a peaceful policy, renouncing conquests, attending to consolidation at home, and protecting the empire against foreign attacks by means of fortifications (Pl. 59, a) and diplomacy. Trajan, like Nerva before him, had attached importance to the primacy of Italy, and organized the system of *Alimenta* for poor children in an attempt to solve the agrarian and pauper problems of Italy. Antoninus Pius stayed permanently in Rome.

Hadrian on the other hand journeyed continually over the provinces to learn their needs. He insisted on bringing them into equality with Italy, granting Roman citizenship with a lavish hand, and founding new towns in every district as bases for civilization and spread of Roman culture. He even divided Italy, as if it were one of the provinces, into a number of districts with a 'consular', dependent on himself, at the head of each. The army had been decimated by Trajan's wars, and its effective strength could not be restored. Hadrian decided on a complete reorganization on new principles, which made it more firmly regional in character: in other words in each province he made use of local recruits, who had greater practical knowledge of the country, and whose patriotism was readier since they were employed in defence of their native lands. It is true that this system increased the centrifugal forces which each province owed to its racial composition and its history. But where these natural tendencies were left to develop freely, without any compulsion or levelling policy promoted by the Roman government, they led to the creation of provinces which were almost nations. Indeed the administration, defence, and economy of every province was so organized that each led something like an autonomous life, adapted to its ethnic composition and the opportunities of the region; and each was allowed to develop spontaneously a definite type of Roman culture peculiar to itself, possessing thereby its own civilization, both national and Roman, at once. It is undoubtedly this decentralizing work above all which made it possible later for many of the western and north-eastern districts, when they separated themselves from the empire, to retain permanently a patina of Latin culture. This was indelible because it was of natural formation and had been freely fused with the innate ways of life found among the various peoples.

Meanwhile the relation of Rome to the new world of Christianity was growing in importance. There was increased friction in Trajan's time, tolerance under Hadrian and Pius, moderate rigidity of policy under Marcus Aurelius.

But during the reign of Marcus' son Commodus (180–192) there was an apparent return to the Neronian pattern, with an emperor who admired Antonius and bent all his energy to secure the sympathies of the praetorians and the people. So the opposition of the senate broke out violently once more, and there was a renewal of conspiracies. In one of them Commodus met his death.[5]

b. *The Severan Age*

In 193 two emperors in Rome were murdered, after eighty-seven and sixty-eight days of rule, leaving three claimants to the empire of whom two were eliminated by the victorious third, the Semitic African Septimius Severus. It was he who gave his name to the thirty years or so which followed, together with his next successor but three, a ruler of Syrian origin called M. Aurelius Severus Alexander. The latter was assassinated in 235 by the Thracian Iulius Verus Maximinus, with whom the period of 'anarchy' begins.

The Severan age is mainly characterized by the growth of violent intervention from both praetorians and legionaries, concerned both to set up emperors and cast them down. A further feature is the renewal of attempts to found a permanent dynasty, in which the moving forces were a series of energetic women, Iulia Domna, Maesa, and Soaemias, ready for every hazard on behalf of the infant rulers they were supporting.

In this period too the process of political advancement of the provinces at the expense of Italy reached fulfilment, with emperors of provincial origin collaborating to that end with great Eastern jurists like Papinian, Paul, and Ulpian. The climax came in 212 with the famous 'Constitutio Antoniniana', promulgated by Caracalla, under which Roman citizenship was granted to 'all *peregrini*', that is to say, with few exceptions, to all communities throughout the empire.[6] This brought Caesar's idea to its final and inevitable conclusion. The precise and immediate aims of this edict were several. It unified legal forms, and so gradually suppressed local law when this could be done. It imposed a uniform system of taxes and increased the yield. Finally it was designed to create an imperial unity in the name of Rome, with Roman language and Roman law, and so to bring together into a single outlook, culture, and even race those peoples which were still to some extent held apart by barriers of race and history.

This period saw great military activity, made necessary by the fact that economic difficulties had complicated the task of frontier defence. Caracalla fought the Rhaeti and Danubian peoples; but the main wars were those of Septimius Severus, and of Caracalla too, against the Parthians. As we have seen, however, it was precisely in these years that the new dynasty of the Sassanids conquered the Arsacids; their powerful spirit of nationalism and their revival of the religion of Zoroaster gave the Parthian empire an energy it had not possessed for many a day.

In matters of religion these emperors, who for the most part came from distant provinces like Africa (Septimius Severus and Macrinus) or the East, were inclined towards the introduction of new and exotic cults into Rome, and were therefore tolerant of religious propaganda. Eventually under

Elagabalus the dynasty made a genuine and peculiar effort at syncretism, in an attempt to invent a universal religion which would include all others, even Judaism and Christianity.

c. *Third-Century Crises*

Despite the astonishing 'recoveries' which various emperors were able to effect in the vast imperial edifice of Rome, it was obvious that this edifice was betraying serious cracks, to which the general state of crisis and the parabolic descent of Roman fortunes bear witness. To give an adequate account of this crisis it may be useful to put forward a number of particular problems, which will be treated more fully in the following chapters to show how each one developed.

In the republican period Italy was successfully unified politically and became in effect a nation. But most statesmen had continued to regard Rome's possessions outside Italy as foreign dominions which formed a source of political power. Caesar and the better among his successors saw the need to relieve the provinces from their position of being simply exploited countries and to elevate them gradually to the level of Italy. This was the process concluded by the 'Constitution' of Caracalla. At the same time, however, for a number of concurrent reasons, the general economic condition of the provinces became more flourishing than that of Italy. Now particularly under Hadrian and Marcus Italy lost even its political and military pre-eminence, while the areas on the periphery attracted more and more of the affairs and life of the empire. Meanwhile the frontier armies with their pronunciamentos were exercising their influence in the appointment of emperors, who were increasingly of non-Italian origin.

So the dualism which Caesar and some of his successors had tried to overcome was made more acute than ever. The two parts of the empire, one Latin or Latinized, the other Greek or Hellenized, differed in traditions, temper, race, way of life, and spiritual outlook; and the hostility which each successive dynasty could show to one part or the other, together with the separatism induced by the civil wars, made the division deeper than ever before. This led first to an administrative and political split between the two parts of the empire, and later to a definite separation.

In every region Rome had tried to found cities, as political and administrative centres: this conformed to its own tradition, which was reinforced by the example set by Hellenistic states. The cities assisted in the collection or exaction of tribute, in the recruitment of legionaries, in promoting commerce, and in spreading Roman language, legal forms, and civilization: their magistrates used normally to acquire Roman citizenship.[7] Romanized towns of this kind were gradually differentiated from the country around them, which was slower in giving up relatively archaic native usages and habits. But with the general decline in the empire's economy the towns lost their vitality and began to decay, partly because the state claimed that the municipal magistrates should still be responsible for the payment of their districts' tribute. Since no one was prepared any longer to submit himself to holding a magistracy, Rome first resorted to the appointment of imperial *curatores*,[8] and then cast the responsibility on to groups of well-to-do inhabitants, who were thus gradually reduced to poverty. Meanwhile in the country districts imperial domains grew in size, and *latifundia* emerged once more; the familiar result was to reduce the small agricultural owners to the status of a proletariate, who eventually were held by the large owners of the so-called *patrocinia* as free serfs, performing the same functions as slaves had done in republican days. In the outcome the land was overworked and became barren; and hordes of famished *coloni*, even as early as Antoninus Pius' time, revolted *en masse*, abandoning their lands and taking to brigandage. The state meanwhile was having to meet vast expenses with a half-empty treasury. It resorted to heavier taxation, abnormal impositions on the well-to-do, and confiscation of the property of those guilty, or supposedly guilty, of *maiestas*. The result, from the time of Marcus Aurelius onwards, was a crop of provincial rebellions.

The spread of *latifundia* led to a closed economy once more, in which consumer goods were directly exchanged among country people. But the state and the cities continued to make use of a monetary economy, so that relations between city and country became more difficult, as did the payment in money of tribute to the state. The situation was made worse by the monetary crisis; and this had a number of causes. Precious metals were going abroad to pay for exotic luxury goods; the mines were yielding less, this factor being only temporarily alleviated by the possession of the mines of Transylvania, eventually abandoned; and there was vast public expenditure to be met from normal budgets, made worse in periods of famine and civil war. The government resorted to the subterfuge of a managed currency, by reducing its weight and debasing the alloy. But this only led to inflation, while the good alloys were hoarded and disappeared from circulation. The poorer classes, salaried workers and soldiers, claimed their pay in terms of raw materials.

Augustus had reduced the number of effectives in the army, making good his loss by the long terms of service of his paid volunteers. But now their recruitment became another source of difficulty, because both pay and pensions were so obviously small. It was now only the country people, from depressed areas, who presented themselves to the legions. Italians disappeared from the ranks, and later even from commands: then Hadrian linked the levy with regional service. So the interests of particular regions, protected by their own people, came to be regarded as more important than those of the central government and of Italy; and the consequences, in the event of military pronunciamentos being made in favour of new emperors, were exceedingly grave. The normal armies, too, were scarcely large enough to garrison the frontiers in time of peace; but even after the costly construction of so many military roads it was always slow and expensive to transfer reinforcements to meet emergencies, and in any case such a course meant denuding another frontier of its garrison. The construction of the *limes* was the plan to which the government, especially in the period from Domitian to Marcus, resorted to meet this failing. But its cost was very high, and it too proved inadequate where an enemy did succeed in passing this single barrier and Rome had no strong body of troops immediately available on the spot to stop the leak. The result was the gradual adoption of a very dangerous practice. First, supposedly friendly barbarian tribes from beyond the frontiers were paid for their help in defending Rome's line; then such tribes were transported as auxiliaries into Roman territory, a course which made the barbarians all the more anxious to cross the imperial frontiers. It should also be noticed that the frontier troops, as well as taking on an increasing number of barbarian auxiliaries, began to make the organization of their regiments more like that of the very barbarians whom they had to fight, and to adopt arms and tactics similar to those of their enemies. Finally cavalry became superior to infantry, and in consequence foreign mercenaries in addition to the Illyrians and Moroccans were indispensable: Germans, Arabs, and Iranians who had grown up with horses.

On the non-material side the most worrying problems were those of legal forms and religious observances. For a long time past it had been the duty of pro-magistrates, and in later days of imperial governors, to face the delicate task of laying down rules to govern the juridical relation between citizens and provincials, although the provincials might have varied traditions and levels of civilization and be continually passing through the different phases of Romanization. The method used at first was that a governor promulgated an edict at the beginning of his term of office: later he had to apply the 'edictum perpetuum', which was compiled by Salvius Iulianus under Hadrian.

Even the edict of Caracalla, which gave citizenship to everyone, did not remove the difficulties, because the adoption of Roman law throughout the empire could be neither immediate nor universal. There were endless obstacles and reasons for resisting it, and there had to be a number of temporary compromises. The result was the appearance of two distinct legal trends. One is seen in the Latinized provinces of the West, when it led later, after the barbarians had settled there, to Romano-German Law. The other, in the Hellenized Eastern provinces, gradually went on to found the Law called Romano-Byzantine. In Egypt the tendency was to compromise between the two.

The faiths and cults of conquered peoples were tolerated by Rome, provided they did not go out of their way to make converts for their gods among Roman citizens. Rome could thus reach a *modus vivendi* even with the Jews, who were monotheists and consequently hostile to the imposition of the cults of Dea Roma and the deified emperors. This form of compromise was for some time a protection to the early Christians, who were not yet clearly distinguishable from the Jews. But from Nero's reign the difference between the two faiths got recognized. Moreover it was established that Christianity started with a man who had been condemned as a rebel against the Caesars, and it was therefore not the traditional religion of a subject people, of which the practice was authorized as such. Indeed it was clearly setting out to make converts throughout the world, and was rapidly spreading not only, as had at first been the case, among the lower orders of society, but even among the upper classes of Roman citizens and members of the government. So there arose the serious problem, political as well as legal, whether the Christians ought to be punished and made to abjure their faith, or whether they should be tolerated: different answers were given in different periods, not only by the central government but also by provincial governors abroad. Meanwhile the new faith was spreading ever more widely, gaining glory from the persecutions (more or less sporadic at first) and by the numbers of martyrs it could boast. Its progress was most rapid in the Eastern provinces, more moderate in Italy, and slowest in the West. It could no longer be either ignored or concealed.

Yet down to the end of the third century it encountered only intermittent interference. It was made supple and resilient by the form of its hierarchy, which was constructed to fit the administrative units of the empire. Its quiet but relentless penetration became more challenging every day.

Although the general crisis of the empire had its repercussions upon culture, resulting in an obvious decline in literary and artistic work, yet the Christians gave the impression of possessing a vitality which was continually becoming more active and productive. This appeared in their theoretical and practical arguments, in their propagandist, apologetic, theological, and literary writings, and in the artistic development seen in their places of worship and burial. It was now clear that this new world, with its ideas which surpassed national boundaries and which aimed at making all men equal, was gradually but inexorably detaching itself from the existing body politic: if it were neither absorbed nor destroyed, it might create a state within a state and become an enemy of the utmost danger. So although several emperors through inertia or patience continued to exert toleration, others like Elagabalus and later Gallienus attempted to absorb Christianity within a religious syncretism, the life of which proved short, and others planned to exterminate it by bloody persecutions. Of those the first which assumed a really general character was that of Decius, the last was that of Diocletian.

d. *The Barbarian Invasions*

The crucial moment in this great crisis which threatened to bankrupt the empire was reached in the so-called period of 'military anarchy' (235–268), when all the northern tribes from across the frontier attacked the empire simultaneously. The anarchy had begun when the ex-herdsman Maximinus Thrax was acclaimed by his fellow-soldiers and took his place as emperor (235–238) without troubling to secure ratification by the senate and without even coming to Rome. He directed the wars against the Germans, Dacians, and Dalmatians, and persecuted the leading figures in the Christian Church.

In thirty-three years of anarchy the Roman world was now ruled by a confused collection of emperors of every sort of origin. One was set up against another by legionaries on the frontiers, by the praetorians, by the senate, or by the people. Some took colleagues or tried to set up ephemeral dynasties. Often their authority spread no farther, and they were recognized over only a limited area. Most of them in the end were deposed or murdered, after they had made their contribution to the exhaustion of the empire's military and economic strength by intestine wars. Their brief and turbulent reigns were weighed down with other cares. Persia was pursuing a policy of formidable expansion, set in motion by the new nationalist dynasty of the Sassanids, which at some moments pressed as far as Antioch with its armies. Meanwhile on the northern frontiers there was pressure from the barbarians, who at several points succeeded in devastating invasions of the Roman provinces.

Few of these rulers managed to reign for any number of years, and even fewer could achieve anything worth recording. Gordian III (238–244) carried out a victorious counter-attack on the Persians. Philip the Arab was tolerant towards the Christians, and defeated the Carpi on the Danube. Decius (247–251), an emperor born in Illyricum, which was still almost closed to Christianity, deceived himself into thinking that he could obliterate the religion altogether; but he then saw the error of his ways. He was eventually the first Roman emperor to fall in battle against the barbarians (this time the Goths). Valerian (252–260) entrusted his son Gallienus, whom he made his colleague, with the defence of the West, against the Franks and Alemanni on the Rhine (who had reached Mauretania and Ravenna respectively), and against the Marcomanni, Quadi, Goths, and other Danubian peoples. Valerian himself took the field in the East against the Persians, but was made a prisoner by treachery. Gallienus was now left as sole emperor. He changed his father's policy towards the Christians, showing toleration once more, and undertook military reforms and the fortification of cities, such as Mediolanum and Verona, which were threatened by German raids. But he had to contend with a formidable number of rivals, who sprang up in every part of the empire, while he found the majority of provinces, in the East as well as the West, being detached from his rule by movements of independence. At the same time the regions which remained loyal (Italy, Narbonensis, the Danube provinces, and Africa) had been largely plundered by the barbarians: the Alemanni reached the walls of Mediolanum, and the Goths penetrated into Greece and Asia Minor.

The two destructive agents, secessionist movements and barbarian thrusts, had a close relationship to each other. The barbarian raids, which the short-lived rival dynasts of Rome, consuming wealth and human lives in their internal struggles, seemed incapable of withstanding, were mainly provoked by causes of an obvious kind. The barbarian populations had increased, and they were pushed forward by other barbarians pressing on their heels. The moment for advance was favourable since the Roman frontier forces were depleted and Rome found difficulty in reinforcing any point that was attacked. A further factor was the practice, first put into force on a large scale by Marcus Aurelius, of employing against the barbarians bands of their own kinsmen who had been transplanted on to Roman soil: these were later frequently ready to make common cause with invaders who had been attracted by the legendary wealth of the empire.

In these difficulties of organizing defence against attacks from barbarians in the north and Persians in the east the threatened areas naturally took measures for their own protection, the central government being incapable. For example one of the army commanders on the Rhine and in Belgica, M. Cassianus Postumus (later backed up by C. Aesuvius Tetricus), was acclaimed by his troops; but instead of attempting to acquire the whole empire, he organized Gaul, Britain, and Spain as a separate unit, his aims being to halt the Germans and restore to his lands the prosperity which Rome seemed no longer able to secure for them (258–273). The same function was assumed in the East, against the Persian and Gothic dangers, by the kingdom of Palmyra. Its rulers were Septimius Odenathus, and later his son Vaballathus under the tutelage of his mother Zenobia (Batzabbai): after the defeat and capture of Valerian they organized the defence of a vast region extending from the Bosporus to Egypt, and gave it an autonomous existence.

Certainly the empire, and above all its economy, seemed to be in ruins. Plagues and wars, both foreign and domestic, were raging; whole provinces had been lost; the population was dwindling and the fields were being deserted, with a return to primitive methods of agriculture and the destruction of hydraulic works; trade was paralysed and the currency was inflated. Everything combined to render conditions of life terrifying to all. They had become altogether intolerable to the mass of the poor and to the agricultural wage-earners, who took to brigandage and piracy; but even the people who had been well-off were oppressed by the treasury, by the heavy burdens of municipal office, and by violent exactions at the hands of the troops and plunder by the bandits, which caused repeated damage to their estates.

e. The Reorganization of the Empire under 'Illyrian' Emperors

To this general collapse of the Roman world there came a reaction, which led to a complete reorganization of the imperial system. The credit belongs to a group of 'Illyrian emperors', so called because several of them came from Illyricum (278–305); Decius had been their precursor. The first was Claudius Gothicus (268–270), who turned the Alemannic hordes out of Italy and the Goths out of Cyprus and Pamphylia; at the same time part of the Gallic empire, namely Spain and Narbonensis, returned into union with the empire of Rome. Aurelian (270–275) was the new champion of the imperial doctrine of absolutism; he built the great wall round Rome for its defence, restored the circulation of the currency, and tried like Elagabalus in earlier days to impose a new syncretist religion of sun-worship; but the Christians rebelled against this move, and later in his last days he decided to persecute them. But his chief concern was the defence of the empire: he recovered such parts of the Gallic empire as were still independent, and also the kingdom of Palmyra; he also defeated the Iuthungi in Rhaetia, and the Vandals and Sarmatians on the Danube. Later he was compelled to evacuate Dacia, creating instead two small provinces called Dacia on the right bank of the Danube. Finally he prepared an expedition against Persia, which was cut short by his death.

Probus (276–282) also deserves mention. He was challenged by many rivals and saw clearly that agricultural work would be upset if he raised more troops. He therefore made use of the system of defending the frontiers by employing the barbarians themselves, and made his soldiers fortify cities, repair roads, and put canals in working order. He defended Gaul from devastation by the Franks and Alemanni, the Balkans from the Vandals, Sarmatians, and Scyths, and Egypt from the Blemmyes. His murder prevented an attack on Persia.

Carus (282–283) was another upholder of absolutist theory, and he attempted to found a dynasty by leaving the West to his son Carinus and the East to Numerian. But both were overcome by the usurpation of Aurelius Valerius Diocletianus (284–305), an ex-freedman from Dalmatia who had spent his entire life in the army. He was convinced that the empire was too large for rule by one man, and that with two Augusti there must be two further collaborators called Caesars, who would be designated for the succession and avoid further usurpations. In 285 therefore he chose M. Aurelius Maximianus as his colleague or Augustus and gave him the West; then in 293 he created two Caesars as well, C. Flavius Valerius Constans and C. Galerius Valerius Maximianus, the one as collaborator in the West, the other in the East. (Pl. 76, a.) Diocletian was an extreme absolutist and champion of theocratic rule. He intended the whole life of the empire to depend on these 'tetrarchs', through the intermediary of the 'consilium principis' and a bureaucracy of officials. To the tetrarchs were subordinated all the provinces, now divided into as many as a hundred units, but grouped into twelve 'dioceses' (six in the East and six in the West). (Map XIII.) To regulate the finances he instituted a general census of the population to take place every fifteen years, together with an 'indictio' or ascertainment of the returns of all property. He also restored the soundness of the currency by a new issue of gold coins. He attempted to fix maximum prices for about a thousand types of foodstuffs and other merchandise, hoping to overcome the rising cost of living; but this measure had later to be rescinded. For eighteen years he tolerated Christianity: then for casual reasons, which are largely unknown

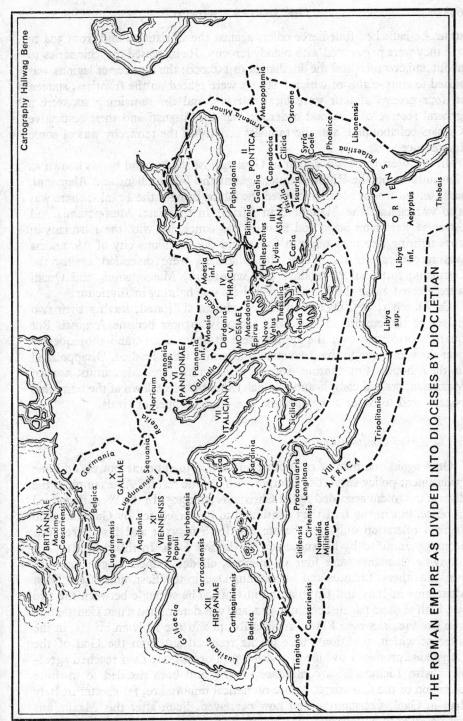

THE ROMAN EMPIRE AS DIVIDED INTO DIOCESES BY DIOCLETIAN

MAP XIII

IX BRITANNIAE
Maxima Caesariensis
Lugdunensis II

X GALLIAE
Germania
Belgica
Lugdunensis II
Sequania
Aquitania

XI VIENNENSIS
Novem Populi
Narbonensis

XII HISPANIAE
Tarraconensis
Carthaginiensis
Lusitania
Baetica
Gallaecia
Tingitana
Caesariensis

VIII AFRICA
Proconsularis
Lengitana
Sitifensis
Cirtensis
Numidia
Militiana
Tripolitania

Corsica
Sardinia
Sicilia

VII ITALICIANA
Dalmatia
Pannonia inf.
Pannonia VI sup.
PANNONIAE
Noricum
Raetia

V MOESIAE
Moesia inf.
Moesia sup.
Dacia
Dardania
Macedonia
Epirus
Nova
Vetus
Thessalia
Achaia

IV THRACIA

Paphlagonia

II PONTICA
Bithynia
Galatia
Cappadocia
Armenia Minor
Mesopotamia
Osroene
Phoenice

III ASIANA
Hellespontus
Lydia
Caria
Pisidia
Isauria
Cilicia
Syria Coele
Libanensis
Palaestina

ORIENS
Aegyptus
Thebais
Libya inf.
Libya sup.

to us, he launched four fierce edicts against the Christians, and from 304 to 312 they were persecuted with bloody ferocity. He increased the legionaries to about 420,000 men and the auxiliaries to 150,000: the number of legions was raised to sixty-eight, of which forty-six were placed on the frontiers, sixteen in four groups of four were local reserves, and the remaining six were a general reserve of a second order. In war the Augusti and their respective Caesars collaborated, and the military activity of the tetrarchy was of some importance.

In the West there was action in Gaul against the brigand bands known as 'Bagaudae',[9] on the Rhine frontier against the Burgundians and Alemanni, and Roman troops actually crossed the Rhine to fight the Franks: there was also war against the Mauretani in Africa. In the East, Mesopotamia and Armenia were won back, and a treaty was concluded with the Parthians in 297: fighting also took place in Syria, and the rebellious city of Alexandria was recovered. In the North the Rhaetians were defended against the Germans; fortifications against the Sarmatians, Marcomanni, and Quadi were erected along the Danube; and there was fighting in Illyricum.

On March 1, 305, Diocletian and Maximian abdicated, leaving their two halves of the empire to the two Caesars, who now became Augusti. But quarrels broke out over the appointment of new Caesars, and subsequently over the succession to the Augustus Constantius when he died. Disappointed in their hopes, Constantine, son of Constantius, and Maxentius, son of Maximian, created complications which led to the breakdown of the tetrarchic system, and to bitter struggles among a large number of rivals.

f. *The Age of Constantine*

Once again one man after another succeeded to supreme power, and one government policy succeeded another with chaotic results. An example is the diverse treatment accorded to the Christians after 305. In the West they lived in peace, but in the East they continued to be persecuted by Galerius, who decreed toleration only just before his death in 311; and his decree was promptly annulled by his successor Maximinus Daia. In this year, 311, the surviving claimants were four in number, all determined to gain mastery over the others, Licinius and Maximinus Daia in the East, and in the West Maxentius in Italy and Constantine in Gaul. The struggle between the two last, both of them pagans, began in 312, and was determined when Constantine won two victories near Rome, at Saxa Rubra and the Milvian bridge, in the latter of which, tradition[10] tells us, he received aid from the God of the Christians, promised to him in a vision or a dream. He then reached agreement with Licinius at a conference in 313, and both decided to institute toleration of the Christians, whose numerical importance, far greater in Italy than in Gaul, Constantine had now perceived. Soon after this Maximinus was defeated in Thrace and took his life by poison.

There was an apparent return to the diarchy originally desired by Diocletian, with Constantine in the West and Licinius in the East. But the choice of Caesars to complete the organization—the young sons of Constantine, Crispus and Constantine II, on one side, and Licinianus, the child of Licinius, on the other—showed that both Augusti were following an undiluted dynastic policy. Soon after this the first period of disagreement between the two began, but a peaceful settlement was reached in 315; and during the ensuing entente the first Constantinian reforms were carried out in the West. The general policy was to reduce the number of legionaries, with recourse once more to barbarian 'foederati' for frontier defence; to improve the finances by devaluing the coinage and substituting forced levies for the abnormal collection of tribute then ruling; and to guarantee the continuity of particular professions by making them hereditary by law. Then the contest between the two Augusti broke out once more, mainly on account of their different religious policies. Licinius was oppressing the Christians, while Constantine showed them favour and was anxious to free them from the difficulties created by the schism. War broke out, and in 323 Licinius was forced to surrender: he was sent into exile and committed suicide. Constantine remained as sole ruler, and elected his third son Constantius II as an additional Caesar. He had now become sovereign of the East as well; and in future days he preferred this region, where he also saw that the Christians formed the majority of the population. That decided him to make Christianity the state religion and to institute an aggressive policy of 'Caesaropapism'.[11] He was determined at all costs to preserve the unity of the Church, and in 325 he had the Arian views condemned at the Council of Nicaea. In 326, by the application of his own laws, he had his son Crispus and his wife Fausta sentenced to death, after which he left Rome, preferring to reside in the East; and there in 324 he consecrated—and dedicated in 330—the new capital of Constantinople (previously called Byzantium). New military and financial reforms then followed, and fresh measures in the Caesaro-papist style, reversing what he had done before and reviving the dignity of the Arian bishops. This led to schism in the Christian world: the Eastern bishops adapted themselves to the fresh measures and accepted the renewed interference, but those of the West, led by the bishop of Rome, were firmly opposed to recognition of the emperor's authority on dogmatic questions.

In the last decade of his reign (327–337) Constantine defeated the Goths and reinforced the defences on the Rhine and Danube frontiers. In 337, while he was preparing a military and diplomatic offensive against Persia, he died, baptized on his death-bed.

g. *Late Developments and the Disintegration of the Empire*

Renewed succession problems followed, for Constantine on his death-bed had enjoined that account be taken of his sons and of two grandsons. The two latter were quickly put out of the way; then Constantine II was defeated by his brother Constans, who in 340 remained sole master of the West; but he in his turn was overcome by a Breton usurper named Magnentius. Up to this time Constantius II had been engaged with Persia, but he now intervened in the West, defeated Magnentius, and became sole master of the empire in 351. Until 359 Constantius remained in the West guarding the lines of the Rhine and Danube. He was at first supported by his nephew Gallus who secured nomination as Caesar; later, however, Gallus was executed and gave place to his brother Julian. For five years Julian fought the Franks and Alemanni with some success and in 357 utterly defeated them at Argentorate (Strasbourg), after which he reorganized the province. But in 361 he was proclaimed emperor, and had to face the armies of Constantius II in Pannonia, securing, however, the position of sole emperor when Constantius died. The two had diverged on religious policy as on other matters. Constantius II aimed to continue Constantine's arrangements and had taken up the cause of the Arians: he went so far as to send the bishop of Rome into exile, and then persecuted the pagans. Julian, on the other hand, though baptized a Christian, got converted to pagan Neoplatonism. When he became emperor (361–363), he was tolerant of the Christians for a time, while he restored pagan temples and made one more attempt to launch on the world a teleological Platonist doctrine based on worship of the sun. But in the period which followed he began to exclude Christians from public affairs, and his governors exceeded his wishes and started persecutions. This let loose a violent reaction against Julian, who was already unpopular for his limitation of expenditure on the court and bureaucracy. But he died prematurely, at the age of 32, during a great offensive against Persia. So the dynasty of Constantine came to an end.

Julian's place was taken by the Illyrian Flavius Iovianus, who annulled his decrees in favour of the pagans and concluded a far from creditable peace with Persia with the surrender of Mesopotamia and Armenia. His successor was Flavius Valentinianus I (364–375), who founded a new dynasty, meanwhile keeping the West for himself and setting up his brother Valens (364–378) in the East. Valentinian was tolerant of all religions, and in social policy was anxious to protect the lower orders (humiles) by posing as 'defender plebis'. But he was compelled to take the field against the Alemanni in their home in Germany, to defend Britain from the Picts and Scots, to deal with a revolt in Mauretania, and to move over to the Danube to protect Pannonia. At his death power passed to his son Gratian, who had his half-brother, the four-year-old Valentinian II, as his colleague.

In the East the emperor Valens, who professed moderate Arianism, found himself in these years confronted with great dangers in the field. With great trouble he had held back the Persians, though compelled to cede them half of Armenia; and he was now surprised by a sudden barbarian attack on the Danube. This came from a section of the Visigoths, who were compelled to seek refuge in Roman territory because a great movement of tribes was pressing them from the other side. The Huns from central Asia had crossed the Rha (Volga) in 374, and were pushing the Alans and the Ostrogoths before them. Valens gave the fleeing Visigoths shelter in Thrace;[12] but very soon they became exasperated by the odious ways of the Roman officials and broke into revolt, aided by parties of Alans and Ostrogoths. The troops of the emperor, who fell beneath the walls of Adrianople in 378, were routed, and the Goths became masters of most of the Balkans.

To prevent further expansion by these barbarians, the Western emperor Gratian sent the Spaniard Theodosius, who was later raised to the position of Augustus, to take the place of the dead Valens in the Eastern provinces. Theodosius I (379–395) took the field against the Visigoths, and concluded a treaty with them, under which they remained in Thrace as *foederati* with the duty of defending the frontiers. In 380 Theodosius had a conference with Gratian at Sirmium; and this was followed by his edict of Thessalonica, confirmed by a Council in 381, which proclaimed the Nicene Christianity of the bishop of Rome to be the religion of the whole empire, and announced that Arians and pagans would be persecuted alike. This was the same line that Gratian had taken under the influence of Ambrosius, bishop of Mediolanum. It naturally provoked a senatorial pro-pagan reaction, led by Symmachus.

On Gratian's death in 383 his place was taken by the Spanish usurper Magnus Maximus, and a difficult and turbulent period began. Theodosius I was occupied with the pagan revolt and with a rebellion of the Antiochenes caused by fiscal exactions: he also had to concern himself with the threat of Persia, and consequently had to recognize the authority of Maximus in Britain, Gaul, and Spain, contenting himself with securing for Valentinian II, who still remained under his protection, the countries of Italy, Illyricum, and Africa. But Maximus, taking advantage of the discontent resulting from Valentinian's Arianism, succeeded in occupying Italy and threatened to invade Illyricum. At this point Theodosius took a hand, defeated Maximus at Aquileia (388) and had him executed, and once more placed all the West under Valentinian II, whose guardian was to be a pagan Frank named Arbogastes. But this general quarrelled with his pupil and had him murdered, transferring his support to a usurping rhetorician, Eugenius, who resumed the reaction against Christianity. Again Theodosius intervened, and the struggle took the shape of a civil war. Strongly supported by the Vandal general Stilicho, Theodosius defeated Eugenius at the Frigidus river (394) and then assumed sole control of the empire, extending his prohibition on pagan cults to West as well as East. But this last unification of the Roman world was short-lived, for in the following year Theodosius died, leaving the East to his son Arcadius under the guardianship of the Gallic praetorian prefect Rufinus, and the West to Honorius who was entrusted to the tutelage of the Vandal Stilicho. The division of the empire into two distinct parts, often at variance with each other, had for long been maturing: it was now made definite, and the barbarians were the first to see how they could take advantage of it.

At the death of Theodosius I Arcadius was seventeen and Honorius ten: the real heads of the two empires were Rufinus and Stilicho. The latter's aim was to reunite all the dominions into one, but before this the ambition of both rulers to acquire Illyricum created a perpetual state of discord. Each tried to tie the hands of the other by fomenting internal dangers, in particular by fostering rebellious subjects and promoting barbarian invasions. This state of affairs was just what the Visigothic leader Alaric wanted, and he made good use of it. He came down with his host to occupy Moesia and Thrace in 395, Macedonia and northern Greece in 397, and secured the recognition of the Visigoths as *foederati* and of himself as general of Illyricum. The Goth Gainas had been sent to Phrygia to fight the Ostrogoths, and it is entirely possible that it was Stilicho who induced him to reach an understanding with them instead and to occupy Constantinople, from which he was then expelled with his Arian barbarians by a rising of the Catholic population. From the other side, both before and after the deaths of the Empress Eudoxia (404) and of Arcadius (408—his successor was Theodosius II), Byzantium fostered and aided a number of troubles for the West. In 396–398, for example, the revolt of Gildo in Mauretania was supported not only by the Donatists but by Arcadius. But the affairs of the West were rapidly going to ruin. In 405 Alaric and his Goths advanced down to Mediolanum, though he was then defeated at Pollentia and Verona; in 405–406 Radagaisus with another Gothic army reached Florentia and was taken prisoner at Faesulae. But in 406, with the Huns who had entered Pannonia pressing at their backs, the Vandals, Alans, and Quadi invaded Gaul and infiltrated as far as Spain; in 407 the Picts and Scots from the island itself, with Saxons from Germany, occupied Britain, and Rome could offer no resistance to them. In the next year there was continuous discord between Stilicho and Honorius, though the emperor had married in succession two of his guardian's daughters, and despite the fact that Alaric was preparing a fresh expedition. The result was a massacre of Stilicho's adherents at Ticinum (Pavia), where Stilicho himself met his death at much the same time. The lowest point in the history of the Western empire was seen in 410, when Alaric succeeded in storming Rome and put it to sack for three days.

h. *Survival of the Eastern Empire*

At this point we must explain the chief reasons why Rome's power crumbled and fell in the Western regions but survived in the East for another thousand years.

To all appearances the two areas still had common foundations: their law, their administrative system, the nomination of annual consuls, one for each part, and so on. But in reality each was following different roads and different destinies. There was almost continuous discord between them, and conditions of life in the two were no longer comparable.

In the West and in the northern provinces population movements had assumed disastrous shape. The peasants, scattered over the countryside, beggared by fiscal exactions, and terrorized by barbarian raids, were taking to brigandage or seeking refuge inside city walls. But in their turn the *curiales* and the city workers, again to escape the *fiscus*, were leaving the towns, and sometimes escaping to live among the barbarians across the frontier. So the social and economic life of the cities was turned upside down, while in the country the only stable points offering a chance of survival were the villas on the great estates. These were owned by capitalists belonging to the senatorial class, and were defended by their own bands of armed men and *coloni*. They were organized as self-contained economies, consisting of a number of cells of feudal type, which had everything to gain if the state were weak and everything to lose if it were strong and firmly unified. These conditions helped the barbarians who found the cities ill defended, and the countryside largely depopulated and ripe for occupation. In the West another factor working for dissolution was the series of struggles between State and Church. The central government was fragile; and political ideas now favoured fragmentation of the centrifugal kind. There was no room for a unification of the *nationes* organized by Rome as overlord, an idea of recent origin which seemed foreign to the area. The centrifugal tendency was fostered by the rival empire of the East for its own advantage; for it wanted to weaken its adversary. But the chief reason for the weakness and decay was the excessive number of barbarians who had penetrated across the frontiers: some had come *en masse* as *foederati*; others were exceptional individuals who came as military leaders or 'duces gentium', and wanted to create principalities for themselves on Roman territory with or without the consent of the imperial government. This penetration was also working rapid changes in Roman culture. The barbarians did to some extent become Romanized by contact with Rome, but Roman citizens were also being barbarized and settling down to live at a lower level than in the past. As to religion, the barbarians were mostly Arians and the Romans Catholics, the difference leading to endless friction.

Compared with this very grave situation in the western and northern provinces, the provinces composing the Eastern empire were in a relatively privileged condition. Their economy was still flourishing on account of the progress made by industry and of the traffic by sea and caravan; their cities were luxurious; and the state was stronger both politically and militarily. The masses shared the government's views on religious matters; and the concept of subordination to an imperial régime was firmly held, for although they had changed their masters, the people of this area had been accustomed to submit to this form of government for thousands of years past. Moreover the Christian bishops were ready to accept the Caesaro-papism of the emperors. All these factors made the Eastern empire readier to withstand the barbarian invasions, and deterred the barbarians themselves from too easily embarking on the dangerous adventure of attacking it.

NOTES TO CHAPTER XIII

1. Hermaeus has sometimes been dated nearly a century earlier. For discussion (with support for Professor Petech's date) see W. Otto, *Realencyclopaedie*, VIII (1912), col. 712.

2. It does not look as though the division between the Aryan culture of the Pallava and the pure Dravidian culture of the Tamil kingdoms was complete. Exchanges were already important between the two cultures although the Pallava had made Sanskrit the dominant language of their official records and had substituted it instead of Prakrit (Sanskrit was a language in general use, as the society that used it was present everywhere).

3. This appellation is not generally accepted by the countries in question, which have a good idea of their own cultural originality breaking out in the differences in their arts and literature in relation to the arts and literature of India, whatever the importance of their borrowings from the latter.

4. Avidius Cassius, who was given charge of all the Eastern provinces after his striking successes against Parthia in 165, was himself of Syrian origin. This brought him wide support in the East when he rebelled in 175, though he was quickly assassinated.

5. One event in the mid-second century which must not be overlooked is the disastrous plague which spread over the empire from the East in the years following 165.

6. Professor Ch. Th. Saricakis emphasizes that Caracalla's edict (see Giessen Papyrus, 40) seems to have made some sort of exception for the class known as 'dediticii'. For the way in which this may have been done (and the exception need not involve any significant modification of Professor Pareti's statement) see A. H. M. Jones, *Studies in Roman Government and Law* (Oxford, 1959), pp. 129 ff.
   For a fuller account, see pp. 804 ff.

7. This was the peculiar privilege of those cities which had what were called 'Latin rights'. The provinces also, of course, contained some cities (Roman colonies, and also 'municipia') in which all the freeborn inhabitants were Romans.

8. These first appear about the time of Trajan (*c.* AD 100).

9. These 'fugitive' peasants (and to some extent perhaps also artisans from the cities) are most significant of the economic distress of the period. Although suppressed by Maximian in 286 they are still active in Gaul a century later. See *Cambridge Ancient History*, XII (1938), p. 267; and for similar movements in other parts of the empire, M. Rostovtzeff, *Social and Economic History of the Roman Empire* (2nd edition, Oxford, 1957), p. 738.

10. The tradition is reflected in certain early coins.

11. Professor H. Hunger criticizes the use of this term (here and in other parts of this work) to describe the relation of the Church either to Constantine or to the later emperors of Byzantium. For Byzantium see Volume III of the *History of Mankind*. As regards Constantine's position see the classic description by N. H. Baynes, 'Constantine the Great and the Christian Church', *Proceedings of the British Academy*, 1929.

12. Valens actually encouraged this settlement, because he hoped the Visigoths would support his Arian policy.

CHAPTER XIV

LANGUAGE AND WRITING

I. LANGUAGE

a. *Chinese in Evolution*

This period coincides approximately with the last stages of 'Archaic Chinese' and with the beginning of 'Ancient Chinese'. It is a transitional period to the Sui and T'ang pronunciations which have been preserved in the *Ch'ieh-yün* dictionary of 601. This will be discussed in the next volume.

The appearance of a foreign element in the vocabulary linked with Buddhism which had penetrated China from the first century AD must be noted. The translation of the sacred texts of the new religion from Sanskrit and from the various Prakrit and central Asian languages created a series of problems in morphology as well as syntax. The technical Buddhist terms were for the most part translated, others were transcribed; but few of the latter became part of the inherited vocabulary of the Chinese language. Syntax struggled between two opposed and irreconcilable ideals: a good Chinese style or the most faithful adherence possible to an original text which was completely different in syntactical outlook. As a result the earlier portions of the great corpus of Buddhist canonical writings (*San-tsang*) consist of very free translations, which often are more like paraphrases of the original Indian text; on the other hand they are nearly always couched in a sort of special jargon and in a style so little related to classical Chinese as to be almost unintelligible to non-Buddhist *literati*. As a result of these peculiarities Buddhist influence on the Chinese language was negligible in vocabulary, style, and syntax.

From the territorial point of view, Chinese language in its various dialects (about which little is known for this period) continued its slow but unceasing advance toward the south-west. It established full dominance in the plains and in the more fertile valleys, and pushed back the local languages into the hills, in zones that were ever poorer and more rugged. The earlier phases of this long-drawn process are little known, as practically no evidence can be extracted from the historical texts. We can only draw inferences from present-day conditions; but of course we have to keep in mind that the latter are the result of another 1,500 years of evolution after the period dealt with here.

The most important of these linguistic relics are Lolo and Moso in Szechwan and Yünnan, both belonging to the Tibeto-Burman group; Miao-tzŭ, a marginal language of the same group, in Kweichow and Yünnan; and Dioi, of the Thai family, in Kweichow and Kwanghsi.

In this period Chinese became the language of culture in Korea and Vietnam. Its use as one of the commercial languages of central Asia is witnessed by documents found in the sands of the Tarim basin by English, Swedish, and French expeditions.

b. *Languages in India*

Sanskrit, having ceased to be a living tongue, continued to be the language of the Hindu religion and the medium and subject of classical education.[1] It rapidly gained ground against the various Prakrit dialects as a literary language. The structure of its morphology and syntax is settled down to the smallest details by the devoted and assiduous work of the great grammarians of the Pāṇini school, of whom Patañjali was the most important. Towards the end of this period even some of the Buddhist schools adopted Sanskrit, though not without giving it a slight special tinge, resulting from peculiarities in syntactic usage, a new technical terminology, and preferential use of certain particles.

The so-called 'hybrid Sanskrit', distinct from Buddhist Sanskrit, was also employed in some of the Buddhist schools. Beneath its ungrammatical appearance, there was concealed a conscious effort to give literary dignity to a Prakrit dialect (perhaps a form of Ardhamāgadhī) by drawing it as close to Sanskrit as possible.[2]

In this epoch Sanskrit gradually but completely replaced the Prakrit dialects as the language of epigraphy throughout all the Aryan-speaking areas; it came to be so used even in the Dravidian zone, though it never succeeded in dispossessing the local languages. It then began its triumphant expansion to the south-east. The first Sanskrit inscription in Indo-China may be the Vo Canh *stele*, possibly of the third century AD, although some authors would place it one century later.

Before the end of this period Sanskrit inscriptions are to be found in Cambodia, the Malay Peninsula, Sumatra, Java, and Borneo. Sanskrit dominated the cultural and religious life of 'Greater India', until its collapse in the fifteenth century.[3]

Inscriptional Prakrit yielded to Sanskrit and disappeared. For a long time the exception was the Prakrit of the Kharoṣṭhī documents of Niya. This was the language used in the community of Indian merchants who had settled in central Asia: in this case it was therefore a question of a language which was really spoken, almost completely free from literary elaborations. It should be noted that the Prakrit languages did not spread at all into south-east Asia.

The literary Prakrit languages, instead, survived either where their use was tied to a particular literary form, in which case they ended by becoming languages of art, or dead languages like Sanskrit, or where they had become the sacred language of particular religious schools.

Among the first category belong the Prakrit dialects used by specific characters in Indian drama—women, servants, clowns, men of low caste, and so on, while kings and Brahmans speak Sanskrit. Saurasenī is the foremost such dialect, Māgadhī and Mahārāṣṭrī are less common. Mahārāṣṭrī on the other hand is employed also outside the theatre in epic poems such as the *Gauḍavaho* and in lyric anthologies such as the *Sattasaī of Hāla*. Paiśācī, a north-western dialect not attested in drama, occupies a particular position since it was used for a great collection of stories, the *Bṛhatkathā* of Guṇāḍhya.

The 'religious' Prakrits are local dialects which in time underwent varying degrees of artificial elaboration. The oldest of these, still very near to Sanskrit, is Pali, whose original home is doubtful. It became the language of a Buddhist school (*Theravāda*), and later, when it had ceased to be a living tongue, accompanied as the sacred language the expansion of Hīnayāna[4] Buddhism to southern Asia (Ceylon, Burma, Thailand, Cambodia, Laos).

Another more advanced form is used in the Jain canon. The oldest parts of this canon, the only ones which are of interest here, are composed in Ardhamāgadhī ('half'-Māgadhī). Other dialects were employed by the two sections of the Jain community for their later canons.

c. *Languages in Iranic Countries*

When the diffusion of Greek and Aramaic had faded in these countries, the Iranic languages reappeared with new vigour: they were now reduced to two groups both called 'Middle Iranic'; one a western or Pehlevīk tongue and the other eastern. The western group appears in two dialect forms, Parthian and the true Middle Persian. Parthian, heavily influenced by Armenian, was spread over the north-west of the country, and is documented in the first century AD about the year 88 by the Graeco-Parthian parchment of *Auraman*, by inscriptions on coins, and later by documents of the Sassanid dynasty. The last were often written in two versions, Parthian and neo-Persian. Parthian was also used in Manichaean literature from the beginning of the third century.

Middle Persian proper (or *Pārsīk*) in the south-west of the zone was the real descendant of Old Persian, with infiltrations of Armenian, Syrian, and Arabian. It was the official language of the Sassanids from 226 onwards. It is attested first by inscriptions and then by papyri, and was used for both religious and profane literature, Mazdean and Manichaean.

In the eastern group a number of dialects were at one time or another used in writing and officially: (1) Sogdian, which in time became the international language of central Asia, appears already in the fourth century in epistolary documents written in cursive letters which were found in the region of the 'Great Wall' (Touen-Houang); (2) the dialects of Khotan (or Śaka) and of Chorasmia, though no written evidence of them has yet been found for this period; (3) the Indo-Scythian, Kuṣāṇa, dialect attested by coin inscriptions of the second–third centuries AD.

d. *Semitic Languages*

We now pass on to the northern Semitic languages. There was neo-Hebrew which was used from the first century AD in the writing of the Qumran sect and, between AD *c.* 190 and *c.* 500, in *Mishnah*, the *Talmuds* and related treatises; it was nearer to the last spoken Hebrew than to the purist form of the language and it was much influenced by Aramaic. In North Africa there was neo-Punic, the last off-shoot of Phoenician, inscriptions in which continue to at least the fourth century AD. But the predominant language of the Middle East was Aramaic in its various forms. For instance there was an Aramaic dialect in Palestine used for translations and paraphrases in popularized versions of the Bible (*Targum* means translation) and for re-editing the *Mishnah* with the additional sections (*Gemara*) which comprised the so-called Palestinian *Talmud*. We can distinguish three regional types of Palestinian Aramaic: (1) Judaean in the Qumran documents and *Targum* earlier than AD 138; (2) Galilean, in the Jerusalem *Talmud* from the School of Tiberias; (3) Samaritan in the *Targum* of the fourth century. In addition we have (4) Nabataean-Aramaic found in recently discovered documents and on second–third century *graffiti* from Sinai; and (5) Palmyrean on inscriptions contemporary with the wars with Rome which ended with Aurelian.

The typical north-eastern Aramaic was Syriac, used particularly in the city of Edessa, which from the third century became one of the focal points for the diffusion of the Christian faith.

Before passing to the southern Semitic or Arabian languages it should be noted that in our period certain northern Arabs changed their homes. A new wave of people was pushed forward north of the Nabataeans in the region of Damascus where Arab *graffiti* are found alongside Greek. Written texts for central Arabia begin with one of AD 128 from En Namara. Finally when the Ethiopians, who had originally been immigrants from Arabia, temporarily conquered the Yemen in the fifth century, there was no noticeable linguistic change.

e. *Egyptian Languages*

A remarkable instance of the resurgence of a national language is found in Egypt. During the Ptolemaic period there were three ethnic groups, native, Hebrew, and Greek. Greek, which was numerically inferior, became dominant and even succeeded in Hellenizing the Hebrew element. This position was maintained even under Roman sovereignty, since the Romans, who formed only a small, though politically dominant, force in the country, kept aloof and abandoned any attempt to Latinize Egypt. Instead they regarded the Greek citizenship of Alexandria as an essential stepping-stone before the inhabitants received Roman citizenship, which was in any case very sparingly granted before Caracalla's edict.

Later when Christianity, spread by Hellenized elements, was sweeping over the indigenous Egyptians, it created a national missionary outlook of its own. In time the Egyptian language, in the new Coptic script derived from Greek (which was used instead of the old demotic), was responsible for a very remarkable literary output, mainly religious, in the last decades of the second century and throughout the third. The Egyptian language maintained its own clear character and full use until the Arab invasions. One of the most marked offshoots of this resurgence was the nationalistic spirit which characterized it. It was completely divorced from the world-wide Greek-Christian, Hellenized-Hebrew ambit.

The movement began, naturally enough, in Upper Egypt where the population was almost entirely indigenous, and it assumed various dialectical forms in particular regions.

f. Survival of Greek Dialects

Greek literary *koiné*, with an Attic and Ionic base, submerged its Achaeo-Doric competitor of western Greece, its victory being complete by about 50 BC. It still had to compete with the local speech of the Dorian islands of the Aegean, which was still alive in the imperial period. But the Attico-Ionic *koiné* ended by becoming the one language not only of literature but of common use.

How much this *koiné* was influenced by the old dialects in each of the affected areas remains to be clarified. On this question the evidence is slight, and scholars' conjectures very different. Thumb, for example, reduces the idea of a combination to its minimum, while Kretschmer gives it great weight. It is true that there are few modern dialects in the Greek world for which clear evidence can be gathered to connect them with the ancient dialects: examples are Tzakonian on the eastern coast of the Peloponnese, Maniot in the southern Peloponnese, and dialects of southern Italy, and the new colonies in Asia Minor. But the uniformity of the other dialects is probably a comparatively recent development. There is very little to prove the contention that about AD 500 the ancient Greek dialects, even in their derivative forms, were dead.

The variety of spoken *koiné* was, naturally, greater in the colonial areas. It must have been most marked in the new Greek settlements in Asia, where foreign words infiltrated, Greek locutions had new meanings, and non-Greek constructions were in use. It would vary too with the proportion of Greeks to barbarians, with the nature of the local languages, and with the use of *koiné* itself, which in some areas was used only for official and literary writing, in others for practical purposes.

But even in the imperial period there were reactions against literary *koiné*. The neo-Attic of the new Sophists took hold not only of the lexicographers of the second century and later, but also of good writers such as Lucian of Samosata. There were also more or less sporadic attempts, attested by epigraphy, to write in Doric (especially Laconian), Ionic, and Aeolic, either out of archaism or through regional pride.

g. *Vulgar Latin and its Survivals*

It was certainly not impossible that there should have been a homogeneous literary and educated Latin language given the great diversity in origin, nature, taste, and culture of the Latin writers, who for many centuries came in increasing numbers from the provinces. But it is even more natural that the 'common and daily speech' (which soldiers and colonists from various parts of Italy, each with its own regional characteristics, introduced into the provinces, which again were ethnically and linguistically distinct), appeared there in very diverse forms.

So for example if the vulgar Latin of the Po valley was very different from that of the Oscan and Umbrian districts, far greater was the difference between the vulgar Latins of Belgica and Spain, when each country ceased to be bilingual and spoke its own 'Latin'—a thorough mixture of Latin and the indigenous pre-Roman tongue.

There remain details of various kinds which give a less general idea of the variety of vulgar Latin over a wide range of space and time. Among these are the texts of authors who used a more popular language in their works, such as the comedians beginning with Plautus; the propagandist Christian writers who addressed the people; the didactic writers on agriculture; the *Satyricon* of Petronius; the grammarians and lexicographers who refer to the vulgar forms; inscriptions cut by common people, and Latin texts transcribed by uneducated copyists; lastly reconstructions of the original vulgar Latin provided in glosses on neo-Latin renderings.

For it is clear that the modern neo-Latin dialects are only the continuation of those regional Latin dialects which history and race have allowed to continue and to develop through the centuries without great upheavals. This continuity was not possible, for example, in north-west Africa which was flooded by the Arab race, nor in those countries which had too many German immigrations. Elsewhere the results were neither uniform nor homogeneous since they depended on variables such as the numerical proportion between the Arab, German, and (later) Slav immigrants and the Romanized inhabitants, as well as the degree of integration achieved, the depth of Romanization in the region, the duration and extent of the invaders' rule.

In other countries such as in the Italian peninsula, the greater part of southern Gaul, Spain (with the exception of the less Romanized Basque country), and in the Alpine belt now called Rhaeto-Romance the bands of immigrants were too thin in comparison with the Romanized inhabitants. The newcomers intermarried little, while they destroyed each other or were destroyed by the Byzantines, Franks, and Arabs. Therefore the earlier racial structure, except for some of the ruling aristocratic class, underwent less decisive modifications, and so the pre-Roman races survived in the main into the succeeding centuries. In other regions such as Flanders, the modern Walloon countries, and some parts of southern Britain the racial mixture achieved a well-balanced compound, and this in time resulted in a balanced hybrid language. At the other end the flood of immigrants was so over-whelming as to make it almost impossible, except to linguistic experts, to detect the traces of Romanization however intense it may once have been.

The spread of Latin in Dacia, and the neo-Latin of modern Rumania, are separate questions. When Trajan conquered Dacia at the beginning of the second century AD he strengthened the indigenous population with a large number of colonists who were drawn from 'all parts of the Roman world'. This resulted in a fairly rapid Romanization of the country, which lasted even when Dacia was lost politically to Rome in the third century. Although in fact Dacia was probably abandoned in 271, we need not take too literally a phrase in Vopiscus (*Life of Aurelian*) that the whole civil population was evacuated south of the Danube. At most it would only have been soldiers and officials. If the survival of Latin in Dacia is not mentioned in succeeding centuries, it is because writers did not mention Dacia at all. At any rate, even if Rumanian neo-Latin was derived wholly from the people who moved south of the Danube (and this is an incredible hypothesis), it would not alter the fact that this Balkan neo-Latin of modern times is linked with the language of the people from the Lower Danube who were deeply Latinized in the second and third centuries AD.

h. *The Germanic Languages*

From the beginning the Germanic languages connect more with the Celtic and Italic than with any other subdivisions of Indo-European. They can be divided for the earliest period into three types. The first can be called 'north-east' in the sense that the people who spoke it, the Goths, lived at one time in the north-east in Scandinavia (so 'Göterland'); from there in the second century AD they descended by the valley of the Vistula and passed south-east to the coast of the Black Sea, dividing into Ostrogoths and Visigoths. This is attested by some inscriptions which may belong to the third century AD but the most important text which proves it is the Gothic version of the Bible by the bishop of Nicopolis in Lower Moesia, Wulfila or Ulfilas, who lived between 311 and about 383. We have some later documents of the sixth century from the Goths who moved into Italy.

The 'northern Germans', after their separation from the Goths, remained in the north and, as one would expect, spoke a language closely linked with Gothic speech. This is attested by a series of brief inscriptions, of which the earliest are from the third century AD, written in Runic letters.

The third or 'western' group in their peripheral areas south of the Danube and west of the Rhine were more intensely influenced by Latin, both in morphology and by the introduction of new agricultural and religious words. Evidence for this group in written texts is much later (see above Part I,

p. 791). But the earliest Germanic personal, religious, and place names
recorded by ancient writers in some glosses on Caesar, Pliny, and Tacitus,
and in numerous Latin and a few Greek inscriptions and papyri, belong to
this group.

i. *North Etruscan Linguistic Derivations*

Unless one has a clear idea of the ancient North Etruscan dialects, of which
Rhaetian was only one among many, one cannot grasp the essence of an
isolated neo-Latin language which derives from those dialects. Equally it
would be impossible to explain the small size of the area to which these
dialects are reduced today, by infiltrations of Germanic speech to the south
and by Celto-Italic speech to the north. The language in question is Ladin
or Romansch, and the area where it is now spoken are the Grisons, the
Dolomite valleys of the Upper Adige, and Friuli. The similarities between
the speech of these three pockets are certainly based on racial affinities; and
all these regions also escaped in varying degrees the sweeping influence of
German and Celtic speech. It seems logical to think that the Ladin dialects
are the survival of those spoken on the Alps before the German and
Celtic immigrations, and are therefore related to the Latinized dialects spoken
in Etruria.

Even in ancient times the Celtic infiltration on the North Etruscan dialects
was strongest south-west of Lugano, less so in Sondrio, and least of all north-
east of Bolzano. It is therefore easy to understand how this process continued
in later generations through the agency of the Celticized cities in the Po
valley.

The area of the western and middle Ladin dialects corresponds in fact
with ancient Rhaetia, but excluding part of the Alpine foothills and also the
great routes across the Alps through which foreign elements from the north
and south had infiltrated.

The greatest difficulties concern Friuli. It has so many peculiarities to
distinguish it from the Ladin of the Grisons or the Trentino. The probable
explanation is that there was an intermediate racial element between proto-
Etruscan and neo-Latin, namely that mixture of Illyrian and Venetic which
is represented by the Euganei of ancient tradition. But this complicated
question certainly cannot be tackled here, and we must simply note the fact
that it exists.

j. *Other Linguistic Groups*

We must refer to the general information given in Part I and to the special
material in Volume III for the penetration into Europe of Asiatic languages
with the emigrations which began in the fourth century and were more fully
developed in the fifth century and later. In the Avars, Huns, and Alans who
carried them out Indo-European (Scythian) elements were mixed with other
races, Caucasians, Mongols, and Turcoids.

In any case it is almost impossible to advance anything better than pro-visional and untested hypotheses because of the scarcity of ancient references, which are themselves often confused and equivocal, the lack of contemporary written material, and the racial admixtures among the migrant peoples.

Some general ideas of a largely hypothetical kind were also put forward in Part I about the languages of countries such as central and southern Africa, Armenia, and Oceania, and to them no further reference need be made.

2. WRITING

a. *Writing and Writing Materials in China*

By this time Chinese writing in its principles and forms was complete. No substantial modifications took place in this period with the exception of the creation of new characters, and the general adoption of *ch'iai-shu*, i.e., of the modern form of writing. The so-called 'grass script' was used at the same time—a cursive form which varied a great deal from one writer to another.

The art of calligraphy in this period boasts some of its most distinguished names, such as Wang Hsi-chih (321–379) and his son Wang Hsien-chih (344–388).

The writing followed the language wherever this became the 'medium of cultural life', for instance in Vietnam and Korea. So Chinese language and script, known in Japan from the fourth century, were adopted for official governmental use from 405. Subsequently Chinese characters were also employed to transcribe the Japanese language, but this is a development which lies outside the limits of our period.

In writing materials the great discovery was paper, which was made with cellulose from rags. Tradition attributes the discovery to Ts'ai Lun (d.114), who presented it to the emperor in 105. However it should be noted that in 1931 F. Bergman found at Edsin-gol a piece of rag-paper together with some pieces of inscribed bamboo; and the dating of the latter (according to Lao Kan) cannot be later than 98, so the paper must therefore be contemporary or very little older. As it is evident that paper was already being made in China and even being sent to such remote outposts of the western frontier on the edge of the desert, it seems probable that, as with the brush, the evolution of paper had been a long process in which Ts'ai Lun only symbolizes the official conclusion. Other datable fragments of paper documents have been found in central Asia: at Lou-lan (*c.*260), Niya (*c.*250–300), and Turfan (*c.*399).

Naturally it was paper alone that made the great development in calli-graphy possible and which provided an easily accessible and cheap material instead of silk. But without printing and the possibility of duplication it provided, the introduction of paper was not altogether a happy event for the preservation of Chinese literary works, since paper was less durable than the parchment and papyri of the West. As a result no early Chinese manuscript

book has survived the ravages of time with the exception of the library that
shortly after 1000 was immured in a cave at Tun-huang, and was opened by
Sir Aurel Stein in 1907; the earliest dated manuscript in it belongs to 406.

b. *Central Asian Writing*

Many alphabets were used in central Asia in addition to Chinese;
Kharoṣṭhī was used to transcribe a Prakrit dialect. There it was somewhat
improved by a better notation of vowels; at the beginning it had made no distinction between short and long. The *Dutreil du Rhins* manuscript, possibly of
the second century, gives a unique example of a literary text of some length
written in Kharoṣṭhī. The last tablets from central Asia in this alphabet are
not later than the seventh century. Brahmī was used for Sanskrit and Prakrit
texts, and (in a form derived from Gupta, itself a form of Brahmī) for
Kuchean and Karashahri (pseudo-Tocharian), and Khotanese Śaka, but
central Asian Brahmī is attested only after the end of this period. The Greek
alphabet survived among the Kuṣāṇa, who used it on their coins to transcribe
their own language. It was retained also on the coinage of the Hephthalites
(fifth–sixth centuries); and we have fragments of texts in which a modified form
of the Greek alphabet was used to write the true Tocharian, the language of
Tokharestan in the north of modern Afghanistan. Later the Aramaic alphabet
penetrated from Iran into central Asia and there it was adapted to write
Sogdian; the enormous success of this language as the language of commerce
from the Caspian to China assured the widest diffusion to the alphabet in
which it was written, and from it the Uigur, Mongol, and Manchu scripts
are derived.

c. *Writing and Writing Materials in India*

Of the two writings in use in India in the preceding period Kharoṣṭhī
became rarer from the second century and the last inscriptions in the north-
west of India belong to the fifth century.

Brahmī was altered and took on variant local forms from which Indian
mediaeval scripts may well have been derived. The Śaka-Kuṣāṇa form in the
north-west was victorious in its competition with Kharoṣṭhī, and is found
in use on central Asian texts. After an evolutionary phase (Andhra and
Kṣatrapa inscriptions) it develops into the Gupta script, one of the most
important stages in Indian palaeographic history. Farther south Brahmī was
the origin of the script in the third–fifth-centuries Pallava inscriptions and in
the somewhat later Cālukya inscriptions. A further development from the
Cālukya script is seen in the Telugu, Kanara, and Tamil alphabets, which
have as a common characteristic the generally rounded form of their letters;
but this was a local fashion, and had nothing to do with the material employed. In the end Brahmī, in its southern form, crossed the sea and from it
derived the various scripts used in south-east Asia and in Indonesia from the
end of this period onwards.

Copper plates (*tāmrapattra*) and stone were the materials for inscriptions. As for manuscripts their Sanskrit name is *pustaka*, from the Iranic *post* meaning skin; but parchment, as far as we know, was never used in India. Apart from the textiles and vegetable fibres the use of which is vaguely implied by Strabo and Quintus Curtius, but for which there is no direct evidence, by far the most important material used in India has always been the palm leaf (*tālapattra*) of which fragments have been found in central Asia going back to the first century AD. The plant used is *Corypha umbraculifera Linn.* or *Borassus flabelliformis Linn.* The leaves, written on both faces lengthwise, were laid one upon the other, and held together by a string which passed through one or two holes in the middle of the leaf. Wood tablets were not used on so large a scale as in central Asia—their use in India is quite incidental. However birch bark (*Betula bhojpattr*) was widely employed in Kashmir and the neighbouring countries. Paper appears in central Asia, to which it had of course been imported from China, and it was used for some of the fourth–fifth-centuries manuscripts in Gupta characters. But paper was not introduced in India until much later and then chiefly by the Muslim invaders.

Writing instruments in the north were for the most part the bamboo pen (*iṣīkā*) and ink (*maṣi*). An iron point (*śalakā*), with which letters were engraved on the surface of the palm leaf, took the place of the pen in the south, and was sometimes used in the north as well.

d. *Aramaic and its Derivations*

The Aramaic alphabet established itself, not only in the Hebrew, Samaritan, Palmyrene, and Nabataean variations as in the preceding period, but also in new areas.

The writing known as Syriac derived, with frequent ligatures, from an Aramaic cursive script. It had its centre at Edessa and is first found on coins and inscriptions of the first century AD. It developed as the Christian Church in Syria grew in importance and spread as far as Mesopotamia, and acquired the name of *estrangelō* or *estrangelā* writing, very probably because it was used for the transmission of the Gospel. In time it developed several regional forms especially in relation to the many Christian sects.

In the Iranic zone Pehlevik (Arsacid) and even more Pārsīk (or Sassanid Pehlevīk) writing continued to be used. So-called Avestic writing, with its fifty signs, developed later from a mixture of the two with other additions.

The Sogdi of eastern Turkestan, who pushed forward into north-west India (the Indo-Scythians) and into Mongolia, continued to develop a writing which was originally Aramaic: the earliest documents are of the second century BC. This writing spread over a wide area in the Middle Ages when Sogdian became the 'lingua franca' of central Asia. We have already spoken of the development of the Aramaic alphabet in India (see p. 377).

The Armenian alphabet according to tradition was derived from two

intentional inventions made to acquire sacred texts independent of the Greek
and the Syrian Church: one invention was by a Syrian bishop, Daniel; the
other, more decisive, invention was by Meśrōp or Mastoc who was born in
the fourth century and died in 441. In fact, however, it is not clear whether
the Armenian alphabet of thirty-six signs derived from Greek or from
Pehlevīk, or whether, as is more probable, its creator took account of both
models and added other elements.

According to tradition the same inventor also created the analogous
writing called 'Albanian'. The two Georgian scripts appear also to have
derived from continuing developments in Pehlevīk with additions from
Greek: one was the 'warrior' writing which goes back to AD 300, the other
was ecclesiastical. The former became the writing which passed into common
use.

e. The Alphabets of Southern Arabia

The alphabets of southern Arabia are attested by many epigraphical
documents: we know many varieties of these alphabets, the principal ones
being Minaean, Sabaean, and Himyaritic. They seem to have descended
from a common prototype nearest to Sabaean, which, in addition to twenty-
two letters from Phoenician and Aramaic, has six additional consonants which
the north Arabian alphabet represents by diacritical marks. The antiquity of
these southern Arabian alphabets is in dispute because the chronology of the
local kingdoms which employed them is inadequately known. These alphabets spread through the colonies which the southern Arabs set up for trade
and in a bid for supremacy in the areas of Dedan, Hegra, and south-east of
Damascus. In those regions three types of writing can be distinguished:
Lihyānitic, Thamūdene, and Safaitic.

About the third century AD southern Arabian writing passed also to
Ethiopia, where the Ethiopian alphabet presents such modifications as were
needed to express the characteristic sounds of the local languages. Gradually
the expansion of Coptic script in this region was halted, and its use reduced
to small proportions.

f. The Latin Alphabet

In the first centuries of the empire the Latin alphabet, with its twenty-three
letters, attained its most elegant form in the epigraphic texts of 'capitalis
epigraphica'; it then sank progressively from the fourth century. At the same
time the elegant writing 'capitalis libraria' was being used for codices. But
quicker and easier systems with cursive tendencies were coming into fashion
as well: the 'capitalis rustica' or 'actuaria', both for writing in public deeds
and for inscribing walls and tablets; the 'capitalis semicursiva' used on stone
or in books; the archaic 'semiuncialis' of the third–fourth centuries; and the
'uncialis' which held the field from the third century onwards. Cursive
proper in many variations—capitals, majuscules, and minuscules—made its

appearance, easy to write but not always so easy to read on account of the ligatures joining several letters together. This became the writing normally employed for documents at the time when the language was most widely diffused.

There was only one temporary modification in the number of signs: in the reign of Claudius new signs were adopted to express the consonant V, Ps, and the sound between U and I.

g. *Runic and Ogam*

There are several problems about Runic, Ogam, and Gothic scripts. The form of writing with which the Germans got acquainted was used first by the North Etruscans and Celts; and both these people derived their writing from the Phocaeans. So the most probable view is that Runic letters were initially a Greek alphabet, which the Germans learned through the intermediary of these two peoples, and that Latin features were later added to it. But many characteristics of Runes, such as the preference for vertical and oblique lines, to the exclusion of the horizontal and rounded ones, are the result of the wooden material on which inscriptions were cut. The order of the twenty-four letters is peculiar. Since Runic writing was spread over an enormous area, from Scandinavia to the Danube valley and Rumania to the south-east, and to England and Ireland on the north-west, there are naturally many variants, of which the earliest can be classified into Germanic and Anglo-Saxon. The earliest texts seem to belong to the third or fourth centuries AD.

The fact is that Runes seem to presuppose a type of writing known as Ogam, employed by the Celts in Ireland and England on inscriptions from the fourth century onwards. This has twenty kinds of stroke, both single and in groups, and both perpendicular and oblique, above and below a straight line. These are the signs for letters, and they read either from bottom to top or from left to right.

In addition the Germanic Runes seem to be connected with the Gothic script which was used by Bishop Wulfila for his Bible translation in the fourth century. The script, however, could not have been evolved without direct knowledge and the use of Greek and Latin alphabets.

NOTES TO CHAPTER XIV

1. Even today Sanskrit can be used in conversation between learned Indians from different provinces. But above all it had been, before the introduction of Persian followed by English, the one language which, throughout the whole of India, had been the object of a classical education. Without being known to all, it was the one language present everywhere and consequently the only definite instrument of communication between people of different mother-tongues whether Dravidian or composed of Prakrits differentiated by the lack of a classic form. This explains its success not only as the religious and literary

language but also its use in official epigraphy in India and abroad. (Cf. J. Filliozat, 'Sanskrit as Language of Communication', Bhandarkar Oriental Research Institute, *Annals*, XXXVI, Parts III–IV [1956], pp. 179–189.)

2. The distinction between 'hybrid Sanskrit' and 'Buddhist Sanskrit' is without doubt justified because hybrid Sanskrit, mixed with Prakrit forms, is not solely Buddhist but is found in secular epigraphy. For its part Buddhist Sanskrit is not always hybrid. It is so, however, in the earliest texts. The theory that hybrid Sanskrit was related to an effort to give literary dignity to a Prakrit dialect is not very likely. A Sanskrit which constantly abused the rules long recognized by purists could not pretend to any literary dignity. This Sanskrit is more likely to correspond to a transitional stage in the first centuries of its usage when it began to be used instead of Prakrits as the language of inter-provincial and international relations. (Cf. *T'oung Pao*, XLIII, 1–2, pp. 164 ff.)

3. There was not a 'collapse' of Greater India in the fifteenth century, but there were political disasters: these did not coincide completely with a cultural change which, beginning earlier, had substituted Pali for Sanskrit as the language of religious culture. Pali has since kept the position it had acquired in Burma, Thailand, Cambodia, and Laos.

4. The term Hīnayāna currently employed to describe the Buddhism of the School of *Theravāda* is injurious; it means: 'the inferior way to advance', or 'the inferior vehicle', and it has the disadvantage of not being precise enough, seeing that many different sects were lumped together under this name by their opponents (see Chapter XVII, p. 833).

CHAPTER XV

COMMERCE, TECHNOLOGY, AND SCIENCE

I. ECONOMICS, TRADE, AND TECHNIQUES

a. *China*

Economic Reforms. Wang Mang's short usurpation (AD 9–23, though in fact the real power was in his hands from 8 BC) was marked by a series of economic and financial reforms, which deeply convulsed Chinese society. In the resulting chaos Wang Mang's régime and his reforms were shipwrecked and not much survived the storm.

And yet this attempt occupies an important place in Chinese history. From one point of view the word 'reforms' is a misnomer. Wang Mang did not want to innovate at all; on the contrary, his aim was to lead China back to the institutions of the earliest antiquity as described in the classics. But since this antiquity was for the most part a reconstruction by the Confucian *literati* in general and the *ku-wen* school in particular, the actual effect was one of startling novelties under an archaic garb.

His experiments with coinage will be mentioned in their context. In AD 6 he coined four new denominations of copper coins; at the same time he nationalized (against compensation) all gold in private possession, thus heavily penalizing the old Han nobility. Between AD 9 and 10 he increased the number of denominations to make twenty-eight in all. These coins were lighter than their nominal value and thus were meant to ensure a profit for the government. The new coinage met with disapproval and passive resistance from the mercantile classes, and in AD 14 it was changed for the third time. It must be recognized that these experiments, whose main purpose was fiscal, did not affect the farmers, i.e. the bulk of the people, overmuch, because they used very little money and merely carried on a small barter trade.

Conditions of land tenure had altered in the last years of the old régime with great loss to imperial finance because of the increase in large holdings, in tenancy, and in landless labourers who turned vagrant. In AD 9 Wang Mang proclaimed the re-establishment of the *ching* system, which according to Confucian tradition had been the rule in early Chou times. The unit (*ching*) was an area one *li* square, divided into nine equal squares. Of these, eight were given to as many farmer families. Each of them also cultivated one-ninth of the central square, the produce of which was handed over to the government as land revenue. The remaining ninth of the central square was for building purposes. The model farmer family was supposed to contain five persons and one male worker. Land was granted when a worker was twenty years old, and withdrawn when he was sixty. In this utopian form the units were much too small: the system required an impossibly fertile soil and was only an antiquarian's dream. Wang Mang, however, enacted it as a means of reducing large holdings and vagrancy. At the same time, in order to prevent any further concentration of land, he nationalized the soil and forbade it to be bought or sold. He also established a maximum amount of land (900 *mou*) which one family of up to nine males could hold. This meant that the possessions of wealthy land-owners were confiscated and that land ceased to have any market value. Private slavery was also abolished as such, and the slaves were turned into 'private dependants' (*ssû-shu*). This measure chiefly hit the households of the great nobles, since private slave-holding in China was mainly domestic, and little if any land-slavery on the Roman pattern existed, though of course penal servitude was widespread and the state owned large numbers of such slaves. The social turmoil arising from these measures was such that after two years the prohibition against the sale of land and slaves had to be rescinded. Things rested here, except for a heavy tax imposed in AD 17 on all slave-owners. There probably had been no actual attempt at parcelling the country into *ching*, and thus the main effect of this short-lived reform was to limit the size of holdings.

Taxation was increased, with the introduction of an income tax, reduction in the salaries of officials, and special levies on their savings.

Another group of reforms concerned state monopolies. Salt and iron monopolies went back at least to the times of the Ch'in dynasty, and although the Confucian *literati* protested against them, they were maintained. Wang Mang, pressed for money, added other monopolies: on liquor, on coinage (this existed already; perhaps it included also mining and smelting of copper), on the products of mountains and marshes (forestry, fishing, hunting, gathering of wild honey, etc.). These five monopolies (or 'controls', *kuan*, as they were called) resulted in the price of certain necessities being stabilized at a high level. They weighed chiefly on the lowest classes of the people, who were compelled to pay in order to obtain a licence to ply their usual simple trades, now covered by the monopolies. A sixth control was the so-called 'Five Equalizations', implying state control of price and distribution of staple goods (chiefly grain), coupled with state loans to farmers. It was an attempt which had precedents in the Warring States period and under the Former Han dynasty. As aptly summarized by H. H. Dubs, *History of the Former Han Dynasty*, p. 532, 'at the imperial capital and at five other large cities . . . storehouses were built. In the middle of each quarter, the Master at each market was to determine a price for equalization for each of three grades of goods (high, middle, low). These prices were to apply to the five kinds of grains (hemp and similar seeds, glutinous millet, paniculed millet, wheat, and beans), linen cloth and silk cloth, thread, and wadding. When any of these goods remained unsold in the market (as they were brought in by farmers), the office for equalization was to buy them at cost or at the market price (provided that price was lower than the price for equalization), so that the people would lose nothing by being compelled to receive a lower price on the market. When the price rose above the price for equalization, the office for equalization was to sell its goods at the price for equalization. Fluctuations of prices in the market were thus to be prevented, merchants were not to be allowed to corner goods or fleece the country people, and the farmers were to be assured of a market for their goods. People who needed money for sacrifices or for mourning ceremonies were to have what they needed lent them, from the payments of the income-tax, without interest respectively for ten days or three months. Others who needed money for working capital were to be given loans, paying interest at 3 per cent per month.' This curiously modern-looking scheme failed because its organization was too crude, and because of mismanagement and corruption. As to the loans, their rate (36 per cent per annum) was much higher than the usual commercial one of 20 per cent, and they were therefore not popular.

On the whole, the 'reforms' of Wang Mang were meant chiefly for fiscal purposes, and were achieved by confiscating the most profitable enterprises on the one hand and by heavily taxing the poorer people on the other. No wonder that they were resented by all classes and that, faced with general revolt, Wang Mang had to rescind all of them in the winter of AD 22, without however being able to save his throne and his life.

Trade with the West. In this period international trade in Asia north of the Himalayas had as its objectives: the gold of Siberia, which was carried as far as India; the horses of Ferghana, which during the second and first centuries BC were in great demand in China, both as a luxury article and as mounts for élite cavalry; various bronze objects produced chiefly in the metallurgical centre of Minusinsk; and, last in time but of an ever-increasing importance, Chinese silk. China had the monopoly of silk production and maintained it during the whole of the period covered by the present volume. Silk became known at Rome in the first century BC (the first reference being in Horace), and it soon became very popular in the fashionable world of the city.

This trade was sharply intensified when, after the embassy of Chang Ch'ien (114 BC), the Chinese entered into direct contact with the Western countries (Hsi-yü), i.e. with the Indo-European peoples of the oases of the Tarim basin and of Transoxiana. The Chinese name for silk (*ssû*, archaic pronunciation *siag*) is perhaps the origin of the term *Seres*, by which the Westerners (the first was Nearchus at the end of the fourth century BC) knew the silk-trading (but not actually silk-producing) peoples of the Eastern countries.

Trade followed a few established routes, starting at Bactra (modern Balkh) in the west and ending on the Chinese *limes* in the east. The earlier direct route (first century BC) followed the string of oases to the south of the Takla-Makan desert, the Southern Route (*nan-lu*) of the Chinese. The cameos and intaglios at Niya and the frescoes of Miran show that one consequence of this flourishing trade was a strong Hellenistic-Roman influence on the local artists. Slightly later the Northern Route (*pei-lu*) came into use, following the string of oases to the north of the Takla-Makan. There were also less frequented variants to these main routes, and the trade of the nomad tribes still followed its old route north of the T'ien-shan to the Caspian.

During the first centuries AD the Chinese more or less effectively dominated the eastern portion of the silk-route, through their outpost of Lou-lan (Kroraimna of the Kharoṣṭhī texts), and the main commercial and military centre of Tun-huang (Drw'n of the Sogdian texts, Throána of Ptolemy). The silk trade and its routes are known both from Chinese itineraries, and from the information gathered by the employees of the rich Macedonian merchant Maes Titianus[1] and embodied in the geographical work of Ptolemy; there is a fair measure of agreement between the two sets of sources.

Sea trade between the Roman world and China was but an extension of the Indian trade. From the Coromandel coast the merchant ships followed the coast of the Gulf of Bengal, or else cut straight through it with the help of the monsoon, as far as Takola, i.e. Takuapa on the Malayan peninsula (now in Siamese territory). The peninsula itself could be circumnavigated, but more often it was covered by a short porterage, after which navigation was resumed as far as Kattigara, the entrepôt of the Sinai, where the latter came to trade; Kattigara was in all probability situated at the mouth of the Mekong.

Trade on this route may be supposed to have been chiefly in the hands of Indians and Indonesians. But several Westerners went with it; one of them was the sea-captain Alexander, whose account is the basis of Ptolemy's information. Another group of enterprising merchants posed as Roman ambassadors and in AD 166 were received as such at the Chinese capital Ch'ang-an. It was the only way to penetrate into the interior lawfully and with full official facilities. But the Chinese became suspicious of this embassy from King An-tun (Marcus Aurelius Antoninus) of Ta-ch'in (the Roman empire), whose tribute consisted of such typically tropical products as ivory, rhinoceros horn, and tortoise-shells, quite evidently picked up in the Malayan peninsula.

This sea trade is well authenticated both from Chinese, Greek, and Latin literary texts, and from actual finds such as the beads found in the Johore river, a Roman lamp at Phong-tük in Thailand, Roman cameos and coins (of Antoninus Pius and Marcus Aurelius) at Oc Eo in the Mekong delta, and Syrian glass in the tombs of the Korean kings of Silla. At the other end of the route a Chinese Huai vase has been found in Rome and a *ku* vessel in the sea off Ostia, while another Chinese vase was unearthed in the south of England.

Thus the first two centuries AD were the first period in world history during which Eurasia may be said to have functioned (with many limitations) as one great commercial area. This did not happen again until the thirteenth century.

(a) *Cerro de los Santos, votive statue.*
    Madrid, Archaeological Museum
(b) *The Lady of Elche,* c. 400 BC.
    Madrid, Prado Museum

(a)   [*photo Mas*

(b)

(a)

58 IBERIAN POTTERY

(a) *Galera, Province of Granada, vase from the necropolis. Madrid, Archaeological Museum*

(b) *Azaila, Aragon, vase. Madrid, Archaeological Museum*

(b)

59   (a) *Section of 'Hadrian's' Wall, Northumberland, Great Britain*

       (b) *Roman city planning: aerial view of Lucca, Italy. Stato Maggiore Aeronautica*
            Militare. Conc. No. 148; *Fotocopia* 8291; 4/*VII*/63

(a)

60　*Pompeii, House of the Vettii*
    (a)　*The Atrium*
    (b)　*The Peristyle*

(b)

61 NAVIGATION, III

Roman ships (a) *Model of a Roman merchant ship, second century AD*
(b) *Ship with a cargo of wine, third-century relief on a tomb*

(b)

62   *Roman crane with a tread-mill. Relief in the Lateran Museum, Rome*
A crane used in building a temple is driven by five men inside a great tread-wheel.
The men on top are decorating the mast for a celebration on the occasion of the completion
of the temple

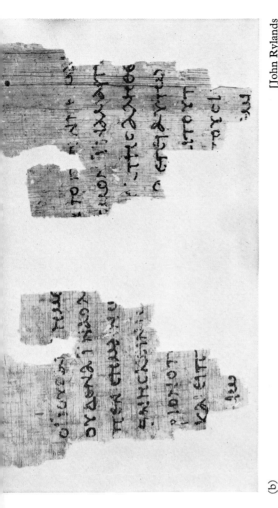

(b)

63 (a) *Papyrus fragments containing passages from an unknown Gospel,*
     British Museum

    (b) *Papyrus fragments containing passages from the Fourth Gospel,*
     John Rylands Library, Manchester

(a)

[Hosaka

(b)

64   *Early Japanese ceramics*
     (a) *Yayoi vase*
     (b) *Haniwa: female figurine*

[N.M.T.

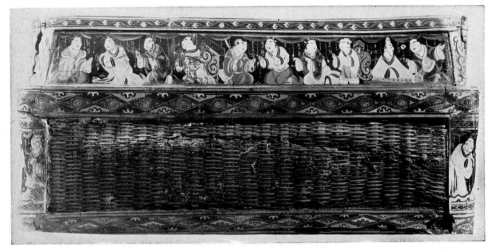

(a)

(b)

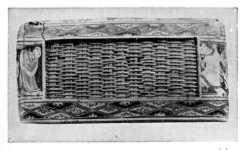

(c)

65 Lacquered basket, Han dynasty,
    National Museum, Seoul.
    Length 0·39 m.; width
    0·18 m.; height c. 0·22 m.

(a) Front view
(b) Side view
(c) End view

(b)

[B.M.

(a)

[L.M.

66

(a) Gandhāra: relief with warriors (the hosts of Maras attacking the Buddha)

(b) Amaravati: relief with warriors, elephants and walls

(a)

67
(a) *Bodhisattva from Shahbazgarhi,
     Paris, Musée Guimet*
(b) *Headless statue of Kaniṣka*

(b)

68
(a) *Gandhāra: Emaciated Buddha,*
     Lahore Museum
(b) *Sarnath: seated Buddha*

(a)

(b)

69 (a) *Begram, ivory casket*
     (b) *Ajanta, India: Cave XVII,
        fresco in the foyer of the
        central shrine; foreigners
        in the congregation of
        Buddha*

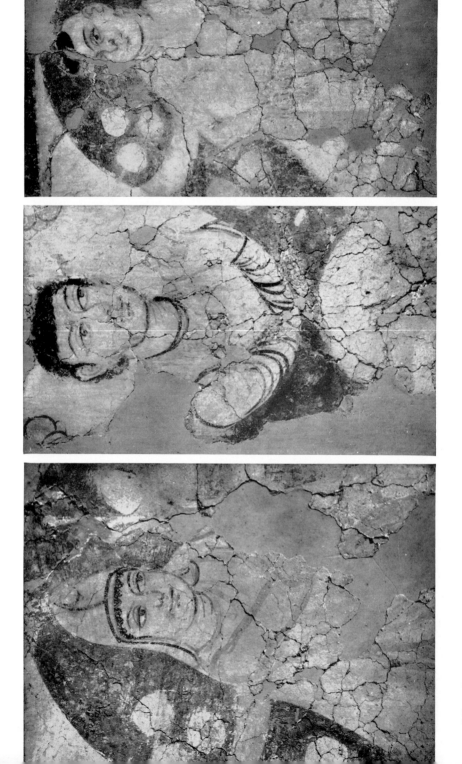

Miran frescoes

[N.M.I.]

71
(a) *Rome: the Colosseum, AD 80.*
    Aerial view
(b) *Rome: Hadrian's mausoleum as*
    reconstructed by Borgatti,
    completed AD 140

(a)

72

(a) *Adamclissi: trophy of Trajan. Metopes*

(b) *The Celtic god Cernunnus between Apollo and Mercury. Rheims, Musée de Saint Rémy*

(b)

Currency. Wang Mang's innovations in the coinage were no less radical than those he introduced in other fields. In AD 7 he introduced three new pieces (two knife-coins and a round coin), meant to circulate along with the 5-*shu* coin. In AD 9 he abolished the knife-coins and the 5-*shu* piece and introduced six types of round coins (*ch'üan*) and ten types of spade coins (*pu*). Further changes were made in AD 14 thus completely upsetting Chinese currency. In the end, people anxiously prayed for the return of the 5-*shu* coin. It was reintroduced after the fall of Wang Mang and remained the standard piece, or at least the basic unit, until about 600. Round coins of very large denominations were issued in the fifth century, but their importance in actual use was slight.

Owing to the shortage of copper in the troubled times after the fall of the Han, attempts were made to use a commodity money instead. Thus the Wei dynasty in 221 abolished copper and ordered that grain and silk should be used. The order was withdrawn in 227, but copper still continued to be scarce and bolts of silk became practically the currency of China for larger transactions during the period 200–600. The country was thus brought back to a sort of natural economy.

Other metals were scarcely used. Gold was not a medium of exchange. Iron coins appeared sporadically in the West, from about the beginning of the Christian era.

Ceramics and Goldsmiths' Work; Japanese Ceramics. Apart from the *ming-ch'i* funerary statuettes, the most characteristic form in Han ceramics is the round *hu* vase and other types imitated as usual from bronze. Their area is more or less restricted to the territory of the two capitals, Ch'ang-an and Lo-yang. Some of the pieces have a glaze of lead silicate, possibly a technique imported from the West, which represents a great advance in ceramic art.[2] Stoneware, too, progressed considerably. We may note the pieces found near Hong Kong, representatives of a local Southern Chinese school; also the Ch'ang-sha pottery, with its strong, coarse character. At Yüeh-chou or Chekiang a new centre appears toward the end of this period; it is the Yüeh pottery (grey stoneware).

But the most important event was the beginning of porcelain, which was brought about by an improvement in stoneware. The earliest record is a local tradition embodied in the *Fou-liang-hsien-chih*, which attributes the manufacture of a sort of porcelain-like ware to the town of Hsi-p'ing near Huai-yang in Honan, during the Late Han period (some think about AD 88). B. Laufer obtained actual specimens from tombs in Shensi near Hsien-yang and Hsi-an, of about the same date; the ware was of porcelain type, but with a coarse, dark body. Perhaps they represent the first experiments of potters toward porcelain.

The most famous manufacturing centre of modern ages is Ch'ing-tê-chên near the Po-yang lake, and its record, the *Ch'ing-tê-chên t'ao-lu*, refers to a blue-green translucent ware produced near Wên-chou in Chekiang during the Chin dynasty (265–420). It was called Tung-ou ware and was much favoured for drinking tea. It is to be noted that early porcelain makers were consciously trying to imitate jade, and therefore their ware was blue-green. But the development of this technique into celadon and then into true porcelain lies outside the limits of the present volume.

Actual finds of Chinese gold work are rarer for this period than for the preceding one. What little remains shows, however, that the same techniques were still followed. Jewellery is more interesting: the objects found in the tomb excavated in the western suburbs of Canton in 1954 include silver hairpins, rings of gold and silver, and gold pieces used as amulets. Other ornaments are known only from paintings, chiefly from the *Ku K'ai-chih* scroll in the British Museum. The *pu-yao*, a gold ornament in the shape of a delicate crown with stalks springing out in spirals from floral buds, is an example. Leaf-shaped plaques in granular work have recently been excavated from Tun-huang. They continue the Han granulation, but their pattern dates them to this period.

Japanese pottery of this period (in which rice-culture and the use of metals began) takes its name from Yayoi, a site in Tokyo. Its style is different from the Jōmon ware, and is somewhat less refined from the artistic point of view. (Pl. 64, a.) The potter's wheel makes its appearance, at least as an instrument for finishing the finer products. About the third century the Yayoi pottery gradually passes into that of the late Kofun period (megalithic). The clay figurines (*haniwa*), found outside the sepulchral mounds (but associated with them), properly belong to the realm of art. (Pl. 64, b.)

b. *India*

Trade with Imperial Rome. Internal trade in India showed very much the same features as during the previous period, though it was subject to increased obstacles from the lack of a widely recognized paramount power such as the Maurya had been. But it is international trade that comes to the fore after the beginning of our era. India tended to become a link in an intercontinental net of trade-routes connecting the Mediterranean with eastern Asia. These routes were by land and by sea.

The land routes started mostly from Antioch, crossed Mesopotamia (where the fair at Batnae played an important regulating role) and Iran, and entered India through the Afghan countries. It was this rich trade that made the fortune of Gandhāra and generally of the Kuṣāṇa territories. There was apparently a close relation between the decay of the Roman trade after the second century and the collapse of the Kuṣāṇa power, just as a passing revival in the fourth century was contemporary with a last flickering of Kuṣāṇa rule. At the worst, when the Sassanids and Rome were at war and the route through Iran was temporarily closed, another way remained open for the Roman-Indian trade: from the northern shores of the Black Sea and of the Caspian to Sogdiana, and hence by the famous trade route from Bactra to Taxila. But whatever route was followed, the Indian centres of the land trade were always Kāpiśi (Begram in Afghanistan) and Taxila; in both places substantial archaeological evidence of commercial relations with the West has been unearthed. (Map XIV.)

Sea trade started from the Red Sea ports of Berenice and Myos Hormos, and at first followed the Arabian coast to the mouth of the Indus and down to the south Indian ports. But about the beginning of our era knowledge of the cycle of the monsoons became current among Egyptian and Syrian sea-captains in the Red Sea; classical writers (Pliny, *N.H.*, VI, 100) attribute this discovery to Hippalus (late second or early first century BC), but it was undoubtedly knowledge that had been accumulating for a number of years. Thus it became safe to cross the Arabian sea directly from Aden to the Indian coast; the ships of the oriental subjects of Rome needed only to entrust themselves to the regular course of the monsoon. The two chief ports to which they sailed were Barygaza (modern Broach) in the north and Muziris (near modern Cranganore) in the south.

Barygaza was the chief port for the trade with northern India, whose merchants flocked there. As such it appears in the handbook of an unknown Levantine sea-captain, the *Periplus of the Erythraean Sea*, of the second half of the first century AD.[3] Bronze statuettes, coins, and other material remains of Roman trade have occasionally come to light in the wider hinterland, but no excavations have as yet been carried out at or near Broach.

Farther down the coast, Muziris was at the same time an outlet for the merchandise of south-western India, an entrepôt on the sea route to the Far East, and the terminus of a land route which crossed the southern tip of the peninsula; this road avoided circumnavigation of the stormy Cape Comorin, and at the same time led through the beryl mines, whose produce was much in demand in the Roman empire. This route was at one time much frequented, as is shown by the numerous hoards of Roman coins found in the area. Muziris may have contained a substantial colony of Roman traders; the *Tabula Peutingeriana* places a Templum Augusti in that region, and Tamil texts of the first centuries AD depict 'sturdy Mlecchas (Westerners) with sinewy round arms and high shoulders, wearing garlands of leaves and flowers round their necks, the ends of their garments hanging loose on both sides, moved to and fro in exuberant spirits, drunk with sweet toddy, through the streets with storeyed buildings, wide and sandy as river-beds, of that prosperous and ancient city, and unmindful of the cold drops of the drizzling rain' (*Nedunalvādai*, 29–35). As a scene in the harbour it could hardly be bettered. From other contemporary Tamil sources we hear of Western mercenaries in the pay of local princes.

On the other side of the peninsula the foremost of those ports open to foreign trade (the ἐμπόρια νόμιμα of the *Periplus*) was Poduce (Πωδούκη), a couple of miles south of Pondicherry. The city itself was washed away

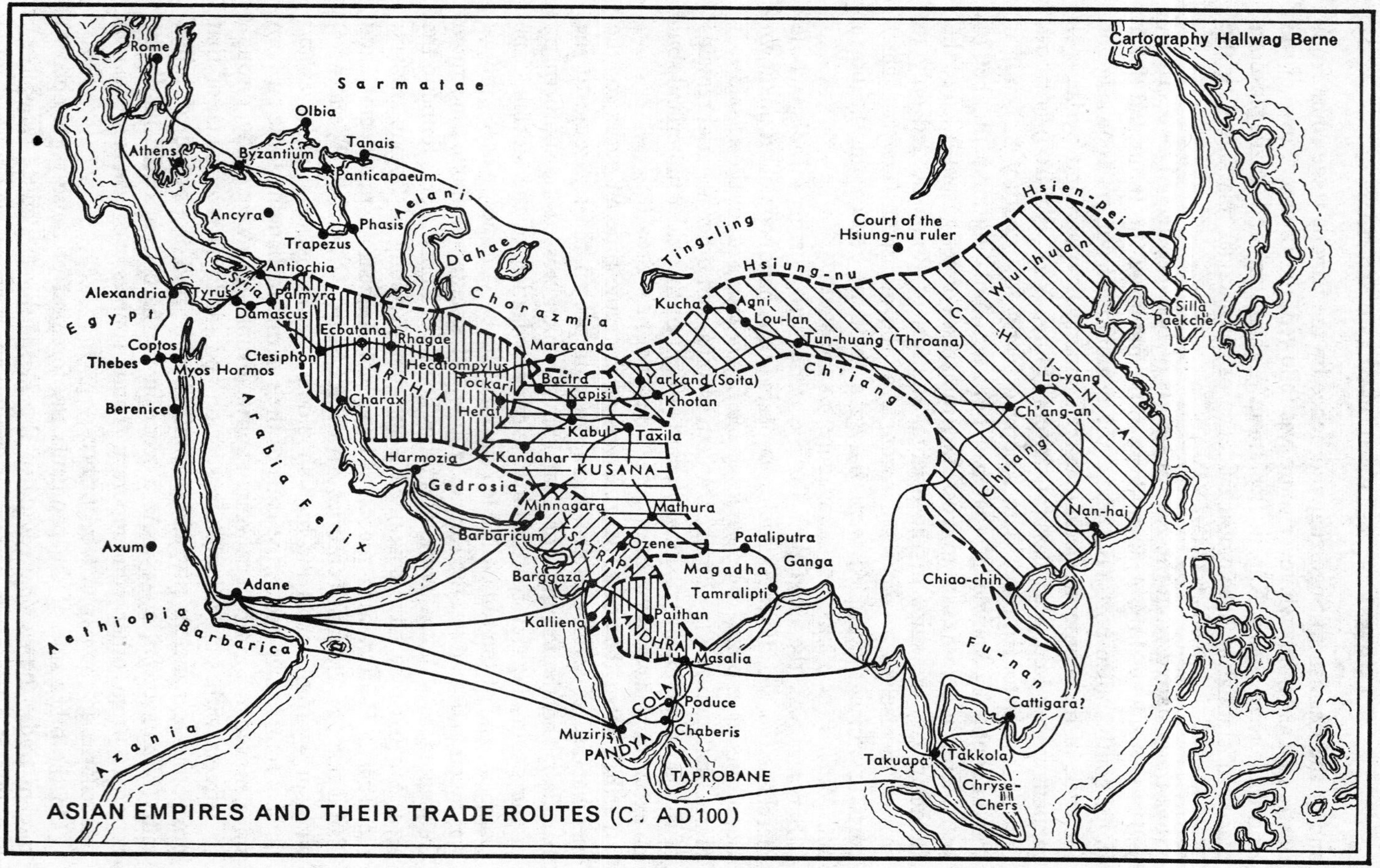

ASIAN EMPIRES AND THEIR TRADE ROUTES (C. AD 100)

MAP XIV

Cartography Hallwag Berne

Hsien-pei

Silla
Paekche

Wu-huan

H S I U N G - N U

Lo-yang

Chang-an

Nan-hai

C h i a n g

Court of the
Hsiung-nu ruler

Hsiung-nu

Tun-huang (Throana)

Lou-lan

Agni

Kucha

Fu-nan

Chiao-chih

Cattigara?

Takkola

Chryse-
Chers

Takuapa

Ting-ling

Yarkand (Soita)

Khotan

Chiang

Taxila

Mathura

Pataliputra

Ganga

Magadha

Tamralipti

Paithan

Masalia

TAPROBANE

Choden

Choraz mlia

Maracanda

Bactra

Kapisi

Kabul

KUSANA

Kandahar

Minnagara

Ozene

Paithan

ANDHRA

COLA

Poduce

Chaberis

PANDYA

Dahae

Tockari

Herat

Barbaricum

Barygaza

Kalliena

Muziris

Aelani

Phasis

Hecatompylus

Rhagae

P A R T H I A

Charax

Harmozia

Gedrosia

Sarmatae

Tanais

Panticapaeum

Olbia

Byzantium

Trapezus

Antiochia

Ecbatana

Ctesiphon

Seleucia

Palmyra

Damascus

Tyrus

Athens

Ancyra

Rome

Arabia Felix

Adane

Alexandria

Coptos

Myos Hormos

Thebes

Berenice

Egypt

Axum

Aethiopia
Barbarica

Azania

by the river but its outskirts (modern Arikamedu or Virapattinam) and a part of the harbour were excavated by French, Indian, and English archaeologists and have yielded a fairly clear idea of what a Roman-Indian trading post looked like. The main buildings appear to have been factories and magazines for the production and storage of the fine cloth (musseline), which was exported to the Mediterranean. Roman imports were mainly represented by statuettes, vases (chiefly Arretine), and wine amphorae, some of which still maintain a sticky deposit on the ground, due to the resin with which the heavy Greek and Italic wines were dressed.

This brings us to the object of this trade. Rome imported costly items, such as beryl and other precious and semi-precious stones, cloth, pepper, cinnamon and other spices, ivory, etc. What it could supply in exchange (wine, glass wares and pottery, bronzes, etc.) was far less valuable, and insufficient to make up the commercial balance. Hard cash had therefore to be exported, and accordingly hoards of Roman coins are quite common both in the extreme north-west (terminus of the land route) and in the far south, where the principal ports were situated. Pliny (VI. 101) complains that the Eastern trade cost Rome about 50 million sesterces annually.

The frequency of the various coin issues shows that the Roman-Indian trade, on both land and sea routes, was very lively during the first two centuries of our era. It decreased with the decline of the Roman empire, the establishment of the Sassanid kingdom, and the increasing insecurity of the routes during the third century. It experienced a short-lived revival during the fourth century, and eventually petered out at the end of the fifth century. But while it lasted, it played a great historical and cultural role, both in itself and as an intermediate step toward the Far East. During the first two centuries of our era there existed a south Eurasian commercial unity, which was revived (except for the short interlude of the Pax Mongolica in the thirteenth–fourteenth centuries) only with the coming of European sailors and traders after 1498.

Currency. From the numismatic point of view, India at the beginning of this period is divided into two great regions. In most of the country the old Indian coins and weight standards still linger on. The devices, however, begin to include short inscriptions, and thus we have scattered coins of local rulers, and above all a substantial series of coins issued by the aristocratic republics of northern India. The second region is represented by modern West Pakistan. It was the seat of several mints working for foreign rulers. The Śaka and Parthian conquerors continued the coinage of the Indo-Greeks in all its essential aspects, but with clumsier execution and an increasingly Indian element in the artistic taste. The Kuṣāṇas introduced a great novelty into India: they were the first (with the exception of some isolated coins of the Bactrian Greeks) to strike gold. Their gold coinage is influenced by that of Rome; Roman coins are found with great frequency in India, but chiefly around the ports and the beryl mines in the far south and in the Kuṣāṇa dominions in the north-west. The new gold coin was struck by Wima Kadphises on the standard of the Roman *aureus* (8·035 gm.). Roman influence was seen also in other coinage, and some copper coins closely imitate issues of Augustus. For a time Greek regained its ascendancy and under Kaniṣka the legends on coins were again in Greek or in Iranian written in Greek characters; but Brahmī and Kharoṣṭhī legends also sometimes occur. With the decline of the Kuṣāṇa empire Greek, no longer understood as a language and increasingly corrupt as a script, disappeared from the coins. The devices on the coins of Kaniṣka and Huviṣka are interesting: they reflect the eclectic tendencies of those rulers and feature Greek, Graeco-Egyptian, Iranian, Vedic, and Brahmanic gods, the Buddha, and perhaps even the Dea Roma.

The Śaka Kṣatrapas, who ruled from the first to the fourth century of our era, minted silver with Indo-Greek standards and type, and their coins have the rare distinction of regularly bearing the name of the ruler and the date (in the Śaka era of AD 78).

Farther south, the Andhra kingdom (first century BC to third AD) struck coins mostly of lead, or of a peculiar alloy of copper, very different in all respects from the northern types.

In numismatics, as in other fields, Gupta rule marked a period of unification, of absorption or rejection of foreign elements, and of high technical skill. Gupta coinage was at first gold and copper only. At the beginning the gold coins followed the Roman standard and even bore a Roman name: *dīnāra* (denarius). But in the middle of the fifth century another class of gold coins appeared, which were an archaizing revival of the ancient Indian weight standard; they are called *suvarṇa* in the inscriptions and represent the coins of the same name (weight 9·48 gm) prescribed in the *Dharmaśāstras*. Silver appears at a late date, after the Gupta conquest of the Kṣatrapa kingdom in Malwa; it is at first a local coinage of that country and continues the coinage of the Kṣatrapas in type and weight. From there it spread to the rest of the empire, although it remained differentiated in two diverging types. Copper is rather rare; from the beginning it is purely Indian and owes little to foreign influence. Workmanship is usually high. At the height of Gupta power, gold and silver coins are marked by great elegance and refinement, and some of them are real works of art. With the decline of the dynasty, however, they decayed very rapidly and in the sixth century were totally worthless from the artistic point of view. The coinage of Hindu India never recovered from this decline.

Agriculture. Agriculture, the livelihood of the majority of the people, was not made the subject of theoretical research by Indian authors. Nor do the inscriptions allow us to give an account of land tenure and connected subjects, as it is possible to do for southern India in the ninth–thirteenth centuries. We know only that irrigation played an important part in the Ganges valley, but above all in the south. Water control in the deltas of the southern rivers

was a complicated and large-scale undertaking; it was made possible only by
the existence of large and well-settled states, which were able to command
and to co-ordinate the efforts of the local people. The barrages (*anicut*) and
canals of the south were a model for all the neighbouring countries, as far as
Indonesia, where the technique of rice-growing by artificial irrigation,
although indigenous, was probably stimulated and influenced by the south
Indian model. Of local agricultural conditions, chiefly in the great Gupta
empire in the north, we know next to nothing. Some information can be
gleaned from the account of the Chinese pilgrim Hsüan-tsang; but his
journey is later than the chronological limits set to the present volume.

Ceramics and Jewellery. Indian pottery of this period is mainly represented
by the Rouletted ware, found in south India only and datable with some
certainty, because it is found at the Roman trading station of Arikamedu
together with Arretine vases of the first half of the first century BC. The
Rouletted ware belongs therefore to the first and second centuries AD. The
most usual shape is a dish with a beaked rim and two or three concentric
rings of rouletted pattern on the flat interior bases; this pattern is almost
certainly derived from the Mediterranean. (Fig. 8.)

In western India the most common type is the red polished ware, which
bears a strong technical resemblance to the Samian vases, although most of
the forms are purely Indian.

In the north, the later levels at Ahicchatrā have yielded a red ware with
red or brownish slip. The vessels bear stamped symbols, which are similar
to those found on the coins of the same period. This pottery forms a remarkably homogeneous series with but minor differences, and it lasts until the
Muslim invasions (twelfth century AD).

Kuṣāṇa pottery is found in many sites in the Punjab and the Ganges-
Jamma Doab: it bears symbols of a religious character, such as the Three
Jewels, the Svastika, etc.

Indian theoretical treatises on jewels (*Ratnaśāstra*) are later than the period
under consideration. The jewellery of ancient India is known from two
sources: actual finds and representations in sculpture.

The jewellery of this period is mainly represented by the abundant finds
at Taxila. As one would expect, strong Hellenistic influence is felt, ranging
from outright copies (bronze figure of Harpocrates, bust of Dionysus) to
more or less Hellenized local produce (bracelets, pendants, ear-rings, anklets,
girdles, etc., mostly of gold, and some interesting ivory combs). Another
influence is the nomad art of the steppes with its rhythmic patterns of
vegetable and animal forms. The Kuṣāṇa dominion was highly conducive
to the blending of Hellenistic, Indian, and central Asian elements in the
jewellery of north-western India. But apart from Taxila, no jewels of this
period have as yet been unearthed from Indian soil. Thus the jewellery of
the Gupta period, which is closely influenced by Gupta art and so shares

with it a climax of refinement at the end of this period, is known only through reproductions on the clay figurines of Ahicchatrā, and above all in the early frescoes of Ajanta; the latter reveal an increasing popularity for the use of precious and semi-precious stones. Jewellery was worn by court ladies in great quantity, the emphasis being placed on quantity rather than on quality, and it tended to cover the parts of the body left exposed by the very scanty clothing.

Ivory carving merits special treatment. The produce of the Indian *danta-kāras* was much appreciated abroad, as shown by the fine ivory statuette of a

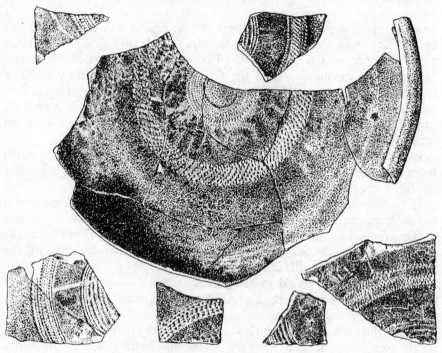

Fig. 8.   Rouletted ware (after a photograph).

Yaksinī (perhaps a mirror handle) found at Pompeii and therefore earlier than AD 79. It is not only a fine piece of carving, but the elaborate ornaments with which the sensuous feminine body is covered gives us perhaps the best available idea of a rich ensemble of jewellery of the first century of our era. Not less finely worked are the fragments of ivory toilet-boxes, probably of the third century AD, found in the hidden store-room (customs-house?) at Begram in Afghanistan. Their delicate, sophisticated, and exquisite work-manship belongs to a very high artistic level and is closely connected with the Mathura school of sculpture.

It must also be remarked that the technique of the Sanchi sculptures certainly owes much to the minute skill of the ivory carvers of the nearby city of Vidiśā.

c. *Rome*

Agriculture under the Empire. In the imperial period Italian agriculture completely lost its superiority over that of the provinces. The methods used in Italy had now spread abroad, as had also the types of crops which were sown, one cause being the assignment of lands to veterans. Moreover all the provinces had now been made self-sufficient in their agricultural output, by cutting down the areas previously under marshland, forest, and semi-desert. So the lands which had earlier been little cultivated and relatively unproductive, such as Africa, Spain, and Gaul, had become valuable, while the lands of Italy, Sicily, and Greece were no longer the most important. Every type of agricultural system was employed, the choice depending on the nature of the adjacent markets, which consisted in the many towns of various size designed by Rome. In the areas nearest the towns there was a cluster of gardens and orchards for the production of vegetables and fruit which would have perished if transported over long distances; and there were also more substantial agricultural undertakings designed for intensive cultivation of cereals, wine, and oil, which could be carried to the neighbouring cities without excessive cost or trouble. At a greater distance more intensive systems of cultivation would flourish, woods and pasture being interspersed with narrow agricultural lands to feed the rural population. So the production and sale of agricultural products responded to local demand, which was regular and was not extended over long distances. Prices were stable; there was no over-production if harvests were good, or under-production if they were bad. Direct relations existed between farmers and consumers, between the country and the city. The people of both classes were harmed by the vicious behaviour of the *fiscus* rather than by the ups and downs of their relations one to another.

The old methods of peasant working still survived. They were supervised by the *pater familias* assisted by one or more slaves, and in the seasons of sowing and harvest by a number of free-born wage-earners who did similar types of work. These old methods were perpetuated by the distribution of land to veterans, and also by the organization of the colonate on the great *latifundia*, both private and imperial. In the past a feature of *latifundia* had been the large-scale use of slaves, whether the estates had been managed directly by their proprietors or by means of *vilici* or *appaltatores* (as normally the case on domain or imperial lands); and the slaves had been trained to specialized work. In this period the tendency was to divide the estates up into small sections, all of them under supervision of *conductores*, and to entrust them to the work of individual families of semi-independent *coloni*, who were bound to pay over a part of the produce and to put in a fixed number of days on corvée work. On the *latifundia*, therefore, there was a return to the small agricultural undertaking, run by families with non-specialist labour.

The improvement of agriculture in the various provinces was of course partly due to the more general use of implements of a specialized and developed kind. Ploughs of various types were developed according to the nature of the soil and the system of agriculture envisaged; and there were harrows, rakes, hoes, shovels and spades, hatchets of metal or wood to deal with the more tender plants, instruments for threshing and sifting cereals, baskets, buckets, and so on. In some cases we find regular agricultural machines of a more complicated sort gaining a wide measure of acceptance: for instance the reaping machine which Pliny says was used in Gaul, and which had metal teeth and was drawn by animals; or the wine-press with a screw (*cochlias*); or the water- and wind-mills.

[*Town Planning and Housing*.* Like Julius Caesar before them, the emperors accepted that municipalities were the basis of social life and administration, and so wherever conditions permitted they founded new colonies and towns. The skill and understanding of the Romans, both in selecting sites and planning the towns, are shown most strikingly by their survival into modern times: in Italy and the western provinces, where such policies were especially applied, many towns were created whose street-plans even today indicate their Roman origins. (Pl. 59, b.) The typical Roman town-plan was derived partly from earlier Greek traditions and partly from their own experience in laying out large military encampments. In its purest form, it was a strictly geometrical design, in which two main streets intersected at right angles, and around these was laid out a network of lesser streets dividing the city into a series of uniform rectangular areas and building-blocks. It is seen most clearly where the builders were able to create a completely new city. The town of Aosta, founded in 24 BC as the colony of Augusta Praetoria, was divided mathematically into sixteen rectangles, each of which was further divided into four; the surrounding town-walls took the form of a larger but similarly-proportioned rectangle. (Fig. 9.) In the Trajanic colony of Timgad in North Africa, one of the best preserved Roman towns, the same precision can be observed. But such perfection could not always be achieved; the plans are sometimes changed to meet the difficulties of a site or to include an earlier settlement.

Roman architects sought to avoid any appearance of monotony by adding secondary features; colonnaded streets, arches and gateways, or ornamental sculpture and fountains could help to soften the sense of geometrical rigour. But by such systematic planning they were able to provide the buildings and amenities that were, for the Romans, of the very essence of city life: the solemn central forum with its temples and public buildings for local magi-

* By M. W. Frederiksen.

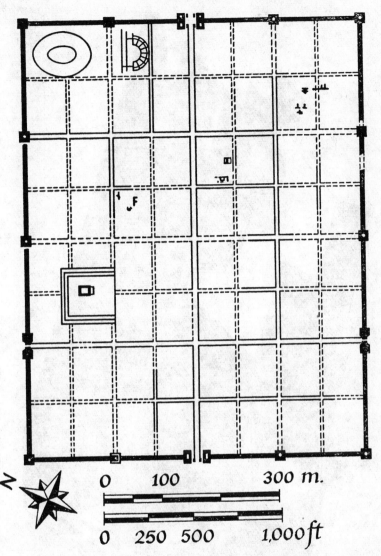

Fig. 9. Plan of Augusta Praetoria (Aosta) after F. Castagnioli.

strates and senate; an adequate drainage system and plentiful water-supply; public baths and theatres; and shops and open markets under official control.

Within a Roman town, private houses followed a variety of patterns. In Italy, where our information is fullest, the earliest houses are of a low-built, spreading form of one or two storeys, which were centred round an open hall (*atrium*) and a colonnaded garden (*peristylium*). (Pl. 60, a, b) (Fig. 10.) These houses are best known from Pompeii, but they were fashionable also in Rome,

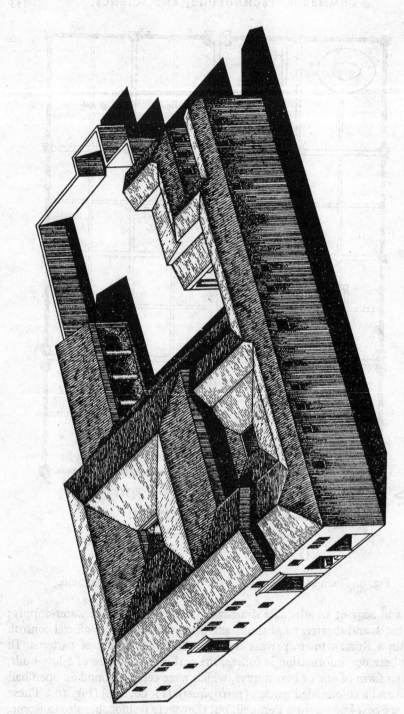

Fig. 10. House of Obelius Firmus, Pompeii (reconstruction), after V. Spinazzola.

and were of a style well suited to the aristocracy and municipal classes of the early empire. In the provinces, housing seems to have kept to local traditions, improved and embellished to suit the prosperity of the times. It was not long before the increasing wealth and social changes in the empire were reflected in architecture. The richest classes began to build luxurious villas with surrounding gardens, often in the countryside or by the sea. But in the largest towns, where space was expensive and a large population of labourers and small craftsmen needed housing, there begins to appear the new style of building known as *insulae*, which were large apartment houses divided into many shops and small flats. Some areas of poor-class tenement housing in this style had existed in Rome from early times; but the new technique of brick-and-concrete architecture had made a revolutionary change, and after the great fire in AD 64 Nero took the opportunity to rebuild Rome systematically in the new style. Of the many cities where these *insulae* were built, our best knowledge comes from the harbour town of Ostia. It is vividly clear how with new building methods spacious apartment houses of five storeys or more could be designed; the *insula*, which had previously been a ramshackle tenement in a slum, was now converted into a safe, pleasant, and almost fire-proof structure. The words in which the historian Tacitus refers to the opponents of Nero's scheme, who defended the unsafe and often insanitary city quarters as they had been before, have a certain ironical flavour to modern readers. This new utilitarian architecture reflected the changed social conditions; it supplied economical housing for a new population who found that only the cities supplied them with their employment and their amusements.]

Artisan Work and Industry. Under the empire very large areas were linked together by regular communications into a peaceful union. In these favourable conditions the industrial organization of Hellenistic times could hold its own in the East, and it became possible to widen and strengthen a similar development in Western countries, along the three recognized systems—work in the household, artisan labour, and large-scale industry. The rapid Romanization of the West, with the emigration of a number of Italians, required a large production of relatively cheap goods; and a great variety were in fact made locally, each city becoming a marketing centre. At first these goods were imitations of the current Italian product, but later they acquired certain local characteristics and even sometimes a reputation for fine work, so that eventually there was a demand for exports to Italy itself, from Gaul and Germany for example.

Household production traditionally was found most in country districts. The families there wanted to be self-sufficient, and to give continuous occupation to the agricultural workers, both slave and free, with labour which was complementary to their agricultural activities in the periods when there was little or no work to be done in the fields. We find these conditions on large and small estates alike: on all of them there was practically a closed economy, in which every sort of article was made, from bread to spun cloth, from furniture to clothing, together with shoes, baskets, rough pottery, bricks, tanned hides, and the more simple utensils of wood or metal.

But in all the towns this kind of production was replaced by artisan labour, and its products, for the most part cheap goods, were marketed over the surrounding country up to a fairly limited distance from the centre. These goods were the output of small factories and shops using mainly general labour, though sometimes there would be a few more specialized craftsmen; and since they were made without the use of machinery they did not take on a standardized appearance. They included utensils, furniture, leather goods, textiles, glass, jewellery, embroidery, scent, and cosmetics. We can also classify under this heading the groups of artisans who worked in villas at the centre of large estates.

These artisans formed new colleges, the shoemakers for instance, or the wine and vegetable merchants. The corporations still kept up their philanthropic ways, giving assistance to workers in time of need, uniting their members in religious and funeral societies, and possessing their own statutes, common funds, protectors, and patrons. Yet we find them increasingly controlled and shaped by the state. In the end the state came to organize all labour, in order to ensure supplies to the cities and the continuity of the necessary trades. Eventually Diocletian made certain professions hereditary by law, under three headings: (1) independent professions, relatively non-essential, but under supervision—the smiths (in metal, and timber), fullers, cloth-workers, innkeepers, boatmen, doctors, and veterinary surgeons; (2) corporations essential for food supplies—bakers for bread, merchants of oxen, pigs, and sheep for their meat, boatmen transporting grain and livestock (especially to Rome by river from Ostia), together with the baggers and dockers of grain; (3) corporations of large industries, independent or monopolized, monopolies being increasingly common in the later empire.

These larger industries often used slave labour and 'chain' methods of production. The following are worthy of mention: (1) the extraction and working of metals. Galleries or mines were dug, and from them the raw or worked material was removed. Silver working was relatively easy: the metal was extracted from argentiferous lead in Sardinia, Spain, Gaul, Epirus, Pannonia, and Dalmatia. Gold and lead came from Africa and Britain, copper was mined in Baetica, Lusitania, Aquitania, Narbonensis, and Britain. The alloying of bronze was also common, rolled or beaten or fused, and fairly advanced methods of soldering were known. The lack of bellows with safety-valves made iron-working very laborious: proper fusion was impossible, and the metal had to be reduced by heating to a spongy form and then hardened on the anvil and tempered in water. However in the course of the second century AD new double bellows made the production of proper steel possible for the first time. Raw iron was mined in Spain, Gaul, Noricum, and other provinces; (2) the furniture industry; (3) textile and fulling industries, found in many parts of Italy (Pollentia, Tarentum, Canusium, etc.), Gaul, and Spain (Tarraco, Emporiae, Saetabis). They turned out cloth made of every sort of material and in all sorts of form, making use both of horizontal and of vertical looms, and then decorating the wares with the most varied finishes; (4) pottery. This was made throughout Italy (e.g. at Arretium, Mutina, Cales, and Cumae), in Gaul, and in Spain (at Saguntum). The most advanced type was the 'sigillata' ware, which was made with punches, and was painted and varnished, very delicately in early times but more roughly as time went on; (5) glass, manufactured in every district (Colonia Agrippinensis is mentioned among others) where suitable sand was available, and worked and ornamented to produce a variety of different articles. There was moulded glass and, since 40 or 30 BC, the recently invented blown glass (see the mention in Seneca); glass in imitation of cameos, or painted with ornamentation or a variety of scenes (the Sidonian glass is typical here), or decorated in *barbotine* style with the twisting threads, or dusted with gold, or iridescent. The articles comprised plate for windows or mirrors, embossed or fluted cups, and vessels with incised ornament or gold inlay (*opus sectile*), sometimes bearing *graffiti* or miniatures of people; (6) the manufacture of scent (used—or misused—even in wines or drinks, and on seats at the circus), chemical mixtures, beauty preparations, cosmetics, dyes, and medicines, now made easier owing to the existence of cheap glass vessels for mixing purposes; (7) jewel-working, including pierced or filigreed gold, incision or carving of semi-precious stones, and the setting of precious stones which have already been partially cut.

In the later empire industry tended to become monopolized. In early times, however, the only monopolies were mines of precious metals, mints, and salt-works (both for evaporated sea-water and for rock salt). Later, goldsmiths, weavers, dyers, and arms manufacturers (when working for the state) were added to the list.

Trade and Communications. The ruling classes, comprising the rich landed proprietors, took no interest in commercial affairs, and the body of traders belonging to the equestrian class or to lower orders in society were markedly left to operate on their own. One result was that commercial monopolies to suit the advantage of Roman citizens did not come into being; it is improper, apart from obviously exceptional examples, to speak of commercial motives exercising a compelling influence on Roman policy before imperial times.[4] Carthage had been a strong contrast.

Nevertheless on their own initiative groups of Roman citizen traders, coming mainly from Campania, Magna Graecia, and the East, had already formed settlements of 'conventus civium Romanorum' at various parts of the Roman world, such as Narbo, Cirta, Vaga, Utica, Sicily, and Delos. They made their fortunes, and also contributed to the Romanization of the

Mediterranean countries; but meanwhile other merchants of provincial origin, particularly Easterners, were freely competing with them in Italy and the provinces alike. The founding of the empire meant the creation of a single vast political and social unit. There was a tendency to uniformity of metric, monetary, and legal systems; internal order was normally maintained, and the early emperors kept the peace with foreign powers; travel by sea was easy, and roads were continually extended and improved. (Map XV.) Moreover there was a minimum of state interference, while new industrial centres and markets were growing up, and the standard of living in the Western lands was rising to the level attained in the Eastern. All these factors were leading to an immense expansion of trade and commerce, not only inside but outside the frontiers. For the countries to north and east and south were slowly reaching some measure of economic equality with the Roman world. (Map XII.)

But Rome never went over to a real policy of mercantilism. Its landed proprietors were always of predominant importance, and trade was still chiefly internal trade. Imports from outside were almost entirely limited to luxury goods, paid for by the exportation of Roman gold and silver; so this trade did more harm than good to the economic development of the empire.

The main factors governing internal trade between province and province were the availability of supplies in one area to meet demands in others, and the cost of transport, which might or might not be economic. The main exporters of grain were North Africa, Egypt, Sicily, occasionally Spain and Britain, and the countries to the north of the Euxine; oil was abundant in Spain and Africa; wine in Gaul, Dalmatia, Asia Minor, Syria, and Sicily; salt meat in Gaul and Britain; smoked and salted fish in Spain, the Bosporus, the Pontus, and Egypt.

Among clothing materials, linen came from Egypt and Africa, cotton from Iran, and silk from China. Hides and leather were to be found in Illyricum, Asia Minor, Arabia, Spain, Gaul, and Britain.

The extraction of metals and minerals depended mainly on the emperor, who owned most of the precious metal mines. Gold came from Dacia, Moesia, Thrace, and Dalmatia, as well as from the older areas in Spain, Gaul, and Britain. There was argentiferous lead from Sardinia, Gaul, Dalmatia, Pannonia, Attic Laurium, and Epirus; tin from Britain; iron from Elba, Etruria, the Pyrenees, and Noricum; copper from Baetica, Lusitania, Aquitania, Narbonensis, and Britain; and lead from Spain, Africa, and Britain. The salt regarded with most favour was found in Italy at Ostia, Volaterrae, and Tarentum, at Gela in Sicily, and at Utica in Africa; and also on the eastern border of Egypt, and in Cyprus, Cappadocia, Phrygia, Thessaly, Illyricum, Epirus, Gaul, and Hither Spain. The marble most in demand came from Greece, Italy, Asia Minor, Iran, and Africa: precious stones from the East, Egypt, and in some measure from Scotland; timber from Africa and Syria, with more valuable woods from India, Iran, and the African caravans, which also carried ivory, a commodity also drawn from India.

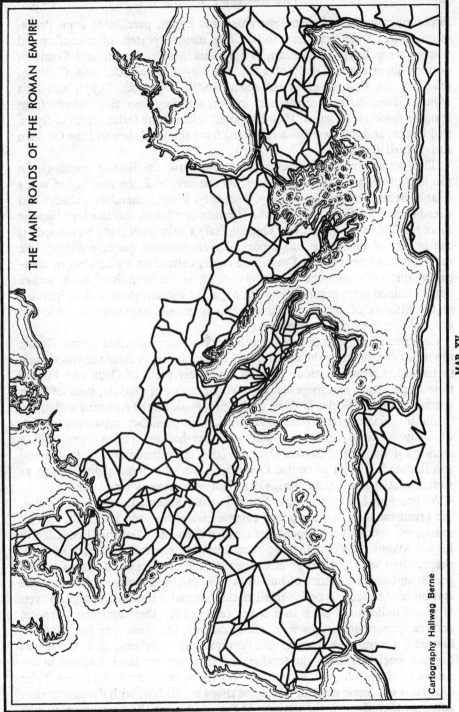

THE MAIN ROADS OF THE ROMAN EMPIRE

Cartography Hallwag Berne

MAP XV

Silphium came from Cyrene, papyrus from Egypt, parchment from Pergamum, spices from Iran and India. The main exporters of manufactured textiles were Egypt, Phoenicia, Syria, Asia Minor, Spain, and Gaul; of pottery Etruria and Gaul; of glassware Egypt, Phoenicia, and Gaul; of jewellery the East generally; of scents India, Phoenicia, Egypt, and Asia Minor. Slaves came from captures in war, but they were also brought from Eastern markets, to which they had been taken from India, Parthia, Syria, and Egypt; and they were also imported from the Black Sea and the German and British frontiers.

This commerce had certain general results for the Roman economy. In the first place, great trading centres, on the sea, or at the meeting of roads inland, became extremely wealthy. Secondly, Eastern merchants always had a lead over those from Italy and the Western provinces, and this lead became more marked as time went on. Thirdly, Italy's balance of trade was based on the import of foodstuffs and export of manufactured goods. Fourthly, we may note the importance of maritime trade, carried on by colleges of *navicularii* through a number of stations which in the periods of fairly secure peace attained great popularity.[5] (Pl. 61, a, b.) Finally, there was an increase in the number of banks providing capital, mainly for wholesale trade and especially in the Eastern provinces.

Commercial organization took on larger and more efficient forms. Rome, the major consumer in the empire, had a commercial structure proportionate to its size. Communications with its two great ports of Ostia and Puteoli were made easier; and there was a growing number of markets, some of them specialized, in particular districts of the city, while on the Aventine and in the forum business quarters were established, with porticoes containing booths, warehouses, shops, granaries, and slaughter-houses. Trajan even built a market for the sale of books. Over all Italy the organization of the capital was imitated, though of course in miniature, in the municipalities, such as Aesernia, Aletrium, Ariminum, Corfinium and many other places.

Archaeology has shown us, at Ostia, Puteoli, Athens, Ephesus, and Delos, the organization of big sea-board commercial towns; and it can also tell us something about what happened at smaller cities like Pompeii, Timgad, and Lepcis Magna. At Pompeii have been found an enormous number of small shops, often with workshops next door for the production of manufactured goods, and also a quantity of buildings to house merchandise sold wholesale and others of bazaar type for retail trade. Normally business in a given type of merchandise took place in a street reserved for that particular purpose, and the appropriate signs were depicted outside. But there were also itinerant hawkers, commission agents, and commercial travellers; and there was distinct specialization in the food trades, of which we have evidence in the names of their colleges. A bas-relief on the monument at Igel near Trier illustrates wholesale trade in cloth: the shops are laid out with the appropriate patterns, then there is the packing of the goods, and their transport by cart or by boat. Reliefs from Noviomagus in the same area illustrate the river transport of casks of wine.

But the commonest means of getting local and retail wares to the agricultural districts was still the institution of markets and fairs at definite dates in the country towns. At the same time the imperial government promoted the rise of larger cities in all parts of the provinces, as an essential means of maintaining control and effecting Romanization. In them there was wholesale trade, sometimes accompanied by factories.

Decay of Commerce. The Roman state never adopted a regular and definite policy of mercantilism or gave any clear encouragement to trade: nor, before Hadrian's time, did it develop state monopolies. Many of the reasons why trade eventually declined and became involved in formidable difficulties were connected with the financial policy of the empire, which was practically always short of money and often invented harmful ways of acquiring it.

A fundamental cause of the obvious decline was inflation of coinage. It was debased in weight and purity, and eventually became a token currency; it found no acceptance in foreign countries, where payment had to be made in precious metal at its face value. The result was a steep fall in the value of money, accompanied by failure of the banks or a rise in their interest rates; but there was a still steeper rise in the cost of essential goods. The state eventually tried to check this by fixed maximum prices, which always bring ruin to producers and merchants.

At the same time large estates were forming, each one becoming a closed economy; and because of the devaluation of the currency the soldiers had to receive their food in kind by means of requisitions. This upset the whole system of trade and exchange, by putting the middlemen out of business.

The system of tax-collection was another important enemy of trade, and it was harmful to the artisan class as well. Tolls and customs dues were maintained at every conceivable point; these had the effect of raising prices and so of gradually making long-distance trade impossible. Then in the third century the continual civil wars and barbarian raids, which interfered with free traffic on the roads, led to a revival of piracy on the sea, and also caused a withdrawal of liquid capital, which was hidden by its terrified owners in hoards underground. Add to this: extensive government interference; the wars on the frontiers, which limited imports from countries outside the empire; the lack of any guarantee behind this international trade, now that commercial treaties were mere words and offered no protection; the general tendency of every district to become self-sufficient with its own agricultural and industrial products, and to carry on only local trade within a narrow radius; and the way in which large-scale enterprises were increasingly falling into the greedy hands of oriental speculators.

The only period when healthy commerce seems to have revived for a few decades was that following the shrewd financial policy of Constantine.

2. SCIENCE

a. *China*

Medicine and Alchemy. No Chinese medical text of this period appears to be extant and the evidence available is fragmentary. Some information can be gleaned about public health. Thus in the Later Han period there were seven epidemics between 37 and 50 AD, and five between 171 and 185. This led the physicians to differentiate between the various infective diseases and to classify their respective symptoms. Malaria, typhoid, cholera are recognized. Smallpox is first mentioned in connection with the Ma Yüan expedition to Chiao-chih (modern Vietnam) between AD 42 and 44. Already in the period 275–279 we hear of people who avoided members of a family struck by epidemic disease, in order not to be contaminated. Hua T'o, the patriarch of Chinese surgery, lived in the second century,[6] and so did Chang Chung-ching, a great physician and the author of the *Shang-han-lun*, an essay on typhoid. The latter was also an ophthalmologist, and mentions several symptoms (lacrymation, exophthalmos, impairment of vision), which were considered, however, as local manifestations of general diseases.

Chinese alchemy is closely connected with Taoism, of which it represents one of the 'technical' aspects. Its aim is immortality. In its quest it starts from man as a unit, not even making a distinction between body and soul. It is based on the theory of the Five Elements (*wu-hsing*: wood, fire, earth, metal, water) and of *yang-yin* (the two opposite but complementary principles of male-female, positive-negative, warm-cold, etc.). The body must be placed in harmony with the *tao*, acquiring its attributes, among them immortality. Alchemy (*lien-tan*, lit. 'pill of transmutation') is divided into the alchemy of prolonging life (*nei-tan*) and the alchemy of transmuting metals (*wai-tan*). It attempts to obtain immortality through a regulated and selective diet and the use as medicine of certain substances containing vitalizing qualities, such as cinnabar, gold, silver, jade, sesamum Indicum, pine, peach, crane, fowl, tortoise; and recipes are compounded with them. The Chinese alchemist tried to make gold because this incorruptible substance was an ingredient of the elixir of immortality, and the Taoist was too poor to make use of natural gold. Alchemic gold was meant to be eaten, not to be spent. The philosopher's stone (*chin-tan*) was also looked for; the basis was always cinnabar, i.e. mercury compounded with various other substances, but the texts are generally vague on the subject of quality, quantity, ingredients, and methods of composition.

The first references to alchemy go back to the end of the second century BC; the *Huai-nan-tzŭ*, although not dealing with alchemic operations, refers to the doctrine underlying the metamorphoses of minerals. Liu Hsing (79–8 BC), a profound student of alchemic lore, tried to make gold with the official support of the emperor, but failed and barely avoided execution. Afterwards nothing more is heard about alchemy for nearly two centuries, perhaps because the prohibition was strictly enforced.

The first alchemic work actually preserved is the *Ts'an-t'ung-ch'i* by Wei Po-yang, the Taoist pseudonym of an unknown author who was living about AD 120–150. This short text, divided into ninety paragraphs, has the apparent form of an application of the cosmic theories of the *I-ching*, but actually it is a treatise on the preparation of the pill of immortality. It is done by heating together *yang* and *yin* in a hermetically closed vessel (the philosopher's egg of Western alchemy), at first on a slow fire and then on a blazing flame.

The classic text of alchemy is the *Pao-p'u-tzŭ* of Ko Hung (*c.*281–361). It is a most important work from many points of view including that of philosophical thought. Its seventy chapters are grouped into two sections: *Wai-p'ien* (politics and government) and *Nei-p'ien* (the Taoist immortals, alchemy proper, exorcism, etc.). Ko Hung was a compiler, not an experimenter. The chief novelty in his work is the increased importance of silver.

The association with Taoism, and soon with its grosser aspects of charlatanry, was hurtful to the development of alchemy in China. Although in time it partly preceded Western alchemy, it was thoroughly despised by the Confucian ruling class and was never able to attain the status of a science and so develop into chemistry.

Knowledge of the Earth and Physics. Geology proper is a modern science, although in China between the second and fifth centuries some hazy ideas on the subject seemed to exist.

Mineralogy was purely descriptive and never theoretical. Still, the theory of the mutations of metal through meteorological and mineralogical exhalations is found already in the *Huai-nan-tzŭ* (122 BC), and goes back at least to 350 BC. As for classification, the Chinese script itself was conducive to it, at least within certain limits. Several mineralogical notions are found also in the various pharmacopoeias (*pên-ts'ao*).

But the one typically Chinese branch of this science is seismology. The Chinese list of earthquakes is the longest and most complete in existence, with precise data for 908 earthquakes beginning from 780 BC down to AD 1644. Chang Hêng (78–139) invented the 'earthquake weather-cock' (*hou-fêng ti-tung-i*), a sort of seismograph consisting of a bronze vessel with a domed cover containing a central column (essentially a pendulum). The latter would move laterally along tracks on the eight directions and was so arranged that it would operate a closing and opening mechanism. Outside the vessel there were eight dragon heads, each of them with a bronze ball in its mouth, and under each was a toad with an open mouth ready to receive it should it fall. The whole was meant to show the epicentre of the earthquake. But the idea was not pursued further and every trace of it was lost after the Han dynasty.

Chinese geographical knowledge in this period marked a rather slow advance in comparison with the great progress of the preceding period. It often felt the harmful influence of religious cosmography, which centred around the legendary K'un-lun mountain, with the Western Countries added as a peninsula jutting out into the ocean. This was supposed to be surrounded by a circular continent, outside which lay another ocean. Several maps of this sort have been found in Korea, but they are very late. They draw most of their names from the *Shan-hai-ching*, and many others from the *Yü-kung, Mu-t'ien-tzŭ-chuan*, etc. Buddhist influence began also to be felt at the end of this period.

Hydrography, of paramount importance in a country like China, where so much depends on the river and on artificial irrigation, saw the reconstruction of the *Shui-ching* ('Water Classic') in the third century; it contains the names of 137 rivers. But far more important than the text is the commentary by Liu Tao-yüan (d. 527), a sober and trustworthy compilation.

Local topography came into existence in this period and was destined to have a very long and rich career. The first example is the *Hua-yang-kuo-chih* (historical geography of Szechwan) by Ch'ang Ch'ü (347).

Cartography was by now a real art. In AD 26 the Emperor Kuang-wu-ti, while campaigning against the rebels, is said to have opened and studied a large silk map of the empire. But the greatest step forward was made when in 116 Chang Hêng presented a map to the emperor which for the first time showed a net of co-ordinates: the squares, however, indicated not meridians and parallels but distances in *li*. Chinese maps were well orientated, but were based on itineraries and not on astronomical determinations; the latter was a step which Chinese science never took. The father of mediaeval Chinese cartography was P'ei Hsiu (224–271), a Minister of Works of the Chin dynasty. Cap. 35 of the *Chin-shu* gives a description of his methods, drawn from the preface to his great atlas *Yü-kung ti-yü-t'u* in eighteen leaves; it was of course a reduction of the *Yü-kung* to map form. It has not come down to us.

Physics never became a science in China, as it never grew beyond the empirical stage. The steelyard and the lever principle underlying it were well known, and we have old specimens, one of which goes back to the time of Wang Mang (*c.* AD 10). In the third century some notion of specific weight and displacement appears: an elephant is weighed by placing it on a boat, noting the boat's immersion and then loading it with known weights down to the same level.

Optics did not remain undeveloped. We have some hints in the *Mo-ching* about shadow and penumbra, definition of the focal point and inversion of the image, mirrors and their combinations, concave and convex mirrors. Burning mirrors were employed from a very early period (sixth century BC) for ceremonial purposes (kindling the new fire). Some of these observations are taken up again in *Huai-nan-tzŭ*. A mere piece of curiosity were the 'magic mirrors' discovered and constructed before the fifth century. When these bronze mirrors reflected the sunlight, the design in relief on the back of the mirror became apparent in its smallest details: this effect was probably due chiefly to small differences in curvature.

The compass came into use very late, not earlier than about 1080. But the magnetic properties of iron were known at an early date. Wang Ch'ung in the *Lun-hêng* (AD 83) speaks of the 'south-controlling spoon' (*ssŭ-nan-chih-shao*), which, when thrown to the ground, came to rest pointing at the south. Probably it was a magnet carved in the form of a spoon, i.e. in imitation of the Great Bear, turning on the ground plate of the diviner's board (*shih*). But for the Chinese of the first centuries of our era all this belonged to the sphere of geomancy and astrology.

Mathematics. The most significant Chinese work of this period on mathematics is the 'Nine Chapters on the Mathematical Art' (*Chiu-chang-suan-shu*), which existed, at least in embryo, in the first century BC. It ranges more widely and shows a more advanced knowledge of mathematics than the 'Classic of Mathematics' (*Chou pei suan ching*), which in this period received its commentary at the hands of Chao Ch'un-ch'ing (end of second century). The 'Nine Chapters' are intended for practical purposes and for dealing with applied problems which were the concern of the administration (land measurement, calculation of the capacity of granaries, planning of dykes and canals, taxation, and so on). Other important texts are the 'Memoirs on the Traditions of the Mathematical Art' (*Shu-shu-chi-i*), written by Hsü Yo about AD 190 and closely connected with Taoist magic; the 'Mathematical Classic of Sun Tzŭ' (*Sun tzŭ suan ching*, c.230); and the 'Mathematical Classic of Chang Ch'iu-chien' (*Chang Ch'iu chien suan ching*, c.500).

An important aid to the everyday use of arithmetic was the gradual acceptance of the abacus (*suan p'an*). It is a frame with twelve iron wires, on each of which seven balls can run. A transverse plank divides it into two unequal parts (two and five). Each of the balls in the upper part is worth as much as the five in the lower part, so that the complete column is equal to fifteen. Each column is equal to ten times the preceding one. In the form so described the abacus appears relatively late, but the *Shu-shu-chu-i* already mentions a more primitive form at the end of the second century. Probably the abacus was invented independently in China and in the West.

At a relatively early date Chinese arithmetic knew the taking of square and cube roots, and negative numbers; eventually it reached the Rule of Three, which appears in the *Chiu-chang-suan-ching*, that is to say a couple of centuries earlier than in India.

The development of algebra was handicapped by the absence of the sign for equality (=), and also of signs showing the exponents and powers. Moreover there was no ordinary algebraic notation; formulae were written out in full, in tabulated columns. The greatest advances in Chinese algebra came only under the Sung dynasty, very much later than the period covered here.

In the early centuries of the Christian era metrology was already completely decimal, at least for measurement of lengths. We find this already in the chapters on acoustics and on the calendar in the *Han-shu* (c. AD 100). Later the decimal system was extended to cover volumes and weights, but for the latter it was given official sanction only in 992.

Geometry continued to be purely empirical and descriptive. Particular study was given to the problems connected with the right-angled triangle, mainly for practical purposes like land-measurement; in this field Liu Hui did useful work with his studies of empirical solid geometry. The first Chinese evaluation of π was given at the beginning of our era by Liu Hsin in a volume measure prepared empirically for the usurper Wang Mang and still preserved at Peking: the figure arrived at is 3·154. The first calculations on this problem are those of Chang Hêng (c. 130). More precise results were obtained in the third century by Liu Hui, making use of inscribed polygons, and arriving at the figure 3·1459. The climax of the Chinese capacity for calculation was reached by Tsu Ch'êng-chih (430–501), with the figure $\frac{355}{113}$, equivalent to 3·1416, a point attained in Europe only a millennium later.

In conclusion it may be said that mathematics, like all scientific studies in China, reflected the positive and practical character of the Chinese people. Their investigations were essentially directed towards practical applications, and there was none of the interest in pure mathematics which is found in Greece.

Engineering and Agriculture. In China engineering always remained on a practical level, without any connotation of theory. Some bits of early information are found in the *K'ao-kung-chi* (artificers' record) chapter of the *Chou-li*: the original was lost and the present one was compiled by the prince of Ho-chien (d. 130 BC). The larger works of mechanical engineering were as a rule connected with the imperial workshops (mostly called *shang-fang*); for the rest engineering was a family and hereditary craft.

Most of our information on mechanical appliances refers to mechanical toys, which were always much appreciated in China. A very famous example of such devices was the south-pointing carriage (*chih-nan ch'ê*), in which a figure was made, by the use of cog-wheels, always to point southward; it certainly had nothing to do with the compass. The '*li*-recording drum carriage' (*chi-li-ku-ch'ê*), a sort of hodometer, is mentioned in the fourth century AD and described in the *Sung-shu*. As perfected later, it beat a drum at every *li* and sounded a gong at every ten *li*; it was a simple problem of reducing cog-wheels. Among these toys there was one destined for a great future, if only the Chinese had guessed its practical use—cardamic suspension. Only known to Europe since the sixteenth century, it seems to be described in the *Hsi-ching tsa-chi* of the sixth century, which attributes it to Ting Huan (c. AD 180): 'a perfume burner for use among cushions. . . ., a contrivance of rings which could revolve in all the four directions [i.e. the three directions of space], so that the body of the burner remained constantly level and could be placed among bedclothes and cushions'. In this connection we may mention a piece of charlatanry which shows an odd element of prophetic divination: about AD 320 Ko Hung speaks of a flying machine on the principle of the helicopter: 'Some have made flying cars [*fei-ch'ê*] with wood from the inner part of the jujube tree, using ox leather straps fastened to returning blades, so as to set the machine in motion' (*Pao-p'u-tzu, Nei-pien*, 15, f. 39a). More solid than these dreams was the fact that an old Chinese toy, the kite, arrived in Europe at the end of the sixteenth century and became the ancestor of modern aviation.

Of simple machines in everyday use, we find that some of them were first manufactured in China. The folding umbrella is one of them, and Wang Mang caused several to be manufactured for magic purposes; some examples have been found in the Lo-lang tombs in northern Korea. The box-bellows (with double effect, like a double pump) was a most efficient instrument, still widely used. A humble but very useful contrivance was the wheel-barrow: the Chinese one, with the wheel in the centre of the box, is much more practical than ours, because the man merely pulls it and holds it in equilibrium, but carries no part of its weight. It was first invented about AD 231 by Chu-ko Liang, for logistic purposes; it was called wooden ox (*mu-niu*).

Cog-wheels are first mentioned in the Han period, and we possess a terracotta mould for a toothed bronze wheel of that epoch. They are the necessary prerequisites for the most typical Chinese hydraulic machine: the square-pallet chain-pump (*fan-ch'ê*). It consists of an endless chain carrying a succession of pallets which, passing upwards through a trough, draw up water. It may lift water up to 16 feet and can be worked by a treadmill, animals, or by a water-mill. Something like this is alluded to in Mencius VIa, 2, 3, but the first certain mention is in *Hou Han-shu*, Cap. 108, f.24b; the invention is attributed to the engineer Pi Lan, who died in AD 186. Water-mills, with both horizontal and vertical axes, are found in China. They first appear in the first century AD, probably as an import from the West; oddly, they were chiefly employed for driving bellows, and seldom for grinding.

But engineering in China was fatally handicapped, in comparison with the West, by the lack of knowledge of some of the simple machines, such as the screw, and also of the crank (with the possible exception of the winnowing fan), and so it could never go farther than the so-called eotechnic stage.

Building engineering employed as its chief technique pisé and raw bricks in wall building. Baked bricks took their place during the Han period. The greatest and most famous feat of Chinese engineering is, of course, the Great Wall, which was formed in the years before 214 BC by connecting already existing stretches of wall. Its main purpose was administrative, fiscal, and, by making the passage of masses of nomad cavalry difficult, also military.

The Chinese road network was started by the first emperor Shih-huang-ti,

who in 220 BC caused two great postal routes (*ch'ih-tao*) to be built, radiating
from the capital Ch'ang-an towards Ch'i and Yen to the east, and towards
the lower Huai to the south-east. They were planted with trees and were
paved with a sort of macadam; no traces of them are left. Several important
roads were built under the Han dynasty. We may mention the one from
Ch'ang-an to Szechwan; it was built, or at least broadened, about 120 BC,
and crossed a very rugged tract of country. About one-third of its 430 miles
consisted of wooden trestles over mountain streams, or high up on the rocks.
The general rule was that road building was the concern of the central
government: in practice the latter took care only of those roads which were
necessary for the transport of taxes in kind.

Suspension bridges are first mentioned in the famous text of the *Han-shu*
concerning the 'Hanging Passages' in the Hindu Kush. They are common
in China, but it is impossible to settle their chronology. The greatest rope-
bridge is that at An-lan in Szechwan: it has five spans, the greatest of which
is 200 feet, the total being over 700 feet. Perhaps it was originally built by
Li Ping in the third century BC, but it is renewed every year.

The most notable innovation in Chinese agriculture of this period was the
'alternance field' (*tai-t'ien*) technique, introduced by Chao Kuo in the middle
of the first century AD. It consisted in ploughing the furrow where in the
previous year the balk had been, coupled with a careful weeding and lopping
of the young plants. This procedure was tried first in the imperial domains,
where it resulted in a double output per surface unit (*mou*); and then it was
officially introduced throughout the empire. It seems, however, that its use
did not last for more than a couple of centuries.

Astronomy. Chinese astronomy now begins to receive its first theoretical
elaboration. The main texts are the 'Memoir on the Calendar' (*Lü-li-chih*)
by Liu Hung (AD 178), and the 'Discussion on the Celestial Sphere' (*Hun-t'ien-
hsiang-shuo*) by Wang Fan (AD 260). From these works we know that at the
end of the second century AD there were three schools of cosmological
astronomy. The first, called *Kai-t'ien* (Heavenly Cover) maintained that
both sky and earth were hemispherical, like inverted bowls. In other words
there were two parallel cupolas, but the bowl of the sky was round, and the
bowl of the earth square. This was a very archaic conception. The second
school, *Hun-t'ien* (Heavenly Sphere) conceived earth and sky as two concentric spheres (like the yolk in an egg). The third school, *Hsüan-yeh*
(Infinite Empty Space), took the view that sun, moon, and all the stars
float freely in the empty space. The heavens are not matter. It was this last
theory which eventually prevailed. The *Hsüan-yeh* and *Hun-t'ien* schools
form the basis of later Chinese thought about astronomy, which is characterized by rigid adherence to the Ptolemaic conception of the spheres, by a strong
observational bias, and by the absence of any use of applied geometry.

Starting from the catalogues of *Shih Shen, Kan Tê,* and *Wu Hsien* mentioned above, Ch'en Cho at the beginning of the fourth century AD prepared a stellar map; and between 424 and 454 Ch'ien Lo-chih made an improved planisphere. Both these are now lost. It should be noticed that the modern system of notation by right ascension and declination, in use since the time of Tycho Brahe, corresponds to that used by the Chinese, and not to the Greek system of ecliptic co-ordinates. The nomenclature was different from that used in the West; and many names are drawn from the bureaucratic hierarchy of the Chinese state.

In this period an instrument made its appearance which was destined to have a greater future in China than elsewhere, the *clepsydra* or water-clock. The first certain mention of it is found in the *Lou-shui-chuan-hun-t'ien-i-chi* ('Method of making an Armillary Sphere rotate by means of Water from a Clepsydra'), a work written by Chang Hêng in AD 90 of which we possess a fragment. Then there appeared the *clepsydra* with a float and an indicator, similar to the one at Alexandria.

The armillary sphere just mentioned was used not only as an instrument for observation, but as a planetarium (orrery or uranorama); it was fundamentally different from its European counterpart because of the system of co-ordinates, which in China was based on declination and the ecliptic. The first mention of it is in the *Fa-yen* ('Discourses on Method') of Yang Hsiung in AD 5, where its first appearance is put in 104 BC. But the earliest description is in the fragment of Chang Hêng referred to above. We are told of diopters, and of the sphere being moved by water and a system of gears, the probable intention being to follow the apparent movement of stars, perhaps like the method of modern telescopes.

In the calendar the ancient sexagenary cycle, derived from the combination of the 10 *kan* and 12 *chih*, hitherto used only for days, came to be applied to years too; but it served only as a subsidiary to the normal means of calculation by years of emperors' reigns, and did not become a substitute.

Knowledge of the mechanics of eclipses grew more elaborate: already in the third century Yang Wei could predict the whereabouts of the first and last contacts in these phenomena. About 390 Chiang Chi predicted whether they would be partial or total.

b. India

Medicine and Alchemy. Indian medicine (*Āyurveda*) reached its highest level during this period. Its classic theory is contained in two famous books. One is the *Suśrutasaṃhitā*, in five sections (*sthāna*) and a supplement (*uttaratantra*); it goes back to the first centuries of our era. The other is the *Carakasaṃhitā*, in eight sections (*sthāna*); its editor Caraka is said to have been the court physician of Kaniṣka, and lived therefore in the second century AD.[7] Both works widely agree, and their body of knowledge and teaching is the same, except that Suśruta attributes much more importance to surgery than Caraka does. The so-called Bower MS from central Asia (fourth–sixth centuries), written in corrupt Sanskrit, is quite separate, and it consists chiefly of pharmaceutical content (curative properties of garlic).

The main tenets of the classic theory of Indian medicine are as follows. The body, like the cosmos, is a compound of five elements (*dhātu*): void (*ākāśa*), wind (*vāyu*), fire (*agni*), water (*jala*), earth (*bhūmi*). Of these, wind, fire, and water (the *tridhātu*) are the most active. Life depends on their harmonious interplay: illness is the effect of a disturbance of their equilibrium, in which case the three elements turn into the 'three evils' (*tridoṣa*). Wind circulates in the respiratory or digestive canals and is divided into five 'breaths' (*prāṇa*), which represent the organic forces. Fire is in a liquid form and is represented above all by the bile (*pitta*), subdivided into five fires (*agni*). Water (*ślesman*) is the common material of all serosities and liquid secretions; it too is divided into five classes. The various substances produced by the action of the three vital elements upon food are formed into organs by the actions of the wind. These organs are studied by direct anatomical observation on corpses, mostly prepared by a long immersion in water; but the knowledge of anatomy and of circulation is rather confused and vague. The network of vessels serves not only for the circulation of the blood, but also for that of the three *dhātu*; and some of them convey the vital principle (*ojas*). Pathology, as mentioned above, is based on the lack of equilibrium due to excitation or to scarcity of one or more *dhātu*. The causes of illness are due to environment, seasonal change, and (most important) food. Therapy is mostly empirical and symptomatic, great importance being attached to hygiene and dietetics. Pharmacology is chiefly vegetable and extremely rich in material. Surgery is fairly well developed. Its most daring operation is perhaps that of suturing wounds of the intestines by a curious process consisting in having the lips of the wound bitten by large ants, whose bodies are at once cut off. Their jaws act as organic sutures, which are more easily absorbed by the body than vegetable or animal threads. Other operations were for the stone (*aśmarī*), embryotomy on a dead foetus, and cataracts.

This theory of Ayurvedic medicine was handed down through generations of physicians (*vaidya*), and is still widely followed in India today.

J. Filliozat has remarked that there are very interesting points of contact with the treatise *Peri physeon* in the Hippocratic Corpus. In addition, the general theory of illness expounded by Plato in the *Timaeus*, while devoid of any Greek antecedent, is exactly parallel to that of the *tridoṣa*, with its three elements represented by breath, bile, and phlegm. The classic texts of the Indian school are more recent, but their body of knowledge is earlier than Plato. An Indian influence (through Iran) on Greek medicine is quite probable, also because no Greek term is found in early Indian pharmacology, while a few Indian names have found their way into the Hippocratic Corpus: *péperi* (from *pippalī*), pepper; *kóstos* (from *kusta*), *Costus speciosus*; *ziggíberis* (from *śṛṅgavera*), ginger; *sakkharon* (from *śarkara*), sugar.

Alchemy in India developed rather late, and then only in the wake of medicine. One section of the *Āyurveda* (the theoretical body of medical knowledge) was supposed to be the *rasāyana*, 'path of the *rasa*', i.e. of the organic humour; it dealt with fortifying and rejuvenating drugs.

Later on the word *rasa* acquired the meaning of mercury, or elemental essence. On this slender basis alchemy was built up, with magical aims: levitation, construction of gold, immortality. The earliest and most famous alchemist was Nāgārjuna, quite distinct from the great Buddhist philosopher. His date is variously given as between the second and the tenth century, and it is even possible that there was more than one alchemist of this name. The *Rasavaiśeṣikasūtra* and the *Rasaratnākara* are attributed to him. The second work is in verse and treats, among other things, of chemical purification (*śodhana*) and of calcination (*māraṇa*).

Astronomy, Mathematics, Architecture. The great new feature about Indian astronomy in the first centuries AD was the Hellenistic and Roman influence, which reached the country over the many trade-routes. It is reflected most of all in certain technical terms: *āpoklima* (ἀπόκλιμα) means 'declination'; *dṛkāna* from δέκανος; *jyāmitra* from διάμετρον; *liptā* from λεπτόν, meaning 'a moment'; *horā* from ὥρα mainly in the sense of 'horoscope'. We suddenly find the solar zodiac of twelve constellations, with the same signs (*raśi*) as those used in Greece; this is a conception which was originally quite foreign to India. Equally unexpected is the appearance of astrology, a science unknown to the Vedic world but destined in later times to have luxuriant developments in India. It would be wrong, however, to speak of a Hellenization of Indian astronomy, which largely continued to follow its own lines sometimes with original results. For instance the application of trigonometry to astronomy is more evident in India than in Greece, and the movement of the equinoxes is explained by the Indian theory of libration rather than by Hipparchus' theory of the precession.

The five main writings of this period are known to us indirectly through the discussion of them by Varāhamihira in his *Pañcasiddhāntikā* at the beginning of the sixth century. They are the *Paitāmaha Siddhānta*, the oldest of the five, still very close to the *Jyotiṣa Vedāṅga*, whose five-year cycle (*yuga*) it retains; then the *Vāsiṣṭha Siddhānta*; thirdly the *Pauliśa Siddhānta*, the name of which in all probability refers to Paul of Alexandria, and which already shows knowledge of an exact method for determining the length of a day and suggests an approximate method for calculating eclipses: fourthly the *Romaka Siddhānta*, or 'Roman System', where for the first time we find a great cycle, that of 2,850, probably the 19-year cycle of Meton of Athens multiplied by 150—the length of a year in the *Romaka* (365 days, 15 hours, 55 minutes, 12 seconds) is the same as that in Hipparchus and Ptolemy, as are various other calculations; and lastly the *Sūrya Siddhānta*, the only one of the five to be preserved, though even here we have it only as a later revision. Today the *Sūrya* is a short work of 500 verses in 14 chapters (*adhikāra*), written in a laconic and obscure style and designed, like all Indian manuals, to provide a mnemonic guide as a summary of what was taught orally. To establish a concordance of the movements of the sun and moon, the equinoxes, planets, and of apsides and nodes, the *Sūrya Siddhānta* uses a 'quadruple period' (*caturyuga*) of 4,320,000 years, divided into four cosmic years. The synodical month is divided into thirty lunar days (*tithi*), the length of which is smaller than that of solar days (*sāvana*); and it is worth noting that in practice mediaeval and modern chronology has made regular use of *tithi* rather than of *sāvana*. The movement of the equinoxes, as has already been stated, is explained by a theory of oscillation, with a theoretical velocity of fifty-four *sāvana* a year. On this theory is based the determination of a fictitious era called Kaliyuga, which is employed in astronomical textbooks with a starting date at 18 February, 3102 BC. This is of course the result of calculations made in the early centuries AD, not of a tradition from pre-Vedic times. The movements of the five planets (Mercury, Venus, Mars, Jupiter, and Saturn) are determined by the cosmic wind (*marut*); so the pneumatic theory has migrated from physiology to astronomy.

Late Vedic mathematics came to a halt in the centuries just preceding and following the beginning of the Christian era. Nevertheless this period saw the definitive completion of the numerical system, and a gradual transition to decimal notation and positional value of digits. The first epigraphic instance of positional value dates back only to 594; and the zero digit appears only in 683 on inscriptions of Cambodia and Sumatra and only in 870 in continental India. But positional and decimal value of digits is known to the *Purāṇas* in the fourth to fifth centuries.

Mathematics are now divided into arithmetic (*pāṭīgaṇita*) and algebra (*bījagaṇita*). The former name derives from the sand-covered table (*pāṭī*) on which the four simple operations were performed. Its earliest monument is the Bakhshali manuscript, written in the eighth or ninth century, but with a content taking us back to the third or fourth. For the first time this contains the word for zero (*bindu*, point), and it shows knowledge of the Rule of Three.

Algebra has ancient origins, but it is difficult to form any clear idea of its development before Āryabhaṭa. It is still a much debated question how much it owed to Greek influence: various Indian writers have strenuously denied such influence in modern times. Perhaps one should speak of stimulus rather than influence.

However that may be, mathematics is primarily an appendage to astronomy, and all the five *Siddhānta* (systematic manuals) on astronomy before Varāhamihira (c. 550), including those cited by that author, contain mathematical material. The first text we possess in its original form is itself part of an astronomical work, the *Āryāṣṭasata* of Āryabhaṭa, written in 499: this section, consisting of thirty-three stanzas, is called *Gaṇita*. It shows knowledge of the indeterminate equations of the first degree $(a + by = c)$, provides a good valuation of π (3·1416), and suggests rules, though they are erroneous, for determining the volumes of the pyramid and the sphere. Indian mathematics reach their zenith with Brahmagupta (born in 598), but his work is outside the limits of this volume.

The theory of Indian architecture (*śilpa*) is known chiefly through the *Mānasāra*, a work in 70 chapters written in barbarous Sanskrit by an unknown practising architect. It goes back, at least in its core, to the post-Gupta age. It begins with an introduction (chapters 1–10) devoted mainly to metrology. The main body of the work deals with architecture in its widest sense (chapters 11–50), and the last part concerns sculpture. But interspersed here and there we find rules concerning various related subjects, such as engineering constructions of every kind, town planning, furniture, and even wearing apparel. Architecture is said to have three main styles: Nāgara, Vesara, and Draviḍa (chapter 18), and houses may have any number of storeys up to twelve, although no actual example of such a tall building is known from ancient India. The *Mānasāra* was followed by several later treatises on this subject, but they do not concern us here.

Philology. Pāṇini and Patañjali reigned undisputed in Indian grammatical studies throughout this period. They were sufficient for all uses over many centuries. The first new works of their school, commentaries only, are not earlier than the seventh century, and thus fall outside the limits set to our study.

A reaction against Pāṇini took place at first in Buddhist and Jain circles, since the language of their sacred texts responded to other requirements and diverged to a greater or lesser extent from classical Sanskrit. And yet the force of tradition was such that the non-Pāṇinean grammars were but pale imitations of the grand old master; they shortened the matter, arranged it differently, but lacked any real originality. The earliest and the most popular of the Buddhist Sanskrit grammars was the *Kātantra* of Śarvavarman; its nucleus goes back to the first century of our era. Another Buddhist grammar is that of Chandragomin (fifth–sixth century) which became the most popular grammar in Nepal, and hence in Tibet. The Jain grammars all seem to be later than this period.

The grammarians of Prakrit and Pali too are late. So are those of the Dravidian languages; but one work may perhaps go back to this period, the *Tolkāppiyam*, a Tamil treatise on literary expressions in which analysis goes down as far as the single words and letters. It is a manual of rhetoric and of grammar at the same time.

The beginning of Sanskrit lexicography goes back to the *Nighaṇṭu*, simple repertories of nouns and verbs compiled on the *Vedas*. But the great dictionaries of later ages responded to another necessity, that of supplying the poets with rare or strange words, or with a large number of synonyms. Thus they contain nouns and adjectives only, but not verbs, and are arranged by various systems of subject-categories. Some fragments of an old dictionary are contained in the Weber manuscript, found in central Asia. But the earliest work still existing in its entirety is the *Nāmaliṅgānuśāsana* or *Amarakośa* by Amarasiṃha, who wrote in the fourth, fifth, or sixth century. It is divided into three sections, and its semantic arrangement was the model for all the later collections of the same kind.

c. *Rome*

Scientific Encyclopaedias. In this period neither Greek nor Roman science, generally speaking, propounded many theoretical problems, but the work of publication which was done by the compilers of collections and manuals had its value. The public interest in this work, so far as Latin writing goes, is shown by the success of the earlier encyclopaedias put out by Cato and Varro.

In Tiberius' time A. Cornelius Celsus, probably a doctor, compiled a large manual, comprising five books on agriculture and eight on medicine, followed by others on the art of war, rhetoric, philosophy, and other subjects. It is written in a plain and agreeable style; and the part which has come down to us, which cites more than seventy authorities, shows the high degree of erudition which lay behind the work.

The natural encyclopaedia (*Naturalis Historia*) of C. Plinius Secundus (AD 23–79), although the author set himself a narrower task, is also the product of wide reading and accurate collection of factual data. It is in thirty-seven books, dealing with nature, the products of nature, and their derivatives or possible derivatives. It draws on earlier authors (146 Roman and 327 Greek are cited) rather than on direct observation, and in its theoretical sections it is little more than a résumé of previous writing. The subjects include geography, mathematics, physics, anthropology, physiology, zoology, and botany, with a digression about the use of animal, vegetable, and mineral matter in artistic production. Where Pliny takes material from earlier systematic works he is relatively orderly and complete; there are more gaps where he has had to do the work of collection himself. But on any estimate his book is of great importance for the information it contains.

The 'Embroideries' or 'Marvels' of Sex. Iulius Africanus (second to third centuries) must also have had a certain encyclopaedic character. We possess fragments dealing with the natural sciences, medicine, magic, commerce, sailing, and the art of war.

Other writers met the demand for encyclopaedic learning with less highly organized work. There were the twenty books of *Noctes Atticae* by Aulus Gellius (*c.* AD 170), which in a series of chapters without order deal with every sort of topic, physical and natural science, grammar, geography, and so on, with many citations of authorities; and the five books *Rerum reconditarum* by Psammetichus Serenus (*fl.* 193–234), who derived information from his vast private library of more than 60,000 volumes. Later, already outside our period, there were similar works, much used in the Middle Ages: the *Disciplinae* (or 'Liberal Arts') of Martianus (Felix) Capella, who wrote in the first decades of the fifth century, and the *Saturnalia* of his contemporary, Macrobius.

Agriculture. Among particular sciences we may start with agriculture. Besides the encyclopaedic writings of Celsus and Pliny mentioned above, first place must be given to the *Res Rustica* of L. Iunius Columella (first century AD), a man of Spanish family who also knew the Eastern countries through his military service and had large estates at Albanum in Italy. His work has come down to us in twelve books, variously arranged: the tenth, on gardening, is in verse, and purports to complete Virgil's *Georgics*. The *Res Rustica* is a complete manual on agricultural economy and technique, with many precepts and a quantity of facts: these are mainly drawn from earlier authors (Greek, Roman, and Carthaginian), but owe something too to his personal experience, as we can see from the central themes. For Columella was used to the types of crop and to the system of slave labour found in Italy in his own day, and consequently attached supreme importance to the cultivation of vines and olives.

Q. Gargilius Martialis, who was born in Mauretania and died in 260, also wrote a book on agriculture, but he gave special attention to arboriculture, to medicines of vegetable origin, and to veterinary questions connected with agricultural operations. A number of extracts have come down to us, and they show that he used data provided by several previous writers.

There still survive fragments of a Greek book on agriculture by Vindonius Anatolius of Berytus. The Latin work of Aggenius Urbicus, *Commentum de agrorum qualitate*, has survived entire; so has the *Opus Agriculturae* of Palladius Rutilius Taurus, a fourth-century writer who was probably a Gaul. Palladius wrote fourteen books (one being preface, twelve treating of cultivation in each of the months, and one in verse on the grafting of plants), and he drew mainly on his own observations rather than on previous writers.

Geography and Cartography. The great geographical works of Augustan times were followed by a series of sketches, which examine the various parts of the inhabited world and indicate their position, climate, conditions of life, and principal products. An example is C. Licinius Mucianus' description of his travels in Armenia, Lycia, and Syria, much used by Pliny in his *Natural History*. Tacitus' *Germania*, which deals with ethnographical questions, is not quite in this genre.

In the first century AD there was also the *Chorographia* of the Spaniard Pomponius Mela, three books of crisp description of the known world following the order of its coasts. There was also the *Periplus Maris Interni* by Menippus of Pergamum.

In the second century Julius Titianus wrote *Provinciarum Libri* in Latin, and there were a number of works in Greek. The *Periplus Maris Erythraei* describes the harbours and trade of the Indian Ocean to the mouth of the Ganges and beyond; Arrian of Nicomedia wrote a *Periplus Ponti Euxini*, drawing partly on his own diaries of his voyages; and the *Periegeseis* of Dionysius Periegetes, written in hexameters at the time of Hadrian, were still read and annotated in the twelfth century. From the second century we may also mention the *Collectanea rerum m·morabilium* of C. Iulius Solinus, which contains a large number of anecdotes and curiosities.

Already in our previous period cartography in the classical world had followed two different systems: one came after the other, and eventually the two were amalgamated. The precursors of Dicaearchus had continued to depict the world as a flat circle, and they had used the few available measurements as the basis for drawing particular countries; in consequence there were enormous distortions, and also very marked variations between the different designs that were made. Dicaearchus altered all this. He traced a rectangular grid, based on one main parallel and one main meridian: his parallel went from the Pillars of Hercules to the Taurus, and then on to the Paropamisus, roughly corresponding to lat. 36° N.; and his meridian passed through Lysimacheia, Rhodes, and Syene. Both lines were divided into stades; and within each rectangle he drew outlines, with measurements proportionate to such actual measurements as were known. Eratosthenes improved on Dicaearchus' approximations, interesting himself mainly in the inhabited countries. He derived his data on latitudes from calculations through the gnomon, and by comparing angles of inclination of the sun's rays to the horizon in various countries and the lengths of their longest days. Hipparchus took the process further, making use of astronomical co-ordinates of longitude.

In the Roman imperial period calculation and drawing could be more accurate and detailed. The countries were better known, and regular itineraries were measured; moreover in Augustus' time the work of land-registration was accompanied by the drawing of appropriate maps; and astronomical computations became much commoner. On the basis of all this work Marinus of Tyre about AD 120 brought out a work accompanied by maps, known to us mainly from the citations and criticisms in Claudius Ptolemaeus. In this *Correctio Tabulae Geographicae* Marinus did his calculations of longitude and altitude in degrees instead of stades. His data were provided by the days taken over journeys, and were therefore not very exact. He calculated the length of the basic parallel to be 70,000 stades, instead of the previously accepted 90,000, and the length of the basic meridian to be 43,500 stades; he then made a grid on which the meridians (or their projection on to a cylinder) were parallel to one another, which led to serious distortions in his drawing of the more northerly and southerly countries.

Claudius Ptolemaeus, who was born in Egypt and flourished at the time of the Antonines, wrote an *Introduction to Geography* in eight books. In the first he was concerned with the foundations of geography—the dimensions of the earth and systems of projection; in Books II–VII he gave co-ordinates for each of the places mentioned; and in Book VIII he dealt mainly with questions of astronomy and climate. Modern scholars are not agreed how far (if at all) Ptolemy himself was responsible for the twenty-seven maps which accompany the text in our manuscripts. It is beyond doubt, however, that the book was based on an immense amount of documentation, and that even though his frequently inadequate assumptions led him into certain errors and failures of method, his work is the climax of ancient geographical writing, bringing together the results of all previous research in this field at the moment when the Roman empire had reached its greatest extent.

Ptolemy calculated the circumference of the earth at 160,000 stades, on the basis of 500 stades to a degree. The size of the inhabited area was 80 degrees or 40,000 stades from north to south, and 180 degrees (instead of Marinus' 225) from east to west. He put two new projections on his map, the conic—with equidistant meridians, but later improved—and the so-called *Homoetera*.

Among Greek geographers of about AD 400 Marcianus of Heraclea is worthy of mention. A number of his works are lost, but we possess a *Periplus Maris Externi* in two books. Menippus of Pergamum wrote an epitome of a *Periplus Maris Interni*.

Latin geography of the fourth century has as its prominent figure Rufus Festus Avienus of Volsinii, who composed a *Descriptio Orbis Terrae* in 1,393 hexameters and an *Orae Maritimae Liber* about the western coasts of Europe. He drew largely on a Greek version of Himilco's ancient Carthaginian geography.

Very soon after this we get the collections of *Itineraries*, designed for use by traveller and trader, but also (as was mentioned earlier) for generals, on which the routes of the more important roads are listed with indications of stages, distances, and other information which might be useful on journeys. The data they provided were later transferred on to pictorial maps (*Tabulae Pictae*). The model must have been the catalogue of stations on Roman roads inscribed on the Golden Milestone, which Augustus set up by the Temple of Saturn in 20 BC. Complex itineraries must also have helped in the construction of the works by Marinus and Ptolemy mentioned above. We possess the *Itinerarium Antonini*, constructed in Caracalla's day, and the incomplete *Itinerarium Maritimum* which describes the sea-routes from Corinth to Carthage and from Rome to Arelate in Narbonensis; there is also an *Itinerarium Alexandri*, dedicated to Constantius II in anticipation of his war against Parthia and describing previous expeditions against that country. We know also of *Itineraries* which deal only with a single road: for example that from Gades to Rome, inscribed on some silver cups found at the watering-place of Aquae Apollinares (Vignanello); the one designed in 333 for the use of Christians making pilgrimage from Burdigala to Jerusalem, known as

Itinerarium Burdigalense or *Hierosolymitanum*; and another late fourth-century document, for use by a woman pilgrim going to the East, called Egeria or some such name. Painted itineraries must have been constructed quite early; the twelfth- or thirteenth-century 'Peutinger Table' derives from an original of the fourth century. Among ancient examples we possess one on the broken frame of a legionary's shield, found at Dura Europus on the Euphrates.

Astronomy and Mathematics. The obstinate propaganda spread by the Chaldeans through all parts of the Roman world was aimed at merging astronomy with astrology and divination; and the struggle between this party and those who wanted to keep the two studies distinct lasted for a great part of the imperial period. Authors like Tacitus and the Elder Pliny are severely critical of astrology: L. Manilius, who wrote his *Astronomica* in the first half of the first century AD, is its strong supporter. Manilius' first book deals with astronomy proper: all the rest is concerned with astrology, the action of the planets and constellations on the life of mankind, and is an attempt to formulate an absolute law governing the celestial and terrestial worlds with immutable order. The treatment is not easy, but the poem contains several fine lyrical episodes, like that on Andromeda and Perseus in Book V.

The union of divination and astrology was expounded by Balbillus in Nero's time, and during several centuries had a vogue in the theories of the neo-Pythagoreans. The most complete work on astrology which has come down to us from antiquity was composed as late as the fourth century, the *Mathesis* of the Neoplatonist Julius Firmicus Maternus. But the Christians rejected astrology, which was proclaimed anathema by the Councils of Laodicea in 366 and Toletum in 400. In particular they could not take the view that human destiny depended on the pagan gods who had been identified with the planets; and the fatalism of astrology was impossible to reconcile with the doctrine of man's free will, which they upheld.

The work which tells us most about astronomical knowledge in the imperial period is, of course, the great *Treatise on Mathematics* or *Great Mathematical Treatise on Astronomy* (the work called *Almagest* by the mediaeval translators of its Arab text), composed by Claudius Ptolemaeus in the second century. This contains the 'Ptolemaic' system, the geocentric doctrine which held the field for fourteen centuries, until the work of Copernicus. Comprising thirteen books, which were completed by lesser authors, it is the work of an advanced mathematician, geometer perhaps rather than astronomer: and on any estimate it represents the greatest achievement of the ancient world in spherical astronomy and the experimental work connected therewith.

In mathematics and geometry, however, the output and progress of the imperial period is smaller than that of previous generations. About AD 100 Menelaus of Alexandria is a figure worthy of mention: besides work on astronomy, he wrote three books of Sphaerica, which have come down to us in Arabic and in a twelfth-century Latin translation, the third book containing some elementary spherical trigonometry.

The first book of Ptolemy's *Almagest* (period of Marcus Aurelius), besides its astronomy, expounds some practical principles of spherical trigonometry; and it contains some tables essential for this study.

Heron of Alexandria was a capable writer on mathematics and mechanics, but views about his date show variations of more than a century: some scholars put him in the first century A D (the more acceptable date), others in the third.[8] For a long time he was regarded as the greatest mathematician of antiquity, but it was later realized that many of his theories derive from his predecessors and that his genius was not so much inventive as expository. He was director of the school of mechanics at Alexandria, the precursor in some sense of our polytechnics, and could therefore treat in an encyclopaedic manner of all branches of the wide discipline he professed. The titles of his writings include *Geometria, Geodesia, Stereometria, Mensurae, Liber Geoponicus, Metrica, Pneumatica,* and he also dealt with algebra. His *Definitions* and his commentary on Euclid are of a more theoretical nature. Towards the middle or end of the fourth century we have Pappus of Alexandria, who in eight books called *Collectio Mathematica* (the first two are mainly lost) gives a complete summary of everything Greek geometry had achieved. He also wrote commentaries on Euclid, Aristarchus, and Ptolemy.

Diophantus of Alexandria wrote thirteen books of *Arithmetica,* of which the first six have survived, and also a book about 'polygonal' numbers. The six books provide a full, but unsystematic, collection of problems about numbers, including indeterminate analysis. The algebraic formulae are more complicated than those used today, and are concerned only with supplying rational solutions to the problems: the algebraic calculus of the Arabs is probably derived from his form of calculus.

In the fourth century Theon of Alexandria was the most famous master. His school produced commentaries and editions of the works of the best-known mathematicians and astronomers, from Aratus through Euclid to Ptolemy.

Mechanics. We have kept the history of Mechanics for the present chapter, having omitted it from Part II. The subject was treated mainly empirically. With Archimedes we shall deal separately in discussing machines of war, but in other respects the theory of mechanics is not formulated in works written before the end of the first century B C. References in so-called 'Aristotelian' treatises are either heavily revised versions of authentic works of Aristotle, for instance the chapters on motion in *Physics,* or else are found in works which have long been recognized as spurious—later in particular than Posidonius—such as the *Mechanica, Peri Ouranou,* and *Peri Kosmou,* the last written in A D 67. In these pseudo-Aristotelian works is found the theory of levers; there is reference to the question of resistance by a weight;

uniform motion in a straight line is examined; there is application of the
principle that velocity is directly proportional to a force and inversely
proportional to resistance; it is shown that the velocity of a falling body is in
proportion to its weight; and there is some understanding of the principle of
inertia. In Heron, whom we have already shown to be not earlier than the
first century AD, we find descriptions of simple machines of a fundamental
type, with the conditions governing their equilibrium: they include the lever,
windlass, pulley-block, wedge, screw, and pulley. Other works of his deal
with the construction of robots, war machines, and so on.

The results of these pseudo-Aristotelian and Heronian works were transmitted, with translations and numerous Greek and Arabic commentaries,
to fourteenth-century Western scholars and were the basis of further work.

Book VIII of Pappus' mathematical work, mentioned above, is another
fundamental feature of the history of mechanics in the fourth century.
Parallel with the development in theoretical mechanics came one in the
practical application of mechanics. This is seen particularly in the field of
hydraulic power and its conveyance over distances; also in the use of pneumatic power to build pumps, organs, and water-clocks; and finally in the
making of machines for war.

Natural Sciences and Medicine. Two general works on natural science from
the imperial period may be mentioned first. In Pliny's *Natural History*
Books VIII–XI are devoted to animals, Books XII–XIX to vegetables, and
Books XXXIII–XXXVII to minerals. Then there are the eight books of
Quaestiones Naturales by L. Annaeus Seneca, who died in AD 65: they treat
of the more important natural phenomena in astronomy, meteorology,
physical geography, and so on.

Two writers called Appian dealt with zoology. The second-century
Appian of Cilicia, in Marcus Aurelius' time, wrote five books on fishing,
with some vivid descriptions; and his namesake from Apamea, under Caracalla, wrote four books on hunting. In the period of Septimius Severus, Aelian
of Praeneste produced seventeen books on the nature of animals, his aim
being to show, with a large number of anecdotes, how animals possess
sentiments, such as affection, love of justice, loyalty, jealousy, and hatred,
which do not put them significantly below the level of mankind.

Botany was treated in the encyclopaedias of Celsus and Pliny, by Columella
and Dioscurides in relation to agriculture and pharmacology respectively,
and by Galen in his medical works. In the third century there was the
agriculturalist Q. Gargilius Martialis, and in the fourth, Palladius. At the
end of the fourth and beginning of the fifth centuries Marcellus Empiricus,
perhaps a native of Burdigala in Gaul, was the author of a work *De Medicamentis*, which gave special attention to Gallic plants and their local names.

Under the empire Rome devoted great attention to the study of medicine,
encouraging the growth of colleges like the *schola medicorum* on the Esquiline

and of *auditoria* for teaching. Under Vespasian these institutions received grants from the state, and the speculation of Greek empiricists, so poorly thought of by Pliny, came to an end. Other schools opened up later in the West, at Massilia, Burdigala, Nemausus, Lugdunum, and Caesaraugusta.

For medicine in the first century the treatment by the encyclopaedists is again of importance. Celsus in Tiberius' time devoted eight of his books to a lucid treatment of medicine: he followed Hippocratic principles with some borrowings from other schools, and paid special regard to surgery (especially dental surgery) and the use of drugs. Pliny's *Natural History*, too, is full of references to physiology and to plants of medicinal value. Certain other scholars should also be remembered. The Stoic Athenaeus of Attalia founded the school of 'pneumatici'. They added to the four traditional elements a fifth called *pneuma*, which had its seat in the heart and was the principle of life, its excessive admixture with other elements being the cause of diseases. Athenaeus wrote a great work on medicine in thirty books, of which only fragments survive; and from him Claudius Agathinus, the eclectic student of hygiene, and Theodorus learned their medicine. Dioscurides must be mentioned for the pharmacology set out in his five books *De Materia Medica*; also Scribonius Largus, especially for his Recipes (*Compositiones*).

In the second century Rufus of Ephesus, a member of the dogmatic school, excelled in anatomy, the most important of his many writings being one on the names of the various parts of the body. Soranus of Ephesus, of the methodical school, was principally concerned with gynaecology, obstetrics, and pediatry: his principal work is entitled *The Diseases of Women*, and he provides some invaluable diagnostic studies and suggested treatments. Marcellus of Side wrote forty books of *Res Medicae* in verse; and Aretaeus of Cappadocia, one of the *pneumatici*, devoted eight books (still preserved) to acute and chronic illnesses, prescribing some very simple remedies of a largely mechanical kind. But the most famous name in this period is that of Claudius Galenus of Pergamum, who lived at Alexandria and for some time also at Rome and Pergamum, and who studied philosophy and rhetoric as well as medicine. His vast scientific output included more than 400 writings in Greek, known to us from two catalogues drawn up by himself. They divide into seven groups, of which five are on medicine: anatomy, pathology, therapy, diagnosis, and prognosis; and his commentary on the writings of Hippocrates. Galen was concerned to collect, in a polemical spirit, everything known about medicine. He stressed the necessity of analysis: in his view disease was due to dislocations of particular organs, and the cure must be adapted to one's understanding of a particular illness. Experimental methods must be constantly applied and anatomical study pressed to the farthest possible point; every kind of dogmatism must be avoided. Yet in the decline in medical studies which followed the second century his advice was disregarded: his own statements were regarded as dogmas because of the enormous reputation he possessed.

From the third century we have Quintus Serenus' *Liber Medicinalis* in hexameters, and the references to medicine in Q. Gargilius Martialis' work on agriculture. From the fourth there are the compilation called *Medicina Plinii*, which collects all the data given by the *Natural History*; an accurate compendium by an admirer of Galen, Oribasius, the doctor of the emperor Julian; and the *De Medicamentis* of Marcellus Empiricus, written under Theodosius I, which is a work full of extravagant superstitions.

A note must be inserted here on surgical instruments, which in their simplest form (probes and needles) go back to much earlier times. In the first decades of the fourth century BC advanced and specialized types could be found in the Greek world, as we can see from the works of Hippocrates—probes of various kinds, knives both sharp and short, or convex in shape, rasps, trepanning saws, dentists' clamps, spectacles, and so on. Similar instruments were known at an early date in Italy by Etruscan doctors, as can be seen from the specimens of pincers, spatulas, knives, and spectacles on show in the Perugia museum.

We know from the works of Celsus that doctors of the Roman period were acquainted with at least fifty types of instrument, including tools for extracting the roots of teeth, scalping instruments, pincers for bones, trepanning and other kinds of saw, catheters, and cystotomes; of many of them examples have been found in excavations, for instance at Pompeii (forceps, pincers, hooks, specula, probes, surgeons' knives, etc.).

About the bandaging of wounds we have precise evidence both in Galen and on monuments, especially in the reliefs on Trajan's Column.

The most characteristic side of Roman medicine under the empire, as in the previous period, was the importance attached to hygiene, which for a long time past had been shown by the construction of water services, including aqueducts and baths. Besides the *ambulatoria* of individual doctors, there grew up hospitals (*valetudinaria*), including particular institutions for soldiers, slaves, and poor people. The state provided sanitary arrangements for the court, and also for individual towns (where free attention was provided for poor persons registered on the list of those exempt from taxation). There were also army doctors in the legions and in the fleets, and these were exempted from ordinary military service. The hospitals had personnel (*accensi*) to give the necessary assistance, *frictores* for massage, and *unguentarii* to rub in ointment and perfume. In the fourth century special hospitals for Christians began to make their appearance.

Veterinary science had a place of its own. Important pages are devoted to it by Pliny and other encyclopaedists, also by Columella, Gargilius Martialis, and Palladius. There were also writings specifically concerned with the subject, especially those of Absyrtus and Pelagonius in the fourth century: these were followed by the anonymous Greek tract, translated into Latin, called 'Mulomedicina Chironis', which was put into more simple terms by Flavius Vegetius Renatus in his *Digestorum artis mulomedicinae libri*.

Besides medicine proper great advances were made in pharmacology. The first important name is that of Pedanius Dioscurides of Taurus, who lived about the middle of the first century AD and wrote five books *De materia medica*. This collects everything known on the subject, and remained a classic for many centuries. The author deals with medicines derived from animals, from about 600 vegetables, and from minerals. Book I is concerned with aromatics, vegetable oils and juices, resins, and balsams; Book II with remedies of animal origin (honey, milk, and fat), with edible vegetables, and garden produce; Books III and IV with herbs, roots, and seeds; Book V with wines and other drinks, and with mineral medicines. Book VI on poisons and antidotes (including animal poisons) is certainly spurious. A contemporary of Dioscurides was Scribonius Largus, who among other writings produced a recipe book (*Compositiones*) in 271 chapters, derived mainly from Greek sources. Galen, of whose medical work we have spoken already, is also important in the history of pharmacology, not only for his writings on food juices, simple medicaments, and antidotes, but for his personal investigations into drugs. These took him on various journeys, and he tells us much about the trade in drugs, by both itinerant merchants and shopkeepers, who are also known to us from archaeological evidence at Pompeii and other places.

Another feature of the first century AD was the growth of alchemy, especially in Egypt and the East, from which it spread to other countries. Its devotees believed that metals extracted from the earth led a real life and then died; and that after their return to mother earth, and after a new period of gestation in which various substances might be mingled with them, they were born again. So the alchemists were confident that with the oven and the crucible, if the crushed 'philosopher's stone' were added, base metals could be transformed into precious ones; and it was their fantastic experiments which accidentally and imperceptibly led to modern chemistry. The first alchemists, of whom some were mystics and others set out to mystify, claimed to derive their secrets from the writings of ancient divinities, such as Hermes Trismegistus (later identified with great biblical figures like Enoch, Adam, Abraham, or Solomon), or Egyptian gods like Ptah, Khnurn and Tiot. They put into circulation apocryphal works, attributed to some of the figures just mentioned, or to Agathodemon, Isis, Chimetes, Cleopatra, Moses, or Mary (whence the name bain-marie). The oldest among these spurious writings were probably those attributed to Democritus, produced in the first or second century AD. On the other hand, alchemistic papyrus recipes from near 300 AD indicate that the early alchemists were often forgers of rare products and not mystics.

Philology. One of the key figures in first century AD philology was the Latin Verrius Flaccus, who taught the grandsons of Augustus. He dealt with orthography, semantics, and lexicography. His *De Significatu verborum* studies all the most obscure words, propounds explanations, and builds a regular storehouse of information about such subjects as language, culture, religion, politics, and law. The original is lost, but we have an epitome in twenty books prepared in the second or third century by Pompeius Festus, and a shorter one by Paulus Diaconus from the eighth century.

Q. Remmius Palaemon of Vicetia, the master of Persius and Quintilian, used the work of his most famous predecessors to compose an *Ars Grammatica*, which is novel in both its content and its outlook. It is no longer Stoic, but Alexandrine, in inspiration; and it gives an unusual degree of importance to syntax. This work was a model for everything written thereafter.

After these two classics came a succession of works on lexicography and grammar in the centuries which followed. Each is less original and more scrappy than the last, and grammar came to cover only the use of the literary language.

In the Greek world of the first century there was much attention paid to the construction of lexicons for particular dialects and particular authors, and for proper names. The *Glosses and Names* of Pamphilus of Alexandria (in ninety-five books) remained famous throughout antiquity; and to Pamphilus' polygraph anti-Semitic contemporary Apion are attributed works on Latin dialect, Homeric glosses, the letters of the alphabet, and similar matters.

In the second century there was Apollonius Dyscolus, another writer in Greek, who produced books on pronouns, adverbs, and conjunctions, as well as on pronunciation, inflection, and prosody. His main contribution, however, was the construction of a theory of syntax which enunciated rules and exceptions, and attempted to explain them. These views dominated the ideas of several centuries.

There were many Latin grammarians in the second century. In the age of Hadrian, Terentius Scaurus studied prepositions, adverbs, and orthography, but above all the history of the Latin language. His contemporary Velius Longus wrote *De Orthographia* and *De Usu Antiquae Lectionis*; Flavius Caper was a student of archaic and classical Latin and wrote *De Latinitate* and *De Dubiis Generibus*; Statilius Maximus produced a work called *De Singularibus* about words only used once; and there was Aulus Gellius who, against the generally accepted opinion, maintained that Greek and Latin were of independent origin.

The Latin writers worth mentioning in the fourth and fifth centuries are Nonius Marcellus, who in his *Compendiosa Doctrina* collected lexical and grammatical examples from Republican Latin; Aelius Donatus, who wrote a grammar (in two parts—elementary and advanced); and Flavius Sosipater Charisius, who also produced an *Ars Grammatica* in five books, dealing with grammar, metric, and style.

The Church Fathers were also led to engage in linguistic researches by their constant meditations on the sacred Hebrew writings and their translations into Greek and Latin: their work was designed to show how far Latin had been affected by Hebraisms and Graecisms.

[d. *Mechanics in Antiquity**

Theory. The 'Mechanical Problems' of Aristotle is the oldest theoretical work on mechanics, whether it was written by Aristotle himself, before 322 BC, or by Strato of Lampsacus, about 285 BC. The effect of the lever is here derived from the nature of the circle and the wheel, and it is then used for

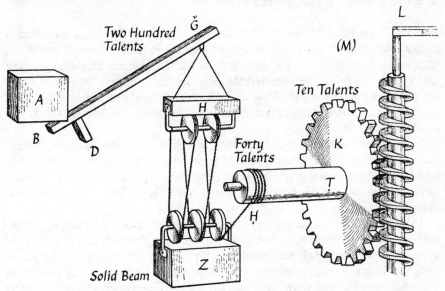

FIG. II.   *Four of the five 'powers' combined.* The figure comes from a manuscript of Heron's *Mechanics*. On the right is a screw engaging a toothed wheel, which turns a drum, which pulls a rope from a pulley, which pulls a lever, which lifts the burden. The burden A weighs 1,000 talents; the power available is 5 talents, but Heron has not been able to compute the effect of the screw. This is just a theoretical example, but all the elements were used in practice. The inscriptions are translated from Arabic.

answering thirty-five questions about mechanics. The centre of gravity is not mentioned.   The book knows the pulley and the wedge, but not the screw.

Archimedes (287–212 BC), mathematician and inventor, defined the centre of gravity and wrote on statics, treating the subject mathematically; fragments of these works are found in Heron's *Mechanics*; preserved are the *Equilibrium of Plane Figures* and the *Floating Bodies*.

Heron of Alexandria, for whose date see above, wrote a work on mechanics, found only in an Arabic translation. He describes the five 'simple powers', that is the winch, the pulley, the lever, the wedge, and the screw. (Fig. II.) He explains that a smaller power will balance or overcome a larger burden if it travels a longer way, or, as he puts it, takes more time. For the first three powers the dimensions cannot be enlarged infinitely, but we can move a

* By A. G. Drachmann.

weight of 1,000 talents with a power of five talents by three toothed wheels
or three sets of pulleys or three levers. Instead of cog-wheels we can use
ropes round drums. The example of the cog-wheels appeared as a separate
work, the *Barulcus*; but it is nothing but theory.

Pappus (300 AD) treats of mechanics in his Book VIII; he is dependent
on earlier authors, especially Heron.

Practice. Two great inventors lived during antiquity: Ctesibius and Archimedes. Heron also seems to have been a capable inventor, though not of the
same class. Ctesibius (270 BC) founded the science of Pneumatics by proving
that the air is a body; he invented the cylinder and plunger, the force-pump,
the water-organ, the water-clock with all sorts of mechanical and pneumatic
parerga, and several catapults and other war engines, which, however, did
not live long. (Fig. 12.)

Archimedes invented the steelyard, the endless screw, and the water-
snail; Oribasius and Tzetzes ascribe to him the invention of the *trispaston*,
which elsewhere means a triple pulley; but the *trispaston* described by Oribasius seems to have been a geared winch (see below). The triple pulley was
known to Aristotle.

Taking the five simple powers we find that the lever was used for wine-
and oil-presses, either with just a winch, or with a winch and a pulley, or
with a screw; the winch was used also for cranes, together with the pulley
and, for heavy burdens, with a gear consisting of ropes round drums of
different size. Pulleys were used also on ships. The wedge was used mostly
for cutting out marble blocks, but Heron describes a perfume-press worked
by wedges; it is pictured in Pompeii. The use of the screw was limited until
a tool was found to cut a female screw in wood; it is described by Heron and
may be his own invention. Then the screw was used first to work the lever of
the press, next to press directly on the mass. For adjusting surgical *specula*
and other instruments, brass screws were used, going through a smooth hole
with a peg to engage the screw-thread.

The endless screw, which may have played a part in the defence of Syracuse
contrived by Archimedes, is later found only in instruments and in the
resetting machine of the surgeon Nymphodorus; in another resetting machine,
that of Andreas, we find the screw moving 'tortoises', blocks running in
grooves, first by means of a smooth hole and a 'tooth', later by a female screw.

Toothed wheels came into use late, because the true form of the teeth
was not calculated till much later (1675 AD). Ctesibius used toothed wheels
and racks for the *parerga* of his clocks; Archimedes used a toothed wheel
with a screw; the first mention of toothed wheels engaging each other at
right angles is in Vitruvius, for the water-mill (see below). An astrological
instrument, the Anticythera instrument, from the first century BC, shows a
number of parallel wheels with triangular teeth engaging each other; it is
unique. The intricate Automatic Theatre of Heron is worked by strings only.

The only power machine known to antiquity was the water-wheel, from the first century BC; it is described by Vitruvius. He wrote a textbook on architecture in 25 BC; the two last of its books deal with cranes and other

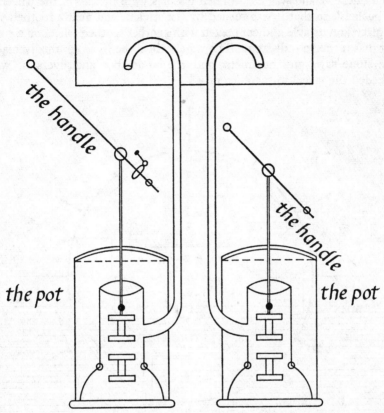

FIG. 12. *The pump of Ctesibius*. This manuscript figure comes from Philo's *Pneumatics*, App. 1, Ch. 2; it shows the pump invented by Ctesibius. The two cylinders, open at the top, are placed in two large 'pots', which must always contain water. The plungers are shown as I-shaped; the two I-shapes under them are the inlet valves. The outlet valves are not shown; according to the text they were placed in the 'bulges' from which the discharge pipes go up. The connecting-rods are hinged to the plungers and the handles. The two separate handles and the two separate discharge pipes show the age of the pump. From MS. Marsh 669, folio 2v, Courtesy of the Curators of the Bodleian Library, Oxford.

engines of interest to the architect, who was also a contractor. We hear of the horizontal water-drum, which will lift water only to the height of its radius, and the water-snail, invented by Archimedes, which will lift water to greater heights; they were turned by men using their bare feet. Next there is the tread-wheel, dipping into the water, with 'square bushels' on its side for scooping up the water and pouring it out at a height not quite that of its diameter. (Fig. 13.) For still greater heights a tread-wheel above the water with a bucket-chain was used. Then paddles were placed on the wheel with the 'bushels', so that it was turned by the stream, and next a toothed wheel was placed on its axle and connected with another toothed wheel on a vertical shaft that turned a mill-stone. The water-wheel then was gradually made to drive stone saws and hammers, and the undershot and overshot wheels succeeded the wheel in the current.

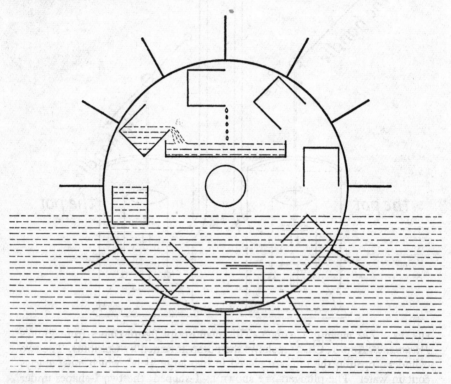

FIG. 13. *Vitruvian water-wheel* with paddles and square buckets. The diagram is made from Vitruvius, Book 10, ch. 5; it shows a wheel, driven by paddles, lifting water from a river by means of 'square bushels'. When two gear-wheels at right angles were added, the water-wheel became a mill-wheel, the first, and for many hundred years, the only power engine used in the Western world.

The gear-wheels at right angles most probably had round sticks for teeth; in Saalburg (about 250 AD) a lantern pinion has been found.

Windmills were unknown to antiquity; hot air or steam is used by Heron to move a few pneumatic toys of no importance.

Except for the water-wheel only the power of animals and men was used. The animals in a horse-walk turned grain mills; for big cranes the men worked inside treed-wheels like great squirrel cages. (Pl. 62.)

The elasticity of wood and horn was used in the bow; when larger engines, catapults, were invented, the elasticity was provided by two bunches of sinews, into which two strong wooden arms were thrust. They carried the string, which was drawn by a winch, and for greater catapults were supplemented with a pulley.]

NOTES TO CHAPTER XV

1. Information about this and other visitors to eastern lands comes from the geographer Ptolemy, often drawing on Marinus of Tyre (early second century AD—see below, p. 756). Maes, 'qui est Titianus' (Ptol. I, 11.7), was probably a Syrian, i.e. a 'Macedonian' settled in Syria, but his date is unknown: M. Cary, *Classical Quarterly*, 1956, pp. 130 ff., argues for the reign of Augustus.

2. It is extremely doubtful whether, as stated here, glazing technique was imported from the West. This was known to the Chinese already during the Yin (see Li Chi, *The Beginning of the Chinese Civilization*, Seattle, 1957, p. 16). (L. S. Vasilyev.)

3. *The Periplus of the Erythraean Sea* appears from the most recent research to be from the third century and not the first century.

4. See also Part II, p. 397, with note.

5. Including many stations on rivers, the Rhine and Danube above all, but also the Save and Drave, the Moselle, and of course the leading rivers of Gaul. Porterage between the main waterways assumed importance and was probably the motive for certain well-known lines of fortification, e.g. the Clyde to the Forth, the Main to the Neckar, or the Dobrudscha 'vallum' from the Danube to the sea: see U. Kahrstedt, *Bonner Jahrb.*, 1940, pp. 62 ff. For grain carried by water between Gaul and Illyricum see a recently discovered inscription published by A. Pflaum, *Libyca*, 1955, p. 135.

6. Professor L. S. Vasilyev notes that Hua T'o, according to some sources, was familiar with skull trepanning: see J. Needham, *Science and Civilisation in China* (Cambridge, 1954), I, p. 204. For similar development in the contemporary Mediterranean world see below, p. 762.

7. Professor J. Filliozat notes that this treatise contains some much earlier teaching, going back to Ātreya (Part II, p. 418).

8. That Heron lived before Ptolemy is cogently argued by A. G. Drachmann, *Centaurus* (1950), I, pp. 117–31. Dr Drachmann also maintains that Heron's *Dioptra* refer to an eclipse of the moon in AD 62: see O. Neugebauer, *The Exact Sciences in Antiquity* (2nd edition, Copenhagen, 1957), p. 178.

CHAPTER XVI

POLITICAL POWER AND PUBLIC ADMINISTRATION

I. CHINA

AFTER the Confucianization of the state during the Former Han dynasty, and after the reforms of Wang Mang had disappeared along with their author, the rule of the Later Han dynasty (22–220 AD) marked a period of calm, but also of stagnation and decay in the administrative field and of slow changes in the social structure.

In the main, the restored dynasty was content with maintaining and continuing the institutions of its ancestors. In the central government the changes were but few. The Three Dukes and the Nine Ministers were retained, but the post of the Counsellor (*ch'êng-hsiang*) was abolished, and the commander-in-chief (*t'ai-wei*) became a regular appointment and took over the functions of Prime Minister. The triad was completed by the resurrection of an old office, that of the *ta-ssü-t'u*, who became an assistant of the *t'ai-wei*. But these changes had little practical importance, since the functions of the Three Dukes and of the Nine Ministers tended more and more to become purely honorific, and theirs were titles without power; actual administrative work tended to be concentrated in the five Secretariats (*ts'ao*). The latter were headed each by a secretary (*shang-shu lang*), assisted by six under-secretaries, *shih-lang*. As said above in Part II, the General Secretary (*shang-shu ling*) was practically the most influential official and the executor of the emperor's will. Since the high officials were recruited according to a fixed routine and therefore were too independent and also too closely knit a class, these posts of trust in the Secretariats were usually given to literati of lesser standing, or even to court eunuchs.

In the provinces the local commander-in-chief was abolished, and the troops of the inner provinces were reduced and placed under the direct command of the governor. For the rest, the Chinese infantry continued to hold its own against the mounted archer of the steppe, thanks mainly to its standard weapon, a powerful crossbow with a most ingenious and clever cocking device.

In financial administration the Privy Treasury of the emperor disappeared and all revenue flowed into the state exchequer; on the other side, the latter had now also to meet the ever-increasing expenses of the court.

Confucian officialdom remained at first paramount in the central administration. But its ascendancy was challenged first by the relatives of the empresses; the foremost instance is that of the Liang family (c. 145–150). Much more dangerous opponents were the eunuchs. Emperors came to lean more and more heavily on them, in an effort to make themselves independent of the bureaucracy. The eunuchs owed everything to the emperor and, coming from low social strata, were usually free of entanglements with the cliques of high officials; but their control of access to the person of the emperor lent itself to many abuses and to wholesale corruption. Thus the second half of the second century AD was marked by savage and often bloody struggles at court between the eunuchs and the Confucian officials (who organized themselves into a regular party). In the end these court intrigues and conflicts merely served to destroy the authority of the central government and to transfer actual power to the commandants of the troops in the frontier provinces. After c. 175 the latter fought for the real power over the heads of the impotent central government. Ts'ao Ts'ao emerged as the strongest, but was not strong enough to eliminate his adversaries; and the empire collapsed and split into three parts.

Neither the Three States nor the Chin dynasty, who for a short spell (280–317) ruled over the whole of the reunited empire, introduced any formal change in the administration. But the old structure was gradually emptied of any substantial meaning by the fact that the emperor usually granted the great offices of state to princes of the imperial family, for whom the actual administrative work was performed by substitutes (ch'êng-shih), usually literati. Hence an atmosphere of mutual suspicion and continuous bickering, which led not to a balance of power, but to inefficiency and stagnation. Military offices increased in number and importance. During the times of the Chin the central government was practically represented by the State Secretariat (shang-shu t'ai), headed by the shang-shu ling. Things came to such a pass that the great officers of the crown caused themselves to be given direction of the State Secretariat, with the title of tu shang-shu shih; this placed the State Secretary under their orders, and by this devious means the old situation was re-established in all but name.

At the same time the recruitment of the bureaucracy underwent a profound change. Proficiency in Confucian studies and selection by examination had become less important than membership of a group of influential families. After the fall of the Han, even the pretence of choice by examination was dropped, being formally replaced in 220 by the so-called 'Nine Classes and the Impartial and Just' (chiu-p'in chung-chêng), i.e. recommendation by government inspectors ('Impartial and Just') sent to the provinces to select suitable candidates. Out of their list, which was divided into nine classes, the government chose its future officials. Since the great families could exert the whole weight of their relations and money in influencing the inspectors, designations became limited to their class only, and had nothing to do with scholarship or merit. This meant the formation of a 'noblesse de toge' at the very moment in which the imperial structure was on the verge of collapsing for more than two centuries and a half.

Shortly afterwards a new nobility was created, with many titles and ranks (from duke to baron); it took the place of the former bureaucratic ranks of Han times. Even before the Hsiung-nu invasion of 313–317 Chinese society was well on the way to a return to feudalism. It should be noted, however, that it was not the title that counted, but membership of an old and established family; a count of an old family was much more respected than a newly-backed duke. The ruling class, chiefly in South China after 317, became a close caste with all the characteristics of economic feudalism.

The social structure of the Later Han dynasty was at first marked by an easing of the social tension. The civil war and the massacres of the time of Wang Mang and of the Red Eyebrows revolt had eliminated many absentee land-owners and had made large areas of land available for the farmer. The trend towards the formation of large estates was sharply checked and for a time reversed. But this did not last. The long internal peace of the first and second centuries caused, it is true, a large increase of national wealth; but it also nearly doubled the population, which was still badly distributed between an over-populated Huang-ho basin and a thinly inhabited south. Pressure on the soil, pauperism, and indebtedness increased, and the concentration of land ownership in a group of great families started again and went on ever more rapidly.

Social tension reached breaking-point with the peasant revolt of the Yellow Turbans (184) and with the internecine wars of the provincial commanders at the end of the second century. The farmers, being exposed without defence to pillage and robbery by soldiers and brigands, abandoned the fields, absconded to the hills or swamps, and turned vagrants (*liu-li-chia*). The only haven of tolerable safety was for those who placed themselves under the protection of the great families; these had taken to self-defence by organizing their relatives and retainers into armed bands (*chia-ping*). Small cultivators joined them in the quality of 'farmer guests' (*tien-k'o*). It is said that about AD 200 five-sixths of the population were thus under the protection of big land-owners. They were, however, not tied to the land like the *coloni* of the Roman world about the same time, but to the lord; and if their protector abandoned his seat and migrated in search of a quieter spot (as occasionally happened), they too went with him. This type of structure has been called, with some reason, 'manorial economy'.

Thus the agrarian problem was becoming paramount in the general breakdown of Chinese society in the third century. The first Wei emperor Wu-ti tried to solve it by the first land regulation of which there is record in Chinese history (280). He limited the number of 'farmer guests' according to the official rank of their host (from a maximum of fifteen families to a minimum of one). Most important was a serious attempt to regulate the relationship of the farmer with the land he tilled. Within the local units (*hsiang*) the soil was distributed among the peasant families according to definite rules; normally only adult males were entitled to a full share, youngsters and old men to something less. This measure met with temporary success; but most of the peasants did not venture to abandon the protection to which they were accustomed. Soon afterwards the barbarian invasion upset the whole organization and brought the earlier process to its logical conclusion. The free peasantry disappeared and were converted into clients (*pu-ch'ü*; originally bodyguards) of the great landed proprietors.[1] The only exception, at least in the early days, lay in the military colonies (*t'un-t'ien*) on the border, a good many of which had been founded by Ts'ao Ts'ao (*c.* 190–220).

Commerce was regarded with suspicion and despised by the bureaucracy; it was restricted by governmental measures and was severely hit by the economic crisis of the third century. Under the Later Han the merchant class began to be affluent and to acquire economic importance, but this was not followed up. Land became once more the only established and recognized form of wealth, the more so because money had become very scarce and the country was lapsing back into a natural economy on a barter basis. In the same way there was no increase in the importance of towns. Practically the only cities in China were the capitals Ch'ang-an and Lo-yang (Fig. 15), with two or three others which were the former headquarters of the old feudal states. All of them were under the strict surveillance of state officials and were divided by walls or closed streets into quarters and wards, passage from one to another being strictly forbidden at night. There was no form of corporate life and the apt synthesis of Max Weber still holds good: 'in China a city was a place with officials and without local autonomy'. To this we may add that the China of this period was one of the purest examples of an agrarian state that ever existed.

2. INDIA

The institutions of the Greek and Iranian invaders of north-western India are little known. There is scarcely any material on the Greeks, except for some vague hints in the *Milindapañha*. It may be, as affirmed by Tarn, that their central and provincial administration was borrowed from Seleucid Asia, including the rise of quasi-autonomous cities. The Śaka and the Parthians formed a very loose confederation of markedly feudal character. Coins and inscriptions show that its supreme head had under him a number of satraps (*kṣatrapa*). Greek titulature lingered on under the Parthians: Gondophernes had a *stratega* called Aspavarman, and the title *meridarkha* also occurs. On the other side the new offices of *kṣatrapa* and *mahākṣatrapa* were created, reviving old Persian institutions. We may, however, note the exaltation of the king's dignity, although his power over the aristocracy was very limited; he bore now the title of Great King of Kings (on the coins:

basileos basileon megalou in Greek, *rājatirajasa mahatasa* in Prakrit). The autonomous cities and other traces of Greek rule disappeared.

Republican states experienced a revival after the decay of Greek power. First the Yaudheya, Ārjunāyana, Rājanya, and Śibi reappeared in the 'limelight in the second and first centuries BC, then the Mālava, Yaudheya, and Kuniṇḍa in the first and second centuries AD; the dedicatory legends on the coins of the Kuniṇḍas seem to refer to a theocratic state. All these republics were situated in the Punjab and Rajasthan. They were reduced into insignificance by the expansion of the Guptas. Their end was perhaps brought about by the headship of the state gradually becoming hereditary and the power of the assembly of the nobles disappearing.

The administration of the Sātavāhana was a continuation of the traditional system with some innovations. The *amātya* took the place of the Mauryan *mahāmātra*; new offices were the minister (*rājāmātya*) and the administrative head of the army (*mahāsenāpati*). Another novelty was the changes in land revenue; it was derived from royal allotments on the villages and not from the usual share of agricultural produce of the cultivators.

Gupta institutions are relatively well known from inscriptions. The king made generous use of his sons, brothers, and relatives. The heir-apparent (*yuvarāja*) had his own separate establishment, and sometimes, when the king was old, took upon himself a large share of responsibilities (as did Skandagupta during the last years of Kumāragupta I). The higher officials seem to have been known under the general name of *kumāramātya*. Within their class there was no basic distinction between civil and military officers; we have instances of counsellors (*mantrin*) being promoted to become army commanders (*mahābalādhikṛta*). There was some tendency for high office to become hereditary, but this was by no means the rule. In Vākāṭaka and Pallava administration there was at the capital a sort of central secretariat, whose chief (*sarvādhyakṣa*) was charged with conveying the orders of the government to the provincial authorities. Routine business was transacted by each minister, but important matters were referred to the council, presided over by the king. When away from the capital, the king communicated his orders to the central secretariat through his private secretaries (*rahasiniyukta*). Other important officials, but with only court duties, were the chamberlains (*pratīhāra*).

The army was commanded directly by the king, often assisted by the heir-apparent; but the head of the military administration was the *mahābalādhikṛta*, corresponding to the *mahāsenāpati* of the Sātavāhana administration. The divisions were led, perhaps on a provincial basis, by generals (*mahāsenāpati*). The *mahādaṇḍanāyaka* were their subordinates. Chariotry having disappeared as a fighting army, the army included cavalry, infantry, and elephants. We know the titles of some officers in the cavalry (*mahā*)*aśvapati*, and in the elephant corps (*mahā*)*pīlupati*. There was a separate police establishment (*cāṭa, bhāṭa*).

Revenue was partly in kind and partly in cash, and forests and mines were the property of the state; so were unreclaimed waste lands, but their actual management and disposal were left in charge of the village in whose jurisdiction they were situated. Public morals in the provinces were subjected to the censorship of the *vinayasthitisthāpika*. Learning and cult were supported by grants of villages (*agrahāra*) to learned Brahmans and to Buddhist and Jain monasteries, such villages being placed under the management of *agrahārikas*.

Foreign affairs were entrusted to a Minister of Peace and War (*mahāsāndhivigrahika*), who appears also to have been in charge of relations with the feudatory states. The degree of dependency of the latter varied according to circumstances. Some of them (e.g. Rudradatta, a feudatory of the Gupta king Vainyagupta) enjoyed no financial autonomy, but had to get imperial sanction for their grants. Larger feudatories (e.g. the Parivrājaka Mahārāja) could do so without permission; and some of them had sub-feudatories of their own.

Provincial administration was well organized on a graded scale. The Gupta empire was divided into provinces (probably called *deśa*), under viceroys whose title is not known; they held wide administrative and even military powers. Provinces were divided into counties (*bhukti*), in charge of governors (*uparika*) appointed directly by the emperor. The counties were divided into districts (*viṣaya*), governed by *viṣayapati*, appointed usually by the *uparikas*, but sometimes by the emperor. Several seals of both *bhukti* and *viṣaya* have come down to us. The *viṣaya* headquarters contained as the most important official a keeper of records (*pustapāla*) with a staff of subordinates (*ākṣapaṭalika*) on the local level. There was a fair amount of decentralization, district authorities being consulted before the alienation of waste lands; the actual grants often bear their seals, apparently in token of registration. The *viṣayapati* was advised by a municipal board (*adhiṣṭhānādhikaraṇa*), or a district council (*viṣayādhikaraṇa*). There were also rural boards (*aṣṭakulādhikaraṇa*). They were headed by elders of districts (*viṣayāmahattara*); and their most prominent members (*puroga*) were the chief banker, the chief trader, the chief artisan, and the chief scribe. We do not know whether they were elected or nominated, but they certainly introduced, for the first time in India, an element of popular participation in provincial administration. This element was urban and not rural, and was dominated by business interests.

The basic unit of the state was, as usual, the village. Its headman (*grāmika*) was assisted by elders (*mahattara*). The latter took care of defence, police, works of public utility, and settlement of minor disputes; and it acted as the fiscal agent of the government. The *mahattaras* were probably not elected, but came to be tacitly recognized as such by common consent on the basis of their age, experience, and character.

Towns were governed by officers who had the status of a *kumāramātya*. They were government officials: the self-governing element is far less conspicuous in the town than in the village. Town councils may have existed (at least halls for public meetings were provided for), but we have no actual mention of them on inscriptions.

Taxation was not too heavy. The traditional number of taxes was eighteen, but their complete list is nowhere given. The land tax was, as always, the mainstay of government revenue. It was collected in kind and cash and seems to have consisted of 16–25 per cent of the actual yield, according to the quality of the land. There were also octroi duties, part of which were assigned in lieu of salary to local officials, under the name of *bhogakara*. A sort of excise duty (*bhūta-pratyāya*) on manufactured goods was also levied.

Indian law was based on the *Dharmaśāstras*. Of the post-Maurya texts, the *Yajñavalkya-smṛti* and the *Nārada-smṛti*, and perhaps also the *Bṛhaspati-smṛti*, belonged to this period. The *Yajñavalkya-smṛti* marks a step forward toward a more systematic arrangement of legal materials, and developed settled rules of procedure (*vyavahāra*). Three kinds of proof are admitted: written documents, witnesses, and possession. Ordeal is also admitted, but only when other evidence is lacking. The *Nārada-smṛti* is based on *Manu*, but shows some original features, chiefly that judicial procedure is much more complex than with *Manu* and *Yajñavalkya*: judgement is pronounced by the *sabhyas*, i.e. the assessors of the judge, and the law of inheritance is more precise and detailed.

Indian (or Indianized) society abroad was organized on the same basis as that of the mother country. Merchants, refugees, and missionaries had exerted a deep cultural influence in south-east Asia. They penetrated into native society by slow stages, intermarrying with the local aristocracy. The latter, struck by the cultural superiority of the newcomers, accepted their theory of life, their religion and, up to a certain point, their social structure. Thus Campa in south Vietnam, Fu-nan in Cambodia, and the various states in Java were ruled by royal houses and aristocracies who were partly of Indian and partly of local descent, but in every case had Sanskrit names, worshipped Hindu gods, and broadly followed the precepts of the *Dharmaśāstras*. The social strata under them, however, were less and less touched by Hinduism the farther down one went in the social scale. But very few inscriptions belong to this period; so an account of the Indian society of Greater India really falls outside the limits set to the present volume. We may only note that the Gupta period in northern India corresponded to a definite and marked increase of Indian cultural (but not political) influence in south-eastern Asia.

3. POPULATION CENSUSES IN THE FAR EAST

In India there existed no system approximating to a census. Neither epigraphic nor literary sources give us any idea of the number of the population. Some modern attempts to determine it are based on purely arbitrary calculations and can be regarded as a complete failure.

In China, on the other hand, a census of the population was taken at more or less regular intervals; and we have even an original though fragmentary list of inhabitants from a village in the Tun-huang district on the north-west frontier. The chapters on geography in the dynastic histories and other sources have preserved the results of censuses of the early Chou period, of 684 BC; and of AD 2, 57, 75, 88, 105, 140, 144, 145, 148, 156, 221 (partial), 280, and 464 (partial). In the various figures, whether complete or incomplete, there are very large oscillations between one census and another, due partly to mistakes in calculation, partly to the varying size of the territory under review, but above all to the employment of two different and irreconcilable systems in the taking of a census: sometimes every individual was counted, at other times only those on the lists of tax-payers, the latter method being preferred for simplicity's sake in the periods of adjustment following great rebellions. Consequently comparison is always difficult. It appears, in any case, that only the figures relating to the censuses of AD 2 and 140 are comparable, being based on the same system and on the same area. These figures are as follows.

Date	Families	Persons
AD 2	12,233,062	59,594,978
140	9,698,630	49,150,220

These figures are very low indeed and show a serious decrease in less than a century and a half, due partly to economic decline, but still more to a disastrous flood of the Huang-ho, which caused countless casualties and resulted in the river mouth being diverted a long distance towards the south. From an analysis of the rough figures by districts it seems that the population was in the early times concentrated in the Great Northern Plain, in the valleys of the Wei and the Fen-ho, and in Szechwan. Fukien is made to appear almost deserted, because it was largely inhabited by non-Chinese populations in a state of *de facto* independence. The Han-kou region, which today is very populous, also seems almost empty, and the reason here may be that before the great banking works carried out in the district it consisted of one enormous area of swamps. We can discern certain main currents of migration, from northern China towards the middle valley of the Yangtze-kiang and towards the estuary of the same great river. The population curve, in so far as it can be reconstructed, is remarkably even: after the heavy decrease mentioned above, the population seems to have become stabilized at about fifty millions down to the eighth century AD.

4. THE PERSIAN STATE UNDER THE SASSANIDS

In AD 224 the Sassanid dynasty, after deposing the Arsacids and taking their place, started on a powerful period in the history of their own house and of the

Persian empire. This was characterized by strong nationalistic and centralizing tendencies. The king concentrated in his own person the running of the army, administration, finance, and the direction of foreign policy, the last especially in relation to the great rival empire of Rome.

Down to the reign of Ardashir II (379–383) each king was, in the normal course of events, designated by his predecessor; but from that time on this process was replaced by a system of election from among the members of the royal family, operated by a college including the heads of the priesthood, the armed forces, and the scribes. The more energetic a king was, the greater his success in bringing affairs under a central control at the expense of the forces of feudalism.

To these powerful Sassanid kings was due the rigorous adoption of a modernized Zoroastrianism as a state religion: other religions were regarded as potential elements of separatism and no toleration was shown them. The kings also regarded it as their main mission to restore the empire's prestige and cause its peculiar culture to be respected once more. The state offices were arranged in a hierarchy, beginning with the viceroys, drawn from royal princes and vassal kings: these were followed by other high posts at court, normally filled by members of seven powerful families, the majority of which were descended from the Arsacids. These upper classes derived their reputation from the part they played in war: and they possessed economic power in their own right as a result of large fiefs, on which they imposed taxes in addition to what the territories in question had to pay to the state. To protect themselves from any possible opposition from these magnates, the kings relied also on a number of lesser potentates (*Vazurkan* or 'grandees', and *Āzātān* or 'nobles'): in return he gave them assistance against encroachments by the feudal lords, and entrusted them with official positions in the administration of the army. Moreover by granting an exclusive position to the Zoroastrian religion the king was assured of the loyalty of the priesthood, which also carried out important functions of a social and cultural nature (the so-called 'purifications' are an example). Besides this the priesthood had judicial duties, since the basis of legal tradition derived from the interpretation of the sacred scriptures.[2]

5. ROME

a. Power Structure

The Emperor. Augustus hoped that he had created a durable system of government, but although the imperial idea persisted, its form was continually changing in detail, and its final outcome was certainly not foreseen by its founder. A number of important factors were responsible for these changes of policy. In three-quarters of a century Rome had experienced many different conceptions of personal rule, each one meeting the more obvious needs of the moment, and each having definite support, at least in principle, from past history. On two occasions, under Caesar and Pompey and under Antony and Octavian, there were duumvirates (derived from previous triumvirates) exercising more or less dictatorial power, one in each of the two distinct parts of the Roman world, the Greek half and the Latin half. Then there had been sole rulers of the whole empire: Caesar, dictator for life, and concentrating almost all powers and duties in his own person; and Augustus, the *princeps*, apparently deriving his powers from the senate, though in fact he too was head of the armed forces and assumed increasing independence and initiative in determining all public policy. But in addition, though this time only in the East, there had been Antony in his last years. He was raised to the level of a god and as King of Kings he had been ruler of a feudal empire, parts of which were divided among the members of his new divine family.

Each of the emperors who followed felt the influence of these predecessors. Some selected one of them as a pattern to fit their own tastes and beliefs; others tried to blend them all within a new formula; some again contributed such innovations as they believed were necessary or suitable for resolving the more urgent problems that they had to face. As early, therefore, as the Julio-Claudian régime, which ruled the empire down to 68, we find an alternation of policies, accompanied by continual evolution in the attitude of each individual emperor.

For example, Tiberius at his accession would have preferred a tripartite division of power,[3] but he gave that up in fear of a military crisis, and later put into force the Augustan system, though he made it into a more genuine diarchy between senate and emperor. In the end, however, he came to rely increasingly on the praetorians and less on the senate, drifting into a lonely despotism which alienated him from his subjects.

Caligula, too, who at the outset had agreed that his powers be determined by the senate and had accepted the senate's co-operation, gradually increased his tendency towards godlike absolutism, which he finally pushed to extremes. This happened under pressure from troubles within his family and from conspiracies, and under the realization of the treacherous part played by the senate during the trials of Tiberius' reign.

Claudius, who had researched deeply into the recent constitutional history of Rome, seems to have genuinely desired to return to the conditions of Augustus' later years. But in the end he, too, was driven in the direction of autocracy: he made more use of his own freedmen than he did of senate and knights, and he placed his reliance on the army—on particular on the praetorian cohorts to whom he owed his proclamation.

Finally Nero, though his teacher Seneca had tried to inculcate in him an admiration for Augustus, first found himself under the influence of his mother Agrippina and the financial expert and freedman Pallas, and later, as his personal experience widened, became increasingly attracted by the examples of Antony and Caligula.[4] From the beginning of his reign he depended on the support of the praetorians, but the value of this was lessened by the conflict between their two commanders, Tigellinus and Faenius Rufus.

In 68–69 came the first crisis, brief but almost fatal. Each one of the elements, both civil and military, which mattered in the life of the empire (senate, knights, people, praetorians, frontier armies, Italians, and provincials) tried to find supporters for their rival interests among the various contenders for the empire; and each of these claimants was following ideas of his own and seeking his own advantage.[5] Galba was proclaimed by the armies in Spain, with support from Gaul, and tried to model himself on Augustus, but forfeited the sympathy of the troops in Rome through parsimony and extreme severity. Otho, who modelled himself on Nero, had the support of the praetorians and the people of Rome, but tried to secure the sympathies of the provinces as well. After him came Vitellius, who attempted to give effect to the dominance of the frontier troops from Germany, even to the point of 'Germanizing'[6] the praetorian guard.

With Vespasian, raised to power by the Eastern armies, we reach the foundation of a new dynasty. It lasted less than thirty years, but its policy was no more consistent than that of the earlier dynasties, and in the reigns of each of its three rulers we can distinguish different phases. On Vespasian, while he was still absent from Rome, the senate had imposed a line of conduct of the 'Augustan' type and had codified his rights and duties. Yet when he had made his position secure, he first gradually enlarged the scope of his interference, and then revived in his own person the office of censor, accompanied by a growing centralization of public affairs into his own hands. He made considerable use of knights and freedmen, and altered the composition of the senate to suit his wishes, expelling any members he regarded as hostile to his ideas.[7] Then under Domitian, who was proclaimed by the praetorians, we find a gradual return to the autocratic conceptions of Antony, closely related to the increasingly serious opposition offered by the senatorial class. To meet these he gave greater prominence to the *consilium principis* and to equestrian and freedmen officials, while as the new Antonius[8] he laid claim in his lifetime to divine worship of 'Deus et Dominus'.

The years from the death of Domitian in 96 to that of Marcus Aurelius in 180 are often called the period of the 'Liberal Empire', in the sense illustrated by Tacitus.[9] They represent a reconciliation between the powers of the ruler and the liberties of the subjects, who for Tacitus mean essentially the members of the senatorial class. It is true that these eighty-four years were in general a period of greater tranquillity in the contest between the main elements in the state, and consequently also in that between the rival systems of government for which these elements stood. It was not that one element or system had won a decisive victory over the others but that some fairly stable equilibrium had been reached between the two powers which had been confronting each other for more than a century: the central government with the emperor at its head had been strengthened and at the same time a number of senatorial prerogatives had been recognized. It is true that the senate, as we shall soon see, had practically nothing in common with the senate of the early empire, which had been largely composed of irreconcilable republicans. The main problem in the relations between the emperor and senate now consisted in that of the imperial succession, which the senate claimed should be governed by the principle of the adoption of the 'best man' (the *Optimus*), while the emperor started by favouring a semi-dynastic system, and later declared for a fully hereditary succession, which was realized with Commodus who succeeded his father. But there were many other very serious problems, to which Trajan and Hadrian, both of them provincials,[10] gave more attention than their successors. It was a question of keeping the government's programme in line with the new situation which was developing with growing clarity in the empire. In general one has the impression that after Hadrian's death the central government of the 'Philosopher Emperors' became markedly less ready to cope with the changes which were taking place and with problems which were becoming more manifest every day. In this way the reigns of Antoninus Pius and (still more) Marcus Aurelius concealed beneath the figures of these two philosopher emperors, with all their moral and cultural excellence, a serious decline or even crisis in government which was not confronted in time. The crisis broke out at the moment of least resistance in the reign of Commodus, who came to power too young, without preparation or proper direction; and it was a crisis which was the logical outcome of the errors of previous reigns.

The 'Dominate' and its Relations with the Army. One of the main features of Roman imperial rule was the concentration of power in the hands of an emperor who controlled a standing army. This made permanent and empire-wide a system which had earlier been achieved at intervals and over limited areas by the grant of *imperium proconsulare maius*. But the firm tendency of most emperors from Commodus onward to assume a power which was absolute and autocratic—to pass, that is to say, from the 'Principate' to the 'Dominate'—cannot simply be due to the fact that they regarded themselves as military emperors, created by and dependent upon the army. Other emperors, such as Caligula, Nero, and Domitian, had shown the same tendency much earlier, quite independently of any military origin or support for their power; on the other hand the tendency was not shared by generals who were specifically proclaimed by the army, like Trajan. Moreover, for more than forty years, from Septimius Severus to Severus Alexander, the army's proclamations were not completely free: they were designed to support the regular succession of members of a single dynasty. The real period of chaotic tyranny by the armies started after Severus Alexander's death.

At first then the Dominate came into being by stages separated by intervals. It was modelled on Caesar and Antony, or sometimes expressed the particular views of individual rulers. Later it began to represent a fairly fixed policy, even when the emperor was as unwarlike as Elagabalus, or had not reached an age at which he could command armies, like Severus Alexander in his early years. So in the early period support from the armies was not the sole or even the main cause of the Dominate so much as a concomitant circumstance; and later on the army's attitude may have embarrassed rather than strengthened the régime, since the *dominus* had to face opposition from counter-emperors, who could draw similar support from dissident groups among the forces.

Under the various emperors who succeeded one another the Dominate assumed a number of different forms; indeed some emperors, like Pertinax, or Balbinus and Pupienus, tried to return to the old ways of government. In fact, like all great phenomena in history, the Dominate was the result of a number of causes working together, some intermittently, others continuously. The following deserve special attention:

(1) Autocratic régimes of the past or of the contemporary kingdoms of the East were taken as models; and this influence was combined with the effect of a repetition of dynasties or near-dynasties exercised by persons who came to power more because they were related to earlier *divi* than because any acknowledged merits of their own could mark them out as *optimi*.

(2) There was an increasingly widespread conviction that to safeguard the dominion of Rome as 'mistress of the world', and to confront the problems and overcome the difficulties of the time, it was essential to concentrate all power in the hands of a single man. He must be a 'monarch', crowned with a mystic halo and supported by a rigid and hierarchical system of government. Such a system was regarded as indispensable for every sphere of human life, eventually including religion, where in any case the concept of a single and omnipotent God was continually gaining ground.

(3) Senatorial magistrates, with their republican tradition of equality, were gradually replaced by bureaucrats drawn from other classes of society and kept dependent on the emperor under close control. Meanwhile the composition of the senate itself had been radically altered, and it was now an assembly of courtiers, ready not only to bestow panegyrics on the ruler but to remove any unruly persons among its own members by use of the *Lex Maiestatis*.

(4) The imperial cult, which had centuries of history behind it but was now enhanced by fresh borrowings from the East, had led to the full-scale deification of emperors in their lifetimes. They were still generally *pontifices maximi* in the ancestral religion, and the Severi were also high priests of oriental cults.

(5) More and more power was centralized in the *consilium principis*, which as early as Hadrian's day contained a preponderance of lawyers, and which Severus Alexander converted into a regular body for the formulation of all legislative proposals. At the same time the *princeps*, who was regarded as above the law, became more and more its real source through his *constitutiones* and other kinds of legislative pronouncements.

(6) Imperial power had been attained by an increasing number of men born in those districts where the concept of a God-king, or a king under divine tutelage and the patron of his people, had an age-long history and had taken deep roots.

(7) The emperor, as head of the army and supreme administrator in the state, possessed unchallenged control of the two main forces supporting the empire, soldiers and money. In fact he had his hands on a most formidable proportion of the empire's means of production, which were scattered throughout all the provinces and had come to him through conquest, confiscation, and inheritance.

It is true that even now, though among an increasingly smaller circle, men looked back with longing to the less autocratic period of the Principate, identified with the name of Augustus, and to a system of government based less on force and on the changing dictates of the *domini*.

At a time when the Dominate had not yet completely destroyed all senatorial aspirations for a share in the power, Philostratus in his *Life of Apollonius of Tyana* (a work commissioned by Julia Domna, the widow of Septimius Severus, and completed soon after 217) expressed in memory of the philosopher emperors of the second century the wish that all rulers should be philosophers and should avoid behaving as autocrats. Soon after 229, in a revision of his History, Dio Cassius inserted two speeches which purport to have been delivered before Augustus by Maecenas and Agrippa, but which really reflect Dio's own thought. He wants the emperor to avoid conducting himself like a *Deus* and giving equality of rights and duties to all peoples and districts of the empire: instead the ruler should preserve the ancient forms of the constitution, govern through the senate, put forward laws which the senate has formulated, display moderation and justice, and shun the use of autocracy and force. In these anachronistic discourses Dio gave shape to longings which by his time were wholly out of date, but which as a senator and the son of a senator he had derived from his study of imperial history. It is certainly wrong, in the present author's opinion, to conclude from his work that in his day there was still a powerful current of political opinion which was pro-senatorial and anti-absolutist.

By now we are dealing with isolated manifestations, which had no practical effects and evoked no complications. Again, from the time of the Philips, there is an oration, probably written by Nicagoras, which contrasts the more autocratic emperors of his generation with those who were more liberal. It prays for a government which is not always exercised arbitrarily through the force of the soldiers and commanders under its orders, but is dutiful, just, merciful, moderate, prudent, virtuous, and paternal: a government ready to curb the will of the soldiers, to avoid war by wise diplomacy, and to improve moral behaviour. Yet the orator no longer asks his ruler to collaborate with any other constitutional power. He is writing at a time when the soldiers were plundering the property of city-dwellers and country-folk alike, and of the great owners of estates along with their *coloni*; a time when the military pronunciamentos of the great crisis period in the third century were turning public life into chaos, and when tyrants and wreckers were taking the place of beneficent *domini*.

*The Period c.*250–400. Two dates can be taken as landmarks in the mid-third century: the death of Decius in battle against the Goths in 251, and Valerian's capture by the Parthians as a prisoner of war in 260. By themselves these two events would show the bankruptcy into which the empire had fallen; and it was in this period that it was split into three sections by the establishment of separate empires in Gaul and in Palmyra. The barbarians were pressing simultaneously on several points in the *limes* which were no longer held; and since the emperor could not be everywhere, individual generals made use of their victories and of the regional outlook of their troops to further their own aspirations to the purple. The methods of the armies were often out of date, their numbers were inadequate, and their units were composed and grouped on too much of a regional basis. The agricultural population was oppressed and discontented. The Christians under persecution were tending to shirk their civil and military obligations. Finally the population was declining under the impact of poverty and war—civil as well as foreign—quite apart from the cataclysms which affected particular areas and a number of plagues which were often of long duration and general throughout the empire.[11]

Even when the catastrophe was at its height there were efforts to stem the tide. One example is the policy of Gallienus as soon as he could rescind his father's arrangements after the latter's capture by the Parthians. He carried out a reform of the army which included new developments in the use of cavalry; he made the first attempt to separate military and civil powers, hitherto granted to the same men; and he showed tolerance to the Christians. His work of recovery was continued and intensified by the three great Illyrian emperors who followed him.

One of these three, Aurelian, succeeded in reuniting the three divisions of the empire. He checked barbarian aggression and improved Rome's defences, although he surrendered the now untenable province of Dacia beyond the Danube. He strengthened the imperial power by undisguised assumption of the position of divine *dominus*; and attempted to consolidate internal unity by imposing sun-worship as the supreme religion.

After Aurelian's murder there followed a curious interregnum, during which legions, praetorians, and senate tossed from one to another the honour of nominating the new emperor, who was eventually chosen by the senate in the person of Tacitus. This however by no means represented a decisive senatorial victory in the matter of imperial nominations, since from the moment of the proclamation of Tacitus' successor Probus all intervention by the senate in these proclamations was finally brought to an end. Probus made further advances on the lines indicated by Aurelian.

The task of reconstruction was firmly carried on by the third great Illyrian emperor, Diocletian, whose measures followed logically from what preceded, even though their outcome was often daring rather than profitable. He studied the needs of imperial defence, together with the precedents for a division of command between two emperors in association and for semi-dynasties built on adoption and on a system whereby selected successors were given training before they acceded to power. All this led him to create the so-called 'Tetrarchy'. This was not a system erected at one moment: it came about gradually, or one might almost say empirically. For a time Diocletian reigned alone: then in March 286 he adopted Maximian and nominated him as Caesar to look after the defence of the West; then in November of the same year Maximian was raised to the status of Augustus; and finally in May 293 he adopted Galerius and made him Caesar, causing Maximian in the West to do the same for Constantius. The two Augusti and the two Caesars in association formed a single dynasty of the adoptive type, constructed hierarchically, the duties of leader being secured solely for the 'Augustus senior', who was called Jovius because his position corresponded to that of Juppiter on Olympus. The system was intended to allow the imperial power to be omnipresent, passing regularly from an Augustus to a Caesar once the latter had served his period of training; and it was thought that thereby usurpations could be prevented and that defence could be rendered speedy and effective against foreign and domestic danger alike. Other measures were intended to serve the same purpose, such as the reform and expansion of the army, the way provinces were split up and then regrouped into dioceses, the financial reforms, and the ruthless attempt to root out Christianity. But the experiment was not conclusive or even lasting. In 305 Diocletian ordained the abdication of himself and Maximian, and Galerius and Constantius became Augusti; Galerius who was Augustus Maior (or Jovius) then chose the two new Caesars, Maximinus Daia under himself in the East and Flavius Valerius Severus for Constantius in the West. In the East the new arrangement was uncontested, but in the West both Constantius' son Constantine and Maximian's son Maxentius had been disappointed in their hopes of becoming Caesars. So the West was troubled by discord and dynastic struggles; and these came to a head on the death of Constantius in 306. Valerius Severus became Augustus and Constantine was chosen as his Caesar, but they found themselves confronted by a rival pair, Maximian, who reassumed power as Augustus, and his son Maxentius, whom he associated with himself as Caesar. Complications grew with Severus' death in 307, since there were now four rulers including L. Domitius Alexander who was newly proclaimed in Africa.

In 307–308 Diocletian intervened as arbiter, and decided that in the West the new Augustus Licinianus Licinius, now elected for the first time, should be the sole Augustus, aided by Constantine as Caesar, and that all other competitors should be removed. But this had no practical effect. In 311 the death of Galerius started a series of struggles for power in the East between Licinius and Maximinus, while in the West the contest between Constantine and Maxentius still continued. After the elimination of Maximinus in the East and Maxentius in the West it seemed for a moment that the situation had returned to where it was in Diocletian's early period between 286 and 293, with one Augustus (now Licinius) in the East and another (now Constantine) in the West. In fact, however, a period of collaboration between the two was followed by war, by the defeat of Licinius, and by the establishment of unified power in the hands of Constantine (323–337).

The institution of two Augusti, one senior to the other and each with his respective Caesar, had been given sanctity by Diocletian, who assumed for himself the title Jovius and gave Maximian the title Herculius; the former name evoked the idea of his own descent from the King of the Gods, while his adopted son entered the family of Hercules, the son of Jove and the greatest of the heroes. Constantine, on the other hand, the monarch of mankind, was as it were the reflection on earth of the heavenly King who had given him the victory, and whose religion had been adopted as the religion given preference by the state in order to give unity to Constantine's subjects in the field of morals. It was for this reason that the emperor, who according to Eusebius liked to be called ἐπίσκοπος τῶν ἐκτός (i.e. 'bishop of the Laity' over against the ecclesiastical hierarchy) felt it right to concern himself with conflicts between Christian doctrines in so far as they might cause moral cleavage among his subjects, and with religious organization in so far as it impacted on the unity of the empire's organization. In this way he came to take up a Caesaro-papist[12] position; moreover when the empire once again had more than one emperor, its rulers could uphold different conceptions of Christianity from one another and so come into conflict.

When Constantine divided the power with Licinius in 317, his two sons Crispus and Constantius II were proclaimed Caesars, and also Licinius' son, Licinius Licinianus. After Licinius' surrender and death a number of steps were taken. Constantine's son Constantius II was made Caesar in 323–324, Crispus was removed from the scene in 326, another son, Constans, was made Caesar in 333, and Licinianus was eliminated in 335. So in that year the only Caesars remaining were the three sons: there was a new type of tetrarchy, with only one Augustus and three Caesars. Constantine, therefore, while retaining general direction of the empire, assigned to each of the three the specific control of one portion; but he created two more districts, one for each of two grandsons, Delmatius and Hannibalianus. It is not easy to see what purpose Constantine thought could be served by all these persons and all these divisions when the moment for succession arrived: perhaps they were intended only as a 'trial team' for practice and eventual selection. However that may be, his arrangements did not prevent attempts by usurpers (Magnus Magnentius, for example), and after his death they led to a series of struggles to the death among his heirs who were all too reluctant to introduce further reforms. In 340 we again find two Augusti, Constans in the West and Constantius II in the East; and religious conflicts resulted, since Constantius supported the Arians and was intolerant of paganism. After the death of Constans in 350 Constantius II once more held united power. He, too, chose a Caesar, his nephew Gallus; but the latter was put out of the way by Constantius' brother Julian, who rebelled in 360 and after the emperor's death in 361 united the whole empire under his own control. The brief reign of Julian, of which the main features were highly beneficial and often enduring administrative reforms and his meteoric restoration of paganism, closed the line of the 'second Flavian' dynasty, which had retained power since the time of Constantius I.

After Julian had died without leaving the throne to any member of his family, two emperors, first Jovian and then in 364 Valentinian I, were proclaimed one after the other by the troops. It was the latter who succeeded in founding a new dynasty, of Pannonian origin. He at once chose his brother Valens as full co-regent and as Augustus in the East, and later designated his son Gratian his successor and made him his own colleague in the West. On the death of Valentinian I in 375 there was a threefold division of power. Valens was still ruler of the East, and in the West the army associated with Gratian his four-year-old son Valentinian II.

On the death of Valens in 378 Gratian replaced him as Augustus in the East by the Spanish general Theodosius I, and on Gratian's death this emperor made himself the protector of the young Augustus of the West, Valentinian II. He rid Valentinian of the usurper Magnus Maximus, who had earlier been recognized as ruler of the provinces of the extreme West. Then, however, Valentinian was murdered; and after the elimination of another usurper, Eugenius, who made a last short-lived attempt to restore paganism, Theodosius became master of the whole empire during the last months of his life. But fate willed that this last sole ruler should be the involuntary author of the empire's final division into two. On his death in 395 he left the East to his son Arcadius, aged seventeen, under the guidance of the praetorian prefect Rufinus, and the West to his ten-year-old second son Honorius, supported by the general Stilicho. An attempt by Stilicho to preserve a unified policy in the two sections was a failure, and from that time on the division was beyond repair. Yet although the Eastern half still possessed enough vitality to survive for many centuries, the decay of the Western half could no longer be arrested. Its provinces were now at the mercy of barbarian inroads and devastations. In 395 the Goths under Alaric invaded Moesia and Thrace, pushed on into Macedonia and Greece in 397, and appeared in Italy in 402, with a further invasion under Radagaisus in the years beginning in 405. Finally in 410 they took and sacked Rome itself. In 406 the Vandals, Alans, Suevi, and Quadi penetrated into Gaul and Spain; and meanwhile the Huns were settling in Pannonia, and the Picts, Scots, and Saxons were taking possession of the Roman portions of Britain.

Roman Jurisprudence. [Our knowledge of Roman Law before the XII Tables is restricted to more or less informed conjecture. The XII Tables themselves, of which the traditional date is 451–450 BC, are founded on custom and did not set out to innovate. Perhaps even more than the substance the precision and terseness of the language show the high degree of skill and the experience of the draughtsmen and testify to a considerable preceding period of development. The Tables are a code but like other early codes they do not set out to give the law in full. To some extent the provisions concentrate on the less usual case and leave out some of the most obvious legal situations.[13] This must cast doubt on the traditional view that under the early system of procedure, the *legis actiones*, the plaintiff had to sue precisely in the words of the statute. The provisions, though often harsh, show the remarkable early development of Roman Law. There is, for instance, already a distinction between deliberate and accidental killing; and a form of contract, *stipulatio*, is well established. Apart from the XII Tables, legislation played a minor role in the development of Roman private law; and the *lex Aquilia*, a plebiscite of 287 BC which regulated damage to property, is probably the only Republican statute of real importance. Development was mainly due to the edicts of the magistrates and the interpretation of the jurists. The main edicts were those of the urban and peregrine praetor though that of the aediles which was concerned with control of the streets and market place was important for the development of sale. No date can be assigned to the introduction of the praetors' edicts though that of the peregrine praetor cannot be earlier than about 242 BC since it was probably only in that year that the office was created. Nor does it seem possible to disentangle the jurisdictions of the two edicts. Thus, the edict on robbery with violence which Cicero tells us was issued as a result of troubles in Italy was issued by the peregrine praetor in 76 BC; and the edict on fraud which so far as we know always included citizens was issued by the holder of that office in 66 BC. Strictly, the praetor could not legislate but could only declare that in certain circumstances he would give or refuse an action. This, of course, did not stop him from making drastic changes in practice in the law, as for instance in succession, but it did mean that in theory the old law continued to exist and to be mentioned by the jurists. Thus we have at times the curious spectacle of the same legal situation having in theory widely differing remedies, as for instance in the case of injuries to the personality; or slightly differing facts being required for a civil or praetorian action which covered in general the same ground, as for example in the case of the actions for cutting down another's trees. Each praetor held office only for one year and each praetor issued his own edict. Naturally, it became usual to re-enact each year the main body of the preceding edict and this permanent part came to be known as the *edictum tralaticium*. Under the empire the edict became of less importance as a source of new law and eventually was revised and stabilized in its final form by the jurist Julian in the reign of Hadrian. The praetors were able to enforce their edicts because they were in charge of legal procedure. Again it is not possible to distinguish the limits of jurisdiction of the *praetor urbanus* and the *praetor peregrinus* though the common opinion is that the former dealt with cases in which all the parties were Romans while the latter was responsible for those in which at least one of the parties was not a Roman citizen. Owing to the praetors the old formal system of procedure, the *legis actiones*, gave way to the flexible *formulae*. The credit for this is given to the peregrine praetor partly on the ground that it was in cases involving peregrines that a flexible system was most needed and it is often said that *formulae* were not available in cases between Roman citizens until the passing of the *lex Aebutia* of about 140 BC. Accordingly, some of the most characteristic and important actions such as those which depend upon good faith—and this includes the important consensual contracts of sale, hire, partnership and mandate—are usually regarded as the creation of the magistrate. But, in fact, it has been shown[14] that *formulae* were available in cases between Roman citizens long before the passing of the *lex Aebutia*. And there is no direct evidence that the peregrine praetor introduced the formulary system or was, indeed, mainly responsible for the important developments arising from that introduction. The praetors also developed the law very considerably by giving *ad hoc* actions (and in time in many situations these came to be taken for granted) where no remedy existed at civil law or under the edict. The evidence suggests that this practice which flourished in the empire was only in its infancy during the last years of the republic.

The jurists were the other main source of law. The first jurists were the pontiffs who among their other functions gave *responsa* (replies to practical problems submitted to them) and this function passed virtually unchanged to the individual private jurist. The pontiff's monopoly of jurisprudence was broken first by the XII Tables, then by the publication of the traditional formulary[15] and the opening of the College of Pontiffs to plebeians by the *lex Ogulnia* of 300 BC. The main importance of the jurists for the development was their interpretation of the XII Tables and other legislation and the edicts. It is often said that originally interpretation was very narrow but came to be relaxed in the course of time. There is, however, no real indication for this and rather, if anything, interpretation tended to become stricter. Thus, for instance, no legislation, so far as we can tell, before the *lex Aquilia* bothered to mention both male and female—the former was automatically taken to include the latter. It is only in this way that we can understand the XII Tables sufficing as a code. Indeed, there are early examples of deliberate misinterpretation in order to widen or change completely the scope of a provision's application.[16] Even in the last century of the republic there is evidence of greater flexibility of interpretation than later became the rule. No doubt there is some connection between the growing disinclination of the jurists to interpret provisions widely and the growth of praetorian *ad hoc* remedies—the jurists would no longer feel that they had to strain the

meaning of a provision so as to enable justice to be done. The republican
jurist in addition to giving his opinion on particular cases and writing
treatises had to advise how a will or contract should be framed in order to
produce the desired effect. Draughtsmanship of this kind would indirectly
be of importance in the development of the law since books were published
in which the form of many of the problems discussed clearly derives from this
cautelary jurisprudence.[17] On the whole, the jurists of note of even the late
republic were men of rank and to a great extent their decisions were followed
because of their personal authority and not because of the reasons, if any,
which they adduced. Augustus increased the authority of selected jurists
by giving them the *ius respondendi*, that is, the right to give opinions publicly
on the authority of the emperor. It is not clear what the precise legal effect
of this was, though it would probably mean that Augustus would gain greater
control over the law. Hadrian in some particular which is also uncertain
altered the *ius respondendi* and there is no later trace of its existence.[18] The
time from about the beginning of the empire until just after the end of the
second century is usually known as the classical period since it was the age
in which Roman law reached maturity. The jurists now were not so much
concerned with new concepts as with refining existing ones and fortunately
they were very prolific in their writings. Their books fall into a number of
classes. First of all, there were treatises on civil law which were usually
named commentaries on Sabinus who was the first to write a systematic work
on the civil law. The most important works in this group are Pomponius',
Paul's and Ulpian's *Commentarii ad Sabinum*. Secondly, there were the
commentaries on the edict—Gaius *ad edictum provinciale* was the earliest
and the most famous were Paul and Ulpian *ad edictum*. Probably Julian's
Digesta should be included in this group. Thirdly, there were books of
discussion of practical or academic problems. The most noted of these were
Papinian's *Quaestiones* and *Responsa*. And fourthly, there were elementary
books intended for teaching of which the famous *Institutes* of Gaius (active
during the reign of Hadrian) was probably the earliest. The teaching of law
itself during the early empire seems to have been carried out in schools of
which we know of two, the Sabinian and the Proculian. The former was
probably founded by the jurist Cassius[19] who was consul in AD 30, the latter
by Proculus[20] who was his contemporary. There was a great deal of rivalry
between the schools and although differences in approach may be discerned
one cannot trace any fundamental cleavage in their opinions.[21] These schools
seem to have died out after Hadrian. From the second century the great
jurists such as Julian, Ulpian, and Papinian were increasingly occupied in
official business.

New sources of law developed in the empire. In the later Principate
Senatusconsulta for the first time had legislative force. More important,
however, were the law-making powers of the emperor. Augustus himself did
not assume legislative powers, but from the first the influence of the emperor

on legal development was very great and by the time of the jurist Gaius at the very latest it was recognized that he could make law. The means at his disposal were numerous. First, like other magistrates, he could issue edicts and since his sphere covered all the business of the state these might be on any subject. Secondly, there were the *decreta*, the sentences which he gave as judge either on appeal or as judge of first instance. As judge he could show considerable freedom of interpretation and could introduce new principles. Thirdly, there were the *epistulae* and *subscriptiones*, replies by the emperor to questions of law raised by officials or public bodies or by private individuals. These could cover all sorts of matters and though perhaps the majority had little influence, many did. In these the emperor could also introduce new law. Fourthly, *mandata*, which were instructions issued to officials and especially to provincial governors. A number of important principles, of which the most famous is the rule allowing soldiers to make wills without the formalities required of civilians, was introduced in this way. The great bureaucratic jurists, of course, would be for the most part the persons really responsible for development by these methods, just as in the republic it was primarily the jurists who were responsible for the edict.

The later third and fourth centuries are generally regarded as a period of decline. The line of great jurists died out with Ulpian who was murdered in 228. In AD 428 was enacted the 'Law of Citations' of Theodosius II under which legal disputes had to be settled by counting the heads of the five great jurists—Papinian, Paul, Ulpian, Modestinus, and Gaius—who were ranged on either side. If, of these jurists, the majority who had considered a particular point of law came to one decision, that view was to prevail. If they were equally divided in numbers between views, the view which had Papinian's support was to prevail. If they were equally divided and Papinian had expressed no opinion, the decision was left to the judge's discretion. This is a recognition of the lack of original jurists and it is often said that it marks the lowest point of Roman law. It should not, however, be regarded as pure innovation. There is very considerable evidence that it is simply imperial recognition of a practice which began shortly after the death of Ulpian. But Diocletian's reign saw the publication of two unofficial collections of imperial constitutions, the *Codex Gregorianus* and *Codex Hermogenianus*. These in turn were to be influential for the publication of an official collection, the *Codex Theodosianus*, in AD 429. And this was to inspire the first *Codex Iustinianus* which itself probably suggested the feasibility of a complete codification of law and resulted in the *Corpus Iuris Civilis*.

Thus developed what is probably the greatest legal system ever known or, if that is too great a claim, at least a system of private law so refined, complex, and flexible that without too much difficulty it could be used as a basis for the law of mediaeval, Renaissance, and modern Europe. Roman criminal law, on the other hand, which tended to be ignored by the jurists until they had become imperial officials, remained rather primitive and has been far less influential.]*

The Emperor in Relation to the Legislative and the Judiciary. For a time Augustus, making use of his tribunician power, put plebiscites before the *comitia*, over which he exercised a confident control. Later he preferred to promote *senatus consulta* through the consuls, or to put out his own *edicta*, *mandata*, *rescripta*, and *decreta*. In the *Lex de Imperio* concerning Vespasian it is stated that Augustus, 'legibus solutus', had the right to take decisions on matters divine and human, public and private, in accordance with what the 'majesty' of the state required. The jurist Gaius[22] asserts that beyond doubt the will of the *princeps* has the force of law; and in the Digest we find that an imperial *constitutio* 'has the power of law' and 'is law'. What is certain is that even the earliest emperors were regarded as having complete freedom to legislate, either by laws which received acclamation by the senate ('oratio principis in senatu habita'), or by *edicta* and *mandata* laying down new rules, or by *edicta* and *decreta* bringing about some modification in the traditional law.

In the period of the Dominate the situation is clear, but we also find this state of affairs being recognized as normal by the jurists of the second century. They keep on saying that 'the *princeps* is freed from the compulsion of the laws' and that 'his will has the force of law'. By Hadrian's time at latest the term 'constitutio principis' had come into general use to describe any type of imperial ordinance, the general binding force of which was therefore recognized. It was also in the time of Hadrian, under whom it became the custom to introduce the most famous legal writers into the *consilium principis*, that increasing use was made of *rescripta*, *decreta*, and *orationes principis in senatu*. At the same time the Praetor's law became a definite institution; and regulations were made about the *ius publice respondendi* which had been introduced under Augustus and named under Tiberius, and about the value attaching to the views of *iuris periti* and the *responsa prudentium*.

In lawsuits the normal procedure in the form of an arbitration, with its two stages *in iure* and *apud iudicem*, was fairly often supplemented as early as Augustus' day by the *cognitio extra ordinem*. In this the *princeps*, and later on his behalf the praetorian prefect, the *iuridici*, or in the provinces the governors, combined the functions of *iudex* and magistrate; in this way they gave judgement on their own after examining the circumstances of the case, without having to draw up a *formula* or nominate a *iudex*. At the same time appeal lay to the emperor or praetorian prefect against the judgement given by any *iudex* outside. Under Diocletian all justice was exercised in the emperor's name and administered by his officials—in the provinces by the *praesides* and in the capital cities by the *praefectus urbi*—though appeal still lay to the imperial *consistorium*, with the praetorian prefect and his deputies acting *vice sacra* in less important cases. Meanwhile the jurisdiction of

* By Alan Watson.

praetors had long since disappeared; and to Constantius II and Constans was due a prohibition on the use of 'formulary' procedure.

Under Constantine criminal law, laid down by imperial edicts to be followed to the letter under pain of grave sanctions, became exceptionally severe. One field in which the government was least inclined to overlook transgression was that of religion, where laws were passed (for example by Gratian, Valentinian II, and Theodosius), against various Christian sects which had been declared heretical, against apostates, and against the Manichaeans (who were regarded as dangerous *magi*).

The Decline of the Senate's Power. Between Augustus' day and the middle of the third century the senate gradually lost not only the greater part of its political importance but also the will to recover it. During the imperial period this importance was at its height in the early years of Tiberius' Principate, when the senate inherited the electoral as well as legislative functions of the *comitia*. Yet already during Tiberius' later years and in the reign of his successor Caligula the process of reducing the senate's power and autonomy had set in, a process which was carried forward at an uneven pace but was never actually reversed. Various methods were employed. Hostile elements were removed from the body by 'purges' or judicial proceedings, being replaced by men from a different social class or new region, who had fewer ties with the traditional aristocracy and with the interests of the capital. Some of the senate's functions were transferred to other assemblies such as the *consilium principis*; and the body's prestige and importance were lowered by a reduction in the number of posts which senators could fill.[23] In the sphere of legislation *senatus consulta*, when use was still made of them, became essentially a means of putting imperial projects into effect. In the choice and proclamation of emperors the senate was often anticipated by the legions or praetorians; and it was unable to establish the principle of choosing the 'best man' among its own members, because the succession was kept within a dynasty or secured in advance by adoptions. An attempt to upset the imperial form of government was no longer practicable, and consequently no such attempt was made at the most favourable moment, namely after the death of Domitian in 96. This despite the fact that as early as the first century there were several autocratic emperors, like Caligula, Nero, Otho, and Domitian, who were markedly anti-senatorial; in the second century Commodus began an almost unbroken series of such rulers; and in addition there were many emperors who, though less autocratic, still displayed an increasing tendency to take a generally harsher line with the senate.

Nevertheless throughout the first century attacks made by emperors on the senate still encountered firm and open senatorial resistance, both because every emperor had his critics and enemies and also because the old aristocratic element in the senate was still significant. Newly admitted members easily allowed their own attitude to be dictated by tradition, by the desire for power, and by the interests of the old families, with whom they established ties of marriage. It was, of course, the literary and philosophical senators who were most given to living in a rhetorical version of the past and to praising its virtues; but this group grew gradually smaller, and many of its members began to find greater satisfaction in praising the present. The gradual extinction of these embers of republicanism was due also to the clever policy of the emperors from Trajan to Marcus Aurelius. By the time of Septimius Severus opponents of the emperor are no longer theorists attacking the imperial idea: they are supporters of alternative claimants to the empire. One might get the impression from histories based on the pro-senatorial and republican tradition, down to the time of the *Scriptores Historiae Augustae*, that the senate of the second and third centuries presented an effective counterweight to the imperial power. This, however, would be a complete illusion.

Of the years 193–217, for which our documentation is fullest, the following picture emerges.[24] The senate contained few *nobiles* from the 'eight families' which had survived from republican days. There were many patricians, belonging to the aristocracy of plebeian origin which had been gradually created in the first and second centuries and which tended to intermarry with the *nobiles*. Finally there was a not unduly large group of *novi homines*, wealthy men but risen from the ranks of the knights or of lower classes in society, who held posts in the provinces, the army, and elsewhere.

This situation explains how the senatorial tradition continued to exist without involving a general decline in senatorial standards of service. It also explains the counterpart of this phenomenon, namely the way in which the general run of senators adapted themselves to circumstances and showed increasing conformity to the imperial régime and its changes. It is an exaggerated view either to regard the senate of the second and third centuries as a body which was still potent and for the most part anti-imperial, or on the other hand to treat it as having by now degenerated into a collection of weak-kneed courtiers.

It is equally sweeping to suppose that the increase in the number of provincial senators was creating a body of barbarians. Once again we can take as a basis the best-known period, that at the end of the second century and the beginning of the third. Of recorded senators about 43 per cent appear to be Italians, 32 per cent Easterners, 15 per cent Africans, and 8 per cent Westerners—mainly Spaniards, with very few men from the Gauls, Britain, Illyricum, or the Danube lands in general. So the great majority of senators still came from Italy or from the provinces of most advanced culture; and most of the provincials were undoubtedly descendants of Italians who had settled abroad. So the average rate of 'barbarization' of the senate cannot have been higher than that to be found in the most civilized classes and districts of the empire.

Under the Illyrian emperors, and to speak more precisely from Probus onwards, the senate lost its last political function, by now almost a dead letter, that of ratifying the proclamation of new emperors. Although in later times it continued to recruit its members from the class of officials, it was practically superseded by the *consistorium sacrum*, and a parallel senate came into being at Constantinople. The senate therefore had now only a symbolic function, recalling its ancient duties of receiving and registering the legal enactments of the emperor; meanwhile the title of senator was still a coveted dignity conferred by the ruler on trusted persons. In the main they were ex-officials who had accumulated wealth and consequently had social and economic importance. Often they were owners of vast estates, living in their fortified villas defended by retainers, slaves and *coloni*, and lording it like feudal chiefs over the people in surrounding territory. Their position set them against the great masses of poor people, whom emperors like Valentinian I defended against their encroachments by creating *defensores plebis* in every city.

The Equites and Lower Classes. The equestrian class was gradually transformed and expanded as a number of Italians, who were Roman citizens, settled for business reasons in provincial towns and became part of the upper bourgeois class, filling magistracies and priesthoods in their cities, and providing a picked section of the army. It became the custom, too, to grant Roman citizenship and equestrian status to men who had done useful work in adminstration or on military service. So in the early days it was a question mainly of Italians who had settled in the provinces, had acquired the necessary wealth to attain the equestrian census, and had sometimes become the owners of substantial landed estates. But in later times the extension of the class came mainly from provincials who had been given citizenship and had then become knights in virtue of their census qualifications.

This was an open class, which was continually growing as the Roman citizenship, a necessary qualification for membership, was extended. It consisted of hard-working men, once members of the common people, who had earned credit in the public service, military or civilian. They were men of action, mainstays of Romanization, who constituted a picked class among the 'citizens' scattered over the Roman world. From Augustus' day onward they were faithful adherents of the emperors: they could use them as devoted officials in posts which were gradually taken away from the senatorial aristocracy or which were answering new needs. These equestrian officials dependent on the emperor or operating under his control became so numerous and performed so many duties that very soon a special equestrian *cursus honorum* was created alongside the senatorial *cursus*. Moreover emperors could introduce favoured members of the equestrian order into the senate and so gradually modify its composition. It is true that there were emperors who preferred to strengthen the senate's power and reduce that of the *equites*, and others who liked to work through freedmen and slaves—some of whom were given equestrian status. But the *equites* constituted one of the most significant props to the imperial power; and their value was appreciated not only by autocratically minded rulers, but also by Claudius, Vespasian, Hadrian, and Marcus Aurelius.

Once it had become a regular custom to introduce knights into the senate, the policy of blending the two orders and obliterating the distinction between them was already there. But under Caracalla and Severus Alexander it was advanced further as the natural result of the general grant of citizenship, combined with a transformation in the senatorial class and frequent transfers, of a voluntary nature, from senatorial to equestrian rank. At the same time we find attempts by wealthy plebeians and freedmen to attain equestrian status, or at any rate to usurp or otherwise acquire the right to display the outward signs of equestrian rank, such as the use of the 'gold ring'.

Naturally, however, the vast majority of the population in all parts of the empire was outside these two orders. The classes into which it was divided are often hard to distinguish, but in modern terminology we can speak of bourgeois (living in the country as well as the city), workers (both artisans and farm labourers), and proletarians or men without property (again both in the cities and in the countryside).

The bourgeoisie was composed of such higher groups among the free population as had not attained to membership of the two top orders. They were owners of lands or other real estate, members of all types of profession, shopkeepers, entrepreneurs, business managers, or high-grade employees— men whose economic and social positions permitted infinite gradations. Except for the owners of medium-sized farms, who lived on their estates, this class lived in Rome or in Italian or provincial towns. They were proud of their superior culture; and they had an affection for their own cities, showing ambition to enter office there and a willingness to bestow public largesse. It was largely to their zeal that these towns owed not only their prosperity and dignified appearance, but their high levels of culture and Romanization.

Free workmen included artisans operating on their own, and also wage-earners employed by city firms, by owners of large estates, and by mining undertakings. In the early centuries this class, though regarded as inferior to those so far mentioned, was able to fend for itself. Artisans were normally associated in *collegia*, which the state would recognize when it considered that a proper case for their existence had been made out, and to some of which it even showed favour, for example when they could assist in maintaining the corn supply. *Coloni* and miners too were mostly formed into groups under the direction of a manager or contractor (*conductor*) or bailiff (*vilicus*).

But the living standards of all this class were entirely altered when the economic position of the empire worsened and the governmental system became more autocratic. Hereditary castes were now introduced, and affected the lives of large sections even of the upper classes. Probably the earliest example of such a caste was that of the municipal *decuriones* who were trying to evade the financial burdens imposed on them as the persons responsible for making advance payments for the *fiscus* on behalf of their fellow-citizens and tax-payers. To prevent these evasions and also secure that *decuriones* should be recruited, the office was made compulsory and hereditary, the sons of *decuriones* being obliged to take on office and its burdens after the deaths of their fathers. The compulsory nature of these obligations was expressed in the description of *decuriones* as *curiae subiecti* or *subnixi*. But later, from Diocletian's time, this system became a general feature of the ordering of society. To keep the various professions going they were gradually transformed into castes, membership of which passed compulsorily from father to son. This applied to state officials, army officers, and members of the colleges which were most essential to the maintenance of the civil and military *annona*, such as the *navicularii* and bakers (*coloni* will be discussed a little later).

Already in the republican period, not only Rome but other cities and smaller country centres had contained fairly large groups of persons without employment or means, and of men unfit for regular work. These men lived partly on casual employment, but mainly from bounty and assistance given them by the government (in later times by the emperors at Rome), and by the bourgeoisie and members of the upper classes at other times. At Rome this mass of 'proletarii' in need of assistance was reduced to between 200,000 and 250,000 in the time of Augustus. It was the portion of the *populus* which caused the government most concern; and at some moments its attitude might be critical, since its members were induced by their poverty to foment riots in the attempt to profit from their outcome. Sometimes the praetorian guard and the police of the city prefect and the *praefectus vigilum* had to be employed against them, but for the most part the government tried to anticipate and relieve their needs by money donations, distributions of food either free or at cut prices, and other forms of bounty. At the same time they sought to distract them with festivals, games, theatrical performances and pantomimes, races, gladiatorial tests, and representations of hunts and sea battles. In this way they instituted the *panem et circenses*, of which Juvenal speaks so much.

Meanwhile, however, the people's political power, which had been significant in the republican period, was gradually removed altogether. Augustus led the way, and handed on the same policy to Tiberius, while at the same time the practice of legislating by plebiscite was being reduced almost to vanishing point. In the outcome, the popular assemblies, though they were not entirely abolished, were reserved for exceptional occasions and lost any real importance. The sporadic interventions by the people in politics were confined to the acclamation of emperors (who had normally been previously proclaimed by the senate or the army), or to riots, which were fairly easily suppressed by the praetorians.

We may add that as early as Augustus' time *libertini*, or liberated slaves (called *liberti* in relation to their patrons) began to acquire increasing right to take part in public life in the municipalities and in Rome itself. From the time of Claudius onwards we find imperial freedmen as powerful members of the secretariat of the *Princeps* or employed in such procuratorships as were not reserved for knights. In late republican times the sons of freedmen and even freedmen themselves had been unable to acquire the rights of free-born citizens (*ingenui*) by means of the 'ius aureorum anulorum'; and during the empire there was added the possibility of *restitutio natalium*, which obliterated the original period of slavery and removed the man's bond to his patron.

[Although their influence was sometimes resented, freedmen played a vigorous role in the municipal society of Italy and the Western provinces. In establishing the imperial cult, Augustus created the annual boards of Augustales, a priesthood which was normally drawn from the important freedmen of a town; this was ostensibly to administer the cult of the emperor, but it was also a means of ensuring the loyalty of these men to the régime. They could not hold civic offices, but the religious duties gave them a comparable social prestige. The priesthoods thus became coveted prizes for a wealthy freedman; and when the cost of providing games, spectacles, or even buildings became too large, his patron might help to defray the expenses. The freedman class thus was given a garb of respectability, but the part they played was an essential one in other ways and especially in economic affairs. While freeborn citizens preferred to own land and compete for public offices, freedmen were overwhelmingly numerous in banking, retail trades, specialized professions and the smaller crafts and industries. In Pompeii the main banker and public auctioneer was a freedman richer than many municipal magistrates. In a commercial town like Ostia, their power was still greater; here the Augustales formed a sort of aristocracy within the freedman class, and were organized into a wealthy corporation whose activities rivalled those of the city magistrates themselves. So long as manumission remained frequent, the cities of the empire were thus supplied with many talented men; even their foreign origins tended to be forgotten, and their sons, who were full citizens, would often desert business to become landowners and prominent members of the local bourgeoisie.]*

Slavery and the Colonate. Slavery under the empire, as in certain parts of the period beginning about 150 BC, undoubtedly reached substantial proportions in certain areas, though the figures must not be exaggerated. The phenomenon was not uniform in every area, but was particularly marked in the city of Rome. One reason lay in great wars of conquest, which provided enormous quantities of prisoners; and the decline which set in by gradual stages in the imperial period is clearly to be related primarily to the reduced number of regular wars of this kind, which were all too often replaced by defensive wars where it was not uncommon to find more Romans than their enemies being taken prisoner. The number of potential slaves, therefore,

* By M. W. Frederiksen.

went down, and eventually we find slaves being commonly replaced by free wage-earners on the imperial estates. But other factors, all of them connected with the growing frequency of manumission, were also contributing to reduce the slave population. Sometimes manumission was to the advantage of a patron, since he preferred to take his share in the profits a manumitted slave could earn. But the chief factor here was a higher conception of ethical and legal standards, allied with Stoic thinking, according to which all men are equal and slavery is contrary to natural rights. Christian ideas tended in the same direction. The Christians did not firmly oppose the use of slaves, but they obliterated any moral difference between slave and free, since for them all men were brothers and 'fellow servants' of God; and of this the main consequence was that slaves were treated more as part of the family.[25,26]

Yet while this process was going on, the hierarchic distinction between rich and poor (*honestiores* and *humiliores*)[27] was becoming increasingly harsh and anti-social under the later empire, and at the same time the caste system was being applied ruthlessly to the rural class of *coloni* or *adscripticii*. In the republican period, as we know for example from Cicero's description of Sicily, farmers were already being driven to abandon their fields by the unhappy treatment they were receiving from society.

Successive governments tried to check the process on account of its adverse effects on output and revenue. Most of our information comes from Egypt, but much the same situation must have obtained elsewhere. Not only did the state make it a punishable offence for farmers to abandon lands they had rented; it also introduced the system known as 'capitatio fugitivorum', under which local communities were obliged to cultivate abandoned property and take over any charges it bore. We now enter on the process which led to serfdom. *Capitatio* was imposed on *dediticii* once the *Constitutio Antoniniana* had made a sharp distinction between this category and the section of the population to which citizenship was granted. Then from Valerian's time well-to-do families, to whom the state granted estates, were obliged to assume responsibility for rendering *capitatio*, in money or kind, in respect of any of their *coloni* who were unable to pay. Finally Diocletian's reforms imposed taxes on *capita* and *iugum*[28] and were a strong incentive to the creation of hereditary castes. All this caused large landowners, with the agreement of the state, to protect themselves against the flight of their tenants by binding them to the soil, and making their occupation hereditary from father to son. So serfdom became an institution with state support, and Constantine among others laid heavy penalties on anyone who had harboured fugitive *coloni*.

b. *Public Administration*

The Central Administration. In the first centuries of the empire the central administration in Rome still comprised all the mechanism needed to look after the life of the capital and the centralized management of other regions. The imperial secretariat, staffed originally by imperial slaves, but from Claudius' time by freedmen and from Hadrian's day by salaried knights as well, was continually made larger and more highly specialized in the regular and permanent services it provided. The assistants of the *princeps* for the discharge of all kinds of administrative tasks (including the management of imperial property) were called 'procuratores' or 'praefecti', the latter being the more important officials with command of troops. The *praefectus urbi* was a senator of consular rank with three 'urban' cohorts under his control, appointed originally to maintain order in the absence of the *princeps* but becoming a permanent official from the last years of Tiberius; his power was extended until he became a judge of first instance, and also of appeal in criminal and civil cases in a radius of a hundred miles from Rome. Also usually of senatorial rank were the presidents of the colleges (*curatores*) for the upkeep of temples and public buildings, of aqueducts, and of the Tiber banks and the drains.

The other *praefecturae* were held by men of equestrian rank. The *praefectus classis* was in command of the imperial fleet; the *praefectus vigilum* with seven cohorts looked after police work at night and the fire services; and the *praefectus annonae* had an organization in Italy and the provinces to supervise the corn supply. But the highest equestrian prefectures were those of the praetorian guard and of Egypt. The latter was the emperor's most important property, and its prefect saw to its administration, presided over criminal and civil jurisdiction, and controlled its defence.

The *praefectura praetorio*, sometimes exercised by a single prefect and sometimes by two, had 9,000 praetorian soldiers at its disposal, regiments of whom, under one of the prefects, would accompany the emperor as a bodyguard on campaigns. In both war and peace the prefect of the guard formed part of the *consilium principis*, and in time he took over criminal jurisdiction in Rome and adjacent areas.

Republican commanders and magistrates had chosen their own counsellors, and Augustus made use of this custom to create the 'consilium principis', later called the 'consistorium'. In early days this consisted of about twenty of his own relatives and other illustrious personages, called together whenever the *princeps* saw fit. Tiberius held more frequent meetings, and included men of equestrian rank and jurists: members of this type increased under Hadrian, when the presence of the *praefectus praetorio* became usual. The importance of the *consilium* was further enhanced under Septimius Severus, Caracalla, and Severus Alexander.

The old republican magistracies, when their duties were not, like those of the censorship, absorbed by the emperors, gradually became honorific posts, involving their holders in great expense. Election to them depended in the main on the emperor, who either designated directly or made a 'recommendation'. As early as Claudius' time the minor offices often remained unfilled. The consulate lost its main functions, those in the military and judicial spheres, and retained only prerogatives of little political significance, with impressive outward trappings and costly burdens. The eponymous consuls, those who gave their names to the year, were those who entered office on 1st January—members of the imperial house and of other illustrious families—but they would remain in office for a short spell and give place to 'suffecti'; and these in their turn would be replaced by a number of later pairs of consuls, who provided the emperor with *consulares* to employ as legates or in all kinds of *curae* and similar tasks.

In the later empire the military career became quite distinct from the civil. The latter was built up around a pyramidal hierarchy of bureaucrats, all dependent on the 'dominus', and among them it was not a man's origin which would determine the job he was assigned; his past would confer on him a certain style and dignity from whatever point he started. So the ruler became head of the *officia* as well as of the *consistorium*. The *officia* were most in evidence in the imperial chancery, with a *magister officiorum* at their head and other persons whom we would call 'ministers' by his side. These were assisted by central bureaux (*memoriae epistularum, libellorum, dispositionum,* etc.), accompanied by a secret service of spies (*agentes in rebus*), who took, under Constantine, the place of similar organizations active in earlier periods, like the *frumentarii* suppressed by Diocletian.

The *consistorium*, corresponding to the earlier *consilium principis*, derived its name from the fact that its members had to remain standing in the presence of their sovereign. It included the *quaestor sacri Palatii*, who presided in the absence of the *dominus*, and the *magister officiorum*, who was also in command of the imperial guards. When the *comitatus* was revived as an institution, various *comites* also formed part of the consistorium, some of them being regular ministers, like the *comes sacrarum largitionum* in charge of finance and the *comes rerum privatarum* who administered imperial property since the time of Septimius Severus.

Many modifications in the administrative machine naturally followed on the partition of the empire into two and on the divisions due to the 'tetrarchic' régime and its attendant circumstances, all of them leading to a multiplication of officials. The creation of a second capital at Constantinople (in addition to cities of imperial residence scattered through the empire) caused two senates to come into being, and a double set of certain older posts, such as the prefecture of the city and the presidency of the senate. Each metropolis had to have its police, corn supply, and judicial system; and each had its praetors and quaestors, the former now confined to preparing programmes for the games. The consulate, on the other hand, being by now entirely an honorific office of imaginary importance, remained a single institution for the whole empire: either the two emperors agreed on nominations or (from 396 onwards) nominations would be made in turn by the emperor of the East and the emperor of the West.

The Administration of Italy. Apart from the Alpine districts and the islands, practically the whole of Italy had Roman citizenship by the end of the republican period. Under the early empire it remained a district on its own, (Map XVI), distinct from the provinces, with a privileged status and unified organization, although the municipalities retained local autonomy. The older municipalities still had their traditional magistrates, and the colonies possessed *duoviri*; the later municipalities were governed by *quattuorviri*,

I   LATIUM-CAMPANIA
II APULIA-CALABRIA
III LUCANIA BRUTTIUM
IV SAMNIUM
V   PICENUM
VI UMBRIA
VII ETRURIA
VIII AEMILIA
IX LIGURIA
X   VENETIA
XI TRANSPADANA

HISTRIA

CORSICA

SARDINIA

SICILIA

Cartography Hallwag Berne   AUGUSTAN ITALY

MAP XVI

two with jurisdiction and two with administrative duties only. Each of these towns had a *curia* with senators, and a territory divided up into *pagi* and *vici*.

But in the imperial period the *municipia* and colonies gradually drew nearer to one another in status, and each lost part of their autonomy. Criminal jurisdiction passed mainly into the hands of the central imperial machine, being exercised by the *praefectus urbi* up to a hundred miles from Rome and by the praetorian prefect for more distant districts. Municipal magistrates were allowed to deal with civil suits of minor importance; but Italy was eventually divided into four districts, similar to the provinces, in which *consulares* in Hadrian's day, and *iuridici* under Marcus Aurelius, were responsible for administering justice. As to finance, after a period of independence which frequently resulted in bankruptcy, the imperial government from the second century onwards imposed on each community a *curator*, whose duties became more complicated as time went on. Other *curatores*, apparently ten in number, were put in charge of whole districts: indeed under Caracalla, and later under Aurelian, we find examples of *correctores totius Italiae*.

Under Diocletian, Italy, together with Rhaetia and the islands, formed two of the 'dioceses', further subdivided into a number of districts (Map XIII): these dioceses were united by Constantine to form a *praefectura* along with Illyria and Africa. But all central and southern Italy, together with Sicily, Sardinia, and Corsica, comprised a diocese on its own, under the superintendence of the *vicarius Romae*.

The Administration of the Provinces. In the early empire the fundamental differences between Italy and the provinces was that in the former the inhabitants were all Roman citizens and in the latter the privilege was confined to small groups. The remaining provincials were still either free citizens of allied cities or 'dediticii' paying a capitation tax.

The inhabitants of self-governing cities were of varying status. Some of them already had Latin or Roman citizenship besides that of their own *polis*, but in Latin towns the majority of inhabitants had local citizenship only. Then there were metics, freedmen, and slaves. Office in all cities was normally confined to the propertied classes; and from the various categories of ex-magistrates were drawn the senators, divided into various grades, though special services by a man towards his fellow-citizens, such as the provision of public works, bounty, or relief measures, might also qualify him for membership of the senate. But city government was becoming gradually more difficult, since magistrates normally had to meet excessive expenditure and there were now few rich citizens willing to take on the responsibility and burden involved. Moreover the more the imperial government granted Roman or Latin citizenship and increased the number of provincial citizens through enrolment in the legions or discharge from other branches of the army, it was at the same time putting the richest of these citizens in a position to aim at posts in Roman service which exempted them from local obligations; other beneficiaries were forming the habit of expecting protection and assistance from Rome. Throughout the second century there was a continual search for ways of reviving the municipal spirit. Minimum age limits for magistracies were lowered; offices were opened to metics, or made obligatory; Latin rights were extended, which implied that ex-magistrates in the cities affected became Roman citizens; and other means were tried.

There was of course a complete change in 212, when Caracalla published his constitution bringing all provincials except *dediticii* up to the level of Roman citizens. From that moment provincial towns, with a few exceptions like Sparta, Athens, or Alexandria, became almost identical with the Italian *municipia*: their new constitutions were modelled on those of Italy, including the system of imperial *curatores* for the control of their administrative machinery. While the nature of this machinery became more uniform, there were changes in the methods of electing *curiales*, or members of the local senates. The main functions of such bodies came to be the appointment of persons fitted to assume the risk of collecting the taxes due to Rome and to undertake liturgies. But it became clear that few men were voluntarily accepting decurionates and that the great majority were making efforts to avoid them. So under the later empire, from the time of Diocletian's introduction of compulsory hereditary castes, decurions as well as other people were compelled to transmit their office to their sons. Office had become essentially a burden rather than an honour, and justly earned the name of 'munus'. From other standpoints too these cities seemed to have lost the purpose they had served for so many centuries: the richer families were gradually retiring to their great 'feuda' on the land.

But under the empire there had also been a great transformation in the methods of governing the provinces themselves. In the Augustan organization the numbers of senatorial and imperial provinces were roughly equal: in the middle of the second century there were twenty-three imperial provinces and only ten senatorial. The ex-consuls and ex-praetors who governed senatorial provinces were still called proconsuls, but as a rule they had no military commands and their judicial authority was directed by imperial edicts. In any case the imperial procurators had intruded into senatorial as well as imperial provinces in order to manage imperial property and to collect tribute due to the imperial and military treasuries. Moreover the emperor had informers to report on the conduct of proconsuls, about which he could take a very stern line, and these informers had to be provided with a bureaucracy of knights, freedmen, and slaves.

In the imperial provinces, on the other hand, there were either senators (*legati Augusti pro praetore*) or knights (*praefecti* or *procuratores*), chosen by the emperor himself. He was responsible for fixing their terms of office, their duties, and the limits within which they could exercise discretion, while all the time he controlled their activity and gave them advice. In any case all provincial governors were now paid officials, with well-defined limits of authority and a continuous relationship with the home government, which may have slowed up their conduct of business but certainly made it more consistent and sure. Being well remunerated, governors were disinterested and efficient, showing fairness in their judicial methods and moderation in matters of taxation. They later had to pay frequent visits to the towns in their provinces to hold assizes and give assistance to the *legati iuridici* in charge of different districts: there they would hold enquiries, settle disputed points, and gradually adapt local customs to Roman law. Against civil verdicts the provincials could appeal to Rome, to the emperor or the senate as the case might be; and criminal questions affecting Roman citizens had to be judged at Rome.[29]

We shall have more to say later about the moderation of the early imperial systems of taxation. In addition it is certain that the provincials were appreciative of the continual outlay of the emperors (Hadrian is the best example) on public works such as aqueducts, roads, and harbours, which furthered provincial interests. The system of provincial assemblies, which had been started by Caesar in Gaul and was later developed throughout the empire to foster the imperial cult, was made to serve other purposes in that it brought the people together and made their own national background seem worth while. For example at the annual meetings it became the custom to vote congratulations or censure in respect of an outgoing governor, thus giving the imperial government a valuable means of control over the behaviour of its officials.[30]

With the development of the empire and the removal of the senate's power the senatorial provinces of course disappeared and their administration became an absolute preserve of the *dominus*. Diocletian carried out an enormous reform in all provincial administration, reducing the size of the provinces and increasing their number from forty-eight to about a hundred. The mass of officials was greatly increased, but their work was speeded up and the defence of the frontiers was improved. Diocletian also united a number of provinces into a single diocese administered by a *vicarius*, an officer acting on behalf of the praetorian prefect (*agentes vices praefectorum praetorii*), and under the military control of a *dux*. By the end of the fourth century there were fifteen dioceses, but at this time there were still twelve: the East, Pontus, Asia, Thrace, Moesia, Pannonia, Italy, Africa, Spain, Viennensis, Gallia, and Britain. Later the dioceses were further grouped together into four *praefecturae*, each under a *praefectus praetorii*; but with the disbanding of the praetorian cohorts this officer no longer had military duties, and instead looked after justice and public order, tax-collection, education, the postal service, and so on. So the four *praefecti*, in the East, Italy, Gaul, and Africa, had under them the *vicarii* of the dioceses; and under these again were the governors of the various kinds of province, with correspondingly various kinds of title —*consulares*, *correctores*, or *praesides*. Outside the system were the two capitals; also Asia, Africa, and Achaea, which were governed by proconsuls.

The Tribute. After he had carried out the necessary censuses and land surveys, Augustus regulated the finances of the empire. Roman citizens in Italy had been exempt from tribute since 167 BC, and Augustus preserved this immunity. But the measure of the resulting burden on the provincials was not increased indiscriminately by his successors; they preferred to work to a budget which was often too tight for the expenditure they had to meet in maintaining the army and administering the provinces concerned. The *stipendium* imposed on provincials was collected through municipalities where they existed, and comprised two main taxes. The *tributum soli*, a land tax, was based on surveys which were started by Augustus and brought to perfection in Trajan's time; and the *tributum capitis*, or poll tax,[31] required regular census lists and the reporting of births at what today would be called register offices, a duty imposed on all parents by Marcus Aurelius. But these were not of course the only sources of revenue. The chief form of indirect taxation (*vectigalia*) lay in customs dues (*portoria*); there was a one per cent duty on public sales and a tax for the upkeep of roads and posting stations; and there was a semi-voluntary contribution called *aurum coronarium* for festivals and great occasions connected with the imperial house, though this was not always exacted and was sometimes in part reimbursed to the contributors. The 5 per cent inheritance tax (*vicesima hereditatum*), which went towards veterans' pensions, was defined as payable by the Roman citizen population.

The revenues of senatorial provinces went to the *aerarium Saturni*; those from the imperial provinces to the provincial *fisci*, which came under the emperor.[32] The latter also had at his disposal the *patrimonium*, into which flowed the returns from his own personal property and from that of the 'Crown', and the *aerarium militare*, employed for pensioning veterans.

One fundamental defect in this system was the unequal division of burdens between Italians and provincials. Another was that a budget was struck on a close balance between revenue and regular expenditure, no adequate margin being left for abnormal outgoings, so that when expenses of that kind were inevitable the funds in hand often very quickly proved insufficient and hard to replenish. Nor was it easy to meet such situations by increasing provincial taxes: the reaction might have been dangerous, and the government felt a sense of fairness and moderation towards its subjects. Already Tiberius, at the time of his accession, found all the treasuries in deficit and had to resort to unpopular economies, as well as reducing various protectorates to the status of provinces in order to get tribute from them. Caligula, despite heavy expenses met mainly from his *patrimonium*, must have left a fair balance, with the result that Claudius was able to undertake a large programme of public works. But the vast expenditure of Nero compelled him to augment his revenues by confiscations, eliciting legacies, imposing contributions on provincials, despoiling temples, and debasing the currency. When his reign had been followed by the disastrous civil wars of 69, Vespasian found the treasuries empty.

The new emperor calculated the minimum annual budget, and apparently arrived at the sum of 4,000 million sesterces.[33] He made certain economies, but at the same time increased the *stipendium* due from various provinces, created new provincial territories, and laid claim both to the regular capitation payment made by the Jews and also to the value of public lands occupied by individuals. Yet he too spent heavily on the corn supply and on building; and his son Titus had to meet extraordinary expenditure in relieving a number of public disasters. So Domitian inherited an almost bankrupt situation from his father and brother. This he met by tightening up tribute collection, and preventing evasion as well as unnecessary outgoings. He increased the revenue of the *patrimonium* from confiscations and legacies, and also had recourse to drastic methods which he later had to forgo, such as reducing the number of legionaries and compelling Italy to grow cereals in support of the corn dole.

The balance was not yet restored by Domitian's death, nor was Nerva able to redress it during his brief reign. Nerva was careful in effecting economies and increasing the revenue, but he expanded the Italian relief programme with a new agrarian law and the institution of 'alimenta' (relief to poor children in Italy). His successor Trajan was therefore troubled by great economic difficulties down to about 104, and met them by selling a large part of the Crown property. Later, however, his Dacian war gave him possession of the mineral wealth of Transylvania, enabling him not only to increase the revenue but to embark on an unlimited programme of public works. So large was the latter that Hadrian on his accession quickly announced that he had inherited an unhealthy financial situation, and at the same time had to write off an enormous sum in credits which the *fiscus* was unable to collect. He reduced army and war expenses to the minimum, kept a vigilant control on income and outgoings, created new towns and gave a proper system of administration to existing ones, improved the management of imperial property, and arranged for a general revision of the finances every fifteen years. Only by these means could he balance his budget, give the Italians an increase in the benefits from the *alimenta*, and provide for the more urgent needs of the provinces, brought home to him in the course of his long journeys.

Antoninus Pius maintained equilibrium by careful management, control of revenues, and limiting public works, without being obliged to abolish any *liberalitates* (imperial bounty). But Marcus Aurelius found his finances burdened by the expense of continual wars, plagues, and cataclysms, as well as by the need to write off bad debts. He had to impose unpopular economies, exact extraordinary contributions from the provinces and municipalities, renew the sales of imperial property, increase the regular provincial tribute, revive taxes which had been previously abolished, and gamble with the purity of the coinage and its face value. All this had grave consequences, of which Marcus seemed unaware but which were soon to show their dangers. They affected the reign of Commodus, during which conditions were in any case complicated by famines and plagues, and rendered worse by the emperor's unreasoning generosities.

Pertinax, who is said to have found only one million sesterces in the *aerarium*, made a sharp distinction between the personal *patrimonium* of the emperor and the property of the Crown, and devoted attention to Italian agriculture in order to provide for the corn dole. But his reign was too short to lay the foundations of a healthy balance once more. The ensuing period of civil war made the situation much worse, and Septimius Severus had to adopt drastic remedies to regulate the currency and prevent financial collapse. He took over practically the whole management of state finances by reducing the part played by the *aerarium*; he created the new imperial treasury of the *res privata*, mainly from enormous political confiscations; he eased the supply of grain to the army by requisitioning foodstuffs and assigning land to the military; he created new outlets for trade; and he built up large stocks of corn to meet any emergency.

Caracalla's *Constitutio Antoniniana* in 212, which effected a large increase in the number of citizens, had financial considerations in mind, even if there were other purposes besides. The *fiscus* profited from the *annona* imposed on farmers, and at the same time the capitation tax was still payable by the *dediticii*, who were excluded from the grant of citizenship. Caracalla tackled the financial situation in other ways. He increased the yield from certain taxes, debased and reformed the coinage, revived measures of economy, and restored the payment of *aurum coronarium*. At his death the treasuries were well stocked, but were then emptied again by the unparalleled extravagance of Elagabalus.

There was a fresh period of recovery under Severus Alexander. He regulated the flow of money, created some new regular taxes of an appropriate kind to meet the expense of maintaining and restoring public works, and increased the range of imperial manufactures and commercial enterprises. He was thus able to be generous with donatives and free distributions, as well as instituting fresh alimentary foundations and improving the economic status of the soldiers.

At this point, however, there supervened the financial chaos resulting from the civil wars. Maximin tried to meet it by confiscations, by the levy of extraordinary contributions, and by forced loans, all of which provoked violent opposition. The results of the monetary reforms attempted by Gordian III were short-lived; they were followed by problems encountered by Philip over the demobilization of troops and by the discontent and rebellion provoked when his brother Perseus, 'rector Orientis', imposed fresh taxes; then there were the expenses of the wars of Decius. So the empire was already bankrupt when under Gallus and Gallienus numerous revolts broke out in several parts of the empire, leading to its temporary dismemberment, to endless wars in which no quarter was given, and to an unhealthy condition throughout the economy. Gradually the 'Illyrian emperors' succeeded in checking the barbarians; Aurelian unified the empire once more, and was able to lay his hands on the wealth of the defeated Palmyra.

But the greatest of these emperors, Diocletian, carried out a radical financial reform, which for good or for ill had far-reaching importance in determining the economics of the Roman world and of later generations as well. He caused an accurate general census to be undertaken of the whole population of the empire together with a detailed survey of all agricultural holdings, including their equipment, cultivable areas, and types of crops. Then, in order to meet the inescapable expenses of the *annona*, both military and civil, he gradually introduced a complete new system of taxation in kind, based on the relationship between the number of 'capita' of population and the area cultivated by each family group, account being also taken of the nature of the crop and the price it fetched locally. These complicated computations, which naturally had to be revised from time to time, enabled him to raise the essential revenue by annual apportionment of quotas payable by individual families, and to let each family know in advance what sum it would have to pay. The system was certainly not perfect, since apart from unavoidable errors in the survey and in calculation it fixed an agricultural tax in advance without any definite relation to what the lands would in fact be able to yield. Moreover the flight of peasants from the land became a regular phenomenon, and led to the *coloni* being converted into serfs. Later on the state effected economies by imposing heavy corvées on its subjects without payment or at cut rates (*munera*), while it obtained other produce from domain land or imperial estates, which in the fourth century were even encroaching on the public lands of the cities.

At first the *capitatio* from all citizen-owned land was naturally collected by decurions, who were made responsible for the entire sum payable to the state. It was for this reason that the decurionate was made hereditary and compulsory. In an attempt to eliminate the hardships resulting from this system Valentinian I arranged for collection by the *officia* of provincial governors; but the state lost by this reform, and the earlier system was reintroduced. There is no doubt that the capitation system was often ruinous to the tax-payer, even though from the government's point of view it guaranteed the corn-supply in a way which saved it trouble.

But the state needed not only provisions in bulk but also money; and this it obtained from every other kind of taxation—such as duties on trade and industry, surtax on large estates, and *aurum coronarium*. Indeed Constantine's revolutionary reform of the coinage, based on the *aureus*, led eventually to friction between that portion of the population which found it more convenient to pay and be paid in kind and the other portion which preferred assessments in gold (*adaeratio*).

c. *The Army, Navy, and Public Order*

The Army under the Empire. The firmest support to the imperial power lay in the emperor's position as the recognized head of a regular standing army which defended Rome's territories. It was a paid army of professional volunteers,[34] and gave the *princeps* the force needed to impose his will abroad and at home. But for various reasons this military basis of his power was hardly ever brought brutally or immoderately out into the open. The *princeps* was temperate in the expression of his wishes, and most rulers showed political ability and a sense of responsibility. Moreover the modest size of the military budget imposed restraint; and in the early stages recruiting was not on a collective basis and was therefore less alarming.

Provinces which were peaceful, or which could not easily be attacked from outside, were denuded of troops even to an embarrassing extent, as Pliny the Younger asserts in writing to Trajan. Furthermore the lack of a reserve force in the early centuries made it necessary, in case of emergency, to deprive one or more frontiers of their garrisons in order to reinforce another. The same thing happened when frontier armies had to send forces to put down internal revolts, or, worse still, when they took part in contests between claimants to the empire. In early times this fortunately happened only at infrequent intervals—in the year 69, then after Domitian's death, and then on the death of Commodus.

The fact that over long periods relatively small forces of defenders along the frontiers were normally able to maintain their positions, pushing Rome's enemies back and even annexing portions of their territory, was due in part to the military efficiency and technical skill of Roman officers and legionaries, but in part also to the courage and ability of the emperors, who were often in command themselves. It also owed much to the measures taken to reinforce the action of the troops, such as the building of a fortified *limes* and of strategic roads, the employment of men and equipment well adapted to local conditions, with auxiliaries trained to mobile warfare in service beside the legionaries, or the formation of vassal buffer-states and alliances with barbarian tribes beyond the frontiers. By trade and other means an attempt was made to promote the prestige of Roman civilization abroad. Besides all this, the government was careful to take on only one war at a time, and by diplomacy would divide its enemies or postpone their action.

A standing army consisting of troops whose numbers were limited, but whose quality, training, and armament were on the highest level, was the most efficient instrument for a defensive system which had to be both permanent and also prompt to meet crises. It was a professional army with fairly long terms of service, corresponding to the most vigorous period of a man's life, and was nothing like the conscript armies which Rome had abolished in Marius' time. It was also designed for defence rather than for conquest; and since there was no longer a continual prospect of booty it was necessary to give the soldiers such minimum guarantee of a sufficient standard of living as would attract recruits from at any rate the poorer elements in the population.

The number of legions was the minimum required by the tasks they had to perform,[35] and the maximum which the normal state budget would permit if there were to be no increases in tribute. Every year it was necessary to recruit a number of men equivalent to the number being discharged, and care was taken to keep the number down by prolonging terms of service. Gratuities payable on discharge were met by a tax on inheritance received by Roman citizens: as such the tax was in early days paid mainly by Italians, who came to be almost permanently excluded from military service.

At the outset legionaries were forbidden to marry; but when they served over long periods in permanent military camps, near which 'canabae' of small traders gradually grew into regular towns, some form of concubinage became common, the issue being recognized at the time of a soldier's discharge. As time went on, this allowed the government to attract soldiers' sons to the army; and veterans were encouraged to settle down near their former camps, where the state would give them plots of land instead of gratuities. Later on, when Septimius Severus allowed serving soldiers to marry, the state had to recognize that there was an even greater need to assign them land which their families could cultivate. There were two corollaries to this. The legionary, who was now transformed into a peasant-soldier, had to be employed locally and not transferred to other sectors. Secondly, it was to the advantage of soldiers' households that their pay should be in kind rather than in money.

The Command. Under the late Republic questions of command had time and again been settled by the decisions of political factions and of such leaders as happened to be in power. Under the Empire an attempt was made to secure a system, but it was impossible to adopt the simple method of selecting the man who seemed most suited for the job and had given proof of most experience and ability in the past. The vested rights of the senatorial, and later also of the equestrian, class were far too strong; so were the preferences shown by particular emperors for senators or *equites*. It became the tradition that, except in connection with the troops in Egypt, members of senatorial families filled the higher posts. They commanded the armies (sometimes containing as many as four legions) of the military provinces, and also the individual legions (as *legati*); and before this they had to hold, for one year or two, the post of *tribunus militum*. This latter did not involve independent command and in some cases senators might be excused; moreover since the tribunate was one of the stages in the senatorial *cursus honorum*, with largely administrative duties, it is clear that too many legionary commanders were without adequate training or proved ability.

Less important commands were normally filled by non-senators, that is to say by knights or by men of lower rank. In particular this applied to the sixty 'centurionates' in each legion (fifty-nine from Hadrian's time), among whom only the senior centurion of the first cohort (*primipilus*) could rise to higher commands. Even when an *eques* was made a senator in reward for his military services, it was only to his sons (who became senatorial too) that access to higher commands was opened.

THE ANCIENT WORLD

The emperor who finally opened the senior military posts to the equestrian order was Septimius Severus. Even, therefore, amid the anarchic outrages of armies struggling for the imperial power, the middle of the third century was the period in which 'merit' became a more important factor than social origin.

Legionaries and Auxiliaries. The strength of the army consisted in two complementary elements, legions and *auxilia*. The former were mainly organized as heavy infantry of the line; the latter were light troops, both on foot and on horseback, employed for such purposes as scouting, to act as outposts on the march, and to make the initial attack in battles. The regular armed forces fluctuated between 330,000 and 450,000 men: a significantly low figure in relation to the 6,000 miles or so of frontier which had to be defended, and to the 100 or so millions of inhabitants in the empire (of whom the army formed between 0·33 and 0·45 per cent). But the proportion was distinctly higher from the third century onwards, when the number of men in arms was increased and the population had gone down. A legion normally contained 5,000 to 6,000 infantry and 100 cavalry, divided into six cohorts or 60 centuries. There were 25 legions after the defeat of Varus, 30 under Trajan, 28 under Hadrian, 30 under Marcus Aurelius, and 33 under Septimius Severus. At the head of each legion was a delegate of the emperor or *legatus Augusti* (in Egypt a *praefectus legionis*); and he was assisted by six tribunes and 60 centurions, among whom the *centurio primipilus* was the most prominent.

The legions, distributed in various ways at different periods, were under the orders of the governors of frontier provinces. From the time when it became the custom for troops to winter in regular camps, each legion's camp was prepared by a *praefectus castrorum*, who also looked after living-quarters, supplies, transport, stores, arms and artillery, watch duties, and sanitation. When later permanent camps for more than one legion were built on the frontiers each camp had its *praefectus*; but its garrison was then reduced to a single legion when Domitian gave orders to this effect, in order to avoid the dangers due to large concentrations of troops.

Being accustomed to citizen armies, the government granted Roman citizenship to provincial recruits who did not already possess it. This, together with the pay and discharge bounties, was one of the attractions of enlistment, at any rate to the population of depressed areas and to proletarians or men in danger of sinking to that status. The system was one which provided soldiers at a reasonable cost, and brought men who might have been a source of disorder on to the side of order: it also brought a higher culture to certain provincials, who would later spread the Roman way of life.

But in the course of time, and by gradual stages, the recruiting system was organized differently. Soldiers who had served for a number of years on the same front, and had established personal ties there, were anxious to avoid being moved; and young men from districts near the frontiers were attracted to the colours by the prospect of bettering their standard of life. All this had advantages for the state. It saved the expense of moving men around, profited from the attachment of recruits to their native country, and saw Romanization furthered in the process. Rome was also able to employ men who knew the ground and customs of the country of their service, and whose military organization could be varied in accordance with the type of enemy they had to encounter. This system was used first for the *auxilia*, but from Hadrian's time it became common for the legionaries too.

Every time the value of money fell, pay had to be increased. Meanwhile the establishment of the military treasury on a permanent footing enabled soldiers who had completed their terms to be discharged more regularly without delays, and to have their gratuities paid in money or in land. The sources show that down to the crises of the third century the troops were reasonably well satisfied with their treatment, even though, especially during long periods of peace, they were employed on construction work as well as on their military exercises. They built camps, roads, forts, and other works on the *limes*, and also civilian works such as city walls and public buildings; and they had their own quarries, woods for timber, and brickworks.

Their major operation was in building the *limes*, a series of fortified works on the frontiers which became necessary once it was recognized that the great rivers, especially when frozen in winter, did not provide an adequate barrier; moreover large sections of the frontier did not follow the river lines. A *limes* was properly a frontier road, to defend which, with some variety as time went on, there would be created a complicated system of trenches, ditches, earthworks, and walls, with fortified posts and fortresses, look-out posts, and advanced blockhouses in enemy territory. Behind would be the regular *castra* for the main bodies of troops. On the northern frontiers fortifications of this kind were designed mainly in the period between Tiberius and the Antonines. In the East and in Africa their construction involved problems of water supplies and of policing the caravan routes.

Alongside each legion, and subordinated to the legionary *legatus*, was an approximately equal body of auxiliary troops, in *turmae* of cavalry grouped together in *alae* and centuries of infantry which together made up cohorts. They were officered in the main by Roman citizens, though sometimes by men of native birth. Their pay was less than that of legionaries and their terms of service (twenty-five years) were longer. On discharge they received Roman citizenship which could be transmitted to their children; their sons therefore could become legionaries. Each regiment bore the name of the country from which it had originated at the outset, but later its ranks were filled up from the country in which it was serving. In the course of the third century AD, the cavalry became more important tactically than the infantry, and therefore got higher pay. Under Gallienus the most important dignitary of the empire was no more the praetorian prefect, the commander of the

Roman legions of infantry, but a general in charge of the imperial crack guard cavalry, the latter being usually destined to become the successor of the reigning emperor.

In Hadrian's day there began to appear a number of light irregular units with special organization. These 'numeri' were either infantry or cavalry, in strength varying between 500 and 1,000, and they used the equipment, tactics, and arms of the barbarian countries from which they were drawn: for instance, the cavalry might carry shock lances, or bows and arrows. These were straightforward mercenaries. They cost little, but were of great value for guerilla warfare, for the dangerous work of advanced patrols, or for encountering fast-moving bands of barbarian cavalry.

Defence and Police Forces. From the beginning of the empire there were special troops in Italy and Rome to deal with defence and public order, and to act as the emperor's bodyguard. These were picked men, Italians, and were better paid than the legionaries, with shorter terms of service (only sixteen years). The praetorian cohorts, nine or ten in number each consisting of between 900 and 1,000 men, were commanded by the *praefectus praetorio* or sometimes by two *praefecti*. At the outset they were all Italians, and it was only after 69 that particular emperors decided to bring in provincials as well. In time of peace they were quartered in the *castrum praetorium*, from which detachments were detailed in turn to guard the *palatium* and the emperor's person. In time of war strong contingents accompanied the emperor wherever he went, and formed the centre of the line in any battle where he was engaged. Senatorial tradition has constructed a murky legend about them, by generalizing unfairly from the violent part they played at certain convulsive moments of Roman history, such as the year 69 or in the aftermaths of the deaths of Domitian and Commodus.

From Hadrian's time the emperor also made use of secret informers called *frumentarii*, who were originally men responsible for requisitioning army food-supplies; and from Flavian times there were the German *equites singulares*, a small body of guards who like the rest were under the command of the praetorian *praefecti*.

Four *cohortes urbanae*, consisting of about 6,000 Italian volunteers, looked after public order and defence in Rome; and seven *cohortes vigilum*, recruited normally from freedmen, each protected two 'regions' of the city from fires and similar catastrophes.

Even in the republican period the fleet, as a permanent force, had not been of any great importance. When under the empire Rome became absolute mistress of the Mediterranean, the sea no longer being significantly troubled by pirate vessels and only in the Euxine containing a small non-Roman squadron, a navy was regarded as almost superfluous. As early as Augustus' day it became practically the emperor's private property, with three main bases, Forum Iulii, Ravenna, and Misenum, of which the first was soon abolished. Crews were recruited from ex-slaves and imperial freedmen, and could receive discharge with Roman citizenship after twenty-six years' service. Under Vespasian the two remaining fleets, now regarded as state forces, found an additional source of recruits in the seaboard districts of the provinces and they were used on occasions to reinforce the land armies. Caracalla enrolled provincials for a twenty-eight year term. The fleets were commanded by *praefecti* and *sub-praefecti* of equestrian rank. In the third century they acquired importance again.

There were some lesser squadrons, also commanded by equestrian *praefecti*, which obtained crews from the more backward peoples. These combined with the armies in operations on the outer seas, the great lakes, and the rivers on the frontier.

Weaknesses of the Army of the Early Empire. Under the early empire the Roman army was never large, and it could not have adequate additions made to it in periods of emergency, mainly because its budgetary allocation was based on the assumption that the empire was to be defended rather than expanded. Its forces often had to be used in civil wars, and external dangers were growing; yet recruitment was becoming more difficult owing both to relatively unattractive conditions of pay, and also to the decline in the population and the necessity of cavalry, which made it necessary to adopt the dangerous expedient of employing barbarians. Rather than speaking of 'the extermination of the fittest' it is preferable to suppose a fall in the population of the Roman world and a rise in that of the non-Roman (both barbarian and non-barbarian), both factors causing outsiders to seek expansion at the empire's expense.[36]

In addition the arrangement of the legionaries on the frontier, protected by the fortified lines of the *limes*, eventually turned out to be less effective than had been supposed. When it came to the point, this was only a single barrier, even though a strong one; and when it was crossed by the enemy, either through a breach in the lines of fortifications or because a sector had been denuded of troops, the interior of the country was left uncovered. This led to repeated raids of provincial territory by the barbarians, increasing in frequency and making the provincials feel the need to wall their cities.

Throughout republican history from Camillus onwards Rome had shown vitality and creative genius in devising new military techniques, and had possessed armies capable of carrying out the most audacious operations of conquest. Under the empire the army did not show either the capacity for improving its methods or the standard of war potential which was required for a lasting policy of expansion. This fact is attested by the repeated instances in which first Augustus himself, and later Tiberius, Domitian, and Hadrian, gave up an operation before it was completed. Meanwhile the civil wars, which began in 69 and later became increasingly frequent (especially in the third century) compelled Rome to put too much trust in the effectiveness of the *limes*.

From Hadrian's day there was some imitation of foreign techniques, such as the mounted catafract, and it became the custom to employ the best recruits obtainable from the frontier districts in their countries of origin. This system was followed by Antoninus Pius and Marcus Aurelius (the latter of whom also made use of slaves and of barbarian auxiliary units). It became a hard and fast rule when Septimius Severus recruited his soldiers from peasants.

As early as the reign of Antoninus Pius Gothic movements started the barbarian attacks, and to these were later added the civil wars, reaching their maximum intensity in the middle of the third century. At this point Rome needed some fundamental innovation to give the legionaries, who were growing very little different from their enemies across the frontier, some means of attaining decisive military superiority. Besides the inadequacy of strength, there was by now a lack of inventive ability and will-power. Various expedients were incapable of achieving decisive results. For example Antoninus Pius attached importance to diplomacy and the support of vassals on the periphery; Caracalla tried to revive the phalanx; the systems of *numeri* and *vexillationes* were developed; and the legionaries took over the arms and cavalry tactics of the *auxilia*, which by this time were those of the barbarians. Even now the government did not create a force for reserve and manœuvre, which had become indispensable when several attacks from outside and more than one internal struggle were taking place at the same time.

Regional Recruitment. Legionary recruitment underwent gradual changes, of which the essential tendency is ascertainable. From Augustus to Caligula Italians were in a distinct majority, though (as in later periods too) most Italians were northerners. Such provincials as there were came mainly from the most highly Romanized Western provinces and from the Eastern provinces with the most advanced Greek culture. In the ensuing period down to 68, Italians and provincials are found in roughly equal proportions, with the provincials including fewer men from Anatolia and more from the Balkans. Between Vespasian and Trajan Italians are only one in five of the provincials, the latter mainly coming from Gaul, the Danubian and northern Balkan countries, Syria, and Asia. From Hadrian to the end of the third century the Italians attested are less than one per cent of the provincials, and the principal areas of recruitment were the Danube lands and the northern Balkans, together with Africa, all countries suitable for recruiting efficient cavalry soldiers.

Until Trajan's time Western recruits normally served in legions stationed in the Western provinces, except for Pannonia, Dalmatia, and Africa; Easterners served in the Eastern provinces and Moesia; and Illyricum was a hybrid zone where the two recruiting areas joined. From the time of Hadrian local recruitment became more and more regular, except for the troops in Britain. For the praetorians (except for the brief period of Vitellius, who made use of men from Germany) it was normal down to the second century to employ Roman citizens from the older districts; but in a few instances as early as Caligula's reign, and later with increasing frequency, it became the practice to transfer individual legionaries, who would mainly be provincials, into the praetorian guard. This practice was adopted wholesale by Septimius Severus, under whom praetorians were mainly chosen from Thracian and Illyrian legionaries, and were accompanied by the Legion II Parthica, a unit of similar composition stationed at Albanum.

Augustus attempted to raise the social background of his legionaries, who as far back as Marius' time had been mainly drawn from 'capite censi'. But the economic position he allowed them was not such as to enable him to fill their ranks without making use of 'inopes et vagi', as Tiberius complained. It was only by increasing provincial recruitment, and later making such recruitment the general rule, that the government was able to attract well-to-do persons into the legions and eventually to induce even members of the provincial nobility to come in. Yet by the time of Septimius Severus the social, and still more the cultural background of the legionary army had sunk significantly, as the result of large enrolments of men from the northern Balkans and Illyricum, men whose rough and lawless behaviour was deplored by Dio Cassius.

The gradual process of social and cultural decline was of course more evident among the auxiliary troops, and still more among the increasingly common units of *foederati* under their native officers and non-commissioned officers. The same was true of Hadrian's *numeri*, of the Germans and Batavians in the imperial bodyguard, of the *equites singulares* employed by Trajan, Caracalla, and other emperors, and of the barbarians who from the time of Marcus Aurelius were paid by Rome, and sometimes even quartered in the frontier districts.

But another system, begun by Severus Alexander, was a further important factor in the 'barbarization' of the army. That emperor, in an attempt to restore the army, tried to revive the phalanx and enrol a legion of Italians; but at the same time he composed the main body of his troops of Illyrians, and was seriously concerned with the development of his cavalry, whom he enrolled not only from Rome's old enemies the Parthians but also from the barbarians recently arriving from the North, the Alans and Goths. So he created a corps of mounted catafracts in imitation of the Parthian horse and with arms captured from them. He took into paid service prisoners and refugees from Armenia, Osroene, and Parthia, and made use of a large number of Mauretanian mounted archers. Maximin added some German deserters, a class later employed freely by Pupienus and Balbinus as a bodyguard and for other purposes. Finally Gordian III took on an even greater risk by employing as mercenaries not only Germans but Goths; and they, when Philip sent them back and refused their promised pay, provoked disastrous reprisals. By this time it can be clearly seen that deliberate barbarization of the army, even though on some occasions it helped to protect the frontiers, could in times of emergency lead to desertion by the 'barbarized' Roman army in collusion with the barbarians themselves.

Reforms of the Late Empire. The most important military reforms in the Roman world between about 250 and 400 can be summarized as follows.

Recruitment. It had now become the custom for sons of soldiers to enter the army. Diocletian, and Constantine after him, in connection with the general policy of compulsion they were applying to the creation of hereditary professions and castes, were concerned to prevent disintegration setting in here any more than in other spheres. They therefore ordained that soldiers' sons who were fit for service must adopt a military career, and by applying the new 'capitation' system of taxation required landed proprietors to send a given proportion of their *coloni* to the levy. These arrangements were extended to allow exemption upon payment of a sum adequate to provide a replacement; and recruits, together with their nearer relatives, were allowed remission from the 'capitation', a concession which was also in part granted to men after discharge.

Numbers. Here all that need be said is that Diocletian raised the number of legions from thirty-nine to sixty-eight, and that about AD 400 the army comprised about 500,000 men.

Distribution. The government at last came to realize that in addition to legions on the frontiers it was essential to have a force for reserve and manœuvre stationed at some appropriate points. This was designed partly to reinforce a threatened section of the frontier without denuding others, partly to meet internal dangers, and partly to enable the various members of the more complicated imperial organizations of this period (tetrarchies and so on) to make use of the new force to help them in their duties. On the one hand, therefore, there were still the frontier troops (*limitanei*), but about two-fifths of the legionaries and auxiliaries were quartered in various cities of the interior, where they made their level of discipline conform to the *civilitas* of their surroundings. These troops were regarded as a continuation of those which in the past had accompanied the emperor on his campaigns; they consequently acquired the name *Palatini*, or alternatively *comitatenses* from the fact that their leaders were *comites*. A further point is that the proportion of cavalry among them was markedly higher than in the past. This had inevitable consequences for tactics and strategy; though it was not enough to prevent Rome's great defeat at Adrianople in 378, achieved by irresistible cavalry charges of the Visigoths.

The Imperial Guard. After the battle of the Milvian Bridge in 312 Constantine disbanded the praetorians, and they are not heard of again. The post of *praefectus praetorio* lost its military duties and was divided among four holders, becoming a civil office for directing the four *Praefecturae* into which the empire was divided.

Military Command. From the time of Diocletian military and civil governors were kept firmly separate from each other. The old senatorial and equestrian orders had lost all importance in both fields; and eventually, at any rate in theory, posts both in the military career and in the hierarchy of *officia* began to depend no longer on a holder's rank but on proved merit: 'dignity' corresponded to the grade a man had attained. At the head of the military forces were a *magister peditum* and a *magister equitum*; and below them were the *duces* of the *limitanei* and the *comites* of the *comitatenses*, all possessing commands which were exclusively military.

Meanwhile the *limes* was continually maintained. As late as the time of Valentinian I large works were being constructed on it, but instead of the continuous barrier of ditches, walls, and the like, the main feature now was a set of forts and camps with a rational lay-out.

At the same time an inordinately large use was being made of the dangerous though inevitable custom of employing barbarians introduced into imperial territory. Under Constantine they were allowed to attain the highest commands. The emperor Julian, in the criticisms he levelled at his great predecessor, was a sound prophet of the consequences soon to follow from this whole system.

6. POPULATION CENSUSES IN ITALY AND THE EMPIRE

It is a probable view that the full lists of the population of both sexes and all ages, compiled from declarations made by *patres familiarum* and guardians (and including childless men and widows), were the source from which was extracted a list of men fit to bear arms, who were then divided into classes and age-groups. Such censuses of the republican period as have come down to us are on this view based on men of military age, including (sometimes explicitly, sometimes not) the small number of orphans declared by their guardians to be reaching military age during the four years of the validity of the census. Moreover, apart from the censuses of the citizen population, the subject peoples who had not yet obtained citizenship must also have been numbered, mainly for fiscal, but partly also for military, reasons; and there must have been a census of Roman citizens living in the provinces—during the Mithradatic Wars we are told that 20,000 could be counted at Delos, and at least 80,000 in Asia. The last known republican census, that of 70–69 BC, gives us the figure of 910,000 men of military age. Yet the censuses recorded in the *Res Gestae* of Augustus give 4,063,000 for 28 BC, 4,233,000 for 8 BC, and 4,937,000 for AD 14. It is impossible that the number of Roman citizens was quadrupled in forty years, and it is therefore clear that imperial data reflect a different method of computation from those of the republican period. In our opinion the best explanation is that Augustus

included not only males of military age but all male citizens, including
children and old men. This may enable us to estimate the number of Roman
citizens of both sexes in Rome, Italy, and the provinces at about double the
figures given by Augustus—without of course including slaves.

But for AD 14 the 'Fasti Ostienses' give 4,100,900 instead of 4,937,000; and
a similar difference is reflected by our sources on the last specifically reported
census, that of AD 47, for which some authorities give 6,944,000 against
Tacitus' figure of 5,984,072. The most likely hypothesis appears to be that
the higher figures for both AD 14 and AD 47 relate to the male citizen population of the whole empire, and the smaller to the male citizen population of
Italy alone. Consequently the balance of 836,100 in AD 14, and 959,928 in
AD 47, represents the male citizens in the provinces. If we add to the Italian
figures a corresponding total for women, and a rough figure of one million
for slaves, we get a global population of Italy amounting to between nine
and nine-and-a-half millions in 14 and between twelve-and-a-half and thirteen millions in 47.

We therefore arrive at a figure approximately double that obtained by
Beloch's invaluable calculations; these were throughout on the low side.
Moreover since every time one re-examines Beloch's calculations of population of the Roman world in the Augustan age one reaches an answer which
is at least twice as high (1,300,000 for Sicily instead of 600,000, or 10,500,000
for the Tres Galliae instead of 3,400,000), it is probably not far from the
truth to put the total for the whole empire at 100 or 110 millions instead of
the 54 million figure at which he arrived.

[This figure is hypothetical but need not be excessive for pre-industrial
conditions. We know that Alexandria in Egypt, the largest city of Hellenistic
times, contained 300,000 free citizens and about the same number of slaves
and non-Greeks; while in Roman times Egypt excluding Alexandria had a
population of 7,500,000. Under the empire, the largest city was Rome itself.
Calculations can be made of its urban population based upon the figures for
corn-distributions under Augustus, the total of corn-distribution under
Severus, and by reckoning the population density within the known built-up
area; the three methods independently agree upon a total of about 1,000,000
inhabitants or more, and the number of food-recipients in the later empire
supports this high figure: see S. Mazzarino, *Aspetti sociali del quarto secolo*
(Rome, 1951), pp. 232 ff. Next to Alexandria, Antioch in Syria and the city
of Seleucia-on-the-Tigris, outside the Roman empire, were of a similar
size, and the latter is known to have had 600,000 inhabitants. For other
cities where we lack direct evidence, the area of city buildings may be used,
especially when excavations have shown the type of architecture employed:
Aquileia can thus be reckoned at well over 100,000, Ostia at 50,000, and
Pompeii at 25,000 inhabitants. But estimates of this kind would be too low
for north Italy and the northern provinces, where many and sometimes
most citizens of a town lived in the surrounding countryside. Exact figures

are unattainable, but a general perspective is not; these considerations would tell rather against Beloch's lower figures for the total citizen and non-citizen populations of the empire.]*

This total figure was a maximum, and it then progressively declined. From the first there was a powerful movement of emigration from areas such as Italy and Greece towards other parts of the empire; later the phenomenon of growing depopulation became more general. There was a long series of causes, sometimes acting in isolation in time and place, at other times working concomitantly. For instance, manpower was destroyed by foreign wars, and in some periods of the third century by civil wars as well. Barbarian invasions and raids brought bloodshed, and to them were added murderous descents on inhabited areas by pirates, brigands, and highlanders. Then there were the devastations caused by prolonged and widespread plagues and the advance of malaria; the malnutrition due to famine, oppressive taxation, soil exhaustion, and the difficulty of securing the necessities of life through trade once civilization had returned to the practice of barter in kind; and finally there were voluntary birth-control, deliberate abortion, and exposure of children.

Further evidence for a continual increase in the extent of deserted areas comes from the practice of settling barbarian peoples on land left untilled: in Augustus' day we hear only of 50,000 Dacians settled near the Danube, but the practice became increasingly common. It is not surprising, therefore, that laws of Septimius Severus' time deplore the 'necessitas penuriae hominum'. Yet the size of this progressive reduction in the population must not be exaggerated (see above p. 815).

* By M. W. Frederiksen.

NOTES TO CHAPTER XVI

1. In Professor L. S. Vasilyev's view two classes of dependants can be identified, (a) the *pu-ch'u*, who were originally bodyguards of the nobles but were eventually issued with land, (b) the dependent peasant proper, known as the *pin-kho*. He also calls attention to the importance of slaves in this period, citing Wang Yi-tung, 'Slaves and other comparable social Groups during the Northern Dynasties', *Harvard Journal of Asiatic Studies*, 1953.

2. On Sassanid organization see F. Altheim, *Ein Asiatischer Staat*, I (1954), *Finanzengeschichte der Spätantike* (1957).

3. Or so Tiberius said. The motives behind his show of reluctance at his accession cannot be determined: our literary sources, especially Tacitus and Suetonius, represent his behaviour as a complete sham, and it certainly became fashionable among new emperors to make a bogus pretence that power was forced upon them. But it is fairly clear that Tiberius tried, initially at least, to enhance the prerogative, as well as the prestige, of the senate.

4. It may perhaps be doubted whether Nero's reign, and his eventual fall, are to be explained by supposing that he aimed at constitutional absolutism. Important reasons were (a) his long-drawn-out attempt to divorce his wife Octavia, married to him for dynastic reasons, (b) the horror caused by his murder of his mother, who had opposed the divorce, (c) his

Hellenizing cultural policy, and his own appearances in the circus and on the stage, (d) the faction struggles occasioned by the rise of Tigellinus at the expense of Seneca and Nero's other earlier advisers, and (e) (probably) acute financial stringency, partly the result of lavish state expenditure in Rome.

5. From Augustus' time the praetorian guard had been a force in politics: the years 68–70 saw the emergence of the provincial armies. The extent to which the generals, the lower officers, or the common soldiers provided the initiative for these disturbances has been much discussed: for a summary see G. E. F. Chilver, *Journal of Roman Studies*, 1957, pp. 29 ff. Another feature of these years was the prevalence of discontent in the provinces, with Gaul, the Rhineland, and Judaea breaking into open rebellion. See P. A. Brunt, *Latomus*, 1959, pp. 531 ff., 1960, pp. 494 ff., and the same writer's low estimate of the integrity of Roman provincial government in this period, *Historia*, 1961, pp. 189 ff.

6. The troops he put into the guard were, of course, not actual Germans, but legionaries (often Italian) from the German armies.

7. In this period several senators were introduced from the Western provinces, as well as from the Po valley of Italy. This probably reflects the growing wealth of the upper classes in those areas; and the process set the pattern for recruitment of senators, largely for political reasons, from the Eastern provinces too. For an analysis of the late first- and early second-century senate see M. Hammond, *Journal of Roman Studies*, 1957, p. 74.

8. There was, of course, no mention of Antonius in Domitian's propaganda; but Domitian, after Caligula, was the first emperor who openly sought divine honours in his lifetime.

9. Writing early in the period (under Trajan, *c.* 106) Tacitus speaks of the 'rara temporum felicitas', when men could think what they wished and say what they thought (*Histories*, I, 1).

10. In the sense that they came from Roman families outside Italy, namely from Spain.

11. The plagues of this period were devastating, and were thought by contemporaries to be more terrifying than the barbarian invasions.

12. See above, p. 704, note 11.

13. Cf. Daube, *Jewish Journal of Sociology*, III (1961), pp. 3 ff. (Alan Watson).

14. Cf. most recently, with references to earlier literature, Watson, *Revue Internationale des Droits de l'Antiquité*, IX (3e sér., 1962), pp. 431 ff. (Alan Watson.)

15. Cf. Schulz, *Roman Legal Science* (Oxford, reprinted 1953), pp. 9 ff. (Alan Watson.)

16. Cf. Daube, *op. cit.* (Alan Watson.)

17. Cf. Daube, *IURA*, XII (1961), pp. 81 ff. (Alan Watson.)

18. Unless one can deduce anything from D. 22.1.32: cf. A. M. Honoré, *Studia et Documenta Historiae et Iuris*, XXVIII (1962), pp. 229 ff. (Alan Watson.)

19. Cf. Honoré, *The Jurist Gaius* (Oxford, 1962), pp. 18 ff. (Alan Watson.)

20. Cf. Honoré, *loc. cit.* (Alan Watson.)

21. Cf. Honoré, *loc. cit.: Tijdschrift voor Rechtsgeschiedenis*, XXX (1962), pp. 491 ff. (Alan Watson.)

22. There is some possibility that Gaius (a somewhat mysterious character, except that he can be shown to have lived in the second century AD) was speaking ironically. See Honoré, *op. cit.*, pp. 117 ff.

23. The developments described in this paragraph proceeded at a varying rate. For the composition of the senate see above, note 7, and the analysis, mainly relating to the Severan age, described in the latter part of the paragraph itself. As regards the functions of senators, it is true that the growth of the central administration caused a great increase, during the first century AD, in the posts open to knights: but even in the mid-second century there was no perceptible reduction in the posts held by senators, who had their earlier financial and administrative duties as well as the all-important commands in the military provinces.

24. See P. Lambrechts, *La Composition du sénat romain* (Antwerp, 1936).

25. It is impossible to agree with the brief account given of slavery under the empire. The author links the transition to other forms of exploitation with the declining role of slave labour, which in his view was the result of the fact that there were no longer masses of prisoners of war coming on to the slave markets, and that an improvement occurred in ethical norms as a consequence partly of Stoicism and partly of Christianity. Although this view is widespread, it is not supported by evidence from the sources. Not one of the Roman writers ever complained that the number of slaves was diminishing, or that slaves were becoming more expensive, as a result of the infrequency of wars. In their view the unprofitability of slave labour was mainly due to the unwillingness of slaves to perform more complex tasks and the necessity to provide continual supervision over their work. Attempts to increase their interest in the work they did by giving them various incentives did not prove very successful, and this led them to seek other forms of economic life that would be more effective than that based on slave labour exclusively. It should not be forgotten that even when wars again became frequent, from the end of the second century onwards, prisoners of war were more frequently made colons rather than slaves. This in itself shows how unprofitable slave labour had become, independently of the supply of slaves and the price they fetched.

The certain change that took place in the treatment of slaves was not the cause but the consequence of the ever-growing unprofitability of slave labour. Moreover, this change was not by any means a general rule: at the same time as an easement occurred in the condition of some slaves, particularly those who occupied privileged positions, cruel laws were applied against other slaves (e.g., the well-known *senatus consultum Silanianum*, the effect of which was felt more widely under the Empire), and a number of writers express their contempt for slaves much more clearly than was the case under the Republic, when there were still traces of patriarchal relationships and so on.

Nor is there any support in the sources for the view expressed by the author that slave labour came to be replaced by hired labour. In the treatise of Columella the landless labourers, who played an important part in Cato's account and are still mentioned by Varro, are no longer to be found at all. The exploitation of slaves gave way, not to exploitation of workers, but of *coloni* and various other groups which fell into a state of dependence of some kind upon large land-owners or tenants of imperial estates. (E. M. Shtaerman.)

26. On these questions see Columella, I, 7.8 and other passages on free *coloni*; A. H. M. Jones, *Economic History Review* (1956), pp. 194 ff.; P. A. Brunt, *Journal of Roman Studies* (1958), pp. 164 ff., reviewing W. L. Westermann, *The Slave Systems of Greek and Roman Antiquity* (Philadelphia, 1955).

It should be added that the provisions of the s.c. Silanianum of AD 10, whereby all the household of a murdered master were executed, were renewed as late as the sixth century by the Christian emperor Justinian I. As Brunt (*cit.*) has shown, the reproduction rate of US slaves in the early nineteenth century was far from low, and it is therefore dangerous to assume that the Roman slave population declined simply because wars of conquest were less common.

27. The legal origin of this distinction is obscure; it appears to start about the middle of the second century AD.

28. The *iugum*, supposed to be the minimum area of land to support a family, was the basis of Diocletian's land tax. It varied according to the nature of the crop and the productivity of the soil, but no other local conditions were taken into account.

29. For criticism of Rome's provincial government under the early Empire, see above, note 5.

30. Yet this practice was attacked, and apparently discontinued for a time, after a speech in AD 62 by Thrasea Paetus, a senator with a high reputation for virtuous ideals. His words (as recorded by Tacitus, *Annals*, XV, 20–1) are peculiarly revealing of the lofty contempt shown by early imperial senators towards the provincials.

31. Although in some provinces, Egypt for example, a simple poll tax was certainly levied, it has seemed to many scholars that *tributum capitis* was in most areas something different, namely a tax on property other than land. See J. Marquardt, *Römische Staatsverwaltung* (2nd edition, 1884), 2, pp. 198 ff.

32. The structure of early imperial finance has been the subject of prolonged controversy. An alternative view is that all regular revenues, including tribute from the 'imperial' provinces, were formally due to the public treasury (*aerarium Saturni*), and that the emperor's *fiscus* was his private property, swollen by his vast accumulation of estates in the provinces. But in any case the emperor exercised a close supervision of all public finance, from Augustus' time on. See A. H. M. Jones, *Studies in Roman Government and Law* (Oxford, 1960), pp. 99 ff.

33. This view (which has been widely held) involves amending the text of Suetonius (*Vespasian*, 8), which gives 40,000 million sesterces as the sum needed to set the state to rights. Others believe that Vespasian referred not to the revenues but to a capital sum required for war damage, new building, and so on. See T. Frank, *An Economic Survey of Ancient Rome*, V (Baltimore, 1940), p. 53, who calculates (probably too conservatively) that the total revenues in Vespasian's time were no more than 1,500 million sesterces.

34. In theory the whole Roman army was still enrolled by conscription (*dilectus*); and the system, to judge from complaints and some revolts, was rigorously applied to the recruitment of subject peoples into the 'auxiliary' units. But the legions, under the early Empire, were filled in practice by volunteers.

35. The number, in the first century AD, varied from 25 to 30 legions, or about 125,000–130,000 men.

36. The view that the population of the Empire declined progressively after the mid-second century, and that this decline was crucial, has been forcefully argued by A. E. R. Boak, *Manpower Shortage and the Decline of the Roman Empire in the West* (London, 1955). See, however, the criticisms of M. Finley, *Journal of Roman Studies*, 1958, pp. 156 ff.

CHAPTER XVII

RELIGION AND PHILOSOPHY:
THE EMERGENCE OF CHRISTIANITY TO
THE FIFTH CENTURY

I. CHINA

CHINESE thought during the Later Han, Three Kingdoms, and Northern Chin periods has little left of the freedom, intellectual curiosity, and variety of the early philosophy. Political conditions were not favourable. The authoritarian government of the Han had no use for anything except supine conformity to its own particular brand of Confucianism. The discussions between the schools of the Old Text of the Classics (*ku-wên*; it was said to have been recovered from oblivion after the 'burning of the books' in 213 BC) and the New Text (i.e., the traditional one) was chiefly of a philological character. But it still bore consequences of weight in the interpretation of the classical texts and even exerted some political influence. Liu Hsin (46 BC–AD 23), the foremost representative of the Old Text School (and as such charged by his opponents with wholesale forgery) was closely connected with Wang Mang and his so-called reforms. The chief result of the Old Text movement was a purging of alien elements, such as the *yin-yang* speculations, from Confucianism. Apart from this, Confucian thought showed no real vitality.

Still later, after the middle of the second century AD, the political decadence and economic stress led thinkers to take refuge in various brands and nuances of pessimism. 'Han thought was often disturbed, frequently apathetic, but seldom vigorous in the sense of being forward-looking and original' (Creel). Philosophers now had little possibility of exerting any influence on government or of escaping from it; they took mostly to a sort of nihilism, i.e. an attempt to flee from reality. The one exception was Wang Ch'ung (*c.*27–97 AD), the author of the *Lun-hêng*, a strong and daring attack on the study of antiquity, on superstition and other matters; he was sharply deterministic or even mechanistic in his conception of life. But his influence was practically nil.

The escapism and nihilism of the years around AD 200 led as a matter of fact to almost complete barrenness in official Confucianism and to a revival of Taoism with some original features (*hsüan-hsüeh*; called Neo-Taoism by Feng Yu-lan). In its rationalistic aspects, it took the shape of commentaries on Chuang-tzǔ by Kuo Hsiang (d. *c.*312) and Hsiang Hsiu (*c.*221–300). They defined *tao* as equivalent to nothingness and maintained that everything is spontaneously produced by itself. The non-action (*wu-wei*) theory is interpreted as allowing the natural abilities to exercise themselves fully and freely. Absolute happiness means transcending the distinction between things: it means absolute freedom. The pure sage lives according to himself but not according to others. The most picturesque representatives of Later Taoism were the Seven Sages of the Bamboo Grove, who in the second half of the third century AD gathered together for convivial conversations. 'They all revered and exalted the Void and Non-Action and disregarded the rites and law; they drank wine to excess and disdained the affairs of this world.' Their eccentricities were of course only a conscious protest against orthodox conformism. The foremost of the seven was Hsi K'ang (223–262). A love of nature, chiefly in its solitary aspects, was a common feature of this trend: later on it was to influence Chinese painting very deeply.

The official religion was rounded off on the lines sketched in Part II: it lost every remnant of a living faith and became a mere state ceremonial. Apart from the very rare sacrifice on the T'ai-shan, its most solemn rites were the imperial sacrifices to the Sovereign Earth, which after 31 BC became localized in the northern suburbs of the capital, and the imperial sacrifice to Heaven, localized in the southern suburbs. Of course here too we find a conscious following of the *yin-yang* pattern. The religious feeling of the masses could not be satisfied by these rites, however imposing. It was catered for chiefly by the development of Taoist religion (as opposed to philosophy) and by the rise of Buddhism.

Taoism absorbed the *yin-yang* elements expelled from Confucianism. Lao-tzu became an increasingly lofty and revered personality as the founder of a recognized religion. There were temples and a liturgy, and even a hereditary chief (the *t'ien-shih* of the Chang family in Szechwan), but no real clergy could be organized, and this was an incurable element of weakness. The main aims were practical and utilitarian, such as invulnerability, the prolongation of life or even immortality; and the means were of a magical kind, such as the elixir of long life, the philosopher's stone, etc. This sort of Taoism soon took political forms in the shape of secret societies, whose usual purpose was religious life and mutual help, but which could, and often did, become the originators and organizers of rebellion. Thus the famous farmer revolt of the Yellow Turbans in AD 184 was led by a Taoist society which employed magic for healing, held a conception of wrongdoing that was very much akin to the Western one of sin, and placed emphasis on public confession. As the influence of Buddhism increased, the Taoist religion borrowed from it a good many institutions and rites, and even the final form of much of its scriptures.

Buddhism was the first foreign religion to enter China. It was introduced during the first years of our era, being perhaps brought over the sea by Indian and Indonesian traders into the Yangtze-kiang valley, but immediately afterwards missionaries began to come in by the land route from the West, even from as far as Parthia. The Buddhism they introduced was mainly that of *Mahāyāna*; the emphasis lay not on its philosophy, but on the moral, disciplinary, and salvational aspects. The new religion gave to the hard-pressed Chinese peasantry and despairing officials what was most needed at that particular moment: a sense of the futility and relativity ('emptiness') of the phenomenal world and a hope for the future; either *nirvāṇa*, or, more grossly, re-birth in one of the numerous paradises. When present life was a hell, Buddhism at least gave a hope of something better in the life after death, about which Chinese thought had never bothered to enquire. Thus the first Indian texts translated into Chinese were manuals of morals and of discipline (e.g. the *Sūtra* in forty-two articles). For much of this Taoism paved the way and supplied the technical terms; indeed the most interesting work of early Buddhist apologetic, the *Mou-tzŭ* of *c.*AD 200, employs Taoist terms and seems to consider Buddhism as another form of Taoism.

The new religion experienced tremendous growth, and during the period of North-South division (317–589) it was the one trend of thought that dominated Chinese spiritual life, first among the masses as a living religion, and somewhat later also among the higher classes and at the various courts as a philosophy of life. Soon it became utterly engrained in Chinese life and was hardly considered any longer as a foreign religion. Its main external characteristic was the existence of a monastic order, i.e. of a clergy. Monasteries became a centre of religious refuge, but also of flourishing economic interests, which contributed to an increasing hold by the new religion on the peasant masses.

2. INDIA

The shift of values in the Indian pantheon went on, slowly but unceasingly. By the time of the Guptas the old Vedic gods had become fossilized remnants of the past, and few people paid service to them. The new pantheon found its glorification in the *Purāṇa*, most of which belong to this epoch. They proclaim the glory of Brahmā, the creator (who remained an abstract figure and never enjoyed popular worship); of Viṣṇu, the preserver; and of Śiva, the destroyer. Puranic mythology replaced the Vedic one for the people.

Brahmanism was developing into Hinduism, and the latter began to crystallize into two main tendencies, Viṣṇuism and Śivaism. However, hostility between the two was seldom violent, and there was no mutual exclusion.[1] The supreme God was worshipped in the form of Viṣṇu by some and in the form of Śiva by others, and that was all. Two essential elements are common to both faiths. One is emotional devotion (*bhakti*) to the god; it can lead to immediate contemplation of the deity (in Viṣṇuism) or to the merging and identification of the devotee with it (in Śivaism). The other is *prasāda*, the grace of the god that brings salvation to the devotee. The first historically recognizable shape assumed by Viṣṇuism is the *Bhāgavata* faith, which began in the Mathura region and was connected with Vāsudeva-Kṛṣṇa. The Besnagar inscription of Heliodorus, the Greek ambassador of the Greek king Antialcidas (second century BC), proclaims his *Bhāgavata* faith. Kṛṣṇa, at first a warrior god (so he appears in the *Mahābhārata* later assumed a dominantly pastoral character. Mathura became a holy place, as the theatre of his sport with the shepherd girls. By the time the *Bhāgavad-gītā* was written, his identification with Viṣṇu was nearly complete.

The accretion of miscellaneous religious material around the central figure of Viṣṇu was systematized during this period in the theory of the incarnations (*avatāra*), by which Viṣṇu descended on earth in various forms in order to free it from some calamity or oppressor. The number of the *avatāra* increased until it was finally fixed at ten. According to the usual list (as finally settled much later), the first three are theriomorphic (Fish, Tortoise, Boar). The next two are half-human or human (Man-Lion, Dwarf). The next three are heroes or gods identified with Viṣṇu (Paraśurāma, Rāma, Kṛṣṇa). The ninth is the Buddha, whose role is to lead wicked men to perdition with false doctrines. The tenth and last has yet to appear: it is Kalkī, who will descend on earth to destroy the wicked and to restore purity, a conception possibly influenced by Iranian ideas. Of course the incarnations were particularly well suited to artistic description and gave rise to a rich iconography.

Another element of the Gupta period is the figure of Lakṣmī (or Śrī), the wife of Viṣṇu and the goddess of beauty and good fortune.

The very ancient god Śiva first became the centre of a definite religious sect with the rise of the Pāśupata (about the first century AD), which has survived to the present day. But more important was the increasing popularity of the cult of Śiva or Mahādeva. It became widely diffused in the north (chiefly in Kashmir), but, the Guptas being Viṣṇuite, it is not surprising that its main centre was rather in the south, mainly around Kāñcipuram, but also farther south.² It was intimately connected with Dravidian beliefs and with the Tamil poetry of the *Nayanar*. Later on, perhaps as the result of a syncretism with a pre-Aryan idea, the phallus (*liṅga*) became Śiva's symbol. The god soon was associated with an originally independent mythological cycle, that of the *śakti*, the energetic female principle. The legends of Śiva now centred around his relation with his *śakti* Umā or Pārvatī, also called in her terrific aspects Durgā and Kālī. Hence the unmistakable sexual element in Śivaite lore: yet this element never became its main characteristic to the same extent as the terrific god who destroys so that new life may arise. Later on, Śivaism developed an independent school of philosophy, based, not on the *Vedas*, but on the revelations of Śiva, the *Āgamas*, but it falls outside the chronological limits of this volume.

Hinduism was carried by emigrants and refugees to Indonesia and to the coastal regions of south-east Asia, where in this period a slow process of Indianization was going on and a Greater India was taking shape. Śivaism became the cult of the royal family in Fu-nan (Cambodia) and in Champa (central Vietnam). But our information on religious conditions in Greater India before AD 400 is too scanty to allow any generalization.

Philosophical speculation went on steadily, and on the basis laid down in the preceding period the six classical systems (*darśana*) came into existence. Each of them centres round a main text (*sūtra*), which is usually very concise and obscure and lends itself to great latitude in interpretation. The *sūtras* go back to different ages that are in no way connected with the antiquity of the respective systems; the *Sāṅkhya-kārikā* is the most recent of them, although the *Sāṅkhya* school is among the earliest and its beginnings are evident already in some *Upaniṣad*. The six *darśanas* are the following.

(1-2) *Sāṅkhya* and *Yoga*. *Sāṅkhya* is a complete system of metaphysics, which postulates one primitive principle, the *prakṛti* (primordial matter). The latter consists of three constituents (*guṇa*), which partake of both the conception of modes of being and of forms: they are *sattva* (lightness, good, intelligence), *rajas* (passion, anger, energy), *tamas* (darkness, fullness, heaviness). The *guṇas* are the foundations of knowledge, action, and rest respectively. The universe consists of the ever-changing relations and combinations in varying quantities of the three *guṇas*. In front of the one *prakṛti* there are the individual souls (*puruṣa*), infinite in number. There is no communication at all between the *puruṣas* and the *prakṛti*, but the latter attracts the soul like a lode-iron, and the soul imagines itself to be drawn into the turmoil of nature; their relation is said to be similar to that of the girl-dancer and of the onlooker. The whole universe and its manifestations are unfolded through a series of twenty-five stages or truths (*tattva*) by this contact. *Prakṛti* is unconscious but dynamic, *puruṣa* is conscious but static. Salvation can be attained through the recognition of the absolute diversity of *puruṣa* and of the complex process evolving from *prakṛti*. The soul then returns to its state of purity and eternal untroubled isolation. God has no part in this, and *Sāṅkhya* is wholly atheistic.

Yoga in a wider sense is a psycho-physiological discipline associated with all sorts of philosophical theories.[3] In its narrower sense, as one of the six classical systems of philosophy, it is supplementary to *Sāṅkhya*. It deals not with metaphysics, but with the psychological technique and discipline through which truth may be comprehended. Its aim is to reach the complete and final quiescence of all the functions and modes of the mind (*citta-vṛtti-nirodha*). This is achieved on the basis of a pneumatic theory, by controlling the breath of life and conveying it into the proper channels of the body through the complete control of mind and muscles, which can be achieved by a series of psycho-physical exercises. *Yoga* admits of a God, but only as an indifferent presence, which serves as the object of meditation.

(3-4) *Nyāya* and *Vaiśeṣika*. *Vaiśeṣika* is an atomistic theory. According to it, the world is real in itself; it is a conglomeration of smaller and smaller parts, ending in indivisible components called *paramāṇu* (atom). It is classified in six categories (*padārtha*): substance (*dravya*), quality (*guṇa*), action

(*karman*), generality (*sāmānya*), particularity (*viśeṣa*), inheritance (*samavāya*).
The souls (*ātman*) exist but are inert; their coming into activity depends on
the contact with the organs of sense by the agency of an atomic, independent,
eternal entity, the mind (*manas*). Salvation is attained when a knowledge of
the *padārthas* causes the soul to return to its primitive inactivity, immobility,
unconsciousness. Early *Vaiśeṣika* was atheistic; but after the commentator
Praśastapāda (fifth century) it came to recognize the existence of a God,
who is the efficient creator of the universe out of the atoms existing *ab
aeterno*. He is also the regulator of *karman*, whose automaticism, usually
absolute in Indian thought, comes thus to be mitigated only in *Vaiśeṣika*.

Nyāya is the theory of logic. It starts from the same premises as *Vaiśeṣika*
(reality of the universe, God, and the soul), but concerns itself almost
exclusively with the sources of knowledge and the means for reaching them
(*pramāṇa*). The sources of knowledge are four: direct perception (*pratyakṣa*),
inference (*anumāna*), analogy (*upamāna*), authority (*śabda*, the *Vedas*). The
mainstay of inference is the syllogism, which is not three-membered as with
Aristotle, but consists of five propositions: premise (*pratijñā*), reason (*hetu*),
example (*udaharaṇa* or *dṛṣṭānta*), application of the example to the argument
under discussion (*upanaya*), conclusion (*nigamana*). The standard example
of a syllogism is the following: 'There is fire in yonder mountain; for there
is smoke in it; wherever there is smoke, there is fire, as in the kitchen; there
is smoke in the mountain; therefore, there must be fire in it.'

(5–6) *Mīmāṃsā* and *Vedānta*, also called *Pūrvamīmaṃsā* and *Uttaramī-
māṃsā*. These are in reality two faces of the same system originally aimed at
interpreting the *Vedas*. *Mīmāṃsā* is really but a continuation of the *Brāhmanas*; it is not a philosophy, but a symbology of ritualism. For it, the
source of all knowledge are the *Vedas*, which are existing '*ab aeterno*'. The
sacrifice is all in all, and *Mīmāṃsā* denies the existence of a creating God
and maintains that the Vedic gods are mere names, mentioned only as an
invitation to the sacrifice, which is valid in itself. The universe is real. The
souls are bound to ceaseless transmigrations, from which only the sacrificial
rite can free them through the complete destruction of *karman*.

Vedānta, on the contrary, is a complete monistic philosophy, reaching
back to the *Upaniṣads* and giving rise to several most important schools in
the Middle Ages, when it became by far the most important school of Indian
thought. In early *Vedānta* the only reality is the *ātman* or *brahman*, who is
ineffable and indefinable. The world is but a mirage and has no existence
of its own. Of course the central problem (as in all monism) is to explain the
relation existing between the absolute and the phenomenal world. And thus
in later developments this monism came to be understood in various forms
and nuances, which cannot concern us here. In its earliest aspects *Vedānta*
is identical with the philosophy of the *Upaniṣads* and of the *Bhagavadgītā*,
of which we have spoken already. At a later date its central text became the
Brahmasūtra of Bādarāyana (third century AD); but they are only the mnem-

onic phrases (and sometimes single isolated catchwords, now incomprehensible) of an oral tradition that has been lost, and thus lend themselves to any sort of interpretation. The classical *Vedānta*, as a complete system, begins only with *Śaṅkara* (c.788–820), and thus its description cannot be included in this volume.

In addition to the six *darśanas*, minor trends of thought also existed. Such were the materialistic, agnostic, and fatalistic currents, survivals from the previous period. Then there were the philosophical theories of the grammarians about word and sound (*śabda*), and the speculations of the medical schools on microcosm and macrocosm; as we had occasion to point out elsewhere, Indian medicine had developed a well-balanced pneumatic theory.

Jainism was always a very conservative creed, and this prevented its expansion, but enabled it to survive in India to the present day. There was no noteworthy doctrinal evolution. What controversies there were, took place around minor points of discipline. Thus the results of the Pāṭaliputra council of the third century BC were not accepted by a part of the community, which under the guidance of Bhadrabāhu had taken refuge in the far south because of a long-protracted famine. Afterwards (first century AD) this led to a partition of the community which has lasted to this day. The followers of Sthūlabhadra and of the Pāṭaliputra council became the *śvetāmbaras*, wearing white robes. The descendants of the dissidents led by Bhadrabāhu became the *Digambara*, who wore no clothes at all (but later they had to abandon this peculiarity), and denied the authenticity of the texts of the other sect; the other points of difference were unimportant. Afterwards (fifth century AD) the *śvetāmbaras* codified their tradition in a canon (*āgama*) written in Ardhamāgadhī, a Prakrit dialect. The original texts, the *puvva* (Skr. *pūrva*), being transmitted orally, were gradually lost, and the canon of the fifth century consisted of 12 *aṅga* (main texts), 5 *uvaṅga* (Skr. *upāṅga*; subsidiary texts), 10 *painna* (Skr. *prakīrṇaka*, i.e. varia) and 6 *cheyasutta* (Skr. *chedasūtra*), mainly on ritual. The *Digambaras* have no canon and rely on systematic treatises of a later period.

The case of Buddhism is quite different. It manifested quite early a lively intellectual activity and a capacity for change and adaptation, which made it a missionary creed and thus a world religion. A few of the early sects maintained their individuality and carried out a good deal of doctrinal and missionary activity (chiefly in central Asia) even in the Gupta period. Such were the *Sarvāstvādin* and the *Sammitīya*. But the most important of them were the *Theravādin*, who passed nearly unchanged through the ages with a conservative capacity which reminds one of Jainism. Having taken definite shape as far back as the third century BC, the sect spread to several regions of India, where it flourished for a long period; its limitation to Ceylon belongs to a later age. *Theravāda* doctrine remained very near to early Buddhism. It based itself on the theory of the twelvefold causal nexus (*pratītya-samut-pāda*), which describes the flowing of thought from one experience to the next. The recognition of this process allows it to be stopped and to realize *nirvāṇa*. There is no Self. Human personality is but a compound of five ingredients (*skandha*): corporeity (*rūpa*), perception (*vedanā*), sensation (*saṃjñā*), psychic coefficients (*saṃskāra*; the traces left by the former *karman*, which influence the character and disposition of man), and conscience (*vijñāna*). Here the problem presents itself: who is the sufferer of the consequences of *karman*, if no self exists? This question was hotly debated by the various schools, but was more circumvented than solved by *Theravāda*. The great systematizer of Ceylonese *Theravāda* was Buddhaghoṣa (fifth century), a most fertile commentator, but not an original thinker. We can here only mention in passing the doctrinal activity of the *Sarvāstivādin*, which culminated in a *magnum opus*, the *Abhidharmakośa* of the younger Vasubandhu (*c.*AD 400—480?).

In a manner largely independent (as it seems) of the old school and their philosophical interests, a quite new way of looking at the Buddha and at the central points of his teaching came into being and formed the base for a development of Buddhism which is called the Great Vehicle (*Mahāyāna*). This is first adumbrated in the apodeictic statements of the *Prajñāpāramitā* literature, around the beginning of our era or even earlier. These works explained and propounded the need of, and the means of attaining, the highest degree (*pāramitā*) of a particular virtue. There were at first six of them: liberality (*dāna*), righteousness (*śīla*), endurance (*kṣānti*), mental energy (*vīrya*), mental concentration (*dhyāna*), intelligence (*prajñā*). Later on four others were added. These supreme perfections of virtue are a necessary requisite for the attainment of Buddhahood. This was the core of *Mahāyāna* ethic.

But even more important were some dialectical elements included in the *Prajñāpāramitā* literature, to which a systematic elaboration was first given by Nāgārjuna, a rather mysterious personality who lived probably in the second century AD. His system, the *Madhyamika* (Middle One), consists in the consequent and pitiless 'reductio ad absurdum' of all existence, by means of a logical process. Nāgārjuna shows that no thing is existent 'per se'; it exists only in so far as it can be brought into relation with other things. Its individuality is imaginary, conventional, apparent (*saṃvṛtti*); every thing is void (*śūnya*), i.e. relative.[4] True knowledge is only that one which discovers the supreme identity beyond all opposites; in this identity *saṃsāra* and Buddha are equivalent. Even thought itself is destroyed.

The *Madhyamika* position was carried one step farther by the *Vijñānavādin* or *Yogācāra* school, whose main representatives were Asaṅga and his brother Vasubandhu the elder (fourth century). According to them, the ultimate reality is not the destruction of thought, but thought itself, the absolute and luminous cosmic conscience. It is *ālaya-vijñāna*, the 'store-knowledge' from which, through a spontaneous manifestation, the individual series or chains of thought arise. This thought is not relative, it is creative. Things are but a non-real projection of pure subjectivity; the latter is void (*śūnya*), not in itself, but in relation with its mode of manifestation, i.e. with its dichotomy of subject and object.

Thus *Mahāyāna* not only rejected the self, like the earlier schools, but also negated the reality of the universe and the existence of God. This was done by the processes of an ever-perfected and refined logic, of which the most famous master was Daināga (*c.*470–530).

Mahāyāna not only developed an original philosophy; it became differentiated from the earlier schools and chiefly from *Theravāda* also on practical grounds, which can be polarized around two main problems. One was the aim of the Buddhist monk. For *Theravāda* it is the old goal of the *arhat*, i.e. of the man who obtains illumination and consequently enters *nirvāṇa*, being thus extinguished. For *Mahāyāna* it is the *bodhisattva*, i.e. the man who has obtained illumination and could enter *nirvāṇa*, but does not; out of compassion (*karuṇā*) for the other things he delays this final act and remains in the *saṃsāra* in order to lead others on the same path by his teaching and example—a fine and novel conception, to which non-Indian influence may have contributed to a certain degree. The other point of difference is the person of the Buddha. For the *Theravāda* he is the Master, the great Teacher, perhaps a super-man, but a man nonetheless. For *Mahāyāna* he becomes the symbol of the absolute; his historical figure fades away and gives place to his hypostasis, the Five Buddhas (*Pañcatathāgata*): *Vairocana*, *Absobhya*, *Ratnasambhava*, *Amoghasiddhi*, *Amitābha*, with a complex symbolism and a rigid but luxuriant iconography. From this beginning a bewildering Pantheon of Buddhas and *Bodhisattvas* developed, to which a solemn and rich cult was rendered with a colourful liturgy.

The followers of *Mahāyāna* claimed that theirs was the shortest way to release, and gave to their opponents (the *Theravāda*, *Sarvāstivādin* and cognate schools) the disparaging name of Little Vehicle (*Hīnayāna*). Still, both belonged to the same faith; and in order to explain their coexistence, the theory of the double truth was invented in *Mahāyāna* circles. The Buddha's revelation was on a twofold plane, a visible, conventional one (*saṃvṛttisatya*) and a higher, absolute one (*paramārthasatya*), *Hīnayāna* corresponding to the former and *Mahāyāna* to the latter.

In the expansion of Buddhism in general and of *Mahāyāna* in particular a great role was played by the Kuṣāṇa kingdom in the first centuries A D. With its tolerance and acceptance of all creeds, with the personal leanings of some kings (chiefly Kaniṣka) toward Buddhism, with its favourable geographic position astride the Hindu Kush, from the Syr-darya to the Ganges, it became the link between India and the outer world and the passage through which Buddhist missionaries brought their faith into central Asia. The oases north and south of the Tarim (Kucha, Karashahr, Kashgar, Khotan, Niya) became seats of flourishing schools both of *Mahāyāna* and of *Hīnayāna*. Texts were translated and even compiled in the local Indo-European languages (Kuchean and Karashahri, Khotanese Śaka). The central Asian communities in their turn played an all-important role in the introduction of Buddhism into China. The first missionaries to northern China came from the Tarim basin, and the prince of the early translators, Kumārajīva (344–413), was the son of an Indian minister; he was born in Kucha and studied in Kashmir, and was brought, rather against his will, from Kucha to China in 401. By the third century Buddhism had flourishing communities throughout China, and by the fifth century it was rapidly becoming the religion of the masses, especially in the north. In 372 Chinese monks first carried it to Korea, and thence it passed into Japan.

The expansion of *Mahāyāna* Buddhism in south-east Asia and Indonesia was not less imposing, although almost all the extant evidence refers to a later period and cannot be used here. In Greater India *Mahāyāna* was dominant; *Hīnayāna* played a secondary role, but was seldom completely absent from the scene.

Foreign influences on Indian religious thought have been often supposed, but seldom demonstrated. One instance might be the *Bodhisattva* doctrine. The other may be a possible influence of the Gnostic schools of western Asia, penetrating in India through the Kuṣāṇa empire and giving birth toward the end of this epoch, to the *Tantra* movement. It is essentially the expression of the religious feeling of the lower classes and was absolutely esoteric in character. To put the case in the most general terms, it aimed at obtaining direct access to ultimate reality or pure consciousness by the medium of the latter's manifestations in the phenomenal world. These manifestations or 'powers' were represented mainly as feminine deities or symbols, and thus the *Tantras* largely resorted to a sexual symbolism even of crude aspects.[5] This current was present in all the great religions of the time, Jainism excepted, and we have Viṣṇuite, Śivaite and Buddhist *Tantras*. But the chronology of this trend and the degree of its connexion (if any at all) with Gnostic thought are very debatable points.

3. PERSIA

We have already explained that the Arsacid kings of Parthia did not pursue a Zoroastrian religious policy of an exclusive kind. They inclined towards tolerance, and allowed syncretistic ideas. This was still their attitude towards religion in the first century A D, when the brother of Vologaeses I came to Rome in 63 and paraded the cult of Mithras. The last Arsacid kings showed more sympathy with the intolerance and exclusiveness of the Magi, and when they fell a similar tendency was shown by the first Sassanid king, Ardashir I, who came to the throne in 224. It was he who devised the idea of making Zoroastrianism a state religion.

But the implementation of this programme was for some time interrupted by the activity of Mani, the creator of a new religion. He was born in 215 of a family related to the Arsacids, and his father, Patek, had been a member of the Gnostic movement known as the 'Baptists'. It was said that his mission had been revealed to him by Parakletos (the Holy Spirit), whereby he became the Messenger or Apostle of Light, 'the seal of the Prophets'. This revelation was supposed to have taken place in 240–241, and it was at this time that he began his reforming propaganda. He claimed to be the last of the Apostles, after Adam, Buddha, and Christ, each of whom had been misunderstood by his successors and had revealed only a part of the Truth. When the twelfth millennium of the world's life was nearing its close, he proposed to reveal the Truth in its entirety. In reality he derived inspiration and ideas from each one of the prophets who had gone before him, or rather from the religions associated with those prophets, in the form which they had assumed after the lapse of time. In regard to Zoroastrianism, for instance, his system reflected the changes brought about by Zervanism, and also the influence of the Mithras cult, the priestly vestments of which were used in his ritual. But he also drew heavily on Gnostic doctrines. He maintained that human life was a temporary union of spirit and matter, good and evil, light and darkness. The human soul is a tiny particle of light, menaced, polluted, and made sickly by evil; but by means of the intellect it can recognize its own nature, attain salvation, and so contribute to the salvation of the God himself of which it is a part (the Saviour saved).

There are three basic ideas behind the religious reform of Mani (Manichaeism). (1) Though other religions are directed essentially at specific and isolated groups of people, Mani's religion, which was designed to comprise and supersede the rest, was to be universal and also adaptable to the needs of individual nations (this gave rise to the various forms of Manichaeism). (2) The new religion was to spread among the peoples by means of missionary work, begun by Mani himself and carried on by his disciples. (3) The faith must be established in writing, to prevent its essential portions being altered or distorted. To this end Mani published seven works: the first was the *Shahbhuragan*, dedicated to King Shahpuhr I (240–271), who had allowed him to preach the new faith in the belief that it might unify the thought of his people and bring their religions into a single whole (in 260 Mani accompanied his king on his campaign against Valerian); the others were the *Living Evangelist*, the *Treasury of Life*, the *Tractatus*, the *Book of Secrets*, the *Book of Giants*, and the *Letters*. To these should perhaps be added a *Book of Conversations and Sermons* and a work entitled *Psalms and Prayers*.

Mani also devised a complete soteriological cosmogony, partly based on earlier ideas. He conceived, for example, that the world's evolution had three stages. In the first the two eternal principles separated from each other: the principle of the Good or of the Father of Greatness (the Christian God the Father and the Mazdean Zerian), whose dominion was in the North, and in the South the principle of the Spirit of Darkness (corresponding to the Devil and to Ahriman). In the second stage the two principles mingled again, and in the third they once more became separate. In the five dwellings of the God of the Good are intelligence, reason, thought, reflection, and will; and in the five abysses of the kingdom of Evil are the smoke which suffocates, the fire which devours, the wind which destroys, the water which poisons, and the darkness. Man passes through three processes which one after another give him some salvation; first, abstinence from many things, then a process of purification, and lastly worship of the divine being by prayer, fasting, and attendance at solemn feasts. The hierarchy of the faithful, in descending order, is composed of Apostles or Masters, Bishops, Priests, the Elect (who live a community life in temple-convents), and the Hearers or catechumens.

Among Mani's disciples Adda, Tomaso, and Herma were active in the East, Egypt, and Syria respectively, and it was largely due to their zealous missions that the religion made rapid ground. But it soon ran into serious difficulties as well. When Bahram I came to the Sassanid throne in 273 the Zoroastrian priests gained acceptance of their view that a state religion was essential. All output of art and literature had been in the hands of these priests, and they had been in charge of the interpretation of those sacred texts on which Persian culture was founded, as well as assuming decisive powers in social and legal matters. So it was of the first importance to them, materially as well as spiritually, that their own religion should be adopted by the state beyond all possibility of challenge. In their view there must be a single cult drawn up in accordance with ancient Persian tradition; and this was to be adopted by all without borrowings from outside. All religions which threatened to dissolve the religious unity of the empire must be stamped out, whereas Mani's policy would have brought such religions into a larger synthesis and so kept them alive. Mani was imprisoned and then martyred, his body being polluted and dismembered; and about twenty years later, in 297, his faith was for the first time persecuted in the Roman world as well, upon orders from Diocletian. Zoroastrianism as a state religion became one of the main principles of government for several of the later Sassanids, such as Hormizd, and the first three Bahrām rulers. It was not in fact a pure form of Zoroastrianism. Some place was allowed to other deities of regional importance, such as Mihr (or Mithra), Anāhitā, Bahrām, Ādhur, and Bēduxt, their introduction being due to Mani's great enemy Kartēr, who was both chief Magus of Ahura Mazda and priest of the Fire. There were of course gradual stages in the process by which the Sassanids imposed a state religion and began to persecute others: for example, the Christians were still tolerated in the days of Hormizd II (302–309), but were persecuted under Shahpuhr II (309–379). But political reasons were in part responsible for this. In the interval Christianity had become the official religion of the Roman empire, and its adherents were seen as the supporters of a power which was Persia's enemy. Later on, when Yezdegert I (395–420) inclined to a policy of tolerance once more, he acquired the reputation of being a thoroughly wicked ruler.

4. RELIGION IN ROMAN IMPERIAL TIMES

During the imperial period the protocol of services connected with the official cult, on the lines laid down by Augustus, became increasingly different from the practices of personal religion. At Rome the priests both of the imperial cult and of the numerous miscellaneous divinities continued to perform their ceremonies, and the ever-increasing number of festivals in honour of these gods were held as before. There was the same regularity of ceremonies in the provinces, at any rate as long as the economic situation permitted. There they were carried out by the priests of the cult of Dea Roma and the deified emperors,[6] to whom temples were set up in the chief cities, such as Ephesus, Miletus, Smyrna, or Lugdunum.[7] Once a year a principal celebration was held in capital towns, to which delegates from all over the province came to sacrifice and so to attest their loyalty to Rome and the empire. To provide evidence of its loyalty every city would erect its own temple to Juppiter Maximus, the guardian of Rome, and every colony had its Capitolium in imitation of that in the metropolis.

In its own turn the Roman government would intervene to protect the most famous homes of the traditional cults in provincial cities, or to preserve and improve religious organizations. In Greece, for example, they modernized the Delphic Amphictiony, and also created the *synedrion* of Zeus Panhellenius with its seat at Athens.

But none of this was more than a formal demonstration of political loyalty and respect for tradition.[8] It did little to touch the minds of either citizens or subjects, both of whom attended to such functions either because they were compelled or because they thought it was in their interest to do so.[9] In every part of the empire, especially in the West, it was not really the official cults which were of serious interest to individuals so much as the old divinities which had been worshipped by their fathers: some of these retained their original names and cult practices, others had altered as the result of syncretism. Moreover some of the ancient shrines still survived and continued to draw their devotees. The people of Latium, for example, continued to worship Silvanus as their principal deity,[10] as well as Juppiter and Hercules, and they still flocked to the temples of Lavinium, Antium, Aricia, Praeneste, and Tibur. In Gaul (as in north Italy, Britain and Spain), many native gods were worshipped, not only under their syncretistic names of Mars and Apollo, but under the names they bore of old, such as Teutates, Caturix, Dunatis, Rigisamus (all these identified with Mars), or Boruo, Grannus, Siannus, and other names which were embraced under the single figure of Apollo.[11]

While, however, these primitive native cults retained local importance in the West, being mainly worshipped by soldiers and traders abroad, there were quite a number of Eastern cults which had much more potentiality for expansion. Not only had they many more means of entry to various parts of the empire, being carried by slaves, itinerant priests, Chaldeans, and the like, as well as by soldiers and traders; even more important were the attractive features of their ritual and the satisfaction they gave to the intimate longings of their catechumens.[12] Many indeed were simply drawn to them by impressive and theatrical ceremonial of an orgiastic kind, which could even excite a state of ecstasy. Or again, there were mysterious performances in 'mime', depicting, for example, the death and resurrection of the god, or his entry to the underworld; and use was made of spectacular devices, such as play with lights, gorgeous clothing, or statues which spoke. There were miracle rites, such as healings, oracles, or divination; rites of violence, like the slaughter of bulls and rams or the drawing of entrails; and mystery rites like purification. Wild songs and dances would be performed, and many other means of attracting worshippers. Yet many came to these cults rather as a means of satisfying more exalted aspirations. They provided a direct relationship between worshippers and their gods, and gave tormented spirits a hope of attaining eternal happiness in another world. They proved the existence of everlasting life and the victory over misfortune and pain by pointing to the example of the dying and resurrected god. Finally they were addressed to all classes and all peoples, without any exclusiveness or differences of race and caste.[13]

These cults, which attained their greatest diffusion and importance in the Severan period, were derived principally from Syria and adjacent areas. The divinities included Hadad of Heliopolis (Juppiter Heliopolitanus), Baal of Damascus (Juppiter Damascenus), Baal of Doliche in Commagene (Juppiter Dolichenus), Atargatis of Bambyce or Hierapolis (Dea Syria), Malakbal of Palmyra, and Baal of Emesa. This last was a nature god worshipped by Elagabalus, who celebrated his ritual marriage with the Carthaginian Tanit (Dea Caelestis). Besides these there were the cults of Teandrius and Manaf, which originated in Arabia; and a number of others were further consolidated, such as the Phrygian cults of Cybele and Attis which Claudius had brought in, or the Egyptian Isis and Osiris who received sanction from Caligula, and Serapis who was fully introduced by Caracalla.[14] These forty years from the accession of Septimius Severus to the death of Severus Alexander, which we have described as the peak period, was one in which the rulers of Rome were Orientals or men with Eastern connections. It was at this time too that the syncretized cult of solar divinities acquired overriding importance in the religious ideas of individual emperors, a phenomenon which reached its climax under Aurelian half a century later. One such cult, that of Mithras, a divinity of Iranian origin, had entered Rome as early as Pompey's day. He was God of Light and of the Sun, the ordainer of the world, and was identified with all the sun-gods of the classical world (Apollo, Helios, Juppiter, Serapis, and so on); but he became of paramount importance when the Babylonian conceptions of astronomy and astrology, after many thousand years of history, found new sponsors among the Chaldean pantheists and the

Stoics. For them the sun was the heart and life-giver of the macrocosm and of the microcosm too; for the human soul was a particle of the sun. As early as Septimius Severus' reign the Augusta, Julia Domna, commissioned Philostratus to write a life of the mythical Apollonius of Tyana, priest of the Sun, a work which may be compared with the Gospels. Then Elagabalus, himself a Sun priest, tried to impose a monotheistic religion of the Sun on the empire, subordinating all other divine figures to his own god; and the same conception was carried on by Severus Alexander, who in his youth had been priest of the Sun at Emesa.[15] But the solar cult with its syncretisms had also very great importance in the Balkan lands. If we can believe Origen, the emperor Maximinus Thrax regarded the sun as the *Deus Maximus*; and some time later Aurelian, whose mother was a priestess of the Sun, assumed the pontificate of this divinity himself and attempted to make his god the supreme god of the empire. This was a mirage which, even after the Christian faith had been victorious for so long, could still move the pagan soul of Macrobius when he composed his *Saturnalia* and his commentary on Cicero's *Somnium Scipionis* in the full tide of the fifth century.

But for the more educated pagans the most attractive forms of religion were the more spiritual and refined ideas provided by the philosophers. Indeed apart from the atheistic Epicureans, who by *c.*AD 150 were decadent and kept at arm's length, all schools liked to make a study of religious problems; and in so doing they moved continually nearer to one another, each doctrine taking on successive doses of contamination. The Platonists, and after them the Neoplatonists, attached great importance to the 'demons' which they interposed between God and the world. The Stoics, although they insisted on the moral purpose of human life, preached obedience to the fate laid down by the divinity which arranges and protects the *cosmos*. Similar tendencies were shown by the neo-Pythagoreans. All these philosophers inclined to belief in a supreme divinity, common to all peoples, who intervened in the life of nations and individuals through the intermediary of certain beings; and these beings were naturally identified with the *numina* of traditional religions, they in turn being syncretized on a variety of principles. It was also widely held by the philosophers that mystic surrender, profound feeling, and fervent faith could enable man to reach his God and obtain divine favour; and there was general belief in a divine providence, which came to the assistance of mankind and was often made manifest in miraculous ways.

The more lofty thinkers were studying the problem of intermediary beings and demonology from a philosophical and theological standpoint. But men who were more excited about practical results were comparing the conclusions of these theories with the old ideas about magic, miracle-working, and oracles. They claimed that a man who was initiated into divine secrets was enabled to be in communion with God, and they thus embarked on a fully-fledged doctrine, the so-called Pagan Gnosis, of 'theurgy' (occultism).

Chaldeans and their like, varying from inspired mystics to rascally busy-bodies, toured the world and approached people who were inclined to their own way of thinking. Their preaching and work was that of astrologers, magicians, and sorcerers; they laid claim to divine men's thoughts and reveal secrets, to be learned in magic practices and understand the speech of animals, to heal sickness and avert cataclysms and plagues. In literature they have left their mark in Apuleius' *Golden Ass* and in the fantastic life which Philostratus wrote about a genuine prototype of such people, namely Apollonius of Tyana. Under Constantine the philosopher Iamblichus wrote praises of the Chaldean Julianus, who had preached the 'religion of the Fire' in Marcus Aurelius' day. Even the severe Neoplatonists who followed Plotinus, men like Porphyry and Iamblichus, put their trust in theurgy. They in their turn influenced the thought of Julian the Apostate.[16]

5. JUDAISM

After Pompey's conquest and the loss of Jewish political independence pagan influence made headway even in Judaea; and as a reaction the most ardent forms of nationalism grew up, whose devotees at times attained a kind of religious and political exaltation. In addition the Jewish people were torn by other divisions, resulting from the formation of castes and parties which differed on the principles to be applied in interpreting the Law and on their attitude to the foreign ruler. The Sadducees were the highest priests, but their beliefs were rather conservative and in favour of an alliance with Parthia, and later of collaboration with the Romans. The Pharisees ('separate') were adherents of novel ethical ideas and ritual, and rigid observers of their interpretation of the Bible and oral tradition; they detested the Romans (though favouring peace) and jealously guarded any form of tradition belonging to the Chosen People.

But within Hebrew religion there existed another much deeper source of conflict, which can be observed in the sacred writings and at times gave rise to dramatic incidents and impressive dénouements. We refer here to the continuous struggle between 'Legalism' and 'Prophetism', the former term implying that scrupulous observance of a vast set of ordinances which is well known to us already, the latter the free response to an irresistible call from heaven to utter preaching, with the object of recalling one's fellow-countrymen to the Lord's service. Both these features are found in Judaism, and it is impossible to dwell on one at the expense of the other if one wants to have an exact conception of Jewish religion. Yet in the period preceding the teaching of Jesus, the adherents of 'Prophetism' were in religious and political opposition against the pro-Roman Jewish governments, while Legalism had gained the upper hand, and had become simply a set of external forms and an arid commentary on the Mosaic Law (we are told of 600 or more commandments or prohibitions collected by the Rabbis in their commentaries, so meticulous that any movement made by a devotee was in danger of being wrong). Apart from anything else the attitude involved a distortion of the Hebrew concept of religion, since the Law was not just a piece of legislation or set of statutes. The Law was the revelation of God's will, to which the faithful must conform, and obedience to it meant fulfilment of the Covenant. So the Hebrew faith[17] was less belief in a Truth than action in accordance with God's word.

In recent years unexpected and unmistakable light has been cast on the state of Jewish religion by a series of fortunate discoveries in some caves in the Desert of Judah, a few miles from the north-west corner of the Dead Sea. Hidden in jars were documents of vast importance written on skins or papyrus in Hebrew, Aramaic, and Greek of the first century BC, and also some miscellaneous objects including coins. Even now the exploration of the district cannot be regarded as complete. We do not propose here to tell the exciting story of these discoveries or to attempt an analysis of the complex critical questions connected with them. The evidence is still too fluid, and not all the material has yet been edited. But it is essential to give a broad outline of some possible conclusions, following the close studies made by a number of scholars in this field, who have competed nobly with one another to further our understanding of the matter. The conclusions in question cannot be considered as absolutely definite, but they embrace what has become the consensus of opinion among many scholars. First we must catalogue the material at our disposal.

a. *The Essenes*

The existence and nature of the Essene sect have long been known from the evidence of Josephus, Philo, and Pliny, but the Dead Sea manuscripts and in particular the 'Manual on Discipline' (the rule of the community in question) have enabled us to penetrate the Essene [18] world more deeply than before, and have made possible a better interpretation of other documents (the so-called Zadokite Fragments or *Document of Damascus*) which have been in our possession for a long time. The caves of Qumrân have also yielded several portions of the Bible, both in fragments and in entire books (in particular two copies of *Isaiah* and a number of parts of *Daniel*), which antedate by fully a thousand years the date of the earliest surviving Biblical manuscripts and, still more important, provide confirmation of the Massoretic text to which we referred in an earlier chapter. These copies also advance the possibilities of solving certain delicate questions concerning the authorship of these works and their dates of composition. Among the manuscripts were found several other religious texts of a non-canonical or apocryphal kind, which formed part of a single specialized library; and at another site, Murabba'at, there have emerged some historical documents, together with letters and contracts, which though interesting in themselves are of less value for our purposes here. Finally, the discovery of the documents must be related to excavations undertaken on sites near the caves, which have revealed the existence of a collective settlement, similar to a monastery (including a dining-hall, *scriptorium*, and reservoirs for water), and also its cemetery, where about a thousand bodies were buried, belonging to men and women between the ages of 20 and 50. We have enough, therefore, to indicate the life and organization of a religious community which was created against a Jewish background and drew on the spiritual heritage of Judaism, but which was governed by its own rules and was in fairly open opposition to the official representatives of the Jewish nation. From its rise to its tragic end we can reconstruct the stages of this historical phenomenon and outline the ideals of those who inspired it, even though we cannot yet exactly identify the meaning of certain figures (such as the 'Master of Justice') nor always understand the reasons for some of the decisions the community took.

From the time of the Seleucid attacks on the Jews and the profanation of the Temple certain small groups became detached from the rest of the people. Their aim was to avoid contact with the infidel, and to enter upon a more perfect form of life, in full observance of God's precepts. Among them there may have been descendants of ancient priestly families (the 'sons of Zadok', tracing their ancestry to a priest of the time of David and Solomon), who claimed to be the authentic guardians of Israel's Covenant with God and regarded Hellenizers and followers of the Maccabees with equal detestation, believing that the latter no less than the former were to blame for forfeiting the rights of the nation's true High Priest. Even when conditions in the country took a general turn for the better, these groups remained hostile to the new order and transformed themselves into regular sects included under the generic term 'the Faithful of the New Covenant'. The organization they built for themselves has been described for us in the *Document of Damascus*; and some of the writings found in the Judah desert (such as the *War of the Children of Light against the Children of Darkness*, the *Hymns of Thanksgiving*, and various commentaries on the Bible) are typical of the literature which emerged from the charged atmosphere of religious exaltation surrounding this community. In contrast to the 'Wicked Priest' or 'Father of Lies', the members of the Covenant took as their hero the 'Master of Justice', the holy priest who was the legitimate heir of the Jewish religious reformers. He had been persecuted by the wicked, but was followed with enthusiasm by all those who had listened to his words and understood the commandments of Moses and the Master's revelations concerning the Law. Very varied interpretations of this personage have been proposed, and he can still be fixed anywhere within a time-span of at least a hundred years (171–65 BC). But at all events it is certain that the author of the Commentary (or perhaps one should say Exegesis) on *Habakkuk* depicted this figure of the 'Master of Justice' with the prime intention of establishing the antithesis between the true and the false follower of the Covenant, between the legitimate beneficiary and the usurper,

Very similar to the one just described, and of the same date, was the 'Essene' movement: the word is of uncertain and much disputed etymology, and may mean 'saints' or 'silent monks' or 'healers'. We have argued that there was an Essene sect in the monastery recently discovered at Qumrân. About the rule there in force we are given minute information in the *Manual on Discipline*, where the regulations and forms of expression are very similar to those contained in the *Document of Damascus*. We see too that these monastic communities had reached an advanced stage of development. They required of their adherents complete detachment from the world, total sharing of property, celibacy, and meticulous observance of community regulations, which by now had become remarkably complicated and exacting. The ideal set before candidates for admission to the monastery was that they should seek God through obedience to his Law and should therefore return to the spirit and letter of the purest Mosaic system. This programme required that God for his part should choose his elect and give them his grace, but that the Children of Light in their turn should undertake to follow a plan of life requiring the practise of many virtues, with the discharge of various cult acts, submission to recognized superiors, and obedience to a series of precepts. A 'postulant' after a certain lapse of time would become a novice for two years, then there followed an examination and an admission ceremony, conducted with a solemn liturgy. The community was ruled by a hierarchy of senior persons, including a president, an inspector of work who was also the treasurer, a council of fifteen, and a priest at the head of each group of ten laymen; but the various sections of the *Manual* are not self-consistent on this subject. There were plenary meetings, at which many matters affecting the community life were discussed and decided by majority vote. Transgressions were punished according to the gravity of the offence by penalties ranging from expulsion to deprivation of a part of the offender's food: about thirty such offences are catalogued in the *Manual*, from lying to unseemly conduct, from fraud to the maintenance of a vendetta, and from yawning at meetings to grumbling about one's fellow-members. Nothing is ever said about regular sacrifices: indeed we are told that expiation of sin and giving pleasure to God are worth more than the flesh of victims. It was compulsory to anoint oneself with lustral water, to confess all sins, to take baths, and to wear white clothing. But although ritual purity is urged most strongly, it was none the less recognized that cleanliness without avails nothing unless there is health within.

But much more than by these and similar details the community of the Covenant was characterized by two features, which are made clear by the nature of the works composed in the monastery of Qumrân or incorporated into its library. One was the deliberate intention of preserving the group as an association of sacerdotal type: the 'Sons of Aaron' (or priests) have a place apart and are always given primacy, while the faithful are constantly called upon to protect the legitimacy of the chief religious office. The second feature is the definite eschatological outlook imposed on the initiates in every department of their lives. Two forces, Good and Evil, are believed to affect mankind, and there is constant appeal to the eternal struggle between good and evil men, which is made the criterion for measuring and evaluating all present and past history and for drawing salutary lessons therefrom.

It was precisely the Sons of Darkness, the 'Kittim' (a term used generally for foreign peoples and nations, but applied particularly, in certain specific contexts, to the Romans),[19] who after having seemed so menacing to the writer of the *Habakkuk* commentary in 65 BC eventually brought about the ruin of the community of Qumrân. During the terrible Jewish War which ended with the destruction of Jerusalem even the remote site in the desert near the Dead Sea was invested by Vespasian's troops in May of AD 68; and the powerful building, within which a few fanatics may have attempted resistance, was destroyed.[20] Yet its cultural heritage had been placed in safety before it was too late, collected into the jars which were hidden in almost inaccessible caves and destined to preserve the material for many centuries. Today, by a series of chances, the treasure has reappeared. It illustrates for us a singular aspect of late Hebrew religious thought and practice, though it provides specialists with a number of disturbing problems.

One of the most difficult of these, undoubtedly, concerns the eventual relationship between the Qumrân community and early Christianity. No full treatment of this question is possible here, much less a definitive answer, but this much may be said. The religious life of this sect on the Dead Sea was certainly on a high level. But no one of their writings is free from the Old Testament system: there is as yet nothing which foreshadows the message of Jesus, or which gives a picture of the personality and work of a Saviour who is at once human and divine.[21] Yet this last is of the essence of the Christian Gospel.

b. *Messianic Thought*

A description of Hebrew religion is not complete without a few words on Messianic doctrine, one of the most interesting features as we come near to the Christian period. We need hardly say that the Hebrew concept of the Messiah was not consistent or unchanging. Moreover the evidence on this subject comes less from the Bible than from extra-canonical literature of the second century BC and later, literature which is not easy to interpret on account of the obscurity of its concepts and definitions. 'Messiah' is the transcription of a Hebrew word meaning 'Anointed', and it originally meant someone holy, a king or a priest or one of those who had a relationship with God. When the Hebrews first lost their independence in the Babylonian Captivity, they centred all their hopes on a better future and so gave the Messianic ideal a definite content, in that they looked forward to the reign of David and to the coming of an era of prosperity and power. At the basis of their hopes were national pride and hatred of the foreigner. But the Messianic idea was not just political: it was also an expression of 'a hunger and thirst after righteousness', and it involved the implementation of the Covenant hallowed between God and Israel. The essential point of this matter was a feeling that the Messiah must be something more than a man. He had to give full realization to the rule of the Law on earth, to restore the power of the Hebrews, and to subdue the Gentiles; for the Gentiles, being heathens, did not believe in the true God and did not practise righteousness. In this connexion we meet the word 'Saviour' in a number of writings, and this was in the future a typical Christian expression. But as yet it had a very worldly and material connotation, and we never find the claim that the Messiah is to be a victim to expiate sin. The Hebrews found it repellent and untenable to say that God's Elect, a man charged with a special mission and destined to restore glory to Israel, could be a man despised and, to all appearance, defeated.

In the course of the first century BC the expectation of a Messiah was spasmodic and fitful. Political conditions became more unhappy, and numerous false Messiahs arose, finding a large following among the people, and evoking currents of fanaticism. The Evangelists, among others, tell us how anxiously Jesus' contemporaries sought to know who was the Messiah, where he was operating, and what his task might be. In fact a variety of evidence makes it easy to see that in the religious sphere confusion and trouble were the rule in Palestine, and that this situation was responsible for the number of apocalyptic visions concerning the Kingdom of God. In those conditions any adventurer could achieve success, but the soil was also well prepared for genuine and earnest preaching of repentance and reform such as was brought by Christianity.

Certain historical facts remain to be added. When Jesus was born Judaea had a king of its own, namely Herod I, who was governing under Roman protection. Being a foreigner (an Idumaean), he sought to gain the favour of the Jewish people by rebuilding the Temple at Jerusalem and by restoring the political unity of the area. In fact he was not a man without stature and sense of greatness, though he lacked moderation: he put three of his sons to death, but divided his kingdom among the remaining three. Herod died in the month of Nisan of 4 BC (but after the birth of Jesus, as we shall see later), and was succeeded by Archelaus, who attempted to gain the goodwill of Augustus and was rewarded with the title of Ethnarch. But after ruling for ten years he was deposed in response to general protests and was exiled to Vienna in Gaul. Meanwhile there had been a continual series of rebellions, and Varus, legate of Syria, was compelled to intervene with two legions. The Roman authorities showed extreme severity in the restoration of order, and then entrusted power to an equestrian procurator, who resided at Caesarea but came frequently to Jerusalem and stayed there for considerable periods. Even from non-Christian sources (Josephus) we know that one of these procurators, Pilate, was cruel and suspicious and that his contemptuous behaviour exasperated the Jews. Nor was there anything much to be hoped for from an appeal to the procurator's superiors, either to the legate at Antioch, who intervened only in extreme circumstances, or to 'Caesar' (the emperor) himself, seeing that approach direct to him was a lengthy process of uncertain outcome. An understanding of this situation throws light on many events in the history of early Christianity and on certain attitudes of political principle adopted in this period. To obtain this understanding we must give the historical phenomenon we have been discussing a more central place than it normally receives in any general picture of the Jewish state and society at the beginning of our era.

c. *Relations between the Roman Government and Jewish Monotheism*

The early history of Christianity and of its relations with the Roman state may be traced more clearly if we preface it with some similar evidence about the profession of Judaism.

It was explained earlier that at the outset, despite the conflict between Jewish monotheism and official polytheism, the Roman government tolerated the profession of Judaism by those who were Jews by birth, but prohibited it among Roman citizens who attempted to become Jewish converts. Under different periods of the empire this policy was often modified, especially when rulers were in power who exacted a greater degree of adherence to the imperial cult.

Augustus attempted to avoid friction, and endeavoured on the whole to maintain the friendship which had prevailed between Julius Caesar and the Palestine and Diaspora Jewries. He was satisfied if the Jews made sacrifices to Yahweh for the emperor's safety and sent the emperor a present from time to time; meanwhile every Jew was allowed to send the traditional 'didrachm' to the Temple at Jerusalem, and the regular Sabbath meetings were tolerated. But the first troubles began at Rome, and in Palestine and Egypt, as early as Tiberius' reign, resulting from the love of autonomy and the refusal of the Jews to stop proselytizing. An enquiry in AD 19 revealed that the number of these catechumens was at least 4,000, and all who refused to recant were punished. The able-bodied among them were sent to Sardinia to fight the mountain brigands, and the remainder went into exile.

Claudius restored full liberty for the Jewish cult at Rome. But the resulting influx of Jews to the city and the revival of proselytizing decided him to institute new measures as early as 41. These were postponed for some while, but a few years later there were riots among the Jews 'impulsore Chresto'. These words of Suetonius imply quarrels between traditionalist Jews and the Christians who were removing themselves from the synagogues. The emperor's answer, in 49, was to banish the Jews from the capital.

In Nero's reign the Jews of the mother country revolted and the great war was declared. Rome under the leadership of Vespasian and Titus took Jerusalem and destroyed the Temple, but such Jews as had remained pro-Roman, or even had not resisted to the last, were given favourable treatment.

RELIGION AND PHILOSOPHY 847

One reason for this was that the Jews of Alexandria had taken part in proclaiming Vespasian emperor. They were allowed to continue professing their national religion, and certain noble Jews were enabled to conduct a school for religious instruction on an imperial estate at Jamnia. Other persons, like the historian Flavius Josephus or King Agrippa and his family, could migrate to Rome and enjoy prestige and power: Agrippa's sister Berenice lived for several years with Titus, the heir to the throne, as if she were his wife. At the same time the cult was given a number of general regulations; and after the fall of the Temple the customary didrachm had to be paid to the temple of Juppiter Capitolinus as a capitation tax on the Jewish race.

The Jews naturally used the relaxation of tension as an opportunity to resume proselytizing, and they eventually succeeded in converting certain members of the imperial house, such as the emperor Domitian's cousins Flavius Clemens and his wife Domitilla, to whose sons the 'dominus' was intending to leave his throne. Domitian had never approved of his father's lenient policy towards the Jews, and still less of Titus' toleration of political interference by Berenice and her family. He therefore now reacted by persecuting the new converts (this is the event which has been mistakenly called Domitian's persecution of the Christians),[22] and by extreme severity in the collection of the *fiscus Iudaicus*, under which a personal examination could be made to identify those who attempted to evade it.

A new and important clash occurred under Trajan, when the communities of Egypt, Cyrenaica, Cyprus, and a Palestinian minority rose against Roman rule to assist their co-religionists in Parthia in their fight against the Roman invaders. Against Hadrian all Palestinian Jewry revolted under Bar-Kochba (AD 132–135) when the emperor had taken measures against circumcision, planted a colony at Jerusalem, and given orders for the erection of a temple of Juppiter Capitolinus there. After their defeat Jews were forbidden to set foot in their former holy city; and there were prohibitions both on circumcision and on the study and observance of the Law.

But all these interdicts were lifted as early as the reign of Antoninus Pius. Two centuries later the emperor Julian ('the Apostate') allowed the rebuilding of the Temple, but the work was arrested by his death. Before the end of the fourth century, in the reign of Theodosius I, legal and economic restrictions at the expense of the Jews were beginning once more.

6. THE BEGINNINGS OF CHRISTIANITY

a. *Jesus and His Work*

It is impossible to write a life of Jesus which conforms to modern conceptions of history. Very little about him can be established with any precision, since the earliest writers to concern themselves with reporting his actions and behaviour did not have interests which were strictly 'historical' in the modern sense of that word. They were simply trying to collect those sayings of their Master and those episodes in his life which contributed most to the proof they were offering of the nature and purpose of his mission, centring their collection around certain main themes and following the literary conventions of their times.

We need not enter upon the endless discussions to which the chronology of the life of Jesus has given rise: we can remain satisfied if we obtain a fair approximation about the dates of his birth and death, and about the start and duration of his preaching. His birth may be set at the end of the Roman year 748 or 6 BC, the discrepancy being due to a well-known arithmetical error made by Dionysius the Less in trying to reconcile two accounts. The beginning of Jesus' preaching very probably followed the news of the Baptist's imprisonment. That would be when Jesus was aged 32 or 33, and the period of his public ministry was brief (two years and a few months at most), divided into two main phases with a crisis, involving the defection of many followers, coming in between. In the early period Jesus preached in Galilee and achieved astonishing successes. He healed a number of sick people, pronounced the famous Sermon on the Mount, and made use chiefly of parables to explain his thinking. He had no fixed headquarters, but moved about from one district to another, accompanied by his Apostles, whom he was educating in preparation for more important tasks.

In the second period the scene changes completely. Jesus moved to Judaea, the home of his chief enemies, who had decided that he was dangerous and were skilfully preparing a *coup* which would destroy him. In the end they were successful in having him convicted of sedition against the Roman power and in obtaining a sentence of death—a matter which was within the competence of the procurator alone, if he was resident at Jerusalem. The execution was carried out at a place called Golgotha, near the city, on the 14th of the month Nisan (roughly identical with our March), probably in the year AD 30.

Various formulae have been used to define the specific content of Jesus' teaching. Some have claimed the point of substance to have been his announcement that he was the Son of God and that God must be worshipped in truth and spirit, independently of any ecclesiastical ordinance. Others have spoken of Jesus as exclusively concerned with 'soteriology', the salvation of the individual human soul. Others again have regarded him as a preacher who was convinced that the end of the world was at hand: this school has given a narrowly eschatological interpretation to his pronouncements, and has consequently had to suppose that the Church was a device substituted by the disciples when they became convinced that their Master's visions had come to nothing. Finally there have been those who have evaluated Jesus' message simply in terms of the political problems of his day, seeing it as an assertion of the rights of the lower classes, or a manifesto in the class war, a message which was very soon deserted and twisted into something quite different. There are those too who deny him practically all claim to originality and reduce the content of his work to ideas, beliefs, and practices already current in his day. Evidence for this view is thought to emerge when the few pages of text containing fundamental Christian doctrine are taken apart piece by piece, the texts themselves being allegedly nothing more than the result of a vast and complicated series of conspiracies and frauds.

What is genuinely novel in the words of Jesus is his definition of the relation between God and man, obtained through the revelation of a majestic plan from the mind of God, which comprised Creation and Redemption, Salvation and the final Glory. From man he demanded a response to the call through a life of faith and good works, together with a confident surrender to celestial providence and detachment from engrossing worldly cares. This explains his insistent invitation to repentance and conversion (*metanoia*, which means 'change of mind'), on the ground that the Kingdom of God is at hand. It explains too his precise assertions about the importance of his own person as the pivot of the new system and as the initiation of a period in history which would never come to an end in terms of time. In this way the national exclusiveness of the Jews was overcome by means of a spiritual interpretation of the promises made by God to his people. The old Covenant was replaced by a new one, open to any man who had faith in the Lord and his Messiah.

Yet one must at once add that, although Jesus preached penitence and transferred the central interest of human life to an existence after death, his was not the bitter form of asceticism which denies temporal values and contests the significance of society and of economic facts. We can see the contrary in his own conduct, so generous towards men's material needs, so unaffected in face of natural things, and so ready to share the aspirations of his people. The same appears in his words. In the new table of the Law (the Sermon on the Mount) he insists on renunciation and sacrifice, but in his teaching couples this with charity, with a lively appreciation of the brotherhood of Man, and with a communion of souls which allows all external differences to be overcome. Lastly, there appears most vividly in Jesus' words an echo of the revolt of a pure and noble spirit against all the formalism and hypocrisy which governs social intercourse. We see his contempt for the casuistries which smother the impulses of men's hearts and distort their sincere intentions of doing good. In short he gives us the highest possible ideal of individual and collective morality, and presents it by enunciating a few clear principles. These are personified in himself as a living model of goodness such as has very rarely been encountered in the history of the world.

It is this reason—the historical facts about its founder—which radically distinguishes the religion founded by Jesus from other religions current at that time,[23] although it is clearly to be classified among the mystery religions on account of its charter of salvation and its initiatory rites. In the religion of Jesus faith rests above all on adherence to a person known to have really existed and does not depend on some mythical personage. Moreover other mystery religions aimed at a physical union with God, an assimilation of the body achieved by various formal acts. Jesus, however, required in a special manner a transformation within, a purification of the heart. His response was to change the lives of individuals and of all mankind by regulating every action in accordance with the law of Love, and by making motive rather than achievement the test of an action's moral quality. This led Jesus to display great understanding even towards sinners (and he has been blamed on this account), but, even more important, it helped to reaffirm the superiority of spiritual values above the chance nature of external circumstances.

b. *The Christian Apostolate*

Although the Apostles were Galileans, they remained at Jerusalem even after Jesus' death, and the life of the young community felt itself dominated by two stupendous facts, the resurrection of their Master and the descent of the Holy Spirit on the first faithful band. To testify to what they had seen and to what they firmly believed, the Apostles began that course of preaching of which the *Acts* have given us a number of examples. The speeches of Peter reported there are obviously not a literal repetition of his words, but in their archaic Semitic style and the simplicity of the ideas presented they reflect a very early phase in the evolution of Christian thought. In this oral teaching very cautious formulae were used on the subject of Jesus: none the less Peter and the rest were several times summoned before the Sanhedrin to account for their statements. The hostility of the Jews to the followers of the new religion became increasingly implacable; and Herod Agrippa too, in order to please the Jews, took savage measures against the sect, including the execution of James (the Greater) and the imprisonment of Peter. In consequence there was a ready wish to break up the closed circle living at Jerusalem and to achieve greater success through settlement elsewhere. James 'the brother of the Lord' remained behind, but the centre of the movement was shifted to Antioch in Syria; and it was in that city that its adherents were first called 'Christians'. Linguistically the term is a curious one, because its suffix is Latin, rather than Greek as one would have expected from the place where the word originated ('Christioi' or 'Christikoi' would have been more natural). The suffix -*anus* means clientship, sonship, or adherence.

Evidence from the *Acts* itself is explicit in showing that internal conflicts had arisen between the various racial groups comprised within the community at Jerusalem, and that the new movement was becoming involved in the nationalistic and social disturbances which were provoked in the area by discontent at the inadequate government conducted by Roman officials. The Galileans were joined by portions of families which had earlier emigrated to Asia Minor and Egypt but had then returned to Jerusalem. These 'Hellenists', as they were generically called, were ignored by the Jewish Christian leaders and put up a protest. The outcome was a general meeting, at which the Apostles declared that they were unwilling to be concerned any longer with administrative duties, since their sole task ought to be preaching and divine services. They therefore invited the whole meeting to choose seven learned and devout persons to undertake works of charity, and on the adoption of this proposal seven deacons were chosen, all of them with Greek names, a circumstance which suggests that the Hellenizing party had gained the upper hand. Among these deacons the first, named Stephen, deserves particular mention. He was stoned to death as the result of popular fury in AD 36, after an inspired speech on the divinity of Jesus; and one of those who was present and who took part in the stoning was Saul, a person upon whom all our attention must now be centred on account of the exceptional importance he later assumed in events related to Christian history.

The evidence about Saul's life is drawn from autobiographical notes of a particularly graphic kind in the Pauline Epistles, and from information contained in the *Acts of the Apostles*. He was born at Tarsus, an important city in Cilicia, in the first years of the Christian era, and belonged to a Jewish family of the tribe of Benjamin; but his father had obtained Roman citizenship, and this was later to be of value to the son at appropriate moments. He had a profitable career open to him and was therefore given a serious education as a boy, entering the school of the celebrated Rabbi Gamaliel. Being zealous in the observance of the Mosaic Law (a Pharisee) he entered with enthusiasm into the attack on the Christians; but while he was on a journey to Damascus to carry orders for pursuing the persecution, he saw a vision and was converted. For three years he lived in the desert, then he made contact with Peter and the rest, after which Barnabas took him to Antioch. He now called himself Paul (his Roman *cognomen*), and carried out various apostolic journeys, in the course of which he visited Cyprus, the Troad, Macedonia, Greece, and Ephesus, often coming into conflict with the Jews. About AD 58 he returned to Jerusalem and was the cause of so serious a riot that he was put in prison and kept there for two years, during which time he continued to expound the Christian doctrine, including persons of high station among his audience. Finally this same Paul appealed to Caesar (the emperor), perhaps because he wanted some means of being transported to Rome and visiting the community there, which for long he had been anxious to get to know. We have little information about the rest of his life, but it is certain that later on he suffered martyrdom in Rome itself, the sentence being carried out by beheading in view of his citizen status.

Thirteen Pauline letters of varying length and importance have come down to us, all composed in the course of a dozen years (53–65) and addressed both to communities and to individual members of the faith. They have given rise to many arguments concerning their authenticity, their doctrinal content, the extent of their author's influence on the religious environment of his day, and the degree of novelty he imported into the Apostolic teaching.

For our purposes it is enough to indicate the main lines of his thought, remembering at the same time that he proclaimed himself throughout to be Christ's minister and that consequently, so far from supposing a conflict between the two, we ought to recognize a continuity of ideas. Paul should be regarded as the most intelligent, the most devoted, and the most enthusiastic among the servants of his predecessor.

In Paul's judgement God's plan for the world rests on two main pillars, the sin of Adam, first ancestor of mankind, and the Redemption of Christ, the new Adam who in his person comprises all humanity. The sacrifice on the Cross was therefore the pivot of the whole order of relations between God and man: though a stumbling-block to the Jews and a piece of folly to the Gentiles, it was a source of pride to the Christians and was what put such force behind them. But once the Redemption had been accomplished, it was man's duty to take possession of the grace which had been put at his disposal with such generosity. This meant that he must enter upon a new life by clinging close to Christ and believing in the salvation achieved by Christ's work. He must not put his trust in the Law, which if wrongly interpreted can be an important cause of sin. The new man must be guided by ideals of purity, chastity, zeal, and obedience, without allowing himself to be enmeshed in a set of barren precepts. All his actions should be inspired by an impetuous freedom; and he should take care to be directed by a sense of spiritual independence, which will bring him also a generous understanding of the various needs of other men.

Now that God has made manifest the mystery which was hidden for centuries, in putting into effect the plan expounded above, we cannot—so Paul goes on to say—have a conception of the further unfolding of history. But this does not mean that the return of the Lord (*parousia*) must necessarily happen soon; and we must not, during the period of waiting, neglect the duties of normal life. On the contrary, there is an institution which preserves and carries on the work of Christ, namely the Church, which occupies so great a part in Pauline doctrine. It is conceived of as being Christ's mystical body, a living and carefully ordered organism in which each man co-operates in an harmonious distribution of duties, according to what God has disposed in his inscrutable but providential designs. The temporal authorities too discharge a valuable function, and for this reason the faithful must pray for them and must co-operate with all men alive, although in their hearts they must be severed from all earthly concerns. Paul's attitude is wholly directed to promoting relations between Christians and non-believers. The Christians were to be an active and useful force in the time and environment in which they lived, in order that they might permeate society with a new spirit, and later, when the moment came, alter society's institutions.

In conclusion, then, we may say that even after taking proper account of (though not interpreting literally) the terrible indictments he sometimes launches at pagan civilization—its literature, its government, and its morals—

yet Paul took a less pessimistic view of the future of the ancient world than is normally believed. Indeed, as a true inheritor of the Christian message, he examined and weighed up what was actual and concrete. Even among the Gentiles, he discovered, there was in secret a sense of waiting, which only in the fullness of Christ's time would be able to find satisfaction.

Confronted with this *Weltanschauung* in all its boldness, we inevitably ask ourselves how much of it was original and how much derived from the culture of the time. The enquiry is all the more legitimate in that Paul's vocabulary is undoubtedly influenced by contemporary philosophical and religious movements. As anyone can readily perceive this is an important problem, since it takes us on to the more general question of the relationship between early Christianity and the ideas which were most widely current in the geographical and cultural area in which Christianity started and flourished. Ancient Christian writers themselves were the first to raise the question, and they gave two opposing answers. One party contemptuously rejected any possibility of contact, and regarded the supposed affinities as diabolical forgeries. The other party was content to establish parallels and discover resemblances, because they constituted a proof that Christianity was responding to the deepest and most healthy needs of the human spirit.

If we ignore purely external similarities, and also avoid hasty conclusions, it still seems correct to recognize that not only the language but the rites of Christianity were adapted from contemporary forms. But this is a very different thing from saying that they were derivative. Adaptation was the product of a deliberate wish to employ the best methods of expression available at the time, forms which were most suited for ensuring that Christian teaching was understood and accepted by a wide public. Even the figure of Christ as it emerges from Paul's writings is not modelled on the type of celestial redeemer previously known to Eastern religions; apart from anything else Paul was too good a Jew to abandon his Jewish outlook completely when he became a Christian. Moreover Paul strenuously opposes all Gnostic interpretations of the Gospel, of the kind which admitted a multiplicity of intermediate beings and saviours between man and his God. But in the actual process of confuting his adversaries he liked to make use of their terminology and to show himself to be in the current of Hellenistic religious vocabulary, although the meanings of the words he borrowed were radically altered in order to give expression to the truth of his new doctrine.

He had discovered a principle of interpretation which was far more exalted than that derived from 'wisdom' based on reason. He had found an explanation of the mysteries of historical reality in a cause hitherto unknown. The wisdom of the sages, though his words censured and rejected it, was in this way given a different set of values by means of *epignosis*, the light that comes through faith.

c. *The Canonical Gospels*

Discussions on the historical value of the sources relating to Christian origins started comparatively recently, in the mid-eighteenth century: for long centuries before that there was no doubt about the divine inspiration of these writings and therefore about their age and authenticity. But once they had embarked on the path of criticism, investigators and 'exegetes' could not be halted. They advanced the most daring hypotheses, created a variety of schools and standpoints, and arrived at largely negative conclusions. But their work laid the foundations of a genuine critical enquiry, which clarified a number of points and uncovered what may be called the 'prehistory' of the historical books of the New Testament. Everyone in fact would now agree that originally there was a system of oral teaching, which was conducted according to definite rules and was used by Christian preachers to expound their good tidings to hearers from different races and classes. The moment came, however, when they wanted to put this evidence into writing, and they therefore prepared a number of short books, still with the purpose of spreading the Gospel and narrating the words and doings of Jesus, in order to show who he was. Only later was this material elaborated and put into shape by the composition of the Gospels as we have them today. This composition followed certain structural rules of literature, namely the forms used by Rabbinical writing[24] of the period. We can see this by comparisons with contemporary and later Jewish writing, which explains how our Evangelists worked.

None of them set out to compose a history of Jesus, that is to say a complete biography with an ordered chronology. Each wanted to present the case from his own particular visual standpoint and to underline things which might be of most interest to a particular class of reader: this they did by adapting themselves to the mentality and speech of their audience. Their mode of composition necessarily awakes many misgivings in the modern critical mind; but no such misgivings will ever impair the documentary value of the Gospels as sources, since they conform perfectly to the geographical and social background of their narratives and are in full harmony with the methods of reasoning and exposition current at the time. The details of their narratives must not be interpreted *stricto sensu* in matters of precise chronology and topography. What interested the authors was the religious basis of their story; their task was to edify the faithful and convince them that Jesus was the Messiah. Nevertheless it is not out of the question to use the data collected in the Gospels to reconstruct the chronology and incidents of Jesus' life, to follow the progress of events, and so to form a precise notion of what occurred at that particular time and place in history.

We may take it as established, then, that the Gospels we possess are the outcome of a fairly long process of elaboration. But to define more closely the significance of their value as history it should also be added that they are an abbreviated version of what Jesus said and did, and of the recollections of him in the minds of the earliest communities. What was put down in writing was what most struck contemporaries—the salient points and the most vigorous phrases—for it is inconceivable that the brief pages of the Evangelists contain everything spoken by a preacher who spoke every day over more than one year. (This holds good even if we admit that Jesus often repeated himself, for obvious reasons, in his discourses, and also that he preferred an 'aphoristic' form because it was more incisive and easy to remember.) We can explain in this way how many sentences got scattered; that is to say how they were not included by the Canonical Evangelists but are found elsewhere, for instance in extra-canonical sayings or in St Paul; and we can understand how the various Evangelists' accounts of the same theme can show formal differences, despite the care they took to adhere faithfully to the Master's words. The Sermon on the Mount is an example: Matthew's version must be a summary of the original,[25] but Luke has the imprecation 'Woe to you', which is not in Matthew; and some of the descriptive features are different. Successive critics are left free to flounder in their conjectures, but it is possible to overcome the various difficulties by employing intelligent principles of source-criticism.

The oral teaching which was the starting-point of testimony about Jesus must originally have been conducted in Aramaic. Soon, however, it was translated into Greek, that being the language most widely employed in all the Mediterranean world. The Greek of the Gospels, like that of other New Testament writings, is the *Koiné* or common tongue, the language of everyday use and speech rather than the literary language of Atticizers. It is not our task to enter upon the complex philological problems which the text and its transmission present to scholars. (If we remember that thousands of manuscripts survive, subdivided into various families and classes, and that besides these there are fragments and citations in the Fathers of the Church, it is easy to understand the labour involved in establishing the most exact version.) Instead we should consider more closely the writings which hitherto we have called *en bloc* the 'Gospels'; and at the start we should note that the corresponding Greek word means the 'good news' preached by Jesus, but passed into current usage to denote the books containing his collected sayings and the narrative of facts related to his life. (Pl. 63, a.)

Many collections or *perikopai* (strictly 'sections' or 'paragraphs'), compiled for particular purposes and never completed, soon started to circulate on the subject of Jesus. Of these, in the course of the slow and delicate process of creating a 'Canon' of sacred books, four were selected to make up what in general (by 'antonomasia') is called 'the Gospel', which is one in substance but fourfold as edited. Among the four there is a further distinction normally made between the first three, known as the 'Synoptic Gospels' because of their very obvious affinities of content and form, and the fourth Gospel, which is attributed to the Apostle John. (Pl. 63, b.) The authors of the Synoptic

Gospels (the term was first introduced into scholarly vocabulary in the eighteenth century) are Matthew, Mark, and Luke. They undoubtedly drew on common written sources, since otherwise the verbal correspondence would be inexplicable; but it is difficult to identify these sources or to define the nature of each writer's dependence. The identity of their general arrangement and of the material they used has not prevented each Synoptist from imprinting a markedly personal character upon his work. Mark is the most shapeless, his Gospel consisting of separate sections pieced together without precise logical or chronological connections; but it is full of picturesque details, and it emphasizes the Humanity of Jesus (in other words the traces of oral preaching are still extremely evident). In Matthew, on the other hand, one notices the didactic character: he groups Jesus' teaching into several series of parables and into discourses concerned with the same subject, and he is still closely tied to the Jewish background (this author had collected in Aramaic the *logia* or sayings of Jesus before composing in Greek the Gospel we possess). Lastly there is Luke, a real writer, elegant and cultivated, who arranges his material with concern for literary style; moreover, since he is addressing the Gentiles, he never forgets to lay special stress on things which might be of special interest to them.

About the dates of composition it is impossible to be precise. But careful examination of several features makes it probable that Matthew (in Greek) is earlier than AD 70, since he does not allude to the fall of Jerusalem, a matter which was so important to a Jew like himself that he could not have passed it over in silence. Mark, who reproduces in part the teaching of St Peter,[26] must have composed about 60; and Luke, whose optimistic view about the Gentiles would surely have been shaken by the Neronian persecution, probably wrote about 63. Luke was also a doctor, and some traces of his knowledge can be found in the text: it is interesting to see the large space he devotes to Jesus' childhood, a subject ignored by the others. We should not forget that Luke was also the author of another important work on Christian origins, the *Acts of the Apostles*, which he wrote directly after his Gospel and then broke off for reasons unknown to us. The *Acts* are divided into two parts, one centred round Peter and the church at Jerusalem, the other wholly devoted to Paul. The latter part contains passages written in the first person plural, because the author was present at the facts he narrates, though for other sections he may have made use of documents and oral information. Luke shows evidence of remarkable literary ability, and even of historical objectivity if the concept is used in the limited sense defined above in relation to this type of writing.

On the Fourth Gospel it is enough to say that it has little material in common with the others and also that there is a different background to the action it describes. When the writer has spoken of the beginnings of Jesus' preaching in Judaea, he passes rapidly over what his predecessors have said about the apostolate in Galilee, and then dwells at length on the journeys to

Jerusalem and in the regions of the south. Moreover in the whole work there is a loftiness of thought very different from the 'aphoristic' form of the other Gospels; and whereas in them the character of Jesus as the Messiah is only adumbrated, in John it is explicitly asserted and defended in a profound piece of thinking. This Gospel, then, is the demonstration of a particular doctrine, the one plainly announced in its preface. The proof is given in a series of facts and discourses, set down in accordance with a thesis or idea which runs through them all. But in addition to all this it provides a number of most valuable legal, topographical, and chronological details, which make it an historical document of the greatest significance.[27] It contains priceless evidence, and is also a work full of humanity and warmth.

d. The Apocrypha

The very keen interest of the early Christians in the life of Jesus and the Apostles explains the origin and diffusion of the so-called 'Apocrypha to the New Testament'. These are a form of religious literature vastly inferior to that of the authentic writings, but one which has some value as an indication of the aspirations and views current at the time. They also provided an inexhaustible source for artistic representations and pious traditions in later ages. The term 'apocryphal' did not then have the pejorative sense inseparable from it today: it simply denoted a sacred and mysterious writing, the meaning of which was inevitably hidden from most readers because it was reserved for the initiated. For this reason many of these compositions were for a long time regarded as inspired, and found their way into the Canons. Eventually, however, their miracle-mongering character and obvious exaggerations, combined with their defects of style, led to their expulsion; and this served to emphasize the amount of falsification which had led to their composition.

The most important apocryphal Gospels include the following: (a) the *Gospel of the Hebrews*, written in Aramaic and translated into Greek and Latin: it was closely related to St Matthew's Gospel and on various occasions gave prominence to James 'the brother of the Lord', the representative of that Christianity which strictly observed Jewish practice; (b) the *Gospel of the Egyptians*, evidently inspired by Gnosticism, and known to the masters of the Christian school at Alexandria; (c) the *Gospel of Nicodemus*, which contains the Acts of Pilate and the account of Christ's descent to the underworld (on Pilate there is a complete literature, designed to vindicate him and make him a witness to the truth of Christianity); and (d) the *Gospel of Thomas*, discovered in Coptic translation recently. Then there are the Gospels of Christ's childhood, the most important being the *Proto-Gospel of James*. Of the texts mentioned so far there survive extensive fragments, including (b) and (d) completely, from translations in a variety of languages. Almost fifty other apocryphal works, Gospels, Epistles, Acts, Apocalypses, and so on, usually of a heretical and Gnostic nature, have now been found (in Coptic) at Al-Hammadi in Egypt. Some other apocryphal Gospels are only vaguely mentioned, and there is no means of describing their features.

The very scanty reliable information about the lives of the various Apostles was supplemented in the second and third centuries by a number of apocryphal Acts, which are a sincere reflection of beliefs widely current among contemporary Christian circles of a popular kind. They contain valuable extracts from prayers, discourses, and rites used in religious services at that time; and in this respect they deserve all the attention which scholars have given them (together with the documents mentioned above) in reconstructing their origins and the history of their texts with patience and acumen, and in separating early material from later additions. The main Acts of which we have evidence are those of Paul (composed by a priest in Asia Minor before 190 and comprising three distinct parts), of Peter (containing the famous stories of Simon Magus and of 'Quo Vadis?'), of Andrew, of Thomas (concerning his apostolate in India), and of Thaddaeus (with the correspondence between Jesus and King Abgar of Edessa). There was also an *Epistula Apostolorum*, written in the middle of the second century, which contained Christ's revelations to the Apostles after his resurrection; and a number of Apocalypses, the earliest being those of Peter (before 150) and Paul (more than a century later).[28]

We have made incidental reference to the Canon of inspired books, which was gradually laid down by the authorities of the Church. Harnack drew attention to the fact that the distinction between Canonical and non-Canonical books of the Bible first appeared at Rome, and that even Eastern manuscripts offer readings of the text which were current in the Roman community. This is easily explicable if every church received a standard text from Rome and corrected its own readings accordingly. Despite this, however, the determination of the official Canon was a slow process, and we cannot follow it in detail here. If we comb the citations of the Bible by Christian writers of the early centuries, we get a valuable indication of the books accepted by that time. We can show by this means that there was a collection of New Testament works in existence as early as the beginning of the second century, and that St Irenaeus cites or alludes to every book of our New Testament except the very short *Third Epistle of John;* and this Epistle is mentioned by Clement of Alexandria about AD 200. Yet down to the fifth century there were still doubts about certain books—the *Epistle to the Hebrews*, the *Second Epistle of Peter*, the *Second* and *Third Epistles of John*, the *Epistles of James* and *Jude*, and above all the *Johannine Apocalypse (Revelation)*. It was this last work which evoked the greatest opposition: St Cyril of Jerusalem and the Apostolic Canons still found difficulty about it, and St Jerome refers to doubts surviving in the East. These uncertainties are explained by the absence of any official decision and by the abuse of certain texts (like *Hebrews* and the *Apocalypse*) by heretics.[29] In time various councils drew up the lists of Canonical books in both Old and New Testaments, and we also find catalogues of this kind in pontifical letters and documents, though the documents are not official and can only serve as an indication of the most reliable and accepted traditions. Special mention should be made of the famous 'Muratorian Fragment', which obtained its name from the great Modenese scholar Lodovico Antonio Muratori, who published it in 1740 from an eighth-century manuscript preserved in the Ambrosian Library at Milan. This is a second-century document containing the oldest list of New Testament books. It enters, though with some reserves, certain books which were decisively rejected later on. But we get the same degree of uncertainty from authors like Tertullian and Origen, who thought that works such as the *Shepherd* of Hermas were inspired but said nothing about other books now considered Canonical.

The question of the transmission of an authentic text and of the translations of the Scriptures is a delicate matter for many believing Christians, because it involves the inspiration and infallibility of the Bible. The earliest Latin translations of the New Testament were made about the middle of the second century in Africa, because from the outset the African Church had a marked stamp of Latinity, which is not encountered even in the Church of Rome. Indeed in the churches of Rome and of other Western cities the Greek element was predominant among Christians, and the earliest literary writings produced by them are all in Greek. The translations follow their Greek original (for the Old Testament this means the Septuagint) unduly literally, so as not to alter the sacred text in any particular. They therefore sounded harsh to Latin ears; and they contained many neologisms and syntactical innovations, drawn freely from the popular use of the language. In general they are documents of that 'Christian Latin', which according to recent studies by the Nijmwegen school (Schrijnen and Mohrmann) had very different features from the 'profane' language because of the generous use made of technical terms needed to express the content of the new faith and its ritual. Though in the past people spoke vaguely and incorrectly about a translation called 'Italian', the distinction now made is between two interdependent forms, the African and the European, the latter being attested from the middle of the third century. It is, however, difficult to determine how the two forms of text got transmitted, for in later times they influenced each other and also suffered infiltrations from outside. Eventually every text had to give way before the translation by St Jerome, known as the 'Vulgate', which was vastly superior to all others in elegance and lucidity.[30] Yet even this text got corrupted by inexpert copyists and wrong readings (there are actually 3,000 manuscripts of it in existence), and at the present time a number of careful scholars deserve great credit for their laborious work in reconstructing Jerome's original form and so giving the Vulgate an edition which conforms to the requirements of modern criticism.

e. *The Letters of the Apostolic Fathers*

After the writings which later found their way into the Canon of inspired biblical books, the oldest Christian literature comprises a group of works by the authors commonly known as 'Apostolic Fathers'. None of them has great profundity of doctrine, but all are marked by a lively faith in Christ; for the authors still retain the memory of him, and are anxiously awaiting his Return.

At the end of the first century a bishop of Rome named Clement wrote a letter for use by the Christian community at Corinth, designed to end the quarrels which had once more broken out in that church. The document acquired more importance than the occasion which had provoked it, on account of the invaluable evidence it contains. Apart from information about the lives of the apostles Peter and Paul and about what happened to the Christians during Nero's persecution, the letter tells us about the structure of the Church, the powers of ecclesiastics, and the return of sacred ceremonies. It also indicates that members of the Church were adopting a very friendly attitude to the Roman government, despite the harsh treatment they had recently undergone at the emperor's hands. Clement must have been of Jewish origin and was a man of some culture: his writings show an excellent knowledge of the Old Testament, but the influence of Stoic philosophy is also plain. As his name implies, he had contact with the aristocratic family of Flavius Clemens, Domitian's cousin, who had been put to death on a charge of Jewish practices and of atheism, his wife Domitilla being exiled to the island of Pandateria.[31] 'First Clement' (as this work is generally called) says nothing about the supremacy of the bishop of Rome. Yet the very fact of the letter's existence and its general tone—quite apart from the veneration with which it was regarded later, as attested in 170 by Dionysius, bishop of Corinth—show that from that time on the Roman community enjoyed a different status from all others and that it was conscious of a duty to concern itself with what was going on in the lives of all parts of the Christian world.

Clement of Rome was credited with other writings, which are later and of doubtful authenticity. There is another letter to the Corinthians, and more than one letter about virginity. Moreover the name 'Pseudo-Clement' is used to describe a long didactic novel, in which a man called Clement, after having sought the truth from various philosophers, is instructed by St Peter in the true doctrine. From this twenty homilies survive, containing Peter's discourses.

In epistolary form are various other writings of the Apostolic Fathers, such as seven letters of St Ignatius of Antioch, the letter of St Polycarp, bishop of Smyrna, and the so-called *Letter of Barnabas*.

When he was taken from Syria to Rome to meet martyrdom about 117, Ignatius directed various writings to the Christians of Ephesus, Magnesia, Tralles, Philadelphia, and Smyrna, also one to his companion Polycarp, and lastly one to the Roman community, full of reverence and praise for that body. In all his letters we can find a Christology based on conviction that Christ was both divine and human, and there are warm expressions of enthusiasm for a life of union with Christ, to be realized through martyrdom. But there is also a firm conception of the Church hierarchy, centred on a number of bishops in communion with the bishop of Rome.

There is little that is new in Polycarp's letter to the Philippians, the only one of his letters which survives. But Polycarp's martyrdom at Smyrna on 22 February 156, soon after his return from a journey to Rome, deserves some mention. His journey was undertaken to discuss with Bishop Anicetus the delicate question of the date of Easter, a matter which was dividing Eastern and Western Christians from each other, both sides following authoritative though different apostolic traditions. The letter of the Smyrnaeans to the church at Philomelium in Phrygia describes Polycarp's resolute behaviour in warm and telling language. They report many of his answers, and put into his mouth a prayer, which is undoubtedly one of the earliest Christian liturgical formulae we know.

The name of Barnabas, St Paul's companion, is given to a letter (which in fact is more like a general theological treatise) composed at Alexandria in the third decade of the second century AD. It provides a crisp refutation of the Old Testament, and describes the effects of the divine adoption obtained through Baptism, which transforms created beings into temples of the Holy Spirit.

An excellent and very early example of primitive Christian letter-writing is the *Didache*, or 'Doctrine of Our Lord transmitted by the Twelve Apostles to the Gentiles', discovered as lately as 1883 by a Greek Metropolitan bishop on a manuscript at Jerusalem.[32] It is a short and composite work divisible into two main parts, one concerned with liturgical instruction, the other with disciplinary rules. It is valuable for the conclusion reached on Our Lord's *parousia*, but also for the abundant information provided about the life of Christians in the sub-apostolic period. The unknown compiler has put together various ecclesiastic rules, probably in use in Syria, concerning Baptism, the Eucharist, Penitence, the duties of charity and brotherly help, the functions of priests, and so on.

There is another short anonymous letter, addressed to a highly-placed pagan named Diognetus (unconvincing attempts have been made to attribute it to the apologist Quadratus, to Hippolytus of Rome, and to Clement of Alexandria). In clear style and with sincere conviction the writer describes the life of a Christian, justifies the late time of the Incarnation, and derides the folly of idolatry. Although he tells us that Christians live a life apart in the world and are strangers in every land, he also claims that they are the vital ferment among mankind and that by love and by wise and unselfish action in society they can, despite misunderstandings and persecutions, bring about the spiritual and temporal salvation of their contemporaries.

This concept is one of the keynotes of early Christian letter-writing, and is a significant indication of the attitude adopted by those who followed the new religion, in relation to the pagan society inside which they had to operate.

Finally there is a much larger work called the *Shepherd*, the significance of which is very obscure. Although it is normally classified with the Apostolic Fathers, it belongs rather to the apocalyptic genre. Parts of it may go back to the late first century, but the completed work is to be attributed to a Roman Christian named Hermas, brother of Bishop Pius, who was in office from 140 to 150. The author gives many autobiographical details and much useful information about the life of the community. But his main aim is to transmit the revelations he has received from an aged lady (the Church) and from an angel in the form of a shepherd (who is Christ); and with this to impart many precepts and illustrate various parables, especially designed to call his brethren to repentance in view of the terrible judgement which will shortly come upon them. The picture of the moral life of Christians of the mid-second century, as it appears in the pages of the *Shepherd*, is extremely sombre. Yet we must not forget that Hermas was a preacher of repentance and a pedantic moralist, one too who had himself been a grave sinner; and that he was consequently conditioned to pessimism. On the other hand his text proves the existence and activity of various Church institutions, which by this time have taken root. It also confirms what we know from other sources about the prevalence of well-to-do people and men of business in the social composition of the Roman community. These were men who did not think they ought to abandon their professions in order to follow Christian precepts; but they gave alms freely, and looked to Baptismal pardon to wash away their sins.

f. *Rome and Christianity*

We have already explained (pp. 546 ff.) how Rome was accustomed to pass decrees of the senate allowing conquered peoples to retain their own religions but prohibiting them from making converts among Roman citizens, the latter being always forbidden to adopt foreign cults of their own accord. We saw too that special difficulties were bound to occur with monotheistic races, who were intolerant of the polytheism practised by the Roman state. This last was the case with Jews and Christians, whom in early times Rome had no means of distinguishing one from the other.

The distinction was forced on them by various stages. First there were what Suetonius calls the riots 'impulsore Chresto', among the sects regarded as Jewish, which led Claudius to banish all concerned from Rome. Then there were the riots and hostility evoked by the Jews against the audacious preaching of Paul; and here, too, after various legal proceedings had taken their course in the East, the matter ended up before the courts in Rome itself. The period was already one in which the government had resumed serious attempts to check the entry of foreign religions and the number of citizens who were becoming converts; even members of the aristocracy, such as Statilius Taurus, Lepida wife of Cassius, Thrasea, and Pomponia Graecina, were attacked on this charge. The Christians were a collection of persons who did not fit into any well-recognized group; their religion was new and was entirely distinct from the Jewish religion; consequently their cult could not be considered legal, not being covered by the various immunities granted to the Jews. So the new superstition was automatically illegal, and it was made all the worse by the fact that the Christians appeared to be followers of one who had been condemned and executed by Roman soldiers for political crimes against the 'majesty' of Rome (a crime more recently imputed to Paul as well). Moreover all Christian propaganda was directed at converting Roman citizens as well as other people.

Therefore no new legislation was required.[33] The actual name of Christian—a man's confession that he was one—was enough to render him guilty under the laws already in force. We are told this continually by the sources, 'Christianos esse non licet . . . non licet esse eos'; and they add that Christians were condemned 'tamquam Christiani'. Tertullian too was later to write 'your sentences say no more than that they declared themselves to be Christians; there is no enquiry into specific crimes; the name itself is regarded as a crime'.

Moreover in the course of litigation and court proceedings involving Jews and Christians it was common to find the Jews, in the excitement of the mutual accusations, tendentiously charging the Christians with ordinary crimes and with engaging in debased and extravagant rites. These charges were readily accepted by the pagan mob, which knew nothing of the concrete facts about this exotic ritual, was disturbed by the secrecy of Christian meetings, and was always ready to see the spread of new religions as the main cause of moral depravity. This accounts for the fact that our sources constantly accuse Christianity of being a 'superstitio nova et malefica', 'superstitio exitiabilis malefica', or 'superstitio prava'.

The sharp distinction between Jews and Christians now had a further effect. It meant that the Christians had no right to have been dispensed hitherto from sacrificing to the Dea Roma and the divinities of emperors. Yet as monotheists they could not perform these sacrifices, and non-observance became a very serious specific charge against those who refused. The danger was all the greater under those emperors who laid most claim to the performance of the cult.

All this helps to explain the sufferings of the Christians in 64. The great fire of Rome was in all probability due to accident, but the people were encouraged by Nero's enemies to blame the emperor himself, and as the days went by the charge was made more openly. Nero did not want to involve himself in argument or threats, which would not have availed to free him from suspicion. It may be too that he was advised by the pro-Jewish Poppaea and through her by the Jews themselves, whom the government now firmly distinguished from the Christians for the first time. He diverted suspicion by accusing the Christians of being the real culprits, regarding them as a body of men so wretched that neither the senate nor the people would have any ground for objecting. All that was needed was to state and get it accepted (perhaps by decree of the senate) that to be a Christian, the follower of an illegal religion, was one and the same thing as to be guilty of crimes against the Empire and against humanity. This, rather than any specific Neronian law condemning and prohibiting Christianity, must be the 'institutum Neronianum' of which Tertullian speaks: the sources mention no such law either on this occasion or at a later time. Nero's concern was not to institute and defend a persecution of a religious character, but to strike without delay at people who could be presumed to hate Rome and the human race, and to have been guilty of extremely serious crimes against the state. He did not want to get immersed in lengthy police enquiries into the possibilities of each defendant's actual complicity in the disaster. He simply proposed to take summary action against those who on their own admission or on the testimony of others were shown to be Christians and who refused to prove the contrary by performing pagan sacrifices. In that case they belonged to a body of men who were generally regarded as criminal and who were in no position to show that they had not secretly committed this new crime in addition to others.

But the punishment of these alleged incendiaries of Rome led to such barbarities that in the end, despite its prejudices, even the mob was moved: 'eventually they felt pity for them, because they were being massacred not for any public benefit, but in order to appease the savagery of a single man' (Tacitus, *Annals*, XV, 44). It turned out, therefore, that Nero's executions, from the moral standpoint, placed an obstacle rather than an incentive in the way of his immediate successors' continuing a persecution which lay outside the religious struggle and was conducted with so little regard for justice and human feeling.

After Nero's execution of Christians as incendiaries it is the opinion of many scholars that the first real persecution directed at citizens who became converts to the new faith took place about thirty years later, in Domitian's time. But, as we have already noted, the literal sense of the sources, if we avoid forced interpretations, is that Domitian punished citizens who were adopting Judaism; and this is the unanimous view of the Jewish tradition. Acilius Glabrio, for example, was regarded as not only a 'molitor rerum novarum' but as an atheist and a follower of Jewish practices (Dio Cassius); and the same charges are made against Flavius Clemens and his wife Domitilla. To this view it is no objection that members of the families concerned, the Acilii and Flavii Clementes, either then or more probably somewhat later, were Christians rather than Jews:[34] passage from one faith to the other was still quite normal in view of the affinity between them and the similar ways in which they were propagated. The *First Letter to the*

Corinthians of Pope Clement alludes to martyrs under Nero but not under Domitian. Christian sources, too, such as Hegesippus (recorded by Eusebius) and Tertullian, though they believed in an edict by Domitian against the Christians, state that he repealed it forthwith 'out of feelings of humanity'. This implies that no genuine Christian martyrs were known to have been condemned by that emperor.

The problem of the treatment of Christians, in fact, seems to have been faced for the first time in Trajan's day, from which period we possess a famous letter from the Younger Pliny as governor of Bithynia requesting the emperor's instructions, together with Trajan's reply.

If we read Pliny's letter carefully we can deduce that there was at that time no explicit law on the subject nor even a set of rules derived from traditional practice. Governors had a free hand and took full responsibility. Every governor therefore was guided by his own sense of law and humanity, by the accusations he received, by imperial complaints about illegal meetings, and by the whims of the mob. On this basis he could be extremely active and strict, or comparatively less so; and this explains why there are strong local differences between all the various persecutions, depending not only on the area affected but on the temper and views of the judges. Even more important is Trajan's reply. It shows first that there were no precise laws to be applied, but secondly that it would have been impossible to draft them, in view of the large number of different types of case that might be envisaged. One must still trust the judgement and common sense of the magistrate to lay down the rules and procedure to be followed from time to time. Nevertheless Trajan requires certain basic rules of law. Offences of thought, like the one in question, must not be sought out unless there is explicit information laid (on the responsibility of the informer); anonymous information must be rejected; and the indictment was to be cancelled if the defendant repented.

A great though temporary advance was made under Hadrian and Antoninus Pius, in whose reigns Christians were not punished for their faith but simply if they transgressed state laws in some other respect. Marcus Aurelius, on the other hand, regarded as heresy the Christian idea that the true life is that beyond the grave, and felt that the fear this doctrine inspired in the weak was against the interests of society. He therefore returned to Trajan's practice of allowing information to be laid by individuals or groups (hence the pressure exercised on magistrates by the mob), of regarding propaganda as sufficient for a conviction, of condemning those who confessed, and discharging unharmed those who performed an act of recantation. His son Commodus, however, when he came under the influence of Perennis and the pro-Christian Marcia, told his governors not to yield to the pressure of the people, who enjoyed seeing bloodshed.

Septimius Severus was an eclectic in religion, and therefore began by showing toleration to the Christians. Soon, however, under the influence of his wife, Julia Domna, who was surrounded by mystics, Pythagoreans, and anti-Christian lawyers like Ulpian, he modified his policy—a further cause of this being the Jewish rebellion. He did not institute any new form of proceedings against Christians and Jews, but he made it clear that pagans who became converts to these religions should be punished. This, quite independently of his wishes, led to harsher treatment of Christians other than converts.

Elagabalus was the head of an oriental solar religion, both monotheist and syncretist in its outlook; and in his Elagabalium he had collected all the sacred and symbolic objects belonging to religions of diverse origin. His biography says that he wanted to concentrate in this temple 'Iudaeorum et Samaritanorum religiones et Christianam devotionem', so that 'omnium culturarum secretum Heliogabali sacerdotium teneret'.

Severus Alexander took a further step in this direction. He admired the controls employed by the Jews and Christians in their selection of priests, and set store by certain moral maxims associated with these religions. He therefore granted privileges to the Jews, allowed the practice of Christianity, and collected into a shrine effigies of the figures he thought were fundamental in the spiritual movements of the world—Apollonius of Tyana, Christ, Abraham, Orpheus, and Alexander. His counsellors are said to have dissuaded him from a proposal 'Christo templum facere . . . eumque inter deos recipere'.

Very different a few years later was the behaviour of the harsh Thracian Maximin, who like later Illyrian emperors, coming as they did from parts of the empire where Christianity had yet made little headway, saw in it (and here the ultra-traditionalists in Italy were with them) a cause of the decline of Roman power. Maximin's decision was not to revive the trials of ordinary Christians (though eventually they too were denounced by informers), but to strike a more direct and systematic blow by prosecuting those mainly responsible for propagating the faith, namely the bishops and priests. One response to this crisis was Origen's *Exhortation to Martyrdom*, in which he implores his fellow-Christians not to let themselves be persuaded into sacrificing to the Sun god and taking oaths by the 'Fortuna Maximini', lest by these sacrifices they should give food to demons. This fresh persecution found victims in the highest ranks of the clergy, but it operated over only a very brief period and area, since few governors carried it out.

Among Maximin's successors an important place belongs to Philip, who although he practised the traditional religion was tolerant of others. He allowed Christians to worship and to preach the faith, considered them fit to occupy public office, and was in correspondence with Origen, who was claiming in his preaching that in time all the empire would be Christian.

Special attention must be given to the religious requirement imposed on all Roman citizens in the empire by Decius. Large-scale action against the Christians began in this reign, being dictated by the growth of Christianity and the large proportion of Christians who were engaged in every field of activity. In complete contrast to Philip's policy, Decius prescribed that every Roman citizen should make proof of his loyalty by sacrificing to the gods and the emperor's genius, before a commission which should give him an attested certificate. Undoubtedly one of the main purposes here was not so much to persecute monotheists as to compel the majority of those who adhered to their faith to enter upon a bargain: by performing a more or less symbolic action they would demonstrate precisely their compromised position. In many cases it was considered enough if the citizen burned a little incense on the altar (*thurificati*); no investigation was directed against people who managed to procure a certificate (*libellus*) without sacrificing (*libellatici*); and no savage measures followed that irreducible minimum of citizens who escaped the test by going into hiding. On the many *libelli* which have survived there is no specific reference to Christianity, nor to any demands that a person should recant his faith; and it is very unlikely that only Christians were required to make the loyal sacrifice, since we possess a *libellus* belonging to an Egyptian priestess of the god Petesuchus. The very fact that proceedings were suspended after a few months shows that there was no desire to press the matter to extremes. The government was satisfied with the broad success it had already achieved, since this seemed to guarantee the general loyalty of the citizen body in preparation for the military campaigns about to begin.

Our sources maintain that after four years of toleration Valerian in 257 launched his first edict against the Christians, and followed this with a second in 258, with the intention of gathering financial resources from the property of the condemned. Other causes doubtless existed, too, in particular the military difficulties created by quite a number of Christians who refused to sacrifice on service or even deserted the army. From what Cyprian says in connexion with the second edict it is clear that it was prominent persons who were chiefly attacked. Bishops, presbyters, and deacons were to be charged without further ado; senators, *egregii viri*, and knights were deprived of their posts and their property (and condemned to death if they were obdurate); matrons were exiled, also with confiscation of property; servants in the imperial household were put to hard labour on the emperor's estates. Christian burial-grounds were also confiscated. That the sufferers were fewer than might have been expected was due chiefly to Valerian's capture by the Persians shortly afterwards. His son Gallienus stopped the persecution and ordered the release of Christian property, sending the bishops copies of his rescript so that no one should encounter further trouble.

In the Eastern provinces, then ruled by the dynasts of Palmyra, we find in this same period the first attempt at an agreed policy between State and Church. It is true that the negotiations were conducted with a dissident Christian dignitary, namely Paul of Samosata. This state official and syncretist-minded bishop had been firmly rejected by two synods, which upheld the claims of his rival Domnus to the see of Antioch; and the controversy was again decided in favour of Domnus, so far as the bishop's house was concerned, by Aurelian in the days when he was still friendly to the Christians. At the end of his reign Aurelian became hostile, and just before he was killed he issued an anti-Christian edict which scarcely had time to be put into practice.

But by this time the importance of the Christians in the Roman world had become so great that an extreme decision was needed to avert the consequences of a dualism which inevitably led to periodical conflicts. A decision of this kind was taken by Diocletian. For nearly twenty years he had ruled the empire without seriously concerning himself with this situation, but he was now won over, probably by Galerius, who is said to have employed deceit and craft in his negotiations. It was now Diocletian's view that the only safe course was to take resolute action to root out Christianity and restore the traditional faith. On February 24, 303, his first decree was issued. This was apparently 'sine sanguine', ordaining that Christians should be sought out, and refrain from attending pagan rituals, on pain of exile and confiscation. Two edicts which followed were more severe, being designed to purge the army and the bureaucracy, and to confiscate Church property and the sacred books used for religious services: the penalty for those who resisted was death. The persecution must have been general, although Constantius did not apply it in the Gallic provinces. But its effect was not so much to strike a blow at the upper classes as to deprive thousands of persons of their livelihood and all too often of their lives as well, with an obvious risk of wrecking all services. The results could be seen in Rome as much as in Africa, and in Palestine (see Eusebius' *Martyrs of Palestine*) no less than in Asia Minor.

The futility of these cruel persecutions must have been recognized by Galerius himself. A few days before his death at Nicomedia, on April 30, 311, he issued an edict of toleration towards such Christians as had not been willing to return to paganism. Its words run 'Whereas very many persons persist in their obstinate ways, now therefore we, yielding to our own clemency, have felt it right to grant these persons too our pardon. We allow that there should be Christians once more and that they should hold their meetings, provided they do nothing contrary to our laws. In return the Christians must pray to their god for the well-being of our State.'

Before Galerius, however, there had been another act of toleration towards Christianity, especially at the time of the election of Pope Miltiades in 311, when confiscated property was restored to the Church. This was done by Maxentius, the emperor who in history has been represented as the extreme defender of paganism and as succumbing before the 'Christian' Constantine.

Constantine was indeed the first emperor to comprehend the real elements of the problem, and the first to possess sufficient drive and perseverance to emerge from a blind alley and open up a new highway in the history of the Empire. In substance what he did was admittedly no more than his duty as a ruler who sought the good of the state, and this many of his predecessors had thought they were doing when they followed the old paths. But to reach his objective he adopted entirely new means. He included the Christians among the active components of society and made them one of the most valuable elements in public life, seeing that they possessed a rich store of fresh and vital forces. This Constantine did neither from Machiavellianism nor from devotion, but because he had full consciousness of his mission and trusted in a divine assistance which could not fail him.[35]

g. *The Martyrs*. The Christian apologetic tradition exaggerates when it speaks of innumerable martyrs in the persecutions, but some moderns exaggerate in an equally polemical way when they try to reduce the numbers to a few hundreds. It is beyond doubt that in the course of two-and-a-half centuries thousands and thousands of men and women, young and old, rich and poor, wage-earners and professional men, soldiers and artisans, priests and laity, Romans and non-Romans, offered up their lives freely and courageously for the freedom of their religious convictions. On the other hand these martyrs were only a small fraction of the Christian community, just as the persecutions, however widely spread, were only the moments of crisis, separated by long periods of toleration and mutual contacts. In these latter periods, since there was no explicit law which drastically prohibited the Christian cult, the two organisms, Christian and pagan, ecclesiastical and civil, spiritual and temporal, slowly encroached on each other and became assimilated each to each. On many occasions the execution of martyrs was not so much the result of edicts as of some outburst of popular indignation or of information laid by interested parties, either of which things might prompt or compel action by local magistrates; or they might simply want to get rid of some eminent persons whose behaviour was disagreeable to them.

Surprising though this may seem, the cult of martyrs among Christians certainly did not go back to a very early date: the first evidence for it comes from the mid-second century. Before this the Christians paid no more than the veneration due to all people after their deaths, something which even pagans normally bestowed. Indeed in this matter Christianity accepted most usages then in force: the exceptions were their avoidance of cremation and the fact that they took the day of a man's death as a date to be recorded (calling it the *dies natalis* because it was the beginning of the true life, whereas pagans regarded it as a day of ill-omen). It was from a collection of these dates that the first martyrologies were formed, the best-known being the *Depositio Martyrum* belonging to the Roman Church. The *Acta Martyrum* are a different matter, being valuable historical sources in that they faithfully reproduce the official reports of cases before the courts. Since such reports were preserved in the archives, the Christians would take pains to obtain copies in order to read them at services celebrated on the anniversaries of martyrs' deaths. These bare records were at least valid and authentic, but later on they would get filled out and embellished by the evidence of people who had been present at the martyrdom; or worse still by the addition of edifying legends, full of fantastic detail and lacking any foundation of truth.

This explains the origin of the many false stories, and also of the various superstitions connected with the cult of Saints. Among the earliest *Acta* (or *Gesta*) *Martyrum* three may be mentioned. The *Acta* of St Justin and his companions relate to men martyred in Marcus Aurelius' reign by order of the prefect Junius Rusticus. Then there are the *Acta* of the martyrs of Scilli in Africa (July 17, 180), the earliest Christian document from Africa in Latin and the earliest evidence about the history of the Church in that province. And thirdly there are the *Acta* of St Cyprian, who was put to death at Carthage on September 14, 258; these comprise three separate documents, his first trial concluding with his exile to Curubis, his arrest and second trial, and finally his execution. Then there are works called *Passiones*, which are not proper court records, but of which some have distinct historical and literary importance. For instance there is the account of St Polycarp's martyr-dom mentioned above, and the story of the martyrs at Lyons in 177 and 178, contained in a long letter to the churches of Asia preserved in Eusebius' *Church History*. The *Acta* of SS. Carpus, Papillus, and Agatonice are another instance of this type: and finally there is the celebrated *Passio* of SS. Perpetua and Felicitas, telling the story of these two women and of three catechumens (Saturus, Saturninus, and Revocatus), who were executed at Carthage on March 7, 202. Of this last there is a Greek version, but the original is Latin and may be from the pen of Tertullian. A large part of the work is Perpetua's own autobiography, which is particularly moving, but there is much theo-logical interest besides.

h. The Spread of the New Religion

The nobility of its doctrine was not the only cause of the growth of Christianity. Among other factors it was of prime importance that the Gospel was spread abroad in a very large area which had already been united politically and culturally by the Roman empire, and which possessed unified (or almost unified) laws, administration, language, and roads. This area was by now governed by emperors and magistrates whose origin gave them few ties with the conservative Roman tradition, and the empire was clearly tolerant of the spread of ideas. Jewish synagogues had been erected in some numbers in practically every district, and acted as the first focal points for the dissemination of the new faith. Finally the people in this great area were already conscious of a common desire to deepen and refresh their religious beliefs, partly as a refuge from the growing troubles which affected their lives.

One thing was of course quite fundamental, namely that the oral Apostolic preaching, which was a constant feature of the first generations of Christian-ity, emphasized the clear superiority of the word of Jesus over all other religious and ethical ideas, and the power of the Gospel to satisfy the longings of men's souls. Christianity could be presented as a religion open to all, without any hidden grades of initiation or secrets which could only be revealed to small groups. Indeed it could be seen that it met the age-long want of the lower orders by bringing together poor and rich in worship, in the *agapé* and in burial, and by making woman the equal of man, and slave of master.

The examples of superhuman devotion to the new faith provided by its martyrs were inspiring, and therefore undoubtedly helped to propagate the Gospel. Similarly the many generations of remarkable 'missionaries' never flagged in their zeal to preach the word in both speech and writing.

Hostile propaganda grew wearisome in its repetition of the old accusation that Christians were a bunch of superstitious criminals. (Fig. 14.) Anyone could get to know them directly and become conscious how false the accusations were and how cruel were the condemnations they produced. Men came to see the Christians in their proper light and found them, in the broad mass, to be a people who were not only normal but lived morally blameless lives. They were dutiful, kept away from worldly pleasures, and were devoted to their faith; the ceremonies for which they came together were proper occasions, concerned with worship and with funeral rites.

Another feature which helped Christianity was one due to the interest awakened among the poorer classes. This was provided by the social organization of Christian communities, with their sense of solidarity among human beings and the unselfish working of their relief measures for the needy. Jesus had said 'Love your neighbour as yourself'; and his words were followed by the Church. The story in the *Acts of the Apostles* (iv. 32 ff.) is evidence of the deep feelings of altruism and brotherhood which were to be found among the well-to-do Christians, when in obedience to the rule of Jesus they placed as much as they could of their property at the disposition of the twelve Apostles in aid of such of the faithful as were in need. In the following chapter (*Acts* v) we have the censure of those who evade, in whole or in part, this obligation of charity. In succeeding centuries it was in truth the general rule that rich catechumens, as well as actual Christians, should bestow a suitable part of their goods upon the community, or should be assessed for the payment of weekly or monthly contributions. Moreover as the numbers of the faithful increased it was the normal thing for donations to be fixed according to definite rules and then entrusted deliberately to the clergy for their alms-boxes (*arcae*, Tertullian, *Apologia*, 39, 1). These boxes provided regular subsistence for widows, orphans, sick persons, prisoners, and hospitals; and we are told that at Rome about 251 approximately 1,500 poor Christians were enjoying regular distributions. Besides these there were exceptional contributions to relief for war damage, or to families which had suffered ruin through persecution, plague, or other public calamity.

A final means of strengthening community life and widening the scope of propaganda lay in the steady improvement of the hierarchical structure of the Church, with its essential emphasis on a combination between communities with individual features and a unified organization of the whole.[36]

It is an easy generalization that the main lines of Christian propaganda

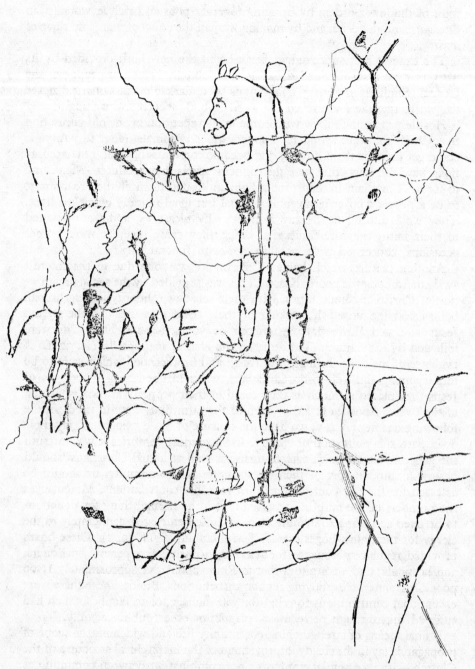

FIG. 14. The Blasphemous Crucifixion, from the Palatine, third-century *graffito*.

followed the roads marked out by trade and commercial expansion. (Map XVII.) The greater part of the audience was therefore composed of persons with whom merchants had previously been in contact and who were relatively accessible, that is to say the inhabitants of the great trading centres of the Mediterranean. Antioch in Syria, Ephesus and other cities of Asia Minor, Corinth and Thessalonica, and Rome itself were the first bases for the religion's rapid spread; from the end of the second century Egypt and Africa too contained important centres of Christian life and preaching; and the periods of peace which the Church enjoyed between about 180 and 250 enabled Christian minorities, of economically powerful persons, to come into being in all the main cities of the recognized world. Nevertheless the intensity of the advance varied from region to region as it grew in the course of time, and only patient study of all the evidence surviving in literature and inscriptions can enable us to fix the proportion of Christians existing in particular districts and periods. In the East the religion expanded fairly early even into outlying and unimportant areas, while in the north-west and in the northern Balkans the spread was for a much longer time confined to the main towns.

But equally important with the number of converts was the average type of person entering the community, the class to which he belonged, and the social influence he could exercise. We must remember here that the second century had seen the early Jewish nucleus converted into a Graeco-Roman one, and also that many people had joined from what today would be called the bourgeoisie—professional men, artisans, managers, merchants, and small farmers. Although the religious fervour and moral purity of the Christian community may have declined, its social importance had grown to the point at which eventually the state could not ignore this powerful organization living inside its territorial borders.

There were few trades in which a Christian was absolutely forbidden to engage. The normal principle was to let each man continue in the profession he was following before his conversion, provided he gave up any dishonest practices, curbed any undue desire for enrichment, and so forth. It was a special question whether a Christian should be allowed to serve in the army or hold public office, but most Christian authors answered this too in the affirmative (so Tertullian's extravagances on the subject must not be taken as the general rule). It is therefore entirely reasonable to depict the Christian communities of the second and third centuries as composed of hard-working peaceful people, who were anxious to be sure of the morrow and found in religion a complement to the morality of their personal lives. Although in theory the distinction between believers and pagans continued (the former being the 'tertium genus' of mankind alongside Jews and Gentiles), in practice everything favoured a meeting and understanding between them. We have already shown that martyrs were in total a very small group compared with the incalculable number of Christians who lived their lives without any necessity of facing the final test, and who actually found means

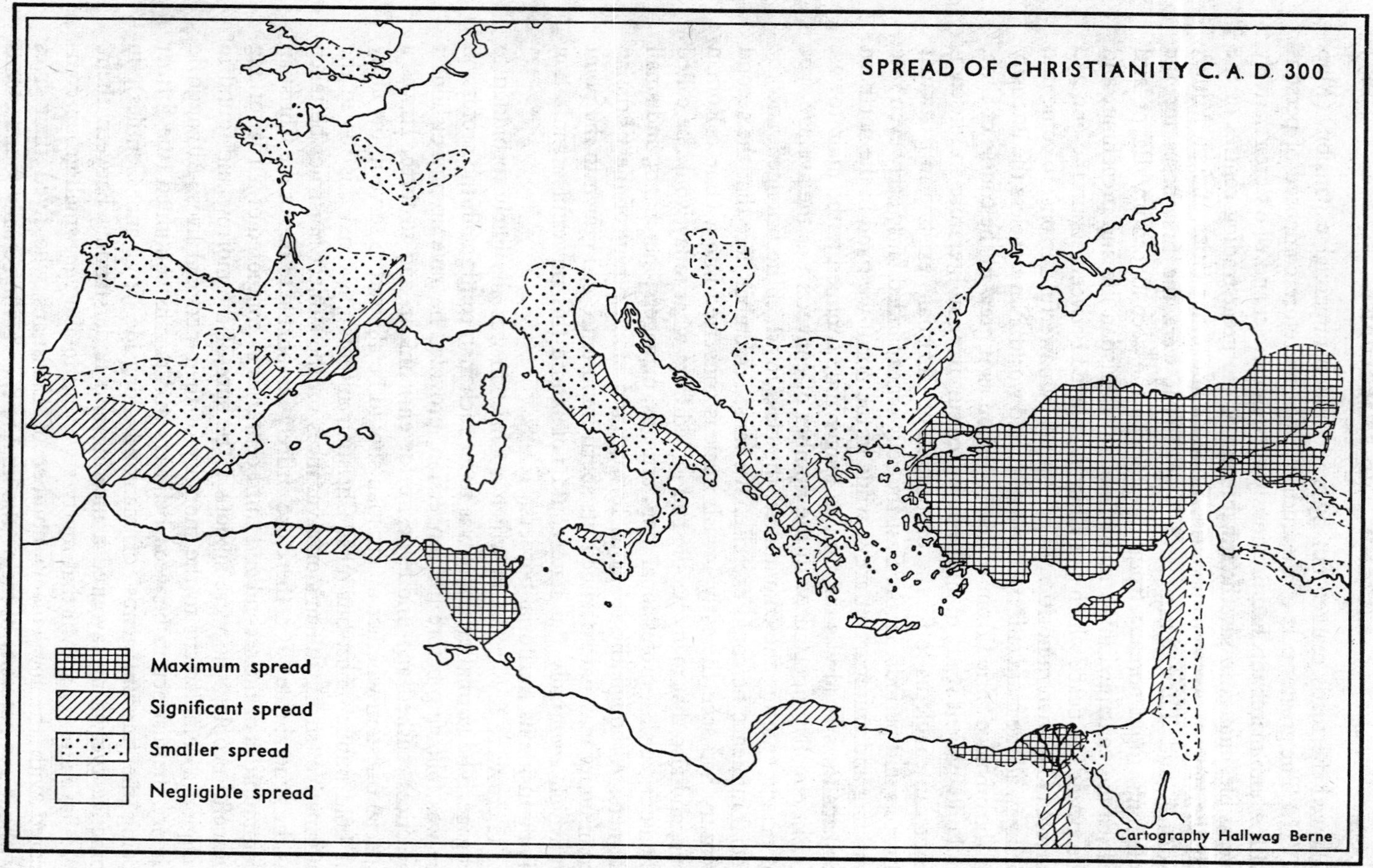

SPREAD OF CHRISTIANITY C. A. D. 300

Maximum spread

Significant spread

Smaller spread

Negligible spread

Cartography Hallwag Berne

MAP XVII

to be a positive force in their environments by working and producing like their contemporaries. In its basic ideas, it is true, Christianity was subversive of the established order, for it proclaimed the equality of all men and the vanity of temporal concerns in comparison with celestial values. Yet in fact it admitted social distinctions as inevitable, and for centuries tolerated slavery (although improving the lot of the slave). It also recognized the beauty of work, adding here a duty to act virtuously; and the Christian took an interest in business, if for no other reason because wealth made charity easier and allowed greater assistance to be given to the needy.

In the early years of the second century we have evidence of Christians at Jerusalem, Damascus, Antioch, Caesarea, Tyre, Sidon, Iconium, Ephesus, Colossae, Laodicea, Hierapolis, Smyrna, Pergamum, Sardis, and Philippi, as well as in certain districts of Arabia, Syria, Cilicia, Galatia, and the Troad. Farther west they are found at Thessalonica, Beroea, Athens, and Corinth, and sporadically in Crete, Dalmatia, and other provinces. Lastly there were the churches at Rome, Puteoli, and Alexandria. By about 180 there were communities as well in Gaul (at Vienna and Lugdunum), Spain, North Africa (at Carthage and Madaura), southern Italy, and Egypt. The list of participants at the Council of Nicaea in 325 provides a complete picture of the spread of Christianity in the East at the beginning of the fourth century. For the West we must supplement this evidence from inscriptions and other texts, since the attendance from the western half of the Empire was very small. Ecclesiastical districts tended to be modelled on the administrative divisions of the empire, but in a number of places they went outside the political boundaries, as in Persia, Arabia, Armenia, and in Gothic territory. However we have little evidence about these Christian communities outside Rome's dominions; they lived a harried existence, being persecuted by the local rulers both for reasons of foreign policy and because the upper class in question could not understand the faith. Yet the perseverance of the Church in these lands, the prosperity of local schools, and the emergence of a number of remarkable personalities, are all significant features worth recording.

. The Church Organization and the Councils

Already by about the end of the Apostles' time Christianity was a 'Catholic Church' in the etymological sense of these two words: that is to say it was a visible association, organized, and universal in its outlook. The essential importance of the earliest ecclesiastical community, within the religious framework instituted by Christ, has become increasingly clear as the result of recent criticism, which completely reverses the earlier emphasis placed upon the individualistic outlook of the new religion. In fact the Church was the middle term, the indispensable intermediary between the faithful and their redeemer; and no action of salvation could be effective unless it was carried out within the Church. Again, Christian promises of a new Kingdom of God on earth could not be implemented without a religious society which transcended the mere collection of persons possessing a common goal; such a society must become an ideal entity and its outlook must be essentially eschatological, directing all its activity with reference to the future. In precise Christian theory even the ecclesiastical hierarchy was not an end in itself. It was ordained to serve a 'communion of saints', the edification of the whole Body of Christ, and the creation of loving unity among believers. It was destined to survive all kinds of external and temporal forms. There are two aspects of the Church in primitive theory, the local community and the transcendent being, the 'charismatic' brotherhood and the organized society; and if we divorce these two aspects, still more if we make them antithetical to each other, we cannot any longer understand Christian origins, where lofty spiritual beliefs and concrete social actions were combined in a single harmonious whole.

To read the *Acts of the Apostles* is to see the importance of the 'Twelve' in the early ordering of the community. Their number, which was that of the old tribes of Israel, was proof of a clear belief in Jesus as the Messiah; and it symbolized the task, which Jesus had entrusted to them, of being witnesses to his resurrection and bearers of the faith confided to their charge. These twelve, having received powers of government and administration, proceeded to teach and perform cult rites. Yet very early we can distinguish in the sources two ways of understanding and carrying out the authority derived from God, namely the preservation of the faith and the performance of ritual services. In other words we must recognize that there was no constant use of *ad hoc* terms, and no precise correspondence between names and functions. The content of ecclesiastical power and the hierarchy employed by the faithful were variously conceived and interpreted according to the needs of the moment in different surroundings. But everyone knew well that a man acting 'as one with authority' must make use of his office not for his own advantage but to perform a service. Such men were 'ministers' in the Latin sense of the word.

Paul regarded himself as bishop of all the churches he had founded. He continued to direct them, passing from one to another; and in his absence there was only an 'alter ego in loco' left to carry out indispensable tasks. Yet in the church of Jerusalem and in the Eastern churches mentioned in the Johannine *Apocalypse* there is a bishop, who is the embodiment of the united community, residing on the spot and taking responsibility. We have already reached the general theory of the monarchical episcopate, which emerges clearly in the letters of St Ignatius of Antioch at the beginning of the second century. He outlines a precise conception of a bishop's position and makes the various pastors the pivot in the working of particular churches. Very similar is the thinking of Cyprian of Carthage (mid-third century), who regarded each community as an organic unity governed by a local bishop with full powers.[37] This bishop derives his authority from legitimate descent from the Apostles, through a regular process of succession.

At this point there arose the problem of relations between the various churches, since there was a pressing danger of fragmentation, a process damaging to Christianity from any point of view. The answer was given by (among others) Irenaeus of Lyons, who insisted that the Roman Church was pre-eminent and that all the faithful would do well to be in agreement with Rome if they wished to preserve intact the true faith handed down by the Apostles. In this way Rome became the witness, the mouthpiece, and the guardian of Christian tradition, not in virtue of priority of foundation (which it did not possess), nor because it was of Apostolic origin (which other illustrious churches could also claim), but as possessing something in greater measure than all the rest. This something was the doctrinal authority of its bishop, the surest weapon for confounding heretics and for establishing religious truth among all Christians. St Cyprian too recognized explicitly and fervently the 'principalitas' of the Roman Church, regarding it as the fountain-head of sacerdotal unity, that is to say as the archetype on which all churches were modelled. Yet he did not infer from this that Rome had the right to intervene in the affairs of other churches: he confined the Roman bishop's action to the achievement of catholic unity. The other sees should conform to Rome's method of procedure and look to it as a point of reference. For the 'Cathedra Petri' was not just a record and a symbol, but a present and working reality in the person of the Apostle's successor.

Ignoring for the moment the intrusions of the civil authority in matters such as nomination of bishops, influence upon conciliar decisions, or grants of temporal power, we can still see the great events at the beginning of the fourth century clearly reflected in the field of ecclesiastical organization. The basic unit was still the bishopric of a city, but above this a growing authority belonged to the metropolitan who presided over a whole province; and from the end of the century onwards we also find patriarchs, who took charge of a number of provinces. Ecclesiastical districts inside the Roman empire tended to be modelled on the administrative divisions of the civil power; but there was no firm organization in outlying regions, and this made Christians tend to disperse at moments of attack by barbarians. The election of bishops was still in the hands of the clergy and city populations, but increasing importance was attained by the 'colleges', which in later times were indispensable for a new prelate's consecration. In addition provincial councils became more frequent as conditions of life became more peaceful and communications more secure (before this time we have full information only about the Carthaginian councils in the mid-third century, which are said to have made decisions on the delicate position of 'lapsed' Christians and on the validity of baptism conducted by heretics). Dioceses were often disturbed by internal struggles, of which the most prolonged and intricate was the Antiochene schism of the third century. This last was brought about by doctrinal differences, conflict of personalities, and irregularities in procedure.

During the reign of Constantine the see of Rome was pushed into the background, but in the course of the fourth century it increased its authority and became an important centre of affairs. As if to underline the bishop's title to priority a new phrase, 'sedes Apostolica', was introduced; this had never taken root earlier because the record of other Apostolic foundations was still fresh, but from that time on the title became the prerogative of Rome. The emperors too were eventually lavish with concessions. Gratian yielded to the bishop the title 'pontifex maximus', which had always been borne by his predecessors, and he put the police force at the bishop's disposal for the execution of ecclesiastical sentences. Theodosius in an edict of 27 February 380, engaged himself to follow the religion 'once taught to the Romans by the Apostle Peter and now proclaimed by the pontiff Damasus'.

Popes Damasus (366–384), Siricius (384–389), and Innocent I (as well as later Leo 'the Great', 440–461) were the main architects of this 'theology of the primacy' by making the weight of their doctrinal authority felt. They declared that no conciliar decision was valid without the approval of the bishop of Rome, 'whose opinion should be asked before that of any others'. To almost every district too they sent 'decretals', letters replying to enquiries put to them by bishops on matters of ordinary administration. In these decretals they discussed questions of discipline and worship in a style which reveals complete awareness that their Apostolic power was supreme and that they exercised a right to which no one could any longer raise objection. Very soon their decisions began to be accepted as authoritative. They were put together in Canonical collections and eventually inserted in the *Corpus Iuris Canonici*. In all pontifical pronouncements on the primacy of Rome we find the notion that Peter is alive and at work in his Church, since the bishop of Rome is identified with him and when seated upon his chair can act as if he were Peter himself. The technical term used for this relationship was 'vicarius', which came to express the concept of substitution of persons between the Apostle and his successors.

Yet it was precisely this period which saw an accentuation of the difference between the two halves of Christendom, West and East; and many pontifical prerogatives and privileges granted to the Roman see were valid only in the western half. Inside this half there is a further distinction to be made between the area immediately subject to Rome (comprising the *ecclesiae suburbicariae* of Latium, Campania, Tuscany, Umbria, Picenum, Apulia, Calabria, and others) and the outer area divided among various metropoleis, such as Carthage, Aquileia, Milan, and Arles. Relations with the East became more strained every day, and the church of Constantinople claimed a patriarchal title which did not belong to it. It was of more recent foundation than other sees, and the claim could also foreshadow a dangerous primacy when exercised by bishops who were closely connected with the imperial court.

The first Oecumenical Council was held at Nicaea in 325 at the wish of the Emperor Constantine, who after his victory over Licinius wanted to give a solemn manifestation of the religious unity obtaining in his dominions. More than 300 bishops assembled in this Bithynian city, brought there by the *cursus publicus*, and held their meetings in the halls of the imperial palace under the presidency of the emperor himself. An incidental reason for the assembly had been provided by a dispute which had broken out at Alexandria between the bishop and one of his priests named Arius, the matter at issue being the nature of the Son of God. Today, however, there is little interest in the doctrinal aspect of the long Arian controversy, since we accord Nicaea, and the councils which followed it, a specific position as ecclesiastical assizes, invested with very precise and substantial functions and powers. The governing principle of these councils may be described as episcopal oligarchy, as opposed to papal monarchy, even though the bishop of Rome was always present through his legates and though the legates were accorded a place of honour in the assembly. Yet it was also true that the final decisions had to be submitted to the pontiff and had no validity unless he promulgated them; and it was precisely during the Arian crisis that a conflict had to be resolved between the conclusions reached by tame councils of court bishops and the vetoes by Rome, sustained by the unshakable faith and iron will of St Athanasius of Alexandria. The Council of Tyre-Jerusalem in 335 is typical, as are those of Sirmium, Arles, Milan, Rimini, and Seleuceia, but at Serdica in 343 the attempt to reconcile Catholics and Arians was a failure. It was recognized there, however, that the bishop of Rome could receive petitions from every part of Christendom and send the cases for examination by a synod. It was only when a fresh Oecumenical Council at Constantinople was summoned by the Emperor Theodosius in 381 that the Arian question could be regarded as resolved, with a complete victory for the dogma of consubstantiality of Father and Son which had been laid down at Nicaea.

j. *Heresies*

Distinctly earlier than political interference engendered by the Arian conflict Christendom had been troubled by 'heretical' movements, and we must now say something about their main course. Strict terminology should prevent us from starting with Gnosticism, since it is now accepted that this was much less a heresy than a general attitude to religious matters which was widespread between the end of the ancient period and the early centuries of the Christian era. But since the first development of ancient Christianity was heavily affected by the existence of this movement, it is essential to say a word about it and especially about the principal known exponents of the doctrine. The complexity and number of the different Gnostic systems make any reconstruction of their chief tendencies a difficult process. The best method of classification is still a geographical one, distinguishing the learned *Gnosis*, with its centre at Alexandria in Egypt, from the vulgar form which was common in Syria and Asia Minor. The one common element was a striving after knowledge of divine mysteries, a knowledge to be acquired not through speculation but through a revelation given by heavenly powers to those who were prepared to receive it in a mystical initiation. This divine communication, which was transmitted by secret messages, was destined to lead to a vision of God and to transform a man in a way that offered him salvation. Yet for the Gnostics the true God was ineffable, and his perfection was unattainable. To bridge the gulf between God and the world they conjured up a complicated mythology and peopled the Universe with intermediate beings. Gnostics also emphasized the dualism between spirit and matter, despising matter and longing to free the soul from it, to enable the soul to reach a higher world. But the dualism in *Gnosis* remained insuperable, and the problem of evil was always the first and most serious problem it had to solve. They multiplied intermediate beings (*aeons*) and attributed the creation to an inferior god (*demiourgos*), but neither these nor their other expedients enabled them to overcome the difficulty; and pessimism became the result of the irreducible antagonism between Light and Darkness, Good and Evil. Nevertheless in those times of restlessness and enquiry complicated speculations of the kind we have outlined were agreeable, because they seemed to satisfy the need for initiation into something higher and for discovering the mysteries of life. So Gnostic doctrines spread widely and exerted a powerful pull on popular imagination, as also on the intellects of the pagan and Christian élite.

About 125 the Syrian Basilides took up residence at Alexandria, and in the same period there was born in that city the greatest and most influential of all second-century Gnostic thinkers, by name Valentinus. The importance of Basilides is his daring theory of pain, which he regarded as exclusively the result of sin. Consequently the martyrs, and even Christ himself, had suffered in expiation of sins they had earlier committed. He also conceived a system of emanations, extending for eight grades down from the Father, who was not begotten; and he supposed that there were at least 365 heavens, born from the unions between different angels.

Valentinus migrated from Egypt to Rome, and there he taught for about thirty years. He took care to reconcile, at least in appearance, his own doctrine with that of the community, and he therefore spoke rarely of the mysteries of *Gnosis*. His literary output is enormous and shows the extraordinary richness of his imagination. In addition he exercised, as head of his school, a remarkable influence on both streams of thought, Italian and Eastern, into which his followers were divided. He peopled the invisible world (*plērōma*) with a number of pairs called *aeons*, each of which generated the next (The Deep and Silence; Cognition and Truth; *Logos* and Life; Man and Church; and so on). The thirtieth *aeon* (*Sophia*) fell when it gave birth to the world, that is to a confused and amorphous mass with all the results one would imagine, such as Sin and Evil.[38]

One of the most controversial points concerned the figure of Christ. The

Gnostics looked on him as the heavenly being who had come to reveal the true God and purify man from the matter that clings to him. For Christians he was above all else the Saviour who had suffered for all mankind; but the Gnostics contested the efficacy of his passion and undermined one of the pillars of the Christian conception by regarding the passion as merely an appearance (this is the theory called 'Docetism'). Equally unacceptable by Christians was the distinction drawn between different categories of men (the *pneumatici*, who were sure of salvation; the *psychichi*, who might or might not attain to the faith; and the *hylici*, who were the majority and who were destined to perdition). This created a grading among the faithful and did not render the benefits of redemption accessible to all.

Finally we may mention the biblical exegesis undertaken by Ptolemy and Heracleon, which took its start from John's *Gospel* and ended by rejecting the letter of that work completely in order to find in it simply a number of hidden meanings. Ptolemy has also left a *Letter to Flora*, explaining the value to be attached to the Mosaic Law. About Bardesanes of Edessa (second half of second century) it is hard to form a judgement, since it is disputed whether he was a heretical Gnostic or simply drew on some portions of Gnostic doctrine; in any case his influence is greater in the history of culture than of religion.39

Another convert to Gnosticism was Marcion, the son of a bishop, who was born at Sinope in Pontus but took up residence at Rome about 140. His considerable wealth and organizing ability enabled him to achieve rapid and marked success. He intensified the opposition between Law and Spirit which was already to be found in Paul, and eventually both repudiated the *Old Testament* and denied any value to the greater part of the *Gospels*, in an attempt to uphold a dualism between the supreme God and the inferior *demiourgos* on the one hand and the God of Evil on the other. Christ was the manifestation of the Good principle, but his manhood was only apparent. Marcion took pleasure in pointing out all the 'Antitheses' or apparent contradictions between different passages in the Bible, since he believed that they provided confirmation of his dualist views and also put the Jews in the worst possible light. Moreover the Apostles, all except Paul, were for him the followers of the *demiourgos* and not of Christ; and from this he concluded that it was essential to found a new Church for the small number of the elect, those who must live as ascetics and stand closely united in their new faith while awaiting salvation. Despite its inconsistencies Marcionism found a large following, because it simplified the exceedingly complex genealogies of the Gnostics and set out a small number of ideas which were both clear and accessible. But Marcionism in turn was later superseded by Manichaeism.

Of quite another type was Montanism, the heresy called 'Cata-Phrygian' from its earliest centre of diffusion. About the middle of the second centruy a neophyte called Montanus, quickly followed by two ladies named Priscilla and Maximilla, began to prophesy and to claim that they saw a number of visions and fell into trances. These effusions of the Spirit, which were not uncommon elsewhere in early Christendom, were held to prepare the way for the Kingdom of the Paraclete, which would follow the Kingdoms of the Father (the *Old Testament*) and the Son (the hierarchy of the Church). It would be manifested in a celestial Jerusalem, which Montanus assured his hearers was about to descend from heaven and come to rest in a plain near the town of Pepuza, where he assembled his disciples. But when their expectation came to nothing, the Montanists organized themselves into a Church and spread widely in Africa and Gaul, though they had little following at Rome. Other features of Montanism included rigorous asceticism, condemnation of second marriages, a call to fasting, and a suggestion that property should be held in common. The Catholic clergy roused powerful opposition to the movement, which was condemned by a number of councils. For a brief period it had seemed really dangerous, on account of the fervour inspiring it and the fact that it was one of the last echoes of the early Christian belief in the end of the world.

To complete this rapid survey of the earliest heresies we must also mention those directly related to the person of Christ. For brevity's sake they may be put into two groups, the Adoptionists and the Monarchianists. Representatives of the former included Theodotus, a leather-worker of Byzantium, another Theodotus who was a banker at Rome, a man called Asclepiodotus, and later one called Artemon of whom nothing is known. The second group was founded by Noetus of Smyrna, and among later members was Praxeas, who after being condemned at Rome migrated to Africa and was attacked by Tertullian in a celebrated pamphlet. The position of the Adoptionists is easy to understand, given the widespread view of antiquity that there were men who for their virtues had been adopted by gods. But it was a view that left the true divinity of Christ hopelessly compromised. Monarchianism, the heresy of the 'unique principle', was quite obviously derived from the rigid monotheism of the Jews. But this view too was fraught with damning consequences, which are summed up in a lapidary phrase of Tertullian, 'Praxeas has exiled the Paraclete and crucified the Father' (hence the custom of calling them Patripassians).

Monarchianism based on philosophical reasoning was carried to extreme conclusions by Sabellius at the beginning of the third century. He is credited with statements of the following order: 'The Word is the Son and the Father, that is to say apart from the name there is only one Being. . . . The One God can be called both Father and Son.' By these means the precise conception of the Trinity and the notion of Christ as both Man and God got lost, and his specific function as Redeemer, achieved through his Incarnation, was distorted. Yet one thing must be underlined, not from the dogmatic but from the more broadly cultural standpoint, about this multiplicity of theories and deep conflict between schools which we find between about 150 and

250 AD. This is the keenness of interest in speculative thought, combined with the influence exerted on Christian theology by classical philosophy. We should also note the uncertainty in the use of terminology, and the numerous errors made in the interpretation of the sacred books by many of those who tried to handle them.

k. *The Greek and Latin Apologists*

The view taken of the Christians by both educated people and the populace in the second century was mainly one of incomprehension accompanied by great contempt. So a number of writers, called Apologists, tried in this period to make known to the pagans the ground for their faith and to clear their brethren of the serious charges made against them. They appealed to the general laws of the Roman empire about matters of religion, and attempted to demonstrate the absurdity of many things in which their adversaries believed, by pointing to the immorality of the ancient gods and to the superiority of Christianity both in doctrine and in personal and social ethics.

The Christian *Apologies* were addressed to rulers, magistrates, or the people at large. They varied in length and nature according to the personal character of the authors and the time at their disposal: they could be erudite or straightforward, didactic or dialectical, satirical or hortatory, violent or serene. During the fifty years between 130 and 180 nearly a dozen Apologists are known, such as Quadratus, Marcianus, Aristides, Athenagoras, Tatian, Melito of Sardis, Theophilus of Antioch, and Miltiades. But the greatest of all was St Justin, who was born in Palestine about 100 and was converted to Christianity after various experiences in philosophy. He later moved to Rome, where he opened a free school and later suffered martyrdom under Marcus Aurelius. In his two *Apologies* he is the champion of a type of Christianity 'ante litteram': the *logos spermaticos* illuminates the pagans and shows them the way to the full revelation of the truth made actual in Christ. He was also very conciliatory of the political authorities, in contrast (for example) to Tatian, who was most bitter in his attacks on everything produced by classical civilization and was practically a rebel against the laws of the state.

In addition the Apologists' writings are full of interest for the amount of information they provide about the life of Christian communities, and about Church organization, pious practices, the moral weaknesses of many members, methods of worship, and so on.

In the course of the second century another form of Christian literature began to appear. This too was polemical, but it was directed not at the external enemies of the faith but at those who fought it from within, the so-called 'heretics'. This term is derived from the Greek word for 'choice', since heretics were those who selected a portion of the truth from the treasury of revealed Christian doctrine, and therefore went outside the rule or canon laid down by the authorities of the Church. In actual fact there was for a long time no clear separation between orthodoxy and heresy since the former gained its precision through dialectical argument with the latter; and in the majority of cases heresy at the outset did not present itself as a deliberate movement of separation, but rather as an attempt to deepen and interpret what existed already. The delicate process of selection and assimilation occupied several centuries before the majestic and harmonious edifice of Christian theology was fully built. But this period is important not only from the standpoint of the history of thought but because of the human interest attaching to the personality of the protagonists, with the intimate drama of their thoughts, the keenness of their disputes, and the multiplicity of views and doctrines they produced.

Here we shall mention only the chief authors of polemic against the heretics, though it should be noted that many other writers of the early centuries (historians, Apologists, and theologians) contain important and valuable information about the various exponents of heretical movements, together with attempts to confute their errors. The greatest champion of the Catholic reaction was St Irenaeus, a native of Asia Minor: he later moved to Gaul, where he became bishop of Lyons during about the last thirty years of the second century. His most important surviving work is the *Adversus haereses* in five books, in which he not only demonstrates the errors of the Gnostics but lays great insistence on the conception of the Incarnation as the summit of divine intentions, designed to give mankind full possession of the life of God. For Irenaeus, Christ summarizes all humanity, being the centre of creation and the explanation of all the workings of providence. In this way the story of the world can be regarded as an educative process, bringing man to the highest ranks of perfection through the many manifestations of God's redeeming love. But Irenaeus was also a great upholder of the value of tradition, as the guarantee that man is adhering to the faith that has been revealed. We have already seen the strength of the claims he makes for the continuity of the Roman bishopric (see above, p. 877).

For all his merits the theological speculation of Irenaeus is not greatly original, being confined almost entirely to references to the Scriptures. Greater heights of thought were reached in the so-called School of Alexandria which directed Christian doctrine into new channels by trying to show that the new religion was able to meet the widespread spiritual needs of the time, and by borrowing formulae and ideas from pagan philosophy to express the content of what had been revealed. The attempt was a bold one and was not free from awkward consequences. But Pantaenus, Clement, and Origen put serious preparation into the task they had set themselves, and for this reason their achievements are enduring.

Pantaenus was a native of Sicily, learned in Indian philosophy, who opened his own school in Alexandria in the last quarter of the second century. He imparted various religious notions to the faithful, and also to any Jews and pagans who wanted instruction on the subject. Clement was his pupil, a man born at Athens about 150, who had already taken up with a number of philosophical schools and mystery religions. He pursued the teaching methods and the doctrines of Pantaenus for more than twenty years, his aim being to act as a sure guide to souls in their search for God and in the way to possess him: this was something they could achieve if they lived in accord with the precepts of true *Gnosis*, which meant revelation. To this end Clement also composed a number of writings, of which some survive. The *Protrepticus* is an exhortation to the Greeks, in twelve chapters. Then there is the *Pedagogus*, in three books, a long moral treatise teaching the way to comport oneself in the various circumstances of daily life without sacrificing one's religious duties. Thirdly the *Stromata*, in eight books, an untidy collection of notes on the nature of true *Gnosis*, on the relation between *Gnosis* and faith, and on the picture of the perfect Gnostic. Another interesting work is his homily entitled 'Quis dives salvetur', which does not take the well-known passage in the Gospels literally and displays great tolerance towards rich Christians.

Clement expressed the Christian faith with feeling and sincerity; he was also deeply concerned with morality, and showed respect for the Church and its sacraments. But his system is defective because he pushed the position of Christ as Redeemer too much into the background, losing it under a vague conception of an illuminating and educative force among mankind. He also uses allegory too much in his interpretation of the data in the Bible, constructing an artificial piece of exegesis on every word and incident. Yet one must recognize that this was the one way to get the Bible text accepted by the non-believers of his day.

From various standpoints Origen was very different from Clement. He was born a Christian, had much more sense of the duties belonging to the life of an ecclesiastical community, and had much wider and more diversified cultural interests. Even under his direction the school at Alexandria had no official status. It was more like a higher institute for sacred studies; and the same continued at Caesarea when Origen was compelled to leave his own city as the result of his excommunication by an episcopal synod (for ordaining a priest outside his own diocese). We shall say more about Origen's thought later on. Here it is enough to add a note about his successors in the Alexandrian *Didaskaleion*, which changed its organization and outlook after his departure, though it always remained a cultural centre of very great significance and distinction. Its teaching began with Dialectic (what we should call formal logic), which trained pupils to reason; then followed Geometry and Astronomy, which gave them rigour and precision, and the Natural Sciences, which taught them to classify, and so to admire God's creation. Then one passed to higher studies, divided into Ethics and Natural Theology. The explanation of the Holy Scriptures was the crown of this *cursus* of encyclopaedic education in which the constant concern was to give a religious tone to everything: science was not to be cultivated for its own sake, but only as a means of raising the student to the level of his Creator and so preparing men who were active and ready to defend their beliefs.

For two years the headship was held by Heraclas, an ex-colleague of Origen who had later abandoned philosophy in order to make himself into a rigid tutor of orthodoxy. When he was then made bishop of Alexandria, the direction of the school passed to another of Origen's pupils, Dionysius, who, following the same path as his predecessor, was himself made bishop down to 264. He conducted a lively series of theological disputes with his namesake the bishop of Rome, since like all Origenists the Alexandrian Dionysius admitted some degree of subordination of the Son to the Father. Later on we have scanty references to the Alexandrian school, and the figures of its chief exponents, such as Theognostus, Pierius, Pietrus, and Achillas, do not stand out with any clarity. Later the one notable thinker was Didymus the Blind, but times had now changed and the heat of the Arian conflict had modified the local situation. Several defects in Origen's system came to light, and a new cycle began both on the theological side and in the problem of relations between Christianity and classical culture.

In Alexandria it was the Hellenistic mentality which Christian thought had encountered and heavily absorbed. Its contacts were different in the towns of Syria and Mesopotamia, but not less important since those countries too were rich in cultural traditions. In this way the Christian religious message took on different forms of expression related to the place in which it was being unfolded; and the situation was complicated by a number of questions of ecclesiastical jurisdiction (such as the authority and precedence of the great patriarchal sees), as well as by the political interests of the Roman empire. This or that body of doctrine would win favour, for reasons which were not always clear (or at any rate not wholly so) and were not entirely the result of speculative thought. The main representative of the trend running counter to that of Alexandria was the so-called School of Antioch in Syria. When Antioch too became Graecized, the role of bulwark of the old native theology current among the Eastern churches was taken over by Edessa, a metropolis of religion and letters in the Euphrates valley and a point of contact between Semites and Westerners. But the time came when even the survival of this theology at Edessa was rendered impossible by the hostility of the emperors at Constantinople, who had political reasons for favouring the Alexandrians. At this point representatives of the Antioch school took refuge at Nisibis, outside the borders of the empire. There they strengthened their position by establishing relations with the Arabs, and for many centuries they exerted a generally beneficial influence.

The main point of divergence lay in the different principles adopted by the two schools over biblical exegesis. In contrast to the Allegorism of Alexandria, which sacrificed the text in order to discover in it some more hidden and spiritual meaning, the prevailing tendency at Antioch was one which may be called historico-grammatical. This was based on solid hermeneutic principles, and was designed to give the maximum value to the letter of the text, without any frills and fantasies. We know little of Antioch's cultural life before the end of the third century, but at that moment a personality of real significance made himself felt. This was Lucian, a native of Samosata educated at Edessa, who was eventually martyred at Nicomedia in 312. He became the centre of a group of churchmen, bound to one another by close ties, who are known as Conlucianists. They ultimately occupied all the main episcopal sees, with Eusebius at Nicomedia, Maris at Chalcedon, Menofas at Ephesus, Theognis at Nicaea, and Leontius at Antioch. But Arius too was one of their number and this may be enough to show the general lines of their theology.

The chief work of Lucian was to edit a text of both *Old* and *New Testaments*. This was called 'Lucianean' after its author, but it was also known as the 'common' text because it circulated so widely in the East. By matter-of-fact methods and constant attention to the sacred writings Lucian presented explanations which were the outcome of patient research and were free from mystical ventures. Yet his teaching aroused great enthusiasm, perhaps because there was need for a return to clarity and precision after the over-daring flights of fancy achieved by the Alexandrians. But it seems that Lucian, following a local tradition which had previously had its greatest exponent in Paul of Samosata, did not explicitly recognize the divinity of Christ. He would not allow the Son of God the same nature as that of the Father, but regarded the Son as a being adopted by God and equipped with exceptional qualities. It may be that this idea, in the form Lucian expounded it, was not an error of dogma but simply a judgement which happened to diverge from what was commonly accepted.[40] It caused great trouble none the less, and a campaign of criticism was unleashed with rapid and unparalleled violence.

The earliest Christian writers in Latin who attained any literary dignity were Tertullian and Minucius Felix, both of them Africans living at the end of the second century. Almost to the middle of the fourth century the principal Christian literature in Latin came almost exclusively from African authors, and for another century after this the contribution of the district was still very marked.

The apologetic works of Q. Septimius Florens Tertullianus are distinguished from those of Greek writers of a slightly earlier date by the legal support he gives to his arguments and by the violence of his invective. This invective is too rhetorical to be convincing, and in general Tertullian's position is strained, although he had undoubted qualities as a controversialist and was completely sincere in his passion as a converted Christian, jealous to preserve in its purity the faith he had attained. Besides the *Apologeticus* and *ad Nationes* he wrote a long list of works: the *de praescriptione Haereticorum, adversus Marcionem, ad Scapulam, adversus Praxeam, de Baptismo, de paenitentia, de spectaculis, de patientia, de cultu feminarum, ad uxorem, de fuga in persecutione, de pudicitia*, and *de pallio*. For the most part these are lively works which touch on very real problems. They show signs of their author's rigid moralism, the quality which towards the end of his life took him outside orthodoxy into the sect of the Montanists. But they also reveal a high level of classical culture, which despite Tertullian's repeated protests that he wanted nothing to do with the fruits of pagan thought yet allowed him to twist his language into the expression of ideas previously unknown and so to forge a new vocabulary.

Minucius, in his dialogue *Octavius*, reveals a completely different character. Although he defends the Christians from false charges and criticizes superstition, he presents a Christianity without Christ, one which is confined to the basic elements of divine justice and natural ethics. Minucius is an elegant writer, but he clings too closely to his classical models and has none of that vigour which despite everything made Tertullian so great.

In the mid-third century another convert, Cyprian, bishop of Carthage (see above p. 876), a man who had also given proof of organizing ability, of apostolic charity on many occasions of calamity, and of understanding for sinners in time of persecution, was able to make a not inconsiderable contribution to literature by publishing thirteen treatises and more than eighty letters. The titles include *ad Donatum*, *ad Demetrianum*, *de Lapsis*, *de Dominica oratione*, *de habitu virginum*, *de opere et eleemosynis*, *de Bono patientiae*, and *de Catholicae Ecclesiae unitate*. Quite apart from the immense importance of these as historical sources, and even if we ignore the full contribution they make to dogmatic and disciplinary questions, they are quite admirable for their stylistic elegance, balanced periods, and the gentleness and lofty harmony which the author's personality has imprinted throughout their pages.

Another African, Arnobius, a late convert to Christianity, wrote very differently (*c.*AD 300). The style of his seven books *adversus Nationes* is pompous and classical in manner; there is no deep Christian feeling behind his violent polemics against the pagans; but his satire can be effective and he is capable of vivid illustration. More learned and more serene was his pupil the 'Christian Cicero', Caecilius Firmianus Lactantius. He again was an African, the author of seven books entitled *Divinae Institutiones*, a systematic presentation of Christianity, and also of the *de Opificio Dei*, the *de Ira Dei*, and an important historical account *de Mortibus Persecutorum*, the reliability of which is not affected by the writer's preconceived thesis. Lactantius lived at the moment of transition between the persecutions and the later favours bestowed on Christianity by the state. He saw that the new religion was a precious feature of civilization and was therefore conscious of its more humane and beneficent aspects. He expressed these views in a finished prose style, though in the search for the elegant phrase he often falls flat. His doctrine too is lacking in depth, though he has clear ideas about theology and ethics.

A further polemic against the pagans was the *de Errore profanarum religionum* of the Sicilian Firmicus Maternus. But by now (in the second half of the fourth century) the main themes of Christian writers had altered, by reason of the changed spiritual background, the development of dogma, and the needs of pastoral teaching. We have reached the golden age of patristic, which saw an exceptional flowering of genius: these were men who combined culture with piety, mastery in writing with the sincere resolve to help their contemporaries through education. In this way not only did the heritage of Christian thought expand miraculously, but literature too had a remarkable revival: even in this part of human activity the new faith could exercise its refreshing power. We need not list all the authors who flourished in this period. A few words about the leading names will give us a clear idea of the type of writing then in vogue and its distinguishing features.

Hilarius, bishop of Poitiers, after being exiled to the East by the Emperor Constans II on account of his opposition to Arianism, brought back to his own country a cultured and polished vocabulary of a kind unknown before in the West, although his own writings (*de Trinitate, de Synodis, contra Constantium*, and a number of sacred hymns) use involved forms and archaic language. But the bringing of Greek Christian thought to the Latin world was even more effectively the work of St Ambrose. In 374 (he died in 397) he was suddenly elected bishop of Milan by the people, having gone there as civil governor to take part in the assembly; and he quickly found it necessary to build up an ecclesiastical culture on the Greek model. His main works, apart from several lengthy letters, are on oratory, exegesis, and dogma; and something is said about his hymns on p. 928. Titles include *Exameron, de Virginitate, de officiis Ministrorum, de Mysteriis, de Excessu fratris, contra Auxentium*, and *de obitu Theodosii*. All his writings have great historical interest, because of the abundance of references to events of his time, but what also emerges most clearly is the author's humanity. He passionately longed to bring moral perfection to his hearers; he was fully conscious of the prerogatives of a bishop, believing them valid even against the highest political authorities; and his noble spirit revolted against social injustice. A judgement on him as a writer is made difficult by our text, which in many cases is a later elaboration of Ambrose's own words based on notes or stenographic reports of his discourses. In general, however, he was cultivated, elegant, and lively; and just as he was always concerned above all else to exalt the ethical ideal of pagan sages in the light of Christianity, so too he brought back to life the language and style of classical writing.

The arduous process whereby the Christians absorbed the culture of earlier times found its greatest practitioner in St Jerome (Eusebius Hieronymus). He was a Dalmatian who had lived at Trier and did most important biblical work at Rome, but who then took refuge in a hermitage at Bethlehem, where he died in 419. As a controversialist he was quick to take offence, but he was a man of rigid moral standards and an untiring scholar. He gave Christianity of the period around 400 what it lacked, a Latin translation of the Bible which was satisfactory from every standpoint. Yet in his opinion this laborious philological work on the Holy Book could not be an end in itself: it had the didactic aim of teaching the spirit of the Christian religion by way of the letter, in order to derive good rules for practical conduct. This explains his continual representation of arguments between Cicero and Christ, of which we find an echo in his *Letters*; and these works are interesting for other reasons, both for their historical references and because they are often regular treatises on asceticism and spiritual guidance. They give great charm to the character of their author, which is full of humanity and intense feeling. Lastly we must mention Jerome's historical works, his *Chronicon*, *de Viris Illustribus*, certain *Lives*, and a number of writings against the heretics of his day. It is right to emphasize the linguistic and stylistic excellences of the author, who had so keen a sense of Latinity but could combine the purest classicism with his spiritual vigour and achieve an original synthesis which was both admirable and productive.

But superior to all earlier Fathers in genius and culture, and in the experience he had endured in relation to the problems he confronts, was Aurelius Augustinus, the greatest doctor of the Latin Church. We shall deal later with his life and philosophical thinking (p. 903), but must say something here about his contribution to literature. To understand their meaning and value we must follow the writings of Augustine step by step, since there are few other authors whose writing expresses so dramatically the stages in his turbulent intellectual and religious experience. Every work, however short and however much confined to particular subjects, has an important place in the evolution of his thought. The vast mass of his writings makes a summary impossible, and we must be content with indicating Augustine's themes. Above all there were the polemics against a number of heretics, the Manichaeans, Donatists, Pelagians, and Arians. The order is both chronological and logical, if we remember that he first confronted questions about God and the universe, then those about the Church and salvation, then passed to Man and freedom, and closed the cycle with the problem of Man, God, and the Redeemer. Next come his works of exegesis and teaching; then his enormous output on theology and philosophy, followed by his moral and pedagogical writings; and finally there is his 'opus magnum et arduum', the *de Civitate Dei*, an encyclopaedia of Apologetic and doctrine. To these must be added his *Sermones*, *Epistulae*, *Retractationes*, and a number of scattered works. One is left astonished at the capacity of this one man, who in addition attended to the affairs of his diocese and of the African Church, administered justice, concerned himself with the spiritual well-being of his friends, ministered to the poor, and so forth. Psychological subtlety, acuteness of speculation, an ardent faith, and zeal for the right cause, all these are qualities to be found in his writings, and even now we have not included his clarity, objectivity, and learning. He is able to adapt his form to his content, availing himself of all the resources coming to him from a consummate knowledge of literature. At the same time he gave his work a personal stamp, which in no way detracts from the elegance and compactness of his style, but yet is better able to express the intensity of feeling in his soul. In other words he is always sincere and convincing as a writer, even though he borrows heavily from rhetorical schemes laid down by the schools and is full of reminiscences from the Bible. Nevertheless, just because his writing is so personal, it is lacking in any order imposed from outside; it is rich in digressions and does not appear to exhaust his themes. Unity in his work must be sought rather in the way he radiates outwards from a central idea. One must always progress upwards from the incidental point which caused Augustine to direct his pen to the general principles to which he repeatedly comes back in his adventurous arguments and which he illustrates with warmth of emotion and even anguish.

1. *Byzantine Caesaro-papism*[41] *and Arianism*

The definitive phase of Constantine's imperial organization saw the triumph of the monarchical idea, supported politically by a hierarchy of lay imperial officials, and also by a hierarchy of churchmen under the leadership of bishops belonging to the triumphant new monotheistic religion. It was the continuous aim of this emperor to prevent his unified system from breaking up, either through the creation of a dualism such as that which later operated with fatal consequences between laity and clergy, or by the dissolution of religious unity as the result of theological disputes. Yet these disputes were inevitable, above all in Constantine's time the 'Arian' controversy. This started about 320 at Alexandria, in the form of a strictly theological argument related to the person of Christ. In the early centuries two sets of doctrine had made their appearance, one at Alexandria the other at Antioch, both tending to subordinate the Son to the Father, although not denying to the Son his exceptional function in the 'economy' of the Redemption. Arius, who was born in Libya, a cultivated and serious-minded priest, said something in a sermon which displeased his bishop Alexander and brought on himself condemnation at the hands of the local synod. In other districts, however, Arius was warmly received, and in this way the movement began to spread and bring itself to the attention of the political authorities. At this time the Emperor Constantine, having defeated his colleague Licinius, had emerged as sole emperor, and was tending to push the centre of gravity of his state farther and farther to the East. It was a good moment for summoning an Oecumenical Council, to show the world the value of imperial protection to the Church, and at the same time to clarify a number of doctrinal and disciplinary points which had not yet been defined with sufficient precision. In this way the causes of conflict might be removed.

In May of 325 the Council met at Nicaea. So far as Arianism was concerned, it established the doctrine of 'consubstantiality' (*Homoousia*) of the Son with the Father, in contrast to the Arian view of the relationship as one of 'similarity' (*Homoiousia*). As a result Arius was sent into exile as a heretic and his followers were removed from any bishoprics they were holding.

But very soon Constantine changed his policy. There may have been family reasons for this, but the real force was a political one, as is proved by the succession of emperors who from that time on were friendly to Arianism. They could not ignore the fact that an oligarchy of bishops at court, ready to obey the political power, was an instrument of government of a kind not provided by the popular mass of Catholics, who were led by bishops out to defend their own independence in religious affairs. So although the new bishop of Alexandria, Athanasius, made himself a rigorous defender of Nicene Catholic orthodoxy, we enter upon a period of many decades marked by a giddy round of councils, protests, condemnations, exiles, and definitions, tending first in one direction and then in the other.

By now, however, Constantine had decided on a policy of supporting Arianism, and this was later followed by his son Constantius II. In 335 a council was held at Tyre at Constantine's wish, to rehabilitate Arius and condemn Athanasius. In 337 both Constantine and Arius died. When the struggle for the imperial succession was over, the victor, Constantius II, thought he could complete his restoration of political unity in the empire by restoring moral unity through the imposition of Arianism. A series of councils was held at Arles, Milan, Rimini, Sirmium, and Seleuceia, at which the will of the *dominus* prevailed and a number of the orthodox (such as Hilarius of Poitiers, Lucifer of Cagliari, Dionysius of Milan, and Eusebius of Vercellae) had to go into exile. Even the bishop of Rome, Liberius, was compelled, by the use of actual force, to retire to Beroea; but a few years later, exhausted by his labours, he pledged himself to lay down an anodyne formula, and was allowed to return to his see. Meanwhile, however, the Arians were splitting up into various parties, ranging from the moderates, like Basilius of Ancyra, to the very extreme 'anomians' such as Aëtius, who by now had little that was Christian in their thought.

m. *Julian's Attempt at Pagan Restoration*

On the death of Constantius II the new ruler, Julian, also possessed unified political power. He had by nature an aversion from Christianity, but to this he added disgust at the endless doctrinal conflicts among the Christians and at the way the imperial power was caught up in them. He wanted to go back in history to the early ideas of Constantine, when Christianity was no more than a tolerated religion and paganism was still the religion of the state.

Hence his twofold action, for the restoration of paganism and the disintegration and abasement of Christianity. To attain the latter aim he stopped all favour for Arianism and even brought Athanasius back from exile. With this move he administered a set-back to the party which did not possess the support of the masses; indeed, to prevent the excesses of the orthodox party, their main spokesmen, and even the bishops returning from exile, undertook the task of pacification. But at the same time Julian fomented their quarrels. He recalled the African Donatists, much beloved by the *humiliores*;[42] he removed Christian teachers from the schools on the ground that they were incompetent to explain the texts of pagan literature; he cancelled privileges granted to the Christians; and he put into circulation once more all the polemic and accusation directed against them by the Jews, and by Celsus, Porphyry, and others.

On the other hand the paganism he proposed to restore was certainly not the paganism of Augustus' day. It had been largely altered by theurgical ideas and Oriental influences,[43] designed to meet the new needs of the human spirit and the religious innovations introduced by the two men who inspired Julian's policy, Maximus of Ephesus and Julianus of Athens. Moreover these cults, partly from conviction and partly in order to compete successfully, were beginning to imitate the Christian hierarchy and social work. Priests, each of whom attended to the cult of all the gods, were subordinated to the emperor as *pontifex maximus*. Austerity, religious preaching, the giving of alms, and even some ceremonies and ritual (such as initiation and penitence) were being copied from Christian practice.

But by now Julian's attempt could only be artificial. Victory over the Persians was intended to bear witness to protection and power of the ancestral gods. When this failed and Julian died, the whole undertaking came to an end, though it had brought ruin to thousands and led to violence its author had never intended.

n. *The Triumph of Catholicism*

With the death of Julian and the accession of Valentinian and Valens the pagan restoration collapsed and Christianity resumed its progress. But at the same time the Arian controversy revived, though in a minor key, in a number of centres. Even at Milan Ambrose as bishop had to face certain obdurate Arians, who were supported by the Empress Justina.

Yet broadly speaking the triumph of the Catholic Church had been achieved by the end of the century. It was sealed in 380 by an edict of Theodosius I imposing the Nicene Creed; and this was proclaimed by an Oecumenical Council convoked by the same emperor at Constantinople, which declared as valid the faith professed by Damasus at Rome and by Peter at Alexandria. Peter had succeeded Athanasius, who had died after a long period of exile in Gaul, where he had introduced monasticism, a practice hitherto unknown in the West though fairly widespread in Egypt.

The Arian affair occupied fully sixty years of the middle of the fourth century, and had repercussions and effects of various kinds in every territory of the Roman empire. If we are to make a complete judgement upon it, we must take account of two factors, the religious or theological aspect, and that related to politics and Church organization. On the first aspect the point to notice is that beyond the various formulae lay two conceptions of divinity.

One was a cold, philosophical, and distant conception of the supreme God, on the Greek model: the other was the more original Christian conception of the Father who was the mysterious giver of life. Here the victory of Catholicism was of advantage to all later progress in the elaboration of doctrine and philosophy. As to the second aspect, it is clear that Arianism gave Caesaro-papism its first test and showed the unhappy consequences that flow from state absolutism when it is applied to personal beliefs and extended to the field of ecclesiastical organization. In its own turn the Church hierarchy, with certain laudable exceptions, showed itself to be lacking in moral energy and unaware of its duties.

But the decline of paganism was given official and decisive recognition during the rule of Gratian (367–383) and Theodosius I (379–395), the latter being the colleague who was originally chosen by Gratian to govern the East but who gained control of the West as well after Gratian's death. It was in this period that the old priestly colleges had their immunities suppressed, and that the dignity of *pontifex maximus*, renounced by the emperors, became a prerogative of the popes. The senate, despite the prayers of Symmachus, removed the statue of Victory. And finally Theodosius ordained the closing of pagan temples and the abolition of their priesthoods, a speech in opposition by Libanius proving of no avail.

The last restoration of paganism was that undertaken by the rival emperor Eugenius (392–394), who had been proclaimed by the Gaul Arbogastes after his destruction of Valentinian II, and was in the paradoxical position of receiving support from both barbarian soldiers and traditionalist Romans. But the attempted restoration was futile and short-lived, as well as being confined to a small area. After Eugenius had been defeated by Theodosius on the Frigidus the official condemnation of paganism became final.

The condemnation could take effect more easily in the populous towns than in the villages and countryside. It naturally did not root up every cult which had thousands of years' history behind it. We can prove the contrary from ancient evidence like that from Maximus at Turin, and also from inescapable survivals of the ancient gods in the cults of saints who took their places: such saints gradually established connections with hilltops, woods, fountains, and caves, the last refuges of pagan worship. It is an open question whether the actual name 'pagan' was coined to distinguish the followers of the ancient religion because they survived only in the *pagi*, or whether it was intended to mark the contrast with the Christians who formed the 'militia Christi'.

o. *The Conflict between Rome and Constantinople*

The bishopric of Constantinople had no right whatever to claim parity with the other great metropolitan sees in the ancient Church. Still less was it in a position to compete with Rome, which boasted an exceptional tradition doubted by no one hitherto. On the other hand it is easy to understand how emperors ruling or residing in the East found it useful to push the bishop of their capital into prominence. He was almost invariably going to be subservient to their wishes, and made an excellent instrument in their hands, especially as he had influence on his fellow bishops. A good instance of this situation is found at the Council of 381, when Theodosius as emperor, though defending orthodoxy against the last Arian efforts at resistance, decided at the same time that the bishop of Constantinople was entitled to 'a primacy after the bishop of Rome, since his city was a second Rome'. This opened a very wide door. It made a city's political position the test of the importance of its ecclesiastical see, disregarding any other type of claim and preparing the way for Byzantium to exercise oecumenical jurisdiction directly the older Rome should have lost all political significance.

The situation became even more complicated at the beginning of the fifth century, when John Chrysostom, a man who was both high-minded and obstinate, became bishop of Constantinople and intervened forcefully in court affairs and in the lives of rich Christians in the city. At least twice he was sent into exile, at the instigation of the Empress Eudoxia and despite the protests of his devoted admirers among the faithful. This shows clearly that the performance of Church business in that city was now wholly dependent on the interests of the state, and that even doctrinal orthodoxy was a matter secondary to the need to win the sympathy of certain influential representatives of the clergy.

Imperial policy was often determined by the conflict between the see of Byzantium and the great sees of Alexandria and Antioch, a conflict which varied in severity but was never far below the surface. Rome would take part in the exercise on occasions, though usually as a moderating and balancing force.

Without going outside the limits of this volume we may sum up the position by saying that every new event made the conflict more fundamental. The dependence of the bishop of Constantinople upon his ruler became more emphatic, and the Byzantine clergy in general had to serve political needs. The result was a Caesaro-papist system of mutual responsibility, which though damaging to religion brought no small gain to the state and was one of the reasons why the Roman imperial organization in the East could survive so long.

The Roman bishop, on the other hand, eventually controlled every activity which went on in his city, and acquired such superiority to every other power that in later days he was able to dispose of thrones in western Europe. Pope Leo, in the mid-fifth century, in his wise and courageous action on behalf of the city when it was menaced by the barbarians and possessed no civil organization, almost seems like a mediaeval pontiff. Rome, he declared, had been 'founded anew by the Apostles, and was destined to be head of an empire which was truly universal'. This explicit pronouncement on Rome's mission shows the conception of history which then prevailed and the interpretation given at that time to the spiritual and temporal primacy of the 'Eternal City', even when confronted with the 'New Rome' on the Bosporus.

7. GRAECO-ROMAN PHILOSOPHY

a. *Stoicism*

Philosophers at Rome in the first century of the empire did not lead a peaceful existence, especially the Stoics, who mostly held republican views.44 Their propaganda against despotism provoked reprisals from a number of emperors, such as Tiberius, Claudius, Nero, Vespasian (who banished all philosophers from Rome in 71), and Domitian—that is to say chiefly, but not exclusively, those who were tending in the direction of the Dominate. This state of affairs, combined with the small interest shown in philosophy by the Italians of those days, helps to explain why, after an initial period in which the figure of the Spaniard Seneca stands out, these studies and speculations were largely left to Greeks and Orientals. Even such Westerners as remained in the field eventually very often wrote in Greek. Moreover the general tendency was for thinkers to concern themselves with moral and religious questions rather than with the improvement of methods of thought.

L. Annaeus Seneca the Younger (*c.* AD 4–65) belonged to the Stoic school, the one which was the most numerous in the first century AD. It counselled and taught its adherents to be indifferent to the external world and to uphold a rigid code of morals. By this time Stoicism was less of a philosophical theory than a guide to a noble life, in which a man was prepared to sacrifice himself to avoid departing from his ideals. Seneca's work showed partiality towards eclecticism and was written in a forceful, though somewhat artificial and rhetorical style. Like other Stoics he was concerned with practical ethics, which he treated in all its aspects in twelve dialogues. He also wrote, on similar subjects, the *Ad Neronem de Clementia*, the *De Beneficiis*, the *Naturales Quaestiones* and the *Epistulae Morales*, the last two addressed to one Lucilius.45

Two other famous Stoics of this period, both of whom wrote in Greek, were also Westerners, namely L. Annaeus Cornutus of Lepcis and C. Musonius Rufus of Volsinii. Cornutus was the teacher of Persius (see below p. 921) and was exiled by Nero: he wrote in both Greek and Latin, and there survives a *Theologia Graeca* containing historical, allegorical, and etymological explanations of myths (the *scholia* to Persius and the very late *Disticha Cornuti* are not his). Musonius was twice exiled, once by Nero, the second time probably by Titus; and each time recalled, first by Galba and then by Titus himself. His writings, consisting of both discourses and letters, are lost; but his work lay less in them than in his very flourishing school, which was attended by both Lucan and Persius. A pupil of his, named Pollio, composed the *Thoughts of Musonius*, a work still read in the fifth century.

At the turn of the century lived Hierocles of Alexandria, described as 'vir sanctus et gravis', from whom there survive on papyri large parts of a work on the guiding duties of life entitled *Elementary Ethical Theory*.

Epictetus of Hierapolis in Phrygia (*c.*AD 60–140), the manumitted slave of a freedman of Nero, was a pupil of Musonius and maintained a school at Rome until he was banished by Domitian to Nicopolis in Epirus. He was a pure Stoic, hostile to eclecticism; his curriculum consisted of logic, reading of philosophical works, and practice exercises in which the pupils criticized their master. He did not publish his writings, but we know of his ideas and methods from his devoted pupil Arrian of Nicomedia, who wrote eight books called the *Diatribes of Epictetus* (four have survived), twelve books of *Homilies*, and an *Encheiridion* which was later re-edited by the Christians and subjected to commentary in the Middle Ages.

Dio Cocceianus, later nicknamed Chrysostomus, from Prusa in Bithynia (*c.*AD 40–115), started by being hostile to philosophy but later became a champion of Stoicism. He made long journeys in the north-eastern provinces of the empire (writing a *Getica*, which has been lost). He had been exiled by Domitian, but was recalled in 97. In his *Diatribes* he tackled serious social and political problems; then he held municipal offices in Bithynia (his *Bithynian Orations* belong to this period); in 105 he was again in Rome, but is last heard of once more in Bithynia in 110–111, when he was put on trial before the Younger Pliny. Of his seventy-six *Orations* the earliest (such as the Rhodian and Trojan) are artificial pieces of rhetoric belonging to the period of his activity as a Sophist; the others were written in his Stoic period (such as the *Diogenic Orations*, the *De Regno*, the *Olympian Oration*, the *Political Questions*, and the *Euboean Oration* on poverty). An admirer of ancient Greece and a critic of Rome, he possessed a style which for all his attempts at polish remained heavy. But he tried to equal the Attic orators (see again below p. 932).

Kebes in his *Pinax* or *Tabula*, a first-century work anticipating Lucian-described a picture on view in a temple, and drew from it a complete alle, gorical interpretation of human life, imagined as a city with bastions (man's duties) all round it. This work circulated widely from the second century onwards, and is a mixture between Stoic thought and that of the Platonists and Pythagoreans.

The last name in this list of Stoics is that of the emperor Marcus Aurelius (121–180), who from his boyhood days, when he heard the orators Herodes Atticus and Fronto, was a follower of the Stoics Apollonius of Chalcedon and Junius Rusticus. We possess some of his Latin letters to Fronto, but for his own satisfaction he wrote the *Meditations (ta eis heauton)*, which have survived in a small collection composed between 166 and 174. This is a marvellously intimate work, consisting not so much of confessions as of daily reflections and thoughts which have been noted down. No special attention has been paid to style or language, but the sensibility and sincerity are such as to make this one of the most exquisite pieces of writing which appeared before the triumph of Christianity. In the *Meditations* we can see not only the melancholy that besets the 'philosopher' emperor, but the whole complex spiritual condition of the most highly educated part of the contemporary pagan world.

b. *Other Schools*

The Peripatetic school still had a few representatives, but we know little more of them than their names.

Among Epicureans may be mentioned Diogenianus (second century) who wrote attacks on the Stoic teaching of Chrysippus, and Diogenes Laertius of Cilicia who wrote a *History of the Philosophers*. The latter is a pedestrian work but it is immensely valuable to us: it contains a list of the principal philosophers in each school, with brief notes on their lives (including anecdotes), their works, and their basic ideas.

The Sceptics and Cynics, who survived into the third century, included one or two men of importance. Favorinus of Arelate in Gaul (born *c.* 70–80, died under Antoninus Pius) was taught Greek by Dio Chrysostom and Epictetus, was a friend of Plutarch, and master of Herodes Atticus, and kept a school of rhetoric and philosophy at Rome. His *Pyrrhonian Speeches* survive in ten books (one for each *Tropos* of Aenesidemus), and are directed to the conclusion that all judgement must be suspended. Sextus Empiricus (end of second century) wrote three books called *Outlines of Pyrrhonism* (*Pyr-rhoneioi hypotyposeis*), and a surviving work entitled *Sceptical Commentaries*. The latter is a repertory of all the innumerable arguments, sometimes serious, sometimes captious and childish, which can be directed against dogmatic philosophy and against the teaching of any form of science. Finally there was Oenomaus of Gadara (second–third century), from whom there survive fragments of a work entitled *The Showing-up of Quacks*, an attack on oracles.

In contrast there was a marked development in neo-Pythagorean theories. About Apollonius of Tyana there is such an accumulation of legend that one ends by doubting the reality of his existence (supposedly AD 4–96). The earliest references to him are found in Lucian and Libanius, but the story goes that his *Bios* was created by Damis and Moiragenes, whose work was advanced further by Philostratus in the third century, under orders from Julia Domna; and only Philostratus' *Life* has come down to us. In it Apollonius is described as a Sophist and Pythagorean, a moral and religious reformer, a worker of miracles during journeys which took him between India and Gades, a friend of philosophers and of Vespasian, and an enemy of Domitian. Neo-Pythagoreans, and Neoplatonists, too, set him up as a figure in challenge to Christ, and in doing so provoked counter-attacks by Christian writers like Eusebius and Lactantius. Many of his works are cited, both on religion (*De Sacrificiis*, *Theologia*), and on oracles and prophecy (*De Divinatione Astrologica*); but they are all of doubtful authenticity. We are apparently better informed about his letters, from references in Philostratus and Photius, and from a separate collection of seventy-seven documents; but there are so many incorrigible contradictions here that they are probably all forgeries by various authors.

From Moderatus of Gades (first–second centuries) we possess fragments of two books called *Pythagorean Teaching*. Nicomachus of Gerasa (early second century) is known to have written on mathematics and philosophy (a *Manual on Harmony*, and the *Arithmeticé Eisagogé*). Finally, Numenius of Apamea in Syria maintained in his various treatises (*The Departure of the Academy from Plato*, *The Good*, and so on) that Platonic thought was fundamentally identical with that of Pythagoras, Moses, the Brahmans, the Eastern Magi, and the Egyptians. He also believed that there were three Gods, one superior God who was independent of matter, one in between, and one below who was himself the World.

For Latin neo-Pythagoreans see below.

c. *The Platonists*

But the school which was destined to produce most writing and to make greatest progress towards new ideas was the Academic or Platonist school. We can ignore lesser figures, who are little more than names to us, and dwell for a moment on Mestrius Plutarchus of Chaeronea (45–117 or later). Plutarch was a pupil of the theologically-minded Academic Ammonius. He studied deeply in medicine, mathematics, rhetoric, and other subjects, journeyed widely, and had a number of illustrious friends, including some at Rome; later he returned to his birthplace at Chaeronea and lived there with a small group of pupils, becoming in his old age a priest of Apollo at Delphi. The *Suda* tell us that he had been consul and had taught Trajan, also that later on he was made general superintendent of Achaea, but all this is very doubtful. He was a great reader and assimilator of knowledge, and his output in Greek was vast (the catalogue made by Lamprias comprises 227 titles); much of it (though not all works attributed to him are authentic) has survived. The normal division of it is into *Moralia*, which are popular writings on subjects like rhetoric and philosophy, and historical works. With the latter (Plutarch's *Lives*) we shall deal in Chapter XVIII, though they too have great interest from the standpoint of moral philosophy. The *Moralia* are sometimes in the form of 'diatribes' or alternating discussions, sometimes dialogues, and sometimes ordinary treatises. They may be classified by subject as follows:

Religion—De Superstitione, De Iside at Osiride, De Sera numinis vindicta, De Pythiae oraculis, De Demone Socratis, etc.
Metaphysics—De Anima.
Physics—Quaestiones naturales, De primo frigido, etc.
Psychology—De sollertia animalium, Bruta ratione uti, De esu carnium.

Hygiene—De tuenda sanitate, De ira cohibenda, etc.

Ethics—Amatorius, De tranquillitate animi, De fortuna, De garrulitate, De fraterno amore, De amore prolis, Praecepta coniugalia, etc.

Education—De liberis educandis, De recta ratione audiendi, etc.

Philosophical doctrine—Platonicae quaestiones, Non posse suaviter vivere secundum Epicuri praecepta, Adversus Colotem, De Stoicorum repugnantiis, etc.

Philology and Literature—De Herodoti malignitate, Comparatio Aristophanis et Menandri.

Music—De musica (Pythagorean in outlook).

Politics—Praecepta gerendae republicae, De unius in republica dominatione, Ad principem ineruditum, etc.

Aetiology—Quaestiones Romanae, Quaestiones Graecae, etc. Various spurious works have also found their way into the Plutarchian collection, mainly because they deal with themes similar to those of the authentic works. Plutarch was a lover of his Greek mother country, but no less of its Roman conqueror; he was an Academic, but had eclectic tendencies. His work was published widely and was very easy to read, being resolutely free from any form of purist mannerism. He has been indeed one of the most widely read authors in the literature of the world, because his writings are among the noblest and most complete examples of 'humanity' in the world of imperial Rome.[46]

d. *The Emergence of Neoplatonism*

The Platonic philosophers of the second century gradually abandoned moral questions for those of religion, metaphysics, and theosophy, thereby entering the orbit of the syncretist tendencies of the period. From Platonism they passed to Neoplatonism. Albinus, who taught at Smyrna and was in 151 the master of Galen, has left fragments of a work on Plato's *Dogmas*, drawing markedly on Peripatetic and Stoic, as well as Academic, doctrine. From Atticus, a commentator on Plato who was alive about 175, we possess part of a commentary on the *Timaeus*. Theon of Smyrna discoursed on Plato's mathematical ideas, and wrote on astronomy. A special place belongs to Celsus, who wrote the first Platonist polemics against Christianity. We learn of his theory of the 'True Word' from citations by Christian Apologists and especially from the full refutation of it made by Origen in his *Contra Celsum* about the middle of the third century.

These hesitating advances reached fruition with Plotinus of Lycopolis in Egypt (204–270), the champion of a new set of philosophico-religious ideas normally known as Neoplatonism. He was the pupil of Ammonius Saccas, and from 244 lived in Rome surrounded by numerous disciples and admirers. He left a number of writings, put together hastily, without much attention to style, clarity, or grammar: these were arranged in six novenas or *Enneads*, concerned respectively with ethics, the world, government, the soul, the reason, and the nature of being. Plotinus believed that man must separate himself from worldly things, which in those years were so full of pain and confusion, and look towards the after-life. He arranged the gods in a graded hierarchy, with a single and abstract God at its head. Man through thought must unite himself with God and live with him. The intelligence can purify itself by crossing over the sensible world to the non-sensible; and where intelligence fails man can substitute intuition, or ecstatic rapture in the vision of God. Plotinus' religion was not lacking in either faith or enthusiasm. But it remained a conception of the learned and the initiated, something which could not be understood by the common man, who was meanwhile being fired by the sacred doctrines of Christianity, so simple and yet so lofty.

Porphyry of Tyre came first under the influence of Origen and Cassius Longinus (the author of *Was Homer a Philosopher?* and works on rhetoric and grammar). Later, during the six years 263–269, he was taught by Plotinus. He wrote many works, among which we may mention his philological studies on Thucydides and Homer, a *History of Philosophy* in four books, and a *Life of Pythagoras*; later he produced *An Introduction to Knowledge of the Intelligible, On Abstinence from Flesh, Philosophy from the Oracles,* and *On the Images of the Gods*. He was continually trying to transform Neoplatonic theory into theosophy and religion, and claimed that divination provided means for a permanent relationship with the divine world. In his fifteen books *Contra Christianos*, of which we possess only fragments, he set this faith up as a challenge to Christianity, whose Apologists regarded him as a formidable enemy.

Iamblichus of Chalcis in Coelesyria (*c.*280–335), was a pupil of Porphyry who maintained a school in his own city. His main work was a *Life of Pythagoras*, which offered a form of Neoplatonism bereft of any rational foundation, and reliant instead on a fantastic ecstasy and unending revelation of the gods, in which everything consists of speech with an infinite number of good and evil spirits in a world where miracles abound. There is attributed to Iamblichus, though it is not certainly authentic, a work called *De mysteriis* (of the Egyptians), which sets out to make known all the inhabitants of the invisible world and the means of evoking them through signs and mysterious rites. This is a typical product of the extreme religious ideas of the non-Christian Hellenic world.

In this setting of ecstatics and men possessed with spirits a number of spurious works of a 'Pagan Gnostic' nature were circulated under the names of the actual pagan divinities, like Hermes Trismegistus, allegedly the author of the *Libri Hermetici*. Similar were the *Poimandres* and the dialogue of 'Asclepius' with King Ammon.

The last resistance of philosophy and pagan religion against the victory of Christianity naturally found its greatest champion in the Emperor Julian, the so-called Apostate. Much of his literary work is concerned with philosophico-religious subjects, or with devotion and meditation (*To the Sun-*

King, reflecting the ideas of Iamblichus, and *To the Mother of the Gods*), or with polemics against Christianity. We know the content of the first of his three books against Christianity from the ten books which Cyril wrote in reply. With great learning and bitter sarcasm Julian set out to prove that the moral and religious ideas of the Bible were inferior to those of the Greek philosophers. Elsewhere, in his *Caesares* (or *Saturnalia*, or *Symposium*), he puts into the mouth of Silenus, as an improvised judge of the various emperors, a severe criticism of the pro-Christian Constantine. Other works treat of moral philosophy, for instance the *Misopogon*, in which he lashes luxury in a series of attacks, and the *Contra Cynicos*. His other writings include his *Orations* (two insincere and conventional panegyrics of Constantius II, and a sincere eulogy of the Empress Eusebia), and a lost historical work on his campaigns in Gaul. There are also about seventy letters, which are sometimes extraordinarily realistic and dramatic; for instance that written in 361 to the Athenians to justify his rebellion against Constantius.

Gradually Neoplatonism lost its main centres of activity one by one, including its famous home in Syria. In the East the only schools which held out for a time were those at Alexandria and Athens. In the former the instructress was Hypatia, daughter of Theon, a woman learned in philosophy and mathematics, who had taught Synesius. But at the beginning of the fifth century she was murdered by the people in a riot stirred up against her by the Christians. The Athenian school survived beyond the chronological limits of this volume under a series of scholars from Nestorius to Proclus. It attempted to improve and widen its work by adding to mathematics and theurgy the study of psychology, dialectic, and the allegorical and pedagogical analysis of texts.

Latin literature in general remained untouched by the more advanced speculation of the Greek neo-Pythagoreans and later of the Neoplatonists also, though it naturally felt the influence of both. We can appreciate such influence as early as the second century in parts of the writings of the 'Magus' Apuleius: for instance in his unfinished *De Platone et eius dogmate*, where Platonic doctrine is markedly distorted; in his *De Deo Socratis* and *De mundo*: and also in the mathematico-astrological ideas contained in his *Naturales quaestiones*.

Cornelius Labeo in the third century was profoundly learned about the various religions of antiquity and tried by means of physical, allegorical and historical interpretations to ennoble and unite them into a single Neoplatonist conception (which drew down on him the attacks of Christian polemic). His works were entitled *De dis Penatibus*, *De oraculo Apollinis Clarii*, *Fasti*, *De dis animalibus*, and *Explanatio disciplinae Tagetis et Bacitidis* (on Etruscan augury).

Three of the last Latin Neoplatonists also deserve mention. Julius Firmicus Maternus of Syracuse, before he became a Christian and delivered his attacks on dying paganism, had been a Neoplatonist. As such he wrote, between 335 and 337, eight books entitled *Mathesis*, in which he tried to bring ethics into line with the astrological ideas he had absorbed from his reading. Parts of this work already show the influence of Christian conceptions.

e. *Christian Philosophy. Origen and St Augustine*

Calcidius' commentary on Plato's *Timaeus* alludes to Christian works, for instance to the Hexapla of Origen. This commentary, dedicated to a certain Hosius (who may have been the famous bishop of Corduba in the first half of the fourth century), was engaged in polemics and exegesis, in theological studies and preaching, then was condemned for being ordained as priest outside his own see, but died as a martyr at Tyre. The aims of his 'apostolate' in cultural matters he expressed in the following terms, 'Nowadays, under the guise of *Gnosis*, heretics are rising up against the Church of Christ, and piling up volumes of commentaries, in which they pretend to interpret the texts of the Evangelists and Apostles. If we remain silent and do not set true and sound dogmas against them, they will get possession of hungry souls; for if these souls find no sound nourishment, they throw themselves eagerly upon these forbidden foods, which are impure and abominable.' So he presented a general picture of reality, starting from the conception of a good God, the Creator of all spiritual beings. Yet between the world and this immutable and unapproachable God he set the *Logos*, consubstantial with the Father but subordinate to him, the pattern of all created things. These things partake also of matter and may allow themselves to be perverted by it and be satisfied with their existence as it stands. In this way they fall into sin. It is essential to free oneself from corporeal things and gather oneself together, in order to return into participation in the Goodness of God; and in this task of making himself perfect every man can take as his pattern and example the events in the life of Christ. Through this striving after purification all reality goes progressively forward to the final 'apocatastasis', which with an end to the punishment of sinners will see the triumph of the good.

The philosophy of Origen emerges mainly from his work in four books entitled *De Principiis*, which have come down to us in a Latin version. It occasioned much controversy, for it involved many dangers for orthodox doctrine; and it is not free from internal contradictions. Yet both for the motives which inspired it and the language in which it is expressed it remains a bold and important achievement, carried out with disinterested enthusiasm by a man who wanted to give a rational basis of support to the Christian religious message.

At the beginning of the fifth century (and here we are compelled by logical necessity to go beyond the limits of our period) Augustinus of Hippo, a man of wider personal experiences and much greater genius, embarked once more on the course marked out by his predecessors and formulated the highest philosophical synthesis attained by ancient Christianity. Born at Tagaste in 354, Augustine studied in various schools and passed through

many currents of thought at Carthage, Rome, and Milan, down to the moment
of his conversion to Catholicism in 386. He then returned to his home town,
but could not realize his dream of a life of study accompanied by a small
band of friends; instead he was called to govern a diocese and found himself
involved in polemic against the heretics. He died in 430 at a moment when
his city of Hippo was being besieged by the Vandals, a people who were
engaged in putting a speedy end to Roman civilization in Africa.

The writings of Augustine are very numerous and varied, including works
of apologetic, pastoral, polemical, exegetical, and theological character.
Four titles at any rate must be mentioned, the *Confessions*, *De vera religione*,
De Trinitate, and *De Civitate Dei*. Yet Augustine was not a systematic
thinker and he did not always hold the same opinions on the greatest problems
of philosophy throughout the long course of his work.

He began with a phase of scepticism, and then derived from the Neoplatonists an awareness of the need to escape from the sensible world. After
this, by a continuous struggle and increasing depth of inward thought, he
strove to attain Truth—or God—by greater knowledge of himself. A true
enquiry, he believed, makes it necessary to transcend all finite things and
encounter the real Being, who is the giver of life and fountain of good.
This Being is found to be in the closest contact with the human soul: it is he
who gives light to the mind and it is he alone who can satisfy that desire for
well-being and peace which is ingrained in individuals and also in societies
throughout history.

There exist no obstacles of a metaphysical kind to prevent the process of
a return to God. So even Evil is not an entity deriving from some principle
which exists: it is simply the absence of Good. Man's will is not wicked
because it has been weakened by sin or vitiated by nature, even though it is
true that every good action already requires divine grace to put it into effect,
a grace which is given freely according to principles unknown to us.

The task of philosophy, after determining the end of existence (namely
God), is to make all men realize the possibilities of their being and to put all
things in their places. By this means there will be a universal order of peace
and joy, in which it is still God whom we serve first of all, but in which the
other activities of man find a way to develop themselves and acquire a
positive (and not 'indifferent') value of their own. Indeed history, which is
guided by Providence, proves that the antagonism between the two Cities
(societies) of good and of bad men can be overcome by the realization of a
just state, one that is supported by Christian religious ideals and is also
directed to the good of humanity in the temporal sphere.

NOTES TO CHAPTER XVII

1. Violent hostilities took place on various occasions in the south of India between Viṣ-
nuites and Śivaites, particularly in the persecutions of the Śivaite King Cola which led
Rāmānuja to exile himself in Mysore for nine years.

2. The localization of important Śivaite centres in Kashmir and in the south (not only around Kāñcipuram but even farther south, Māmallapuram, Cidambarum, Madura, etc.) is final, but the flowering of Śivaism was very great in the west too where Kālidāsa contributed to it, and where it is attested by the monuments at Ellora and Elephanta.

3. It would be interesting to note from the point of view of scientific history that the theoretical conceptions at the base of *Yoga* rest on the physiological pneumatic doctrines of the *Āyurveda* and on a psychology of the unconscious. In this theory psychic acts leave latent but active impressions in the individual which govern his subsequent situations, and which can be methodically chosen by the discipline of action and meditation to guide the individual to given situations, including liberation from mundane attachments, and salvation.

4. One can be more precise in explaining the burden of the assertion that all is empty, by saying that it is a question of being 'devoid of existence of a thing's own right' (*svabhāvaśūnya*); this means that things have no existence or essence by themselves or in themselves, no absolute consistency of their own (which is why Stcherbatsky called them 'relative'). Things not being natural autonomous beings are reduced to images surrounding the fundamental reality (*paramārthasatya*), the essential existence.

5. The elaborating movement of the *Tantras* appears mostly to correspond with a formalizing of rituals and religious practices associated with the beliefs of various religions—Śivaite, Viṣṇuite, Buddhist; beliefs recorded in the canonical and instructional literature which contains the edifying legends (*Jātaka, Purāṇa*, etc.). *Tantra* is practically synonymous with *Āgama*. The general character of the *Tantra* and *Āgama* do not tend towards sexual symbolism. That is limited to certain sects. Their general feature is to prescribe a ritual, linking rites properly so called, and formulae (*mantra*); this ritual being different from Vedic ritual in having as its crowning achievement the obtainment of salvation (*mukti*), rather than the Vedic ritual which essentially aims at procuring prosperity (*bhukti*).

6. Emperor worship in its earliest phase still had a definite connexion with the divinity it honoured. A distinction should be drawn in this respect between the East, where the tradition of the *Dea Roma* was strong, and the West, where in certain of the imperial provinces, such as Tarraconensis, the emperor was acknowledged as *Deus praesens* (R. Etienne, *Le culte impérial dans la péninsule ibérique d'Auguste à Dioclétien*, Paris, 1958, Bibl. des Écoles françaises Athènes et Rome, 191, pp. 374–5). Nor was the worship of the *Divi* accepted immediately; it did not become widespread until the reign of Vespasian. The worship of Rome did not extend to all the provinces until Hadrian's time. But in Tarraconensis it was associated with the worship of the deified emperors and of their living successors. (Robert Etienne.)

7. This enumeration takes too much account of the East and passes over the very active centres of Tarragona and Merida; provincial emperor worship was not established in the senatorial provinces of Narbonensis, Baetica, and Proconsular Africa until Vespasian's reign. (Robert Etienne.)

8. The empire transfigured the concept of loyalty, by centring it upon the emperor—the August One. The Lares of Augustus became the 'august' Lares and the Apollo of Augustus became the 'august' Apollo; *Augustus* was also appended to the title of *Iuppiter Optimus Maximus*. No property, real or ideal, was denied to the emperor; every god and goddess was decked with the epithet of *augustus*, which conferred increased authority without altering the original significance. Thus the whole pantheon united to acclaim the imperial divinity, so that under the empire the real religious centre of a city was the temple dedicated to the imperial worship. (Robert Etienne.)

9. We entirely dissociate ourselves from this political, realistic, and pessimistic view of emperor worship; or rather, we maintain that its manifestations should be examined in their chronological perspective. It is incorrect to say that it began as an expression of political loyalty and respect for tradition. On the contrary, it would not be improper to speak of it as a form of 'imperial mysticism'. Though Augustus and Tiberius objected to some manifestations of it, which they considered to be ill-timed or dangerous, the fact

remains that the provincial population believed in certain divine symbols: the palm-tree, rising from the imperial altar at Tarragona, contributed to the mystique of victory, and the emperor on his coinage announces his eternity, just as his presence was felt in the cities he founded and his virtues perpetuated for praise by his deification. Later on— chiefly as a third-century development—the individual sank back into the collective, and impersonal sovereignty found expression in the triple concept of Rome, the *Divi*, and the *Augusti*. Persons were gradually making way for institutions; the foundations of the state were defined and given expression in the titles of priests and public officials alike. The state had become an object of worship, and at that epoch, naturally, political loyalty gained precedence over mystical fervour. (Robert Etienne.)

10. Silvanus, the Latin god of woods, acquired exceptional popularity in the Po valley, in Illyricum, and in other Western provinces, doubtless through syncretism with local divinities. Cf. J. Toutain, *Les cultes païens dans le monde antique* (Paris, 1907), I, pp. 261 ff.; G. E. F. Chilver, *Cisalpine Gaul* (Oxford, 1941), p. 193.

11. In point of fact there was a limit to this fidelity to the native worship, in Gaul and else-where in the Celtic territories. Most of the local divinities were dubbed *Augustus*, which paved the way, so to speak, for their official recognition. Epona, one of the most revered goddesses of Gaul, is sometimes referred to as *Epona augusta*. Although not many Gallic divinities were admitted to the Augustan pantheon, their subjection to its influence must not be overlooked. (Robert Etienne.)

12. Stress should again be laid here on the links between oriental forms of religion and the worship of the emperors—illustrated, for example, by the taurobolical altars at Lectoure (R. Etienne, 'La chronologie des autels tauroboliques de Lectoure', in *Gascogne gersoise, archéologie, histoire, économie*, Auch, 1960, pp. 35–43), particularly on December 8, 241, by the city fathers in honour of the emperor Gordian, the Empress Sabina Tranquillina, and the whole divine house (*C.I.L.*, XIII, 511 = *I.L.S.*, 4126). It should also be noted that in this city of the Lactorates a certain Valeria Gemina observed the Blood Feast of the primitive myth by dedicating the *vires* of Eutyches (*C.I.L.*, XIII, 510 = *I.L.S.*, 4127) and that once on the day set aside for the imperial worship she took part in a tauroboly in honour of the emperor (*C.I.L.*, XIII, 518 = *I.L.S.*, 4128). The same clergy and the same worshipper are thus present at ceremonies held for two different purposes; this unity transcends the differences between the two religious calendars and bears witness to the cementing influence of the imperial religion in the Roman world. (Robert Etienne.)

13. This 'catholic' aspect of the congregation is not confined to the eastern religions. Finan-cial, social, and legal differences were swept away in the emperor worship. Anyone could be a votary of the imperial divinity; the priesthood and the religious communities were open to the rich and to the humble without distinction; the *augustales*, in particular, rescued freedmen from the contempt attaching to their origin and condition. (Rober Etienne.)

14. Serapis may rather be said to have been introduced by Septimius Severus, after being associated under Commodus with the theology of imperial victory. The triumphal arch at Lepcis Magna, erected to honour the family of Severus, depicts the Capitoline triad with the emperor enthroned as Juppiter Capitolinus in a replica of the Serapis of Bryaxis; indeed, from the year 204 onwards, Serapis was the favourite form of portrayal for emperors, as on the arch of the money changers (*argentarii*). It must be remembered that when Septimius Severus visited Egypt in the year 200, his curiosity was aroused by the worship of Serapis (*Script. Historiae Augustae, V. Sev.*, 17). The ideology of the sovereign as a god upon earth reaches its culmination with Septimius Severus-Serapis; the divine apotheosis is no longer reserved for the person of the emperor, but extends to his whole family group. The solar, Serapidian aspect of Septimius Severus is strengthened by his Jovian character. A Tripolitanian inscription (*Inscript. of Roman Tripolitania*, 295) is addressed to 'the benevolent Lar of Severus, my sun, born of Juppiter'. In the *Septizonium*, a monument dedicated to the seven planets and completed at the end of 203, the emperor occupies the central niche, in the place of the sun-god, and in the pose of the cosmocratic god, which resembles that of Serapis. At this stage Serapis was promoted to the rank of tutelary deity of the imperial family. Caracalla took

the sobriquet of 'philoserapis', and during his reign he made a zealous display of devotion to the Alexandrian divinities; but his father had pointed the way and in this respect the son was merely a follower. (Robert Etienne.)

15. Despite all evidences of syncretism, the sun-worship of the Severi masked a rivalry between Sol-Serapis and Sol-Baal which has been suggested as an explanation of the enmity between Caracalla and Geta. Geta was the first to issue coins in the name of Sol-Baal, and he was undoubtedly the favourite of his mother, Julia Domna, daughter of the High Priest of Baal at Emesa. Not until Geta had been murdered was Caracalla's Serapian empire able to express itself freely. The triumph of Baal, prepared by Julia Soemias and Elagabalus after the death of Caracalla, might be regarded as the revenge of the Syrian worship. The accession of Severus Alexander would also seem to have marked a return of Serapian orthodoxy, in a setting of religious equivalence. In any case, this emperor adorned the temple of Isis and Serapis in a befitting manner (*Script. Historiae Augusta, V. Sev. Alex.*, 26. According to *Roman Imperial Coinage*, IV, 2, forty-eight designs of coins illustrate his devotion to the sun. (Robert Etienne.)

16. It is very important to grasp more precisely the attitude of Julian the Apostate towards the gods. Though regarding himself as chosen by God for his position as leader of the empire, he never fell into the excesses of oriental mysticism, as his pagan and even his Christian predecessors had done. His rejection of the deification of rulers is exemplified by his attitude towards the monarchical ceremony then customary at court and the honours which the populations of the towns through which he passed were eager to lavish on him, by his refusal of the title of *dominus et deus* which his forerunners had accepted, and by his ironical manner when the dead emperor was to be deified. The ruler is no god, but he must imitate God by following the purest Platonic tradition, for he has to show by his actions that he is really the elect of the gods. Divinity is in him the source of morality. Helios had given Julian a programme: 'it is necessary that thou set forth, that thou cleanse the earth of all these impieties, and that thou call upon my name, with those of the goddess Athena and all the other gods'. He was *pontifex maximus*, he became the head of the pagan Church, and his portraits show him with the stephané of the archiereus. So Julian should not be represented as a rationalist in the same sense as Libanius. For him, reason was a means of access to mysticism; he was very close to the early Neoplatonists in his way of thinking; Plotinus, too, had argued against theories that exaggerated the mystic aspect of power. But he never felt called upon to choose between the cause of Hellenism and that of Rome, for to him the Romans were a Hellenic race and the sun swayed the destinies of Rome as of Greece. The gods venerated in Rome were identified with the sun, so there could be no dispute between the Hellenistic and Roman tendencies in the empire. Above all, the designs of Julian the Apostate had nothing in common with the theocratic systems of Egypt or Assyria. (Robert Etienne.)

17. At any rate of the Legalists, who may be regarded as a pro-Roman faction.

18. Professor Brezzi's account of the 'Dead Sea Scrolls' is close to that of A. Dupont-Sommer, *The Essene Sect of Qumrân* (Oxford, 1961, translated from an earlier French edition). There are, of course, several points still argued among scholars. For instance, among many attempts to identify the sect, the view is still held that they were Zealots, i.e. nationalists and revolutionaries, rather than Essenes (who were pacifistic): see (e.g.) G. Roth, *The Discovery of the Dead Sea Scrolls* (Oxford, 1958).

19. This view is defended by Dupont-Sommer in an appendix to his book.

20. The coin evidence which has been used to support the date AD 68 is not entirely conclusive, and some scholars believe that the site was destroyed in Bar Kochba's rebellion (AD 132–135).

21. Although some scholars claim to have found allusions to the personality and work of a crucified mediator and leader of a sect.

22. It has often been believed that Clemens and Domitilla, together with the other members of the aristocracy at this time, were Christian. See, however, pp. 864 ff.

23. In describing the history of Christianity, there is a manifest tendency on the author's part not only to demonstrate the absolutely exceptional nature of Christian teaching

(for example, by comparison with the Essenes and the members of the Qumrân community, or with the Hellenistic and Roman philosophical systems of the time), but also to clear it of any taint of suspicion that it was in opposition to the Roman government and the existing order. It is not fortuitous that the author attempts to sow doubt in the reader's mind as to the canonical character of the *Apocalypse* of John, which was a strongly anti-Roman work. Nor is there any justification for the author's denial of the fact that Christianity originated and at first spread among the lower oppressed classes: the references to the fact that already at an early date Christianity was accepted by individual members of the nobility, in the first place is not founded on completely reliable evidence, and in the second place does not refute the clearly social orientation of early Christianity, as an ideology of the labouring poor. Nor does the author mention the 'heresies' which appeared as a result of dissatisfaction on the part of the democratic elements in the Christian communities at the modifications introduced by members who joined them from the upper classes. Thus he does not even mention Commodianus, who expressed with unusual vigour the hatred of the popular masses for their oppressors.

The author links Christianity exclusively with Judaism, dismissing all other influences upon it on the grounds that they only introduced the terminology employed by the Christian writers. Like any other doctrine that has captured the minds of millions, Christianity absorbed those ideas that had previously appealed to various classes and social groups and which had arisen in their midst as the fruit of their attitude towards different phenomena in their environment. If this had not been so, the success of Christianity and its victory over other religious and philosophical tendencies would be inexplicable. (E. M. Shtaerman.)

24. And surely also (as Professor Heichelheim points out) by Hellenistic and Latin authors.

25. This original was very probably the Aramaic or Hebrew version provided by the early *Gospel of the Hebrews*: see below.

26. It is commonly held that Mark drew on Peter's oral recollections when the Apostle took up residence in Rome near the end of his life.

27. A recently discovered papyrus fragment (now in the British Museum) makes it likely that 'John' used a lost Gospel which was as old as the Synoptists. For John itself the earliest evidence is a small papyrus fragment (in Manchester) of *c.* AD 100.

28. Among apocryphal works should now be added the *Epistles of Paul to the Corinthians* of which a recently discovered Greek text has been published as *Pap. Bodmer* X (ed. M. Testuz, Cologne, 1959).

29. As Dr E. M. Shtaerman points out, one reason for misgiving about the *Apocalypse* is likely to have been its bitterly anti-Roman character.

30. Moreover it used excellent Hebrew and Greek manuscripts of the second century AD.

31. This inference is questionable: the name (*cognomen*) Clemens was extremely common among Roman citizens of the period.

32. Now known also from other finds.

33. Although Professor Pareti's views at this point take account of most recent literature, it may be worth calling attention to discussion of the legal questions by H. Last, *Journal of Roman Studies*, 1937, pp. 80 ff., and by A. N. Sherwin-White, *Journal of Theological Studies*, 1952, pp. 199 ff.

34. I.e. that the Catacombs near Rome contain a Coemeterium Domitillae and a Coemeterium Acilianum (Acilius Glabrio, consul AD 91, is also supposed to have been a Christian); but see P. Styger, *Die Antiken Katakomben* (Berlin, 1933).

35. Dr E. M. Shtaerman insists that the changes of policy described in this section were not due simply to the whims of particular emperors. Yet Professor Pareti did not intend to imply anything of the kind. Probably Dr Shtaerman is right in maintaining that the strength of the Christian communities, 'harbouring widely different elements of the opposition', was responsible for the violence of the reaction under Decius and Valerian, as contrasted with previous periods.

36. A further factor, as Professor F. M. Heichelheim notes, was the attraction which Christian theology exercised over intellectuals, especially after *c.* AD 150.

37. Cyprian, who was put to death by the Roman government in 258, is described by Dr E. M. Shtaerman as 'the founder of potent episcopal authority'. He was concerned with the treatment of 'lapsed' Christians, with the question of baptism of heretics, and with the unity of the Church. Yet it appears misleading to regard the resulting controversies as part of the issue of the authority of bishops—much less, though Dr Shtaerman seems to hint this, as part of a conflict between rich and poor. For Cyprian's writings see p. 888.

38. A whole library of mainly Valentinian writings has lately been discovered at Al Hammadi in Egypt: see W. C. van Unnik, *Newly Discovered Gnostic Writings* (London, 1958), with full bibliography on these and related finds.

39. An acute analysis of this remarkable figure was made by F. C. Burkitt, *Cambridge Ancient History*, XII (1938), pp. 496 ff.

40 *Forse . . . non un errore dogmatico, ma un giudizio divergente da quelli più communemente accolti.* The distinction has no doubt often been useful to benevolent inquisitors.

41. See above p. 704, note 11.

42. The Donatist schism began as a protest against the hurried election in 311 of a bishop of Carthage who had, it was claimed, given in to the secular powers and surrendered Christian texts. After prolonged negotiations the issue was submitted to a synod of Gallic bishops, who adjudicated against the Donatists. They continued their protest: Constantine in 316 condemned them and confiscated their property, but he later relented and his successors continued to show them tolerance. The schism survived into the fifth century, and was of concern to Augustine. An interesting feature is the support given to the Donatists by the *circumcelliones* (or Agonistics), a populist group which embraced fugitive slaves and other poorer elements. The ecclesiastical issues were consequently often subordinated to the class struggle.

43. Julian himself had undergone the bloody Mithraic ceremonies of the *taurobolium*; see above, pp. 838 ff.

44. To this there were important exceptions. Seneca, for example, believed that the best form of government was 'ideal kingship', and criticized Caesar's murderers for not understanding this (*de Beneficiis*, II, 20, 3). His *de Clementia* (addressed to Nero near the beginning of his reign) sets out the qualities which distinguish the just king from the tyrant, in a manner followed by many later writers (e.g Dio Chrysostom under Trajan —see below). In fact some scholars have described the Stoicism of this period as the 'official philosophy of monarchy'. It remains a problem why Stoics like Helvidius Priscus attacked 'good' emperors like Vespasian. For discussion of this and kindred questions see Ch. Wirszubski, *Libertas as a Political Idea at Rome* (Cambridge, 1950) pp. 124 ff.

45. For Seneca's career and other writings, see below, pp. 919, 930, 967 ff.

46. On Plutarch's *Lives*, which he wrote as a contribution to ethics more than to history, see below, p. 942.

CHAPTER XVIII

LITERATURE AND ART TO *c.* AD 500

I. LITERATURE

a. *China*

Chinese poetry of the Later Han period (23–220) is at first a continuation of that of the Former Han. The *fu* is almost the only cultivated form, and all the great littérateurs, such as the historian Pan Ku (32–92) and the astronomer Chung Hêng (78–139) delighted in it. But erudition more and more took the place of lyric feeling; and the *fu* became, and remained, a court poetry in every sense.

A contact with music, which was so intimately connected with the ancient Odes but had been practically lost with the Elegies of Ch'u and with the *fu*, was re-established through the work of the Imperial Music Office (*yüeh-fu*), which had to supply the tunes and the words for songs on ceremonial occasions. For this purpose it delved into the rich treasure of anonymous folk poetry, and did not spurn even foreign motifs (mostly of central Asian origin). This led to the rise of a new kind of poetry, meant at first to be sung and not recited, although the importance of the words soon overcame that of the tune. It employed a new verse of popular origin, in five syllables, which later became the most widely used metre of Chinese prosody. The *yüeh-fu* poetry grew very popular during the Three Kingdoms period and under the short-lived unification of the empire by the Chin. Some of the best poets of the epoch of turmoil (the Chien-an period, 196–219) which accompanied the fall of the Han were indeed Ts'ao Ts'ao and his sons Ts'ao P'ei and Ts'ao Chih, the founders of the new Wei dynasty. A place of honour is also occupied by Ts'ai Yen, a woman who was carried away by the Hsiung-nu and had to stay with them for twelve years; she related her experiences in her poems 'on the measure of the Hsiung-nu horn', which are among the gems of Chinese lyric. The contents of these poems were strongly influenced by the pessimism of the age and by Taoism, as expressed chiefly by the group of the Seven Sages of the Bamboo Grove. One theme which originated with them was wine, and the spiritual (more than material) enjoyment it gave to thinkers who were withdrawn from a world run mad. This poetry reached its summit after the barbarian invasion of the North, with T'ao Yüan-ming (365–427). We cannot deal with him here; suffice it to say that the wine poems became one of the most outstanding features in Chinese literature.

Historiography followed in the track set down once and for all by Ssǔ-ma Ch'ien. The outstanding production of this period was the History of the

---

* The passages within square brackets were contributed by Professor Pierre Grimal, to supplement the original text, after the death of Professor Pareti.

(Former) Han dynasty (Han-shu) by several members of the Pan family, headed by Pan Ku (32–92).

Apart from history, prose mostly took the form of the essay, the interest of which is at least as much philosophical as literary. The best prose writer of the Later Han is perhaps Wang Ch'ung (*c.* 27–96), whose *Lun-hêng*, with its corrosive and destructive criticism of all and sundry, reminds us forcibly (as pointed out by Demiéville) of the nearly contemporary Lucian of Samosata.[1] The new philosophy of the Chien-an period also gave rise to a natural, delicate prose, unstilted, and devoid of affectation.

In the meantime the new religion, Buddhism, confronted by other problems and other trends of thought, developed for its translation from Indian languages an original prose style of its own, not very far from the colloquial speech of the day, and intended for a much wider circle of readers than the classical prose. Beginning with the fourth century this new style began to exert its influence even among non-Buddhist writers. The latter, however, being drawn almost exclusively from court circles, during most of this period patronized a highly artificial style, the symmetric prose (*p'ien-wen*), in which clarity of expression was sacrificed in favour of alternate sentences of four or six syllables, balanced expressions, and a constant use of allusions to classical texts. After the fourth century literary prose became a game to be played and understood by connoisseurs only.

b. *India*

This period is marked by the victorious advance of Sanskrit as the written language of the court and of official documents on the one hand, and of secular literature on the other. This did not take place without a stubborn contest with the local Prakrits. The only advantage of the latter, confronted with a sacred language spread all over India, was their quality as spoken tongues. When the Prakrits lost contact with the spoken word and became just another half-dead and highly artificial language, their fate was sealed. By the end of this) period the secular literature of Aryan India was almost wholly couched in Sanskrit.

In making this statement we leave out of consideration the *dharmaśāstra* literature; it is too closely connected with religion in its social aspects to be a case in point. A better example for the secular progress of Sanskrit is represented by the drama. Its origin is still a controversial point, the influence of the Greek stage being asserted or denied on equally strong (or feeble) grounds. One element in favour of a connexion with Greece is the name of the curtain, *yavanikā*, i.e. the Greek 'cloth'. This is, however, a merely external element, and on inner grounds a connexion with or derivation from the dialogue hymns in the Vedas is possible and likely. The most balanced opinion seems to be that 'the Sanskrit drama came into being shortly after, if not before, the middle of the second century BC, and that it was evoked by the combinations of epic recitations with the dramatic moment of the Krsna legend' (Keith).

At the beginning of Indian drama we find the name of the great Buddhist poet Asvaghoṣa (second century AD), who was also the author of three dramas discovered in central Asia. They are religious in content and already show the most peculiar characteristic of Indian drama, namely the rule that the language should differ according to the social status of the characters of a play. Kings and Brahmans speak Sanskrit, persons of lesser status and all women various kinds of Prakrit.

Bhāsa seems to be slightly later (third century?): thirteen plays attributed to him were found in 1912 in southern India. If the attribution is sure (not all doubts have yet disappeared), they show a dramatist of no mean powers, chiefly in those plays (e.g. Svapnavāsavadatta, Cārudatta), of which the subject matter is drawn not from epic but from current story literature. Bhāsa's Sanskrit is already of classical purity, conforming on the whole with Pāṇini's rules.

An isolated place belongs to the legendary figure of King Śūdraka, very variously dated, but perhaps a fourth-century writer. His Mṛccha-kaṭika is the most pleasant, vivacious, and realistic product of India's dramatic literature. It is written in a simple and effective style, and gives a direct and clear-cut picture of life in that period.

We may close this rapid sketch with the name of Kālidāsa. This greatest of Indian poets was also a playwright of the first order. He wrote little in this field, but one of his three plays, the Śākuntala, is one of the greatest dramatic works of all time.

Dramaturgy found its theoretical codification in the Nāṭyaśāstra of Bhārata, probably earlier than Kālidāsa.

The writers of fables, in which amusement is always coupled with a moral intent, indulge in a peculiar process on 'House that Jack built' lines: a character in a story may support his statements by relating another fable, which is therefore enframed in the first one. A character in this secondary fable may do the same, and the process can be carried very far. The simplest and earliest work of this kind is the Pañcatantra, the original core of which seems to go back to this period. It was exceedingly popular in India and its fame soon over-stepped the boundaries of the sub-continent: in the sixth century it was translated into Pehlevi and thence, somewhat later, into Arabic and Syriac. Another tradition of tales was represented by the Bṛhatkathā of Guṇāḍhya (fifth century?), written in a Prakrit language, the Paisācī; it is lost, and we can gain an idea of its contents only from later compilations. The question of the relation of this literature to Aesop and the Greek fables has been keenly debated, but the issue remains open and is not likely ever to be definitely settled.

Indian lyric oscillated for a while, in its choice of language, between Sanskrit and Prakrit. An early anthology of Prakrit poems has come down to us, the *Sattasaī* of Hāla (third or fourth century). It is bucolic poetry of a simple and tender nature, portraying mainly the simple joys of love, wedded life, and motherly affection in the villages of the Deccan.

But here, too, Sanskrit soon won the field. Sanskrit poetry seems to have started from the lyrical portions of epic. It soon took the form of artistic poetry (*kāvya*), subjected to severe rules and employing an elaborate set of rhetorical ornaments (*alaṃkāra*). This brought in its wake a certain artificiality and almost baroque luxuriance, though from this the greater poets were able to steer clear. The chronology here is very vague, but at least we have one fixed point: one of the earliest *kāvya* poets, the Buddhist Asvaghoṣa, was a contemporary of Kaniṣka ánd therefore lived (according to the chronology here adopted) around the middle of the second century AD. He is the author, among other works, of two poems: the *Saundarananda* and the *Buddhacarita*. The latter, a life of the Buddha in thirteen cantos (fifteen more are preserved in Chinese translation), is a piece of fervent and deeply felt religious poetry, with charming imagery, and a simple and somewhat archaic style. But Buddhist religious poetry soon died out. We need only mention in passing Āryaśūra, the author of the *Jātakamālā*, a collection of legends on the former lives of the Buddha. It is in prose, intermingled with verse, written in a careful and polished Sanskrit. Āryaśūra was the first to make consistent use of long nominal compounds, a device the abuse of which was to become an unpleasant feature in later works.

Of court poetry of the Gupta age we have two fair examples in the panegyric (*prasāsti*) of Samudragupta inscribed on the Allahabad pillar and composed by Hariṣena (*c.* 350) and in Vatsabhaṭṭi's inscription in the temple of the sun at Mandasor, written in 473–474. Hariṣena's work reveals a poet of some merit, fully conversant with the rules of *alaṃkāra* and enjoying his struggle against serious difficulties.

Even the date of India's greatest poet Kālidāsa is highly uncertain and keenly debated, opinion ranging over a span of nearly one thousand years. The bulk of the available evidence points, however, to the Gupta period, possibly to the reign of Chandragupta II, i.e. about 400 AD. Great as a playwright, Kālidāsa is even greater as a *kāvya* poet. His works are the *Kumārasambhava* (eighteen cantos, only eight of which are genuine) on the birth of Kumāra, the god of love and son of Śiva and Pārvatī; the *Raghuvaṃsa* (nineteen cantos), a collection of biographies of some thirty kings of the race of Raghu; the *Ṛtusaṃhāra* (six cantos), a description of the six Indian seasons, marked by some superb descriptions of natural phenomena; and, perhaps his crowning achievement, the *Meghadūta*, a short lyrical poem of slightly more than 100 verses, in which a Yakṣa requests a cloud to carry his message of passion to his faraway beloved. Kālidāsa is a sovereign master of Indian poetical style, conversant with all the technicalities of his art, and yet completely free from the extravagances and artificialities which mar the works of later *kāvya* authors. In the words of A. B. Keith, he prefers suggestion to elaboration. His Olympian serenity, removed from the contingencies of life, reminds one of Goethe, to whom he shows a striking spiritual affinity. Kālidāsa represents the fullest maturity of Indian poetry, between the archaism of Asvaghoṣa and the decadent preciosity of later poets.

The Dravidian literatures begin independently and come only very gradually under the influence of Sanskrit literature in subject matter, aesthetic outlook, and technique. Early Tamil literature, the only one which goes back to this period, is classified by tradition under the head of three successive *Sangam*, or societies of learned men, patronized by the Pāṇḍya kings in the farthest south. They are endowed with impossibly long lives, and absurdly high numbers of members. A conservative estimate places them in the thousand years between 500 BC and AD 500; but none of the works now extant belongs to the centuries before our era. Of the first *Sangam* nothing is left. Of the second, only a grammatical treatise, the *Tolkāppiyam*. The bulk of the production of the third *Sangam* is included in three anthologies: *Pattuppāṭṭu* (Ten Idylls), *Eṭṭuttokai* (Eight Collections), *Patinenkīlkaṇakku* (Eighteen Minor Didactic Poems). The best and most famous piece included in the third collection is the *Kural*, comprising eleven sections of ten couplets each; it is a collection of aphorisms on every possible aspect of social life. Apart from the three anthologies, we have three epics on south Indian themes, already touched in subjects, metres, and vocabulary by northern influence: *Silappadikāram*, *Maṇimēkalai*, and *Sīvakacintāmaṇi*. It is interesting to note that Tamil literature, and chiefly the idylls, has several stray references to the Westerners (*Yāvanas*) frequenting south Indian ports in the heyday of Roman-Indian trade during the first two or three centuries of our era.

c. Persia

We said something in the appropriate context about the *Gātha* which go back to Zarathustra, but given the complex way in which the *Avesta* was created we have preferred to reserve references to its later editions for this single point in our story. Parsee tradition, preserved in the tenth-century Pehlevīk work known as *Dēnkart*, attributes the first collection of the sacred texts (the *Gātha*) to a supporter of Zarathustra named Viśtasp. Of this it is supposed that Darius III (the king defeated by Alexander) had two copies made. (Darius, we are told, revived the cult of Anāhitā and the use of sacred statues, and there is actually an allusion to a statue of this king in the Yaśt dedicated to the goddess Ardoī Sūrā Anāhitā.) About the copies there is further evidence in the *Book of Artāk Virāz*. One was destroyed in the burning of Persepolis after it had been stormed by the Macedonian victor; the other was carried to Greece and there translated. To this a notice in Pliny (*Nat. Hist.*, XXX, 1, 4) is relevant: he speaks of one Hermippus the follower of Callimachus who (in the third century BC) set down the work of Zarathustra in two million lines.

[Alinari]

(b)

[Alinari]

(a)

73 Roman sculpture
   (a) Trajan sailing from Ancona. Details from Trajan's Column, Rome, AD 113
   (b) Marcus Aurelius taking part in the apotheosis of Sabina, the Empress. Rome, Museo dei Conservatori

(a)

[Alinari

74
(a) *The Good Shepherd.*
    Rome, Lateran Museu
(b) *Christian sarcophagus*
    with St Anastasius an
    scene from the Passion
    of Christ

(b)

[A.S.

(a)   [Alinari

75
(a) *Bust of the Young*
       Octavian. Modena,
       Museo Estense
(b) *Head of Vespasian*

(b)
[M.N.B.

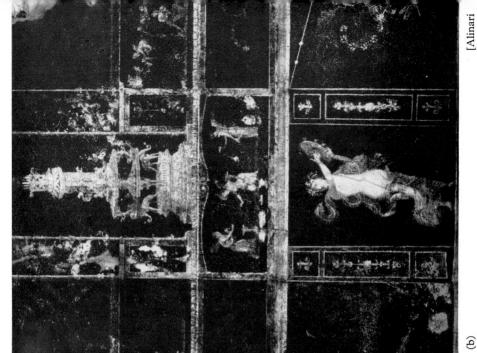

[Alinari]

(b)

[Alinari]

(a)

76 (a) *Constantine's family, cameo. Stadtbibliothek, Trier*
(b) *Pompeii: Casa of the Vettii, detail of the wall painting*

(a) [A.S.

77 *Early Christian Painting*
   (a) *Catacomb of Priscilla, the Greek Chapel: the institution of the Eucharisty*
   (b) *The Good Shepherd, fourth century AD*

(b)
[A.S.

(a)

[Berlin

78 *Roman Painting III (portraiture)*
    (a) *Septimus Severus with his family*
    (b) *Portrait of a man, from the Catacomb of Pamphilius*

(b)

[A

(a)

[B.F.M.

(b)

9 *Roman sculpture*

(a) *Venice, St Marco: the Tetrarchs*

(b) *Barletta, Puglie: statue believed to represent Theodosius I*

[Alinari

80 *The Catacombs*
    (a) *Gallery in the Catacombs of Domitilla*
    (b) *Tombstone of Marianus, Catacomb of Domitilla*
    (c) *Tombstone of Saprocattus and Nice, Catacomb of Domitilla*

[A.S.]

[A.S.]

[A.S.]

[A.S.]

Later, in the time of the Arsacid Vologaesus III (AD 148–190), a new collection is said to have been made of all texts concerning Zarathustra; evidently this was the work of the Magi, and was done in Persian Aramaic. Then, after the Sassanids had come to power, Ardashir III (377–383) is credited with causing the priest Tausar to undertake a final edition of the sacred texts in twenty-one *nask*. Of this the *Dēnkart* gives us a brief summary. The twenty-one writings were divided into three groups—*gāsān* (the revelation), *dāt* (legal and moral literature), and *hātāk mānsarik* (liturgical ritual). From all this only about a quarter survives, unevenly distributed among the three groups:

(1) *Yasna*: seventy-two chapters of prayers, celebrations, and divine services. These include the *Gātha* of Zarathustra (capp. 28–34, 43–51, 53) in archaic language, and also a single *Yasna* (capp. 35–41), of which the language is similar: all the rest is in late language and in a monotonous priestly style.

(2) *Visprat* (=all the Judges), twenty-four chapters of formulae to complete the *Yasna*.

(3) *Kuartak Apastak*, the 'small *Avesta*' for use by the profane, consisting of litanies, prayers, hymns, and benedictions (twenty-one prayers being addressed to individual divinities).

The loss of the rest of the collection is attributed to the Arabs. The *Zend* (or *Zand*) was the literature expounding Zoroastrianism in Pehlevīk, on the basis of a literal translation of the *Avesta* into that language.

As well as these sacred texts from the *Avesta* we know of other Persian literary documents. Popular literature took shape at this period, and some of its products were still used in the tenth or eleventh century by Firdūsī in the *Shānāmeh* (*Book of Kings*), one example being the epico-religious legend of Gōderz (Gotarzes, AD 40–51). Linguistic considerations give a similar Late Arsacid date for the earliest editions of certain novels transmitted in later texts, for instance the religious ballad called *The Tree of Babylon* and the short epic romance entitled *History of Zarēr*.

The use of Greek came to an end with the Sassanids, the last Greek text being one by Shahpuhr I (241–272). The established language was now Medo-Persian or Pārsīk, which forms a bridge between the ancient language of the Achaemenids and modern Persian. Several of the Sassanids, such as Shahpuhr I, Shahpuhr II, and Ardashir II (see above) were thought well of by religious tradition, and historical inscriptions of them have been preserved. A famous inscriptional text (in Greek, Medo-Persian, and Parthian) commemorates Shahpuhr I's achievements, among them his victory over the Roman emperor Valerian; and there is a text in Medo-Persian and Parthian relating to Narses II (293–302).

d. *Greek and Latin*

The Epic. In the bilingual world of letters during the earlier part of this period Latin poetry was much more prolific and rewarding than Greek. Greek epic was written during the first three centuries, but it has gradually got lost: in any case, whether mythological or historical in type, it must have been a poor affair. Mythological poetry included the *Heroicae Theogamiae* by Peisander of Laranda (in sixty books), and the Dionysiac poems of Dionysius of Samos and Soterichus of Oasis; on historical subjects there were Arrian's twenty-four books on Alexander, and the thirty books of an *Antoniniade* (on Antoninus Pius and Marcus Aurelius) by Gordian I.

In the fourth century the influence of sophistic brought about a final flowering of Greek epic. Historical and eulogistic work included the poems of Callistus on Julian's Persian Wars, and the works of Eusebius and Ammonius on Gainas. We know more about the mythological type, represented by the *Gigantomachia* of Claudian. Quintus Smyrnaeus, probably still in the fourth century, wrote fourteen books of *Posthomerica* (which survive), narrating what happened between the end of the *Iliad* and the return of the Achaeans to their homes. The material is drawn more from pictures than from original poems, but his stylistic models are the archaic and classical epics. The versification is faultless, the style is simple and not unduly epigrammatic, and the handling of the plot is well proportioned. What is missing is poetical inspiration and inventive fancy: the characters lack personality, the descriptions dramatic force, and the episodes cohesion.

Nonnus of Panopolis in Egypt, for all his shortcomings, was a distinctly better poet. At the end of the fourth century he wrote an enormous work in forty-eight books called 'Dionysiaca', the central motif being the combat of the heroes against the Giants of India, representing Hellenism against barbarism. Into this narrative the poet introduces a large number of fables, and passes from episode to episode in a style which is bombastic, rhetorical, and epigrammatic. Despite this he has a wealth of fancy and vivid colour; his versification is forceful and sonorous; and he makes daring use of surprising neologisms in his diction. His epic is the last spontaneous product of the union between Hellenistic Greece and Asia, coming from the very gateway to Byzantium's Middle Age.

Latin epic of the first century AD, both the verse histories of the type written by Lucan and Silius and the rhetorical myth on Statius' model, is distinctly better than anything produced in Greek at this period.

[Latin epic composition was then dominated by Virgil, and much that was written in that form followed his manner, which was regarded as classic. Side by side with his influence, however, was another school, bent upon bringing fresh blood into the epic, both in its form and its subject-matter. We connect this attempt with the name of Lucan.

Lucan (M. Annaeus Lucanus, of Corduba, AD 39–65) was the nephew of

Seneca and, like him, imbued with the Stoic philosophy. He belonged to the
same generation as Nero, and became the latter's friend and constant companion after his uncle had introduced him into the imperial palace. He had
been a child prodigy, and soon won a place in the circle of youths who
surrounded the emperor and assisted him in his literary and musical activities.
Lucan is a typical example of the spirit of the ardent generation, passionately
interested in philosophy and art, which saw the last years of the Claudian
dynasty. Like many of his contemporaries, he was drawn into the catastrophe
that involved the élite of the senatorial class in the year 65.] He took part in
Piso's conspiracy against Nero and though he denounced his accomplices
when the conspiracy was betrayed he was forced to commit suicide at a very
early age.

[The only one of his works to have come down to us is *Pharsalia*, an epic
in ten cantos, but unfinished. Its real title is *Bellum Civile* (Civil War), and
its theme the struggle between Caesar and the Republican Party, which
began in 49 BC and ended in victory for Caesar. It seems strange to us nowadays that this subject should have been chosen by a poet on terms of close
friendship with Nero, who owed his throne to Caesar's success; and we
hardly feel that Lucan could have handled it in a spirit of independence.
And yet, perhaps with the rashness of youth or perhaps because Nero himself made a great show of broad-mindedness regarding what already belonged
to ancient history, Lucan had the audacity to side with the republicans
against Caesar. His Stoic principles led him to consider civil war as an
episode in the fated course of events, a symbol of the periodical cosmic
conflagration proclaimed in the doctrine of Chrysippus. Caesar thus becomes
the instrument of Destiny, and it is possible to censure the man himself
without regretting the developments he brought about. Contrasted with
Caesar is the figure of Cato, symbolizing the human conscience, which rejects
all compromise and maintains its liberty in defiance of Destiny, by willingly
accepting death. This turns the epic into a tremendous tragedy with a cosmic
setting. Its actors are the helpless toys of *Fatum*, and the gods take no hand
in the matter. Hence there is no supernatural element in *Pharsalia* and this,
again, differentiates it strongly from the *Aeneid*. It is more tragic than the
earlier work, because it leaves less scope for human free-will to influence
history. Less 'human', too, for there is little tenderness or pity in it. Lucan
is carried away by his own inner logic, despite his attempt to be objective,
and ends by developing an enthusiastic admiration for Cato and expressing
himself in explicitly republican terms. Tradition has it that this spiritual
development was hastened, if not caused, by a quarrel with Nero, who is
said to have grown jealous of Lucan's talent.] That is why *Pharsalia* is
usually considered to have been composed in two distinct periods. The first
three books, before his quarrel with Nero, deal with the opening of the Civil
War in a manner relatively friendly to Caesar: in the remaining seven,
published after Lucan's death, passionate republicanism gains the upper

hand. The whole work (incomplete when the poet died) is Livy's narrative put into epic form: it is a medley of rhetorical speeches and pathetic descriptive scenes, and throughout the story we see *casus* intervening in human affairs.

The other epic poets of this period were all disciples of Virgil.

C. Valerius Flaccus Setinus Balbus spent about twenty years (*c.* 70–90) on his *Argonautica*, which won little popularity, although it is undoubtedly superior to many contemporary poems. The material is drawn from Apollonius Rhodius, but it is in part abridged and in other places interspersed with fancies of the poet's own or elements from other sources. Flaccus was influenced not only by Virgil but by the rhetorical schools. He showed a fondness for pathetic episodes, and handled them with skill.

Ti. Catius Silius Italicus, whose family may have originated at Italica in Spain, was taught by Stoic philosophers, but became consul in 68 and was a supporter of Vitellius. In the years following 92 he published the seventeen books of his *Punica*, a work about the Hannibalic War. This too is the Livian narrative reduced to epic, with the insertion of frequent episodes of divine intervention together with some brilliant passages describing scenery and a number of rhetorical speeches. Many sections are imitated from Homer and Virgil, such as the descriptions of funeral games, journeys to the lower world, battle pieces, and catalogues of peoples.

P. Papinius Statius (*c.* 55–100), a native of Neapolis but son and pupil of a poet from Velia, devoted himself first to *Silvae*, then between AD 79 and 91 to the twelve books of his *Thebais*, and finally after 95 to his *Achilleis*, which was broken off in the tenth book by his death. The *Thebais* tells once again the story of the Seven against Thebes, ignoring the many times it had found favour in the past. It is a poem without poetic fire. It follows the *Aeneid* too slavishly, is crammed to excess with divine intervention and divine personification of human beings, and is tinged throughout with rhetoric. In the *Achilleis* the main subject is still more heavily diluted, and even in the tenth book the hero has not reached Troy. Briefly mentioned should be the fragments from a Latin epic about the war between Octavian and Antony which were rediscovered at Herculaneum.

Although a certain amount of epic, of both the historical and the mythological type, still continued to be written in later years, the genre can now be regarded as worked out. For fanciful narrative it was superseded by the romance.

Tragedy. In tragedy, too, at any rate in the early empire, Latin work was much more notable than Greek. Tragedians still existed in the Greek world, such as Philostratus (I), who wrote forty-three tragedies and fourteen comedies in Nero's time, or Isagoras, or Antiphon of Athens. We also hear of Romans, like Asinius Pollio or the Younger Pliny, writing tragedies in Greek as an exercise. All these works are lost, and the loss may not be all that grave.

It is certain that down to the third century the old Athenian plays were still recited, though abridged to become simple recitatives, the choral and sung passages being cut. New tragedies must have been written mainly to be read rather than acted, and by the time of Libanius reading was to become tragedy's only function.

There were still, however, some reputable works of Latin tragedy, which became more independent of Greek tragedy than in the preceding period. The poet expresses his own political and philosophical ideas, stitches together some religious and moral disquisitions, and puts into the mouths of his characters a number of rhetorical speeches, which are then interspersed with moving lyrics.

L. Annaeus Seneca the Younger (*c.* AD 5–65), son of the Seneca who wrote on rhetoric, was born at Corduba and migrated to Rome.[2] After he had held the early posts in a senator's career he was exiled to Corsica, where he remained for part of Claudius' reign (41–49). He returned at the wish of Agrippina and became tutor to Nero, but then fell into disgrace and retired into private life. He committed suicide after having been implicated in the Pisonian conspiracy.[3] He was a versatile writer, and besides his plays he composed philosophical dialogues, letters, and satire. Eight of the. nine tragedies ascribed to him are certainly his (the only one about which there is reasonable doubt is the *Hercules Oetaeus*), and together they form the only complete set of works which has come down to us from a Roman tragedian. The *Hercules Furens* is inspired by Euripides, but both the plot and some of the episodes have been substantially altered. The *Phoenissae* consists now only of two fragmentary episodes. The *Medea* contains a number of scenes not in Euripides, and probably drew on the lost work of Ovid bearing the same name. The origins of the *Phaedra* cannot be traced with any confidence; but the *Oedipus* is based on Sophocles' play, though with considerable abridgement and revision. The differences between the *Agamemnon* and Aeschylus' work, especially at the beginning and end, may derive from an intervening play by Livius Andronicus. With the *Thyestes* we have no model for comparison, since all earlier tragedies of this name have been lost. So far as their plots and dialogues go, Seneca's plays could certainly have been recited on the stage, as we know was done for plays of similar type by Pomponius Secundus. But it is also beyond doubt that they could not have been understood or appreciated by a popular public, but only by a select class of persons. This means that they must mainly have been used for public readings, in halls for declamation. Their influence on mediaeval and modern literature was enormous.

The manuscripts are certainly wrong in attributing to Seneca a tragedy called *Octavia*, the only surviving example of a *praetextata* (tragedy on a Roman subject). It is concerned with the unhappy life of Octavia, daughter of Claudius and Messalina, who was compelled to marry Nero, and was then put to death in banishment after having been supplanted by Poppaea. The tragedy alludes by 'post eventum' prophecy to Nero's death; it therefore cannot have been written earlier than 68, and by then Seneca was no longer alive.

Of Publius Pomponius Secundus, who lived under Tiberius and Claudius, we are told that he wrote tragedies, one at least of which was a *praetextata*, and that he engaged in controversy with Seneca. His tragedies caused riots to break out in the theatre. More *praetextatae*, on the subject of Cato Uticensis and on one of the Domitii, were written by Curiatius Maternus in Vespasian's time, and we know the names (but very little else) of other Latin tragedies. But by now this form of poetry seems to have exhausted itself as far as the West is concerned.

In the fourth century the sources speak once more of tragedy in Greece, the authors including Andronicus of Hermopolis, Apollinaris of Laodicea (who wrote comedy too), and Synesius. But their works were beyond doubt written for declamation in schools, following the custom described by Libanius. Performances, which Christians and priests were forbidden to attend, were still given in the theatre; but these, as we said earlier, were largely improvised scenes, which could give delirious pleasure to people whose taste was easily satisfied.

Comedy. We have little to go on about comedy in Greek, simply a few names of authors, including some like Germanicus Caesar and the emperor Claudius who were famous politically. Nor is our information about Latin comedies any better. M. Pomponius Bassulus of Aeclanum (between AD 50 and 100) translated Menander and wrote some comedies of his own. Vergilius Romanus started by writing comedies of Menander's type, then turned to Aristophanic composition, and finally devoted himself to mimiambics. Lastly there was Annianus in Hadrian's time, who is said to have written 'Fescennines', 'ludicra carmina', and 'Falisca', which are probably all the same kind of composition.

What is certain is that the public of imperial times preferred mime and pantomime to comedy. We can tell what Greek mimes of this period were like, partly from references in ancient texts to writers such as Nicostratus and Alciphron, but still more from the fragments found on Egyptian papyri. Among other discoveries there is a 'hypothesis' of a mime for eight characters, with the title *Charition*, dealing with the liberation of a courtesan whom an Indian prince is about to sacrifice to the moon. This is a prose parody of Euripides' *Iphigeneia in Tauris*, with some verse and musical notation scattered through its pages. Papyri have also revealed a scene from a work called *Moicheutria*, inspired by a mime of Herondas, in which a slave is saved from a mistress who has condemned him to death. Then there is a fragment of Euripos and Sarapas concerning a festival of Cronos, and a number of other works.

But throughout the empire, as we know from the diatribes of philosophers and from imperial interdicts, the general public developed a passion for 'pantomimes', which were mimic dances to musical accompaniment, based on plots commonly derived from mythology. These were composed not only by Greeks (such as Pylades, Bathyllus, Lucianus, Libanius, and Corycius) but by Latins too: we know, for example, of 'fabulae salticae' written by Lucan.

In the last phase of the empire Latin comedy underwent a new and curious development, in which the comedies of Plautus were turned into prose with rhythmic clausulae. This was probably done simply for purposes of declamation. We have an example in the *Querolus*, a prose adaptation of the *Aulularia* by an anonymous Gaul; and we know that the same was done to the *Amphitruo*.

Satire. Even in Horace's later period Latin satire was no longer a spirited attack on personalities, and it had lost its contact with daily life. In the hands of Persius and Juvenal it became even more abstract and rhetorical. Sometimes however, its content became fuller, as in the 'Menippean' satire used by Seneca, Petronius, and Demetrius of Troezen. In addition the iambic side of satire gave place to epigram: Martial's poems, for instance, were justly called 'abbreviated satires'.

A. Persius Flaccus (34–62), a man of equestrian family from Volaterrae, spent the whole of his very short life between his school and his books, leaving the latter to his master, the philosopher Cornutus, after his death. His six satires were published posthumously. The prologue and the first satire are in the style of Lucilius and Horace, treating literary criticism without much originality. The remaining five are impersonal pieces of philosophizing about customs; they derive from the school rather than from real life, being flat and somewhat shallow.

D. Iunius Iuvenalis of Aquinum (55/60–*c*. 140) began his active life with a creditable military career; then for twenty years or so he occupied himself with rhetoric at Rome; then he held municipal offices at Aquinum; finally he returned to Rome. Not much confidence can be placed in the story that he was exiled under Hadrian. His sixteen satires were composed between 98 and (at earliest) 126. Although he wrote at a time when free speech was allowed, and although he was of an impassioned character and had promised his readers to treat of all kinds of human action, he made it impossible for himself to deal with contemporary matters by deciding to mention only people who were dead. His satire, therefore, seems flat directly one sees that it looks to the past, mainly indeed to the period of Domitian, the emperor Juvenal detested. But it is also often exaggerated and artificial, containing sententiousness and artificial pathos, even though the breadth of his personal experience at times gave greatness to his verse. His various themes include an attack on the mythological type of epic, the vexations of city life, Domitian's court, the miseries of clients; and there are various philosophical subjects, as well as an onslaught on women.[4]

We now pass to writers of Menippean satire. One example of bitter parody is the Menippean piece of prose and verse satirizing the death of Claudius, which tradition has identified with the 'Pumpkinification of Claudius' allegedly written by Seneca.5 We also know, mainly from Tacitus, of a particularly refined Roman noble named Petronius, who had been proconsul of Bithynia and then consul, and who was called by Nero his 'arbiter elegantiarum'. Though Nero's friend he was prosecuted as an accomplice in the Pisonian conspiracy, and committed suicide after sending the tyrant a letter accusing him of his crimes. This is the personage to whom we should ascribe authorship of one of the finest pieces of imperial literature, a great Menippean work in prose and verse, which our manuscripts describe as *Satirae* or *Satiricon*. Only small portions remain, perhaps belonging to books XIV–XVI. This was a fanciful romance, of which both the prose and the verse sections were composed in a most agreeable style. The surviving fragments describe a spectacular feast at the house of an exceedingly wealthy freedman named Trimalchio, and they describe the background in vivid, colourful, and also biting terms.6

The Greek work of Demetrius of Troezen must have been another example of Menippean satire. He wrote in early imperial times, and dealt with philosophical criticism by way of parody.

Lyric Poetry. In Greek literature the favourite form of lyric was still the epigram; and the collections gradually grew larger, starting with the work of Philippus in the time of Caligula, who was followed by Diogenianus in Hadrian's day. Collections were also made of special types of epigram; Strato of Sardis, for example, assembled a number of poems about boys, and included with them several pleasing efforts of his own. These lyrics were mainly concerned with love, but some too are hymns to the gods. We also know of several poets' names from inscriptions. There were still epigram-matists of note in the fourth century, like Palladas of Alexandria, whose 150 surviving epigrams are sometimes gay and sometimes bitter. Then there were the *Anacreontea*, slight pieces of verse on continually recurring topics, which were designed to be sung at banquets. Many of these were composed in the second and third centuries, but still more in the fourth.

Latin lyric was much more extensive and important. The *Silvae* of Statius were written between 88 and 95, in five books of which the last is unfinished. These are occasional poems, congratulations on births of children and on birthdays, *epithalamia*, invitations, comfort to invalids and celebrations of their recovery, dirges and condolences to the afflicted, gratitude for presents, panegyrics to emperors, and descriptions of festivals and other events or of magnificent buildings and statues. This sort of purpose gives a number of them a marked degree of spontaneity and directness, even though the ideas they contain are repeated time and again. In others the futility of the subject blocked any inspiration, and Statius' skill in handling verse was no substitute.

Yet throughout the collection one is struck by the pleasant and clear-cut pictures of Roman life.

M. Valerius Martialis (44–104) came to Rome from Bilbilis in Spain, and had to adapt himself in the capital to living as a poor 'client' of well-to-do 'patrons', who were also Spaniards (of the type of Seneca or Quintilian). After he had attained a relatively comfortable existence and some degree of reputation, he became poor again and set out on his wanderings, first to Forum Cornelii, then to Rome again, and finally back to Bilbilis where someone gave him the cottage in which he died. His earliest epigrams, like those of Statius, were written only for occasions: the *Liber spectaculorum* describes the games inaugurating the Flavian Amphitheatre in AD 80, and his *Xenia* and *Apophoreta* in 84–86 are epigrams to accompany the gifts and invitations which used to be exchanged at the festival of the *Saturnalia*. But the real Martial is to be found in the twelve books of 1,200 *Epigrammata* which he wrote between 85 and 102. His three preferred metres are the choliambus, the hendecasyllable, and the elegiac couplet. He was a poet who lived in the midst of the world, observing what he saw; so his poems speak of everything and of every type of person, and he touches on their humorous side with an astonishing measure of variety. He knew earlier literature, both Greek and Roman, in his own genre, but he is no imitator: even when he takes ideas from other people he transforms them. The power and clarity of his expression are often inimitable: his verse, though he polished it with the most delicate care, looks as if it were turned out impromptu; he never gives way to rhetoric, and mythology is excluded from his list of subjects. There are only two things to offend us in this marvellous poetry: one is Martial's excessive servility, the other the obscenity which pervades his pages.

A number of other lyric poets were writing at the end of the first and beginning of the second century. There have also survived some largely anonymous pieces, of varying purpose and poetical value, from the late second and the third centuries, such as the *Pervigilium Veneris*, the *Vespae iudicium*, or the sententious work known as the *Dicta Catonis*. With these may be classed the *De concubitu Martis et Veneris* of Reposianus and the elegies of Pentadius.

The fourth century, however, is marked by a strong group of lyricists. The African poet Publilius Optatianus Porphyrius, prefect of Rome in 329 and 333, wrote verse panegyrics of Constantine. He also composed 'figured' poems (*Technopaignia*), which are mostly palindrome verses capable of being read equally from the top or the bottom, or sometimes verses forming a pattern.

Decimus Magnus Ausonius (*c*. 310–395), was a Gallic *rhetor*, who taught Gratian and Paulinus, was a friend of Symmachus, and became consul in 379. He wrote much 'occasional' verse of every kind, largely devoid of poetical inspiration but important for its content. There were 120 epigrams, an *Ephemeris* describing life from morning to evening, *Parentalia* on the deaths of relations and friends, *Epitaphia heroum*, *Caesares*, *Ordo nobilium urbium*, *Ludus septem sapientium*, *Idyllia* (the delightful piece called *Mosella*, written in 371, stands out among this group), *Epistulae*, and perhaps also the *Periochae Homeri* (partly prose, partly verse). In general the poetry of Ausonius shows the influence of the 'Neoterics' of the golden age, but it certainly did not receive the polish they had given to their work. What we feel throughout is a tone of friendliness, tenderness, and even paganism.

But if Ausonius was a Christian who thought like a pagan, Claudius Claudianus was a pagan outright: 'pervicacissimus paganus' Orosius called him later, and there is only the barest allusion to the fact that he professed Christianity at all. He was born at Alexandria, and in his early days wrote in Greek; but most of his poetry was done in Latin after he migrated to Rome in 395. He died soon after 404, while still a young man. The more important among Claudian's poems are largely concerned with contemporary events, and are written under the influence of passionate affection for Honorius and Stilicho and passionate hatred of Rufinus and Eutropius. But he also composed poems on mythological subjects, such as the *De Raptu Proserpinae*, written in the years 395–397 but left unfinished; this contains a description of the Sicilian spring of considerable lyrical merit. His minor works include poetical letters, epigrams, and descriptive pieces about animals, places, and so on.

Finally we should mention the two books of elegiacs by Claudius Rutilius Namatianus, a Gaul who was *praefectus urbi* in 414. These are noteworthy for their content and deep patriotism. Rutilius' *De reditu suo* describes a journey from Rome to Gaul along the coast.

Pastoral and Story-telling. Certain Latin bucolic poems have come down to us, written by a Sicilian poet called T. Calpurnius Siculus (having been adopted by the famous Calpurnius Piso who conspired against Nero). Seven poems are preserved under his name, but he probably also wrote two pieces celebrating Nero's musical talent and his policies, and also a *Panegyric of Piso* said to be the work of a poet who was young and poor. The *De ruralibus* of Septimius Serenus, who lived in Hadrian's day, were probably also pastoral poems; and included in the collection of Calpurnius are two pieces of the same type written by Nemesianus, who lived about 284 and will be mentioned later as a didactic poet.

Among writers of fables in verse we may mention an Oriental who wrote in Latin and an Italian who wrote in Greek. Phaedrus, a Thracian slave freed by Augustus, composed much more than the five books of *Aesop's Fables* transmitted by our manuscript, as we know from three prose collections made in the Middle Ages. In his first book, written before 31 BC, Phaedrus began by translating Aesop; but in later books he inserted more and more fables of his own, and he also shows increasing independence in his style. The work we possess has been re-edited in various ways, particularly as regards the 'Morals' which accompany the fables at their beginning or end: these are often ill suited to the fables in question, and in several editions they actually contradict them.

Valerius Babrius, an Italian resident in Asia, wrote before the end of the second century; his ten books of fables were still intact at the time the *Suda* were compiled. Many of these fables still survive in verse (123 on a single manuscript), and many others in prose paraphrase. The language contains some curious Ionisms; the style is that of sophistic writing; the metre is the choliambus, quite elegantly handled. Babrius derives his fables from all kinds of source—Aesop, the philosophers, and various story-tellers—but he has also added much of his own.

Finally there was a collection of poetic fables by the pagan Avienus in the fourth or fifth century. Drawing on Babrius' material he put forty-two fables of Aesop into fairly pure Latin elegiacs. The collection was used as a school text and consequently suffered much re-editing and interpolation.

Didactic poetry is represented by a few Latin writers of the first century AD, some Greeks in the second century and early third, and finally some more Latins from the second to the fourth. M. Manilius, whose origin is unknown (possibly a provincial), was a writer at the time of Tiberius. His five unfinished books of *Astronomia* show a lofty, though at times nebulous, conception of the absolute law which governs the celestial and terrestrial worlds and gives them eternal order. The treatment is difficult, but it is often illuminated by polished lyrical episodes, like that of Andromeda and Perseus in Book V. Claudius Caesar Germanicus (15 BC–AD 19), the adopted son of Tiberius, wrote some comedies as a young man and also an *Aratea*. This last was based on the *Phaenomena* of Aratus (previously translated by Cicero), but Germanicus altered the format; for example he substituted an invocation to Tiberius for the original invocation to Zeus and added a section called *Prognostica* which he did not find in Aratus. Here too we should mention Book X of Columella's *De Agricultura*, which he put into verse without any poetic inspiration: the book is the one devoted to arboriculture, written with the laudable intention of completing the *Georgics* of Virgil.

Among Greek didactic poets of the second and third centuries we may first mention Dionysius Periegetes, who wrote a *Periegesis* of the world in 1,187 hexameters, published in Hadrian's day. In later centuries this was a standard treatise on geography, and as such was transmitted also in two Latin versions by Avienus and Priscian. It received a Greek commentary by Eustathius as late as the twelfth century.

Oppianus of Cilicia (*c.* 192–212) followed his father into exile on the island of Malta and died at a very early age soon after his recall by Caracalla in 211. He left five books of a poem on fishing, the *Halieutica*, most elegant in diction, style, and metre, but wholly derivative in content. Oppian is also credited with a *Cynegetica* in five books and with a work on bird-catching

(*Ixeutica*), of which the former survives entire and the latter in a summary; but they are in fact the work of a Syrian writer from Apamea, whose style, metre, and language are very different from Oppian's and greatly inferior in quality. This Pseudo-Oppianus (sometimes called Oppianus II) also drew all his information from books, and much of it is absurd. Another writer of this period, this time on medicine, was Marcellus of Side, who wrote forty-two books of *Iatrica* in Marcus Aurelius' day: of these only fragments survive.

In Latin, Terentianus Maurus and Juba wrote at the end of the second century on metric. In addition Nemesianus, whom we mentioned above, was the author of poems called *Cynegetica*, *Halieutica*, and *Nautica*, from the first of which 325 lines are preserved, datable to 283/4.

But the most flourishing period of Latin didactic and learned poetry was the fourth century, and the work which stands out was that of the pagan Rufius Festus Avienus of Volsinii, who lived around AD 360 and is possibly identical with a proconsul of Achaea of that name. His renderings of Livy's history and Virgil's myths into iambics are now lost, but he also once again translated the *Phaenomena* and *Prognostica* of Aratus (into 1325 and 533 hexameters respectively), making use of earlier translations but also adding erudite data of his own. Besides this he drew on Dionysius' *Periegesis*, not without some misunderstanding, for a *Descriptio orbis terrae* in 1,393 hexameters; and another Greek *Periplus*, based largely on data supplied by Himilco the Carthaginian, was his source for an *Orae maritimae liber* about the western and southern coasts of Europe (from this there survive 700 trimeters on the coasts from Britain to the territory of Massilia).

Sacred Poetry. On the pagan side we need only mention a number of anonymous 'Orphic' poems which happen to have survived. The most notable examples are the *Argonautica*, supposedly spoken by Orpheus and including a number of ritual hymns and prayers, and the *Lithica*, which describe the propitiatory and amuletic properties of precious stones.

Among Christian sacred poems we must pass over the ancient liturgical hymns, of which too little is known. Our account may start from Apollinaris, bishop of Laodicea in Syria and the well-known founder of the heresy bearing his name. He wrote various exegetical works on the Scriptures and thirty books against the Neoplatonist Porphyry, but also some paraphrases of the Bible in verse. A *Sacred History to Saul's day* is cited by our sources, and we actually possess the *Paraphrases of the Psalms*, a strange medley of Biblical texts and reminiscences of Homer.

From Gregory of Nazianzus (died *c.* 380) we possess some moral and religious 'poems' for the young. These are divided into historical and theological poems, the most important of the former being an autobiographical work of about 2,000 lines. He also left some 'epitaphs' and ninety-four gnomic 'epigrams' in a great variety of metres, including two examples of accentual (as opposed to quantitative) verse. All these are full of fine sayings, lengthy pieces of reasoning, and subtle distinctions, but they are, in the opinion of the present author, almost wholly devoid of poetic inspiration.

We should also mention a few epigrams by Claudian to his God, and ten hymns by Synesius in Doric dialect and anacreontic or logaoedic metre. All the latter are inspired by a deep mysticism, though some are addressed to Christ, and others, written before his conversion, to the pagan gods.

Christian Poets. The remains of ancient Christian poetry in Latin are very scanty. In the first place it was not much in the nature of the practical Roman to express in poetry the new ideas and sentiments and way of life conveyed by the Christian message. Secondly poetry at that time was used in the liturgy; and liturgies were still composed in Greek for Western as well as for Eastern Christians. We may pass over the few references to Church hymns and canticles in Latin, and also over the earliest metrical inscriptions, in order to say something at greater length about the more important poets.

Commodianus of Gaza (probably the African rather than the Palestinian town of that name) began as a pagan, then became a Jewish proselyte, and was finally converted to Christianity. He lived in the West and wrote in Latin. His poetry is rugged but effective: despite his learning it was to the populace that he addressed his hexameters, which are a mixture of accentual and quantitative versification. His *Carmen apologeticum adversus Iudaeos* was probably written about 250, because it seems to allude to the Decian persecution and the appearance of the Goths on the Danube, although some scholars date the poem much later. It admonishes both Jews and pagans with severity, and is a succinct though imprecise exposition of doctrine with a manifestly polemical purpose. There is marked satirical power behind it, animated though it is by genuine religious feeling. Against the same opponents Commodianus wrote for the benefit of Christian catechumens eighty acrostic poems, which are collected into two books under the title *Instructions*.

C. Vettius Aquilinus Iuvencus, a Spanish poet writing about 330, composed a paraphrase of the Gospels in verse, following first Luke and then Matthew. The action in these *Evangeliorum Libri Quattuor* never comes to life in dramatic form, though the poet is faithful to the text and writes in smooth verses reminiscent of Virgil.

Somewhat earlier, at the beginning of the fourth century, though certainly after his conversion to Christianity, L. Caecilius Firmianus Lactantius composed eighty-five distichs on the fable of the phoenix (*De ave phoenice*), which he took as the symbol of the Christian soul (for other writings of Lactantius see p. 888).

Hilarius of Pictavium (Poitiers) is the first Latin hymnographer we know (c. 315–367; see above p. 889). Of his hymns to be sung in church we possess those for morning and evening, and fragments of three others about the

Redemption. Damasus (306–384, Pope from 366) has left sepulchral epigrams for martyrs' tombs which he had restored, some dedicatory verses for sanctuaries, a few hymns for saints and martyrs, and a prose-verse composition about virginity. Proba, wife of the *praefectus urbi* of 361 and authoress of a lost poem on the war between Constantius and Magnentius, produced a curious composition in Virgilian half-lines, entitled *Cento ex Vergilio de fabrica mundi et Evangeliis*: its 694 hexameters describe the Creation, the Fall, the Flood, and the Life of Christ. Ausonius' *Versus rhopalici* are mere word-plays, in which each word has one syllable more than the last; they contain no echo of Christian thought. Finally there are two anonymous poems against the pagans, composed in Gaul during Eugenius' attempted restoration of paganism in 394.

The real inventive genius in hymnography was St Ambrose (340–397; see above p. 889). His hymns, antiphonal chants, *Horae*, and *Vigiliae* were composed to meet practical needs of Church propaganda, but he found the way to create genuine works of art within the brief measure of his strophes. They have great variety as well as sincerity, avoid both abstruseness and banality, and succeed in conforming to high poetic standards without becoming precious. Many of the 'Ambrosian hymns' are undoubtedly his— for example *Aeterne rerum conditor*, *Deus creator omnium*, *Iam surgit hora tertia*, *Veni redemptor gentium*, and the hymn to Gervasius and Protasius: others, and above all the famous *Te Deum*, must be later.

But the greatest Latin Christian poet of this era is undoubtedly Aurelius Prudentius Clemens (348–after 405), a native of Caesaraugusta in Spain who after holding high offices retired to a life of meditation and published the seven books of his works in 404/5. Written under stress of deep emotion, Prudentius' poetry is sometimes fanciful and impetuous, sometimes logical and compelling, but always genuinely lyrical and personal, even when its forms are traditional. In his style, too, though he is at times obscure, he is second only to Claudian. His themes are extremely varied. The *Cathemerinon liber* contains twelve hymns in nine different metres for given days and hours of the day; the *Peristephanon* has fourteen hymns for martyrs with horrifying descriptions of their martyrdom; the *Apotheosis* is a defence of the divinity of Christ; the *Hamartigeneia* is about the evil which is born of the human will; the *Contra Symmachum* is directed at paganism in general, and at Symmachus in particular over the restoration of the altar of Victory in the senate; the *Psychomachia* concerns the hesitation of the soul between Christian virtues and pagan vices. In these writings the lyrical element is blended with epic and dramatic features, and the descriptive power is sustained by the poet's complete command of diction and metre. Enthusiasm and doctrine, vigour and grace, confidence in Rome's destiny and admiration for nature as God's work—all these qualities and sentiments are found in Prudentius; and they raise his work to the highest plane, even if on occasions he can be prolix and rhetorical. In general the sensibility and artistic talent of this poet are quite remarkable. They show what wealth Latin literature could still command, once both its inspiration and its forms had been given new life by Christian ideals.

It is a far cry from the violence of Prudentius' poetry to the calm and composed verses of Meropius (Paulinus of Nola) which recall the Horatian and Virgilian models he employed. Meropius Pontius Anicius Paulinus (353–431) was a rich senator from Burdigala, who passed through the regular career of honours (becoming consul in 378), and was then baptized. For a long while he retired to a life of meditation, then from 394 he was bishop of Nola, in Campania, where he lived near the tomb of San Felice. His poems contain much information about his life and the events of his time. The *Poetic Letters* to his teacher Ausonius are written to justify his retirement into asceticism; and he also composed Epigrams on Damasus' model, a nuptial song intended as a contrast to the songs written by pagans, and fourteen *Carmina Natalicia* to celebrate each birthday of his chosen patron Felix. There is a sameness about Meropius' themes, and his verbosity is combined with a tendency to rest content with rhetorical devices. Yet the art is there, and amid his unmistakable reminiscences of classical poetry there is genuine religious enthusiasm.

Oratory and the Neo-Sophists. We have explained already how in the early imperial period Latin oratory, and later Greek oratory too, was mainly to be found only in *suasoriae* and scholastic controversies. It had been divorced from public life and the popular courts, and instead became the artificial form of eloquence provided in schools, or at banquets, and the audiences of magistrates. The orator of those days who wanted to call himself a 'sophist' had to be an encyclopaedia of learning, trained not only to perceive all tenable sides of every argument but to sustain them with dexterity and with the voice and gestures of an actor. Like the sophists of old he would travel from city to city declaiming at banquets the imaginary discourses of some ancient personality whose part he was playing, or engaging in discussions about his own views on philosophy and ethics, or delivering ceremonial orations, panegyrics, and palinodes related to fictitious and often paradoxical occasions.

The style and tone of the sophists predominated in almost every school in the empire, and sophistic rhetoric had a vast influence on the creation of a prevailing type of common culture. Almost every writer in every genre of literature succumbed to this culture and tried to propagate it further. [But this literature, though predominantly rhetorical, is not without its value. It has been shown that the schools of rhetoric, in which the Ciceronian tradition was preserved, made it their aim to teach young men the art of persuasion, and consequently to give them the habit of 'putting themselves in someone else's place', which is the very essence of humanistic culture. (See *The Roman Rhetorical Schools as a preparation for the Courts under the Early*

Empire, by Brother E. Patrick Parks, the Johns Hopkins University Studies in Historical and Political Sciences, Series LXIII, No. 2, 1945.) In any case they considerably accentuated the oratorical character of classical prose. One of the most typical bodies of writing from this angle is that of Seneca the Philosopher (whose life is described above, p. 919, and in note 3).

Seneca's first prose composition was a consolation addressed to a patrician Roman lady named *Marcia*, who had just lost a son. Marcia was the daughter of the historian Cremutius Cordus, a senator belonging to the 'Stoic' opposition, which had been disapproved by Sejanus; and it is by invoking the Stoic principles that Seneca tries to comfort the bereaved mother. At this period philosophy was no longer confined to the schools, as a source of material for dialectical exercises; it had been brought in to help people in practical life. This intention is displayed in the greater part of Seneca's surviving philosophical writings, which include few purely theoretical treatises. In fact, that description only applies to the *Naturales Quaestiones* he wrote in his old age—and even those were an attempt to interpret the laws of the universe and thus elucidate the intentions of the divine Providence which was the supreme law of the Sage.

This first consolation was followed by two more, one addressed by Seneca to his own mother, Helvia, to comfort her in her grief for her son's banishment. The other, dedicated to Claudius' freedman, Polybius, who had just lost his brother, is really an attempt at ingratiation by which Seneca hoped to induce the all-powerful minister to plead for him and have him brought back from exile. For the most part, however, Seneca's treatises take the form of 'dialogues' which can fairly be described as 'exhortations to philosophy'. Soon after his return from banishment, Seneca advised his father-in-law Paulinus, then Prefect of the *Annona* (Minister of Food Supply), to ask permission to retire and lead a life of contemplation. Seneca himself seems to have intended to devote himself entirely to philosophy. But he was driven in another direction by Agrippina's wishes and the pressure of life in Rome, and he was soon entrusted with heavy responsibilities. He thereupon resolved to govern the empire according to Stoic principles, and of the 'dialogues' he wrote at this time for a younger friend, Annaeus Serenus, Prefect of the Vigiles, the earlier ones show great optimism. In his treatises *On the Constancy of the Wise Man* and *On Tranquillity of Soul*, Seneca admits the possibility of leading a life of wisdom without renouncing the world of action. Gradually, however, his confidence is undermined by experience. In the dialogue *On Leisure*, he reverts to more pessimistic ideas, and is forced to acknowledge that political life compels a man to make compromises which are inconsistent with virtue. As time goes on, his inner experience is whetted still further and his conscience becomes more clamorous. When, after the premature death of Serenus, he becomes the spiritual adviser of another of his younger friends, Lucilius, his guidance takes a more direct line. Instead of formal treatises, he usually resorts to letters. Most of the *Letters to Lucilius* have survived, and they constitute one of the most moving documents left to us by the pagan world in spiritual matters. They are genuine letters, written by one friend to another, yet they form a progression by which Lucilius is gradually led to a perception of spiritual truths, and then to the firm possession of them. It is here that Seneca puts forth his most 'modern' ideas—his assertion that even slaves have their human dignity, his condemnation of violence in every form (including the cruelties of the circus), his almost mystical aspiration for direct union with God, his serene acceptance of death, etc.

The rhetorical aspect of Seneca's writings is always in evidence, the dominant feature of his 'art of persuasion'; but he made it his aim to break away from conventional methods, and introduced innovations, liberating himself from the Ciceronian style which in those days had an iron grip on the majority of schools. We are told that he had many pupils, and for a time he was the idol of the young. In the next generation, however, Quintilian led teaching back on to more traditional lines. Still, it would be unjust to rank Seneca purely and simply with the 'sophists' and 'rhetoricians'. The demands of conscience and the inner life meant more to him than sheer virtuosity, which was the great concern of the writers associated with the 'second Sophistic'. This latter was at first represented in Rome itself by foreign philosophers, Orientals, such as Euphrates—a friend of the younger Pliny and a bitter enemy to Apollonius of Tyana—who treated moral preaching as though it were a branch of art.]

There was of course some reaction against this movement especially in the early stages, and even later there were a few artists of merit who stood out as exceptions, to say nothing of Christian literature. An early Greek reaction is probably to be found in the anonymous treatise *On the Sublime* (wrongly attributed to Longinus, but datable in the opinion of the present author to the first century AD) which requires all orators to have a proper sense of grandeur. The acute and well-reasoned observations of this admirable writer are evident allusions to the neo-Sophistic school in its early days. At Rome a reaction was attempted by both Quintilian and Tacitus, but on very different lines from each other.

M. Fabius Quintilianus from Calagurris in Spain had studied at Rome and returned there in 68 until his death in 95/6, being first a paid state professor of rhetoric and then the tutor of Domitian's young cousins. In his lost work *De causis corruptae eloquentiae* he attributed the decline of oratory to the fashion for empty declamation on fictitious and futile themes. His *Institutiones Oratoriae*, on which he spent the years between 68 and 95, deal with the education of an orator, the composition and structure of a speech, the choice of arguments, elocution, and the moral and practical aims of a perfect orator. Quintilian was an admirer of Cicero, though he was still an eclectic in his tastes and doctrines: a great gulf separates him from the writers of *suasoriae*.

The same problem of the decay of oratory was faced by Cornelius Tacitus in his *Dialogus de Oratoribus* a little later than 96.[7] This is a conversation imagined to have taken place in the year 74 between the supporters of the old, intermediate, and modern forms of oratory; and the suggested cause of degeneration is tyrannical government. Much of this dialogue is a masterpiece of dialectic. It is composed in a clear, crisp, Ciceronian style, different from that of Tacitus' historical works because it is employed for a different literary genre.

But these counter-attacks, whether by Greek or by Latin writers, could do nothing to check the neo-Sophistic movement, which during the first and second centuries obtained complete mastery in the literatures of both languages. A few examples follow.

From the many works of Dion Cocceianus of Prusa (Dio 'Chrysostom', 40–c. 115, whom we mentioned as a philosopher in the preceding chapter) there survive seventy-six orations, from two periods of his life. The earlier, such as the *Rhodian* and *Trojan* speeches, are pieces of rhetoric on imaginary themes, and can be classified as sophistic: the later are important for understanding the ideas and the life of the second century AD and belong to Dio's Stoic period, including the 'Diogenic' speeches, the *Olympic* and *Euboean*, the *Political Questions*, and speeches *On Kingship* and *On Poverty*. Next comes Nicetas of Smyrna, who flourished in Nerva's period, and who betrays the connexion between the sophistic trend and the bombastic Asianic school of oratory found at an earlier period. An indirect pupil of Nicetas (by way of Scopelianus) was Antonius Polemon of Laodicea, who later became head of the Smyrna school in the reigns of Hadrian and Antoninus Pius. Contemporary opinion regarded Polemon as one of the real glories of his times, but the two surviving examples of his speeches, which are for two Marathon runners, are grotesque by modern standards.

One of the most famous Sophists was Herodes Atticus of Marathon (*c.* 103–179), consul, friend and teacher of emperors, one of the richest men of his time, and a noted builder of public works in Greece and Italy; but his oration *On the State* seems from its surviving fragments to have been of little significance. One of his pupils was P. Aelius Aristides (129–189), son of a priest of Hadrianu Thera in Mysia. After a long period of study with several teachers and after many travels (he was at Rome in 155–156) he spent seventeen years as a sick man partly at Smyrna and partly at Pergamum. Fifty-five of his speeches have survived, some for particular occasions (such as the *Panathenaic*, or the *Praise of Rome*), others of a scholastic type, including exercises on imaginary themes of literary criticism and politics. He also wrote treatises on rhetoric. He was a learned man, who knew the Attic classics well especially from the linguistic standpoint, and was a clever dialectician; but he wasted much of his culture and ability on a distressing form of rhetoric, in which he mingles the most specious arguments with serious ones and devotes himself to words rather than to ideas. We should also mention Maximus of Tyre, who had pretensions as an academic philosopher in the time of Commodus and composed his philosophical ideas into a number of ornamental stanzas. Forty-one *Dialexeis* survive on these lines, containing a medley of absurdity and truth, set out with the greatest affectation and verbosity.

Roman oratory and rhetoric in this period starts as something rather more serious, but before long it rivalled Greek in its emptiness. Pride of place belongs to the *Gratiarum Actio* (or *Panegyric of Trajan*), delivered in the senate in AD 100 by C. Plinius Caecilius Secundus (the Younger Pliny—see below p. 948). It was long when delivered, but has come down to us in an even longer version which he elaborated later, and comprises eulogies on all the events of Trajan's early years, combined with continual attacks on Domitian.

There have survived two collections of nineteen long and 145 short orations on fantastic themes, wrongly attributed by some sources to Quintilian and by others to Postumus Iunior. Yet a third collection contains about fifty items, which are probably of the early second century and are attributed to a certain Calpurnius Flaccus.

But the greatest monstrosity of Latin sophistic was M. Cornelius Fronto (*c*. 100–after 175), a rich African who taught Marcus Aurelius and Verus; he was a senator, and became consul in 143. He won great repute as an orator and letter writer, and composed some historical and antiquarian sketches, as well as a *Consolatio*. The letters he exchanged with the emperors and with his friends are of a quite depressing futility; the same applies to some declamations which have survived, such as the *Praises of Smoke and Dust* or the *Praise of Negligence*. Fronto was interested only in erudition and collecting rare words. His mind was full of old quotations, but what was lacking was thought, even though he had Marcus Aurelius as a friend.

These neo-Sophists, though they were given an exaggerated reputation, were mediocre figures, but among them were a few persons of more considerable stature; Lucian was one and so to some extent was Apuleius. Lucian of Samosata in Syria (*c*. 125–192) learned Greek late, after which he toured round the Mediterranean as a Sophist, staying for longer periods in two places, first at Athens from 165 to 185, and then in Egypt where he became a court official until his death. Of the eighty-two works attributed to him the authentic ones may be divided into those written before and after his residence in Athens. In his early period, after a few declamations in the prevailing fashion on imaginary and empty themes (*The two men called Phalaris, In praise of the fly*, and so on), his treatises became more serious and artistic, his dialectic more agile, and his language more supple (the works of this period include *The Dream, The defence of portraiture*, and *The way to write History*). But the real Lucian is the polemical and satirical writer of his later years. The comic dialogues and parodies of this period mock unmercifully the rascally and childish rhetoricians, the dogmatic philosophers, the bogus moralists, the untenable myths and creeds, together with the literary absurdities of his day—exaggerated Atticism, wild work on grammar, dreary novels, and grotesque tragedies. In the philosophy, religion, and ethics which lie behind his satire he came increasingly under the influence of the Cynics, the Epicureans, and the New Comedy; but he is essentially a great humorist with a biting wit, a supple style, and a brilliant command of fancy. In him dialogue takes on a fresh and easy flow, and the polemical pamphlet attains a lively pungency which it would be difficult to surpass.

L. (?) Apuleius of Madaura in Numidia (c. 125–170) studied dialectic, music, mathematics, and philology in his home town, and also at Carthage, Athens, and Rome, learning to speak and write equally in Greek and Latin. He was initiated into various cults and mysteries. When he returned to Africa he became involved in a serious charge of fraud, connected with a rich elderly widow whom he had married. Later on we find him made *sacerdos provinciae* and honoured with statues at Carthage. Tradition called him a magician: certainly his complex nature and culture enabled him to write as a poet, novelist, philosopher or theosopher, naturalist, and mathematician. Many of his speeches are lost, but we can judge him as an orator and rhetorician from the *Apology* which he wrote in his defence against the charges connected with his marriage, and which does much to tell us about the systems of magic current in his day. We also possess the *Florida*, a collection of excerpts from twenty-three speeches, some written for actual occasions, the rest on imaginary themes. Apuleius is still a sophist after the archaizing manner of Fronto. But he has much more breadth of vision than most sophists, his works are more varied and interesting, and his style is loftier and more personal (on Apuleius' *Golden Ass* see p. 950).

After Lucian Greek sophistic continued its decline into emptier and more fantastic pieces of nonsense, with its erudition becoming increasingly disorganized and often a sham.

In the third century we meet the second of the Philostrati of Lemnos, who lived at Athens and then, from 211 to 244, at Rome. This Philostratus was the author of letters and of the *Lives of the Sophists*, and he was the essential inventor of the story of the Sophist and magician Apollonius of Tyana, whom he depicted as a rival to Christ.[8] Then there was the third Philostratus, nephew to the second, who probably wrote the *Heroicus*, containing lives of heroes in a rural setting, and the *Icones*, an imaginative description of sixty-four pictures in a villa. Mention must also be made of Claudius Aelianus of Praeneste, who prided himself on being able to speak Attic like an Athenian and published elegant descriptions of 'curious' matters in science and scholarship under the titles *The Nature of Animals* and *Miscellaneous stories*, as well as writing a number of letters and two lost works on *Providence* and *Divine Evidence*. Between 193 and 228 appeared the *Deipnosophistae* of Athenaeus of Naucratis, an account of an imaginary banquet attended by twenty-nine diners—jurists, poets, grammarians, philosophers, rhetoricians, doctors, and musicians. This is almost an encyclopaedia of sophistic learning, though it is valuable too for its description of settings and its citation of continuous passages from literature.

Also in the second and third centuries there were writers who collected 'preparatory exercises' (*progymnasmata*), and there appeared several treatises on rhetoric, some more complete than others. Hadrianus Alexander, son of Numenius, wrote a *General Rhetoric* and a book on *Figures of Thought and Speech*. Aelius Theon of Alexandria wrote *Rhetorical Hypotheses* and *Researches into Syntax*, as well as collecting exercises. Hermogenes of Tarsus, an infant prodigy of Marcus Aurelius' day, astonished the world with his speeches, and later wrote *Progymnasmata*, together with works on *Composition, Style*, and *The Method of Eloquence*, providing a complete series of prescriptions, definitions, and examples. Apsines of Gadara, who became consul under Maximin, wrote a work called *Techne*; Menander of Laodicea produced a tract on *Epideictic Speeches*; and Cassius Longinus (220–273), the teacher of Porphyry and counsellor of Zenobia, a man later executed at Rome, was a philosopher, lexicographer, and author of a *Treatise on Rhetoric*.

There was a regular renaissance of Greek rhetoric and sophistic in the fourth century, with Athens as the main centre of its production. Libanius (*c.* 314–393) was born at Antioch and became professor at Athens, Nicaea, Constantinople, and finally (from 354) at Antioch itself. He was a friend of the Emperor Julian (himself a considerable writer) and taught important Christians like John Chrysostom, Theodorus, Basileius, and Gregory Nazianzenus, as well as such pagans as Ammianus Marcellinus. He himself was a convinced pagan, and was distressed at the neglect and scorn shown for the ancient religion. He wrote treatises and scholastic models, but there is more spontaneity and information in his sixty-five orations on topics of the day, including panegyrics, court speeches, descriptions of towns, speeches to the emperor, and speeches in defence of pagan temples. Equally important are his 1,605 letters to every class of person on every kind of topic. Although he was a schoolmaster who lived on erudition and the little happenings in his school, and although as an orator and dialectician he was commonplace, he is still a genuine character with a certain appeal.

Himerius of Prusa (*c.* 315–386) spent most of his life as master of a flourishing school at Athens. His eighty speeches, of which twenty-four survive entire, are concerned with school subjects and particular occasions. They are not impressive either for their ideas or for their dialectical skill, being a collection of fancies, mythical traditions, and poetical quotations, strung together in a mannered, ornamental, and melodious style.

A much superior writer was Themistius of Paphlagonia (310/20–390/5), who kept a school at Constantinople from 347 but also rose to the highest offices in the state (he was prefect of the city in 384) and was the tutor of Flavius Arcadius. An ardent pagan, he begged the emperors to allow religious freedom, but to no avail. In his school he dealt with ethical questions among others. He has left us an abridged but clear *Paraphrase of Aristotle* and thirty-five speeches, some official and others occasional. The most noteworthy are the speech to Flavius Iovianus on *Religious Toleration*, the

Sophist (an apology for his life), and the speech on *Humanity*. His writings are important for their content, but their style too, though ornate and academic, is not lacking in grace and power.

In the Latin world too the fourth century was a flourishing period for rhetoric and oratory. From court speeches of the eulogistic kind there survive twelve extremely servile *Panegyrics*, some from the end of the previous century and all of them written in Gaul. They are modelled on the style of Cicero and are in the genre of Pliny's *Panegyric* to Trajan; for the most part they are in a reasonably pure and smooth classical Latin. Some of them are anonymous, others bear the names of Eumenius, Nazarius, Mamertinus, and Drepanius Pacatus; and they are addressed to various emperors, from Maximian to Theodosius.

But the most eminent figure in this branch of literature was Q. Aurelius Symmachus (340-405), proconsul of Africa in 373-375, *praefectus urbi* in 384/5, consul in 391. Eight of his orations, all of the panegyric type, survive as a single 'corpus'. Symmachus, too, was a devoted pagan, and his letters, which are of great interest, show how he implored in vain for respect, or at least toleration, to be extended to the old religion of Rome's ancestors.

In the Latin part of the empire the fourth century also produced several writers of more or less elementary works on rhetoric. Aquila Romanus wrote *De figuris sententiarum et elocutionis*, which was used, with additions, for a work of the same name by Julius Rufinianus. Messius Arusianus published *Exempla elocutionum* in 395; and a little before 400 C. Chirius Fortunatianus produced three books *Artis Rhetoricae* in the form of questions and answers.

Historical Writing. Historians, both in Greek and in Latin, were conspicuous in the first two centuries of the empire.

a. *Latin*

C. Velleius Paterculus had a long and gallant military career which was crowned by his participation in Tiberius' triumph in AD 12. He was engaged on the preparation of a history from the Civil Wars down to Tiberius, but in 29 he composed, on the spur of the moment, a short historical work as a compliment to a friend who had been designated consul. This is his *Historia Romana* in two books, which have survived with some gaps. The style is ungainly, and Velleius' attempts at the pointed phrasing of post-Augustan prose are seldom successful. The history is extremely cursory from the origins of Rome down to Tiberius, but he spreads himself more fully on Tiberius himself and, without allowing too much detail to emerge, attacks the critics of his emperor's achievements and methods of government, thereby providing us with an excellent corrective to the account of Tacitus. For the early history Velleius uses a variety of sources; and he includes sections on literary and cultural history, and on the colonies and provinces, which were unusual in historians of the period.

The contemporary work of Valerius Maximus, nine books on *Facta et dicta memorabilia* composed between about 28 and 31, had very different purposes. He aimed at providing rhetoricians with a collection of facts, sayings, and historical examples: they are drawn from every kind of source, and compiled with some attention to style. Probably very similar were the *Historiae diversae exempla Romana* collected by an anonymous author (probably of Augustan date) and later abridged by C. Titius Probus.

Probably to Claudius' time belong the ten books of *Historiae Alexandri Magni* by Q. Curtius Rufus. This work has no historical value of its own, and includes statements which are incredible and reasoning which is absurd. It is written in an easy and agreeable style by a rhetorician who wanted to compose a pleasant work on an historical subject of the semi-romantic kind.

Much Latin historiography of this century has been lost; such as the memoirs and autobiographies of Tiberius, Claudius, Vespasian, and Domitian, and also of Agrippina, Domitius Corbulo, L. Antistius Vetus, Suetonius Paulinus, and Vipstanus Messalla. There were biographies of Cato Uticensis by P. Clodius Thrasea Paetus, of Thrasea Paetus and Helvidius Priscus by Junius Arulenus Rusticus, and of L. Annius Bassus by Ti. Claudius Pollio. There were monographs on the Civil Wars by A. Cremutius Cordus, on the German wars down to Nero's time by Aufidius Bassus (continued by Pliny the Elder's twenty books on the same subject), by Fabius Rusticus on the British wars, by M. Antonius Iulianus on the Jews, and by Pompeius Planta on the year 69. But more considerable works have also perished, such as the *Histories* of Cluvius Rufus, consul about AD 40 and governor of Hither Spain in 68, and the Universal Chronicle of L. Cornelius Bocchus, probably a Lusitanian, on whom Pliny the Elder drew for his work *The Marvels of Spain.*

Cornelius Tacitus (*c.* 55–*c.* 120), who perhaps came from Interamna,[9] studied rhetoric when young and then in 78 married the daughter of Agricola, the conqueror of Britain. He pursued the public career of a senator under Vespasian, Titus, and Domitian, became consul under Nerva in 97, and in 100 took on the defence of the province of Africa against Marius Priscus. After that he devoted himself solely to his literary publications (for the *Dialogus de Oratoribus* see p. 931 above).

The *De vita et moribus Iulii Agricolae* belongs to 98, the beginning of the reign of Trajan, and its style still shows signs of Ciceronian influence. It is a eulogistic biography of Tacitus' own father-in-law, telling the story of his achievements in Britain (with long digressions on geography and ethnology) and contrasting his virtues with the vices of Domitian (who was now dead). The short work ends with a fine passage addressed to the dead Agricola.

To the same year 98 belongs the *Germania*, or *De origine, situ, moribus, ac populis Germanorum*, a work written in rhetorical style with Sallustian undertones. Tacitus uses the original sources, both oral and written, to deal first with the region in general—its boundaries, climate, and products, and the military, religious, political, and private life of its inhabitants—and then with individual peoples. The work was written at a time when Trajan was consolidating Rome's possessions in Germany, and it seeks to make better known the country and tribes against which Rome was fighting and to give his readers an idea of the right policy to adopt. Sometimes too Tacitus, following a technique which was becoming increasingly common, idealizes the primitive customs of the barbarians to point a contrast with the advanced but corrupt customs of his own people.

Tacitus had planned a history of the emperors, dividing the work in a way which departed from chronological order. First would come the emperors from Galba to Domitian (69–96), then those from Tiberius to Nero (14–68), thirdly Nerva and Trajan (96–117), and finally the rule of Augustus (27 BC–AD 14). But he was able to complete only the first two parts of this work. His *Historiae* covers the period from 69 to 96 in fourteen books,[10] of which there survive only the first four and part of the fifth, dealing with the events of 69 and part of 70. This work was written between 104 and 109. The *Annales* or *Ab excessu divi Augusti*, written some ten years later, run from AD 14 to 68. From them there survive Books I–IV, parts of V–VI, and Books XI–XVI, the last section being incomplete at its beginning and its end: this gives us almost all the reign of Tiberius and parts of the reigns of Claudius and Nero.

Tacitus made use of all available written sources—documents, the *Acta Diurna*, proceedings of the senate, tracts, memoirs, autobiographies, and regular histories. He also drew on personal recollections by himself and others, especially for later events. We should know more about his use of sources if we could decide with certainty, and in detail, the reasons for the parallels between passages in the *Histories* and three other texts, namely Plutarch's *Lives* of Galba and Otho, Suetonius' biographies, and the *History* of Dio Cassius. These parallels sometimes amount to verbal correspondence, and would seem to prove not only the use of common sources but the actual transcription of them, even by Tacitus, with what in many cases is close adherence to their words. There are other reasons for thinking that Tacitus' research was not particularly scholarly, especially over details.

He was a passionate aristocrat and convinced admirer of free institutions, detesting tyrannically-minded emperors; and his long experience of men and life had led him to put a pessimistic interpretation on human actions. Being richly endowed with the power to construct hypotheses about the psychological reasons for the behaviour of his characters, he tended unconsciously to turn these hypotheses into factual data, and managed to extract from the sources information which best accorded with his own largely *a priori* beliefs. He was a supreme master of dramatic exposition of a kind that impresses and even fascinates the reader; and this makes his histories, while immensely interesting, also extraordinarily suggestive. They must therefore be used with quite exceptional caution. His undertaking to write 'sine ira et studio' must be regarded with the fullest reserve, and his prejudice and character too often make his judgements excessively rosy or gloomy.

His style is both intimate and powerful. Refinement in rhetoric is in his case combined with daring efforts at dramatization and epigrammatic brevity. His language is highly coloured and poetical, and possesses an astringency which is all his own (though in other respects he was influenced by Thucydides and Sallust).[11]

C. Suetonius Tranquillus (*c.* 75–*c.* 140) was already a man of note in Trajan's reign and became a high official in the Imperial Archives, the 'scrinium a studiis', and thereafter *ab epistulis Latinis* to Hadrian. Later, however, he devoted himself entirely to his literary work. We possess no clear idea of his lost work, especially of the *Prata*, which may have been a systematic encyclopaedia, or possibly just an assembly of miscellaneous pieces of research. We do not know if certain other writings formed part of the *Prata* or were separate works, though the former seems more probable. These include the *De naturis rerum, De animantium naturis, De anno Romanorum, De notis,* and *De Roma et institutis legibusque Romanorum.*

In the *De viris illustribus* Suetonius made use of all kinds of authors and documents to write the lives of Roman literary figures from the time of Cicero to that of Domitian, divided into poets, orators, historians, philosophers, grammarians and rhetoricians. We know something of its contents under each of these heads from Jerome and later biographers, who drew heavily on Suetonius' work.

On the other hand his eight books *De vita Caesarum*, published between 119 and 121, have survived almost entire. These contain Lives of the twelve emperors from Caesar to Domitian. The information is largely anecdotal and of very varying value, drawn from every possible source without even the minimum of discrimination. It is then put, with little critical sense or psychological insight, into a stereotyped scheme which Suetonius borrowed from his biographies of literary figures. The standard paragraphs in each Life are therefore 'forma, habitus, cultus, mores, civilia, bellica, studia'. The work has no artistic finish, but it is valuable because excellent and unusual sources are often used and because the political prejudices behind it are less factious and one-sided than those of other authors.

In Hadrian's time (more precisely in 116/17) the African poet and professor of rhetoric, P. Annius Florus, wrote his *Epitome de Tito Livio bellorum omnium* in two books, interpolating data from Sallust and Caesar into those provided by Livy. This is a careless, rhetorical, and poetical work, which was very popular in later centuries. In the same period or slightly later Justinus composed his epitome (mentioned in Part II) of the *Philippica* of Pompeius Trogus; and L. Ampelius wrote an historical and geographical handbook for schools under the title *Liber Memorialis*, designed to instruct pupils 'quid sit mundus, quid elementa, quid orbis terrarum ferat, vel quid genus humanum peregerit'.

The last great attempt to write a complete Roman History in Latin was made by Granius Licinianus at the time of the Antonines. Using Livy, but supplementing and correcting his account from other sources, he wrote thirty-eight books, from which there survive only a few fragments of the latter portion, mainly referring to events of the years 165, 108, and 78 BC. These make us greatly regret the loss of the remainder. It is a disputed question whether the surviving fragments come from Licinianus' original work or from an epitome.

There were numerous continuators and imitators of Suetonius' *Lives of the Caesars*, but they have unfortunately been lost almost without exception. One of the most important was Marius Maximus, possibly to be identified with the consul of 223 and 232, who wrote biographies of the more out-standing emperors from Nerva to Elagabalus, omitting the minor figures. He was very painstaking in transcribing documents and ransacking the *Acta Urbis*, but was too fond of scandal and legend, and becomes tedious on account of long-windedness. Aelius Iunius Cordus, who was still alive at the time of the Philips, wrote the lives of the 'obscurer' emperors omitted by Marius Maximus, and also of the later emperors, from Elagabalus to Gordian III. He was often satisfied with frivolities and gossip, and goes into the most trivial details.

In contrast the work of the so-called *Scriptores Historiae Augustae* has been preserved almost intact. This is a 'corpus' of the lives of the emperors from 117 to 284, attributed by our manuscripts to six different authors, Aelius Spartianus, Julius Capitolinus, Vulcacius Gallicanus, Aelius Lampridius, Trebellius Pollio, and Flavius Vopiscus, who are said to have lived in the period of Diocletian and Constantine. This traditional view of the *Scriptores* has been challenged in various ways, and we cannot here refer to all the discordant views. Given the uniformity of style many scholars suppose that the 'writers' never existed, and that the lives were written *en bloc* at a later date (some say in the age of Julian, others in the reign of Theodosius, others at some point between the two): at one or more other dates there was a further process of re-editing. It is worth noting that most of the documents contained in these lives are beyond doubt forgeries, often of the clumsiest kind.

If we leave aside biographies, Latin historical work of this period (the fourth century included except for Ammianus) mainly consists of simple epitomes adapted to a lazy public and containing little of interest. In the time of Constantius II, Aurelius Victor, an African who was prefect of Rome in 389, wrote a well-informed work with some imprint of personality about it, which was called the *Caesares* and dealt with the emperors from Augustus to AD 360. To this an unknown scholar added two short prefaces, designed to complete the story and make it an 'Historia tripertita': one is called *Origo gentis Romanae*, the other *De viris illiustribus urbis Romae* (from Romulus to M. Antonius). There is also an *Epitome de Caesaribus* covering imperial history from Augustus to the death of Theodosius in 395: this follows Victor's *Caesares* at its outset, but is by a different author.

Eutropius, the *magister memoriae* of Valens (364–378), wrote ten short books called *Breviarium ab urbe condita*, for which he drew on Livy, Suetonius, an imperial chronicle, and his own recollections. This was a work much read: it was several times translated into Greek and often added to (from Paulus Diaconus onwards). Also for the use of Valens was Rufius Festus' *Breviarium* (*rerum gestarum populi Romani*), based for the earlier sections on Livy or an *Epitome* of that historian,[12] with the addition of some other sections badly constructed and badly put together. A Livian *Epitome* was also used by the pagan Julius Obsequens for a *Liber prodigiorum* covering the years 190–12 BC, although the record of prodigies in Livy begins at the year 249.

We may finally mention the first of the historical scholars in the rich Sicilian family of the Nicomachi, the only one who falls within the limits of this volume. This was Virius Nicomachus Flavianus, *vicarius* of Africa in 377 and *quaestor sacri Palatii* to Theodosius I, to whom he dedicated an historical work with the title *Annales*.

But the most important Latin historical work of the fourth century was that of Ammianus Marcellinus (*c.* 330–400), a Greek of Antioch, who after a long and gallant military career, during which he got to know many people, lands, and types of human being, finally retired and devoted himself to writing thirty-one books of *Res Gestae*, a continuation of the *Histories* of Tacitus from 96 to 378. The surviving books are XIV–XXXI, covering the years 353 to 378, and they show Ammianus to have been a genuine historian, shrewd at understanding men and events, well informed, and unprejudiced and balanced in his judgements—for example on Julian, whose virtues and defects he appreciates equally. He avoided being overwhelmed by rhetoric, although his style is often obscure and bizarrely Tacitean, and although he inserts into his history a number of curious excursuses on geography, physico-mathematics, philosophy, religion, and social matters, which are neither very original nor very accurate, and are collected from every kind of source. A portion of Ammianus' history, relating to Constantinople, was re-edited about 390 by a pagan, and interpolations were later made by a Christian editor. This constitutes the first of two fragments known as the *Anonymus Valesianus*.

b. *Greek*

Flavius Josephus of Jerusalem (37–*c.* 100) was an anchorite in his youth, but then sided with the pro-Roman section of the Pharisees. In 64 he came on an embassy to Rome, where Poppaea thought well of him. In the Romano-Jewish War he was taken prisoner, and he remained in Titus' camp during the siege of Jerusalem. Later he lived at Rome, having been made a Roman citizen, and died in Trajan's reign. His plan was to make known the history of the Jews in the Graeco-Roman world, in ancient as well as in modern times. He therefore wrote first (between 70 and 79) seven books *On the Jewish War* (then just completed) with a preface on the earliest contacts between Rome and Judaea. Then, before 94, he composed twenty books of *Jewish*

Antiquities, from the creation of the world down to AD 66. He dwelt at length on the most recent history, for which his narrative, though tendentious, is extremely valuable, and drew on the Bible for the remainder. When his two works were greeted with disbelief and criticism by certain Greeks, notably by Apion, Josephus went on to write his *Contra Apionem*, in which he demonstrates the antiquity of the Hebrew people, brings together references to them from ancient Greek writers, and defends the Jewish Law against attacks by Greeks. The style of Josephus has rhetorical flourishes, but one must bear in mind that he wrote in Hebrew and then translated his works into Greek with the help of a friend.

A man of opposing views, an anti-Roman 'zealot' named Justus from Tiberias, wrote a hurried chronicle from Moses to Herod Agrippa II (down to AD 100). Josephus deplored the tendentious character of this work, which appeared slightly before his death.

The rest of Greek historical writing from the first century AD, before we reach Plutarch, is almost entirely lost, but some of these writers deserve a mention. We may start with Claudius, who before he became emperor in 41 had devoted himself to historical and grammatical studies, and had composed in Greek twenty books of *Tyrrhenica* and eight of *Carchedoniaca*. In Latin he wrote the early part of a Roman history from the death of Caesar, resuming it again in forty-one books from the restoration of Augustus. He also wrote an autobiography in Latin.

Then there was the Samaritan Thallus, a freedman of Tiberius, who produced three books on chronology with synchronisms between the histories of Greece, Rome, the Orient, and Judaea. This was much used by Christian chronographers. In addition we find a series of writers of local history, Teucer on Cyzicus, Hippocrates on Sicily, Memnon on Heraclea, Apion on Egypt, Theagenes on Macedonia, and so forth.

From Plutarch we possess forty-six 'Parallel Lives' in pairs, and also four on their own (Artaxerxes II, Aratus, Galba, and Otho), all written between 105 and 115. We know, however, that others existed and that the author had still more in mind. Varro and Cornelius Nepos had already made comparisons between illustrious Romans and foreigners, but Plutarch limited his scope to generals, statesmen, and legislators. The pairing, sometimes successful but sometimes forced, was emphasized by the writing of a *Comparison* at the end of each one. The *Lives* were published by the author directly he had them ready, the degree of elaboration depending on the number of sources he had available. When earlier writers provided him with a large number of anecdotes he stretched them out over practically the whole of the Life in question; when the anecdotes were few, he dwelt more on the historical events connected with his hero. Since he was a great reader and took many notes, it is difficult to reconstruct his precise sources: they are more numerous in the Greek *Lives* (although many citations may be derived at second hand from earlier biographies), less numerous in the Roman. Plutarch's purpose was more moral than historical: he wanted to edify, though he is often silent about the defects of his heroes, and also to produce a psychological analysis of a set of 'characters', a difficult enough task when he had to use anecdotes of any sort of value and from any sort of source. The *Lives* of Plutarch are a great mine of information for the historian, information which is good or bad according to the value of the sources he was using.

Flavius Arrianus of Nicomedia, a prosperous Roman citizen, was a pupil of Epictetus and set himself to publish his master's theories. But after the death of his master, whom he compared with Socrates, he became a second Xenophon and passed from philosophy to soldiering. He served in various provinces, was consul in 130, and afterwards governor of Cappadocia when it was menaced by the Alani, this being the period in which he wrote his works on geography and tactics. Then we find him at Athens, holding important municipal posts; during old age he was still able to hunt, and must have been generally affluent. Many of the historical works of Arrian's Athenian period have been lost: the *Lives* of Timoleon and Diocles of Syracuse, eight books of *Bithyniaca* from the origins to 75 BC, his personal memoirs entitled *Alanica*, and his *Parthica* down to the time of Trajan (in seventeen books). What survives is, first, his work *On India*, written in Ionic dialect in imitation of Herodotus, and based mainly on the *Periplus* of Nearchus; secondly the *Anabasis of Alexander*, for which he used Ptolemy and Aristobulus, attempting to compare them critically; and thirdly the *Succession to Alexander*, known to us from a résumé by Photius. Although his style is commonplace, his language, like Lucian's, is one of the better examples of Attic during this period. We have already spoken about his epic poetry.

Appian of Alexandria was *advocatus fisci* at Rome under Hadrian and Antoninus Pius, then a procurator down to the time of Marcus Aurelius. A great admirer of the empire, he wrote a vast *Roman History* in twenty-four books, divided on the lines adopted by Pompeius Trogus into sections related to each of the peoples conquered by Rome. In this way it got split into a number of separate monographs piled one on top of another, which in certain portions were even given irrational titles. There survive only fragments of Books I–V, with Books VI–IX and XI–XVII entire. Throughout the work there is no serious attempt to explain the dominion of Rome. The form is simple, and shows no sophistic influence.

Phlegon of Tralles, a freedman of Hadrian, composed a collection of *Olympic victors and chronological data* in sixteen books. These were later reduced to eight and used by Julius Africanus.

Herennius Philon of Byblus, born about 70, wrote various historical works which have since been lost: *The Reign of Hadrian, Important cities and men* (a work in thirty books, much used by the lexicographers Stephanus of Byzantium and Hesychius), *Paradoxical Stories* (about contradictions among historians), and a *History of the Phoenicians* in nine books of which Eusebius preserves fragments. In this last work he gives a Euhemerist explanation of

Phoenician mythology, adducing a supposed work by Sanchoniathon of Tyre, a probably non-existent or apocryphal writer assigned to the period before Homer.

Cassius Dio Cocceianus (c. 155–235) may be regarded as the last great Greek historian before the age of Justinian. Born at Nicaea in Bithynia and descended from Dio Chrysostom, he was a senator and advocate in Rome, praetor in 194, and companion of Caracalla on his campaigns of 211–217. In 218 he was imperial commissioner at Smyrna and Pergamum, then governor in Africa in 224, and consul in 229. He spent his last years in Bithynia, having withdrawn from public life. His first work was a monograph on Commodus, written in 194. Then he put in hand his *Roman History* for which he collected material between 200 and 209, elaborating it down to 221 and returning to it once more after 229. Of its eighty books those numbered XXXVI–LX (68 BC–AD 47) and LXXIX–LXXX (Caracalla to Elagabalus) have survived in entirety: for the rest there are extracts made by order of Constantine Porphryogenitus, and the works based on Dio by Xiphilinus and Zonaras (eleventh and twelfth centuries). Dio tried once again, by comparing the versions given by earlier writers, to reconstruct a sound and reasoned history: he took the work of Thucydides as his model, though he could not begin to approach it. His style is notable for the clarity and agreeable nature of his exposition, which becomes tiresome only in his oratorical passages and in his lists of prodigies. The better part of the work, naturally, is that which concerns events near his own day.

Aelius Herodianus, an official at Rome, wrote the history of the successors of Marcus Aurelius down to 238, drawing mainly on his personal recollections, though he was also familiar with Dio and other historians. He was remarkably impartial, and was knowledgeable about men and political parties; but he is less careful in his references to chronology, geography, and warfare. Herodian's language is easy and his style presentable, but he too is a writer who wearies one with an excess of discursive and sophistic passages.

P. Herennius Dexippus was an Athenian who took part in the defence of Athens against the Heruli in 269. He wrote a *History of the Successors of Alexander the Great, The War against the Scythians* (his personal reminiscences), and an *Historical Chronicle*. This last was used by Eusebius, who also drew on a chronicle by the Neoplatonist Porphyry (mentioned earlier for his philosophy).

Pagan Greek historiography in the fourth century, apart from a few autobiographical narratives like the lost commentaries of Julian on the Gallic War, was the work of court panegyrists. This applies both to short lives of emperors (these too are lost) and also to the writings of Eunapius of Sardis (346–after 414), a pagan pupil of Neoplatonists and rhetoricians, who kept a school of rhetoric himself and wrote fourteen books of chronicles continuing Dexippus from 270 to 404. This work, the *Historical Records*, is written in pompous style, its central part, even more pompous than the rest, being five books of eulogy dedicated to Julian, which was widely used by Zosimus, though only fragments survive today. Eunapius also wrote a series of twenty-three *Lives of Sophists and Philosophers* (his own contemporaries), a peculiarly wordy and futile piece of work.

Christian Chronographers Hippolytus, whose *Philosophoumena* were mentioned earlier, and who is said to have been martyred in the Decian persecution, wrote a concise *Chronicle* from the origin of the world to 234. This is preserved in part in Armenian, and was an important source for later Chroniclers.

The *Chronographiai* of Sextus Iulius Africanus (died *c.* 240) are in five books from the origins of the world to AD 221, with synchronisms between the Bible story, which is taken as a base, and the events of the pagan world. The work has survived in fragments. According to Africanus the world was destined to last 6,000 years; Christ had come to earth in the year 5,500, and therefore there would be 500 years of the world's life after his birth. The considerable use made of this work by Byzantine historians has enabled scholars to give a satisfactory reconstruction of it both in its general lines and also in some of its details.

Eusebius, born at Caesarea in Palestine between 260 and 265, was so devoted a pupil of Pamphilus that he took his name just as if he had been his adopted son. He learned from his master a veneration for Origen and a love of erudition. He became bishop of his own city about 313, and died some time before 340, after having taken an active part in the theological struggles which disturbed Christianity after 325. He was present at councils and important religious ceremonies, and has left descriptions of them in his writings. The latter include, first, some commentaries on the Bible with revisions of the sacred text; secondly some apologetic works, such as the *Contra Hieroclem*, and the *Contra Porphyrium* in twenty-five books; but thirdly and most important his histories, which have gained him the honourable title of 'Father of Ecclesiastical History'. His service was in fact confined to the labour of collecting material. He enriched his own text with many extracts from earlier authors, and also cited passages which would undoubtedly have been lost if he had not reported them. For this reason his pages are particularly precious and represent an inexhaustible mine of information.

He composed a *Chronological Canon* and an *Epitome of World History of Greeks and Barbarians*. The latter has two parts, the first a date-table for the history of particular peoples, the second a set of chronological rules and synchronisms, from 2016 BC, in which he interweaves sacred and profane history together very closely. The original Greek is lost, but it can be constructed on the basis of the Latin version (with additions) by Jerome, and of two other versions, Armenian and Syriac; help is also given by the chronological work of Syncellus, though all these various texts show noticeable

variations between one another. The same idea inspires two other works of
Eusebius, the *Praeparatio Evangelica* and the *Demonstratio Evangelica*, where
with his customary erudition he illustrates his thesis that Christianity has
crowned all that was good in the ancient world, whether pagan or Jewish,
and that we cannot therefore deny its truth or condemn the religion which
has been revealed. Other historical works of Eusebius include *The Martyrs
of Palestine*, *The Acts of the ancient Martyrs*, and a *Life of Constantine*, the
last a sickening piece of eulogy including a number of documents which some
have held to be spurious. These works, and more particularly the *Ecclesiastical History* which we come to next, have always been the subject of lively
argument; and even now it cannot be said that scholars have reached agreement upon their degree of reliability.

The *Ecclesiastical History* of Eusebius consists today of ten books covering
the period from the birth of Jesus down to 323. But it was composed in
sections and not as a single work. First came Books I–VII and an early edition
of Book VIII, taking the story down to the events of 312; then Book IX,
published in 315; and Book X, together with a revision of the whole work,
came out in 324. The manuscript tradition itself reveals the alterations which
were made. These revisions led to inconsistencies in the author's judgements,
and sometimes serious ones, since he changed his opinions accordingly as
particular persons fared in relation to Constantine, who remains the guiding
star of the whole work. The *Life of Constantine* presents even greater difficulties: it is not a genuine biography, but (as we indicated above) a eulogistic
speech in four books, with sixteen documents inserted which purport to come
from the imperial chancellery and other archives. The *Life* too had two
editions, since it had to be brought up to date in the light of the political
situation and the fortunes of its protagonist. But the most striking thing is the
difference in the tone of this work as compared with the *History*. Facts are
presented in different ways in the two Eusebian works, and there is no doubt
that the *Life* is not so much an historical narrative as a piece of apology, shot
through with pure invention. The two documents, however, are quite
certainly authentic as transcribed: there has been no tampering.

Eusebius' conception of history and politics started with an ingenious idea.
He would not use theoretical arguments for defending Christianity but take
his stand on history, showing what struggles and what victories the religion
had undergone and what glorious traditions and forms of organization it had
achieved. Yet the undertaking required powers which Eusebius did not
possess. The disparity between his promise and performance accordingly led
to contradictions, incoherence, disorder, and arbitrary judgements, of the
kind found so often in the *History* despite the sincere enthusiasm and
religious ardour which inspired it. Moreover the author was convinced that
there was a parallelism between Christianity and the Roman empire: he
made that empire, especially as governed by the absolute monarchy of
Constantine's time, into the expression on earth of the government in

heaven, the rule of God. According to him the emperor was the new Moses leading the Christian people to salvation, and it is not surprising that he was impressed by the complete revolution which in the course of a few years had transformed Christianity from a persecuted faith to a religion actually promoted by the state. For the same reason he approved of Constantine's ecclesiastical policy over the Arian controversy, disregarding the serious menace to religious freedom because he maintained that Constantine's way provided the only means of safeguarding the true faith—or the faith Eusebius believed to be true.

Eusebius was openly hostile towards belief in the millennium. This too is to be explained by his conviction that any such belief contradicted his ideal, which was based on a longing for the establishment of God's temporal Kingdom and for a religion which brought civilization through the support afforded it by the political authorities. This was the line imprinted by Eusebius on all his Church History, and it left an indelible mark on that branch of study for all time. Again and again histories were composed with the purpose of discovering external signs of Christian progress, despite the fact that this progress is something which takes place within, and cannot be in any way determined or measured.

After Eusebius the Latin tradition in Church History, with a few exceptions, turned to the compilation of chronological works. The so-called 'Chronographer of 354' is a handbook of chronology and history, comprising the official calendar, the consular *Fasti* down to 354, the tables for determining Easter between 312 and 411, the list of *praefecti urbi* between 254 and 354, the dates on which bishops of Rome and martyrs were buried, and the list of bishops of Rome down to Liberius (352–356). Down to 334 it has a chronicle of events in two different hands, and it also includes a chronicle of Rome to 324 and the *Notitia Regionum* of the same city.

The Church father Athanasius wrote a biography of St Antony the Great which was used as a model for Greek and Latin biographies and lives of saints during the Western and Byzantine Middle Ages.

The Latin version of Josephus, in part abridged and in part enlarged, may be the work of Ambrose, though it was for a long time wrongly called the edition by Hegesippus. Jerome has given us a Latin translation of the second part of Eusebius' *Chronicle*, which he prolonged down to 380. He also made the first attempt at a history of Christian literature in his *Viri Illustres*, which was written in 392 and includes 135 authors from St Peter to Jerome himself. We should also mention his various lives of monks and saints, such as St Paul of Thebes and Malchus.

The Aquitanian Sulpicius Severus, a lawyer turned monk, has left us two books of *Chronici* composed in 403. These are a history of the Jews and Christians from Adam to AD 400, with especial emphasis on the earliest parts of sacred history and on events near to the author's own day. The style is that of Sallust or Tacitus.

Finally there is Julius Hilarianus, bishop of Africa, who in 397 wrote *De mundi duratione* and on the date of Easter.[13]

Letter-writing. Letter-writing had a number of different aspects during the imperial period. Sometimes we find correspondence which really took place, even though it may have been edited at the time of publication, as Cicero's had been: here the examples are Pliny and Fronto. In other cases the letters are fictitious, and serve either as the dressing for treatises, especially treatises on philosophy (as with Seneca) or as exercises in sophistic (as with Alciphron, Julius Titianus, Philostratus, or Claudius Aelianus). Sometimes the latter as well as the former kind are arranged in complete collections. We have already noticed too the importance of 'Epistulae' in the Christian world from the Apostolic period onward.

In Latin letter-writing the sophistic genre came later than the use of letters for treatises (see p. 930 on the Younger Seneca as a philosopher) or the genuine letters produced by the Younger Pliny. C. Plinius Caecilius Secundus (61/2–114) was born at Comum and was named C. Caecilius until his adoption by the Elder Pliny, who was his uncle. He was taught by Quintilian, and followed the full *cursus honorum* down to a consulate in 100 and a legateship in Bithynia in 111–113. On his death he left his books and a foundation for *alimenta* (upkeep of poor children) to the people of Comum. As a young man he had written poems described as 'lusus et ineptiae' and in 100 he composed the *Panegyric* to Trajan (mentioned above). But his main literary work was his twofold collection of letters, the nine books of letters to his friends written between 97 and *c.* 109, and his correspondence with Trajan. The letters to his friends are at once different from the letters of Cicero in that they were conceived and written with a view to publication. They enable us to get to know all sides of their author, at any rate in the way that he wanted to be known. More interesting from the historical standpoint are the 121 letters exchanged with Trajan, mainly during the governorship of Bithynia. Pliny turns to the *princeps* for his views on every kind of question; and Trajan replies clearly, briefly, and with judgement, though he is sometimes evasive. The style of the *Letters*, like those of Cicero, is simpler and more everyday than that of the *Panegyric*.

We have already alluded to the correspondence of Fronto with Antoninus Pius, Marcus Aurelius, and Verus. A contrast to him in style was Julius Titianus, who composed letters imagined to have been written by women—like Ovid's *Heroides*. He was so successful in reproducing the style of Cicero's *Letters* that he earned the nickname of 'ape'.

Among Greek letters of sophistic type, we may mention the 108 written by Lucian's friend Alciphron of Athens between 160 and 190. They were intended to be like a series of little mimes reproducing the background of Athens in the fourth century BC, and as such they owe much to comic poetry. From Philostratus we possess seventy-three letters which are mainly scholastic exercises, or love letters full of witticisms and little epigrams. Claudius Aelianus produced letters which imitate the rustic speech of peasants.

Once the fashion for this genre had started in sophistic circles people started fabricating both single letters and whole collections, and attributing them to literary figures or philosophers or statesman of the past, such as Phalaris, Anacharsis, Solon, Themistocles, Socrates, or Apollonius of Tyana.

Collections of letters, both genuine and fictitious, in both Greek and Latin, were much in vogue in the fourth century. The most interesting are those by a number of Fathers of the Greek Church (Athanasius, Basil, Gregory Nazianzenus, Gregory of Nyssa, Synesius, John Chrysostom, and Theodoret of Cyrrhus), and those by the pagans Libanius and Julian. The 159 letters of Synesius, written between 399 and 413, are full of facts and evidence, and are the most important document we possess on the political, economic, religious, and cultural condition of Cyrenaica at the end of the fourth and beginning of the fifth century. Julian's letters lay bare the tragic conflict which was never absent from that emperor's mind.

In the Latin world of the late fourth century the most notable set of letters is that by the pagan Symmachus, collected by his son into ten books in 403–408. Even in Symmachus' lifetime they were much sought after, and are a most valuable source of information about dying paganism. But still more remarkable are the forty-nine letters he wrote to the emperor when he was *praefectus urbi* in 384–385. These are collected under the title of *Relationes*, and the third of them, which is requesting the restoration of the altar of Victory in the hall of the senate, shows feeling and life of a kind that make it a real masterpiece: we may call it the last despairing cry of the pagan soul.

In Greek literature there is a fair amount of information about the treatment of myths and paradoxes. A work called *Bibliotheca*, which has survived in three books, is attributed by the manuscripts and by Photius to Apollodorus of Athens, but the edition we possess is certainly to be dated to the first century AD, two centuries later than his lifetime. It is a systematic exposition of the genealogies and deeds of gods and heroes, and it is not impossible that it is a late revision, containing substantial alterations, of an authentic work of Apollodorus called *About the gods*. We also possess a collection of *Metamorphoses* by Antoninus Liberalis (Antonine period), largely derived from Nicander.

As to paradoxes, a manuscript has preserved the so-called *Paradoxographus Florentinus*, written about AD 100, on the subject of *Marvellous fountains, lakes and streams*. We also know of some *Paradoxa* assembled by Aristocles and of a work on *Earthquakes* by Artemon of Miletus. In Latin there was the *Marvels of Spain* by Cluvius Rufus.

There are some writings in which myth and paradox are combined. Ptolemy Chennus of Alexandria (*c*. AD 100), among a number of works with strange titles, wrote a *Paradoxical History* and a *New History*, in both of which he assembled mythical and paradoxical curiosities. Citations are also made from a poem of his called *Sphinx* and an epic poem called *Anthomerus*.

The Novel. Among Latin romances pride of place belongs to the *Satyricon* of Petronius which we discussed earlier. A more regular form of novel is to be found in the *Metamorphoses* of Apuleius, which according to Augustine was also known as the *Golden Ass*. This tells of the adventures of one Lucius, who was transformed into an ass and after many changes of owner succeeded in getting back his human shape by devouring the roses intended for a festival of Isis. The theme is not new: we find its broad outlines in a short story by Lucian (or pseudo-Lucian) entitled *Lucius and the Ass*, and it seems that both writers derived it from another short work by Lucius of Patrae (AD 90?), which was known to Photius. But the Greek story was altered considerably by Apuleius. He put in new episodes and fables, some of which were his own and others derived from a great variety of sources, such as the famous story of Cupid and Psyche; and he handled the whole thing in the style he had made his own.[14]

Perhaps the earliest known Greek novel of this period is the Romance of Ninus (probably AD 50–100). This has a very rhetorical colouring but uses simple diction (like that of Diodorus), and it tells of the adventures in the love of Ninus for the renowned Semiramis. We know of this from papyrological finds, which have also revealed parts of a work entitled *The Loves of Metiochus and Parthenope*.

Antonius Diogenes, apparently at the end of the first century AD, wrote an imaginary journey called *On the marvels beyond Thule*: this was in twenty-four books, a summary of which is given by Photius. At the same time or perhaps rather later a lawyer's scribe, Chariton of Aphrodisias in Caria, wrote eight books describing *The Adventures of Chaireas and Callirrhoe*, the love story (full of anachronisms) of the daughter of the Syracusan Hermocrates, who lived in the fifth century BC. The work contains monologues, letters, and continuous passages quoted from Homer; its style is reasonably straightforward, though there is an obvious tendency to rhetoric and a striving after erudition.

The romantic plots of some of Lucian's shorter works we can pass over. Between 166 and 180 came the *Babyloniaca* of the Syrian Iamblichus, a work in thirty-nine books known from Photius' summary, and one which is notable for its psychological analyses and ingenious selection of characters. It tells how Rhodanes and the fair Sinonis were crossed in love and how they were then victorious over the king of Babylon.

Between 200 and 250 there were published the *Ephesiaca* of Xenophon of Ephesus. These were based partly on the legend of Penelope, and recounted the loves of Habrokomes and the fair Anthea, who were pledged in marriage but were then separated by a thousand adventures. Very similar in background and form is the anonymous *History of Apollonius of Tyre*, known to us from a Christianized version in Latin, in which a prince of Tyre loses his wife and daughter but later finds them again and becomes king of Antioch, Tyre, and Cyrene.

Perhaps before the end of the second century Longus of Lesbos composed his pastoral romance of *Daphnis and Chloe*, whose adventures take place on Lesbos without much movement or great drama. The descriptions of scenery are charming, and many of the small episodes are graceful and true to life; but the characters in the story are unreal, and the love scenes show a decadent and highbrow kind of taste.

In the time of Aurelian, or perhaps as late as Diocletian, Heliodorus of Emesa wrote his *Aethiopica*, in which an Ethiopian princess named Charicleia and her lover Theagenes have a series of dramatic adventures—storms, brigands, persecution, and imprisonment by a jealous queen—but at last triumph when they are just on the point of being sacrificed. The plot is clever, the characters well handled, and the descriptions agreeable, but these virtues do not make up for the excess of erudition and the emptiness of the sophistic ornamentation.

Still probably in the fourth century appeared *The Adventures of Leucippe and Cleitophon* by Achilles Tatius, in which Cleitophon tells of his own adventures and those of his beloved in a series of episodes which recall those in Heliodorus' novel. It seems strange that this hotch-potch, in which the story is continually interrupted by descriptive scenes, speeches, and letters, should have been taken as a model of style throughout the Byzantine period.

It is true, however, that two extremely poor Latin works were equally popular, each of them a rehash of a Greek text. One was L. Septimius' translation entitled *Ephemeris of the Trojan War*, written in the style and language of Sallust but in a flat matter-of-fact manner which makes the work most tedious. The story purports to be told by Dictys, a Cretan of remote antiquity, who took part in the Trojan War; and another participant named Dares of Phrygia is the supposed narrator in the other work, the *History of the Fall of Troy*, which was translated anonymously.

2. ART

a. *China*

The art of the Later Han (23–220), and Three Kingdoms (220–280), is a continuation of that of the Former Han, and, like it, is almost wholly a funeral art. The best relief work is found on the pillars that marked the entrance to the Spirit Road which led to the tomb of rich people. We may cite as an outstanding example those from the Shen tomb at Ch'ü-hsien in Szechwan. The decoration consists of mythological animals (tiger, dragon, phoenix). Many more sculptures of this kind, as well as gilt-bronze animal figures, are extant. So are large stone lions, the earliest (AD 147) in Shantung; this sort of stylized, heraldic animal of large proportions continued to be set up in the Yangtze-kiang valley even later, throughout the period of division (317–589). They are often matched by winged, horned, and tiger-like creatures, which we conventionally call chimaeras; the earliest is that from the tomb of Kao I in Szechwan (209). Lions and chimaeras are the noblest guardians one can imagine for the imperial or princely tombs of old China.

The art of casting bronze mirrors reached perfection under the Former, and even more under the Later Han. At the side of an ever more fantastic geometric décor, we also find human figures, such as Taoist sages, etc.

For the architecture of this period we are still limited to literary remnants and drawings on funeral plaques. No actual buildings are left, and the results of recent excavations at Lo-yang are more important for the history of town planning than for architecture.

Painting consisted of frescoes on the walls of the imperial palaces and of portraits and scenes from the classics on silk. All these are lost, but we can gain a faint idea of them from the rough and sketchy imitations on pressed pottery tiles from tombs, as well as from decorated lacquers from the Korean tombs of Lo-lang (Pl. 65) and from Yang-kao-hsien in northern Shansi. Of lesser aesthetic value are the painted tombs, e.g. those at Liao-yang in Manchuria. Of course imitations for the use of the deceased were never carefully done, and they can only give an inadequate idea of what court painting of the Later Han period was like.

The elaborate tombs of Hsiao-t'ang-shan in Shantung have yielded a fair collection of specimens of that peculiar production of the Han period, the funeral stone. Even more refined are those from the Wu family shrines, also in Shantung.

As to the central Asian influence, it was intimately connected with Buddhism, which was percolating into China from the beginning of this period. But no Chinese work of art inspired by Buddhism is earlier than the fifth century; and so this influence, which revolutionized Chinese sculpture, must be left to be dealt with in the following volume.

b. *India*

The artistic, like the political, history of northern India is dominated during the first two and a half centuries of our era by the influence exerted by the foreign invaders: Greeks, Śakas, Parthians, Kuṣāṇas. The Greek kingdoms left no trace (except for numismatics) in the artistic field; at least none has been recognized down to the present day, atlhough this statement may possibly be subjected to revision in the near future. At Taxila, which was the main centre of Greek rule, only the foundations of the royal palace are still extant. The Śakas, too, passed unnoticed. The Parthians were more active, and to their dominance (first century AD) we owe the so-called First Temple in the Jandial site at Taxila; it shows a Mazdaean form, coupled with Hellenistic decorative elements.

Then the Kuṣāṇa came, and around the court of their kings an art arose that has been called by various names (Gandhāra, Indo-Greek, Roman-Buddhist); it can be best defined as a Graeco-Roman form for an Indian iconography. (Pl. 66, a) The subjects of the reliefs and statues, as far as they are not secular (royal) portraits, are always Buddhist. But here the Buddha (and this is the great novelty) is represented in human form; credit for this development is disputed between Gandhāra and Mathura art, but it was probably arrived at by both schools independently and at the same time. The Buddha images are imitated, in their anatomy and chiefly in their drapery, from Roman-Greek originals of the imperial period. We have Zeus-like Buddhas, Apollo-like Bodhisattvas (Pl. 67, a); to give an example, the head of the famous standing Buddha, formerly in the Guides' Mess at Hoti Mardan, bears a striking resemblance to the Apollo of Belvedere in the Vatican. The inner development of this art is still under dispute, as is the complicated question of its chronology and its relationship with contemporary artistic currents in the Roman empire. It is certain that an earlier period (second and third centuries), in which the material was stone (blue schist), was followed by another (fifth century), in which the images were chiefly made of stucco. In the latter period the aesthetic ideal slowly changed toward an increased naturalism and spirituality of expression which is strongly reminiscent of European Gothic art (Pl. 68, a); the best examples are the stuccoes of Hadda in Afghanistan. At the same time the full-size statuary culminated with the two colossi of Bamiyan (Afghanistan): a Buddha image of 120 feet (fourth century) and another of 170 feet (fifth century) of which only the armatures, cut from the sandstone cliffs, are still preserved, while the features and drapery, modelled in clay mixed with straw, have long since crumbled away. But although the statues are still Gandhāra in their conception, the badly ruined remnants of paintings that decorate the top of the niche above the smaller Buddha are Sassanian in style, while other paintings point rather to India, and still others to central Asia. Bamiyan was indeed a cross-road of all the artistic currents of the East.

As Sassanid political dominance increased, so the artistic influence from Iran became paramount; and this same territory saw the rise of the Irano-Buddhist art (stucco of Fondukistan), in which there is nothing Indian beyond the subject.

The whole art of Gandhāra was essentially a foreign element on the fringe of India, exactly as it was a foreign element on the fringe of the Western world. It exerted a deep influence on Indian art, but far less directly than as a challenge to which India nobly responded in its own ways. Gandhāra was the typical product of the twin-bodied, twin-faced, twin-souled Kuṣāṇa empire between Iran and India, and of the flourishing Indo-Roman trade that played an outstanding role in its economy.

As to Gandhāra architecture, little has survived except the ravaged core of some *stūpas*, e.g. that at Ali Masjid, or the pitiful remnants of the great *stūpa* of Kaniṣka at Shahji-ki-dheri near Peshawar.

A somewhat isolated position is occupied by the statues of Wima Kad-phises, Kaniṣka, and Caṣṭana found at Mathura but not belonging to the local school of art. In their rigid and hieratic expressiveness, the barbaric majesty of their quaint heavy central Asian clothing and accoutrement, they occupy a place apart, perhaps not devoid of Parthian influences (Pl. 67, b).

While the Kuṣāṇa court and the mercantile circles around it patronized Gandhāra art, the Indian provinces of the empire witnessed the rise of a purely indigenous school, that of Mathura. It starts with massive and heavy statues of the Buddha, which appear to show a direct descent from the squat Yakṣas of Mauryan art. As said above, they are the first ones, together with the Hellenizing Buddhas of Gandhāra, to give human representation to the figure of the Buddha. Mathura soon outgrew this phase and developed a religious sculpture that was idealized and crystallized into a self-imposed abstraction of the elements of traditional iconography. It is an art more spontaneous, less artificial, perhaps more sympathetic and human than Gandhāra; and although not completely devoid of Hellenistic elements, its spirit and its technique are wholly independent of the West. Nor was its expansion confined to India. Ivory carvings in this style, portraying ladies at their toilet, have been found at Kāpiśi (Begram in Afghanistan); their glorious sensuality shows an art that has reached the climax of perfection in that particular material, both in technique and in inspiration (Pl. 69, a). With Mathura, and not with Gandhāra, Indian art starts definitely on its own original paths.

Outside the Kuṣāṇa empire, in central and southern India, artistic activity did not wholly escape the ubiquitous Western influence, making itself felt either through the Kuṣāṇa territory or directly from the sea and by way of the Roman trading posts on the coast. The territories concerned were mainly under the rule of the Andhras (first to third centuries A D). In the north-western fringe of their kingdom the old type of architecture continued to produce its fine rock-cut *caityas*, culminating perhaps with the powerful structures of Karli. But creative artistic activity tended to shift to the eastern coast. Here between the mouths of the Krishna and of the Godavary, we find the most important group of early monuments in south India, those at and around Amaravati. The great *stūpa* of Amaravati has been destroyed, but its sculptural décor is partly preserved. The art of Amaravati at first avoided the human representation of the Buddha, but later, after the rise of Mahāyāna Buddhism, gradually accepted the great conquest of the north, the iconic representation. Its figures are heavy and massive; and drapery, although reminiscent of Gandhāra, has a new aesthetic value, based on the ordered rhythm of its undulating lines; rhythm characterizes also the composition of the reliefs and rises sometimes to dynamic and even frenetic movement (Pl. 66, b). The preference of these artists for complicated composition led to a consistent use of chiaroscuro and foreshortening motifs, with a decorative effect that exerted a profound influence on the later sculpture of south India.

In art, as in many other fields, the Gupta period (320–550 AD) reached a pinnacle of attainment. The Gupta renaissance rejuvenated the local schools; what grew up in the Ganges valley was the true classical art of India. Architectural monuments have suffered from the lapse of time and from Muslim destructions; they are rare and not very conspicuous. Such are, for example, some of the Ajanta caves, and chiefly the *caitya* of Cave XIX, with its extremely rich, almost baroque, ornamentation of foliate reliefs. But above all, architecture frees itself from cliffs and rocks and takes the form of free-standing temples, built in stone or brick. We may cite the *caityas* at Ter and at Chezarla, now reduced to Hindu temples, as well as two buildings at Sanchi, and the temple at Aihole in what was later Cālukya territory. The finest surviving temple of Gupta times is that of Deogarh (fifth century), consisting essentially of a cubic block of masonry surmounted by a pyramidal tower, and surrounded by four porticoes, with richly ornamented portals. Other temples of the Gupta period (Bhitargaon, Bhumara) are too ruinous to give us more than a glimpse of their original appearance.

Gupta sculpture shows an unexhausted luxuriant fantasy in the decorative panels of the temples. But it is with the free-standing statues that it reaches its climax. It continues both the Mathurā and the Gandhāra schools, but either rejects or completely assimilates all non-Indian elements. Gupta art is Indian through and through, and 'is marked by a finished mastery in execution and a majestic serenity in expression that have seldom been equalled in any other school of art' (B. Rowland). Its Buddhist figures (chiefly those from the workshops of Sarnath near Benares), with their truly classical composure, devoid of naturalism as well as of conventionalism, vie with Brahmanical and Jain images in giving the same supremely refined impression (Pl. 68, b).

Painting of the Gupta age seems to be concentrated rather at the end of the period (sixth century), when, politically speaking, the dynasty had lost its ascendancy outside Magadha. It too does not break with tradition, but achieves its culmination. It is chiefly represented by the frescoes of Ajanta (Caves I, II, XVI, XVII, XIX) and Bagh: later (and outside Gupta territory) there were Badami and Sittanavasal. Ajanta, with its frescoes of Buddhist subjects, portrays a refined world of gentlemen and of voluptuous beautiful women, through a perfectly adapted technique and with a psychological balance that is truly Olympian (Pl. 69, b). The lovely feminine figures of the royal fortress of Sigiriya in Ceylon are also influenced by Ajanta.

Gupta art was not only the climax of Indian art, but exerted a deep influence on the statuary and the architecture of the Greater India that was slowly coming into existence beyond the seas.[15]

c. *Central Asia*

The caravan cities of the Tarim basin, flourishing through the rich trade on the silk route from China to Parthia, India, and Rome, were subjected to direct and indirect artistic influences coming from all these countries. These influences sometimes completely inspired the local artists, but much more frequently they intermingled and interacted, giving rise to a composite art that shows many aspects of originality and was capable in turn of influencing the neighbouring countries. All this belongs to a world long since dead, that of the oasis peoples of central Asia, speaking Indo-European languages and believing in Buddhism, and later in Manichaeism and Nestorian Christianity. The Turkization and Islamization of eastern Turkestan destroyed this flourishing civilization in the course of three centuries after 1000 AD; it was utterly forgotten and was only recovered for us by the great English, Swedish, German, French, Russian, and Japanese expeditions during the present century.

The art of central Asia seems to start with the first or second century AD. In some sites (carvings at Niya, and chiefly the Miran frescoes (Pl. 70), third century) Roman influence is so strong as to render it likely that Romans or Romanized artists were at work in that lost corner of the world. Elsewhere (Qyzyl; also Rawak) the influence of Gandhāra and of the Irano-Buddhist art of Bamiyan is as strongly felt; but these centres belong already to the middle of the fifth century at their earliest, falling outside the limits of the present volume. Chinese influence, too, comes later, and the Persian begins in earnest only after the fall of the Sassanid empire and the Arab conquest. India, on the other hand, is present in Turkestan from the very earliest time, at first through Gandhāra and then by the direct influence of Gupta art and the paintings of Ajanta (frescoes of Dandan Oiliq).

d. Neo-Persian Art

For clarity's sake we are dealing briefly here with everything that seems to matter about the typical forms of art in the Persian zones from the Macedonian conquest to about AD 400. At first the direct rule of the Macedonians encouraged Hellenization in local art, and in some places imposed it, the process being more marked in the field of decoration. We find this more in the Eastern districts, where we should least expect it; and from these districts came many of the influences which affected India and China. In the Western districts there was a more complicated admixture of types and techniques, since the new Greek elements had there to contend with survivals not only from Iranian but from Mesopotamian culture, many of the larger cities of the Parthian kings' dominions (both ancient and modern foundations) being situated in Mesopotamia.

When by gradual stages they liberated themselves from the Seleucids, the Iranian countries preserved many of the artistic features they had borrowed from the Greeks, but they modified them fairly radically to suit their own tastes. At the same time a revival of native artistic traditions is attested in remains of art of Achaemenid type. This revival was in part accidental and spontaneous, but in part deliberate.

In architecture we find the old Babylonian technique of building in brick combined with the Greek construction of stone walls consisting of a core of irregular, unbleached stones with a facing of regular blocks. Much use was made of vaulting both in barrel shape and in domes. In palaces, too, the most typical feature is seen in the great domed throne-rooms (*Līwān*), sometimes more than 30 yards long and 20 wide, which are open on one side; they were sometimes used for summer and sometimes for winter residence. These are flanked by more modest buildings with two floors; or they may lie in the middle of a group of buildings arranged round a central court in a harmonious structural plan.

Greek influence, as we said earlier, is most noticeable and permanent in the decorative sections of buildings, where the walls are found covered with stone facings carved in relief (as at Hatra), or with coloured and painted stucco tablets (as at Ashur), or with frescoes (as at Dura Europus). The painted stucco became a more frequent feature in the Sassanid period. Important tombs usually consist of *tumuli*, or of rooms to which there is access by a corridor.

In sculpture we find busts (at Kish there are several copies of the same model arranged in the niches of a hall); and there are also masks, for instance at Hatra. But the commonest form is the relief. A typical example is the set of sculpture on the tomb of Antiochus I of Commagene (AD 34) at Nimrūd Dag; and there are others with hunting and battle scenes, such as those on the palace at Ctesiphon. The figures assume once more the hieratic rigidity which had been characteristic of art in the Achaemenid period, and it was the rock carving of the Achaemenids, with their accompanying historical inscriptions, that the Sassanids tried to imitate and rival in their own monuments.

Another notable feature, especially in the Sassanid period, is the artistic work in gem-cutting (the incision of semi-precious stones) and in metal-carving. Cups, bowls, and other forms of silver vase were decorated, in relief or by incision, with human figures (especially kings) and ornamental and linear animals or plants, sometimes realistically designed and sometimes stylized. In the Arsacid period the pottery shapes are elegant, and a green or greenish-blue glaze becomes typical; Sassanid production shows a falling-off. The clay sarcophagi are of interest; they are made with a bright varnish and sometimes with plastic decoration on their lids.

Under the Sassanids glass moulding made progress as an independent art; and the same is true of the weaving of valuable cloth, which is decorated with geometric or plant designs.

e. *The Graeco-Roman World*

Architecture. The dangers arising from barbarian raids compelled the Romans, from the second century onwards, to confront once more the old problem of defending large cities with circuits of walls. These are sometimes

very large and imposing, like the walls constructed by Aurelian at Rome or
the work undertaken at Byzantium/Constantinople first by Septimius
Severus, then by Constantine, and later still by Theodosius. They display
great variety of building systems in their towers, circular corridors, storehouses and so on, and equal variety of architectural forms in their gates.
Of very great interest, too, are the remains of guard-posts and forts which
strengthened the frontiers of the empire along the line of the fortified *limes*.

Temple architecture presents a contrast between different districts. In the
West the commonest type was that which met Roman taste, either in rectangular shape or with buildings grouped round a central chamber. In Greece,
even in work undertaken by Roman emperors, the old Hellenic methods were
followed, for example a colossal temple of Zeus Olympius at Athens erected
by Hadrian. In the East, on the other hand, new and fairly characteristic
Graeco-Oriental methods made their appearance, as in the 'baroque' temple
at Heliopolis (Baalbek), the great circular colonnades at Gerasa (Dierach)
in Palestine, and the temple-grotto at Petra in Arabia.

Imperial palaces assumed very large proportions: they were vast enclosures
with buildings inside. Severus and Celer, the architects of Nero's enormous
Golden House, and Rabirius, who built the Flavian palace, were Italians.
Inside these great constructions, for instance in the palaces on the Palatine
hill, there were temples, circuses, hippodromes, and so forth. Diocletian's
palace at Salonae (Split) is 206 metres long and 165 metres wide, with
four gates, and looks from outside like a great fortress: the monumental
buildings inside include a temple, porticoes, and a mausoleum. Hadrian's
villa near Tibur is even larger, and looks like a regular collection of architectural styles, including bold experiments in polygonal rooms and domed
ceilings.

Basilicas for forensic purposes became larger all the time. Some contained
enormous halls, of the kind still to be found in the basilica of Maxentius at
Rome. Others—so Vitruvius tells us, and he is confirmed by the remains of
the Flavian palace—were constructed in private houses and used for meetings
and declamations. Sometimes libraries were placed in these basilicas, a
practice which became increasingly common both at Rome and in the other
leading cities of the empire.

To the earliest Imperial *Fora*, constructed by Caesar and Augustus, others
were gradually added by later emperors; and *fora* in imitation of the Roman
model were built in all districts, not only in the cities of the West but
eventually in Greece as well (such as the imperial *Agorā* at Athens and the
Schola Romanorum at Delos).

Theatres, too, were continually being built in the imperial period, both
closed and open varieties, in every district from Gaul (Orange for example)
to Crete (the Odeum of Gortyn), and Pamphylia (at Aspendus). But still
commoner was the Roman type of 'double theatre' or amphitheatre used for
gladiatorial shows. These were large elliptical-shaped buildings closed on the

outside with walls containing tiers of columns, while inside the arena was surrounded by steps supported on a set of substructures. The largest example is the Flavian amphitheatre (or Colosseum) at Rome (Pl. 71, a), but amphi-theatres were soon being built in other parts of Italy—at Pola, Verona, Augusta Praetoria, Ferentinum, Casinum, Capua, Puteoli, and Pompeii, and also outside Italy (outstanding examples are at Vindonissa in the Hel-vetian country and at Sabratha in Tripolitania). There was a still further growth in the number of circuses and hippodromes in both Italy and the provinces, and the hippodrome at Constantinople, of which there are important remains, is said to have seated 100,000 persons.

Triumphal arches, too, became very numerous in every part of the empire. At Rome there were the arches of Claudius, Titus, Septimius Severus, and Constantine. In Italy arches are found at Tergeste, Spoletium, Beneventum (with extremely interesting ornamental reliefs dedicated to Trajan), Capua, and Canusium; and in the provinces they are found at Nemausus in Gaul (to Tiberius), at Thamugadi, Oea, and Theveste in Africa (to Trajan, Marcus Aurelius, and Caracalla, respectively), and in Greece at Athens (to Hadrian). Their forms vary according to the tastes of different periods and districts, but in general they developed from simple types of architecture and decoration to an increasing complication in both directions.

In addition the old practice of erecting commemorative columns saw a further development in the great sculpted columns covered from head to foot with reliefs. At Rome the first example is Trajan's column, with its twenty-three spirals carrying a pictorial description of the Dacian Wars of 101–106; and this was imitated in 176 when the Antonine column was set up to depict the achievements of Marcus Aurelius against the Germans and Sarmatians. Outside Rome we find at Moguntiacum, as early as Nero's reign, a sculpted column nearly 40 feet high, crowned with a statue of Jove. Then at Adamclissi in Moesia Trajan erected a magnificent monument 90 feet high, the *Tropaeum Traiani*, decorated with crude reliefs of provincial workmanship which seem to foreshadow the techniques and forms of medieval art (Pl. 72, a).

Road works have left traces in all parts of the Roman world, including bold constructions like the tunnel in the Furlo pass across the Apennines, which was executed in the time of Vespasian. Both literary and archaeological evidence attests the building of bridges across the great rivers, for example the bridge over the Danube erected by Trajan's architect Apollodorus of Damascus.

The construction of aqueducts continued, and in the building of baths one emperor after another—Nero, Titus, Trajan, Caracalla, Severus Alexander, Gallienus, Diocletian, and Constantine—seems to have rivalled his predeces-sor with works of astonishing size and grandeur, which can be seen in their ruins today. But bath construction was also eagerly pursued by every municipality, and in some places, such as Lepcis in Trajan's time, the baths were of considerable proportions. In some of these bath buildings we find further examples of the bold forms of architectural construction mentioned earlier, for instance in the polygonal halls of Caracalla's baths at Rome or in the building (also at Rome) wrongly known as the 'Temple of Minerva Medica', which must have been a central portion of the baths of Gallienus.

Emperors and members of great families received large tombs of circular construction, like those of the Flavians, Hadrian (Pl. 71, b), and Caecilia Metella at Rome, or the tombs found at Attalia. More simple types were erected for the burial societies of the poorer classes—little buildings along the roads outside cities, or 'columbaria' with a large number of niches. But besides these we find some quite original constructions, which at times are the product of interesting local forms. We may mention here the small pyramid of Egyptian style which constitutes the tomb of C. Cestius at Rome, the *tumulus* at Neumagen in Belgica which depicts a ship carrying casks (Pl. 61, b), and the tomb at Poetovio in Pannonia which is decorated with remarkable bas-reliefs of Orphic significance.

The subterranean cemeteries used by the Christians, who in this matter followed a precedent set by the Jews and other Eastern peoples, have special features of their own. In early days they were constructed inside private burial grounds, like those of Priscilla, Lucina, and Domitilla, and were therefore protected by property rights; later they were *coemeteria* or *dormitoria* belonging to brotherhoods of the faithful. They consisted of galleries (*ambulacra* or *criptae*) dug in the rock, with separate rooms (*cubicula*) containing tiers of tombs (*loci*) (Plate 80). Each room had a rectangular aperture, which could be closed with a flat stone held in a vertical position. Some of the more important tombs were placed under arches (*arcosolia*), and eventually halls or chapels might be constructed for the funeral *agapae* and meetings of the faithful. Besides the enormous range of catacombs near Rome they are also to be found in a number of other districts: in central Italy at Chiusi, Sutri, Nepi, Bolsena, Otricoli, Vulci, and Anagni; in southern Italy at Suessa Aurunca, Pozzuoli, Naples, Nola, Canosa, Venosa, and Tropea; in Sicily at Messina, Taormina, Syracuse, Ragusa, Agrigento, and Palermo; in Sardinia; in France at Poitiers, Rheims, and Ste Victoire; in Germany at Trier; in Spain at Saragossa, Seville, and Elvira; in Hungary at Pécs; and in Egypt, Numidia, the Syrtes, Cyrene, and elsewhere. The Jews, some Christian heretics, and certain other religious sects, also had their catacombs. A typical example is an underground chamber with four arms (in the shape of a cross) datable to AD 259 at Palmyra.

Sculpture. A fondness for reliefs of historical character, and a special competence in executing them, are attested by the evolution of the art in a long series of examples during the first three centuries of the empire. From Tiberius' time we have the reliefs on silver vessels, especially those from Boscoreale, the incised cameo depicting the departure of Germanicus for the East, and other unusual incised cameos like the Camée de France in Paris and the Gemma Augustea in Vienna; from the period between Claudius and Domitian there are the figured reliefs on triumphal arches; for the reigns of Trajan and Marcus Aurelius the marvellous scenes which wind round their two columns (Pl. 73, a) (from Trajan's time also the reliefs on the *Rostra* and on the Arch at Beneventum); and finally for Constantine's reign there are the contemporary portions of the reliefs on his arch. After Trajan the figures begin to look more rigid, and the rendering of expression and feeling is less successful. Under Marcus Aurelius less detail is shown in landscapes, (Pl. 73, b), and with Constantine the emperor's figure is detached from the crowd and takes on a hieratical attitude.

From the time of Hadrian and for a long period thereafter there is a large collection of carved sarcophagi of Roman workmanship. These carry mythical scenes and it is obvious that their distant ancestry lies both in Etruria and in Greece. Equally evident, however, are their Roman features. The spaces are filled with crowd scenes or personified types of deities, or with narrative pictures in continuous bands without any division into episodes; and there are often distinctive Roman subjects, such as legionaries fighting barbarians, magistrates with subject peoples, sacrifices, or marriage scenes. Later on, but still before the time of Constantine, the Christians, too, adopted this form of sarcophagus. At first they retained the pagan designs, but later selected such of these as were capable of being 'allegorized' on Christian lines (Pl. 74, b). Eventually they used scenes from the Bible, or Christian symbols like the Good Shepherd (Pl. 74, a). Here we may note that even for these early symbols the models used in early Christian art are still always pagan: the Good Shepherd, for example, is clearly derived from the Alexandrian *Criophorus* (the Bearer of the Ram), and saints and Apostles are equally clearly drawn from classical statues of philosophers and orators.

Portraiture remained one of the most typical departments of Roman sculpture. Fashions changed, and at some periods one finds, for example, a vogue for colossal statues like those of the Neronian age; attempts were also sometimes made to idealize characters and poses in heroic guise. Yet the heads of emperors, in regular statuary as well as on cameos (Pl. 76, a) and coins, retain throughout the period a magnificent realism; and it is often possible to use imperial portraits as a better means of getting to understand an individual's psychology than is provided by biographies written by court historians (Pl. 75). This tendency towards realism is also very clear in the way women's headdress is drawn to correspond with prevailing fashions, and in the particular treatment given to barbarian personages. The latter are found both on reliefs like Trajan's column and in full-standing statues like the 'Dacian' of the Lateran Museum or the 'German prisoner' in the Loggia dell'Orcagna at Florence.

Yet outside Italy monuments so far discovered are enough to show, in sculpture as in architecture, the blending of native styles with those imported from Rome, and the consequent appearance of 'provincial' characteristics which help to clarify those found in later periods. We can begin to identify some of the features of Ibero-Roman art, for example in a curious statue of a priestess; or of Gallo-Roman art in the bas-relief of the stag-god Cernunnus (Pl. 72, b) or of Romano-British in a group depicting a lion and a stag; or of Romano-Dacian in the extremely peculiar reliefs of the *Tropaeum Traiani* mentioned earlier (Pl. 72, a). But we already possess evidence suggesting that the same situation existed in the Eastern provinces, for instance in Lycia and in the territory of Palmyra (where reliefs in many ways foreshadow the methods and styles of the Byzantine period).

We mentioned stuccoes in relation to the period covered in Part II: this art became very popular and attained great perfection during the first two centuries AD. It was used to cover the uneven stone and brick surfaces of walls and ceilings in both houses and tombs, and later in the Christian catacombs. Stuccoes were moulded on to cornices, friezes, or panels, and consisted of floral designs, mythical scenes, or impressionist landscapes. The fineness of their detail, which is at times extremely intricate, must have required a most delicate touch.

Painting and Mosaic. The early part of this period coincides with the last two 'Pompeian styles' of wall-painting, the Third (c. AD 14–63) and the Fourth (c. AD 50–79). The Third or 'Real Wall' style is simpler than the Second, using fewer and less vivid colours. The architectural designs in the painting have become a smaller proportion of the whole, and are used, together with a stylized decoration of flowers, to create rectangular panels, or friezes and wainscots (Pl. 76, b). The pictures in the middle are usually no longer landscapes but mythical scenes. In contrast the Fourth style, or 'Architectural Illusionism' (the *Thermae Stabianae* provide an example) tends to exaggerate the optical illusions which had been attempted in the Second style, and makes use of pavilions, niches, and the like. The architectural features become more slender, consisting of threadlike columns, arabesques, and what the Renaissance called 'grotesques', all in strident colours. This taste is also found in the Neronian *Domus Aurea* of the same period, which was decorated by Fabullus. Sometimes we also find a new method of painting, which Petronius, who deplored it, called the 'short cut' (*compendiaria*) and which we should call Impressionist. In this the painter confines his colours to large masses and does not attempt to delineate details; but with light and shade he makes an effort to depict the elusive appearance of moving objects. For later examples in portraiture see Pl. 78, a, b.

The lack of secure chronological references and our scanty knowledge of the phases in late-first-century pagan painting make it difficult to give any precision to the phases of Christian painting in the catacombs. This was painting in tempera on Impressionist lines, a tendency favoured by the special light conditions in which the artist was working; and there was a preference for landscape backgrounds. Down to the time of Constantine its history can be approximately divided into two phases. The first corresponds roughly to the first half of the second century and includes the very graceful decoration on the ceiling of the crypt of Lucina in the cemetery of Callistus. It shows a fondness for shaded masses of bright and transparent colours, with delicate floral ornament and a number of features derived from pagan art. The second phase starts in the latter half of the second century, with a preference for even more distinctly Impressionist drawing and for a fusion of colours against an off-white background. Examples are the paintings in the Greek chapel of Priscilla (Pl. 77, a, b), and in the chamber of *Coronatio* in Praetextato.

In painting as in other arts one can detect regional styles in the various provinces. In those farthest to the East, as for example those from both the Synagogue and the Christian Church of Dura-Europus, those from elsewhere in Syria and in the underground chambers at Palmyra, we find methods and types of painting which foreshadow Byzantine art. In Egypt of the same period there is a series of stuccoes, and of paintings on cloth and wooden tablets, which are inserted in the coverings of mummies. The portraiture on these is of Hellenistic origin, but it was employed throughout the empire and possessed an astonishing realism.

Mosaics, too, had Hellenistic origins, and for a long time retained their original features, not only at Rome and in adjacent areas (such as the temple at Praeneste or Hadrian's villa near Tibur), but also, through Roman influence, in the provinces (as in those found at Zliten in Tripolitania). They are delicately made out of tiny *tesserae* (as many as sixty to the square centimetre) of a great number of colours; and they depict exotic scenes, mainly of a 'Nilotic' or 'genre' variety (Pl. 43). But with the growing use of mosaics for paving very large halls the colours became less varied and the attention to detail diminished. *Tesserae* became larger, and instead of about 150 colours only three (white, black, and red) were normally employed: later there were only two (white and black). Designs, too, were gradually altered, and instead of making genuine pictures, which could rival painting, artists took to simple decoration, which often had to be executed along purely copybook lines. Larger spaces were left uniform as background, and designs were confined to borders and panels, with medallions in the corners, rosettes or stars in the panels, and occasional scenes in the middle. Among a very large number of examples, two, which contain portraits of poets, are worthy of note: one at Augusta Trevirorum with the figures of Ennius and Virgil, the other at Hadrumetum depicting Virgil among the Muses.

One of the earliest large Christian mosaics, derived from Roman models, was found near the cathedral at Aquileia.

In the first and second centuries we also find some daring experiments in *opus sectile*, or inlay in a variety of marbles. Examples are found in the Flavian palace at Rome, and there is another at Maxino portraying Romulus and Remus.

Local Changes. The fourth century saw a number of marked changes in artistic production resulting from certain environmental factors, chief among which were the transfer of the capital to Constantinople, the new ascendancy of the Eastern provinces over the West, and the establishment of Christianity as a state religion. Art was also profoundly affected, especially in Greek districts, by the influence of the older ideas and techniques of the Orient, which had been stifled by Hellenism but not annihilated. In the West it was not so much Oriental and Byzantine influences as the growing barbarization that made itself felt, and there was a rapid development of regional styles, which hitherto had remained beneath the surface.

In architecture the recognition of the Church, and the consequent gradual decline and extinction of paganism, brought a need to provide a proper number of imposing homes for the new cult. No uniform method of temple construction was developed in the different parts of the empire, for one thing because the various architectural styles already in vogue were taken over for this new purpose. In many cases in East and West alike old temples, like the Parthenon at Athens, the Athenaeum at Syracuse, or one of the temples at Agrigentum, were made to serve, with appropriate adaptations, as Christian churches. Sometimes they were enlarged by the filling-in of the external columns, which were then included as an inset to the perimeter of the new church. At other times pagan temples were pulled down, and their materials were used to build churches. Another possibility was to make churches out of rooms in palaces or baths, as happened with the two Roman churches Santa Croce in Gerusalemme and Santa Maria degli Angeli, both later than the fourth century but cited here to illustrate the point. Generally, however, although modifications were made to meet the needs of the new cult, the new buildings were in shape the same as the rectangular basilicas of the pagans, with an entrance on the shorter side; or they took over the form of the basilical halls in palaces, which had *atria* in front of them. The various models therefore produced Christian basilicas with one nave, or three, or five. Santa Maria Maggiore and Santa Sabina, both Roman churches of the fifth century, have three: but there were five in the 'Church of the Nativity' at Bethlehem, the core of which goes back to the first half of the fourth century. There would be pilasters and columns holding up flat architraves or arches; and some churches had apses, either inside or outside the rectangular line of the basilica.

In other cases the Christian temple owed its shape to the fact that it was a replacement or copy of some circular pagan temple or hall, possibly a set of baths. Santa Costanza at Rome and San Sepolcro at Jerusalem, both of the fourth century, are of this kind. Some too had cruciform arms and a hemispherical dome, like the fifth-century Mausoleum of Galla Placidia at Ravenna; others were polygonal, a shape perpetuated in the various kinds of 'Baptistery'.

In the East the origin of the architectural methods employed in certain

Byzantine churches, such as Santa Sophia, is not yet entirely clear. But it is becoming increasingly likely that one important influence came from the Oriental temples of previous generations, which we examined earlier.

Naturally the construction of large buildings and works of a practical nature, such as baths, aqueducts, roads, and cemeteries, proceeded regularly in the fourth century as before. But special importance attaches to the great villas of noblemen, the centres of large estates. One example is the famous *Villa del Casale* discovered near Piazza Armerina in Sicily. This is laid out in a most complex fashion and possesses a number of magnificent mosaic pavements and elegant colonnades.

The triumph of Christianity also brought a change in sculpture. This was more rapid in the East, where the features we call 'Byzantine' began to make their appearance. In the West the classical tradition was more enduring, but it was also distorted by 'barbarian' influences, sometimes affecting particular regions.

The tendencies of a general kind which contributed most to the transformation of Roman into Byzantine art were—in painting as well as sculpture —tendencies which had for a long time been manifest in the works produced in the Eastern regions of the empire. They include the pervading hieratical solemnity and impressive rigidity of their figures, symmetry and the standardization of iconographic types (Pl. 79, a), the isolation of figures in painting, the use of colour instead of plastic, and general stylization.

At Rome and in the West innovation and distortion came in more slowly. Gradually the standard types of preceding generations were altered, but a few artists were still capable of producing masterpieces in the old style. One example is the famous ivory diptych celebrating a marriage alliance between the Nicomachi and the Symmachi: this was carved between 392 and 394. The historical relief remained a remembered form, and examples were still made; but gradually there came a change. Figures became more rigid and less expressive, and bas-reliefs were made flatter on a raised surface. The figure of an emperor is detached from the throng of his subjects, as becomes a divine despot, and takes on a cold and formal appearance.

The same is true of Christian sculpture. The figure of Christ, once youthful and smiling, becomes stern and formal; and the sarcophagi, instead of animated scenes from the *Old* and *New Testaments*, carry much more stylized reliefs, lacking any life. An example is a well-known porphyry tomb, once at Santa Costanza, on which the humna scenes are enclosed within large but rigid festoons of flowers and vine-leaf spirals.

Only the portrait was destined to retain its traditional features for a relatively long period after Constantine's day, before it too became stiffer and less rounded. One or two key examples will illustrate the point: a cameo with the figures of Julian and Ceres, a head of Constans I with the motionless gaze of a hieratical ruler, and a colossal bronze statue from Barletta which some say represents Theodosius I (Pl. 79, b), others Theodosius II. In this

last the artist has used vast size and hieratical formalism to express the
grandeur of a sovereign who requires reverence from his subjects.

The same tendencies were working in painting and mosaic, but the sharp
distinction between colours now that mosaic stones were larger also imposed
a simplification in design. Once again we find that the change came faster
in the 'Byzantine' districts: in the West the contrast between pagan (or
classical) and Christian forms is both slower and less complete. At the same
time painting tends to give way to mosaic, which was better adapted for
portraying the vast size of the scenes the triumphant Church required—and
was also less perishable. Sometimes, however, a painter found a way of giving
his picture an imposing quality which matched the great apsidal mosaics:
take, for instance, the scene of *Christ amid the Apostles*, a mid-fourth-century
fresco in the apse of a chamber in the cemetery of Domitilla.

Among large Christian mosaics we may mention the scenes adorning the
vault of Santa Costanza at Rome, and the apsidal mosaic of Santa Pudentiana,
executed at the time of Pope Siricius (385–398) and depicting the *Preaching
of Jesus*. The Santa Pudentiana mosaic is the last real masterpiece of Romano-
Christian art, magnificent in the pose of its figures, the harmony of its
colours, and the depth of perspective. But the marvellous mosaics of the
Villa of Piazza Armerina, vast and daring works of art which have no equal
in the whole Mediterranean area, show how even at the end of the fourth
century certain artists retained their skill, quite independently of any inspiration to be derived from Christianity.

3. MUSIC

During the Han dynasty the contact with the Western countries brought
foreign tunes and foreign instruments into China; such was the *p'i-p'a*, a
short lute with four strings and twelve frets. But Chinese music made little
progress during the troubled centuries prior to the rise of the T'ang dynasty.

Indian theory of music during this period is known only from fragments
included in the *Purāṇas*, from which no detailed picture can be gained.

In the area of Greek culture we see as early as the second century BC,
from the evidence of the 'Delphic hymns' (Chapter XII), how archaism was
the prevailing tendency behind the solo performance of *nomoi*, and how
diatonic rather than chromatic scales were in fashion. But in raising the
frequency of modulation there was also a tendency towards innovation, and
it was music based on the latter tendency which gradually gained the upper
hand.

It was during this period that people ceased to feel the quantities of the
words they were singing. This is proved by the fact that it was found necessary
to give written indication of the length of syllables, as is seen in the epitaph
of Seikilos, which was found at Tralles and dates from the second century
AD. Later documents with musical notations include three hymns of Meso-

medes, also of the second century (published in the sixteenth century), and a text from Oxyrhynchus which belongs somewhere between the second century and the fourth.

Christian writing was affected by the Jewish custom of setting to music all recited texts, even those written in prose. We find the Christians adopting this practice not only with the very numerous liturgical texts which derived from Jewish origins, but also with other writings coming from a variety of sources. Their scoring followed musical rhythm rather than syllabic quantities; but they also came under the influence of Graeco-Oriental culture in the East and of Graeco-Italian culture in the West, for example in their use of *accentus* and *concentus*.

Meanwhile the volume of writing on musical theory and the history of music was constantly growing. From the time of Augustus we have some notes by the Latin writer Vitruvius (V, 104), and from the first century AD two Greek works have survived, the *Problemata* of Pseudo-Aristotle and the *De Musica* of Pseudo-Plutarch. From the second century, besides certain allusions in Pausanias and in the *Onomasticon* (Book IV) of Julius Pollux, there are a number of treatises on the subject: the *Harmonica* of Claudius Ptolemaeus, the seven books *De Musica* by Aristides Quintilianus, the *Encheiridion Harmonices* of Nicomachus of Gerasa, a work by Theon of Smyrna ('Mathematical aids to the reading of Plato'), and the *Eisagogae Harmonicae* of Gaudentius and Cleomeides.

The third century produced the Latin *De die natali* by Censorinus, and in Greek the fourteenth book of the *Deipnosophistae* by Athenaeus of Naucratis and the *Commentary on Ptolemy* by Porphyrius. Finally from the fourth century we have in Latin the *Commentary on Cicero's Somnium Scipionis* by Macrobius, and also three Greek works: the anonymous treatise which was edited by Bellermann in 1841; Baccheius' *Eisagoge technices mousices*; and the *Eisagoge Mousice* by Alypius, which contains notes on musical scoring.

NOTES TO CHAPTER XVIII

1. Professor L. S. Vasilyev calls attention also to Liu Hsiang, one of the earliest masters of the Chinese short story.

2. See also above, p. 617.

3. Seneca the Philosopher, born at Corduba, was brought to Rome when only a few months old and brought up there together with his two brothers—all most carefully educated by their father, Seneca 'the Rhetorician' (see above, p. 617). The younger Seneca was born about the year 4 BC. He showed great precocity, and was attracted by philosophy to such an extent that in adolescence he took up Neo-Pythagorean practices. From these, however, he was dissuaded by his father, a sensible man who feared that his son's delicate constitution might suffer from the excesses involved. Seneca was never a man of strong health; he was acquainted with illness and pain, a fact which undoubtedly influenced his ideas and philosophical attitude. At the age of twenty he had to go to Egypt for reasons of health, and his career was thus interrupted for several years. On his return (about

AD 30) he soon made up for lost time and became celebrated for his eloquence—so much so as to arouse the jealousy of Caligula, who was at one time on the point of having him sentenced to death. Seneca was already one of the hopes of the senatorial party. At the beginning of Claudius' reign the freedmen of the imperial household gained the upper hand and set up a tyranny in opposition to the senate. Seneca was among the victims of this 'palace revolution'; accused of committing adultery with one of the royal princesses, (a sister of Caligula), he was banished to Corsica. He was recalled, however, when, after Messalina's death and Claudius' marriage to Agrippina, another palace revolution brought the Senate Party back to power. Agrippina made use of him to win support for her son, the youthful Nero, among the section of the public which had remained faithful to the senatorial oligarchy and the 'liberal' policy introduced by Augustus. She appointed Seneca as Nero's tutor, and he was the real power behind the throne after Claudius died and was succeeded by Nero (AD 54). But Seneca did not prove to be the obedient tool for which Agrippina had hoped. Faithful to the programme of his own party, he got rid of the freedmen and of Agrippina herself. After her death, however, his influence began to decline. Nero was tiring of his early mentors and wished to exert his own authority. The empire turned away from liberalism. Seneca tried to leave the court, but Nero, still reluctant to displease the senators, would not let him go. Thereupon, Seneca joined the opposition, allowing the malcontents to make use of his name and perhaps relishing the thought that if the 'tyrant' were assassinated he might regain power. But the conspiracy was betrayed before it struck, and Seneca was too heavily compromised for Nero to spare his life.

Seneca was a prolific writer, and in addition to many philosophical treatises (see below, p. 930) he left tragedies, his authorship of which was questioned for a long time, but with no real justification. Modern critics have often declared that these tragedies are not real plays, but declamatory verse compositions which it would be impossible to perform on a stage. That opinion is now disproved. The tragedies were meant for stage performance, and they (and they alone) give us some idea of the nature of Roman tragic drama. This was directly derived from Hellenistic tragedy (see above, pp. 578 ff.) and laid considerable stress on spectacle, singing, and music. They were by no means 'realistic', but more in the nature of operas. Each 'act' opens with a kind of prologue, chanted by the chorus. Then come two or three scenes consisting of long speeches with very little action. Sometimes there is a more lively scene, between two characters, recalling the spirit of the *agon* which was such a feature of Greek tragedy.

Like all Roman theatrical works, Seneca's tragedies draw simultaneously upon several different branches of Greek drama. His *Phaedra*, for instance, contains outright imitations of at least three separate models—Euripides' *Hippolytus Veiled* (which, though now lost, can be reconstructed, at least in part), the same author's *Hippolytus the Crown-bearer* (extant), and Sophocles' *Phaedra* (lost). Seneca does not write in this way from lack of imagination, but in the attempt to put fresh life into a hackneyed subject; and does this very successfully. For example, the character of Phaedra, which Euripides handles very differently in his two plays (in *Hippolytus Veiled*, Phaedra seems to have been a 'shameless' woman who boldly demanded the love of Hippolytus; in *Hippolytus the Crown-bearer*, she is the victim of Aphrodite and dies of her torment yielding to it only in spite of herself) emerges in Seneca's as a complex one, his heroine being at odds with herself, sometimes indulging her passion, sometimes determinedly resisting it, and killing herself in the end to preserve her honour and her freedom. Psychological analysis is thus carried a long way, and Seneca's characters have their own moral universe which is quite different from that of Sophocles or Euripides, for instance.

We do not know at what period of his career Seneca wrote his tragedies. He is not likely to have intended them for his pupil, Nero, though the latter was, as we know, a fervent addict of the stage. They are generally assumed to date from his period in exile, or at least from a time when he had not completely worked out his philosophy, and was still sometimes attracted by Epicurean ideas. It is particularly curious to note that the 'wisdom' proffered by his choruses is very similar to that propounded by Horace—consisting of moderation, the happy medium, human considerations—and differs widely from the themes of Seneca's philosophical treatises, which call for heroism, self-denial, and 'elevation towards God'. It seems as though the theatre provided Seneca with an experience of moral life which he later absorbed into his philosophy. (Pierre Grimal.)

4. The interesting feature of Juvenal's sixteen satires, from our point of view, is that they draw a picture of the Rome of that day as seen by a man resolutely hostile to every departure from the old national traditions. Juvenal's unquestionable narrow-mindedness made him exceptionally alert to new developments in Rome, which was now the spiritual as well as the political capital of the Mediterranean world. Juvenal is infuriated by the changes taking place in religious views under the influence of the oriental beliefs, by the increase in luxury, by the emancipation of women, now determined to take their place in intellectual life and, even at the cost of provoking scandal, to achieve material independence, and by the improvement in the social status of freedmen—'new' citizens who have emerged from slavery by their own merits. He is furious and he says so; but if he had not been so, we should not have his testimony. As it is, his Satires remain as an invaluable document on daily life and morals in the age of the Antonines —provided we are not hoodwinked by an attitude which we may suspect to be occasionally subject to deliberate exaggeration.

At the same time, however, the attitude adopted by Juvenal was one that he shared with a great proportion of the population of the empire, especially the 'provincials' in the average Italian municipium. Rome, the modern, cosmopolitan city, was far ahead of the smaller towns, with their old-fashioned, middle-class ideas. The gap is evident when we study provincial life from the inscriptions, and Juvenal throws a bright light on it; in this respect, too, his writings have outstanding documentary value. (Pierre Grimal.)

5. This satire, published under the Greek title of *Apocolocynthosis*, contains a violent criticism of Claudius, in which the writer is obviously seeking to revenge himself on the emperor who had banished him (see above, note 3). But this negative aspect of the work should not blind us to Seneca's true purpose; he is less interested in criticizing Claudius than in praising Nero by contrast. This little pamphlet was written just when young Nero came to the throne, after Agrippina had assassinated Claudius, and by describing the youthful ruler as the spiritual heir of Augustus, it won him the sympathy of the aristocracy (see above, p. 930). So this is a piece of political propaganda—a type of writing of which not very much has come down to us, but which is known to have been highly popular in Rome at all periods. Unfortunately, it usually took the form of short pieces, which were passed surreptitiously from hand to hand, and soon disappeared from circulation. This example survived, perhaps because its author was a famous man, but more probably because it was an item of official government propaganda. (Pierre Grimal.)

6. The *Satiricon* is the earliest prose romance to have survived from ancient times in reasonably complete form. The Greeks had historical romances, and also folk tales, known as 'Milesian tales' (after the city of Miletus, where the style seems to have been especially popular). The 'Milesian tales' were brought to Rome in Sulla's time, at the end of the republican period. The *Satiricon* seems to be a combination of the old national *satura* (see above, p. 584) and the narrative styles imported from the Orient. From the *satura* it derives its mixture of verse and prose (for instance, the portions that have survived include an entire epic poem on the Civil War, probably intended as a 'classical' counterpart to Lucan's *Pharsalia*); from the historical romance comes the actual plot, with its shipwrecks, abductions, and so forth; while the 'Milesian tales' are responsible for the interpolation of 'short stories', not always very skilfully embodied in the main structure. One such episode is 'Trimalchio's Feast', which has been preserved in full. Set in Campania, it gives a picture of everyday life in a small, southern Italian town which has been invaded by Orientals, some of whom have prospered there, while others can scarcely make both ends meet. We hear their speech, which differs appreciably from classical Latin and already foreshadows the turns of speech of the Romance languages. Petronius introduces us to a branch of literature intended for a lower-class public. (Pierre Grimal.)

7. Recent investigations concur in attributing the dialogue to the period between 105 and 107, when Tacitus was beginning to write his *Histories*. See K. Barwick, *Der Dialogus de Oratoribus . . .* (Leipzig, 1954); R. Syme, *Tacitus* (Oxford, 1958); J. Frot, in *Revue des Études Latines*, XXXIII (1955), pp. 130 ff. (Pierre Grimal.)

8. This view derives from the Christian apologists, and in particular from Eusebius of Caesarea; but it is entirely without foundation. The Life of Apollonius makes no mention of Christ. Apollonius was a real man, who lived in the reigns of Nero and Domitian and the people who are brought into his life-story actually existed. We know of some of them from other sources, and what Philostratus says about them is quite consistent with the other evidence. The story of Apollonius gives valuable information about spiritual life at the end of the first century AD, outside the Christian Church. It shows that the Pythagorean doctrines were still practised, with all their religious severity, and also that some thinkers, at least, were curious about spiritual life outside the Roman empire. One of the most important passages in the book describes Apollonius' voyage to visit the gymnosophists—the Brahmans of India—whom he regarded as his masters and the masters of Pythagoras. (Pierre Grimal.)

9. R. Syme, *Tacitus*, pp. 611–24, makes a strong case for believing that Tacitus came from Narbonese Gaul, perhaps from Vienne. Cisalpine Gaul (North Italy) is also a possibility.

10. Or possibly only twelve, see Syme, *op. cit.*, p. 686.

11. Tacitus belonged to the class of senators of provincial origin who had been called by the Flavians to share the responsibilities of government. He shared the prejudices of the aristocracy, setting all the more store on his nobility because of its recent origin. In his historical writings he represents Roman policy as the pawn of rivalry between the nobility—alone entitled to govern the city—and the emperors, surrounded by their courtiers whom Tacitus clearly mistrusts. He interprets events as the effect of the passions to which his characters are a prey—Tiberius being a hypocrite, Nero a monster, etc. The course of history is dominated by Destiny, which finds expression in various very general tendencies, but does not affect minor developments. The *Annales* and *Historiae* are almost entirely concerned with events in Rome—in the city and at court. Economic matters and provincial happenings are seldom mentioned. It should also be remembered that Tacitus was writing in Trajan's reign and that his criticism of previous rulers was a way of flattering the emperor. But despite such reservations, no reader of Tacitus can resist the power of persuasion generated by his highly dramatic writing. (Pierre Grimal.)

12. A number of *Epitomes* (summaries) of the great historians were made in this period and later. The existing Epitome of Livy (the *Periochae*) probably belongs to the sixth century.

13. The author exaggerates the influence of Christianity in the third and fourth centuries, its victory being by no means complete in the latter. For some time afterwards pagan elements continued to occupy a leading place in literature and art, and at the end of the fourth century there developed in the Roman empire a bitter struggle between paganism and Christian teaching. The pagans were still so strong that it was not certain what the fate of Christianity would be. The radical changes that took place in the ideological sphere during the fourth century are attributable in the first instance to the economic and social changes that resulted from the crisis of the slave-owning mode of production. (N. I. Golubtsova.)

14. The aim—and the result—of the additions made by Apuleius to the tale of Lucius of Patras is to bring about the radical transformation of what had begun as a mere fantasy into a 'symbolical' romance. It must be remembered that Apuleius was not merely a rhetorician, that he was above all a philosopher, versed in the doctrine of Platonism as it was understood during that period—that is, as a doctrine involving belief in a world of demons who occupied an intermediate position between mortals and the primordial divinities, and who could be influenced by human action. Apuleius believed in magic and in all probability he practised it. He was an initiate of all the great religious mysteries, including those of the worship of Isis, which was then in great vogue. The *Metamorphoses* offered him a theme admirably suited to symbolic treatment. Isis was the 'Lady of becoming', the divinity who presided over earthly change. The story of the man who is changed into an ass, then restored to human shape by the favour of Isis, and subsequently initiated into the loftiest mysteries, which teach him the secret of the universe, is symbolic of the soul which emerges from the animal state and, thanks to Isis, comes to understand the purpose of creation. Within this wider framework the story of Eros and Psyche treats

the same theme, that of knowledge acquired through love, with the addition of gnostic elements and even, perhaps, of allusions to magic practices, such as the conjuring-up of demons by means of the lamp. (It will be remembered that Psyche, loved by a husband she never sees, who comes to her only by night, has the idea of concealing a lamp which she uncovers when he has fallen asleep. She thus discovers that she is loved by the God of Love. But the 'sin of curiosity' has terrible consequences for her; she has to pass through ordeals in which she is helped by the complicity of the gods; and finally she wins immortality and happiness.) The last book of the *Metamorphoses*, which describes the miracle wrought by Isis and the restoration of the ass to human shape, was added by Apuleius to the original story by Lucius of Patras. And so was the story of Cupid and Psyche. (Pierre Grimal.)

15. One can differ about Gupta art considered as the 'climax of Indian art' and as having exercised a profound influence on the art of south-east Asia. Pallava and other arts can be preferred to it. Moreover it is after the Gupta period that Indian influences are most marked in south-east Asia and the originality of the treatment of Indian themes in this so-called 'Greater India' is such that it is difficult to determine the Indian regions or periods from which they originated.

SELECTED BIBLIOGRAPHY

The bibliographical material in this volume is divided into three parts: I: The principal sources for the history of Greece, Rome, and of the Near East, compiled by Dr Barbara Levick of St Hilda's College, Oxford, who used bibliographical annotations prepared by Professor Luigi Pareti himself (it was subsequently revised by Professor Pierre Grimal); II: Selected titles on the history of the Hebrews and of the origins of Christianity, by Professor Paolo Brezzi; and III: Selected titles on Oriental history (India, the Far East, Japan), prepared by Professor Luciano Petech.

In so far as possible, Dr Levick and Professor Petech organized their bibliographical materials along the plan of each section of this volume, viz. general history, language and writing, social conditions, technological and scientific life, religion, and artistic expression.

A

I. THE ANCIENT WORLD

1. *Works of Reference; General Histories*

F. BILABEL, *Geschichte Vorderasiens und Ägyptens vom 16–11 Jahrhundert v. Chr.* (Heidelberg, 1927).

J. B. BURY *et al.*, eds., *The Cambridge Ancient History* (Cambridge, 1923–39), 12 vols., 5 vols. plates (revised ed., I. E. S. Edwards *et al.*, eds. (Cambridge, 1961–), fasc. 1–).

L. DELAPORTE, *Les peuples de l'Orient méditerranéan, I: Le proche-orient asiatique* (Paris, 1938).

G. GLOTZ, ed., *Histoire générale: Histoire ancienne* (Paris, 1925–47), 10 vols.

A. GOETZ, *Kulturgeschichte des alten Orients: Kleinasien* (München, 1957).

H. R. HALL, *The Ancient History of the Near East* (11th ed., London, 1950).

H. HASSINGER, *Geographische Grundlagen der Geschichte* (2nd ed., Freiburg, 1953).

P. E. VAN DER MEER, *The Chronology of Ancient Western Asia and Egypt* (2nd ed. Leiden, 1955).

E. MEYER, *Geschichte des Altertums* (2nd–4th eds., Stuttgart, etc., 1907–58), 8 vols.

Paulys Real-Encyclopädie der classischen Altertumswissenschaft (neue Bearbeitung unter Mitwerkung zahlreicher Fachgenossen herausgegeben von G. Wissowa, Stuttgart, 1894–), Vol. I– .

H. SCHMÖKEL, *Kulturgeschichte des alten Orients: Mesopotamien, Hethiterreich, Syrien, Palästina, Urartu* (Stuttgart, 1961).

2. *Language and Writing*

D. DIRINGER, *The Alphabet* (London, 1948).

I. J. GELB, *Von der Keilschrift zum Alphabet* (Stuttgart, 1958).

G. HOWARDY, *Clavis Cuneorum* (London, etc., 1933).

A. MEILLET and M. COHEN, eds., *Les Langues du Monde* (2nd ed., Paris, 1952).

3. *Science and Technology*

L. AITCHISON, *A History of Metals* (London, 1960–   ), Vol. I.

O. BECHER, *Das mathematische Denken der Antike* (Göttingen, 1957).

M. CARY and E. WARMINGTON, *The Ancient Explorers* (London, 1929).

H. H. COGHLAN, *Notes on Prehistoric and Early Iron in the Old World* (Oxford, 1956).

R. J. FORBES, 'Bibliographia antiqua'; Section 2: *Philosophia Naturalis* (Leiden, 1948–50), 10 vols.; Supplement I (1952).

R. J. FORBES, *Man the Maker, A History of Technology and Engineering* (New York, 1950).

R. J. FORBES, *Metallurgy in Antiquity* (Leiden, 1950).

R. J. FORBES, *Studies in Ancient Technology* (Leiden, 1955–59), 6 vols.

H. FRANKFORT et al., *The Intellectual Adventure of Ancient Man* (Chicago, 1946).

W. GIESECKE, *Antikes Geldwesen* (Leipzig, 1938).

I. L. HEIBERG, *Geschichte der Mathematik und Naturwissenschaften im Altertum* (München, 1960).

W. KUBITSCHEK, *Grundriss der Antiken Zeitrechnung* (München, 1927).

O. NEUGEBAUER, *Quellen und Studien zur Geschichte der Mathematik, Astronomie, und Physik* (Berlin, 1932–38), 5 vols.

O. NEUGEBAUER, *The Exact Sciences in Antiquity* (Copenhagen, etc., 1957).

C. SINGER et al., *A History of Technology* (Oxford, 1954–56).

P. TANNERY, *Recherches sur l'histoire de l'astronomie ancienne* (Paris, 1893).

A. P. USHER, *A History of Mechanical Inventions* (2nd ed., Cambridge, Mass., 1954).

4. *Economics*

R. GÜNTHER and G. SCHROT, *Sozialökonomische Verhältnisse im alten Orient und im klassischen Altertum* (Berlin, 1961).

F. M. HEICHELHEIM, *An Ancient Economic History from the Palaeolithic Age to the Migrations of the Germanic, Slavic and Arabic Nations* (revised ed., tr. by J. Stevens, Leiden, 1958).

E. SPECK, *Handelsgeschichte des Altertums* (Leipzig, 1900–6), 5 vols.

M. WEBER, 'Agrarverhältnisse im Altertum' in *Gesammelte Aufsätze zur Sozial- und Wirtschaftsgeschichte* (Tübingen, 1924).

5. *Social Life*

R. C. ANDERSON, *Oared Fighting Ships* (London, 1962).

L. CASSON, *The Ancient Mariners* (London, 1959).

H. DELBRÜCK, *Geschichte der Kriegskunst im Rahmen der politischen Geschichte; I: Das Altertum* (Berlin, 1909).

A. KÖSTER, *Das antike Seewesen* (Berlin, 1923).

C. H. KRAELING and M. R. ADAMS, *City Invincible* (Chicago, 1960).

E. MEYER. 'Sklaverei im Altertum', in *Kleine Schriften zur Geschichtstheorie und zur wirtschaftlichen und politischen Geschichte des Altertums* (Halle, 1910), Vol. I.

R. VON PÖHLMANN, *Geschichte der Sozialen Frage und des Sozialismus in der antiken Welt* (3rd ed., durchgesehen von F. Oertel, München, 1925), 2 vols.

6. Religions

W. F. ALBRIGHT, *From the Stone Age to Christianity: Monotheism and the Historical Process* (Baltimore, 1946).

F. BOLL, *Sternglaube und Sterndeutung* (3rd ed., herausgegeben von W. Gundel, Leipzig, etc., 1926).

A. BOUCHÉ-LECLERQ, *Histoire de la divinisation dans l'antiquité* (Paris, 1879–82), 4 vols.

E. DRIOTON *et al.*, *Les religions de l'Orient ancien* (Paris, 1956).

H. FRANKFORT, *Kingship and the Gods* (Chicago, 1948).

C. J. GADD, *Ideas of Divine Rule in the Ancient Near East* (London, 1948).

T. H. GASTER, *Thespis: Ritual, Myth, and Drama in the Ancient Near East* (New York, 1950).

S. H. HOOKE, *Myth, Ritual, and Kingship* (Oxford, 1958).

E. O. JAMES, *Myth and Ritual in the Ancient Near East* (London, 1958).

J. LIEPOLDT and S. MORENZ, *Heilige Schriften* (Leipzig, 1953).

F. TAEGER, *Charisma: Studien zur Geschichte des antiken Herrscherkultes* (Stuttgart, 1957–60), 2 vols.

7. Literature and Art.

R. H. BAINTON *et al.*, *The Idea of History in the Ancient Near East* (New Haven, etc., 1955).

F. BEHN, *Musikleben im Altertum und frühen Mittelalter* (Stuttgart, 1954).

A. W. BYVANCK, *Die Kunst der Oudheid* (Leiden, 1947), Vol. I.

G. CONTENAU, *L'art de l'Asie occidentale ancienne* (Paris, etc., 1928).

N. DAVEY, *A History of Building Materials* (London, 1961).

L. DELAPORTE, *L'art de l'Asie antérieure* (Paris, 1932).

H. FRANKFORT, *The Art and Architecture of the Ancient Orient* (Harmondsworth, 1954).

C. SACHS, *The History of Musical Instruments* (New York, 1940).

E. SCHMIDT *et al.*, *Die orientalischen Literatur* (Berlin, etc., 1906).

II. EGYPT FROM 1200 BC TO AD 400

1. General Works and History

E. BEVAN, *A History of Egypt under the Ptolemaic Dynasty* (London, [1927]).

J. H. BREASTED, *Ancient Records of Egypt* (Chicago, etc., 1906–7), 5 vols.

J. H. BREASTED, *A History of Egypt from the Earliest Times to the Persian Conquest* (2nd ed., London, etc., 1905).

E. BRECCIA, *Alexandrea ad Aegyptum* (Bergamo, 1922).

E. DRIOTON and J. VANDIER, *Les peuples de l'Orient méditerranéen;* II: *L'Egypte* (3rd ed., Paris, 1952).

W. J. EDGERTON and J. A. WILSON, *Historical Records of Ramses III: The Texts in Medinet Habu* (Chicago, 1936), 2 vols.

R. ENGELBACH, *Introduction to Egyptian Archaeology* (Cairo, 1946).

H. GAUTHIER, *Le livre des rois d'Egypte* (Le Caire, 1907–17), 7 vols.

S. R. K. GLANVILLE, ed., *The Legacy of Egypt* (Oxford, 1942).

J. M. JANSSEN, *Ramses III* (Leiden, 1948).

H. JUNKER, 'Die Völker des Antiken Orients: Die Aegyptier', in H. Finke *et al.*, *Geschichte der führenden Völker* (Freiburg, 1933), Vol. III.

W. KAMMERER *et al.*, *A Coptic Bibliography* (Ann Arbor, 1950).

J. P. MAHAFFY, *A History of Egypt under the Ptolemaic Dynasty* (London, 1899).

J. G. MILNE, *History of Egypt under Roman Rule* (3rd ed., London, 1924).

L. MITTEIS und U. WILCKEN, *Grundzüge und Chrestomathie der Papyruskunde* (Leipzig, 1912).

P. MONTET, *Byblos et l'Égypte* (Paris, 1928–29), 2 vols.

A. MORET, *Le Nil et la civilisation égyptienne* (2nd ed., Paris, 1937).

G. POSNER, *La première domination perse en Égypte* (Le Caire, 1936).

E. REVILLOUT, *L'ancienne Égypte d'après les papyrus et les monuments* (Paris, 1907–9), 4 vols.

A. SCHARFF, 'Geschichte Ägyptens von der Vorzeit bis zur Gründung Alexandreias', in A. Scharff and A. Moortgat, *Ägypten und Vorderasien im Altertum* (München, 1950).

G. STEINDORFF and K. C. STEELE, *When Egypt Ruled the East* (Chicago, 1942).

J. STURM, 'Der Hethiterkrieg Ramses II', *Wiener Zeitschrift für die Kunde des Morgenlandes*, Beiheft IV (Wien, 1939).

H. VOLKMANN, *Kleopatra, Politik und Propaganda* (München, 1953).

R. WEILL, *Bases, méthodes et résultats de la chronologie égyptienne* (Paris, 1926); Compléments (1928).

J. A. WILSON, *The Burden of Egypt: An Interpretation of Ancient Egyptian Culture* (Chicago, 1951).

W. H. WORRELL, *A Short Account of the Copts* (Michigan, 1945).

2. *Language and Writing*

W. E. CRUM, *A Coptic Dictionary* (Oxford, 1939).

A. ERMAN and S. GRAPOW, *Wörterbuch der Ägyptischen Sprache* (Leipzig, 1928–50), 6 vols.

A. H. GARDINER, *Egyptian Grammar* (3rd ed., London, 1957).

G. LEFEBVRE, *Grammaire de l'égyptien classique* (Le Caire, 1940).

F. LEXA, *Grammaire démotique* (Praha, 1948–49), 2 vols.

J. M. PLUMLEY, *An Introductory Coptic Grammar* (Sa'idic Dialect) (London, 1948).

B. PORTER and R. L. B. MOSS, *Topographical Bibliography of Ancient Egyptian Hieroglyphic Texts, Reliefs, and Paintings* (Oxford, 1927–51), 7 vols. (Vol. VIII in preparation).

C. E. SANDER-HANSEN, *Altägyptische Grammatik* (Wiesbaden, 1962).

G. STEINDORF, *Kurzer Abriss der koptischen Grammatik* (Berlin, 1921).

G. STEINDORFF, *Lehrbuch der koptischen Grammatik* (*Sa'idic Dialect*) (Chicago, 1951).

T. W. THACKER, *The Relationship of the Semitic and Egyptian Verbal Systems* (Oxford, 1954).

W. TILL, *Koptische Dialektgrammatik* (2nd ed., München, 1961).

W. H. WORRELL, *Coptic Sounds* (Michigan, 1934).

3. *Science and Technology*

R. A. PARKER, *The Calendars of Ancient Egypt* (Chicago, 1950).

T. E. PEET, 'Mathematics in Ancient Egypt', John Rylands Library, Manchester, *Bulletin*, obtainable separately (1931).

J. W. WILSON, 'Egyptian Technology, Science, and Lore', *Journal of World History*, II, 1 (1954).

4. *Economics*

J. CARCOPINO, 'Le gnomon de l'idiologue et son importance historique', *Revue des études anciennes*, XXIV (1922).

J. ČERNÝ, 'Prices and Wages in Egypt in the Ramesside Period', *Journal of World History*, I, 4 (1954).

K. FITZLER, *Steinbrüche und Bergwerk im ptolemäischen und römischen Aegypten* (Leipzig, 1910).

F. HEICHELHEIM, *Wirtschaftliche Schwankungen der Zeit von Alexander bis Augustus* (Jena, 1930).

W. S. LEROY WALLACE, *Taxation in Egypt from Augustus to Diocletian* (Princeton, 1938).

N. LEWIS, *L'industrie du papyrus dans l'Égypte gréco-romaine* (Paris, 1934).

A. LUCAS, *Ancient Egyptian Materials and Industries* (3rd ed., London, 1948).

V. MARTIN, *La fiscalité romaine en Égypte aux trois premiers siècles de l'empire* (Genève, 1926).

T. REIL, *Beiträge zur Kenntnis des Gewerbes im hellenistischen Aegypten* (Leipzig, 1910).

E. SACKEL *et al.*, *Der Gnomon des Idios Logos* (Berlin, 1919), 2 vols.

J. VOGT, *Die alexandrinischen Münzen* (Stuttgart, 1924).

5. *Administration, Law, and Social Life*

W. M. FLINDERS-PETRIE, *Social Life in Ancient Egypt* (London, etc., 1923).

A. H. GARDINER, *Ramesside Administrative Documents* (London, 1940).

M. GELZER, *Studien zur byzantinischen Verwaltungs Aegyptens* (Leipzig, 1909).

W. HELCK, *Zur Verwaltung des mittleren und neuen Reichs* (Leiden, 1958).

L. LESQUIER, *L'armée romaine d'Égypte d'Auguste à Dioclétien* (Le Caire, 1918).

P. M. MEYER, *Juristische Papyri: Erklärung vom Urkunden zur Einführung in die juristische Papyri* (Berlin, 1920).

P. MONTET, *La vie quotidienne en Égypte au temps des Ramsès* (*XIII–XIIe siècles avant J. C.*) (Paris, 1946).

H. A. MUSURILLO, *The Acts of the Pagan Martyrs* (Oxford, 1952).

J. PIRENNE, 'Le statut de la femme dans l'ancienne Égypte', extrait des *Recueils de la Société Jean Bodin*, XI (1959).

R. TAUBENSCHLAG, *The Law of Graeco-Roman Egypt in the Light of the Papyri* (2nd ed., Warsaw, 1955).

J. G. WINTER, *Life and Letters in the Papyri* (Ann Arbor, 1933).

6. *Religion*

H. I. BELL, *Cults and Creeds in Graeco-Roman Egypt* (Liverpool, 1953).

J. H. BREASTED, *The Dawn of Conscience* (New York, 1934).

J. H. BREASTED, *The Development of Religion and Thought in Ancient Egypt* (New York, 1912).

J. ČERNÝ, *Ancient Egyptian Religion* (London, 1952).

A. ERMAN, *Die Religion der Ägypter* (Berlin, etc., 1934).

W. M. FLINDERS-PETRIE, *Religious Life in Ancient Egypt* (London, 1924).

J. GWYN GRIFFITHS, *The Conflict of Horus and Seth* (Liverpool, 1960).

T. HOPFNER, 'Fontes Historiae religionis Aegyptiacae', in C. Clemen, ed., *Fontes Historiae Religionum* (Bonn, etc., 1922–25), 7 fasc., 3 vols.

DE L. O'LEARY, *The Saints of Egypt* (London, 1937).

W. OTTO, *Priester und Tempel im hellenistischen Ägypten* (Leipzig, etc., 1905–8), 2 vols.

R. T. RUNDLE CLARK, *Myth and Symbol in Ancient Egypt* (London, 1959).

A. W. SHORTER, *The Egyptian Gods, A Handbook* (London, 1937).

J. VANDIER, *La religion égyptienne* (Paris, 1949).

H. WADDELL, *The Desert Fathers* (London, 1946).

7. *Literature and Art*

a. *Literature*

E. DRIOTON, *Le théâtre égyptien* (Le Caire, 1947).

A. ERMAN, *The Literature of the Ancient Egyptians* (London, 1927).

P. GILBERT, *La poésie égyptienne* (2nd ed., Bruxelles, 1949).

T. GRASSI, 'Musica, mimica e danza secondo i documenti papiracei greco-egizi', Scuola Papirologica, *Studi*, III (Milano, 1920).

G. LEFEBVRE, *Romans et contes égyptiens de l'époque pharaonique* (Paris, 1949).

T. E. PEET, *A Comparative Study of the Literatures of Egypt, Palestine, and Meso-potamia: Egypt's Contribution to the Literature of the Ancient World* (Oxford, 1931).

S. SCHOTT, *Altägyptische Liebeslieder* (Zürich, 1950).

b. *Art*

J. CAPART, *L'art égyptien; II: Choix de documents* (Bruxelles, 1942–47), 3 vols.

S. CLARKE and R. ENGELBACH, *Ancient Egyptian Masonry* (Oxford, 1930).

N. M. DAVIES, *Ancient Egyptian Paintings* (Chicago, 1936).

C. DECROCHES-NOBLECOURT, *Le style égyptien* (Paris, 1946).

W. M. FLINDERS-PETRIE, *Arts and Crafts of Ancient Egypt* (Edinburgh, etc., 1909).

C. M. KAUFFMANN, *Ägyptische Terrakotten* (Cairo, 1913).

P. MONTET, *Les reliques de l'art syrien dans l'Égypte du nouvel empire* (Paris, 1937).

H. RANKE, *The Art of Ancient Egypt* (Vienna [1937]).

E. D. ROSS, *The Art of Egypt through the Ages* (London, 1931).

E. B. SMITH, *Egyptian Architecture as a Cultural Expression* (New York, 1938).

J. VANDIER, *Egyptian Sculpture* (London, 1951).

W. WEBER, *Die Ägyptisch-griechischen Terrakotten* (Berlin, 1914).

K. WESSEL, *Koptische Kunst* (Recklinghausen, 1963).

III. AFRICA

A. J. ARKELL, *A History of the Sudan from the Earliest Times to 1821* (London, 1961).

J. BENT, *The Sacred City of the Ethiopians* (London, 1893).

C. CONTI ROSSINI, *Storia d'Ethiopia; I: Dalle origini all'avventuto della dinastia Salomonide* (Bergamo, 1928).

J. GARSTAND, *Meroë* (Oxford, 1911).

A. KAMMERER, *Essai sur l'histoire antique d'Abyssinie* (Paris, 1926).

G. A. REISNER, 'The Meroite Kingdom of Ethiopia: A Chronological Outline', *Journal of Egyptian Archaeology*, IX (1923).

A. WYLDE, *Modern Abyssinia* (London, 1901).

IV. ARABIA

E. GLASER, *Skizze der Geschichte Arabiens von den ältesten Zeiten bis zum Propheten Muhammad* (München, 1889).

E. GLASER, *Skizze der Geschichte und Geographie Arabiens* (Berlin, 1890).

A. GROHMANN, *Kulturgeschichte des alten Orients: Arabien* (München, 1963).

P. K. HITTI, *A History of the Arabs* (4th ed., London, 1949).

M. HÖFNER, 'Die Kultur des vorislamischen Südarabien', *Zeitschrift der Deutschen Morgenländischen Gesellschaft*, XCIX (1945–49).

A. JAMME, 'Le Panthéon sud-arabe préislamique d'après les sources épigraphiques', *Le Muséon*, LX (1947).

A. KAMMERER, *Pétra et la Nabatène* (Paris, 1929–30), 2 vols.

R. LE BARON BOWEN et al., *Archaeological Discoveries in South Arabia* (Baltimore, 1958).

D. NIELSEN, *Handbuch der altarabischen Altertumskunde; I: Die altarabische Kultur* (Copenhagen, 1927).

G. RYCKMANS, *Les religions arabes préislamiques* (2nd ed., Louvain, 1951).

J. RYCKMANS, *L'institution monarchique en Arabie méridionale avant l'Islam (Maîn et Saba)* (Louvain, 1951).

A. SPRENGER, *Die alte Geographie Arabiens* (Bern, 1875).

V. THE HITTITES

1. *General Works and History*

K. BITTEL, 'Hethiter und Proto-Hattier', *Historia*, I (1950).

E. CAVAIGNAC, *Les Hittites* (Paris, 1950).

G. CONTENAU, *La civilisation des Hittites et des Hurrites du Mitanni* (2nd ed., Paris, 1948).

L. J. DELAPORTE, *Les Hittites* (Paris, 1936).

R. DUSSAUD, *Prélydiens, Hittites et Achéens* (Paris, 1935).

J. GARSTANG, *The Hittite Empire* (London, 1929).

A. GOETZE, *Hethischer, Churriter und Assyrer* (Oslo, 1936).

O. R. GURNEY, *The Hittites* (Harmondsworth, 1952).

E. MEYER, *Reich und Kultur der Chetiter* (Berlin, 1914).

F. SCHACHERMAYR, 'Hethiter und Achäer', *Mitteilungen der altorientalischen Gesellschaft*, IX, 1–2 (1935).

F. SOMMER, 'Aḫḫijavāfrage und Sprachwissenschaft', *Abhandlungen der Bayerischen Akademie der Wissenschaften, Philosoph.-historische Abt.*, Neue Folge, IX (1934).

F. SOMMER, 'Die Aḫḫijavā-Urkunden', *ibid.*, VI (1932).

F. SOMMER, *Hethiter und Hethitisch* (Stuttgart, 1947).

2. *Language*

E. BENVENISTE, *Hittite et Indo-européen, études comparatives* (Paris, 1962).

J. FRIEDRICH, *Hethitisches Wörterbuch* (Heidelberg, 1952–61) (in progress).

I. J. GELB, *Hittite Hieroglyphs* (Chicago, 1931–42), 3 vols.

C.-J. S. MARSTRANDER, *Caractère indo-européen de la langue hittite* (Christiania, 1919).

P. MERIGGI, *Hieroglyphisch-hethitisches Glossar* (2nd ed., Wiesbaden, 1962).

H. PEDERSEN, *Hittitisch und die anderen indo-europäischen Sprachen* (Copenhagen, 1938).

E. A. SPEISER, "Introduction to Hurrian", *American School of Oriental Research, Annual*, XX (1941).

E. H. STURTEVANT and E. A. HAHN, *A Comparative Grammar of the Hittite Language* (2nd ed., New Haven, 1951).

F. J. TRITSCH, "Lycian, Luwian, and Hittite", *Archiv Orientalní*, XVIII (1950).

3. *Religion*

G. FURLANI, *La religione degli Hittiti* (Bologna, 1936).

4. *Art*

E. AKURGAL, *Spaethetitische Bildkunst* (Ankara, 1949).

E. POTTIER, *L'art hittite* (Paris, 1926).

VI. ASSYRIA AND BABYLON

1. *General Works and History*

W. ANDRAE, *Das Wiederstandene Assur* (Leipzig, 1938).

A. S. ANSPRACHER, *Tiglath Pileser III* (New York, 1912).

V. CHRISTIAN, *Altertumskunde des Zweistromlandes von der Vorzeit bis zum Ende der Achämenidenherrschaft* (Leipzig, 1940).

G. CONTENAU, *La civilisation d'Assur et de Babylone* (Paris, 1951).

L. DILLEMAN, *Haute Mésopotamie orientale et pays adjacents* (Paris, 1962).

R. P. DOUGHERTY, *Nabonidus and Belshazzar: A Study of the Closing Events of the Neo-Babylonian Empire* (New Haven, 1929).

E. EBELING and B. MEISSNER, *Reallexikon der Assyriologie* (Berlin, etc., 1928–59), 3 vols.

C. FOSSEY, *Manuel d'Assyriologie* (Paris, 1904–26), 2 vols.

G. FURLANI, *La Civiltà babilonese e assira* (Roma, 1929).

C. J. GADD, *The Stones of Assyria* (London, 1936).

C. H. W. JOHNS, *Assyrian Deeds and Documents* (Cambridge, 1898–1923), 4 vols.

J. LAESSØE, *People of Ancient Assyria, their Inscriptions and Correspondence* (tr. by F. S. Leigh Browne, London, 1963).

S. H. LANGDON, *Die neubabylonischen Königsinschriften* (tr. by R. Zehnpfund, Leipzig, 1912).

F. M. T. DE LIAGRE BÖHL, 'Het Tijdvak der Sargonieden volgens Brieven uit het koninklijk archief te Nineve', *Meddelingen der Konikl. Nederlandsche Akad. van Wetenschappen*, Afd. Letterkunde, Nieuwe Reeks, Deel XII, no. 8 (1949).

S. LLOYD, *Twin Rivers* (2nd ed., Oxford, 1950).

B. MEISSNER, *Babylonien und Assyrien* (Heidelberg, 1920–25), 2 vols.

B. MEISSNER, *Könige Babyloniens und Assyriens* (Leipzig, 1926).

A. T. OLMSTEAD, *A History of Assyria* (New York, 1923).

A. H. SAYCE, *Babylonians and Assyrians* (New York, 1899).

W. VON SODEN, *Der Aufstieg des Assyrerreichs als geschichtliches Problem* (Leipzig, 1937).

L. WATERMAN, *Royal Correspondence of the Assyrian Empire* (Michigan, 1930–36), 4 vols.

2. Language and Writing

F. DELITZSCH, *Assyrisches Handwörterbuch* (Leipzig, etc., 1896).

I. GELB *et al.*, *The Assyrian Dictionary of the Oriental Institute of the University of Chicago* (Chicago, 1956–   ) (in progress).

G. RYCKMANS, *Grammaire accadienne* (Louvain, 1938).

A. UNGNAD, *Grammatik des Akkadischen* (3rd ed., München, 1949).

3. Science and Technology

R. CAMPBELL THOMPSON, *A Dictionary of Assyrian Botany* (London, 1949).

R. CAMPBELL THOMPSON, *A Dictionary of Assyrian Chemistry and Geology* (Oxford, 1936).

G. CONTENAU, *La médicine en Assyrie et en Babylonie* (Paris, 1938).

F. K. GINZEL, *Die astronomischen Kenntnisse der Babylonier* (Leipzig, 1902).

P. JENSEN, *Die Cosmologie der Babylonien* (Strassburg, 1890).

F. X. KUGLER, *Die babylonische Mondrechnung* (Freiburg, 1900).

F. X. KUGLER, *Sternkunde und Sterndienst in Babel* (Münster, 1907–35), 3 vols. (Ergänzungsheft 3 von J. Schlumberger).

M. LEVEY, *Chemistry and Chemical Technology in Ancient Mesopotamia* (Amsterdam, etc., 1959).

T. G. PINCHES *et al.*, *Late Babylonian Astronomical and Related Texts* (Providence, 1955).

M. RUTTEN, *La science des Chaldéens* (Paris, 1960).

4. *Social Life*

G. CONTENAU, *Everyday Life in Babylonia and Assyria* (tr. by K. R. and A. R. Maxwell-Hyslop, London, 1954).

I. MENDELSOHN, *Legal Aspects of Slavery in Babylonia, Assyria and Palestine* (Williamsport, 1932).

5. *Religion*

E. DHORME, *Les religions de Babylonie et d'Assyrie* (Paris, 1945).

G. FURLANI, *La religione babilonese e assira* (Bologna, 1928–29), 2 vols.

S. H. HOOKE, *Babylonian and Assyrian Religion* (London, 1953).

L. W. KING, *Babylonian Religion and Mythology* (London, 1899).

W. KROLL, *De Oraculis Chaldaicis* (Hildesheim, 1962).

H. LEWY, *Chaldean Oracles and Theurgy: Mysticism, Magic, and Platonism in the Later Roman Empire* (Le Caire, 1956).

H. LEWY, 'The Late Assyro-Babylonian Cult of the Moon and its Culmination at the Time of Nabonidus', Hebrew University College, *Annual*, XIX (1945–46).

6. *Literature and Art*

W. ANDRAE, *Coloured Ceramics from Assur* (London, 1925).

C. BEZOLD, *Kurzgefasster überblick über die babylonische assyrische Literatur* (Leipzig, 1886).

E. D. VAN BUREN, *Clay Figurines of Babylonia and Assyria* (New Haven, 1930).

H. FRANKFORT, *Cylinder Seals* (London, 1939).

C. F. JEAN, *La littérature des Babyloniens et des Assyriens* (Paris, 1924).

B. MEISSNER, *Die babylonisch-assyrische Literatur* (Wild Park-Potsdam, 1928).

A. PARROT, *Nineveh and Babylon* (tr. by S. Gilbert and J. Emmons, Paris, 1961).

A. PARROT, *Ziggurats et tour de Babel* (Paris, 1949).

O. WEBER, *Die Literatur der Babylonier und Assyrier* (Leipzig, 1907).

C. ZERVOS, *L'art de la Mésopotamie* (Paris, 1935).

VII. SEMITIC CIVILIZATION IN GENERAL

G. A. BARTON, *Semitic and Hamitic Origins* (Philadelphia, 1934).

W. W. BAUDISSIN, *Studien zur semitischen Religionsgeschichte* (Berlin, 1911), 2 vols.

Corpus inscriptionum Semiticarum (Paris, 1881–1951), Parts I–V.

G. R. DRIVER, *Semitic Writing* (Oxford, 1948).

S. MOSCATI, *Storia e civiltà dei Semiti* (Bari, 1949).

Répertoire d'épigraphie sémitique (Paris, 1900–), Vol. I–   (in progress).

R. C. THOMPSON, *Semitic Magic* (London, 1908).

VIII. CANAAN AND THE JEWS

1. *General Works and History*

W. F. ALBRIGHT, *The Archaeology of Palestine* (Harmondsworth, 1949).

A. BEA, 'La Palestina preisraelitica', *Biblica*, XXIV (1943).

F. BÖHL, *Kanaanäer und Hebräer* (Leipzig, 1911).

F. HELLING, *Die Frühgeschichte des jüdischen Volkes* (Frankfurt-am-Main, 1947).

R. KITTLE, *Geschichte des Volkes Israel* (Stuttgart, 1923–29), 3 vols.
(Vols. I and II eds. 5 and 6; Vol. III (in two parts) eds. 1 and 2.)

R. LARGEMENT, *La religion cananéenne* (n.p., n.d.).

R. A. S. MACALISTER, *A Century of Excavation in Palestine* (London, 1925).

T. J. MEEK, *Hebrew Origins* (2nd ed., New York, 1950).

M. NOTH, *Geschichte Israels* (Göttingen, 1950).

W. O. E. OESTERLEY and T. H. ROBINSON, *A History of Israel* (Oxford, 1932), 2 vols.

E. ROBERTSON, 'The Period of the Judges', John Rylands Library, Manchester, *Bulletin*, XXX (1946).

H. H. ROWLEY, *From Joseph to Joshua* (London, 1950).

E. F. SELLIN, *Geschichte des israelitisch jüdischen Volkes* (Leipzig, 1924), Vol. I.

R. P. H. VINCENT, *Canaan* (2nd ed., Paris, 1914).

R. P. H. VINCENT, *Canaan d'après l'exploration récente* (Paris, 1907).

A. C. WELCH, *Kings and Prophets of Israel* (ed. by N. W. Porteous, London, 1952).

J. WELLHAUSEN, *Israelitische und jüdische Geschichte* (4th ed., Berlin, 1901).

J. WELLHAUSEN, *Prolegomena zur Geschichte Israels* (6th ed., Berlin, 1927).

2. *Language and Writing*

H. BAUER and P. LEANDER, *Historische Grammatik der hebräischen Sprache des alten Testamentes* (Halle, 1918–22).

G. BERGSTRÄSSER, ed., *W. Gesenius' Hebräische Grammatik* (29th ed., Leipzig, 1918–29), 2 vols. in 3.

S. MORAY, *The Vocalization Systems of Arabic Hebrew and Aramaic* ('s Gravenhage, 1962).

3. Religion and Law

H. GRESSMAN, *Altorientalische Bilder zum alten Testament* (2nd ed., Berlin, etc., 1926–27).

H. GRESSMAN et al., eds., *Altorientalische Texte zum alten Testament* (2nd ed., Berlin, etc., 1926).

P. HEINISCH, *Geschichte des alten Testaments* (Bonn, 1950).

J. B. PRITCHARD, *Ancient Near Eastern Texts relating to the Old Testament* (2nd ed., Princeton, 1955).

Recueil Edouard Dhorme: Études bibliques et orientales (Paris, 1951).

E. F. SELLIN, *Einleitung in das alte Testament* (9th ed., bearb. von L. Rost, Heidelberg, 1959).

J. M. P. SMITH, *The Origin and History of Hebrew Law* (Chicago, 1931).

Testament Presentation of History (Uppsala, etc., 1951).

C. TOUSSAINT, *Les origines de la religion d'Israel; I: L'ancien Jahvisme* (Paris, 1931).

IX. SYRIA

H. T. BOSSERT, *Altsyrien* (Tübingen, 1951).

P. K. HITTI, *A History of Syria* (London, 1951).

T. NÖLDEKE, *A Compendious Syriac Grammar* (London, 1904).

A. OLMSTEAD, *A History of Palestine and Syria to the Macedonian Conquest* (New York, 1931).

X. AMURRU

T. BAUER, *Die Ostkanaanäer: eine philologisch-historische Untersuchung über die Wanderschicht der sogenannten 'Amoriter' in Babylonien* (Leipzig, 1926).

A. T. CLAY, *Amurru, the Home of the Northern Semites* (Philadelphia, 1909).

A. T. CLAY, *The Antiquity of Amorite Civilization* (New Haven, 1924).

A. T. CLAY, *The Empire of the Amorites* (New Haven, 1919).

P. DHORME, 'Les Amorrhéens', *Revue Biblique*, XXXVII (1928).

XI. THE PHOENICIANS

D. BARAMKI, *Phoenicia and the Phoenicians* (Beirut, 1961).

W. BORGEAUD, *Dieux indo-européens et dieux phéniciens* (Damas, 1960).

H. T. BOSSERT, 'Die Phoenizisch-hethitischen Bilinguen vom Karatepe', *Oriens*, I (1948), II (1949).

G. CONTENAU, *La civilisation phénicienne* (2nd ed., Paris, 1949).

R. DUSSAUD, *Les religions des Phéniciens et des Syriens* (Paris, 1945).

C. H. GORDON, 'Azitawadd's Phoenician Inscription', *Journal of Near Eastern Studies*, VIII (1949).

D. HARDEN, *The Phoenicians* (London, 1962).

Z. S. HARRIS, *A Grammar of the Phoenician Language* (New Haven, 1936).

G. LEVI, della Vida 'Osservazioni all'iscrizione fenicia di Karatepe', *Atti della Accademia nazionale dei Lincei, Rendiconte*, Series VIII, Vol. IV (1949).

M. NOTH, 'Zum Ursprung der phönikischen Küstenstädte', *Die Welt des Orients*, I (1947).

J. OBERMANN, *The New Discoveries at Karatepe* (New Haven, 1949).

R. T. O'CALLAGHAN, 'The Great Phoenician Portal Inscriptions from Karatepe', *Orientalia*, New Series, XVIII (1949).

A. POIDEBARD, *Un grand port disparu: Tyr* (Paris, 1939), 2 vols.

A. POIDEBARD et J. LAUFFRAY, *Sidon: Aménagements antiques du Port de Saida* (Beyrouth, 1951).

G. RAWLINSON, *History of Phoenicia* (London, 1889).

R. WEILL, *La Phénice et l'Asie occidentale des origines à la conquête macédonienne* (Paris, 1939).

C. L. WOOLLEY, 'La Phénice et les peuples égéens', *Syria*, II (1921).

XII. THE ARAMEANS

F. ALTHEIM and R. STIEHL, *Die aramäische Sprache unter den Achaimeniden* (Frankfurt-am-Main, 1962), Vol. I.

H. BAUER and P. LEANDER, *Grammatik des Biblisch-Aramäischen* (Halle, 1927).

A. E. COWLEY, ed., *Aramaic Papyri of the Fifth Century* BC (Oxford, 1923).

A. DUPONT-SOMMER, *Les Araméens* (Paris, 1949).

K. ELLIGER, 'Sam'al und Hamat in ihrem Verhältnis zu Hattina, Unki, und Arpaf', in J. Fück, ed., *Festschrift O. Eissfeldt* (Halle, 1947).

H. INGHOLT, *Rapport préliminaire sur sept campagnes de fouilles à Hama en Syrie* (1932–38), (København, 1940).

B. LANDESBERGER, *Sam'al: Studien zur Entdeckung der Ruinenstätte Karatepe* (Ankara, 1948).

F. ROSENTHAL, *A Grammar of Biblical Aramaic* (Wiesbaden, 1961).

F. ROSENTHAL, *Die aramäistische Forschung seit Th. Nöldeke's Veröffentlichungen* (Leiden, 1939).

S. SCHIFFER, *Die Aramäer* (Leipzig, 1911).

XIII. THE PHILISTINES

O. EISSFELDT, *Philister und Phönikier* (Leipzig, 1936).

R. A. S. MACALISTER, *The Philistines* (London, 1943).

XIV. UGARIT

J. AISTLEITNER, *Wörterbuch der ugaritischen Sprache* (Berlin, 1963).

H. BAUER, *Das Alphabet von Ras Schamra* (Halle, 1932).

C. H. GORDON, tr. and ed., *The Loves and Wars of Baal and Anat, and other Poems from Ugarit* (Princeton, 1943).

C. H. GORDON, 'The Ugaritic "ABC"', *Orientalia*, XIX (1950).

C. H. GORDON, *Ugaritic Handbook* (Rome, 1947).

C. H. GORDON, *Ugaritic Literature* (Rome, 1949).

ANDRÉE HAERTNER, *Corpus des tablettes en cunéiforme alphabétique de Ras Shamra* (Paris, 1963).

A. JIRKU, *Kanaanäische Mythen und Epen aus Ras Schamra-Ugarit* (Gutersloh, 1962).

R. DE LANCHE, *Les textes de Ras Shamra-Ugarit et leurs rapports avec le milieu biblique de l'Ancient Testament* (Paris, 1945), 2 vols.

M. LIVERANI, *Storia di Ugarit nell'età degli archivi politici* (Roma, 1962).

J. OBERMANN, *Ugaritic Mythology* (New Haven, 1948).

C. F. A. SCHAEFFER, *Ugaritica*, Série I—(*Bibliothèque archéologique et historique*, tomes 31, 47, 64) (Paris, 1939–   ).

C. VIROLLEAUD, 'Les nouvelles tablettes de Ras Shamra (1948–9)', *Syria*, XXVIII (1951).

C. L. WOOLLEY, *A Forgotten Kingdom* (London, 1953).

XV. ARMENIA: URARTU

C. LEHMANN-HAUPT, *Armenia einst und jetzt* (Berlin, 1926), 2 vols.

A. H. SAYCE, 'The Cuneiform Inscriptions of Van', Royal Asiatic Society of Great Britain and Ireland, *Journal*, XIV (1882), XX (1888), XXIV (1893), XXVI (1894), XXXIII (1901), XXXVIII (1906), XLIII (1911).

XVI. ANATOLIAN STATES

H. T. BOSSERT, *Altanatolien* (Berlin, 1942).

E. CHAPUT *et al.*, *Phrygie* (Paris, 1941–51), 3 vols.

R. DUSSAUD, *La Lydie et ses voisins* (Paris, 1930).

A. ERZEN, *Kilikien bis zum Ende der Perserherrschaft* (Leipzig, etc., 1940).

R. GUSMANI, *Lydisches Wörterbuch* (forthcoming).

S. LLOYD, *Early Anatolia* (Harmondsworth, 1956).

G. RADET, *La Lydie et le monde grec au temps des Mermnades* (687–546) (Paris, 1893).

F. SARTIAUX, *Les civilisations anciennes de l'Asie Mineure* (Paris, 1928).

O. TREUBER, *Geschichte der Lycier* (Stuttgart, 1887).

XVII. AEGEAN CIVILIZATION:
THE PEOPLES OF THE SEA, CRETE, MYCENAE, AND TROY

1. *General Works*

J. BÉRARD, 'Recherches sur la chronologie de l'époque mycénienne', *Comptes Rendus de l'Académie des inscriptions et belles-lettres* (1946).

C. W. BLEGEN, 'New Evidence for Dating the Settlement at Troy', *Annual of the British School at Athens*, XXXVII (1936–37).

C. W. BLEGEN and K. KOUROUNIOTIS, 'Excavations at Pylos, 1939', *American Journal of Archaeology*, XLIII (1939).

C. W. BLEGEN *et al.*, eds., *Troy: Excavations Conducted by the University of Cincinnati, 1932–38* (Princeton, 1950–58), 8 vols.

A. H. BURN, *Minoans, Philistines, and Greeks, 1400–900 BC* (London, 1930).

J. L. CASKEY, 'Notes of Trojan Chronology', *American Journal of Archaeology*, LII (1948).

C. DUGAS, *La céramique des Cyclades* (Paris, 1925).

F. FIMMEN, *Die kretisch-mycenische Kultur* (Leipzig, etc., 1921).

E. GJERSTAD, *Studies in Prehistoric Cyprus* (Uppsala, 1926).

G. GLOTZ, *La civilisation égéenne* (Paris, 1923).

H. R. HALL, *Aegean Archaeology* (London, 1915).

H. R. HALL, *The Civilization of Greece in the Bronze Age* (London, 1928).

H. R. HALL, 'The Peoples of the Sea', in *Recueil d'études égyptologiques dédié à la mémoire de J.-F. Champollion* (Paris, 1922).

W. A. HEURTLEY, 'Excavations in Ithaca; IV: Summary', *Annual of the British School at Athens*, XL (1940).

W. A. MCDONALD, 'Where did Nestor Live?', *American Journal of Archaeology*, XLVI (1942).

F. MATZ, *Kreta, Mykene, Troja* (Stuttgart, 1962).

O. MEY, *Das Schlachtfeld von Troja* (Berlin, etc., 1926).

G. E. MYLONAS, *Ancient Mycenae* (London, 1957).

L. R. PALMER, *Mycenaeans and Minoans* (London, 1961).

W. K. PRENTICE, 'The Achaeans', *American Journal of Archaeology*, XXXIII (1929).

J. SUNDWALL, 'Knossisches in Pylos', *Acta Academiae Aboensis*, XIII (1940).

G. THOMPSON, *Studies in Ancient Greek Society; I: The Prehistoric Aegean* (London, 1949).

C. TSCUNTAS and J. A. NISUATT, *The Mycenaean Age* (Boston, 1890).

C. VELLAY, *Les Nouveaux aspects de la question de Troie* (Paris, 1930).

G. A. WAINWRIGHT, 'Keftiu: Crete or Cilicia?', *Journal of Hellenic Studies*, LI (1931).

2. Language and Writing

J. CHADWICK, *The Decipherment of Linear B* (Cambridge, 1958).

L. R. PALMER, *The Interpretation of Mycenaean Greek Texts* (Oxford, 1962).

L. R. PALMER and J. BOARDMAN, *On the Knossos Tablets; Independent Studies* (Oxford, forthcoming).

G. P. SHIPP, *Essays in Mycenaean and Homeric Greek* (Melbourne, 1961).

M. VENTRIS and J. CHADWICK, *Documents in Mycenaean Greek* (London, 1956).

3. Religion

M. P. NILSSON, *The Minoan-Mycenaean Religion and its Survival in Greek Religion* (2nd ed., Lund, 1950).

A. W. PERSSON, *The Religion of Greece in Prehistoric Times* (Berkeley, etc., 1942).

4. Art

H. T. BOSSERT, *Alt-Kreta* (Berlin, 1923).

J. CHARBONNEAUX, *L'art égéen* (Paris, etc., 1929).

G. A. S. SNIJDER, *Kretische Kunst* (Berlin, 1936).

5. Homer and the Aegean World

W. LEAF, *Homer and History* (London, 1923).

H. L. LORIMER, *Homer and the Monuments* (London, 1950).

J. L. MYRES, *Homer and his Critics* (ed. D. F. H. Gray, London, 1958).

M. P. NILSSON, *Homer and Mycenae* (London, 1933).

D. L. PAGE, *History and the Homeric Iliad* (Berkeley, etc., 1959).

L. PARETI, *L'epica e le origini greche* (Firenze, 1942).

T. B. L. WEBSTER, *From Mycenae to Homer* (London, 1958).

XVIII. INDO-EUROPEAN MIGRATIONS; THE DORIAN INVASION

1. General Works

M. ANDRONIKOS, 'The "Dorian Invasion" and Archaeology', *Hellenika*, XIII (1954) (in Greek).

P. BOSCH-GIMPERA, *El Problema indoeuropeo* (Mexico, 1960).

V. GORDON CHILDE, *The Aryans* (London, 1926).

R. A. CROSLAND, 'Indo-European Origins, the Linguistic Evidence', *Past and Present*, XII (November, 1957).

J. F. DANIEL *et al.*, 'The Dorian Invasion', *American Journal of Archaeology*, LII (1948).

G. DEVOTO, *Origini indoeuropee* (Firenze, 1962).

N. G. L. HAMMOND, 'Prehistoric Epirus and the Dorian Invasion', *Annual of the British School at Athens*, XXXII (1931–32).

H. KRAHE, *Die Indogermanisierung Griechenlands und Italiens* (Heidelberg, 1949).

F. MATZ, 'Die Indogermanisierung Italiens', *Neue Jahrbücher für Antike und Deutsche Bildung* (1938).

J. MELLAART, 'The End of the Early Bronze Age in Anatolia and the Aegean', *American Journal of Archaeology*, LXII (1958).

V. MILOJČIĆ, 'Die dorische Wanderung im Lichte der vorgeschichtlichen Funde', *Archäologischer Anzeiger* (Beiblatt zum *Jahrbuch des deutschen archäologischen Instituts*), LXIII–IV (1948–49).

F. MILTNER, 'Die dorische Wanderung', *Klio*, XXVII (N.F., IX) (1934).

J. L. MYRES, *Who Were the Greeks?* (Berkeley, 1930).

G. PATRONI, 'L'indoeuropeizzazione d'Italia', *Athenaeum*, N.S., XVII (1939).

F. SCHACHERMEYR, 'Das Problem der griechischen Nationalität', *X Congresso internazionale di scienze storiche, Relazioni* VI (Roma, 1955).

C. SCHUCHHARDT, 'Die Indogermanisierung Griechenlands', *Forschungen und Fortschritte*, IX (1933).

C. SCHUCHHARDT, 'Die Urillyrier und ihre Indogermanisierung', *Abhandlungen der Preussischen Akademie der Wissenschaften* (1937, no. 4).

T. C. SKETT, *The Dorians in Archaeology* (London, [1934]).

2. *Language*

K. BRUGMANN and B. DELBRÜCK, *Grundriss der vergleichenden Grammatik der indogermanischen Sprachen* (2nd ed., Strassburg, 1897–1916), 4 vols. in 8.

H. KRAHE, *Indogermanische Sprachwissenschaft* (3rd ed., Berlin, 1958–59), 2 vols.

A. MEILLET, *Introduction à l'étude comparative des langues indo-européennes* (8th ed., Paris, [1949]).

A. MEILLET, *Les origines indo-européennes des mètres grecs* (Paris, 1923).

3. *Religion*

F. CORNELIUS, *Indogermanische Religionsgeschichte* (München, 1942).

G. DUMÉZIL, *Les dieux des Indo-européens* (Paris, 1952).

XIX. IRAN: THE MEDES AND PERSIANS; THE ARSACID AND SASSANIAN PERIODS

1. *General Works and History*

F. ALTHEIM and R. STIEHL, *Ein asiatischer Staat* (Wiesbaden, 1954), Vol. I.

A. R. BURN, *Persia and the West* (London, 1962).

G. G. CAMERON, *History of Early Iran* (Chicago, 1936).

A. CHRISTENSEN, *Die Iranier* (*Handbücher der Altertumswissenschaft, Kulturgeschichte des alten Orients*, III, 1) (München, 1933).

A. CHRISTENSEN, *L'Iran sous les Sassanides* (Copenhagen, etc., 1936).

G. COUSIN, *Kyros le jeune en Asie Mineure* (Paris, etc., 1905).

N. C. DEBEVOISE, *A Political History of Parthia* (Chicago, 1938).

R. GHIRSHMAN, *Iran: Parthians and Sassanians* (Tr. by S. Gilbert and J. Emmons, Paris, 1962).

H. HENNING VON DER OSTEN, *Die Welt der Perser* (Stuttgart, 1956).

E. E. HERZFELD, *Archaeological History of Iran* (London, 1935).

E. E. HERZFELD, *Iran in the Ancient East* (London, etc., 1941).

E. HONIGMANN and J. MARICQ, 'Recherches sur les Res Gestae Divi Saporis', Académie Royale de Belgique, *Mémoires*, XLVII, fasc. 4 (1953).

K. A. INOSTRANZEV, *Sassanian Studies* (St. Petersburg, 1909) (in Russian).

P. J. JUNGE, *Dareios I* (Leipzig, 1944).

F. W. KÖNIG, *Aelteste Geschichte der Meder und Perser* (Leipzig, 1934).

P. LOZINSKI, *The Original Homeland of the Parthians* ('s-Gravenhage, 1959).

A. J. OLMSTEAD, *History of the Persian Achaemenid Period* (Chicago, 1948).

J. V. PRÁŠEK, *Kambyses* (Leipzig, 1913).

J. V. PRÁŠEK, *Kyros der Grosse* (Leipzig, 1912).

R. W. ROGERS, *A History of Ancient Persia* (London, 1939).

E. D. ROSS, *The Persians* (Oxford, 1931).

2. *Language and Writing*

O. HANSEN, *Mittelpersiches Lesebuch* (Berlin, 1962).

R. G. KENT, *Old Persian* (New Haven, 1950).

J. OPPOERT, *Le peuple et la langue des Mèdes* (Paris, 1879).

H. H. SCHAEDER, 'Ein parthischer Titel im Sogdischen', School of Oriental Studies, *Bulletin*, VIII (1936).

F. H. WEISSBACH, *Die Keilinschriften der Achämeniden* (Leipzig, 1911).

3. *Religion*

F. C. BURKITT, *The Religion of the Manichees* (Cambridge, 1925).

C. CLEMEN, *Die griechischen und lateinischen Nachrichten über die persische Religion* (Giessen, 1920).

K. ERDMANN, *Das iranische Feuerheiligtum* (Leipzig, 1941).

R. REITZENSTEIN and H. H. SCHAEDER, *Studien zum antiken Synkretismus aus Iran und Griechenland* (Leipzig, 1926).

R. C. ZAEHNER, *Zoroastrianism* (London, 1961).

4. Literature and Art

F. W. VON BISSING, "Die Kunst Irans zur Zeit der Sassaniden", *Die Welt des Orients*, I (1947).

E. DIENST, *Iranische Kunst* (Wien, 1944).

K. ERDMANN, *Die Kunst Irans zur Zeit der Sassaniden* (Berlin, 1943).

A. GODARD, *L'art d'Iran* (Paris, 1962).

P. HORN and G. STEINDORFF, *Sassanidische Siegelsteine* (Berlin, 1891).

E. A. READ, *Persian Literature Ancient and Modern* (Chicago, 1893).

XX. CLASSICAL GREECE

1. General Works and History

K. J. BELOCH, *Griechische Geschichte* (2nd ed., Strassburg, etc., 1912–27), 4 vols.

K. J. BELOCH, *Griechische Geschichte seit Alexander* (2nd ed., Leipzig, etc., 1914).

J. BÉRARD, *La colonisation grecque de l'Italie méridionale et de la Sicile dans l'antiquité: l'histoire et la légende* (2nd ed., Paris, 1957).

H. BERVE, *Das Alexanderreich* (München, 1926), 2 vols.

A. BOUCHÉ LECLERQ, *Histoire des Séleucides* (Paris, 1913–14), 2 vols.

A. R. BURN, *The Lyric Age of Greece* (London, 1960).

A. R. BURN, *The World of Hesiod* (London, 1936).

J. S. CALLAWAY, *Sybaris* (Baltimore, 1950).

M. CARY, *The Geographic Background of Greek and Roman History* (Oxford, 1949).

M. O. B. CASPARI, 'The Revolution of the 400 at Athens', *Journal of Hellenic Studies*, XXXIII (1913).

F. CHAMOUX, *Cyrène sous la monarchie des Battiades* (Paris, 1953).

E. CIACERI, *Storia della Magna Grecia* (Milano, etc., 1927–32), 3 vols.

M. CLERC, *Massalia* (Marseille, 1927–29), 2 vols.

P. CLOCHÉ, *Démosthène et la fin de la démocratie athénienne* (Paris, 1937).

P. CLOCHÉ, *Histoire de la Macédoine* (Paris, 1960).

P. CLOCHÉ, *Thèbes de Béotie* (Namur, etc., n.d.).

R. M. COOK, 'Ionia and Greece in the Eighth and Seventh Centuries BC', *Journal of Hellenic Studies*, LXVI (1946).

R. M. COOK, *The Greeks in Ionia and the East* (London, 1962).

G. N. CROSS, *Epirus* (Cambridge, 1932).

C. DAREMBERG and E. SAGLIO, *Dictionnaire des antiquités grecques et romaines d'après les textes et les monuments* (Paris, 1877–1919), 10 vols.

G. DAUX, *Delphes au IIe et au Ier siècle* (Paris, 1936).

G. DOWNEY, *A History of Antioch in Syria from Seleucus to the Arab Conquest* (Princeton, 1961).

T. J. DUNBABIN, 'The Greeks and their Eastern Neighbours', Society for the Promotion of Hellenic Studies, *Supplementary Papers*, no. 8 (1957).

V. EHRENBERG, *Alexander and the Greeks* (tr. by R. F. von Velsen, Oxford, 1938).

W. S. FERGUSON, *Hellenistic Athens* (London, 1911).

R. FLACELIÈRE, *Les Aitoliens à Delphes* (Paris, 1937).

K. FREEMAN, *The Life and Work of Solon* (Cardiff, 1926).

A. GARCIA Y BELLIDO, *Hispania Graeca* (Barcelona, 1948), 2 vols.

N. G. L. HAMMOND, *A History of Greece* (Oxford, 1959).

E. V. HANSEN, *The Attalids of Pergamum* (New York, 1947).

J. HATZFELD, *Alcibiade* (Paris, 1940).

B. W. HENDERSON, *The Great War between Athens and Sparta* (London, 1927).

C. HIGNETT, *Xerxes' Invasion of Greece* (Oxford, 1963).

D. G. HOGARTH, *Philip and Alexander of Macedon* (London, 1897).

G. HUXLEY, *Early Sparta* (London, 1962).

W. JAEGER, *Demosthenes* (Cambridge, 1938).

J. KESSLER, *Isokrates und die panhellenische Idee* (Paderborn, 1911).

J. A. O. LARSEN, 'Sparta and the Ionian Revolt: A Study of Spartan Foreign Policy and the Genesis of the Peloponnesian League', *Classical Philology*, XXVII (1932).

J. A. O. LARSEN, 'The Constitution of the Peloponnesian League', *Classical Philology*, XXVIII (1933).

P. LÉVÊQUE, *Pyrrhos* (Paris, 1957).

E. MANNI, *Demetrio Poliorcete* (Roma, 1951).

P. MELONI, *Perseo e la fine della monarchia Macedone* (Roma, 1953).

H. MICHELL, *Sparta* (Cambridge, 1952).

A. MOMIGLIANO, *Filippo il Macedone* (Firenze, 1934).

A. K. NARAIN, *The Indo-Greeks* (Oxford, 1957).

M. P. NILSSON, *The Age of the Early Greek Tyrants* (Belfast, 1939).

H. NOETHE, *Der delische Bund* (progr. Magdeburg, 1889).

A. OLIVERI, *Civiltà greca nell' Italia meridionale* (Napoli, 1931).

J. G. O'NEILL, *Ancient Corinth* (Baltimore, 1930).

H. G. PAYNE, *Necrocorinthia* (Oxford, 1931).

G. RADET, *Alexandre le Grand* (7th ed., Paris, 1950).

C. ROEBUCK, *Ionian Trade and Colonization* (New York, 1959).

G. E. M. DE STE CROIX, 'The Character of the Athenian Empire', *Historia*, III (1954–55).

G. DE SANCTIS, *Historia dei Greci dalle origini alla fine del secolo V* (Firenze, 1939), 2 vols.

G. DE SANCTIS, *Pericle* (Milano, etc., n.d.).

M. SORDI, *Timoleonte* (Palermo, n.d.).

K. F. STROHEKER, *Dionysios I* (Wiesbaden, 1958).

W. W. TARN, *Alexander the Great* (Cambridge, 1948), 2 vols.

W. W. TARN, *Antigonus Gonatas* (Oxford, 1913).

W. W. TARN, *Hellenistic Civilization* (3rd ed., rev. W. W. Tarn and G. T. Griffith, London, 1952).

W. W. TARN, *The Greeks in Bactria and India* (Cambridge, 1938).

V. TCHERIKOWER, *Hellenistic Civilization and the Jews* (tr. by S. Applebaum, Philadelphia, 1959).

G. VITUCCI, *Il regno di Bitinia* (Roma, 1953).

F. W. WALBANK, *Aratos of Sicyon* (Cambridge, 1933).

F. W. WALBANK, *Philip V of Macedon* (Cambridge, 1940).

G. WELTER, *Aegina* (Berlin, 1938).

P. WENDLAND, *Die hellenistisch-römanische Kultur* (3rd ed., Tübingen, 1912).

E. WILL, *Doriens et Ioniens* (Paris, 1951).

E. WILL, *Korinthiaka* (Paris, 1955).

A. G. WOODHEAD, *The Greeks in the West* (London, 1962).

2. *Language and Writing; Education*

C. D. BUCK, *Comparative Grammar of Greek and Latin* (Chicago, 1959).

C. D. BUCK, *Introduction to the Study of the Greek Dialects* (2nd ed., Boston, 1928).

K. J. FREEMAN, *Schools of Hellas* (2nd ed., London, 1912).

P. GIRARD, *L'éducation athénienne* (2nd ed., Paris, 1891).

L. H. JEFFERY, *The Local Scripts of Archaic Greece* (Oxford, 1961).

F. G. KENYON, *Books and Readers in Ancient Greece and Rome* (2nd ed., Oxford, 1951).

A. KIRCHHOFF, *Studien zur Geschichte des griechischen Alphabets* (4th ed., Gutersloh, 1887).

J. VAN LEEUWEN and M. B. MENDES DA COSTA, *Der Dialekt der homerischen Gedichte* (aus dem holländischen übersetzt von E. Mehler, Leipzig, 1886).

H. I. MARROU, *Histoire de l'éducation dans l'antiquité* (Paris, 1948).

A. MEILLET, *Aperçu d'une histoire de la langue grecque* (3rd ed., Paris, 1930).

M. P. NILSSON, *Die hellenistische Schule* (München, 1955).

W. SCHUBART, *Das Buch bei den Griechen und Römern* (3rd ed., by E. Paul, Leipzig, 1961).

A. THUMB, *Handbuch der griechischen Dialekte* (2nd ed., by E. Kieckers and A. Scherer, Heidelberg, 1959).

3. *Science and Technology*

H. BERGER, *Geschichte der wissenschaftlichen Erdkunde der Griechen* (2nd ed., Leipzig, 1903).

F. BOLL, *Studien zur Geschichte des antiken Weltbildes und der griechischen Wissenschaft* (Leipzig, 1914–21), 6 vols.

G. E. BROCHE, *La première en date des explorations polaires: Pythéas le Massaliote* (Nîmes, 1928).

H. DIESS, 'Hippokratische Studien', *Hermes*, XLV (1910); 'Hippokratische Forschungen', *Hermes*, XLVI, XLVIII, LIII (1911, 1913, 1918).

A. G. DRACHMANN, *The Mechanical Technology of Greek and Roman Antiquity* (Copenhagen, 1963).

B. FARRINGTON, *Greek Science and its Meaning For Us* (Harmondsworth, 1953).

T. HEATH, *Aristarchus of Samos* (2nd ed., Oxford, 1913).

T. HEATH, *Greek Mathematics* (Oxford, 1921).

J. L. HEIBERG, *Naturwissenschaften und Mathematik im klassischen Altertum* (Leipzig, 1912).

C. MUGLER, *La physique de Platon* (Paris, 1960).

S. SAMBURSKY, *Physics of the Stoics* (London, 1959).

S. SAMBURSKY, *The Physical World of the Greeks* (London, 1956).

G. SARTON, *A History of Science* (Oxford, 1953), 2 vols.

C. SINGER, *Greek Biology and Greek Medicine* (Oxford, 1922).

C. SINGER, 'The Herbal in Antiquity', *Journal of Hellenic Studies*, XLVII (1927).

F. SOLMSEN, *Aristotle's System of the Physical World* (New York, 1960).

P. TANNERY, *La géométrie grecque* (Paris, 1887).

4. *Economics, Agriculture, Trade and Industry; Coinage*

E. ARDAILLON, *Les mines du Laurion dans l'antiquité* (Paris, 1897).

E. BABELON, *Traité de monnaies grecques et romaines* (Paris, 1901–32), 9 vols.

K. J. BELOCH, *Die Bevölkerung der griechisch-römischen Welt* (Leipzig, 1886).

G. M. CALHOUN, *The Business Life of Ancient Athens* (Chicago, 1926).

L. EINAUDI, *Greatness and Decline of Planned Economy in the Hellenistic World* (tr. by R. H. F. Dalton, Berne, 1950).

H. FRANCOTTE, *L'industrie dans la Grèce ancienne* (Bruxelles, 1900).

G. GLOTZ, *Le travail dans la Grèce ancienne* (Paris, 1920).

P. GUIRAUD, *La main-d'œuvre industrielle dans l'ancienne Grèce* (Paris, 1900).

J. HASEBROEK, *Griechische Wirtschafts- und Gesellschaftsgeschichte bis zur Perserzeit* (Tübingen, 1931).

B. V. HEAD, *A Guide to the Principal Coins of the Greeks from circa 700 to 270 AD* (2nd ed., rev. by G. F. Hill and J. Walker, London, 1959).

B. V. HEAD, *Historia Numorum: A Manual of Greek Numismatics* (2nd ed., Oxford, 1911).

W. E. HEITLAND, *Agricola: A Study of Agriculture and Rustic Life in the Graeco-Roman World, from the Point of View of Labour* (Cambridge, 1921).

G. F. HILL, *Historical Greek Coins* (London, 1906).

H. MICHELL, *The Economics of Ancient Greece* (2nd ed., Cambridge, 1957).

J. G. MILNE, *Greek Coinage* (Oxford, 1931).

L. A. MORITZ, *Grain-mills and Flour in Classical Antiquity* (Oxford, 1958).

F. OERTEL, *Die Liturgie* (Leipzig, 1917).

M. ROSTOVTZEFF, *The Social and Economic History of the Hellenistic World* (2nd ed., Oxford, 1953), 3 vols.

C. T. SELTMAN, *Greek Coins* (2nd ed., London, 1955).

E. ZIEBARTH, *Beiträge zur Geschichte des Seeraubs und Seehandels im alten Griechenland* (Hamburg, 1929).

5. *Political Theory and Institutions, Law and Social Life; War*

F. E. ADCOCK, *The Greek and Macedonian Art of War* (Berkeley, 1959).

A. AYMARD, *Les assemblées de la confédération achéenne* (Paris, 1938).

M. BIELER, *Griechische Kleidung* (Berlin, etc., 1928).

E. BIKERMAN, *Institutions des Séleucides* (Paris, 1938).

H. BLUEMNER, *Griechische Privataltertümer* (Vol. IV of K. F. Hermann, *Lehrbuch der griechischen Altertümer*) (3rd ed., Fribourg, etc., 1882).

G. BUSOLT, *Griechische Staatskunde* (3rd ed. of *Die griechischen Staats- und Rechtsaltertümer*, München, 1920–26), 2 vols.

J. CARCOPINO, *L'ostracisme athénien* (Paris, 1935).

M. CLERC, *Les métèques athéniens* (Paris, 1893).

W. ERDMANN, *Die Ehe im alten Griechenland* (München, 1934).

H. FRANCOTTE, *De la condition des étrangers dans les cités grecques* (Liège, etc., 1910).

E. A. FREEMAN, *A History of Federal Government in Greece and Italy* (22nd ed., by J. B. Bury, London, 1893).

K. FREEMAN, *Greek City-States* (London, 1950).

E. N. GARDINER, *Athletics of the Ancient World* (Oxford, 1930).

P. GERHARDT, *Die attische Metoikie im vierten Jahrhundert* (Königsberg, 1933).

G. GLOTZ, *La cité grecque* (2nd ed., Paris, 1953).

C. HIGNETT, *A History of the Athenian Constitution* (Oxford, 1952).

A. H. M. JONES, *The Greek City from Alexander to Justinian* (Oxford, 1940).

J. W. JONES, *The Law and Legal Theory of the Greeks* (Oxford, 1956).

F. KAMPERS, *Alexander der Grosse und die Idee des Weltimperiums in Prophetie und Sage* (Freiburg, 1906).

J. KROMAYER et al., *Heerwesen und Kriegsführung der Griechen und Römer* (*Handbücher der Altertumswissenschaft*, IV, 3, 2), (München, 1928).

M. LAUNEY, *Recherches sur les armées hellénistiques* (Paris, 1949–50), 2 vols.

R. MARTIN, *L'urbanisation dans la Grèce antique* (Paris, 1956).

V. MARTIN, *La vie internationale dans la Grèce des cités* (Paris, 1940).

C. MASSÉ, *La fin de la démocratie athénienne* (Paris, 1962).

M. H. E. MEIER and G. F. SCHÖNEMANN, *Das attische Recht und Rechtsverfahren* (dargestellt von J. H. Lipsius, Leipzig, 1905–15), 3 vols.

I. VON MÜLLER, *Griechische Privataltertümer* (*Handbücher der klassischen Altertumswissenschaft*, IV, 1, 2), (München, 1893).

W. L. RODGERS, *Greek and Roman Naval Warfare* (Annapolis, 1937).

T. A. SINCLAIR, *A History of Greek Political Thought* (London, 1952).

W. W. TARN, *Hellenistic Military and Naval Developments* (Cambridge, 1930).

M. N. TOD, *International Arbitration among the Greeks* (Oxford, 1913).

R. F. WILLETTS, *Aristocratic Society in Ancient Crete* (London, 1955).

E. WOLF, *Griechisches Rechtsdenken* (Frankfurt, 1950–56), 3 vols. in 4.

P. ZANCAN, *Il monarcato ellenistico nei suoi elementi federativi* (Padova, 1934).

A. ZIMMERN, *The Greek Commonwealth* (5th ed., Oxford, 1931).

6. *Religion and Astrology*

F. BÖMER, "Untersuchungen über die Religion der Sklaven in Griechenland und Rom", Mainz, *Akademie der Wissenschaften und der Literatur* (1957, nr. 7; 1960, nr. 1; 1961, nr. 4).

F. BROMMER, *Herakles* (Münster, etc., 1953).

L. CERFAUX and J. TONDRIAU, *Le culte des souverains dans la civilisation gréco-romaine* (Louvain, 1956).

A. B. COOK, *Zeus* (Cambridge, 1914–40).

F. CUMONT, *Astrology and Religion among the Greeks and Romans* (New York, 1912).

M. DELCOURT, *L'oracle de Delphes* (Paris, 1955).

E. R. DODDS, *The Greeks and the Irrational* (Berkeley, etc., 1951).

E. J. and L. EDELSTEIN, *Asclepius* (Baltimore, 1946), 2 vols.

L. R. FARNELL, *The Cults of the Greek States* (Oxford, 1896–1909), 5 vols.

A. J. FESTUGIÈRE, *La révélation d'Hermès Trismégiste* (Paris, 1944–54), 4 vols.

A. J. FESTUGIÈRE, *Personal Religion among the Greeks* (Berkeley, etc., 1954).

F. C. GRANT, *Hellenistic Religions* (New York, 1953).

H. GRESSMANN, *Die orientalischen Religionen im hellenistisch-römischen Zeitalter* (Berlin, etc., 1930).

W. K. C. GUTHRIE, *The Greeks and their Gods* (London, 1950).

R. HERBIG, *Pan* (Frankfurt, 1949).

H. JEANMAIRE, *Dionysos* (Paris, 1951).

V. MAGNIEN, *Les mystères d'Eleusis* (3rd ed., Paris, 1950).

L. MOULNIER, *Orphée et l'orphisme à l'époque classique* (Paris, 1955).

G. MURRAY, *Four Stages of Greek Religion* (London, 1912).

M. P. NILSSON, *Geschichte der griechischen Religion* (München, 1941).

M. P. NILSSON, *The Dionysiac Mysteries of the Hellenistic and Roman Age* (Lund, 1957).

M. P. NILSSON, *The Rise of Astrology in the Hellenistic Age* (Lund, 1943).

K. PFEIFF, *Apollon* (Frankfurt, 1943).

L. PRELLER, *Griechische Mythologie* (4th ed., by C. Robert, Berlin, 1894–1921), 2 vols.

L. RADERMACHER, *Mythos und Sage bei den Griechen* (Baden, etc., 1938).

R. REITZENSTEIN, *Die hellenistischen Mysterienreligionen* (3rd ed., Berlin, 1927).

W. H. ROSCHER, *Ausführliches Lexikon der griechischen und römischen Mythologie* (Leipzig, 1884–1937), Vols. I–VI, and Supplement 1–4.

H. J. ROSE, *A Handbook of Greek Mythology* (6th ed., London, 1958).

J. RUDHARDT, *Notions fondamentales de la pensée religieuse et actes constitutifs du culte dans la Grèce classique* (Genève, 1958).

7. *Philosophy*

A. W. H. ADKINS, *Merit and Responsibility* (Oxford, 1960).

A. H. ARMSTRONG, *Introduction to Ancient Philosophy* (3rd ed., London, 1957).

C. BAILEY, *The Greek Atomists and Epicurus* (Oxford, 1928).

E. BEVAN, *Stoics and Sceptics* (Oxford, 1913).

E. BIGNONE, *Empedocle* (Torino, 1916).

F. BUFFIÈRE, *Les mythes d'Homère et la pensée grecque* (Paris, 1956).

F. M. CORNFORD, *Plato and Parmenides* (London, 1939).

F. M. CORNFORD, *Principium Sapientiae* (Cambridge, 1952).

D. R. DUDLEY, *A History of Cynicism* (London, 1937).

A. J. FESTUGIÈRE, *Epicurus and his Gods* (tr. by C. W. Chilton, Oxford, 1955).

P. FRIEDLÄNDER, *Plato, an Introduction* (tr. by H. Meyerhoff, London, 1958).

T. GOMPERZ, *Greek Thinkers* (tr. by L. Magnus and G. Berry, London, 1901–12), 4 vols.

W. K. C. GUTHRIE, *A History of Greek Philosophy* (Cambridge, 1962), Vol. I.

W. JAEGER, *Aristotle* (tr. by R. Robinson, 2nd ed., Oxford, 1948).

W. JAEGER, *Paideia* (tr. by G. Highet from the 2nd German ed., Oxford, 1939–49), 3 vols.

C. H. KAHN, *Anaximander and the Origins of Greek Cosmology* (New York, 1910).

G. S. KIRK and J. E. RAVEN, *The Presocratic Philosophers* (Cambridge, 1957).

I. LÉVY, *Recherches sur les sources de la légende de Pythagore* (Paris, 1927).

N. R. MURPHY, *The Interpretation of Plato's Republic* (Oxford, 1951).

L. PEARSON, *Popular Ethics in Ancient Greece* (Oxford, 1962).

K. REINHARDT, *Parmenides und die Geschichte der griechischen Philosophie* (Bonn, 1916).

L. ROBIN, *La pensée grecque* (2nd ed., Paris, 1948).

R. ROBINSON, *Plato's Earlier Dialectic* (2nd ed., Oxford, 1953).

W. D. ROSS, *Aristotle* (5th ed., London, 1949; repr. 1956).

W. D. ROSS, *Plato's Theory of Ideas* (Oxford, 1951).

M. SOLOVINE, *Démocrite* (Paris, 1928).

J. STENZEL, *Zahl und Gestalt bei Plato und Aristoteles* (3rd ed., Bad Hamburg vor der Höhe, 1959).

M. VAN STRAATEN, *Panétius* (Amsterdam, 1946).

R. STRÖMBERG, *Theophrasten* (These, Göteborg, 1937).

A. E. TAYLOR, *Aristotle* (2nd ed., London, etc., 1919).

A. E. TAYLOR, *Plato, the Man and his Work* (4th ed. rev., London, 1937).

H. THESLEFF, *An Introduction to the Pythagorean Writings of the Hellenistic Period* (Åbo, 1961).

F. ÜBERWEG *et al.*, *Grundriss der Geschichte der Philosophie* (12th ed., 1926), Vol. I.

G. VALLAURI, *Origine e diffusione dell' evemerismo nel pensiero classico* (Torino, 1960).

C. J. DE VOGEL, *Greek Philosophy* (Leiden, 1950–59), 3 vols.

U. VON WILAMOWITZ-MOELLENDORFF, *Der Glaube der Hellenen* (Berlin, 1931–32), 2 vols.

U. VON WILAMOWITZ-MOELLENDORFF, *Platon* (2nd ed., Berlin, 1920).

E. ZELLER, *Die Philosophie der Griechen in ihrer geschichtlichen Entwicklung dargestellt*, II, 1: *Sokrates und die Sokratiker. Plato und die alte Akademie* (3rd ed., Leipzig, 1875).

A. N. ZOUMPOS, *Herakleitos von Ephesos als Staatsmann und Gesetzgeber* (Athens, 1956).

8. Literature

a. *Homer* (see also under Aegean Civilization)

P. BAUER, *Grundfragen der Homerkritik* (3rd ed., Leipzig, 1923).

V. BÉRARD, *Introduction à l'Odyssée* (Paris, 1924–25), 3 vols.

C. M. BOWRA, *Homer and his Forerunners* (Edinburgh, 1955).

G. S. KIRK, *The Songs of Homer* (London, 1962).

D. PAGE, *The Homeric Odyssey* (Oxford, 1955).

K. REINHARDT, *Die Ilias und ihr Dichter* (Göttingen, 1961).

G. P. SHIPP, *Studies in the Language of Homer* (Cambridge, 1953).

U. VON WILAMOWITZ-MOELLENDORFF, *Die griechische und lateinische Literatur und Sprache* (2nd ed., Berlin, 1907).

U. VON WILAMOWITZ-MOELLENDORFF, *Die Heimkehr des Odysseus* (Berlin, 1927).

U. VON WILAMOWITZ-MOELLENDORFF, *Die Ilias und Homer* (2nd ed., Berlin, 1920).

W. J. WOODHOUSE, *The Composition of Homer's Odyssey* (Oxford, 1930).

b. *Poetry*

C. M. BOWRA, *Early Greek Elegists* (Cambridge, Mass., 1938).

C. M. BOWRA, *Greek Lyric Poetry* (Oxford, 1936).

R. W. B. BURTON, *Pindar's Pythian Odes* (Oxford, 1962).

E. HARRISON, *Studies in Theognis* (Cambridge, 1902).

A. KÖRTÉ, *Die hellenistische Dichtung* (2nd ed., by P. Händel, Stuttgart, 1960).

G. NORWOOD, *Pindar* (Berkeley, 1945).

D. PAGE, *Sappho and Alcaeus* (Oxford, 1955).

F. SCHWENN, *Die Theogonie des Hesiodes* (Heidelberg, 1934).

F. SOLMSEN, *Hesiod and Aeschylus* (New York, 1949).

U. VON WILAMOWITZ-MOELLENDORFF, *Hellenistische Dichtung in der Zeit des Kallimachos* (Berlin, 1924), 2 vols.

U. VON WILAMOWITZ-MOELLENDORFF, *Pindaros* (Berlin, 1922).

U. VON WILAMOWITZ-MOELLENDORFF, *Sappho und Simonides* (Berlin, 1913).

F. A. WRIGHT, *A History of Later Greek Literature* (London, 1932).

c. *Theatre*

i. *General*

M. BIEBER, *The History of the Greek and Roman Theatre* (Princeton, 1961).

H. D. F. KITTO, *Greek Tragedy* (London, 1939).

P. E. LEGRAND, *The New Greek Comedy* (tr. by J. Loeb, London, 1917).

A. LESKY, *Die griechische Tragödie* (2nd ed., Stuttgart, 1958).

O. NAVARRE, *Le théâtre grec* (Paris, 1925).

G. NORWOOD, *Greek Comedy* (London, 1931).

A. PICKARD-CAMBRIDGE, *Dithyramb, Tragedy, and Comedy* (2nd ed., by T. B. L. Webster, Oxford, 1962).

A. PICKARD-CAMBRIDGE, *The Theatre of Dionysus at Athens* (Oxford, 1946).

R. REICH, *Der Mimus* (Berlin, 1903).

T. B. L. WEBSTER, *Greek Theatre Production* (London, 1956).

U. VON WILAMOWITZ-MOELLENDORFF, *Einleitung in die griechische Tragödie* (Berlin, 1907).

ii. *Sophocles*

C. M. BOWRA, *Sophoclean Tragedy* (Oxford, 1944).

T. B. L. WEBSTER, *An Introduction to Sophocles* (Oxford, 1936).

H. WEINSTOCK, *Sophokles* (3rd ed., Wuppertal, 1948).

T. VON WILAMOWITZ, *Die dramatische Technik des Sophokles* (Berlin, 1917).

iii. *Euripides*

W. H. FRIEDRICH, *Euripides* (München, 1953).

W. NESTLE, *Euripides* (Stuttgart, 1901).

iv. *Aristophanes*

V. EHRENBERG, *The People of Aristophanes* (Oxford, 1951).

P. MAZON, *Essai sur la composition des comédies d'Aristophane* (Paris, 1904).

G. MURRAY, *Aristophanes, a Study* (Oxford, 1933).

v. *Aeschylus*

G. MURRAY, *Aeschylus* (Oxford, 1940).

d. *History, Biography, Criticism*

J. W. H. ATKINS, *Literary Criticism in Antiquity* (London, 1952), 2 vols.

G. L. BARBER, *The Historian Ephorus* (Cambridge, 1935).

O. CUNTZ, *Polybius und seine Werke* (Leipzig, 1902).

J. F. DOBSON, *The Greek Orators* (London, 1919).

A. W. GOMME, *A Historical Commentary on Thucydides* (Oxford, 1945–56), 3 vols.

F. JACOBY, *Atthis* (Oxford, 1949).

F. LEE, *Die griechisch-römische Biographie* (Leipzig, 1901).

E. MEYER, *Theopomps Hellenika* (Halle, 1909).

J. L. MYRES, *Herodotus, Father of History* (Oxford, 1933).

E. NORDEN, *Die antike Kunstprosa* (2nd ed., Leipzig, 1909).

L. PEARSON, *The Early Ionian Historians* (Oxford, 1939).

E. ROHDE, *Der griechische Roman und seine Vorläufer* (3rd ed., Leipzig, 1914).

M. UNTERSTEINER, *I Sofisti* (Torino, 1949).

9. *Art*

a. *General*

R. CARPENTER, *Greek Art* (Pennsylvania, 1962).

G. M. A. RICHTER, *Archaic Greek Art* (New York, 1949).

D. SCHLUMBERGER, *Descendants non méditerranéens de l'art grec* (Paris, 1960).

b. *Architecture and City Planning*

W. B. DINSMOOR, *The Architecture of Ancient Greece* (London, 1950).

W. DÖRPFELD, *Alt-Olympia* (Berlin, 1935), 2 vols.

J. DURM, *Die Baukunst der Griechen* (3rd ed., Leipzig, 1910).

T. FYFE, *Hellenistic Architecture* (Cambridge, 1936).

E. N. GARDINER, *Olympia, its History and Remains* (Oxford, 1925).

A. VON GERKAN, *Griechische Städteanlage* (Berlin, etc., 1924).

I. C. T. HILL, *The Ancient City of Athens* (London, 1953).

D. S. ROBERTSON, *Greek and Roman Architecture* (2nd ed., Cambridge, 1943).

R. E. WYCHERLEY, *How the Greeks Built Cities* (2nd ed., London, 1962).

c. *Sculpture*

J. D. BEAZLEY and B. ASHMOLE, *Greek Sculpture and Painting* (Cambridge, 1932).

C. BLINKENBERG, *Polykleitus* (Kjøbenhavn, 1920).

S. CASSON, *The Technique of Early Greek Sculpture* (Oxford, 1933).

J. CHARBONNEAUX, *Les bronzes grecs* (Paris, 1958).

G. DICKENS, *Hellenistic Sculpture* (Oxford, 1920).

E. A. GARDINER, *Handbook of Greek Sculpture* (3rd ed., London, 1920).

F. P. JOHNSON, *Lysippos* (Durham, N.C., 1927).

W. LAMB, *Greek and Roman Bronzes* (London, 1929).

A. W. LAWRENCE, *Classical Sculpture* (London, 1929).

A. W. LAWRENCE, *Later Greek Sculpture* (London, 1927).

G. LIPPOLD, *Griechische Porträtstatuen* (München, 1912).

G. M. A. RICHTER, *Kouroi* (2nd ed., New York, 1960).

G. M. A. RICHTER, *Three Critical Periods in Greek Sculpture* (Oxford, 1951).

G. E. RIZZO, *Prassitele* (Milano, etc., 1932).

G. RODENWALDT, *Das Relief bei den Griechen* (Berlin, 1923).

d. *Pottery and Painting*

J. D. BEAZLEY, *Attic Black-figure Vase-Painters* (Oxford, 1956).

J. D. BEAZLEY, *Attic Red-figure Vase-Painters* (2nd ed., Oxford, 1962).

J. D. BEAZLEY, *Attische Vasenmaler des rotfigurigen Stils* (Tübingen, 1925).

J. D. BEAZLEY, *The Development of Attic Black-figure* (Berkeley, etc., 1951).

V. R. d'A. DESBOROUGH, *Protogeometric Pottery* (Oxford, 1952).

A. LANE, *Greek Pottery* (London, 1948).

G. LIPPOLD, *Gemmen und Kameen des Altertums und der Neuzeit* (Stuttgart, 1922).

E. LÖWY, *Polygnot* (Wien, 1929).

E. PFUHL, *Masterpieces of Greek Drawing and Painting* (tr. by J. D. Beazley, London, 1926).

S. REINACH, *Répertoire des peintures grecques et romaines* (2nd ed., Paris, 1929).

XXI. CARTHAGE

G. and C. CHARLES-PICARD, *La vie quotidienne à Carthage au temps d'Hannibal* (Paris, 1958).

V. EHRENBERG, *Karthago* (Leipzig, 1927).

A. GARCIA Y BELLIDO, *Fenicios y Carthaginenses en occidente* (Madrid, 1942).

E. GROAG, *Hannibal als Politiker* (Wien, 1929).

S. GSELL, *Histoire ancienne d'Afrique du nord* (Paris, 1920–28), 8 vols. (3rd ed. of Vol. I).

A. LÉZINÉ, *Architecture punique* (Paris, n.d.).

H. R. PALMER, *The Carthaginian Voyage to West Africa, 500 BC* (Bathurst, 1931).

XXII. PRE-ROMAN SPAIN AND GAUL: GERMANY AND EASTERN EUROPE

1. *History and General Works*

F. ALTHEIM, *Geschichte der Hunnen* (Berlin, 1959–62), 5 vols.

J. C. BAROJA, *España primitiva y romana* (Barcelona, 1957).

P. BOSCH-GIMPERA, *Etnologia de la península iberica* (Barcelona, 1932).

P. BOSCH-GIMPERA, *Two Celtic Waves in Spain* (*Proceedings of the British Academy*, XXVI) (London, 1940).

P. BOSCH-GIMPERA, 'La formazione dei popoli della Spagna', *La parola del passato*, IV (1949).

W. CAPELLE, *Das alte Germanien* (Jena, 1929).

V. G. CHILDE, *The Danube in Prehistory* (Oxford, 1929).

A. GARCÍA Y BELLIDO, *La península iberica* (Madrid, 1953).

S. HOMMERBERG, *Hallstattidens Relativa Kronologi* (Lund, etc., 1946).

H. HUBERT, *Les Celtes et l'expansion celtique jusqu'à l'époque de la Tène* (Paris, 1932).

H. HUBERT, *Les Celtes depuis l'époque de la Tène et la civilisation celtique* (2nd ed., Paris, 1950).

H. HUBERT, *Les Germains* (Paris, 1952).

C. JULLIAN, *Histoire de la Gaule* (Paris, 1920–26), 8 vols.

G. KAZAROW, *Beiträge zur Kulturgeschichte der Thraker* (Sarajevo, 1916).

N. KONDAKOF *et al.*, *Antiquités de la Russie méridionale* (Paris, 1891).

G. KOSSINA, *Ursprung und Verbreitung der Germanen in vor- und frühgeschichtlicher Zeit* (Leipzig, 1928).

J. MARKWART, "Iberia und Hyrkanier", *Caucasia*, VIII (1931).

E. MINNS, *Scythians and Greeks* (Cambridge, 1913).

J. MOREAU, *Die Welt der Kelten* (Stuttgart, 1959).

E. and J. NEUSTUPNÝ, *Czechoslovakia before the Slavs* (London, 1961).

F. C. OXENSTIERNE, *Die Nordgermanen* (Stuttgart, 1957).

V. PARVAN, *Dacia, an Outline of the Early Civilizations of the Carpatho-Danubian Countries* (Cambridge, 1928).

H. PEAKE, *The Bronze Age and the Celtic World* (London, 1922).

R. M. PIDAL, *Historia d'España* (Madrid, 1947–54), Tome I, Vols. 1–3.

R. PITTIONI, 'Zum Herkunftsgebiet der Kelten', *Österreichische Akademie der Wissenschaft*, Phil.-Hist. Klasse, *Sitzungsberichte*, 233, Band III (1959).

J. POKORNY, *Zur Urgeschichte der Kelten und Illyrier* (Halle, 1938).

A. RANDA, *Der Balkan, Schlüsselraum der Weltgeschichte: von Thrake zu Byzanz* (Graz, etc., 1949).

M. I. ROSTOVTZEFF, *Iranians and Greeks in South Russia* (Oxford, 1922).

M. I. ROSTOVTZEFF, *Scythien und der Bosporus* (tr. by E. Pridik, Berlin, 1931), vol. I.

L. SCHMIDT, *Geschichte der Wandalen* (2nd ed., München, 1942).

H. SCHNEIDER, *Germanische Altertumskunde* (München, 1951).

A. SCHULTEN, *Tartessus* (2nd ed., Hamburg, 1950).

M. STENBERGER, *Sweden* (London, n.d.).

T. TALBOT RICE, *The Scythians* (London, 1957).

E. TÄUBLER, "Zur Geschichte der Alanen", *Klio*, IX (1909).

E. WAHLE, *Deutsche Vorzeit* (Basel, 1952).

2. *Language and Writing*

H. ARNTZ, *Handbuch der Runenkunde* (2nd ed., Halle, 1954).

A. HOLDER, *Alt-celtischer Sprachschatz* (Leipzig, 1896–1913), 2 vols.

L. JACOBSEN and E. MOLTKE, *Danmarks Runeindskrifter* (København, 1941–42), 2 vols.

3. *Science and Economics*

J. D. G. CLARKE, *Prehistoric Europe: the Economic Basis* (London, 1952).

H. DELBRÜCK, *Geschichte der Kriegskunst im Rahmen der politischen Geschichte*, II: *Die Germanen* (3rd ed., Berlin, 1921).

A. RIETH, *Die Eisentechnik der Hallstattzeit* (Leipzig, 1942).

4. Religion

J. M. BLASQUEZ MARTINEZ, *Religiones primitivas de Hispania*, I: *Fuentes literarias y epigrafias* (Madrid, 1962).

C. CLEMEN, *Altgermanische Religionsgeschichte* (Bonn, 1934).

P. M. DUVAL, *Les dieux de la Gaule* (Paris, 1957).

J. GRIMM, *Deutsche Mythologie* (Berlin, 1875–78), 3 vols.

P. LAMBRECHTS, *Contributions à l'étude des divinités celtiques* (Bruges, 1942).

E. PETERICH, *Götter und Helden der·Germanen* (5th ed., Olten, etc., 1955).

M. L. SJOESTEDT, *Dieux et héros des Celtes* (Paris, 1940).

J. VENDRYÈS et al., *Les religions des Celtes, des Germains et des anciens Slaves* (Paris, 1948).

J. DE VRIES, *Altgermanische Religionsgeschichte* (2nd ed., Berlin, 1956–57), 2 vols.

J. DE VRIES, *Keltische Religion* (Stuttgart, 1961).

5. Art

M. ALMAGRO et al., *Ars Hispaniae* (Madrid, 1947), 2 vols.

J. C. AZNAR, *Los artes y los pueblos de la España primitiva* (Madrid, 1954).

P. JACOBSTHAL, *Early Celtic Art* (Oxford, 1944), 2 vols.

H. PICTON, *Early German Art and its Origins* (London, 1939).

A. VARAGNAC et al., *L'art gaulois* (Paris, 1956).

XXIII. PRE-ROMAN ITALY

1. General Works

G. DEVOTO, *Gli antichi Italici* (2nd ed., Firenze, 1951).

G. DEVOTO, 'Illiri, Tirreni, Piceni', *Studi Etruschi*, XI (1937).

F. VON DUHN, *Italische Gräberkunde* (Heidelberg, 1924–39), 2 vols.

G. PATRONI, 'Intorno alle popolazioni dell'Italia preromana', *Antiquitas* (1946).

G. PATRONI, *La preistoria (Storia politica d'Italia)*, (2nd ed., Milano, 1951), 2 vols.

D. RANDALL-MACIVER, *Italy before the Romans* (Oxford, 1928).

J. WHATMOUGH, *The Foundations of Roman Italy* (London, 1937).

2. Language and Writing

M. BEELER, *The Venetic Language* (Berkeley, 1949).

C. D. BUCK, *A Grammar of Oscan and Umbrian* (2nd ed., Boston, etc., 1928).

R. S. CONWAY, *The Italic Dialects* (Cambridge, 1897), 2 vols.

A. ERNOUT, *Le dialecte ombrien: lexique du vocabulaire des 'Tables Eugubines' et des inscriptions* (Paris, 1961).

J. WHATMOUGH, *The Prae-Italic Dialects of Italy* (London, 1933).

3. *Social Life*

L. E. W. ADAMS, *A Study in the Commerce of Latium from the early Iron Age through the Sixth Century* (Menasha, Wisconsin, c. 1917).

E. ROSENBERG, *Der Staat der alten Italiker* (Berlin, 1913).

4. *Religion*

F. ALTHEIM, *Terra Mater: Untersuchungen zur altitalischen Religionsgeschichte* (Giessen, 1931).

XXIV. THE ETRUSCANS

1. *General Works and History*

F. ALTHEIM, *Der Ursprung der Etrusker* (Baden-Baden, 1950).

J. BÉRARD, 'La question des origines étrusques', *Revue des études anciennes*, LI (1949).

P. BOSCH-GIMPERA, 'Le relazioni mediterranee postmicenee ed il problema etrusco', *Studi Etruschi*, III (1929).

P. DUCATI, *Etruria antica* (Torino [1925]), 2 vols.

M. PALLOTTINO, *Etruscologia* (3rd ed., Milano, 1955).

M. PALLOTTINO, *L'origine degli Etruschi* (Roma, 1947).

L. PARETI, *Le origini etrusche* (Firenze, 1926).

A. PIGANIOL, 'Les Etrusques, peuple d'orient', *Cahiers d'histoire mondiale*, I (1953-54).

A. SCHULTEN, 'Die Tyrsener in Spanien', *Klio*, XXXIII, 1-2 (1940).

2. *Language and Writing*

A. J. CHARSEKIN, *Zur Deutung etruskischer Sprachdenkmäler* (forthcoming).

Corpus Inscriptionum Etruscarum (Lipsiae, 1893), 2 vols. and supplement.

S. P. CORTSEN, 'L'inscription de Lemnos', *Latomus*, II (1928).

M. PALLOTTINO, *Epigrafia e lingua etrusca* (Roma, 1950).

M. PALLOTTINO, *Testimonia linguae etruscae* (Firenze, 1954).

3. *Political and Social Life*

J. HEURGON, *La vie privée chez les Etrusques* (Paris, 1962).

G. PAPSÀOGLI, *L'agricoltura degli Etruschi e dei Romani* (Roma, 1942).

L. PARETI, 'La disunione politica degli Etruschi e suoi riflessi storici ed archeologici', *Atti de la pontifica romana di archeologia, Rendiconti*, Ser. III, Vol. VIII, *annate accademiche 1929-1931* (1932).

4. *Religion*

C. CLEMEN, *Die Religion der Etrusker: Untersuchungen zur allgemeinen Religionsgeschichte* (Bonn, 1936).

C. O. THULIN, *Die etruskische Disciplina; I: Die Blitzlehre* (Göteborg, 1906).

5. *Art*

J. D. BEAZLEY, *Etruscan Vase-painting* (Oxford, 1947).

P. DUCATI, *Storia dell'arte etrusca* (Firenze, 1927), 2 vols.

L. GOLDSCHEIDER, *Etruscan Sculpture* (London, 1941).

M. PALLOTTINO, *Etruscan Painting* (tr. by M. E. Stanley and S. Gilbert, Geneva, 1952).

M. PALLOTTINO, *Etruskische Kunst* (tr. by F. Hindermann, Zürich, 1955).

P. J. RIIS, *An Introduction to Etruscan Art* (Copenhagen, 1953).

P. J. RIIS, *Tyrrhenika* (Copenhagen, 1941).

O.-W. VON VACANO, *Die Etrusker* (Stuttgart, 1955).

XXV. ROME AND THE ROMAN EMPIRE
(for works covering both Classical Greece and Rome, see under CLASSICAL GREECE)

1. *General Works and History* (see also under Constitution, etc.)
A. Early History and the Republic

F. ALTHEIM, *Italien und Rom* (3rd ed., Amsterdam, etc., n.d.), 2 vols.

A. AYMARD, *Les premiers rapports de Rome et de la Confédération achaienne* (Paris, 1938).

E. BADIAN, *Foreign Clientelae (264–70 BC)* (Oxford, 1958).

R. L. BEAUMONT, 'The Date of the First Treaty between Rome and Carthage', *Journal of Roman Studies*, XXIX (1939).

J. CARCOPINO, *Autour des Gracques* (Paris, 1928).

J. CARCOPINO, *Les secrets de la correspondence de Cicéron* (Paris, 1947), 2 vols.

J. CARCOPINO, *Sylla ou la monarchie manquée* (Paris, 1931).

E. CIACERI, *Cicerone e i suoi tempi* (Milano, etc., 1926–30), 2 vols.

W. DRUMANN, *Geschichte Roms in seinem Übergange von der republikanischen zur monarchischen Verfassung* (2nd ed., by P. Groebe, Berlin, etc., 1899–1929), 6 vols.

B. FERRO, 'Le origini della II guerra macedonica', *Atti della Accademia di scienze, lettere e arti di Palermo*, Ser. IV, vol. XIX, parte II, lettere, anno 1958–9 (1960).

M. GELZER, *Caesar der Politiker und Staatsmann* (2nd ed., München, 1940).

A. GRENIER, *Le génie romain* (Paris, 1926).

E. G. HARDY, *The Catilinarian Conspiracy in its Context* (Oxford, 1924) (reprinted from the *Journal of Roman Studies*, VII (1917)).

M. HOLLEAUX, *Rome, la Grèce et les monarchies hellénistiques* (Paris, 1921).

M. LEVI, *Ottaviano capoparte* (Firenze, 1933), 2 vols.

J. MARQUARDT and T. MOMMSEN, *Handbuch der römischen Altertümer* (Leipzig, 1879–88), 9 vols.

S. MAZZARINO, *Dalla monarchia allo stato repubblicano* (Catania, 1945).

S. MAZZARINO, *Introduzione alle guerre puniche* (Catania, 1947).

E. MEYER, *Caesars Monarchie und das Principat des Pompejus* (2nd ed., 1919).

T. MOMMSEN, *Römische Geschichte* (various ed., Berlin, 1865–1954), 5 vols.

E. PAIS, *Storia di Roma dall' età regia alle vittorie su Tarento e Pirro* (Torino, 1934).

E. PAIS, *Storia di Roma durante le guerre puniche* (2nd ed., Torino, 1935).

L. PARETI, *Storia di Roma e del mondo romano* (Torino, 1952–61), 6 vols.

R. PARIBENI, *Le origine e il periodo regio* (*Storia di Roma*, I) (Bologna, 1954).

S. M. PUGLISI et al., 'Gli abitatori primitivi del Palatino attraverso le testimonianze archeologiche e le nuove stratigrafiche sul Germalo', *Monumenti antichi*, XLI (1951).

L. DE REGIBUS, *La repubblica romana e gli ultimi re di Macedonia* (Genova, 1951).

M. REINHOLD, *Marcus Agrippa* (Geneva, N.Y., etc., 1933).

T. RICE HOLMES, *Caesar's Conquest of Gaul* (2nd ed., Oxford, 1911).

A. ROSENBERG, 'Zur Geschichte des Latinerbundes', *Hermes*, LIV (1919).

G. DE SANCTIS, *Storia dei Romani* (Torino, etc., 1907–57), 4 vols. in 6.

M. L. SCEVOLA, 'Una testimonianza trascurata di Livio sul più antico trattato romano-cartaginese', *Athenaeum*, N.S., XXI (1943).

H. H. SCHMIDT, *Rom und Rhodos* (München, 1957).

H. H. SCULLARD, *From the Gracchi to Nero* (London, 1959).

H. H. SCULLARD, *Roman Politics 220–150 BC* (Oxford, 1951).

H. H. SCULLARD, *Scipio Africanus in the Second Punic War* (Cambridge, 1930).

J. W. SPAETH, *A Study of the Causes of Rome's Wars from 343 to 265 BC* (Diss., Princeton, 1926).

H. E. STIER, *Roms Aufstieg zur Weltmacht und die griechische Welt* (Köln, 1957).

R. SYME, *The Roman Revolution* (Oxford, 1939; corrected reprint, 1952).

J. VOGT, 'Pergamon und Aristonikos', *Atti del terzo Congresso internazionale di epigrafia greca e latina* (Roma, 1959).

H. WILLRICH, *Cicero und Cäsar* (Göttingen, 1944).

B. The Empire

E. ALBERTINI, *L'empire romain* (Paris, 1929).

F. ALTHEIM, *Die Krise der alten Welt* (Berlin, etc., 1943), 3 vols.

F. ALTHEIM, *Niedergang der alten Welt* (Frankfurt, 1952).

F. ALTHEIM, *Die Soldaten Kaiser* (Frankfurt, 1939).

P. E. ARIAS, *Domiziano* (Catania, 1945).

J. P. V. D. BALSDON, *The Emperor Gaius* (Oxford, 1934).

G. M. BERSANETTI, *Vespasiano* (Roma, 1941).

J. BIDEZ, *La vie de l'empereur Julien* (Paris, 1932).

A. CALDERINI, *I Severi (Storia di Roma*, VII) (Bologna, 1949).

F. CARRATA THOMES, *Gli Alani nella politica orientale di Antonino Pio* (Torino, 1958).

F. CARRATA THOMES, *Il regno di Marco Aurelio* (Torino, 1953).

G. E. F. CHILVER, 'The Army in Politics, A.D. 68–70', *Journal of Roman Studies*, XLVII (1957).

E. CIACERI, *Tiberio, successore di Augusto* (Milano, etc., 1934).

P. DAMARAU, 'Kaiser Claudius Goticus', *Klio*, Beiheft, XXXIII (Leipzig, 1934).

H. DESSAU, *Geschichte der römischen Kaiserzeit* (Berlin, 1924–30), 2 vols. in 3.

A. VON DOMASZEWSKI, *Geschichte der römischen Kaiserzeit* (Leipzig, 1909).

H. DÖRRIES, *Konstantin der Grosse* (Stuttgart, 1958).

A. S. L. FARQUHARSON, *Marcus Aurelius, his Life and his World* (ed. by D. A. Rees, Oxford, 1951).

M. FORTINA, *L'imperatore Graziano* (Torino, etc., 1953).

M. FORTINA, *L'imperatore Tito* (Torino, etc., 1955).

A. GARZETTI, *Nerva* (Roma, 1950).

J. GEFFCKEN, *Kaiser Julianus* (Leipzig, 1914).

E. GIBBON, *The History of the Decline and Fall of the Roman Empire* (ed. by J. B. Bury, London, 1896–1900), 7 vols.

S. GSELL, *Essai sur le règne de l'empereur Domitien* (thèse, Paris, 1893).

A. GÜLDENPENNING, *Geschichte des oströmisches Reiches unter den Kaisern Arcadius und Theodosius II* (Halle, 1885).

M. HAMMOND, *The Antonine Monarchy* (Roma, 1959).

M. HAMMOND, *The Augustan Principate* (Harvard, 1933).

H. HASEBROEK, *Untersuchungen zur Geschichte des Kaisers Septimius Severus* (Heidelberg, 1921).

R. HEINZE, *Die Augusteische Kultur* (2nd ed., Leipzig, etc., 1933).

B. W. HENDERSON, *Five Roman Emperors* (Cambridge, 1927).

B. W. HENDERSON, *The Life and Principate of the Emperor Hadrian*, AD *76–138* (London, 1923).

B. W. HENDERSON, *The Life and Principate of the Emperor Nero* (London, 1903).

W. HERING, *Kaiser Valentinian I* (Magdeburg, 1927).

T. HODGKIN, *Italy and her Invaders* (Oxford, 1880–99), 8 vols.

L. HOMO, *De Claudio Gotico* (Paris, 1903).

L. HOMO, *Essai sur le règne de l'empereur Aurélien (270–275)* (Paris, 1904).

R. V. N. HOPKINS, *The Life of Alexander Severus* (Cambridge, 1907).

W. HÜTTL, *Antoninus Pius* (Prague, 1936), 2 vols.

A. JARDÉ, *Études critiques sur la vie et le règne de Sévère Alexandre* (Paris, 1925).

U. KAHRSTEDT, *Kulturgeschichte der römischen Kaiserzeit* (2nd ed., Bern, 1958).

E. KLEBS, *et al.*, *Prosopographia Imperii Romani* (Berlin, 1897–8), 3 vols.; (2nd ed. by E. Groag *et al.*, Berlin, etc., 1933–58), Vols. I–IV (in progress).

E. KORNEMANN, *Augustus, der Mann und sein Werk* (Breslau, 1937).

E. KORNEMANN, *Tiberius* (Stuttgart, 1960).

K. F. W. LEHMANN, *Kaiser Gordian III* (Berlin, 1911).

F. A. LEPPER, *Trajan's Parthian War* (Oxford, 1948).

M. LEVI, *Nerone e i suoi tempi* (Milano, etc., 1949).

M. LEVI, *Il tempo di Augusto* (Firenze, 1951).

F. LOT, *La fin du monde antique* (Paris, 1927).

E. MANNI, *L'impero di Gallieno* (Roma, 1949).

F. B. MARSH, *The Reign of Tiberius* (Oxford, 1931).

H. MATTINGLY, *Roman Imperial Civilization* (London, 1957).

P. MELONI, *Il regno di Caro, Numeriano e Carino* (Cagliari, 1948).

A. MOMIGLIANO, *Claudius, the Emperor and his Achievement* (Oxford, 1934).

L. B. MOSS, *The Birth of the Middle Ages* (Oxford, 1935).

G. J. MURPHY, *The Reign of the Emperor L. Septimius Severus from the Evidence of the Inscriptions* (Philadelphia, 1945).

M. P. NILSSON, *Imperial Rome* (tr. by G. C. Richards, London, 1926).

D. D'ORGEVAL, *L'empereur Hadrien* (Paris, 1950).

R. PARIBENI, *Optimus Princeps* (Messina, 1926), 2 vols.

H. M. PARKER, *A History of the Roman World, AD 138–337* (2nd ed., by B. H. Warmington, London, 1958).

K. PFISTER, *Der Untergang der antiken Welt* (Leipzig, 1943).

D. M. PIPPIDI, *Autour de Tibère* (Bucharest, 1944).

B. RAPPAPORT, *Die Einfälle der Goten in das römische Reich* (Leipzig, 1899).

T. RICE HOLMES, *The Architect of the Roman Empire* (Oxford, 1928–31), 2 vols.

O. T. SCHULZ, *Leben des Kaisers Hadrian* (Leipzig, 1904).

O. T. SCHULZ, *Der römische Kaiser Caracalla* (Leipzig, 1909).

V. M. SCRAMUZZA, *The Emperor Claudius* (Cambridge, etc., 1940).

O. SEECK, *Geschichte des Untergangs der antiken Welt* (Stuttgart, 1921–22), 4 vols. (4th ed., Vol. I; 2nd ed., Vols. II–IV).

O. SEECK, *Regesten der Kaiser und Päpste für die Jahre 311 bis 476 n. Chr.* (Stuttgart, 1919).

W. SESTON, *Dioclétien et la tétrarchie* (Paris, 1946), vol. I.

E. STEIN, *Histoire du Bas-empire*, tr. by J.-R. Palanque (Paris, etc., 1949–59), 2 vols. in 3.

R. SYME, *Tacitus* (Oxford, 1958), 2 vols.

W. THIELE, *De Severo Alexandro imperatore* (Berlin, 1909).

G. VITRUCCI, *L'imperatore Probo* (Rome, 1952).

J. VOGT, *Constantin der Grosse und sein Jahrhundert* (München, 1949).

F. W. WALBANK, *The Decline of the Roman Empire in the West* (London, 1946).

G. WALSER and T. PÉKARY, *Die Krise des römischen Reiches* (Berlin, 1962).

W. WEBER, *Untersuchungen zur Geschichte des Kaisers Hadrian* (Leipzig, 1907).

E. VON WIETERSHEIM, *Geschichte der Völkerwanderung* (2nd ed., by F. Dahn, Leipzig, 1880–81).

U. VON WILAMOWITZ-MOELLENDORFF, *Kaiser Marcus* (Berlin, 1931).

P. ZANCAN, *La crisi del principato nell' anno 69 d.c.* (Padova, 1939).

C. The Eastern Empire

N. H. BAYNES, *The Byzantine Empire* (London, 1925).

N. H. BAYNES and H. ST. L. B. MOSS, *Byzantium, an Introduction to East Roman Civilization* (Oxford, 1948).

L. BRÉNIER, *Le monde byzantin* (Paris, 1948–50), 3 vols.

C. DIEHL, *History of the Byzantine Empire* (tr. by G. B. Ives, Princeton, 1925).

J. M. HUSSEY, *The Byzantine World* (London, 1957).

M. V. LEVTCHENKO, *Byzance des origines à 1453* (Paris, 1949).

G. OSTROGORSKY, *History of the Byzantine State* (tr. by J. Hussey, Oxford, 1956).

D. TALBOT RICE, *The Byzantines* (London, 1962).

2. *Language and Writing: Education*

J. COUSIN, *Bibliographie de la langue latine, 1880–1948* (Paris, 1951).

A. DRÄGER, *Historische Syntax der lateinischen Sprache* (2nd ed., Leipzig, 1878–81), 2 vols.

A. ERNOUT and A. MEILLET, *Dictionnaire étymologique de la langue latine* (4th ed., Paris, 1959–60), 2 vols.

C. H. GRANDGENT, *An Introduction to Vulgar Latin* (Boston, 1908).

A. GWYNN, *Roman Education from Cicero to Quintilian* (Oxford, 1926).

T. HAARHOFF, *Schools of Gaul: a Study of Pagan and Christian Education in the Last Century of the Western Empire* (Oxford, 1920).

H. B. VAN HOESEN, *Roman Cursive Writing* (Princeton, 1915).

W. M. LINDSAY, *A Handbook of Latin Inscriptions* (London, etc., 1937).

W. M. LINDSAY, *The Latin Language* (Oxford, 1894).

E. LÖFSTEDT, *Syntactica* (Lund, etc., 1933–42), 2 vols. (2nd ed., vol. I).

A. MEILLET, *Esquisse d'une histoire de la langue latine* (5th ed., Paris, 1948).

L. R. PALMER, *The Latin Language* (London, 1954).

P. PETIT, *Les étudiants de Libanius* (Paris, 1956).

O. RIEMANN, *Syntaxe latine* (7th ed., by A. Ernout, Paris, 1927).

F. SOMMER, *Handbuch der lateinischen Laut- und Formenlehre* (2nd ed., Heidelberg, 1915).

F. STOLZ and J. H. SCHMALZ, *Lateinische Grammatik* (*Handbücher der Altertumswissenschaft*), II, 2 (5th ed., by M. Leumann and J. B. Hoffmann, München, 1926–28).

3. *Science and Technology*

C. ALLBUTT, *Greek Medicine in Rome* (London, 1921).

W. ALY, *Strabonis Geographica, IV: Strabo von Amaseia, Untersuchungen über Text, Aufbau und Quellen der Geographika* (Bonn, 1957).

D. DETLEFSEN, *Untersuchungen über die Zusammensetzung der Naturgeschichte des Plinius* (Berlin, 1899).

J. SVENNUNG, *Untersuchungen zu Palladius* (Uppsala, etc., [1935]).

E. A. THOMPSON, ed., *A Roman Reformer and Inventor, Being a New Text of the Treatise De Rebus Bellicis* (Oxford, 1952).

4. *Economics: Finance, Agriculture, Industry, Trade, and Coinage*

F. ALTHEIM, *Finanzgeschichte der Spätantike* (Frankfurt, 1957).

A. ASHLEY, 'The Alimenta of Nerva and his Successors', *English Historical Review*, XXXVI (1921).

D. VAN BERCHEM, *Les distributions de blé et d'argent à la plèbe romaine sous l'empire* (Genève, 1939).

A. E. R. BOAK, *Manpower Shortage and the Decline of the Roman Empire in the West* (London, 1955).

H. BOTT, *Die Grundzüge der diokletianischen Steuerverfassung* (Frankfurt, 1928).

A. BURDESE, *Studi sull'ager publicus* (Torino, 1952).

J. CALMETTE, *Le monde féodal* (Paris, n.d.).

M. P. CHARLESWORTH, *Trade Routes and Commerce of the Roman Empire* (2nd ed., Cambridge, 1926).

O. DAVIES, *Roman Mines in Europe* (Oxford, 1935).

J. G. FÉVRIER, *Essai sur l'histoire politique et économique de Palmyre* (Paris, 1931).

T. FRANK, *An Economic History of Rome* (2nd ed., Baltimore, 1927).

T. FRANK, ed., *An Economic Survey of the Roman Empire* (Baltimore, 1933–40), 6 vols.

J. HATZFELD, *Les trafiquants italiens dans l'Orient hellénique* (Paris, 1919).

W. E. HEITLAND, 'Agriculture', in C. Bailey, ed., *The Legacy of Rome* (Oxford, 1923).

E. J. HOLMBERG, *Zur Geschichte des Cursus publicus* (Inaug.-Diss., Uppsala, 1933).

S. J. DE LAET, *Portorium* (Brugge, 1949).

F. LOT, *L'impôt foncier et la capitation personnelle sous le Bas-empire et à l'époque franque* (Paris, 1928).

F. LOT, *Nouvelles recherches sur l'impôt foncier* (Paris, 1955).

H. MATTINGLY and E. A. SYDENHAM, *The Roman Imperial Coinage* (London, 1923–51), 6 vols. in 9.

J. MAURICE, *Numismatique constantinienne* (Paris, 1908–12), 3 vols.

G. MICKWITZ, *Geld und Wirtschaft in römischen Reich des vierten Jahrhunderts n. Chr.* (Helsingfors, 1932).

T. MOMMSEN and H. BLÜMNER, *Edictum Diocletiani de pretiis rerum venalium* (Berlin, 1893).

M. ROSTOVTZEFF, *Caravan Cities* (Oxford, 1932).

M. ROSTOVTZEFF, 'Geschichte der Staatspacht in der römischen Kaiserzeit bis Diocletian', *Philologus*, Suppl. IX (1901–4, No. 3).

M. ROSTOVTZEFF, *The Social and Economic History of the Roman Empire* (2nd ed., by P. M. Fraser, Oxford, 1957), 2 vols.

M. ROSTOVTZEFF, *Studien zur Geschichte des römischen Kolonates* (Leipzig, etc., 1910).

V. A. SIRAGO, *L'Italia agraria sotto Traiano* (Louvain, 1958).

C. H. V. SUTHERLAND, *Coinage in Roman Imperial Policy, 31 BC–AD 68* (London, 1951).

R. SYME, 'The Imperial Finances under Domitian, Nerva, and Trajan', *Journal of Roman Studies*, XX (1930).

J. P. WALTZING, *Étude historique sur les corporations professionnelles chez les Romains* (Louvain, 1895–1900), 4 vols.

E. H. WARMINGTON, *The Commerce between the Roman Empire and India* (Cambridge, 1928).

R. M. WHEELER, *Rome Beyond the Imperial Frontiers* (London, 1954).

5. *Institutions, Administration, Law, and Social Life; the Army*

A. The Roman State and the Roman Constitution

F. ALTHEIM, *Lex Sacrata; die Anfänge der plebeischen Organisation* (Amsterdam, 1940).

J. ANDERSON, 'Augustan Edicts from Cyrene', *Journal of Roman Studies*, XVII (1927).

G. BARBIERI, *L'albo senatorio da Settimio Severo a Carino* (Roma, 1952).

U. COLI, *Regnum* (Roma, 1951).

J. CROOK, *Consilium Principis* (Cambridge, 1955).

M. GELZER, *Die Nobilität der römischen Republik* (Leipzig, 1912).

M. GRANT, *From Imperium to Auctoritas* (Cambridge, 1946).

A. W. HUNTZINGER, *Die diokletianische Staatsreform* (diss., Rostock, 1899).

E. KORNEMANN, *Doppelprinzipat und Reichseinteilung* (Leipzig, etc., 1930).

J. MARQUARDT, *Römische Staatsverwaltung* (2nd ed., Leipzig, 1881–85,) 3 vols.

H. MATTINGLY, *The Imperial Civil Service of Rome* (Cambridge, 1910).

T. MOMMSEN, *Römisches Staatsrecht* (Leipzig, 1887–88), 3 vols. (3rd ed., vols. I and II).

F. MÜNZER, *Römische Adelsparteien und Adelsfamilien* (Stuttgart, 1920).

A. VON PREMERSTEIN, 'Vom Werden und Wesen des Prinzipats' (ed. H. Volkmann), *Abhandlungen der bayerischen Akademie der Wissenschaften*, Phil.-Hist. Abteilung, N.F., Heft XV (1937).

O. T. SCHULZ, *Vom Principat zum Dominat* (Paderborn, 1919).

H. SIBER, *Die plebejischen Magistraturen bis zur Lex Hortensia* (Leipzig, 1936).

A. STEIN, *Der römische Ritterstand* (München, 1927).

C. S. WALTON, 'Oriental Senators in the Service of Rome', *Journal of Roman Studies*, XIX (1929).

C. WIRSZUBSKI, *Libertas as a Political Idea at Rome* (Cambridge, 1950).

B. The Provinces and the Empire

F. F. ABBOTT and A. C. JOHNSON, *Municipal Administration in the Roman Empire* (Princeton, 1926).

A. ALFÖLDI, *A Conflict of Ideas in the Late Roman Empire* (tr. by H. Mattingly, Oxford, 1952).

T. ASHBY, *The Roman Campagna in Classical Times* (London, 1927).

E. BICKERMANN, *Das Edikt des Kaisers Caracalla* (diss., Berlin, 1926).

A. W. BYVANCK, *Nederland in den romeinschen Tijd* (Leiden, 1945), 2 vols.

J. CARCOPINO, *Points de vue sur l'impérialisme romain* (Paris, 1934).

G. E. F. CHILVER, *Cisalpine Gaul* (Oxford, 1941).

R. G. COLLINGWOOD and J. N. L. MYRES, *Roman Britain and the English Settlements* (2nd ed., Oxford, 1937).

P. M. DUVAL, *Le vie quotidienne en Gaule pendant la paix romaine* (Paris, 1952).

B. M. FELLETTI MAJ, *Siria, Palestina, Arabia settentrionale nel periodo romano* (Roma, 1950).

A. J. FESTUGIÈRE, *Antioche païenne et chrétienne* (Paris, 1959).

L. HARMAND, *L'Occident romain* (Paris, 1960).

J. HATT, *Histoire de la Gaule romaine* (Paris, 1959).

R. HEUBERGER, *Rätien im Altertum und Frühmittelalter* (Innsbruck, 1932), vol. I.

O. HIRSCHFELD, *Die kaiserlichen Verwaltungsbeamten bis Diokletian* (2nd ed., Berlin, 1905).

J. JUSTER, *Les Juifs dans l'empire romain* (Paris, 1914).

D. MAGIE, *Roman Rule in Asia Minor* (Princeton, 1950), 2 vols.

R. MEIGGS, *Roman Ostia* (Oxford, 1960).

T. MOMMSEN, *The Provinces of the Roman Empire* (tr. by W. P. Dickson from *Römische Geschichte*, vol. V, London, 1909), 2 vols.

M. PAVAN, *La provincia romana della Pannonia Superior* (Roma, 1955).

P. PETIT, *Libanius et la vie municipale à Antioche au IVᵉ siècle après J. C.* (Paris, 1955).

I. A. RICHMOND, *Roman Britain* (Harmondsworth, 1955).

A. N. SHERWIN-WHITE, *The Roman Citizenship* (Oxford, 1939).

F. STÄHELIN, *Die Schweiz in römischer Zeit* (2nd ed., Basel, 1931).

G. H. STEVENSON, *Roman Provincial Administration* (Oxford, 1939).

C. H. V. SUTHERLAND, *The Romans in Spain* (London, 1939).

R. SYME, *Colonial Elites* (London, 1958).

F. VITTINGHOFF, *Römische Kolonisation und Bürgerrechtspolitik unter Caesar und Augustus*, Akademie der Wissenschaften und der Literatur in Mainz, *Abhandlungen der Geistes- und Sozialwissenschaftlichen Klasse* (1951, nr. 14).

F. WAGNER, *Die Römer in Bayern* (4th ed., München, 1928).

C. Roman Law

V. ARANGIO-RUIZ, *Instituzioni di diritto romano* (7th ed., Napoli, 1943).

V. ARANGIO-RUIZ, *Storia del diritto romano* (6th ed., Napoli, 1950).

A. BERGER, *Encyclopaedic Dictionary of Roman Law* (Philadelphia, 1953).

P. BONFANTE, *Corso di diritto romano* (Roma, 1925–36), 4 vols. (4th ed., Vols. I and II).

C. C. BRUNS, *Fontes Iuris Romani* (7th ed., Strassburg, 1908).

P. E. CORBETT, *The Roman Law of Marriage* (Oxford, 1930).

E. U. F. L. CUQ, *Manuel des institutions juridiques des Romains* (2nd ed., Paris, 1928).

D. DAUBE, *Forms of Roman Legislation* (Oxford, 1956).

P. DE FRANCISCI, *Storia del diritto romano* (Roma, 1926–38), 3 vols.

P. F. GIRARD, *Manuel élémentaire de droit romain* (8th ed., by F. Senn, Paris, 1929).

A. M. HONORÉ, *Gaius* (Oxford, 1962).

A. H. M. JONES, *Studies in Roman Government and Law* (Oxford, 1960).

P. JÖRS, *Römisches Privat Recht* (3rd ed., by W. Kunkel, Berlin, etc., 1949).

B. G. A. KÜBLER, *Lesebuch des römischen Rechts* (3rd ed., Leipzig, etc., 1925).

T. MOMMSEN, *Römisches Strafrecht* (Leipzig, 1899).

R. MONIER, *Manuel élémentaire de droit romain* (5th ed., Paris, 1945–54), 2 vols.

F. SCHULZ, *Classical Roman Law* (Oxford, 1951).

F. SCHULZ, *History of Roman Legal Science* (Oxford, 1946).

E. WEISS, *Grunzüge der römischen Rechtsgeschichte* (Reichenberg, 1936).

D. Social Conditions

R. H. BARROW, *Slavery in the Roman Empire* (London, 1929).

C. COGENTINI, *Studi sui liberti* (Catania, 1948–50), 2 vols.

A. M. DUFF, *Freedmen in the Early Empire* (reissued with addenda, Cambridge, 1958).

L. FRIEDLÄNDER, *Darstellung aus der Sittengeschichte Roms* (9th and 10th eds. by E. Wissowa, Leipzig, 1919–21).

A. PIGANIOL, *Recherches sur les jeux romains* (Strasbourg, 1923).

W. WARDE FOWLER, *Social Life at Rome in the Age of Cicero* (London, 1908).

E. The Military

P. K. BAILLIE-REYNOLDS, *The Vigiles of Imperial Rome* (Oxford, 1926).

D. VAN BERCHEM, *L'armée de Dioclétien et la réforme constantinienne* (Paris, 1952).

A. VON DOMASZEWSKI, *Die Rangordnung des römischen Heeres* (Bonn, 1908).

G. FORNI, *Il reclutamento delle legioni da Augusto a Diocleziano* (Milano, etc., 1953).

R. GOSSE, *Römische Militärgeschichte von Gallienus bis zum Beginn der byzantinischen Themenverfassung* (Berlin, 1920).

H. M. D. PARKER, *The Roman Legions* (Oxford, 1928).

R. E. SMITH, *Service in the Post-Marian Roman Army* (Manchester, 1958).

J. H. THIEL, *A History of Roman Sea-power before the Second Punic War* (Amsterdam, 1954).

J. H. THIEL, *Studies in the History of Roman Sea-power in Republican Times* (Amsterdam, 1946).

6. *Religion and Astrology*

A. ALFÖLDI, *The Conversion of Constantine and Pagan Rome* (Oxford, 1948).

F. ALTHEIM, *Römische Religionsgeschichte* (Baden-Baden, 1951–53), 2 vols.

J. CARCOPINO, *Aspects mystiques de la Rome païenne* (Paris, 1942).

F. CUMONT, *After-life in Roman Paganism* (New Haven, 1922).

F. CUMONT, *Lux Perpetua* (Paris, 1949).

F. CUMONT, *Les religions orientales dans le paganisme romain* (Paris, 1929).

F. CUMONT, *Textes et monuments figurés relatifs aux mystères de Mithra* (Bruxelles, 1896–99), 2 vols.

A. VON DOMASZEWSKI, *Die Religion des römischen Heeres* (Trier, 1895).

J. G. FERNIER, *La religion des Palmyréniens* (Paris, 1931).

J. GEFFCKEN, *Der Ausgang des griechisch-römischen Heidentums* (Heidelberg, 1920).

W. R. HALLIDAY, *The Pagan Background of Early Christianity* (Liverpool, 1925).

A. H. M. JONES, *Constantine and the Conversion of Europe* (London, 1948).

G. LEIPOLDT, *Die Religionen in der Umwelt der Urchristentums* (Leipzig, 1926).

A. MOMIGLIANO, ed., *The Conflict between Paganism and Christianity in the Fourth Century* (Oxford, 1963).

D. M. PIPPIDI, *Recherches sur le culte impérial* (Paris, n.d.).

H. J. ROSE, *Ancient Roman Religion* (London, n.d.).

M. I. ROSTOVTZEFF, *Mystic Italy* (New York, 1927).

E. SCHWARZ, *Kaiser Constantin und die Christliche Kirche* (Leipzig, etc., 1936).

K. SCOTT, *The Imperial Cult under the Flavians* (Stuttgart, etc., 1931).

K. STADE, *Der Politiker Diokletian und die letzte grosse Christenverfolgung* (Wiesbaden, 1926).

L. R. TAYLOR, *The Divinity of the Roman Empire* (Middleton, 1931).

H. WAGENVOORT, *Roman Dynamism* (Oxford, 1947).

W. WARDE FOWLER, *The Religious Experience of the Roman People* (London, 1922).

G. WISSOWA, *Religion und Cultus der Römer* (2nd ed., München, 1912).

7. *Philosophy*

J. BIDEZ, *Vie de Porphyre* (Gand, etc., 1913).

I. HEINEMANN, *Poseidonios' metaphysische Schriften* (Breslau, 1921), Vol. I.

R. HIRZEL, *Plutarch* (Leipzig, 1912).

R. HIRZEL, *Untersuchungen zu Ciceros philosophischen Schriften* (Leipzig, 1877–83), 3 vols.

H. A. K. HUNT, *The Humanism of Cicero* (Melbourne, 1954).

K. REINHARDT, *Poseidonius* (München, 1921).

A. WEISCHE, *Cicero und die neue Akademie* (Münster, 1961).

T. WHITTAKER, *Apollonius of Tyana and other Essays* (London, 1909).

T. WHITTAKER, *The Neo-Platonists* (Cambridge, 1918).

8. *Literature*

A. General Works

F. ALTHEIM, *Literatur und Gesellschaft im ausgehenden Altertum* (Halle, 1948–50), 2 vols.

M. BARDIRESI, *Nevio epico* (Padova, 1962).

N. H. BAYNES, *The Historia Augusta* (Oxford, 1926).

A. BERGER and G. CUCHEVAL, *Histoire de l'éloquence latine* (3rd ed., Paris, 1892).

T. R. GLOVER, *Life and Letters in the Fourth Century* (Cambridge, 1901).

J. HUBAUX, *Les thèmes bucoliques dans la poésie latine* (Bruxelles, 1930).

F. LEO, *De Tragoedia romana* (Göttingen, 1910).

F. LEO, *Geschichte der römischen Literatur* (Berlin, etc., 1913), Vol. I.

W. M. LINDSAY, *Early Latin Verse* (Oxford, 1922).

E. LÖFSTEDT, *Roman Literary Portraits* (tr. by P. M. Fraser, Oxford, 1958).

G. H. E. LUCK, *The Latin Love Elegy* (London, 1959).

R. PICHON, *Histoire de la littérature latine* (5th ed., Paris, 1912).

K. QUINN, *Latin Explorations* (London, 1963)

W. Y. SELLAR, *The Roman Poets of the Augustan Age* (2nd ed., Oxford, 1883–99), 2 vols.

W. Y. SELLAR, *The Roman Poets of the Republic* (3rd ed., Oxford, 1889).

W. C. SUMMERS, *The Silver Age of Latin Literature* (London, 1920).

R. Y. TYRRELL, *Latin Poetry* (London, etc., 1895).

V. USSANI, *Storia della letteratura latina* (Milano, 1929).

J. WIGHT DUFF, *A Literary History of Rome* (3rd ed., by A. M. Duff, 1953).

J. WIGHT DUFF, *A Literary History of Rome in the Silver Age* (London, 1927).

J. WIGHT DUFF, *Roman Satire* (Cambridge, 1937).

B. Individual Authors

F. ARNALDI, *et al.*, *Studi ovidiani* (Roma, 1959).

H. VON ARNIM, *Leben und Werke des Dio von Prusa* (Berlin, 1898).

H. BARTHOLOMÉ, *Ovid und die antike Kunst* (Borna, etc., 1935).

A. BOULENGER, *Aelius Aristide et la sophistique dans la province d'Asie au 2 ème siècle de notre ère* (Paris, 1923).

K. BÜCHNER, *Studien zur römischen Literatur, II: Cicero* (Wiesbaden, 1962).

J. COLLART, *Varron, grammairien latin* (Paris, 1954).

M. CROISET, *Essai sur la vie et les œuvres de Lucien* (Paris, 1882).

H. DAHLMANN, *Varro und die Hellenistische Sprachtheorie* (Berlin, 1932).

T. FRANK, *Catullus and Horace* (New York, 1928).

C. GIUSSANI, *Studi Lucreziani* (Torino, 1945).

N. I. HERESCU, *Ovidiana* (Paris, 1958).

G. HIGHET, *Juvenal the Satirist* (Oxford, 1954).

L. LAURAND, *Cicéron* (Paris, 1933–34), 2 vols.

P. LEGRAS, *Les légendes thébaines en Grèce et à Rome: étude sur la Thébaïde de Stace* (thèse, Paris, 1905).

F. LEO, *Plautinische Forschungen* (2nd ed., Berlin, 1912).

C. MARCHESI, *Seneca* (3rd ed., Milano, etc., 1944).

I. MARIOTTI, *Introduzione a Pacuvio* (Urbino, 1960).

I. MARIOTTI, *Studi Luciliani* (Firenze, 1960).

J. MÜLLER, *Der Stil des aelteren Plinius* (Innsbruck, 1883).

G. NORWOOD, *The Art of Terence* (Oxford, 1923).

R. PICHON, *Lactance* (Paris, 1901).

K. QUINN, *The Catullan Revolution* (Melbourne, 1959).

C. ROBERT, *Pausanias als Schriftsteller* (Berlin, 1909).

H. TRÄNKLE, *Die Sprachkunst des Properz und die Tradition der lateinischen Dichtersprache* (Wiesbaden, 1960).

P. VILLENEUVE, *Essai sur Perse* (Paris, 1918).

O. WEINREICH, *Studien zu Martial* (Stuttgart, 1928).

i. *Virgil*

C. BAILEY, *Religion in Virgil* (Oxford, 1935).

T. FRANK, *Virgil, a Biography* (Oxford, 1922).

H. HEINZE, *Virgils epische Technik* (3rd ed., Leipzig, 1915).

V. PÖSCHL, *The Art of Virgil* (tr. by G. Seligson, Ann Arbor, 1962).

H. ROSE, *The Eclogues of Virgil* (Berkeley, 1942).

ii. *Horace*

K. BÜCHNER, *Studien zur römischen Literatur, III: Horaz* (Wiesbaden, 1962).

E. FRAENKEL, *Horace* (Oxford, 1957).

W. WILI, *Horaz und die augusteische Kultur* (Basel, 1948).

L. P. WILKINSON, *Horace and his Lyric Poetry* (Cambridge, 1945).

T. ZIELIŃSKI, *Horace et la société romaine du temps d'Auguste* (Paris, 1938).

iii. *The Historians*

H. BORNECQUE, *Tite-Live* (Paris, 1935).

W. SCHUR, *Sallust als Historiker* (Stuttgart, 1934).

W. SOLTAU, *Livius' Geschichtswerk, seine Komposition und seine Quellen* (Leipzig, 1897).

R. SYME, *Tacitus* (Oxford, 1958), 2 vols.

H. ST. J. THACKERAY, *Josephus, the Man and the Historian* (New York, 1929).

E. A. THOMPSON, *The Historical Work of Ammianus Marcellinus* (Cambridge, 1947).

P. ZANCAN, *Tito Livio* (Milano, 1940).

9. *Art*

T. ASHBY, *The Aqueducts of Ancient Rome* (ed. by I. A. Richmond, Oxford, 1935).

T. BREASTED, *Oriental Forerunners of Byzantine Painting* (Chicago, 1924).

H. J. CHARLESTON, *Roman Pottery* (London, n.d.).

C. DIEHL, *Manuel d'art byzantin* (Paris, 1910).

E. ESPÉRANDIEU, *Recueil général des bas-reliefs, statues et bustes de la Gaule romaine* (Paris, 1907–38), 11 vols.

A. IPPEL, 'Römische Porträts', in H. Schaal, *Bilderhefte zu Kunst und Kunstgeschichte des Altertums* (Bielefeld, etc., 1927).

C. ISINGS, *Roman Glass from Dated Finds* (Groningen, etc., 1957).

G. LUGLI, *I monumenti antichi di Roma e suburbio* (2nd ed., Roma, 1931).

F. OSWALD and T. DAVIES PRYCE, *An Introduction to the Study of Terra Sigillata* (London, 1920).

S. B. PLATNER, *A Topographical Dictionary of Ancient Rome* (rev. by T. Ashby, Oxford, 1929).

W. M. RAMSAY, *Studies in the History and Art of the Eastern Provinces of the Roman Empire* (Aberdeen, 1906).

I. A. RICHMOND, *The City Wall of Imperial Rome* (Oxford, 1930).

G. T. RIVOIRA, *Roman Architecture and its Principles of Construction under the Empire* (tr. by G. McN. Rushforth, Oxford, 1925).

E. STRONG, *Art in Ancient Rome* (2nd ed., London, 1929).

J. M. C. TOYNBEE, *The Hadrianic School* (Cambridge, 1934).

A. J. B. WACE, 'Studies in Roman Historical Reliefs', *Papers of the British School at Rome*, IV (1907).

R. WEST, *Römische Porträt-Plastik* (München, 1933–41), 2 vols.

F. WICKHOFF, *Roman Art* (tr. by S. A. Strong, London, 1900).

XXVI. THE AMERICAS

C. A. BURLAND, *Art and Life in Ancient Mexico* (Oxford, 1948).

J. R. GRIFFIN, ed., *The Archaeology of the Eastern United States* (Chicago, 1952).

P. A. MEANS, *The Ancient Civilizations of the Andes* (New York, etc., 1931).

J. H. PARRY, 'The Native Cultures of the Americas', in J. Bowle, ed., *The Concise Encyclopaedia of World History* (London, 1958).

T. PROSKOURIAKOFF, *A Study of Classic Maya Sculpture* (Washington, 1950).

J. G. THOMPSON, *The Archaeology of South America* (Chicago, 1936).

J. G. THOMPSON, *The Rise and Fall of Maya Civilization* (2nd ed., Norman, Oklahoma, 1956).

H. UBBELOHDE-DOERING, *The Art of Ancient Peru* (London, 1952).

G. C. VAILLANT, *The Aztecs of Mexico* (Harmondsworth, 1950).

XXVII. THE PACIFIC

T. S. FOSTER, *Travels and Settlements of Early Man* (London, 1929).

R. HEINE GELDERN, 'Heyerdahl's Hypothesis of Polynesian Origins: a Criticism', *The Geographical Journal*, CXVI (1950).

T. HEYERDAHL, *American Indians in the Pacific* (London, 1952).

A. MÉTRAUX, *Easter Island* (tr. by M. Bullock, London, 1957).

M. W. SMITH, 'The Theory behind the Kon-Tiki Expedition', *The Geographical Journal*, CXIX (1953).

D. R. H. TAYLOR, *A Pacific Bibliography* (Wellington, 1951).

B.

HEBREWS

Encyclopaedia Judaica (Berlin, 1928–).

The Jewish Encyclopaedia (New York, 1901–6), 12 vols.

J. HASTINGS, *A Dictionary of the Bible* (Edinburgh,), 5 vols.

F. VIGOUROUX, *Dictionnaire de la Bible* (Paris, 1895–1925). Supplements under the direction of L. Pirot and A. Robert (Paris, 1928–).

F. M. ABEL, *Géographie de la Palestine* (Paris, 1933), 2 vols.

S. W. BARON, *A Social and Religious History of the Jews* (New York, 1952–58), 8 vols. Partly transl. into French: *Histoire d'Israël, Vie sociale et religieuse* (Paris, 1952).

J. BONSIRVEN, *Le Judaïsme palestinien au temps de Jésus-Christ* (Paris, 1953), 2 vols.

W. BOUSSET, *Die Religion des Judentums in späthellenistischen Zeitalter* (3rd ed. Tübingen, 1926).

M. DU BUIT, *Géographie de la Terre Sainte* (Paris, 1958).

A. CAUSSE, *Les pauvres d'Israël* (Strasbourg, 1922).

J. DANIÉLOU, *Théologie du Judéo-Christianisme* (Tournai-Paris, 1958).

D. W. FORESTER, *Neutestamentliche Zeitgeschichte*, vol. I: *Das Judentum Palästinas zur Zeit Jesu und der Apostel* (Hamburg, 1955).

J. DE FRAINE, *L'aspect religieux de la royauté israélite* (Rome, 1954).

A. GELIN, *Les pauvres de Yahwé* (3rd ed., Paris, 1955).

L. GOPPELT, *Christentum und Judentum im ersten und zweiten Jahrhundert* (Gütersloh, 1954).

C. GUIGNEBERT, *Le monde juif vers le temps de Jésus* (Paris, 1935).

J. JUSTER, *Les juifs dans l'empire romain* (Paris, 1914), 2 vols.

G. KITTEL, *Urchristentum, Spätjudentum, Hellenismus* (Stuttgart, 1926).

H. J. KRAUS, *Le peuple de Dieu dans l'Ancien Testament* (Neuchâtel, 1960).

M. J. LAGRANGE, *Le Judaïsme avant Jésus-Christ* (Paris, 1931).

S. LIEBERMAN, *Hellenism in Jewish Palestine* (New York, 1950).

A. LODS, *Israël des origines au milieu du VIIIe siècle* (Paris, 1957).

R. MARTIN-ACHARD, *Israël et les nations* (Neuchâtel, 1959).

G. F. MOORE, *Judaism in the First Centuries of the Christian Era* (Cambridge, Mass., 1927), 3 vols.

S. MOSCATI, *Le antiche civiltà semitiche* (Bari, 1958).

M. NOTH, *Histoire d'Israël* (Paris, 1954), trans. into English, 1958.

W. O. E. OESTERLEY, *A History of Israel* (Oxford, 1932), 2 vols.

R. H. PFEIFFER, *Il Guidaismo nell'epoca neotestamentaria* (Rome, 1951).

A. RAVENNA, *L'Ebraismo postbiblico* (Brescia, 1958).

G. RICCIOTTI, *Storia d'Israele* (Turin, 1934), 2 vols.

H. J. SCHOEPS, *Theologie und Geschichte des Judenchristentums* (Tübingen, 1949).

H. J. SCHONFIELD, *The History of Jewish Christianity* (London, 1936).

E. SCHÜRER, *Geschichte des jüdischen Volkes im Zeitalter Jesu Christi* (4th ed., Leipzig, 1901–), 4 vols.

M. SIMON, *Verus Israël. Étude sur les relations entre Chrétiens et Juifs dans l'Empire romain* (Paris, 1948).

M. SIMON, *Les sectes juives au temps de Jésus* (Paris, 1960).

F. SPADAFORA, *Collettivismo e individualismo nel Vecchio Testamento* (Rovigo, 1953).

J. STEINMANN, *Histoire du prophétisme biblique* (Paris, 1959).

C. TRESMONTANT, *La doctrine morale des prophètes d'Israël* (Paris, 1958).

R. DE VAUX, *Les institutions de l'Ancien Testament, I: Le nomadisme et ses survivances; institutions familiales, civiles; II: Institutions militaires, religieuses* (Paris, 1958–60).

J. WELLHAUSEN, *Israelitische und jüdische Geschichte* (Berlin, 1894; 7th ed., 1914; 9th ed., Berlin, 1958).

P. WENDLAND, *Die hellenistisch-römische Kultur in ihren Beziehungen zu Judentum und Christentum* (3rd ed., Tübingen, 1912).

G. WIDENGREN, *Sakrales Königtum im Alten Testament und im Judentum* (Stuttgart, 1955).

'*Judentum, Urchristentum, Kirche*' Festschrift f. J. Jeremias (Berlin, 1960).

THE DEAD SEA SCROLLS

M. BURROWS, *The Dead Sea Scrolls* (New York, 1956).

M. BURROWS, *Lumières nouvelles sur les manuscrits de la Mer Morte* (Paris, 1959).

J. DANIÉLOU, *Les manuscripts de la Mer Morte et les origines du Christianisme* (Paris, 1957).

H. E. DEL MEDICO, *L'énigme des manuscrits de la Mer Morte* (Paris, 1957).

A. DUPONT-SOMMER, *Aperçus préliminaires sur les manuscrits de la Mer Morte* (Paris, 1950).

A. DUPONT-SOMMER, *Les écrits esséniens découverts près de la Mer Morte* (Paris, 1959).

W. S. LASOR, *Bibliography of the Dead Sea Scrolls 1948–1957* (Pasadena, 1958).

T. MILIK, *Dieci anni di scoperte nel deserto di Giuda* (Turin, 1957).

I. SCHREIDEN, *Les énigmes des manuscrits de la Mer Morte* (Wetteren, Belgique, 1961).

K. SCHUBERT, *Die Gemeinde vom Toten Meer. Ihre Entstehung und ihre Lehren* (München-Basel, 1958).

G. VERMÈS, *Les manuscrits du désert de Juda* (Paris-Tournai, 1954).

A. VINCENT, *Les manuscrits hébreux du désert de Juda* (Paris, 1955).

E. WILSON, *The Scrolls from the dead Sea* (London, 1955).

Revue biblique (a systematic bibliography on the question, Paris, 1956).

Revue de Qumrân (since 1958, Paris).

'La secte de Qumrân et les origines du Christianisme', *Recherches bibliques* IV (Bruges, 1959). (Matter: 12 studies presented to the Colloquy of Louvain).

CHRISTOLOGY

E. B. ALLO, *L'évangile spirituel de Saint Jean* (Paris, 1944).

F. AMIOT, *Les idées maîtresses de Saint Paul* (Paris, 1959).

J. BONSIRVEN, *L'Évangile de Paul* (Paris, 1948).

L. BOUYER, *La spiritualité du Nouveau Testament et des Pères* (Paris, 1960).

F. M. BRAUN, *Jean le théologien et son évangile dans l'église ancienne* (Paris, 1959).

P. BREZZI, *Da Tarso a Roma. Significato dell'itinerario paolino* (Milan, 1962).

L. CERFAUX, *La théologie de l'église suivant Saint Paul* (Paris, 1948).

O. CULLMAN, *Saint Pierre, disciple, apôtre, martyr* (Neuchâtel-Paris, 1952).

O. CULLMAN, *Christologie du Nouveau Testament* (Neuchâtel-Paris, 1958).

M. DIBELIUS and W. G. KUMMEL, *Paulus* (Berlin, 1951).

J. DUPONT, *Gnosis: la connaissance religieuse dans les épîtres de Saint Paul* (Louvain, 1949).

J. DUPONT, *Les Problèmes du Livre des Actes d'après les travaux récents* (Louvain, 1950).

J. DUPONT, *Les Béatitudes* (Louvain, 1954).

J. DUPONT, *Les sources du Livre des Actes* (Paris, 1960).

P. GAECHTER, *Petrus und seine Zeit* (Innsbrück-Vienna, 1958).

F. C. GRANT, *The Gospels, their Origin and Growth* (London, 1957).

J. GUITTON, *Le problème de Jésus* (Paris, 1956).

E. HAENCHEN, *Die Apostelgeschichte* (Göttingen, 1956).

E. HENNECKE, *Neutestamentliche Apokryphen* (3rd ed., Tübingen, 1959).

J. HERMANN, *Kyrios und Pneuma. Studien zur Christologie der paulinischen Hauptbriefe* (München, 1961).

J. HUBY, *L'Evangile et les évangiles* (Paris, 1954).

J. JEREMIAS, *Das Problem des historischen Jesus* (Stuttgart, 1960).

E. A. JUDGE, *The Social Pattern of the Christian Groups in the First Century* (London, 1960).

E. KIRSCHBAUM, *Les fouilles de Saint Pierre de Rome* (Paris, 1961).

D. LAZZARATO, *Chronologia Christi seu discordantium fontium concordantia ad juris normam* (Rome, 1952).

H. LIETZMANN, *Petrus und Paulus in Rom* (Berlin, 1927).

A. H. MCNEILE, *An Introduction to the Study of the New Testament* (Oxford, 1927).

J. MUNCK, *Paulus und die Heilsgeschichte* (Copenhagen, 1954).

A. RICHARDSON, *The Gospel According to St. John* (London, 1958).

J. RUYSSCHAERT, *Réflexions sur les fouilles vaticanes* (Louvain, 1954).

K. TH. SCHÄFER, *Grundriss der Einleitung in das Neue Testament* (Bonn, 1952).

H. J. SCHOEPS, *Paulus, die Theologie des Apostels im Lichte der Jüdischen Religions-geschichte* (Tübingen, 1959).

H. J. SCHONFIELD, *The Jew of Tarsus, an Unorthodox Portrait of Paul* (London, 1950).

E. SCHWEIZER, *Gemeinde und Gemeindeordnung im Neuen Testament* (Zürich, 1959).

I. N. SEVENSTER, *Paul und Seneca* (Leyden, 1961).

M. SIMON, *St. Stephen and the Hellenists in the Primitive Church* (London, 1958).

A. SOUTER, *The Text and Canon of the New Testament* (London, 1954).

N. B. STONEHOUSE, *Paul before the Areopagus and Other New Testament Studies* (London, 1957).

J. TOYNBEE and J. W. PERKINS, *The Shrine of St. Peter and the Vatican Excavations* (London, 1956).

E. TROCMÉ, *Le livre des Actes et l'histoire* (Paris, 1957).

L. VAGANAY, *Le problème synoptique* (Paris, 1954).

A. WIKENHAUSER, *Das Evangelium nach Johannes* (Ratisbon, 1957).

M. F. WILES, *The Spiritual Gospel* (London, 1960).

Esplorazioni sotto la Confessione di S. Pietro in Vaticano eseguite negli anni 1940–49 (Vatican City, 1952).

'L'évangile de Jean, Études et problèmes', *Recherches bibliques III* (Paris-Louvain, 1958).

'La formation des évangiles. Problème synoptique et Formgeschichte', *Recherches bibliques II* (Bruges, 1957).

'Littérature et théologie pauliniennes', *Recherches bibliques V* (Paris-Bruges, 1960).

A. BAUDRILLART, Ed., *Dictionnaire d'Histoire et de Géographie ecclésiastiques* (Paris, 1912–   ). At ENZ ... in 1960.

F. CABROL, H. LECLERCQ, Eds., *Dictionnaire d'Archéologie chrétienne et de Liturgie* (Paris, 1907–58), 30 vols.

L. CROSS, Ed., *The Oxford Dictionary of the Christian Church* (Oxford, 1957).

HERZOG, HAUCK, Eds., *Realencyklopädie für Protestantische Theologie und Kirche* (Leipzig, 1896–   ).

KITTEL, Ed., *Theologisches Wörterbuch zum Neuen Testament* (Stuttgart, 1933–   ). Up to the letter *p*.

Reallexicon für Antike und Christentum (Leipzig, 1942).

A. VACANT, E. MANGENOT, E. AMANN, Eds., *Dictionnaire de Théologie catholique* (Paris, 1902–50), 15 vols.

H. VILLIER, J. DE GUIBERT, Eds., *Dictionnaire de Spiritualité* (Paris, 1937–   ). Up to the letter *e* in 1960.

K. ALAND, *Die religiöse Haltung Kaiser Konstantins* (Gütersloh, 1960).

K. ALAND, *Kaiser und Kirche von Konstantin bis Byzanz* (Gütersloh, 1960).

D. ATTWATER, *St. John Chrysostom Pastor and Preacher* (London, 1959).

G. BARDY, *L'église et les derniers romains* (Paris, 1948).

R. BEAUPÈRE, *Atlas de la Bible* (Brussels, 1955).

A. BENOIT, *Saint Irénée. Introduction à l'étude de sa théologie* (Paris, 1960).

G. BETZ, *Die Eucharestie in der Zeit der griechischen Väter* (Fribourg, 1955 and 1961), 2 vols.

P. BREZZI, *Analisi ed interpretazione del De Civitate Dei di S. Agostino* (Tolentino, 1960).

P. BREZZI, *Dalle persecuzioni alla pace di Costantino* (Rome, 1960).

H. VON CAMPENHAUSEN, *Lateinische Kirchenväter* (Stuttgart, 1960).

H. VON CAMPENHAUSEN, *Tradition und Leben* (Tübingen, 1960).

J. CHAIX-ROY, *Saint Augustin. Temps et histoire* (Paris, 1956).

H. CHIRAT, *L'assemblée chrétienne à l'âge apostolique* (Paris, 1949).

J. COLSON, *Les fonctions ecclésiales aux deux premiers siècles* (Paris, 1956).

S. COTTA, *La città politica di sant' Agostino* (Milan, 1960).

P. COUSIN, *Précis d'histoire monastique* (Paris, 1956).

H. CROUZEL, *Origène et la connaissance mystique* (Paris, 1961).

L. DALOZ, *Le travail selon Saint Jean Chrysostome* (Paris, 1959).

H. M. DIEPEN, *Aux origines de l'anthropologie de Saint Cyrille d'Alexandrie* (Paris, 1957).

G. L. ELLSPERMANN, *The Attitude of the Early Christian Writers toward Pagan Literature and Learning* (Washington, 1949).

CH. FAVEZ, *Saint Jérôme peint par lui-même* (Brussels, 1958).

A. J. FESTUGIÈRE, *Antioche païenne et chrétienne: Lybanius, Chrysostome,* etc. (Paris, 1959).

A. J. FESTUGIÈRE, *Les moines d'Orient. Culture ou sainteté* (Paris, 1960).

E. L. FORTIN, *Christianisme et culture philosophique au Ve siècle* (Paris, 1959).

J. GAUDEMET, *L'église dans l'empire romain* (Paris, 1958).

R. M. GRANT, *Gnosticism and Early Christianity* (New York, 1959).

A. GRILLMEIER and H. BACHT, *Das Konzil von Chalkedon. Geschichte und Gegenwart* (Würzburg, 1951–54), 3 vols.

TR. JALLAND, *The Life and Times of St. Leo the Great* (London, 1941).

E. A. JUDGE, *The Social Pattern of Christian Groups in the First Century* (London, 1960).

J. N. D. KELLY, *Early Christian Creeds* (London, 1950).

W. KRAUSE, *Die Stellung der frühchristlichen Autoren zur heidnischen Literatur* (Vienna, 1958).

K. S. LATOURETTE, *A History of Christianity* (New York, 1953).

F. LEFHERS, *Studien zu Gregor von Nazianz* (Bonn, 1958).

F. G. MAIER, *Augustin und das antike Rom* (Stuttgart, 1955).

J. L. MAIER, *Les missions divines selon Saint Augustin* (Fribourg, 1960).

F. VAN DER MEER and CH. MOHRMANN, *Atlas of the Early Christian World* (London, 1958).

J. MESOT, *Die Heidenbekehrung bei Ambrosius von Mailand* (Beckenried, 1958).

R. METZ, *La consécration des vierges dans l'église romaine* (Paris, 1954).

C. C. MIEROW, *St. Jerome, the Sage of Bethlehem* (Milwaukee, 1959).

CH. MOHRMANN, 'Études sur le latin des chrétiens', *Storia e Letteratura*, LXV (Rome, 1958).

J. MOREAU, *La persécution du Christianisme dans l'Empire romain* (Paris, 1956).

H. MULLER, *Christians and Pagans from Constantine to Augustine. The Religious Policies of the Roman Emperors* (Pretoria, 1946).

J. H. NEWMAN, *Essay on the Development of Christian Doctrine* (3rd ed., London, 1878).

A. ORBE, 'Los primeros herejes', *Analecta Gregoriana*, LXXXIII (Rome, 1956).

A. PAREDI, *S. Ambrogio e la sua età* (Milan, 1960).

M. PELLEGRINO, *Le 'Confessioni' di Sant' Agostino. Studio introduttivo* (Rome, 1956).

E. PETERSON, *Frühkirche, Judentum und Gnosis. Studien und Untersuchungen* (Fribourg, 1959).

K. PIEPER, *Atlas Orbis christiani antiqui* (Düsseldorf, 1936).

A. PIGANIOL, *L'empire chrétien (313-395)* (Paris, 1947).

S. PRETE, *Pelagio e il Pelagianesimo* (Brescia, 1961).

J. QUASTEN, *Patrology* (Utrecht, 1954) 2 vols.

G. QUISPEL, *Gnosis als Weltreligion* (Zürich, 1954).

T. A. ROBERTS, *History and Christian Apologetic* (London, 1960).

M. SCHMAUS and H. RAHNER, *Handbuch der Dogmengeschichte* (Freiburg-im-Breisgau, 1951-   ).

R. SEEBERG, *Lehrbuch der Dogmengeschichte* (4th. ed., Leipzig, 1933), 4 vols.

W. SEIBEL, *Fleisch und Geist beim heiligen Ambrosius* (Munich, 1958).

K. M. SETTON, *The Christian Attitude toward the Emperor in the Fourth Century* (New York, 1941).

E. STAUFER, *Le Christ et les Césars* (Paris, 1956).

E. STEIN, *Histoire du Bas Empire* (Brussels, 1949).

J. TIXERONT, *Histoire des dogmes* (Paris, 1930), 3 vols.

G. TURBESSI, *Ascetismo e monachesimo prebenedettino* (Rome, 1961).

L. VISCHER, *Basilius der Grosse* (Basel, 1953).

L. VOELKL, *Der Kaiser Konstantin* (München, 1956).

J. VOGT and W. SESTON, 'Die Constantinische Frage', Congresso storico internazionale, Roma, 1955, *Atti VI* (Florence, 1955).

W. VOLKER, *Gregor von Nyssa als Mystiker* (Wiesbaden, 1955).

D. S. WALLACE-HADRILL, *Eusebius of Caesarea* (London, 1960)

R. MCL. WILSON, *The Gnostic Problem* (London, 1958).

Augustinus Magister. Congrès International Augustinien (Paris, 1954), 3 vols.

Die Religion in Geschichte und Gegenwart (Tübingen, 1927).

Le Concile et les Conciles. Contribution à l'histoire de la vie conciliaire de l'église (Gembloux, 1960).

'Il monachesimo orientale', *Orientalia christiana Analecta*, CXXXV (Rome, 1958).

C

CHINA AND NEIGHBOURING COUNTRIES

1. *General*

D. BODDE, *China's First Unifier: A Study of the Ch'in Dynasty as Seen in the Life of Li Ssu* (Leiden, 1938).

CHENG TE-K'UN, *Archaeology in China* (Cambridge, 1959–60), Vols I and II.

W. EBERHARD, *China's Geschichte* (Bern, 1948), available also in English (London, 1950), and in French (Paris, 1952).

FAN WEN-LAN, *Drevnjaja isorija Kitaja* (Moscow, 1958).

C. P. FITZGERALD, *China: A Short Cultural History* (London, 1954).

O. FRANKE, *Geschichte des chinesischen Reiches* (Berlin, 1930–52), 5 Vols.

2. *Language and Writing*

W. A. C. DOBSON, *Late Archaic Chinese: A Grammatical Study* (Toronto, 1959).

R. A. D. FORREST, *The Chinese Language* (London, 1948).

B. KARLGREN, 'Compendium of Phonetics in Ancient and Archaic Chinese', Museum of Far Eastern Antiquities, Stockholm, *Bulletin*, XXVI (1954), pp. 211–367.

B. KARLGREN, 'Grammata serica recensa', *Ibid.*, XXIX (1957), pp. 1–332.

E. G. PULLEYBLANK, 'The Consonantal System of Old Chinese', *Asia Major*, IX (1962), pp. 58–144, 206–65.

3. *Social and Economic Conditions*

E. BALAZS, 'La propriété foncière en Chine', Primo congresso internazionale di diritto agrario, *Atti* (Milan, 1955), II, pp. 37–43.

E. BALAZS, 'Transformations du régime de la propriété dans la Chine Tartare et dans la Chine chinoise aux IVe–Ve siècles, AD', *Journal of World History*, I (1953), pp. 417–26.

H. BIELENSTEIN, 'The Census of China during the Period 2–742 AD', Museum of Far Eastern Antiquities, Stockholm, *Bulletin*, XIX (1947), pp. 125–63.

H. G. CREEL, *The Birth of China: A Study of the Formative Period of Chinese Civilization* (New York, 1954).

M. GRANET, *La féodalité chinoise* (Oslo, 1952).

M. GRANET, *Fêtes et chansons anciennes de la Chine* (Paris, 1929).

HO TZU-CH'ÜAN, 'Early Development of Manorial Economy in Wei and Tsin' in E-tu Zen Sun and J. De Francis, *Chinese Social History* (Washington, D.C., 1956, pp. 137–41.

H. MASPERO, *La Chine antique* (2nd ed., Paris, 1955).

H. MASPERO, 'Le régime féodal et la propriété foncière dans la Chine antique', *Mélanges posthumes* (Paris, 1950), Vol. III, pp. 102–46.

H. MASPERO, 'Les régimes fonciers en Chine des origines aux temps modernes', *Ibid*, pp. 147–92.

H. MASPERO and J. ESCARRAT, *Les institutions de la Chine* (Paris, 1952).

WANG YÜ-CH'ÜAN, *Early Chinese Coinage* (New York, 1951).

WANG YÜ-CH'ÜAN, 'An Outline of the Central Government of the Former Han Dynasty', Harvard University, *Journal of Asiatic Studies*, XII (1949), pp. 134–87.

C. M. WILBUR, *Slavery in China during the Former Han Dynasty* (Chicago, 1943).

WU CH'I-CH'ANG, 'The Chinese Land System before the Ch'in Dynasty', in E-tu Zen Sun and J. De Francis, *Chinese Social History* (Washington, D.C., 1956), pp. 55–81.

L. S. YANG, *Money and Credit in China* (Cambridge, Mass., 1952).

4. *Technical and Scientific Life*

J. C. ANDERSSON, 'The Goldsmith in Ancient China', Museum of Far Eastern Antiquities, Stockholm, *Bulletin*, VII (1935), pp. 1–38.

H. H. DUBS, 'Wang Mang's Economic Reforms', in *History of the Former Han Dynasty* (Baltimore, 1955), Vol. III, pp. 506–36.

W. HOCHSTADTER, 'Pottery and Stonewares of Shang, Chou and Han', Museum of Far Eastern Antiquities, Stockholm, *Bulletin*, XXIV (1952), pp. 81–108.

KI CH'IAO-P'ING, *The Chemical Arts of Old China* (Easton, 1948).

LEE TAO, 'Achievements of Chinese Medicine in the Ch'in and Han Dynasties', *Chinese Medical Journal*, LXXI (1953), pp. 380–96.

J. NEEDHAM, *Science and Civilization in China* (Cambridge, 1954–62), 4 vols.

WONG MAN, 'Nei-ching, the Chinese Canon of Medicine', *Chinese Medical Journal*, 68 (1950), pp. 1–33.

5. *Religious Life, Philosophy*

E. BALAZS, 'Entre révolte nihiliste et évasion mystique', *Études Asiatiques* 1/2 (1948), pp. 27–55.

H. G. CREEL, *Chinese Thought from Confucius to Mao Tse-tung* (London, 1954).

E. ERKES, *Credenze religiose della Cina antica* (Rome, 1958).

FUNG Y-LAN, *A History of Chinese Philosophy* (Princeton, 1952), 2 vols.

M. GRANET, *La religion des chinois* (2nd ed., Paris, 1951).

E. ZÜRCHER, *The Buddhist Conquest of China* (Leiden, 1959).

6. *Artistic Expression: Literature, the Fine Arts, etc.*

E. FEIFEL, *Geschichte der chinesischen Literatur* (Hildesheim, 1960).

C. S. GARDNER, *Chinese Traditional Historiography* (Cambridge, Mass., 1936).

B. GRAY, *Early Chinese Pottery and Porcelain* (London, 1953).

R. GROUSSET, *La Chine et son art* (Paris, 1951).

LI CHI, *The Beginnings of Chinese Civilization* (Seattle, 1957).

L. PICKEN, 'The Music of Far Eastern Asia, I, China', in *New Oxford History of Music* (Oxford, 1957), I, pp. 83–96.

L. SICKMAN and A. SOPER, *The Art and Architecture of China* (Harmondsworth, Middlesex, 1956).

O. SIRÉN, *Chinese Painting* (London, 1956).

INDIA AND INDIAN CIVILIZATION

1. *General*

D. B. DISKALKAR, 'Classification of Indian Epigraphical Records', *Journal of Indian History*, XXXV (1957), pp. 177–220.

R. C. MAJUMDAR and A. D. PULSAKER, *The History and Culture of the Indian People* (Bombay, 1951–60), Vols I to VI.

K. A. NILAKANTA SASTRI, *The Mauryas and Satavahanas* (Calcutta, 1957).

L. RENOU and J. FILLIOZAT, *L'Inde classique* (Paris, 1947).

B. SUBBARAO, *The Personality of India* (2nd ed., Baroda, 1958).

2. *Language and Writing*

J. BLOCH, *Structure grammaticale des langues dravidiennes* (Paris, 1946).

C. C. DASGUPTA, *The Development of Kharoṣṭhī Script* (Calcutta, 1958).

L. RENOU, *Histoire de la langue sanscrite* (Paris, 1956).

3. *Social and Economic Conditions*

J. ALLAN, *Coins of Ancient India* (London, 1936).

A. S. ALTEKAR, *State and Government in Ancient India* (3rd ed., Delhi, 1958).

U. N. GHOSHAL, *A History of Indian Political Ideas* (Bombay, 1959).

U. N. GHOSHAL, 'Some Aspects of Ancient Indian Political Organization', *Journal of World History*, VI, 2 (1960), pp. 223–34.

K. M. SEN, *Jatibheda* (Calcutta, 1948).

N. C. SEN GUPTA, 'Comparative View of Law in Ancient India', *Journal of World History*, II, 2 (1954), pp. 283–302.

R. S. SHARMA, 'La vie et l'organisation économiques dans l'Inde ancienne', *Journal of World History*, VI, 2 (1960), pp. 235–64.

4. *Technical and Scientific Life*

B. B. DATTA and A. N. SINGH, *History of Hindu Mathematics* (Lahore, 1935–38), 2 vols.

J. FILLIOZAT, *La doctrine classique de la médecine indienne* (Paris, 1949).

J. FILLIOZAT, 'India and Scientific Exchanges in Antiquity', in Guy S. Métraux and François Crouzet, *The Evolution of Science: Readings in the History of Mankind* (New York, 1963), pp. 88–105.

R. C. MAJUMDAR, 'Scientific Spirit in Ancient India', in Guy S. Métraux and François Crouzet, *The Evolution of Science: Readings in the History of Mankind* (New York, 1963), pp. 77–8).

P. RAY, *History of Chemistry in Ancient and Medieval India* (Calcutta, 1956).

B. P. SINHA, 'The Art of War in Ancient India', *Journal of World History*, IV, 1 (1957), pp. 123–60.

5. *Religious Life, Philosophy*

S. N. DASGUPTA, *A History of Indian Philosophy* (Cambridge, 1932).

A. B. KEITH, *Religion and Philosophy of the Vedas and Upanishads* (Cambridge, Mass., 1925).

E. LAMOTTE, *Histoire du bouddhisme indien* (Louvain, 1958), Vol. I.

R. C. MAJUMDAR, 'L'antiquité et l'importance du Rgveda', *Journal of World History*, VI, 2 (1960), pp. 215–22.

G. TUCCI, *Storia della filosofia indiana* (Bari, 1957).

6. *Artistic Expression: Literature, The Fine Arts, etc.*

K. P. ACHARYA, *An Encyclopaedia of Hindu Architecture* (Allahabad, 1941).

J. B. BHUSHAN, *Indian Jewellery, Ornaments, and Decorative Designs* (Bombay, n.d.).

ARNOLD BLAKE, 'The Music of India', in *New Oxford History of Music* (Oxford, 1957), I, pp. 195–227.

S. N. DASGUPTA and S. K. DE, *A History of Sanskrit Literature: The Classical Period* (Calcutta, 1947).

V. V. MIRASHI, 'Recent Theories on the Date of Kalidasa', *Journal of World History*, VI, 2 (1960), pp. 303–30.

B. ROWLAND, *The Art and Architecture of India* (Harmondsworth, Middlesex, 1954).

SIR R. E. M. WHEELER, *Early India and Pakistan* (London, 1959).

M. WINTERNITZ, *A History of Indian Literature* (Calcutta, 1927), 2 vols.

SOUTH-EAST ASIA

G. COEDÈS, *Les États hindouinisés d'Indochine et d'Indonésie* (Paris, 1948).

LE THANH KHOI, *Le Viet-Nam* (Paris, 1955).

JAPAN

K. ENOKI, 'Les origines de l'empire du Japon dans leurs rapports avec l'histoire générale de l'Extrême Orient', *Journal of World History*, II, 1 (1954), pp. 26–37.

C. HAGUENAUER, *Les origines de la civilisation japonaise* (Paris, 1956).

Y. KOBAYASHI, 'La culture préhistorique du Japon', *Journal of World History*, IV, 1 (1957), pp. 161–82.

CIVILIZATIONS OF THE STEPPES

R. GROUSSET, *L'empire des Steppes* (Paris, 1939).

K. JETTMAR, 'The Karasul Culture and its South-Eastern Affinities', Museum for Far Eastern Antiquities, Stockholm, *Bulletin*, XXII (1950), pp. 83–126.

O. LATTIMORE, *Inner Asian Frontiers of China* (New York, 1951).

GREEK AND ROMAN CIVILIZATION AND THE ORIENT

J. FILLIOZAT, 'Les échanges de l'Inde et de l'empire romain aux premiers siècles de l'ère chrétienne', *Revue Historique* (1949), pp. 1–29.

R. GHIRSHMAN, *Bégram, recherches archéologiques et historiques sur les Kouchans* (Cairo, 1946).

J. E. VAN LOHUIZEN-DE LEEUW, *The 'Scythian' Period* (Leiden, 1949).

L. MALLERET, *L'archéologie du delta du Mékong* (Paris, 1959–60), Vols. I and II.

A. K. NARAIN, *The Indo-Greeks* (Oxford, 1957).

C. G. SELIGMAN, 'The Roman Orient and the Far East', *Antiquity*, II (1937), pp. 5–30.

W. W. TARN, *The Greeks in Bactria and India* (2nd ed., Cambridge, 1951).

SIR R. E. M. WHEELER, *Rome Beyond the Imperial Frontiers* (London, 1954).

INDEX

aborigines, Australian, 85

abortion, 150

Abu Howan, 'Thessalian' pottery finds at, 18

Academy, the (Plato's), 534–6

Acarnanian dialect, 67

Accadian language, 80

Achaeans, 7, 11, 27, 29, 67, 68

Achaemenid dynasty, 37, 39; astronomy, 144; influence in Central and Western Asia, 321; languages, 60, 80; and Parthia, 681–2; and Persia, 447–9; religion, 230, 231; writing, 88

Actium, battle of, 356

Adad-apaliddiu (Aramean prince), 19–20

Adad Nirari II (Assyrian king), 13

Adad Nirari III (Assyrian king), 20

adzes, 118

Aegean islands
'Cycladic' communities in, 6, 7; historical movements in, 22 ff.; Phoenicians and the area, 18; the tyrants in, 27

Aemilianus, Scipio: see Scipio, Aemilianus

Aeolians and Aeolian dialects, 6, 7–8, 66–8

Aequi (people), 344, 345

Aeschylus of Eleusis, 576–7

Aesclepius and the Aesclepiaeum, 151

Aetolian dialect, 67

Africa
'black' and 'white' zones, 48–9; Julius Caesar and, 355; Cato and, 486; Phoenician colonies in, 18, 31, 92; Rome and, 349: see also Carthage; Egypt; Libya

Africanus the Elder: see Scipio, Publius

after-life, concepts of the, 224, 227, 231, 235, 237, 243, 244

Agaiwasha (tribe), 11

Agathocles of Syracuse, 343

Agnean language, 58

agriculture, 110 ff., 117–21, 318, 382–7, 477, 728–9, 731–2, 748, 755: see also under entries for individual countries

Ahicchatrā (India), 441

Ainu (people), 45, 85, 324

Ajryana Vaejo (the 'home of the Aryans'), 57

Akhiram (Phoenician king), 81, 92

Akhlâmu (anti-Assyrian alliance), 19

Alalia, battle of, 30, 31

Alaric (Visigoth king), 702

Alarodians (people), 59

Albania, 65; language, 64

alchemy, 742–3, 749–51, 763

Alcmaeon (Greek scientist), 151, 418

Aleppo, 15

Alexander the Great, 451; and Armenia, 358; conquests, explorations and empire of, 337–9, 460–2, 416; and India, 325; and Persia, 330, 448, 449

Alexandria (Egypt), 425, 467, 471

alliances and coalitions, international, 198–9

Almerian culture, 33

Al Mina, 95, 135, 136

alphabets, 18, 31, 89, 92–100, 377, 714–17: see also under entries for individual countries and peoples

Altaic languages, 57

Alyattes (king of Lydia), 11, 37

Amarna: see Tell el Amarna

Amasis (Pharaoh), 12

amber, 35, 128, 133

America
pre-Columbian period, 48; irrigation, 122; language, 85–6; mathematics, 148; ancient writing, 100–1

Ammon (deity), 11

Amorites, 13, 15

Amphictionies (Greek history), 196, 336, 451

Anatolia, 6–10, 37; alphabet, 96; coinage, 138; and the Hittites, 10; languages, 58, 59, 63; and Phoenicia, 15

anatomy, 417–19 passim, 761

Anaxagoras (Greek philosopher), 530

Anaximander of Miletus (Greek philosopher), 142, 145, 249, 282

Anaximenes (Greek philosopher), 145, 151–2, 249

Andronicus, L. Livius (Greek philosopher), 563, 585

animals
domestication of, 110, 112–14, 118, 129; in spirit cults, 238; trade in, 35; worship of, 225: see also sacrifices

'Annales Maximi' (Roman history), 71

Antigonus Doson (king of Macedonia), 341

Antigonus Gonatas (king of Macedonia), 339, 341

Antioch, 465

Antiochus III (king of Syria), 349–50, 357, 358

Antonius, Marcus, 355–6, 503–4

Antony, Mark: see Antonius, Marcus

Anyang (China), 42, 89, 173

Anzan (Persia), 37

Apollo, temple of, 196

Apollonius Pergaeus (Apollonius Perge; Greek mathematician), 411, 414

Apollonius of Rhodes (Greek writer), 563